Metropolitan Phoenix Area

The Thomas Guide®
Street Guide & Directory

Contents | Page

For more information regarding licensing and copyright permission, please contact us at:
licensing@thomas.com
call: 1 (800) 899-MAPS (6277)
Printed in the United States

PHOENIX

INTRO

How To Use this Street Guide & Directory
Modo De Empleo Del Thomas Guide

To Find a City or Community:
Manera de Localizar una Ciudad o Comunidad:

Start with the Key Map to Detail Pages, then turn to the Detail Page indicated.

Empiece con el mapa clave de páginas detalladas, luego pase a la página detallada que se indica.

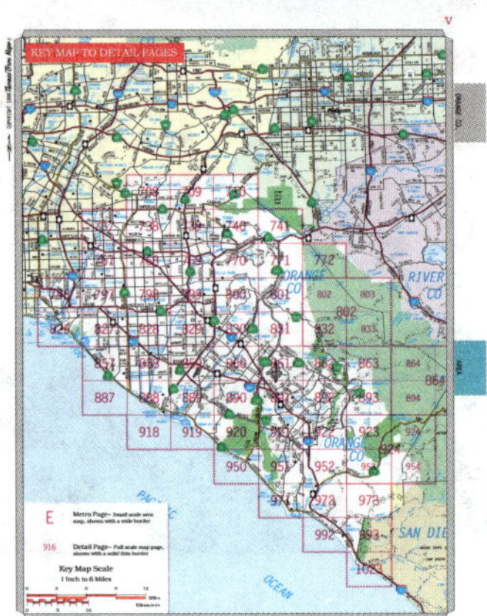

or

o

Community Name	CITY ABBR	ZIP CODE	MILES TO SA	EST. POP	MAP PAGE
ALISO VIEJO		92656	27.00		921
* ANAHEIM	ANA	92801	6.20	293,200	768
ANAHEIM HILLS		92807	7.00		771
ATWOOD		92811	10.60		740
BALBOA		92661	11.50		919
BALBOA ISLAND		92662	10.10		919
* BREA	BREA	92821	12.10	34,800	709
* BUENA PARK	BPK	90620	11.00	72,700	767
CAPISTRANO BEACH		92624	25.30		972
CORONA DEL MAR		92625	10.20		919
COSTA MESA	CMSA	92626	8.20	102,100	859
COTO DE CAZA		92679	39.00		893
COWAN HEIGHTS		92705	6.10		800
* CYPRESS	CYP	90630	12.30	46,400	797
* DANA POINT	DAPT	92629	26.00	36,000	971
DOVE CANYON		92679	39.00		893

Look up the name in the Cities and Communities Index, then turn to the Detail Page indicated.

Busque el nombre en el Indice de Ciudades y Comunidades, luego pase a la página detallada que se indica.

To Find an Address:
Manera de Localizar una Dirección:

1. Look up the street name in the Street Index. If there are multiple listings, choose the proper city and/or address. (All city abbreviations are listed in the Cities and Communities Index).

Localice el nombre de la calle en el Indice de Calles. Si aparecen varias listas, seleccione el área apropiada de la ciudad y/o el domicilio. (Todas las abreviaturas de las ciudades figuran en la lista del Indice de Ciudades y Comunidades).

2. The street name will include a Thomas Bros. Maps Page and Grid where the address is located.

El nombre de la calle incluye un cuadro de Thomas Bros. Maps Page and Grid con el número de página y de coordenadas que indican la ubicación del domicilio.

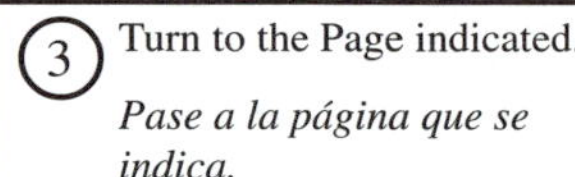

COWAN
17600 IRVN 92614 859-G3

3. Turn to the Page indicated.

Pase a la página que se indica.

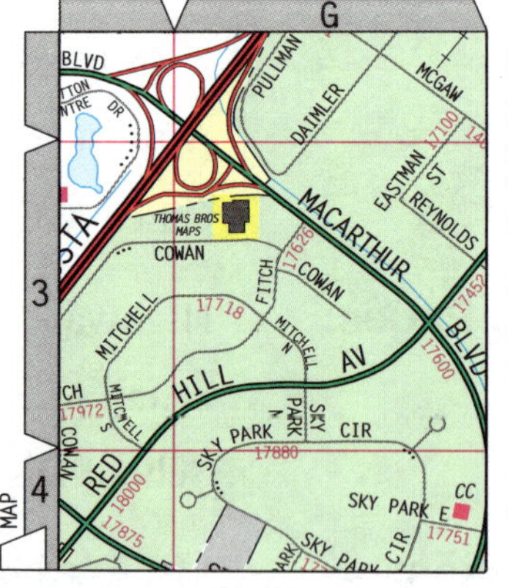

4. Locate the address by following the indicated Letter column and Number row until the two intersect. The street name is within this Grid area.

Localice el domicilio siguiendo la columna con letras y la hilera con números indicadas hasta que intersecten. El nombre de la calle se encuentra dentro de dicho cuadro.

Thomas Bros. Maps Page and Grid

The pages in this Thomas Guide® are part of our national Page and Grid layout and our new digital mapping system. Each page number is unique, enabling you to have precise page information when looking up a city, community, or street address.

En estas páginas Thomas Guide es parte de nuestra página nacional y arreglo de coordenados y nuestro nuevo mapa de sistema digital. Cada numero de página es única, lo abilidad de tener informacion precisa en una página cuando usted busca una ciudad, comunidad o calle.

Grids are 1/2 Mile Square

The map Grids (shown in magenta on your map) are 1/2 mile square, and go from Grid A1 through Grid J7. This gives you the ability to quickly locate cities, streets, addresses, and points of interest. If you have any questions about the Thomas Bros. Maps Page and Grid, please call us at 1-800-899-6277 (1-800-899-MAPS)

Los coordenados del mapa (indican en color morado de su mapa) son media milla cuadrada e indican del coordenado A1 hasta el coordenado J7. Esto le da la abilidad de poder encontrar ciudades, calles, domicilios y puntos de interés. Si usted tiene alguna pregunta en referencia a Thomas Bros. Maps "Page & Grid", ó página y coordenados, favor de llamar al 1-800-899-6277 (1-800-899-MAPS).

How to Use the Key Maps to Detail Pages

Como Usar el Mapa Clave de las Páginas Detalladas

Key to Map Pages
Clave de las Páginas del Mapa

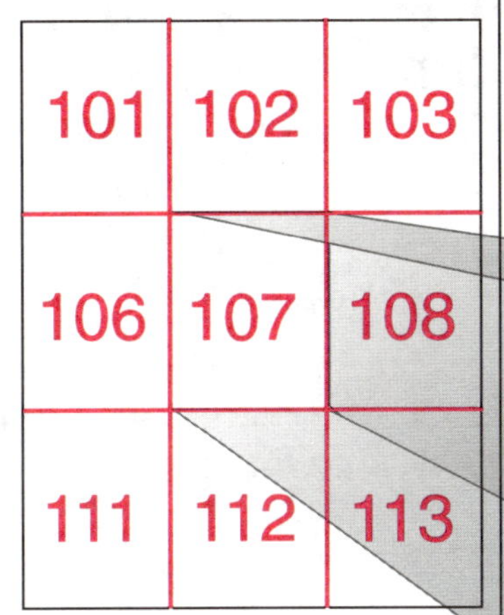

If you know the general area in which the city or community is located, start with the ***Key to Map Page***. Find the general area, then turn to the ***Highway Page*** indicated.

Si Ud. conoce la zona general en que la ciudad o la comunidad está localizada, vea la página Clave de la Página del Mapa. Encuentre la zona general, después vaya a la Página del Highway que se Indica.

Highway Page
Página del Highway

767	768	769	770
797	798	799	800
827	828	829	830
857	858	859	860
887	888	889	890
917	918	919	920
947	948	949	950

Once on the ***Highway Page***, find the area in which the city or community is located, then turn to the ***Detail Page*** indicated.

Una vez que esté en la Página del Highway, busque la zona en que ciudad o la comunidad está localizada, después busque la Página Detallada que se indica.

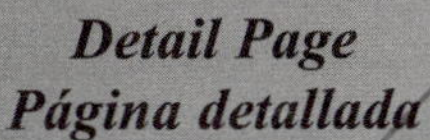

Detail Page
Página detallada

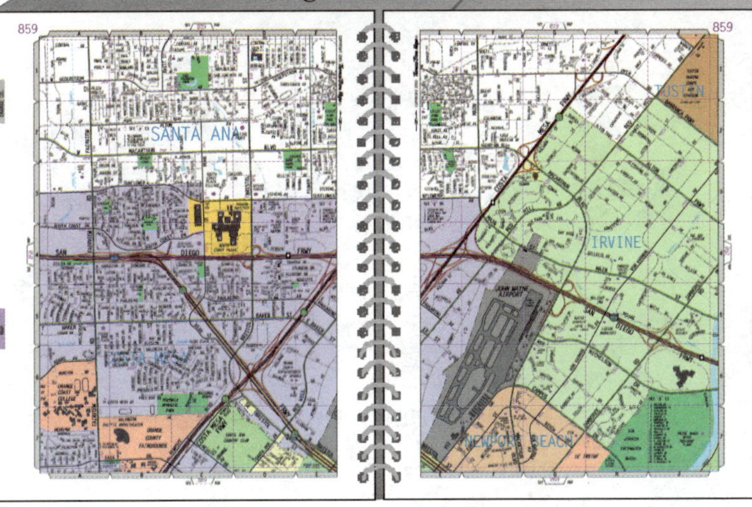

From the ***Highway Page***, turn to the ***Detail Page*** indicated. This page should have the street you are trying to locate. If you know the address, you can look it up in the ***Street Index*** located in the back of this Thomas Guide.

Desde la Página del Highway, vaya a la Página Detallada que se Indica. Esta página debe tener la calle que Ud. quiere localizar. Si Ud. sabe la dirección puede buscarla en el Indice de Calles que está en las páginas de atrás del Thomas Guide.

PHOENIX

INTRO

LEGEND OF MAP SYMBOLS

- Freeway
- Interchange/Ramp
- Highway
- Primary Road
- Secondary Road
- Minor Road
- Restricted Road
- Alley
- Unpaved Road
- Tunnel
- Toll Road
- High Occupancy Veh. Lane
- Stacked Multiple Roadways
- Proposed Road
- Proposed Freeway
- Freeway Under Construction
- One-Way Road
- Two-Way Road
- Trail, Walkway
- Stairs
- Railroad
- Rapid Transit
- Rapid Transit, Underground
- City Boundary
- County Boundary
- State Boundary
- International Boundary
- Military Base, Indian Resv.
- Township, Range, Rancho
- River, Creek, Shoreline
- Ferry
- 85231 ZIP Code Boundary

- 5 Interstate
- 5 Interstate (Business)
- 3 U.S. Highway
- 8 Arizona State Highway
- 4 County, Indian Res. Highway
- Carpool Lane
- A Street List Marker
- Street Name Continuation
- Street Name Change
- Airport
- Station (Train,Bus)
- Building (see List of Abbr. page)
- Building Footprint
- Public Elementary School
- Public High School
- Private Elementary School
- Private High School
- Shopping Center
- Fire Station
- Library
- Mission
- Winery
- Campground
- H Hospital
- Mountain
- Section Corner
- Boat Launch
- Gates, Locks, Barricades
- Lighthouse

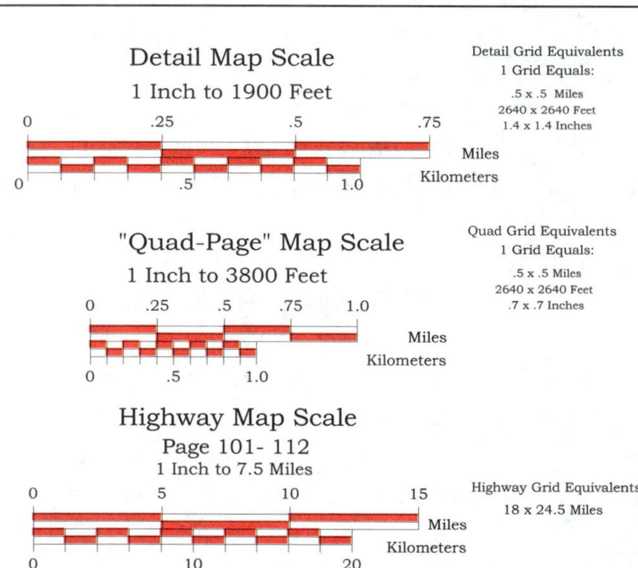

Detail Map Scale

1 Inch to 1900 Feet

0 .25 .5 .75 Miles

0 .5 1.0 Kilometers

Detail Grid Equivalents
1 Grid Equals:
.5 x .5 Miles
2640 x 2640 Feet
1.4 x 1.4 Inches

"Quad-Page" Map Scale

1 Inch to 3800 Feet

0 .25 .5 .75 1.0 Miles

0 .5 1.0 Kilometers

Quad Grid Equivalents
1 Grid Equals:
.5 x .5 Miles
2640 x 2640 Feet
.7 x .7 Inches

Highway Map Scale

Page 101- 112

1 Inch to 7.5 Miles

0 5 10 15 Miles

0 10 20 Kilometers

Highway Grid Equivalents
18 x 24.5 Miles

- Dry Lake, Beach
- Dam
- Point of Interest
- Golf Course, Country Club
- Cemetery
- Military Base
- City, County, State Park
- National Forest, Park
- Water
- Intermittent Lake, Marsh
- Airport
- Parking Lot
- Structure Footprint
- Regional Shopping Center
- S Major Dept. Store (List of Abbr. page)

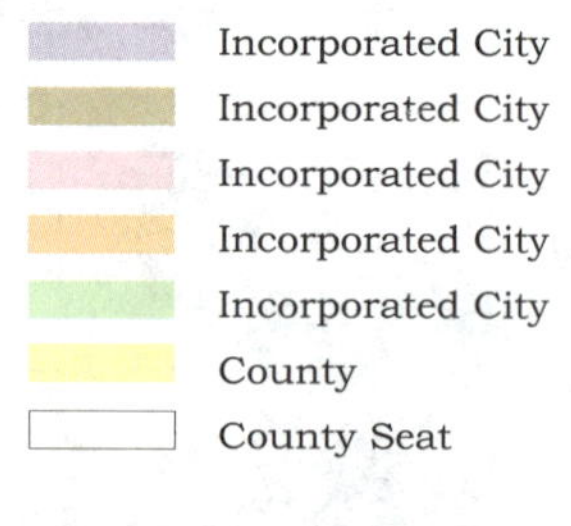

- Incorporated City
- Incorporated City
- Incorporated City
- Incorporated City
- Incorporated City
- County
- County Seat

Public Land Survey

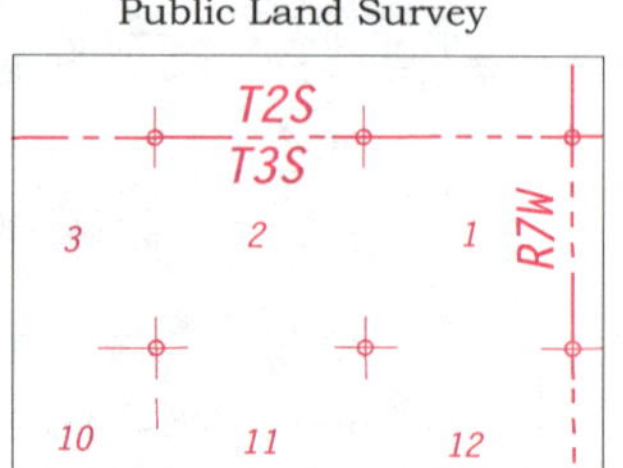

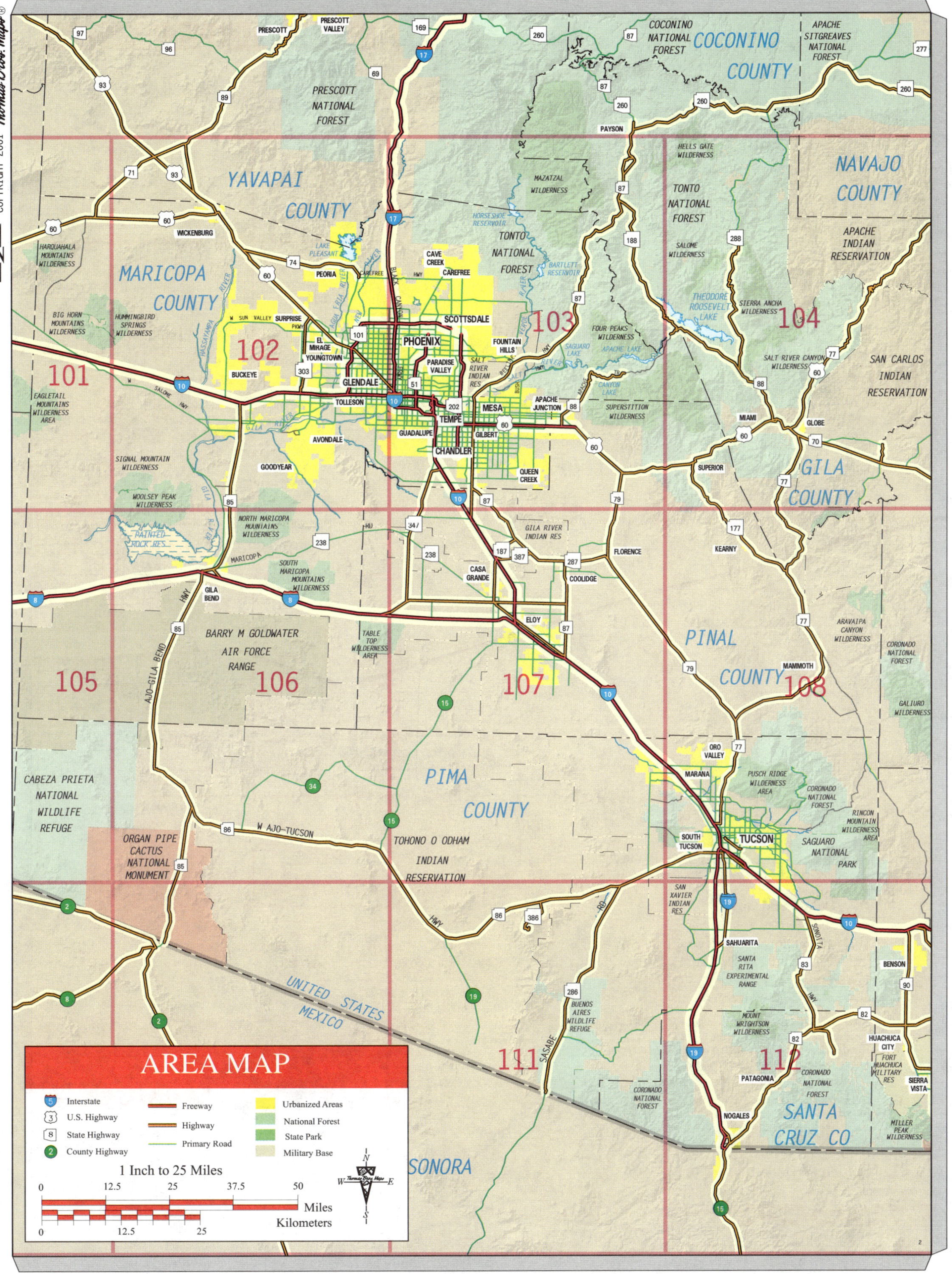

PHOENIX
INTRO

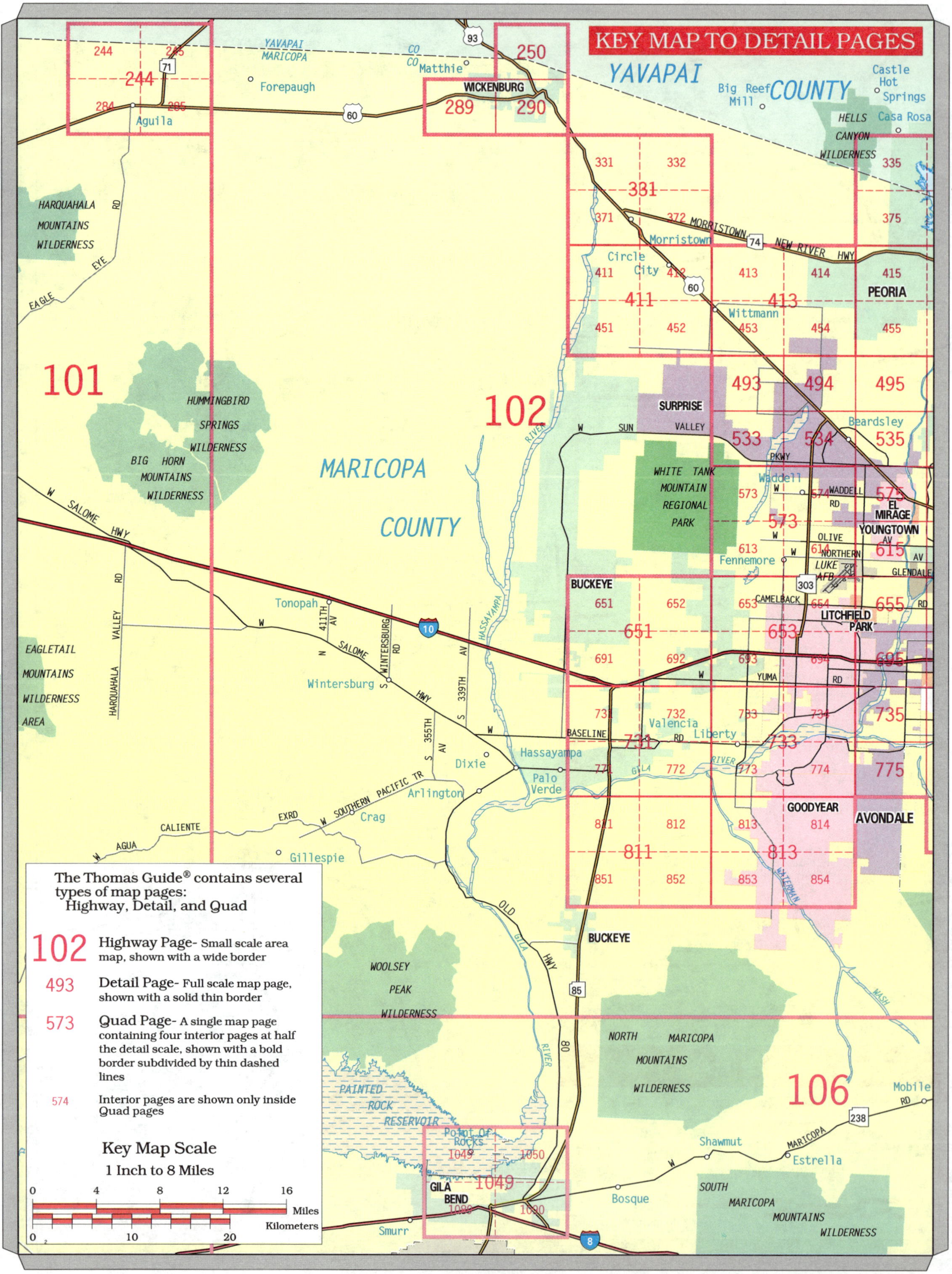

KEY MAP TO DETAIL PAGES

The Thomas Guide® contains several types of map pages: Highway, Detail, and Quad

102 Highway Page- Small scale area map, shown with a wide border

493 Detail Page- Full scale map page, shown with a solid thin border

573 Quad Page- A single map page containing four interior pages at half the detail scale, shown with a bold border subdivided by thin dashed lines

574 Interior pages are shown only inside Quad pages

Key Map Scale

1 Inch to 8 Miles

0 4 8 12 16 Miles

0 2 10 20 Kilometers

YAVAPAI COUNTY

MARICOPA COUNTY

101

102

106

WICKENBURG

SURPRISE

PEORIA

EL MIRAGE

YOUNGTOWN

LITCHFIELD PARK

GOODYEAR

AVONDALE

BUCKEYE

GILA BEND

PHOENIX

INTRO

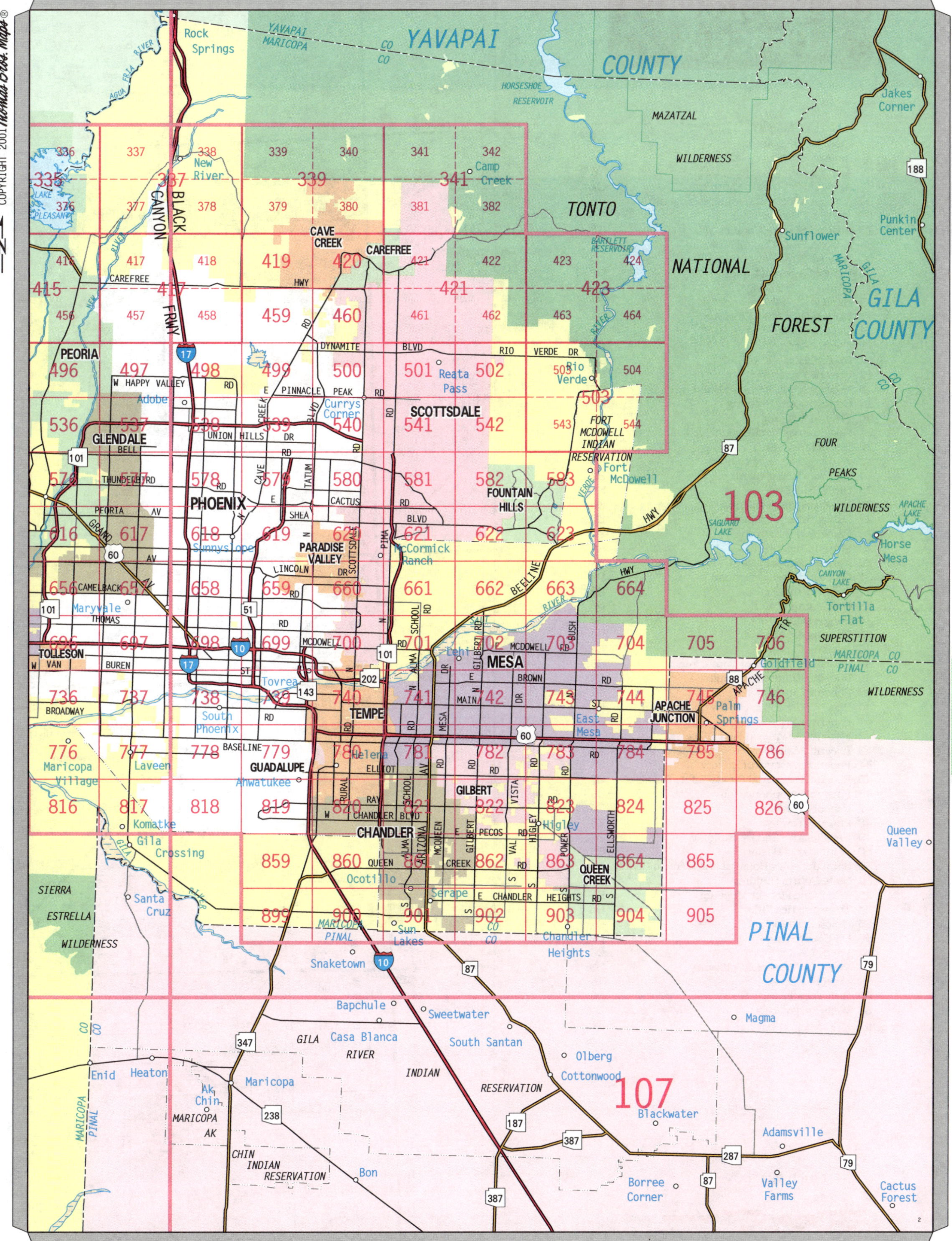
YAVAPAI
COUNTY
YAVAPAI
MARICOPA
Rock Springs
HORSESHOE RESERVOIR
MAZATZAL
WILDERNESS
TONTO
NATIONAL
FOREST
GILA COUNTY
Jakes Corner
Sunflower
Punkin Center
New River
Camp Creek
BLACK CANYON FRWY
CAVE CREEK
CAREFREE
BARTLETT RESERVOIR
PEORIA
GLENDALE
Adobe
Currys Corner
SCOTTSDALE
Reata Pass
Rio Verde
FORT MCDOWELL INDIAN RESERVATION
Fort McDowell
FOUNTAIN HILLS
FOUR PEAKS
WILDERNESS
103
SAGUARO LAKE
APACHE LAKE
Horse Mesa
CANYON LAKE
Tortilla Flat
SUPERSTITION
WILDERNESS
PHOENIX
Sunnyslope
PARADISE VALLEY
McCormick Ranch
Maryvale
TOLLESON
Tovrea
TEMPE
MESA
Lehi
APACHE JUNCTION
Goldfield
Palm Springs
East Mesa
South Phoenix
Maricopa Village
Laveen
GUADALUPE
Ahwatukee
Helena
GILBERT
CHANDLER
Higley
QUEEN CREEK
Komatke
Gila Crossing
Ocotillo
Serape
Sun Lakes
Chandler Heights
Queen Valley
SIERRA ESTRELLA WILDERNESS
Santa Cruz
Snaketown
PINAL COUNTY
Bapchule
Sweetwater
Magma
GILA RIVER INDIAN RESERVATION
Casa Blanca
South Santan
Olberg
Cottonwood
107
Blackwater
Adamsville
Enid
Heaton
Maricopa
Ak Chin
MARICOPA AK CHIN INDIAN RESERVATION
Bon
Borree Corner
Valley Farms
Cactus Forest

PHOENIX

INTRO

Downtown Phoenix

Points of Interest

No.	Name	Grid
1	America West Arena	E7
2	Arizona Center	E6
3	Arizona Department of Health Services	A6
4	Arizona Hall of Fame Museum	C7
5	Arizona Mining and Mineral Museum	B6
6	Arizona Public Service	E6
7	Arizona Science Center	E7
8	Arizona State Capitol Museum	A7
9	Arizona State Fairground	A3
10	Bank of America Building	D6
11	Bank One Building	E6
12	Bank One Ballpark	F7
13	Burton Barr Main Library	E4
14	Capital Center	B7
15	Capitol Annex	B6
16	Central Bus Station	E6
17	Crowne Plaza Hotel	E6
18	County Administration Building	D7
19	County Court Building	D7
20	Federal Building	D6
21	Good Samaritan Regional Medical Center	G4
22	Heard Museum	E3
23	Herberger Theater Center	E6
24	Highway Department	B7
25	Hilton Suites	E1
26	Hyatt Regency Phoenix	E6
27	Luhrs Tower Complex	E7
28	Municipal Building	D7
29	Museo Chicano	E6
30	National Bank Plaza	E1
31	Office of Attorney General	B7
32	Old Courthouse	D7
33	Orpheum Theater	D6
34	Phelps Dodge Tower	E2
35	Phoenix Art Museum	E4
36	Phoenix Center	E4
37	Phoenix Chamber of Commerce	E6
38	Phoenix Children's Hospital	G4
39	Phoenix City Hall	D7
40	Phoenix Civic Plaza Convention Center	E6
41	Phoenix Corporate Tower	E1
42	Phoenix Downtown Post Office	E6
43	Phoenix Main Department of Motor Vehicles	A7
44	Phoenix Museum of History	E6
45	Phoenix Police and Public Safety Building	C7
46	Phoenix Symphony Hall	E6
47	Phoenix Theater	E4
48	Phoenix Towers	E3
49	Renaissance Square Building	D7
50	Saint Marys Basilica	E6
51	Saint Joseph's Hospital and Medical Center	D1
52	State Courts Building	B7
53	Telephone Pioneer Museum	E1
54	Transamerica Title	D6
55	Union Station	D7
56	US Courthouse	D6
57	Valley Center	E6
58	Veterans Memorial Coliseum	B3
59	Visitors Bureau	E6
60	Web Theater	F6
61	Wells Fargo Plaza	D7
62	YMCA	D6

Map Scale

1 Inch to 1600 Feet

0 .125 .25 .375 .50 Miles

0 .25 .50 Kilometers

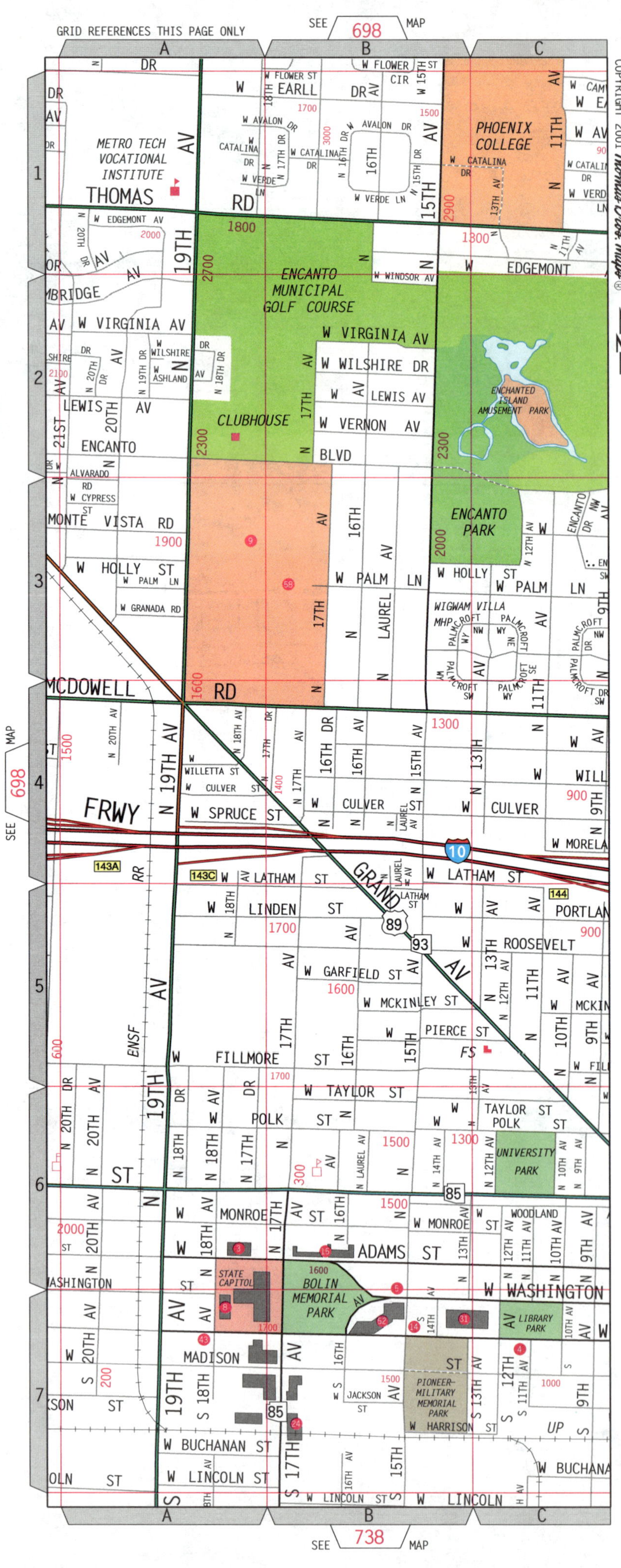

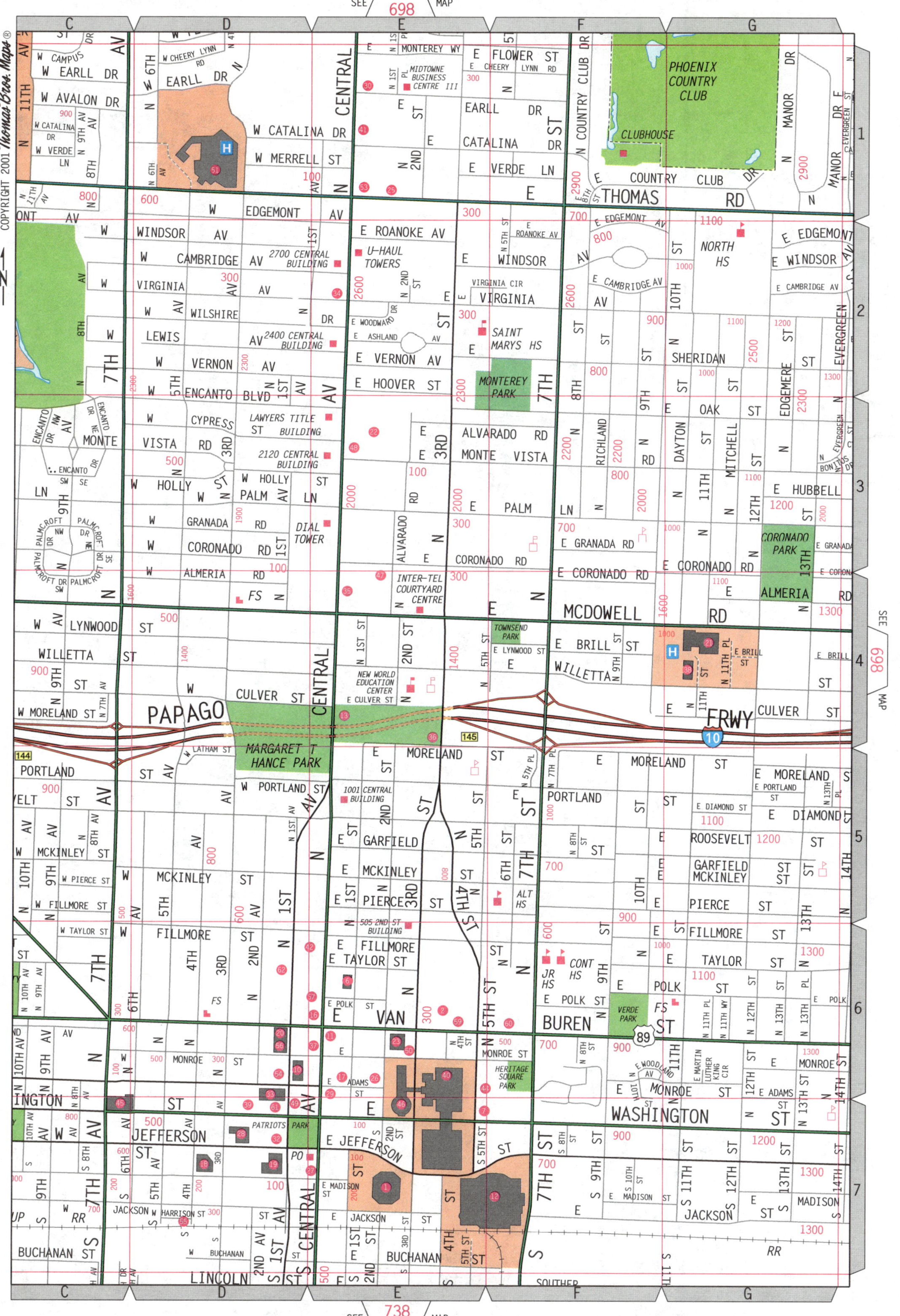

PHOENIX

INTRO

Phoenix Sky Harbor International Airport

Phoenix Sky Harbor International Airport is located approximately 4 miles from Downtown Phoenix. Sky Harbor International Airport is served by 18 major airlines and three commuter airlines. Nonstop service is available from Phoenix to 105 cities in the U.S. and around the world. America West and Southwest Airlines have major hub operations in Phoenix providing convenient connections to virtually any city in the U.S. Phoenix Sky Harbor International Airport has three passenger terminal buildings - Terminal 2, Terminal 3, and Terminal 4. Each terminal has its own parking garage, car rental facilities, shops, restaurants, services and ground transportation facilities. Convenient and no cost transportation between terminals is provided by an inter-terminal shuttle bus system.

SEE PAGE & GRID 739 D1

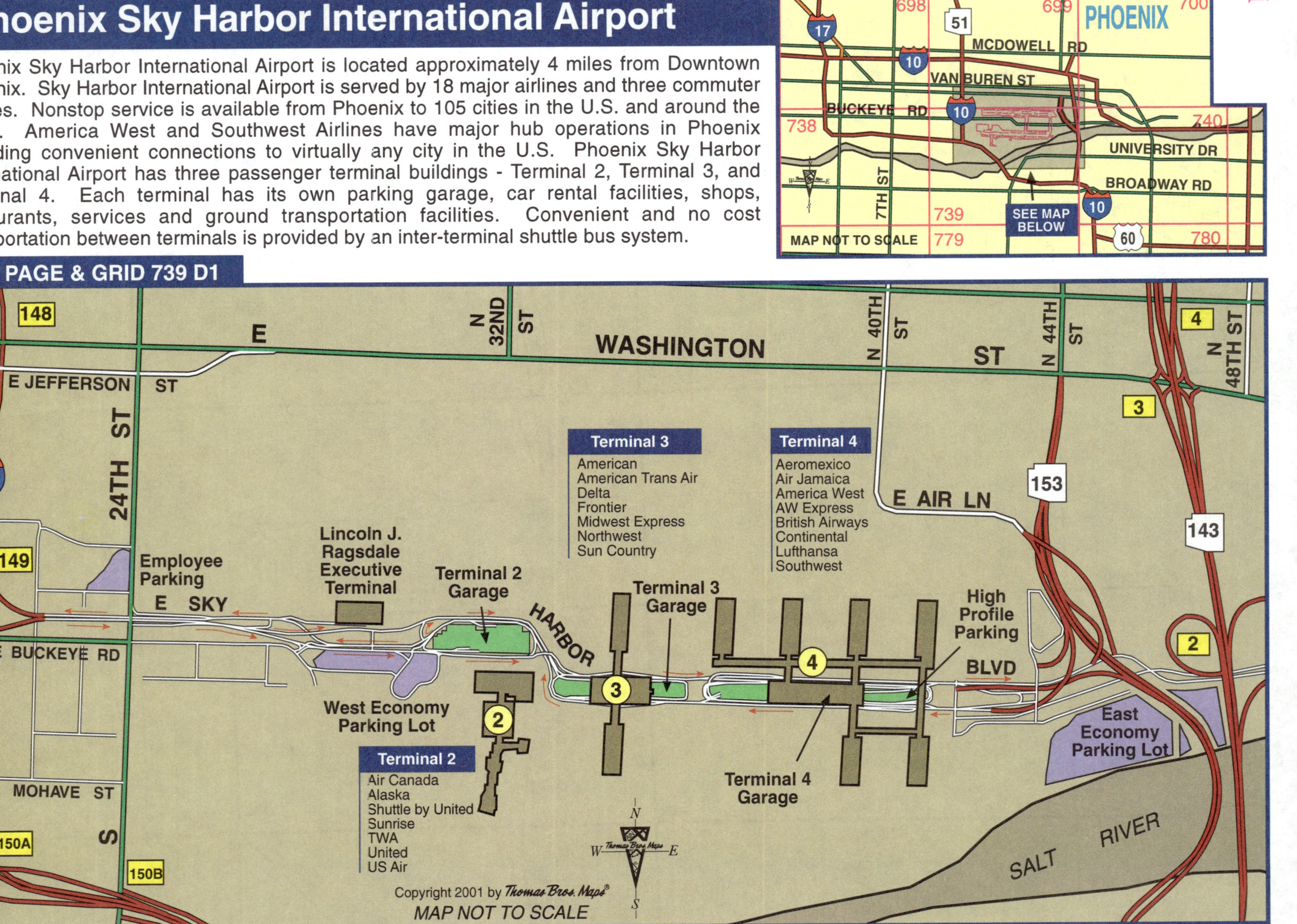

PHOENIX
Cities And Communities Index

Community Name	City Abbr.	County	ZIP Code	Page
ADOBE		MarC	85027	538
AHWATUKEE		MarC	85044	819
AGUA CALIENTE		MarC		105
AGUA FRIA		MarC	85335	575
AGUILA		MarC	85320	284
ALHAMBRA		MarC	85019	657
ANTHEM		MarC	85087	337
❖ APACHE JUNCTION	APJT	PinC	85220	745
ARLINGTON		MarC	85322	102
❖ AVONDALE	AVON	MarC	85326	813
BEARDSLEY		MarC	85375	534
BIG HORN		MarC		106
BOSQUE		MarC		106
❖ BUCKEYE	BUCK	MarC	85373	751
BUCKHORN		MarC	85206	743
BUMSTEAD		MarC	85335	615
CACTUS		MarC	85032	579
CAMEL		MarC		105
CAMP CREEK		MarC	85377	342
❖ CAREFREE	CARE	MarC	85377	420
CASHION		MarC	85353	735
❖ CAVE CREEK	CVCK	MarC	85337	420
❖ CHANDLER	CHAN	MarC	85224	821
CHANDLER HEIGHTS		MarC	85242	903
CITRUS PARK		MarC	85355	614
CIRCLE CITY		MarC	85342	412
COTTON CENTER		MarC		106
CRAG		MarC		102
CURRYS CORNER		MarC	85255	540
DIXIE		MarC		102
EAST MESA		MarC	85208	744
❖ EL MIRAGE	ELMG	MarC	85335	575
ESTRELLA		MarC		106
FALFA		MarC	85233	781
FENNEMORE		MarC	85355	614
FOREPAUGH		MarC		102
FORT MCDOWELL		MarC	85264	583
❖ FOUNTAIN HILLS	FTNH	MarC	85268	583
FOWLER		MarC	85043	697
FREEMAN		MarC		106
GERMANN		MarC	85242	863
❖ GILA BEND	GBND	MarC	85337	1090
GILA CROSSING		MarC		102
❖ GILBERT	GIL	MarC	85233	782
GILLESPIE		MarC		102
GLADDEN		MarC		101
❖ GLENDALE	GLEN	MarC	85304	617
GOLDFIELD		PinC	85290	706
❖ GOODYEAR	GDYR	MarC	85338	774
❖ GUADALUPE	GUAD	MarC	85283	780
HAMILTON CORNER		MarC	85249	861
HARMONY VILLA		MarC	85215	703
HARQUA		MarC		102
HASSAYAMPA		MarC		102
HELENA		MarC	85283	780
HIGHTOWN		MarC	85226	820
HIGLEY		MarC	85236	823
HORSE MESA		MarC		103
KAKA		MarC		106
KOMATKE		MarC	85339	817
KYRENE		MarC	85284	820
LAVEEN		MarC	85339	777
LEHI		MarC	85203	702
LIBERTY		MarC	85236	773
LITCHFIELD JUNCTION		MarC	85338	734
❖ LITCHFIELD PARK	LP	MarC	85340	655
-- MARICOPA COUNTY	MarC	MarC		
MARICOPA VILLAGE		MarC	85339	776
MARYVALE		MarC	85031	657
MATTHIE		MarC		102
MCCORMICK RANCH		MarC	85258	620
❖ MESA	MESA	MarC	85205	743
MIDWAY		MarC		106
MOBILE		MarC	85239	106
MONTEZUMA		MarC		105
MORRISTOWN		MarC	85342	371
NEW RIVER		MarC	85087	338
NORTON		MarC	85338	734
NORTONS CORNER		MarC	85296	822
OCOTILLO		MarC	85248	901
PALM SPRINGS		PinC	85220	745
PALO VERDE		MarC	85343	102
PAPAGO		MarC		105
❖ PARADISE VALLEY	PVAL	MarC	85253	660
❖ PEORIA	PEOR	MarC	85345	616
PERRYVILLE		MarC	85326	693
❖ PHOENIX	PHX	MarC	85201	618
PIEDRA		MarC		106
-- PINAL COUNTY	PinC	PinC		
POINT OF ROCKS		MarC	85337	1049
❖ QUEEN CREEK	QC	MarC	85242	864
REATA PASS		MarC	85255	501
RIO VERDE		MarC	85263	503
ROCKY POINT		MarC		106
SADDLE		MarC		101
SAN LUCY VILLAGE		MarC	85337	1090
SANTA MARIA		MarC	85043	737
❖ SCOTTSDALE	SCTS	MarC	85251	700
SENTINEL		MarC		105
SERAPE		MarC	85249	901
SHAWMUT		MarC		106
SMURR		MarC		106
SONORA TOWN		MarC	85296	822
SOUTH PHOENIX		MarC	85041	738
STANWIX		MarC		105
SUN CITY		MarC	85351	576
SUN CITY WEST		MarC	85375	535
SUNDAD		MarC		101
SUNFLOWER		MarC		103
SUN LAKES		MarC	85248	901
SUNNYSLOPE		MarC	85020	618
❖ SUPERIOR	SUPR	PinC	85273	104
❖ SURPRISE	SURP	MarC	85387	534
❖ TEMPE	TEMP	MarC	85282	740
❖ TOLLESON	TOL	MarC	85353	694
TONOPAH		MarC	85354	102
TOVREA		MarC	85034	739
TORTILLA FLAT		MarC	85290	103
TOTPITK		MarC		106
VALENCIA		MarC	85326	732
WADDELL		MarC	85379	574
WAYNE		MarC	85355	614
WEEDVILLE		MarC	85381	576
WEST CHANDLER		MarC	85226	820
WEST END		MarC	85037	656
WHITE TANKS		MarC	85335	575
❖ WICKENBURG	WICK	MarC	85390	290
WINTERSBURG		MarC		102
WITTMANN		MarC	85361	453
-- YAVAPAI COUNTY	YavC	YavC		
❖ YOUNGTOWN	YNTN	MarC	85335	575

❖ - Indicates Incorporated City

PHOENIX

INTRO

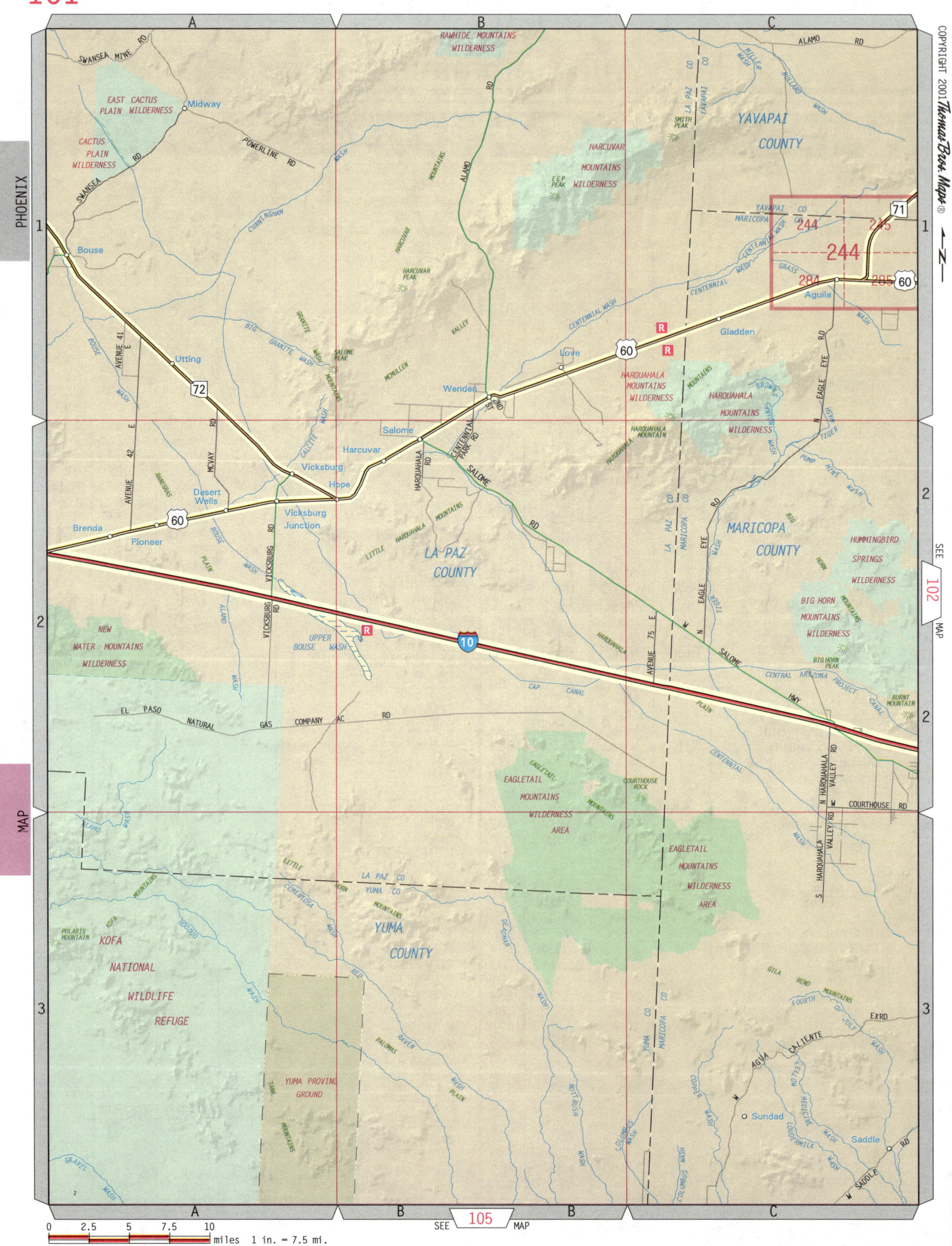
PHOENIX
MAP
RAWHIDE MOUNTAINS WILDERNESS
EAST CACTUS PLAIN WILDERNESS
Midway
CACTUS PLAIN WILDERNESS
POWERLINE RD
SWANSEA MINE RD
HARCUVAR MOUNTAINS WILDERNESS
ECP PEAK
SMITH PEAK
YAVAPAI COUNTY
ALAMO RD
Bouse
Utting
Wenden
Salome
Harcuvar
Vicksburg
Hope
Desert Wells
Vicksburg Junction
Brenda
Pioneer
Love
Gladden
Aguila
HARQUAHALA MOUNTAINS WILDERNESS
MARICOPA COUNTY
LA PAZ COUNTY
HUMMINGBIRD SPRINGS WILDERNESS
BIG HORN MOUNTAINS WILDERNESS
BIG HORN PEAK
BURNT MOUNTAIN
NEW WATER MOUNTAINS WILDERNESS
UPPER BOUSE WASH
EL PASO NATURAL GAS COMPANY RD
CENTRAL ARIZONA PROJECT CANAL
SALOME HWY
EAGLETAIL MOUNTAINS WILDERNESS AREA
COURTHOUSE ROCK
COURTHOUSE RD
YUMA COUNTY
KOFA NATIONAL WILDLIFE REFUGE
POLARIS MOUNTAIN
YUMA PROVING GROUND
GILA BEND MOUNTAINS
AGUA CALIENTE
Sundad
Saddle
60
72
10
71
244
245
284
285
SEE 102 MAP
SEE 105 MAP
0 2.5 5 7.5 10 miles 1 in. = 7.5 mi.

SEE 101 MAP

SEE 103 MAP

SEE 106 MAP

YAVAPAI COUNTY

MARICOPA COUNTY

PINAL COUNTY

Congress
Stanton
Richhill
Weaver Mountain
Sugarloaf Mountain
Wades Butte
Seal Mountain
Hassayampa River Canyon Wilderness
Sam Powell Peak
Prescott National Forest
Minnehaha
Wasson Peak
Twin Peaks
East Fort
South Fort
Castle Creek Wilderness
Lane Mountain
Watson Peak
Silver Mountain
Malpais Hill
Copperopolis
Table Mountain
Smallow Mountain
Morgan Butte
Denver Hill
Rock Hill
Sheep Mountain
Columbia
Flores
Forepaugh Peak
Matthie
Forepaugh
WICKENBURG
Castle Hot Springs
Dutch Butte
White Picacho
Big Reef Mill
Casa Rosa
Lake Pleasant Park
Lake Pleasant
Vulture Peak
Diamond Mountain
Morristown
Circle City
Wittmann
Black Canyon
PEORIA
Sun City West
Beardsley
SURPRISE
Trilby Wash Basin
EL MIRAGE
White Tank Mountain Regional Park
Waddell
YOUNGTOWN
Agua Fria
White Tanks
Sun City
Weedville
GLENDALE
Hummingbird Springs Wilderness
Fennemore
Wayne
Bumstead
Citrus Park
Alhambra
BUCKEYE
LITCHFIELD PARK
Maryvale
Tonopah
West End
PHOENIX
Saddle Mountain
Wintersburg
TOLLESON
Cashion
Fowler
Perryville
Litchfield Junction
Santa Maria
Palo Verde Nuclear Generating Station
Valencia
Liberty
Dixie
Norton
Hassayampa
Palo Verde
Arlington
Maricopa Village
Laveen
Estrella Mountain Park
Crag
Buckeye Hills Park
Komatke
Gila Crossing
Gillespie
Harqua
AVONDALE
Gila River Indian Reservation
Sierra Estrella Wilderness
Butterfly Mountain
Signal Mountain Wilderness
GOODYEAR
BUCKEYE
Santa Cruz
Montezuma Peak
Woolsey Peak
North Maricopa Mountains Wilderness
Woolsey Peak Wilderness

0 2.5 5 7.5 10 miles 1 in. = 7.5 mi.

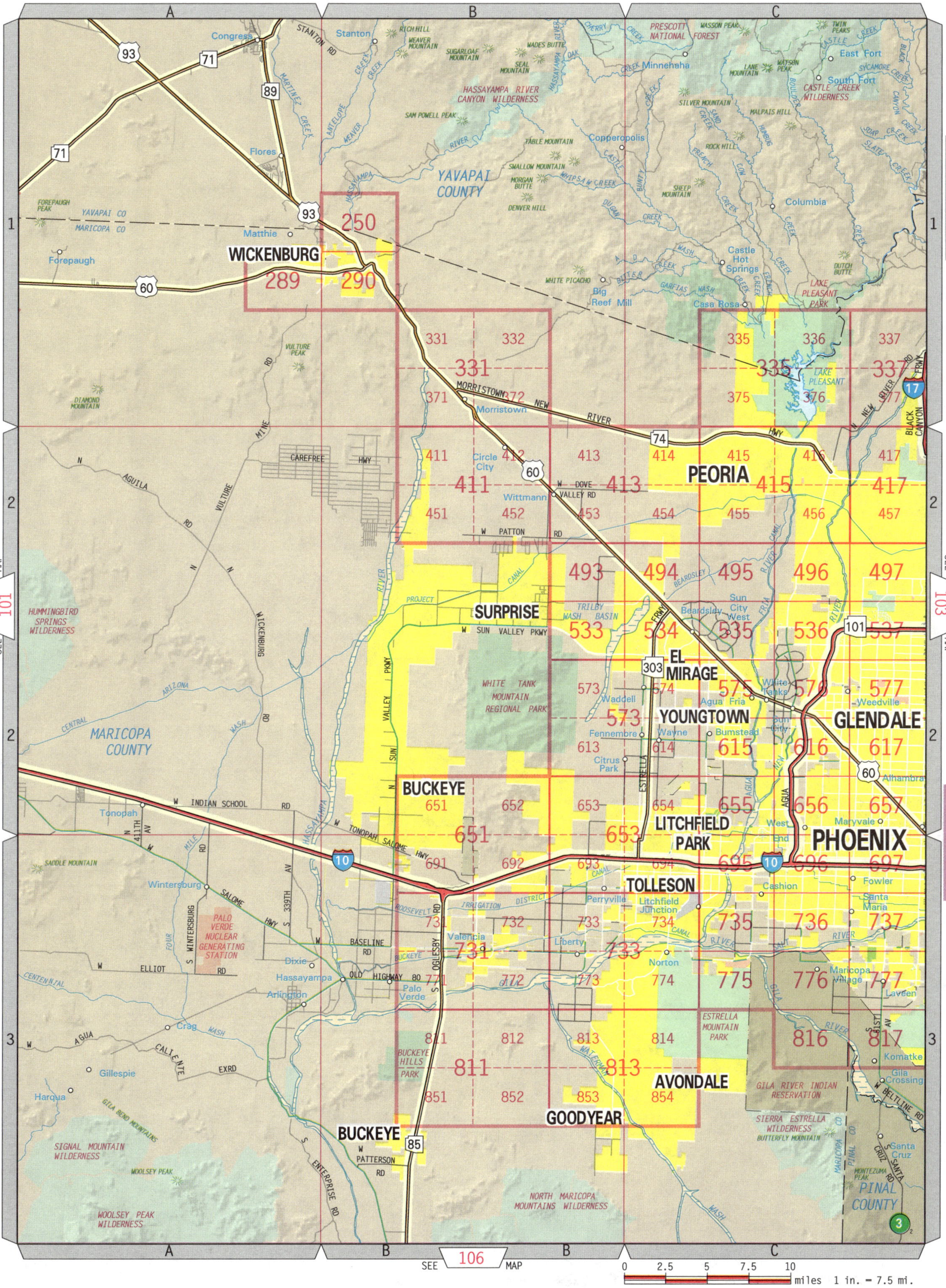

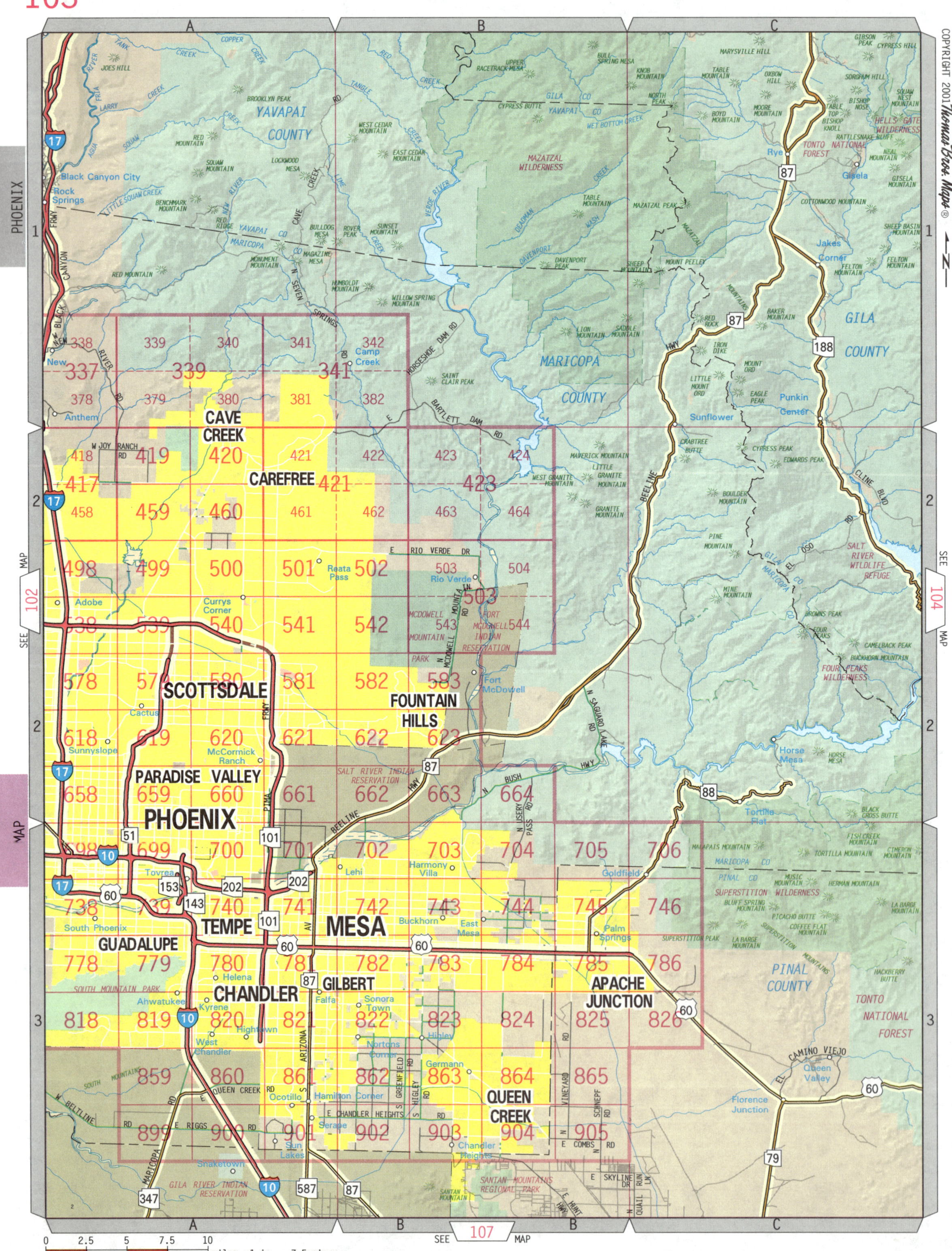

PHOENIX
MAP
COPYRIGHT 2001 Thomas Bros. Maps®
SEE 102 MAP
SEE 104 MAP
SEE 107 MAP
YAVAPAI COUNTY
MARICOPA COUNTY
GILA COUNTY
PINAL COUNTY
MAZATZAL WILDERNESS
TONTO NATIONAL FOREST
HELLS GATE WILDERNESS
FOUR PEAKS WILDERNESS
SUPERSTITION WILDERNESS
SALT RIVER WILDLIFE REFUGE
FORT McDOWELL INDIAN RESERVATION
SALT RIVER INDIAN RESERVATION
GILA RIVER INDIAN RESERVATION
SANTAN MOUNTAINS REGIONAL PARK
SOUTH MOUNTAIN PARK
McDOWELL MOUNTAIN PARK
Black Canyon City
Rock Springs
New River
Anthem
Camp Creek
Rye
Gisela
Jakes Corner
Punkin Center
Sunflower
Rio Verde
Fort McDowell
Reata Pass
Currys Corner
Adobe
Cactus
Sunnyslope
McCormick Ranch
Tortilla Flat
Horse Mesa
Goldfield
Lehi
Harmony Villa
Tovrea
South Phoenix
Buckhorn
East Mesa
Palm Springs
Helena
Falfa
Sonora Town
Kyrene
Ahwatukee
Hightown
West Chandler
Nortons Corner
Higley
Germann
Hamilton Corner
Ocotillo
Serape
Sun Lakes
Chandler Heights
Snaketown
Queen Valley
Florence Junction
CAVE CREEK
CAREFREE
SCOTTSDALE
FOUNTAIN HILLS
PARADISE VALLEY
PHOENIX
TEMPE
MESA
GUADALUPE
GILBERT
CHANDLER
APACHE JUNCTION
QUEEN CREEK
BEELINE HWY
RIO VERDE DR
BARTLETT DAM RD
HORSESHOE DAM RD
SEVEN SPRINGS RD
BLACK CANYON FRWY
PIMA FRWY
N BUSH HWY
N SAGUARO LAKE RD
E QUEEN CREEK RD
E RIGGS RD
E CHANDLER HEIGHTS RD
E COMBS RD
E SKYLINE DR
W BELTLINE RD
CAMINO VIEJO
17
87
188
88
60
101
202
51
153
143
10
587
347
79
0 2.5 5 7.5 10 miles 1 in. = 7.5 mi.

A B C

PHOENIX

MAP

SEE 103 MAP

Young
TONTO NATIONAL FOREST
HELLS GATE WILDERNESS
LOST CAMP MOUNTAIN
FULLER MESA
DIAMOND BUTTE
WOLVERTON MOUNTAIN
MCDONALD MOUNTAIN
SOLDIER CAMP MOUNTAIN
HOUDON MOUNTAIN
POTATO BUTTE
BREADPAN MOUNTAIN
ROBBERS ROOST MOUNTAIN
JIM SAM BUTTE
SQUAW PEAK
CHALK MOUNTAIN
JERKY BUTTE
PINE MOUNTAIN
LOOKOUT POINT
JUNIPER MOUNTAIN
MIDDLE MOUNTAIN
COPPER MOUNTAIN
PICTURE MOUNTAIN
MISTAKE PEAK
BEAR HEAD MOUNTAIN
BUCK PEAK
MCFADDEN PEAK
MCFADDEN HORSE MOUNTAIN
SALOME WILDERNESS
BONEYBACK PEAK
GREENBACK PEAK
RED BLANKET PEAK
HORSE MESA
THREE SISTERS MOUNTAIN
HOPKINS MOUNTAIN
TANNER PEAK
JACK MOUNTAIN
CENTER MOUNTAIN
BAKER MOUNTAIN
BLUE PEAK
CHUBB MOUNTAIN
SALOME MOUNTAIN
VICTORIA PEAK
METHODIST MOUNTAIN
THOMPSON MESA
CARR MOUNTAIN
CARR PEAK
GRANTHAM PEAK
AZTEC PEAK
SIERRA ANCHA WILDERNESS
ZIMMERMAN POINT
DUTCHWOMAN BUTTE
ASBESTOS POINT
COON CREEK BUTTE
SALT RIVER WILDLIFE REFUGE
HACKBERRY MOUNTAIN
THEODORE ROOSEVELT LAKE
Roosevelt
Grapevine
Hill
188
288
88
GLOBE-YOUNG HWY
CHERRY CREEK RD
YOUNG-HEBER
APACHE TR
CHERRY CREEK RD F S 203 RD
ROUND MOUNTAIN
CHERRY CREEK HILL
CROUCH MESA
GENTRY MOUNTAIN
SHELL MOUNTAIN
CATHOLIC PEAK
VOSBURG MESA
MIDDLETON MESA
COW FLAT MOUNTAIN
PENDLETON MESA
HOBBLE MESA
CASTLE PEAK
GUNSIGHT BUTTE
HORSE CAMP MESA
SOMBRERO PEAK
SALT RIVER CANYON WILDERNESS
REDMOND MOUNTAIN
GRANITE PEAK
ROCKINSTRAW MOUNTAIN
SALT RIVER MOUNTAINS
SQUAW PEAK
SALT RIVER PEAK
MARICOPA COUNTY
PINYON MOUNTAIN
CASTLE DOME
TWO BAR MOUNTAIN
GRANITE MOUNTAIN
SUPERSTITION WILDERNESS
APACHE HILL
BLACK MOUNTAIN
MARICOPA CO
PINAL CO
MOUND MOUNTAIN
PINTO PEAK
BARNES PEAK
WEBSTER MOUNTAIN
MURPHY RANCH MOUNTAIN
NUGGET MOUNTAIN
RICHMOND MOUNTAIN
BULL HILL
CRASH-UP MOUNTAIN
IRON MOUNTAIN
J.K. MOUNTAIN
MONTANA MOUNTAIN
GOVERNMENT HILL
GRIZZLY MOUNTAIN
CAMELBACK MOUNTAIN
FLAT TOP MOUNTAIN
MOONSHINE HILL
DAY PEAKS
JEWELL HILL
NEEDLE MOUNTAIN
MANITOU HILL
Radium
Burch
RAMBOZ PEAK
QUARTZITE PEAK
BLACK PEAK
BUCKEYE MOUNTAIN
Central Heights
Claypool
Inspiration
Miami Gardens
Midland City
COPPER HILL
Little Acres
MIAMI
GLOBE
GRANITE POINT
PEACHVILLE MOUNTAIN
FORTUNA PEAK
SIGNAL MOUNTAIN
KINGS CROWN PEAK
FIVE POINT MOUNTAIN
60
SUPERIOR
HUTTON PEAK
PINAL COUNTY
TONTO NATIONAL FOREST
MADERA PEAK
EAST MOUNTAIN
SIGNAL PEAK
PINAL PEAK
ICE HOUSE CANYON RD
SIX SHOOTER CANYON RD
RUSSELL RD
PICKETPOST MOUNTAIN
RAY RD
177
SLEEPING BEAUTY MOUNTAIN
TEAPOT MOUNTAIN
Ray
Sonora
WHITE CANYON WILDERNESS
GRANITE MOUNTAIN
SCOTT MOUNTAIN
HALEYS MOUNTAIN
PIONEER MOUNTAIN
OLD BALDY
EL CAPITAN MOUNTAIN
77
SWAMP CREEK MOUNTAIN
CHEDISKI PEAK
THE PYRAMIDS
CHEDISKI MOUNTAIN
HORSE CAMP MESA
GRASSHOPPER BUTTE
Grasshopper
NAVAJO COUNTY
Cibecue
LONELY MOUNTAIN
INDIAN ROUTE 12
NAVAJO CO
GILA CO
SPOTTED MOUNTAIN
BRUSH MOUNTAIN
BLUE HOUSE MOUNTAIN
Carrizo
BURKE MOUNTAIN
APACHE INDIAN RESERVATION
BLACK HILL
CIBECUE PEAK
DOUBLE BUTTES
BRUSHY TOP MOUNTAIN
INDIAN BUTTE
BEAR MOUNTAIN
ROCK HOUSE BUTTE
RAGGED TOP MOUNTAIN
WILD DOVE BUTTE
COYOTE BUTTE
BLACK MESA
COW PASTURE BUTTE
CANYON CREEK BUTTE
BECKERS BUTTE
ASH MOUNTAIN
PICACHO COLORADO
Seneca
GILA COUNTY
BULL BUTTE
HAYSTACK BUTTE
LITTLE BUTTE
TONTO NATIONAL FOREST
CAROL SPRING MOUNTAIN
BLACK MOUNTAIN
TIMBER CAMP MOUNTAIN
JACKSON BUTTE
STEER MOUNTAIN
ROCK SPRINGS BUTTE
CHALKY BUTTE
INDIAN LOOKOUT
DADS LOOKOUT
APACHE PEAKS
Bear Canyon Junction
CHROME BUTTE
CASSADORE MOUNTAIN
SONTAG MESA
GRANITE BUTTE
SAN CARLOS INDIAN RESERVATION
ANTELOPE HILLS
GILA CO
GRAHAM CO
OLD SAN CARLOS RD
INDIAN ROUTE 6
Cutter
HACKBERRY
MOUNT TRIPLET
INDIAN ROUTE 8
170
Peridot
BUCKET MOUNTAIN
HOG MOUNTAIN
HAYES MOUNTAINS
SAN CARLOS RESERVOIR
GRAHAM COUNTY
Coolidge Dam
COOLIDGE DAM RD

SEE 108 MAP

0 2.5 5 7.5 10 miles 1 in. = 7.5 mi.

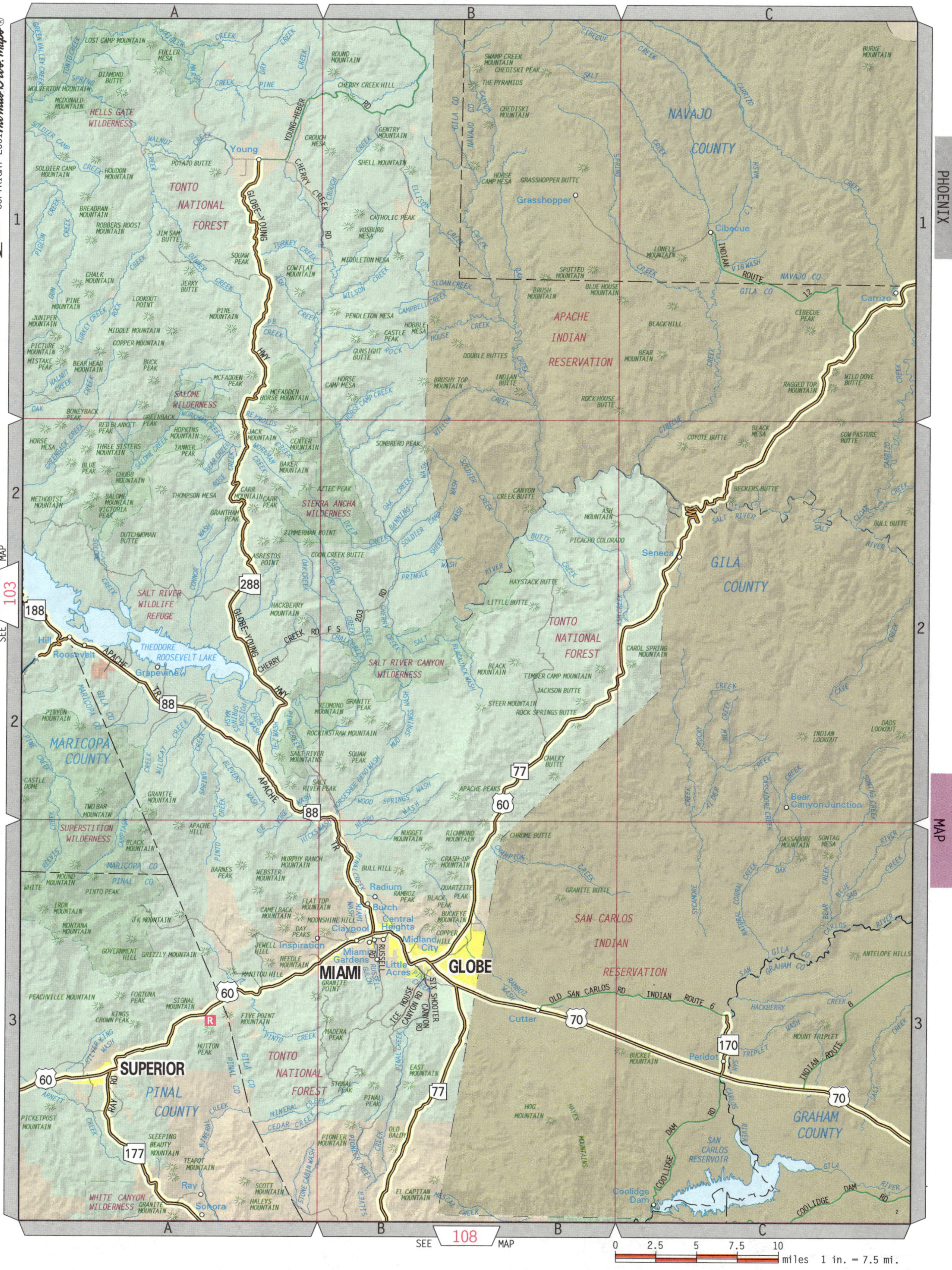

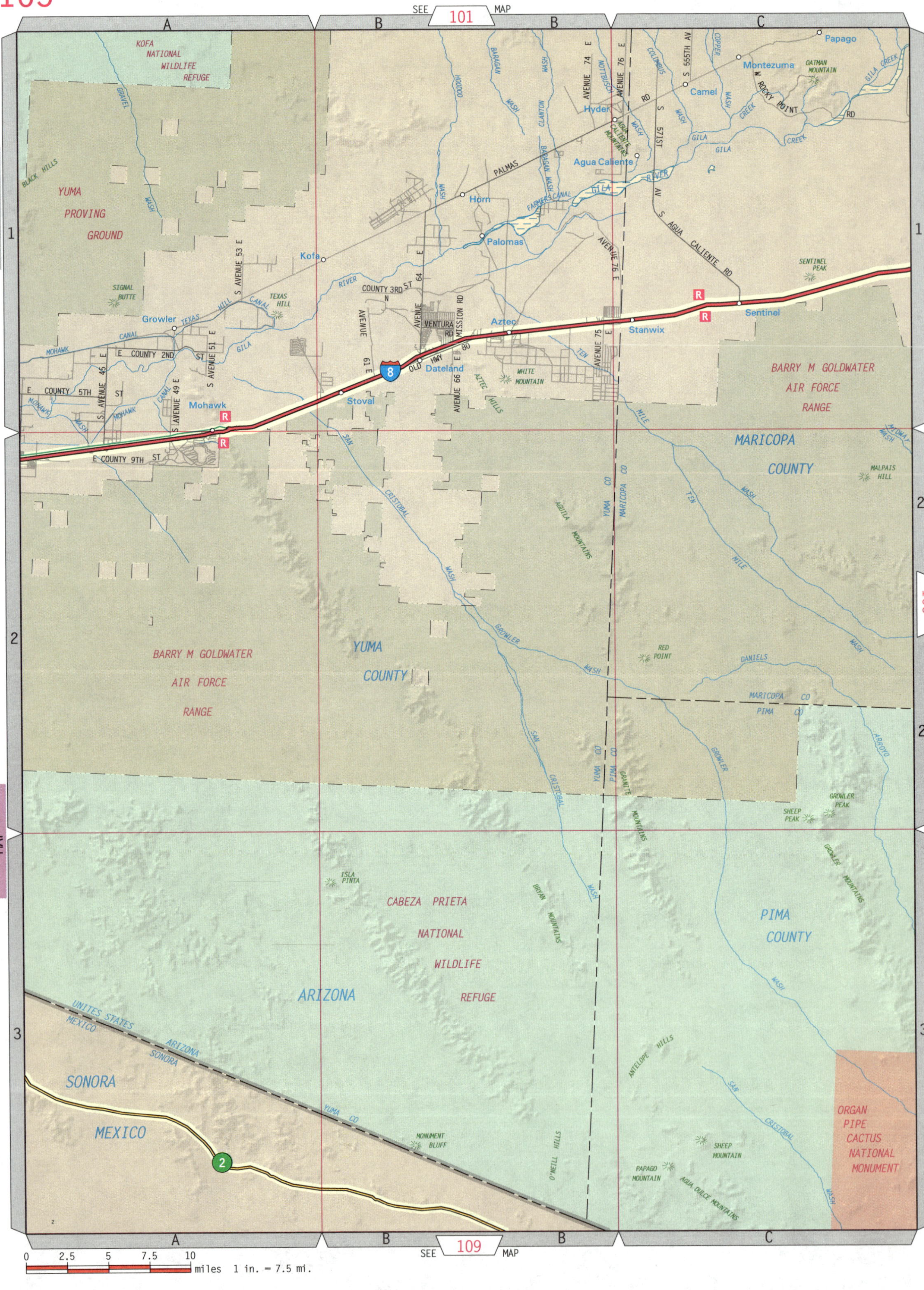

SEE 101 MAP

A B B C

PHOENIX

MAP

1

KOFA NATIONAL WILDLIFE REFUGE

GRAVEL

BLACK HILLS

YUMA PROVING GROUND

WASH

SIGNAL BUTTE

Growler

TEXAS HILL

S AVENUE 53 E

CANAL

MOHAWK

E COUNTY 2ND ST

S AVENUE 51 E

GILA

E COUNTY 5TH ST

S AVENUE 45 E

S AVENUE 49 E

MOHAWK

WASH

Mohawk

E COUNTY 9TH ST

Kofa

RIVER

COUNTY 3RD ST

N

AVENUE 61 E

AVENUE 64 E

VENTURA RD

MISSION RD

OLD HWY 80

Dateland

AVENUE 66 E

Stoval

8

AZTEC HILLS

WHITE MOUNTAIN

Aztec

HOODOO

BARAGAN WASH

WASH

CLANTON

PALMAS

Horn

BARAGAN WASH

FARMERS CANAL

Palomas

AVENUE 74 E

NOTTBUSCH

AVENUE 76 E

Hyder

AGUA CALIENTE MOUNTAINS

Agua Caliente

GILA RIVER

AVENUE 76 E

AVENUE 75

TEN MILE

Stanwix

COLUMBUS

S 555TH AV

COPPER WASH

Camel

Montezuma

Papago

OATMAN MOUNTAIN

W ROCKY POINT RD

GILA CREEK

S 571ST AV

S AGUA CALIENTE RD

Sentinel

SENTINEL PEAK

BARRY M GOLDWATER AIR FORCE RANGE

MARICOPA COUNTY

MOHAWK WASH

MALPAIS HILL

2

SAN CRISTOBAL WASH

AGUILA MOUNTAINS

YUMA CO

MARICOPA CO

TEN MILE WASH

WASH

GROWLER WASH

RED POINT

DANIELS

SEE 106 MAP

BARRY M GOLDWATER AIR FORCE RANGE

YUMA COUNTY

MARICOPA CO

PIMA CO

SAN CRISTOBAL

YUMA CO

PIMA CO

GRANITE MOUNTAINS

GROWLER

ARROYO

GROWLER PEAK

SHEEP PEAK

GROWLER MOUNTAINS

ISLA PINTA

CABEZA PRIETA NATIONAL WILDLIFE REFUGE

BRYAN MOUNTAINS

WASH

PIMA COUNTY

ARIZONA

3

UNITES STATES MEXICO

ARIZONA SONORA

SONORA

MEXICO

2

YUMA CO

MONUMENT BLUFF

O'NEILL HILLS

ANTELOPE HILLS

SAN CRISTOBAL

WASH

SHEEP MOUNTAIN

PAPAGO MOUNTAIN

AGUA DULCE MOUNTAINS

ORGAN PIPE CACTUS NATIONAL MONUMENT

SEE 109 MAP

0 2.5 5 7.5 10 miles 1 in. = 7.5 mi.

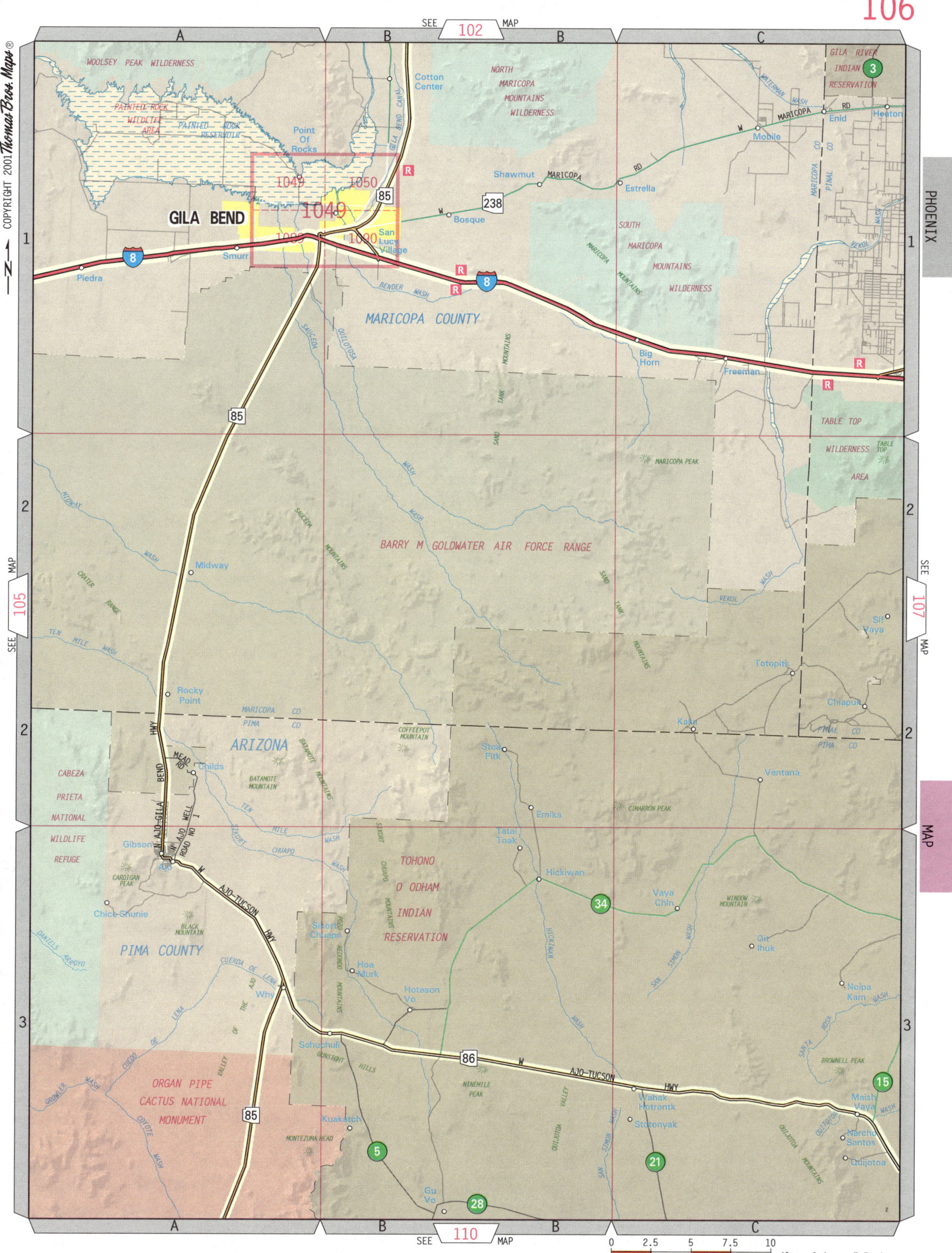

SEE 102 MAP
GILA BEND
WOOLSEY PEAK WILDERNESS
PAINTED ROCK WILDLIFE AREA
PAINTED ROCK RESERVOIR
Point Of Rocks
Cotton Center
NORTH MARICOPA MOUNTAINS WILDERNESS
GILA RIVER INDIAN RESERVATION
Mobile
Enid
Heaton
Shawmut
Estrella
Bosque
Smurr
Piedra
San Lucy Village
SOUTH MARICOPA MOUNTAINS WILDERNESS
BENDER WASH
MARICOPA COUNTY
Big Horn
Freeman
TABLE TOP WILDERNESS AREA
MARICOPA PEAK
BARRY M GOLDWATER AIR FORCE RANGE
Midway
CRATER RANGE
TEN MILE WASH
Rocky Point
SEE 105 MAP
SEE 107 MAP
PHOENIX
Sif Vaya
Totopitk
Chiapuk
Kaka
MARICOPA CO
PIMA CO
PINAL CO
ARIZONA
COFFEEPOT MOUNTAIN
BATAMOTE MOUNTAIN
Childs
Stoa Pitk
Ventana
Emika
CIMARRON PEAK
CABEZA PRIETA NATIONAL WILDLIFE REFUGE
Gibson
Ajo
CARDIGAN PEAK
Tatai Toak
Hickiwan
TOHONO O ODHAM INDIAN RESERVATION
Vaya Chin
WINDOW MOUNTAIN
Chico Shunie
BLACK MOUNTAIN
Sikort Chuapo
Oit Ihuk
PIMA COUNTY
Hoa Murk
Why
Hotason Vo
Noipa Kam
Schuchuli
AJO-TUCSON HWY
ORGAN PIPE CACTUS NATIONAL MONUMENT
NINEMILE PEAK
BROWNELL PEAK
Wahak Hotrontk
Maish Vaya
Kuakatch
Stotonyak
Narcho Santos
MONTEZUMA HEAD
Quijotoa
Gu Vo
SEE 110 MAP
0 2.5 5 7.5 10 miles 1 in. = 7.5 mi.

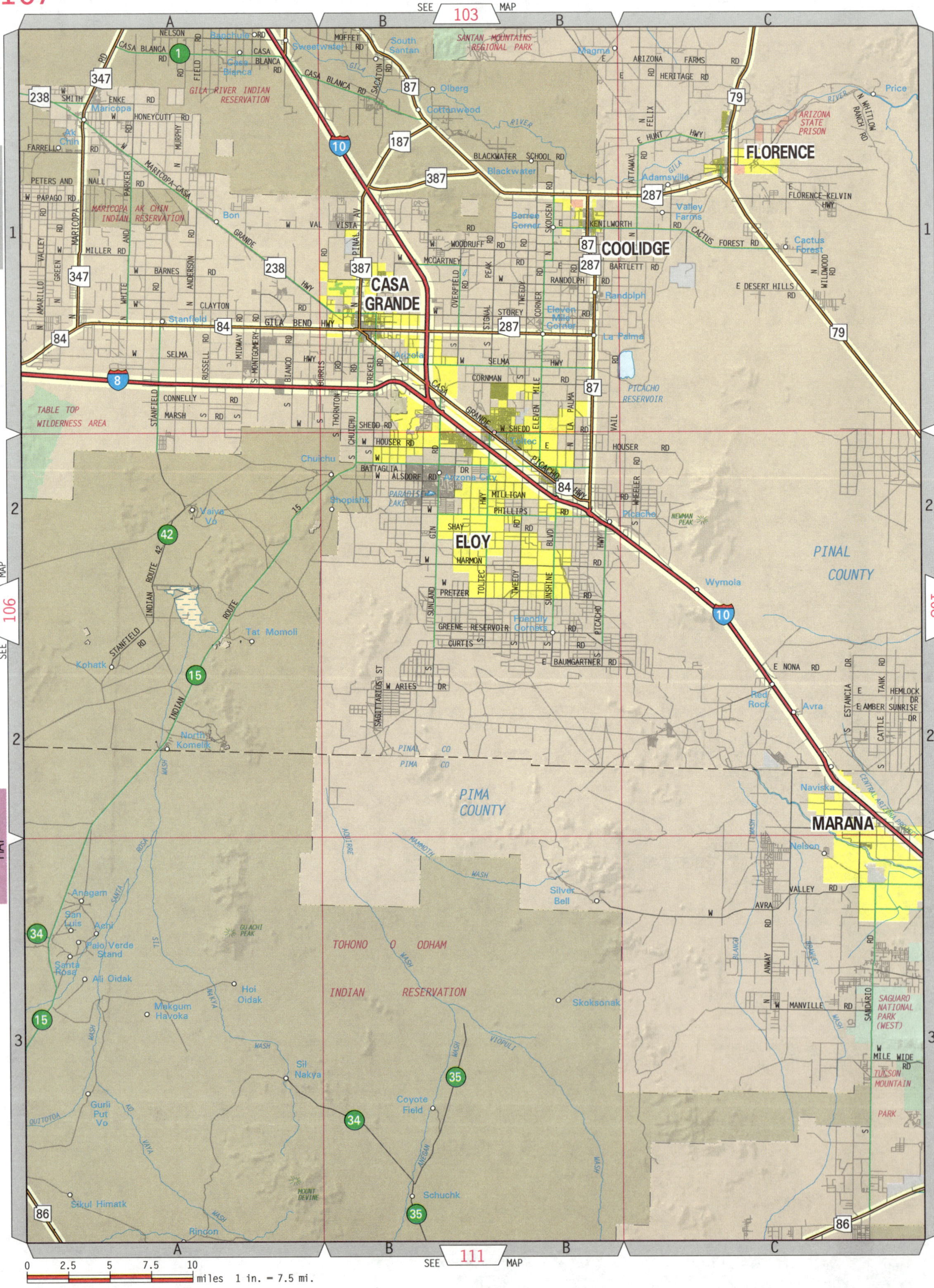

SEE 103 MAP

PHOENIX

FLORENCE

COOLIDGE

CASA GRANDE

ELOY

MARANA

PINAL COUNTY

PIMA COUNTY

GILA RIVER INDIAN RESERVATION

MARICOPA AK CHIN INDIAN RESERVATION

SANTAN MOUNTAINS REGIONAL PARK

ARIZONA STATE PRISON

TABLE TOP WILDERNESS AREA

PICACHO RESERVOIR

TOHONO O ODHAM INDIAN RESERVATION

SAGUARO NATIONAL PARK (WEST)

TUCSON MOUNTAIN PARK

Nelson, Casa Blanca, Sacaton, South Santan, Sweetwater, Olberg, Cottonwood, Magma, Price, Maricopa, Ak Chin, Blackwater, Bon, Adamsville, Valley Farms, Cactus Forest, Bonee Corner, Randolph, Stanfield, Eleven Mile Corner, La Palma, Arizola, Toltec, Arizona City, Chuichu, Shopishk, Paradise Lake, Picacho, Newman Peak, Wymola, Vaiva Vo, Tat Momoli, Kohatk, North Komelik, Friendly Corners, Red Rock, Avra, Naviska, Nelson, Silver Bell, Anegam, San Luis, Achi, Palo Verde Stand, Santa Rosa, Ali Oidak, Hoi Oidak, Makgum Havoka, Skoksonak, Sil Nakya, Coyote Field, Gurli Put Vo, Guachi Peak, Mount Devine, Schuchk, Sikul Himatk, Rincon

Roads: Interstate 10, Interstate 8; routes 1, 15, 34, 35, 42, 79, 84, 86, 87, 187, 238, 287, 347, 387; Casa Blanca Rd, Smith Enke Rd, Honeycutt Rd, Farrell Rd, Peters and Nall Rd, W Papago Rd, Miller Rd, W Barnes Rd, Clayton Rd, Gila Bend Hwy, Selma Hwy, Connelly Rd, Marsh Rd, Maricopa-Casa Grande Hwy, Val Vista Rd, Woodruff Rd, McCartney Rd, Storey Rd, Blackwater School Rd, Arizona Farms Rd, Heritage Rd, Hunt Hwy, Kenilworth Rd, Bartlett Rd, Florence-Kelvin Hwy, Cactus Forest Rd, E Desert Hills Rd, Cornman Rd, Shedd Rd, Houser Rd, Battaglia Dr, Alsdorf Rd, Milligan Rd, Phillips Rd, Shay Rd, Harmon Rd, Pretzer Rd, Greene Reservoir Rd, Curtis Rd, Baumgartner Rd, W Aries Dr, Sagittarius St, Casa Grande-Picacho Hwy, E Nona Rd, E Amber Sunrise Dr, Hemlock Dr, Valley Rd, Avra Valley Rd, Manville Rd, Sandario Rd, W Mile Wide Rd, Indian Route 15, Indian Route 42, Stanfield Rd, Central Arizona Project

Washes: Gila River, Santa Rosa Wash, Aguirre Wash, Mammoth Wash, Vaiva Wash, Viopuli Wash, Quitotoa Wash, Brawley Wash, Blanco Wash, Los Robles Wash

SEE 106 MAP

SEE 108 MAP

SEE 111 MAP

0 2.5 5 7.5 10 miles 1 in. = 7.5 mi.

SEE 104 MAP

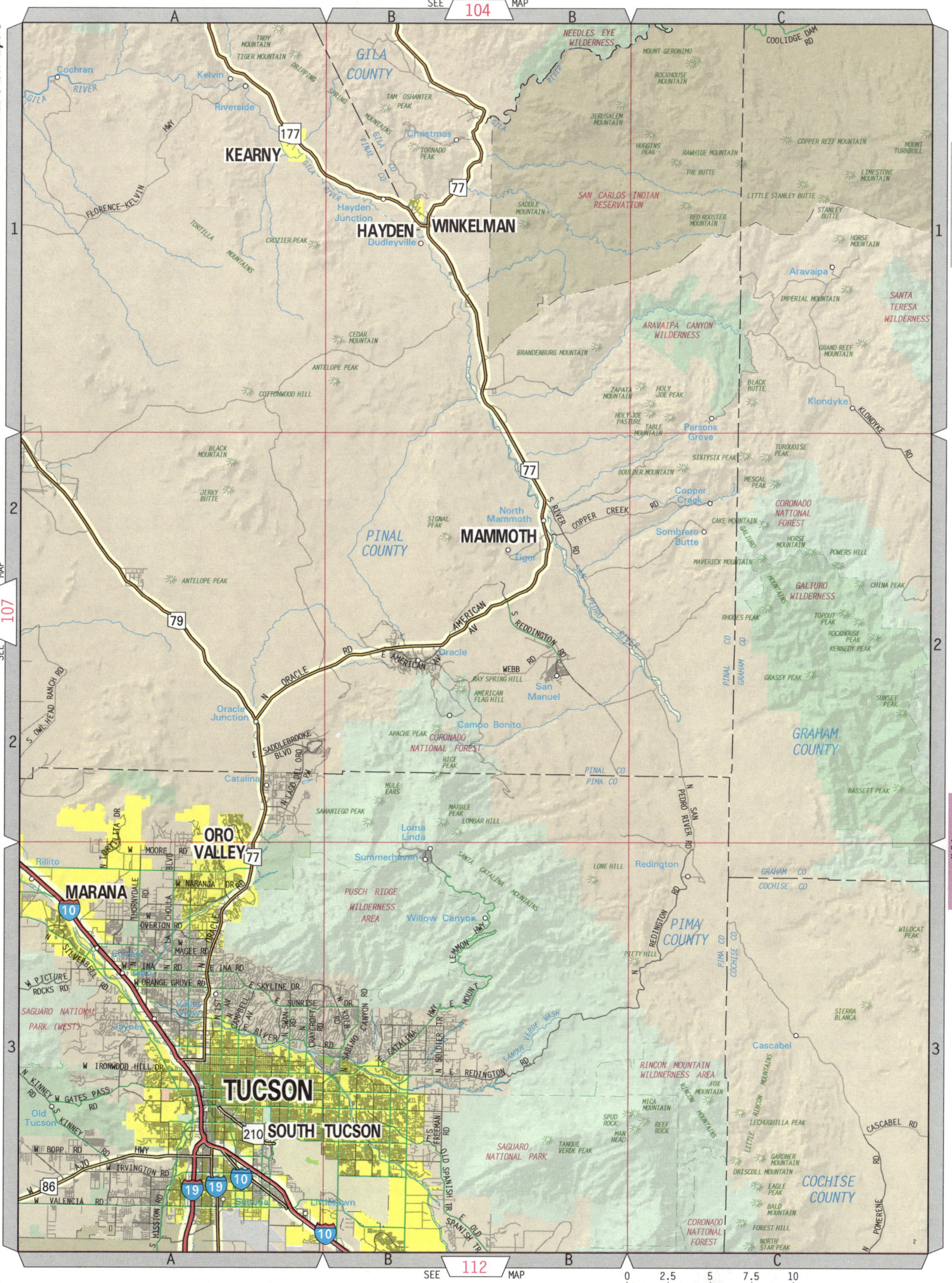

SEE 107 MAP

PHOENIX

MAP

A B B C

1 2 2 3

KEARNY
HAYDEN
WINKELMAN
MAMMOTH
ORO VALLEY
MARANA
TUCSON
SOUTH TUCSON

GILA COUNTY
PINAL COUNTY
PIMA COUNTY
GRAHAM COUNTY
COCHISE COUNTY

Cochran
Kelvin
Riverside
Christmas
Hayden Junction
Dudleyville
Aravaipa
Klondyke
Parsons Grove
Copper Creek
Sombrero Butte
North Mammoth
Tiger
Oracle
San Manuel
Oracle Junction
Camp Bonito
Catalina
Loma Linda
Summerhaven
Redington
Willow Canyon
Rillito
Cortaro
Valley View
Jaynes
Old Tucson
Cascabel
Littletown

GILA RIVER
SAN PEDRO RIVER
NEEDLES EYE WILDERNESS
SAN CARLOS INDIAN RESERVATION
ARAVAIPA CANYON WILDERNESS
SANTA TERESA WILDERNESS
CORONADO NATIONAL FOREST
GALIURO WILDERNESS
PUSCH RIDGE WILDERNESS AREA
RINCON MOUNTAIN WILDERNESS AREA
SAGUARO NATIONAL PARK
SAGUARO NATIONAL PARK (WEST)
SANTA CATALINA MOUNTAINS
GALIURO MOUNTAINS
RINCON MOUNTAINS
LITTLE RINCON MOUNTAINS
TORTILLA MOUNTAINS

TROY MOUNTAIN
TIGER MOUNTAIN
TAM O'SHANTER PEAK
TORNADO PEAK
CROZIER PEAK
CEDAR MOUNTAIN
ANTELOPE PEAK
COTTONWOOD HILL
BLACK MOUNTAIN
JERKY BUTTE
SIGNAL PEAK
APACHE PEAK
RICE PEAK
MULE EARS
SAMANIEGO PEAK
MARBLE PEAK
LOMBAR HILL
RAY SPRING HILL
AMERICAN FLAG HILL
MOUNT GERONIMO
ROCKHOUSE MOUNTAIN
JERUSALEM MOUNTAIN
HUGGINS PEAK
RAWHIDE MOUNTAIN
THE BUTTE
SADDLE MOUNTAIN
RED ROOSTER MOUNTAIN
COPPER REEF MOUNTAIN
MOUNT TURNBULL
LIMESTONE MOUNTAIN
LITTLE STANLEY BUTTE
STANLEY BUTTE
HORSE MOUNTAIN
IMPERIAL MOUNTAIN
GRAND REEF MOUNTAIN
BRANDENBURG MOUNTAIN
ZAPATA MOUNTAIN
HOLY JOE PEAK
HOLY JOE PASTURE
TABLE MOUNTAIN
BLACK BUTTE
SIXTYSIX PEAK
TURQUOISE PEAK
BOULDER MOUNTAIN
MESCAL PEAK
CAKE MOUNTAIN
POWERS HILL
MAVERICK MOUNTAIN
CHINA PEAK
RHODES PEAK
TOPOUT PEAK
ROCKHOUSE PEAK
KENNEDY PEAK
GRASSY PEAK
SUNSET PEAK
BASSETT PEAK
LONE HILL
PIETY HILL
WILDCAT PEAK
SIERRA BLANCA
FOX MOUNTAIN
MICA MOUNTAIN
SPUD ROCK
MAN HEAD
REEF ROCK
TANQUE VERDE PEAK
LECHUGUILLA PEAK
GARDNER MOUNTAIN
DRISCOLL MOUNTAIN
EAGLE PEAK
BALD MOUNTAIN
FOREST HILL
NORTH STAR PEAK

177 77 79 77 210 86 10 19 19 10 10

COOLIDGE DAM RD
FLORENCE-KELVIN HWY
COPPER CREEK RD
S RIVER RD
S REDDINGTON RD
WEBB RD
AMERICAN AV
N ORACLE RD
E SADDLEBROOKE BLVD
N LAGO DEL ORO PKWY
S OWLHEAD RANCH RD
KLONDYKE RD
N SAN PEDRO RIVER RD
N REDINGTON RD
CASCABEL RD
POMERENE RD
N TORTOLITA DR
W MOORE RD
W NARANJA DR
N THORNYDALE RD
W OVERTON RD
W MAGEE RD
W INA RD
W ORANGE GROVE RD
W PICTURE ROCKS RD
N SILVERBELL RD
E SKYLINE DR
E SUNRISE DR
E RIVER RD
N SWAN RD
N CRAYCROFT RD
N KOLB RD
N SABINO CANYON RD
CATALINA HWY
N SOLDIER TR
E REDINGTON RD
E MOUNT LEMMON HWY
TANQUE VERDE WASH
W IRONWOOD HILL DR
N KINNEY RD
W GATES PASS RD
S KINNEY RD
W BOPP RD
AJO HWY
W IRVINGTON RD
W VALENCIA RD
S MISSION RD
S FREEMAN RD
OLD SPANISH TR

PINAL CO
PIMA CO
GRAHAM CO
COCHISE CO

SEE 112 MAP

0 2.5 5 7.5 10 miles 1 in. = 7.5 mi.

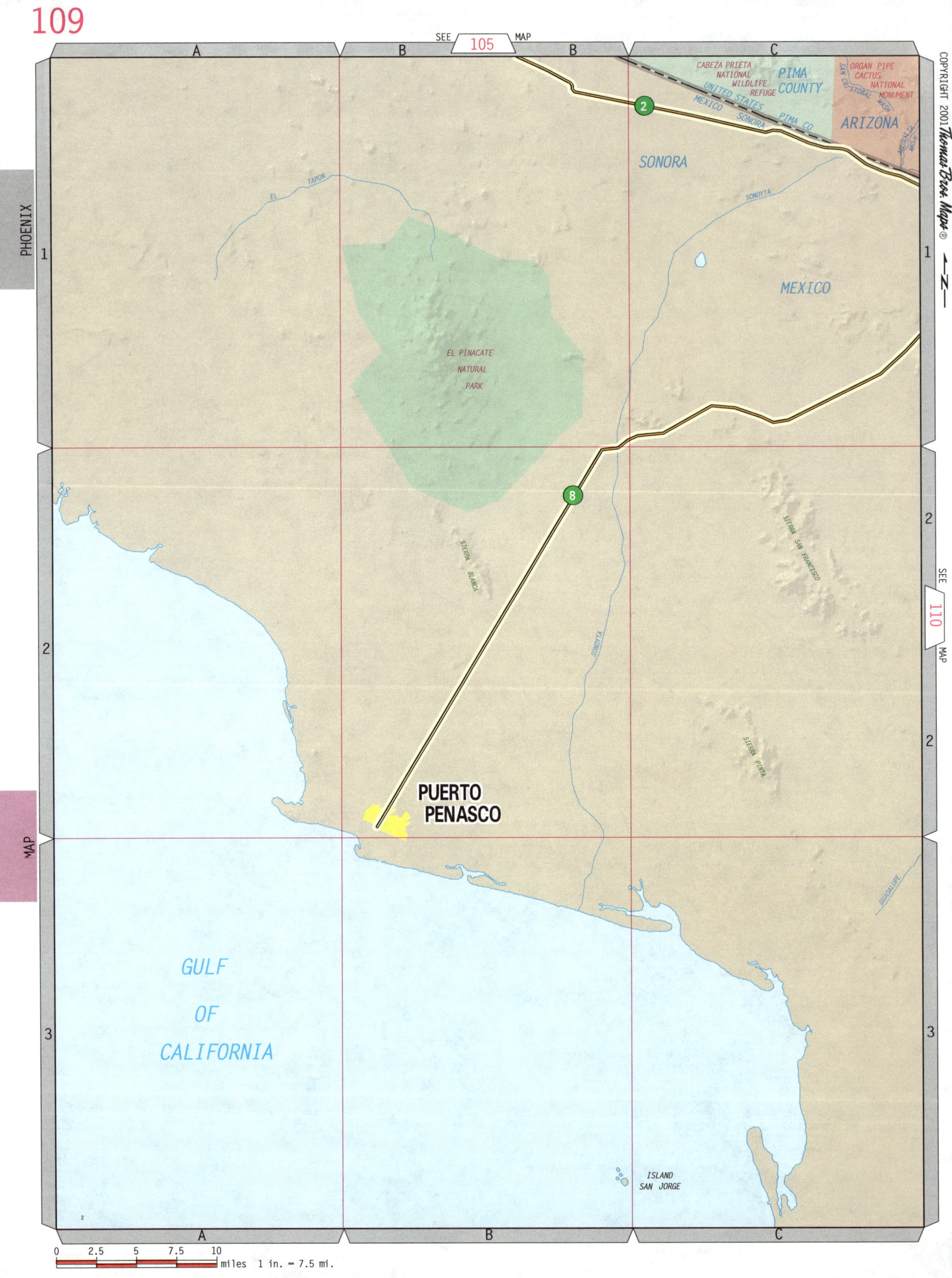
SEE 105 MAP
A
B
B
C
CABEZA PRIETA NATIONAL WILDLIFE REFUGE
PIMA COUNTY
ORGAN PIPE CACTUS NATIONAL MONUMENT
UNITED STATES
MEXICO
SONORA
PIMA CO
ARIZONA
2
SONORA
EL TAPON
SONOYTA
MEXICO
PHOENIX
1
EL PINACATE NATURAL PARK
8
SIERRA BLANCA
SIERRA SAN FRANCISCO
SEE 110 MAP
SONOYTA
2
SIERRA PINTA
PUERTO PENASCO
MAP
GUADALUPE
GULF OF CALIFORNIA
3
ISLAND SAN JORGE
A
B
C
0 2.5 5 7.5 10
miles 1 in. = 7.5 mi.

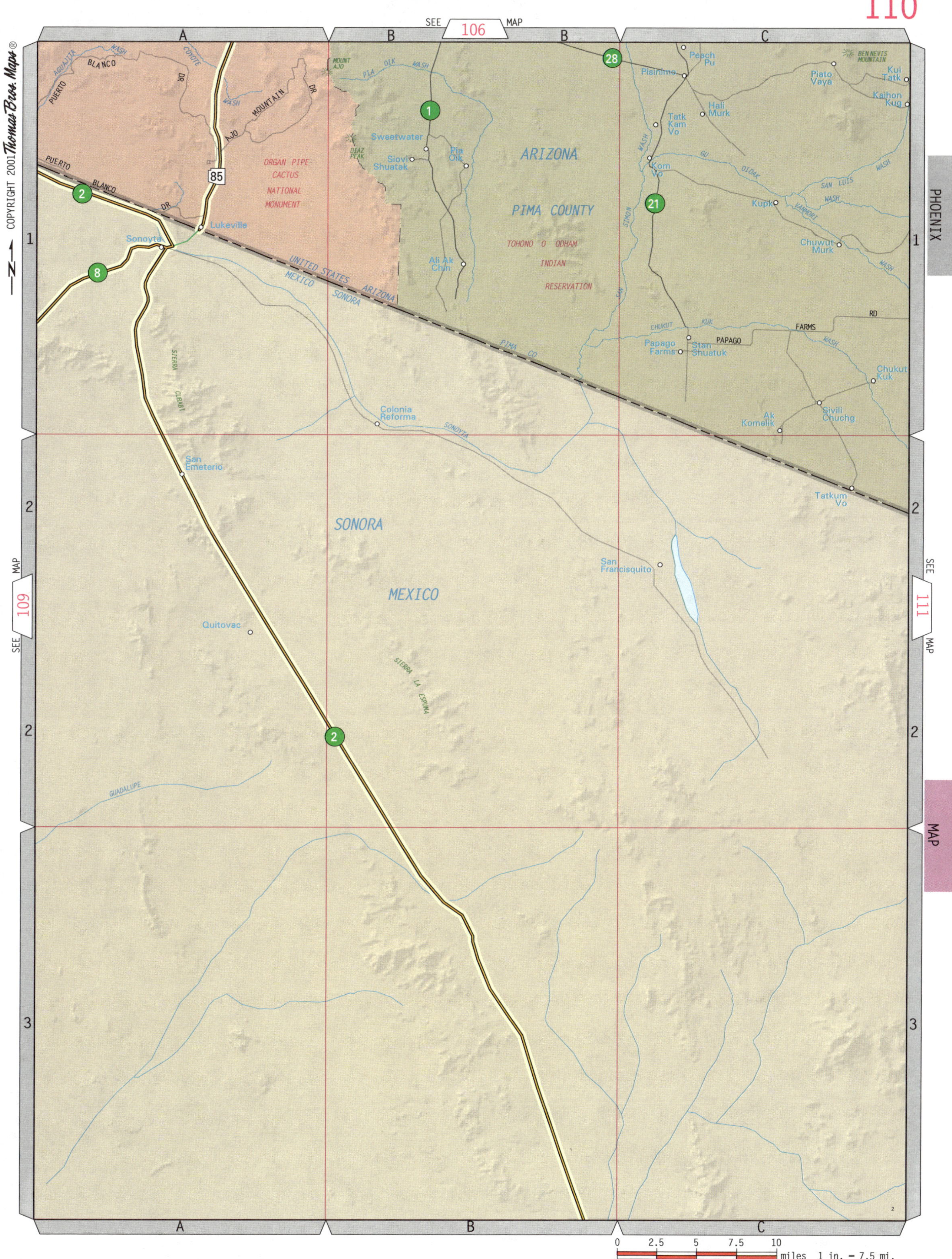
SEE 106 MAP
A
B
B
C
AGUAJITA
WASH
BLANCO
PUERTO
COYOTE
DR
WASH
AJO
MOUNTAIN
DR
MOUNT AJO
PIA OIK WASH
28
Peach Pu
Pisinimo
Pisinimo
Pirato Vaya
BEN NEVIS MOUNTAIN
Kui Tatk
Kaihon Kug
1
Sweetwater
Hali Murk
Tatk Kam Vo
DIAZ PEAK
Siovi Shuatak
Pia Oik
ARIZONA
WASH
Kom Vo
GU
OIDAK
WASH
PUERTO
BLANCO
DR
85
ORGAN PIPE
CACTUS
NATIONAL
MONUMENT
2
PIMA COUNTY
21
SAN LUIS
WASH
Kupk
VAMORI
Lukeville
Sonoyta
TOHONO O ODHAM
INDIAN
RESERVATION
SIMON
Chuwut Murk
WASH
8
Ali Ak Chin
UNITED STATES
ARIZONA
MEXICO
SONORA
SAN
RD
CHUKUT
KUK
FARMS
PAPAGO
Papago Farms
Stan Shuatuk
WASH
PIMA CO
Chukut Kuk
SIERRA
CUBABI
Colonia Reforma
SONOYTA
Ak Komelik
Sivili Chuchg
San Emeterio
Tatkum Vo
SONORA
San Francisquito
MEXICO
SEE 109 MAP
SEE 111 MAP
Quitovac
SIERRA LA ESPUMA
2
GUADALUPE
PHOENIX
MAP
1
2
3
0
2.5
5
7.5
10
miles 1 in. = 7.5 mi.

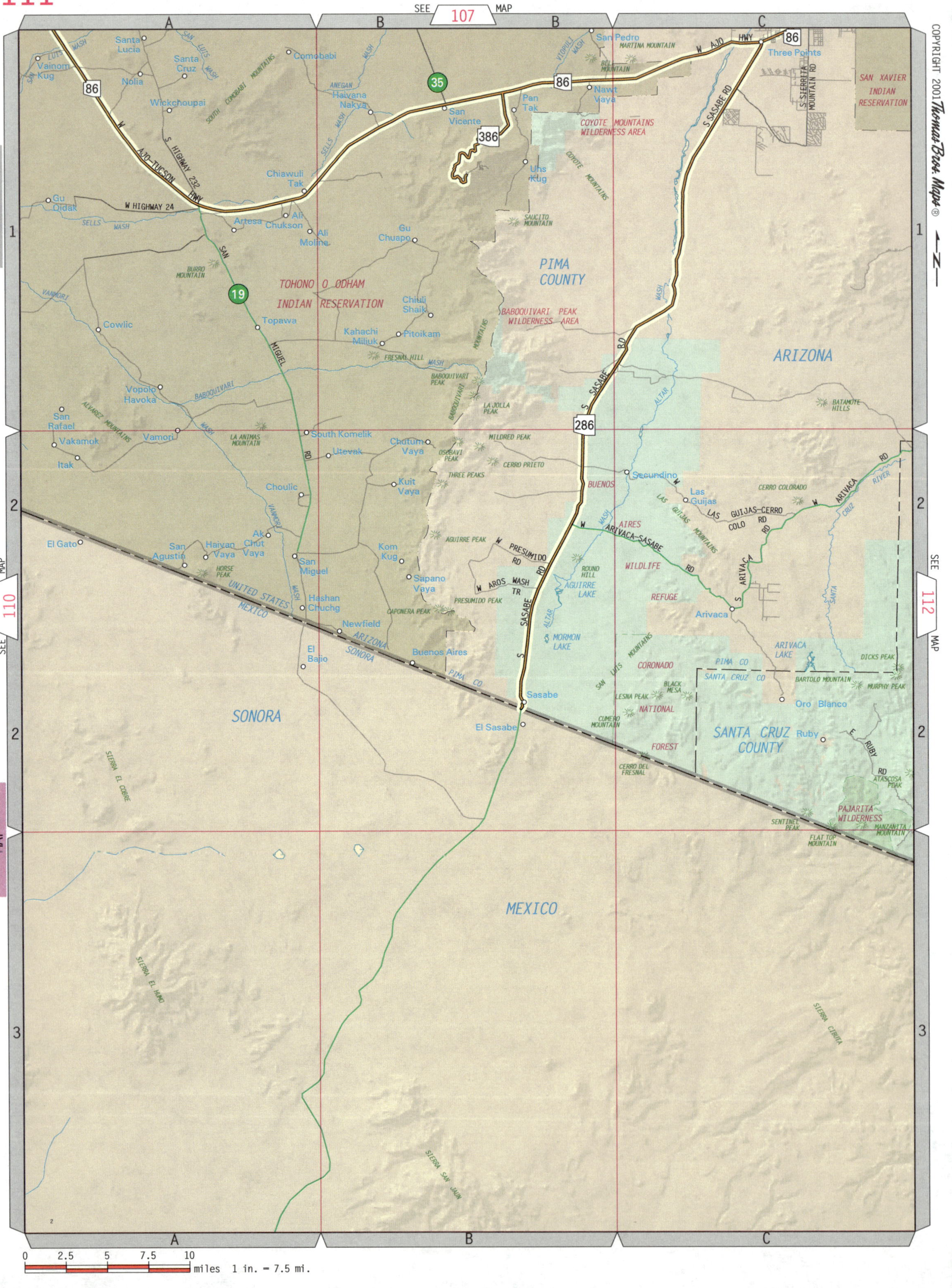

SEE 107 MAP

PHOENIX

SEE 110 MAP

SEE 112 MAP

MAP

TOHONO O ODHAM INDIAN RESERVATION

PIMA COUNTY

ARIZONA

SANTA CRUZ COUNTY

SAN XAVIER INDIAN RESERVATION

COYOTE MOUNTAINS WILDERNESS AREA

BABOQUIVARI PEAK WILDERNESS AREA

BUENOS AIRES NATIONAL WILDLIFE REFUGE

CORONADO NATIONAL FOREST

PAJARITA WILDERNESS

SONORA

MEXICO

UNITED STATES

Santa Lucia
Santa Cruz
Vainom Kug
Nolia
Comobabi
Wickchoupai
Anegan
Haivana Nakya
San Vicente
San Pedro
Three Points
Pan Tak
Nawt Vaya
Uhs Kug
Chiawuli Tak
Gu Oidak
Artesa
Ali Chukson
Ali Molina
Gu Chuapo
Chiuli Shaik
Topawa
Cowlic
Kahachi Miliuk
Pitoikam
Vopolo Havoka
San Rafael
Vakamok
Itak
Vamori
South Komelik
Utevak
Chutum Vaya
Kuit Vaya
Choulic
El Gato
San Agustin
Haivan Vaya
Ak Chut Vaya
San Miguel
Kom Kug
Sapano Vaya
Hashan Chuchg
Newfield
El Bajio
Buenos Aires
Secundino
Las Guijas
Arivaca
Sasabe
El Sasabe
Oro Blanco
Ruby

W AJO HWY
W AJO-TUCSON HWY
S HIGHWAY 232
W HIGHWAY 24
SAN MIGUEL RD
S SASABE RD
S SIERRITA MOUNTAIN RD
W ARIVACA-SASABE RD
W LAS GUIJAS-CERRO COLO RD
W ARIVACA RD
S ARIVACA RD
W PRESUMIDO RD
W AROS WASH TR
E RUBY RD
86
386
286
35
19

SAN LUIS WASH
SELLS WASH
VAMORI WASH
BABOQUIVARI WASH
VAMORI WASH
FRESNAL WASH
VIOPULI WASH
ALTAR WASH
CRUZ RIVER
SANTA CRUZ

MARTINA MOUNTAIN
BELL MOUNTAIN
SOUTH COMOBABI MOUNTAINS
COYOTE MOUNTAINS
SAUCITO MOUNTAIN
BURRO MOUNTAIN
BABOQUIVARI MOUNTAINS
FRESNAL HILL
BABOQUIVARI PEAK
ALVAREZ MOUNTAINS
LA JOLLA PEAK
LA ANIMAS MOUNTAIN
MILDRED PEAK
OSOBAVI PEAK
CERRO PRIETO
THREE PEAKS
BATAMOTE HILLS
CERRO COLORADO
LAS GUIJAS MOUNTAINS
AGUIRRE PEAK
HORSE PEAK
PRESUMIDO PEAK
CAPONERA PEAK
ROUND HILL
AGUIRRE LAKE
MORMON LAKE
SAN LUIS MOUNTAINS
ARIVACA LAKE
DICKS PEAK
BARTOLO MOUNTAIN
MURPHY PEAK
BLACK MESA
LESNA PEAK
CUMERO MOUNTAIN
CERRO DEL FRESNAL
ATASCOSA PEAK
SENTINEL PEAK
MANZANITA MOUNTAIN
FLAT TOP MOUNTAIN
SIERRA EL COBRE
SIERRA EL HUMO
SIERRA CIBUTA
SIERRA SAN JUAN

ARIZONA
SONORA
PIMA CO
SANTA CRUZ CO

A B B C
1 2 3

0 2.5 5 7.5 10 miles 1 in. = 7.5 mi.

SEE 108 MAP

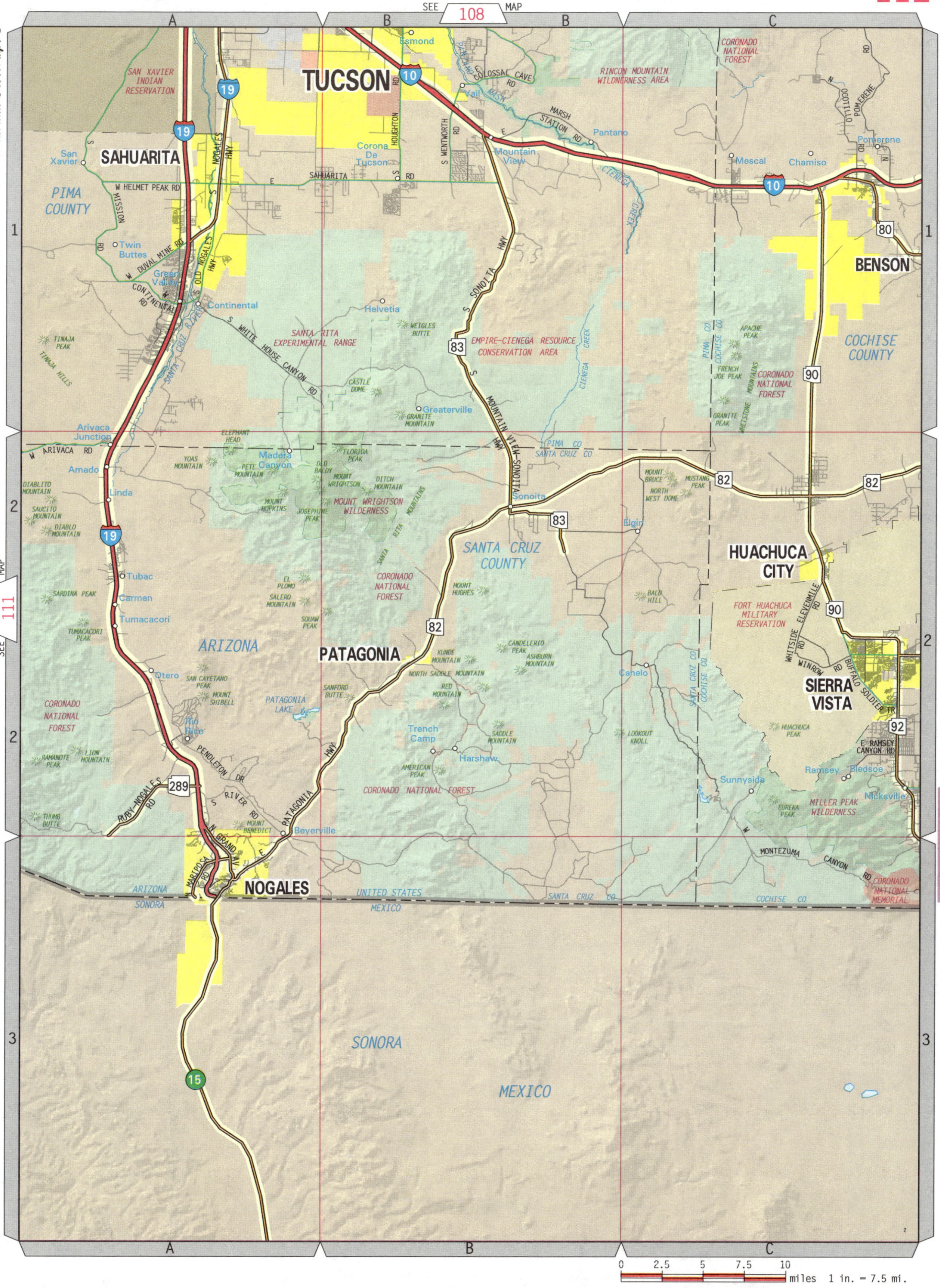

SEE 111 MAP

PHOENIX MAP

A B B C

1 2 3

TUCSON
SAHUARITA
BENSON
HUACHUCA CITY
SIERRA VISTA
PATAGONIA
NOGALES

Esmond
Vail
Corona De Tucson
Mountain View
Pantano
Mescal
Chamiso
Pomerene
San Xavier
Twin Buttes
Green Valley
Continental
Helvetia
Greaterville
Arivaca Junction
Amado
Linda
Madera Canyon
Sonoita
Elgin
Tubac
Carmen
Tumacacori
Otero
Rio Rico
Beyerville
Trench Camp
Harshaw
Canelo
Sunnyside
Ramsey
Bledsoe
Nicksville

PIMA COUNTY
COCHISE COUNTY
SANTA CRUZ COUNTY
ARIZONA
SONORA
MEXICO
UNITED STATES
ARIZONA SONORA
PIMA CO
SANTA CRUZ CO
COCHISE CO

SAN XAVIER INDIAN RESERVATION
CORONADO NATIONAL FOREST
RINCON MOUNTAIN WILDERNESS AREA
SANTA RITA EXPERIMENTAL RANGE
EMPIRE-CIENEGA RESOURCE CONSERVATION AREA
MOUNT WRIGHTSON WILDERNESS
FORT HUACHUCA MILITARY RESERVATION
MILLER PEAK WILDERNESS
CORONADO NATIONAL MEMORIAL

TINAJA PEAK
TINAJA HILLS
WEIGLES BUTTE
CASTLE DOME
GRANITE MOUNTAIN
ELEPHANT HEAD
YOAS MOUNTAIN
PETE MOUNTAIN
OLD BALDY
FLORIDA PEAK
MOUNT WRIGHTSON
DITCH MOUNTAIN
MOUNT HOPKINS
JOSEPHINE PEAK
SANTA RITA MOUNTAINS
DIABLITO MOUNTAIN
SAUCITO MOUNTAIN
DIABLO MOUNTAIN
EL PLOMO
SALERO MOUNTAIN
SQUAW PEAK
SARDINA PEAK
TUMACACORI PEAK
SAN CAYETANO PEAK
MOUNT SHIBELL
SANFORD BUTTE
PATAGONIA LAKE
MOUNT HUGHES
KUNDE MOUNTAIN
NORTH SADDLE MOUNTAIN
RED MOUNTAIN
CANDELERIO PEAK
ASHBURN MOUNTAIN
SADDLE MOUNTAIN
AMERICAN PEAK
MOUNT BENEDICT
RAMANOTE PEAK
LION MOUNTAIN
THUMB BUTTE
MOUNT BRUCE
NORTH WEST DOME
MUSTANG PEAK
BALD HILL
LOOKOUT KNOLL
APACHE PEAK
FRENCH JOE PEAK
WHETSTONE MOUNTAINS
GRANITE PEAK
HUACHUCA PEAK
EUREKA PEAK
CIENEGA CREEK
SANTA CRUZ RIVER
PANTANO WASH

I-10
I-19
80
82
83
90
92
289
15

COLOSSAL CAVE RD
MARSH STATION RD
S HOUGHTON RD
S WENTWORTH RD
E SAHUARITA RD
W HELMET PEAK RD
MISSION RD
W DUVAL MINE RD
CONTINENTAL RD
S NOGALES HWY
S OLD NOGALES HWY
S WHITE HOUSE CANYON RD
S SONOITA HWY
S MOUNTAIN VIEW RD
SONOITA HWY
W ARIVACA RD
OCOTILLO RD
POMERENE RD
WHITSIDE RD
ELEVENMILE RD
WINROW RD
BUFFALO SOLDIER TR
E RAMSEY CANYON RD
PENDLETON DR
S RIVER RD
RUBY-NOGALES RD
PATAGONIA HWY
N GRAND AV
N MARIPOSA RD
W MONTEZUMA CANYON RD

0 2.5 5 7.5 10 miles 1 in. = 7.5 mi.

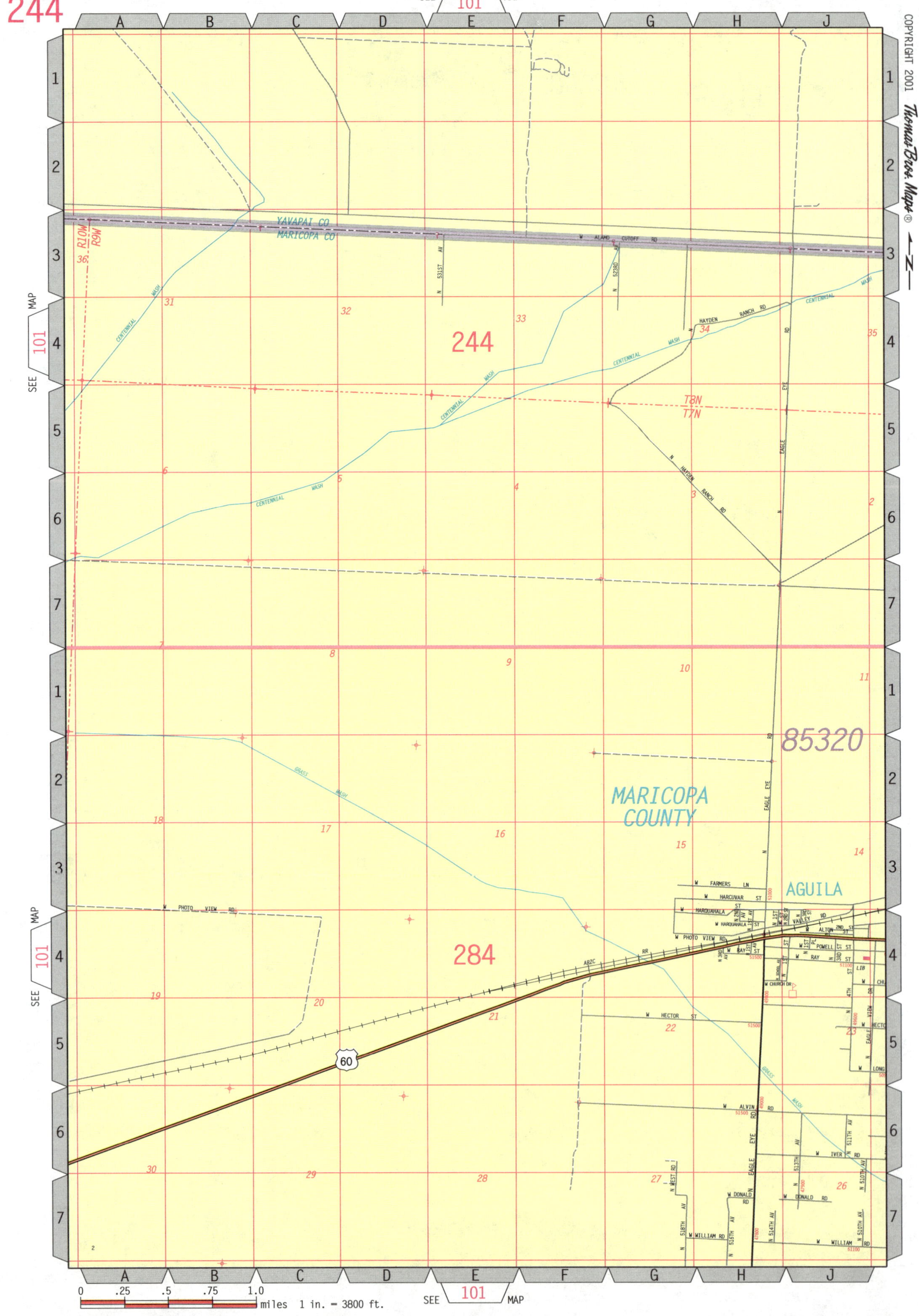

SEE 101 MAP
A B C D E F G H J
1 2 3 4 5 6 7
COPYRIGHT 2001 Thomas Bros. Maps®
YAVAPAI CO
MARICOPA CO
R10W
R9W
W ALAMO CUTOFF RD
N 531ST AV
N 523RD AV
CENTENNIAL WASH
HAYDEN RANCH RD
N EAGLE EYE RD
N HAYDEN RANCH RD
244
T8N
T7N
GRASS WASH
85320
MARICOPA COUNTY
AGUILA
W FARMERS LN
W HARCUVAR ST
W HARQUAHALA ST
W PHOTO VIEW RD
VALLEY RD
ALTON ST
POWELL ST
RAY ST
W CHURCH DR
LIB
W HECTOR ST
W ALVIN RD
W IVER RD
W DONALD RD
W WILLIAM RD
N 518TH AV
N 516TH AV
N 514TH AV
N 513TH AV
N 511TH AV
N 510TH AV
N 510TH AV
N WEST RD
RR
ABZC
60
284
SEE 101 MAP
0 .25 .5 .75 1.0 miles 1 in. = 3800 ft.

MAP

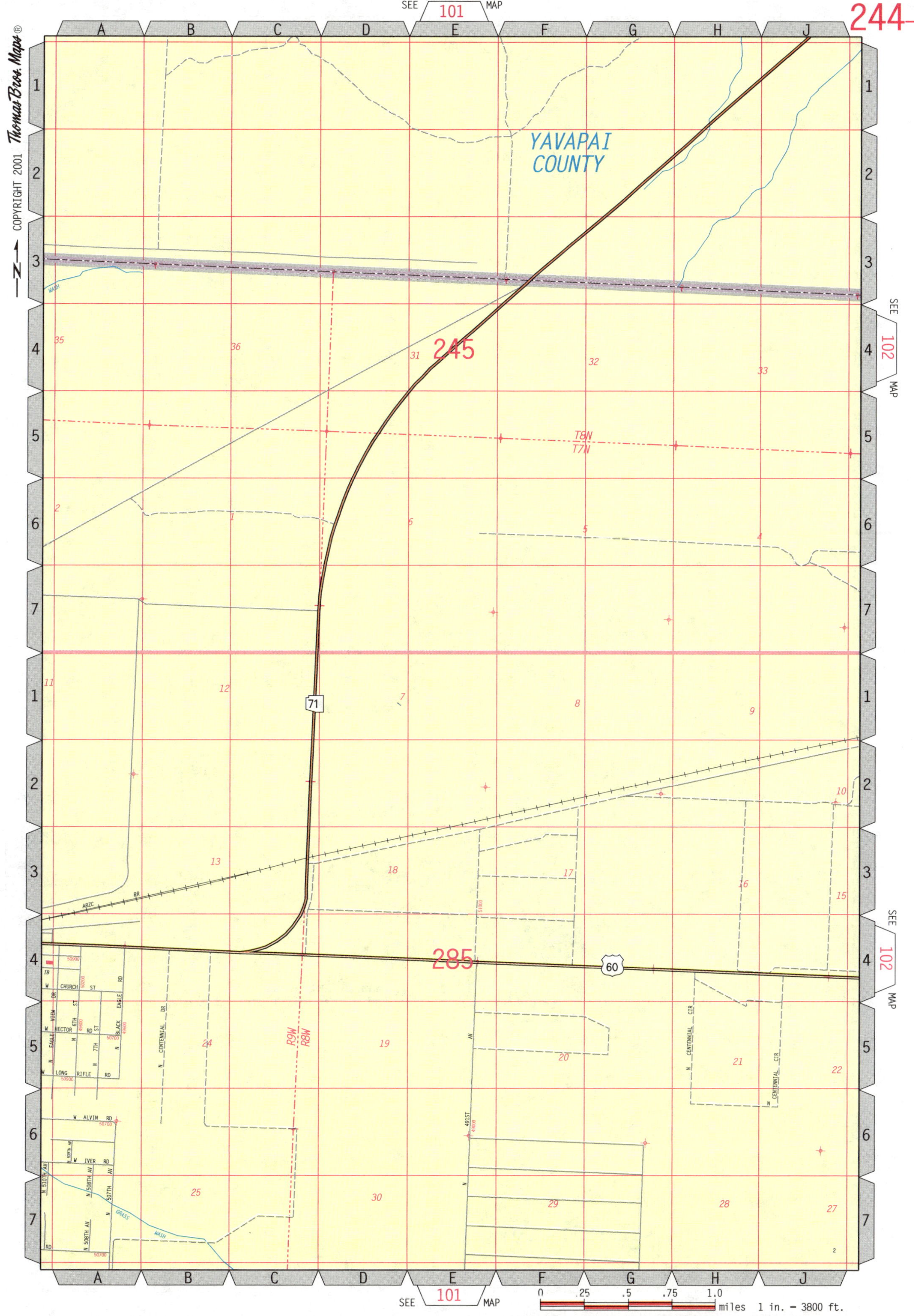

0 .25 .5 .75 1.0 miles 1 in. = 3800 ft.

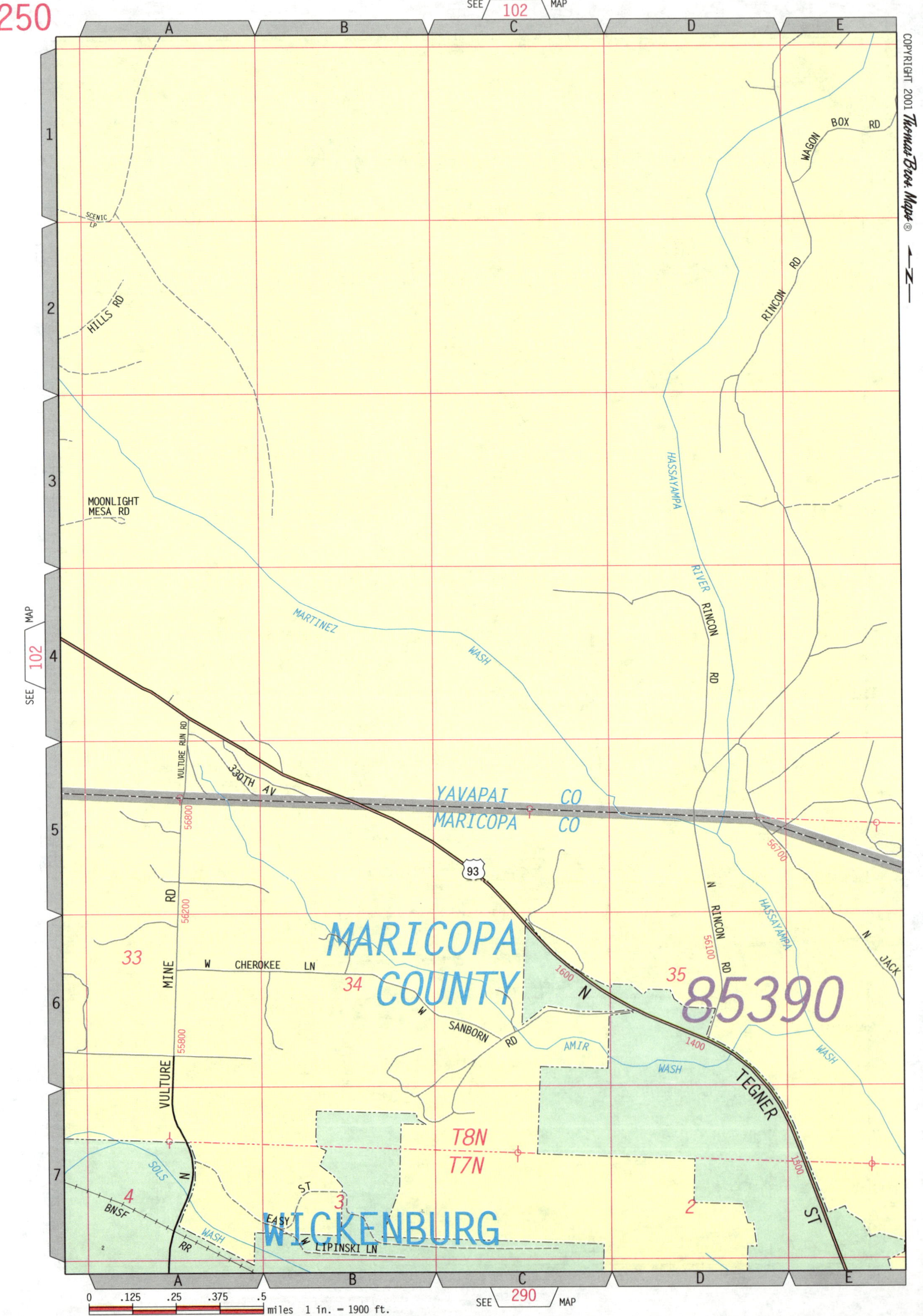

SEE 102 MAP
COPYRIGHT 2001 Thomas Bros. Maps
WAGON BOX RD
RINCON RD
SCENIC LP
HILLS RD
MOONLIGHT MESA RD
HASSAYAMPA RIVER
MARTINEZ WASH
RINCON RD
VULTURE RUN RD
330TH AV
YAVAPAI CO
MARICOPA CO
93
56800
56700
56200
56100
N RINCON RD
HASSAYAMPA WASH
N JACK
MARICOPA COUNTY
33
34
35
85390
W CHEROKEE LN
VULTURE MINE RD
55800
1600
1400
W SANBORN RD
AMIR WASH
N
TEGNER ST
T8N
T7N
1500
SOLS WASH
4
3
2
BNSF RR
EASY ST
W LIPINSKI LN
WICKENBURG
SEE 290 MAP
SEE 102 MAP
PHOENIX
MAP
0 .125 .25 .375 .5 miles 1 in. = 1900 ft.

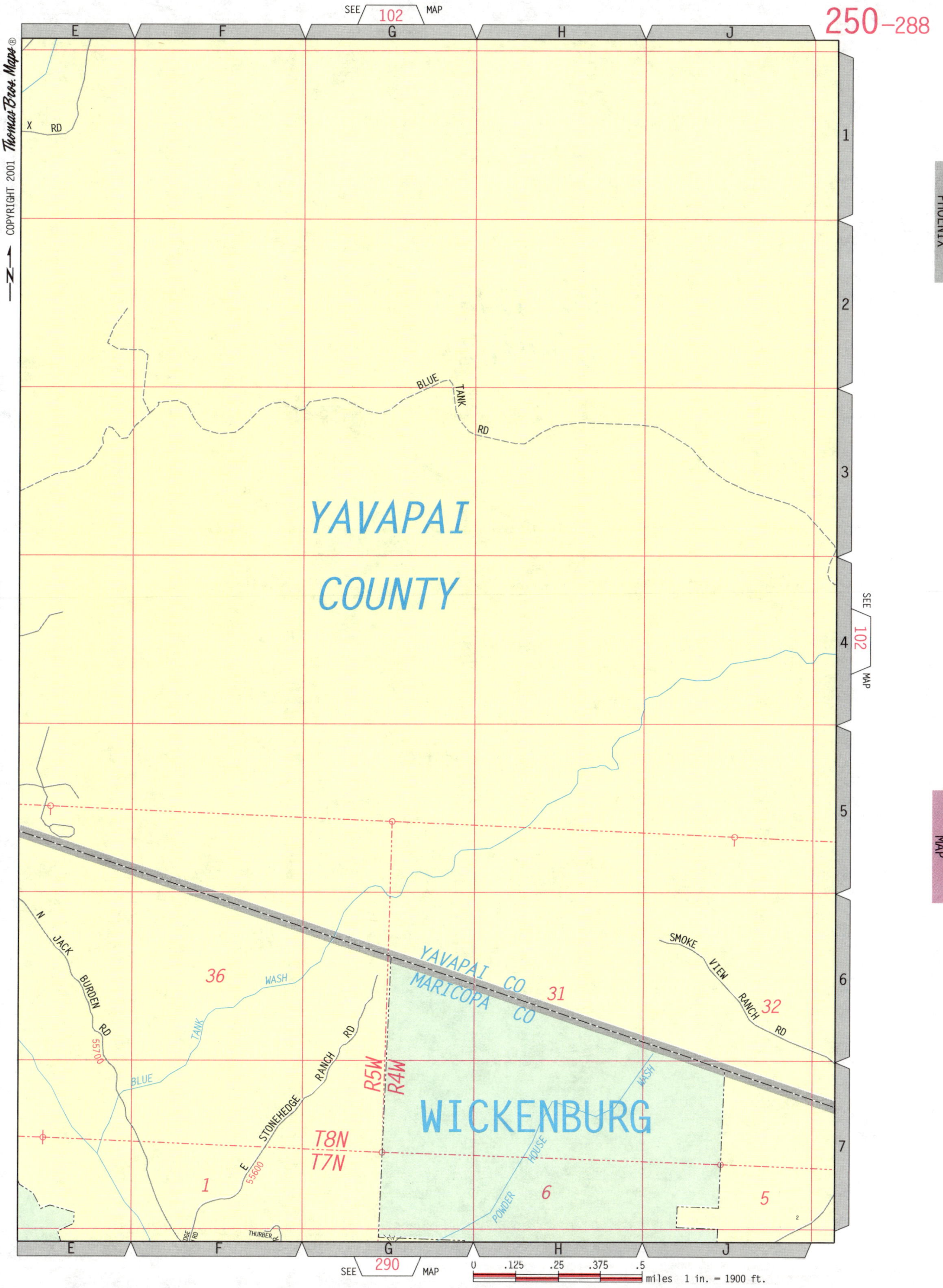

SEE 102 MAP

E F G H J

1 2 3 4 5 6 7

N

PHOENIX

MAP

X RD

BLUE TANK RD

YAVAPAI COUNTY

SEE 102 MAP

N JACK BURDEN RD

55700

36

WASH

TANK

BLUE

YAVAPAI CO

MARICOPA CO

31

SMOKE VIEW RANCH RD

32

E STONEHEDGE RANCH RD

55600

R5W
R4W

T8N
T7N

WICKENBURG

WASH

POWDER HOUSE

1

6

5

THURBER

SEE 290 MAP

0 .125 .25 .375 .5 miles 1 in. = 1900 ft.

SEE 102 MAP

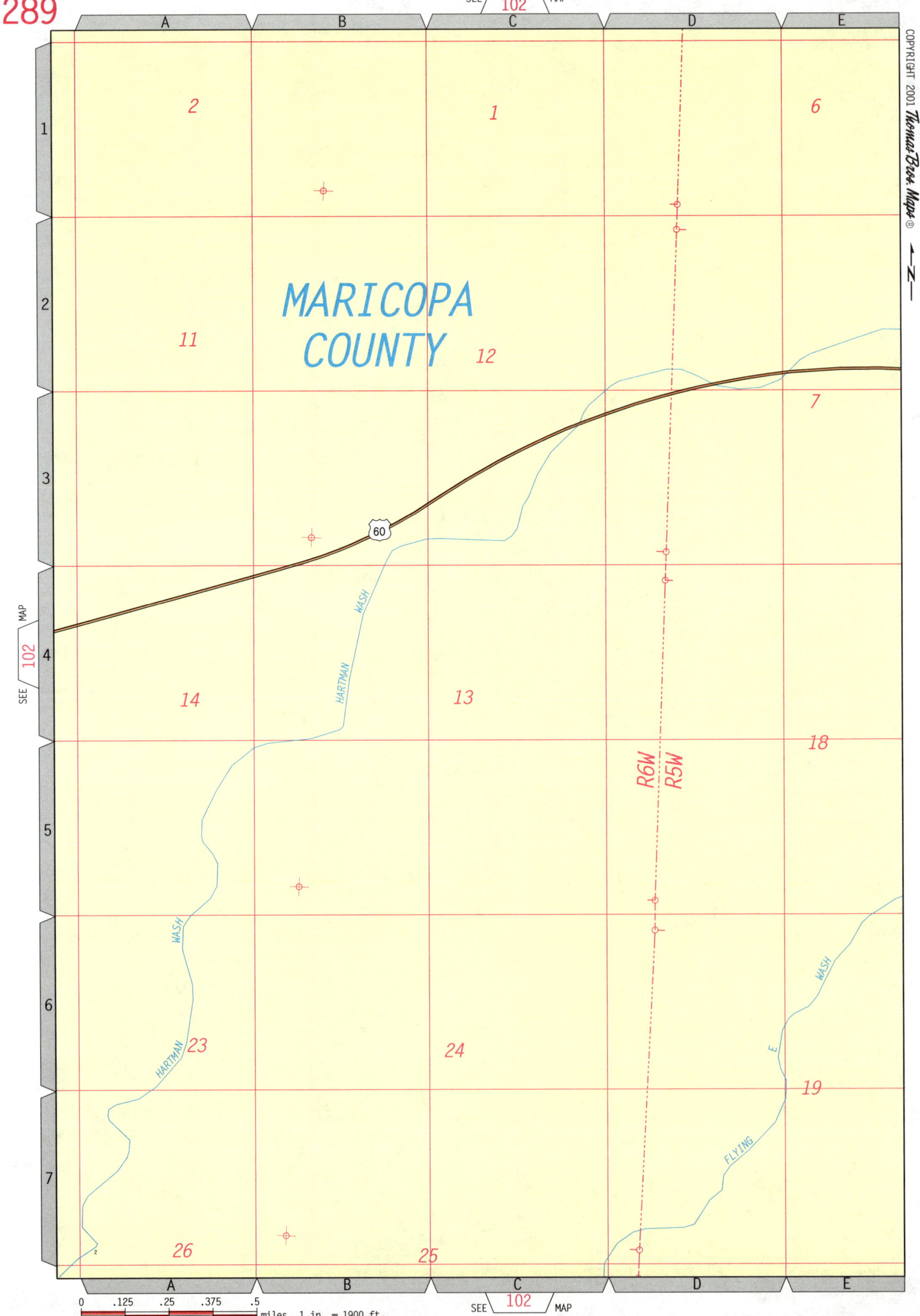

PHOENIX

MAP

SEE 102 MAP

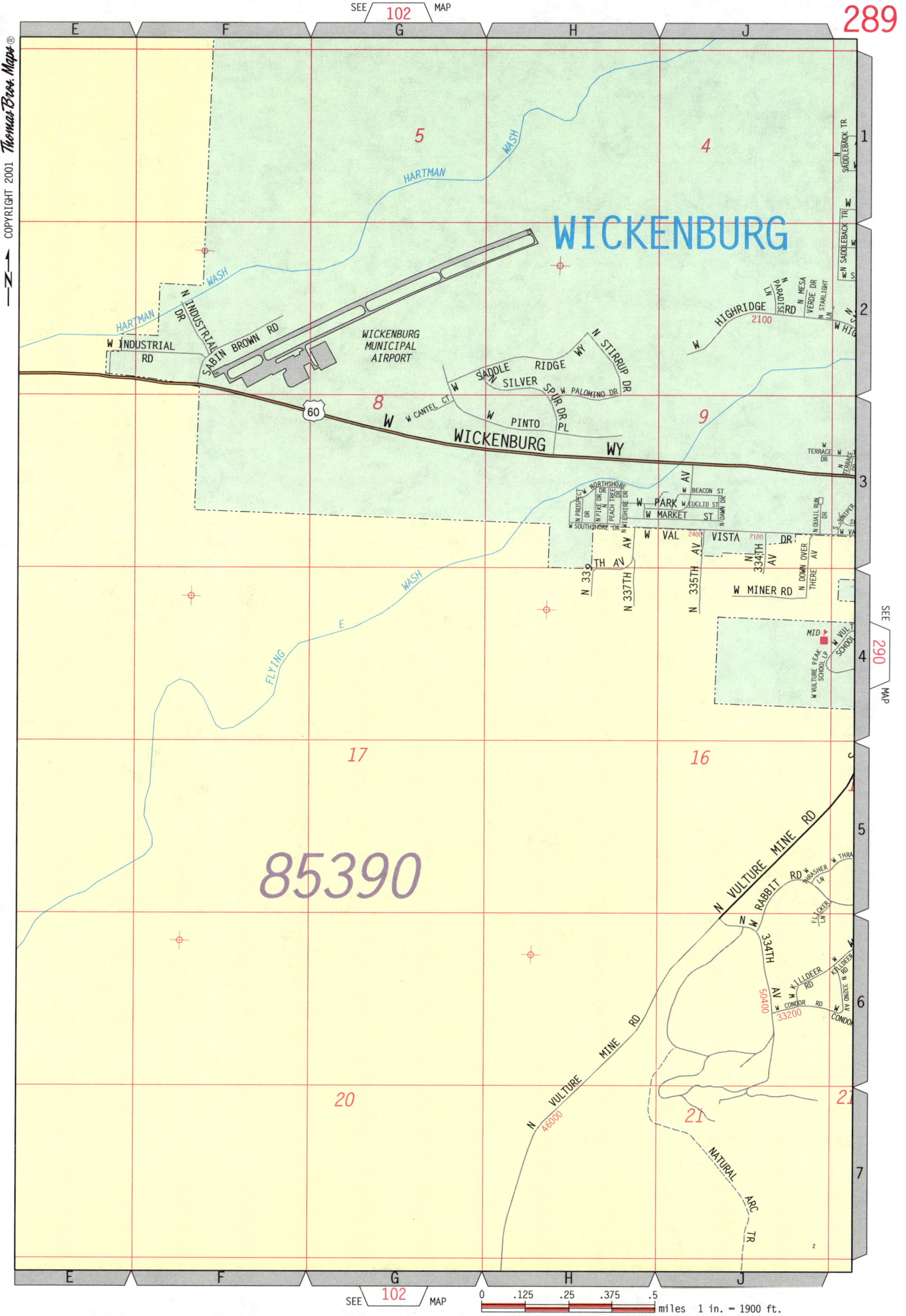

0 .125 .25 .375 .5 miles 1 in. = 1900 ft.

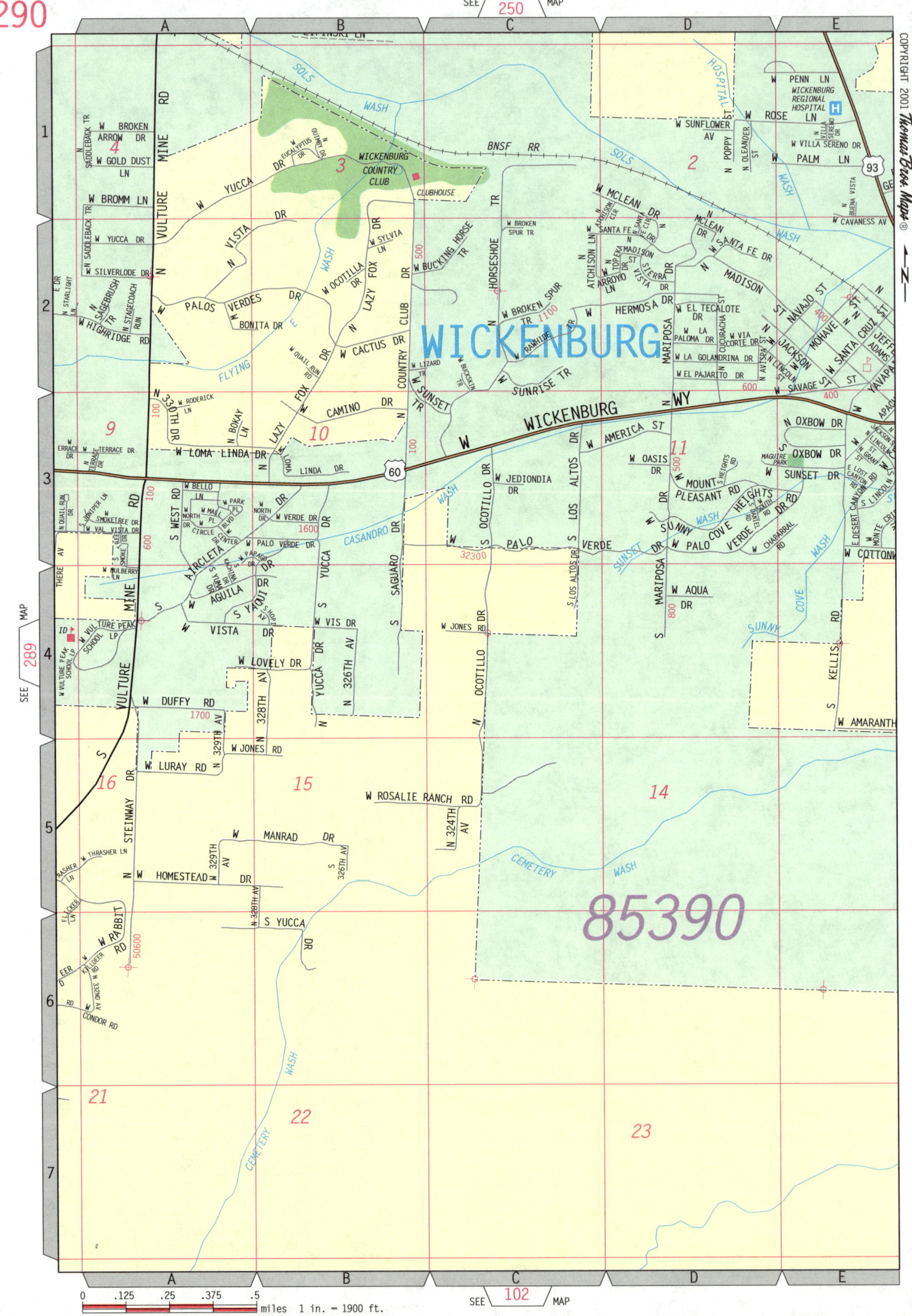
SEE 250 MAP
WICKENBURG
85390
WICKENBURG REGIONAL HOSPITAL
WICKENBURG COUNTRY CLUB
CLUBHOUSE
W WICKENBURG WY
BNSF RR
N VULTURE MINE RD
S VULTURE MINE RD
W YUCCA DR
W VISTA DR
N COUNTRY CLUB DR
W CACTUS DR
N LAZY FOX DR
W LOMA LINDA DR
W PALO VERDE DR
W BROKEN ARROW DR
W GOLD DUST LN
W BROMM LN
W SILVERLODE DR
W HIGHRIDGE RD
W PALOS VERDES DR
W BONITA DR
W CAMINO DR
W AMERICA ST
W JEDIONDIA DR
N OCOTILLO DR
S LOS ALTOS DR
S MARIPOSA DR
W HERMOSA DR
W SUNRISE TR
W MCLEAN DR
W SANTA FE DR
W MADISON ST
W SUNFLOWER AV
W ROSE LN
W PALM LN
W PENN LN
W CAVANESS AV
W VILLA SERENO DR
W OXBOW DR
W SUNSET DR
W MOUNT PLEASANT RD
W SUNNY COVE DR
W SUNSET HEIGHTS RD
W COTTONWOOD
W AMARANTH
S KELLIS RD
W AQUA DR
W JONES RD
W VIS DR
W LOVELY DR
W DUFFY RD
W LURAY RD
W ROSALIE RANCH RD
W MANRAD DR
W HOMESTEAD DR
S YUCCA DR
N STEINWAY DR
W RABBIT RD
CONDOR RD
N 324TH AV
S 326TH AV
N 326TH AV
N 328TH AV
N 329TH AV
N 330TH DR
W VULTURE PEAK SCHOOL LP
SOLS WASH
FLYING E WASH
CASANDRO WASH
SUNSET WASH
SUNNY COVE WASH
CEMETERY WASH
HOSPITAL WASH
60
93
1 2 3 4 9 10 11 14 15 16 21 22 23
SEE 289 MAP
SEE 102 MAP
0 .125 .25 .375 .5 miles 1 in. = 1900 ft.
COPYRIGHT 2001 Thomas Bros. Maps ®

PHOENIX
MAP

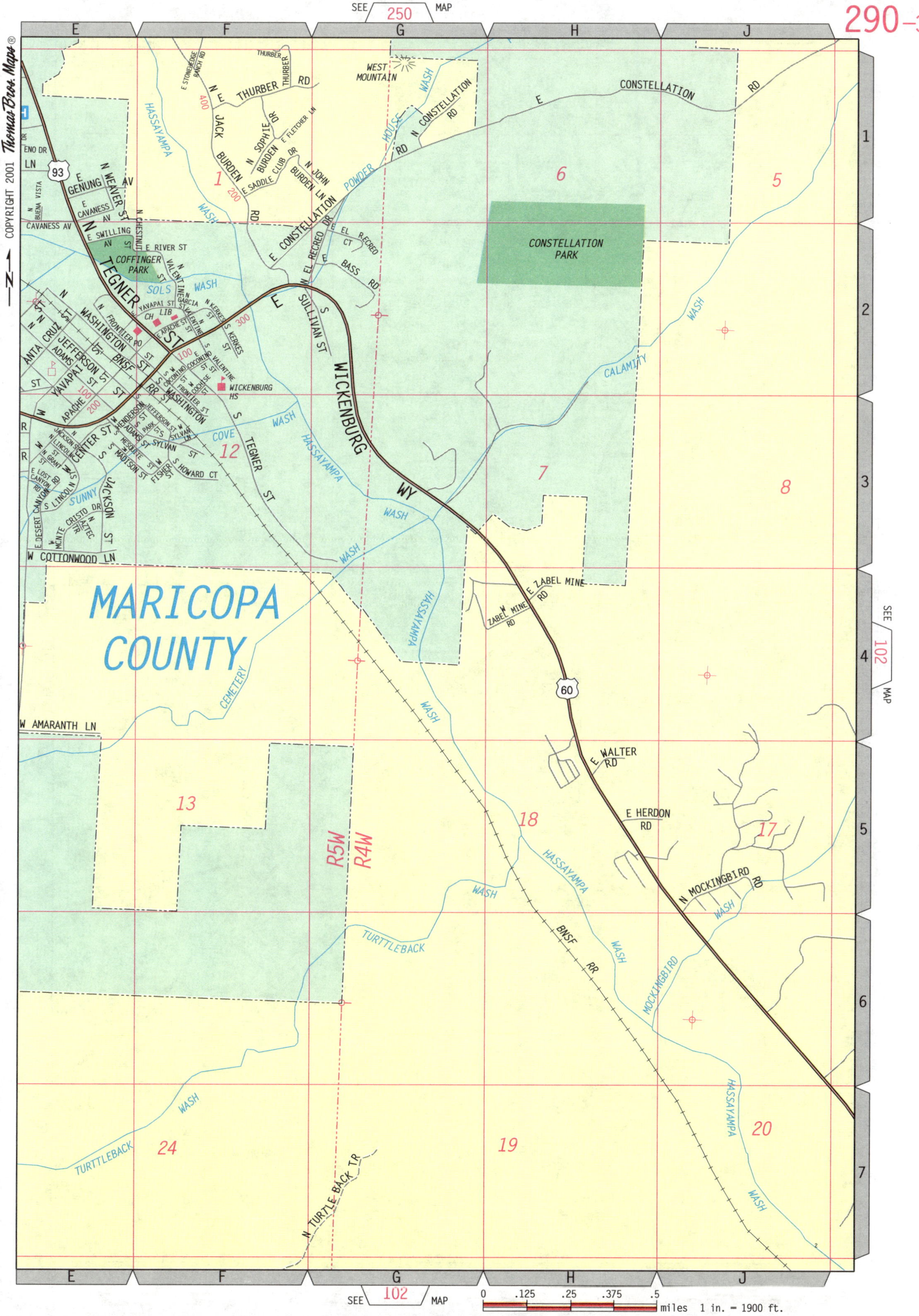
SEE 250 MAP
MARICOPA COUNTY
CONSTELLATION PARK
COFFINGER PARK
WICKENBURG WY
CONSTELLATION RD
WEST MOUNTAIN
HASSAYAMPA WASH
SOLS WASH
COVE WASH
CALAMITY WASH
CEMETERY WASH
TURTLEBACK WASH
MOCKINGBIRD WASH
BNSF RR
E ZABEL MINE RD
E WALTER RD
E HERDON RD
N MOCKINGBIRD RD
N TURTLE BACK TR
W AMARANTH LN
W COTTONWOOD LN
R5W
R4W
WICKENBURG HS
PHOENIX
MAP
SEE 102 MAP
0 .125 .25 .375 .5 miles 1 in. = 1900 ft.

SEE 102 MAP

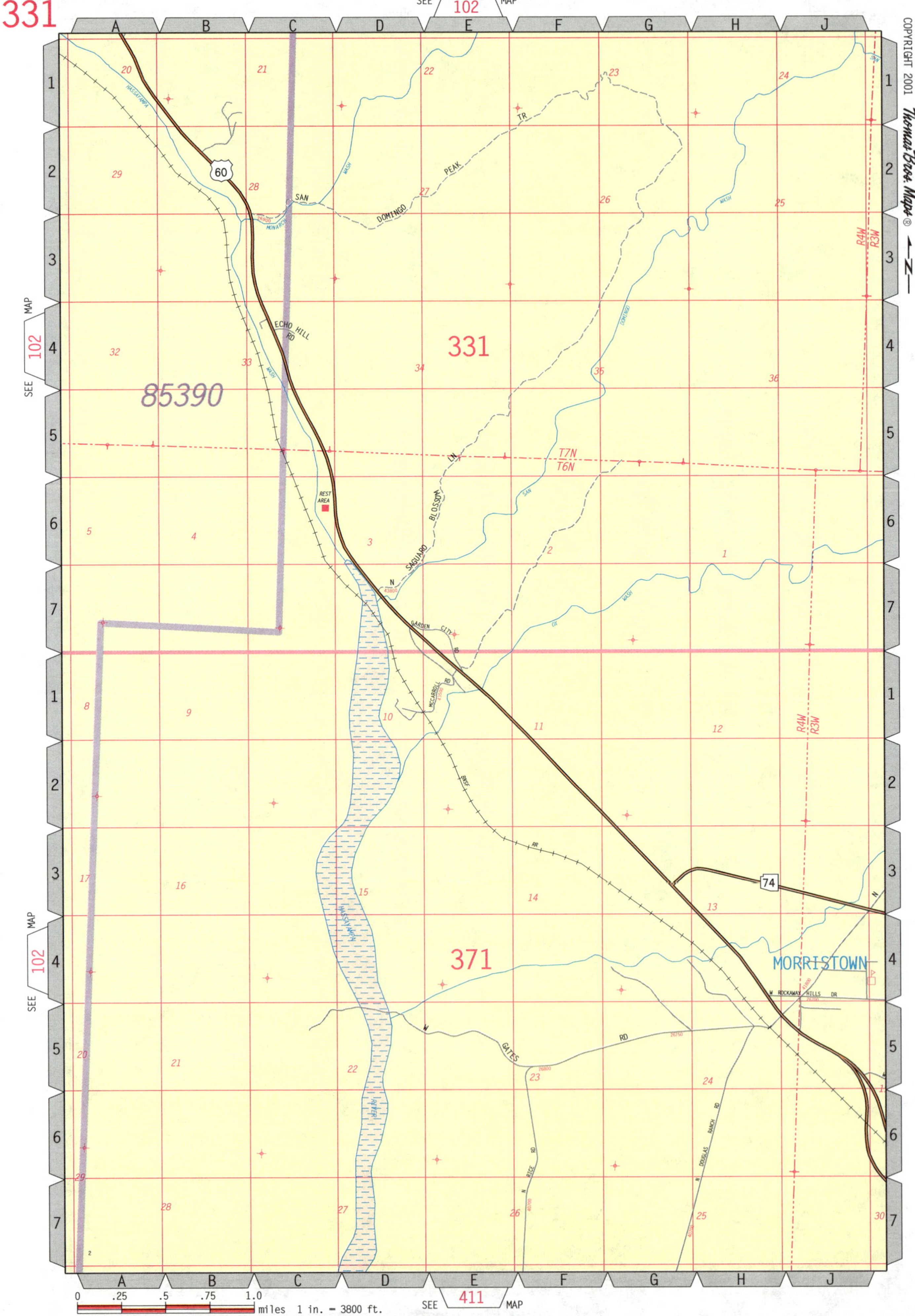

SEE 102 MAP
SEE 411 MAP

0 .25 .5 .75 1.0 miles 1 in. = 3800 ft.

PHOENIX

MAP

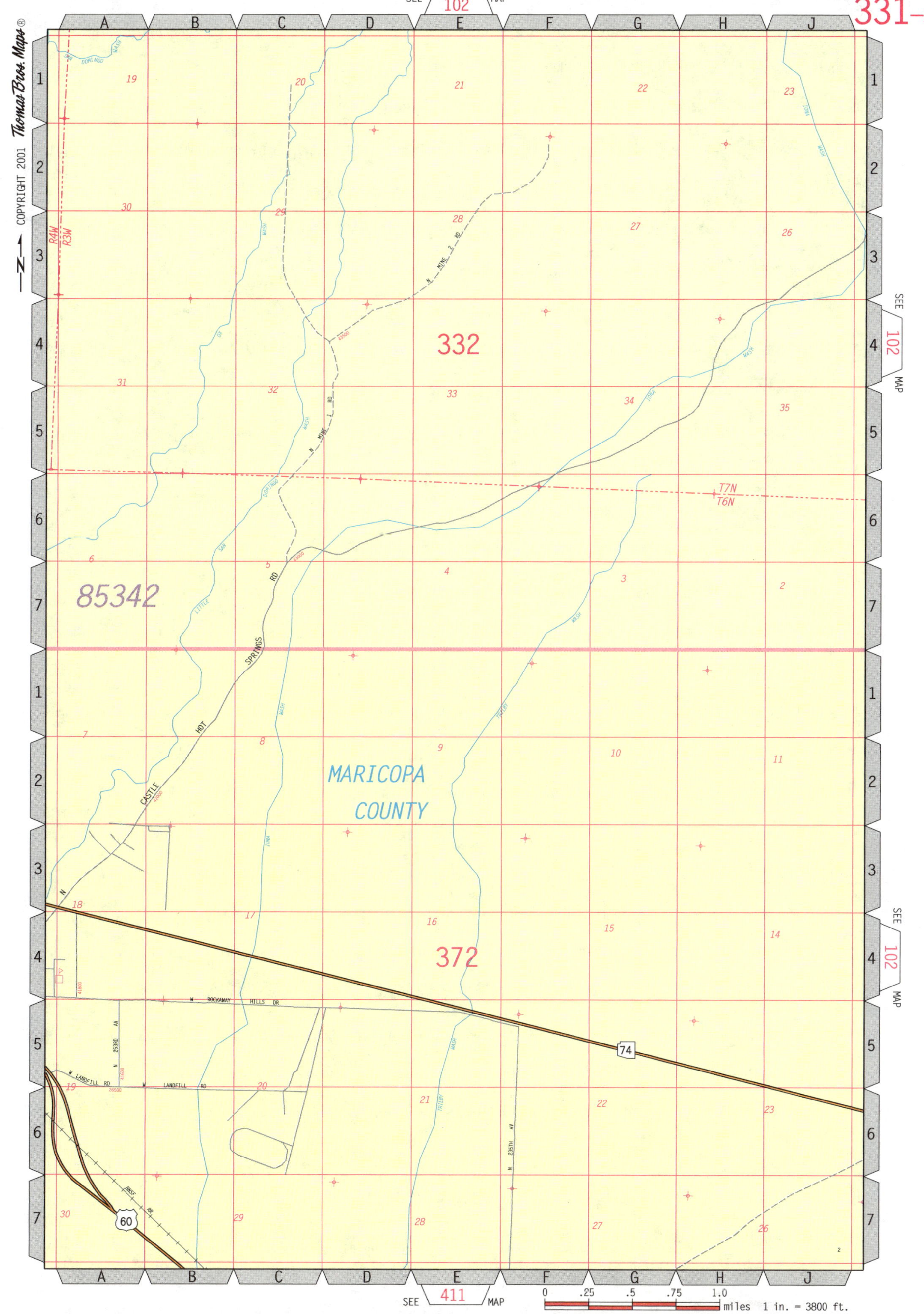

SEE 102 MAP
332
372
85342
MARICOPA
COUNTY
T7N
T6N
R4W
R3W
CASTLE HOT SPRINGS RD
N MINE 1 RD
N MINE 2 RD
W ROCKAWAY HILLS DR
W LANDFILL RD
N 253RD AV
N 235TH AV
IOWA WASH
TRILBY WASH
LITTLE SAN DOMINGO WASH
SAN DOMINGO WASH
BNSF RR
74
60
SEE 411 MAP
0 .25 .5 .75 1.0 miles 1 in. = 3800 ft.
PHOENIX
MAP

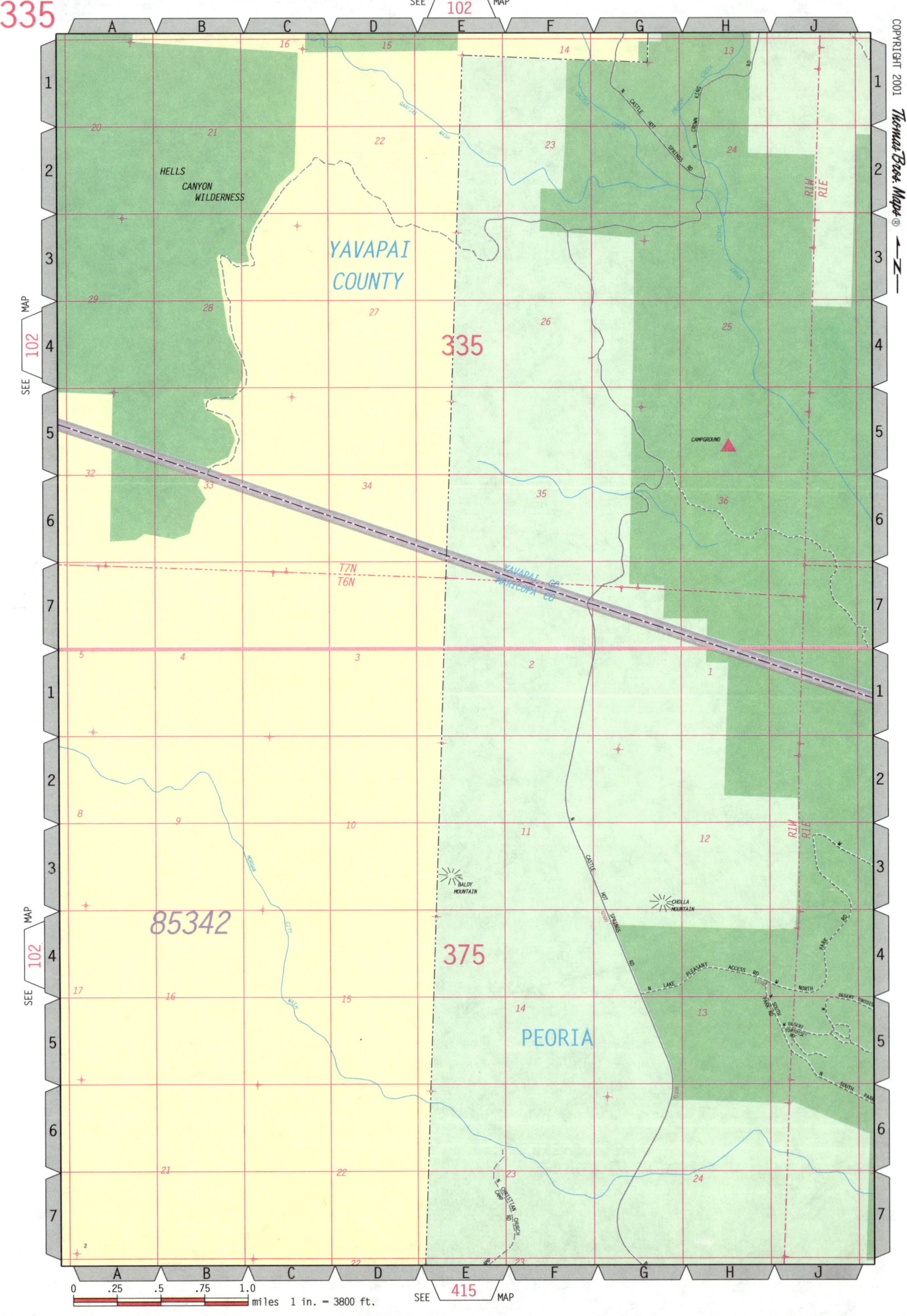

SEE 102 MAP
HELLS CANYON WILDERNESS
YAVAPAI COUNTY
335
N CASTLE HOT SPRINGS RD
N CROWN KING RD
CAMPGROUND
T7N
T6N
YAVAPAI CO
MARICOPA CO
R1W
R1E
BALDY MOUNTAIN
CHOLLA MOUNTAIN
85342
375
N LAKE PLEASANT ACCESS RD
PEORIA
N CHRISTIAN CHURCH CAMP RD
SEE 415 MAP
0 .25 .5 .75 1.0 miles 1 in. = 3800 ft.
PHOENIX
MAP

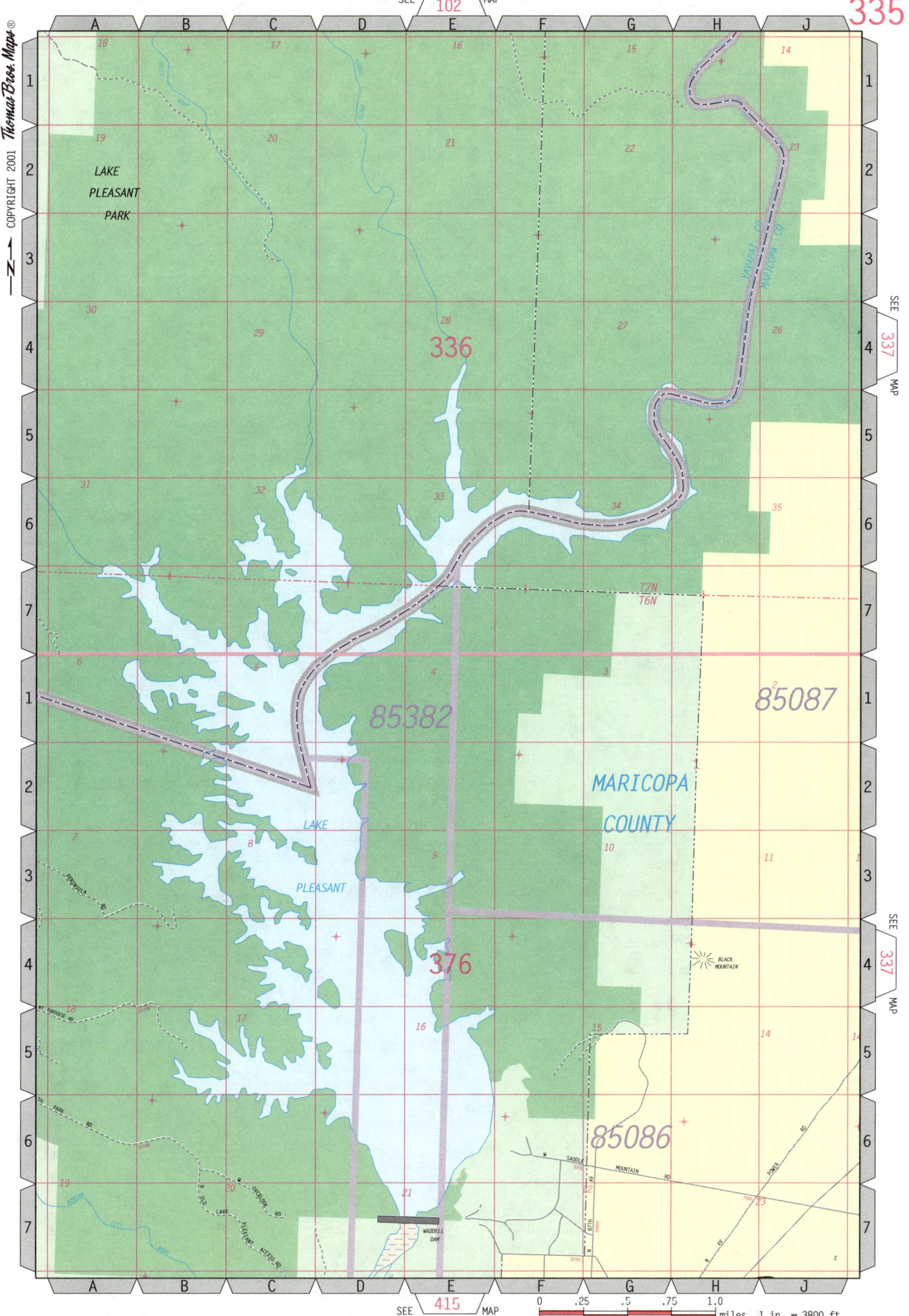

SEE 102 MAP
LAKE PLEASANT PARK
336
YAVAPAI CO
MARICOPA CO
T7N
T6N
85382
85087
MARICOPA COUNTY
LAKE PLEASANT
376
BLACK MOUNTAIN
85086
SADDLE MOUNTAIN RD
POWER RD
OVERLOCK RD
OLD LAKE PLEASANT ACCESS RD
PENINSULA RD
PARK RD
WADDELL DAM
87TH AV
SEE 337 MAP
SEE 415 MAP
0 .25 .5 .75 1.0 miles 1 in. = 3800 ft.

PHOENIX
MAP

SEE 102 MAP

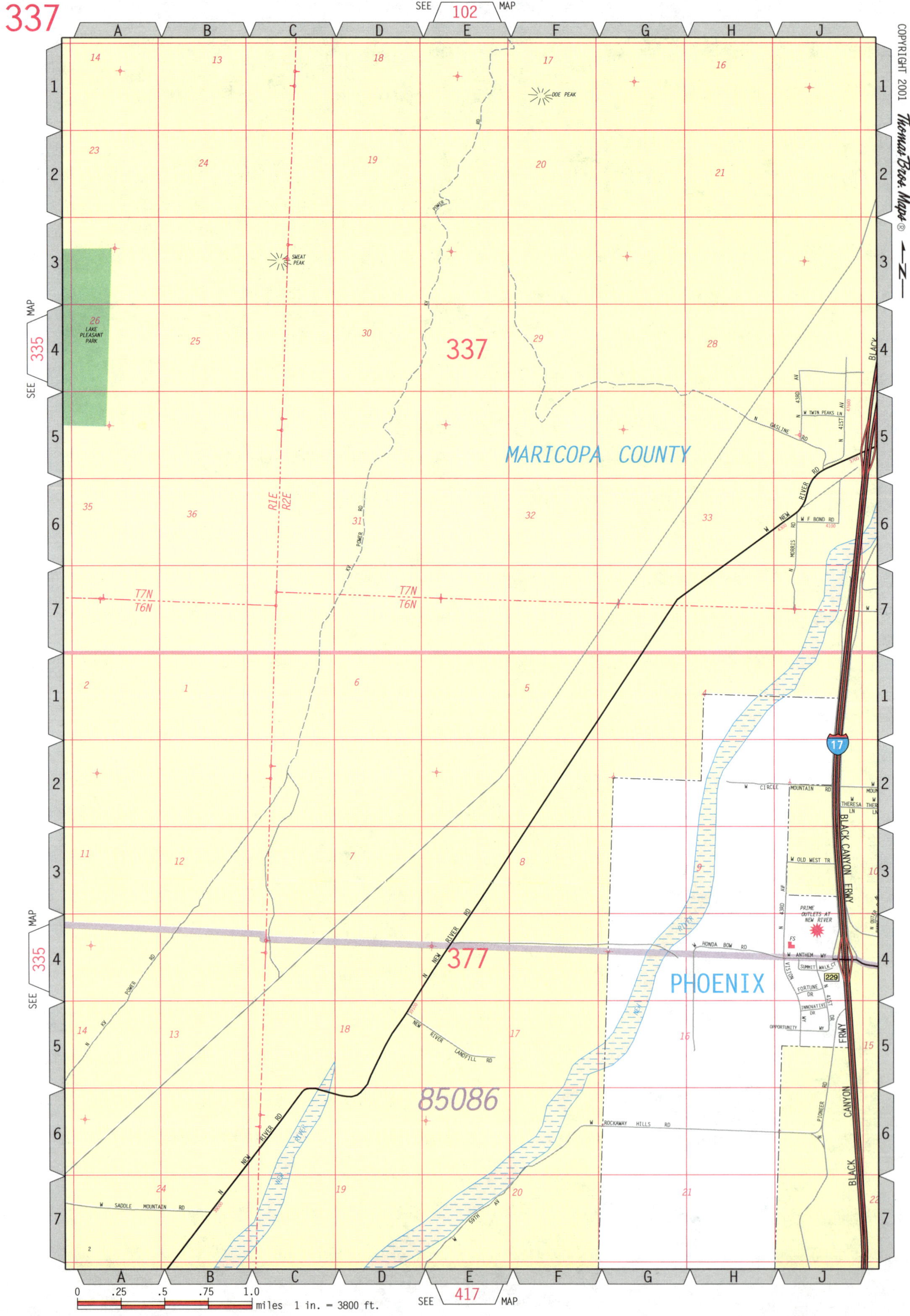

SEE 417 MAP

0 .25 .5 .75 1.0 miles 1 in. = 3800 ft.

PHOENIX

MAP

SEE 103 MAP
NEW RIVER
85087
GAVILAN PEAK
DAISY MOUNTAIN
ANTHEM
ANTHEM COMMUNITY PARK
ANTHEM GOLF & COUNTRY CLUB
BLACK CANYON FRWY
17
232
T7N
T6N
R2E
R3E
W PHOTO VIEW RD
W ESTRELLA RD
W CHIRICAHUA RD
W WHITE SPAR RD
W MINGUS DR
N FIG SPRINGS RD
W LAZY K RANCH RD
COMMUNITY PARK RD
NEW RIVER RD
W SUNSET DR
W TWIN PEAKS LN
W LAZY G RANCH RD
W WANDER LN
W COUNTRY RD
W WOLFTRAP RD
W 14TH AV
W GIBBONS
W MEANDER RD
N JENNY LIN RD
W JENNY LIN RD
W VENADO DR
E VENADO DR
E SABROSA DR
W CIRCLE MOUNTAIN RD
E CIRCLE MOUNTAIN RD
W LEANN RD
W CAVALRY RD
W HONDA BOW RD
E HONDA BOW RD
E LINDA LN
W ROCKAWAY HILLS RD
W SADDLE MOUNTAIN RD
W RIDGECREST RD
E RIDGECREST RD
GAVILAN PEAK PKWY
W ANTHEM WY
W DAISY MOUNTAIN DR
SKUNK CREEK
RODGER CREEK
CLINE CREEK
DEADMAN WASH
338
378
SEE 339 MAP
SEE 339 MAP
PHOENIX
MAP
SEE 417 MAP
0 .25 .5 .75 1.0 miles 1 in. = 3800 ft.

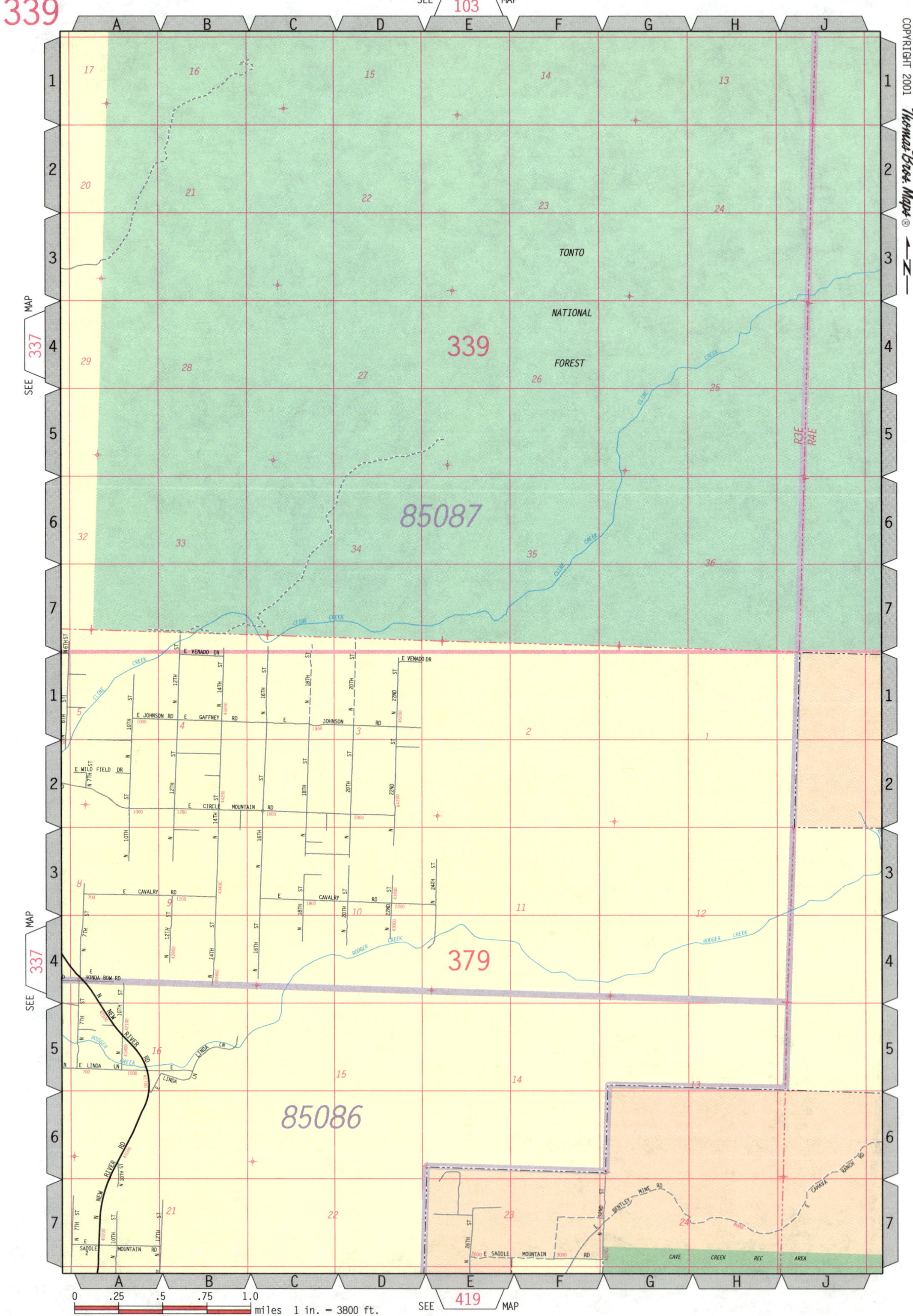

SEE 103 MAP
SEE 337 MAP
SEE 419 MAP
TONTO
NATIONAL
FOREST
339
85087
379
85086
CLINE CREEK
RODGER CREEK
E VENADO DR
E JOHNSON RD
E GAFFNEY RD
E WILDFIELD DR
E CIRCLE MOUNTAIN RD
E CAVALRY RD
HONDA BOW RD
N NEW RIVER RD
E LINDA LN
E SADDLE MOUNTAIN RD
BENTLEY MINE RD
E CAHAVA RANCH RD
CAVE CREEK REC AREA
N 7TH ST
N 10TH ST
N 12TH ST
N 14TH ST
N 16TH ST
N 18TH ST
N 20TH ST
N 22ND ST
N 24TH ST
N 26TH ST
N 32ND ST
R3E
R4E
miles 1 in. = 3800 ft.

PHOENIX
MAP

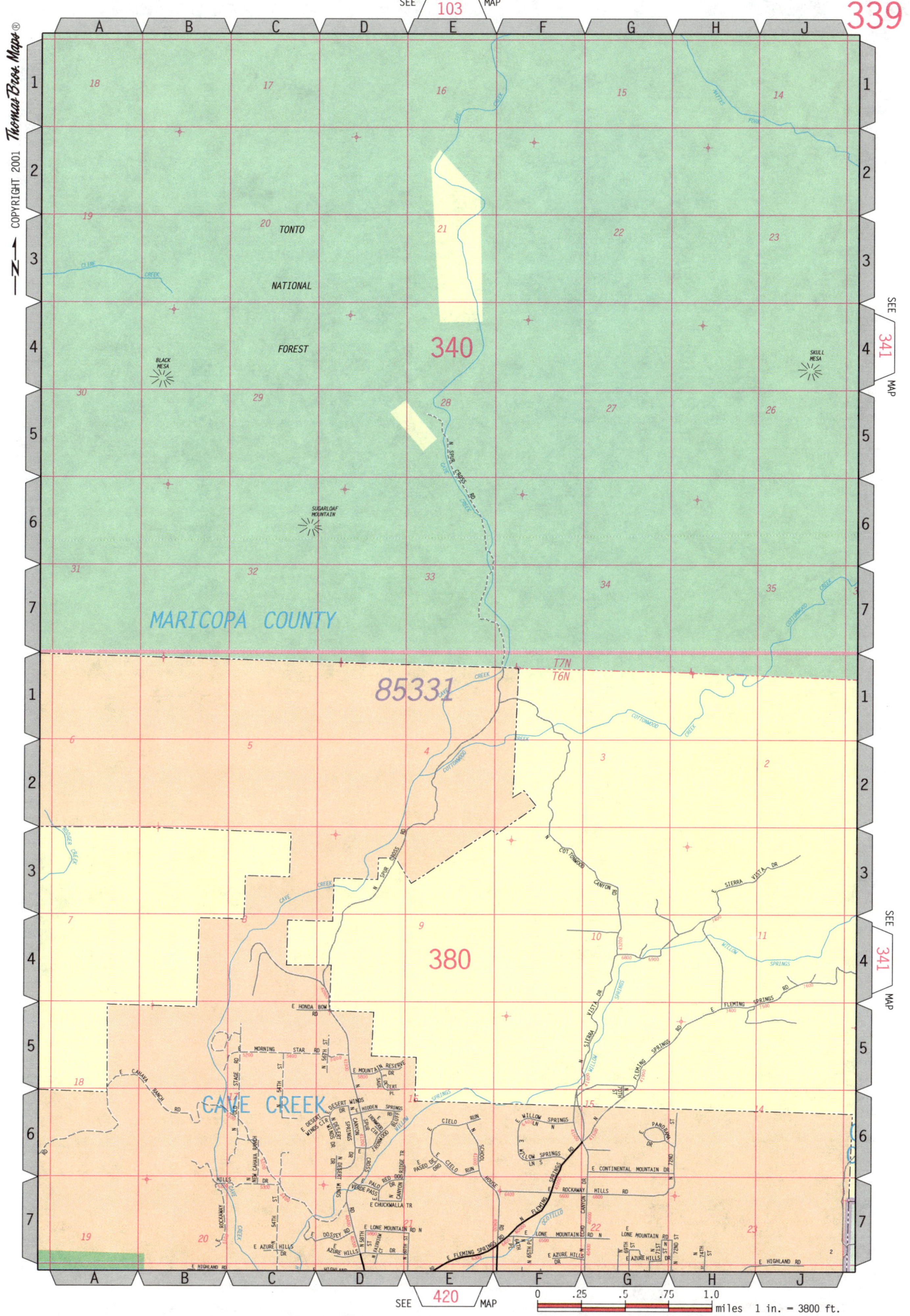

SEE 103 MAP
TONTO
NATIONAL
FOREST
340
BLACK MESA
SKULL MESA
SUGARLOAF MOUNTAIN
MARICOPA COUNTY
T7N
T6N
85331
380
CAVE CREEK
CAVE CREEK
COTTONWOOD CREEK
N SPUR CROSS RD
N COTTONWOOD CANYON RD
E SIERRA VISTA DR
N SIERRA VISTA DR
E FLEMING SPRINGS RD
WILLOW SPRINGS
E HONDA BOW RD
MORNING STAR RD
E MOUNTAIN RESERVE DR
E CAHAVA RANCH RD
DESERT WINDS
HIDDEN SPRINGS
CIELO RUN
E WILLOW SPRINGS LN
E CONTINENTAL MOUNTAIN DR
ROCKAWAY HILLS RD
E CHUCKWALLA TR
E LONE MOUNTAIN RD
E AZURE HILLS DR
E HIGHLAND RD
N SCHOOL HOUSE RD
N 72ND ST
PANORAMA DR
SEE 341 MAP
SEE 420 MAP
PHOENIX
MAP
Thomas Bros. Maps®
© COPYRIGHT 2001
0 .25 .5 .75 1.0 miles 1 in. = 3800 ft.

PHOENIX

MAP

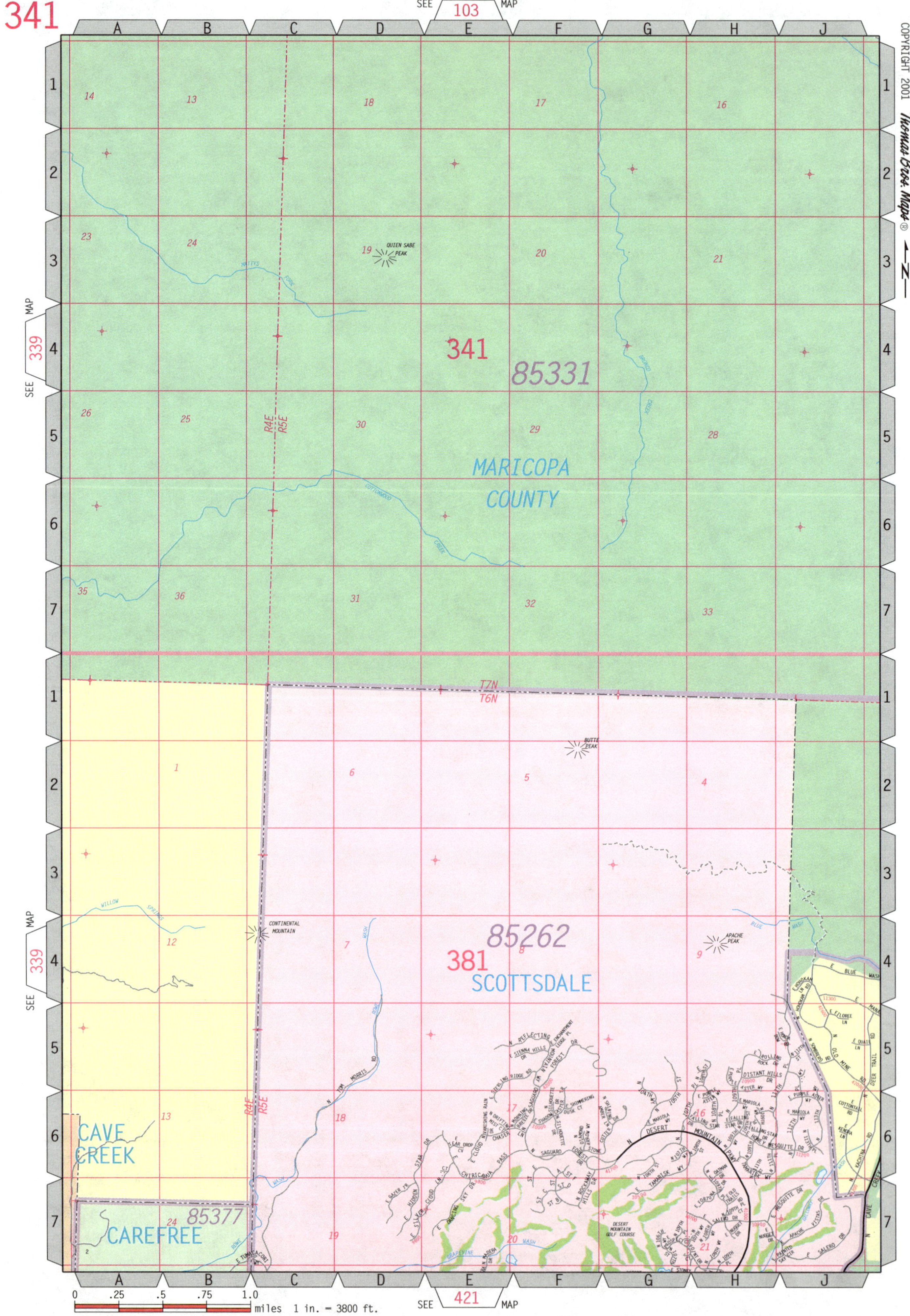

SEE 103 MAP
SEE 339 MAP
SEE 421 MAP
COPYRIGHT 2001 Thomas Bros. Maps®
N
QUIEN SABE PEAK
NATIVS FORK
341
85331
MARICOPA COUNTY
COTTONWOOD CREEK
R4E R5E
T7N T6N
BUTTE PEAK
CONTINENTAL MOUNTAIN
WILLOW SPRINGS
BLUE WASH
APACHE PEAK
85262
381
SCOTTSDALE
CAVE CREEK
CAREFREE
85377
DESERT MOUNTAIN PKWY
DESERT MOUNTAIN GOLF COURSE
N TOM MORRIS RD
CHIRICAHUA PASS
GRAPEVINE WASH
0 .25 .5 .75 1.0
miles 1 in. = 3800 ft.

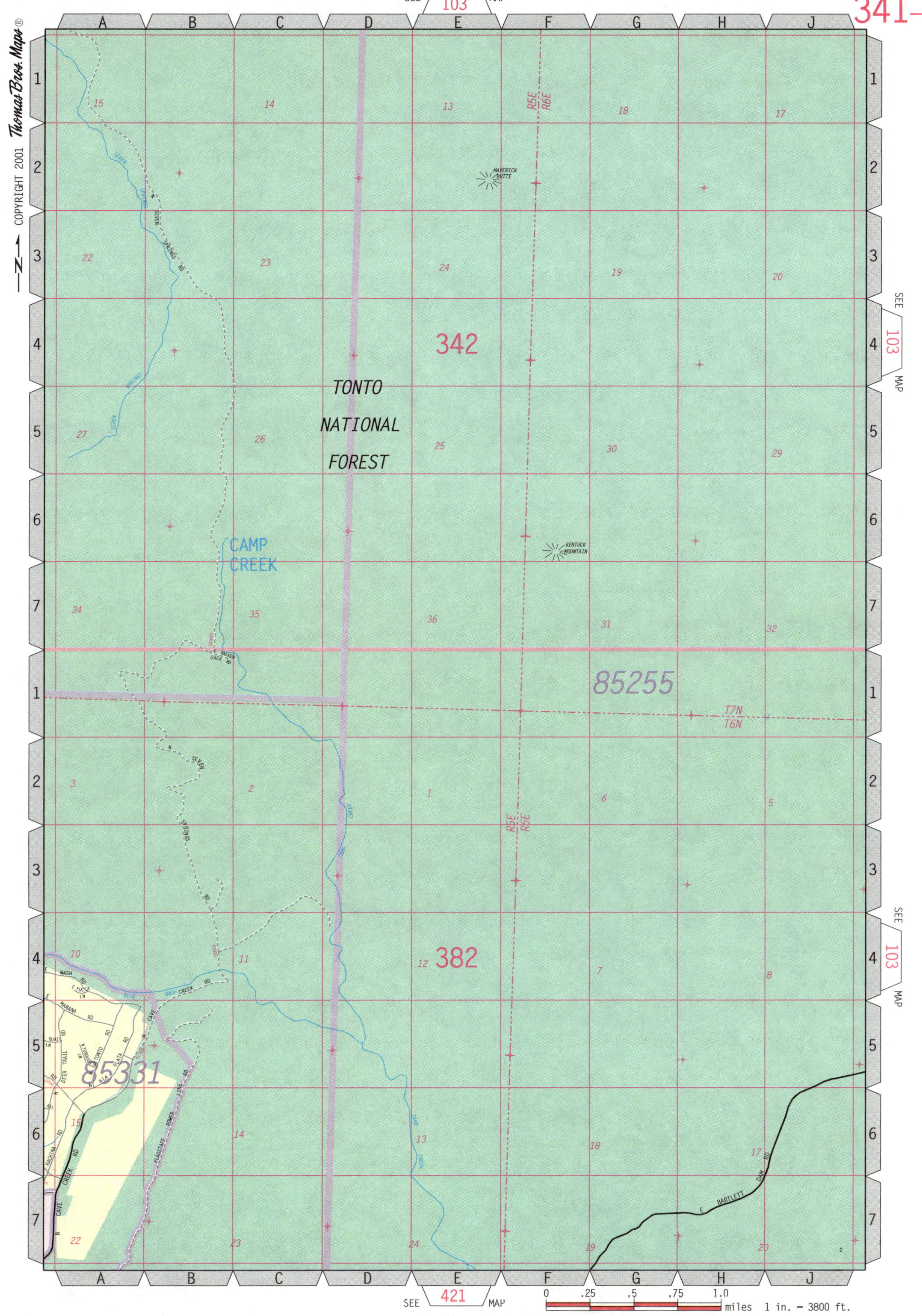
SEE 103 MAP
342
TONTO
NATIONAL
FOREST
MAVERICK BUTTE
KENTUCK MOUNTAIN
CAMP
CREEK
R5E
R6E
T7N
T6N
85255
85331
382
SEVEN SPRINGS RD
CAVE CREEK RD
FLAGSTAFF POWER LINE RD
BLUE WASH CREEK RD
E BARTLETT DAM RD
E MANANA LN
DEER TRAIL
TONTO
KACHINA
SEE 421 MAP
SEE 103 MAP
0 .25 .5 .75 1.0 miles 1 in. = 3800 ft.

PHOENIX

MAP

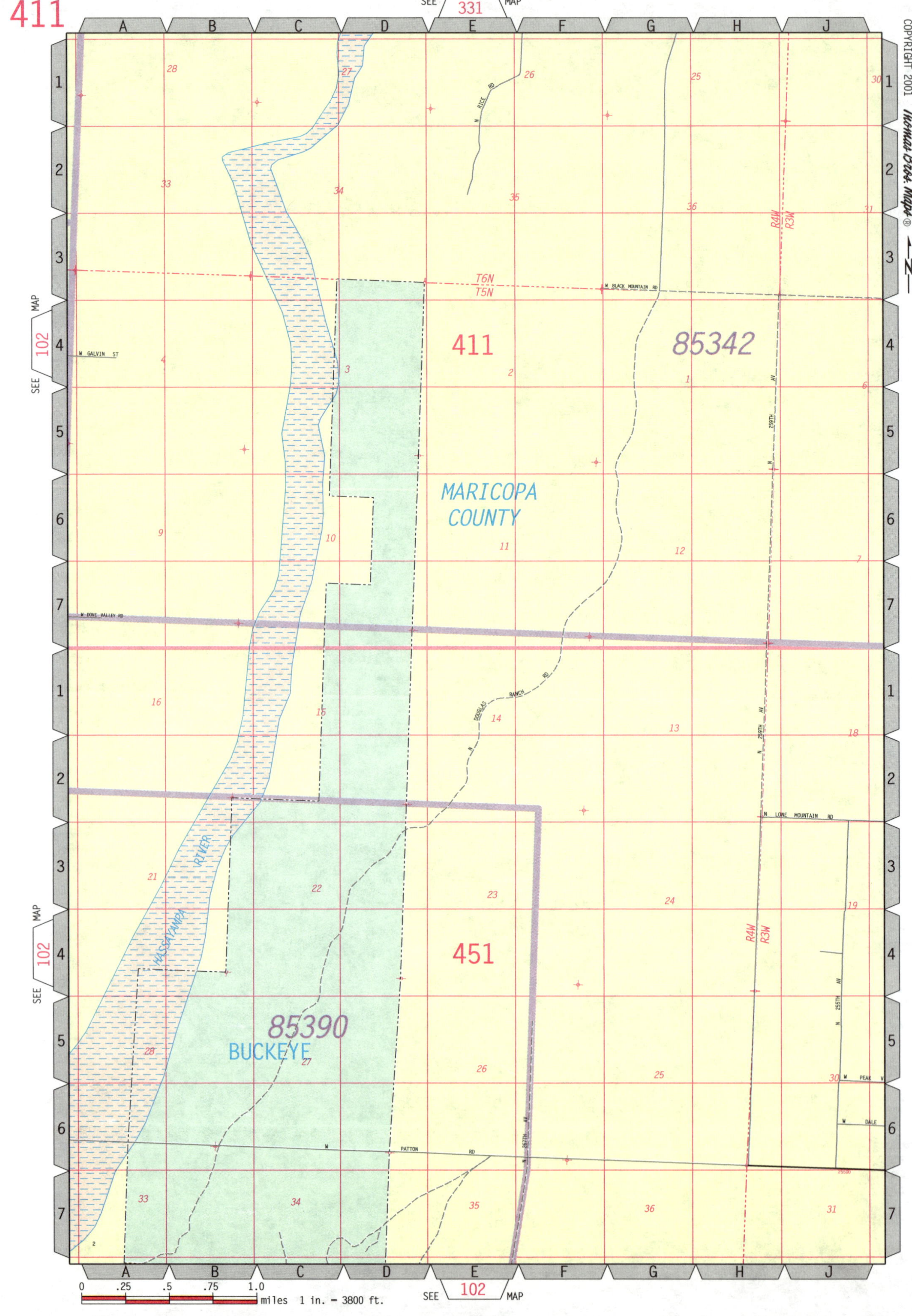
SEE 331 MAP
SEE 102 MAP
SEE 102 MAP
SEE 102 MAP
411
451
85342
85390
MARICOPA COUNTY
BUCKEYE
HASSAYAMPA RIVER
T6N
T5N
R4W R3W
W BLACK MOUNTAIN RD
W GALVIN ST
W DOVE VALLEY RD
N RICE RD
N DOUGLAS RANCH RD
N 259TH AV
N LONE MOUNTAIN RD
N 267TH AV
W PATTON RD
N 255TH AV
W PEAK V
W DALE
miles 1 in. = 3800 ft.

PHOENIX
MAP

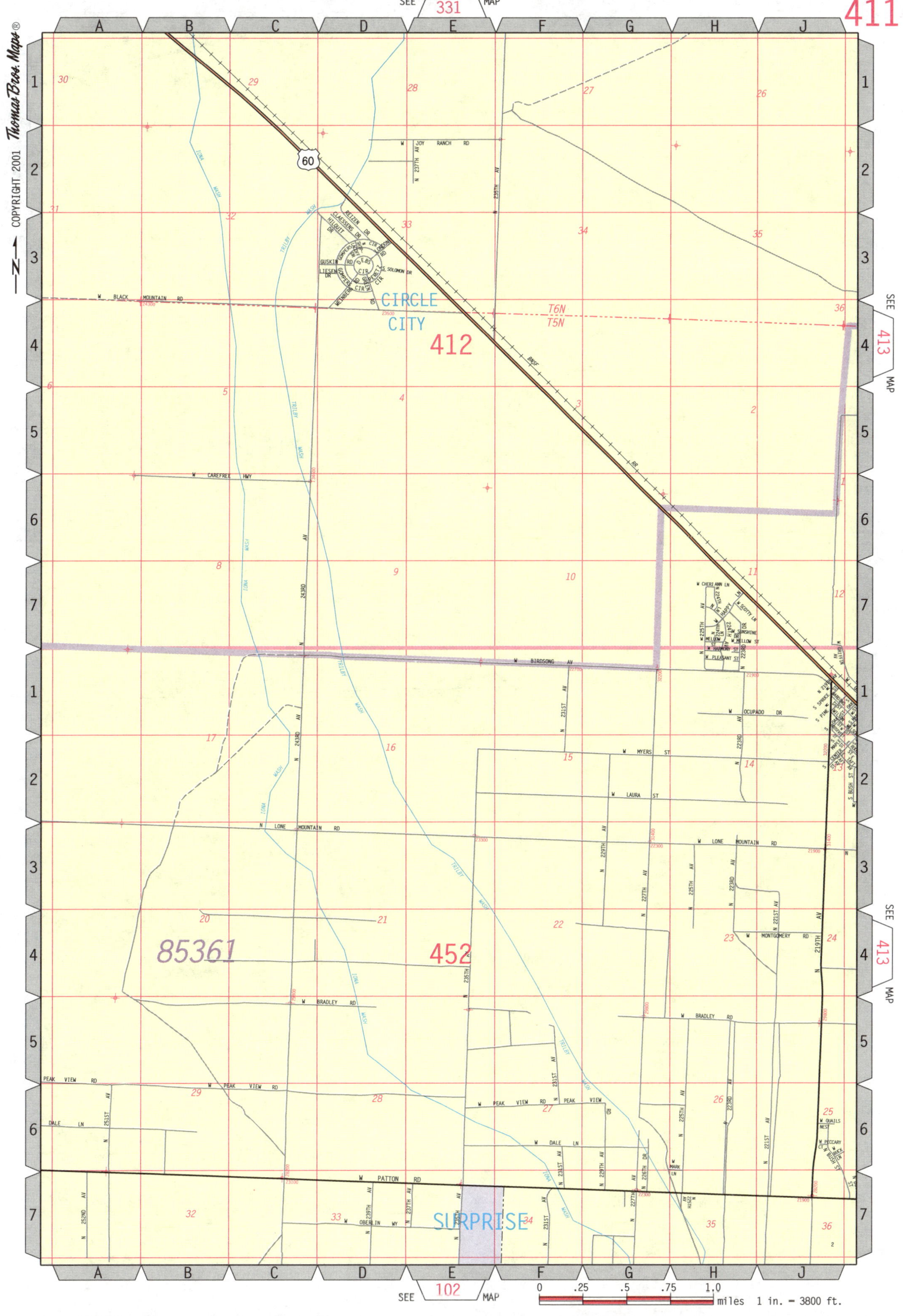

SEE 331 MAP
SEE 413 MAP
SEE 102 MAP
PHOENIX
MAP
CIRCLE CITY
SURPRISE
412
452
85361
T6N
T5N
W JOY RANCH RD
W BLACK MOUNTAIN RD
W CAREFREE HWY
W BIRDSONG AV
W OCUPADO DR
W MYERS ST
W LAURA ST
N LONE MOUNTAIN RD
W LONE MOUNTAIN RD
W MONTGOMERY RD
W BRADLEY RD
PEAK VIEW RD
W PEAK VIEW RD
DALE LN
W DALE LN
W PATTON RD
W OBERLIN WY
N 243RD AV
N 235TH AV
N 231ST AV
N 229TH AV
N 227TH AV
N 225TH AV
N 223RD AV
N 221ST AV
N 219TH AV
N 251ST AV
N 252ND AV
N 237TH AV
N 239TH AV
IONA WASH
TRILBY WASH
BNSF RR
60
0 .25 .5 .75 1.0 miles 1 in. = 3800 ft.

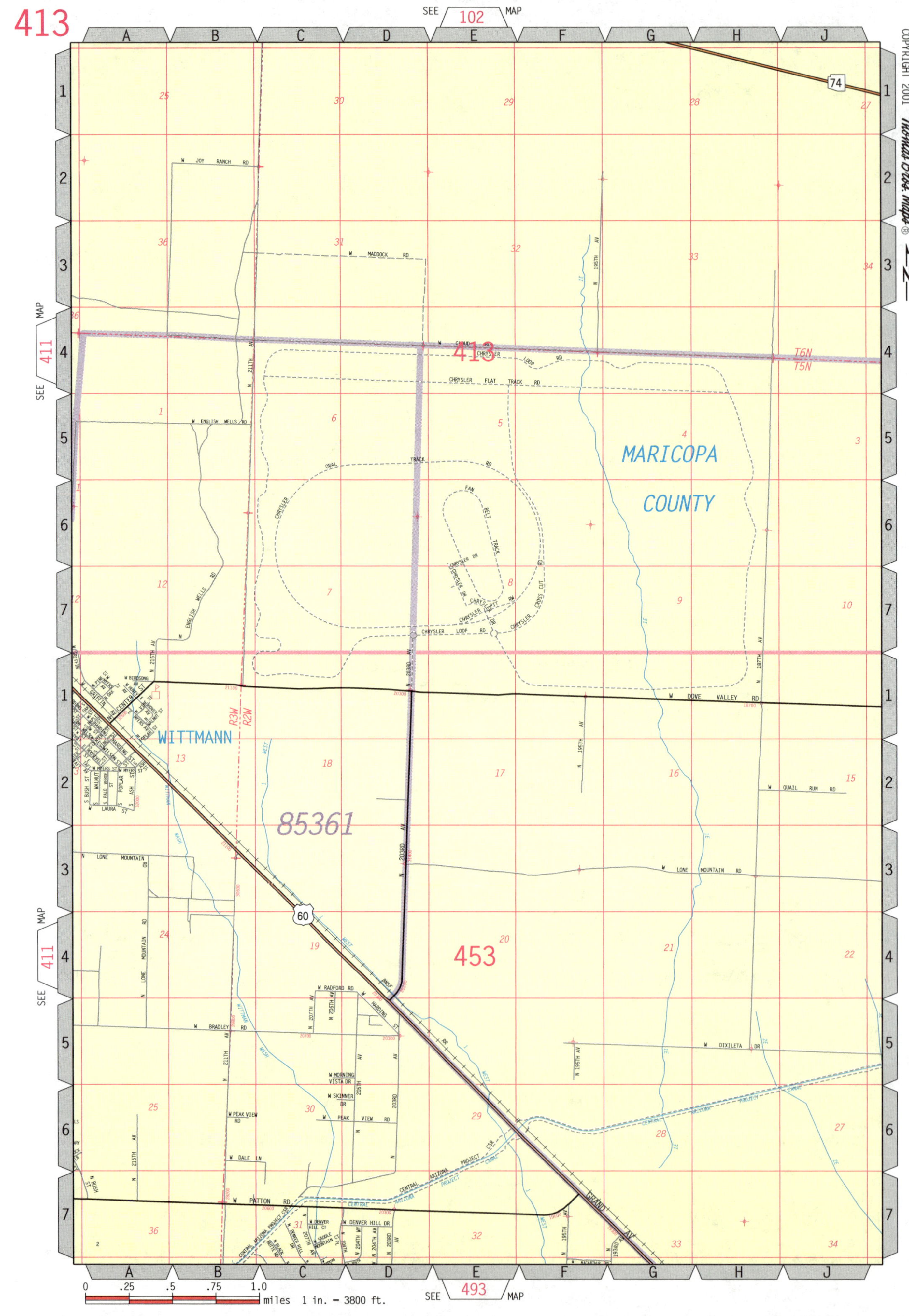

0 .25 .5 .75 1.0 miles 1 in. = 3800 ft.

PHOENIX

MAP

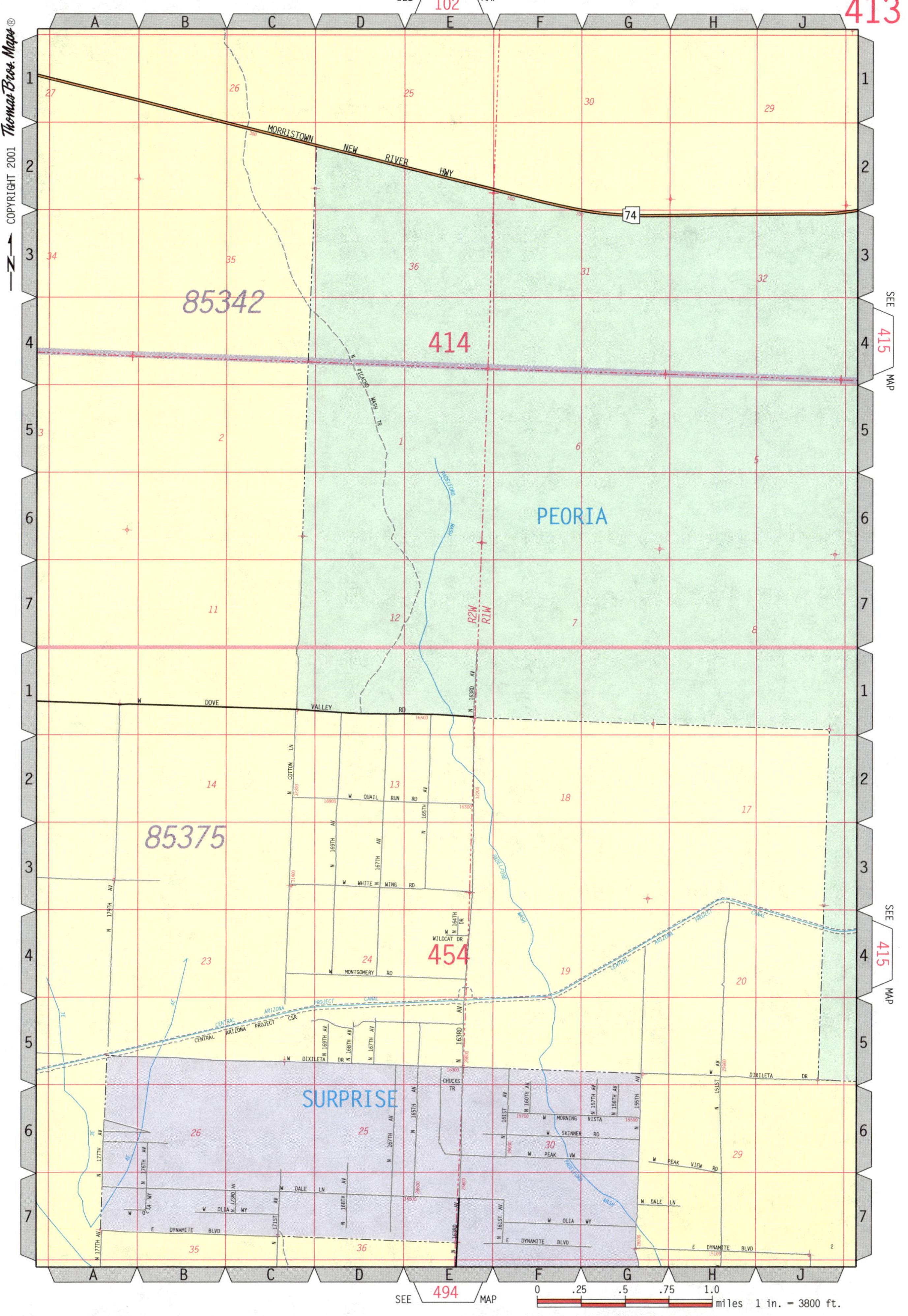
SEE 102 MAP
85342
414
PEORIA
MORRISTOWN NEW RIVER HWY
74
N PICACHO WASH TR
R2W R1W
W DOVE VALLEY RD
N 163RD AV
N COTTON LN
W QUAIL RUN RD
N 165TH AV
N 169TH AV
N 167TH AV
W WHITE WING RD
85375
N 179TH AV
N 164TH DR
WILDCAT DR
454
W MONTGOMERY RD
CENTRAL ARIZONA PROJECT CANAL
CENTRAL ARIZONA PROJECT CSR
W DIXILETA DR
N 168TH AV
SURPRISE
CHUCKS TR
N 161ST AV
N 160TH AV
N 157TH AV
N 156TH AV
N 155TH AV
N 151ST AV
W MORNING VISTA
W SKINNER RD
W PEAK VW
W PEAK VIEW RD
N 177TH AV
N 176TH AV
W DALE LN
N 173RD AV
W OLIA WY
N 171ST AV
E DYNAMITE BLVD
SEE 415 MAP
SEE 494 MAP
miles 1 in. = 3800 ft.

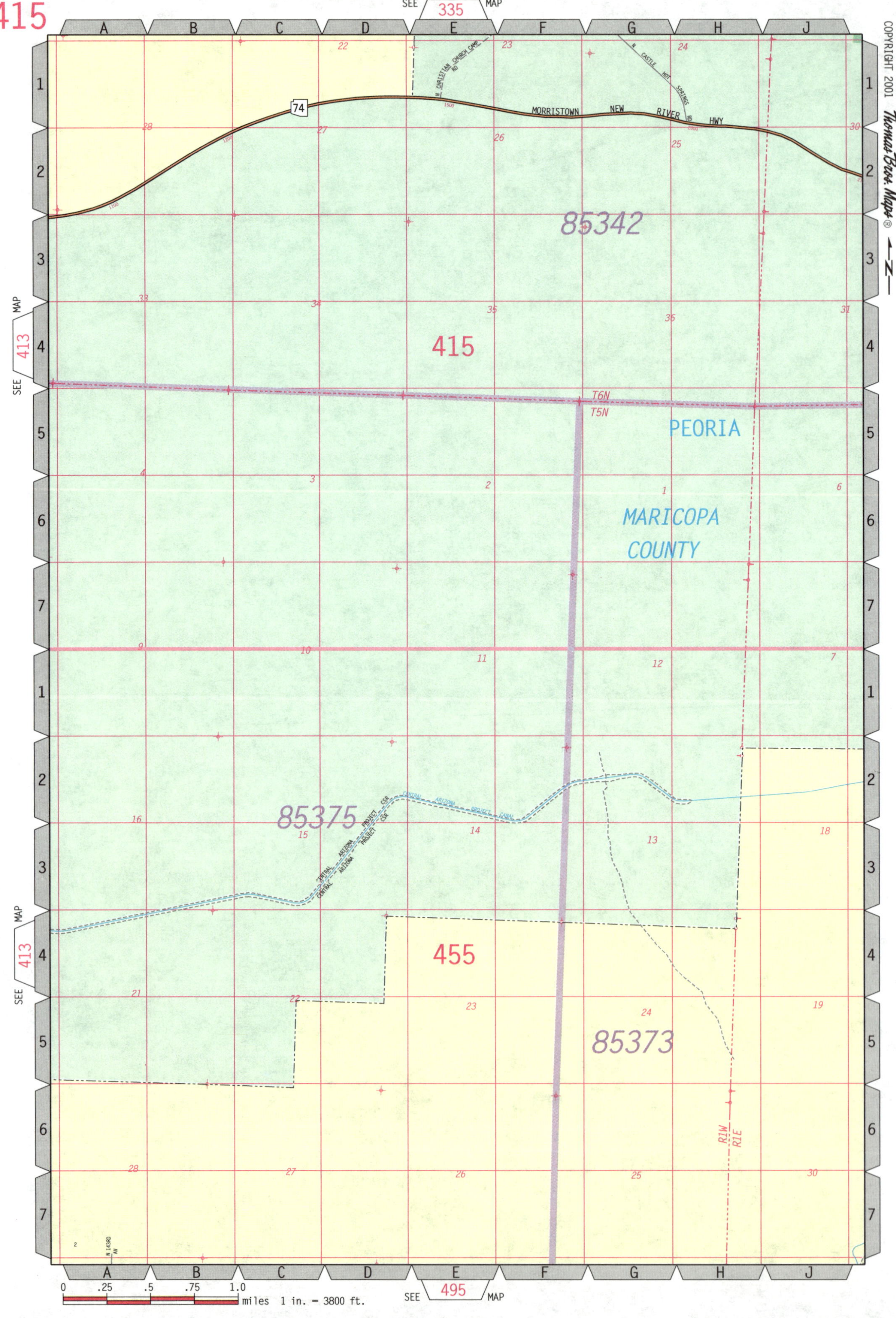
SEE 335 MAP
A
B
C
D
E
F
G
H
J
1
2
3
4
5
6
7
N CHRISTIAN CHURCH CAMP RD
N CASTLE HOT SPRINGS RD
74
MORRISTOWN NEW RIVER HWY
85342
SEE 413 MAP
415
T6N
T5N
PEORIA
MARICOPA
COUNTY
CENTRAL ARIZONA PROJECT CANAL
CENTRAL ARIZONA PROJECT CSR
85375
455
85373
R1W
R1E
N 143RD AV
SEE 495 MAP
0 .25 .5 .75 1.0 miles 1 in. = 3800 ft.
COPYRIGHT 2001 Thomas Bros. Maps®
N

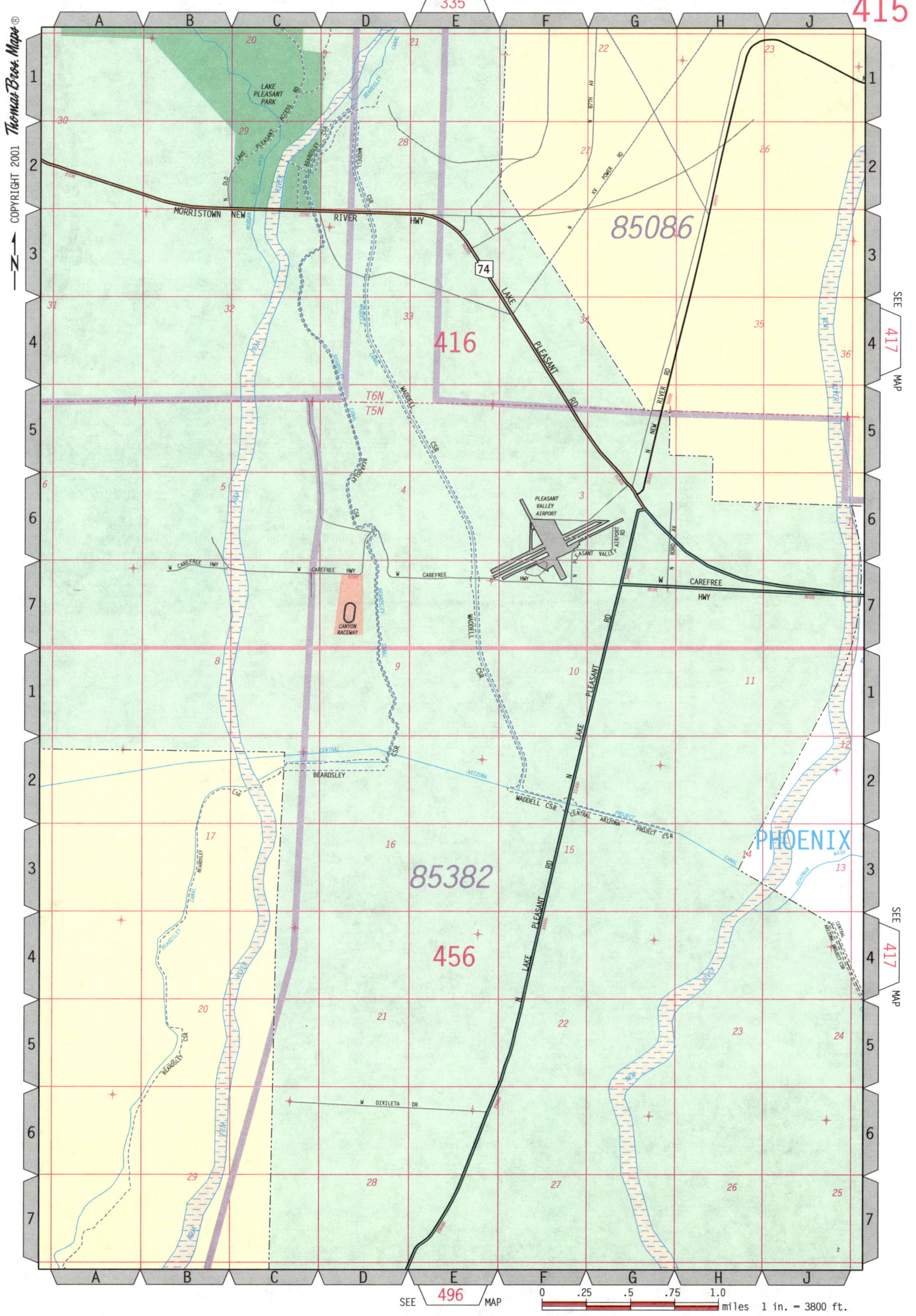

SEE 335 MAP
SEE 417 MAP
SEE 496 MAP
PHOENIX
MAP
LAKE PLEASANT PARK
MORRISTOWN NEW RIVER HWY
74
LAKE PLEASANT RD
N NEW RIVER RD
85086
416
T6N
T5N
PLEASANT VALLEY AIRPORT
W CAREFREE HWY
CAREFREE HWY
CANYON RACEWAY
WADDELL CSR
BEARDSLEY CANAL
BEARDSLEY CSR
CENTRAL ARIZONA PROJECT CSR
N LAKE PLEASANT RD
85382
456
PHOENIX
W DIXILETA DR
AGUA FRIA RIVER
NEW RIVER
0 .25 .5 .75 1.0 miles 1 in. = 3800 ft.

SEE 337 MAP

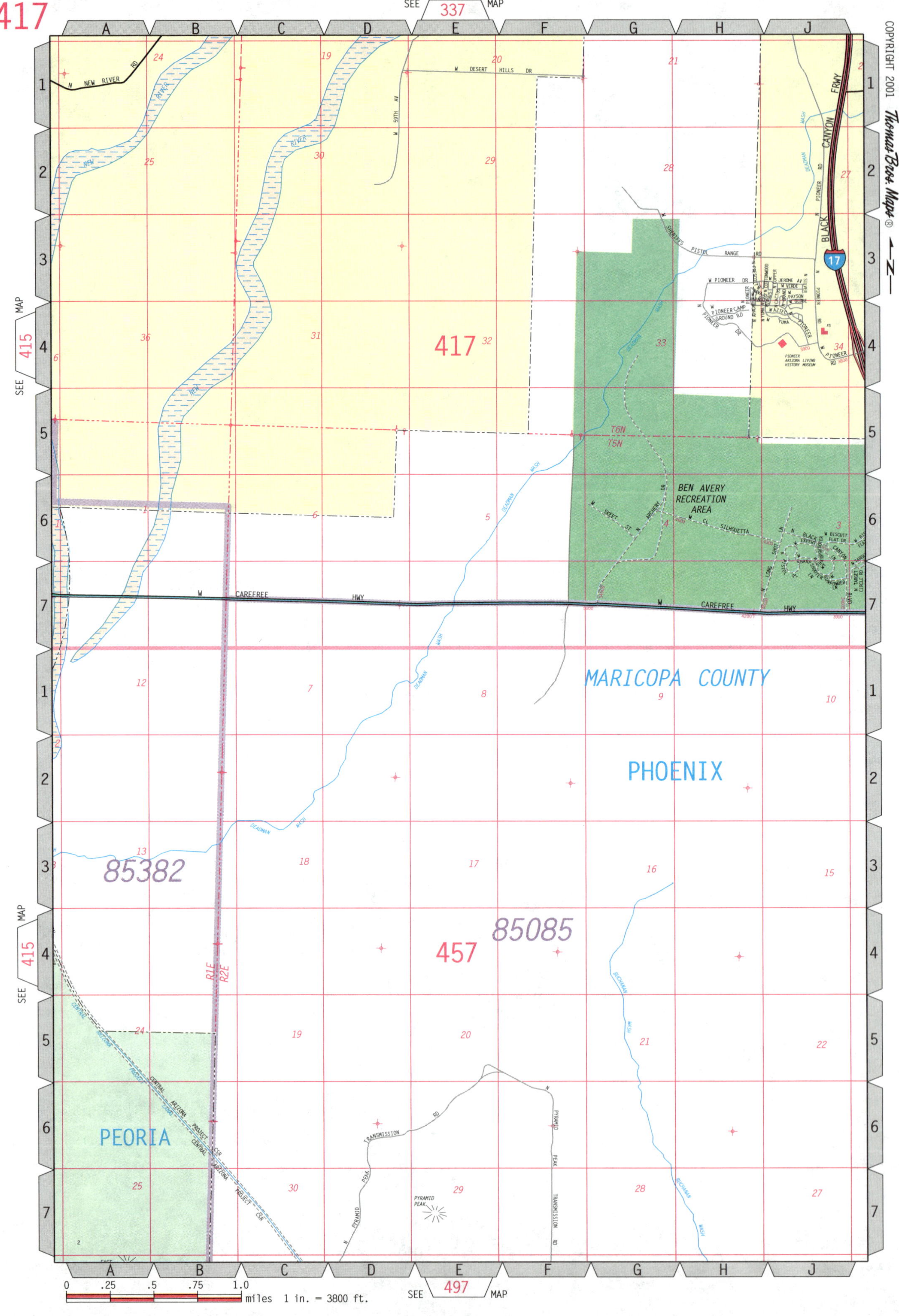

SEE 415 MAP

SEE 415 MAP

PHOENIX

MAP

0 .25 .5 .75 1.0 miles 1 in. = 3800 ft.

SEE 497 MAP

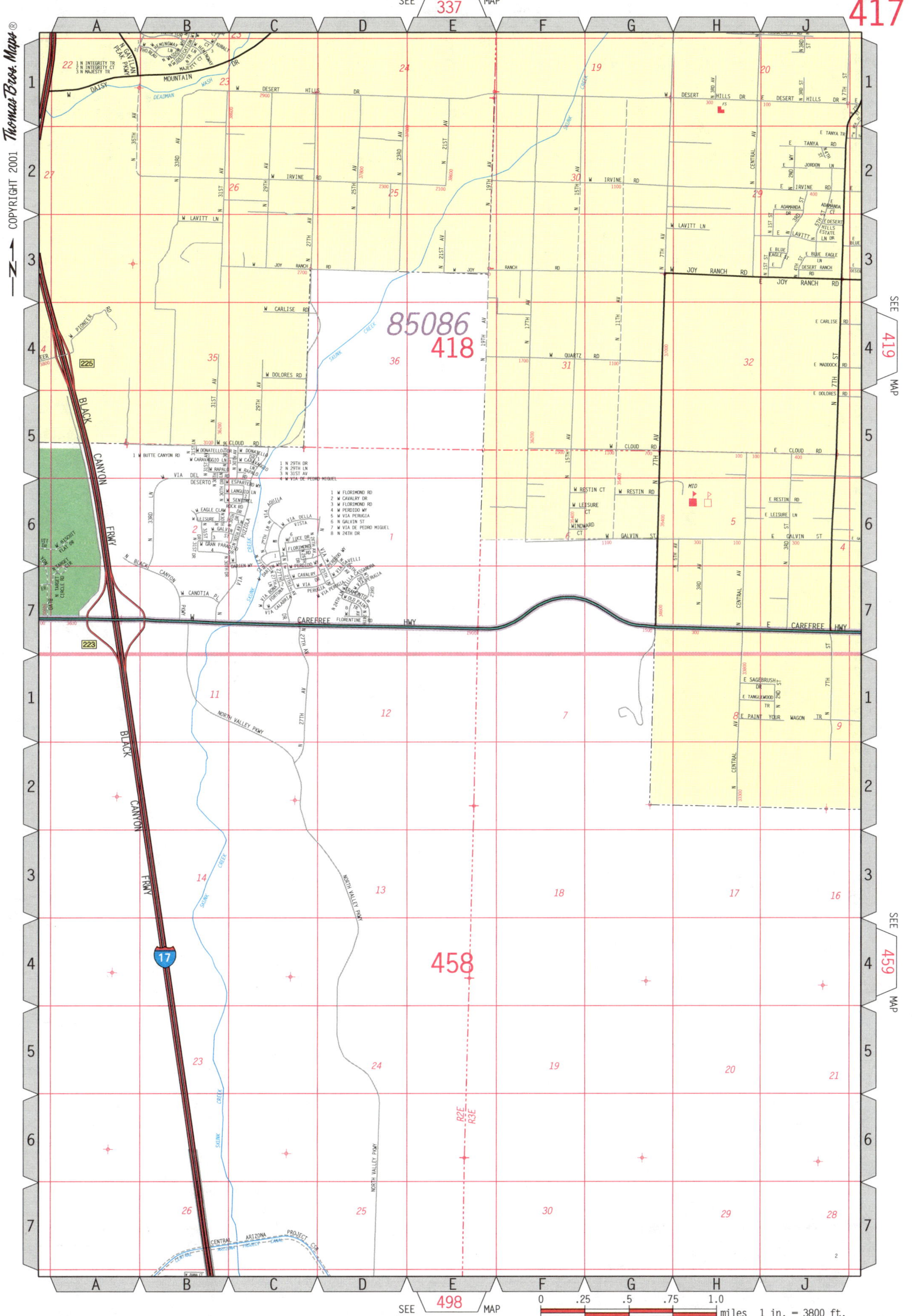
SEE 337 MAP
SEE 419 MAP
SEE 459 MAP
SEE 498 MAP
PHOENIX
MAP
85086
418
458
W DESERT HILLS DR
W IRVINE RD
W LAVITT LN
W JOY RANCH RD
W CARLISE RD
W DOLORES RD
W QUARTZ RD
W CLOUD RD
E CLOUD RD
W RESTIN RD
W GALVIN ST
CAREFREE HWY
E CAREFREE HWY
BLACK CANYON FRWY
NORTH VALLEY PKWY
SKUNK CREEK
DEADMAN WASH
MOUNTAIN DR
W DAISY
W PIONEER RD
CENTRAL ARIZONA PROJECT CANAL
17
225
223
R2E
R3E
0 .25 .5 .75 1.0 miles 1 in. = 3800 ft.

SEE 339 MAP

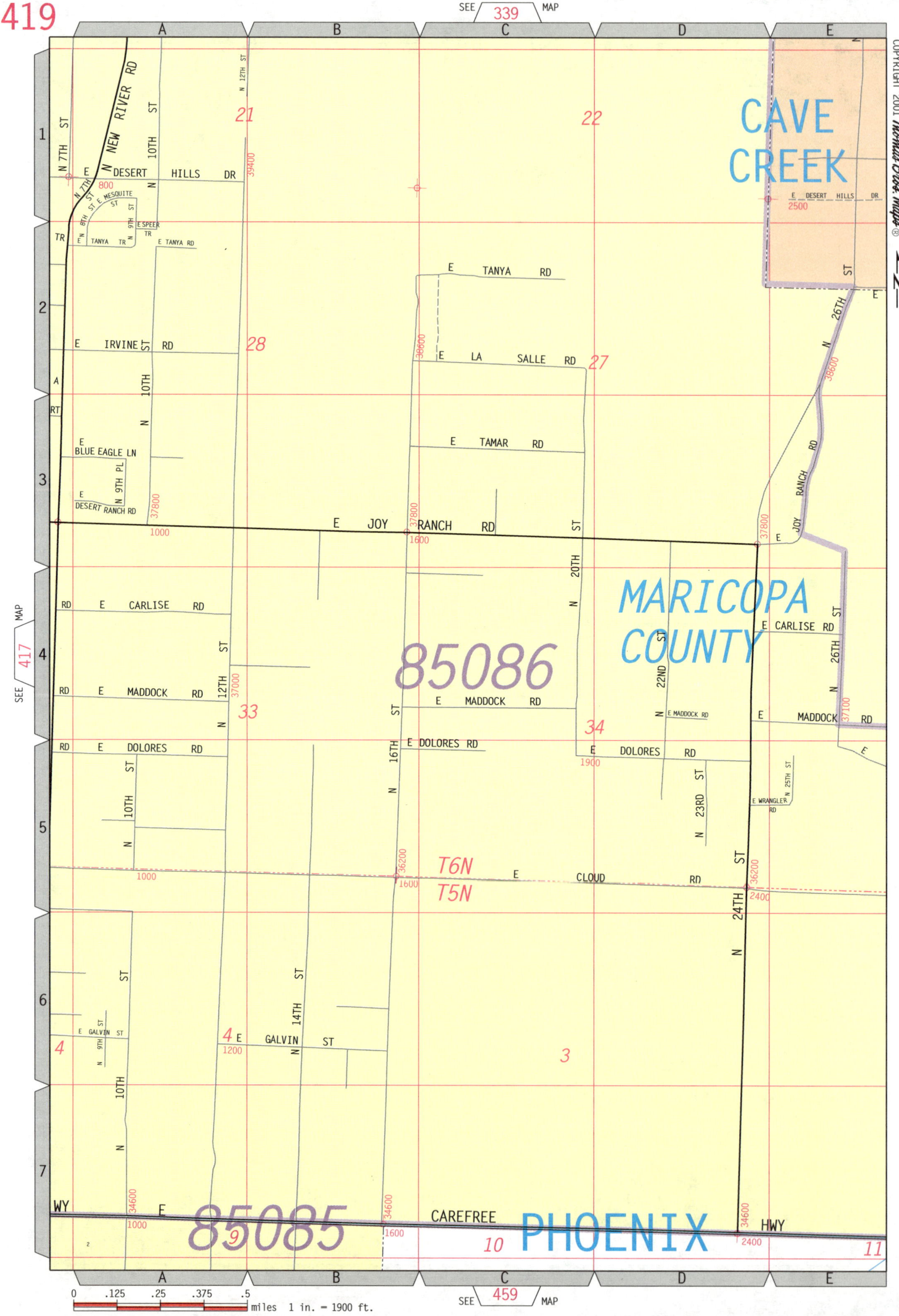

SEE 417 MAP

0 .125 .25 .375 .5 miles 1 in. = 1900 ft.

SEE 459 MAP

PHOENIX

MAP

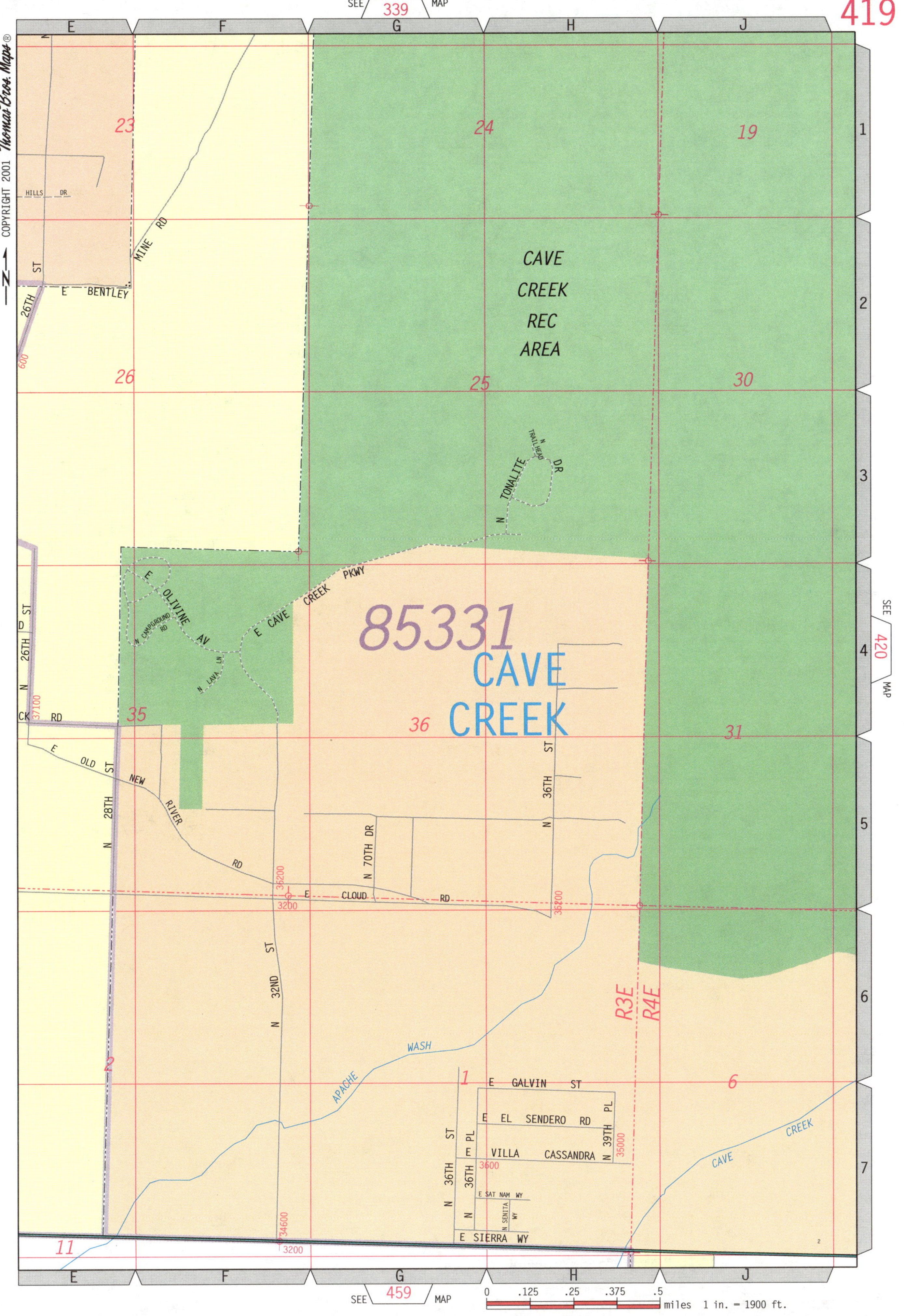
SEE 339 MAP
E
F
G
H
J
1
2
3
4
5
6
7
23
24
19
HILLS DR
MINE RD
ST
26TH
E BENTLEY
CAVE
CREEK
REC
AREA
26
25
30
600
N TRAILHEAD DR
TONALITE
N
E OLIVINE AV
N CAMPGROUND RD
N LAVA LN
E CAVE CREEK PKWY
85331
CAVE
CREEK
D ST
26TH
N
37100
CK RD
35
36
31
E OLD ST
NEW RIVER
RD
N 28TH
36TH ST
N
N 70TH DR
36200
E CLOUD RD
3200
36200
N 32ND ST
R3E
R4E
APACHE WASH
2
1
E GALVIN ST
6
E EL SENDERO RD
N 39TH PL
35000
N 36TH ST
36TH PL
E VILLA CASSANDRA
3600
E SAT NAM WY
N SENITA WY
N
E SIERRA WY
CAVE CREEK
34600
3200
11
SEE 420 MAP
SEE 459 MAP
0 .125 .25 .375 .5 miles 1 in. = 1900 ft.
PHOENIX
MAP

SEE 339 MAP

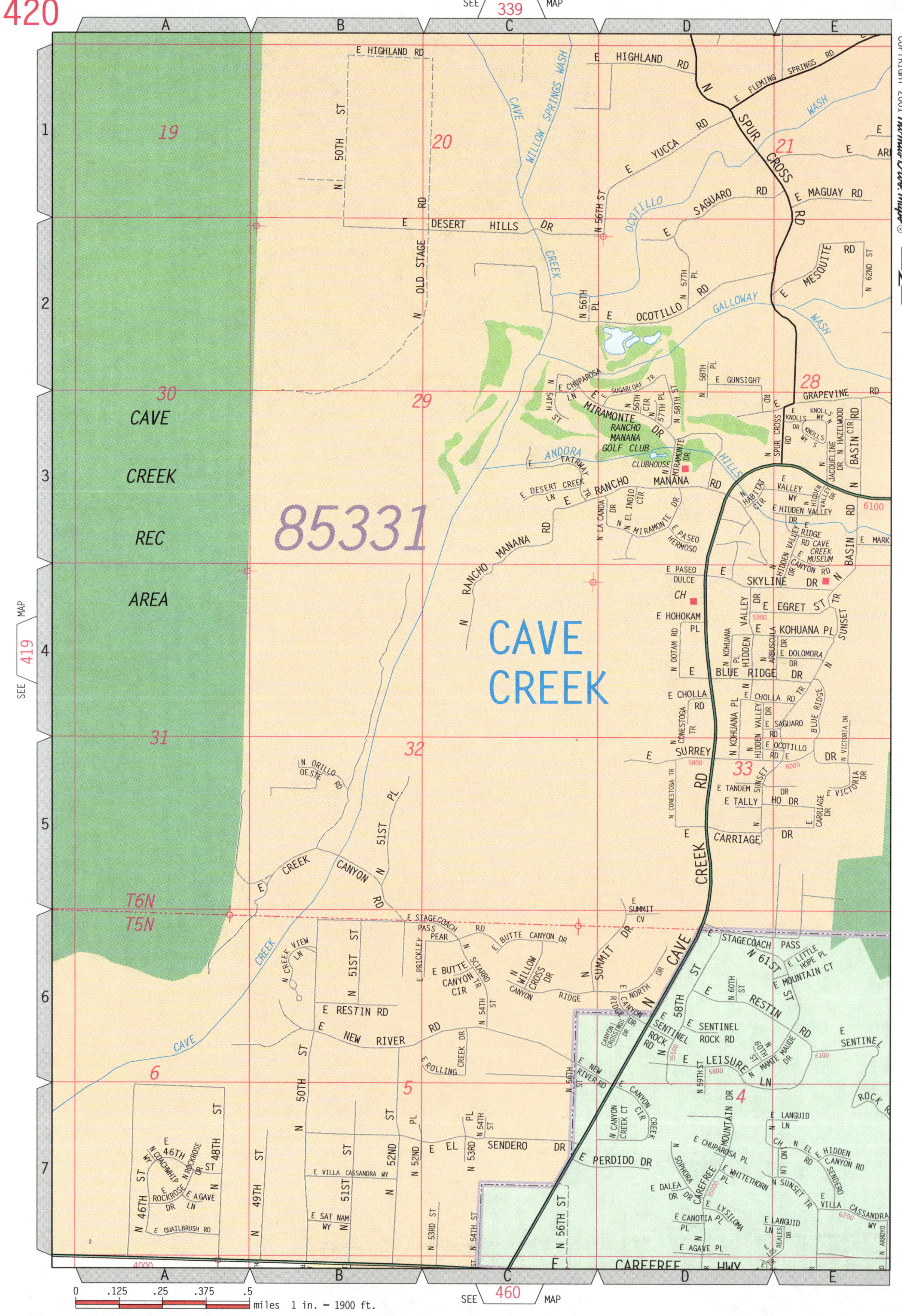

SEE 419 MAP

SEE 460 MAP

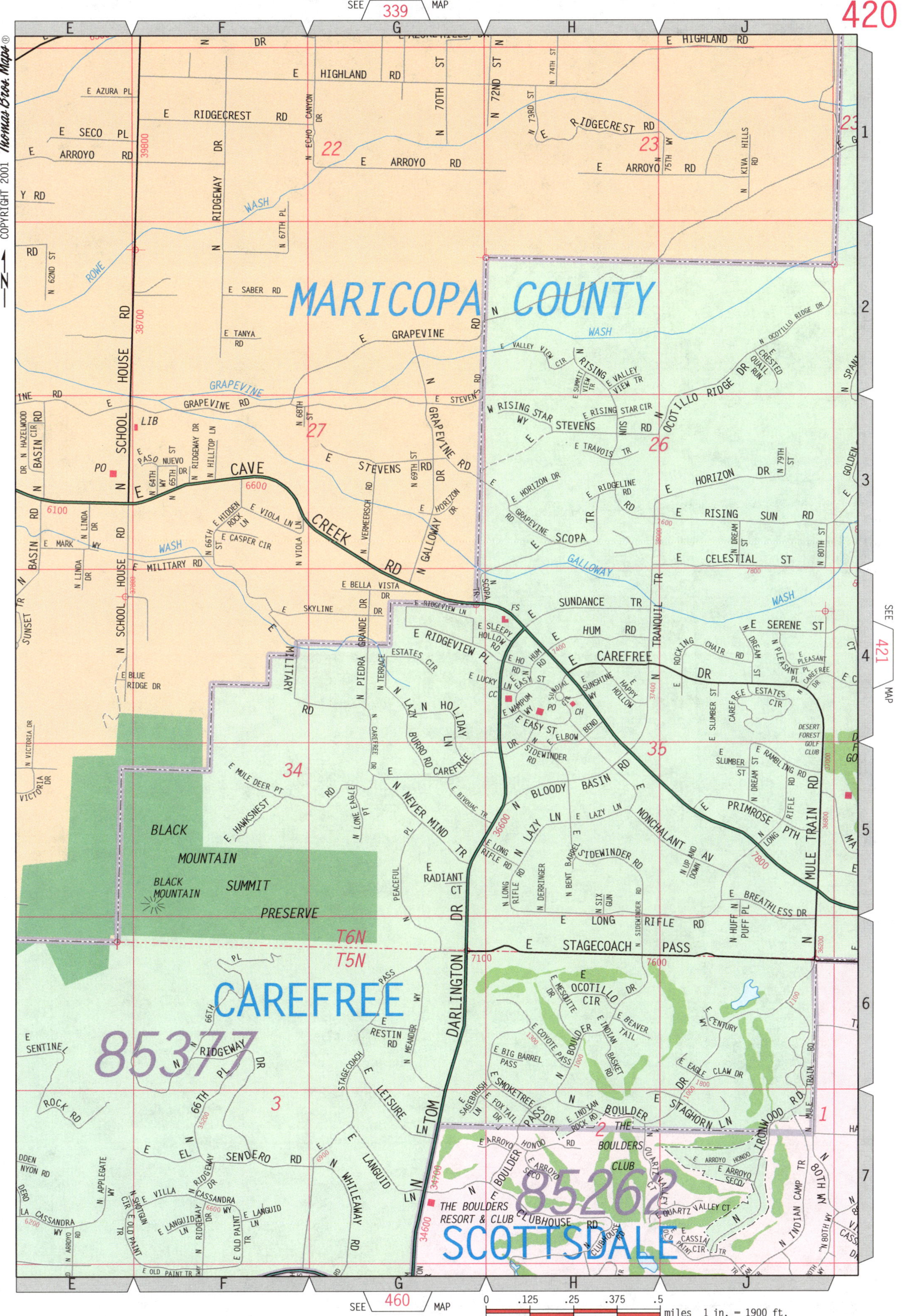

SEE 339 MAP
SEE 421 MAP
SEE 460 MAP
PHOENIX
MAP
Thomas Bros. Maps
COPYRIGHT 2001
MARICOPA COUNTY
CAREFREE
85377
85262
SCOTTSDALE
BLACK MOUNTAIN SUMMIT PRESERVE
BLACK MOUNTAIN
THE BOULDERS RESORT & CLUB
THE BOULDERS CLUB
DESERT FOREST GOLF CLUB
T6N
T5N
E HIGHLAND RD
E RIDGECREST RD
E ARROYO RD
E SECO PL
E AZURA PL
N RIDGEWAY DR
N ECHO CANYON DR
N 70TH ST
N 72ND ST
N 73RD ST
N 74TH ST
N 75TH WY
N KIVA HILLS RD
N 62ND ST
N 67TH PL
ROWE WASH
E SABER RD
E TANYA RD
N SCHOOL HOUSE RD
E GRAPEVINE RD
GRAPEVINE WASH
E STEVENS RD
N 68TH ST
N GRAPEVINE RD
E CAVE CREEK RD
N HAZELWOOD DR
N BASIN CIR
N 64TH WY
N 65TH DR
E PASO NUEVO ST
N RIDGEWAY DR
N HILLTOP LN
E HIDDEN ROCK LN
E VIOLA LN
N VIOLA DR
N 66TH ST
E CASPER CIR
N VERMEERSCH RD
N 69TH ST
N GALLOWAY DR
E HORIZON DR
E MARK WY
N LINDA DR
N BASIN RD
E MILITARY RD
E BELLA VISTA DR
E SKYLINE DR
N SUNSET TR
E BLUE RIDGE DR
N VICTORIA DR
E VALLEY VIEW CIR
N RISING SUN TR
E RISING STAR CIR
W RISING STAR WY
E TRAVOIS TR
E RIDGELINE RD
N OCOTILLO RIDGE DR
E CRESTED QUAIL RUN
E HORIZON DR
N 79TH ST
E RISING SUN RD
N DREAM ST
E CELESTIAL ST
N 80TH ST
N SCOPA TR
GALLOWAY WASH
E SUNDANCE TR
E HUM RD
N TRANQUIL TR
E SERENE ST
E ROCKING CHAIR RD
N PLEASANT PL
E CAREFREE DR
E RIDGEVIEW PL
E SLEEPY HOLLOW RD
E HO HUM RD
E EASY ST
E LUCKY LN
N PIEDRA GRANDE
N TERRACE
ESTATES CIR
N LAZY BURRO RD
N HOLIDAY LN
N CAREFREE DR
E SUNSHINE WY
E HAPPY HOLLOW
E WAMPUM WY
SUNDIAL CIR
E ELBOW BEND
E SIDEWINDER RD
N SLUMBER ST
CAREFREE ESTATES CIR
E RAMBLING RD
N RIFLE RD
E PRIMROSE PTH
N MULE TRAIN RD
E MULE DEER PT
E HAWKSNEST RD
N LONE EAGLE PT
N NEVER MIND TR
E CAREFREE
E BIVOUAC TR
N BLOODY BASIN RD
N LAZY LN
E LAZY LN
E NONCHALANT AV
E LONG RIFLE RD
N DERRINGER
N BENT BARREL
N SIX GUN RD
N UP AND DOWN
E BREATHLESS DR
N HUFF N PUFF PL
E RADIANT CT
N PEACEFUL PL
E LONG RIFLE RD
E STAGECOACH PASS
N DARLINGTON DR
E OCOTILLO CIR
E OCOTILLO DR
N MESQUITE DR
N BOULDER DR
E BEAVER TAIL
E INDIAN BASKET RD
E COYOTE PASS
E BIG BARREL PASS
E CENTURY WY
E EAGLE CLAW DR
E STAGHORN LN
E RESTIN RD
N MEANDER WY
E SENTINEL
N 66TH PL
E RIDGEWAY PL
E ROCK RD
N 66TH ST
E LEISURE LN
N TOM DARLINGTON DR
E SMOKETREE DR
E FOXTAIL DR
E SAGEBRUSH LN
E INDIAN ROCK RD
E BOULDER DR
E ARROYO HONDO
E ARROYO SECO
E ARROYO HONDO RD
N IRONWOOD RD
N MULE TRAIN RD
N INDIAN CAMP TR
N 80TH WY
E QUARTZ VALLEY CT
E CASSIA CIR
E CLUBHOUSE RD
N BOULDER DR
E EL SENDERO RD
N APPLEGATE WY
E VILLA CASSANDRA
LA CASSANDRA WY
N RIDGEWAY DR
E LANGUID LN
N WHILEAWAY RD
N LANGUID LN
E OLD PAINT TR
miles 1 in. = 1900 ft.

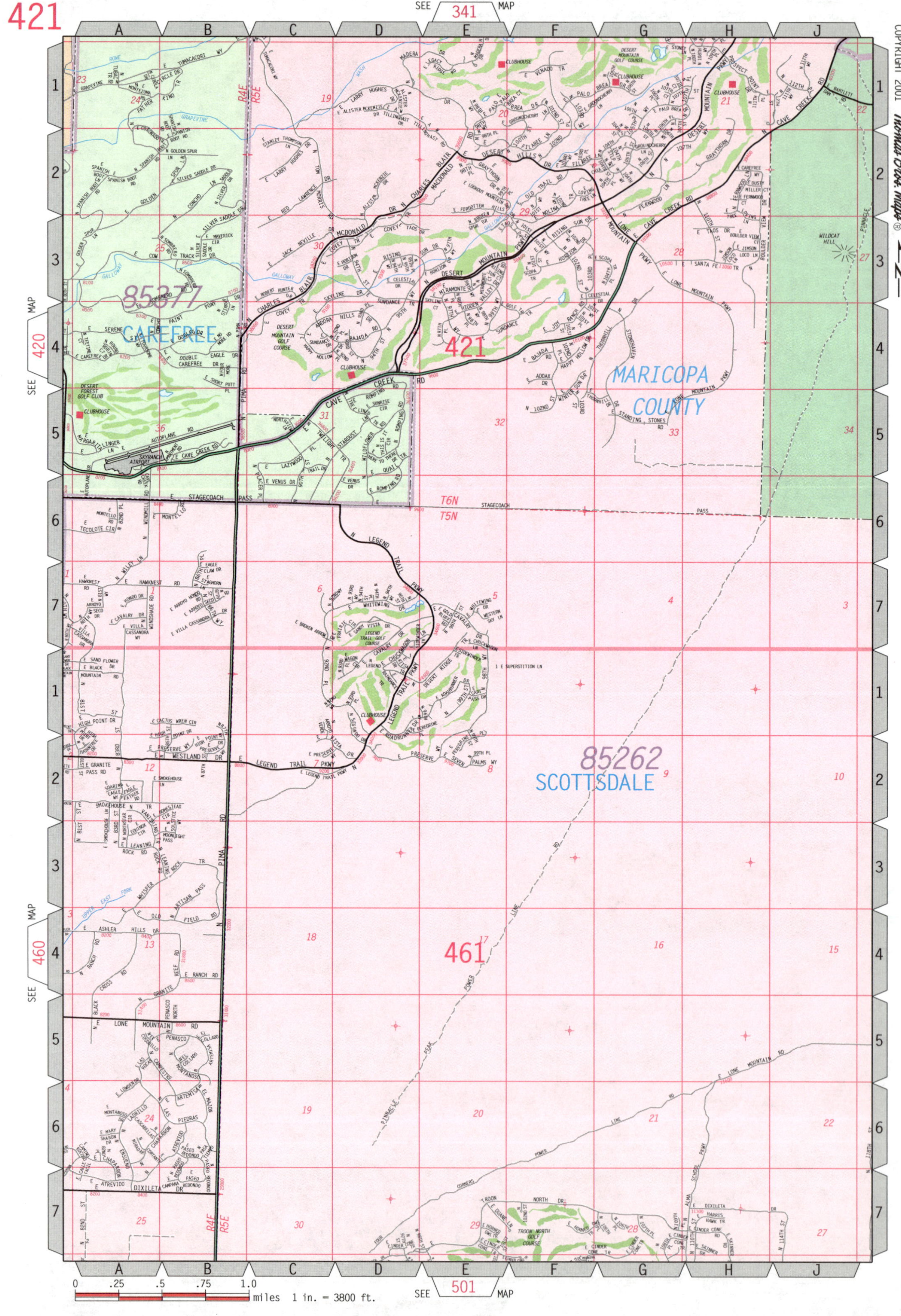

0 .25 .5 .75 1.0 miles 1 in. = 3800 ft.

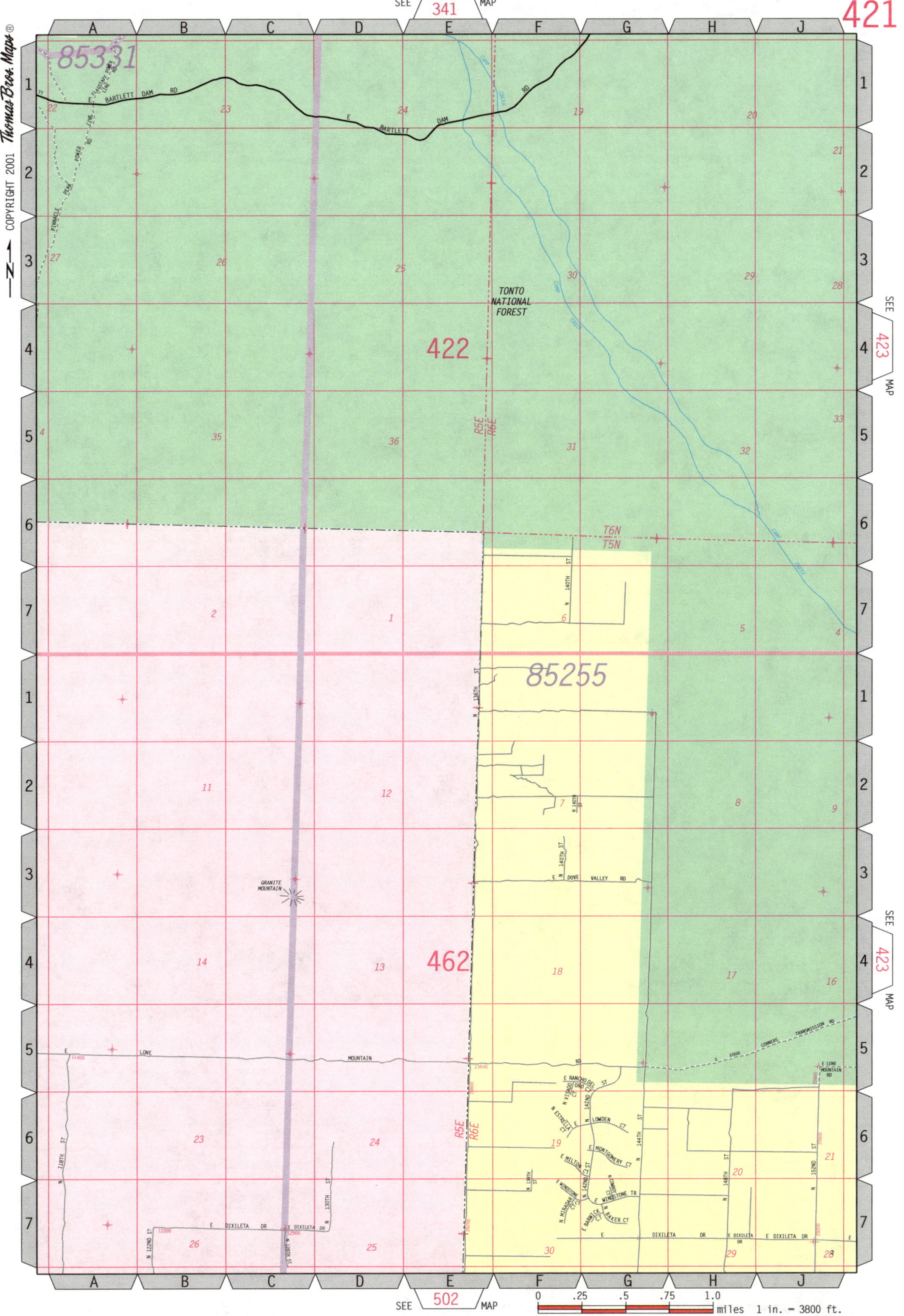

SEE 341 MAP
SEE 423 MAP
SEE 502 MAP
PHOENIX
MAP
Thomas Bros. Maps®
COPYRIGHT 2001
85331
85255
422
462
E BARTLETT DAM RD
TONTO NATIONAL FOREST
CAVE CREEK
R5E
R6E
T6N
T5N
N 140TH ST
N 138TH ST
E DOVE VALLEY RD
GRANITE MOUNTAIN
E LONE MOUNTAIN RD
E FOUR CORNERS TRANSMISSION RD
E RANCHO DEL ORO CT
N 142ND ST
N 144TH ST
E LOWDEN CT
N ESTRELLA CT
E MONTGOMERY CT
E MILTON CT
E WINDSTONE TR
E BARWICK CT
E BAKER CT
N 118TH ST
N 122ND ST
N 130TH ST
N 148TH ST
N 152ND ST
E DIXILETA DR
0 .25 .5 .75 1.0 miles 1 in. = 3800 ft.

SEE 103 MAP

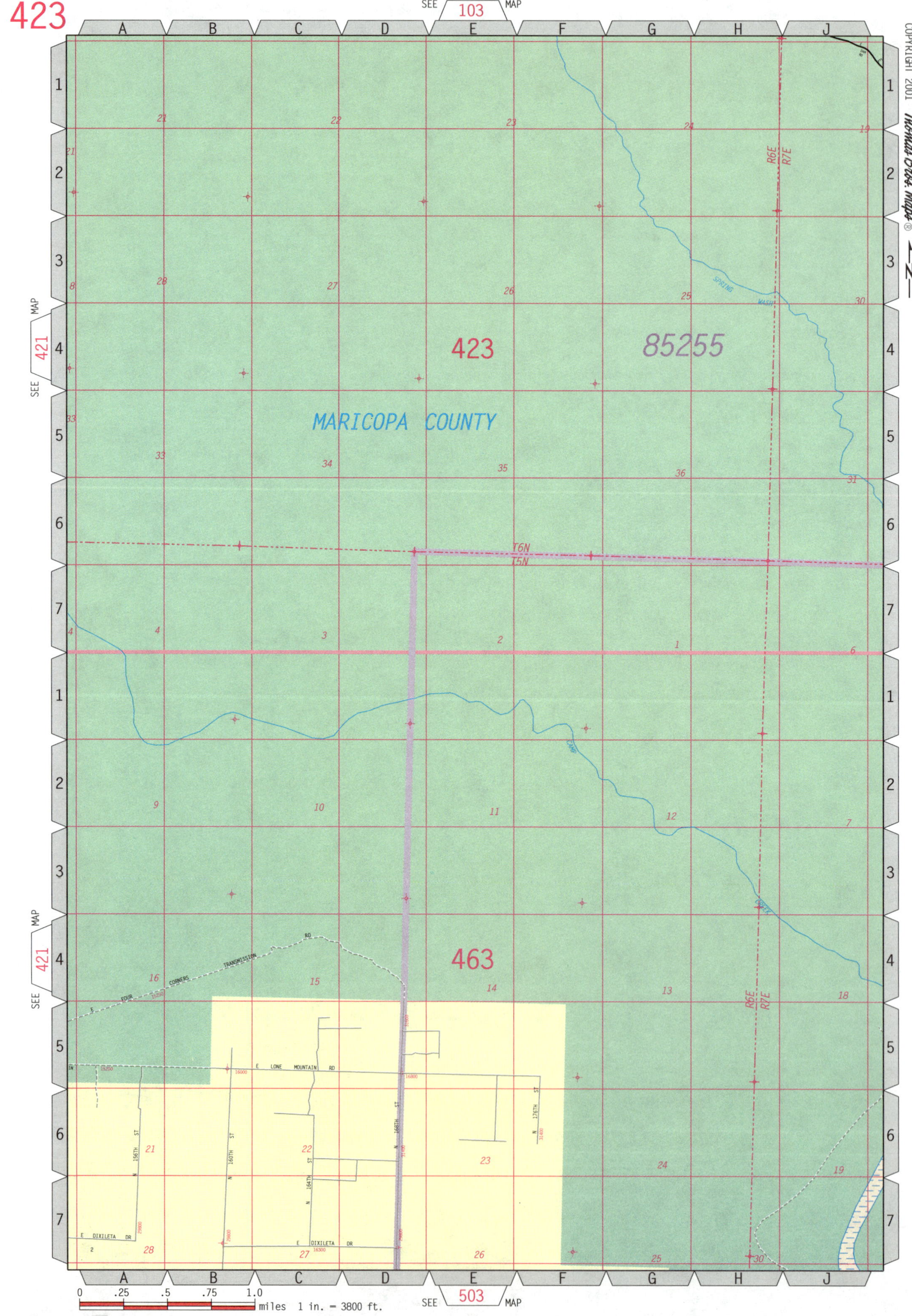

SEE 421 MAP
SEE 421 MAP
SEE 503 MAP

0 .25 .5 .75 1.0 miles 1 in. = 3800 ft.

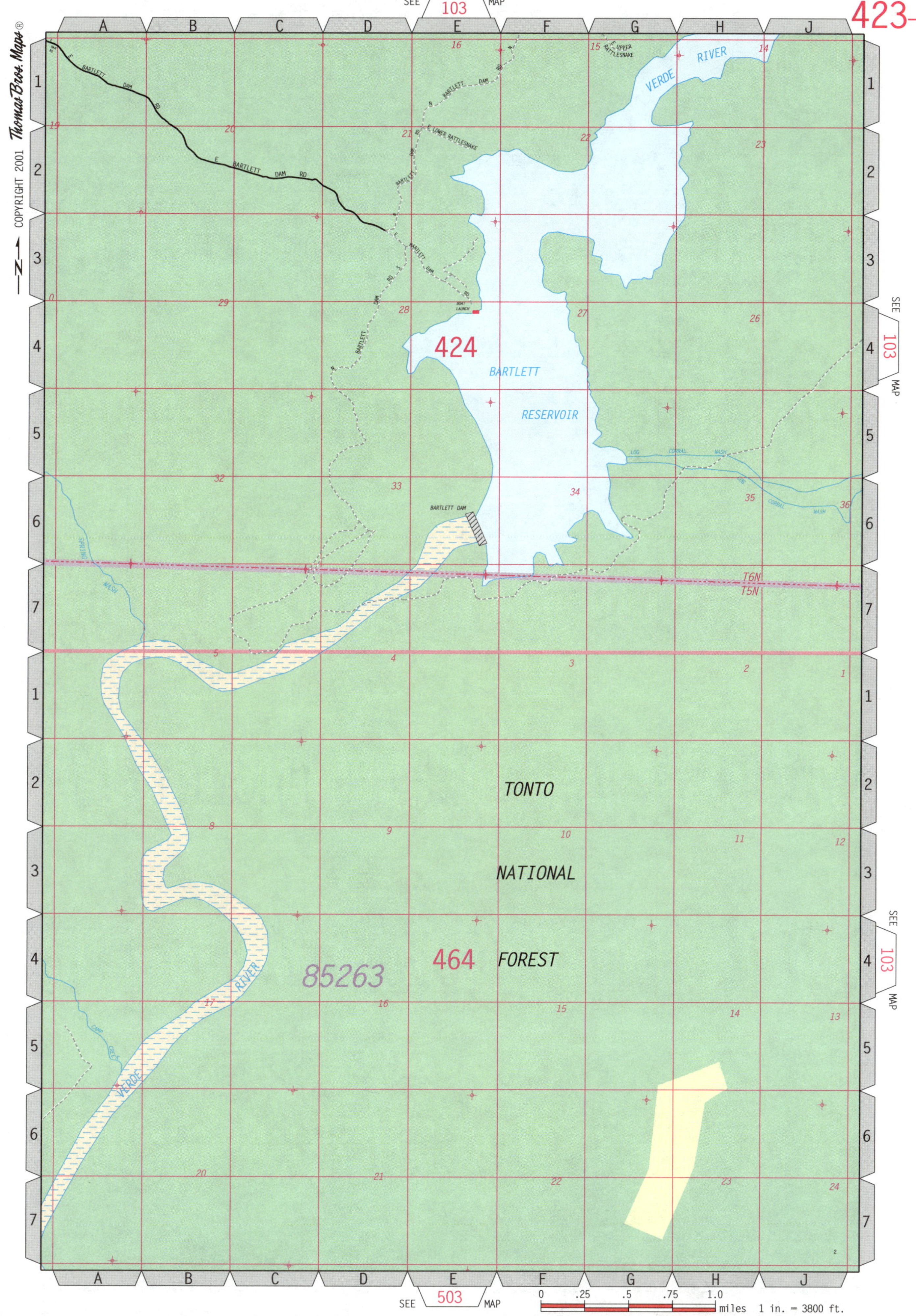
SEE 103 MAP
A
B
C
D
E
F
G
H
J
Thomas Bros. Maps®
© COPYRIGHT 2001
E BARTLETT DAM RD
N BARTLETT DAM RD
E LOWER RATTLESNAKE
E UPPER RATTLESNAKE
S BARTLETT DAM RD
VERDE RIVER
BOAT LAUNCH
424
BARTLETT
RESERVOIR
LOG CORRAL WASH
BARTLETT DAM
SPRING WASH
T6N
T5N
TONTO
NATIONAL
FOREST
464
85263
VERDE RIVER
CAVE CREEK
SEE 103 MAP
SEE 503 MAP
0 .25 .5 .75 1.0 miles 1 in. = 3800 ft.
PHOENIX
MAP

SEE 419 MAP

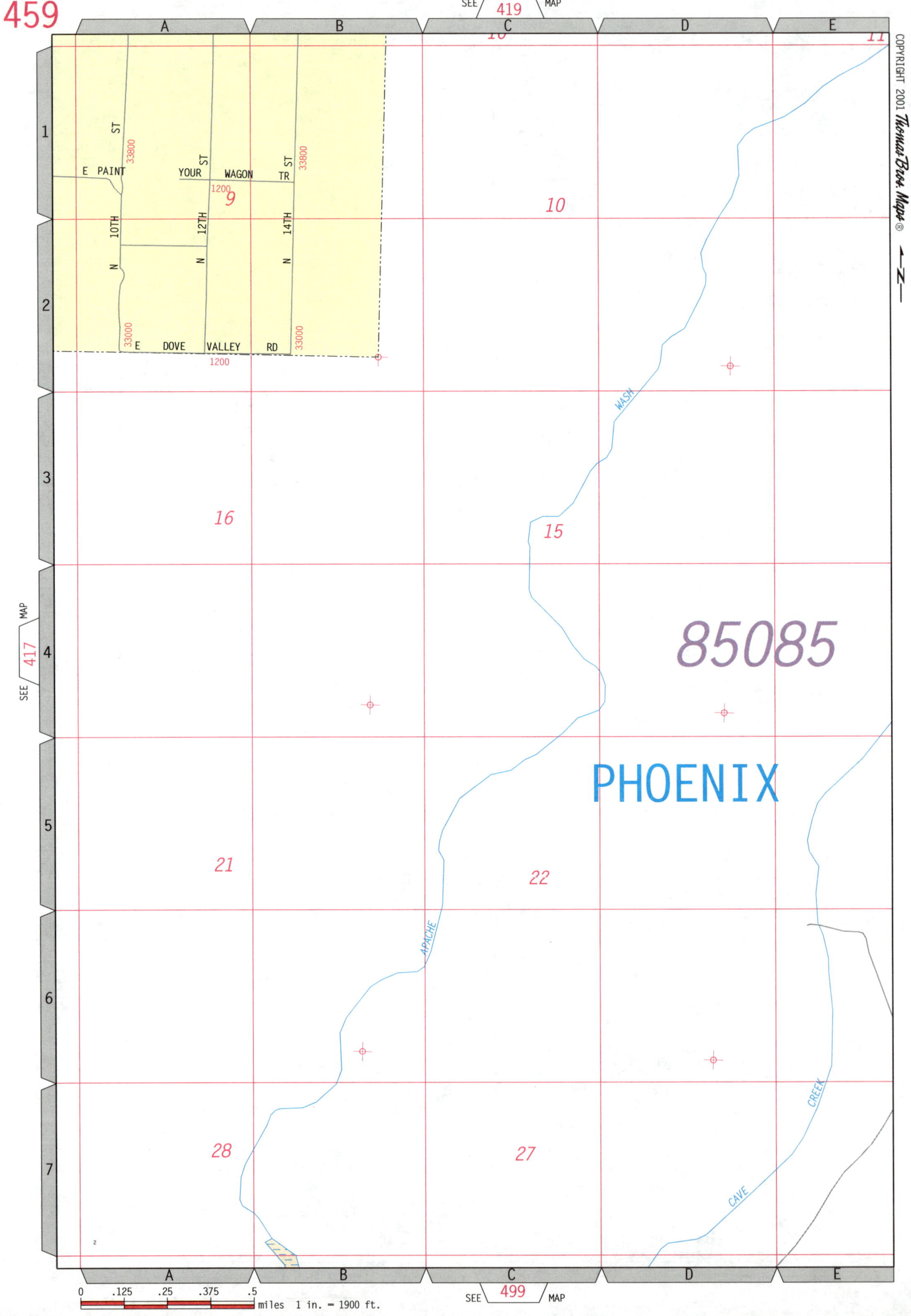

SEE 417 MAP

SEE 499 MAP

0 .125 .25 .375 .5 miles 1 in. = 1900 ft.

SEE 419 MAP

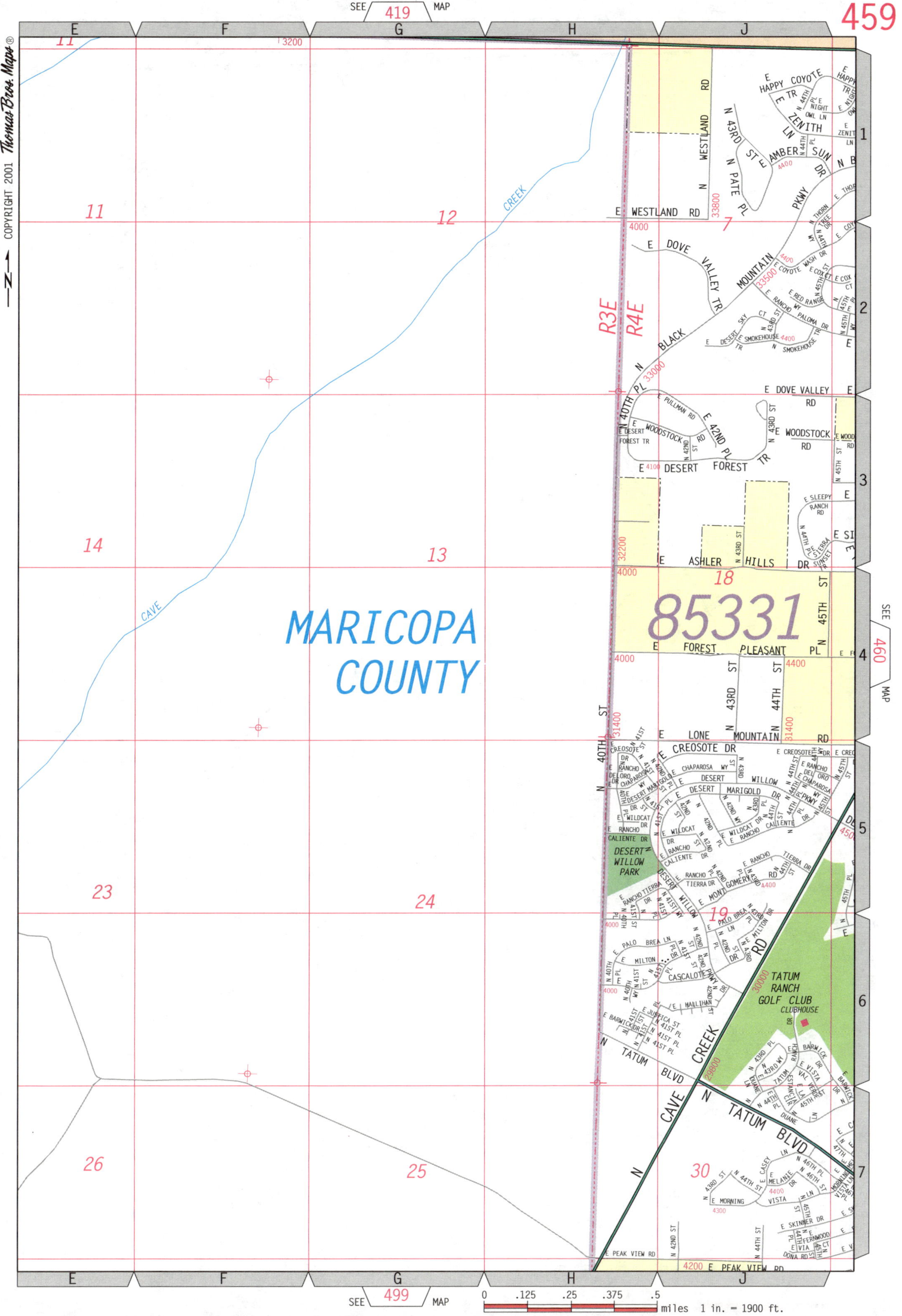

SEE 460 MAP

SEE 499 MAP

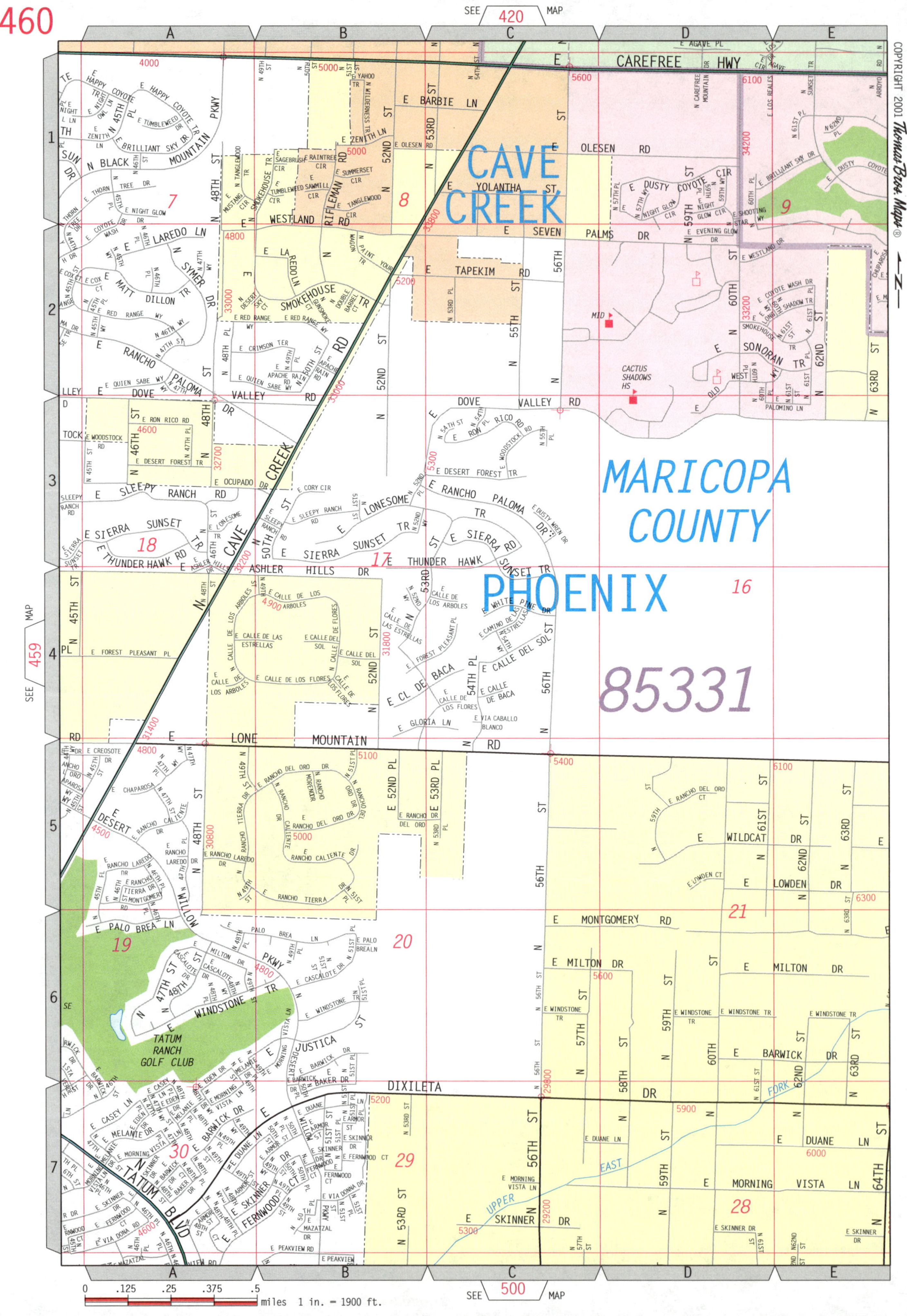
SEE 420 MAP
CAVE CREEK
MARICOPA COUNTY
PHOENIX
85331
CAREFREE HWY
DOVE VALLEY RD
LONE MOUNTAIN RD
DIXILETA DR
TATUM BLVD
TATUM RANCH GOLF CLUB
CACTUS SHADOWS HS
MID
UPPER EAST FORK
SEE 459 MAP
SEE 500 MAP
miles 1 in. = 1900 ft.

PHOENIX
MAP

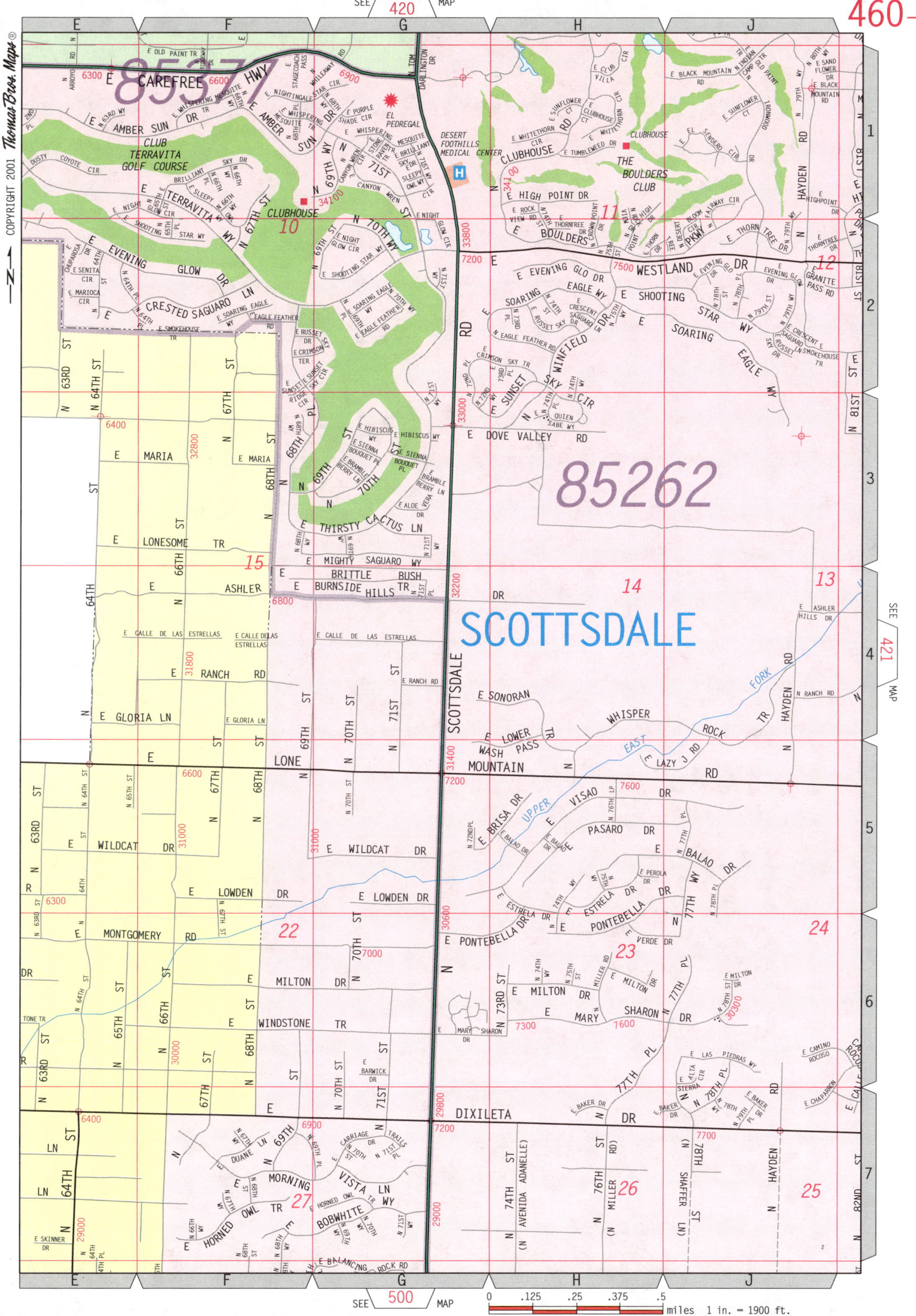

SEE 420 MAP
85377
85262
SCOTTSDALE
CAREFREE HWY
CLUB TERRAVITA GOLF COURSE
CLUBHOUSE
EL PEDREGAL
DESERT FOOTHILLS MEDICAL CENTER
THE BOULDERS CLUB
SCOTTSDALE RD
HAYDEN RD
WESTLAND DR
DOVE VALLEY RD
LONE MOUNTAIN RD
DIXILETA DR
UPPER EAST FORK
SEE 421 MAP
SEE 500 MAP
PHOENIX
MAP
0 .125 .25 .375 .5 miles 1 in. = 1900 ft.

SEE 413 MAP

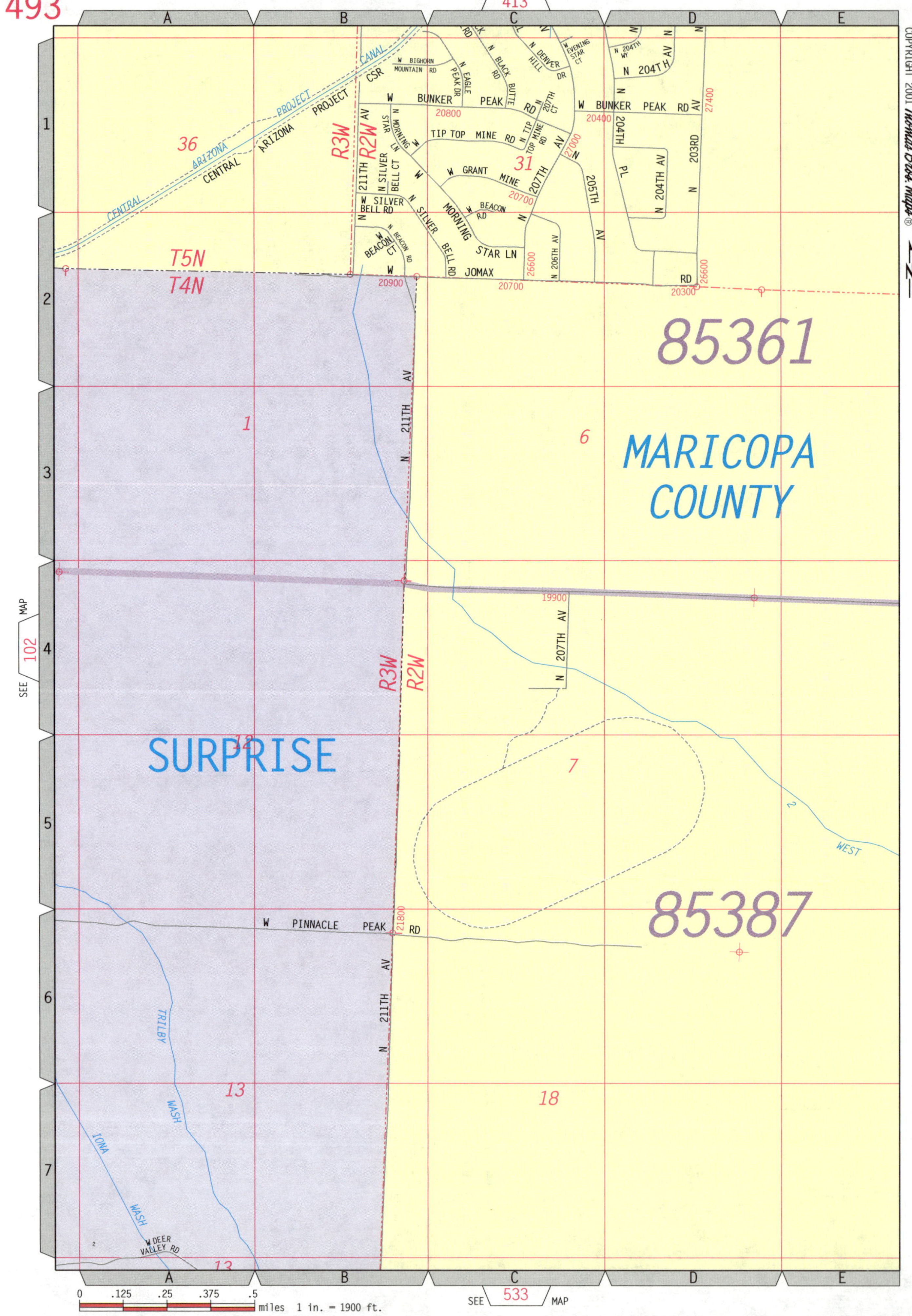

SEE 533 MAP

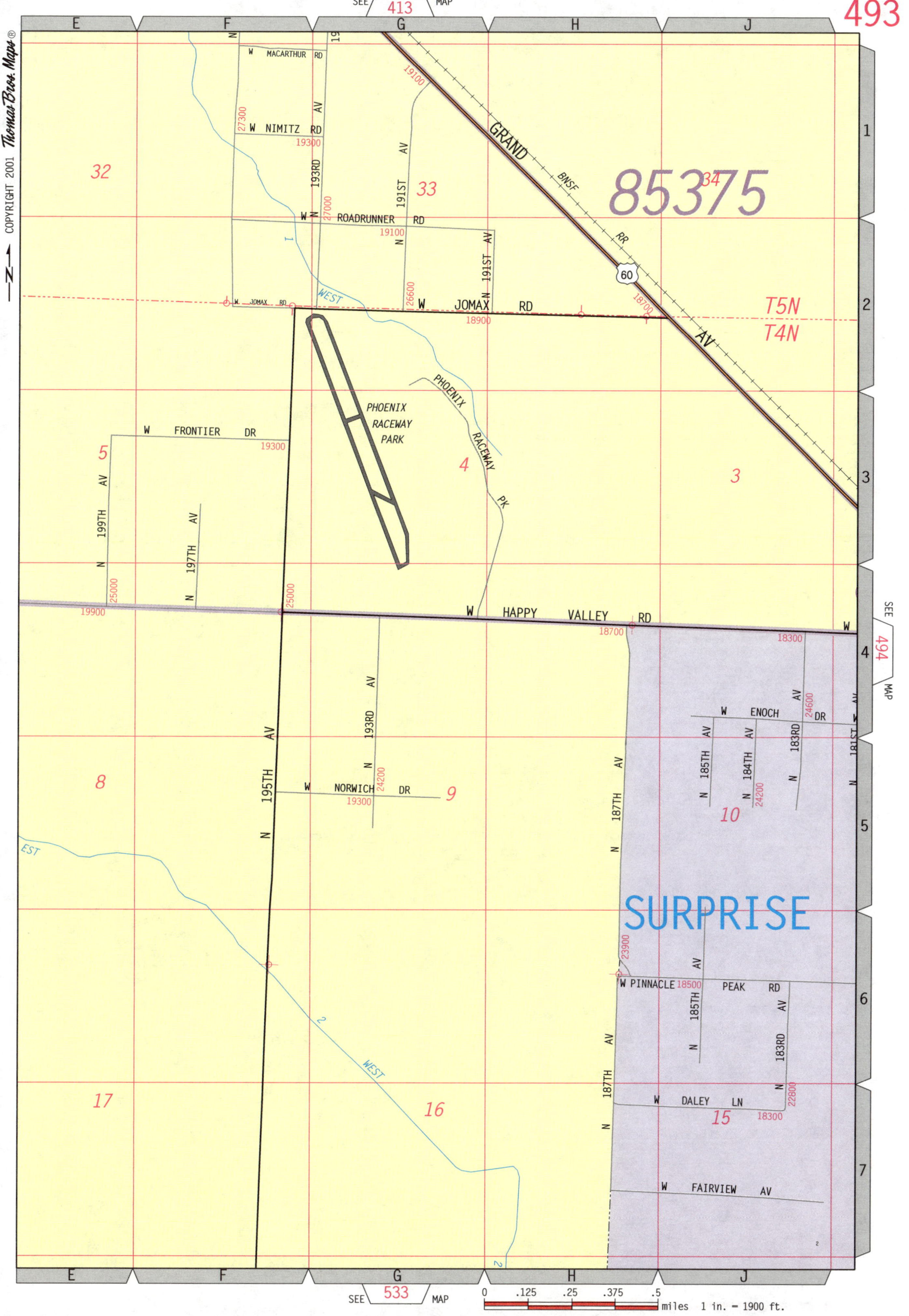

SEE 413 MAP
SEE 494 MAP
SEE 533 MAP
Thomas Bros. Maps®
COPYRIGHT 2001
85375
SURPRISE
PHOENIX RACEWAY PARK
W MACARTHUR RD
W NIMITZ RD
W ROADRUNNER RD
W JOMAX RD
GRAND AV
BNSF RR
60
T5N
T4N
W FRONTIER DR
PHOENIX RACEWAY PK
W HAPPY VALLEY RD
W ENOCH DR
W NORWICH DR
N 195TH AV
N 199TH AV
N 197TH AV
N 193RD AV
N 191ST AV
N 187TH AV
N 185TH AV
N 184TH AV
N 183RD AV
W PINNACLE PEAK RD
W DALEY LN
W FAIRVIEW AV
WEST
PHOENIX
MAP
0 .125 .25 .375 .5 miles 1 in. = 1900 ft.

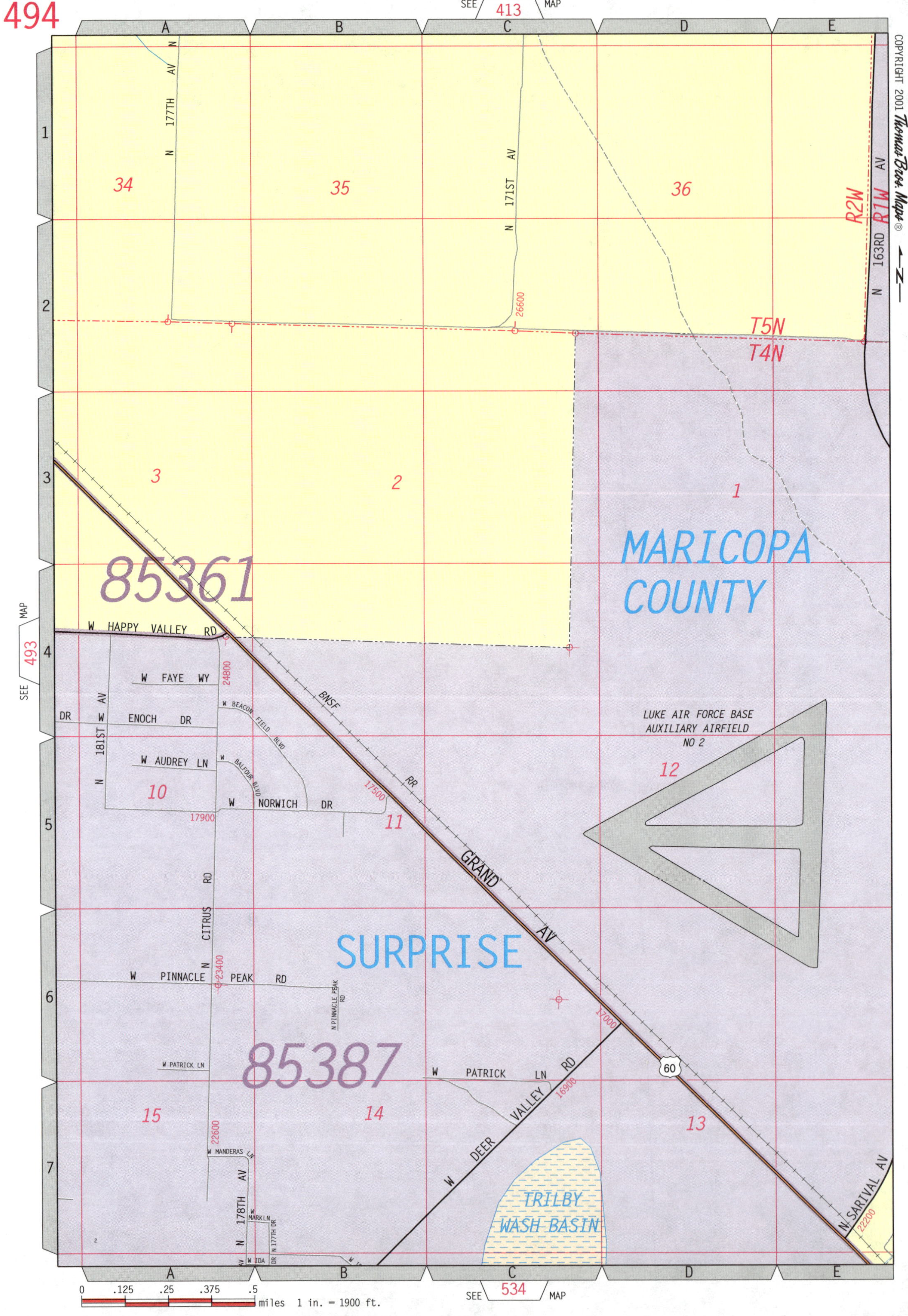
SEE 413 MAP
SEE 493 MAP
SEE 534 MAP
PHOENIX
MAP
A B C D E
1 2 3 4 5 6 7
N 177TH AV
N 171ST AV
N 163RD AV
34
35
36
3
2
1
R2W R1W
T5N
T4N
26600
85361
MARICOPA COUNTY
W HAPPY VALLEY RD
W FAYE WY
24800
W BEACON FIELD BLVD
N 181ST AV
ENOCH DR
W AUDREY LN
W BALFOUR BLVD
BNSF RR
LUKE AIR FORCE BASE AUXILIARY AIRFIELD NO 2
12
10
W NORWICH DR
17900
17500
11
GRAND AV
N CITRUS RD
SURPRISE
W PINNACLE PEAK RD
23400
N PINNACLE PEAK RD
17000
60
85387
W PATRICK LN
W PATRICK LN
W DEER VALLEY RD
16900
15
14
13
22600
W MANDERAS LN
N 178TH AV
W MARK LN
N 177TH DR
W IDA DR
TRILBY WASH BASIN
N SARIVAL AV
22200
0 .125 .25 .375 .5 miles 1 in. = 1900 ft.

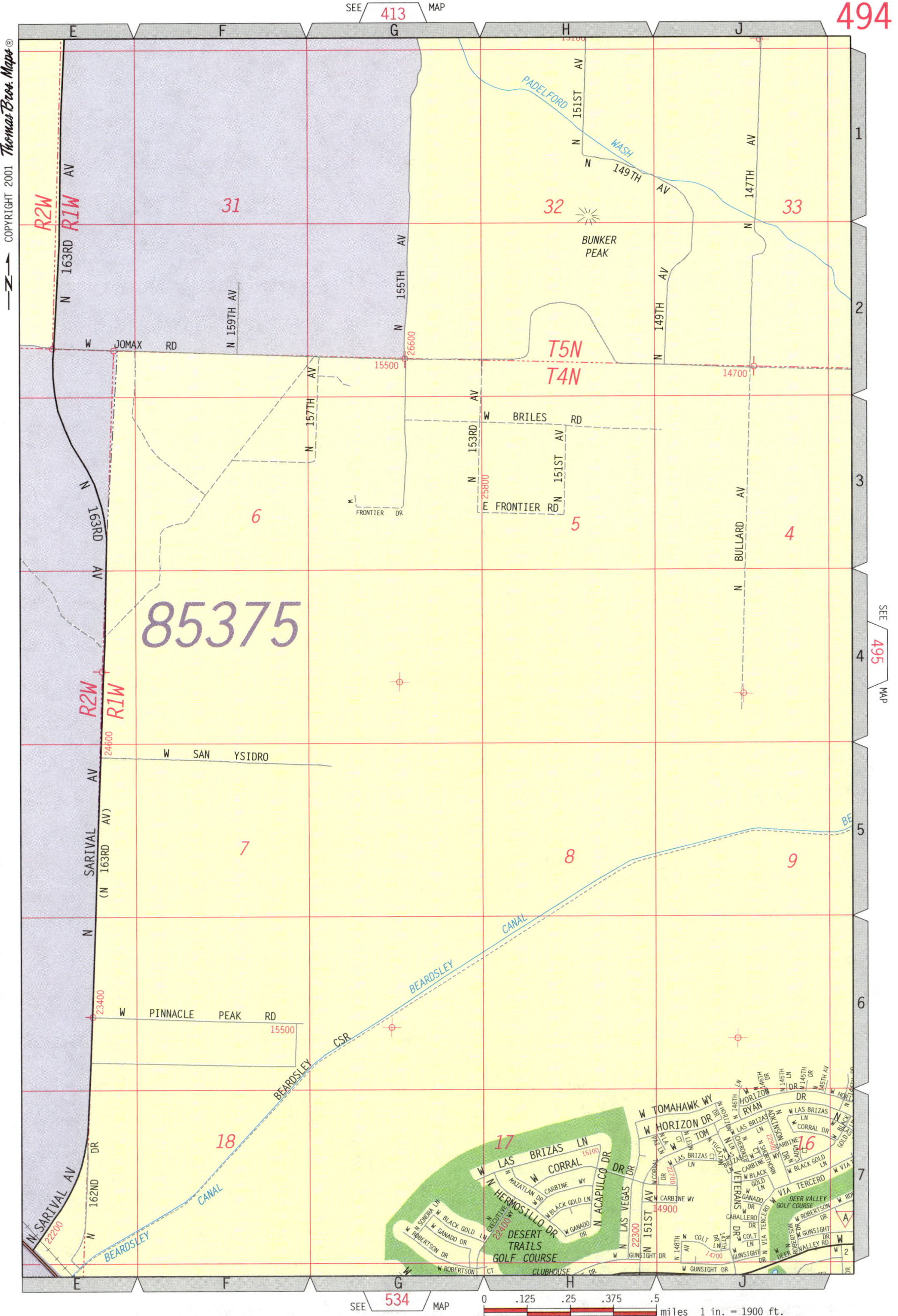

SEE 413 MAP
SEE 495 MAP
SEE 534 MAP
PHOENIX
MAP
85375
T5N
T4N
R2W
R1W
PADELFORD WASH
BUNKER PEAK
N 151ST AV
N 149TH AV
N 147TH AV
N 163RD AV
N 159TH AV
N 155TH AV
W JOMAX RD
N 157TH AV
W BRILES RD
N 153RD AV
N 151ST AV
FRONTIER DR
E FRONTIER RD
N BULLARD AV
W SAN YSIDRO
N SARIVAL AV (N 163RD AV)
BEARDSLEY CANAL
W PINNACLE PEAK RD
BEARDSLEY CSR
N 162ND DR
N SARIVAL AV
W TOMAHAWK WY
W HORIZON DR
W LAS BRIZAS LN
W CORRAL DR
N HERMOSILLO DR
N ACAPULCO DR
N LAS VEGAS DR
N 151ST AV
N VETERANS DR
W VIA TERCERO
DEER VALLEY GOLF COURSE
DESERT TRAILS GOLF COURSE
CLUBHOUSE DR
W GUNSIGHT DR
W ROBERTSON CT
0 .125 .25 .375 .5 miles 1 in. = 1900 ft.

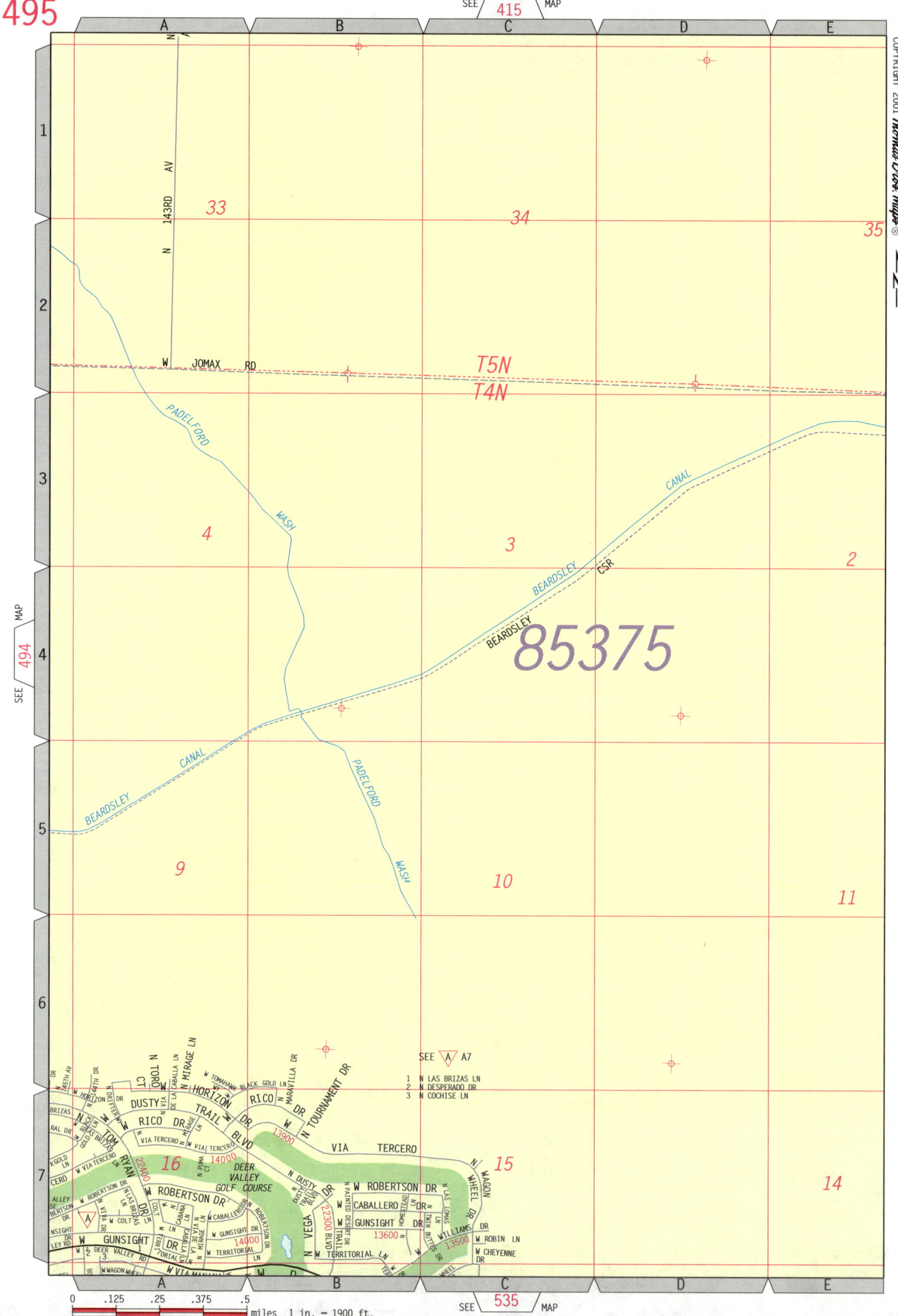

SEE 415 MAP
N 143RD AV
W JOMAX RD
T5N
T4N
33
34
35
PADELFORD WASH
BEARDSLEY CANAL
CSR
4
3
2
85375
9
10
11
SEE 494 MAP
SEE A A7
1 N LAS BRIZAS LN
2 N DESPERADO DR
3 N COCHISE LN
W HORIZON TRAIL BLVD
W DUSTY DR
W RICO DR
N TOURNAMENT DR
VIA TERCERO
N TOM RYAN DR
16
15
14
DEER VALLEY GOLF COURSE
W ROBERTSON DR
W CABALLERO DR
W GUNSIGHT DR
W TERRITORIAL LN
N VEGA BLVD
N WAGON WHEEL DR
W WILLIAMS DR
W ROBIN LN
W CHEYENNE DR
W DEER VALLEY RD
13900
14000
13600
13500
22400
22300
SEE 535 MAP
0 .125 .25 .375 .5 miles 1 in. = 1900 ft.

PHOENIX

MAP

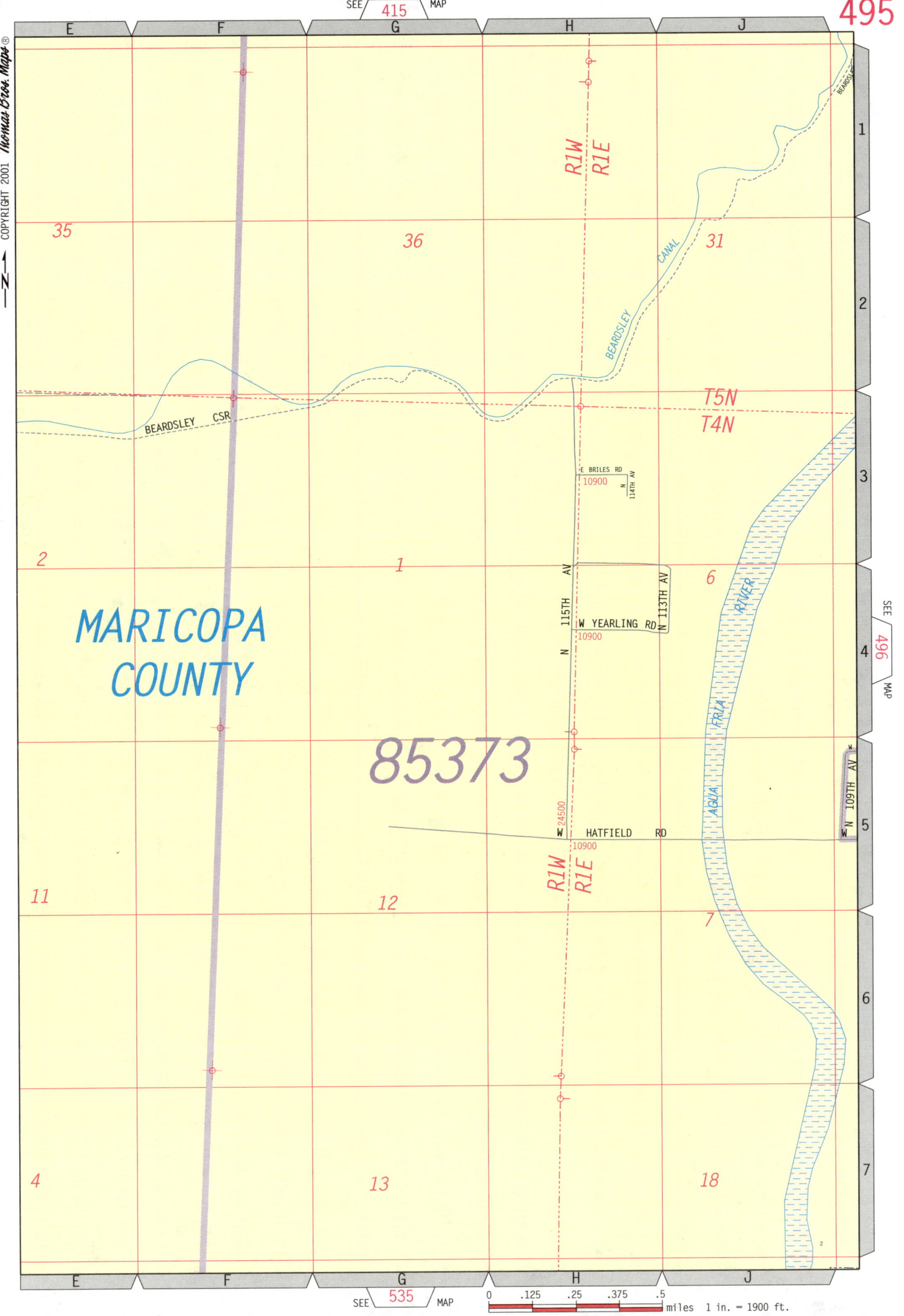
SEE 415 MAP
E
F
G
H
J
1
2
3
4
5
6
7
35
36
31
2
1
6
11
12
7
4
13
18
R1W
R1E
T5N
T4N
BEARDSLEY CANAL
BEARDSLEY CSR
E BRILES RD
10900
N 114TH AV
N 115TH AV
W YEARLING RD
N 113TH AV
MARICOPA
COUNTY
85373
AGUA FRIA RIVER
N 109TH AV
24500
W HATFIELD RD
10900
SEE 496 MAP
SEE 535 MAP
PHOENIX
MAP
0 .125 .25 .375 .5 miles 1 in. = 1900 ft.

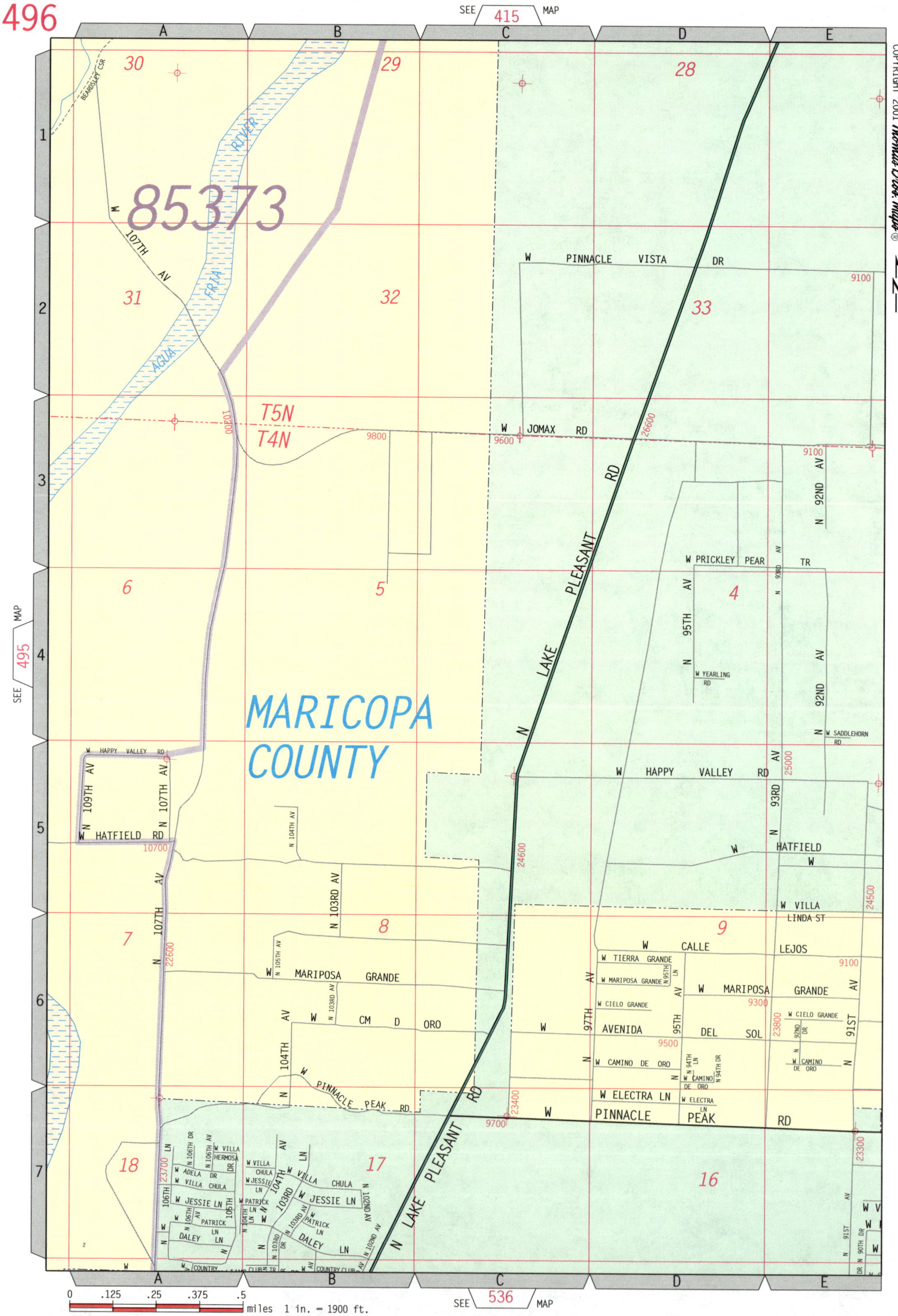
SEE 415 MAP
SEE 495 MAP
SEE 536 MAP
PHOENIX
MAP
85373
MARICOPA
COUNTY
AGUA FRIA RIVER
T5N
T4N
W JOMAX RD
W PINNACLE VISTA DR
N LAKE PLEASANT RD
W HAPPY VALLEY RD
W HATFIELD RD
W PRICKLEY PEAR TR
W YEARLING RD
W SADDLEHORN RD
N 92ND AV
N 93RD AV
N 95TH AV
N 97TH AV
N 107TH AV
N 109TH AV
N 103RD AV
N 104TH AV
N 105TH AV
W VILLA LINDA ST
W CALLE LEJOS
W TIERRA GRANDE
W MARIPOSA GRANDE
W CIELO GRANDE
W AVENIDA DEL SOL
W CAMINO DE ORO
W CM D ORO
W ELECTRA LN
W PINNACLE PEAK RD
W VILLA CHULA
W JESSIE LN
W PATRICK LN
W DALEY LN
W ADELA DR
W VILLA HERMOSA
W COUNTRY CLUB TR
BEARDSLEY CSR
N 91ST AV
COPYRIGHT 2001 Thomas Bros. Maps ®
0 .125 .25 .375 .5 miles 1 in. = 1900 ft.

SEE 415 MAP

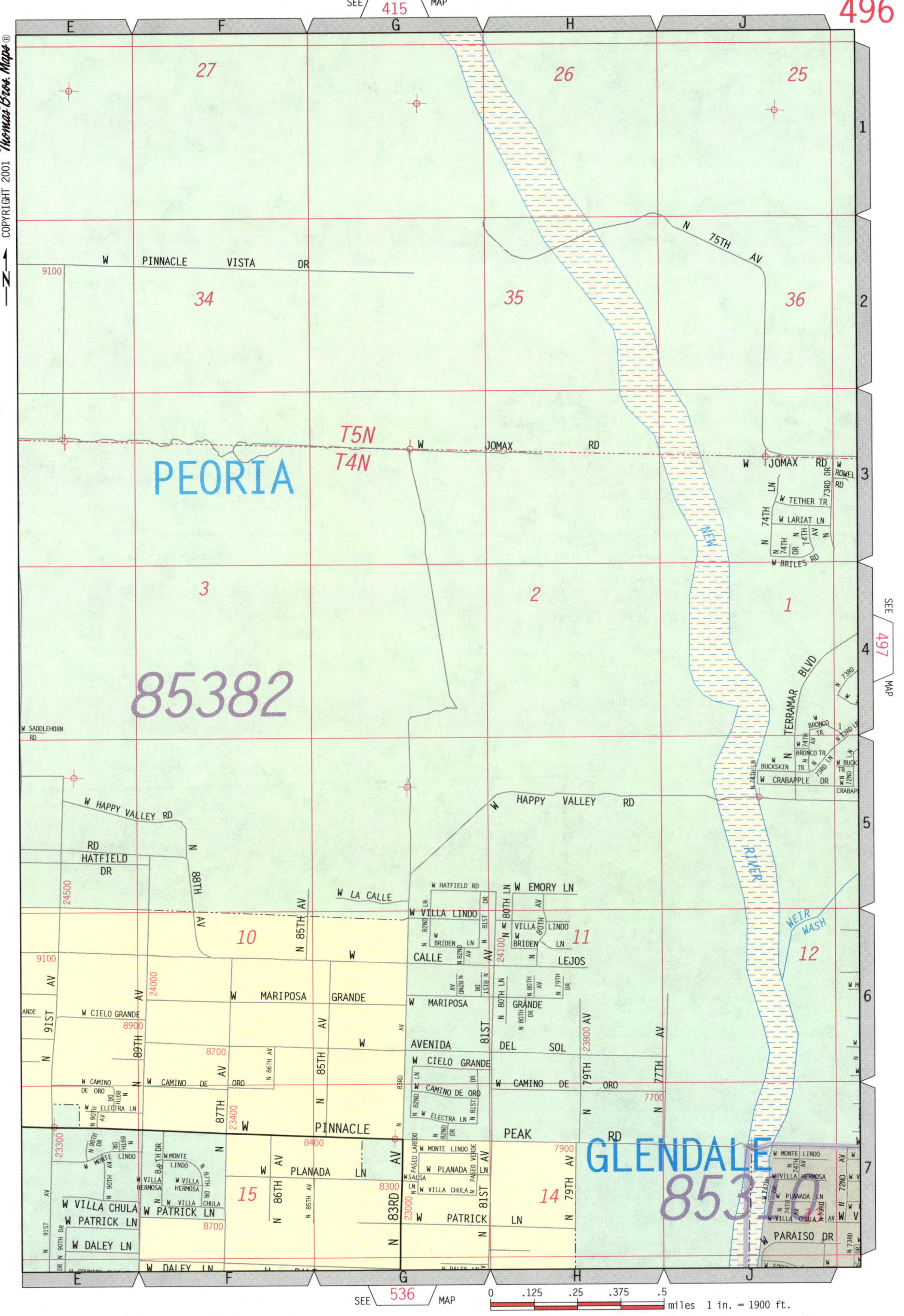

SEE 497 MAP

SEE 536 MAP

0 .125 .25 .375 .5 miles 1 in. = 1900 ft.

PHOENIX

MAP

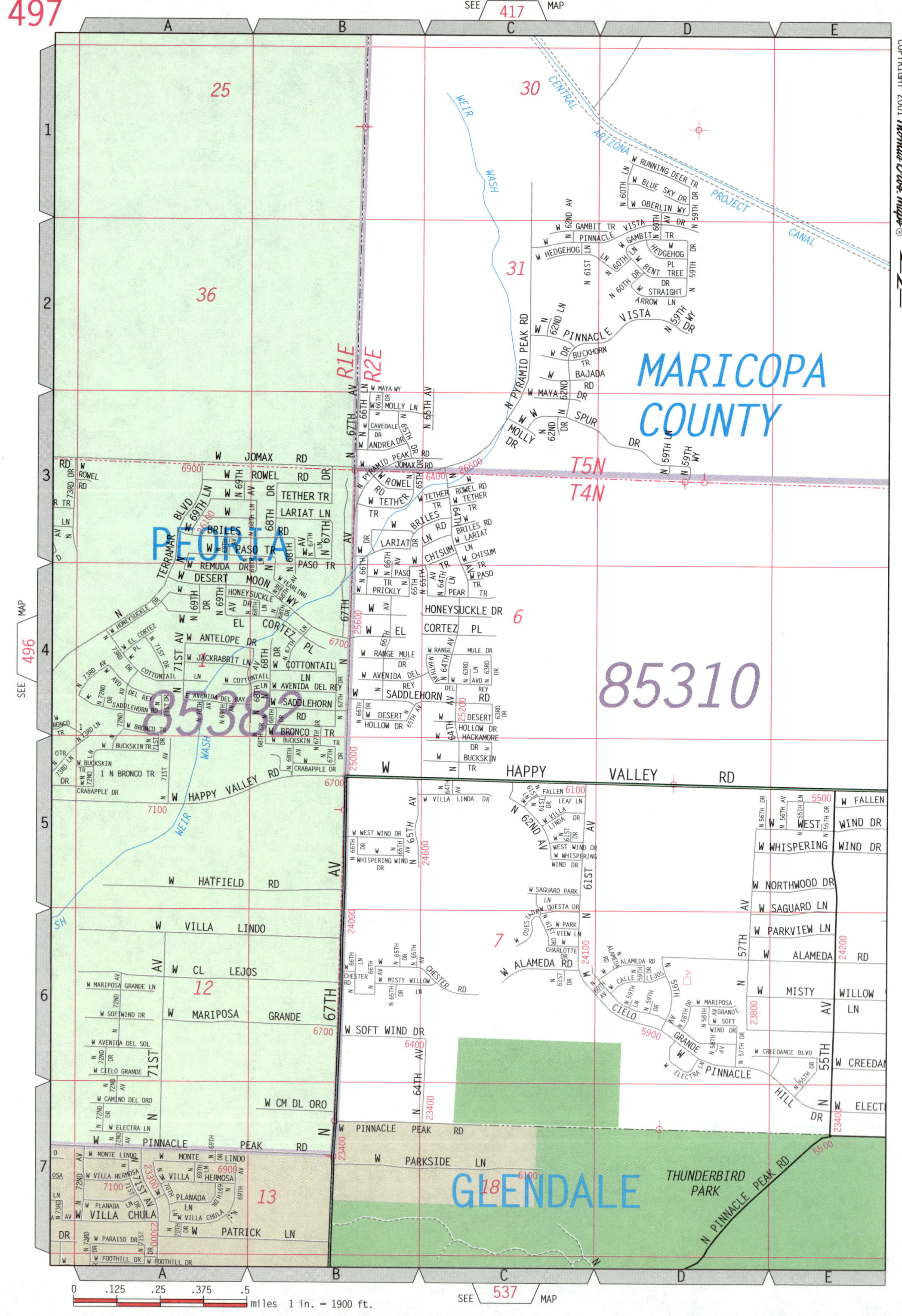

SEE 417 MAP
SEE 496 MAP
SEE 537 MAP

0 .125 .25 .375 .5 miles 1 in. = 1900 ft.

PHOENIX

MAP

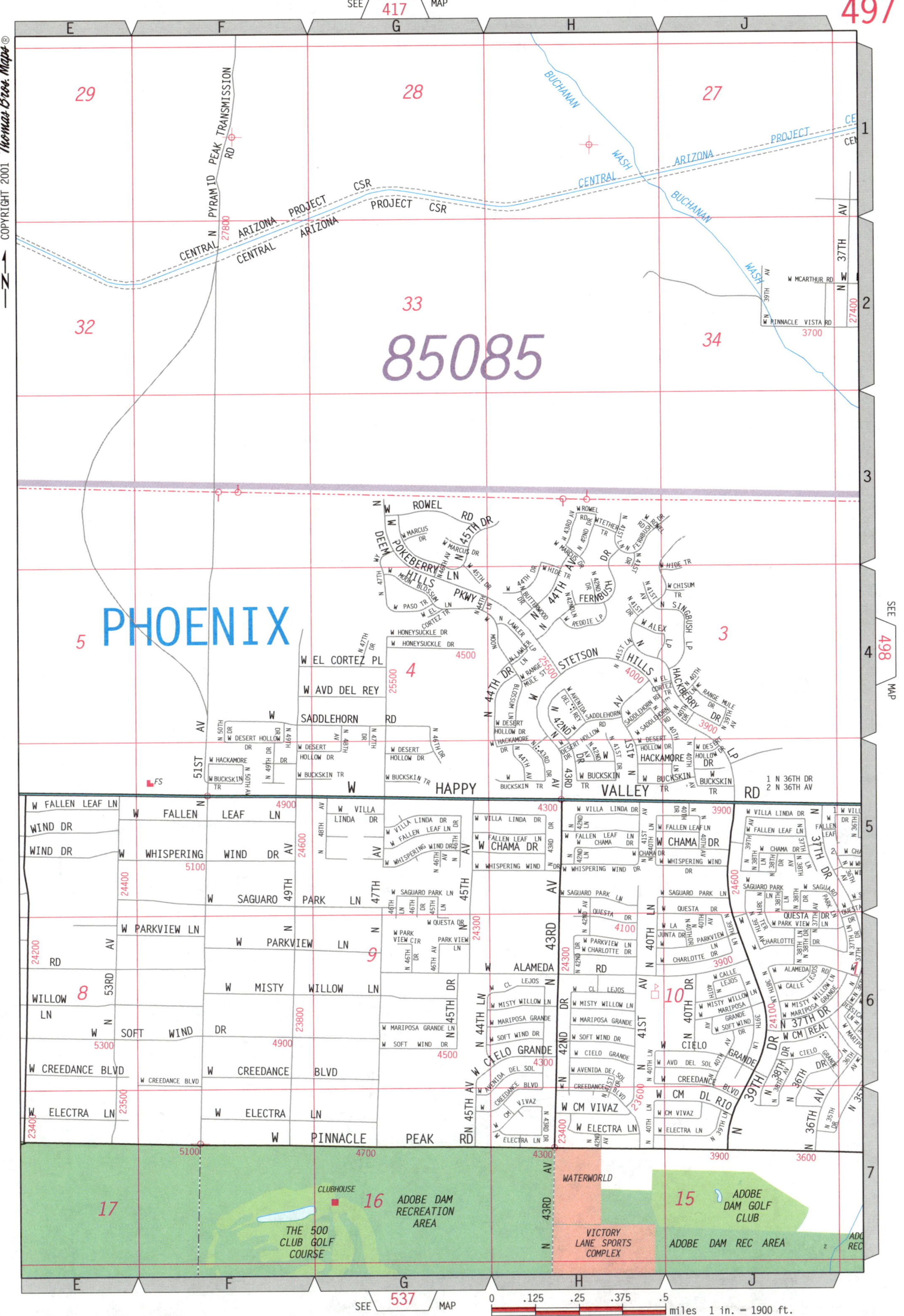
SEE 417 MAP
SEE 498 MAP
SEE 537 MAP
85085
PHOENIX
CENTRAL ARIZONA PROJECT CSR
PYRAMID PEAK TRANSMISSION RD
BUCHANAN WASH
W ROWEL RD
W POKEBERRY LN
HILLS PKWY
STETSON HILLS LP
W SADDLEHORN RD
W EL CORTEZ PL
W AVD DEL REY
W HAPPY VALLEY RD
W FALLEN LEAF LN
W WHISPERING WIND DR
W SAGUARO PARK LN
W PARKVIEW LN
W ALAMEDA RD
W MISTY WILLOW LN
W SOFT WIND DR
W CREEDANCE BLVD
W ELECTRA LN
W PINNACLE PEAK RD
W CIELO GRANDE
W CM VIVAZ
CM DL RIO
W CHAMA DR
W HACKAMORE DR
W BUCKSKIN TR
51ST AV
43RD AV
39TH DR
37TH AV
36TH AV
40TH AV
41ST AV
42ND DR
44TH DR
45TH AV
47TH AV
49TH AV
53RD AV
W PINNACLE VISTA RD
W MCARTHUR RD
WATERWORLD
VICTORY LANE SPORTS COMPLEX
ADOBE DAM RECREATION AREA
THE 500 CLUB GOLF COURSE
CLUBHOUSE
ADOBE DAM GOLF CLUB
ADOBE DAM REC AREA
FS
0 .125 .25 .375 .5 miles 1 in. = 1900 ft.

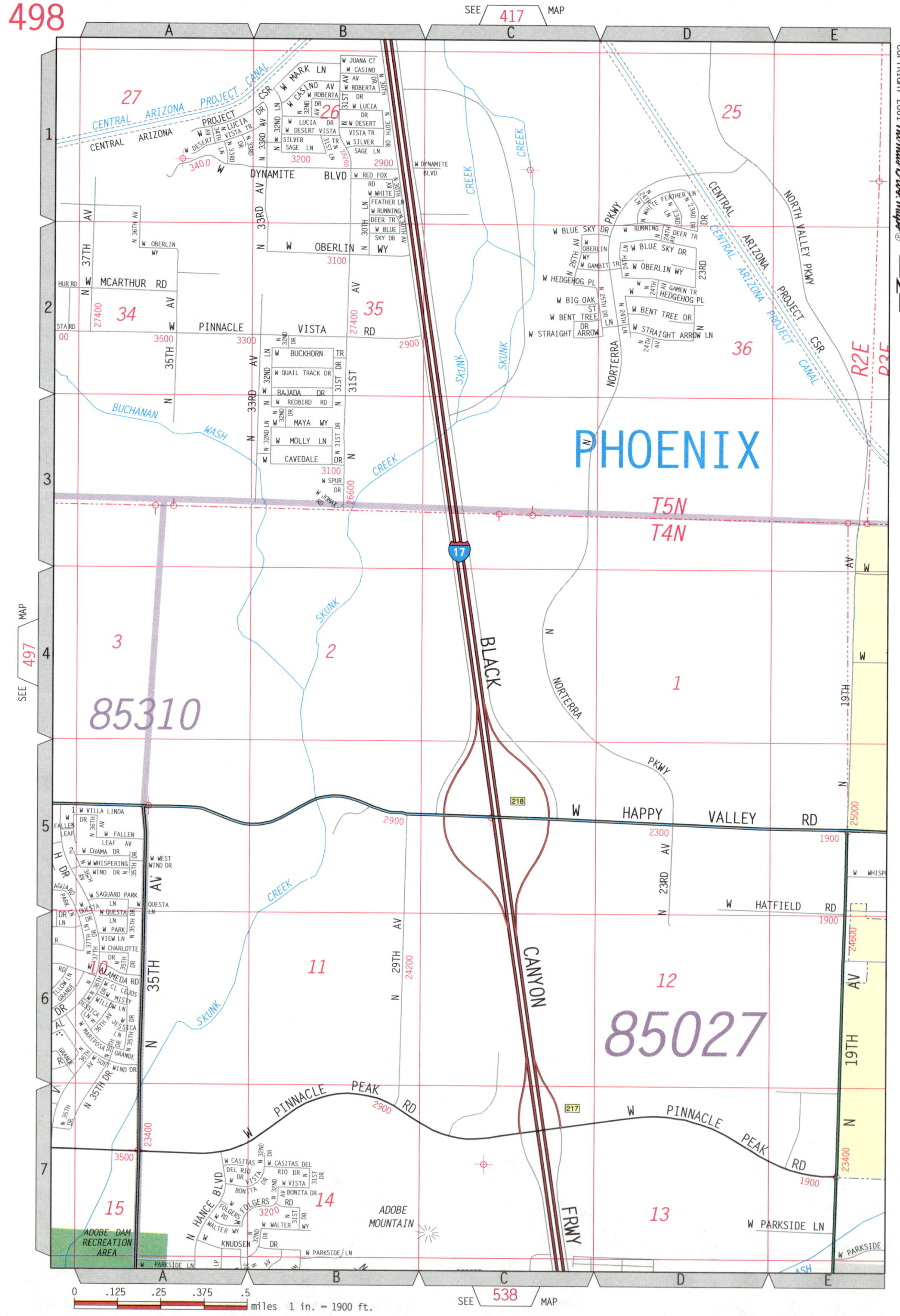

0 .125 .25 .375 .5 miles 1 in. = 1900 ft.

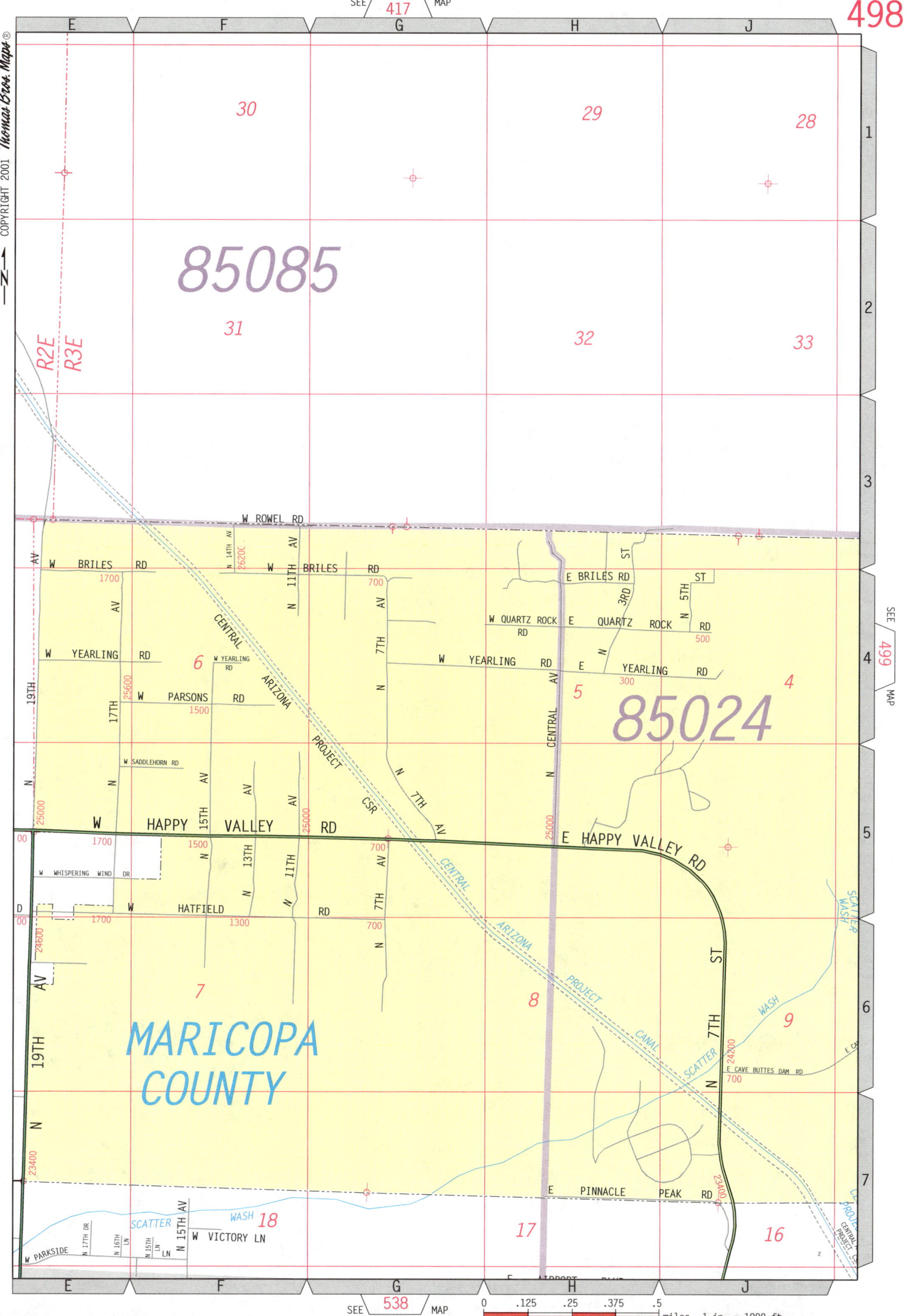

SEE 417 MAP
E
F
G
H
J
1
2
3
4
5
6
7
30
29
28
31
32
33
85085
R2E
R3E
W ROWEL RD
W BRILES RD
W BRILES RD
E BRILES RD
W QUARTZ ROCK RD
E QUARTZ ROCK RD
W YEARLING RD
W YEARLING RD
E YEARLING RD
W PARSONS RD
W SADDLEHORN RD
CENTRAL ARIZONA PROJECT CSR
6
5
4
85024
W HAPPY VALLEY RD
E HAPPY VALLEY RD
W WHISPERING WIND DR
W HATFIELD RD
N 19TH AV
N 17TH AV
N 15TH AV
N 13TH AV
N 11TH AV
N 7TH AV
N CENTRAL AV
N 3RD ST
N 5TH ST
N 7TH ST
7
8
9
MARICOPA COUNTY
CENTRAL ARIZONA PROJECT CANAL
SCATTER WASH
E CAVE BUTTES DAM RD
E PINNACLE PEAK RD
18
17
16
W VICTORY LN
W PARKSIDE
SEE 499 MAP
SEE 538 MAP
PHOENIX
MAP
0 .125 .25 .375 .5 miles 1 in. = 1900 ft.

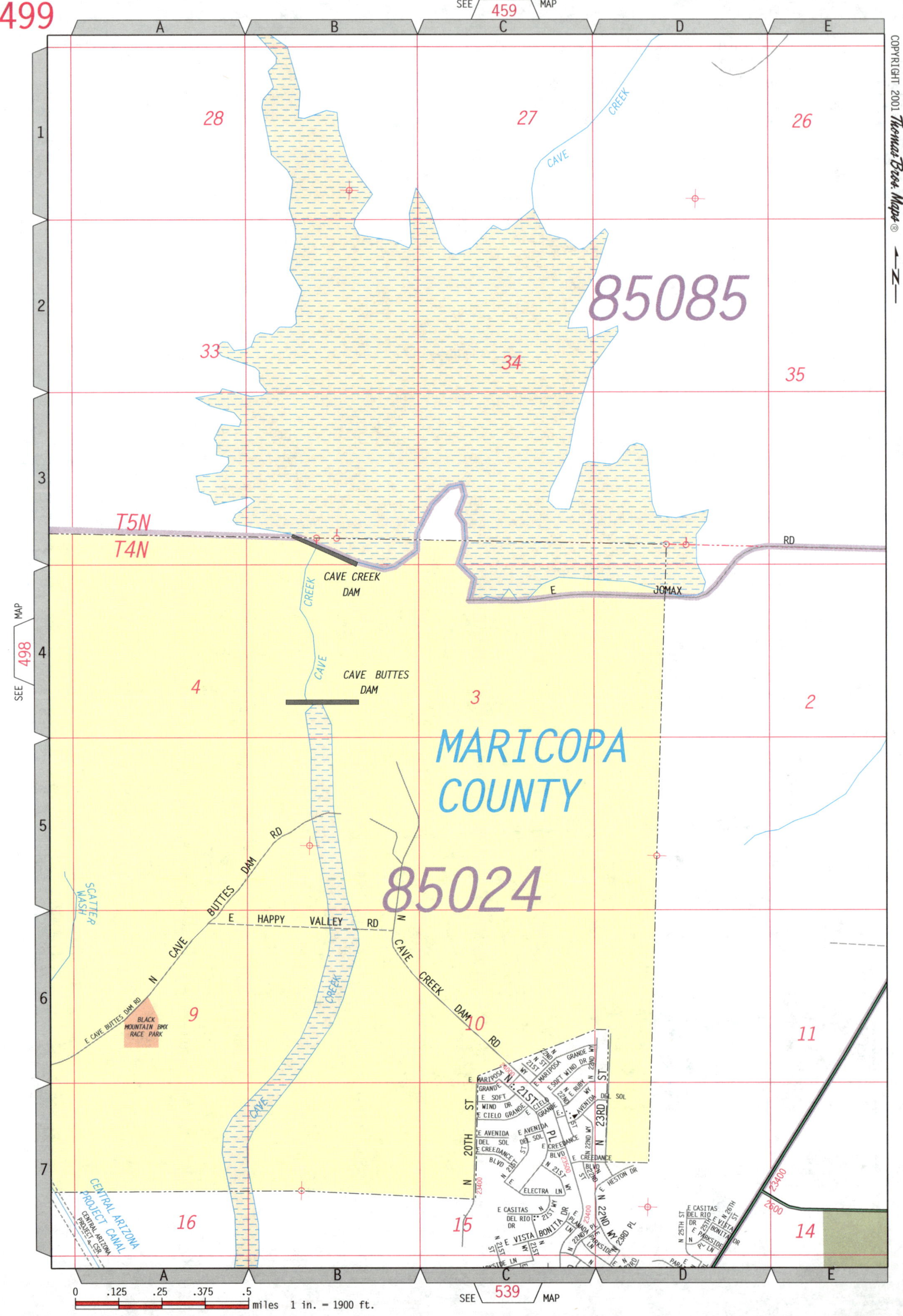

SEE 459 MAP
SEE 498 MAP
SEE 539 MAP
PHOENIX
MAP
85085
85024
MARICOPA
COUNTY
T5N
T4N
CAVE CREEK
CAVE CREEK DAM
CAVE BUTTES DAM
E JOMAX RD
N CAVE BUTTES DAM RD
E CAVE BUTTES DAM RD
E HAPPY VALLEY RD
N CAVE CREEK DAM RD
SCATTER WASH
BLACK MOUNTAIN BMX RACE PARK
CENTRAL ARIZONA PROJECT CANAL
N 20TH ST
N 21ST PL
N 23RD ST
E MARIPOSA GRANDE
E SOFT WIND DR
E CIELO GRANDE
E AVENIDA DEL SOL
E CREEDANCE BLVD
E ELECTRA LN
E HESTON DR
E CASITAS DEL RIO DR
E VISTA BONITA DR
N 22ND WY
N 23RD PL
28
27
26
33
34
35
4
3
2
9
10
11
16
15
14
0 .125 .25 .375 .5 miles 1 in. = 1900 ft.

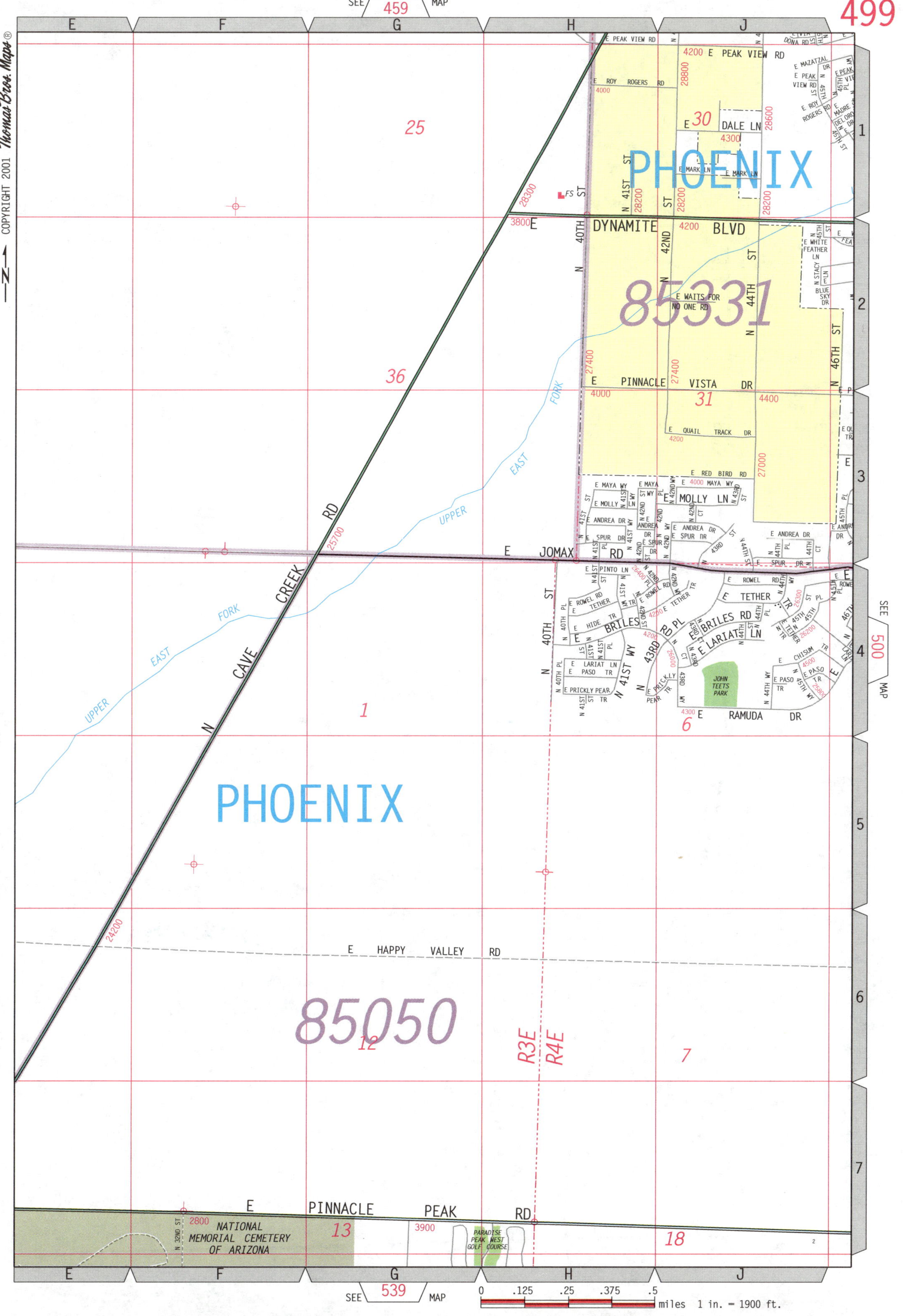
SEE 459 MAP
PHOENIX
85331
PHOENIX
85050
E DYNAMITE BLVD
E JOMAX RD
N CAVE CREEK RD
E HAPPY VALLEY RD
E PINNACLE PEAK RD
E PINNACLE VISTA DR
E PEAK VIEW RD
N 40TH ST
N 42ND ST
N 44TH ST
N 46TH ST
UPPER EAST FORK
NATIONAL MEMORIAL CEMETERY OF ARIZONA
JOHN TEETS PARK
PARADISE PEAK WEST GOLF COURSE
E RAMUDA DR
R3E
R4E
SEE 500 MAP
SEE 539 MAP
miles 1 in. = 1900 ft.

PHOENIX
MAP

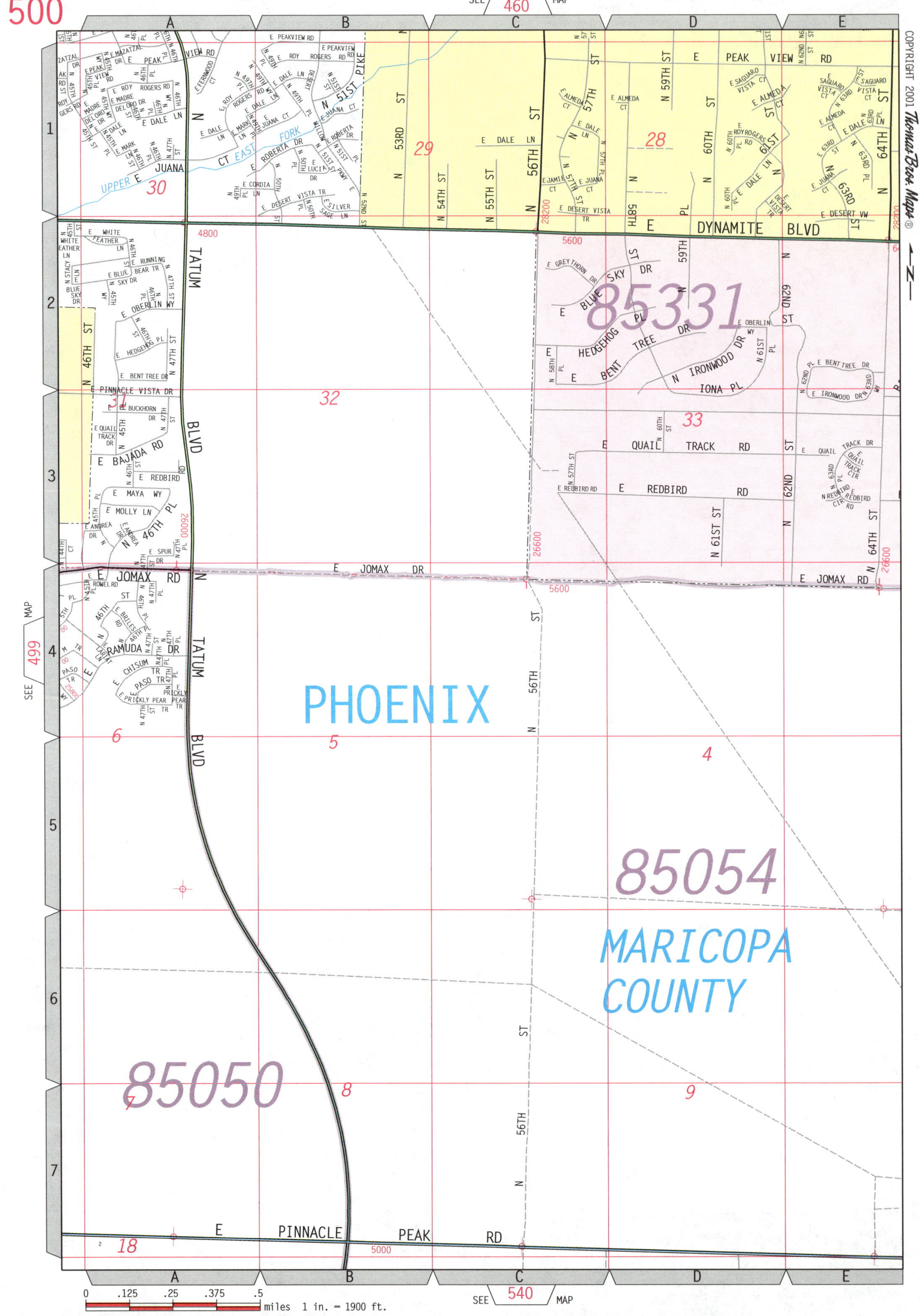
SEE 460 MAP
SEE 499 MAP
SEE 540 MAP
PHOENIX
MARICOPA COUNTY
85331
85054
85050
E PEAK VIEW RD
E DYNAMITE BLVD
E JOMAX RD
E JOMAX DR
E PINNACLE PEAK RD
TATUM BLVD
N 56TH ST
UPPER EAST FORK
E JUANA CT
E DALE LN
E ROY ROGERS RD
E DESERT VISTA TR
E BLUE SKY DR
E HEDGEHOG PL
E BENT TREE DR
N IRONWOOD DR
E IONA PL
E QUAIL TRACK RD
E REDBIRD RD
E PINNACLE VISTA DR
E BAJADA RD
E MAYA WY
E MOLLY LN
E RAMUDA DR
E CHISUM TR
E PASO TR
E PRICKLY PEAR TR
N 46TH ST
N 53RD ST
N 54TH ST
N 55TH ST
N 58TH ST
N 59TH ST
N 60TH ST
N 61ST ST
N 62ND ST
N 64TH ST
N 51ST PKWY
miles 1 in. = 1900 ft.
COPYRIGHT 2001 Thomas Bros. Maps®
PHOENIX
MAP

SEE 460 MAP

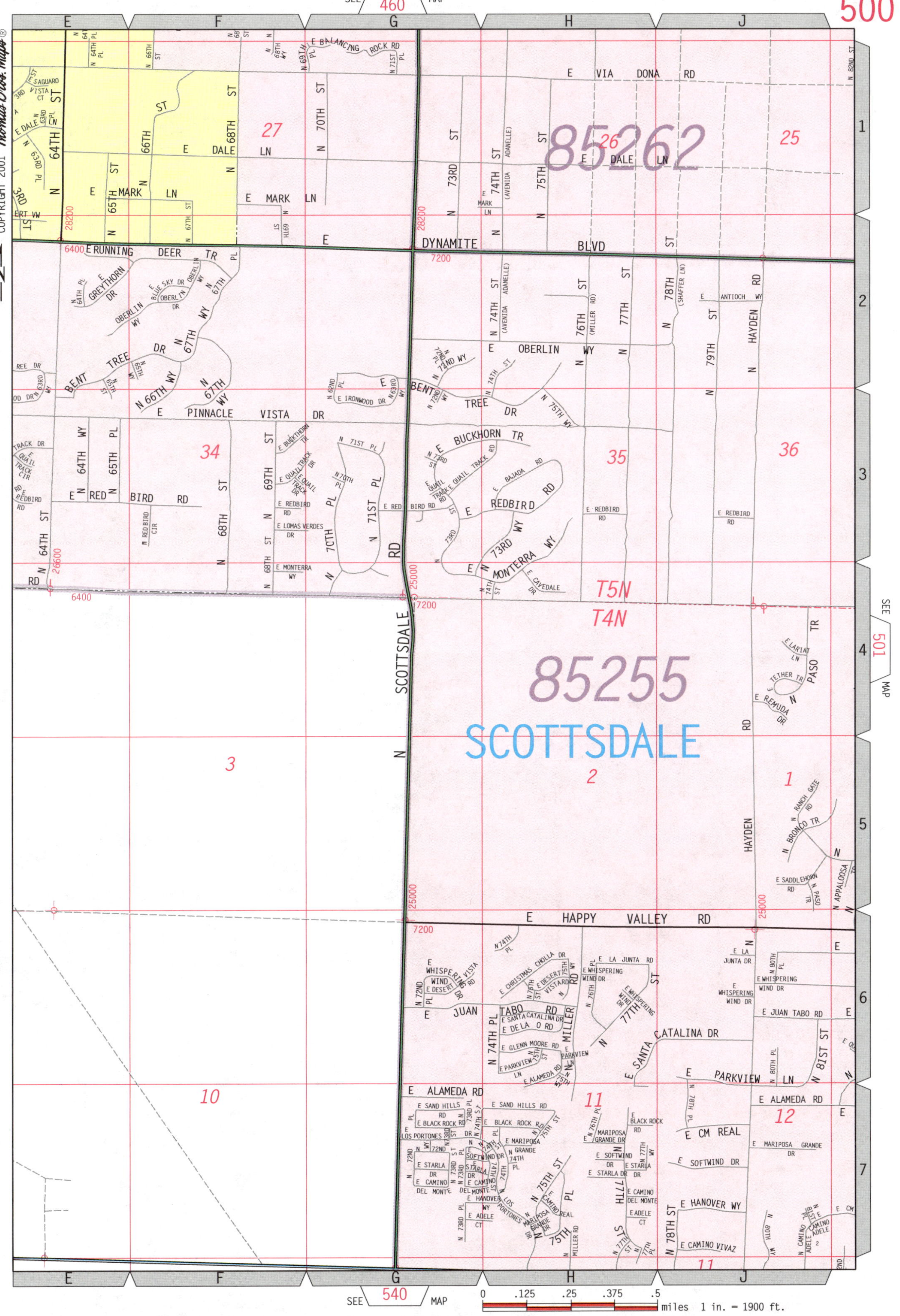

SEE 501 MAP

SEE 540 MAP

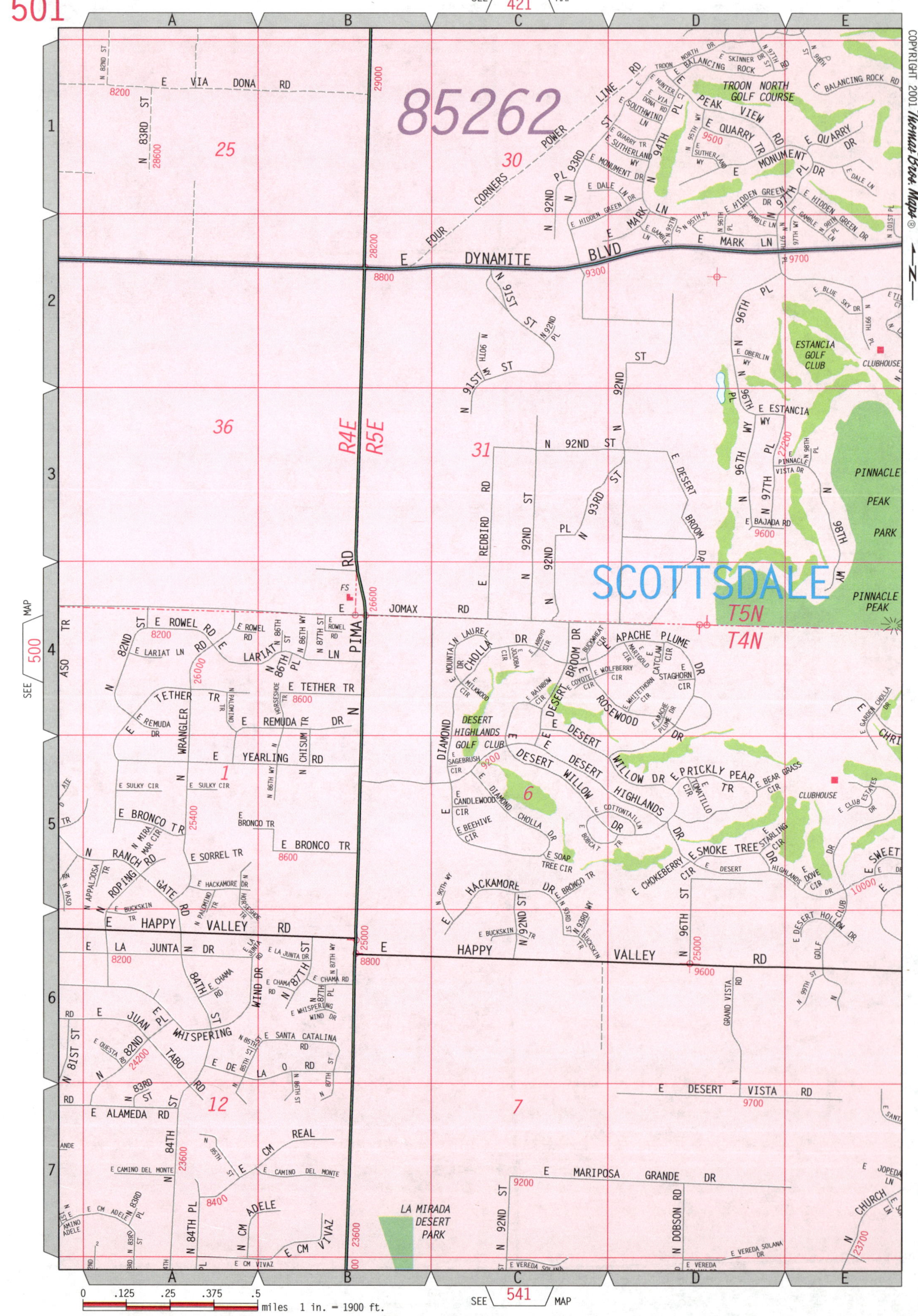
SEE 421 MAP
85262
SCOTTSDALE
TROON NORTH GOLF COURSE
ESTANCIA GOLF CLUB
PINNACLE PEAK PARK
PINNACLE PEAK
DESERT HIGHLANDS GOLF CLUB
LA MIRADA DESERT PARK
CLUBHOUSE
E DYNAMITE BLVD
E JOMAX RD
E HAPPY VALLEY RD
N PIMA RD
E FOUR CORNERS POWER LINE RD
E DESERT VISTA RD
E MARIPOSA GRANDE DR
N DOBSON RD
R4E
R5E
T5N
T4N
SEE 500 MAP
SEE 541 MAP
PHOENIX
MAP
miles 1 in. = 1900 ft.
COPYRIGHT 2001 Thomas Bros. Maps ®

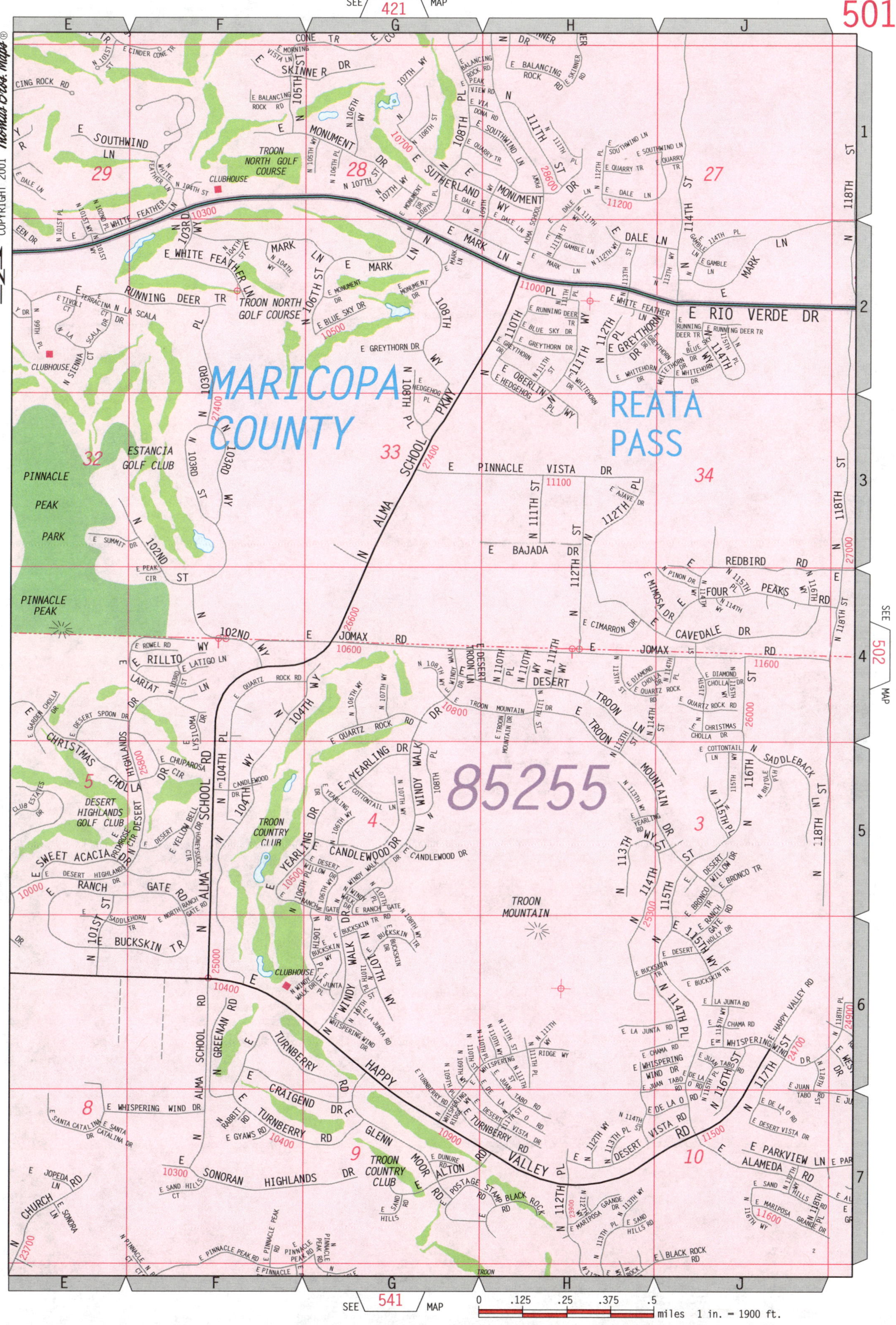
SEE 421 MAP
E
F
G
H
J
1
2
3
4
5
6
7
PHOENIX
MAP
SEE 502 MAP
SEE 541 MAP
Thomas Bros. Maps®
COPYRIGHT 2001
MARICOPA COUNTY
REATA PASS
85255
TROON NORTH GOLF COURSE
CLUBHOUSE
ESTANCIA GOLF CLUB
PINNACLE PEAK PARK
PINNACLE PEAK
DESERT HIGHLANDS GOLF CLUB
TROON COUNTRY CLUB
TROON MOUNTAIN
E RIO VERDE DR
E DALE LN
E MARK LN
E WHITE FEATHER LN
RUNNING DEER TR
E SOUTHWIND LN
E SKINNER DR
E SUTHERLAND WY
N ALMA SCHOOL PKWY
N ALMA SCHOOL RD
E PINNACLE VISTA DR
E BAJADA DR
E REDBIRD RD
FOUR PEAKS
E CAVEDALE DR
E JOMAX RD
E DESERT TROON LN
TROON MOUNTAIN DR
E HAPPY VALLEY RD
E DESERT VISTA RD
E SONORAN HIGHLANDS DR
E TURNBERRY RD
E CRAIGEND DR
E WHISPERING WIND DR
E BUCKSKIN TR
E SWEET ACACIA DR
E CHRISTMAS CHOLLA DR
E SADDLEBACK ST
N 118TH ST
N 108TH ST
N 112TH ST
N 114TH ST
N 116TH ST
E ALAMEDA RD
E PARKVIEW LN
TROON COUNTRY CLUB
0 .125 .25 .375 .5
miles 1 in. = 1900 ft.

SEE 421 MAP

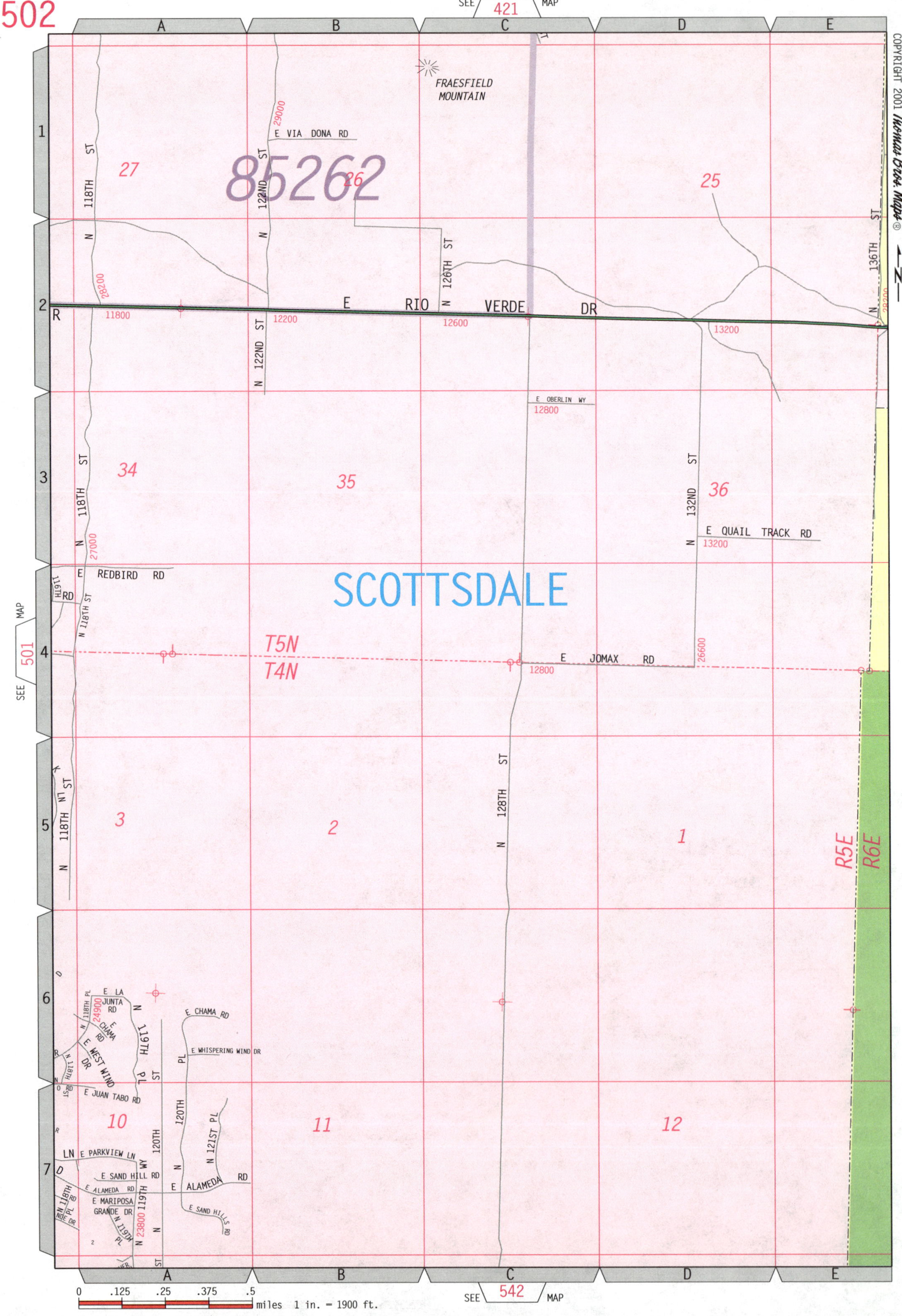

SEE 501 MAP

SEE 542 MAP

0 .125 .25 .375 .5 miles 1 in. = 1900 ft.

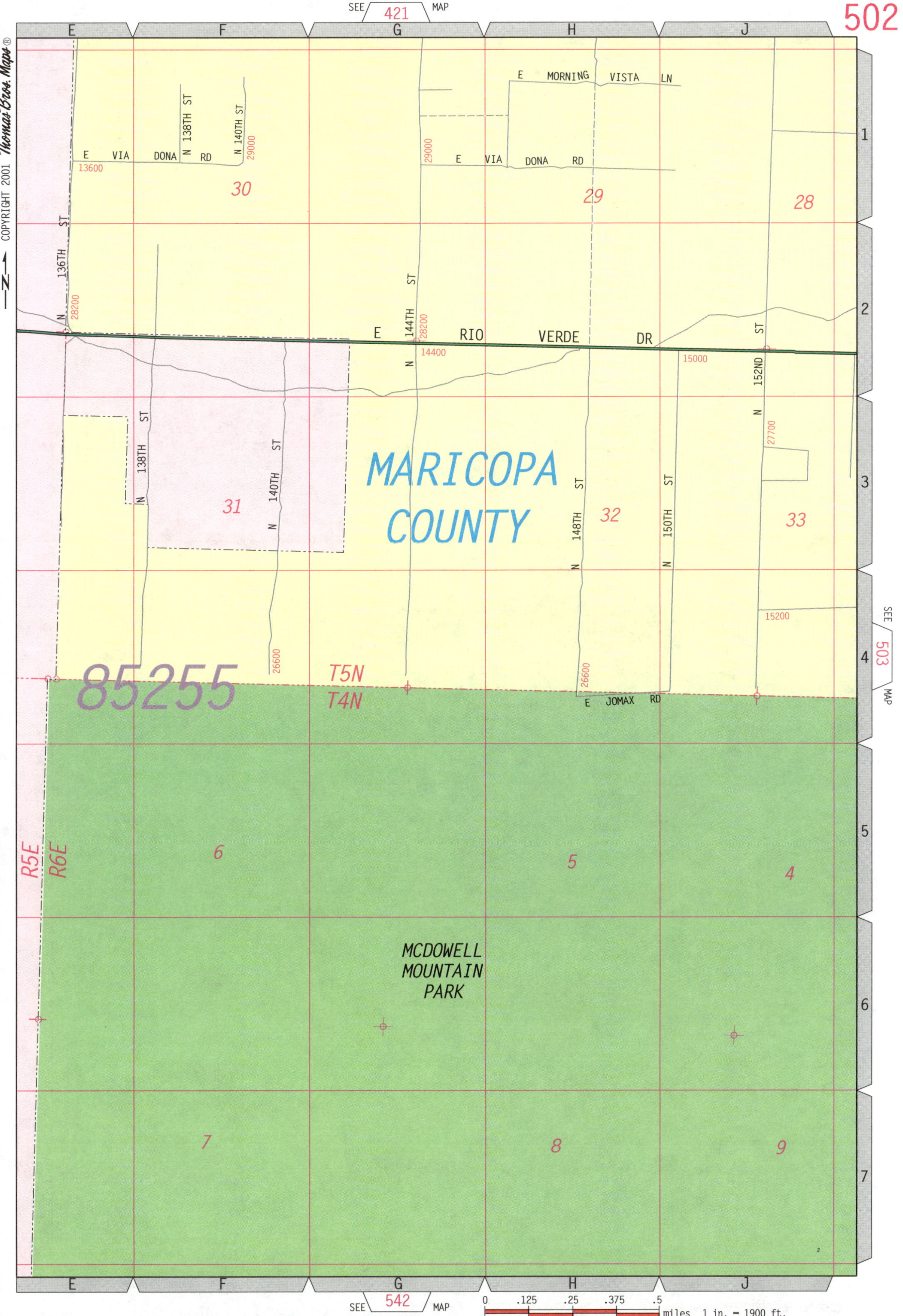

SEE 421 MAP
E
F
G
H
J
E MORNING VISTA LN
N 138TH ST
N 140TH ST
E VIA DONA RD
13600
29000
30
29
28
N 136TH ST
28200
N 144TH ST
E RIO VERDE DR
14400
15000
N 152ND ST
N 138TH ST
N 140TH ST
MARICOPA COUNTY
31
N 148TH ST
32
N 150TH ST
33
27700
15200
26600
85255
T5N
T4N
E JOMAX RD
R5E
R6E
6
5
4
MCDOWELL MOUNTAIN PARK
7
8
9
1
2
3
4
5
6
7
SEE 503 MAP
SEE 542 MAP
0 .125 .25 .375 .5 miles 1 in. = 1900 ft.
PHOENIX
MAP

SEE 423 MAP

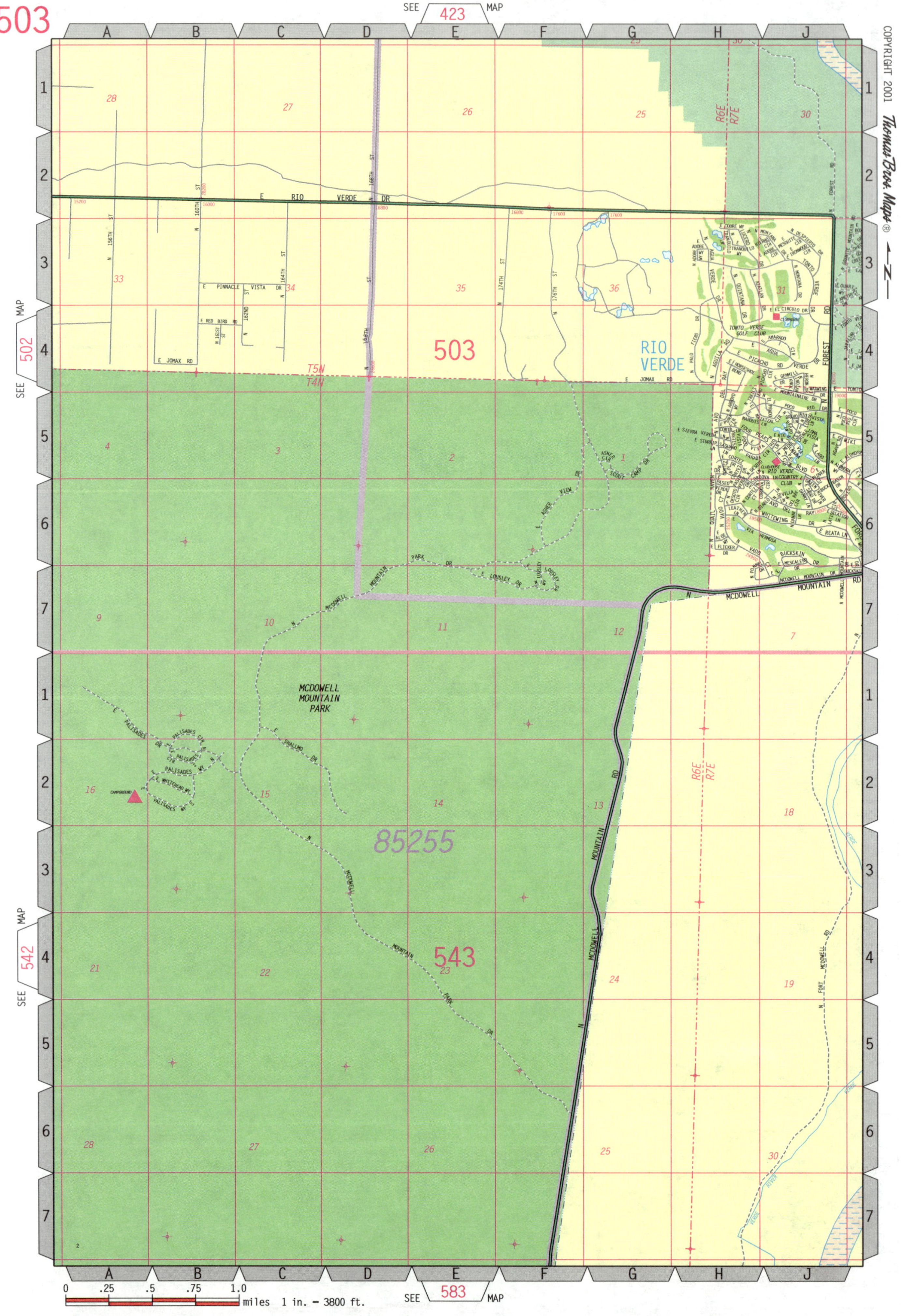

SEE 502 MAP

SEE 542 MAP

SEE 583 MAP

0 .25 .5 .75 1.0 miles 1 in. = 3800 ft.

PHOENIX

MAP

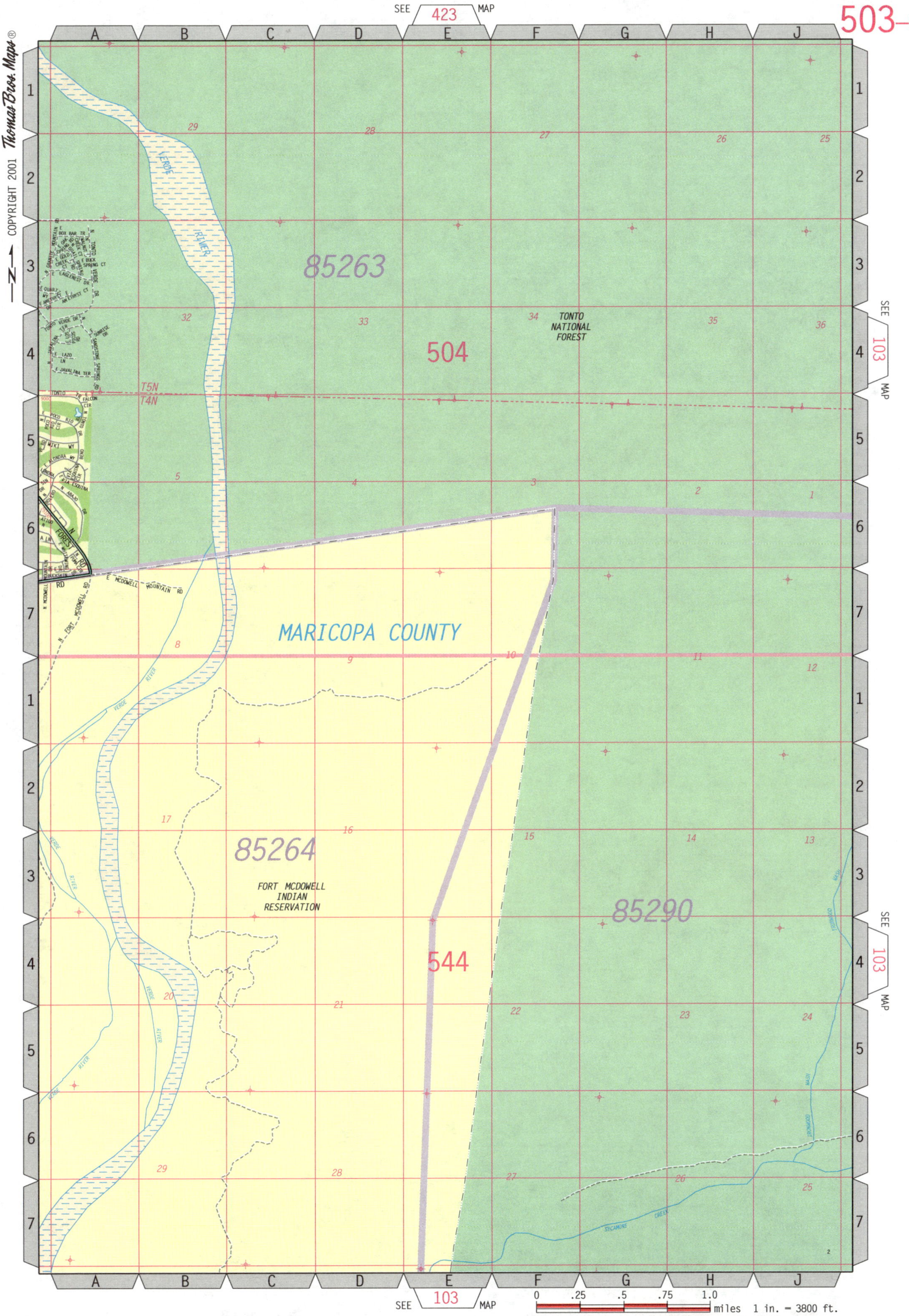

SEE 423 MAP
85263
504
TONTO NATIONAL FOREST
VERDE RIVER
T5N
T4N
MARICOPA COUNTY
85264
FORT MCDOWELL INDIAN RESERVATION
85290
544
E MCDOWELL MOUNTAIN RD
N FORT MCDOWELL RD
SYCAMORE CREEK
SEE 103 MAP
0 .25 .5 .75 1.0 miles 1 in. = 3800 ft.

PHOENIX

MAP

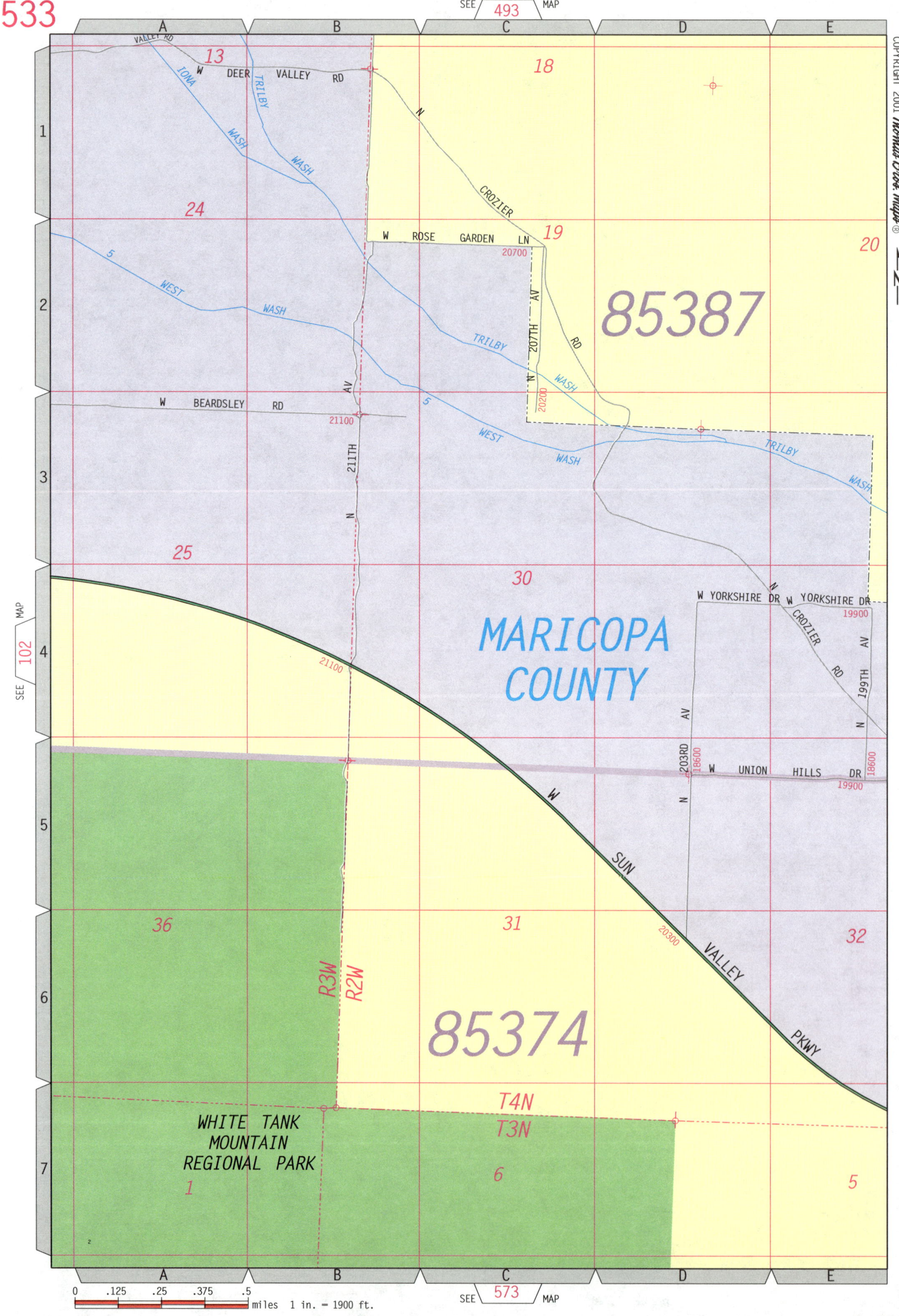

SEE 493 MAP
A
B
C
D
E
1
2
3
4
5
6
7
SEE 102 MAP
SEE 573 MAP
VALLEY RD
W DEER VALLEY RD
IONA WASH
TRILBY WASH
N CROZIER RD
W ROSE GARDEN LN
20700
N 207TH AV
20200
5 WEST WASH
TRILBY WASH
W BEARDSLEY RD
21100
N 211TH AV
W YORKSHIRE DR
W YORKSHIRE DR
19900
N CROZIER RD
N 199TH AV
N 203RD AV
18600
W UNION HILLS DR
19900
18600
21100
W SUN VALLEY PKWY
20300
13
18
19
20
24
25
30
31
32
36
1
6
5
85387
85374
MARICOPA COUNTY
R3W
R2W
T4N
T3N
WHITE TANK MOUNTAIN REGIONAL PARK
0
.125
.25
.375
.5
miles 1 in. = 1900 ft.
PHOENIX
MAP

SEE 493 MAP

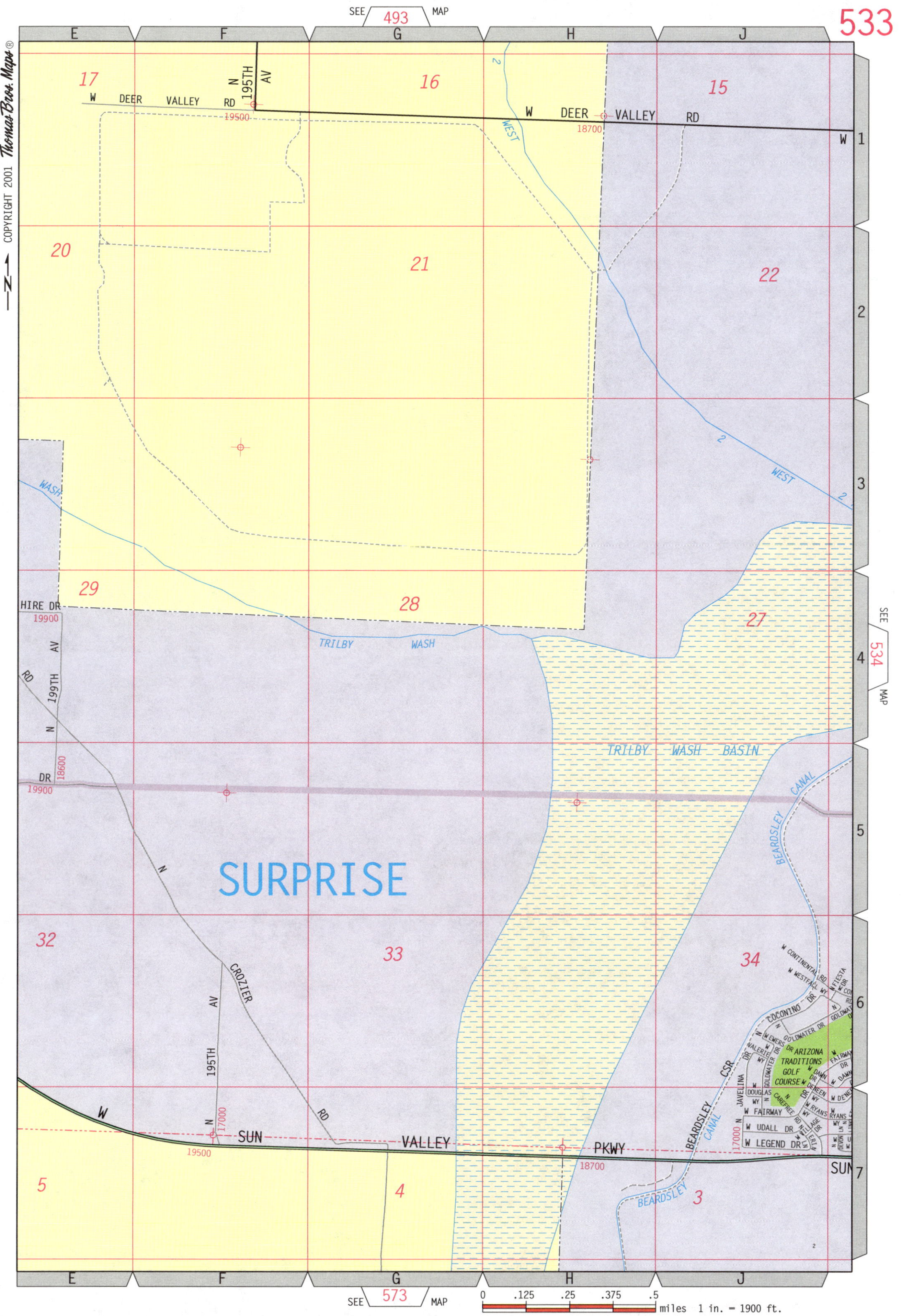

SEE 534 MAP

SEE 573 MAP

0 .125 .25 .375 .5 miles 1 in. = 1900 ft.

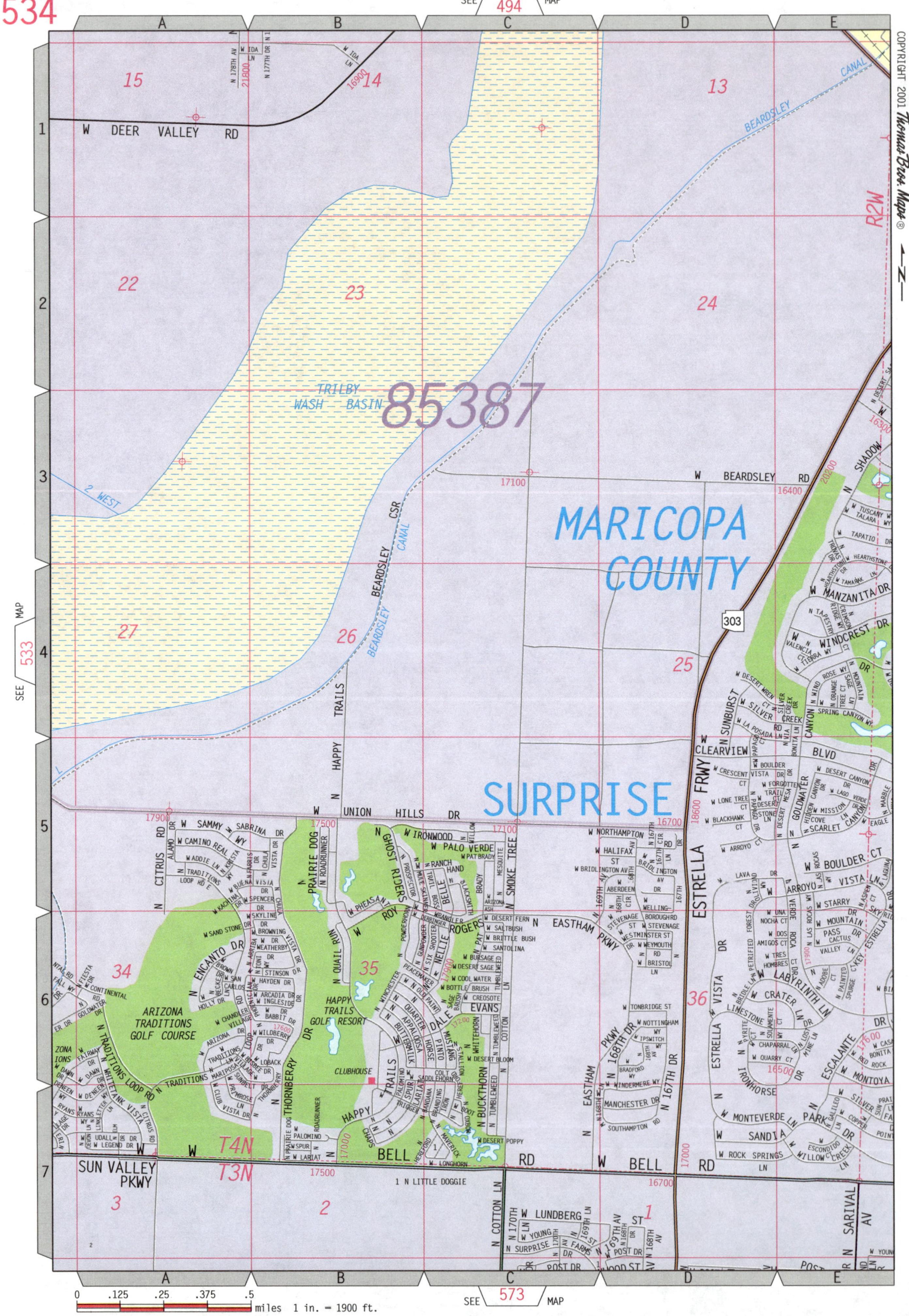
SEE 494 MAP
SEE 533 MAP
SEE 573 MAP
85387
MARICOPA COUNTY
SURPRISE
TRILBY WASH BASIN
W DEER VALLEY RD
W BEARDSLEY RD
BEARDSLEY CANAL
BEARDSLEY CSR
W UNION HILLS DR
N HAPPY TRAILS
ESTRELLA FRWY
303
W CLEARVIEW BLVD
W BELL RD
SUN VALLEY PKWY
ARIZONA TRADITIONS GOLF COURSE
HAPPY TRAILS GOLF RESORT
CLUBHOUSE
T4N
T3N
R2W
N CITRUS RD
N SMOKE TREE
EASTHAM PKWY
N 167TH DR
W MANZANITA DR
W WINDCREST DR
N SARIVAL AV
W LUNDBERG ST
N COTTON LN
1 N LITTLE DOGGIE
15
14
13
22
23
24
27
26
25
34
35
36
3
2
1
17900
17500
17100
16700
16400
17000
miles 1 in. = 1900 ft.

SEE 494 MAP

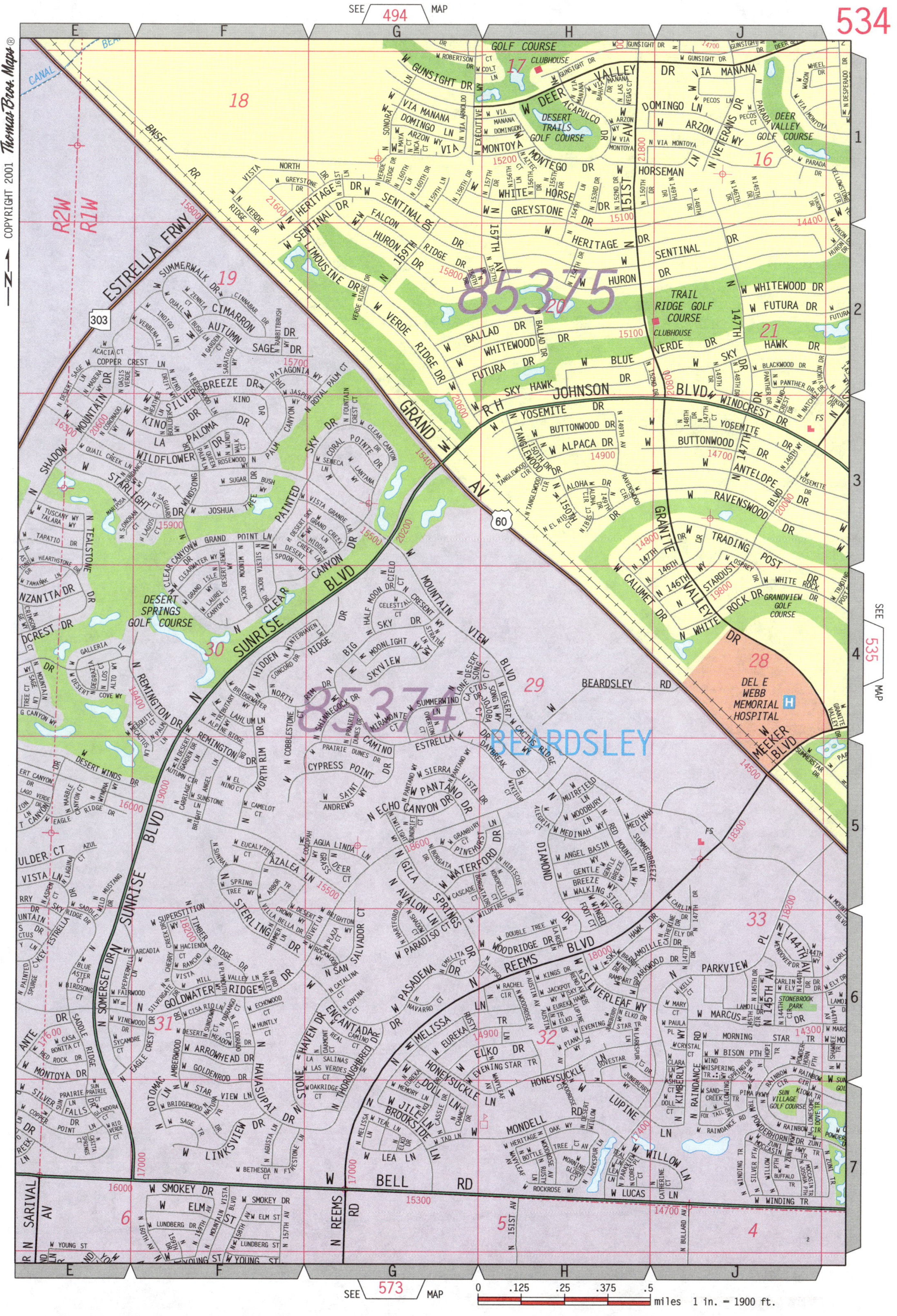

SEE 573 MAP
0 .125 .25 .375 .5 miles 1 in. = 1900 ft.

SEE 495 MAP

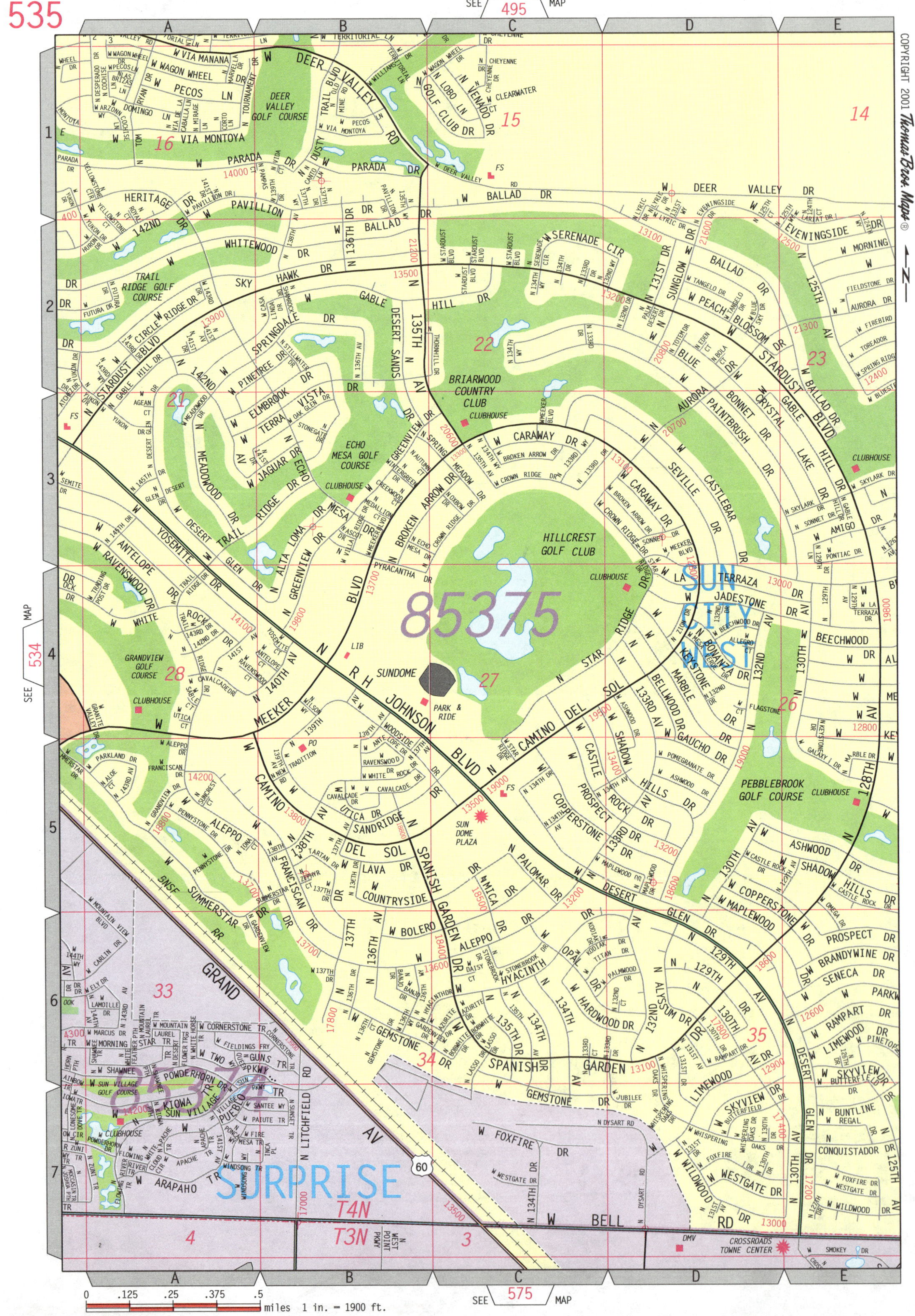

SEE 534 MAP

SEE 575 MAP

0 .125 .25 .375 .5 miles 1 in. = 1900 ft.

PHOENIX

MAP

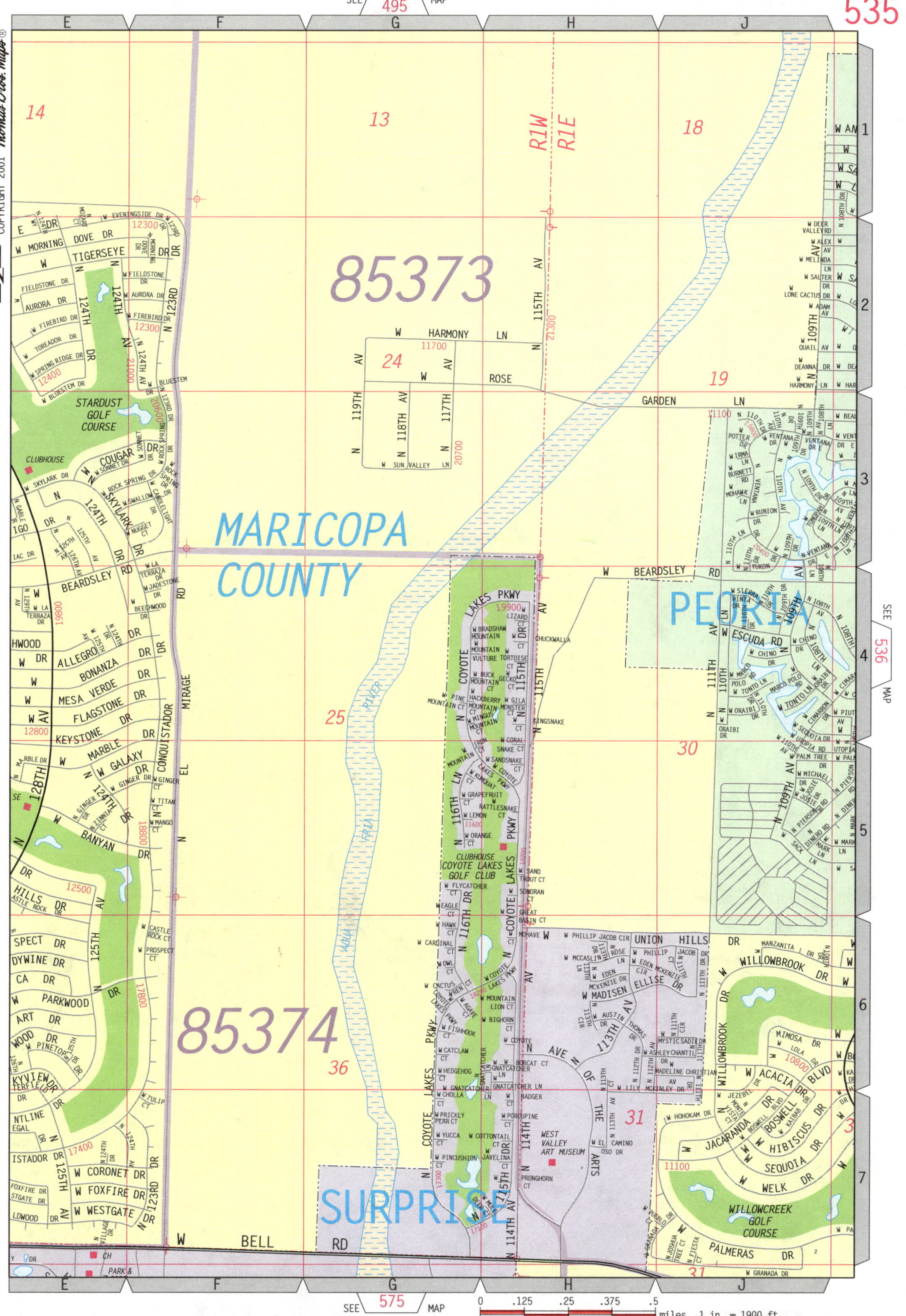
SEE 495 MAP
85373
85374
MARICOPA COUNTY
PEORIA
SURPRISE
STARDUST GOLF COURSE
COYOTE LAKES GOLF CLUB
WILLOWCREEK GOLF COURSE
WEST VALLEY ART MUSEUM
AGUA FRIA RIVER
R1W R1E
W BELL RD
W BEARDSLEY RD
N EL MIRAGE RD
W GARDEN LN
W HARMONY LN
W ROSE
N 115TH AV
N 111TH AV
N 109TH AV
COYOTE LAKES PKWY
N 114TH AV
UNION HILLS DR
PHOENIX
SEE 536 MAP
SEE 575 MAP
miles 1 in. = 1900 ft.

SEE 496 MAP
SEE 535 MAP
SEE 576 MAP
PHOENIX
MAP
PEORIA
85382
85373
W DEER VALLEY RD
W LAKE PLEASANT PKWY
W BEARDSLEY RD
W UNION HILLS DR
N LAKE PLEASANT RD
N OLD LAKE PLEASANT RD
N 107TH AV
N 99TH AV
N 91ST AV
W WILLIAMS RD
W COUNTRY CLUB TR
W ANGELS LN
W CARLOTA LN
W SANDS DR
W LOUISE DR
W VIA DEL SOL
W ALEX AV
W MELINDA LN
W SALTER DR
W LONE CACTUS DR
W ADAM AV
W QUAIL AV
W DEANNA DR
W HARMONY LN
W ROSE GARDEN LN
W ROSS AV
W POTTER DR
W IRMA LN
W MOHAWK LN
W RUNION DR
W TONOPAH DR
W YUKON DR
W PONTIAC DR
W ALBERT LN
N DOVE VALLEY RANCH DR
W MARY ANN DR
W CLARA LN
W WILLOWCREEK CIR
W CONCHO CIR
W PONDEROSA CIR
W SADDLE RIDGE
N PALO VERDE DR
N CONESTOGA DR
W EDGEWATER DR
W ESCUDA DR
W MARCO POLO RD
W TONTO LN
W ORAIBI DR
W WESTBROOK PKWY
W LAKEVIEW DR
N 96TH LN
N 96TH AV
W KERRY LN
W TARO LN
THE LAKES AT WESTBROOK VILLAGE
CLUBHOUSE
W GARNETTE DR
W MANZANITA DR
W WILLOWBROOK DR
W MIMOSA DR
W BOSWELL BLVD
W SEQUOIA DR
WILLOWCREEK GOLF COURSE
UNION HILLS COUNTRY CLUB
W SPANISH MOSS LN
W COUNTRY CLUB DR
W LINDGREN AV
N 107TH AV
N DEL WEBB BLVD
W HIGHWOOD LN
N BOSWELL BLVD
W WHEATRIDGE DR
W CALICO DR
W APPALOOSA DR
W COTTONWOOD DR
W MOCKINGBIRD DR
W TERRACE LN
W WRANGLER DR
W GRANADA DR
N PALO VERDE DR
W ATHENS
FS
1
2
3
4
5
6
7
A
B
C
D
E
16
17
18
19
20
21
28
29
30
31
32
33
0 .125 .25 .375 .5 miles 1 in. = 1900 ft.

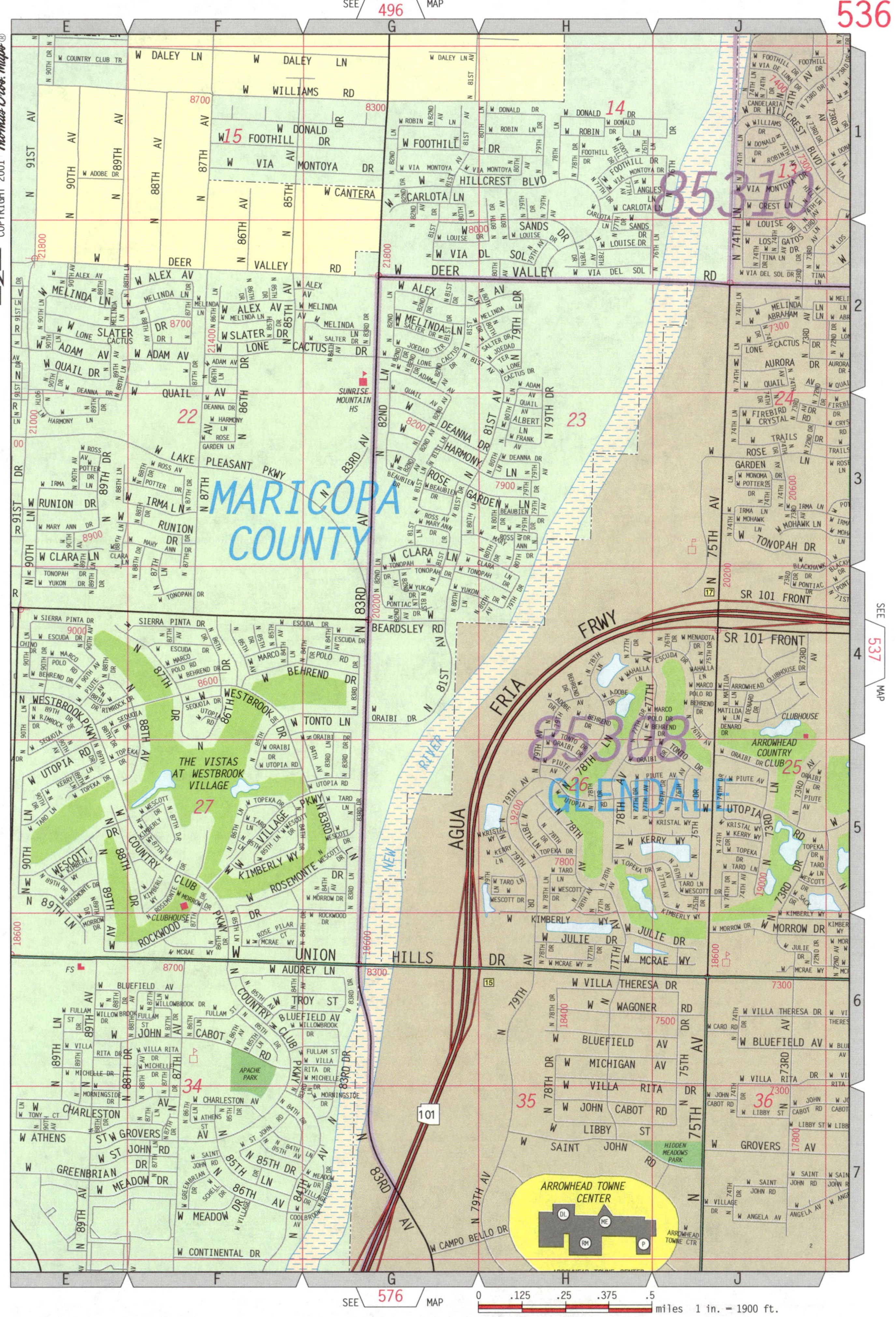
SEE 496 MAP
SEE 537 MAP
SEE 576 MAP
PHOENIX
MAP
Thomas Bros. Maps®
COPYRIGHT 2001
MARICOPA COUNTY
GLENDALE
85310
85308
AGUA FRIA FRWY
NEW RIVER
101
SR 101 FRONT
W DALEY LN
W WILLIAMS RD
W DONALD DR
W FOOTHILL DR
W VIA MONTOYA DR
W CANTERA
W HILLCREST BLVD
W CARLOTA LN
W SANDS DR
W LOUISE DR
W VIA DEL SOL
W DEER VALLEY RD
W ALEX AV
W MELINDA LN
W SLATER DR
W LONE CACTUS DR
W ADAM AV
W QUAIL DR
SUNRISE MOUNTAIN HS
W DEANNA DR
W HARMONY LN
W ROSE GARDEN LN
W LAKE PLEASANT PKWY
W RUNION DR
W IRMA LN
W CLARA LN
W TONOPAH DR
W SIERRA PINTA DR
W BEARDSLEY RD
W BEHREND DR
W WESTBROOK PKWY
W TONTO LN
W ORAIBI DR
W UTOPIA RD
THE VISTAS AT WESTBROOK VILLAGE
CLUBHOUSE
W COUNTRY CLUB PKWY
W KIMBERLY WY
W ROSEMONTE DR
W ROCKWOOD DR
W UNION HILLS DR
W AUDREY LN
W TROY ST
W BLUEFIELD AV
W JOHN CABOT RD
APACHE PARK
W CHARLESTON AV
W ATHENS
W GROVERS AV
W ST JOHN RD
W GREENBRIAN
W MEADOW DR
W CONTINENTAL DR
W VILLA THERESA DR
W WAGONER RD
W MICHIGAN AV
W VILLA RITA DR
W LIBBY ST
W SAINT JOHN RD
HIDDEN MEADOWS PARK
ARROWHEAD TOWNE CENTER
W CAMPO BELLO DR
ARROWHEAD COUNTRY CLUB
W JULIE DR
W MCRAE WY
W MORROW DR
W KERRY WY
N 75TH AV
N 83RD AV
N 91ST AV
0 .125 .25 .375 .5 miles 1 in. = 1900 ft.

SEE 497 MAP

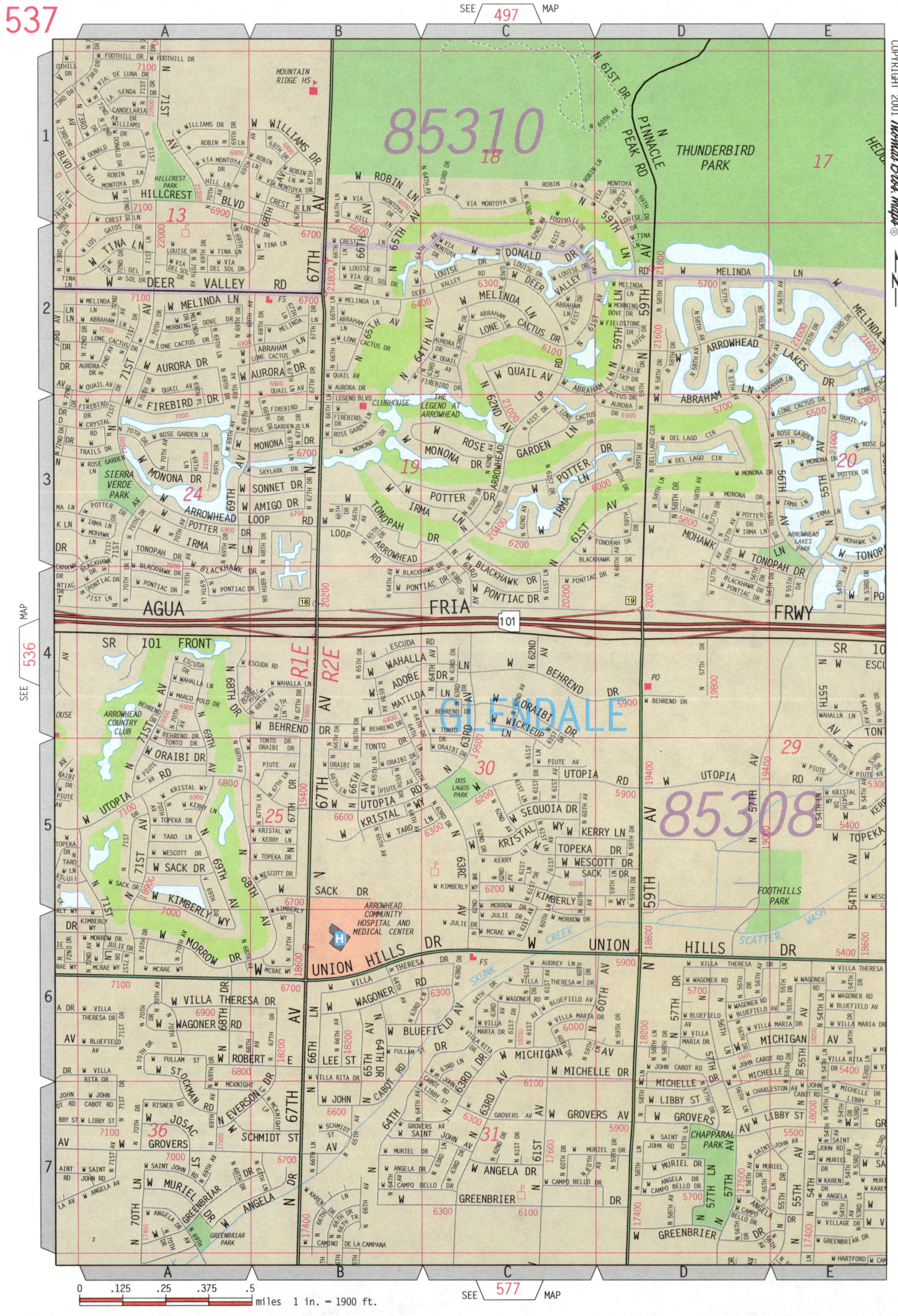

SEE 577 MAP

SEE 497 MAP

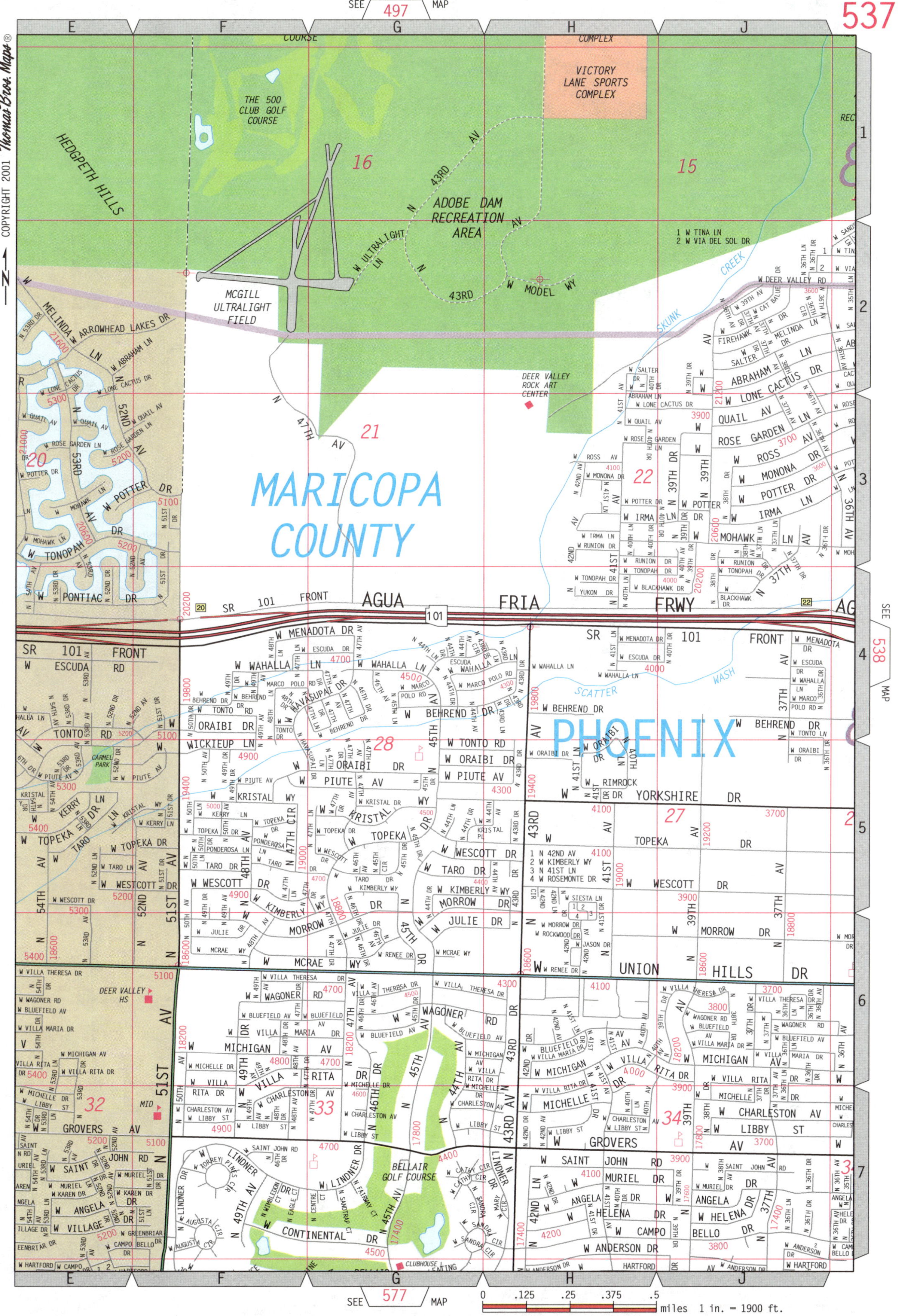

SEE 538 MAP

SEE 577 MAP

0 .125 .25 .375 .5 miles 1 in. = 1900 ft.

PHOENIX

MAP

SEE 498 MAP

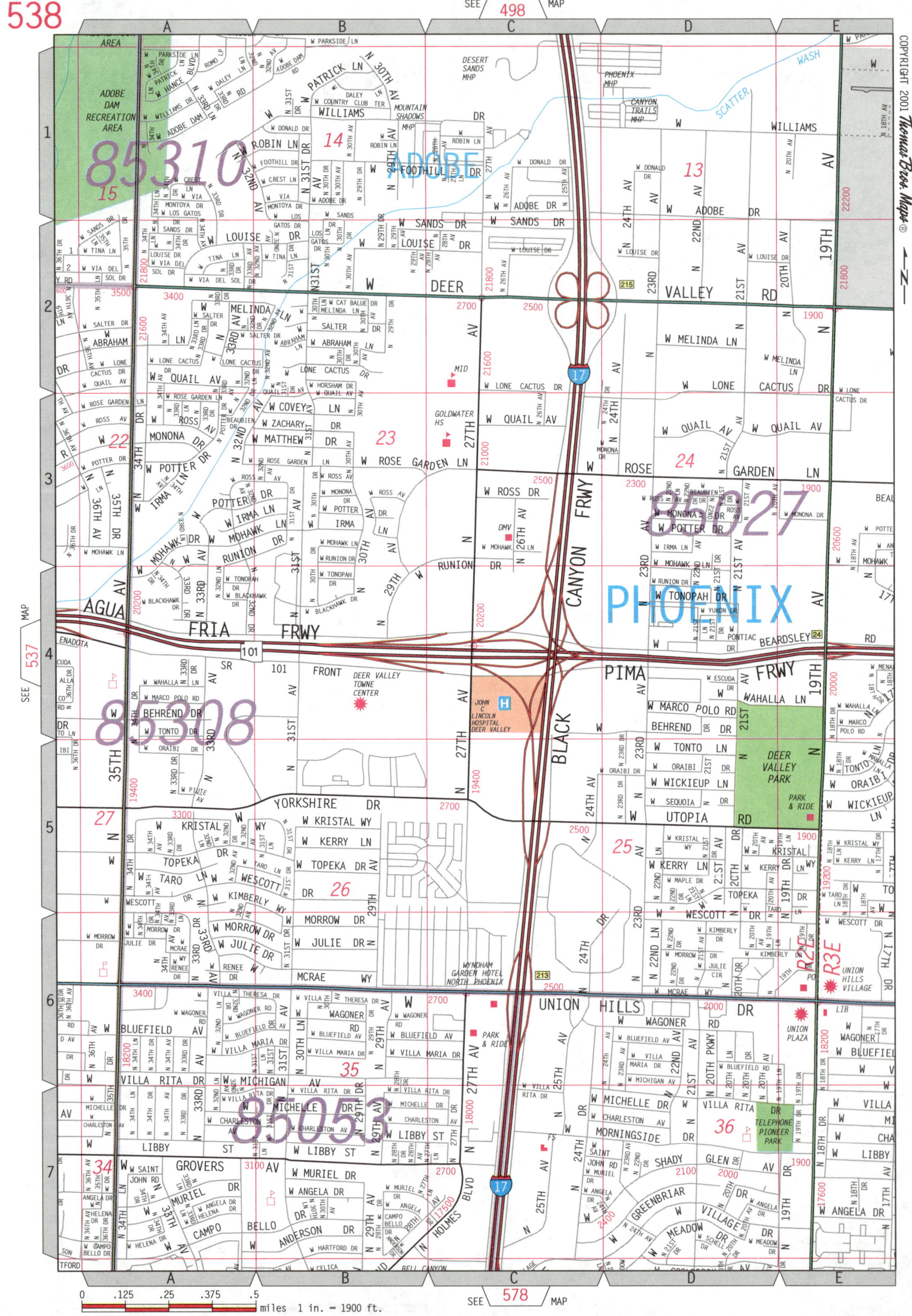

SEE 537 MAP

SEE 578 MAP

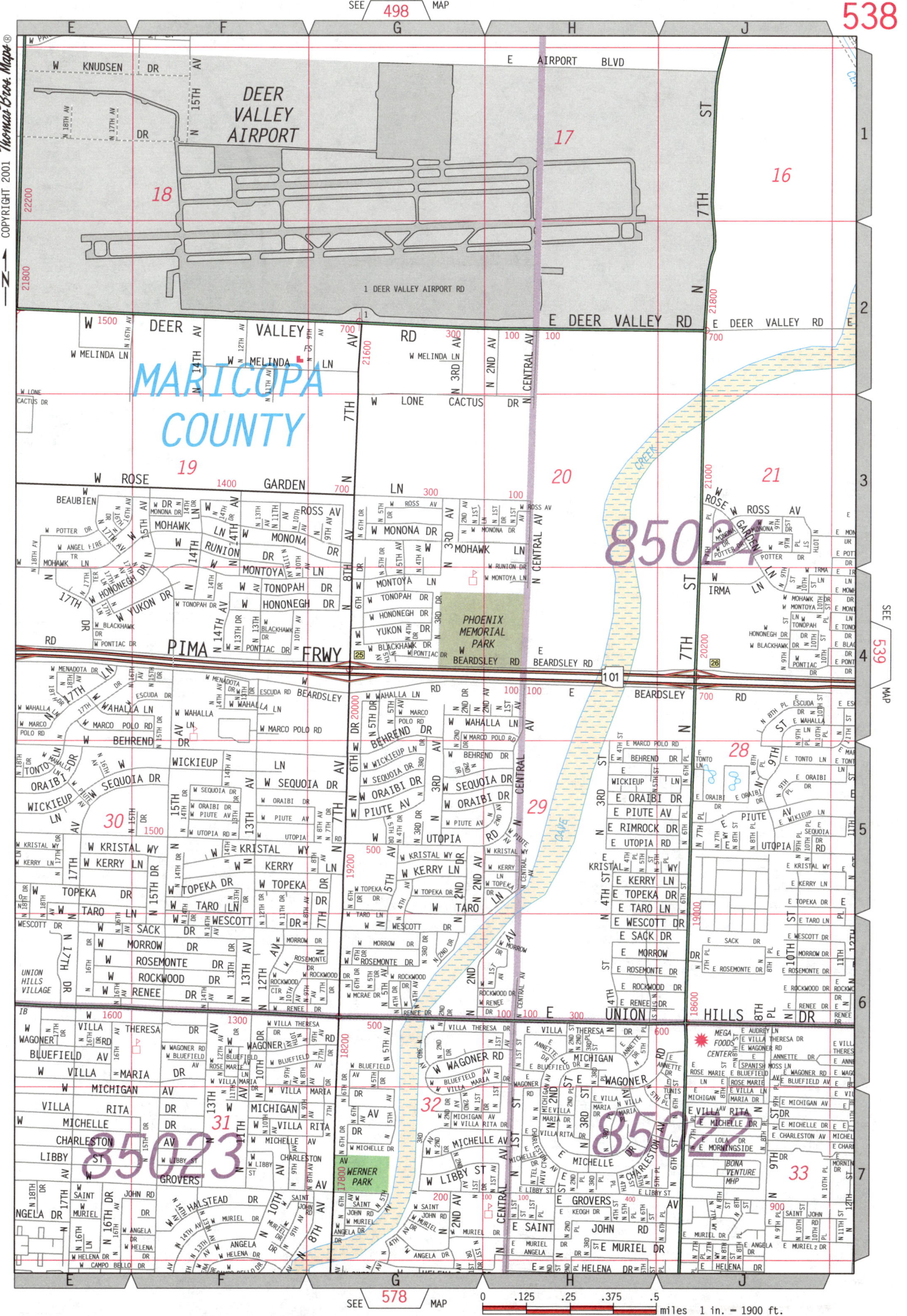
SEE 498 MAP
DEER VALLEY AIRPORT
E AIRPORT BLVD
W KNUDSEN DR
1 DEER VALLEY AIRPORT RD
E DEER VALLEY RD
W DEER VALLEY RD
MARICOPA COUNTY
W MELINDA LN
W LONE CACTUS DR
W ROSE GARDEN LN
N 7TH AV
N 7TH ST
N CENTRAL AV
PHOENIX MEMORIAL PARK
PIMA FRWY
101
E BEARDSLEY RD
W BEARDSLEY RD
CAVE CREEK
85024
85022
85023
W UTOPIA RD
E UNION HILLS DR
UNION HILLS VILLAGE
WERNER PARK
MEGA FOODS CENTER
BONA VENTURE MHP
E GROVERS AV
E MURIEL DR
W HALSTEAD DR
E HELENA DR
16
17
18
19
20
21
28
29
30
31
32
33
PHOENIX
SEE 539 MAP
SEE 578 MAP
0 .125 .25 .375 .5 miles 1 in. = 1900 ft.

SEE 499 MAP

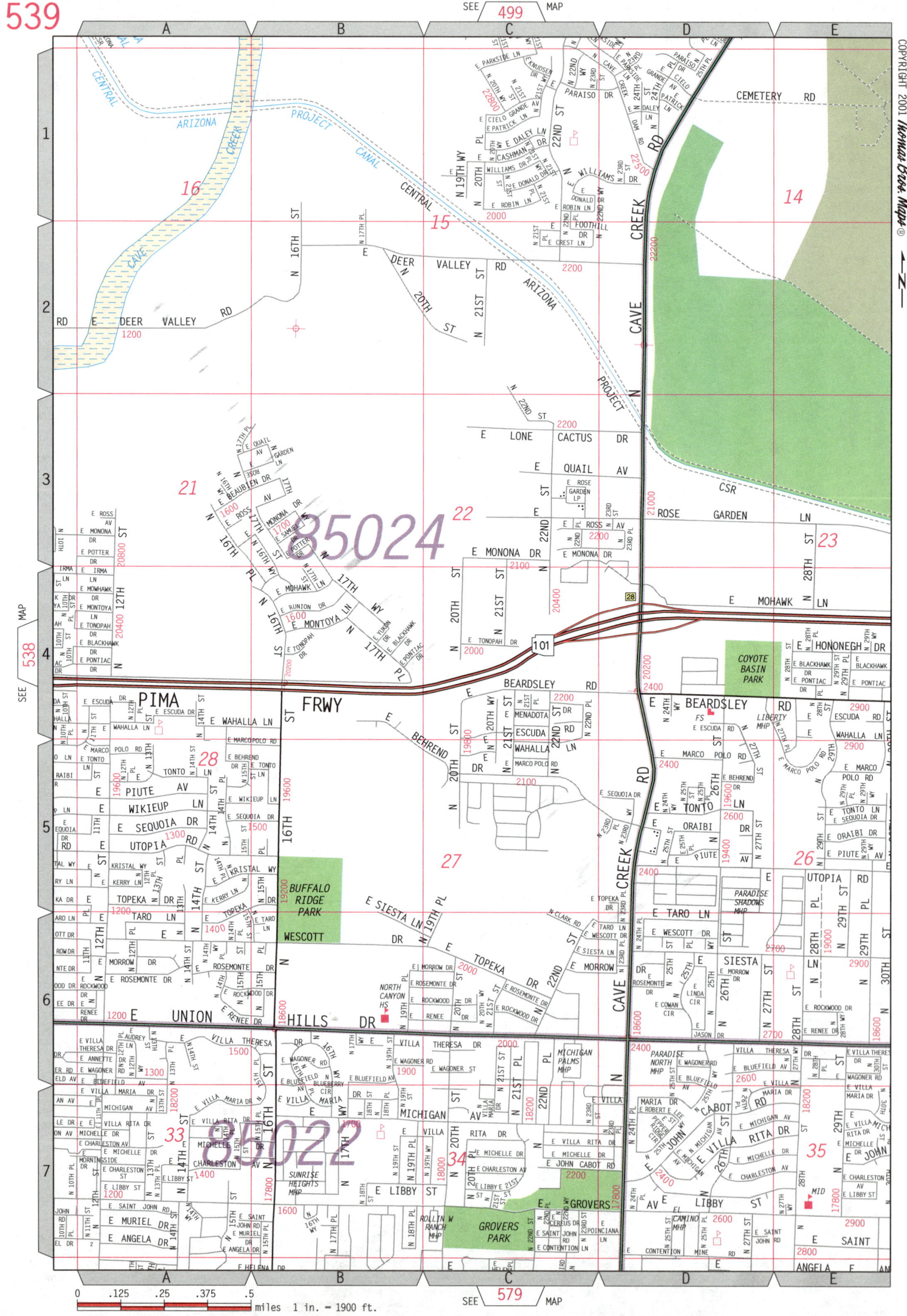

SEE 538 MAP
SEE 579 MAP

SEE 499 MAP

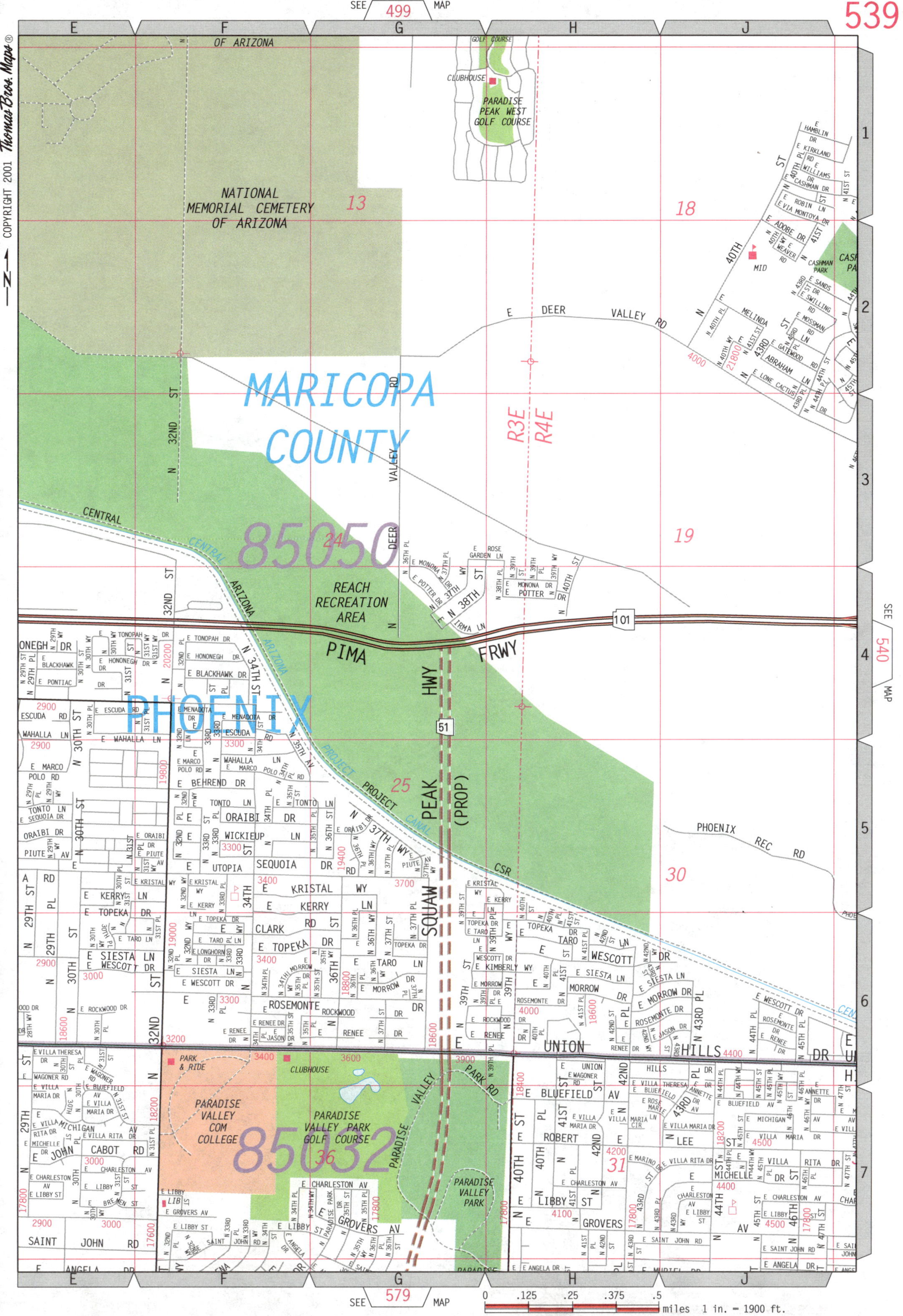

SEE 540 MAP

SEE 579 MAP

0 .125 .25 .375 .5 miles 1 in. = 1900 ft.

PHOENIX

MAP

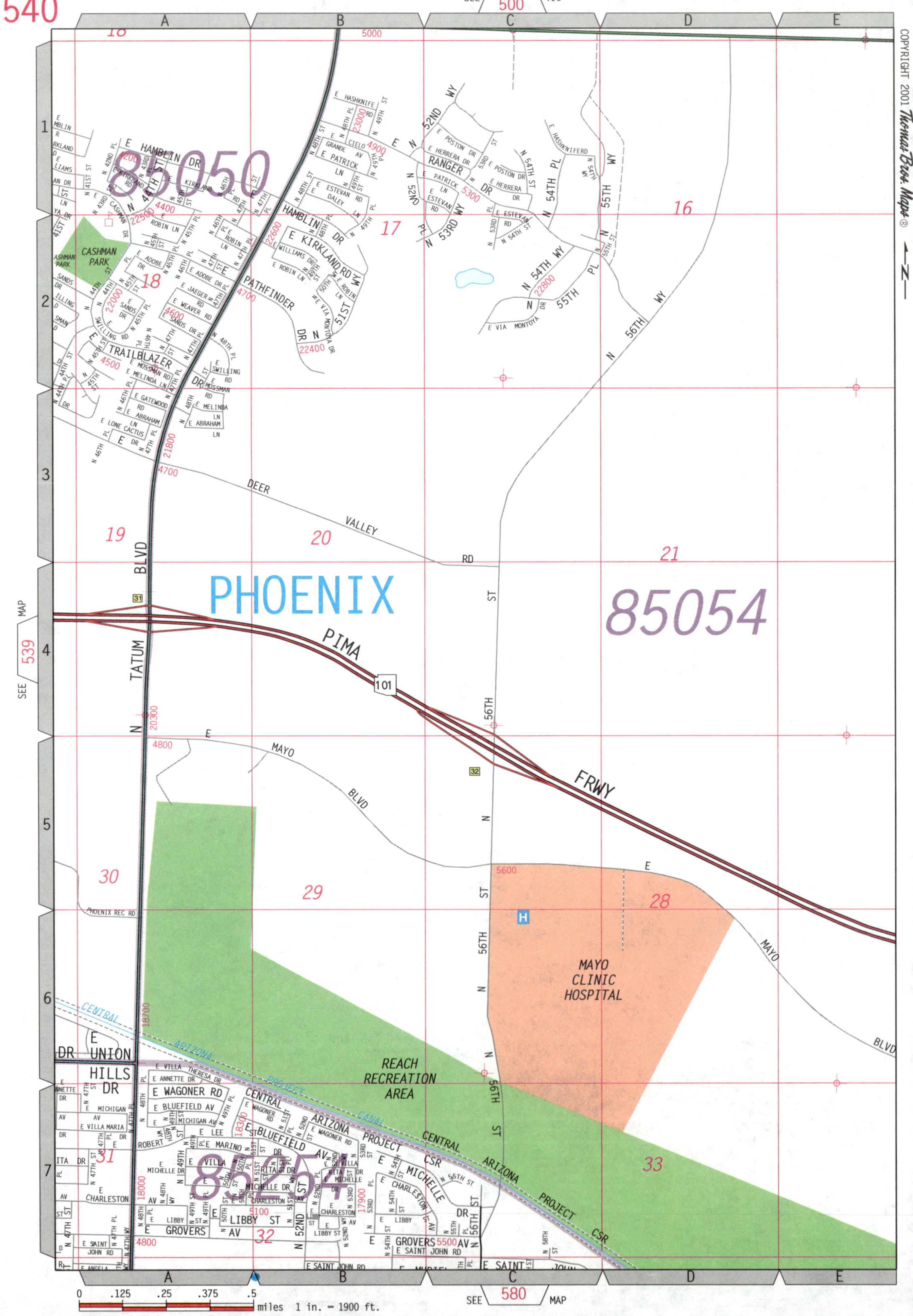

0 .125 .25 .375 .5 miles 1 in. = 1900 ft.

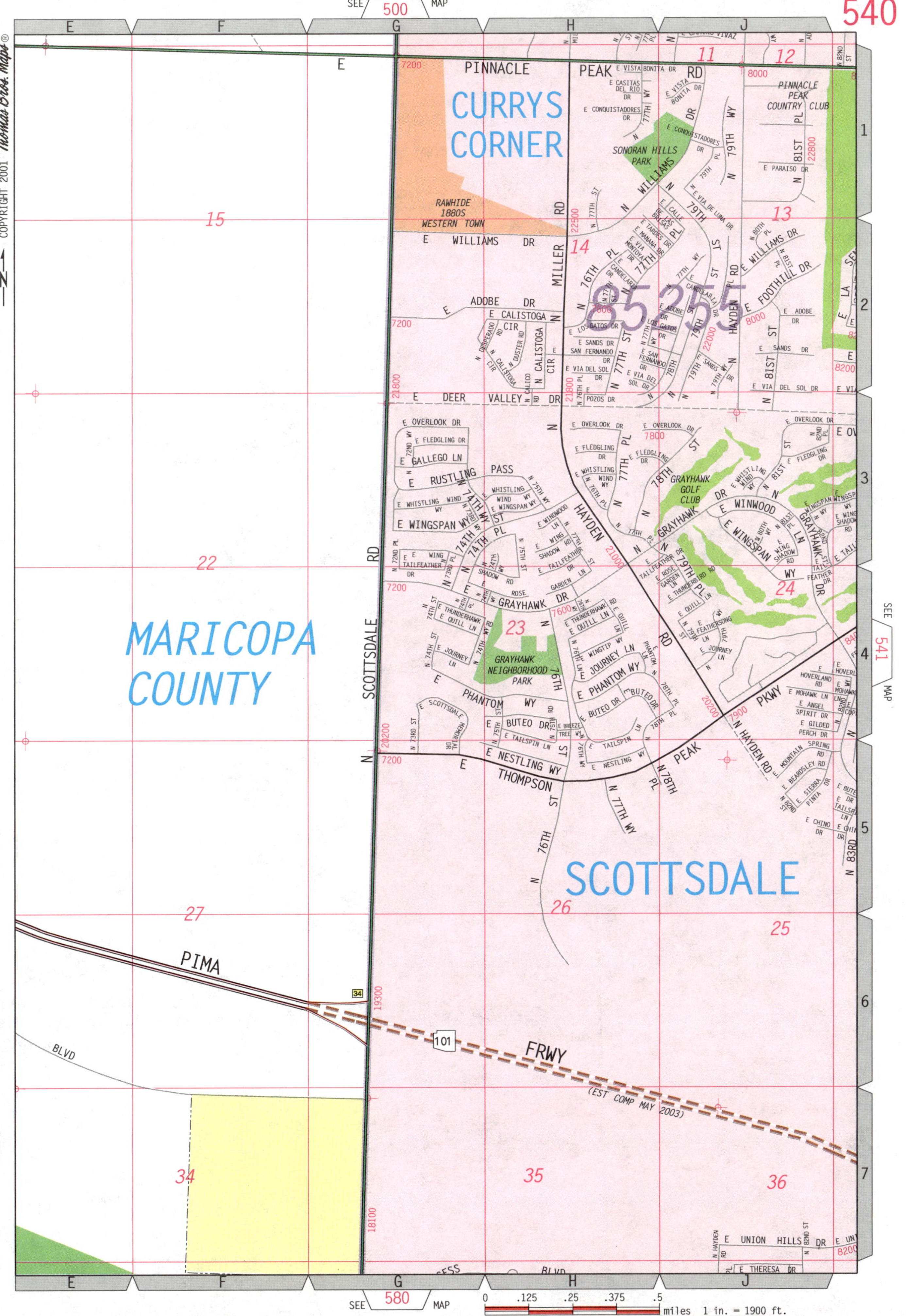

SEE 500 MAP
CURRYS CORNER
RAWHIDE 1880S WESTERN TOWN
PINNACLE PEAK RD
E WILLIAMS DR
SONORAN HILLS PARK
PINNACLE PEAK COUNTRY CLUB
85255
E ADOBE DR
E DEER VALLEY DR
MILLER RD
HAYDEN RD
GRAYHAWK GOLF CLUB
GRAYHAWK NEIGHBORHOOD PARK
E GRAYHAWK DR
E PHANTOM WY
E THOMPSON PEAK PKWY
N SCOTTSDALE RD
MARICOPA COUNTY
SCOTTSDALE
PIMA
BLVD
101
FRWY
(EST COMP MAY 2003)
E UNION HILLS DR
SEE 541 MAP
SEE 580 MAP
PHOENIX
MAP
miles 1 in. = 1900 ft.

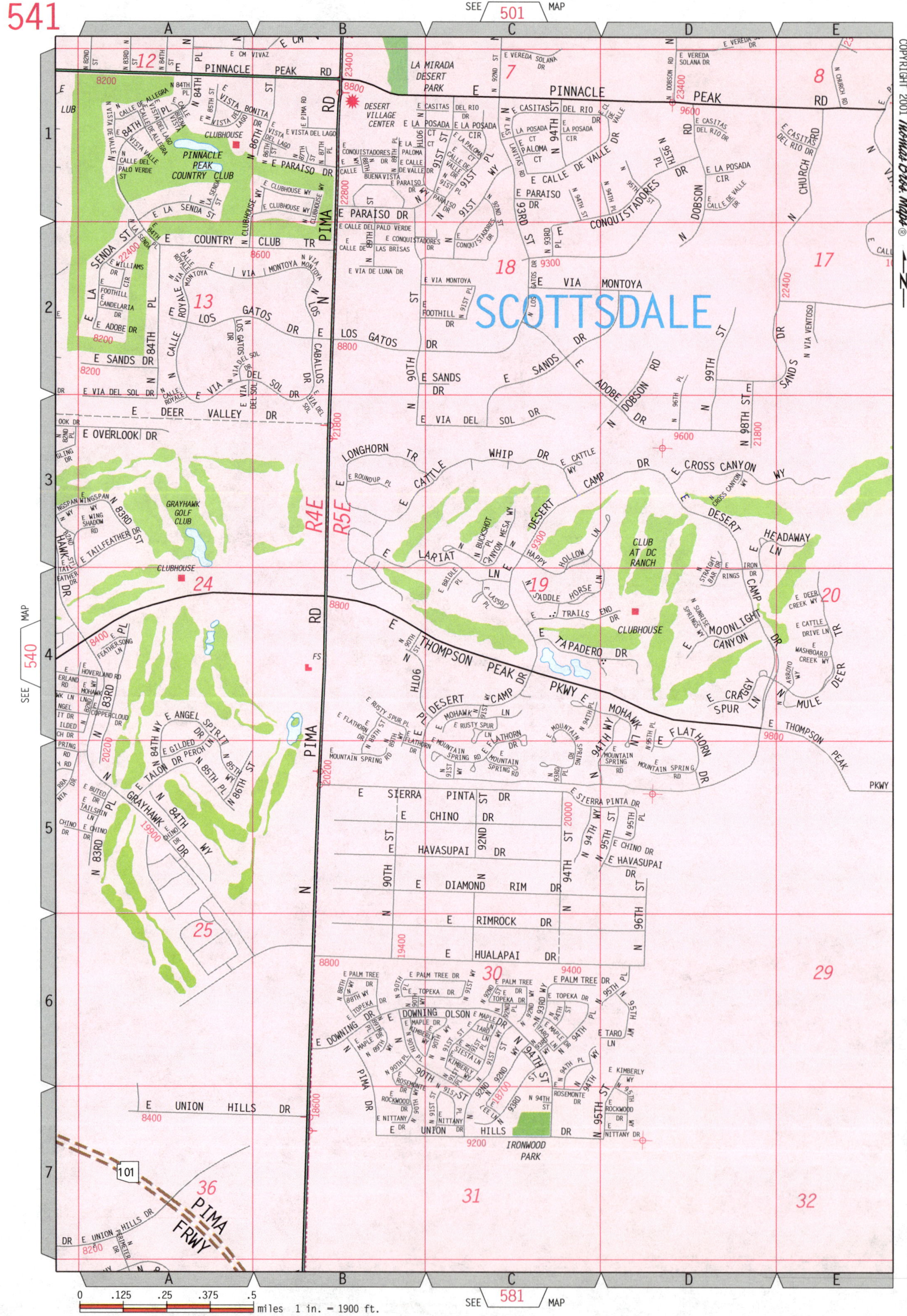
SEE 501 MAP
SCOTTSDALE
PHOENIX
MAP
SEE 540 MAP
SEE 581 MAP
PINNACLE PEAK COUNTRY CLUB
GRAYHAWK GOLF CLUB
CLUB AT DC RANCH
LA MIRADA DESERT PARK
DESERT VILLAGE CENTER
IRONWOOD PARK
E PINNACLE PEAK RD
E DEER VALLEY DR
E THOMPSON PEAK PKWY
E UNION HILLS DR
N PIMA RD
PIMA FRWY
101
R4E
R5E
0 .125 .25 .375 .5 miles 1 in. = 1900 ft.

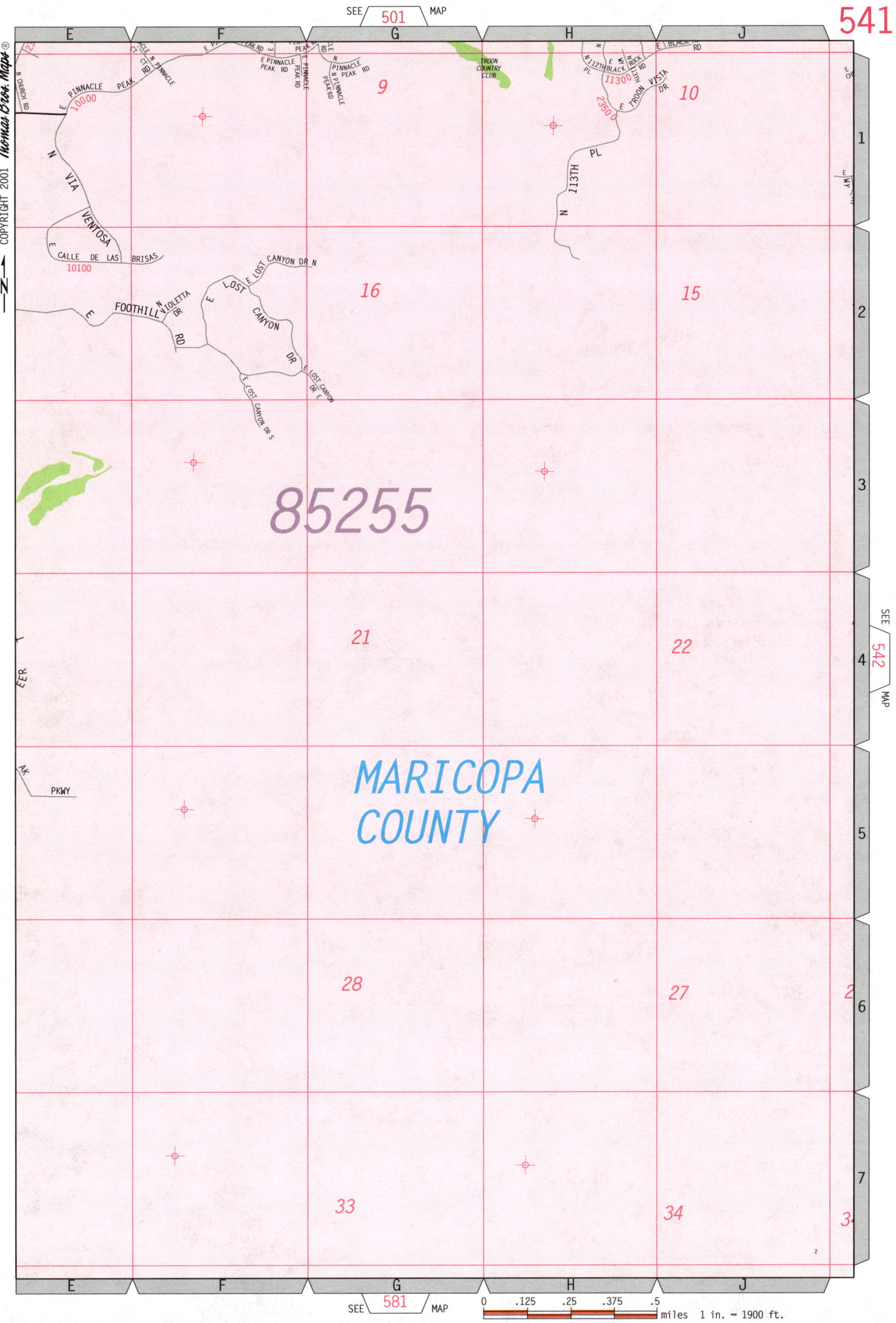

SEE 501 MAP
E
F
G
H
J
E PINNACLE PEAK RD
N VIA VENTOSA
E CALLE DE LAS BRISAS
10000
10100
E FOOTHILL DR
N VIOLETTA DR
RD
E LOST CANYON DR N
E LOST CANYON DR
E LOST CANYON DR E
E LOST CANYON DR S
N PINNACLE PEAK RD
TROON COUNTRY CLUB
N 112TH PL
E BLACK ROCK RD
N 113TH PL
11300
2350
E TROON VISTA DR
9
10
16
15
21
22
28
27
33
34
85255
MARICOPA COUNTY
PKWY
1
2
3
4
5
6
7
SEE 542 MAP
SEE 581 MAP
0 .125 .25 .375 .5 miles 1 in. = 1900 ft.
PHOENIX
MAP

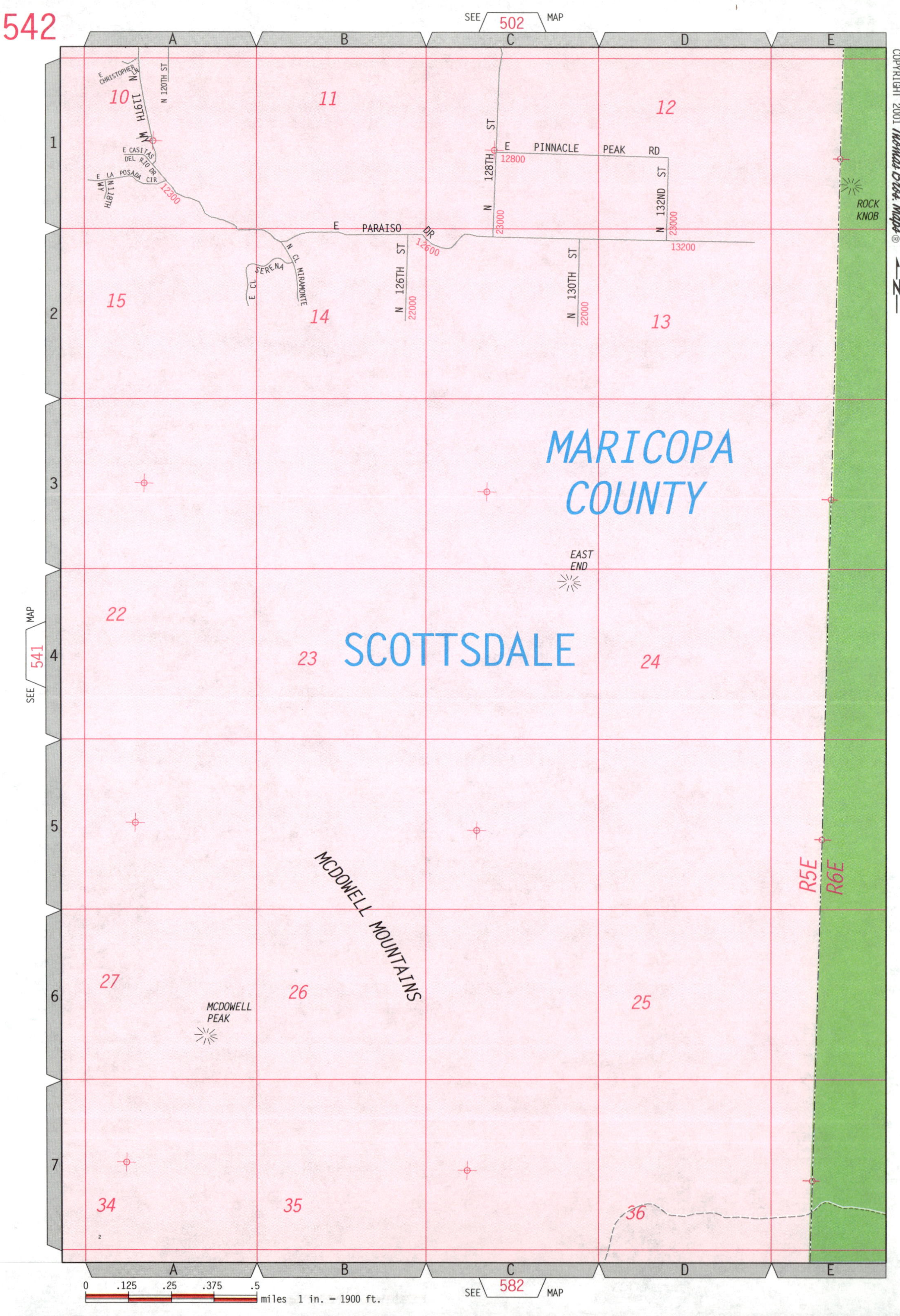
SEE 502 MAP
A
B
C
D
E
1
2
3
4
5
6
7
E CHRISTOPHER LN
N 119TH WY
N 120TH ST
E CASITAS DEL RIO DR
E LA POSADA CIR
N 118TH WY
12300
E PINNACLE PEAK RD
N 128TH ST
12800
N 132ND ST
23000
E PARAISO DR
12600
13200
N CL MIRAMONTE
E CL SERENA
N 126TH ST
22000
N 130TH ST
22000
ROCK KNOB
10
11
12
15
14
13
MARICOPA COUNTY
EAST END
22
23
SCOTTSDALE
24
SEE 541 MAP
MCDOWELL MOUNTAINS
R5E
R6E
27
26
25
MCDOWELL PEAK
34
35
36
0 .125 .25 .375 .5
miles 1 in. = 1900 ft.
SEE 582 MAP
PHOENIX
MAP

SEE 502 MAP

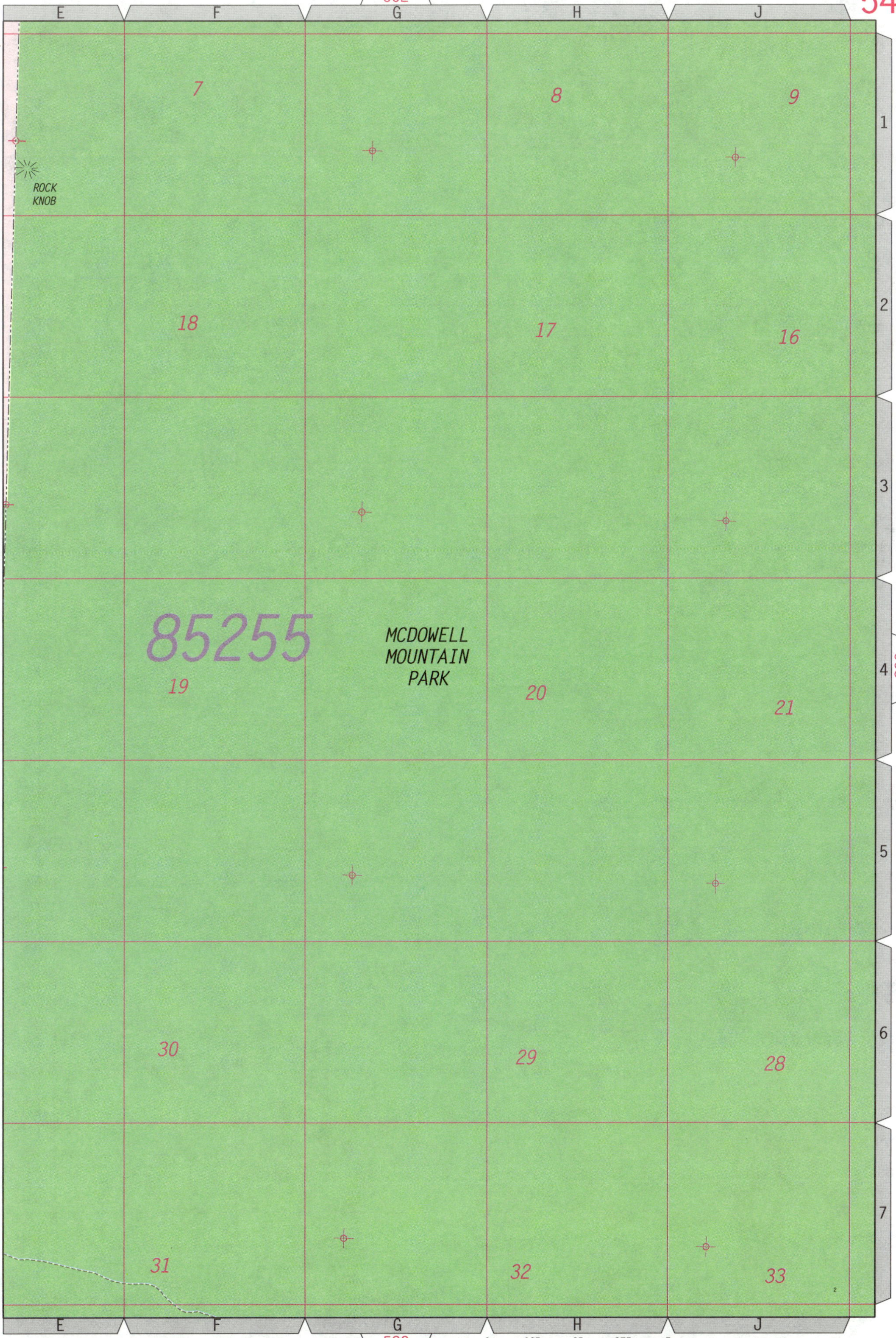

E F G H J

1 2 3 4 5 6 7

ROCK KNOB

7 8 9

18 17 16

85255

MCDOWELL MOUNTAIN PARK

19 20 21

30 29 28

31 32 33

SEE 503 MAP

SEE 582 MAP

0 .125 .25 .375 .5 miles 1 in. = 1900 ft.

PHOENIX

MAP

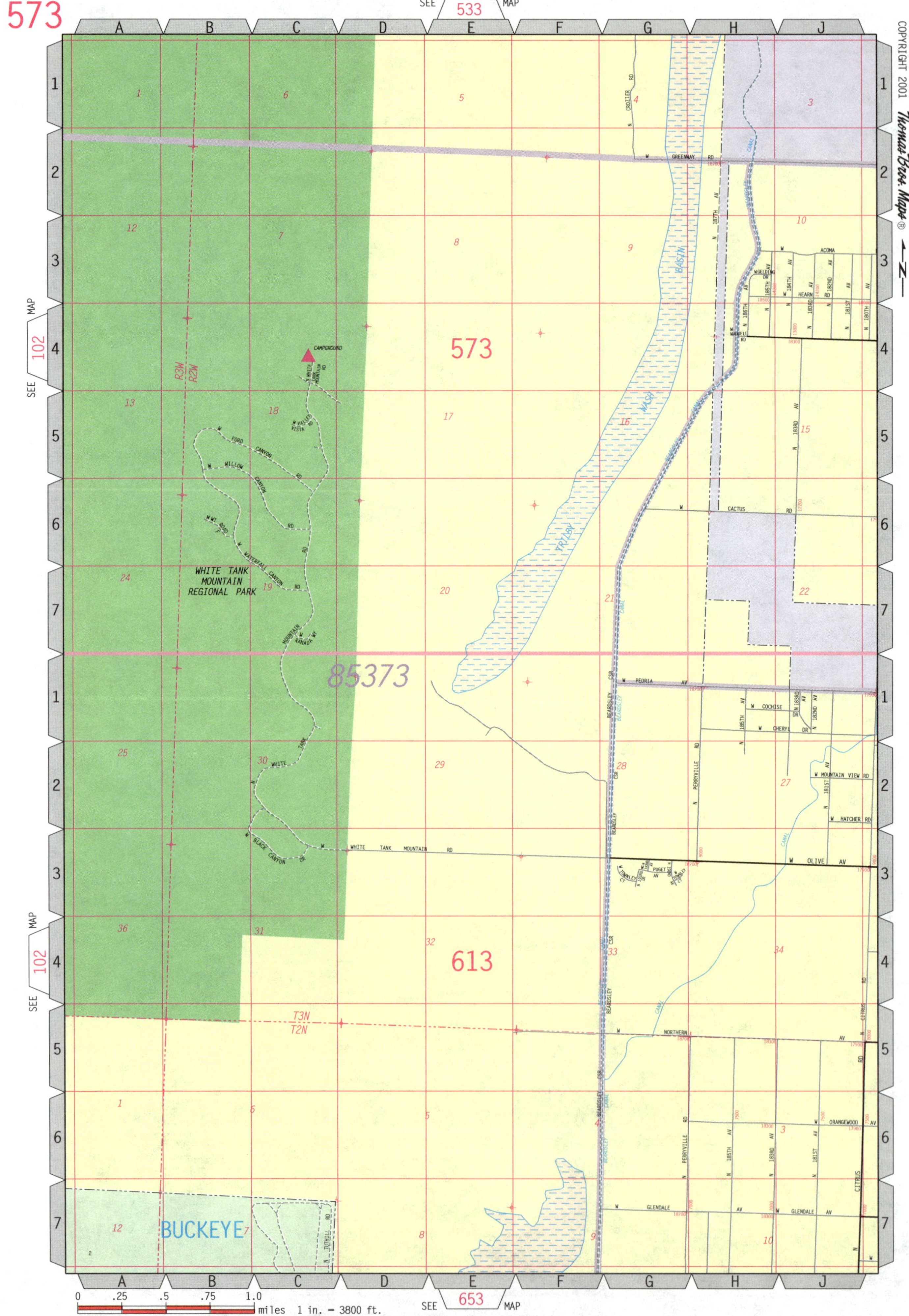

SEE 533 MAP
SEE 102 MAP
SEE 653 MAP
573
613
85373
WHITE TANK MOUNTAIN REGIONAL PARK
CAMPGROUND
BUCKEYE
GREENWAY RD
CACTUS RD
PEORIA AV
OLIVE AV
NORTHERN AV
GLENDALE AV
ORANGEWOOD AV
WHITE TANK MOUNTAIN RD
BEARDSLEY CANAL
TRILBY WASH BASIN
PERRYVILLE RD
CITRUS RD
COCHISE
CHERYL DR
MOUNTAIN VIEW RD
HATCHER RD
ACOMA
HEARN RD
WADDELL RD
PUGET AV
TOWNLEY CT
W FORD CANYON RD
W WILLOW CANYON RD
W WATERFALL CANYON RD
W BLACK CANYON DR
N WHITE TANK MOUNTAIN RD
N VALLEY VISTA RD
MOUNTAIN RAMADA WY
N TUTHILL RD
N CROZIER RD
187TH AV
186TH AV
185TH AV
184TH AV
183RD AV
182ND AV
181ST AV
180TH AV
T3N
T2N
R3W
R2W
0 .25 .5 .75 1.0
miles 1 in. = 3800 ft.

PHOENIX
MAP

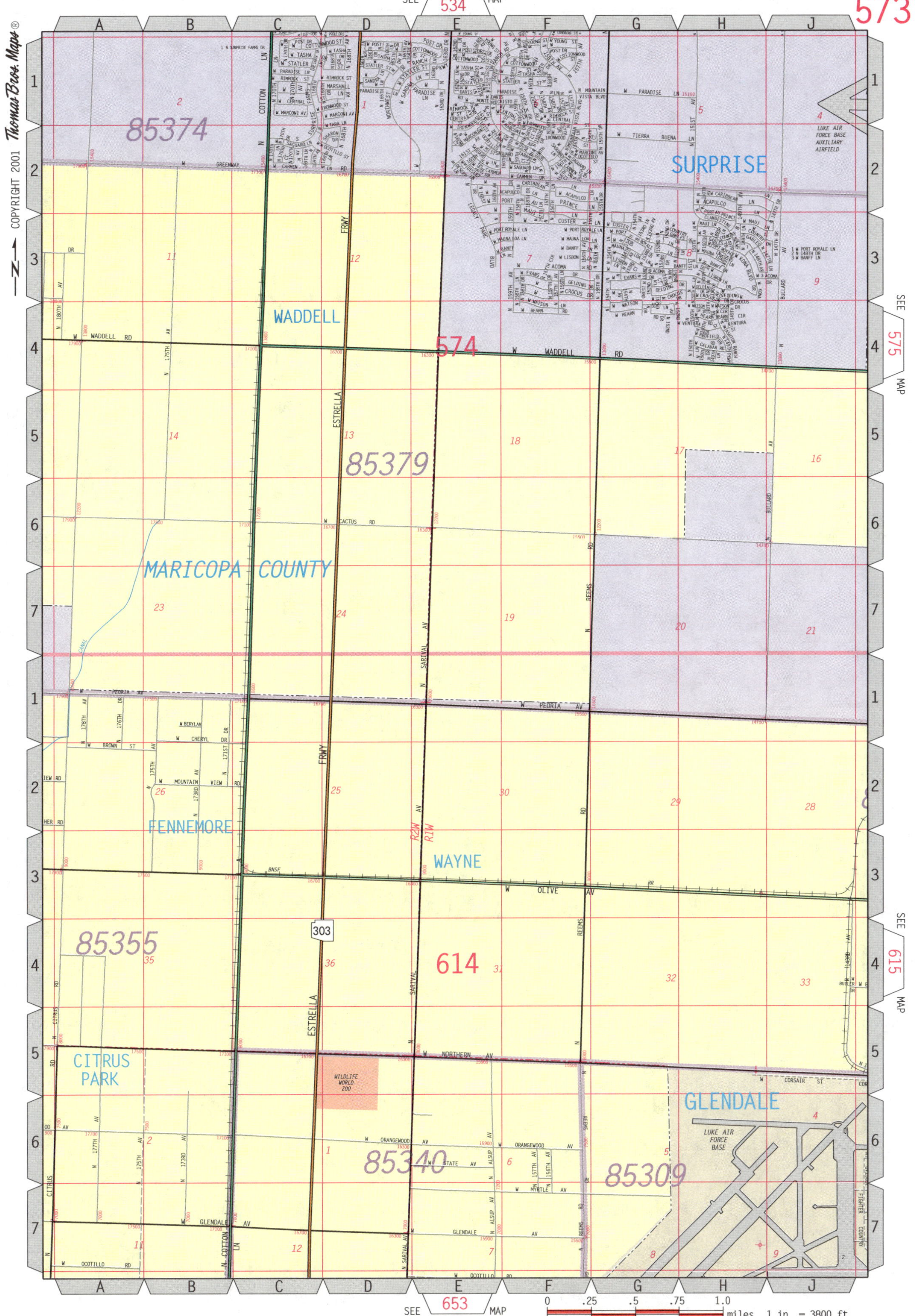

0 .25 .5 .75 1.0 miles 1 in. = 3800 ft.

SEE 535 MAP

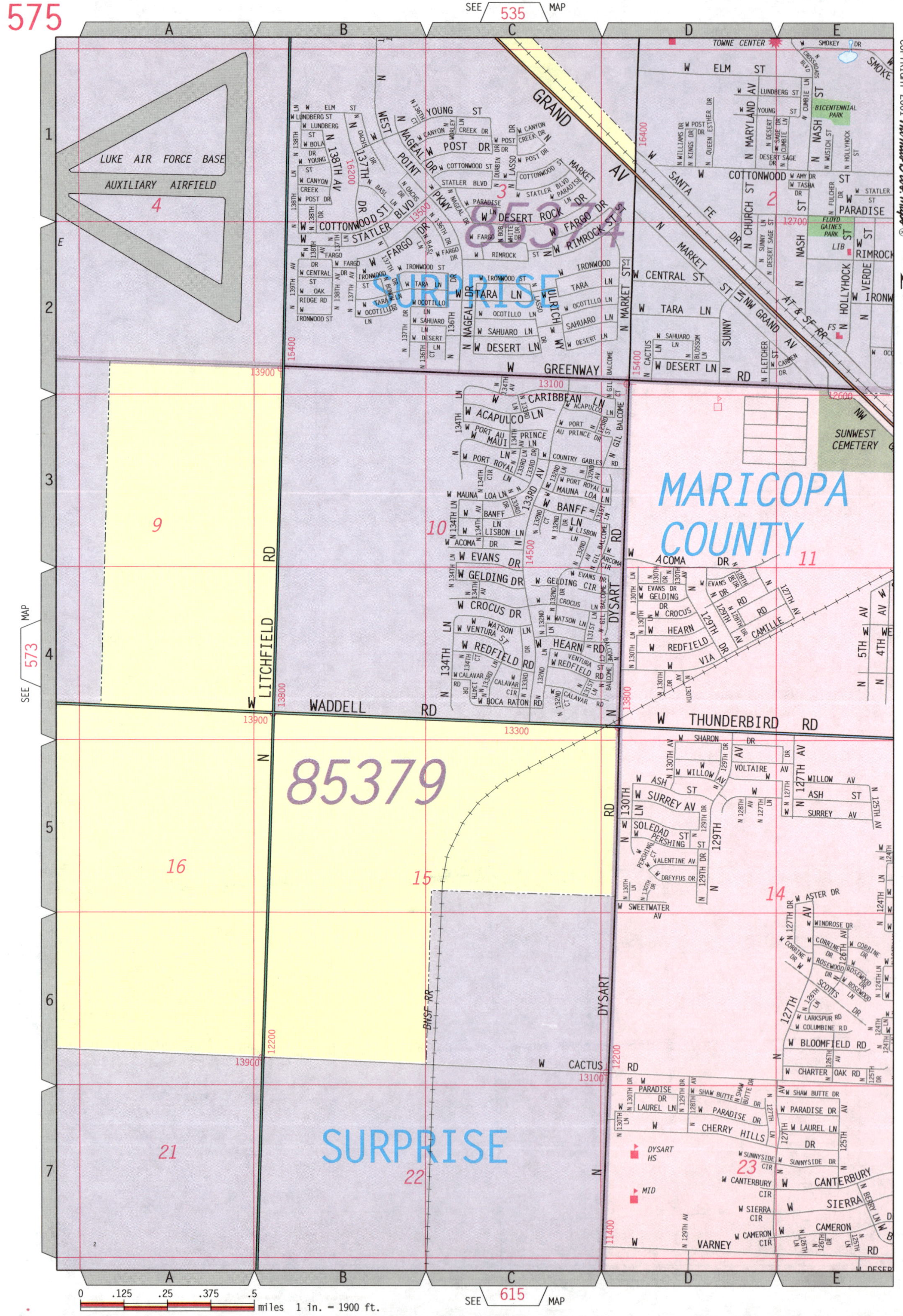

SEE 573 MAP

SEE 615 MAP

0 .125 .25 .375 .5 miles 1 in. = 1900 ft.

PHOENIX

MAP

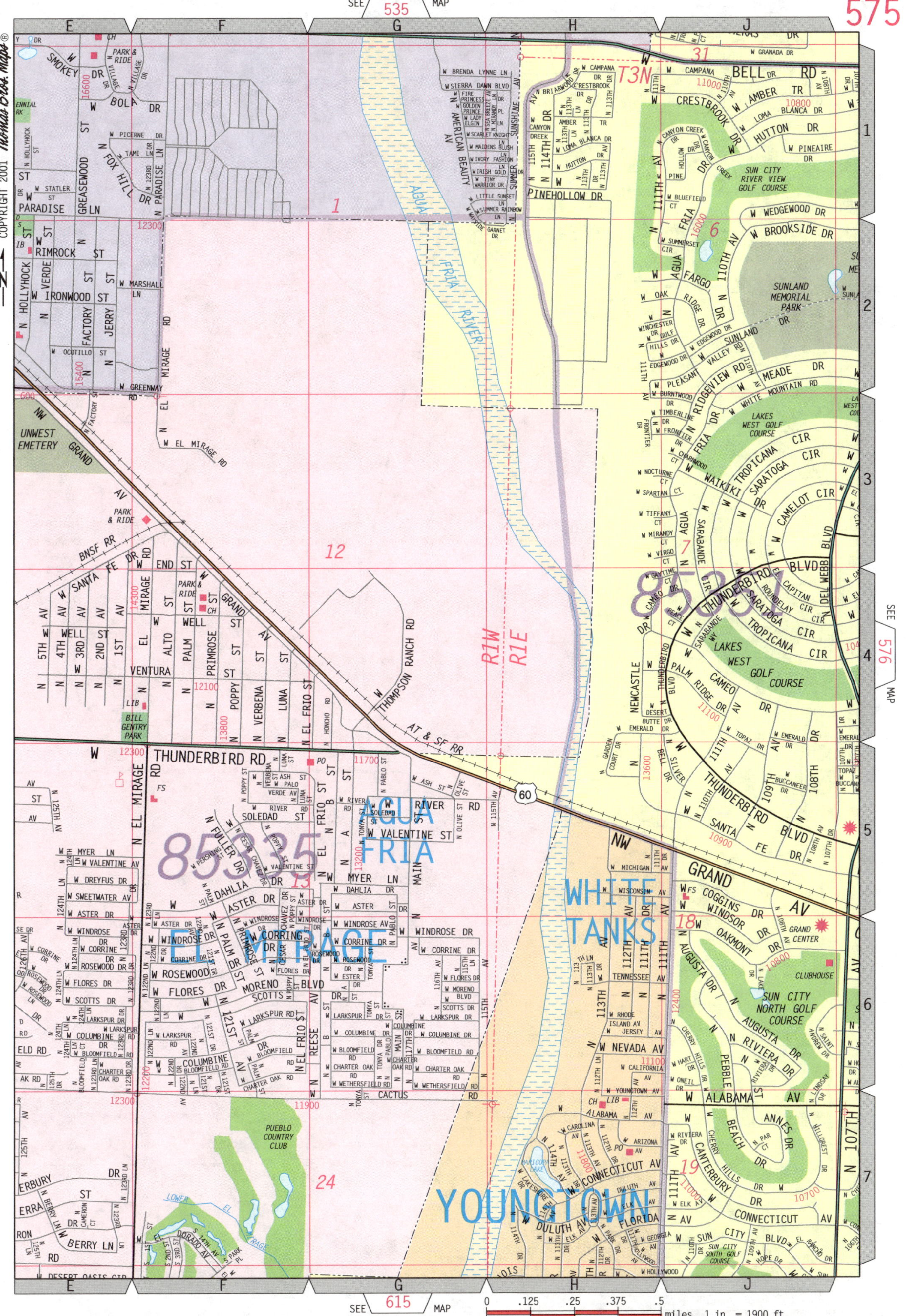

SEE 535 MAP
SEE 615 MAP
SEE 576 MAP
PHOENIX
MAP
COPYRIGHT 2001 Thomas Bros. Maps
E
F
G
H
J
1
2
3
4
5
6
7
T3N
R1W
R1E
85335
EL MIRAGE
AGUA FRIA
WHITE TANKS
YOUNGTOWN
AGUA FRIA RIVER
SUN CITY RIVER VIEW GOLF COURSE
SUNLAND MEMORIAL PARK
LAKES WEST GOLF COURSE
SUN CITY NORTH GOLF COURSE
SUN CITY SOUTH GOLF COURSE
PUEBLO COUNTRY CLUB
BILL GENTRY PARK
UNWEST EMETERY
GRAND CENTER
CLUBHOUSE
PARK & RIDE
BNSF RR
AT & SF RR
60
W THUNDERBIRD RD
NW GRAND AV
BELL RD
N EL MIRAGE RD
THOMPSON RANCH RD
W CACTUS RD
W ALABAMA AV
W CONNECTICUT AV
N 107TH AV
N 111TH AV
N 115TH AV
0 .125 .25 .375 .5 miles 1 in. = 1900 ft.

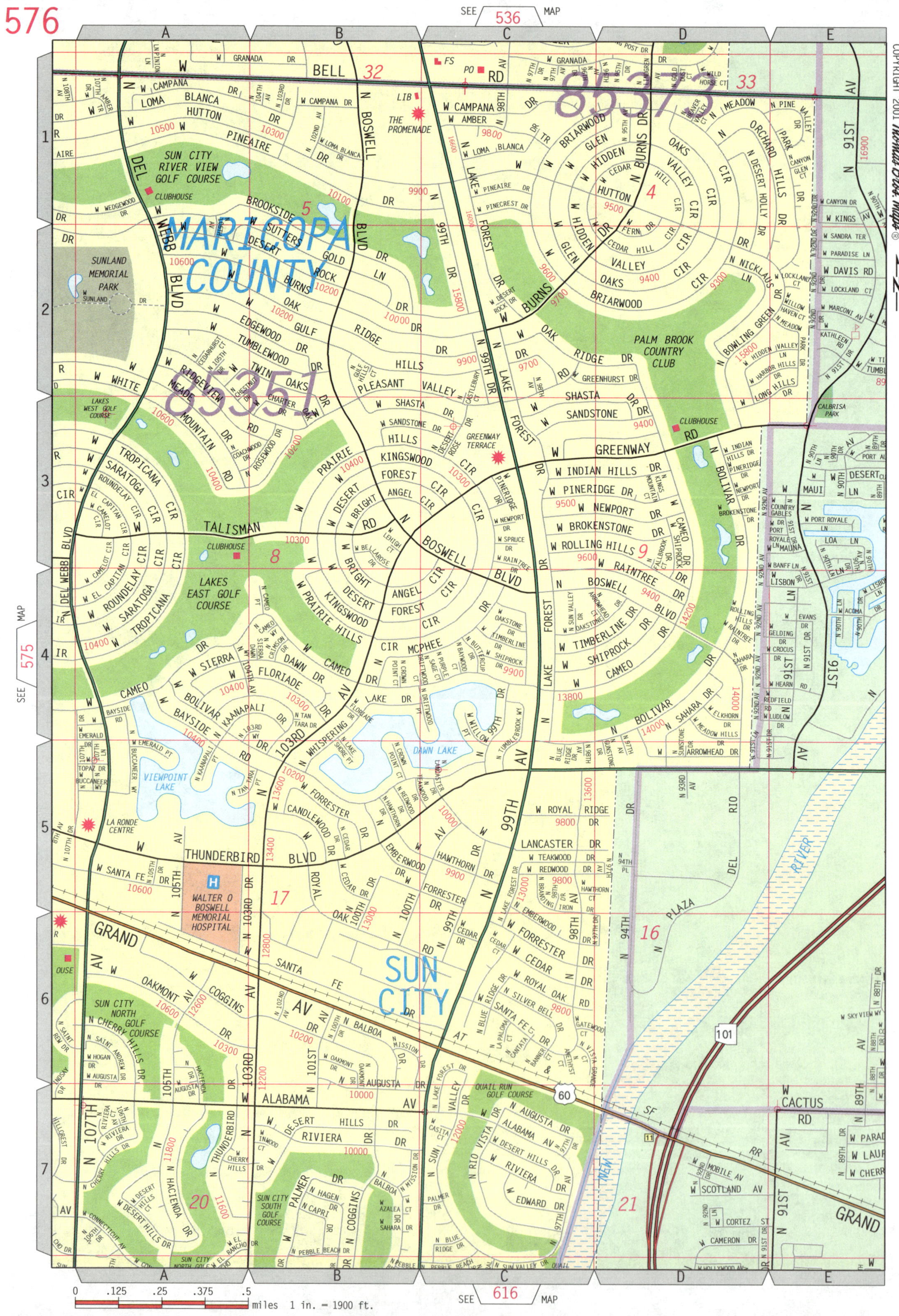

SEE 536 MAP
SEE 575 MAP
SEE 616 MAP
PHOENIX
MAP
MARICOPA COUNTY
SUN CITY
85373
85351
SUN CITY RIVER VIEW GOLF COURSE
SUNLAND MEMORIAL PARK
LAKES WEST GOLF COURSE
LAKES EAST GOLF COURSE
CLUBHOUSE
THE PROMENADE
GREENWAY TERRACE
PALM BROOK COUNTRY CLUB
CALBRISA PARK
VIEWPOINT LAKE
DAWN LAKE
LA RONDE CENTRE
WALTER O BOSWELL MEMORIAL HOSPITAL
SUN CITY NORTH GOLF COURSE
SUN CITY SOUTH GOLF COURSE
QUAIL RUN GOLF COURSE
BELL RD
GREENWAY RD
TALISMAN
THUNDERBIRD BLVD
GRAND AV
ALABAMA AV
W CACTUS RD
DEL WEBB BLVD
BOSWELL BLVD
99TH AV
103RD AV
107TH
N 91ST AV
LAKE FOREST DR
N 94TH DR
DEL RIO PLAZA
NEW RIVER
101
60
COPYRIGHT 2001 Thomas Bros. Maps ®
0 .125 .25 .375 .5 miles 1 in. = 1900 ft.

SEE 536 MAP

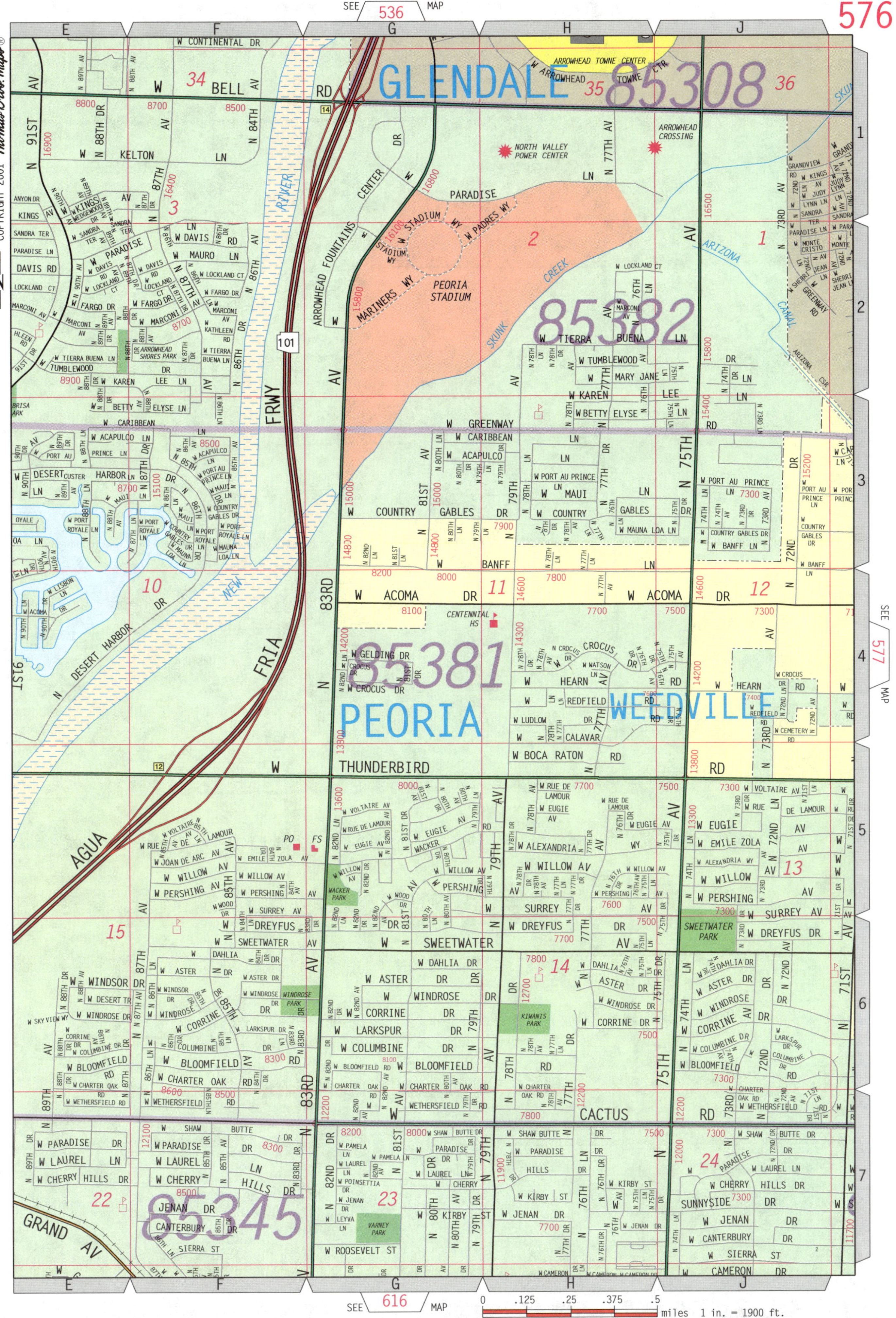

SEE 577 MAP

SEE 616 MAP

0 .125 .25 .375 .5 miles 1 in. = 1900 ft.

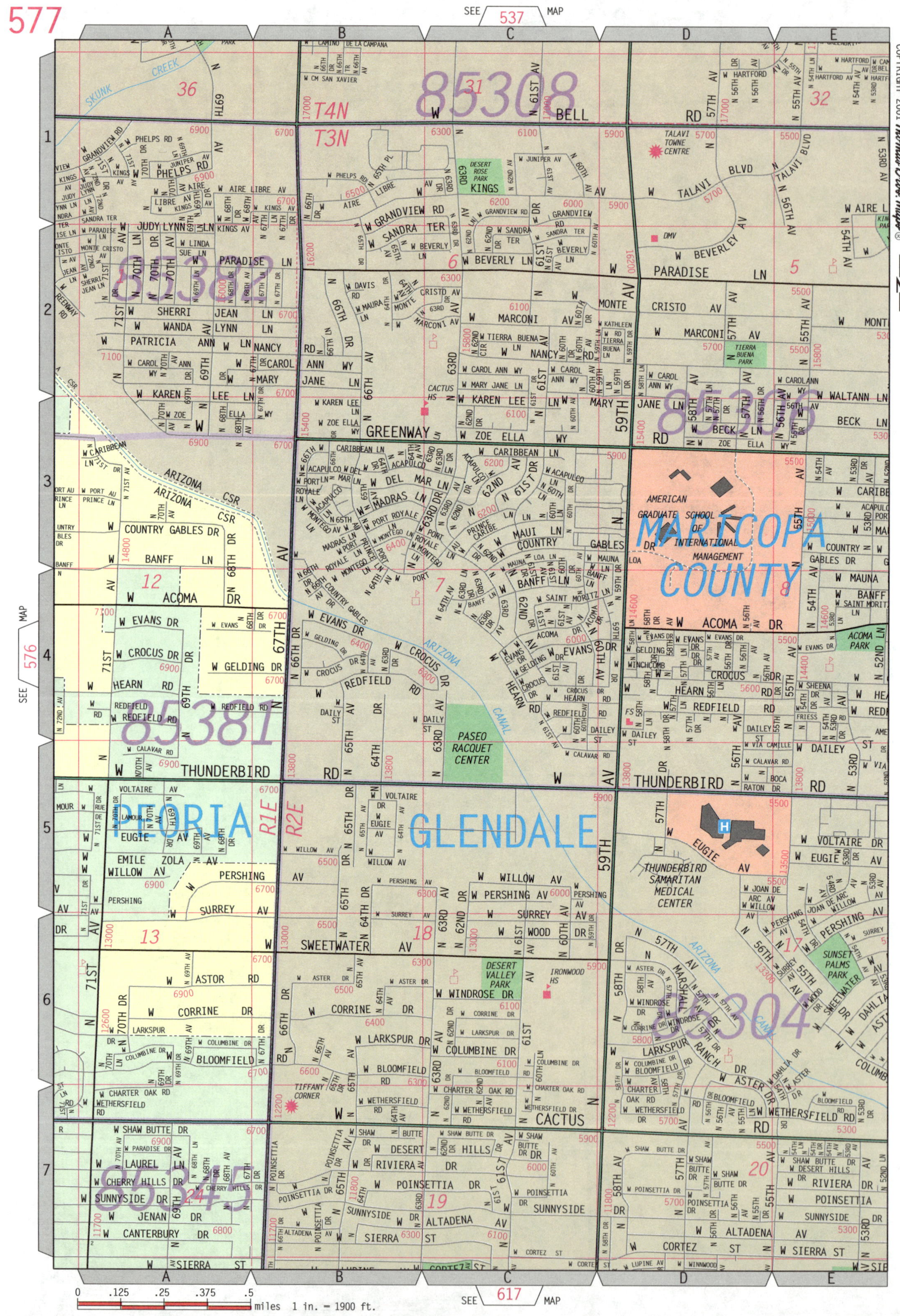

SEE 537 MAP
SEE 576 MAP
SEE 617 MAP
PHOENIX
MAP
85308
85382
85381
85306
85304
85345
T4N
T3N
R1E
R2E
PEORIA
GLENDALE
MARICOPA COUNTY
SKUNK CREEK
ARIZONA CANAL
TALAVI TOWNE CENTRE
DMV
DESERT ROSE PARK
TIERRA BUENA PARK
CACTUS HS
AMERICAN GRADUATE SCHOOL OF INTERNATIONAL MANAGEMENT
ACOMA PARK
PASEO RACQUET CENTER
THUNDERBIRD SAMARITAN MEDICAL CENTER
SUNSET PALMS PARK
DESERT VALLEY PARK
IRONWOOD HS
TIFFANY CORNER
W BELL RD
W GREENWAY RD
W THUNDERBIRD RD
W SWEETWATER AV
W CACTUS RD
N 67TH AV
N 59TH AV
N 51ST AV
N 55TH AV
0 .125 .25 .375 .5 miles 1 in. = 1900 ft.

SEE 537 MAP

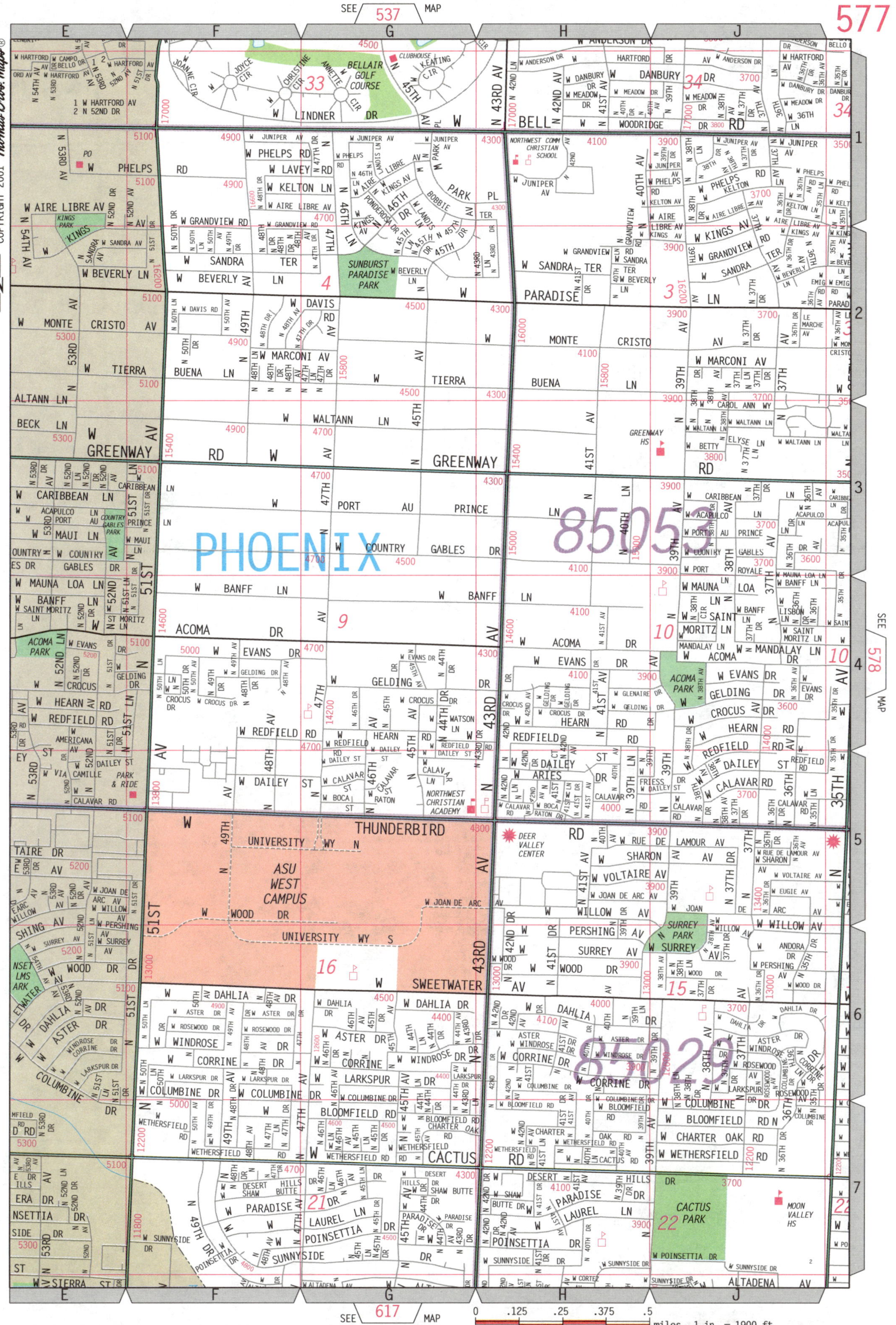

SEE 578 MAP

SEE 617 MAP

SEE 538 MAP

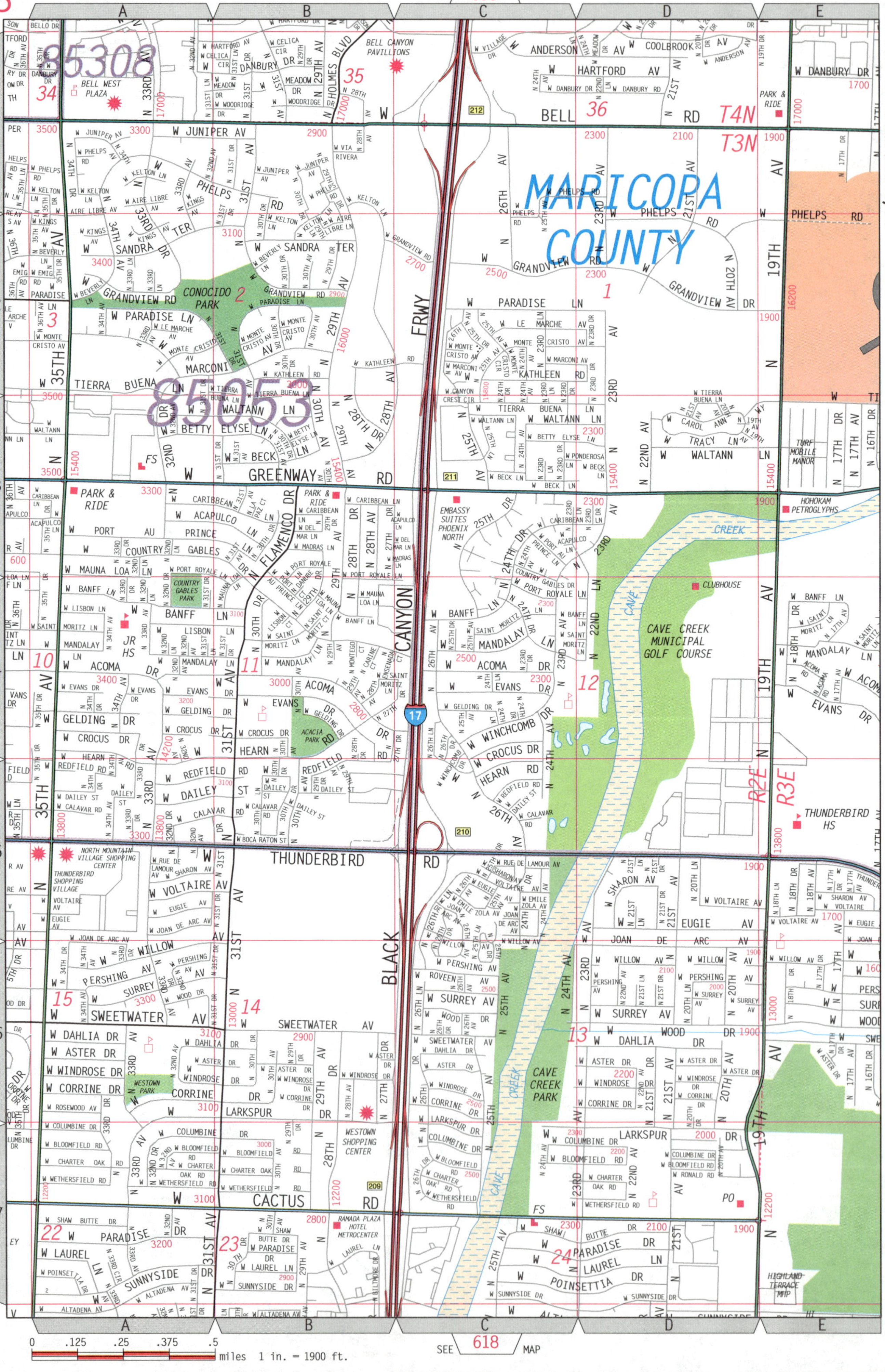

SEE 577 MAP

PHOENIX

MAP

A B C D E

1 2 3 4 5 6 7

85308

85053

MARICOPA COUNTY

BELL RD

W JUNIPER AV

PHELPS RD

GRANDVIEW RD

W PARADISE LN

TIERRA BUENA LN

W WALTANN LN

BETTY ELYSE LN

GREENWAY RD

W PORT AU PRINCE

COUNTRY GABLES

MAUNA LOA LN

BANFF LN

LISBON LN

MANDALAY LN

ACOMA DR

EVANS DR

GELDING DR

CROCUS DR

HEARN RD

REDFIELD RD

DAILEY ST

CALAVAR RD

THUNDERBIRD RD

VOLTAIRE AV

EUGIE AV

JOAN DE ARC AV

WILLOW AV

PERSHING AV

SURREY AV

SWEETWATER AV

DAHLIA DR

ASTER DR

WINDROSE DR

CORRINE DR

LARKSPUR DR

COLUMBINE DR

BLOOMFIELD RD

CHARTER OAK RD

WETHERSFIELD RD

CACTUS RD

PARADISE DR

LAUREL LN

SUNNYSIDE DR

35TH AV

31ST AV

29TH AV

BLACK CANYON FRWY

17

23RD AV

19TH AV

BELL CANYON PAVILLIONS

BELL WEST PLAZA

CONOCIDO PARK

PARK & RIDE

COUNTRY GABLES PARK

JR HS

ACACIA PARK

EMBASSY SUITES PHOENIX NORTH

HOHOKAM PETROGLYPHS

CAVE CREEK

CLUBHOUSE

CAVE CREEK MUNICIPAL GOLF COURSE

TURF MOBILE MANOR

THUNDERBIRD HS

NORTH MOUNTAIN VILLAGE SHOPPING CENTER

THUNDERBIRD SHOPPING VILLAGE

WESTOWN PARK

WESTOWN SHOPPING CENTER

CAVE CREEK PARK

RAMADA PLAZA HOTEL METROCENTER

HIGHLAND TERRACE MHP

T4N T3N R2E R3E

0 .125 .25 .375 .5 miles 1 in. = 1900 ft.

SEE 618 MAP

SEE 538 MAP

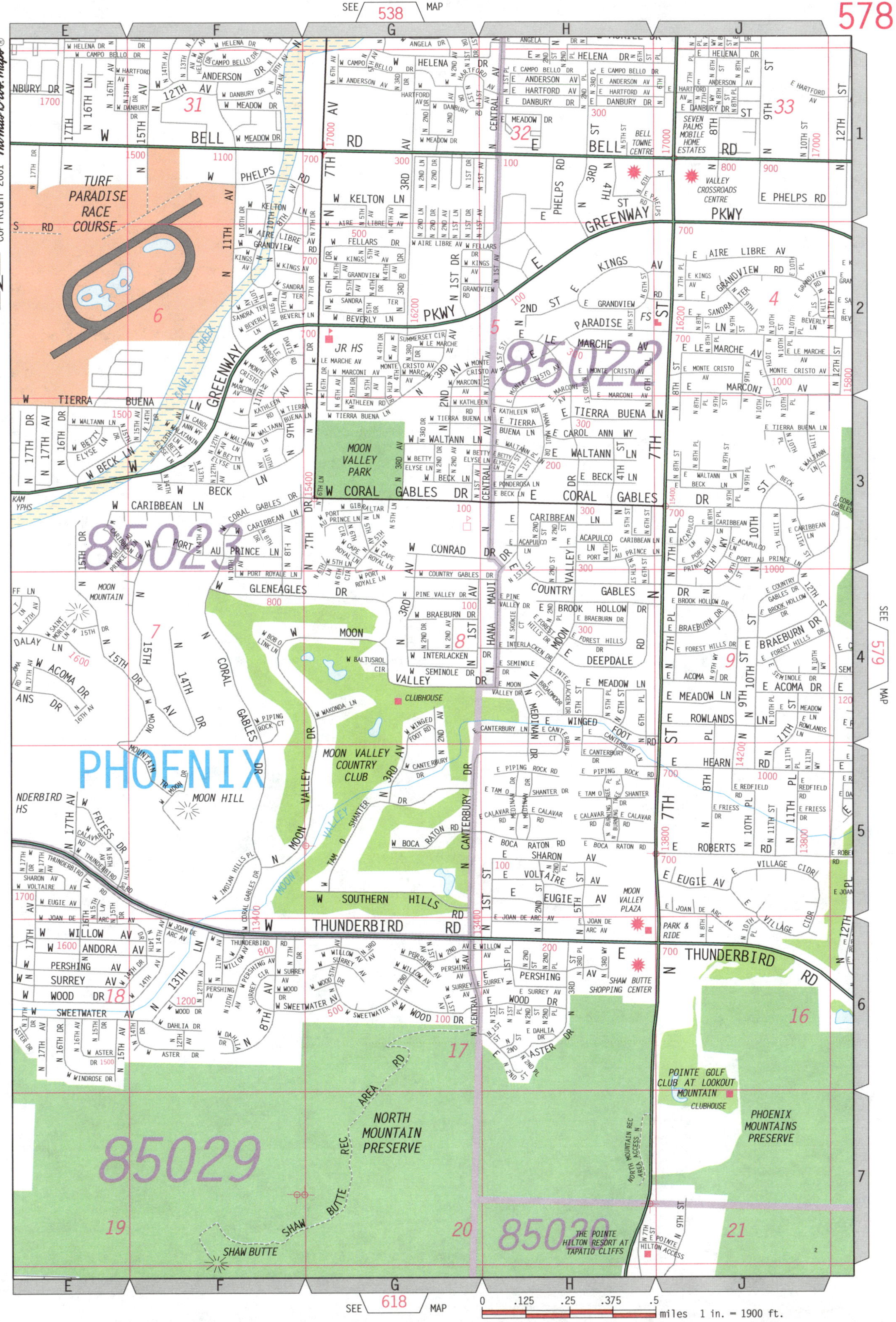

SEE 579 MAP

SEE 618 MAP

0 .125 .25 .375 .5 miles 1 in. = 1900 ft.

PHOENIX

MAP

SEE 539 MAP

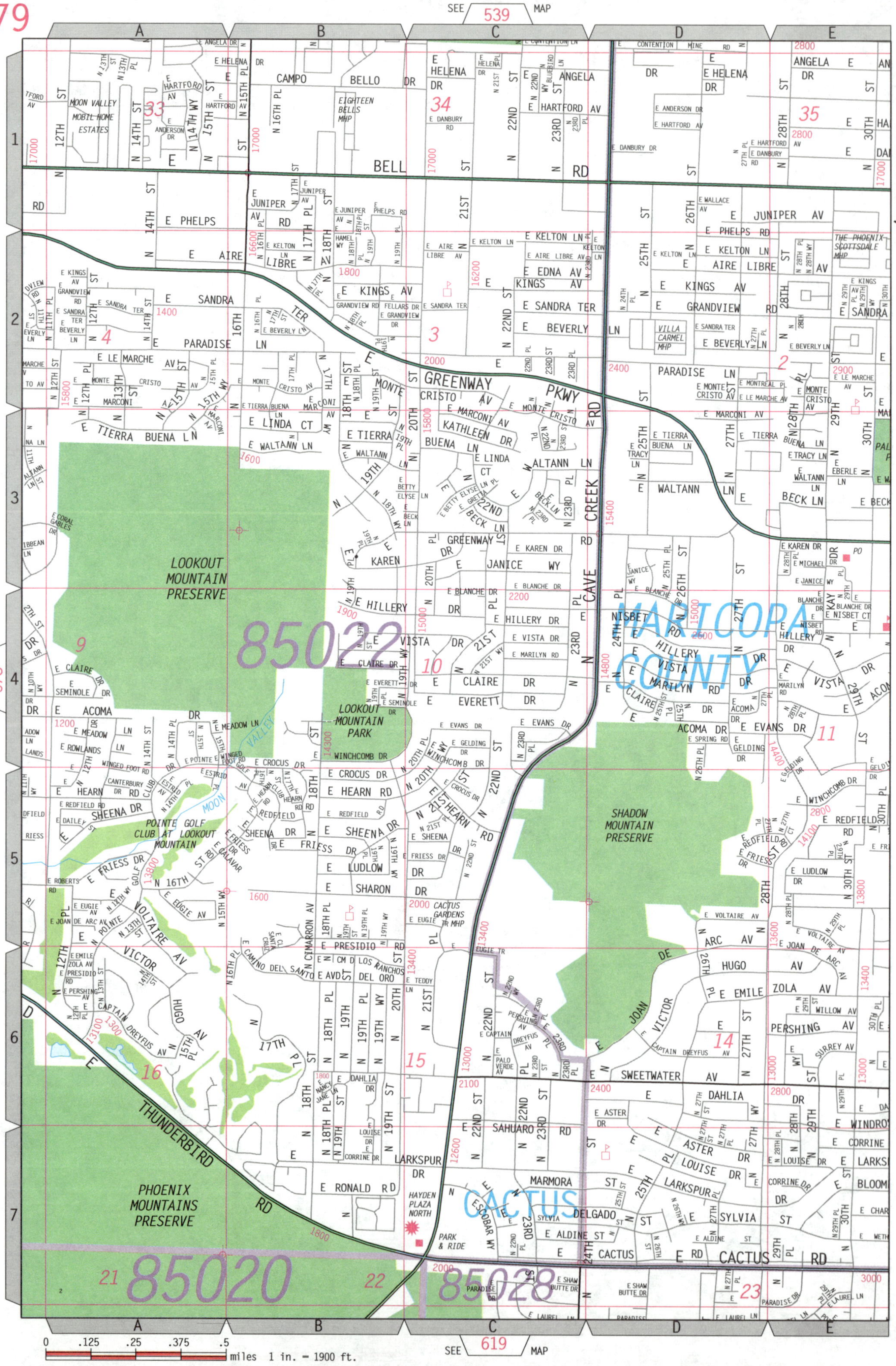

LOOKOUT MOUNTAIN PRESERVE

LOOKOUT MOUNTAIN PARK

SHADOW MOUNTAIN PRESERVE

POINTE GOLF CLUB AT LOOKOUT MOUNTAIN

PHOENIX MOUNTAINS PRESERVE

MOON VALLEY MOBILE HOME ESTATES

EIGHTEEN BELLS MHP

VILLA CARMEL MHP

THE PHOENIX SCOTTSDALE MHP

CACTUS GARDENS MHP

HAYDEN PLAZA NORTH

PARK & RIDE

MARICOPA COUNTY

CACTUS

85022

85020

85028

GREENWAY PKWY

N CAVE CREEK RD

THUNDERBIRD RD

BELL RD

CACTUS RD

SEE 578 MAP

SEE 619 MAP

0 .125 .25 .375 .5 miles 1 in. = 1900 ft.

PHOENIX

MAP

SEE 539 MAP

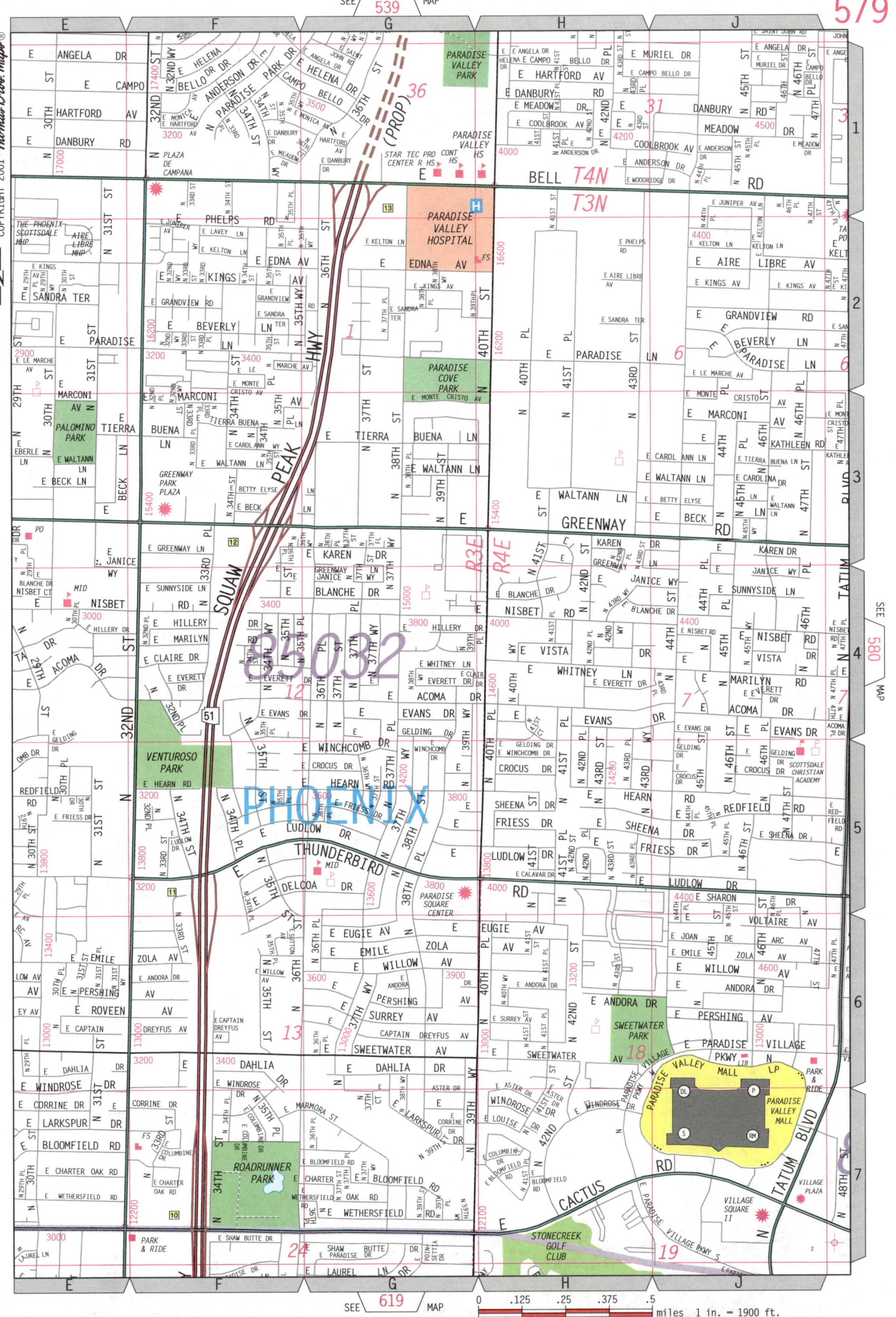

SEE 580 MAP

SEE 619 MAP

0 .125 .25 .375 .5 miles 1 in. = 1900 ft.

PHOENIX

MAP

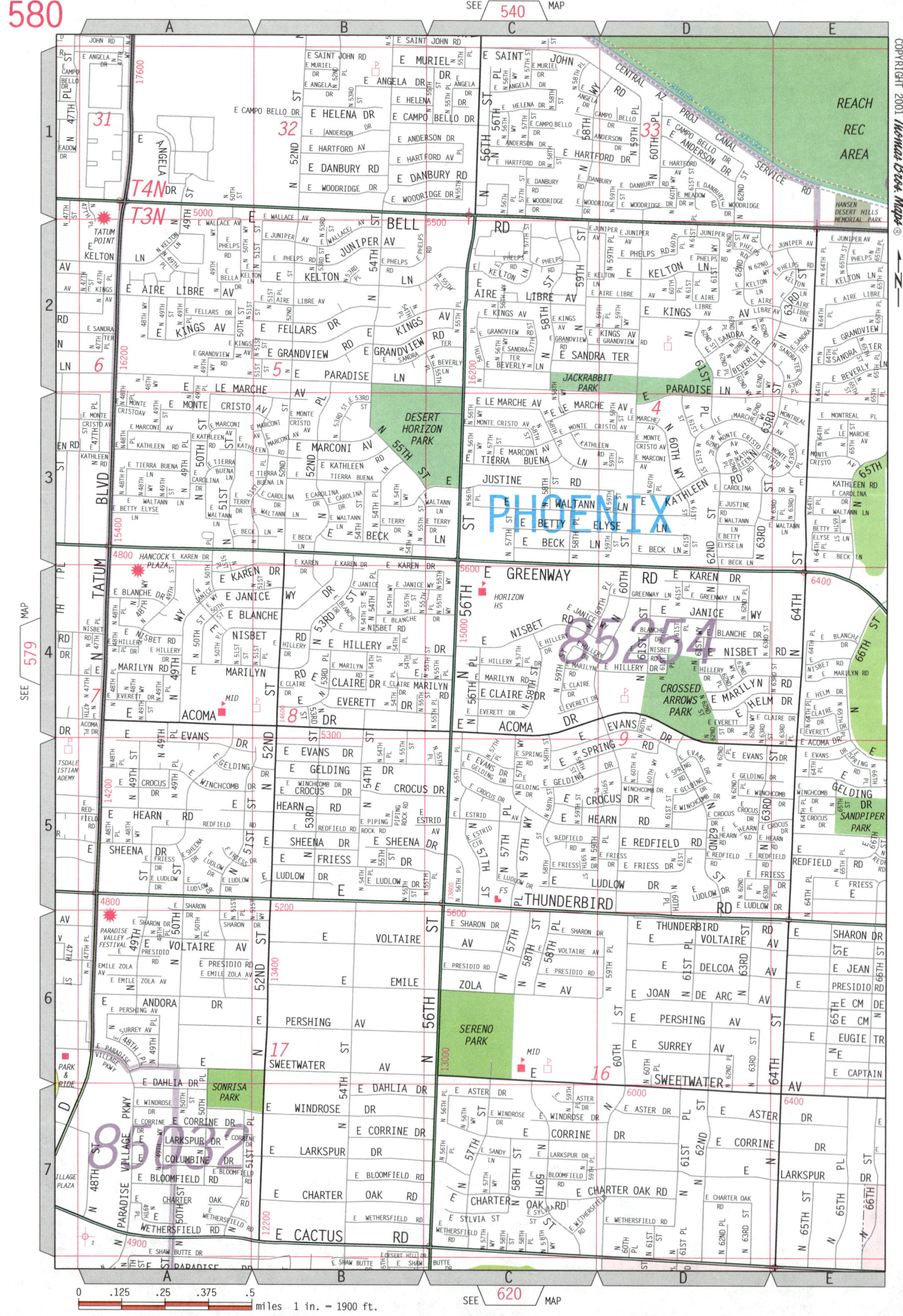
SEE 540 MAP
SEE 579 MAP
SEE 620 MAP
PHOENIX
T4N
T3N
REACH REC AREA
CENTRAL AZ PROJ CANAL
SERVICE RD
HANSEN DESERT HILLS MEMORIAL PARK
TATUM POINT
DESERT HORIZON PARK
JACKRABBIT PARK
HANCOCK PLAZA
HORIZON HS
CROSSED ARROWS PARK
SANDPIPER PARK
PARADISE VALLEY FESTIVAL
SONRISA PARK
SERENO PARK
PARK & RIDE
VILLAGE PLAZA
85254
85032
N TATUM BLVD
E BELL RD
E GREENWAY RD
E THUNDERBIRD RD
E CACTUS RD
N 56TH ST
N 64TH ST
N 52ND ST
PARADISE VILLAGE PKWY
E ACOMA DR
E MARILYN RD
E KELTON LN
E AIRE LIBRE AV
E KINGS AV
E FELLARS DR
E GRANDVIEW RD
E PARADISE LN
E LE MARCHE AV
E MONTE CRISTO AV
E MARCONI AV
E KATHLEEN RD
E WALTANN LN
E BECK LN
E KAREN DR
E JANICE WY
E BLANCHE DR
E NISBET RD
E HILLERY DR
E CLAIRE DR
E EVERETT DR
E EVANS DR
E GELDING DR
E CROCUS DR
E HEARN RD
E REDFIELD RD
E SHEENA DR
E FRIESS DR
E LUDLOW DR
E VOLTAIRE AV
E EMILE ZOLA AV
E PERSHING AV
E SWEETWATER AV
E DAHLIA DR
E WINDROSE DR
E CORRINE DR
E LARKSPUR DR
E BLOOMFIELD RD
E CHARTER OAK RD
E WETHERSFIELD RD
E SAINT JOHN RD
E MURIEL DR
E ANGELA DR
E HELENA DR
E CAMPO BELLO DR
E ANDERSON DR
E HARTFORD AV
E DANBURY RD
E WOODRIDGE DR
E JUNIPER AV
E PHELPS RD
E SANDRA TER
E BEVERLY LN
E JUSTINE RD
E SPRING RD
E SHARON DR
E DELCOA AV
E JOAN DE ARC AV
E SURREY AV
E ASTER DR
E SHAW BUTTE DR
FS
MID
0 .125 .25 .375 .5 miles 1 in. = 1900 ft.

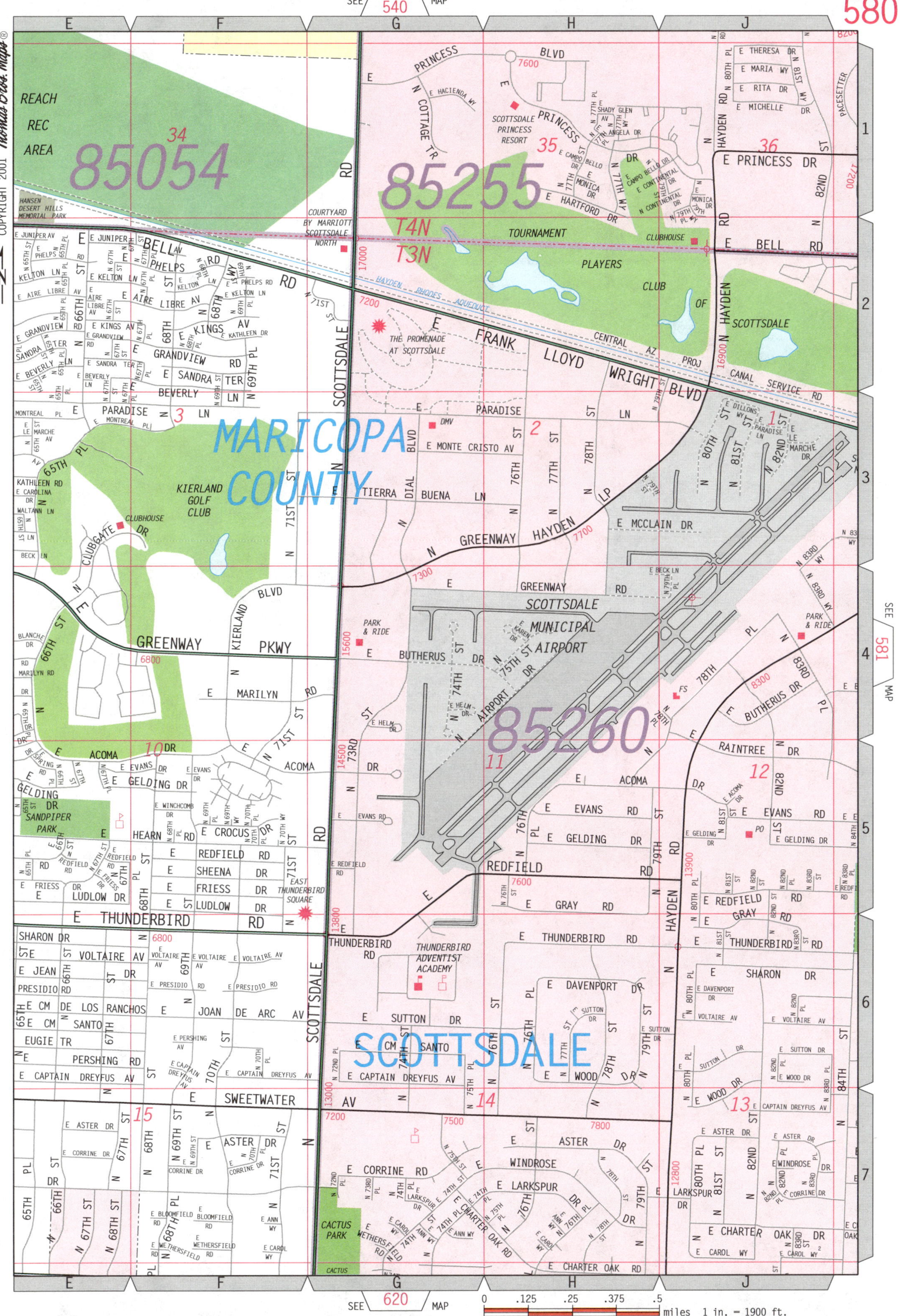
SEE 540 MAP
85054
85255
85260
MARICOPA COUNTY
SCOTTSDALE
PHOENIX
REACH REC AREA
TOURNAMENT PLAYERS CLUB OF SCOTTSDALE
KIERLAND GOLF CLUB
SCOTTSDALE MUNICIPAL AIRPORT
SCOTTSDALE PRINCESS RESORT
THE PROMENADE AT SCOTTSDALE
THUNDERBIRD ADVENTIST ACADEMY
SANDPIPER PARK
CACTUS PARK
HAYDEN RHODES AQUEDUCT
CENTRAL AZ PROJ CANAL SERVICE RD
E FRANK LLOYD WRIGHT BLVD
E BELL RD
E THUNDERBIRD RD
N SCOTTSDALE RD
N HAYDEN RD
GREENWAY PKWY
SEE 581 MAP
SEE 620 MAP
miles 1 in. = 1900 ft.

SEE 541 MAP

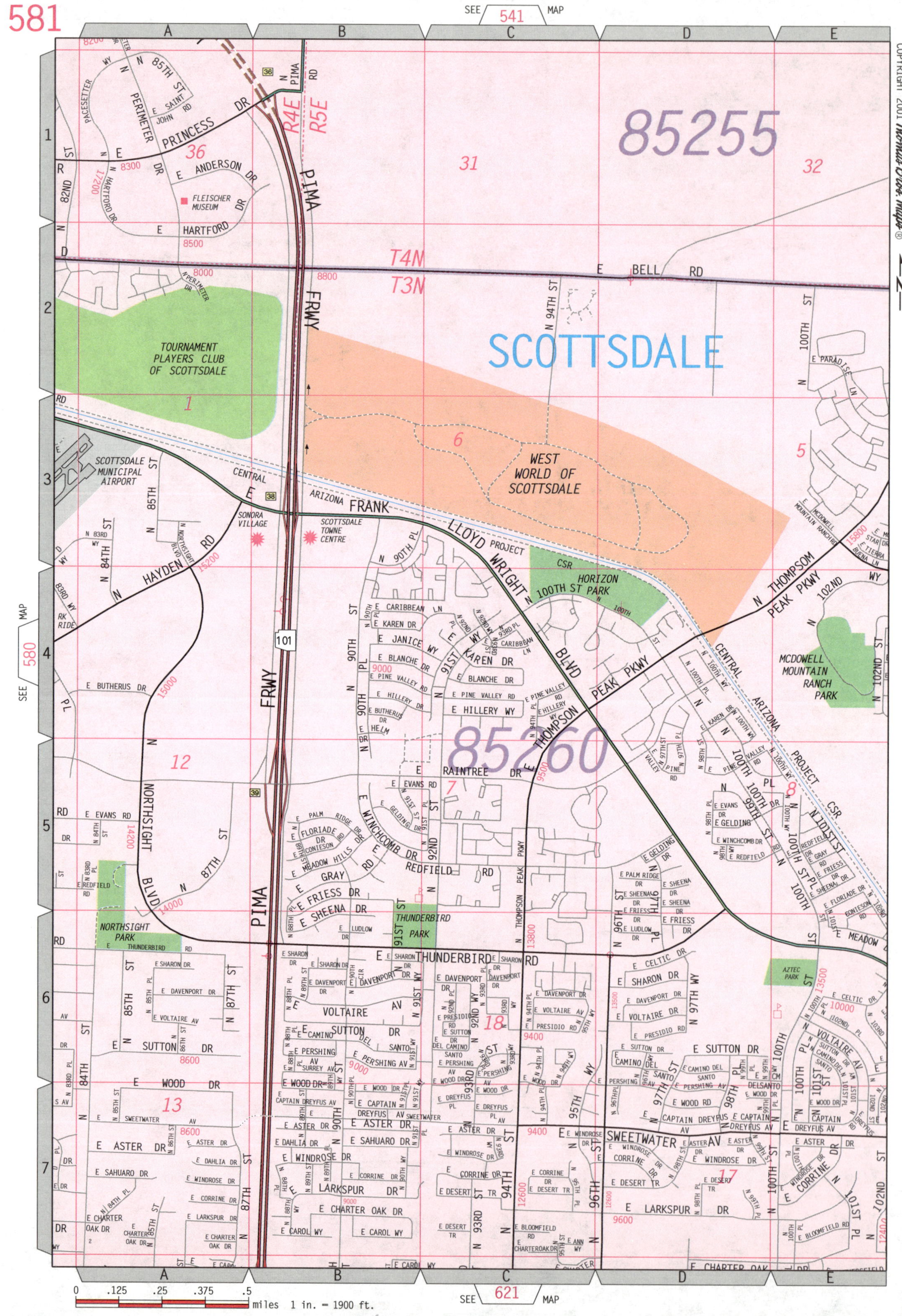

0 .125 .25 .375 .5 miles 1 in. = 1900 ft.

SEE 621 MAP

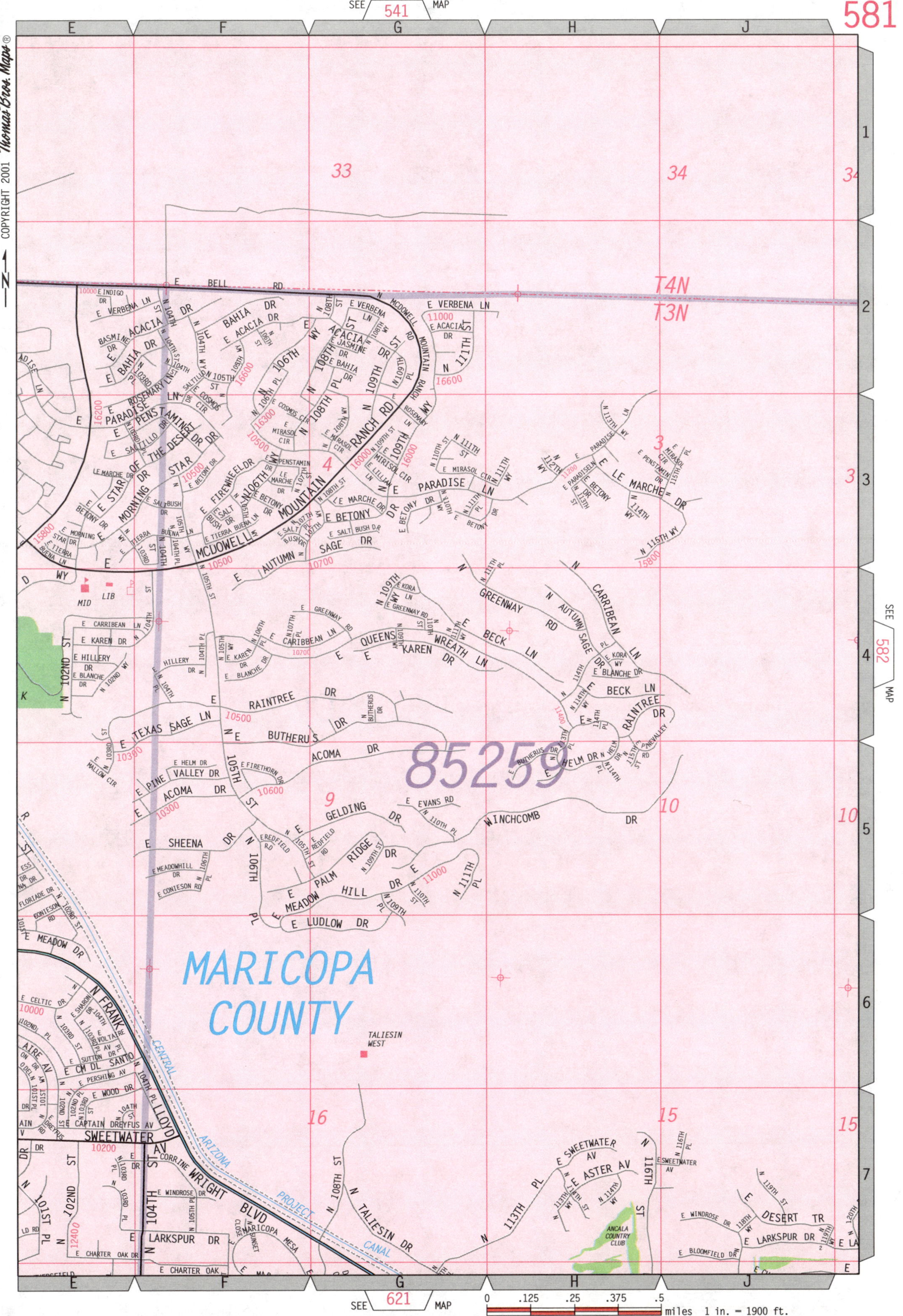
SEE 541 MAP
E
F
G
H
J
1
2
3
4
5
6
7
33
34
T4N
T3N
E BELL RD
E VERBENA LN
N MCDOWELL MOUNTAIN RANCH RD
N 104TH ST
E ACACIA DR
E BAHIA DR
N 105TH ST
N 106TH WY
N 108TH ST
N 109TH ST
N 111TH ST
E PARADISE LN
E STAR OF THE DESERT DR
E MORNING STAR
E BETONY DR
E LE MARCHE DR
E SALT BUSH DR
E SAGE DR
E AUTUMN SAGE DR
E MCDOWELL
MID
LIB
N 102ND ST
E CARRIBEAN LN
E KAREN DR
E HILLERY DR
E BLANCHE DR
E CARIBBEAN LN
E QUEENS WREATH LN
E GREENWAY RD
E BECK LN
N CARRIBEAN LN
E RAINTREE DR
E TEXAS SAGE LN
E BUTHERUS DR
E ACOMA DR
E PINE VALLEY DR
E HELM DR
E SHEENA DR
E GELDING DR
E EVANS RD
E WINCHCOMB DR
E PALM RIDGE DR
E MEADOW HILL DR
E LUDLOW DR
N 106TH PL
N 105TH ST
N 111TH PL
85259
9
10
MARICOPA COUNTY
TALIESIN WEST
E MEADOW DR
N FRANK LLOYD WRIGHT BLVD
ARIZONA PROJECT CANAL
CENTRAL
E SWEETWATER AV
E CAPTAIN DREYFUS AV
E CORRINE DR
E LARKSPUR DR
E CHARTER OAK DR
N TALIESIN DR
N 108TH ST
N 113TH PL
N 116TH ST
E ASTER AV
E DESERT TR
E WINDROSE DR
E BLOOMFIELD DR
ANCALA COUNTRY CLUB
16
15
SEE 582 MAP
SEE 621 MAP
PHOENIX
MAP
0 .125 .25 .375 .5 miles 1 in. = 1900 ft.

SEE 542 MAP

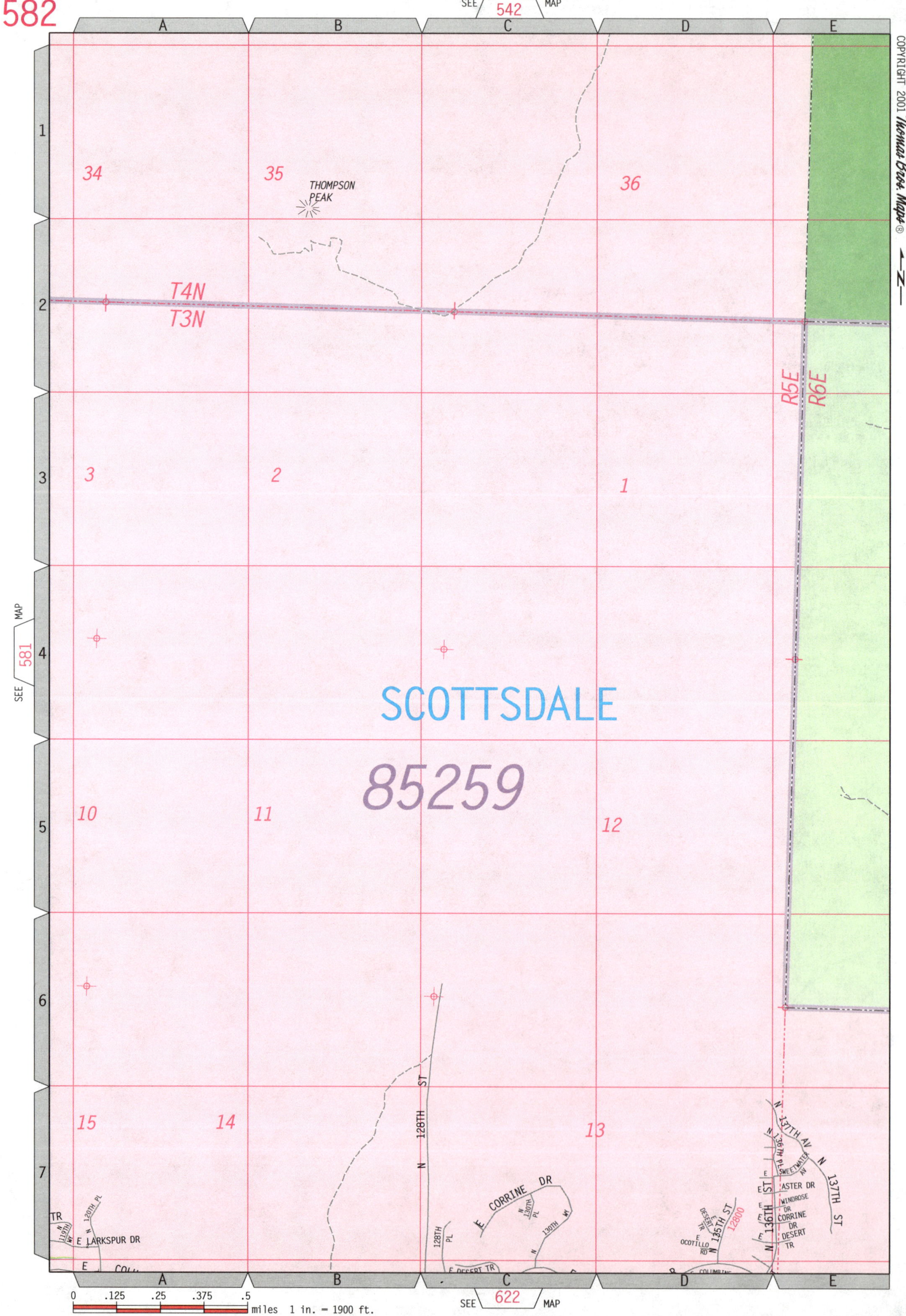

SEE 581 MAP

SEE 622 MAP

0 .125 .25 .375 .5 miles 1 in. = 1900 ft.

PHOENIX

MAP

SEE 542 MAP

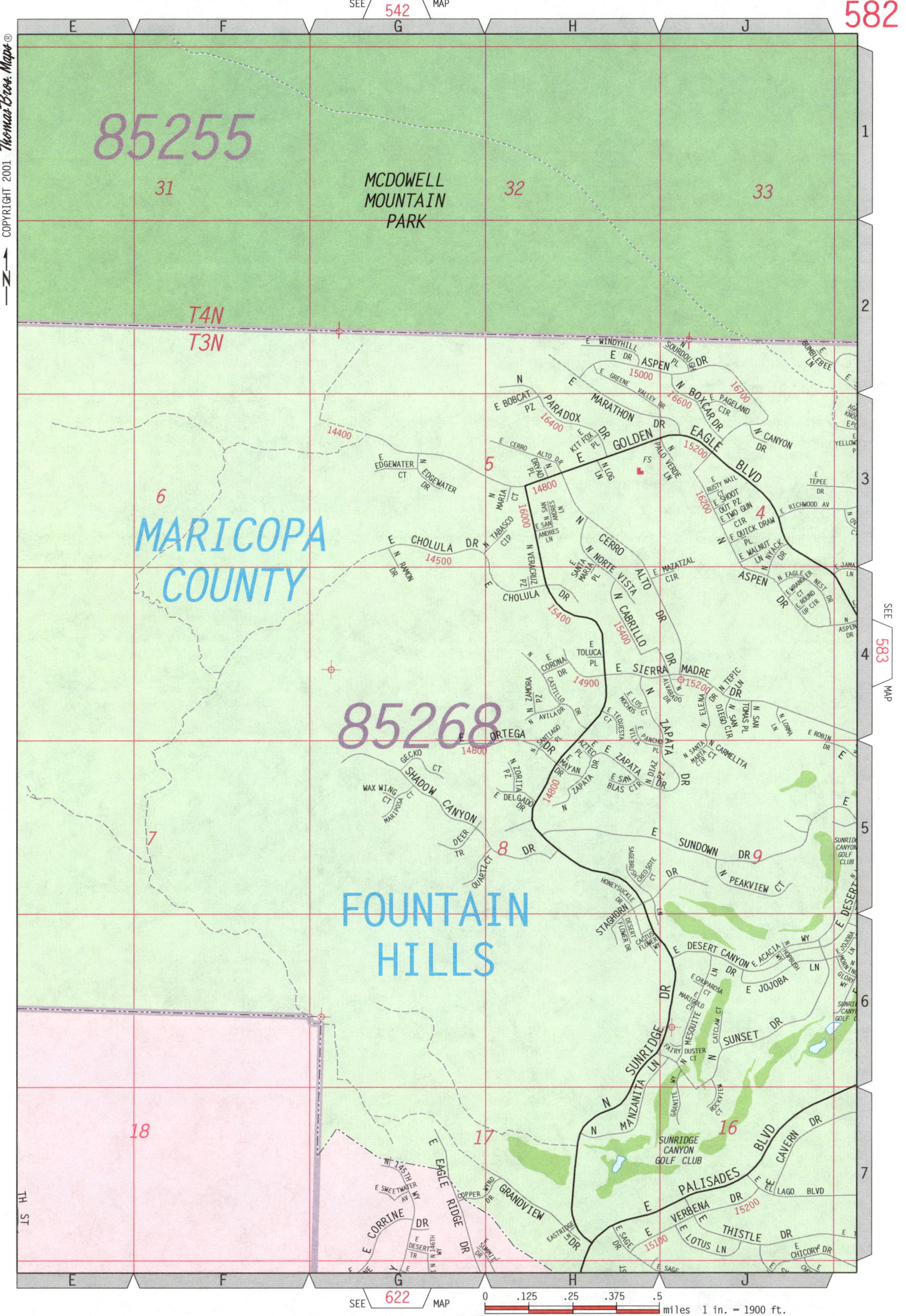

SEE 583 MAP

SEE 622 MAP

0 .125 .25 .375 .5 miles 1 in. = 1900 ft.

SEE 503 MAP

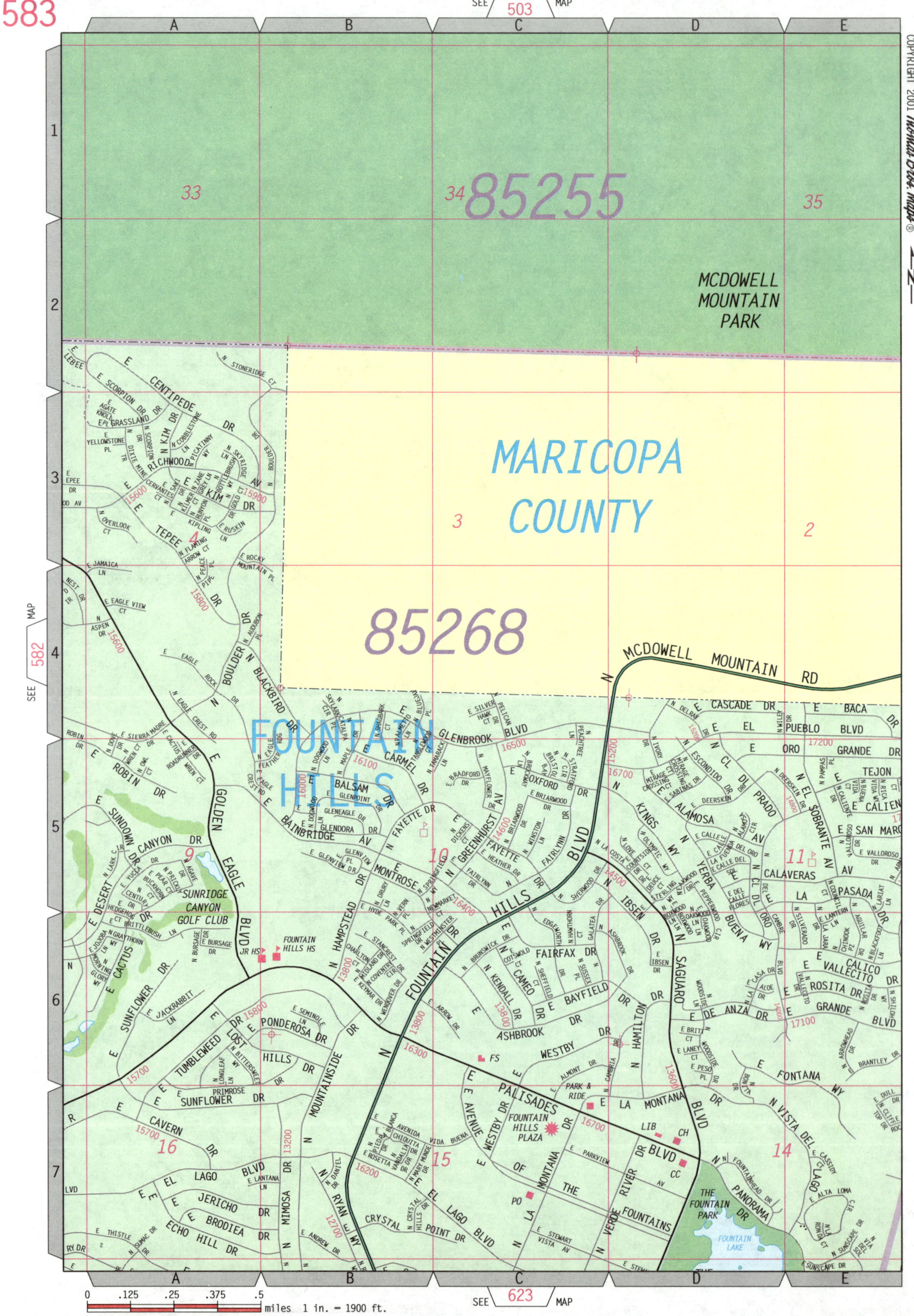

SEE 582 MAP

SEE 623 MAP

0 .125 .25 .375 .5 miles 1 in. = 1900 ft.

PHOENIX

MAP

SEE 503 MAP

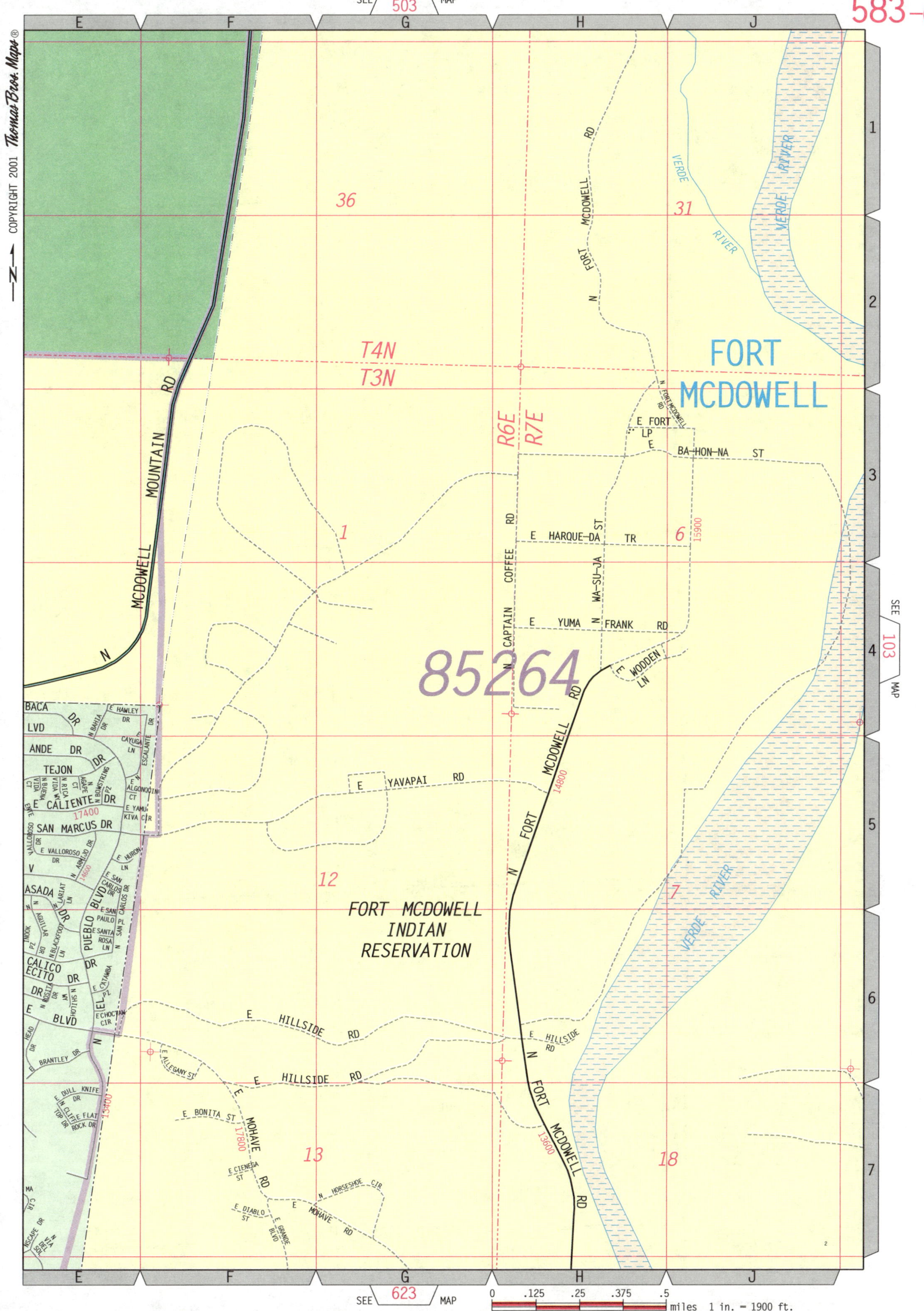

SEE 103 MAP

SEE 623 MAP

0 .125 .25 .375 .5 miles 1 in. = 1900 ft.

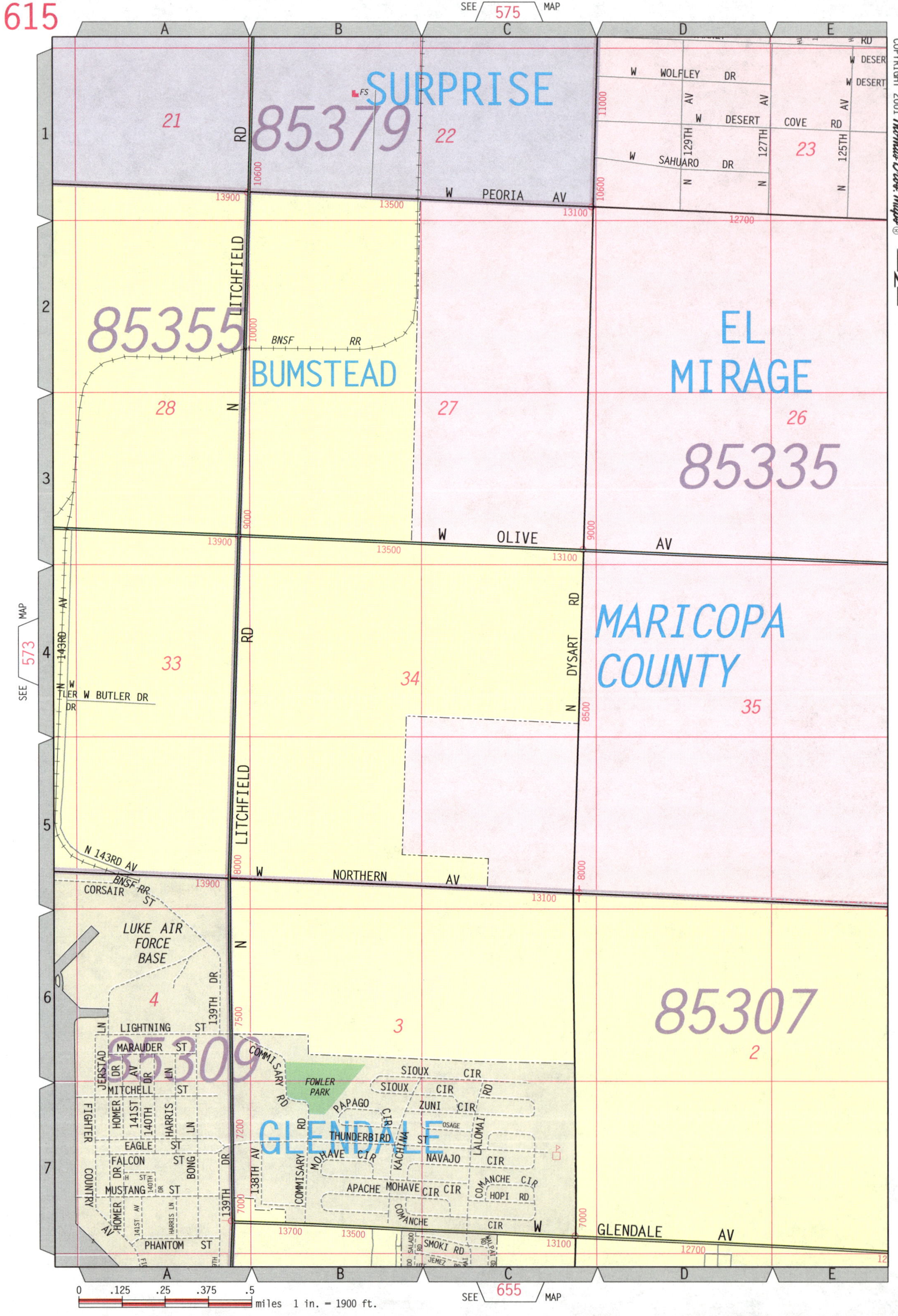

SEE 575 MAP
SURPRISE
85379
85355
BUMSTEAD
EL MIRAGE
85335
MARICOPA COUNTY
85309
GLENDALE
85307
LUKE AIR FORCE BASE
FOWLER PARK
W PEORIA AV
W OLIVE AV
W NORTHERN AV
W GLENDALE AV
N LITCHFIELD RD
N DYSART RD
N 143RD AV
BNSF RR
W WOLFLEY DR
W DESERT COVE RD
W SAHUARO DR
N 129TH AV
N 127TH AV
N 125TH AV
W BUTLER DR
CORSAIR ST
LIGHTNING ST
MARAUDER ST
MITCHELL ST
EAGLE ST
FALCON ST
MUSTANG ST
PHANTOM ST
FIGHTER COUNTRY AV
JERSTAD LN
HOMER DR
141ST AV
140TH DR
HARRIS LN
BONG DR
139TH DR
138TH AV
COMMISARY RD
SIOUX CIR
ZUNI CIR
PAPAGO CIR
THUNDERBIRD ST
OSAGE
KACHINA CIR
NAVAJO CIR
LALOMAI RD
MOHAVE CIR
APACHE CIR
COMANCHE CIR
HOPI RD
SMOKI RD
JEMEZ
SALADO
21
22
23
28
27
26
33
34
35
4
3
2
SEE 573 MAP
SEE 655 MAP
PHOENIX
MAP
0 .125 .25 .375 .5 miles 1 in. = 1900 ft.

SEE 575 MAP

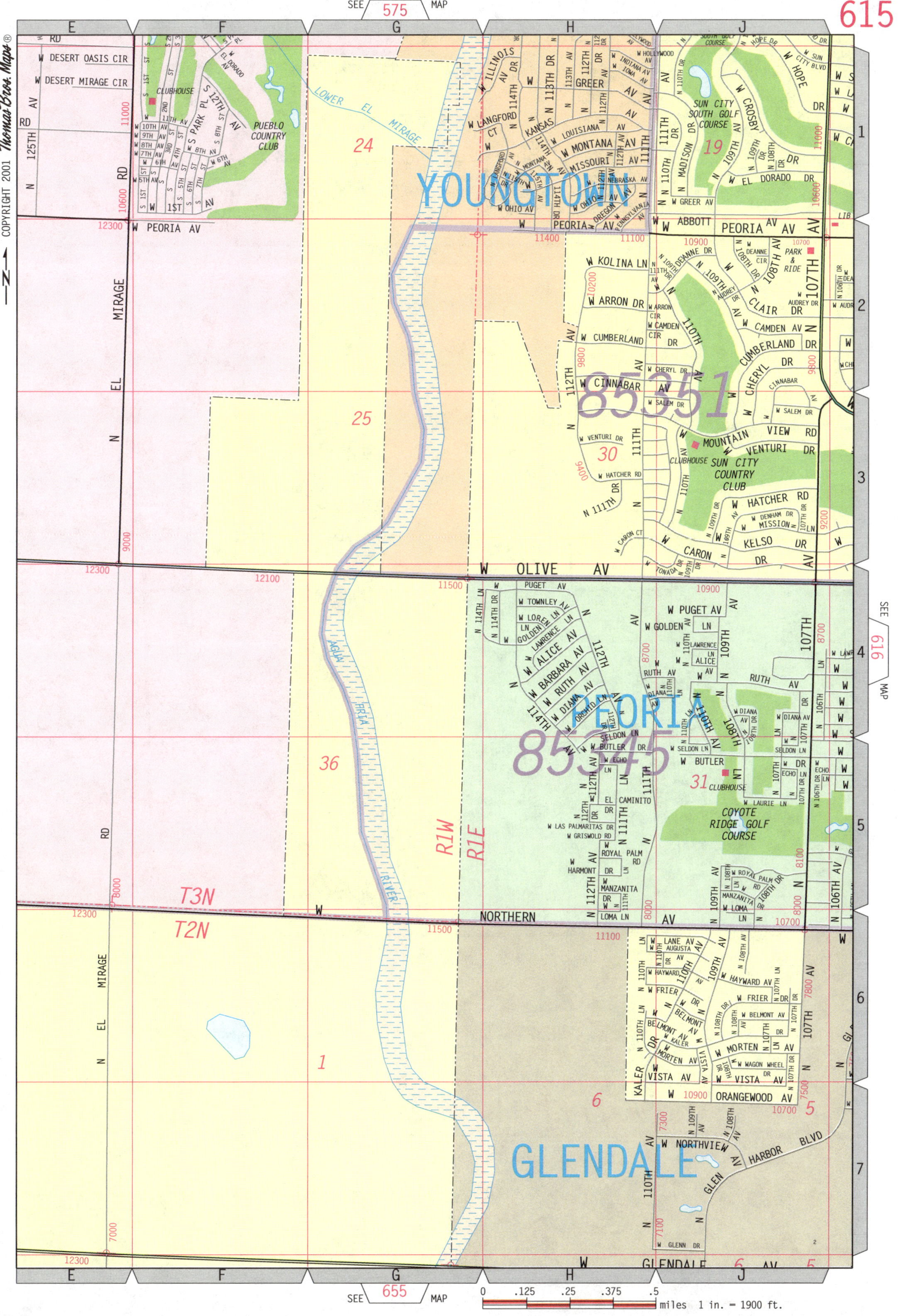

SEE 616 MAP

SEE 655 MAP

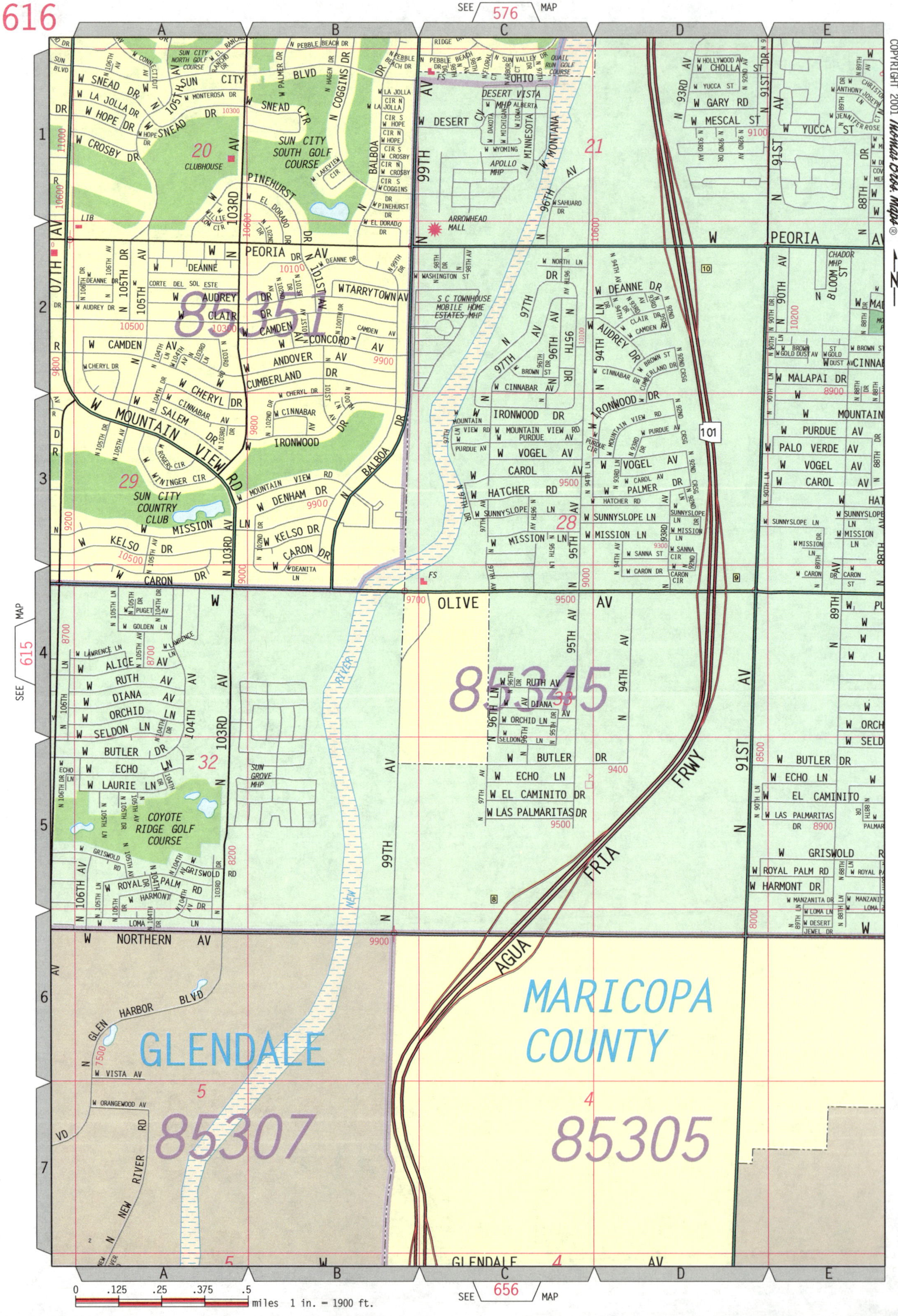
SEE 576 MAP
PHOENIX
SUN CITY NORTH GOLF COURSE
20
CLUBHOUSE
SUN CITY SOUTH GOLF COURSE
85351
21
ARROWHEAD MALL
DESERT VISTA MHP
APOLLO MHP
S C TOWNHOUSE MOBILE HOME ESTATES MHP
29
SUN CITY COUNTRY CLUB
28
W PEORIA AV
W MOUNTAIN VIEW RD
OLIVE AV
85345
33
32
SUN GROVE MHP
COYOTE RIDGE GOLF COURSE
AGUA FRIA FRWY
101
NEW RIVER
W NORTHERN AV
GLENDALE
MARICOPA COUNTY
85307
85305
GLEN HARBOR BLVD
W GLENDALE AV
SEE 615 MAP
SEE 656 MAP
MAP
COPYRIGHT 2001 Thomas Bros. Maps ®
0 .125 .25 .375 .5 miles 1 in. = 1900 ft.

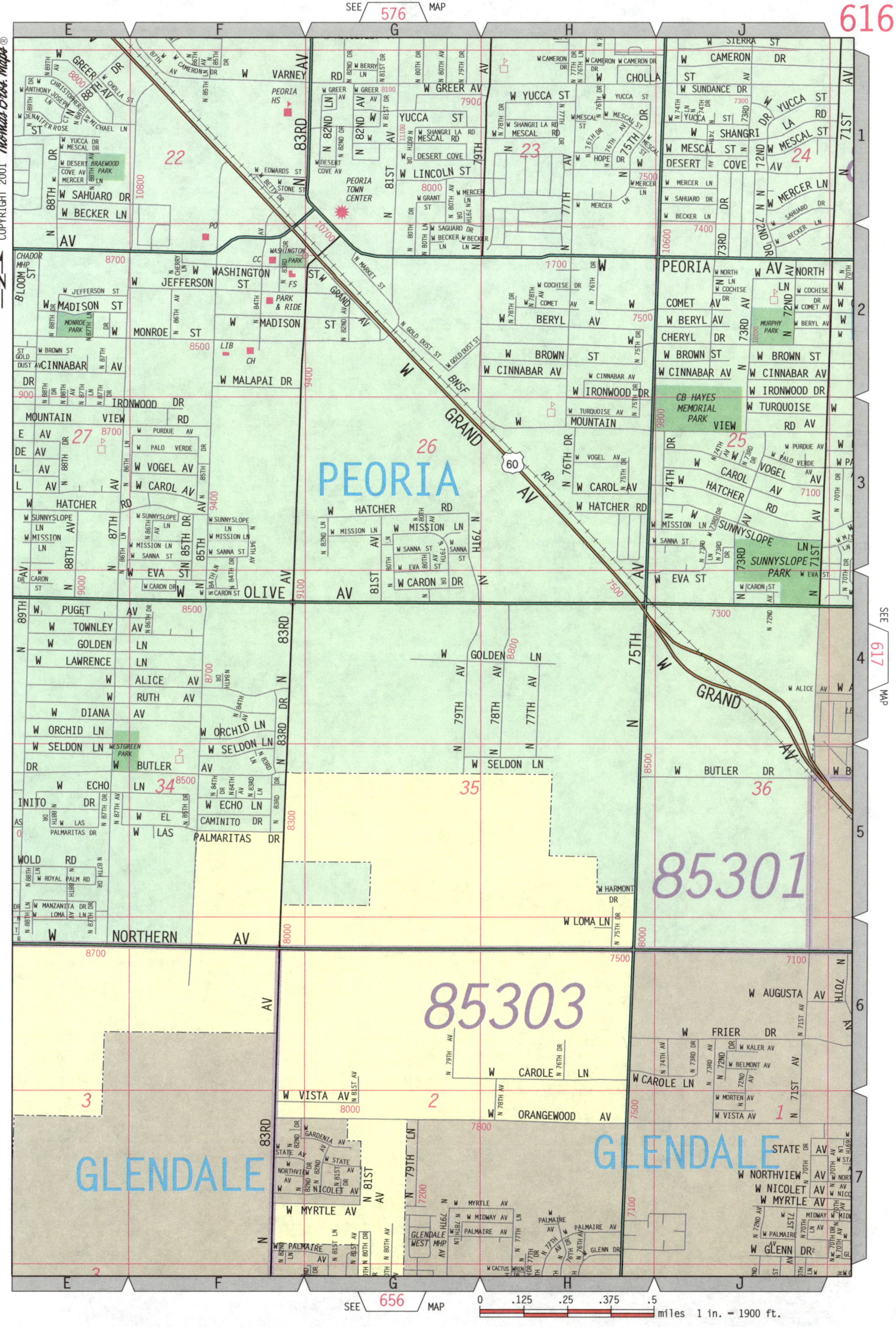
SEE 576 MAP
E
F
G
H
J
PEORIA
GLENDALE
85301
85303
W PEORIA AV
OLIVE AV
NORTHERN AV
W GRAND AV
BNSF RR
60
83RD AV
N 75TH AV
N 79TH AV
N 71ST AV
N 81ST AV
W GREER AV
W YUCCA ST
W MESCAL ST
W LINCOLN ST
W CACTUS WREN
W VARNEY RD
W WASHINGTON ST
W JEFFERSON ST
W MADISON ST
W MONROE ST
W BROWN ST
W CINNABAR AV
W MALAPAI DR
IRONWOOD DR
MOUNTAIN VIEW RD
W VOGEL AV
W CAROL AV
W HATCHER RD
W SUNNYSLOPE LN
W MISSION LN
W EVA ST
W CARON DR
W PUGET AV
W TOWNLEY AV
W GOLDEN LN
W LAWRENCE LN
W ALICE AV
W RUTH AV
W DIANA AV
W ORCHID LN
W SELDON LN
W BUTLER DR
W ECHO LN
W EL CAMINITO DR
W LAS PALMARITAS DR
W LOMA LN
W AUGUSTA AV
W FRIER DR
W CAROLE LN
W VISTA AV
W ORANGEWOOD AV
W STATE AV
W NORTHVIEW AV
W NICOLET AV
W MYRTLE AV
W PALMAIRE AV
W GLENN DR
PEORIA HS
PEORIA TOWN CENTER
BRAEWOOD PARK
MONROE PARK
WASHINGTON PARK
CB HAYES MEMORIAL PARK
MURPHY PARK
SUNNYSLOPE PARK
WESTGREEN PARK
GLENDALE WEST MHP
CHADOR MHP
PO
LIB
CH
CC
FS
PARK & RIDE
22
23
24
25
26
27
34
35
36
1
2
3
SEE 617 MAP
SEE 656 MAP
PHOENIX
MAP
0 .125 .25 .375 .5 miles 1 in. = 1900 ft.

SEE 577 MAP

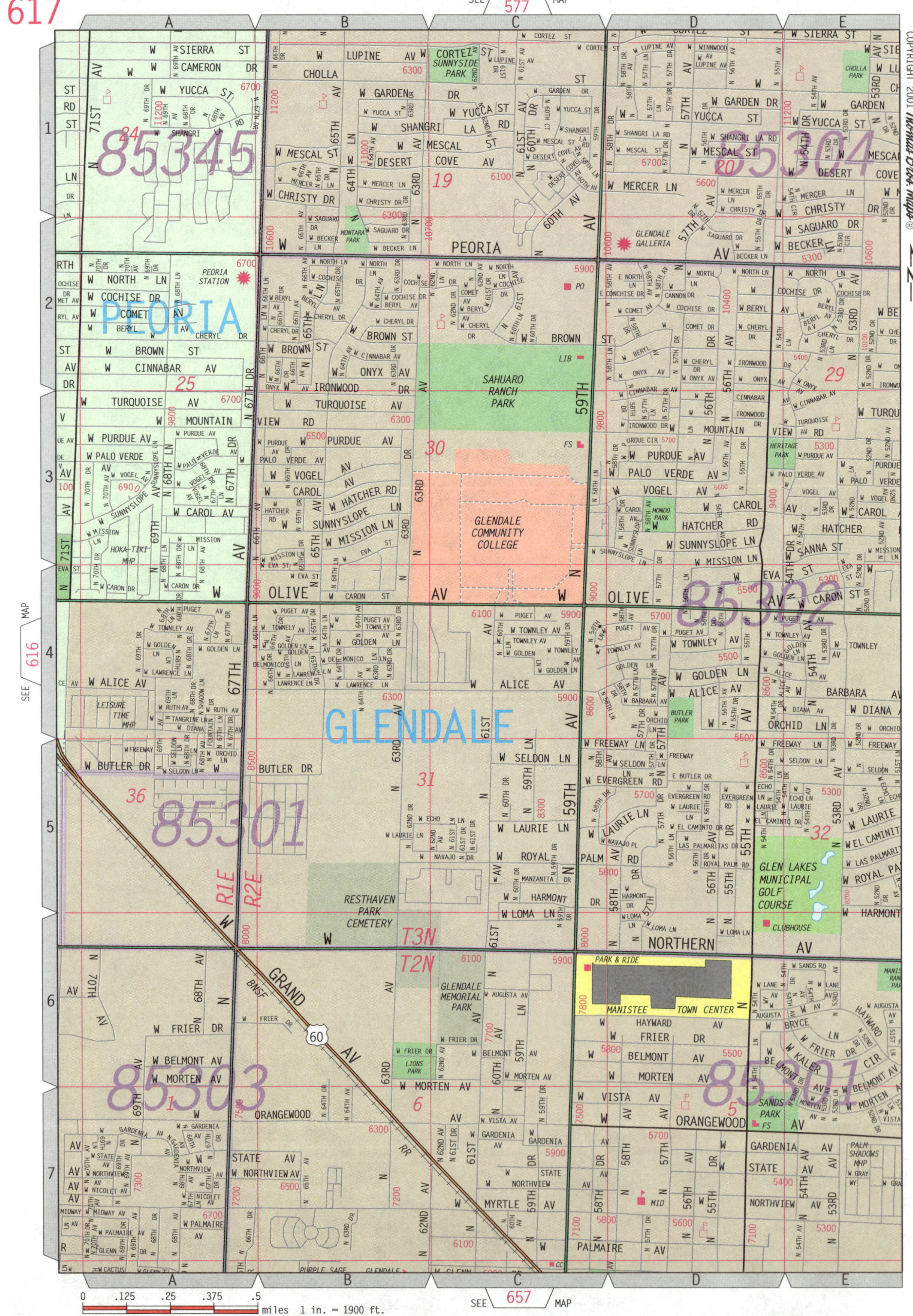

SEE 616 MAP

SEE 657 MAP

0 .125 .25 .375 .5 miles 1 in. = 1900 ft.

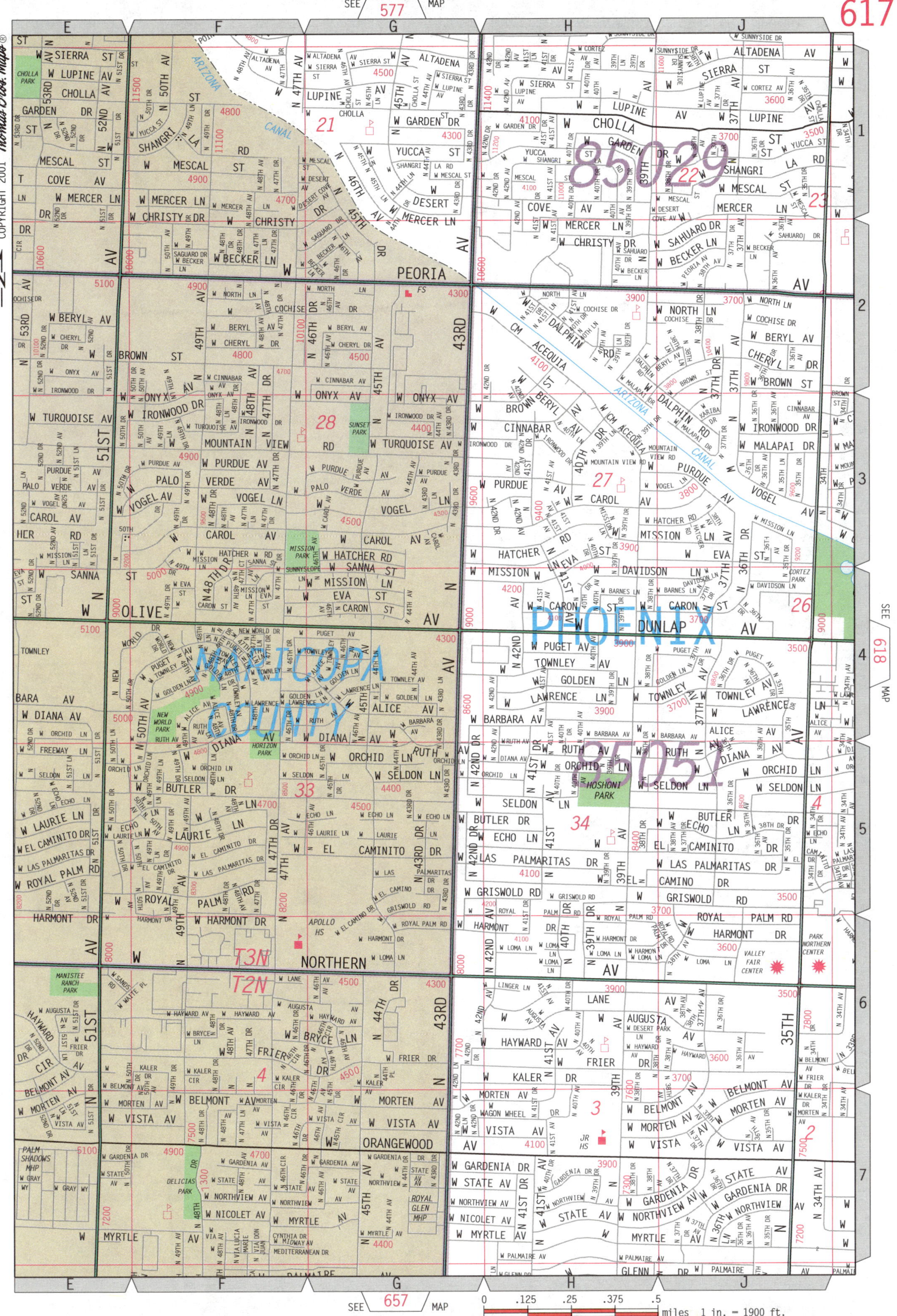
SEE 577 MAP
SEE 618 MAP
SEE 657 MAP
E F G H J
1 2 3 4 5 6 7
85029
85051
PHOENIX
MARICOPA COUNTY
ARIZONA CANAL
T3N
T2N
W CHOLLA
PEORIA AV
OLIVE AV
DUNLAP AV
NORTHERN AV
ORANGEWOOD AV
51ST AV
43RD AV
35TH AV
SUNSET PARK
MISSION PARK
NEW WORLD PARK
HORIZON PARK
HOSHONI PARK
CHOLLA PARK
MANISTEE RANCH PARK
DELICIAS PARK
CORTEZ PARK
PALM SHADOWS MHP
ROYAL GLEN MHP
APOLLO HS
JR HS
VALLEY FAIR CENTER
PARK NORTHERN CENTER
0 .125 .25 .375 .5 miles 1 in. = 1900 ft.
PHOENIX
MAP

SEE 578 MAP

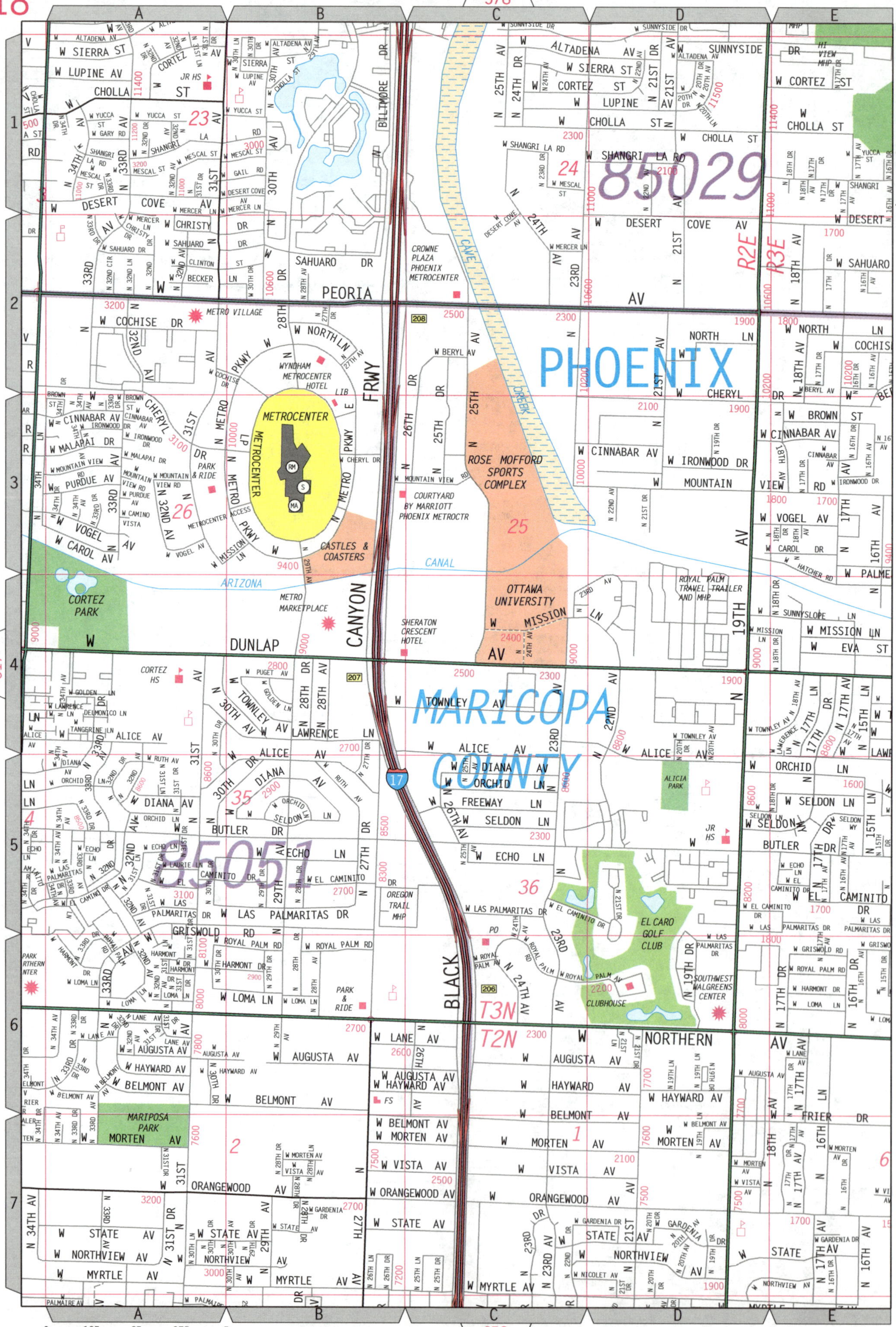

SEE 617 MAP

SEE 658 MAP

PHOENIX

MARICOPA COUNTY

85029

85051

R2E R3E

T3N T2N

METROCENTER

METRO VILLAGE

WYNDHAM METROCENTER HOTEL

CROWNE PLAZA PHOENIX METROCENTER

ROSE MOFFORD SPORTS COMPLEX

COURTYARD BY MARRIOTT PHOENIX METROCTR

CASTLES & COASTERS

METRO MARKETPLACE

SHERATON CRESCENT HOTEL

OTTAWA UNIVERSITY

ROYAL PALM TRAVEL TRAILER AND MHP

CORTEZ PARK

CORTEZ HS

JR HS

ALICIA PARK

EL CARO GOLF CLUB

CLUBHOUSE

SOUTHWEST WALGREENS CENTER

OREGON TRAIL MHP

PARK & RIDE

MARIPOSA PARK

ARIZONA CANAL

CAVE CREEK

BLACK CANYON FRWY

17

PEORIA AV

DUNLAP AV

NORTHERN AV

ORANGEWOOD AV

0 .125 .25 .375 .5 miles 1 in. = 1900 ft.

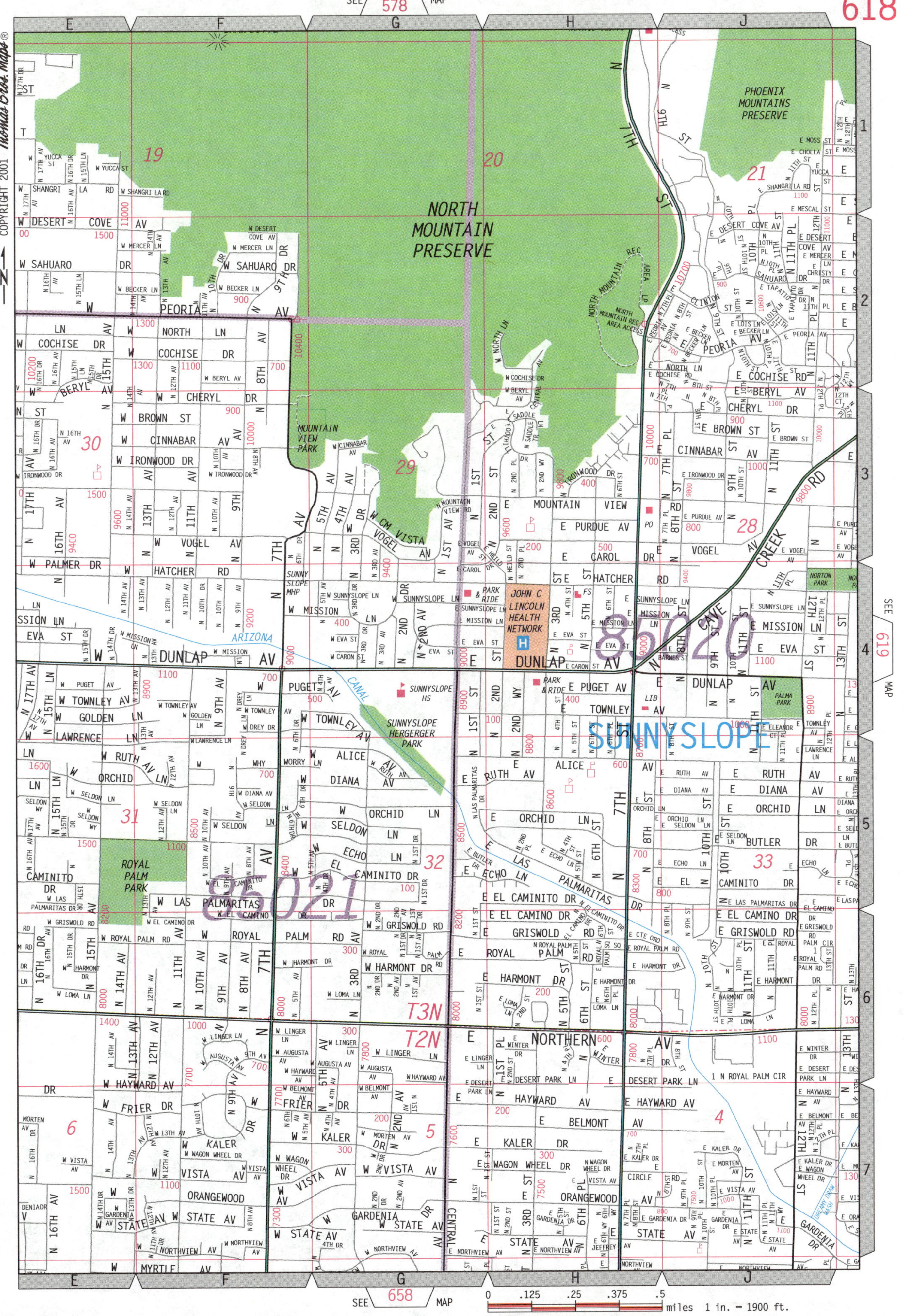
SEE 578 MAP
NORTH MOUNTAIN PRESERVE
PHOENIX MOUNTAINS PRESERVE
MOUNTAIN VIEW PARK
SUNNYSLOPE HERGERGER PARK
ROYAL PALM PARK
PALMA PARK
NORTON PARK
JOHN C LINCOLN HEALTH NETWORK
SUNNYSLOPE HS
SUNNYSLOPE MHP
SUNNYSLOPE
ARIZONA CANAL
CAVE CREEK RD
NORTH MOUNTAIN REC AREA LP
W PEORIA AV
E PEORIA AV
W DUNLAP AV
E DUNLAP AV
W NORTHERN AV
E NORTHERN AV
N CENTRAL AV
N 7TH AV
N 7TH ST
85020
85021
T3N
T2N
PHOENIX
SEE 619 MAP
SEE 658 MAP
miles 1 in. = 1900 ft.
COPYRIGHT 2001 Thomas Bros. Maps®

SEE 579 MAP

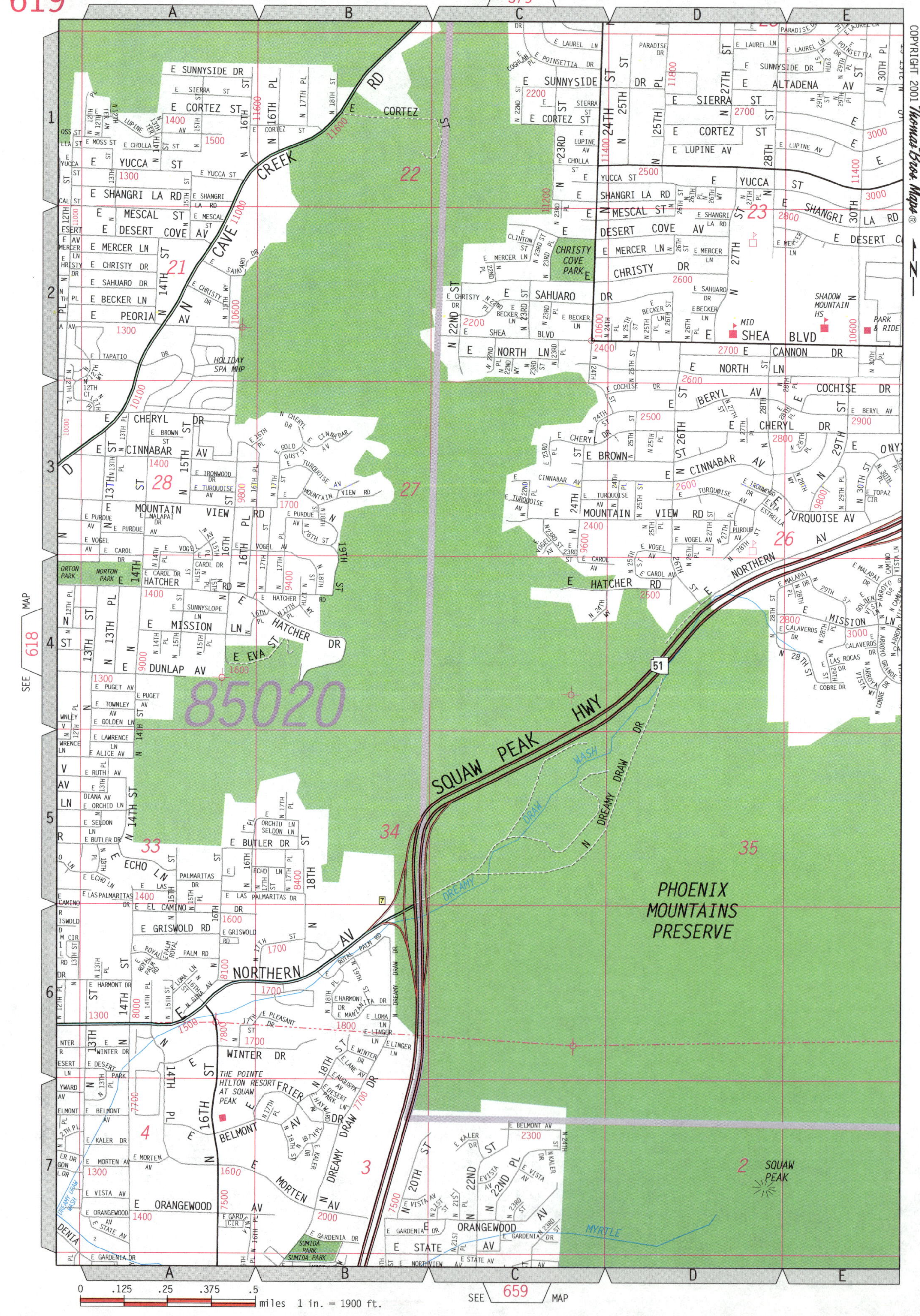

SEE 618 MAP

SEE 659 MAP

0 .125 .25 .375 .5 miles 1 in. = 1900 ft.

PHOENIX

MAP

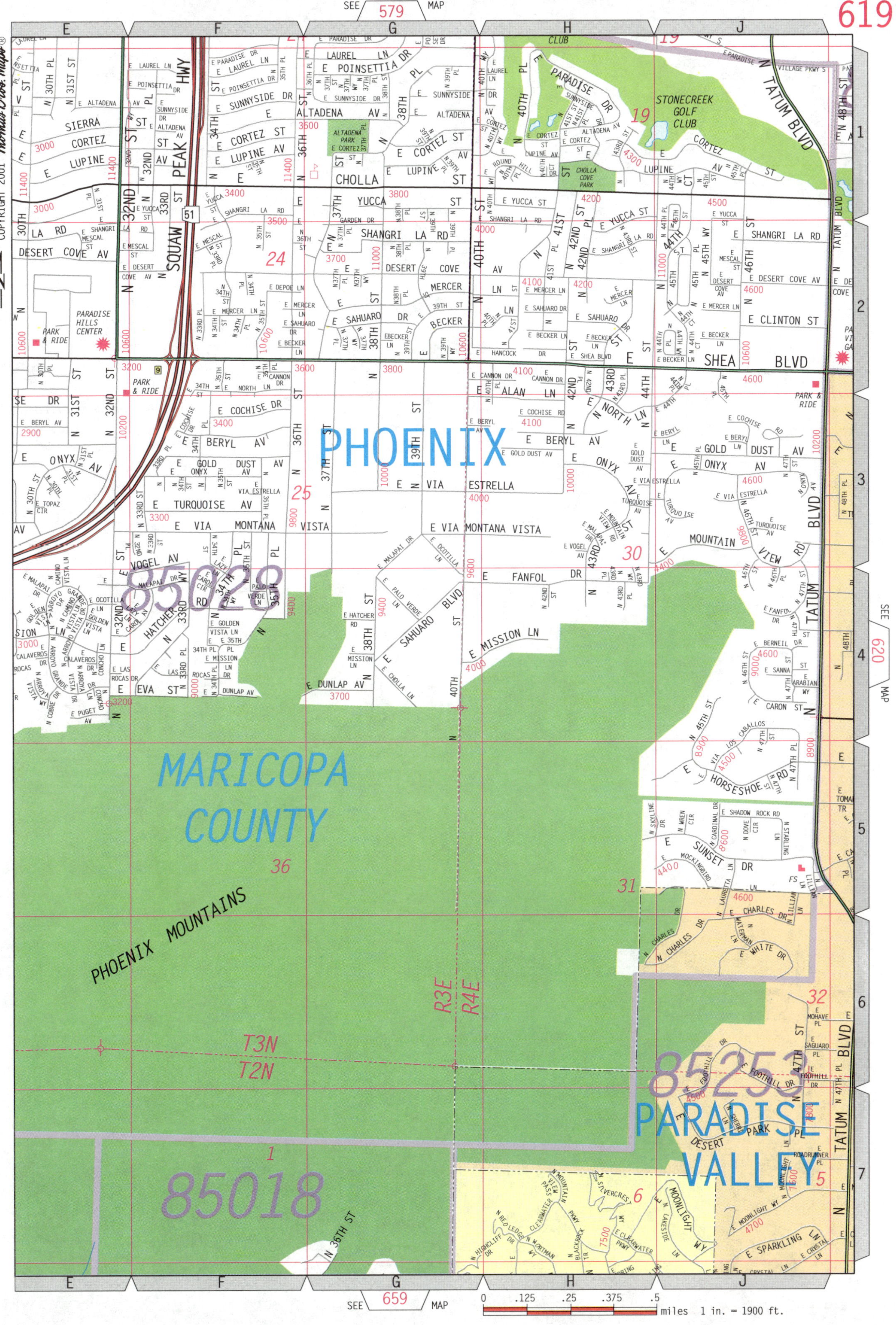
SEE 579 MAP
PHOENIX
MARICOPA COUNTY
PHOENIX MOUNTAINS
PARADISE VALLEY
STONECREEK GOLF CLUB
PARADISE HILLS CENTER
SHEA BLVD
TATUM BLVD
SQUAW PEAK HWY
85028
85018
85253
R3E R4E
T3N T2N
SEE 620 MAP
SEE 659 MAP
miles 1 in. = 1900 ft.
PHOENIX
MAP

SEE 580 MAP

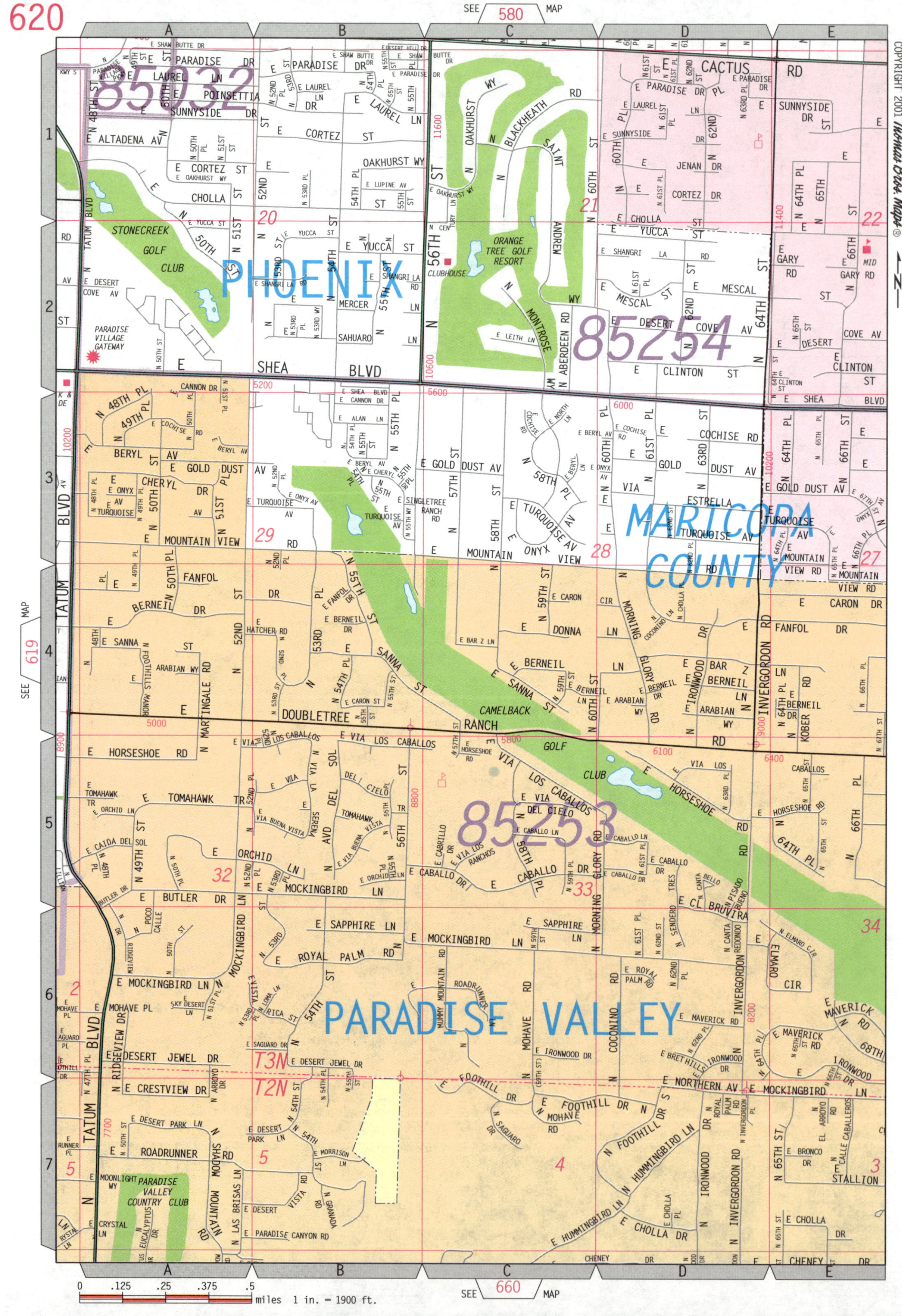
PHOENIX
PARADISE VALLEY
MARICOPA COUNTY
85032
85254
85253
STONECREEK GOLF CLUB
ORANGE TREE GOLF RESORT
CLUBHOUSE
PARADISE VILLAGE GATEWAY
CAMELBACK GOLF CLUB
PARADISE VALLEY COUNTRY CLUB
TATUM BLVD
SHEA BLVD
CACTUS RD
DOUBLETREE RANCH RD
MOCKINGBIRD LN
INVERGORDON RD
NORTHERN AV
T3N
T2N
SEE 619 MAP
SEE 660 MAP
PHOENIX
MAP
COPYRIGHT 2001 Thomas Bros. Maps®
0 .125 .25 .375 .5 miles 1 in. = 1900 ft.

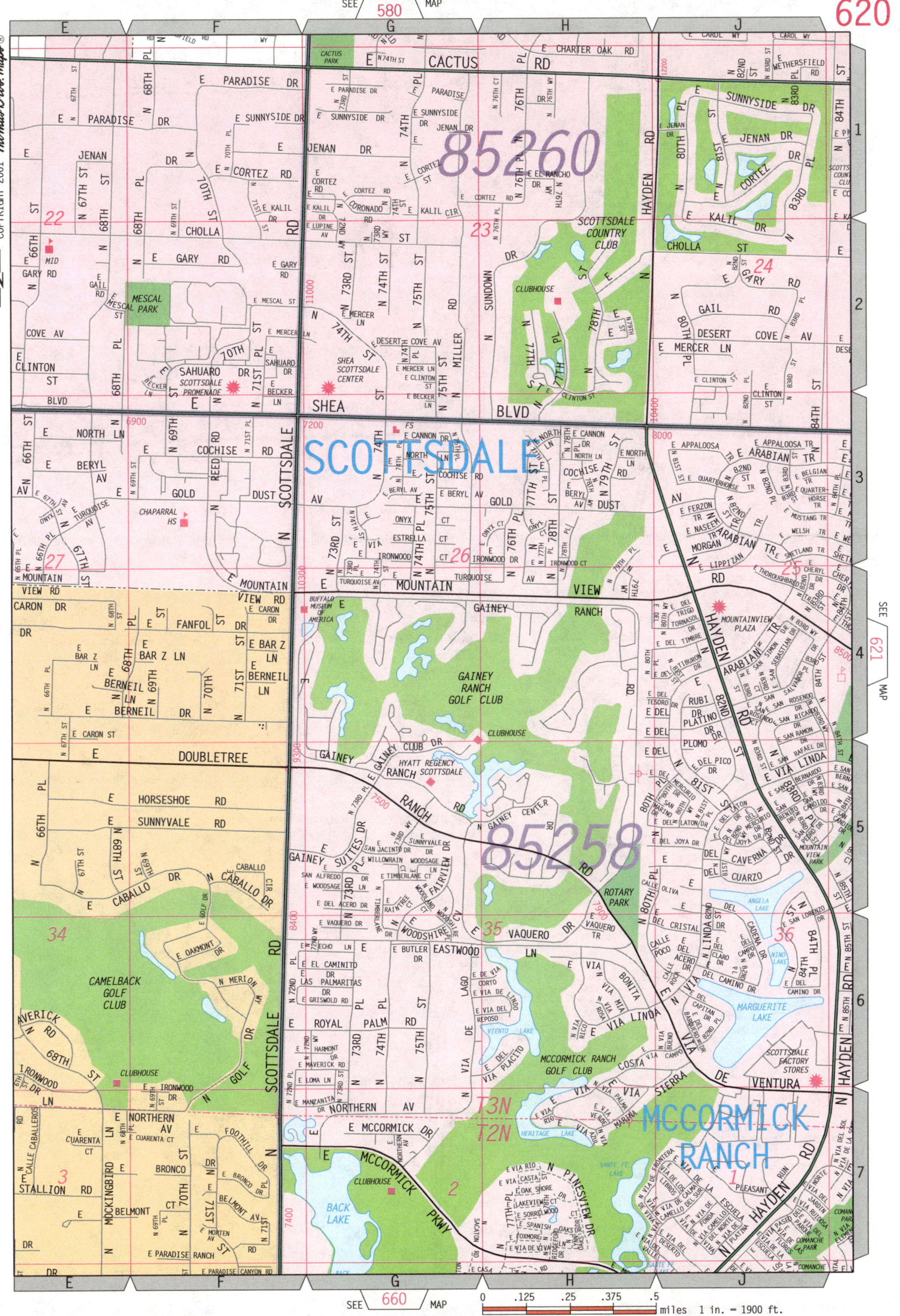
SEE 580 MAP
E
F
G
H
J
85260
SCOTTSDALE
85258
MCCORMICK RANCH
PHOENIX
SEE 621 MAP
E CACTUS RD
E SHEA BLVD
E MOUNTAIN VIEW RD
E DOUBLETREE RANCH RD
N SCOTTSDALE RD
N HAYDEN RD
E GAINEY RANCH RD
N MCCORMICK PKWY
E VIA DE VENTURA
SCOTTSDALE COUNTRY CLUB
GAINEY RANCH GOLF CLUB
CAMELBACK GOLF CLUB
MCCORMICK RANCH GOLF CLUB
HYATT REGENCY SCOTTSDALE
SHEA SCOTTSDALE CENTER
SCOTTSDALE PROMENADE
MOUNTAINVIEW PLAZA
SCOTTSDALE FACTORY STORES
BUFFALO MUSEUM OF AMERICA
CHAPARRAL HS
MESCAL PARK
CACTUS PARK
ROTARY PARK
BACK LAKE
MARGUERITE LAKE
ANGELA LAKE
HERITAGE LAKE
VIENTO LAKE
T3N
T2N
SEE 660 MAP
0 .125 .25 .375 .5 miles 1 in. = 1900 ft.

SEE 581 MAP

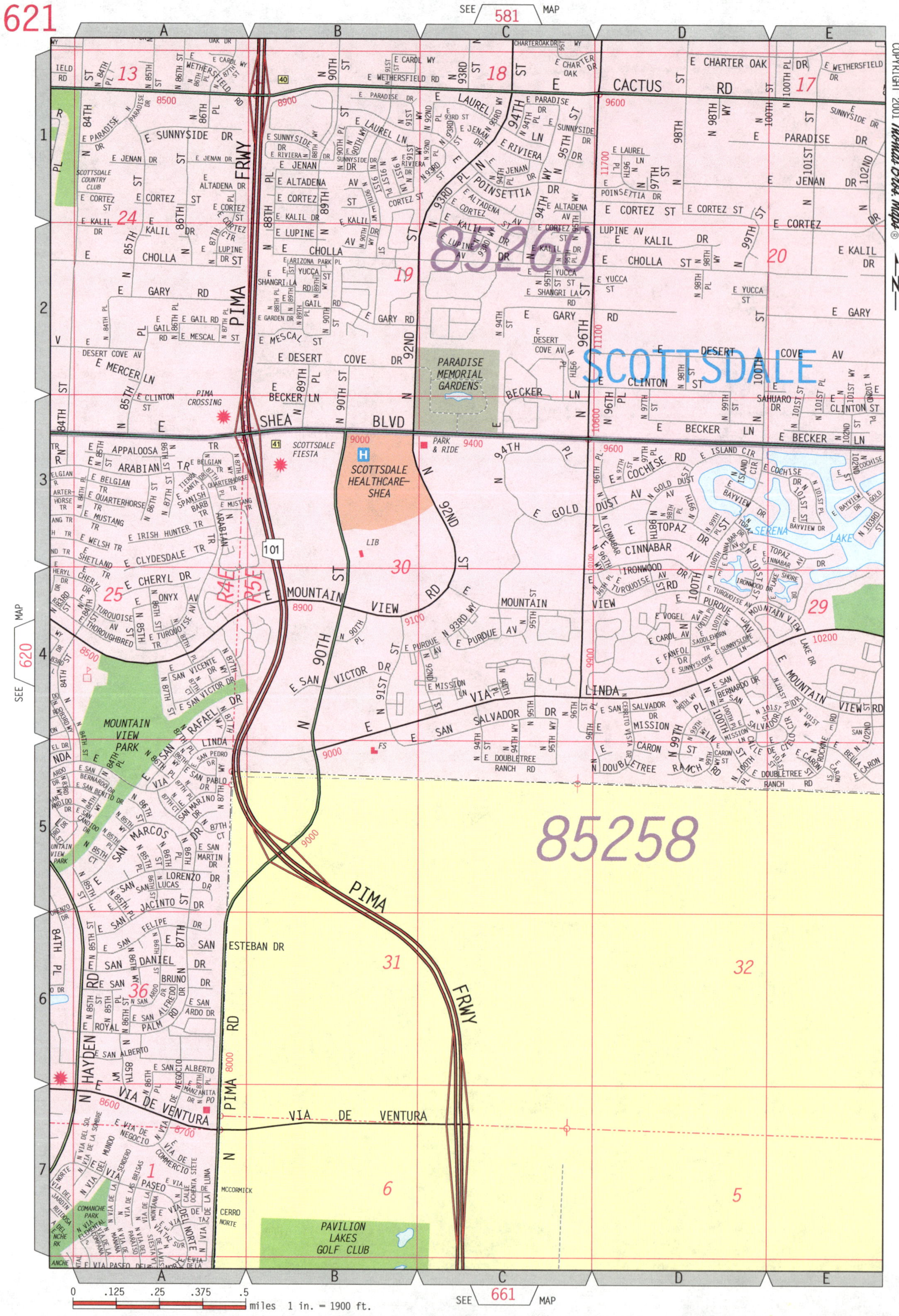

SEE 620 MAP

SEE 661 MAP

MAP

SEE 581 MAP

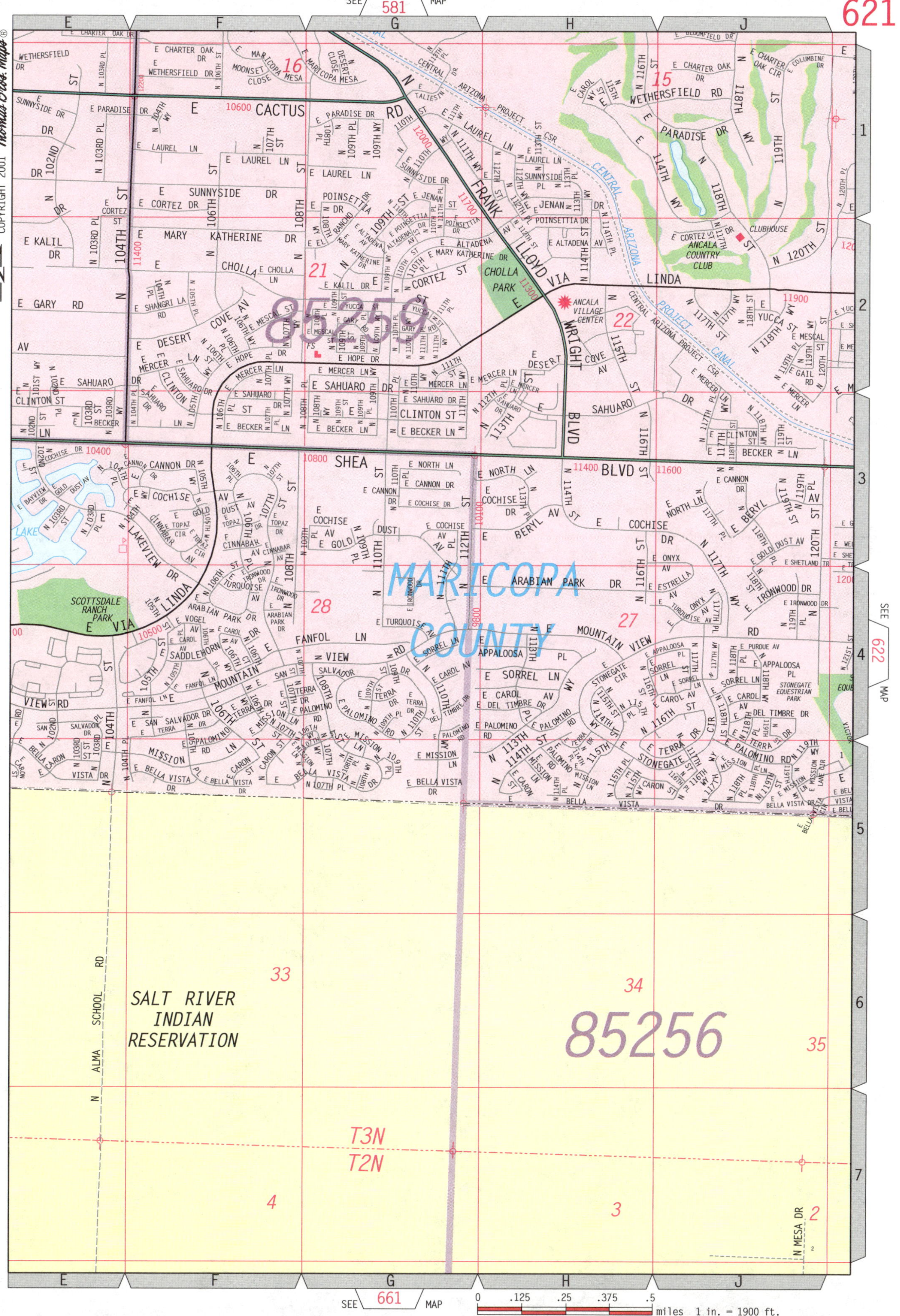

SEE 622 MAP

SEE 661 MAP

SEE 582 MAP

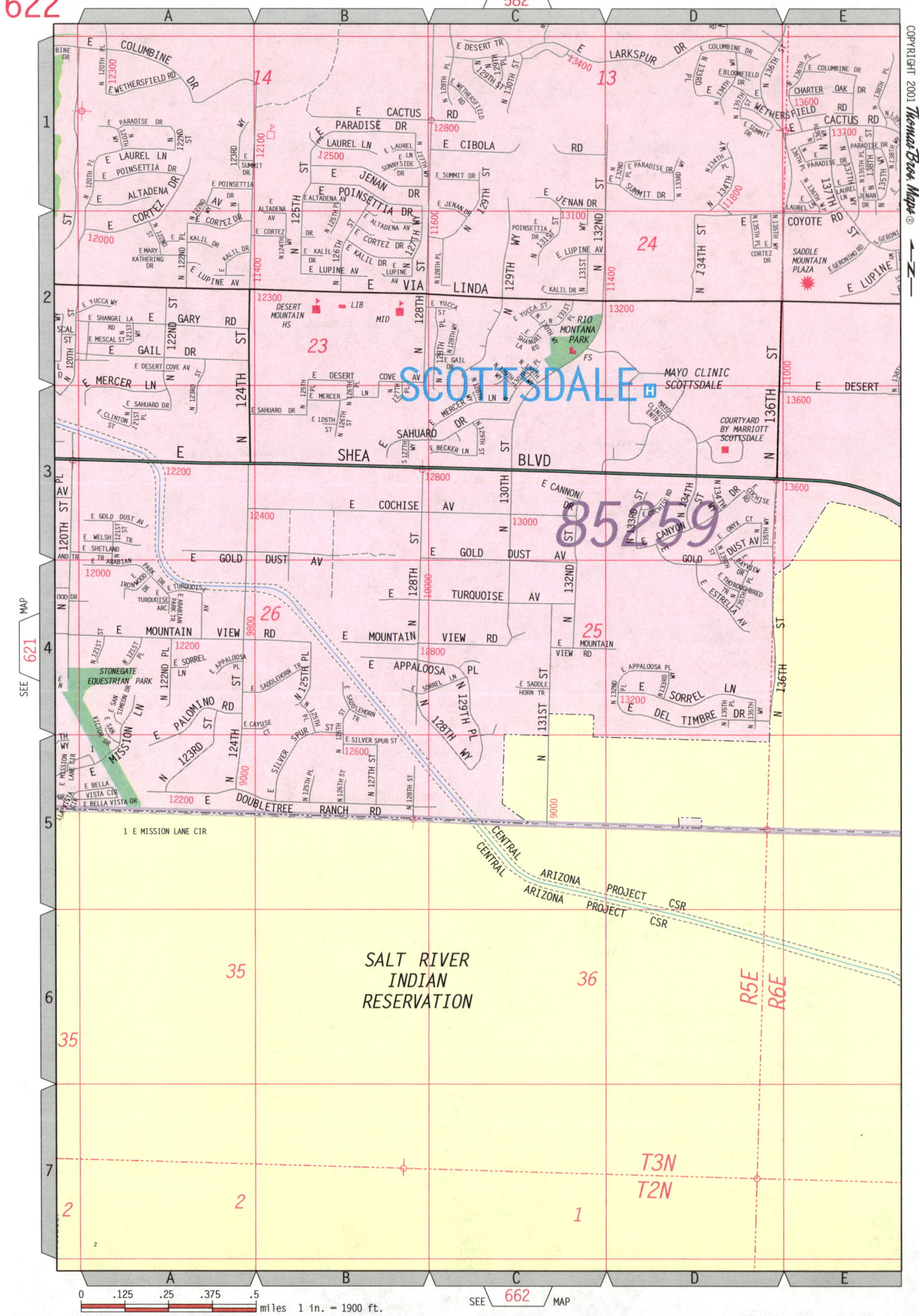

SEE 621 MAP

SEE 662 MAP

SEE 582 MAP

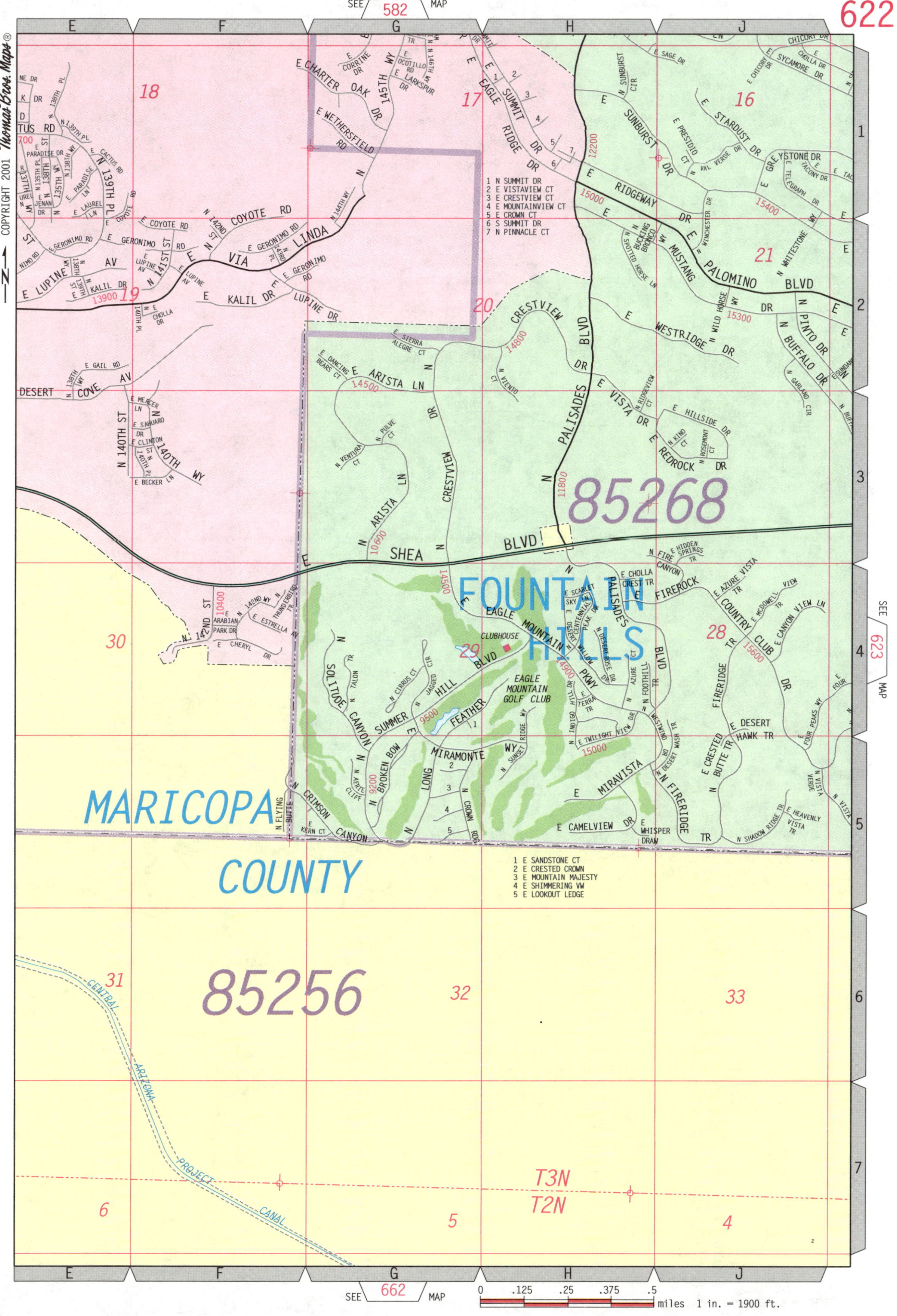

SEE 623 MAP

SEE 662 MAP

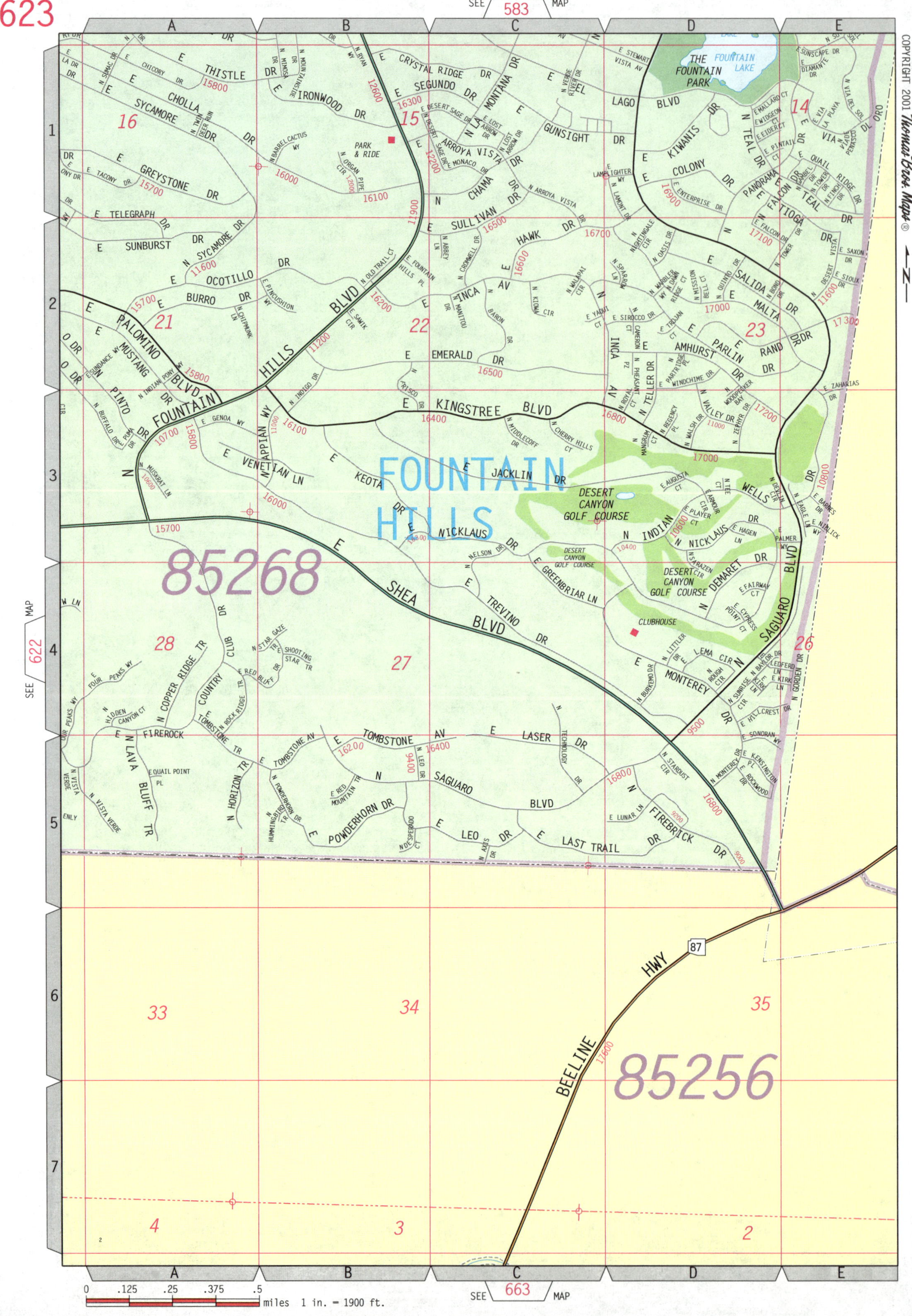

0 .125 .25 .375 .5 miles 1 in. = 1900 ft.

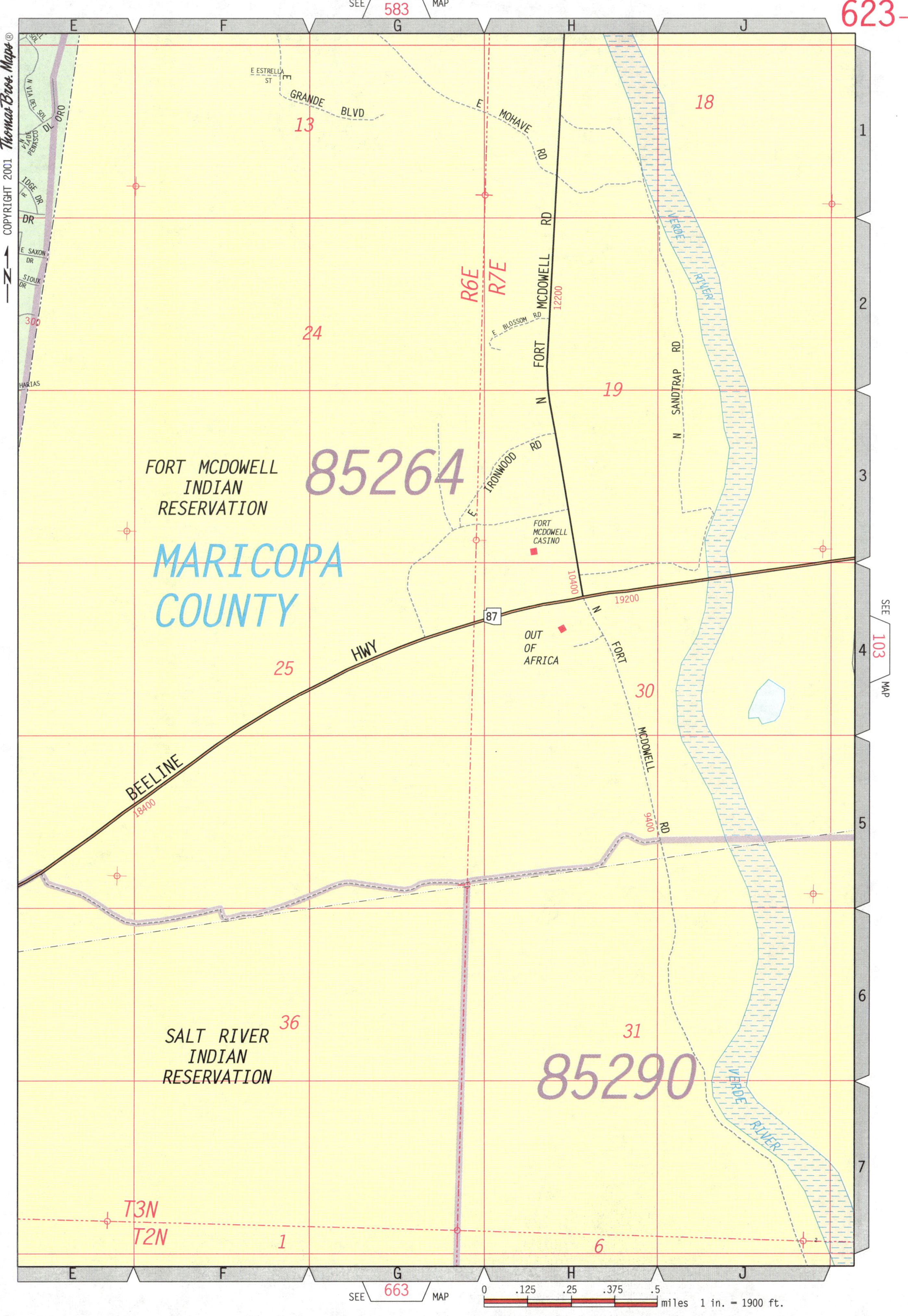
SEE 583 MAP
FORT MCDOWELL INDIAN RESERVATION
85264
MARICOPA COUNTY
BEELINE HWY
87
N FORT MCDOWELL RD
FORT MCDOWELL CASINO
OUT OF AFRICA
N SANDTRAP RD
E IRONWOOD RD
E BLOSSOM RD
E MOHAVE RD
E GRANDE BLVD
E ESTRELLA ST
VERDE RIVER
R6E
R7E
SALT RIVER INDIAN RESERVATION
85290
T3N
T2N
SEE 103 MAP
SEE 663 MAP
PHOENIX
MAP
0 .125 .25 .375 .5 miles 1 in. = 1900 ft.

SEE 102 MAP

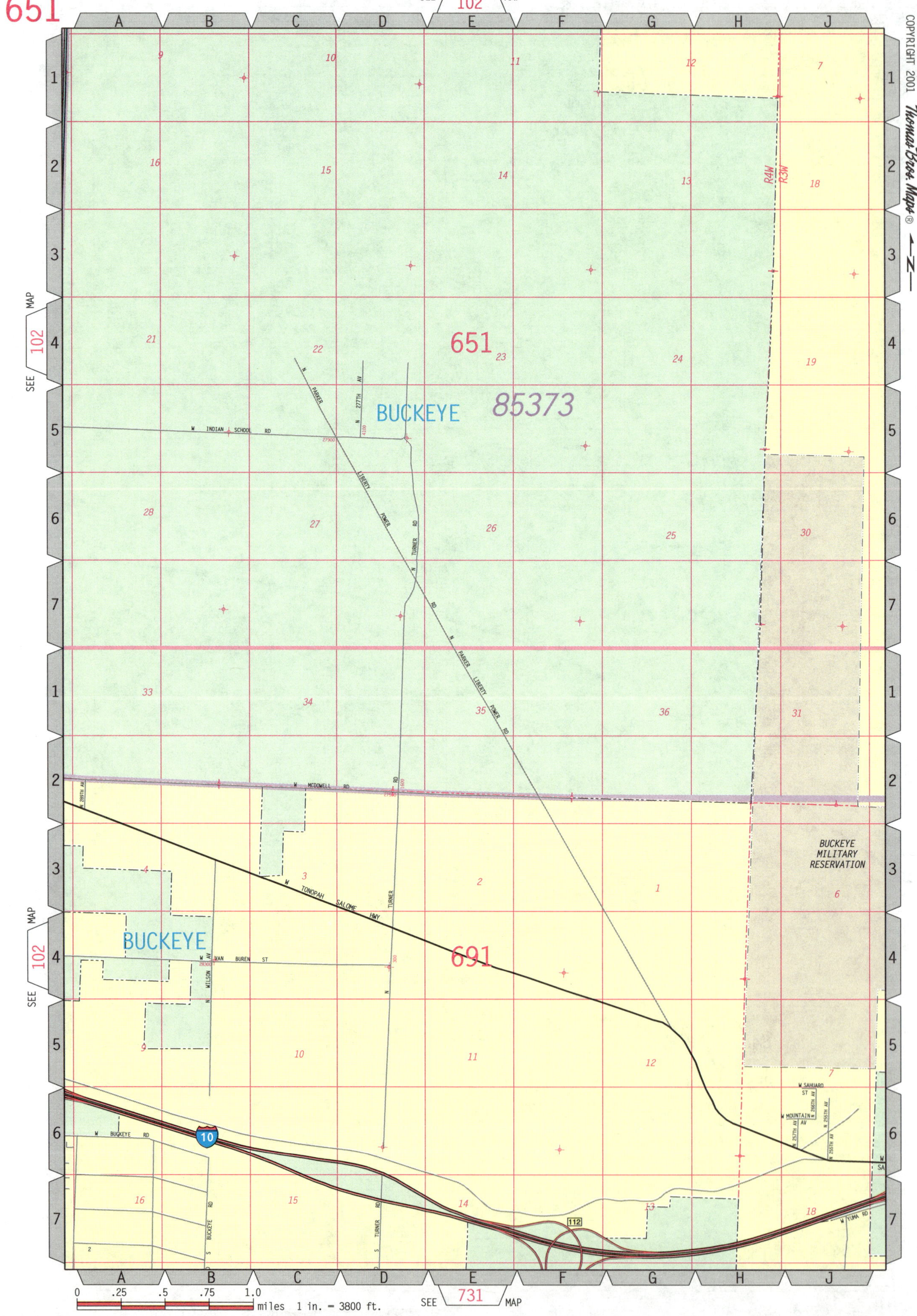

PHOENIX

MAP

SEE 102 MAP

SEE 102 MAP

0 .25 .5 .75 1.0 miles 1 in. = 3800 ft.

SEE 731 MAP

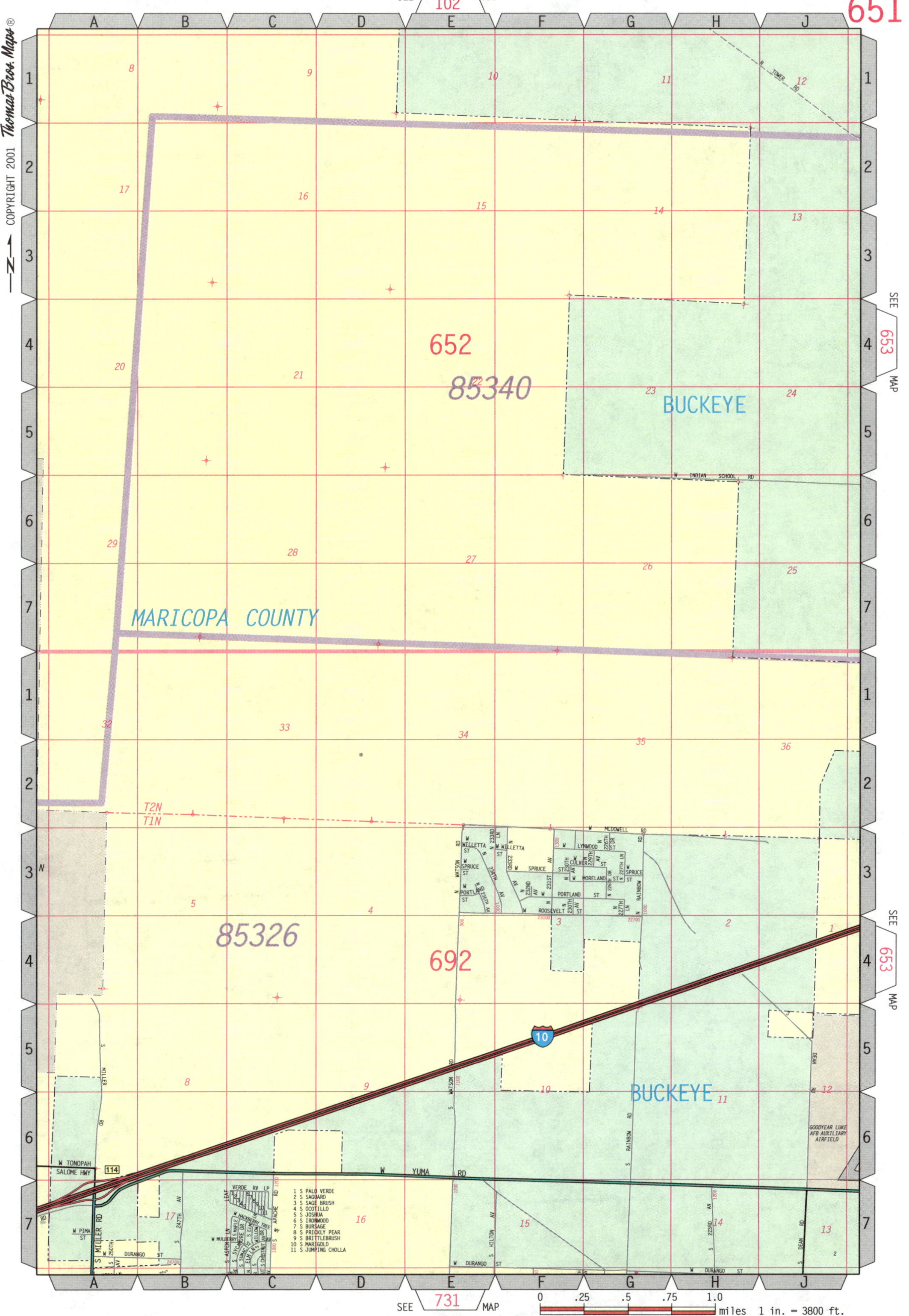
SEE 102 MAP
SEE 653 MAP
SEE 731 MAP
652
85340
BUCKEYE
MARICOPA COUNTY
W INDIAN SCHOOL RD
N TOWER RD
T2N
T1N
W MCDOWELL RD
85326
692
10
BUCKEYE
W YUMA RD
W TONOPAH SALOME HWY
114
S MILLER RD
S WATSON RD
S RAINBOW RD
S DEAN RD
GOODYEAR LUKE AFB AUXILIARY AIRFIELD
W DURANGO ST
1 S PALO VERDE
2 S SAGUARO
3 S SAGE BRUSH
4 S OCOTILLO
5 S JOSHUA
6 S IRONWOOD
7 S BURSAGE
8 S PRICKLY PEAR
9 S BRITTLEBRUSH
10 S MARIGOLD
11 S JUMPING CHOLLA
0 .25 .5 .75 1.0 miles 1 in. = 3800 ft.

PHOENIX

MAP

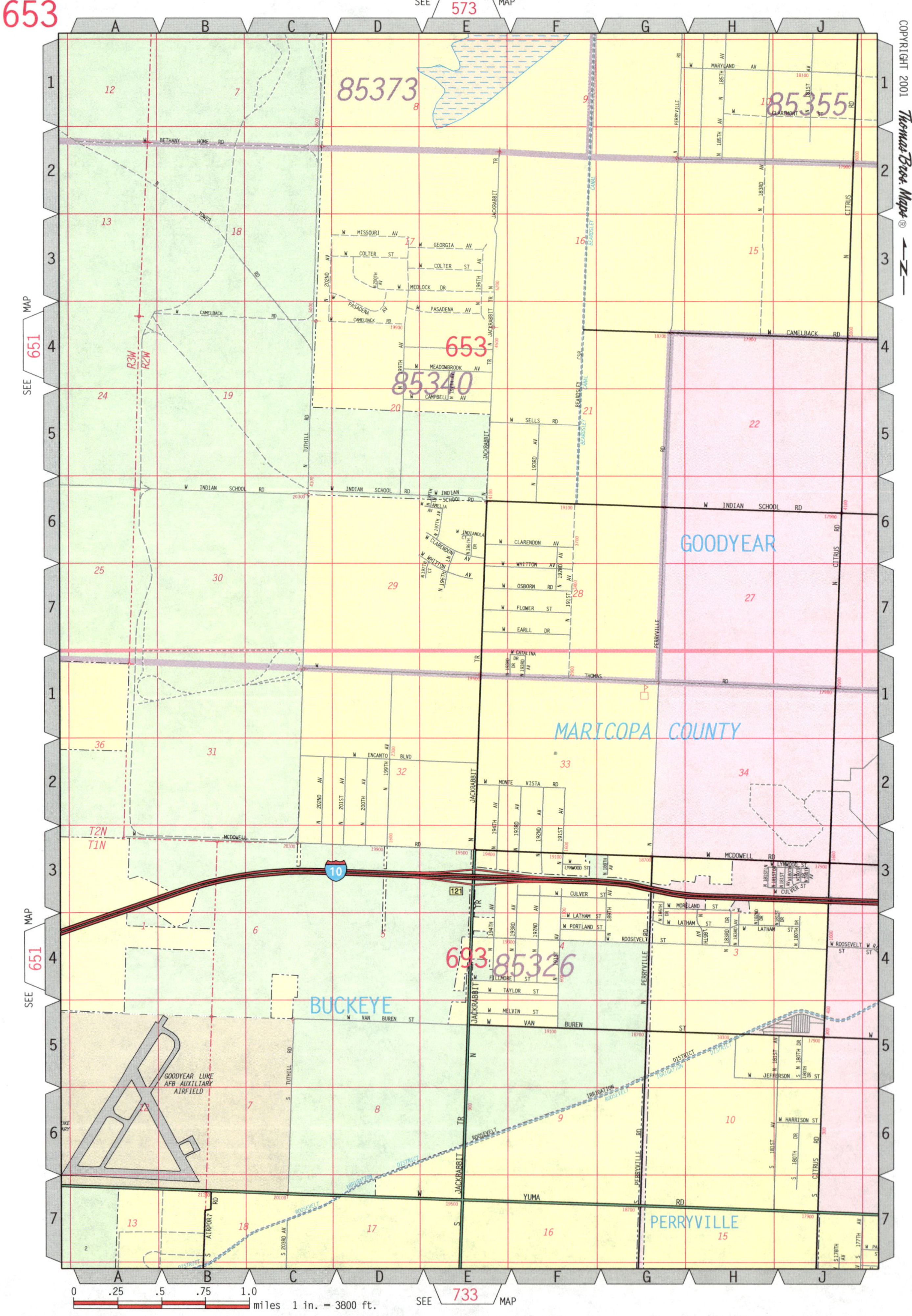

0 .25 .5 .75 1.0 miles 1 in. = 3800 ft.

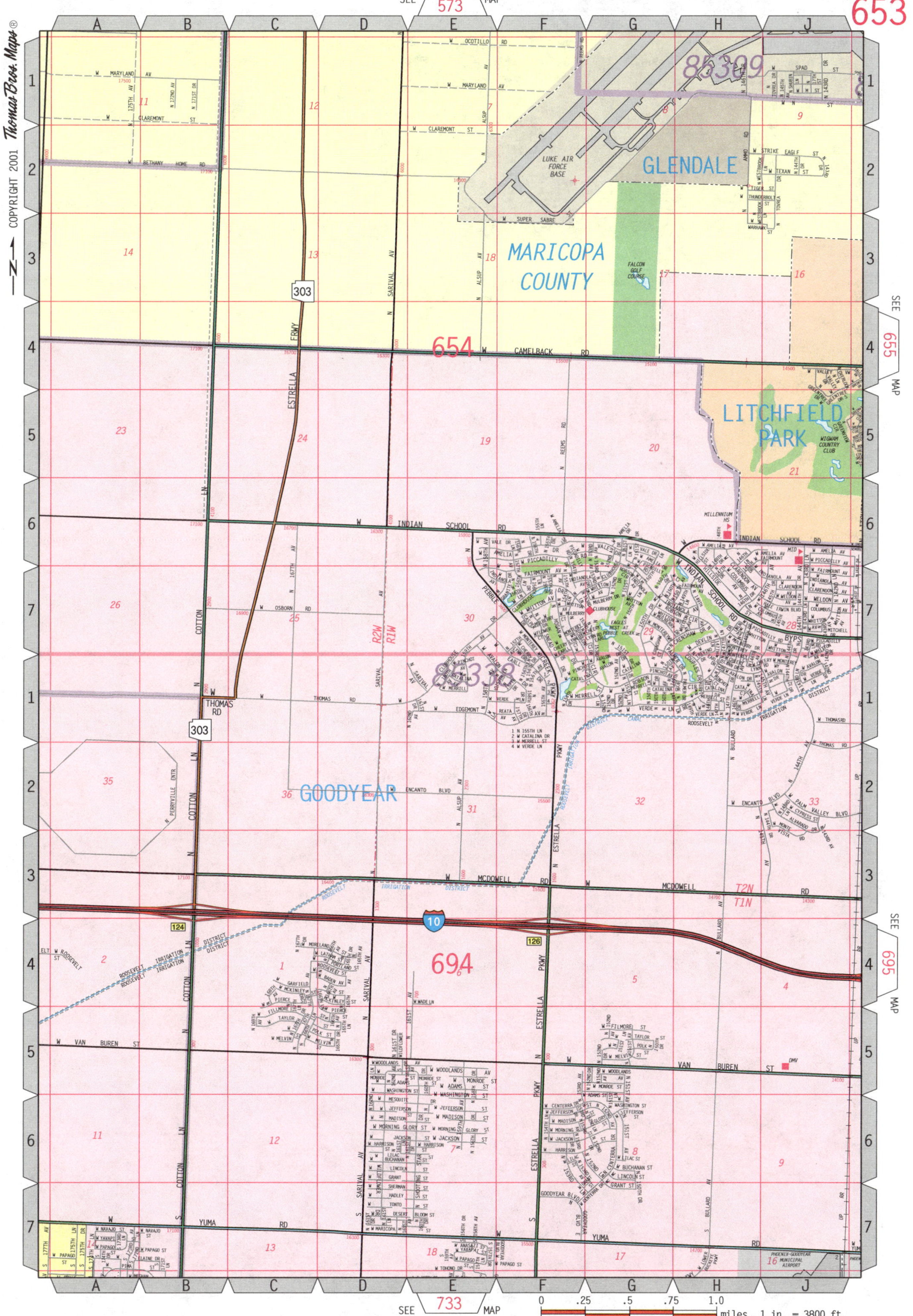
SEE 573 MAP
SEE 655 MAP
SEE 695 MAP
SEE 733 MAP
654
694
LUKE AIR FORCE BASE
GLENDALE
MARICOPA COUNTY
LITCHFIELD PARK
WIGWAM COUNTRY CLUB
GOODYEAR
FALCON GOLF COURSE
85309
85338
W CAMELBACK RD
W INDIAN SCHOOL RD
W MCDOWELL RD
W VAN BUREN ST
W YUMA RD
W THOMAS RD
ESTRELLA FRWY
ESTRELLA PKWY
COTTON LN
SARIVAL AV
BULLARD AV
PHOENIX-GOODYEAR MUNICIPAL AIRPORT
PHOENIX
MAP
0 .25 .5 .75 1.0 miles 1 in. = 3800 ft.

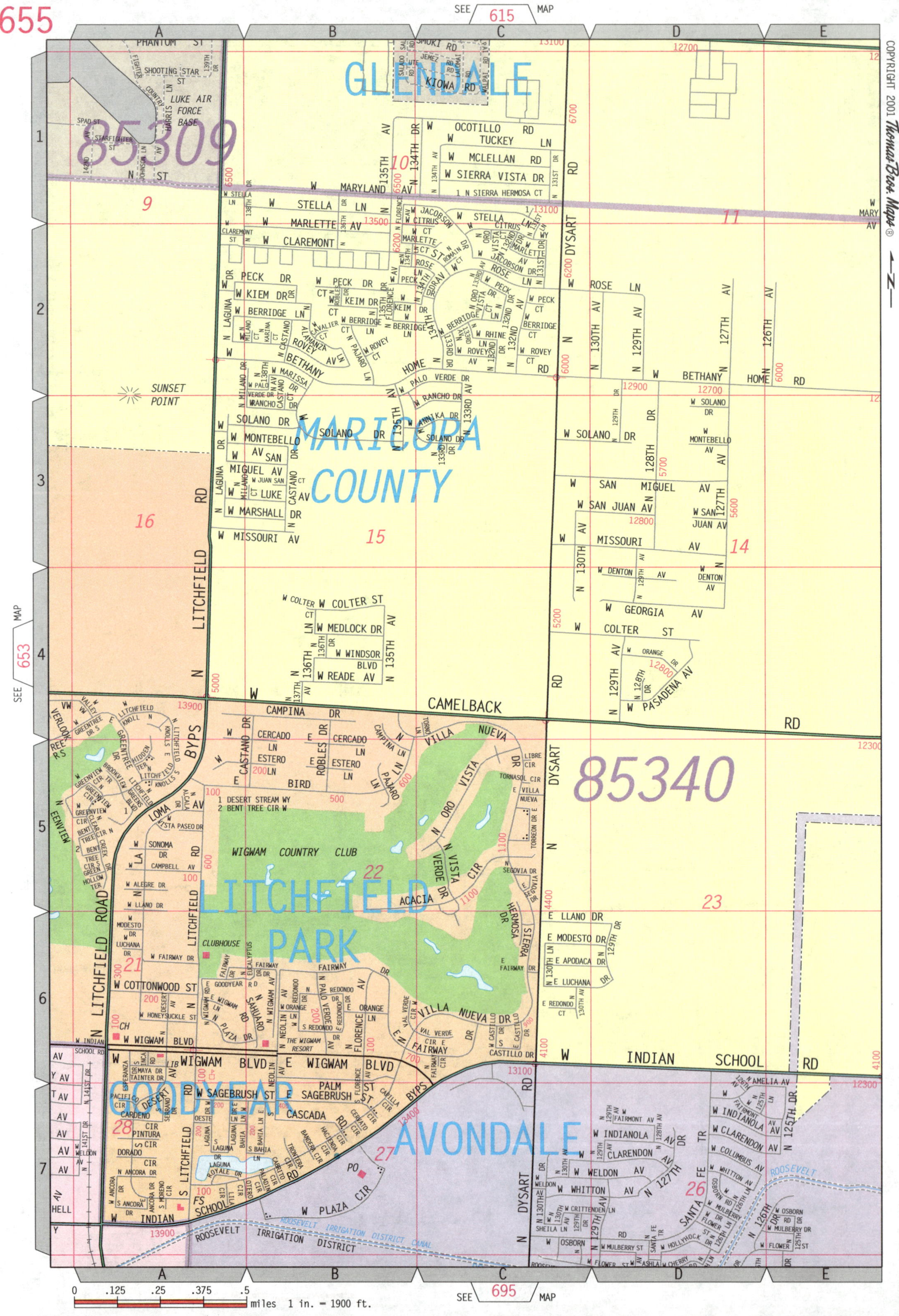
SEE 615 MAP
GLENDALE
85309
LUKE AIR FORCE BASE
MARICOPA COUNTY
SUNSET POINT
85340
LITCHFIELD PARK
WIGWAM COUNTRY CLUB
CLUBHOUSE
GOODYEAR
AVONDALE
W MARYLAND AV
W BETHANY HOME RD
W CAMELBACK RD
W INDIAN SCHOOL RD
N LITCHFIELD RD
N LITCHFIELD ROAD
N DYSART RD
ROOSEVELT IRRIGATION DISTRICT
ROOSEVELT IRRIGATION DISTRICT CANAL
SEE 653 MAP
SEE 695 MAP
PHOENIX
MAP
miles 1 in. = 1900 ft.

SEE 615 MAP

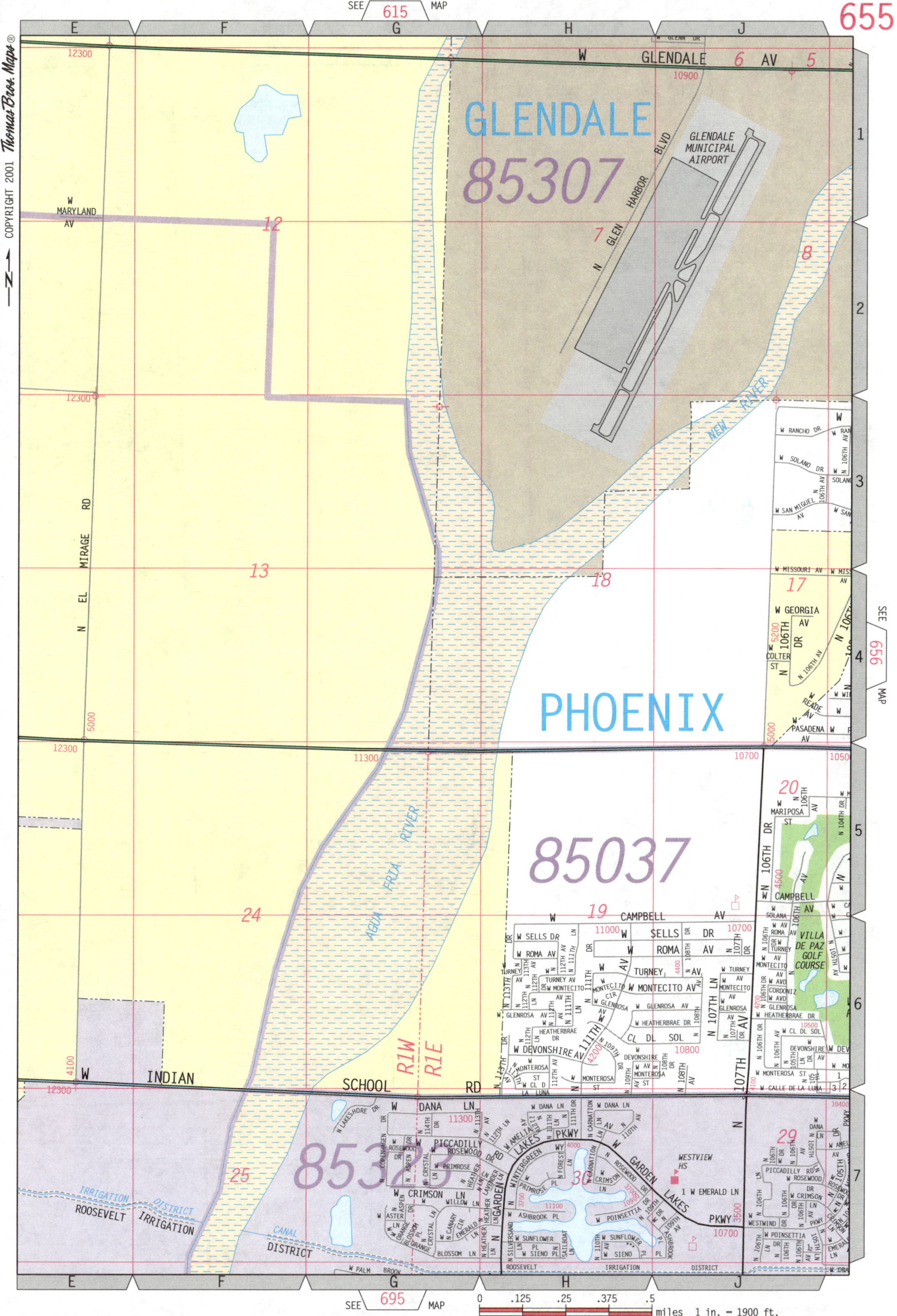

SEE 656 MAP

SEE 695 MAP

0 .125 .25 .375 .5 miles 1 in. = 1900 ft.

PHOENIX

MAP

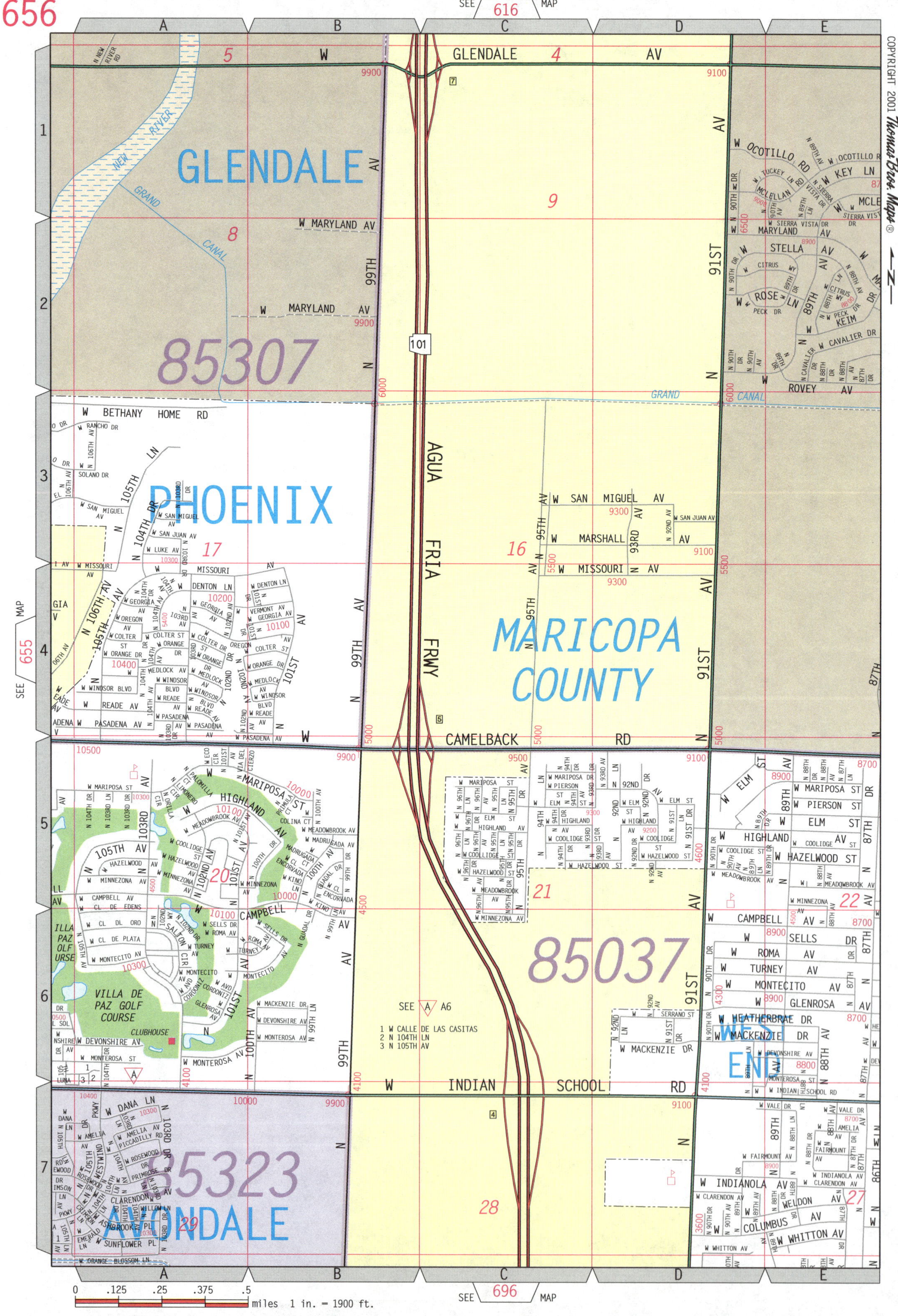

SEE 616 MAP
SEE 655 MAP
SEE 696 MAP
PHOENIX
MAP
GLENDALE
PHOENIX
MARICOPA COUNTY
AVONDALE
WEST END
85307
85037
85323
W GLENDALE AV
W MARYLAND AV
W BETHANY HOME RD
W CAMELBACK RD
W INDIAN SCHOOL RD
N 99TH AV
N 91ST AV
AGUA FRIA FRWY
101
NEW RIVER
GRAND CANAL
N NEW RIVER RD
W MISSOURI AV
W SAN MIGUEL AV
W MARSHALL AV
W OCOTILLO RD
W STELLA AV
W ROVEY AV
W CAVALIER DR
W CAMPBELL AV
W HIGHLAND AV
W MARIPOSA ST
W MONTECITO AV
W GLENROSA AV
W MACKENZIE DR
W DEVONSHIRE AV
W MONTEROSA ST
W INDIANOLA AV
W COLUMBUS AV
W WHITTON AV
W WELDON AV
W SUNFLOWER PL
W ORANGE BLOSSOM LN
W DANA LN
VILLA DE PAZ GOLF COURSE
CLUBHOUSE
SEE A A6
1 W CALLE DE LAS CASITAS
2 N 104TH LN
3 N 105TH AV
0 .125 .25 .375 .5
miles 1 in. = 1900 ft.

SEE 616 MAP

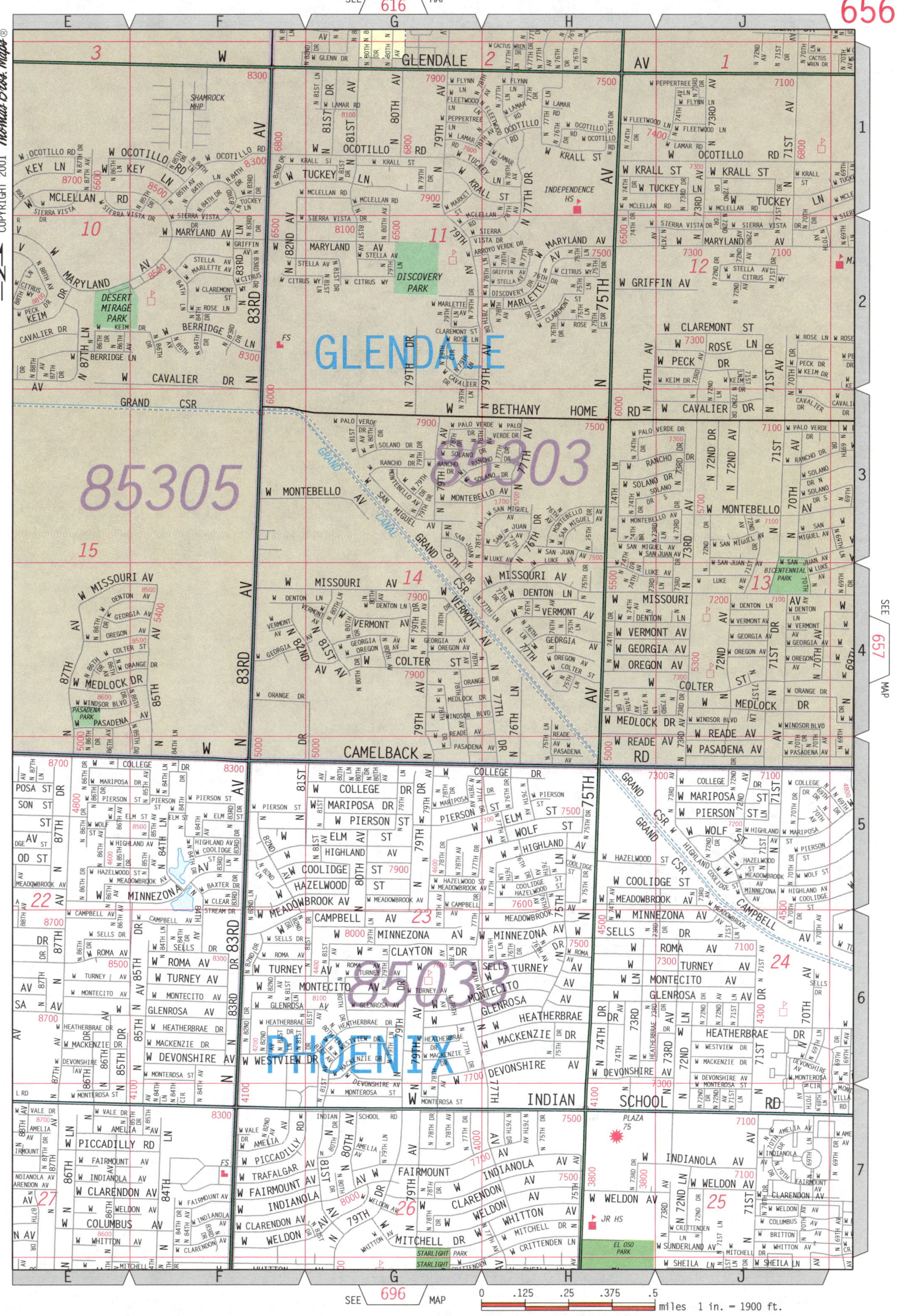

SEE 657 MAP

SEE 696 MAP

SEE 617 MAP

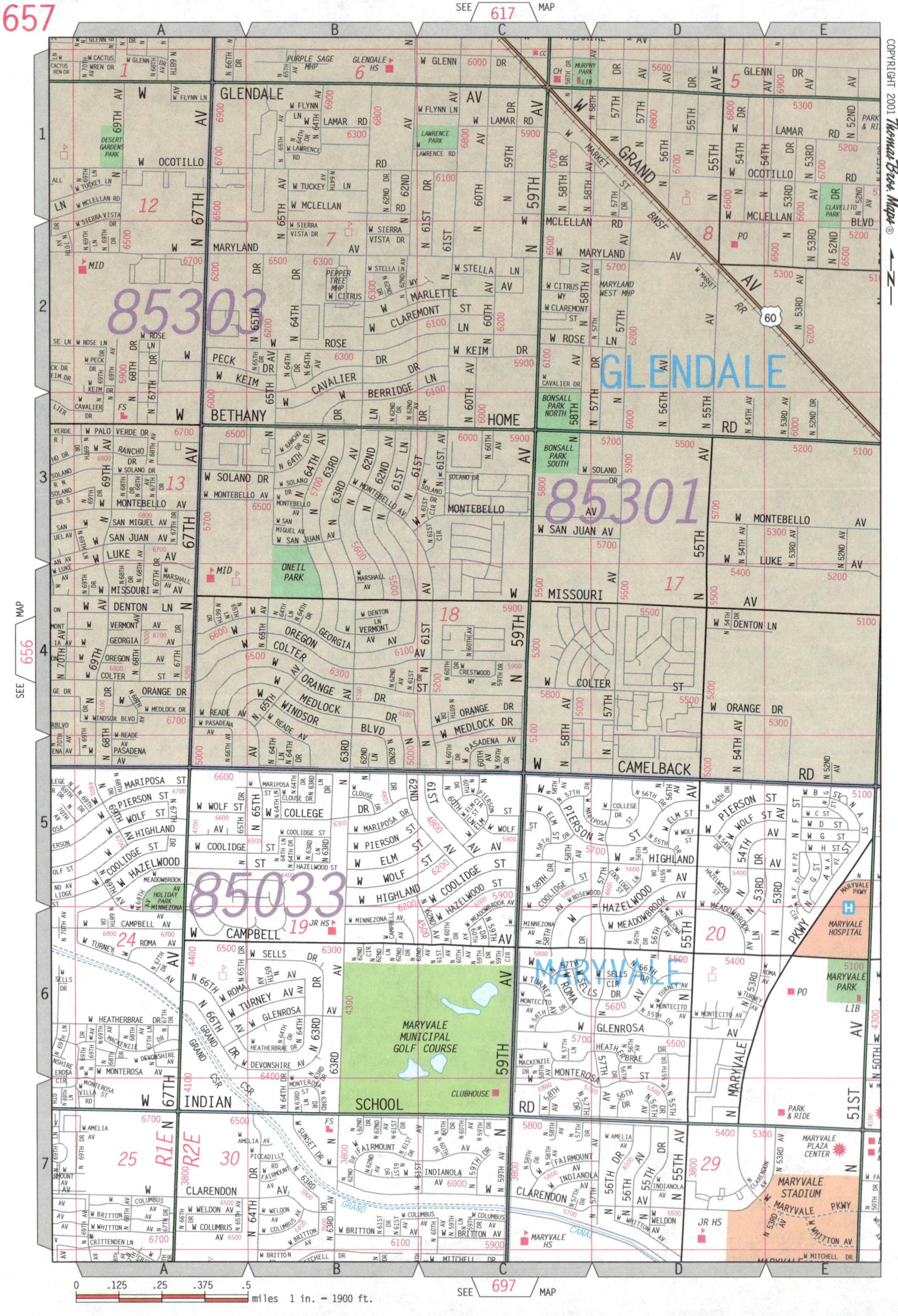

SEE 697 MAP

SEE 617 MAP

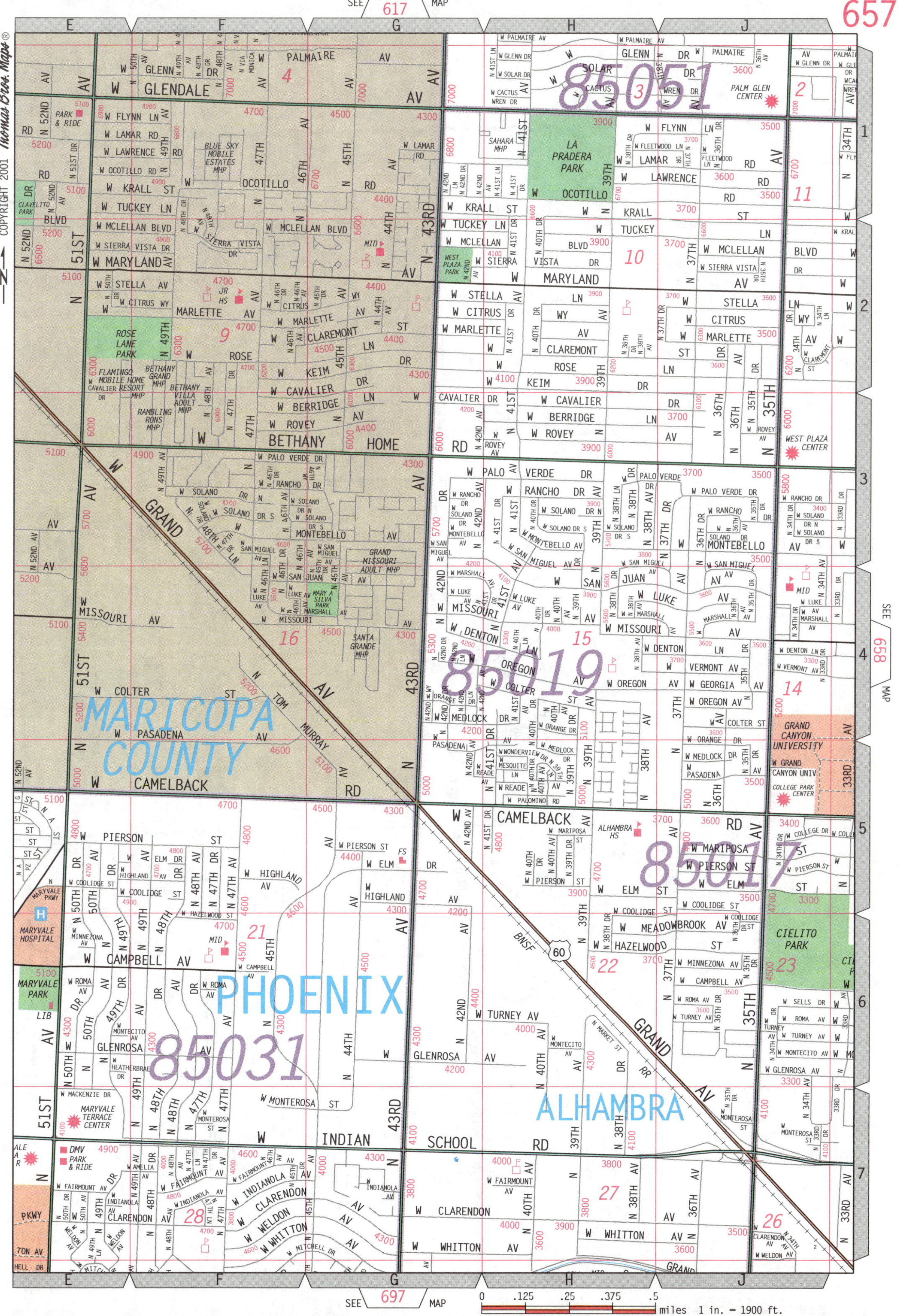

SEE 658 MAP

SEE 697 MAP

0 .125 .25 .375 .5 miles 1 in. = 1900 ft.

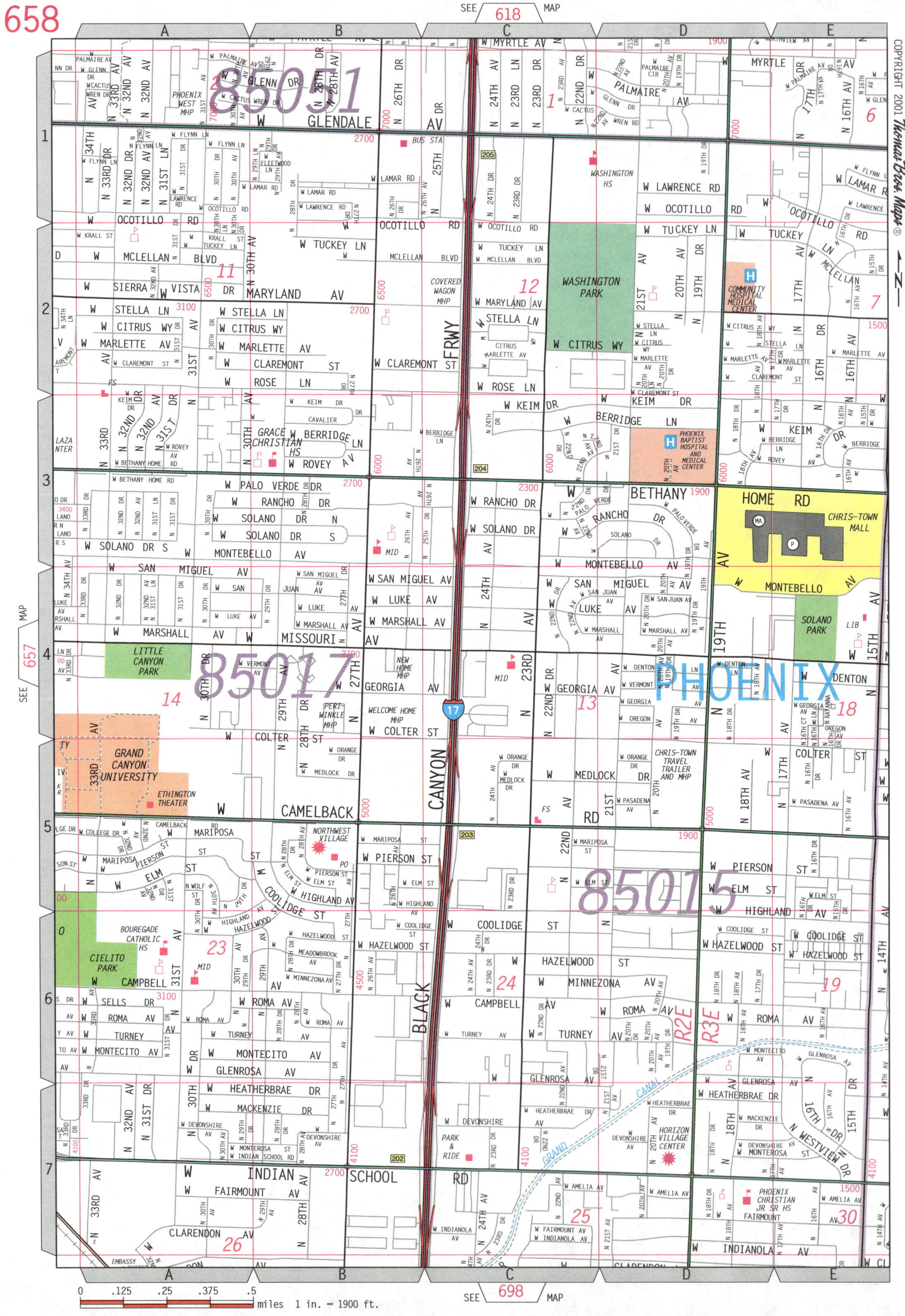

SEE 618 MAP
SEE 657 MAP
SEE 698 MAP
85051
85017
85015
PHOENIX
GLENDALE AV
CAMELBACK RD
INDIAN SCHOOL RD
BETHANY HOME RD
BLACK CANYON FRWY
MARYLAND AV
MISSOURI AV
WASHINGTON PARK
LITTLE CANYON PARK
GRAND CANYON UNIVERSITY
ETHINGTON THEATER
CIELITO PARK
BOUREGADE CATHOLIC HS
GRACE CHRISTIAN HS
WASHINGTON HS
COMMUNITY HOSPITAL MEDICAL CENTER
PHOENIX BAPTIST HOSPITAL AND MEDICAL CENTER
CHRIS-TOWN MALL
SOLANO PARK
CHRIS-TOWN TRAVEL TRAILER AND MHP
NORTHWEST VILLAGE
HORIZON VILLAGE CENTER
PHOENIX CHRISTIAN JR SR HS
PHOENIX WEST MHP
COVERED WAGON MHP
NEW HOME MHP
WELCOME HOME MHP
PERIWINKLE MHP
PARK & RIDE
GRAND CANAL
R2E
R3E
0 .125 .25 .375 .5 miles 1 in. = 1900 ft.

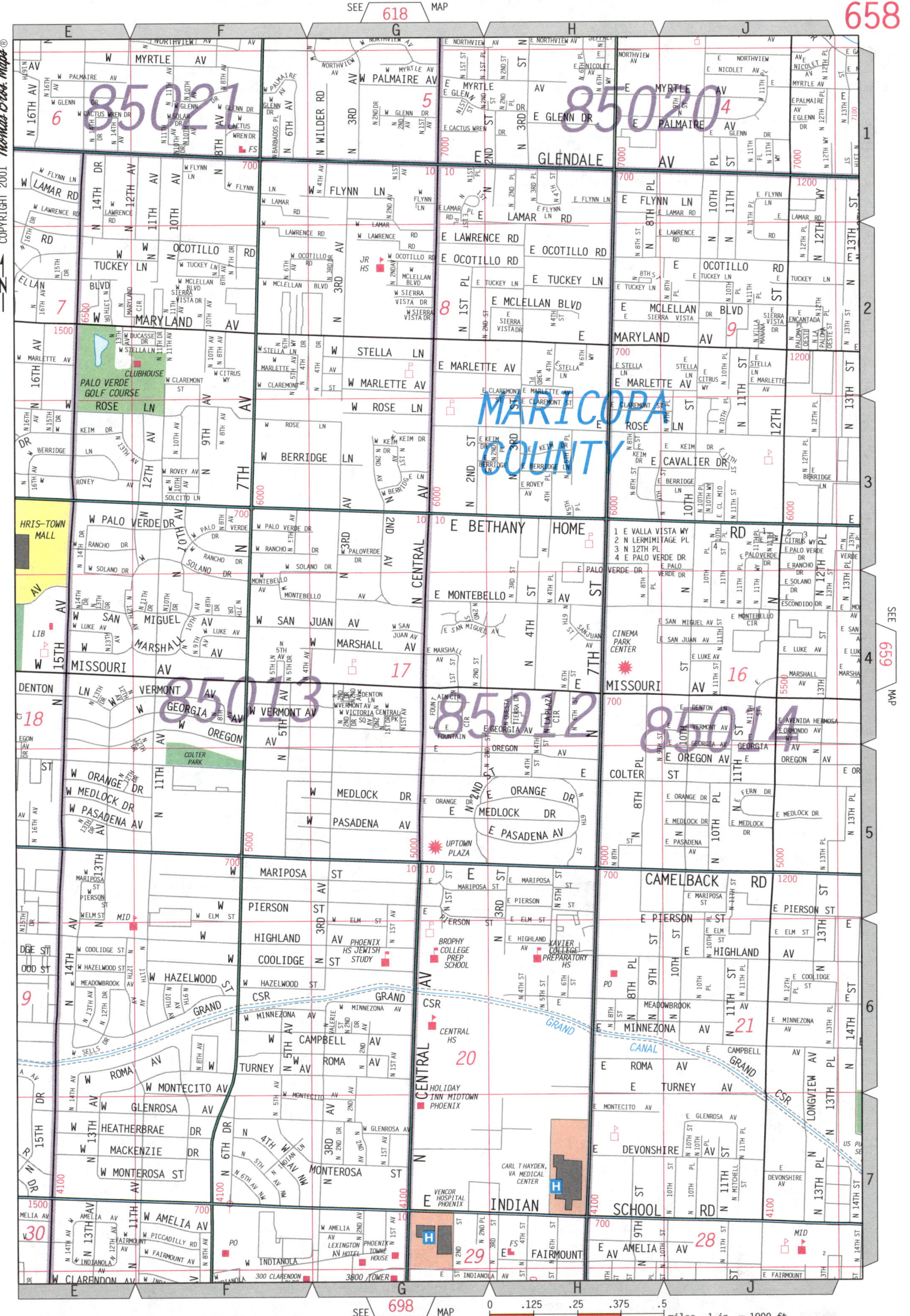
SEE 618 MAP
E
F
G
H
J
85021
85020
85013
85012
85014
MARICOPA COUNTY
PHOENIX
MAP
SEE 659 MAP
W MYRTLE AV
W PALMAIRE AV
W GLENN DR
GLENDALE AV
E GLENN DR
E MYRTLE AV
E PALMAIRE AV
W LAMAR RD
W FLYNN LN
E FLYNN LN
E LAMAR RD
W OCOTILLO RD
E OCOTILLO RD
E LAWRENCE RD
W TUCKEY LN
E TUCKEY LN
E MCLELLAN BLVD
W MARYLAND AV
E MARYLAND AV
W STELLA LN
E MARLETTE AV
W MARLETTE AV
W ROSE LN
E ROSE LN
W BERRIDGE LN
E CAVALIER DR
PALO VERDE GOLF COURSE
CLUBHOUSE
JR HS
E BETHANY HOME RD
W PALO VERDE DR
W SAN MIGUEL AV
W SAN JUAN AV
W MARSHALL AV
W MISSOURI AV
E MISSOURI AV
E MONTEBELLO AV
CHRIS-TOWN MALL
LIB
CINEMA PARK CENTER
W VERMONT AV
W GEORGIA AV
W OREGON AV
E OREGON AV
COLTER PARK
COLTER ST
W ORANGE DR
W MEDLOCK DR
W PASADENA AV
E ORANGE DR
E MEDLOCK DR
E PASADENA AV
UPTOWN PLAZA
CAMELBACK RD
W MARIPOSA ST
W PIERSON ST
E PIERSON ST
W HIGHLAND AV
E HIGHLAND AV
W COOLIDGE ST
W HAZELWOOD ST
PHOENIX HS JEWISH STUDY
BROPHY COLLEGE PREP SCHOOL
XAVIER COLLEGE PREPARATORY HS
GRAND CANAL
W MINNEZONA AV
E MINNEZONA AV
W CAMPBELL AV
CENTRAL HS
W ROMA AV
E ROMA AV
W TURNEY AV
E TURNEY AV
W MONTECITO AV
W GLENROSA AV
W HEATHERBRAE DR
W MACKENZIE DR
W MONTEROSA ST
HOLIDAY INN MIDTOWN PHOENIX
CARL T HAYDEN VA MEDICAL CENTER
VENCOR HOSPITAL PHOENIX
E DEVONSHIRE AV
INDIAN SCHOOL RD
W AMELIA AV
E AMELIA AV
W INDIANOLA AV
W CLARENDON AV
LEXINGTON HOTEL
PHOENIX TOWNE HOUSE
300 CLARENDON
3800 TOWER
E FAIRMOUNT AV
N CENTRAL AV
N 7TH ST
N 7TH AV
N 15TH AV
N 16TH ST
SEE 698 MAP
0 .125 .25 .375 .5 miles 1 in. = 1900 ft.
Thomas Bros. Maps®
COPYRIGHT 2001

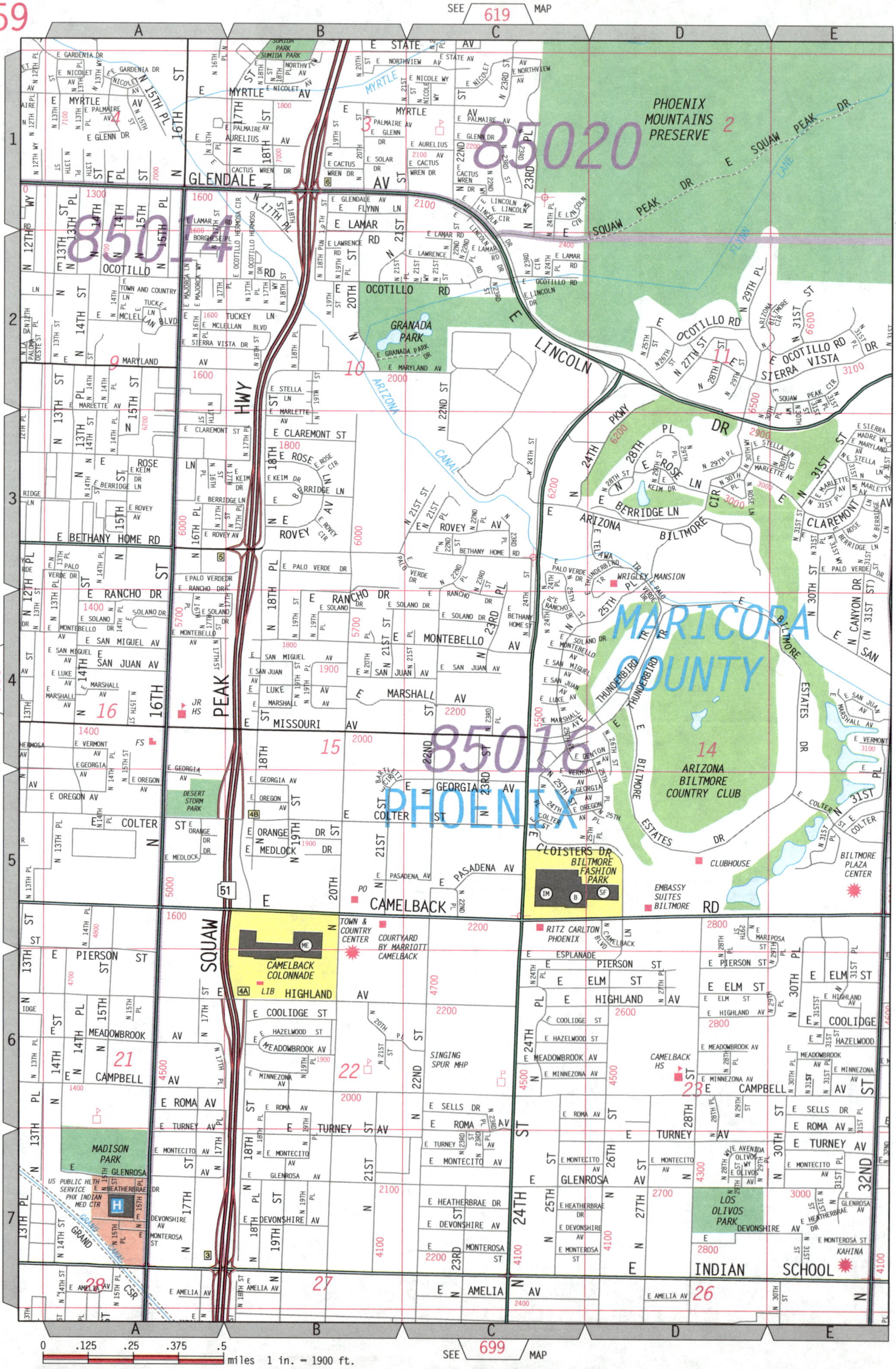

SEE 619 MAP

SEE 658 MAP

SEE 699 MAP

PHOENIX MOUNTAINS PRESERVE

85020

85014

85016

PHOENIX

MARICOPA COUNTY

ARIZONA BILTMORE COUNTRY CLUB

GRANADA PARK

DESERT STORM PARK

MADISON PARK

LOS OLIVOS PARK

SUMIDA PARK

BILTMORE FASHION PARK

CAMELBACK COLONNADE

BILTMORE PLAZA CENTER

TOWN & COUNTRY CENTER

COURTYARD BY MARRIOTT CAMELBACK

RITZ CARLTON PHOENIX

EMBASSY SUITES BILTMORE

WRIGLEY MANSION

CLUBHOUSE

CAMELBACK HS

JR HS

SINGING SPUR MHP

US PUBLIC HLTH SERVICE PHX INDIAN MED CTR

KAHINA

ARIZONA CANAL

GRAND CANAL

E GLENDALE AV

E LINCOLN DR

E SQUAW PEAK DR

SQUAW PEAK HWY

E OCOTILLO RD

E BETHANY HOME RD

E MISSOURI AV

E CAMELBACK RD

E INDIAN SCHOOL RD

E MYRTLE AV

E LAMAR RD

E ROSE LN

E MARSHALL AV

E COLTER ST

E HIGHLAND AV

E CAMPBELL AV

E TURNEY AV

E AMELIA AV

N 16TH ST

N 20TH ST

N 24TH ST

N 32ND ST

N 40TH ST

BILTMORE ESTATES DR

0 .125 .25 .375 .5 miles 1 in. = 1900 ft.

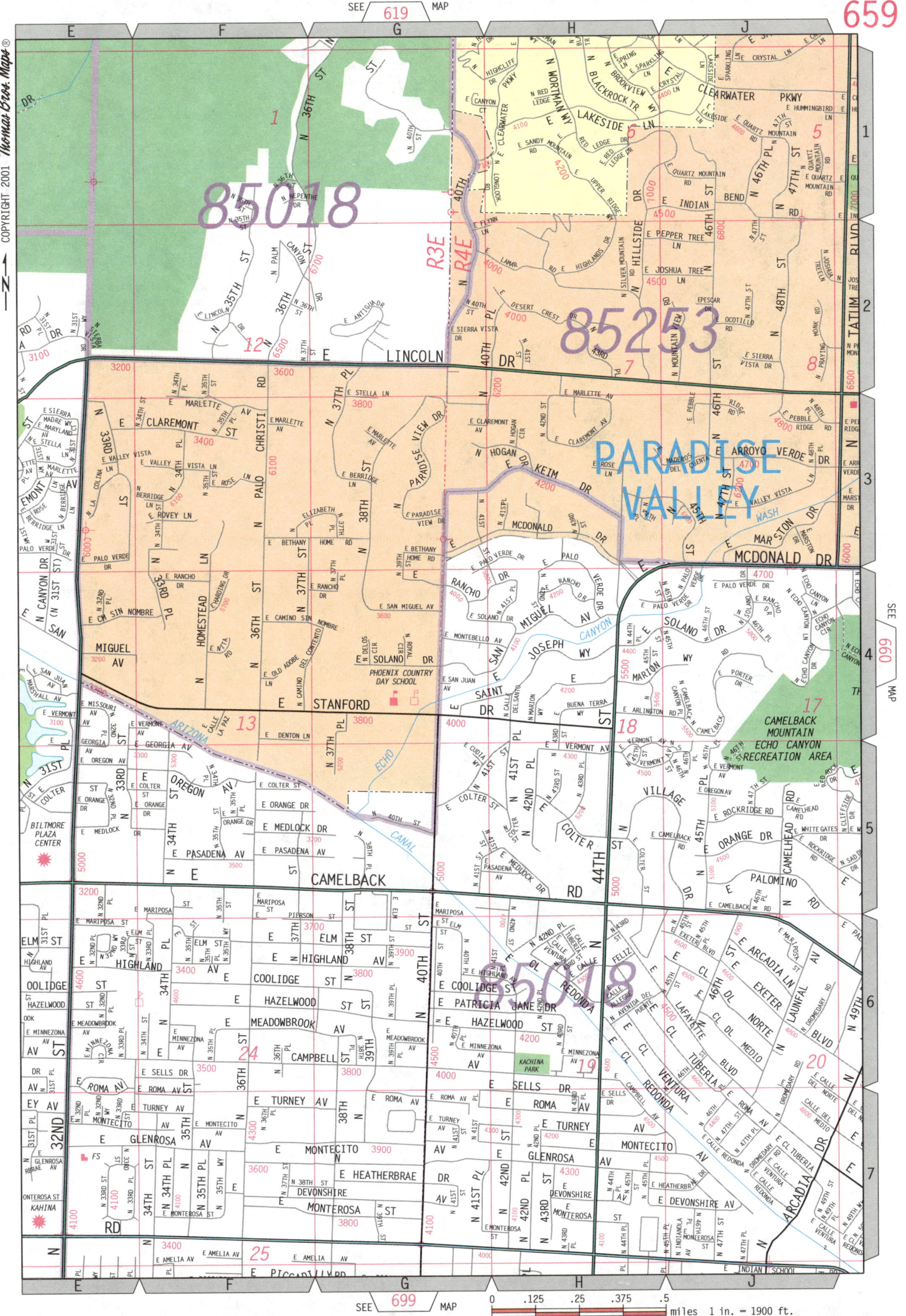
SEE 619 MAP
SEE 699 MAP
SEE 660 MAP
PHOENIX
MAP
85018
85253
PARADISE VALLEY
R3E
R4E
E LINCOLN DR
CAMELBACK RD
E MCDONALD DR
TATUM BLVD
E CLEARWATER PKWY
E STANFORD DR
ARIZONA CANAL
PHOENIX COUNTRY DAY SCHOOL
CAMELBACK MOUNTAIN ECHO CANYON RECREATION AREA
BILTMORE PLAZA CENTER
KACHINA PARK
0 .125 .25 .375 .5 miles 1 in. = 1900 ft.

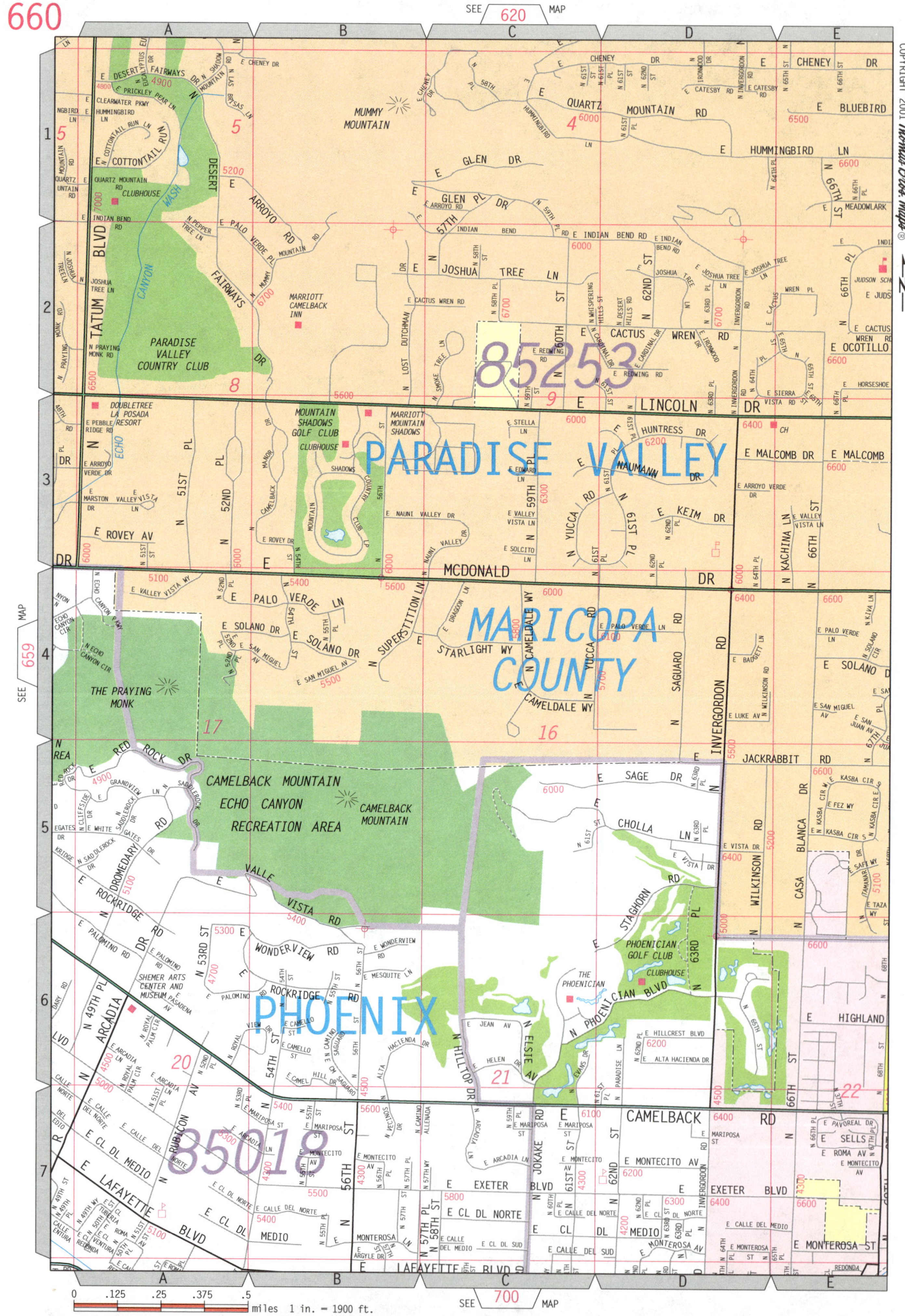
SEE 620 MAP
SEE 659 MAP
SEE 700 MAP
PHOENIX
MAP
MUMMY MOUNTAIN
PARADISE VALLEY COUNTRY CLUB
MARRIOTT CAMELBACK INN
QUARTZ MOUNTAIN RD
HUMMINGBIRD LN
INDIAN BEND RD
JOSHUA TREE LN
CACTUS WREN RD
LINCOLN DR
85253
DOUBLETREE LA POSADA RESORT
MOUNTAIN SHADOWS GOLF CLUB
MARRIOTT MOUNTAIN SHADOWS
PARADISE VALLEY
MCDONALD DR
MARICOPA COUNTY
THE PRAYING MONK
CAMELBACK MOUNTAIN ECHO CANYON RECREATION AREA
CAMELBACK MOUNTAIN
JACKRABBIT RD
PHOENICIAN GOLF CLUB
THE PHOENICIAN
SHEMER ARTS CENTER AND MUSEUM
PHOENIX
CAMELBACK RD
85018
TATUM BLVD
INVERGORDON RD
HIGHLAND
LAFAYETTE BLVD
0 .125 .25 .375 .5 miles 1 in. = 1900 ft.

SEE 620 MAP
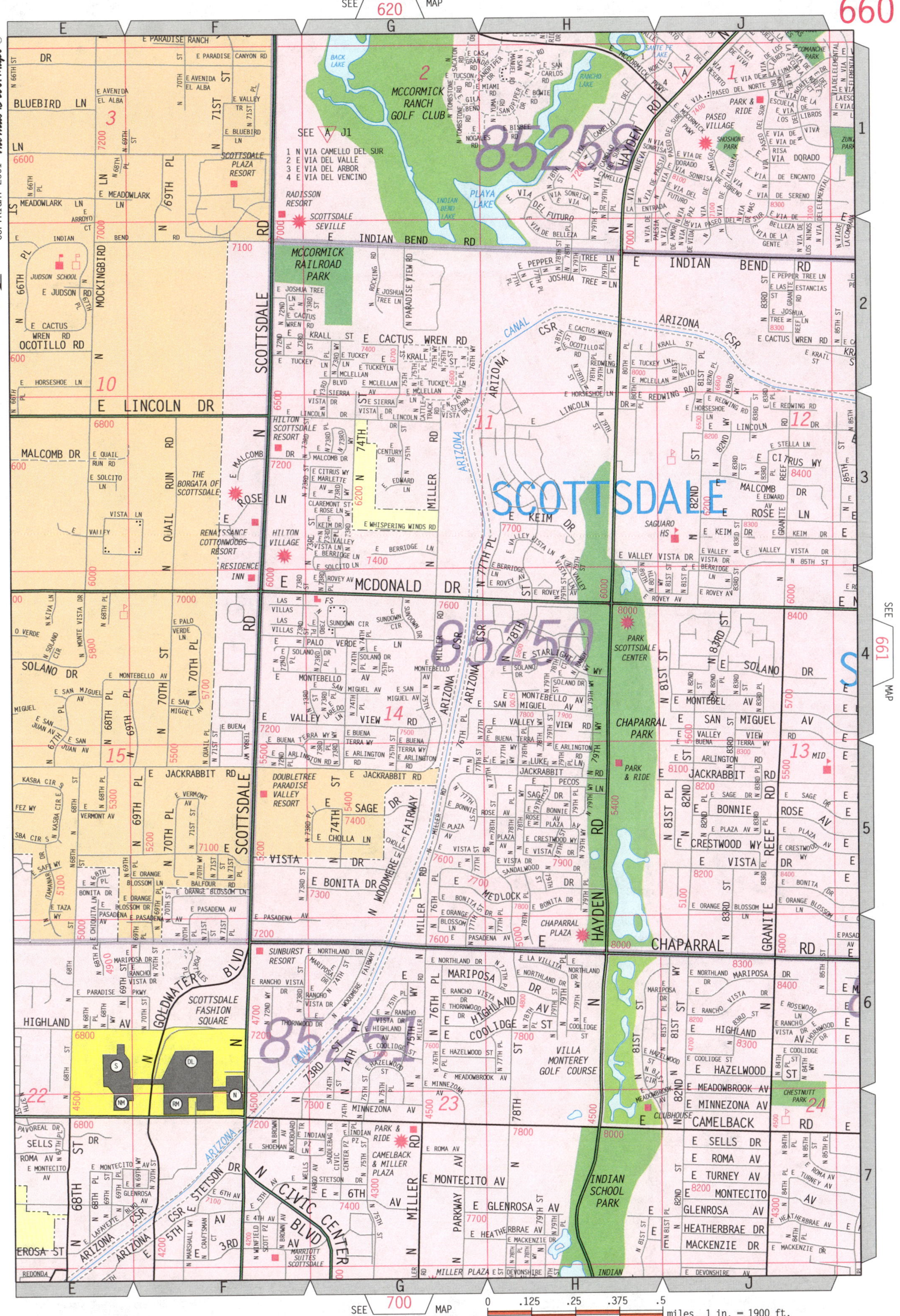

SEE 700 MAP

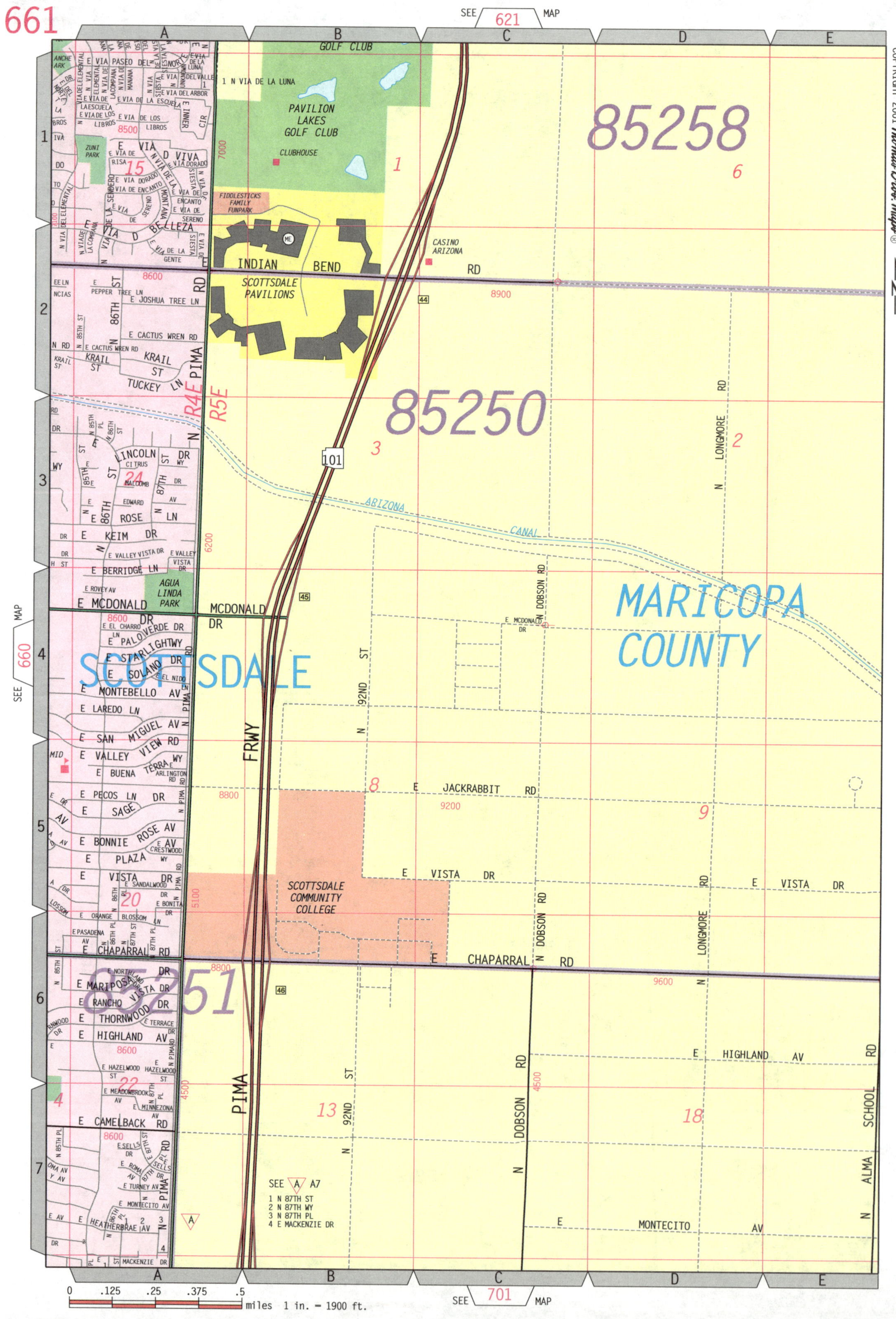

SEE 621 MAP
85258
85250
85251
PAVILION LAKES GOLF CLUB
CLUBHOUSE
FIDDLESTICKS FAMILY FUNPARK
CASINO ARIZONA
INDIAN BEND RD
SCOTTSDALE PAVILIONS
ZUNI PARK
AGUA LINDA PARK
E MCDONALD DR
MCDONALD DR
SCOTTSDALE
MARICOPA COUNTY
ARIZONA CANAL
R4E
R5E
101
PIMA FRWY
N PIMA RD
N DOBSON RD
N LONGMORE RD
N 92ND ST
E JACKRABBIT RD
E VISTA DR
SCOTTSDALE COMMUNITY COLLEGE
E CHAPARRAL RD
E HIGHLAND AV
E MONTECITO AV
N ALMA SCHOOL RD
E CAMELBACK RD
SEE A A7
1 N 87TH ST
2 N 87TH WY
3 N 87TH PL
4 E MACKENZIE DR
SEE 660 MAP
SEE 701 MAP
miles 1 in. = 1900 ft.

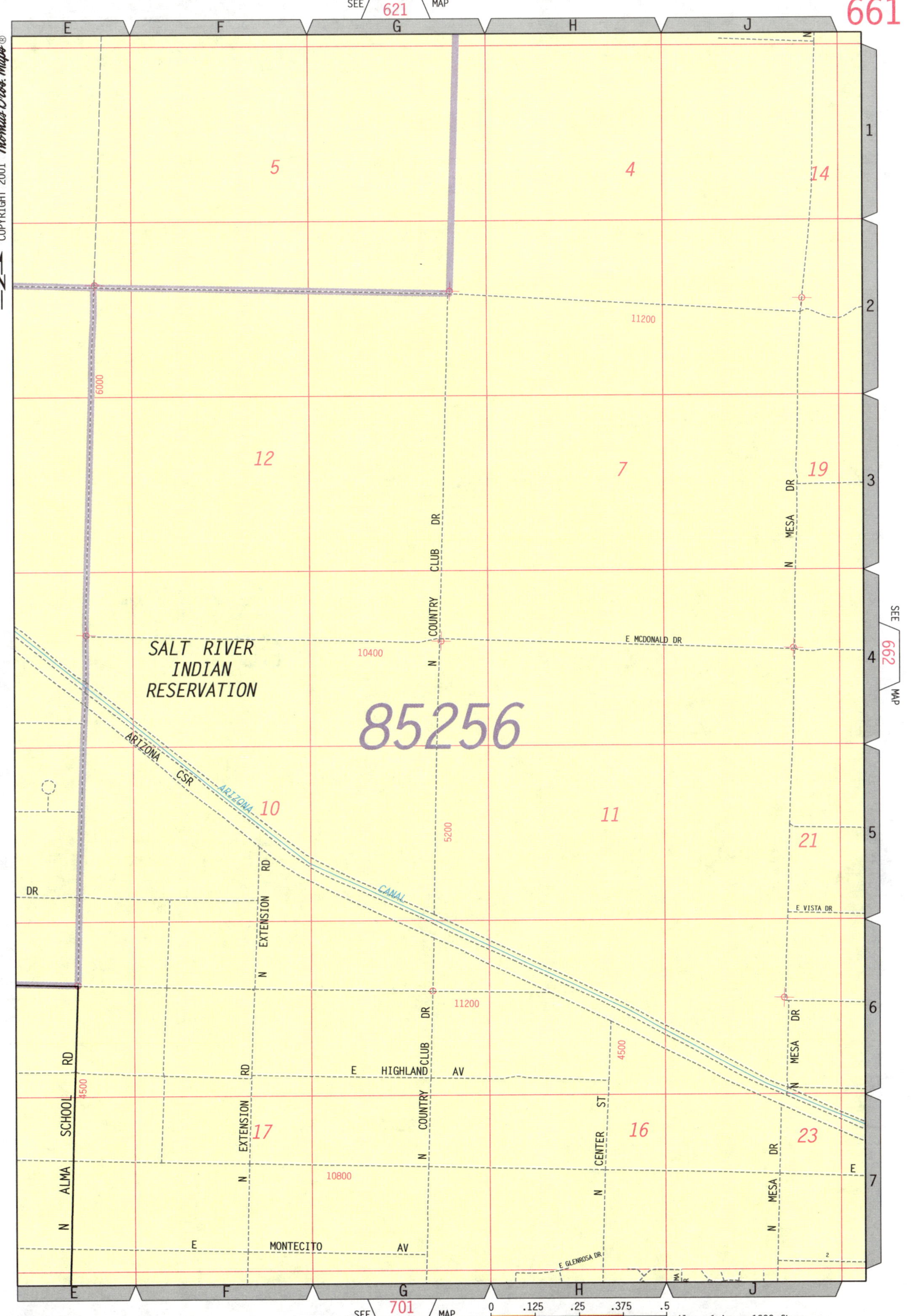
SEE 621 MAP
E
F
G
H
J
1
2
3
4
5
6
7
5
4
14
12
7
19
10
11
21
17
16
23
11200
6000
N MESA DR
N COUNTRY CLUB DR
E MCDONALD DR
10400
SALT RIVER
INDIAN
RESERVATION
85256
ARIZONA CSR
ARIZONA
CANAL
5200
N EXTENSION RD
DR
E VISTA DR
11200
4500
E HIGHLAND AV
N ALMA SCHOOL RD
4500
N CENTER ST
10800
E MONTECITO AV
E GLENROSA DR
SEE 662 MAP
SEE 701 MAP
0 .125 .25 .375 .5
miles 1 in. = 1900 ft.
PHOENIX
MAP

SEE 622 MAP

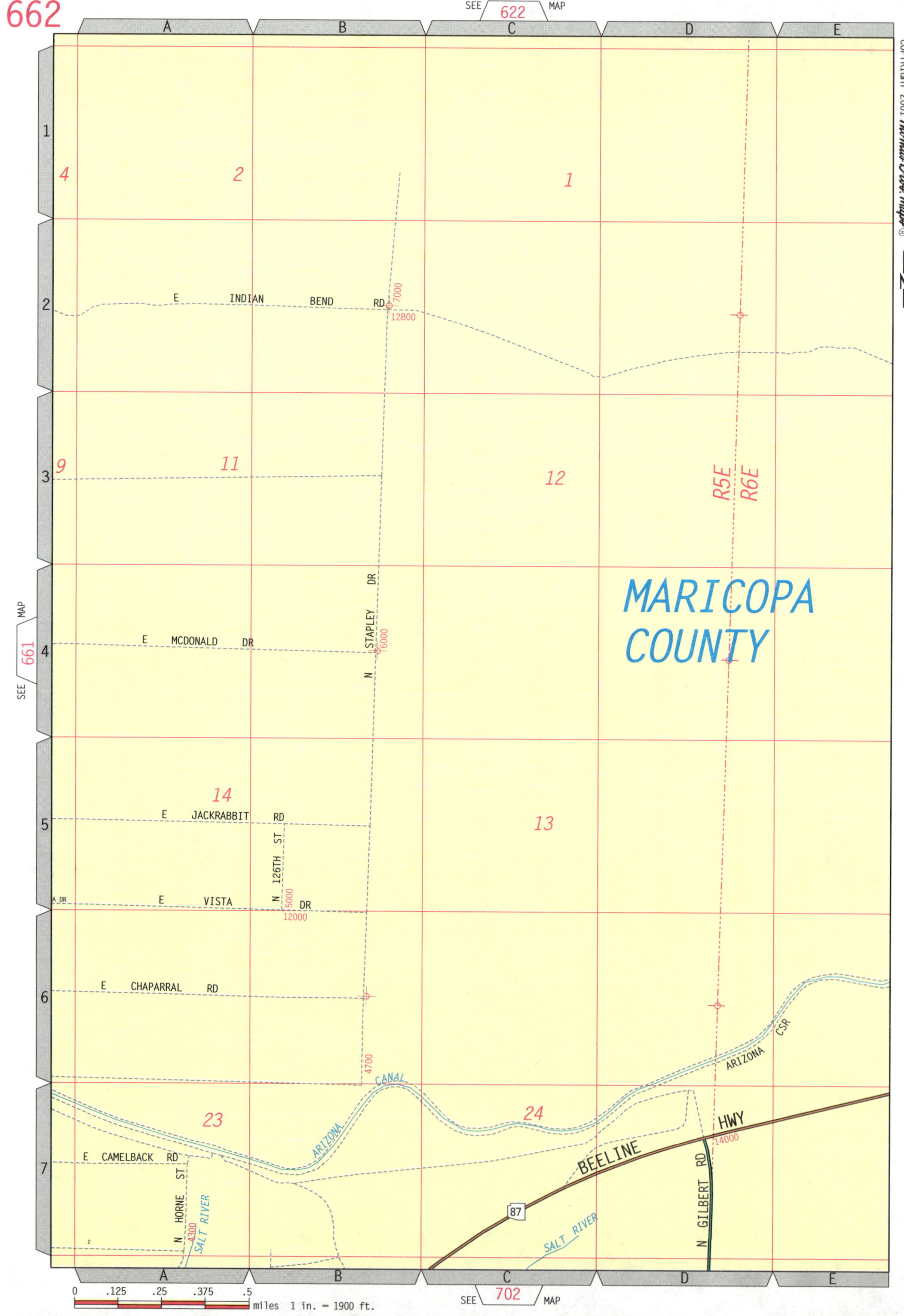

SEE 661 MAP

SEE 702 MAP

PHOENIX

MAP

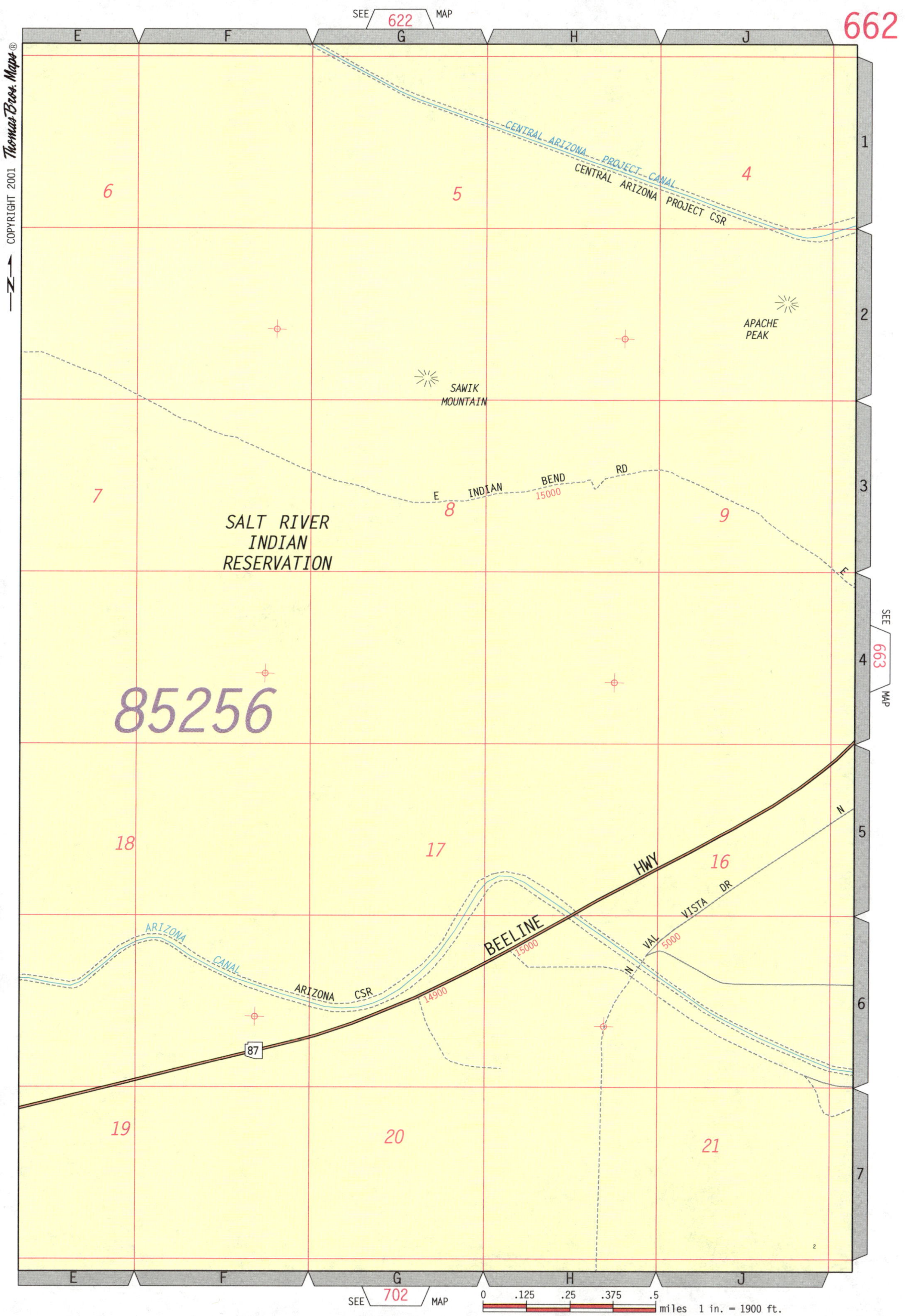
SEE 622 MAP
E
F
G
H
J
1
2
3
4
5
6
7
CENTRAL ARIZONA PROJECT CANAL
CENTRAL ARIZONA PROJECT CSR
APACHE PEAK
SAWIK MOUNTAIN
E INDIAN BEND RD
15000
SALT RIVER INDIAN RESERVATION
85256
SEE 663 MAP
BEELINE HWY
N VISTA DR
N VAL
5000
15000
14900
ARIZONA CANAL
ARIZONA CSR
87
6
5
4
7
8
9
18
17
16
19
20
21
SEE 702 MAP
0 .125 .25 .375 .5 miles 1 in. = 1900 ft.
PHOENIX
MAP

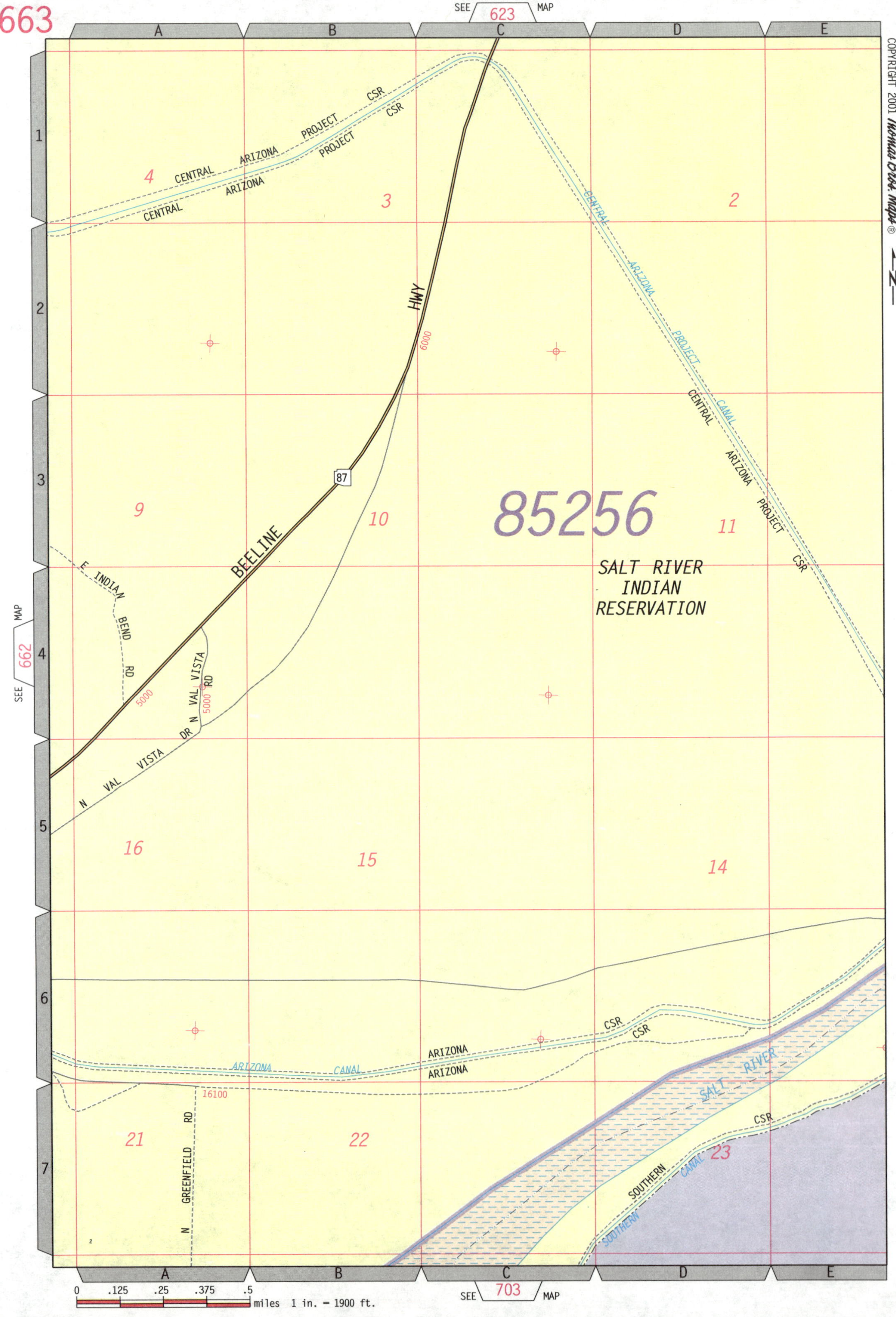

SEE 623 MAP
SEE 662 MAP
SEE 703 MAP
85256
SALT RIVER
INDIAN
RESERVATION
CENTRAL ARIZONA PROJECT CSR
CENTRAL ARIZONA PROJECT CANAL
BEELINE HWY
87
E INDIAN BEND RD
N VAL VISTA RD
N VAL VISTA DR
ARIZONA CANAL
ARIZONA CSR
N GREENFIELD RD
SALT RIVER
SOUTHERN CANAL
CSR
16100
6000
5000
4
3
2
9
10
11
16
15
14
21
22
23
A
B
C
D
E
1
2
3
4
5
6
7
0 .125 .25 .375 .5
miles 1 in. = 1900 ft.

PHOENIX

MAP

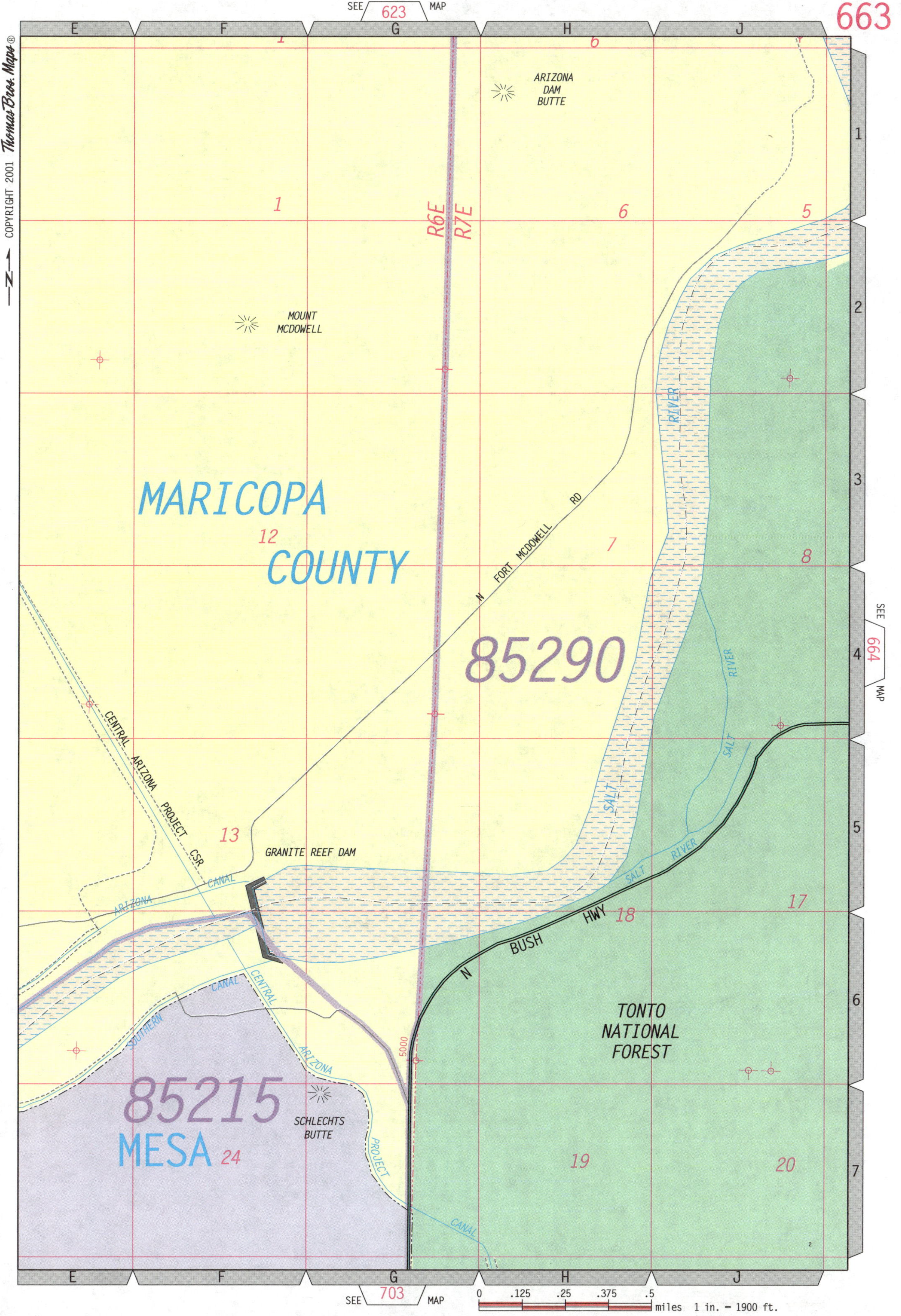
SEE 623 MAP
E
F
G
H
J
ARIZONA
DAM
BUTTE
MOUNT
MCDOWELL
R6E
R7E
MARICOPA
COUNTY
N FORT MCDOWELL RD
85290
RIVER
SEE 664 MAP
SALT
CENTRAL ARIZONA PROJECT CSR
GRANITE REEF DAM
ARIZONA
CANAL
N BUSH HWY
TONTO
NATIONAL
FOREST
SOUTHERN
CANAL
CENTRAL
ARIZONA
PROJECT
85215
MESA
SCHLECHTS
BUTTE
5000
SEE 703 MAP
0 .125 .25 .375 .5 miles 1 in. = 1900 ft.
PHOENIX
MAP

SEE 103 MAP

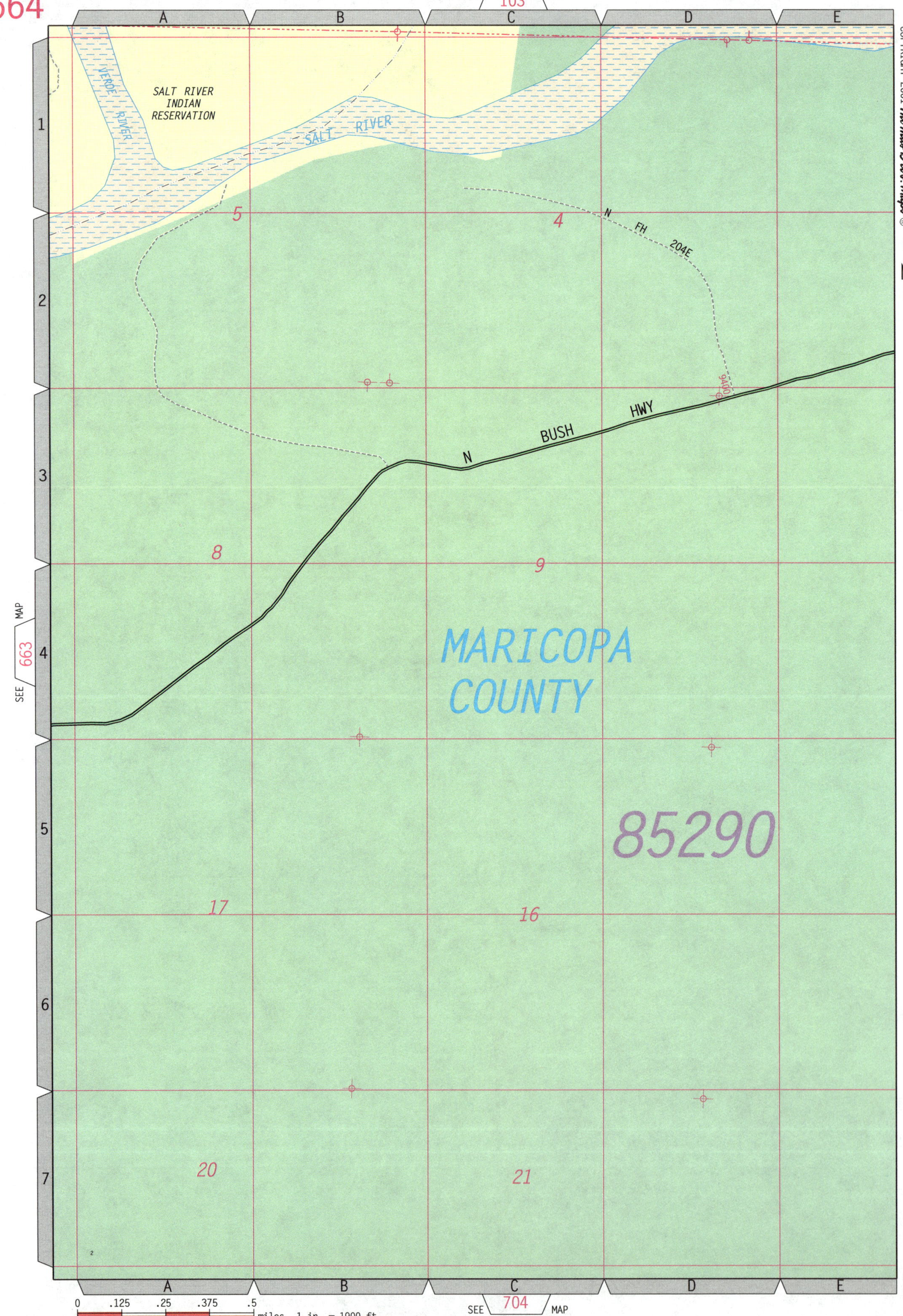

SEE 663 MAP

SEE 704 MAP

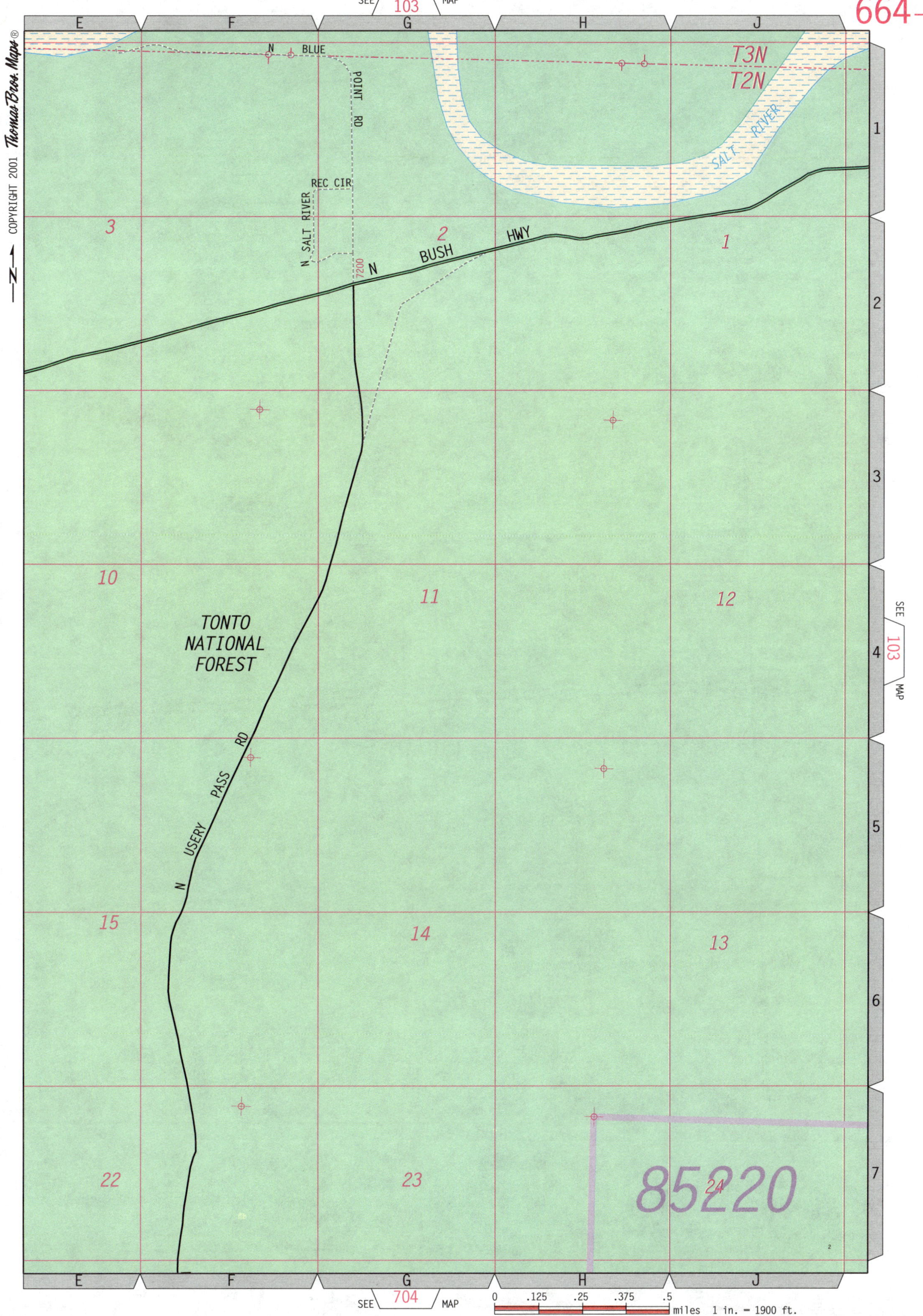
SEE 103 MAP
E
F
G
H
J
N BLUE
POINT RD
T3N
T2N
SALT RIVER
REC CIR
N SALT RIVER
1
2
3
4
5
6
7
3
2
1
N BUSH HWY
7200
10
11
12
TONTO
NATIONAL
FOREST
SEE 103 MAP
N USERY PASS RD
15
14
13
22
23
24
85220
SEE 704 MAP
0 .125 .25 .375 .5
miles 1 in. = 1900 ft.
PHOENIX
MAP

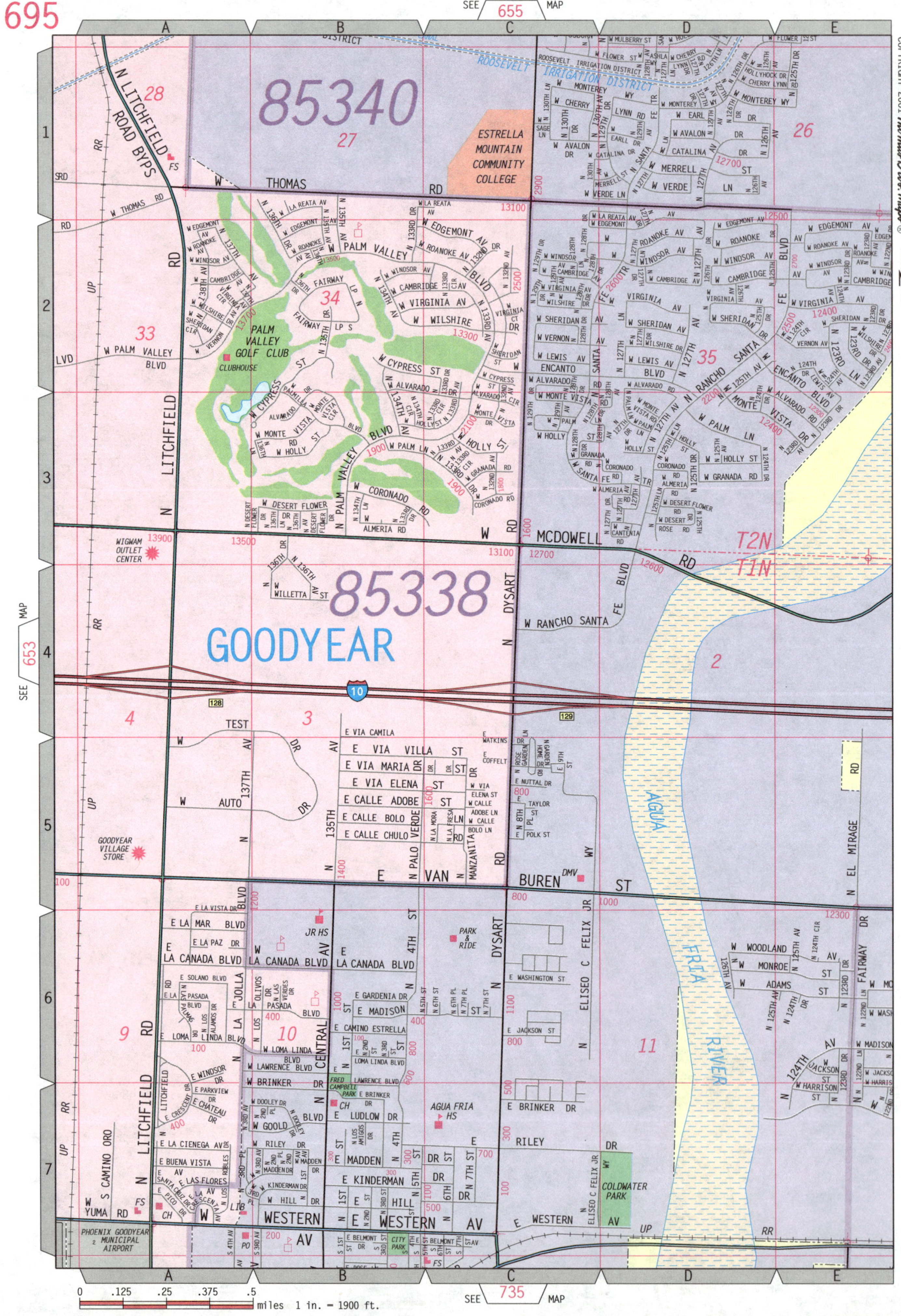

SEE 655 MAP
SEE 653 MAP
SEE 735 MAP
A
B
C
D
E
1
2
3
4
5
6
7
85340
85338
GOODYEAR
PHOENIX
ESTRELLA MOUNTAIN COMMUNITY COLLEGE
PALM VALLEY GOLF CLUB
CLUBHOUSE
WIGWAM OUTLET CENTER
GOODYEAR VILLAGE STORE
PHOENIX GOODYEAR MUNICIPAL AIRPORT
COLDWATER PARK
FRED CAMPBELL PARK
CITY PARK
AGUA FRIA HS
JR HS
PARK & RIDE
DMV
AGUA FRIA RIVER
ROOSEVELT IRRIGATION DISTRICT
N LITCHFIELD ROAD BYPS
W THOMAS RD
W PALM VALLEY BLVD
MCDOWELL RD
N DYSART RD
W RANCHO SANTA FE BLVD
E VAN BUREN ST
W WESTERN AV
N LITCHFIELD RD
N CENTRAL AV
N ELISEO C FELIX JR WY
N EL MIRAGE RD
T2N
T1N
10
128
129
28
27
26
33
34
35
4
3
2
9
10
11
COPYRIGHT 2001 Thomas Bros. Maps®
0 .125 .25 .375 .5
miles 1 in. = 1900 ft.

MAP

SEE 655 MAP

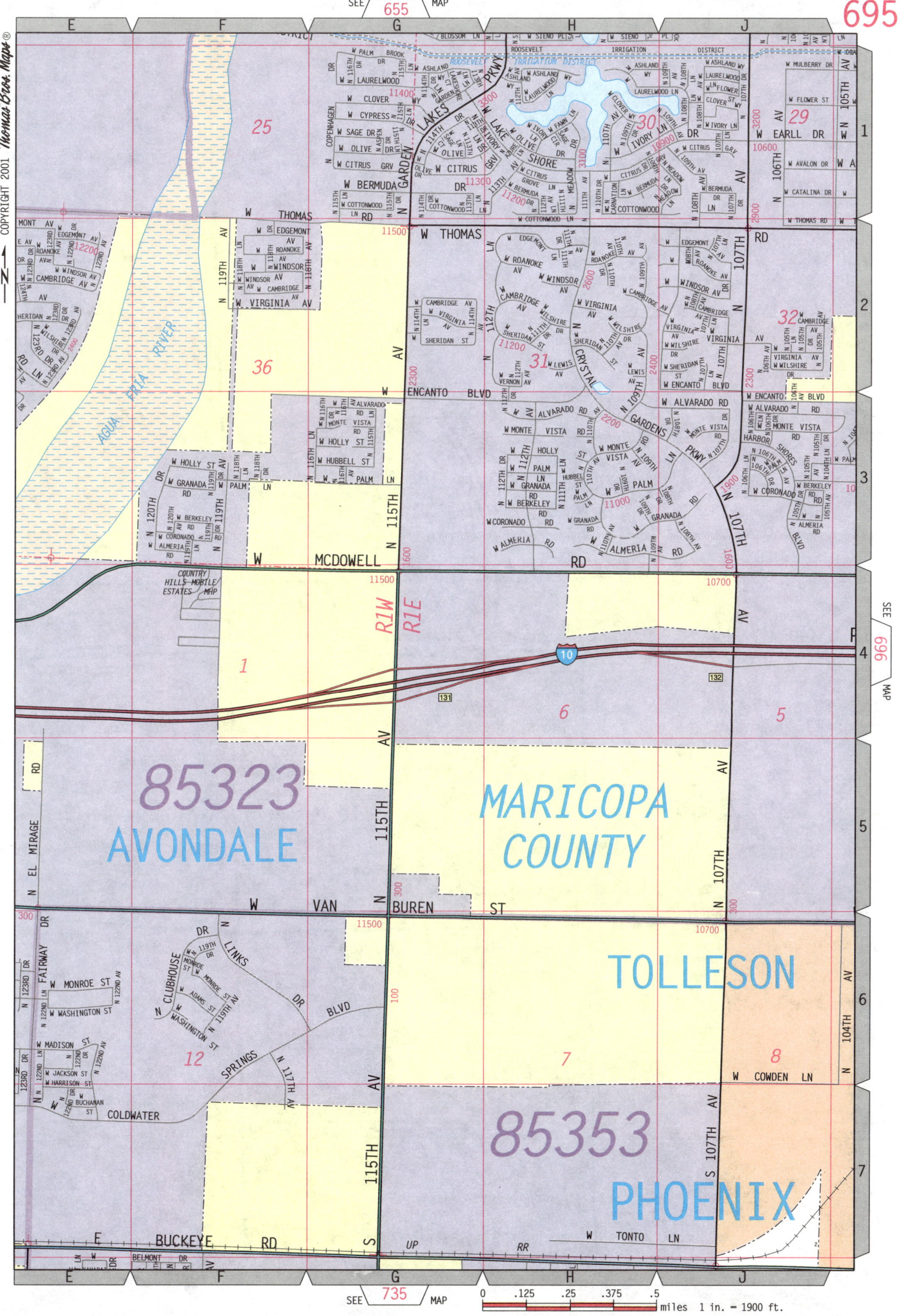

SEE 696 MAP

SEE 735 MAP

0 .125 .25 .375 .5 miles 1 in. = 1900 ft.

PHOENIX

MAP

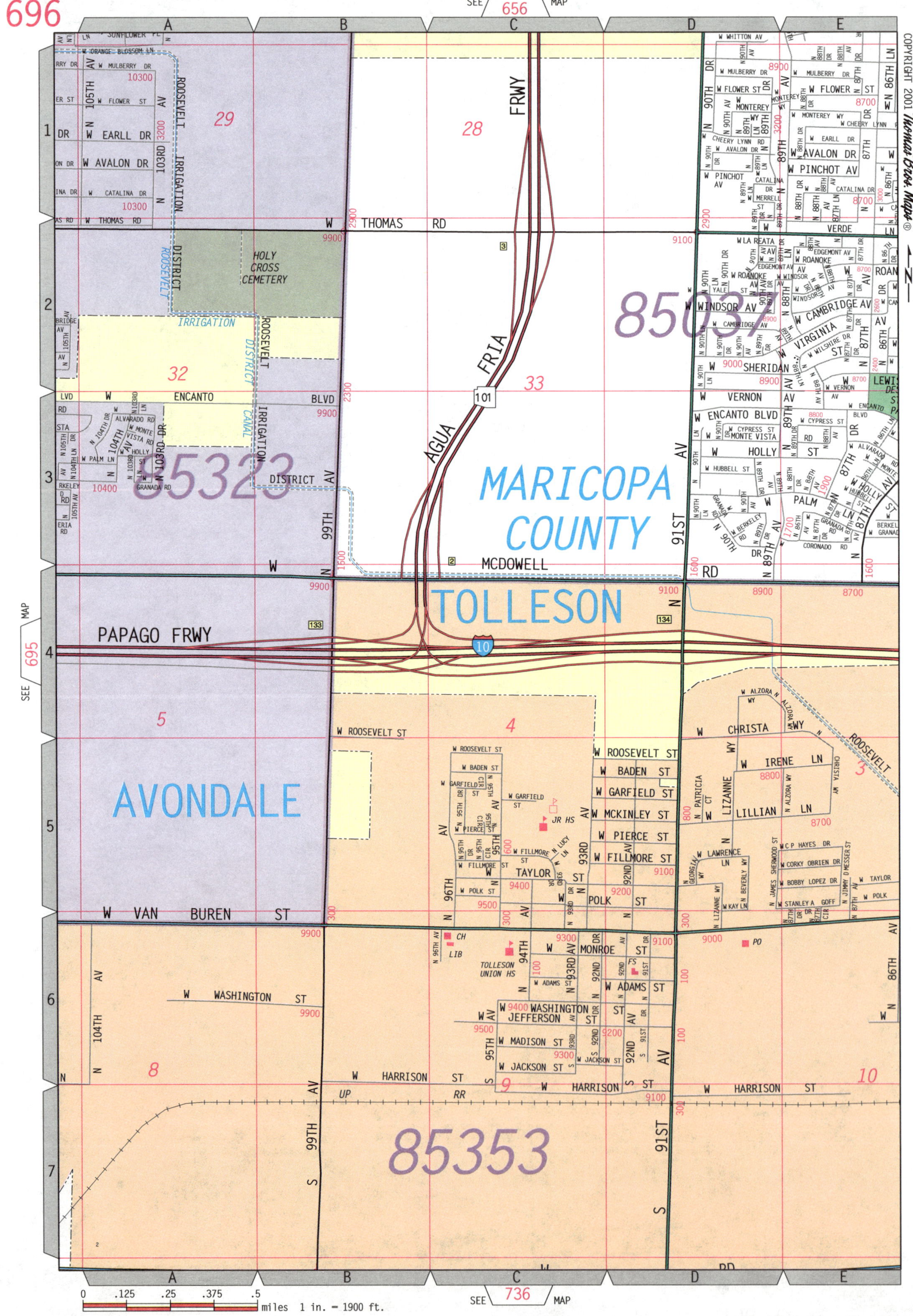
SEE 656 MAP
PHOENIX
MAP
SEE 695 MAP
W THOMAS RD
W ENCANTO BLVD
W MCDOWELL RD
PAPAGO FRWY
W ROOSEVELT ST
W VAN BUREN ST
W WASHINGTON ST
W HARRISON ST
UP RR
AGUA FRIA FRWY
101
10
ROOSEVELT IRRIGATION DISTRICT
ROOSEVELT DISTRICT IRRIGATION CANAL
HOLY CROSS CEMETERY
MARICOPA COUNTY
TOLLESON
AVONDALE
85323
85037
85353
99TH AV
91ST AV
104TH AV
103RD AV
105TH AV
W AVALON DR
W EARLL DR
W CATALINA DR
W MULBERRY DR
W FLOWER ST
W CAMBRIDGE AV
W VIRGINIA
SHERIDAN
VERNON AV
ENCANTO BLVD
HOLLY ST
PALM
W CHRISTA WY
W IRENE LN
LIZANNE WY
LILLIAN LN
W LAWRENCE LN
W BADEN ST
W GARFIELD ST
W MCKINLEY ST
W PIERCE ST
W FILLMORE ST
TAYLOR ST
POLK ST
MONROE ST
W ADAMS ST
JEFFERSON ST
W MADISON ST
W JACKSON ST
93RD AV
92ND AV
95TH AV
96TH AV
94TH AV
JR HS
TOLLESON UNION HS
CH
LIB
FS
PO
0 .125 .25 .375 .5 miles 1 in. = 1900 ft.
SEE 736 MAP

SEE 656 MAP

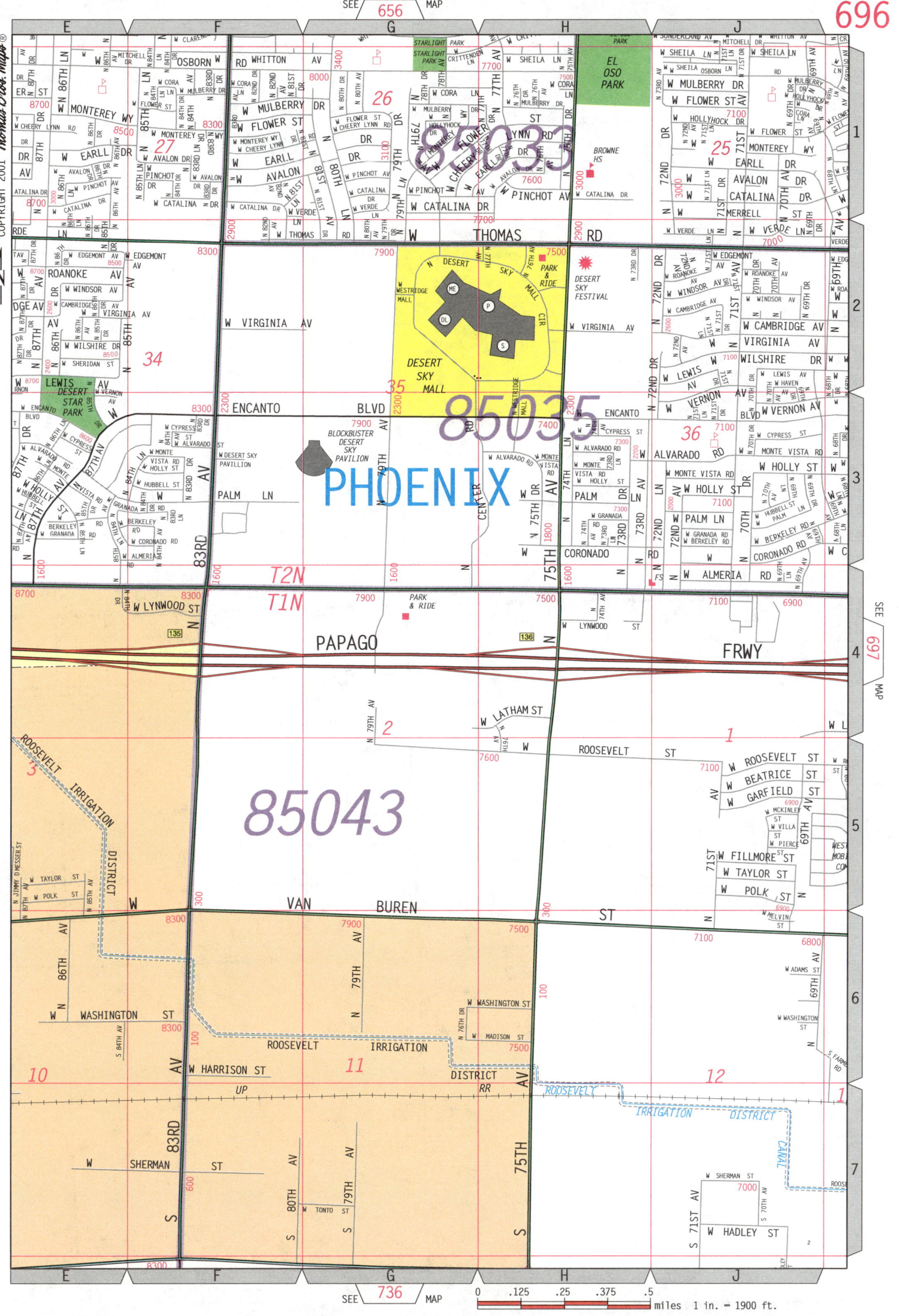

SEE 697 MAP

SEE 736 MAP

PHOENIX

MAP

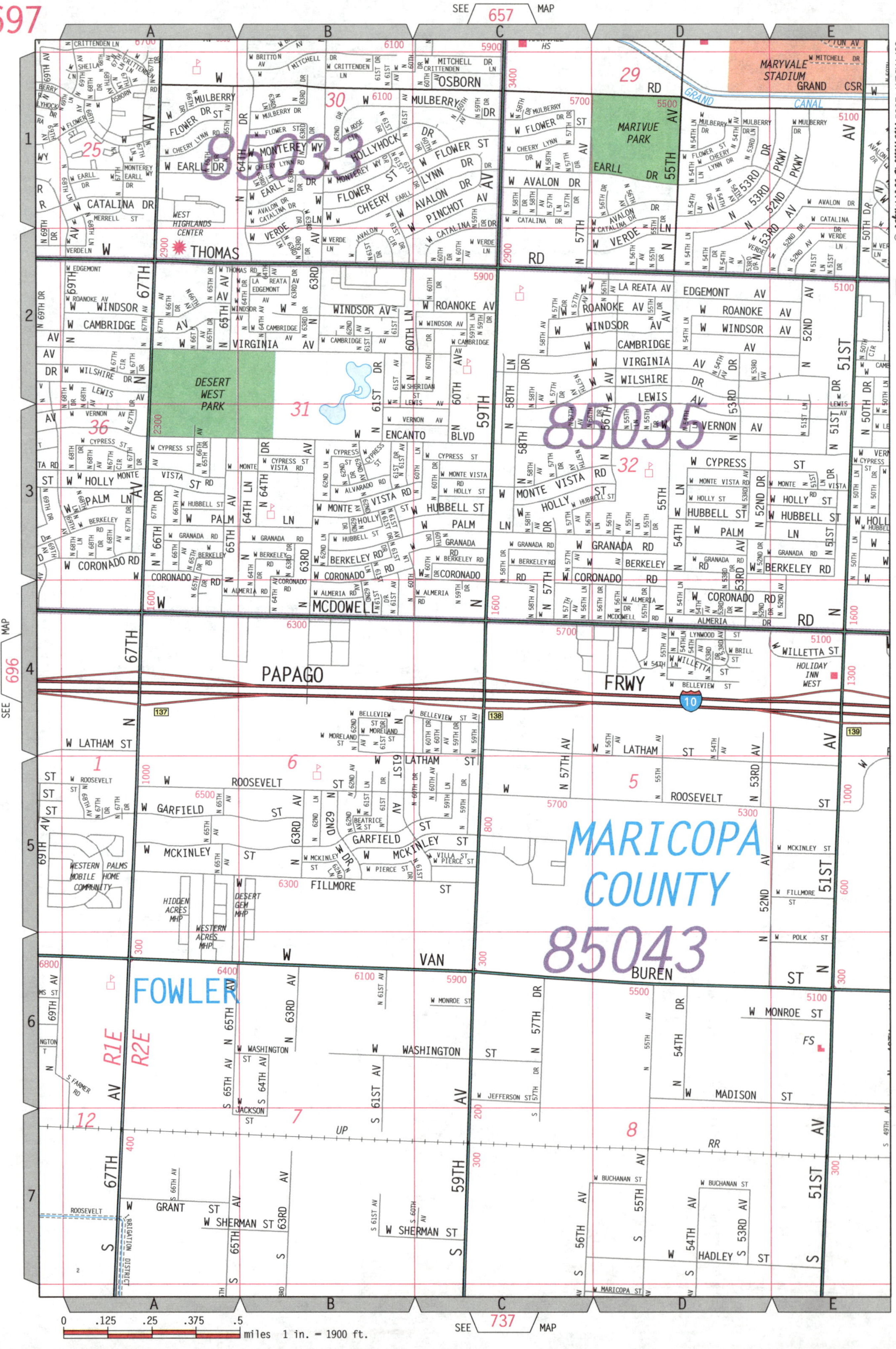

SEE 657 MAP

SEE 696 MAP

SEE 737 MAP

PHOENIX

MAP

A B C D E

1 2 3 4 5 6 7

MARYVALE STADIUM

GRAND CANAL

MARIVUE PARK

DESERT WEST PARK

WEST HIGHLANDS CENTER

HOLIDAY INN WEST

WESTERN PALMS MOBILE HOME COMMUNITY

HIDDEN ACRES MHP

DESERT GEM MHP

WESTERN ACRES MHP

FOWLER

MARICOPA COUNTY

85033

85035

85043

R1E R2E

OSBORN RD

THOMAS RD

MCDOWELL RD

PAPAGO FRWY

10

VAN BUREN ST

W LATHAM ST

ROOSEVELT ST

W GARFIELD ST

MCKINLEY ST

FILLMORE ST

W WASHINGTON ST

MADISON ST

W MONROE ST

GRANT ST

W SHERMAN ST

HADLEY ST

67TH AV

59TH AV

51ST AV

UP RR

IRRIGATION DISTRICT

0 .125 .25 .375 .5 miles 1 in. = 1900 ft.

SEE 657 MAP

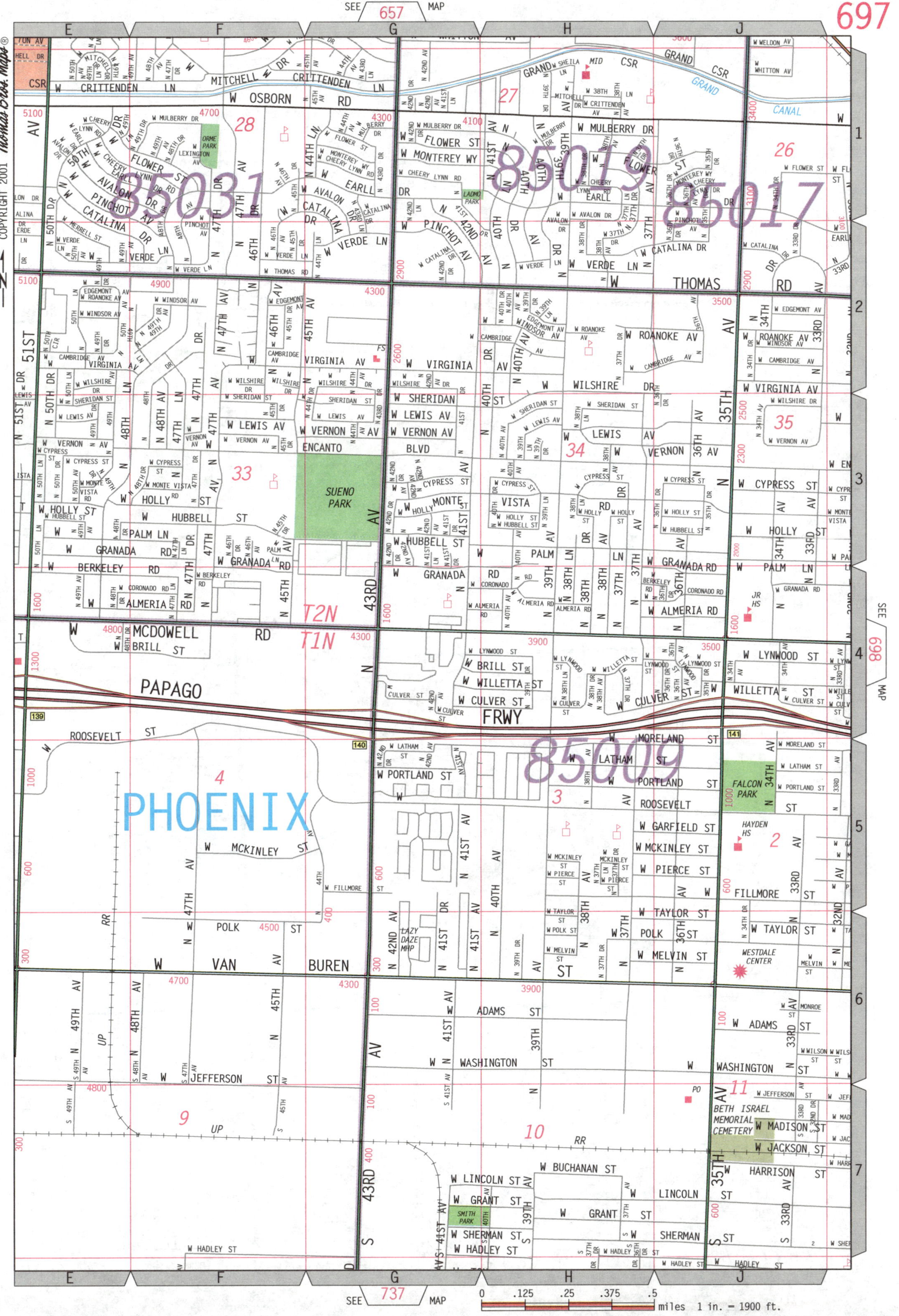

SEE 698 MAP

SEE 737 MAP

miles 1 in. = 1900 ft.

SEE 658 MAP

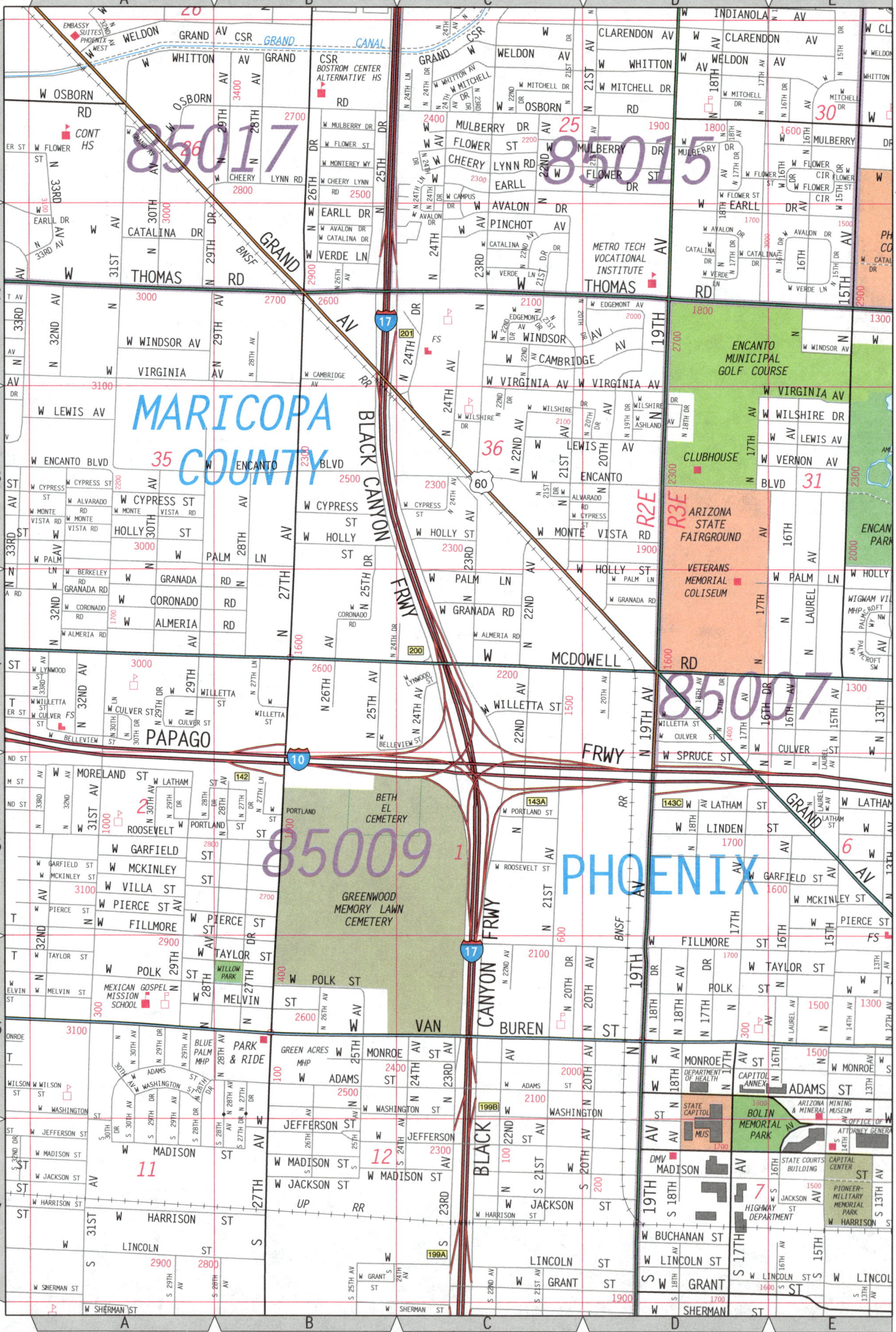

SEE 697 MAP

PHOENIX

MAP

A B C D E

1 2 3 4 5 6 7

85017

85015

85007

85009

MARICOPA COUNTY

PHOENIX

R2E R3E

W OSBORN RD
W THOMAS RD
W ENCANTO BLVD
MCDOWELL RD
PAPAGO FRWY
VAN BUREN ST
BLACK CANYON FRWY
GRAND AV
GRAND CANAL
W INDIANOLA AV
W CLARENDON AV
W WELDON AV
W WHITTON AV
W MULBERRY DR
W FLOWER ST
W CHEERY LYNN RD
W EARLL DR
W AVALON DR
W CATALINA DR
W VERDE LN
W WINDSOR AV
W VIRGINIA AV
W LEWIS AV
W CYPRESS ST
W HOLLY ST
W PALM LN
W GRANADA RD
W CORONADO RD
W ALMERIA RD
W WILLETTA ST
W CULVER ST
W MORELAND ST
W LATHAM ST
W ROOSEVELT ST
W GARFIELD ST
W MCKINLEY ST
W VILLA ST
W PIERCE ST
W FILLMORE ST
W TAYLOR ST
W POLK ST
W MELVIN ST
W MONROE ST
W ADAMS ST
W WASHINGTON ST
W JEFFERSON ST
W MADISON ST
W JACKSON ST
W HARRISON ST
W BUCHANAN ST
W LINCOLN ST
W GRANT ST
W SHERMAN ST

EMBASSY SUITES PHOENIX WEST
CONT HS
BOSTROM CENTER ALTERNATIVE HS
METRO TECH VOCATIONAL INSTITUTE
ENCANTO MUNICIPAL GOLF COURSE
CLUBHOUSE
ENCANTO PARK
ARIZONA STATE FAIRGROUND
VETERANS MEMORIAL COLISEUM
BETH EL CEMETERY
GREENWOOD MEMORY LAWN CEMETERY
WILLOW PARK
MEXICAN GOSPEL MISSION SCHOOL
BLUE PALM MHP
PARK & RIDE
GREEN ACRES MHP
DEPARTMENT OF HEALTH
CAPITOL ANNEX
STATE CAPITOL MUS
ARIZONA MINING & MINERAL MUSEUM
BOLIN MEMORIAL PARK
OFFICE OF ATTORNEY GENERAL
STATE COURTS BUILDING
CAPITAL CENTER
PIONEER-MILITARY MEMORIAL PARK
HIGHWAY DEPARTMENT
DMV
WIGWAM VILLAGE MHP

0 .125 .25 .375 .5 miles 1 in. = 1900 ft.

SEE 738 MAP

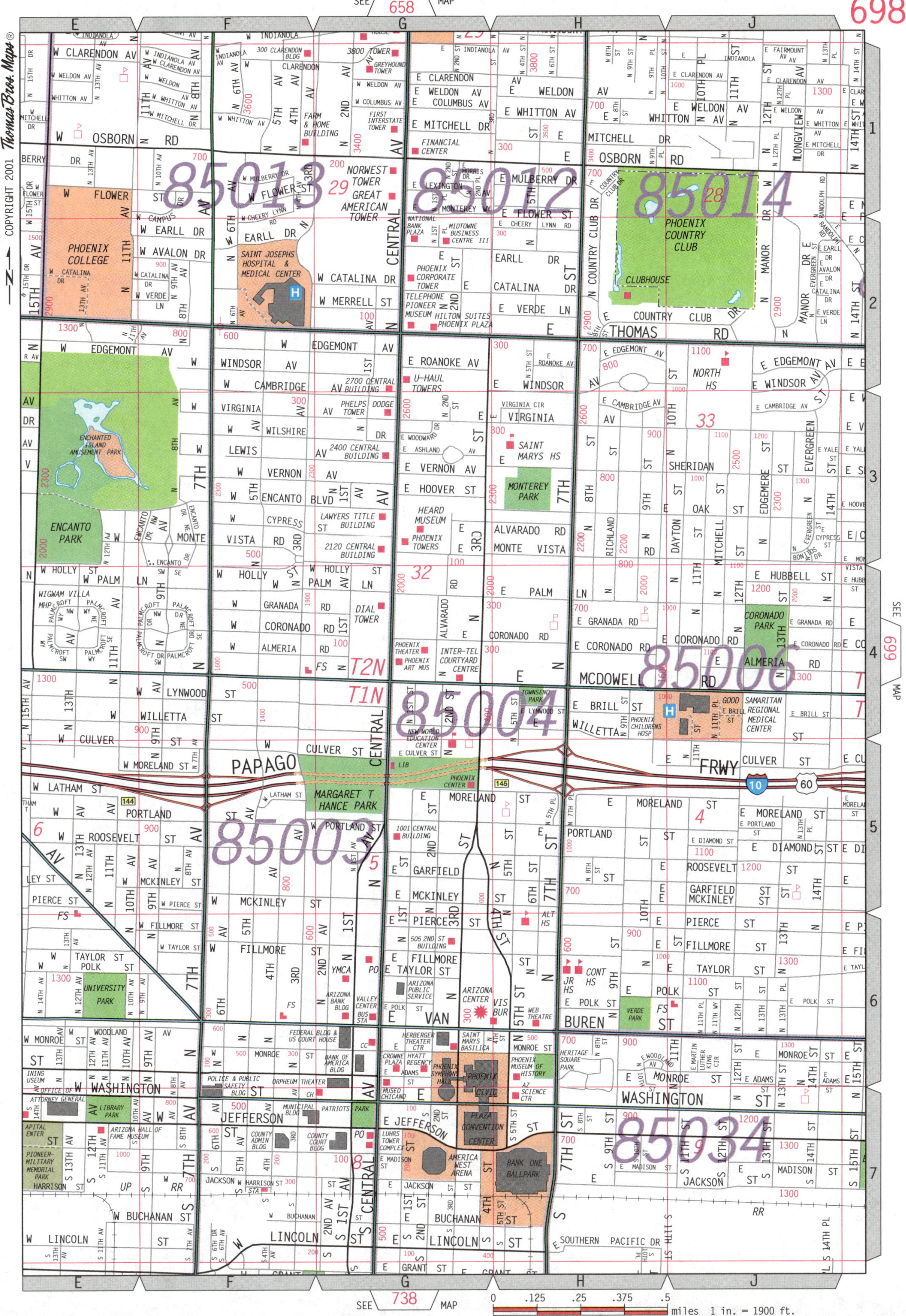
SEE 658 MAP
SEE 738 MAP
SEE 699 MAP
COPYRIGHT 2001 Thomas Bros. Maps
85013
85012
85014
85006
85004
85003
85034
T2N
T1N
W CLARENDON AV
W OSBORN RD
OSBORN RD
W FLOWER ST
W EARLL DR
W AVALON DR
W CATALINA DR
W MERRELL ST
THOMAS RD
W EDGEMONT AV
WINDSOR AV
W CAMBRIDGE AV
VIRGINIA AV
W VERNON AV
W ENCANTO BLVD
W HOLLY ST
W PALM LN
GRANADA RD
CORONADO RD
ALMERIA RD
MCDOWELL RD
W LYNWOOD ST
W WILLETTA ST
W CULVER ST
PAPAGO FRWY
W LATHAM ST
PORTLAND ST
W ROOSEVELT ST
W MCKINLEY ST
W FILLMORE ST
TAYLOR ST
POLK ST
VAN BUREN ST
W MONROE ST
W WASHINGTON ST
JEFFERSON ST
W BUCHANAN ST
W LINCOLN ST
GRANT ST
SOUTHERN PACIFIC DR
CENTRAL AV
7TH AV
7TH ST
15TH AV
N COUNTRY CLUB DR
PHOENIX COLLEGE
SAINT JOSEPHS HOSPITAL & MEDICAL CENTER
PHOENIX COUNTRY CLUB
CLUBHOUSE
ENCANTO PARK
ENCHANTED ISLAND AMUSEMENT PARK
MONTEREY PARK
SAINT MARYS HS
NORTH HS
HEARD MUSEUM
CORONADO PARK
TOWNSEND PARK
SAMARITAN REGIONAL MEDICAL CENTER
PHOENIX CHILDRENS HOSP
MARGARET T HANCE PARK
PHOENIX CENTER
UNIVERSITY PARK
VERDE PARK
ARIZONA CENTER
PHOENIX CIVIC PLAZA
PHOENIX CONVENTION CENTER
AMERICA WEST ARENA
BANK ONE BALLPARK
HERITAGE SQUARE PARK
PHOENIX MUSEUM OF HISTORY
AZ SCIENCE CTR
LIBRARY PARK
PIONEER-MILITARY MEMORIAL PARK
ARIZONA HALL OF FAME MUSEUM
COUNTY ADMIN BLDG
COUNTY COURT BLDG
FEDERAL BLDG & US COURT HOUSE
POLICE & PUBLIC SAFETY BLDG
ORPHEUM THEATER
PATRIOTS PARK
SAINT MARYS BASILICA
HERBERGER THEATER CTR
PHOENIX SYMPHONY HALL
10
60
17
0 .125 .25 .375 .5 miles 1 in. = 1900 ft.
PHOENIX
MAP

SEE 659 MAP

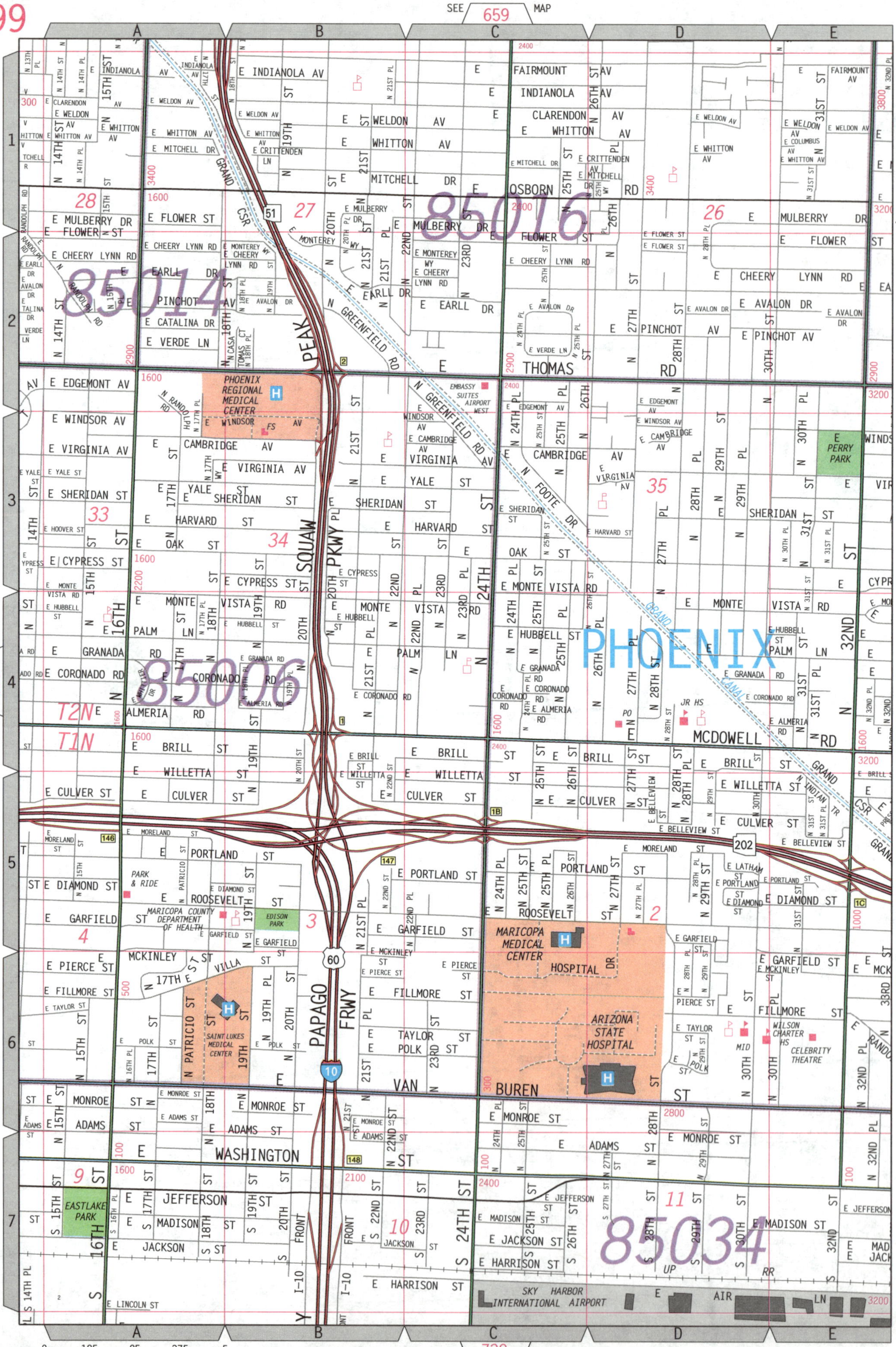

SEE 698 MAP

A B C D E

1 2 3 4 5 6 7

85014 85016 85006 85034

PHOENIX

T2N T1N

28 27 26 33 34 35 4 3 2 9 10 11

PHOENIX REGIONAL MEDICAL CENTER

EMBASSY SUITES AIRPORT WEST

E PERRY PARK

MARICOPA COUNTY DEPARTMENT OF HEALTH

PARK & RIDE

EDISON PARK

SAINT LUKES MEDICAL CENTER

MARICOPA MEDICAL CENTER

ARIZONA STATE HOSPITAL

WILSON CHARTER HS

CELEBRITY THEATRE

JR HS

PO

EASTLAKE PARK

SKY HARBOR INTERNATIONAL AIRPORT

SQUAW PEAK PKWY

PAPAGO FRWY

GRAND CANAL

N GREENFIELD RD

N FOOTE DR

E INDIANOLA AV · E WELDON AV · E WHITTON AV · E MITCHELL DR · E OSBORN RD · E MULBERRY DR · E FLOWER ST · E CHEERY LYNN RD · E EARLL DR · E AVALON DR · E PINCHOT AV · E CATALINA DR · E VERDE LN · E THOMAS RD · E EDGEMONT AV · E WINDSOR AV · E CAMBRIDGE AV · E VIRGINIA AV · E YALE ST · E SHERIDAN ST · E HARVARD ST · E OAK ST · E CYPRESS ST · E MONTE VISTA RD · E HUBBELL ST · E PALM LN · E GRANADA RD · E CORONADO RD · E ALMERIA RD · E MCDOWELL RD · E BRILL ST · E WILLETTA ST · E CULVER ST · E MORELAND ST · E PORTLAND ST · E DIAMOND ST · E ROOSEVELT ST · E GARFIELD ST · E MCKINLEY ST · E PIERCE ST · E FILLMORE ST · E TAYLOR ST · E POLK ST · E VAN BUREN ST · E MONROE ST · E ADAMS ST · E WASHINGTON ST · E JEFFERSON ST · E MADISON ST · E JACKSON ST · E HARRISON ST · E LINCOLN ST · E AIR LN

N 14TH ST · N 15TH ST · N 16TH ST · N 17TH ST · N 18TH ST · N 19TH ST · N 20TH ST · N 21ST ST · N 22ND ST · N 23RD ST · N 24TH ST · N 25TH ST · N 26TH ST · N 27TH ST · N 28TH ST · N 29TH ST · N 30TH ST · N 31ST ST · N 32ND ST · N PATRICIO ST

51 60 10 202 146 147 148

SEE 739 MAP

0 .125 .25 .375 .5 miles 1 in. = 1900 ft.

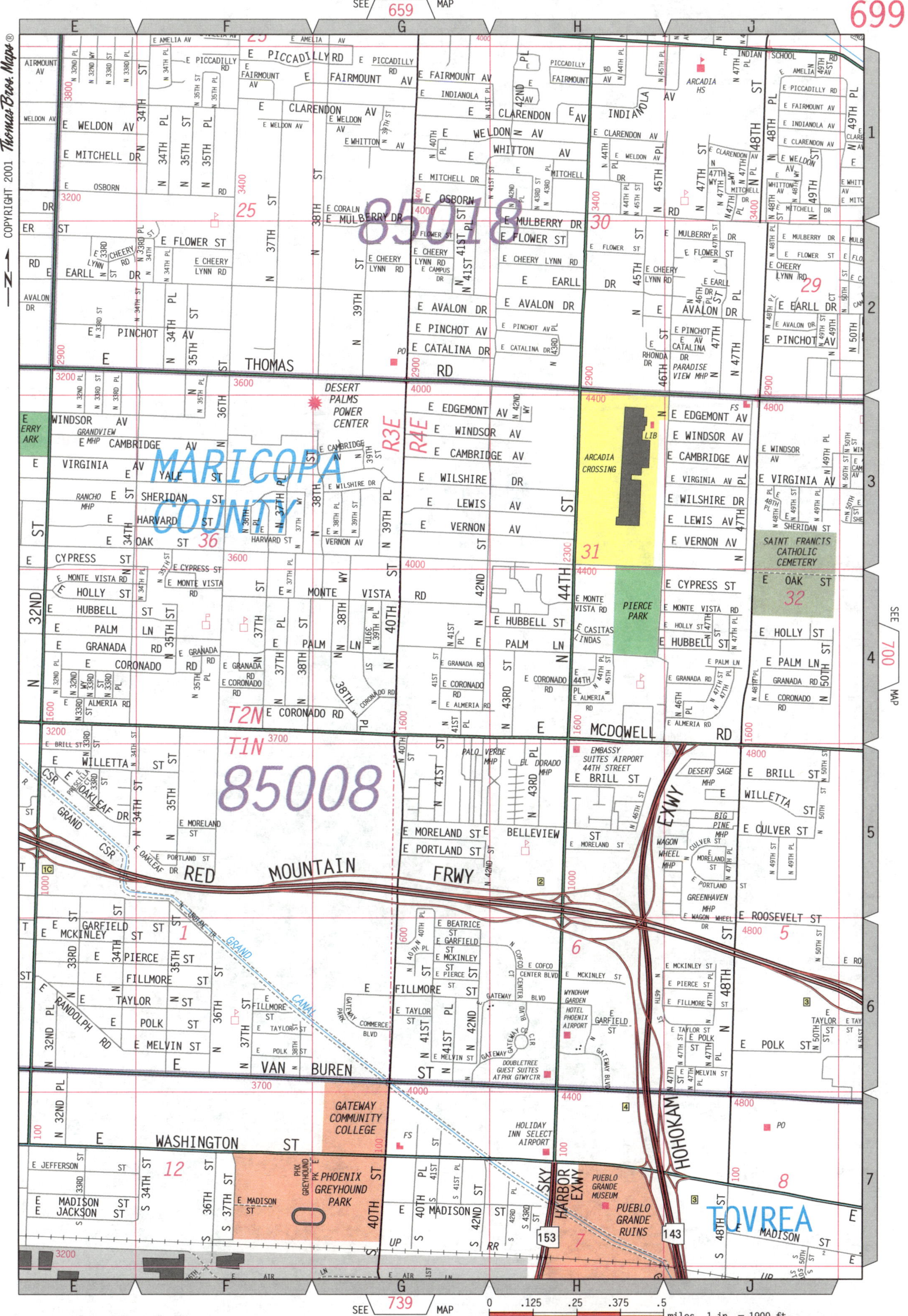
SEE 659 MAP
SEE 739 MAP
SEE 700 MAP
PHOENIX
MAP
85018
85008
MARICOPA COUNTY
R3E
R4E
T2N
T1N
E PICCADILLY RD
E FAIRMOUNT AV
E CLARENDON AV
E WELDON AV
E MITCHELL DR
E OSBORN RD
E MULBERRY DR
E FLOWER ST
E CHEERY LYNN RD
E EARLL DR
E AVALON DR
E PINCHOT AV
E CATALINA DR
THOMAS RD
INDIANOLA AV
ARCADIA HS
E INDIAN SCHOOL RD
DESERT PALMS POWER CENTER
E EDGEMONT AV
E WINDSOR AV
E CAMBRIDGE AV
E VIRGINIA AV
E WILSHIRE DR
E LEWIS AV
E VERNON AV
E CYPRESS ST
E MONTE VISTA RD
E HUBBELL ST
E PALM LN
E GRANADA RD
E CORONADO RD
E HOLLY ST
E OAK ST
ARCADIA CROSSING
LIB
PIERCE PARK
SAINT FRANCIS CATHOLIC CEMETERY
PARADISE VIEW MHP
GRANDVIEW MHP
RANCHO MHP
MCDOWELL RD
E BRILL ST
E WILLETTA ST
E MORELAND ST
E PORTLAND ST
BELLEVIEW ST
PALO VERDE MHP
EL DORADO MHP
EMBASSY SUITES AIRPORT 44TH STREET
DESERT SAGE MHP
BIG PINE MHP
WAGON WHEEL MHP
GREENHAVEN MHP
E CULVER ST
RED MOUNTAIN FRWY
HOHOKAM EXWY
GRAND CSR
GRAND CANAL
E ROOSEVELT ST
E GARFIELD ST
E MCKINLEY ST
E PIERCE ST
E FILLMORE ST
E TAYLOR ST
E POLK ST
E MELVIN ST
RANDOLPH RD
VAN BUREN ST
GATEWAY CENTER BLVD
GATEWAY PARK COMMERCE BLVD
WYNDHAM GARDEN HOTEL PHOENIX AIRPORT
DOUBLETREE GUEST SUITES AT PHX GTWYCTR
E WASHINGTON ST
GATEWAY COMMUNITY COLLEGE
HOLIDAY INN SELECT AIRPORT
E JEFFERSON ST
E MADISON ST
E JACKSON ST
PHX GREYHOUND PK
PHOENIX GREYHOUND PARK
SKY HARBOR EXWY
PUEBLO GRANDE MUSEUM
PUEBLO GRANDE RUINS
TOVREA
153
143
N 32ND ST
N 34TH ST
N 35TH ST
N 36TH ST
N 37TH ST
N 38TH ST
N 40TH ST
N 42ND ST
N 44TH ST
N 48TH ST
miles 1 in. = 1900 ft.

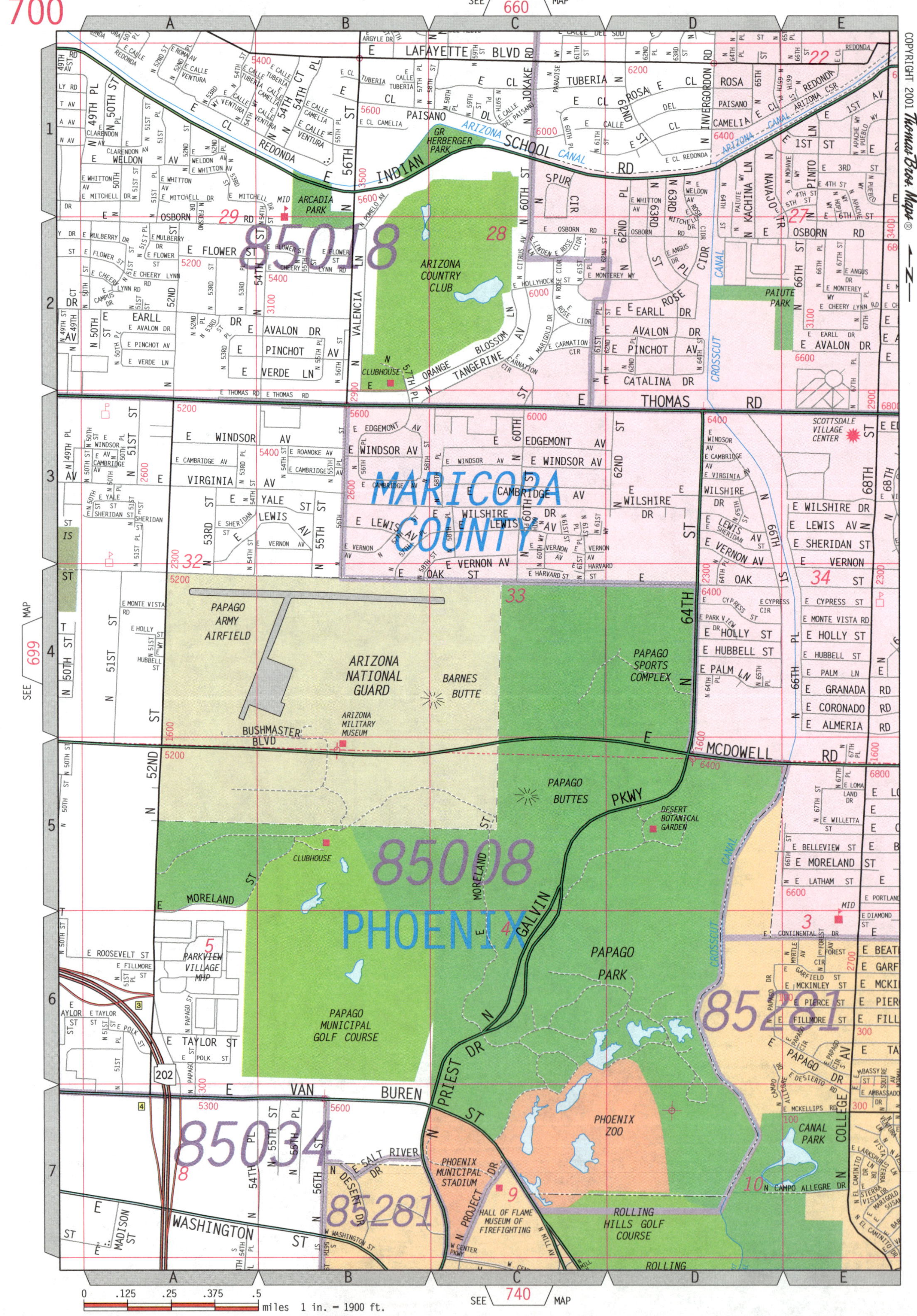
SEE 660 MAP
SEE 699 MAP
SEE 740 MAP
PHOENIX
MAP
COPYRIGHT 2001 Thomas Bros. Maps ®
85018
85008
85034
85281
MARICOPA COUNTY
PHOENIX
E LAFAYETTE BLVD
INDIAN SCHOOL RD
ARIZONA CANAL
CROSSCUT CANAL
E THOMAS RD
E MCDOWELL RD
E VAN BUREN ST
WASHINGTON ST
N GALVIN PKWY
PRIEST DR
N 52ND ST
N 56TH ST
VALENCIA LN
N 64TH ST
N 68TH ST
N 66TH ST
N 60TH ST
N JOKAKE RD
N INVERGORDON RD
E OSBORN RD
E FLOWER ST
E EARLL DR
E AVALON DR
E PINCHOT AV
E VERDE LN
E WINDSOR AV
E VIRGINIA AV
E YALE ST
E LEWIS AV
E VERNON AV
E OAK ST
E EDGEMONT AV
E CAMBRIDGE AV
E WILSHIRE DR
E HOLLY ST
E HUBBELL ST
E PALM LN
E GRANADA RD
E CORONADO RD
E ALMERIA RD
E MORELAND ST
E ROOSEVELT ST
E TAYLOR ST
E MADISON ST
N COLLEGE AV
N PAPAGO DR
E MCKELLIPS RD
N CAMPO ALLEGRE DR
ARCADIA PARK
GR HERBERGER PARK
ARIZONA COUNTRY CLUB
CLUBHOUSE
PAIUTE PARK
SCOTTSDALE VILLAGE CENTER
PAPAGO ARMY AIRFIELD
ARIZONA NATIONAL GUARD
BARNES BUTTE
ARIZONA MILITARY MUSEUM
BUSHMASTER BLVD
PAPAGO SPORTS COMPLEX
PAPAGO BUTTES
DESERT BOTANICAL GARDEN
PARKVIEW VILLAGE MHP
PAPAGO MUNICIPAL GOLF COURSE
PAPAGO PARK
PHOENIX ZOO
PHOENIX MUNICIPAL STADIUM
HALL OF FLAME MUSEUM OF FIREFIGHTING
ROLLING HILLS GOLF COURSE
CANAL PARK
202
0 .125 .25 .375 .5
miles 1 in. = 1900 ft.

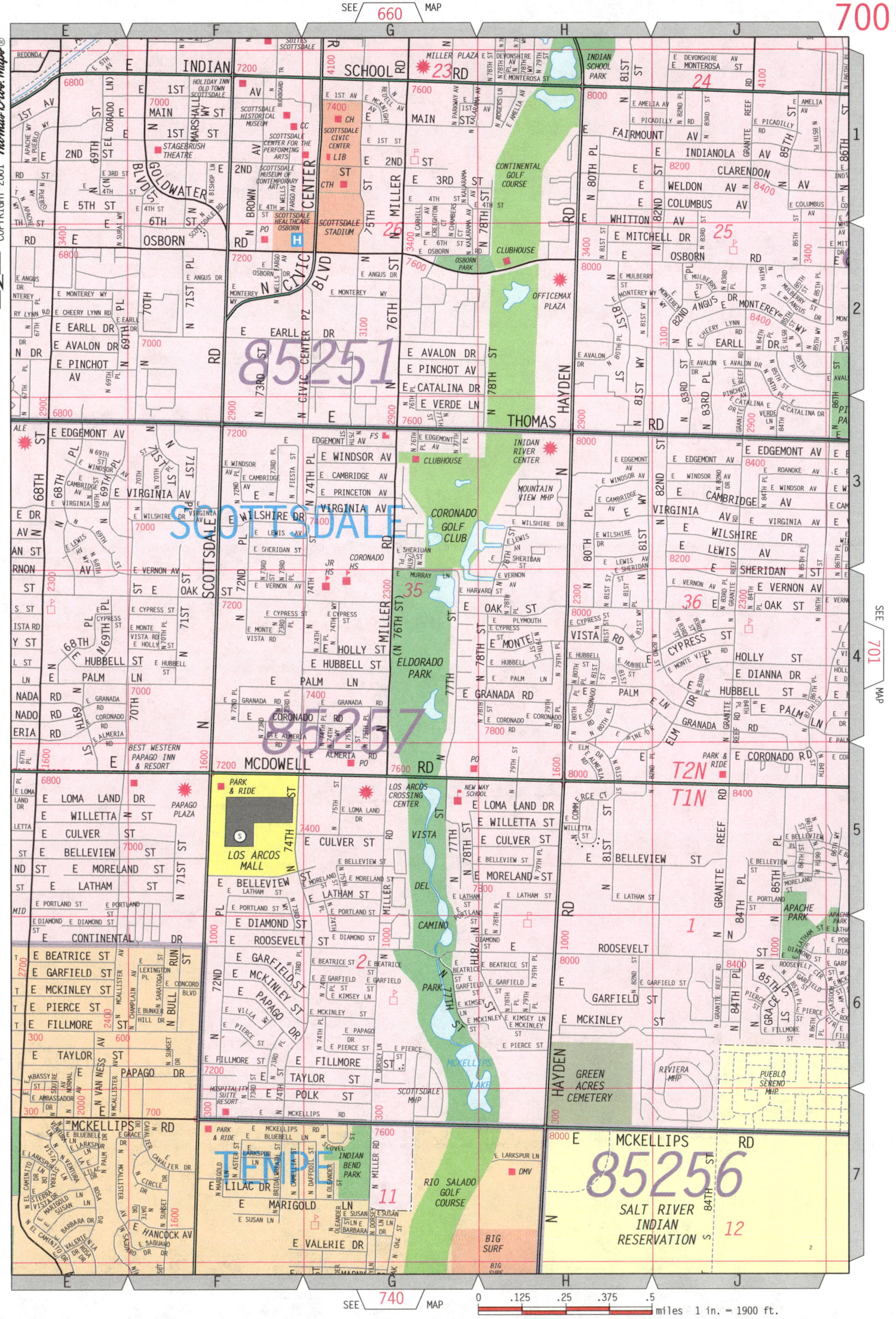

SEE 660 MAP
SEE 701 MAP
SEE 740 MAP
PHOENIX
MAP
Thomas Bros. Maps
COPYRIGHT 2001
SCOTTSDALE
TEMPE
85251
85257
85256
INDIAN SCHOOL RD
THOMAS RD
MCDOWELL RD
MCKELLIPS RD
HAYDEN RD
SCOTTSDALE RD
MILLER RD
OSBORN RD
CIVIC CENTER BLVD
GOLDWATER BLVD
SCOTTSDALE CIVIC CENTER
SCOTTSDALE STADIUM
SCOTTSDALE HEALTHCARE OSBORN
SCOTTSDALE HISTORICAL MUSEUM
SCOTTSDALE CENTER FOR THE PERFORMING ARTS
SCOTTSDALE MUSEUM OF CONTEMPORARY ARTS
STAGEBRUSH THEATRE
HOLIDAY INN OLD TOWN SCOTTSDALE
SUITES SCOTTSDALE
CONTINENTAL GOLF COURSE
CLUBHOUSE
OSBORN PARK
OFFICEMAX PLAZA
INDIAN SCHOOL PARK
INDIAN RIVER CENTER
MOUNTAIN VIEW MHP
CORONADO GOLF CLUB
CORONADO HS
JR HS
ELDORADO PARK
BEST WESTERN PAPAGO INN & RESORT
PAPAGO PLAZA
PARK & RIDE
LOS ARCOS MALL
LOS ARCOS CROSSING CENTER
NEW WAY SCHOOL
VISTA DEL CAMINO PARK
APACHE PARK
GREEN ACRES CEMETERY
RIVIERA MHP
PUEBLO SERENO MHP
SCOTTSDALE MHP
HOSPITALITY SUITE RESORT
MCKELLIPS LAKE
INDIAN BEND PARK
RIO SALADO GOLF COURSE
BIG SURF
DMV
SALT RIVER INDIAN RESERVATION
T2N
T1N
0 .125 .25 .375 .5 miles 1 in. = 1900 ft.

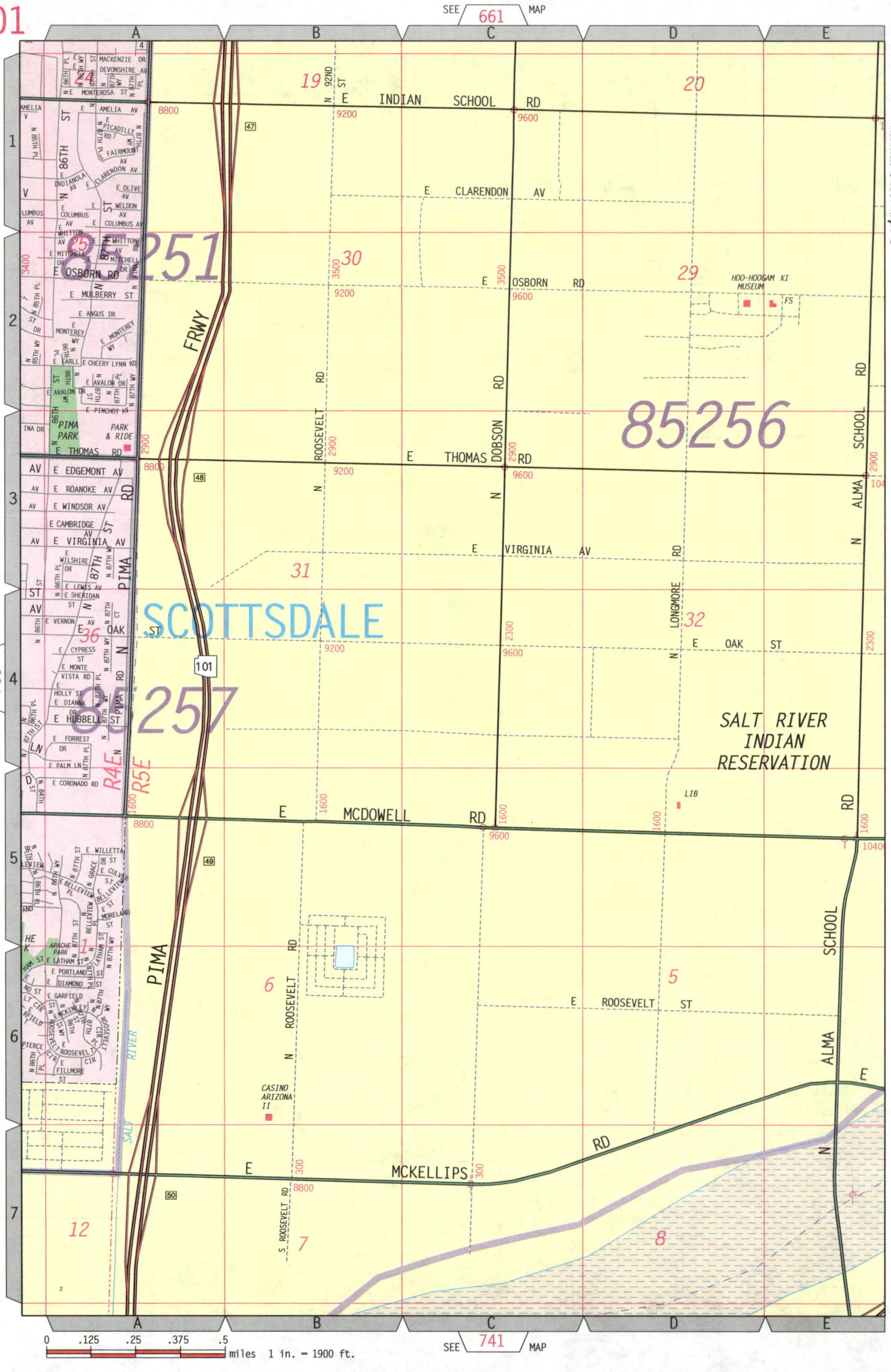
SEE 661 MAP
SEE 700 MAP
SEE 741 MAP
A
B
C
D
E
1
2
3
4
5
6
7
E INDIAN SCHOOL RD
E CLARENDON AV
E OSBORN RD
E THOMAS RD
E VIRGINIA AV
E OAK ST
E MCDOWELL RD
E ROOSEVELT ST
E MCKELLIPS RD
N 92ND ST
N ROOSEVELT RD
S ROOSEVELT RD
N DOBSON RD
N LONGMORE RD
N ALMA SCHOOL RD
PIMA FRWY
101
N PIMA RD
SALT RIVER
SCOTTSDALE
85251
85256
85257
SALT RIVER INDIAN RESERVATION
HOO-HOOGAM KI MUSEUM
FS
LIB
CASINO ARIZONA II
PIMA PARK
PARK & RIDE
APACHE PARK
R4E
R5E
19
20
24
25
29
30
31
32
36
1
5
6
7
8
12
8800
9200
9600
3500
2900
2300
1600
300
3400
10400
47
48
49
50
E MACKENZIE DR
E DEVONSHIRE AV
E MONTEROSA ST
E AMELIA AV
E PICADILLY RD
E FAIRMOUNT AV
E CLARENDON AV
E INDIANOLA AV
E OLIVE AV
E WELDON AV
E COLUMBUS AV
E WHITTON AV
E MITCHELL DR
E MULBERRY ST
E ANGUS DR
E MONTEREY WY
E EARLL DR
E CHEERY LYNN RD
E AVALON DR
E PINCHOT AV
E EDGEMONT AV
E ROANOKE AV
E WINDSOR AV
E CAMBRIDGE AV
E VIRGINIA AV
E WILSHIRE DR
E LEWIS AV
E SHERIDAN ST
E VERNON AV
E OAK ST
E CYPRESS ST
E MONTE VISTA RD
E HOLLY ST
E DIANNA DR
E HUBBELL ST
E FORREST DR
E PALM LN
E CORONADO RD
E WILLETTA ST
E CULVER ST
E BELLEVIEW PL
E MORELAND ST
E LATHAM ST
E PORTLAND ST
E DIAMOND ST
E GARFIELD ST
E MCKINLEY ST
E ROOSEVELT CIR
E FILLMORE ST
N 86TH ST
N 86TH PL
N 86TH WY
N 87TH ST
N 87TH PL
N 87TH WY
N 85TH PL
N 85TH WY
N 84TH ST
0 .125 .25 .375 .5 miles 1 in. = 1900 ft.

PHOENIX
MAP

SEE 661 MAP
SEE 702 MAP
SEE 741 MAP
PHOENIX
MAP
E INDIAN SCHOOL RD
E CLARENDON AV
E OSBORN RD
E EARLL DR
E THOMAS RD
E VIRGINIA AV
E MCDOWELL RD
N BEELINE HWY
N ALMA SCHOOL RD
N EXTENSION RD
N COUNTRY CLUB DR
N CENTER ST
N MESA DR
MARICOPA COUNTY
85203
85201
MESA
T2N
T1N
SALT RIVER
CLUBHOUSE
CYPRESS GOLF COURSE
E MCKELLIPS RD
RED MOUNTAIN FRWY
W MCKELLIPS RD
E LEHI RD
E LELAND ST
E LYNWOOD ST
E NANCE ST
E CLUFF LN
N PIONEER
N BRIMHALL ST
N SPRING ST
HAWAIIAN VILLAGE MHP
COUNTRY CLUB VILLAGE MHP
SUNDIAL MHP
KAY-BEE MOBILE VILLA MHP
EASTWAY MHP
LA CASITA MHP
MID
W JUNIPER
W JASMINE ST
E JUNE ST
E JASMINE ST
E JACARANDA
E JUNIPER ST
W INGLEWOOD ST
WHITMAN PARK
N ROBSON
N GRAND
N PIMA
N PASADENA ST
JUNE ST
0 .125 .25 .375 .5 miles 1 in. = 1900 ft.

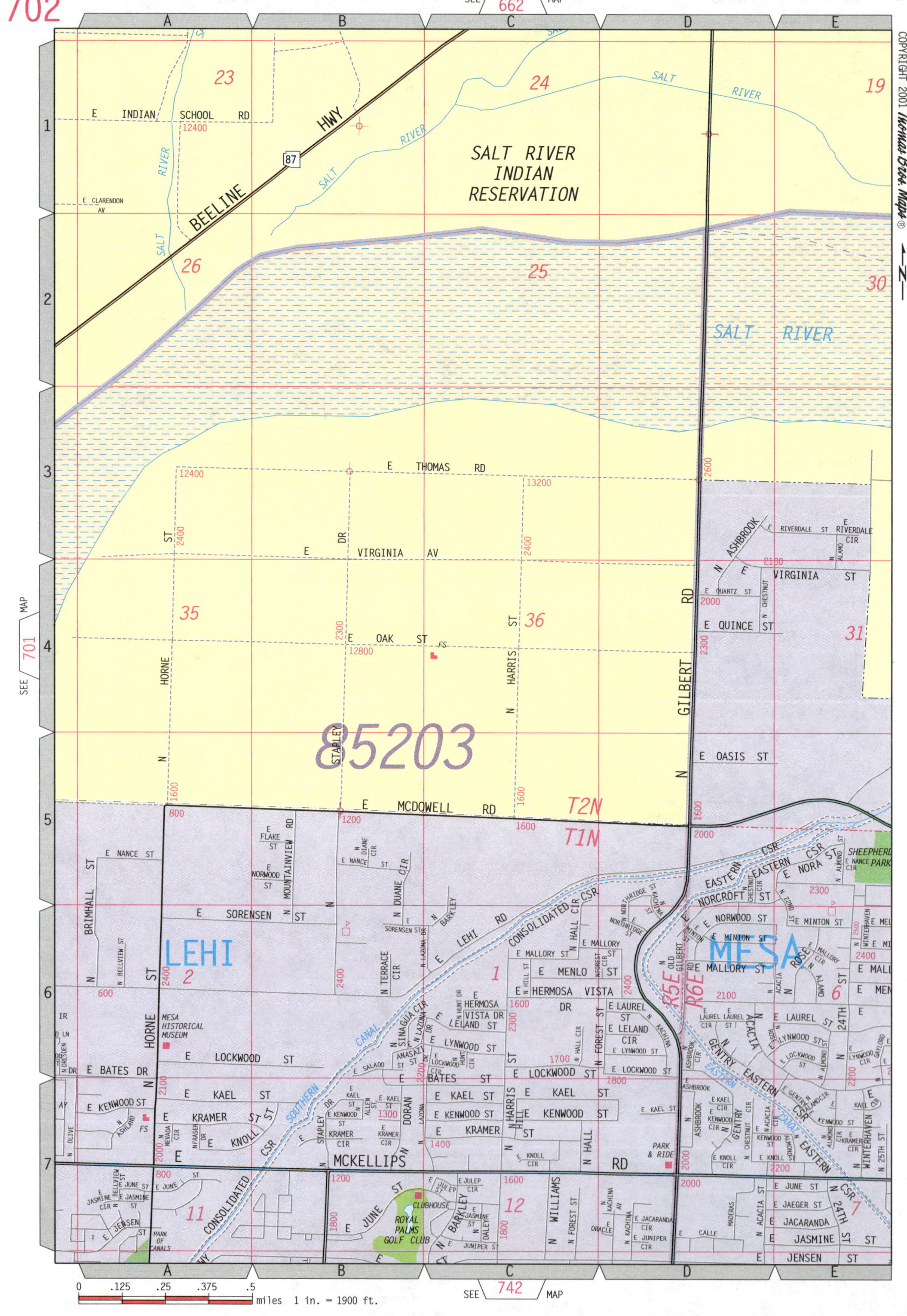
SEE 662 MAP
SALT RIVER INDIAN RESERVATION
E INDIAN SCHOOL RD
BEELINE HWY
87
SALT RIVER
E THOMAS RD
E VIRGINIA AV
E OAK ST
N HORNE ST
N STAPLEY DR
N HARRIS ST
N GILBERT RD
85203
E MCDOWELL RD
T2N
T1N
LEHI
MESA
R5E
R6E
MESA HISTORICAL MUSEUM
E LEHI RD
CONSOLIDATED CANAL
SOUTHERN CANAL
EASTERN CANAL
E MCKELLIPS RD
ROYAL PALMS GOLF CLUB
SHEEPHERD PARK
SEE 701 MAP
SEE 742 MAP
miles 1 in. = 1900 ft.

PHOENIX
MAP

SEE 662 MAP

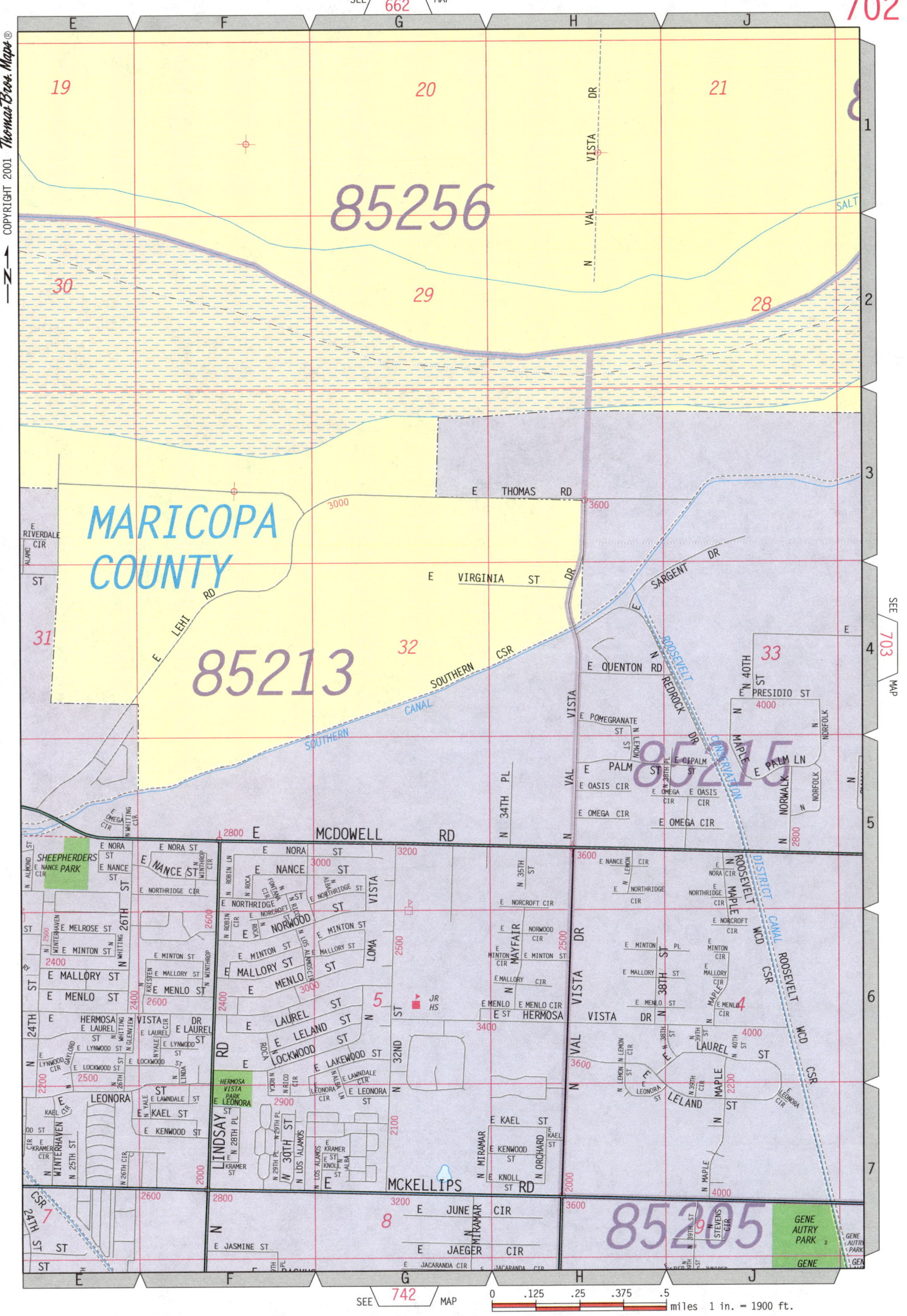

SEE 703 MAP

PHOENIX

MAP

SEE 742 MAP

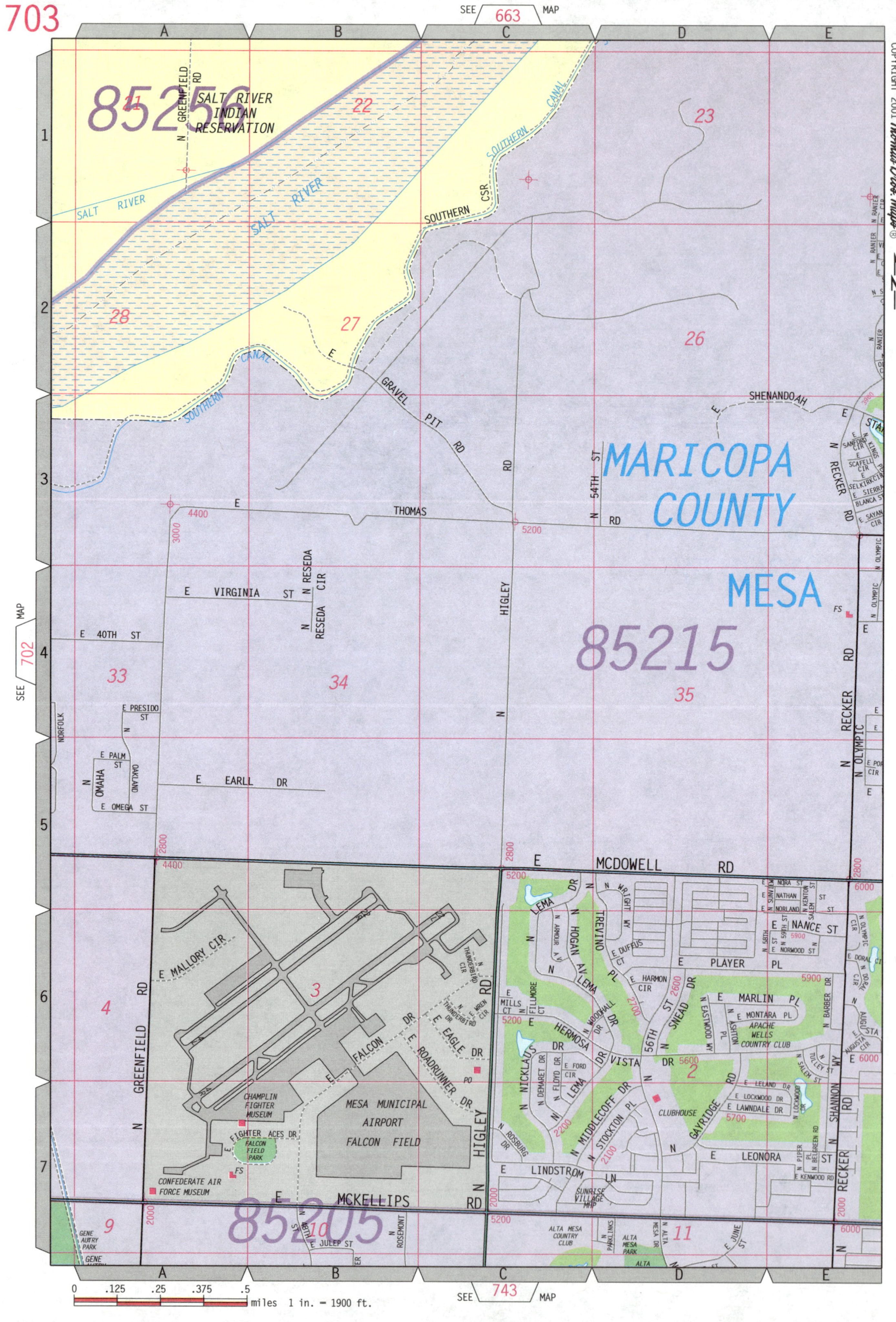

SEE 663 MAP
85256
SALT RIVER INDIAN RESERVATION
N GREENFIELD RD
SALT RIVER
SOUTHERN CANAL
SOUTHERN CSR
E GRAVEL PIT RD
E THOMAS RD
N HIGLEY RD
N 54TH ST
E SHENANDOAH
MARICOPA COUNTY
MESA
85215
E VIRGINIA ST
N RESEDA CIR
E 40TH ST
E PRESIDO ST
NORFOLK
E PALM ST
N OMAHA
OAKLAND
E OMEGA ST
E EARLL DR
N RECKER RD
N OLYMPIC
E MCDOWELL RD
E MALLORY CIR
N GREENFIELD RD
THUNDERBIRD CIR
FALCON DR
E EAGLE DR
E ROADRUNNER DR
MESA MUNICIPAL AIRPORT FALCON FIELD
CHAMPLIN FIGHTER MUSEUM
E FIGHTER ACES DR
FALCON FIELD PARK
CONFEDERATE AIR FORCE MUSEUM
N HIGLEY RD
E MCKELLIPS RD
85205
E JULEP ST
N ROSEMONT
GENE AUTRY PARK
N LEMA DR
N HOGAN AV
N TREVINO PL
N WRIGHT WY
E DUFFUS CT
E HARMON CIR
E PLAYER PL
E NANCE ST
E MARLIN PL
E MONTARA PL
APACHE WELLS COUNTRY CLUB
E HERMOSA VISTA DR
N 56TH ST
N SNEAD DR
N NICKLAUS DR
N DEMARET DR
N FLOYD DR
E FORD CIR
N MIDDLECOFF DR
N STOCKTON PL
CLUBHOUSE
N GAYRIDGE RD
E LELAND DR
E LOCKWOOD DR
E LAWNDALE DR
E LEONORA ST
E LINDSTROM LN
SUNRISE VILLAGE MHP
N ROSBURG DR
N SHANNON WY
N BARBER DR
N AUGUSTA CIR
ALTA MESA COUNTRY CLUB
ALTA MESA PARK
N ALTA MESA DR
N PARKLINKS
E JUNE ST
SEE 702 MAP
SEE 743 MAP
0 .125 .25 .375 .5 miles 1 in. = 1900 ft.

SEE 663 MAP

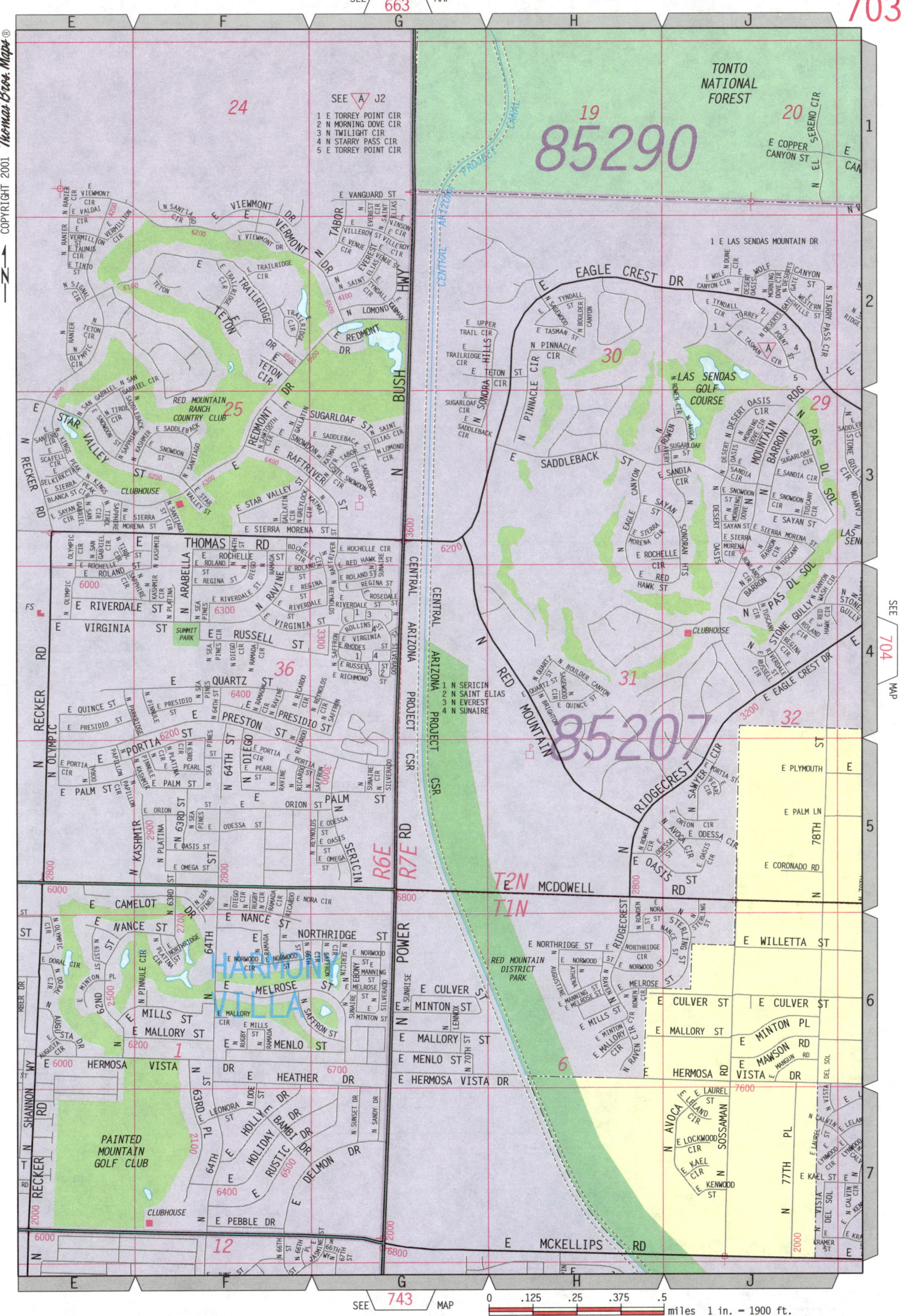

SEE 704 MAP

SEE 743 MAP

PHOENIX

MAP

SEE 664 MAP

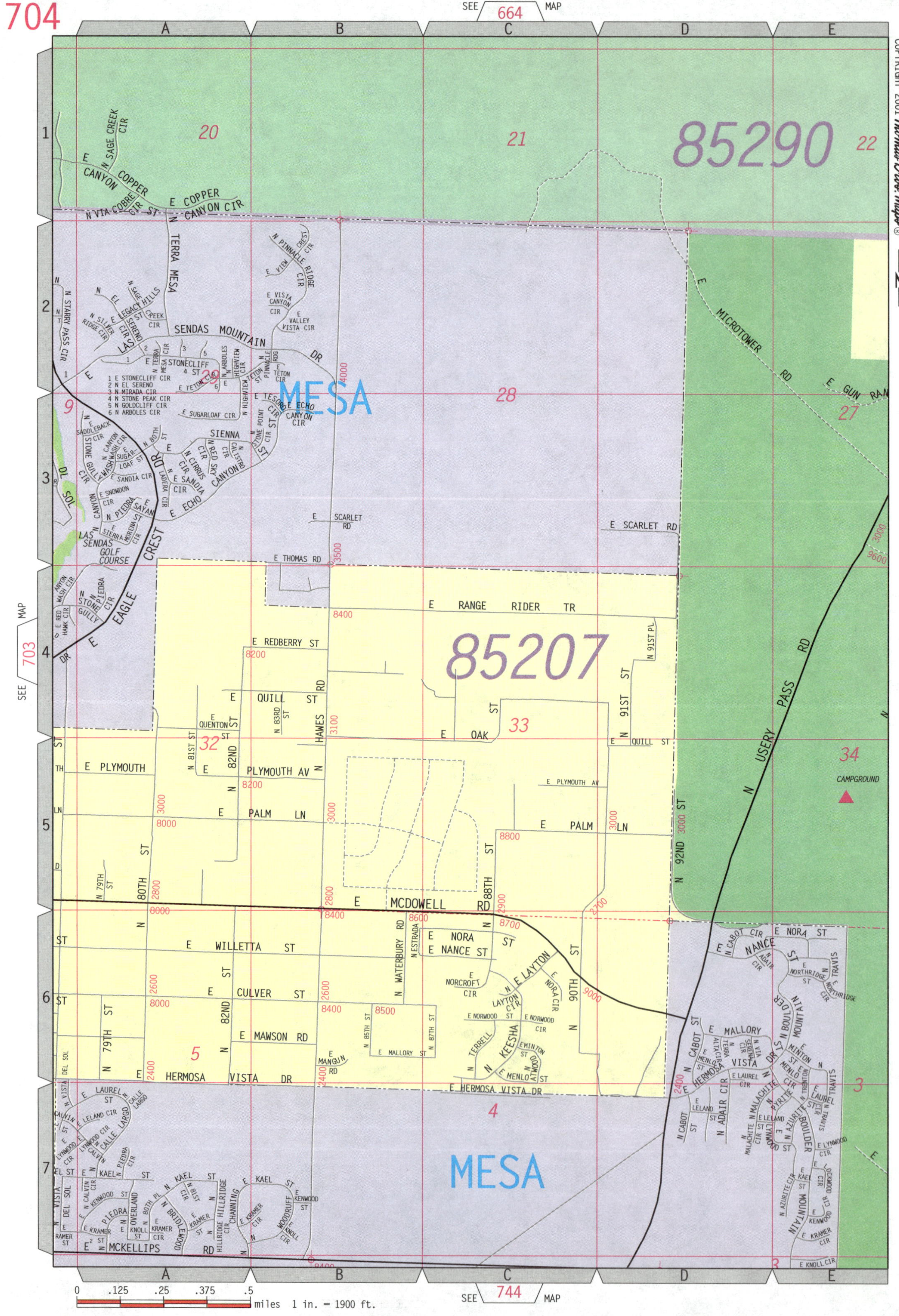

SEE 703 MAP

SEE 744 MAP

0 .125 .25 .375 .5 miles 1 in. = 1900 ft.

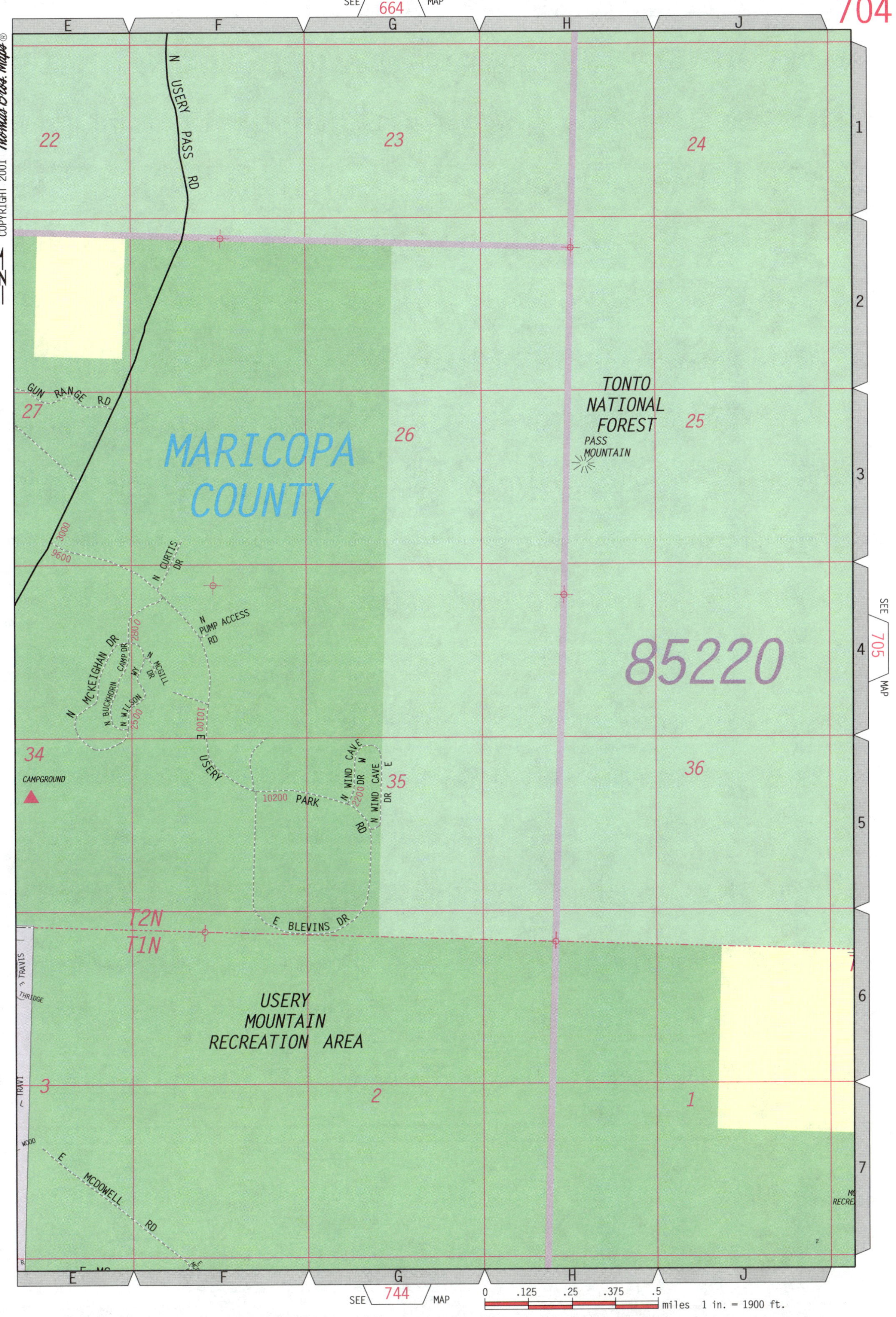

SEE 664 MAP
E
F
G
H
J
1
2
3
4
5
6
7
N USERY PASS RD
22
23
24
GUN RANGE RD
27
MARICOPA
COUNTY
26
TONTO
NATIONAL
FOREST
25
PASS
MOUNTAIN
N CURTIS DR
N PUMP ACCESS RD
N MCKEIGHAN DR
N BUCKHORN CAMP DR
N WILSON
N MCGILL DR
E USERY PARK RD
10100
10200
9600
3000
2800
2500
2200
N WIND CAVE DR
E BLEVINS DR
85220
34
CAMPGROUND
35
36
T2N
T1N
USERY
MOUNTAIN
RECREATION AREA
TRAVIS
THRIDGE
3
2
1
E MCDOWELL RD
WOOD
SEE 705 MAP
SEE 744 MAP
0 .125 .25 .375 .5 miles 1 in. = 1900 ft.
PHOENIX
MAP

SEE 103 MAP

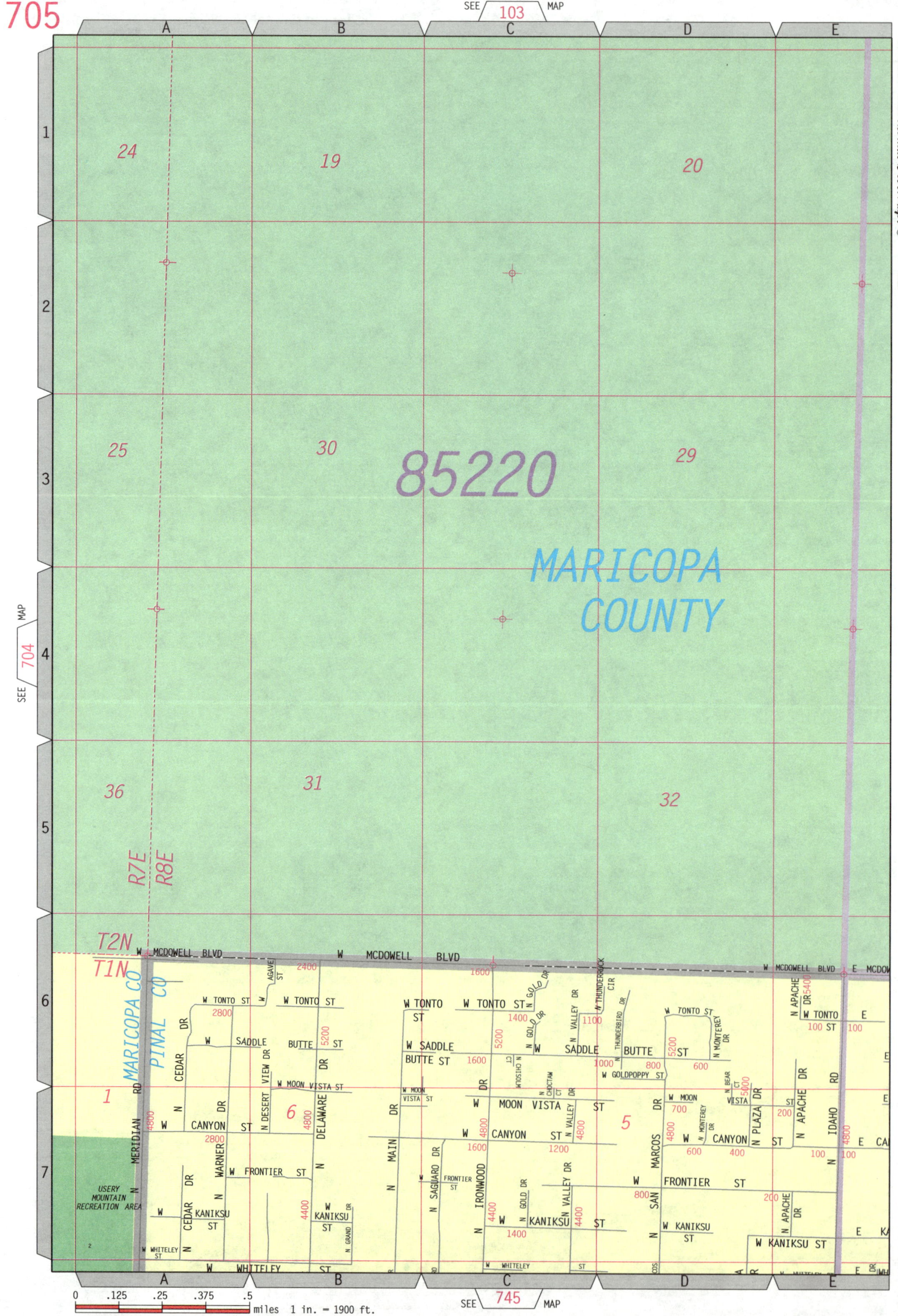

SEE 704 MAP

SEE 745 MAP

0 .125 .25 .375 .5 miles 1 in. = 1900 ft.

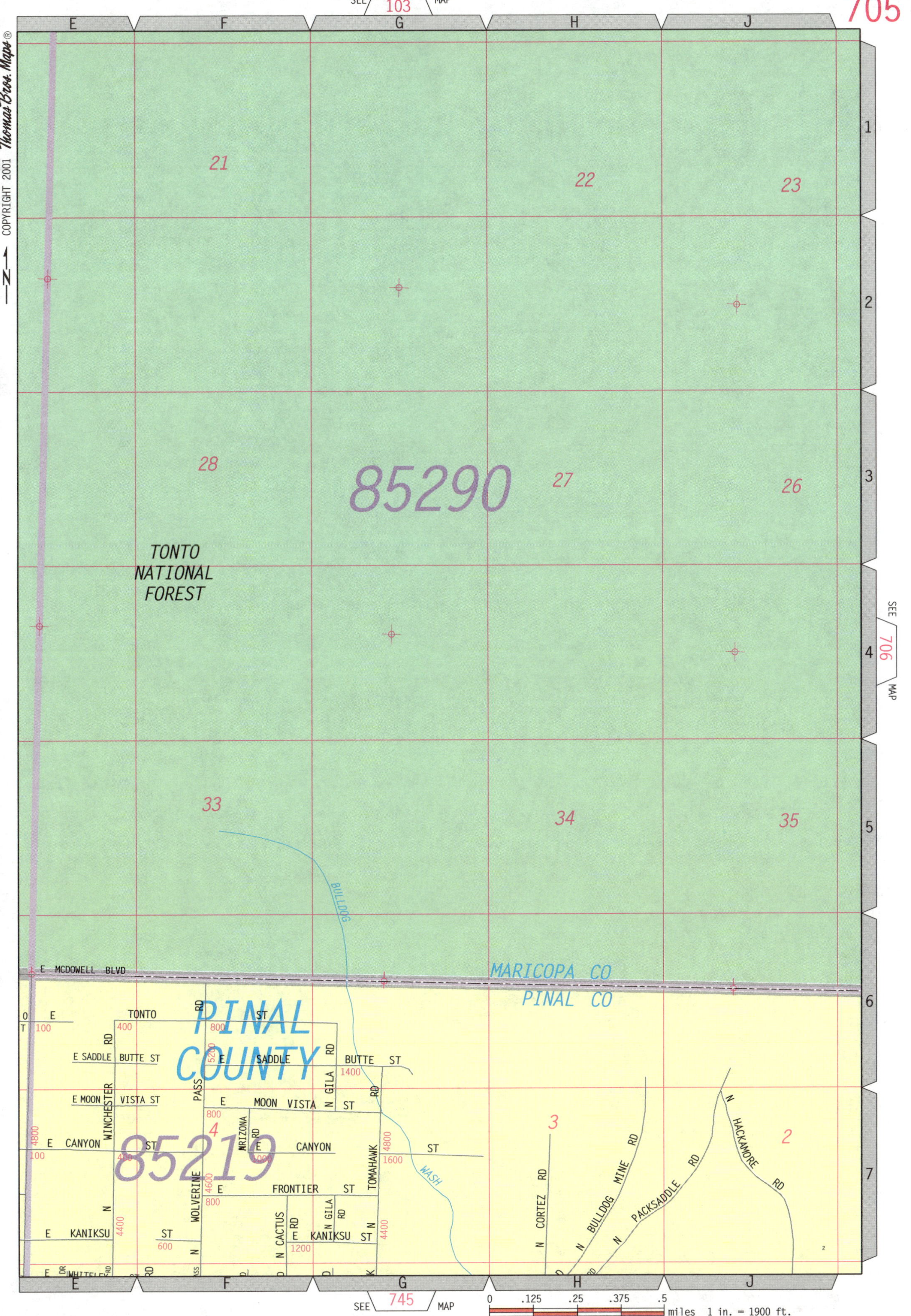
SEE 103 MAP
E
F
G
H
J
1
2
3
4
5
6
7
21
22
23
28
85290
27
26
TONTO
NATIONAL
FOREST
SEE 706 MAP
33
34
35
BULLDOG
E MCDOWELL BLVD
MARICOPA CO
PINAL CO
PINAL
COUNTY
E TONTO ST
E SADDLE BUTTE ST
E SADDLE BUTTE ST
E MOON VISTA ST
E MOON VISTA ST
E CANYON ST
E CANYON ST
WINCHESTER RD
PASS RD
GILA RD
TOMAHAWK RD
WASH
85219
E FRONTIER ST
WOLVERINE
E KANIKSU ST
E KANIKSU ST
N CACTUS RD
N GILA RD
N CORTEZ RD
N BULLDOG MINE RD
N PACKSADDLE RD
N HACKAMORE RD
3
2
4
SEE 745 MAP
0 .125 .25 .375 .5 miles 1 in. = 1900 ft.
PHOENIX
MAP

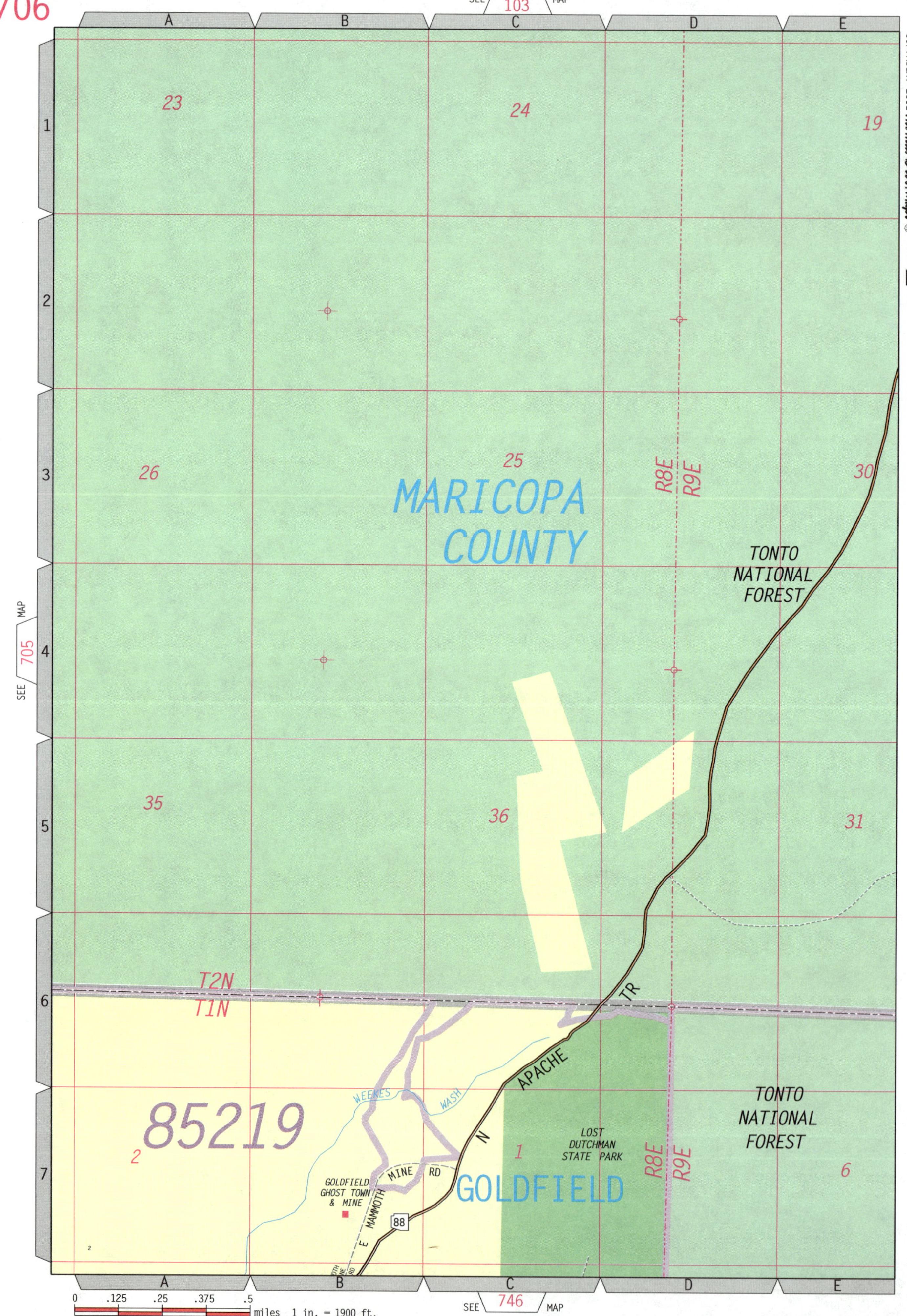
SEE 103 MAP
A
B
C
D
E
1
2
3
4
5
6
7
23
24
19
26
25
30
35
36
31
MARICOPA
COUNTY
R8E
R9E
TONTO
NATIONAL
FOREST
SEE 705 MAP
T2N
T1N
TR
APACHE
N
WEEKES
WASH
85219
2
1
6
LOST
DUTCHMAN
STATE PARK
GOLDFIELD
GOLDFIELD
GHOST TOWN
& MINE
MINE
RD
E MAMMOTH
88
SEE 746 MAP
0
.125
.25
.375
.5
miles 1 in. = 1900 ft.
PHOENIX
MAP

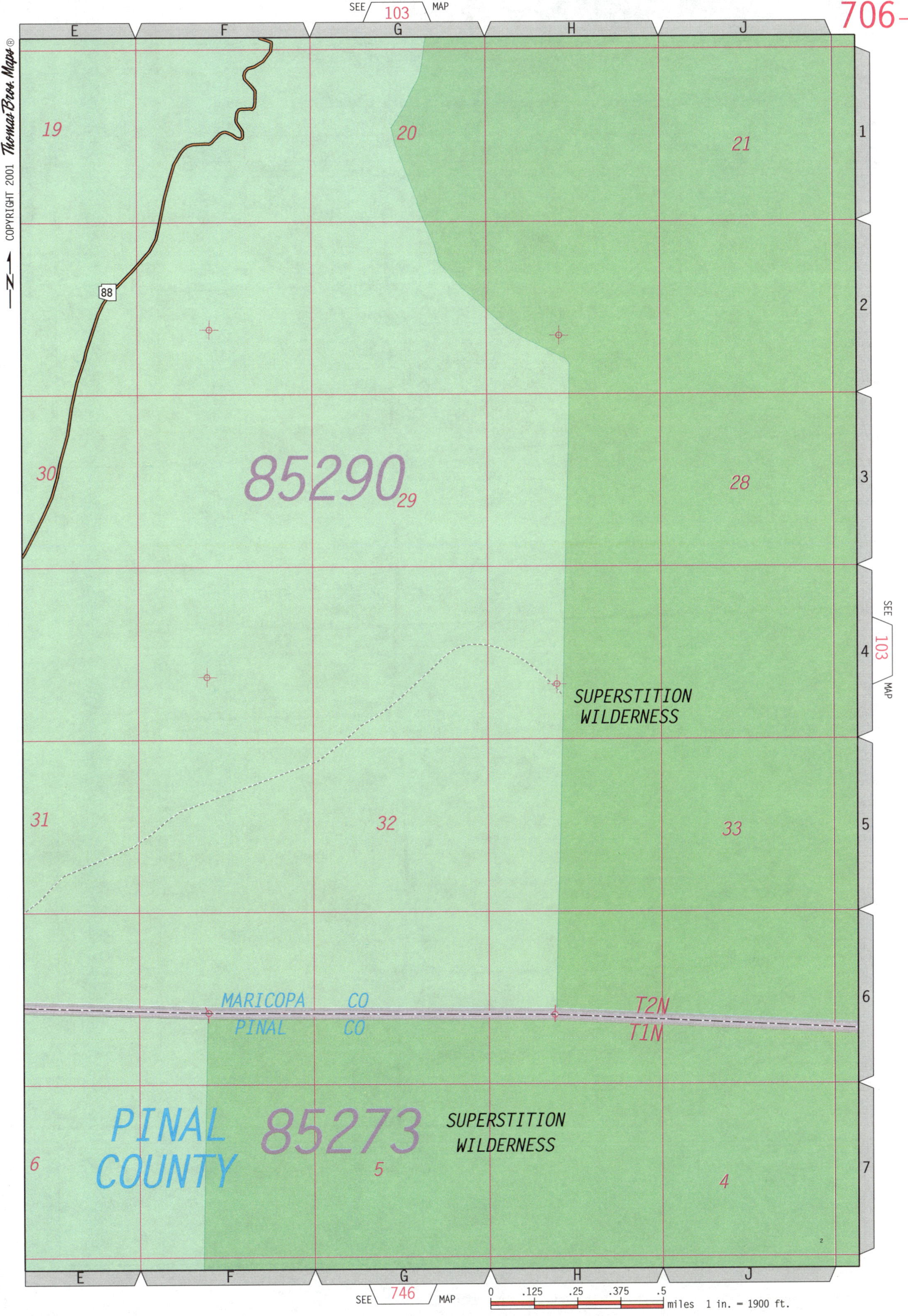
SEE 103 MAP
E
F
G
H
J
1
2
3
4
5
6
7
19
20
21
88
30
85290
29
28
SUPERSTITION
WILDERNESS
31
32
33
MARICOPA CO
PINAL CO
T2N
T1N
PINAL
COUNTY
85273
SUPERSTITION
WILDERNESS
6
5
4
SEE 103 MAP
SEE 746 MAP
0 .125 .25 .375 .5 miles 1 in. = 1900 ft.
PHOENIX
MAP

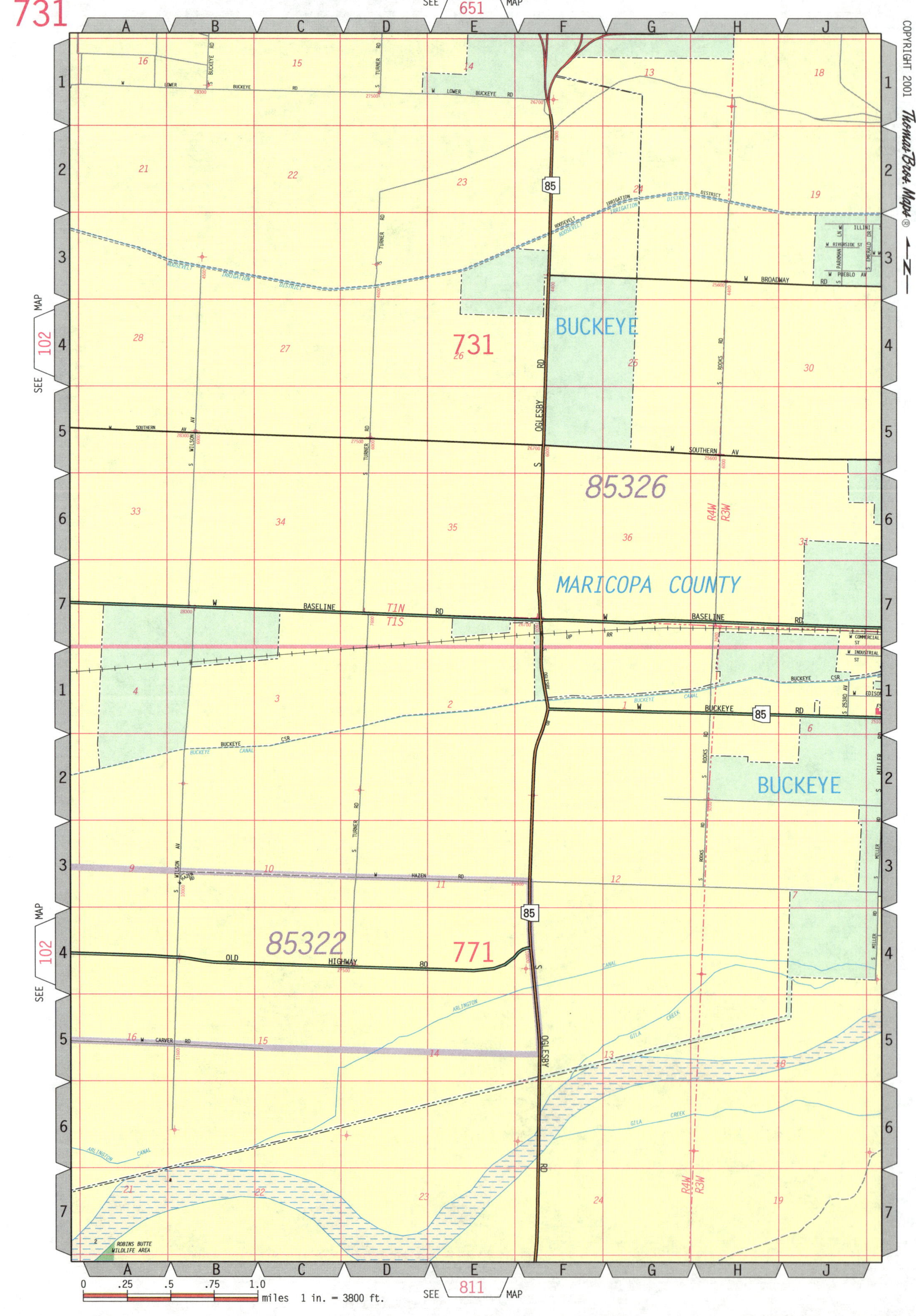

SEE 651 MAP
BUCKEYE
731
85326
MARICOPA COUNTY
BASELINE RD
SOUTHERN AV
OGLESBY RD
TURNER RD
WILSON AV
ROCKS RD
BROADWAY RD
LOWER BUCKEYE RD
ROOSEVELT IRRIGATION DISTRICT
BUCKEYE CANAL
HAZEN RD
CARVER RD
OLD HIGHWAY 80
85322
771
ARLINGTON CANAL
GILA CREEK
ROBINS BUTTE WILDLIFE AREA
T1N
T1S
R4W
R3W
SEE 102 MAP
SEE 811 MAP
0 .25 .5 .75 1.0 miles 1 in. = 3800 ft.

PHOENIX

MAP

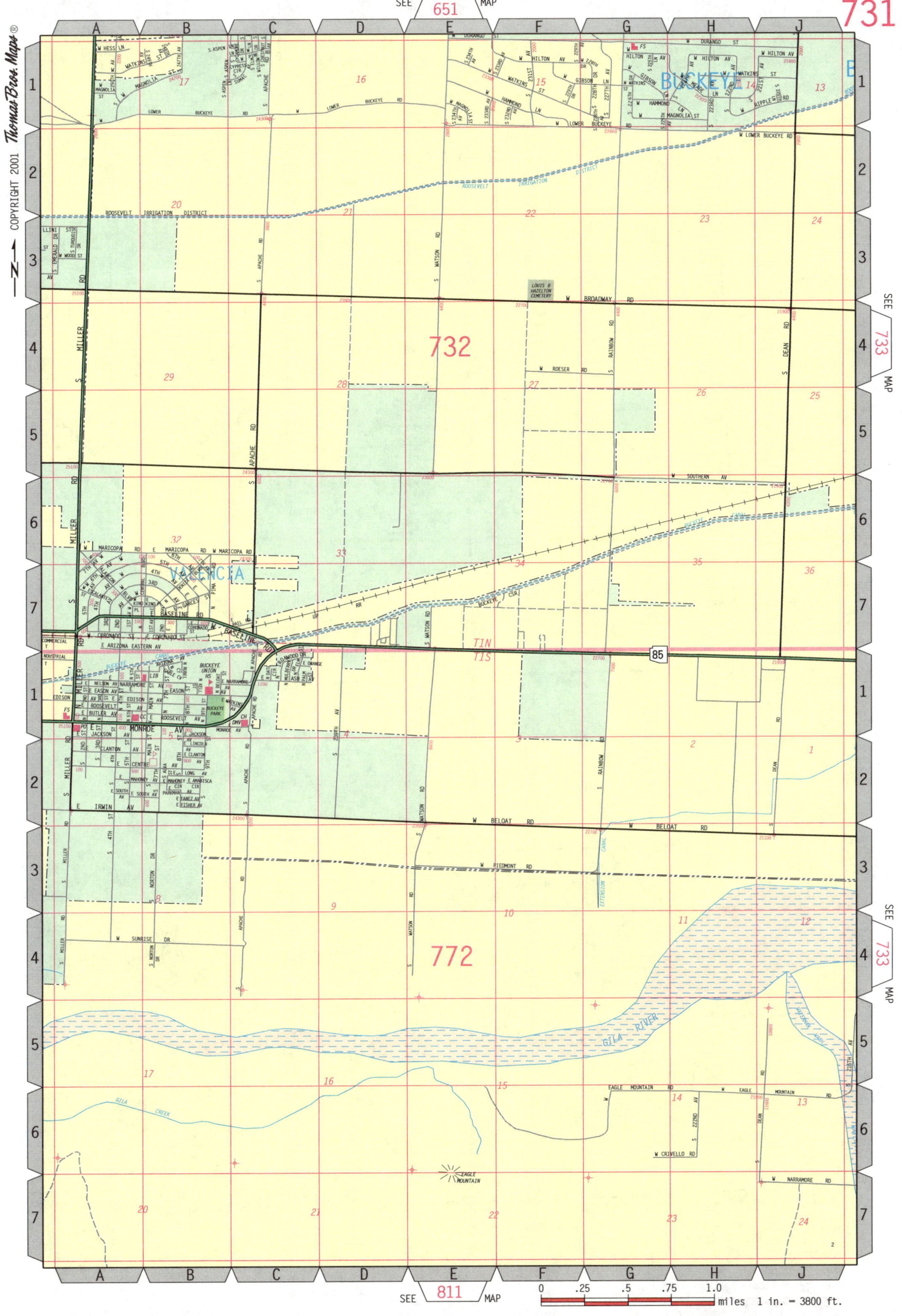

SEE 651 MAP
BUCKEYE
VALENCIA
732
772
ROOSEVELT IRRIGATION DISTRICT
W BROADWAY RD
LOUIS B HAZELTON CEMETERY
W SOUTHERN AV
W BELOAT RD
W PIEDMONT RD
W LOWER BUCKEYE RD
S MILLER RD
S APACHE RD
S WATSON RD
S RAINBOW RD
S DEAN RD
W ROESER RD
BASELINE RD
MONROE AV
BUCKEYE PARK
BUCKEYE UNION HS
GILA RIVER
GILA CREEK
EAGLE MOUNTAIN
W EAGLE MOUNTAIN RD
W CRIVELLO RD
W NARRAMORE RD
W SUNRISE DR
85
SEE 733 MAP
SEE 811 MAP
PHOENIX
MAP
0 .25 .5 .75 1.0 miles 1 in. = 3800 ft.

SEE 653 MAP

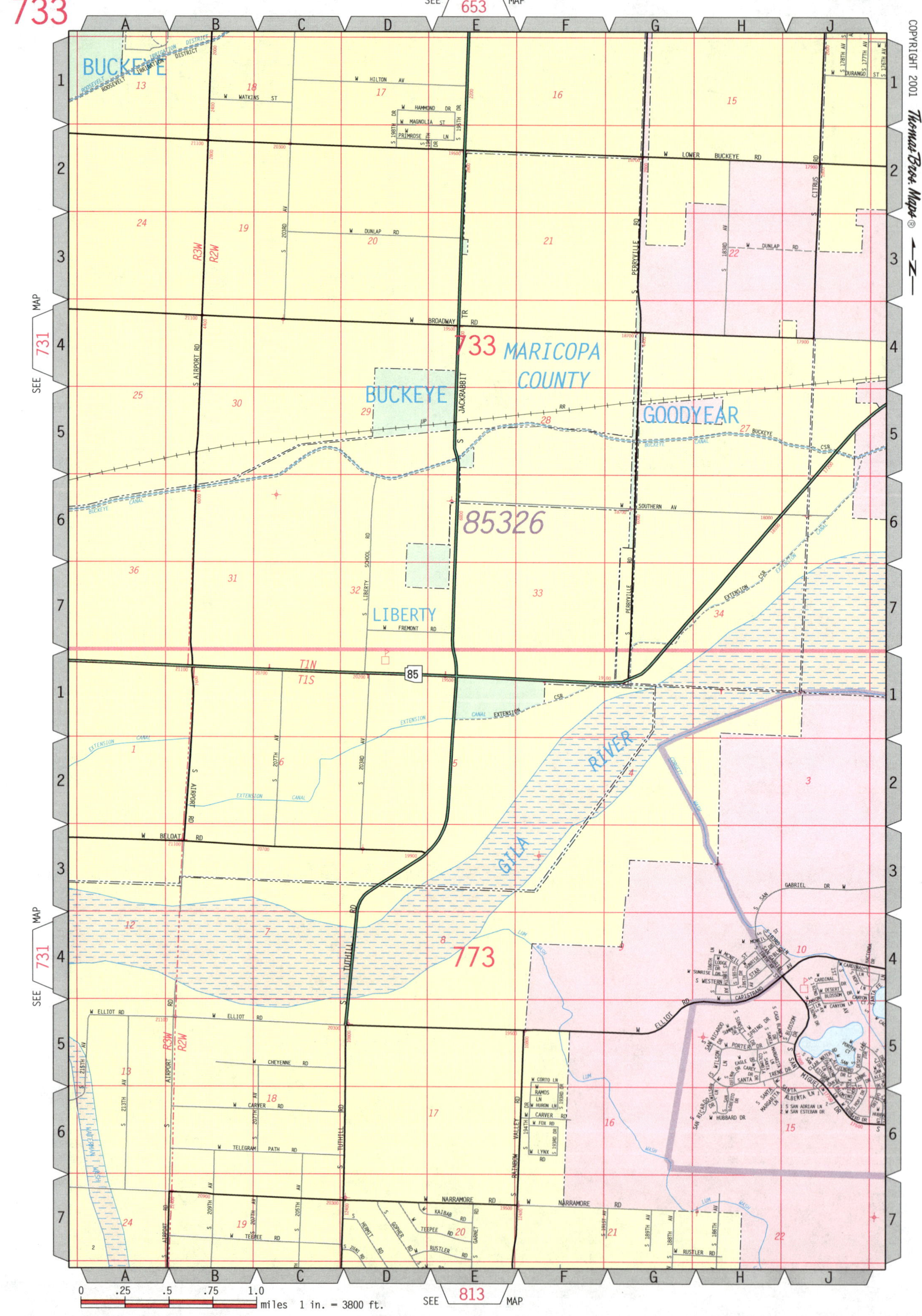

SEE 731 MAP

SEE 813 MAP

0 .25 .5 .75 1.0 miles 1 in. = 3800 ft.

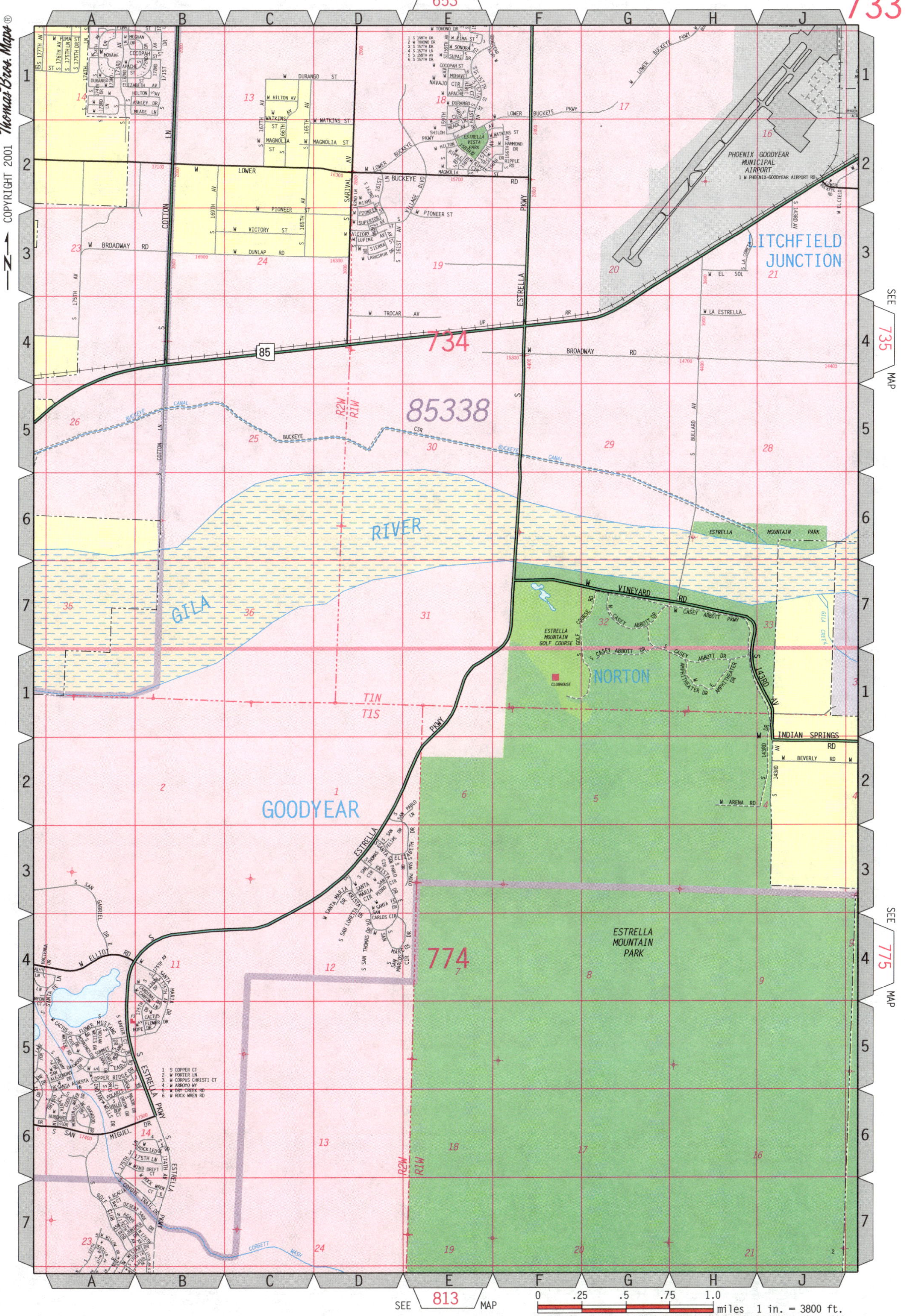

SEE 653 MAP
SEE 735 MAP
SEE 775 MAP
SEE 813 MAP
PHOENIX GOODYEAR MUNICIPAL AIRPORT
LITCHFIELD JUNCTION
85338
734
774
GILA RIVER
ESTRELLA MOUNTAIN PARK
ESTRELLA MOUNTAIN GOLF COURSE
NORTON
GOODYEAR
ESTRELLA VISTA PARK
LOWER BUCKEYE PKWY
ESTRELLA PKWY
W BROADWAY RD
W VINEYARD RD
W INDIAN SPRINGS RD
COTTON LN
BUCKEYE CANAL
0 .25 .5 .75 1.0 miles 1 in. = 3800 ft.

PHOENIX
MAP

SEE 695 MAP

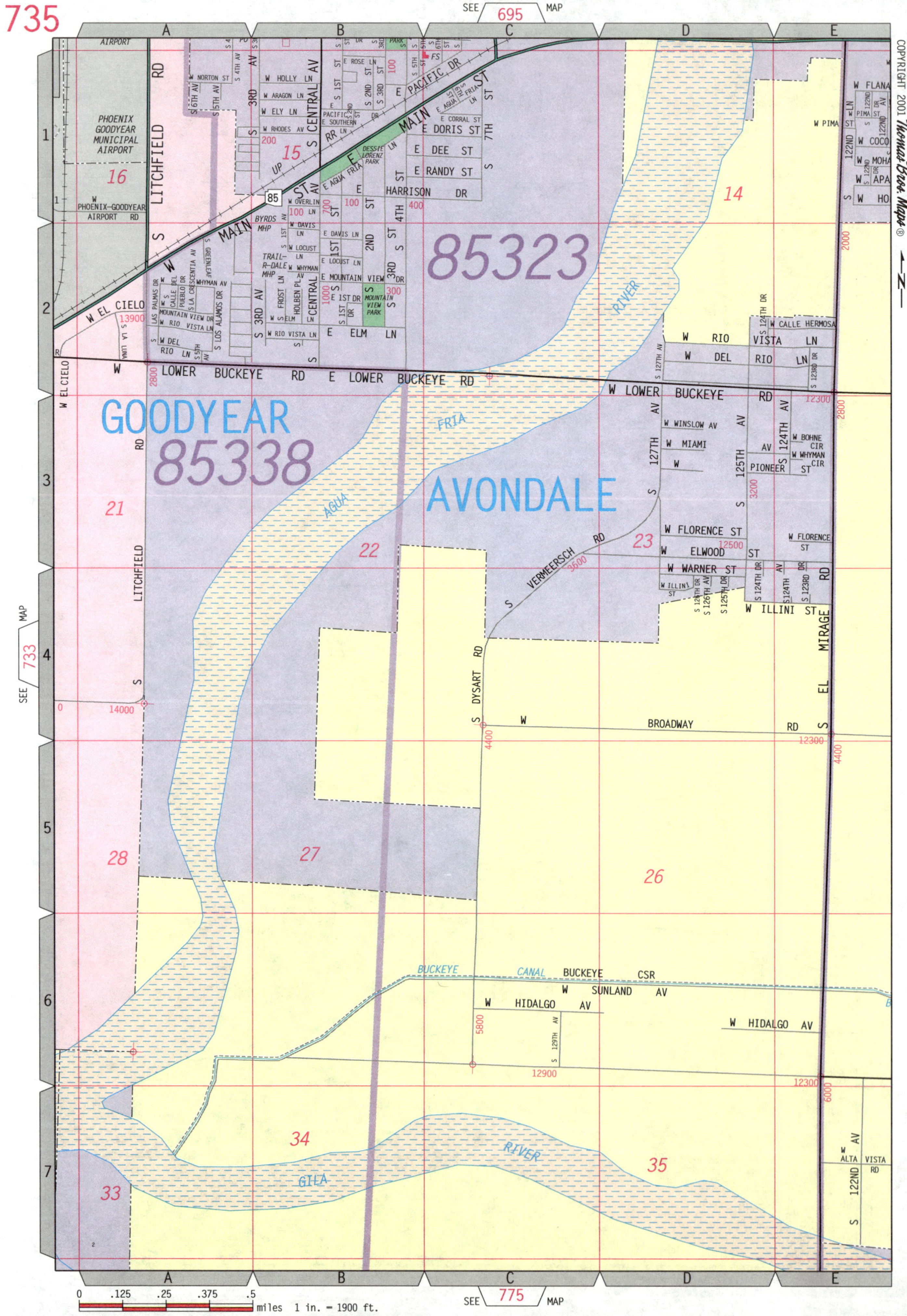

SEE 733 MAP

SEE 775 MAP

0 .125 .25 .375 .5 miles 1 in. = 1900 ft.

PHOENIX

MAP

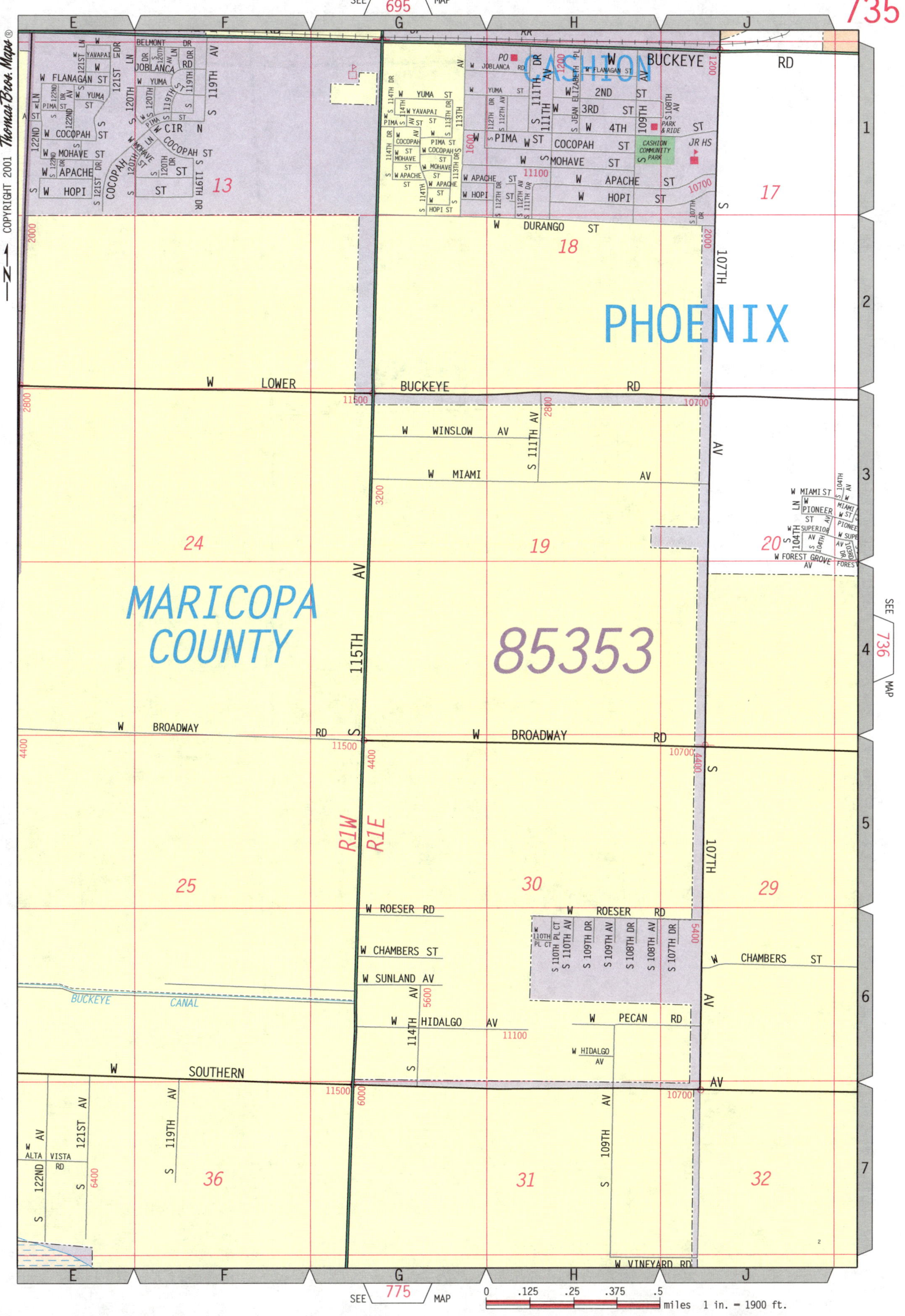
SEE 695 MAP
CASHION
PHOENIX
MARICOPA COUNTY
85353
W LOWER BUCKEYE RD
W BROADWAY RD
W SOUTHERN AV
S 115TH AV
S 107TH AV
W DURANGO ST
W WINSLOW AV
W MIAMI AV
W ROESER RD
W CHAMBERS ST
W SUNLAND AV
W HIDALGO AV
W PECAN RD
W VINEYARD RD
BUCKEYE CANAL
CASHION COMMUNITY PARK
JR HS
R1W R1E
SEE 736 MAP
SEE 775 MAP
miles 1 in. = 1900 ft.

PHOENIX

MAP

SEE 696 MAP

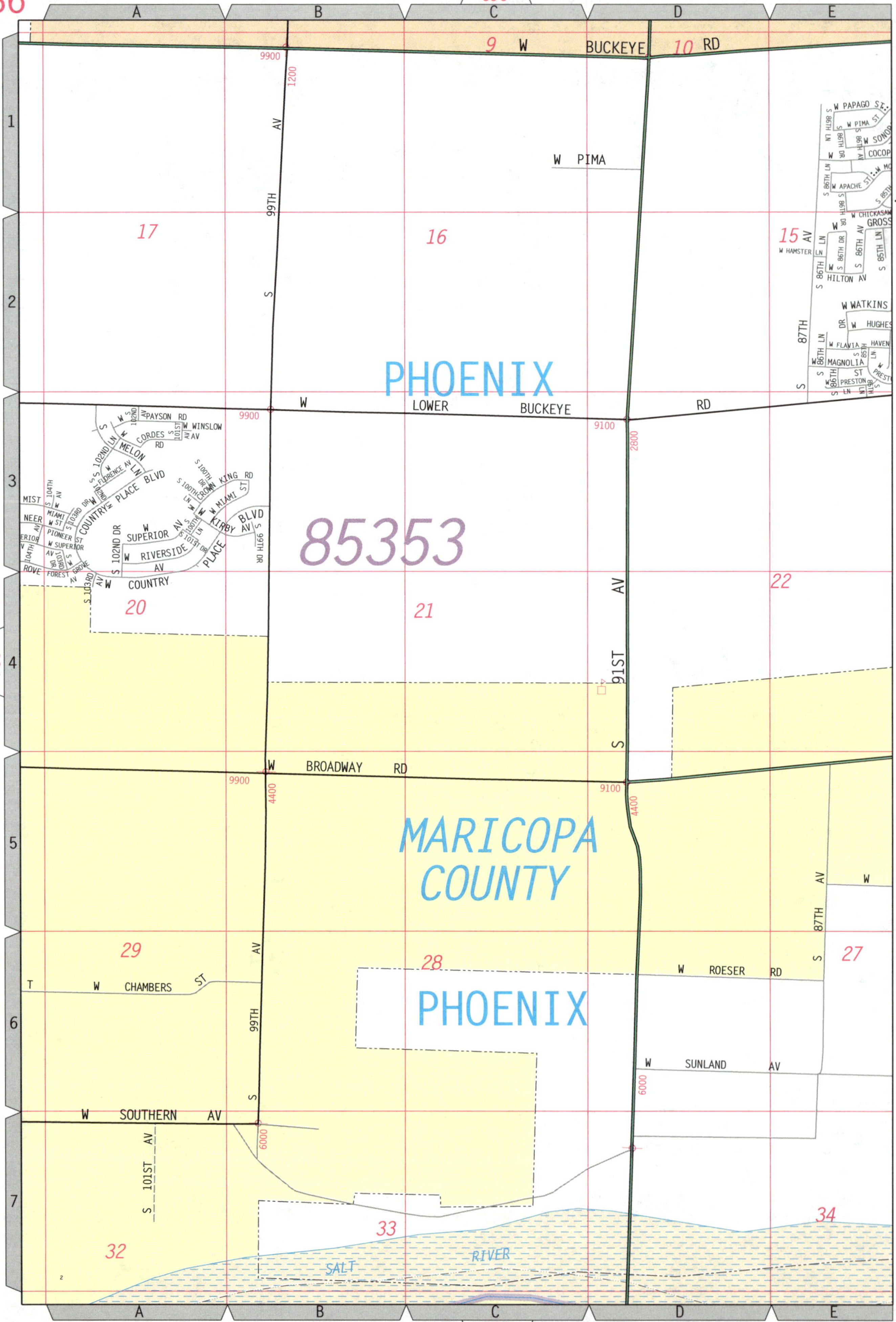

SEE 735 MAP

SEE 776 MAP

0 .125 .25 .375 .5 miles 1 in. = 1900 ft.

PHOENIX

MAP

SEE 696 MAP

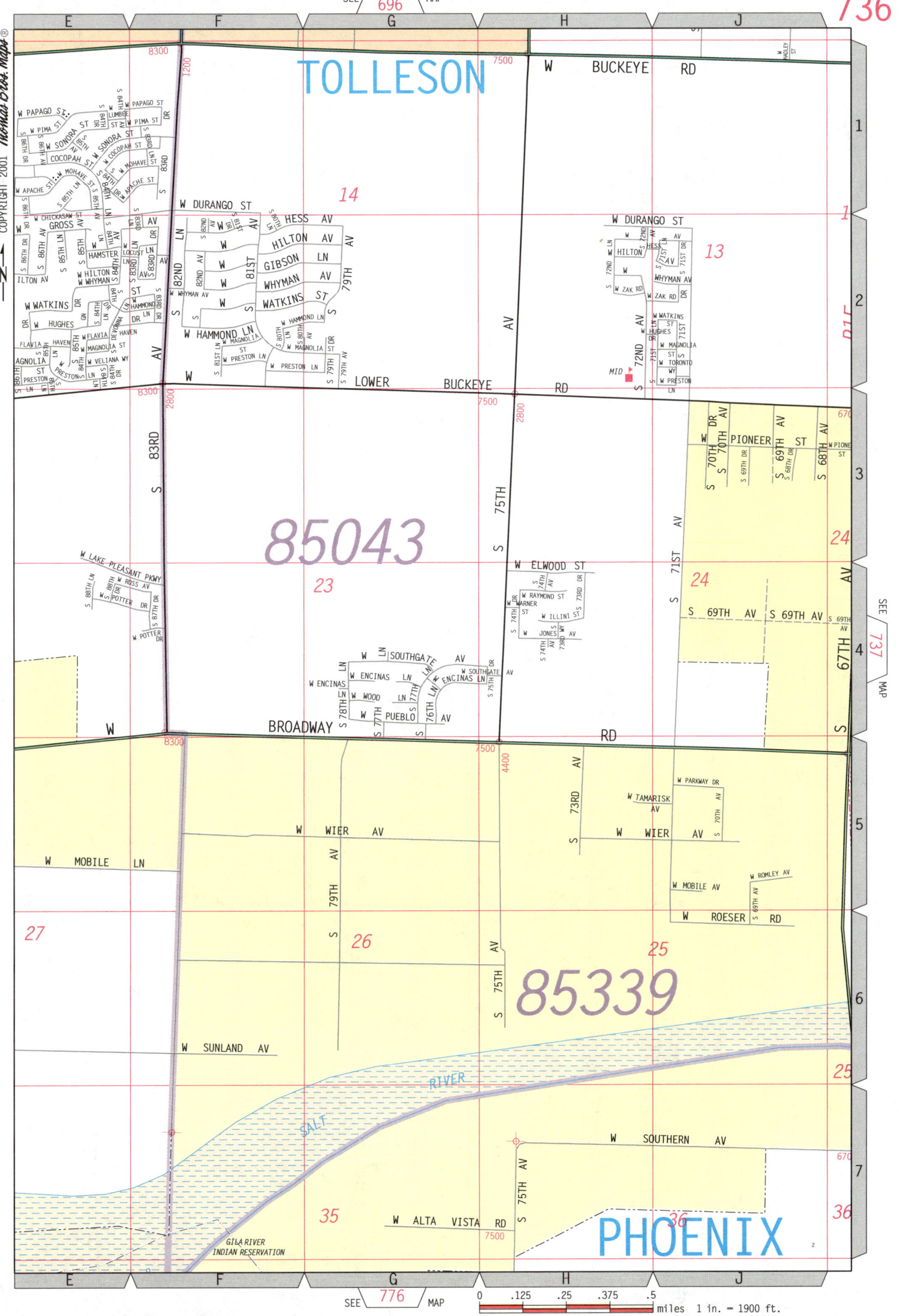

SEE 776 MAP

0 .125 .25 .375 .5 miles 1 in. = 1900 ft.

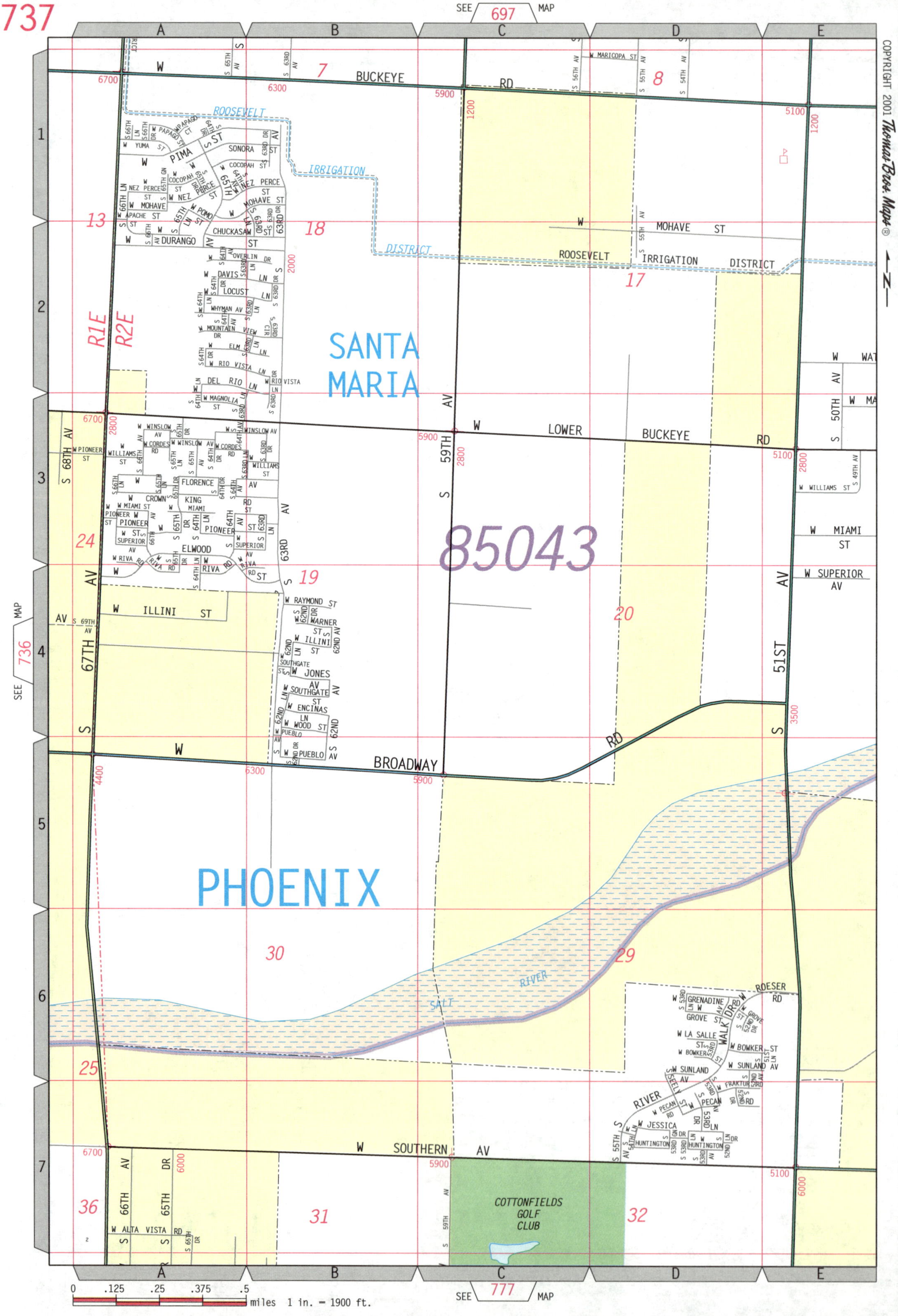
SEE 697 MAP
SEE 736 MAP
SEE 777 MAP
A B C D E
1 2 3 4 5 6 7
SANTA MARIA
PHOENIX
85043
R1E R2E
W BUCKEYE RD
W LOWER BUCKEYE RD
W BROADWAY RD
W SOUTHERN AV
S 67TH AV
S 59TH AV
S 51ST AV
ROOSEVELT IRRIGATION DISTRICT
SALT RIVER
COTTONFIELDS GOLF CLUB
W MOHAVE ST
W ILLINI ST
W MARICOPA ST
S 56TH AV
S 55TH AV
S 54TH AV
S 65TH AV
S 63RD AV
S 68TH AV
W PIMA ST
W SONORA ST
W COCOPAH ST
W NEZ PERCE ST
W YUMA ST
W PAPAGO CT
W APACHE ST
W DURANGO ST
W CHUCKASAW ST
W POMO ST
W OVERLIN DR
W DAVIS LN
W LOCUST LN
W WHYMAN AV
W MOUNTAIN VIEW DR
W ELM LN
W RIO VISTA LN
W DEL RIO LN
W MAGNOLIA ST
W WINSLOW AV
W CORDES RD
W WILLIAMS ST
W PIONEER ST
W FLORENCE AV
W CROWN KING RD
W MIAMI ST
W SUPERIOR AV
W ELWOOD ST
W RIVA RD
W RAYMOND ST
W WARNER ST
W JONES AV
W SOUTHGATE AV
W ENCINAS LN
W WOOD ST
W PUEBLO AV
S 62ND DR
S 62ND AV
W ROESER RD
W GRENADINE RD
W GROVE ST
W LA SALLE ST
WALK DR
W BOWKER ST
W SUNLAND AV
RIVER ST
S SEELY ST
W PECAN RD
W FRAKTUR RD
W JESSICA LN
W HUNTINGTON DR
S 53RD AV
S 52ND DR
W ALTA VISTA RD
S 66TH AV
S 65TH DR
S 50TH AV
W WATKINS
W MARICOPA
S 49TH AV
1 2 7 8 13 17 18 19 20 24 25 29 30 31 32 36
6700 6300 5900 5100
1200 2000 2800 3500 4400 6000
COPYRIGHT 2001 Thomas Bros. Maps ®
0 .125 .25 .375 .5 miles 1 in. = 1900 ft.

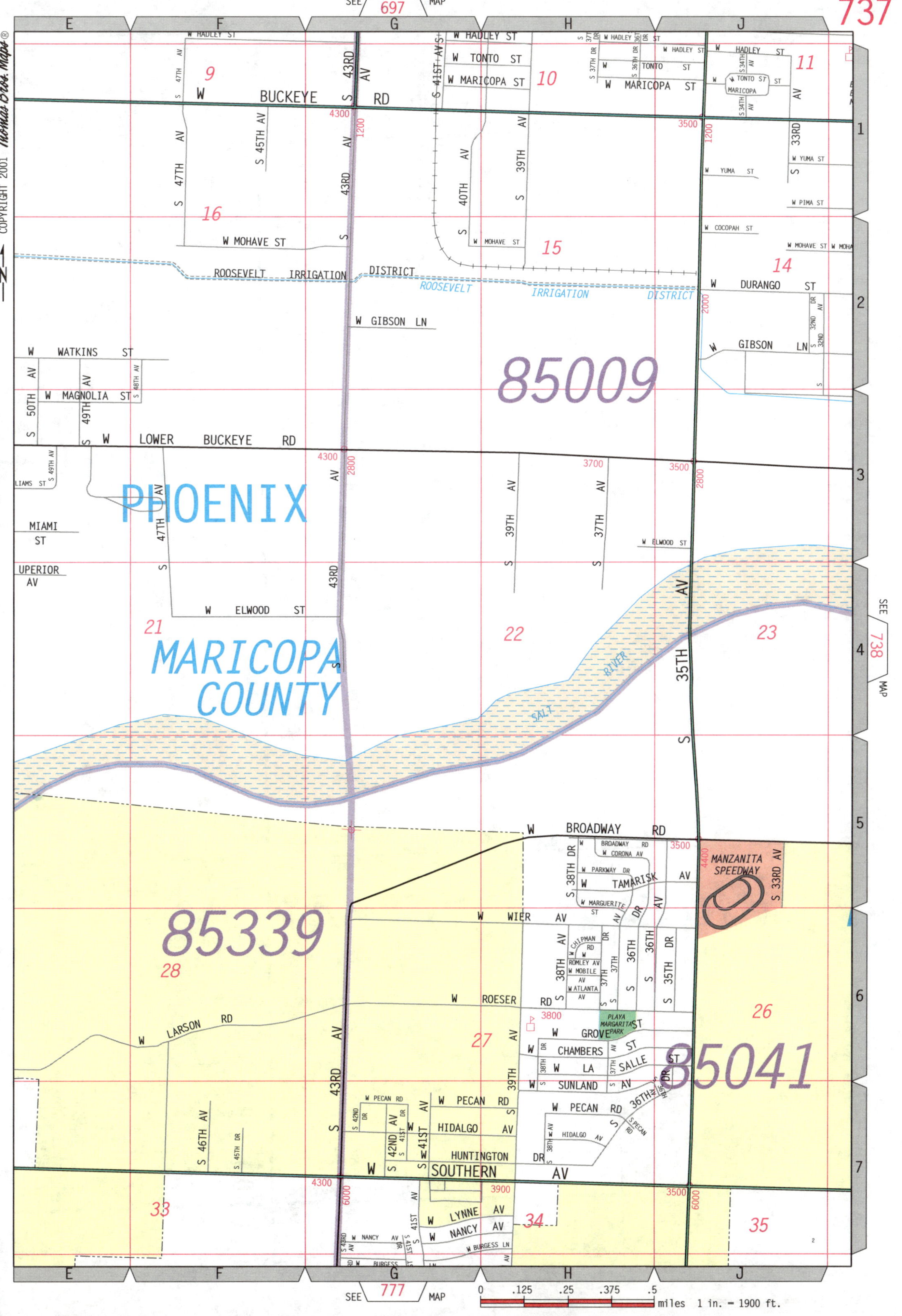
SEE 697 MAP
85009
PHOENIX
MARICOPA COUNTY
85339
85041
W BUCKEYE RD
W LOWER BUCKEYE RD
W BROADWAY RD
W SOUTHERN AV
W ROESER RD
W LARSON RD
W WIER AV
S 43RD AV
S 35TH AV
S 39TH AV
S 47TH AV
ROOSEVELT IRRIGATION DISTRICT
SALT RIVER
MANZANITA SPEEDWAY
PLAYA MARGARITA PARK
W MOHAVE ST
W GIBSON LN
W DURANGO ST
W WATKINS ST
W MAGNOLIA ST
W ELWOOD ST
W PECAN RD
HIDALGO AV
HUNTINGTON DR
W LYNNE AV
W NANCY AV
W BURGESS LN
SEE 738 MAP
SEE 777 MAP
miles 1 in. = 1900 ft.

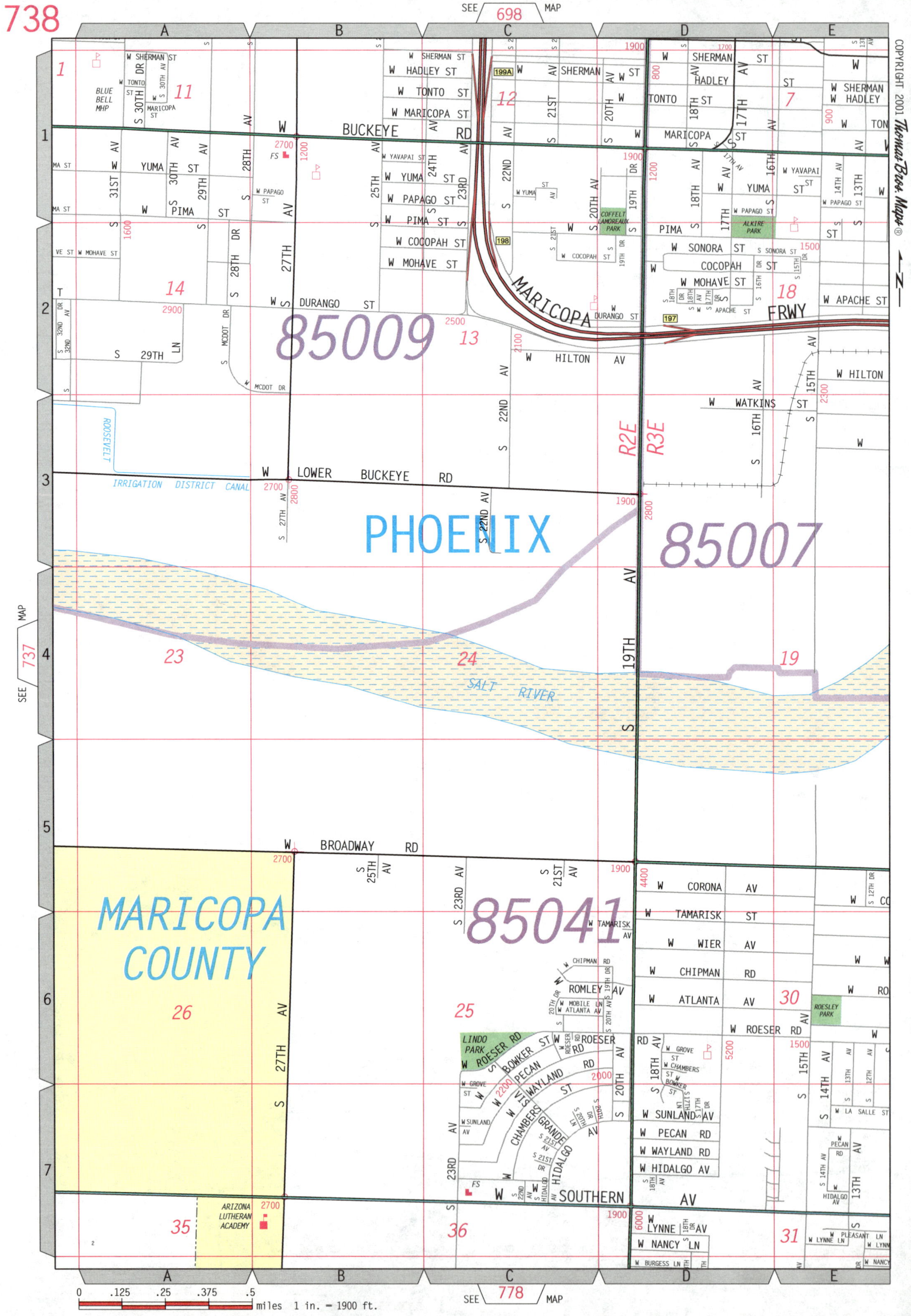

SEE 698 MAP

PHOENIX

85009

85007

85041

MARICOPA COUNTY

W BUCKEYE RD

W LOWER BUCKEYE RD

W BROADWAY RD

W SOUTHERN AV

MARICOPA FRWY

SALT RIVER

ROOSEVELT IRRIGATION DISTRICT CANAL

R2E R3E

W SHERMAN ST
W HADLEY ST
W TONTO ST
W MARICOPA ST
W YAVAPAI ST
W YUMA ST
W PAPAGO ST
W PIMA ST
W SONORA ST
W COCOPAH ST
W MOHAVE ST
W APACHE ST
W DURANGO ST
W HILTON AV
W WATKINS ST
W CORONA AV
W TAMARISK ST
W WIER AV
W CHIPMAN RD
W ROMLEY AV
W MOBILE LN
W ATLANTA AV
W ROESER RD
W GROVE ST
W CHAMBERS ST
W BOWKER ST
W SUNLAND AV
W PECAN RD
W WAYLAND RD
W HIDALGO AV
W LA SALLE ST
W LYNNE LN
W NANCY LN
W PLEASANT LN
W BURGESS LN

S 32ND DR
S 32ND AV
S 31ST AV
S 30TH DR
S 30TH AV
S 29TH AV
S 29TH LN
S 28TH DR
S 28TH AV
S MCDOT DR
S 27TH AV
S 25TH AV
S 24TH AV
S 23RD AV
S 22ND AV
S 21ST AV
S 20TH AV
S 19TH AV
S 19TH DR
S 18TH AV
S 18TH DR
S 17TH AV
S 17TH DR
S 16TH AV
S 16TH DR
S 15TH AV
S 15TH DR
S 14TH AV
S 13TH AV
S 12TH DR
S GRANDE AV

BLUE BELL MHP
COFFELT LAMOREAUX PARK
ALKIRE PARK
ROESLEY PARK
LINDO PARK
ARIZONA LUTHERAN ACADEMY
FS

197
198
199A

1 11 12 7 14 13 18 23 24 19 26 25 30 35 36 31

1900 2700 2900 2500 2100 2800 1200 1600 1700 800 900 1500 2300 4400 5200 6000 2200 2000

A B C D E
1 2 3 4 5 6 7

SEE 737 MAP

SEE 778 MAP

0 .125 .25 .375 .5 miles 1 in. = 1900 ft.

PHOENIX

MAP

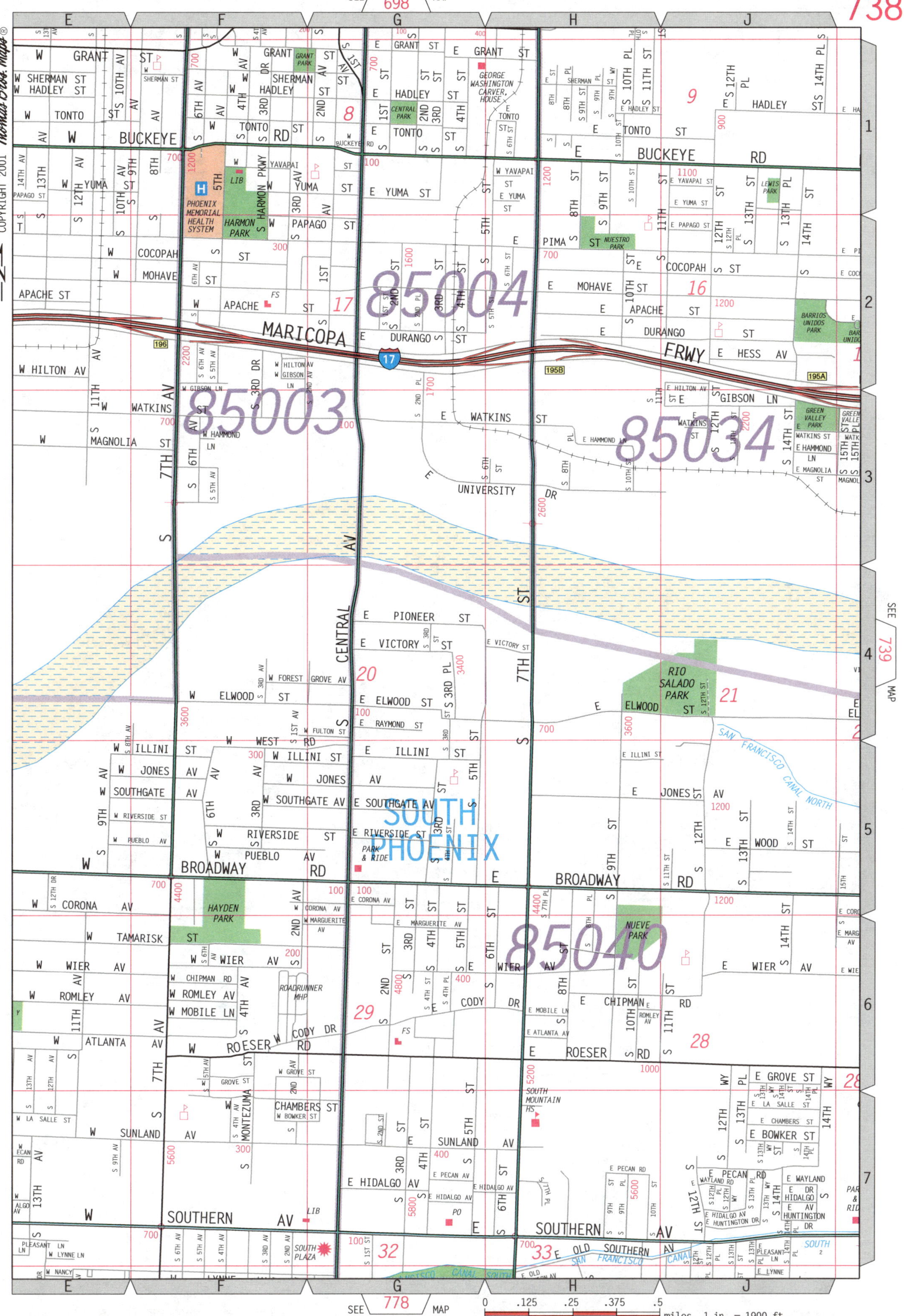

SEE 698 MAP
SEE 778 MAP
SEE 739 MAP
PHOENIX
MAP
Thomas Bros. Maps
COPYRIGHT 2001
85004
85003
85034
85040
MARICOPA FRWY
W GRANT ST
W BUCKEYE RD
E BUCKEYE RD
W YUMA
E YUMA ST
W PAPAGO ST
W COCOPAH ST
E COCOPAH ST
W MOHAVE ST
E MOHAVE ST
W APACHE ST
E APACHE ST
E DURANGO ST
W HILTON AV
E HESS AV
E WATKINS ST
W MAGNOLIA ST
E UNIVERSITY DR
S CENTRAL AV
S 7TH AV
S 7TH ST
E PIONEER ST
E VICTORY ST
W ELWOOD ST
E ELWOOD ST
W ILLINI ST
E ILLINI ST
W JONES AV
W SOUTHGATE AV
E SOUTHGATE AV
W RIVERSIDE ST
W PUEBLO AV
W BROADWAY RD
E BROADWAY RD
W CORONA AV
W TAMARISK ST
W WIER AV
E WIER AV
W ROMLEY AV
W MOBILE LN
W ATLANTA AV
W ROESER RD
E ROESER RD
E CHIPMAN RD
E CODY DR
W SUNLAND AV
E SUNLAND AV
E HIDALGO AV
W SOUTHERN AV
E SOUTHERN AV
E OLD SOUTHERN AV
SOUTH PHOENIX
PHOENIX MEMORIAL HEALTH SYSTEM
HARMON PARK
CENTRAL PARK
GEORGE WASHINGTON CARVER HOUSE
NUESTRO PARK
LEWIS PARK
BARRIOS UNIDOS PARK
GREEN VALLEY PARK
RIO SALADO PARK
HAYDEN PARK
NUEVE PARK
ROADRUNNER MHP
SOUTH MOUNTAIN HS
SOUTH PLAZA
PARK & RIDE
SAN FRANCISCO CANAL NORTH
0 .125 .25 .375 .5 miles 1 in. = 1900 ft.

SEE 699 MAP

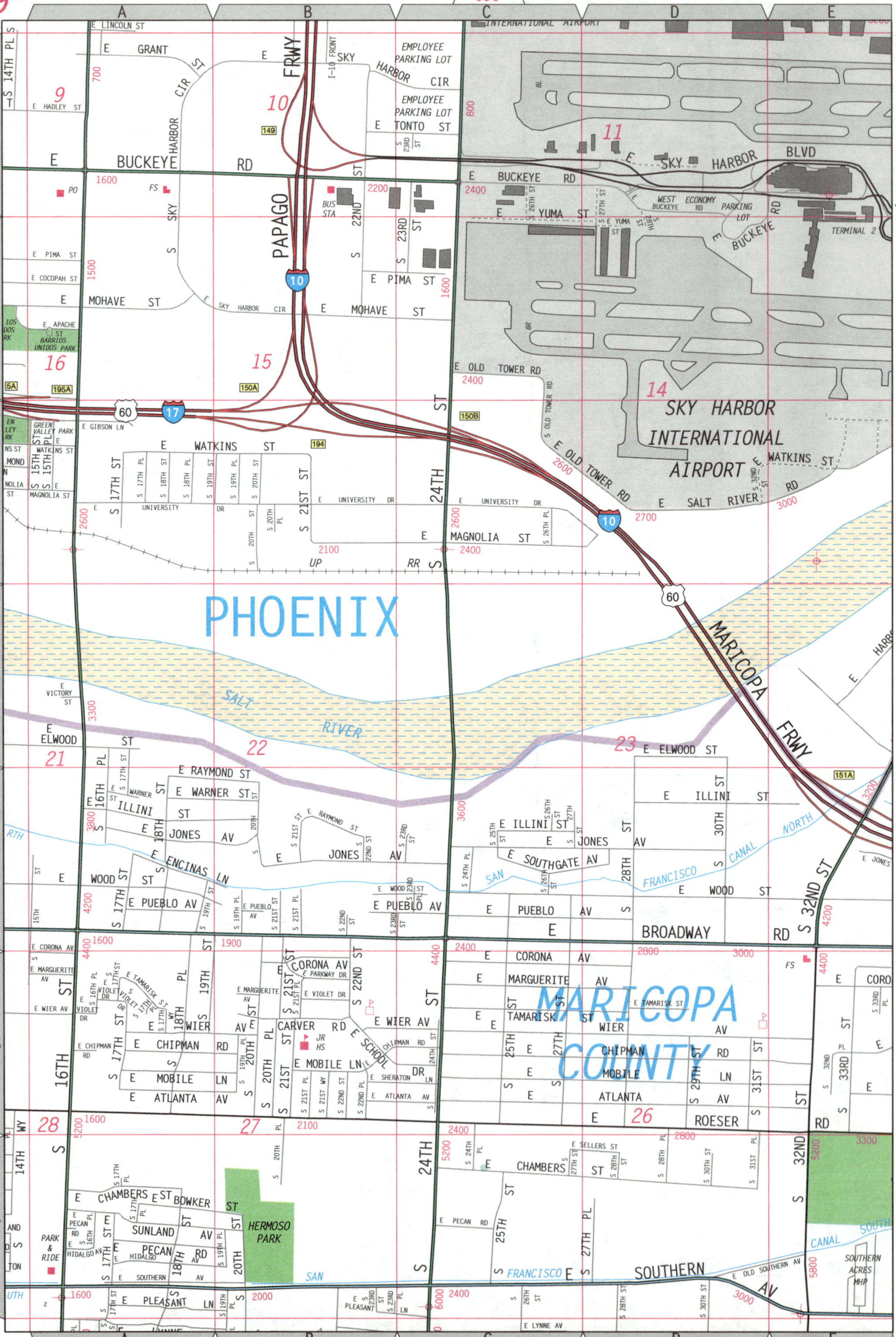

PHOENIX

SKY HARBOR INTERNATIONAL AIRPORT

MARICOPA COUNTY

E BUCKEYE RD

PAPAGO FRWY

MARICOPA FRWY

SALT RIVER

E SKY HARBOR BLVD

BROADWAY RD

SOUTHERN AV

S 16TH ST

S 24TH ST

S 32ND ST

HERMOSO PARK

SEE 738 MAP

SEE 779 MAP

0 .125 .25 .375 .5 miles 1 in. = 1900 ft.

See Page viii for Detail Airport Map

SEE 699 MAP

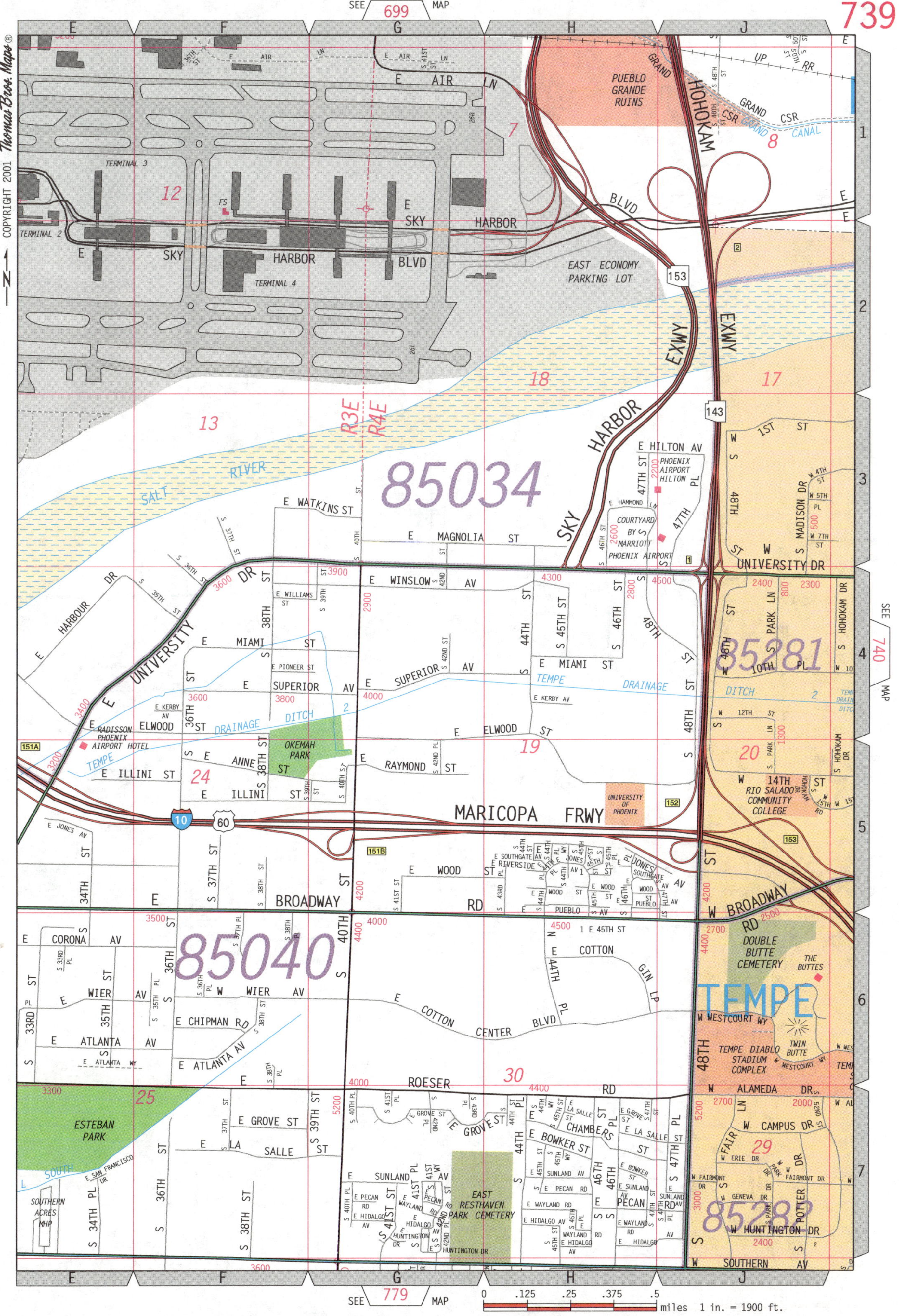

SEE 740 MAP

SEE 779 MAP

SEE 700 MAP

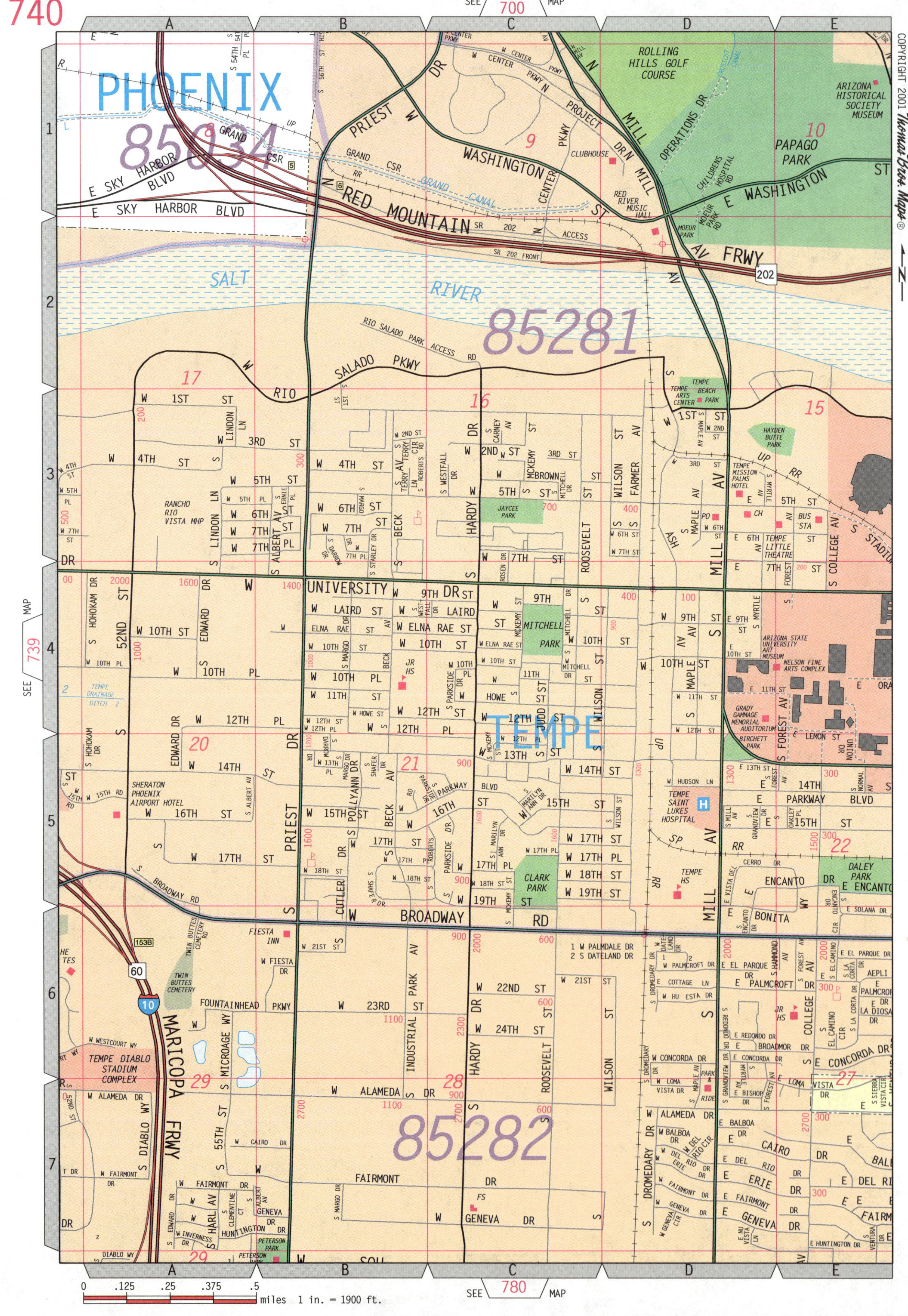

SEE 739 MAP

SEE 780 MAP

SEE 700 MAP

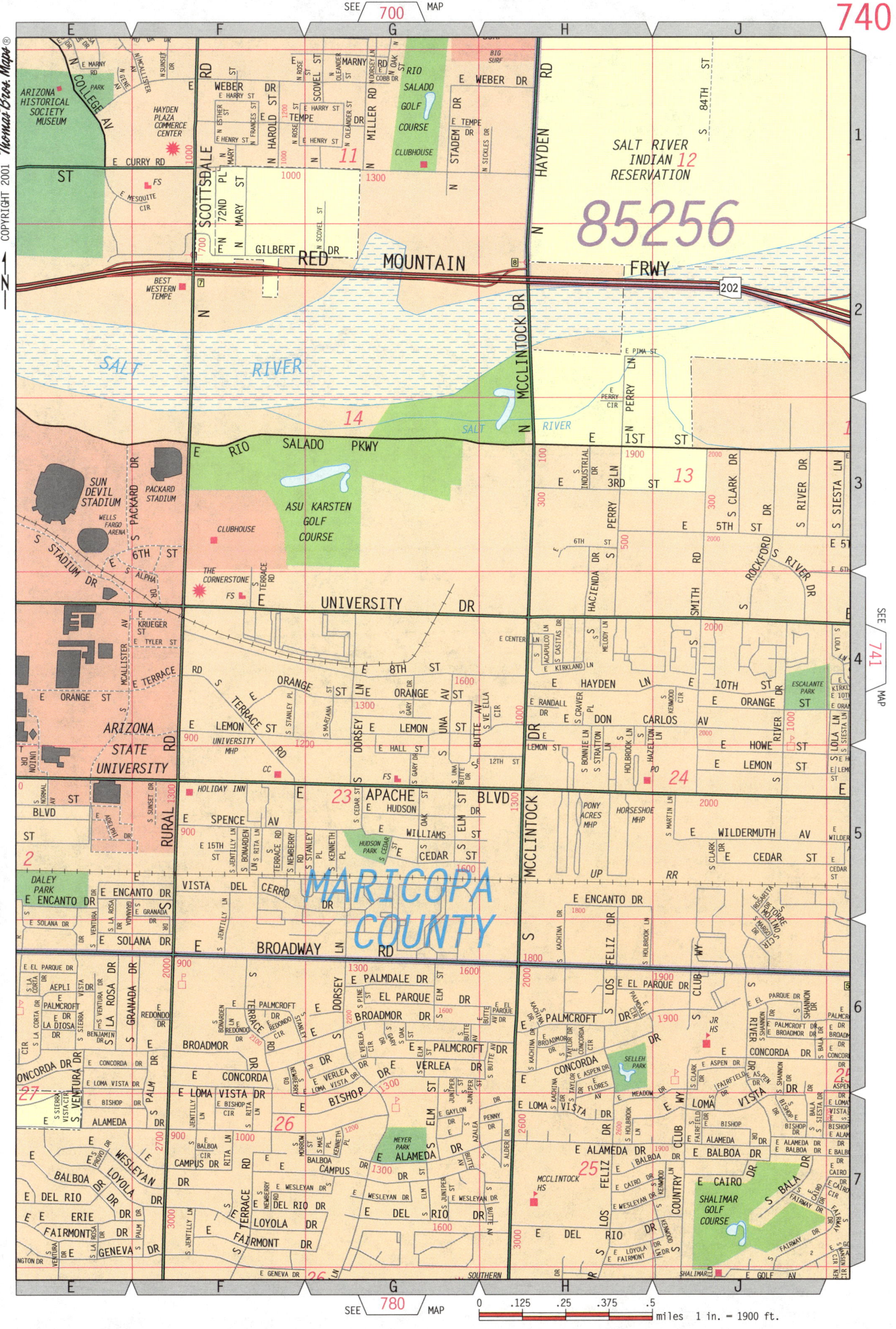

SEE 741 MAP

SEE 780 MAP

0 .125 .25 .375 .5 miles 1 in. = 1900 ft.

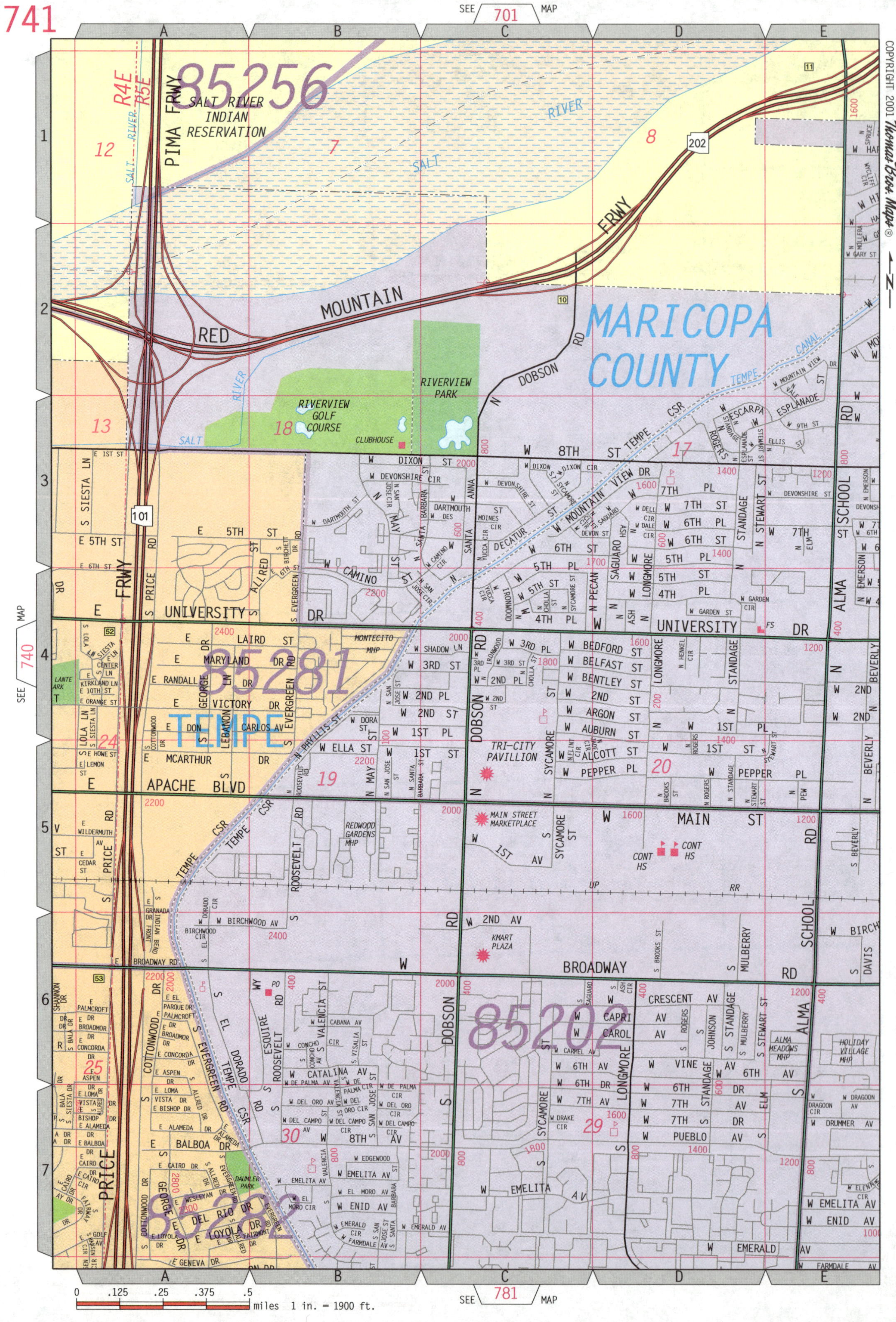

SEE 701 MAP
85256
SALT RIVER INDIAN RESERVATION
PIMA FRWY
RED MOUNTAIN
FRWY
202
MARICOPA COUNTY
RIVERVIEW GOLF COURSE
RIVERVIEW PARK
CLUBHOUSE
DOBSON RD
TEMPE CANAL
85281
TEMPE
UNIVERSITY DR
APACHE BLVD
MAIN ST
BROADWAY RD
TRI-CITY PAVILLION
MAIN STREET MARKETPLACE
KMART PLAZA
MONTECITO MHP
REDWOOD GARDENS MHP
ALMA MEADOWS MHP
HOLIDAY VILLAGE MHP
DAUMLER PARK
85202
85282
ALMA SCHOOL RD
PRICE FRWY
101
SEE 740 MAP
SEE 781 MAP
COPYRIGHT 2001 Thomas Bros. Maps®
PHOENIX
MAP
0 .125 .25 .375 .5 miles 1 in. = 1900 ft.

SEE 701 MAP

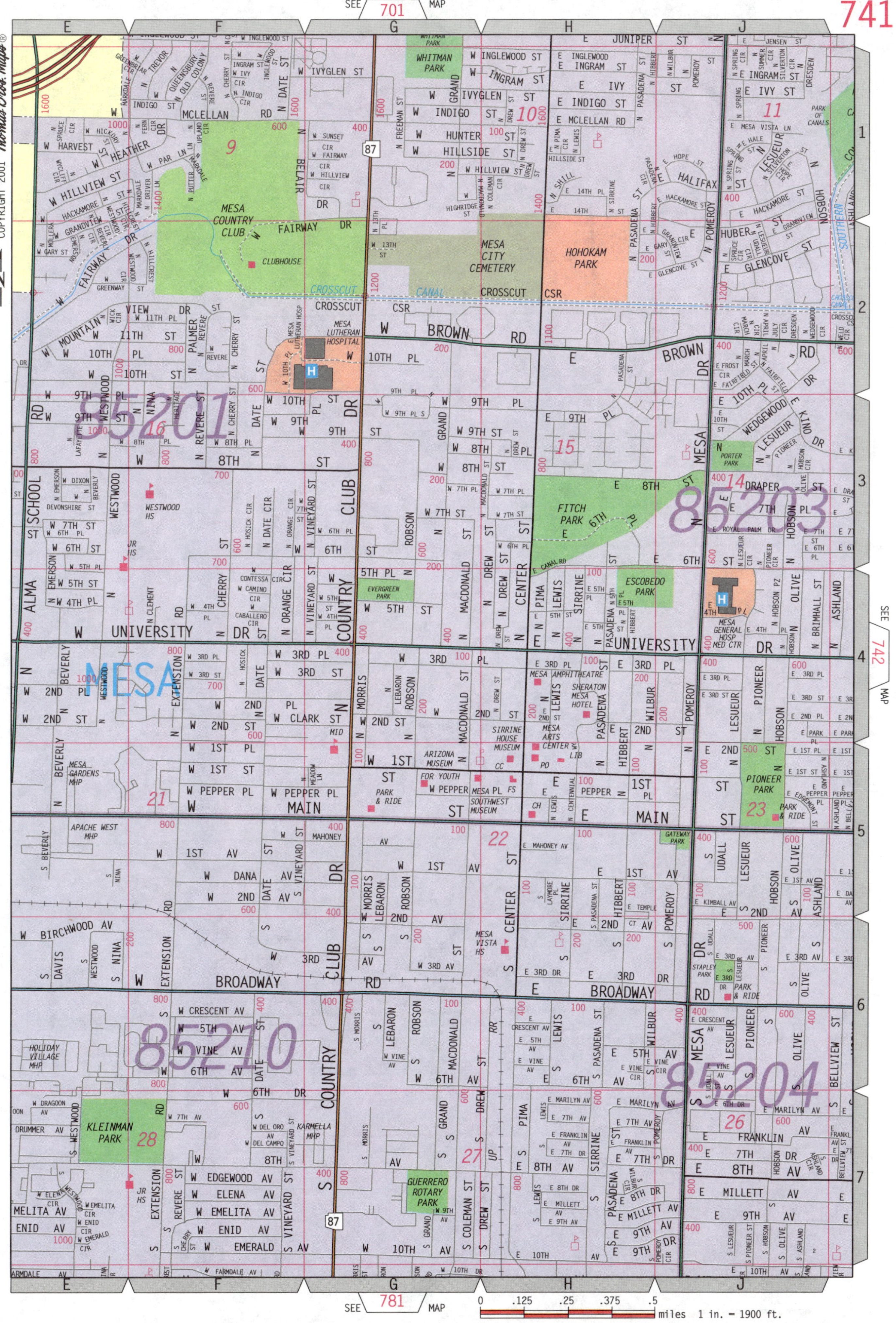

SEE 742 MAP

SEE 781 MAP

0 .125 .25 .375 .5 miles 1 in. = 1900 ft.

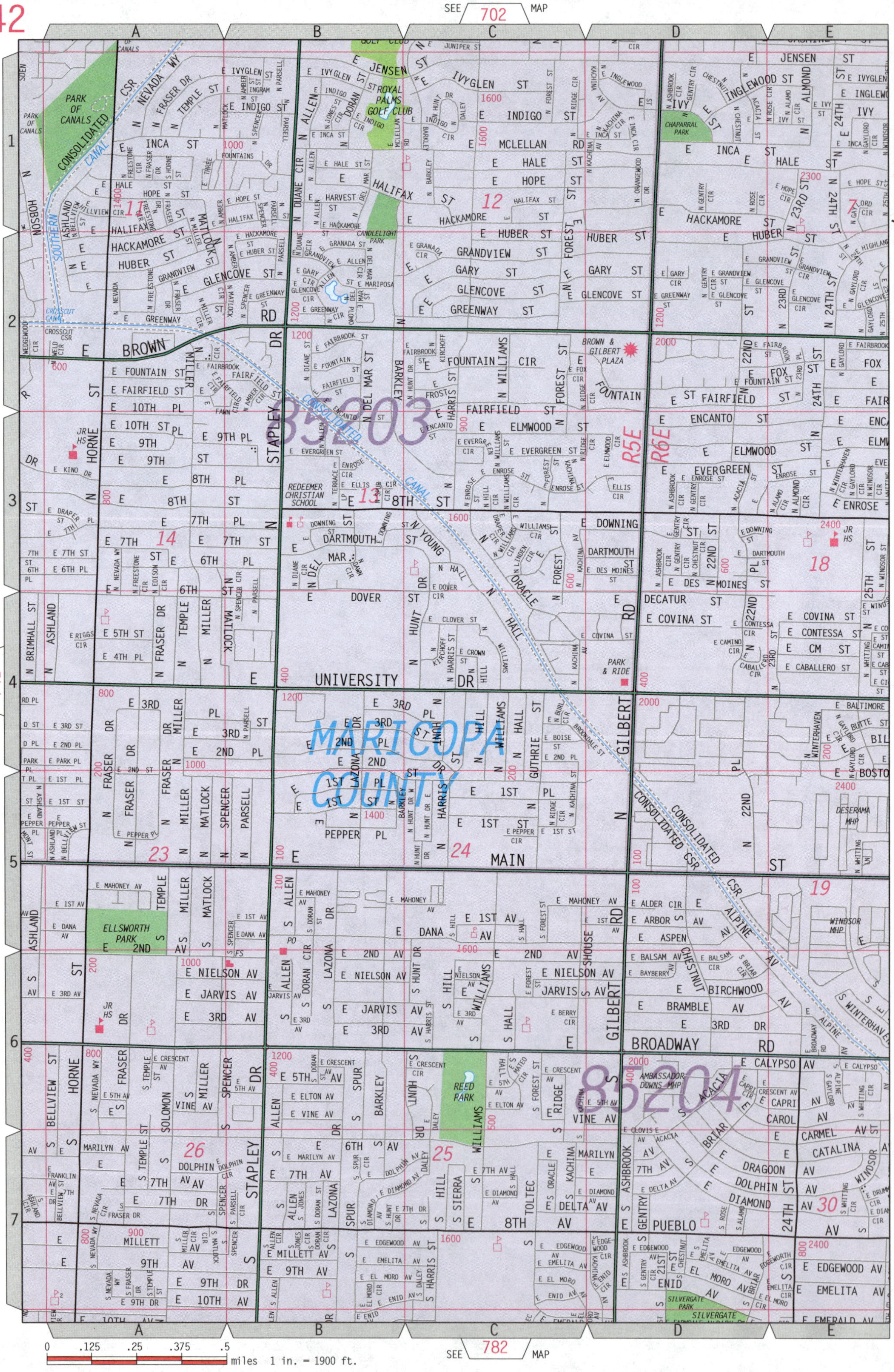

SEE 702 MAP

SEE 741 MAP

SEE 782 MAP

PHOENIX

MAP

A B C D E

1 2 3 4 5 6 7

PARK OF CANALS

CONSOLIDATED CANAL

SOUTHERN CANAL

CROSSCUT CANAL

ROYAL PALMS GOLF CLUB

CHAPARRAL PARK

CANDLELIGHT PARK

BROWN & GILBERT PLAZA

REDEEMER CHRISTIAN SCHOOL

JR HS

PARK & RIDE

MARICOPA COUNTY

85203

85204

R5E R6E

DESERAMA MHP

WINDSOR MHP

ELLSWORTH PARK

REED PARK

AMBASSADOR DOWNS MHP

SILVERGATE PARK

E JENSEN ST

E IVYGLEN ST

E INDIGO ST

E MCLELLAN RD

E INCA ST

E HALE ST

E HOPE ST

E HALIFAX ST

E HACKAMORE ST

E HUBER ST

E GRANDVIEW ST

E GARY ST

E GLENCOVE ST

E GREENWAY ST

E BROWN RD

E FOUNTAIN ST

E FAIRFIELD ST

E ENCANTO ST

E ELMWOOD ST

E EVERGREEN ST

E 8TH ST

E DOWNING ST

E DARTMOUTH ST

E DOVER ST

E DES MOINES ST

E DECATUR ST

E COVINA ST

E UNIVERSITY DR

E 3RD PL

E 2ND PL

E 1ST PL

E PEPPER PL

E MAIN ST

E DANA AV

E 2ND AV

E NIELSON AV

E JARVIS AV

E 3RD AV

E BROADWAY RD

E 5TH AV

E VINE AV

E 6TH AV

E 7TH AV

E 8TH AV

E DOLPHIN AV

E DIAMOND AV

E PUEBLO AV

E MILLETT AV

E 9TH AV

E 10TH AV

E EDGEWOOD AV

E EMELITA AV

N STAPLEY DR

N GILBERT RD

N HORNE

N MILLER

N MATLOCK

N SPENCER

N PARSELL

N FRASER DR

N TEMPLE

N FOREST ST

N HARRIS

N HUNT DR

N WILLIAMS

N HALL ST

N ASHBROOK

N 22ND

N 24TH ST

S HORNE

S ALLEN

S LAZONA

S SPUR

S BARKLEY

S HUNT DR

S HILL

S WILLIAMS

S SHOUSE

S ASHBROOK

S GENTRY

S 24TH ST

0 .125 .25 .375 .5 miles 1 in. = 1900 ft.

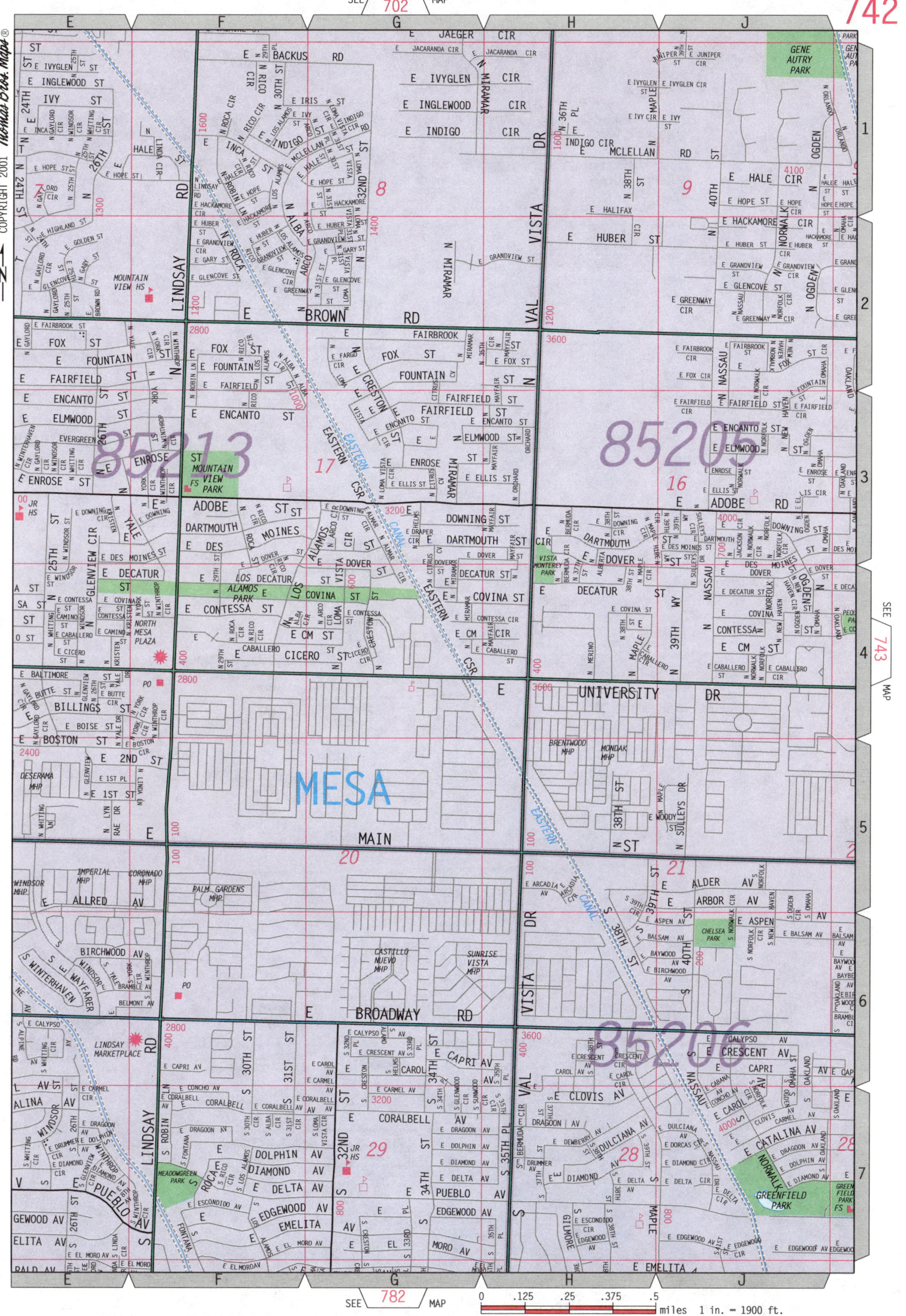
SEE 702 MAP
Thomas Bros. Maps®
COPYRIGHT 2001
PHOENIX
MAP
SEE 743 MAP
SEE 782 MAP
MESA
85213
85205
85206
GENE AUTRY PARK
MOUNTAIN VIEW HS
MOUNTAIN VIEW PARK
LOS ALAMOS PARK
NORTH MESA PLAZA
VISTA MONTEREY PARK
EASTERN CANAL
BRENTWOOD MHP
MONDAK MHP
DESERAMA MHP
IMPERIAL MHP
CORONADO MHP
WINDSOR MHP
PALM GARDENS MHP
CASTILLO NUEVO MHP
SUNRISE VISTA MHP
CHELSEA PARK
LINDSAY MARKETPLACE
MEADOWGREEN PARK
GREENFIELD PARK
E BROWN RD
E ADOBE RD
E UNIVERSITY DR
MAIN ST
E BROADWAY RD
LINDSAY RD
VAL VISTA DR
0 .125 .25 .375 .5 miles 1 in. = 1900 ft.

SEE 703 MAP

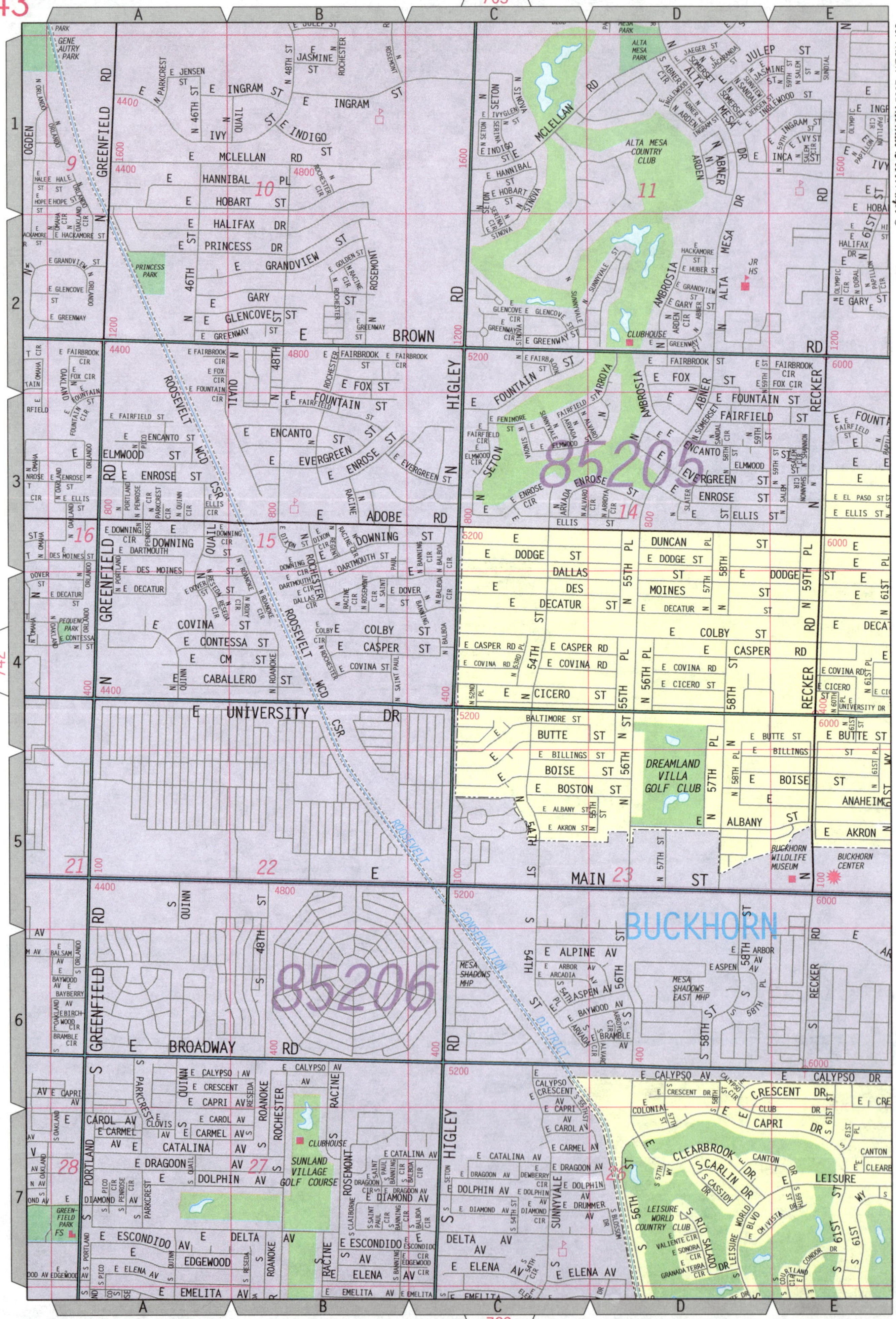

SEE 742 MAP

A B C D E

1 2 3 4 5 6 7

GENE AUTRY PARK
PRINCESS PARK
ALTA MESA PARK
ALTA MESA COUNTRY CLUB
CLUBHOUSE
JR HS
PEQUENO PARK
DREAMLAND VILLA GOLF CLUB
BUCKHORN WILDLIFE MUSEUM
BUCKHORN CENTER
BUCKHORN
MESA SHADOWS MHP
MESA SHADOWS EAST MHP
SUNLAND VILLAGE GOLF COURSE
GREENFIELD PARK FS
LEISURE WORLD COUNTRY CLUB

85205
85206

GREENFIELD RD
HIGLEY RD
RECKER RD
E BROWN RD
E UNIVERSITY DR
E MAIN ST
E BROADWAY RD
E MCLELLAN RD
E INGRAM ST
ROOSEVELT WCD CSR
ROOSEVELT CONSERVATION DISTRICT
E ADOBE RD
E CALYPSO AV
E DRAGOON AV
E DOLPHIN AV
E ESCONDIDO AV
E ELENA AV
E EMELITA AV
E COVINA ST
E CONTESSA ST
E CABALLERO ST
E DOWNING ST
E DECATUR ST
E COLBY ST
E CASPER RD
E CICERO ST
E BUTTE ST
E BOISE ST
E BOSTON ST
E ALBANY ST
E AKRON ST
E FOUNTAIN ST
E FAIRFIELD ST
E ENCANTO ST
E EVERGREEN ST
E ENROSE ST
E ELLIS ST
E HANNIBAL PL
E HOBART ST
E HALIFAX DR
E PRINCESS DR
E GRANDVIEW ST
E GARY ST
E GLENCOVE ST
E GREENWAY ST
E FAIRBROOK ST
E FOX ST
E DODGE ST
E DALLAS ST
E DES MOINES ST
E DUNCAN ST
E BALTIMORE ST
E BILLINGS ST
E ALPINE AV
E ARBOR AV
E ASPEN AV
E BAYWOOD AV
E CRESCENT DR
E CAPRI DR
E CLEARBROOK DR
E CARLIN DR
E LEISURE WORLD BLVD
E RIO SALADO DR
N ALTA MESA DR
N AMBROSIA
N ABNER
N ARDEN
N SOMERSET
N SUNNYVALE
N SETON
N SINOVA
N QUAIL
N ROCHESTER
N ROSEMONT
N RACINE
N 46TH ST
N 48TH ST
N 54TH ST
N 55TH PL
N 56TH ST
N 57TH ST
N 58TH ST
N 59TH PL
N 61ST ST

A B C D E

0 .125 .25 .375 .5 miles 1 in. = 1900 ft.

SEE 783 MAP

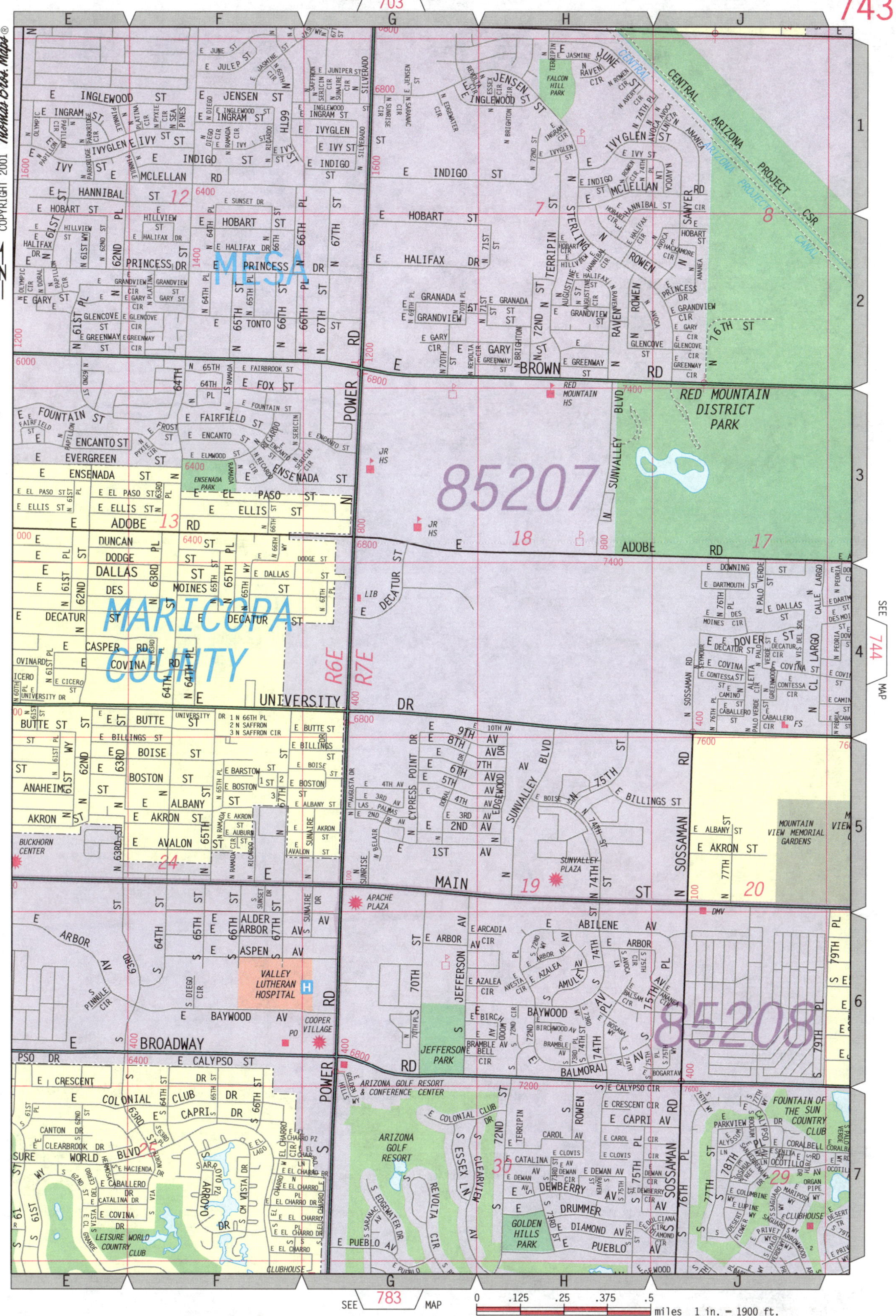
SEE 703 MAP
SEE 744 MAP
SEE 783 MAP
PHOENIX
MAP
MESA
MARICOPA COUNTY
85207
85208
R6E
R7E
E INGLEWOOD ST
E JENSEN ST
E INDIGO ST
E HOBART ST
E HALIFAX DR
PRINCESS DR
E BROWN RD
E FOX ST
E FOUNTAIN ST
E FAIRFIELD ST
E ENCANTO ST
E EVERGREEN
E ENSENADA ST
E EL PASO ST
E ELLIS ST
E ADOBE RD
E DALLAS ST
DES MOINES ST
E DECATUR ST
E CASPER RD
COVINA RD
E UNIVERSITY DR
BUTTE ST
E BOISE ST
BOSTON ST
E ALBANY ST
E AKRON ST
E AVALON ST
E MAIN ST
E ARBOR AV
E ASPEN AV
E BAYWOOD AV
E BROADWAY RD
E CALYPSO ST
E COLONIAL CLUB DR
E CAPRI DR
LEISURE WORLD BLVD
POWER RD
SUNVALLEY BLVD
SOSSAMAN RD
STERLING ST
TERRIPIN
CENTRAL ARIZONA PROJECT CSR
ARIZONA PROJECT CANAL
FALCON HILL PARK
RED MOUNTAIN HS
RED MOUNTAIN DISTRICT PARK
ENSENADA PARK
JR HS
LIB
FS
BUCKHORN CENTER
SUNVALLEY PLAZA
MOUNTAIN VIEW MEMORIAL GARDENS
DMV
APACHE PLAZA
VALLEY LUTHERAN HOSPITAL
COOPER VILLAGE
PO
JEFFERSON PARK
ARIZONA GOLF RESORT & CONFERENCE CENTER
ARIZONA GOLF RESORT
GOLDEN HILLS PARK
LEISURE WORLD COUNTRY CLUB
FOUNTAIN OF THE SUN COUNTRY CLUB
CLUBHOUSE
0 .125 .25 .375 .5 miles 1 in. = 1900 ft.

SEE 704 MAP

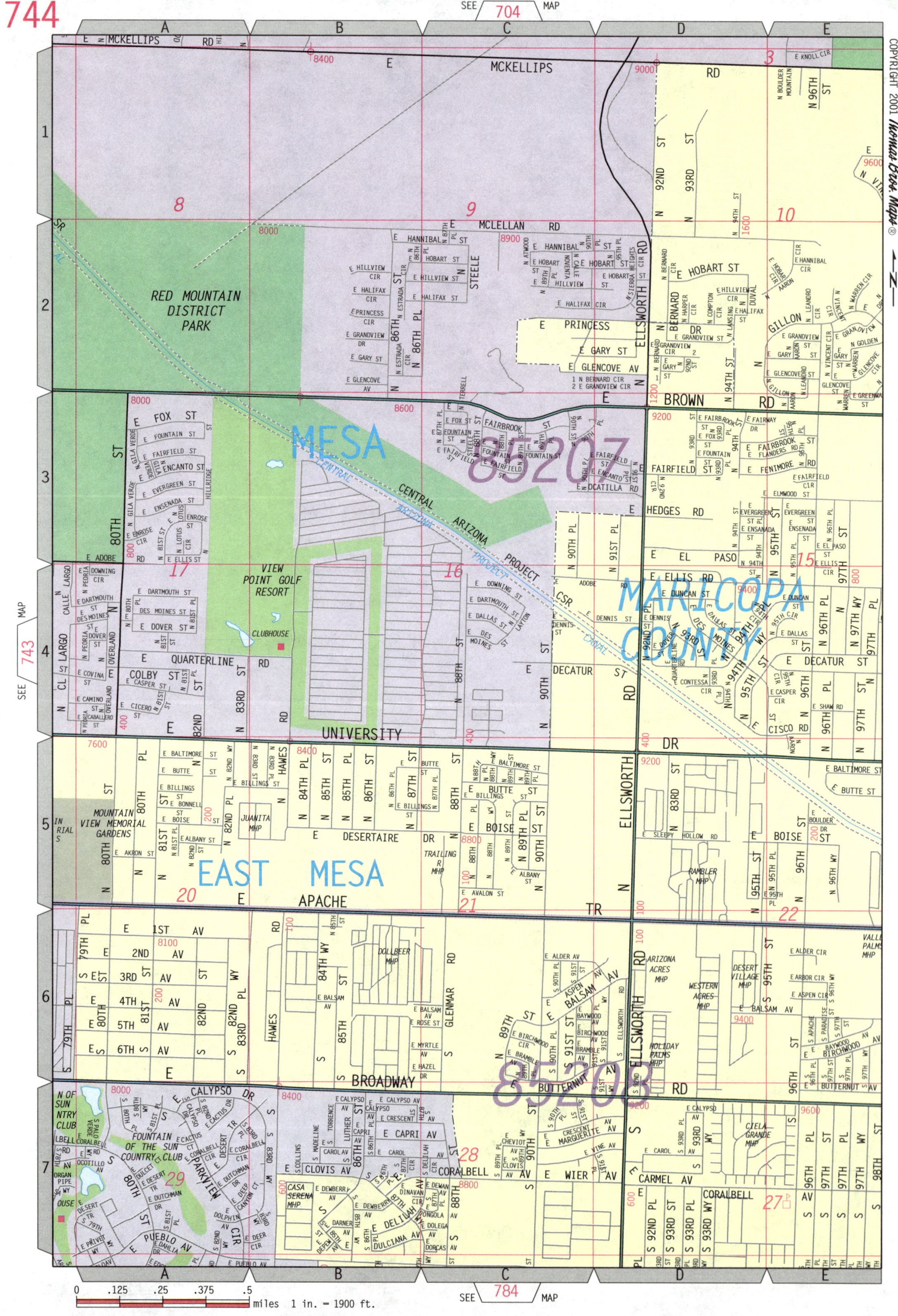

SEE 743 MAP

SEE 784 MAP

0 .125 .25 .375 .5 miles 1 in. = 1900 ft.

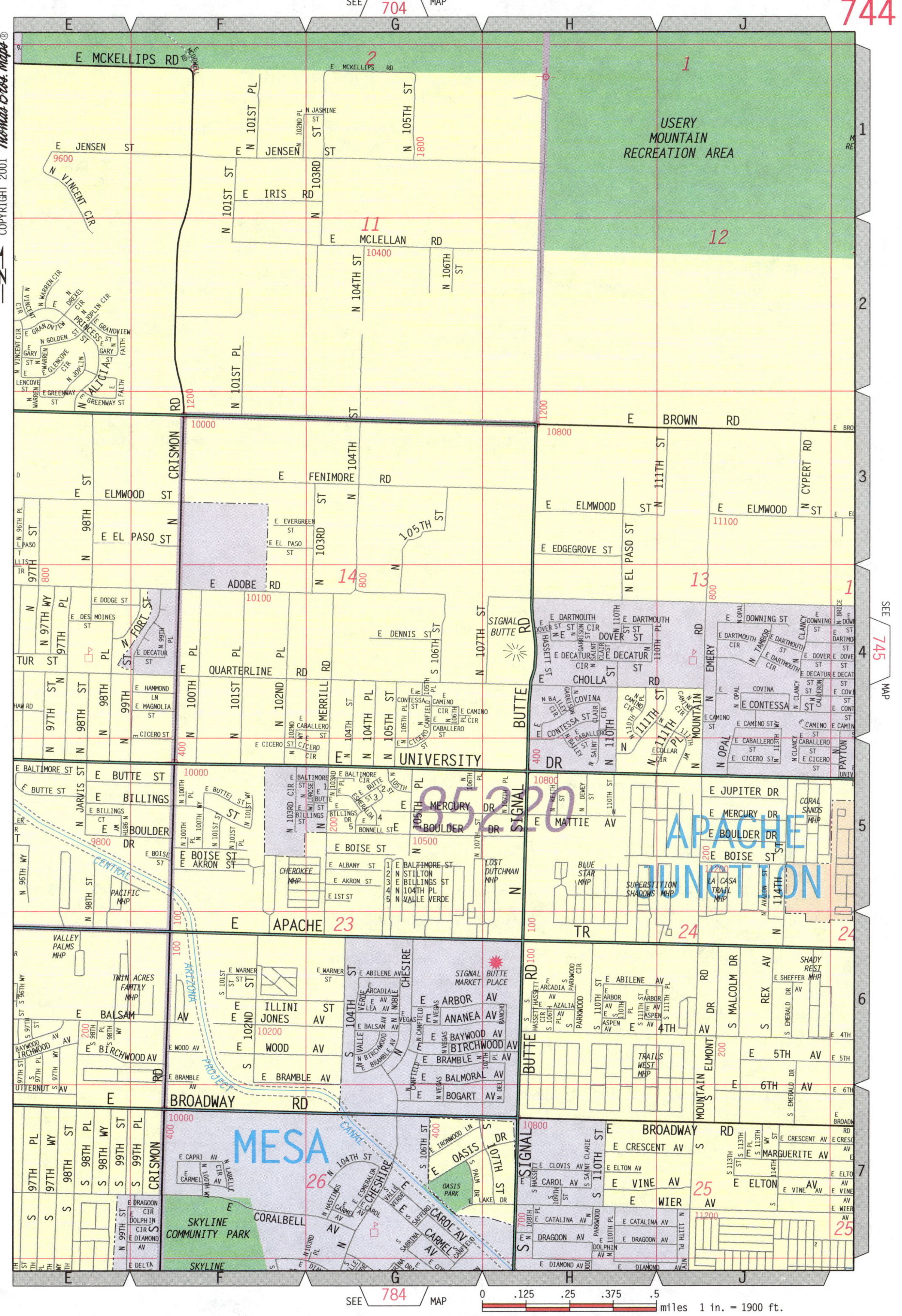
744
SEE 704 MAP
SEE 745 MAP
SEE 784 MAP
PHOENIX
MAP
COPYRIGHT 2001 Thomas Bros. Maps
E MCKELLIPS RD
E JENSEN ST
E IRIS RD
E MCLELLAN RD
USERY MOUNTAIN RECREATION AREA
E BROWN RD
E FENIMORE RD
E ELMWOOD ST
E EL PASO ST
E EDGEGROVE ST
E ADOBE RD
E DENNIS ST
QUARTERLINE RD
SIGNAL BUTTE RD
E UNIVERSITY DR
CRISMON RD
85220
E MERCURY DR
E BOULDER DR
E BOISE ST
E MATTIE AV
E JUPITER DR
APACHE JUNCTION
CORAL SANDS MHP
BLUE STAR MHP
SUPERSTITION SHADOWS MHP
LA CASA TRAIL MHP
CHEROKEE MHP
LOST DUTCHMAN MHP
PACIFIC MHP
CENTRAL ARIZONA PROJECT CANAL
E APACHE TR
VALLEY PALMS MHP
TWIN ACRES FAMILY MHP
SIGNAL BUTTE MARKET PLACE
SHADY REST MHP
TRAILS WEST MHP
E BALSAM AV
E ARBOR AV
E ANANEA AV
E BIRCHWOOD AV
E BRAMBLE AV
E BALMORAL AV
E BOGART AV
E ABILENE AV
E 4TH AV
E 5TH AV
E 6TH AV
BROADWAY RD
MESA
E CRESCENT AV
E MARGUERITE AV
E OASIS
OASIS PARK
E VINE AV
E ELTON AV
E WIER AV
E CORALBELL AV
SKYLINE COMMUNITY PARK
E CATALINA AV
E DRAGOON AV
E DIAMOND AV
SKYLINE
0 .125 .25 .375 .5 miles 1 in. = 1900 ft.

SEE 705 MAP

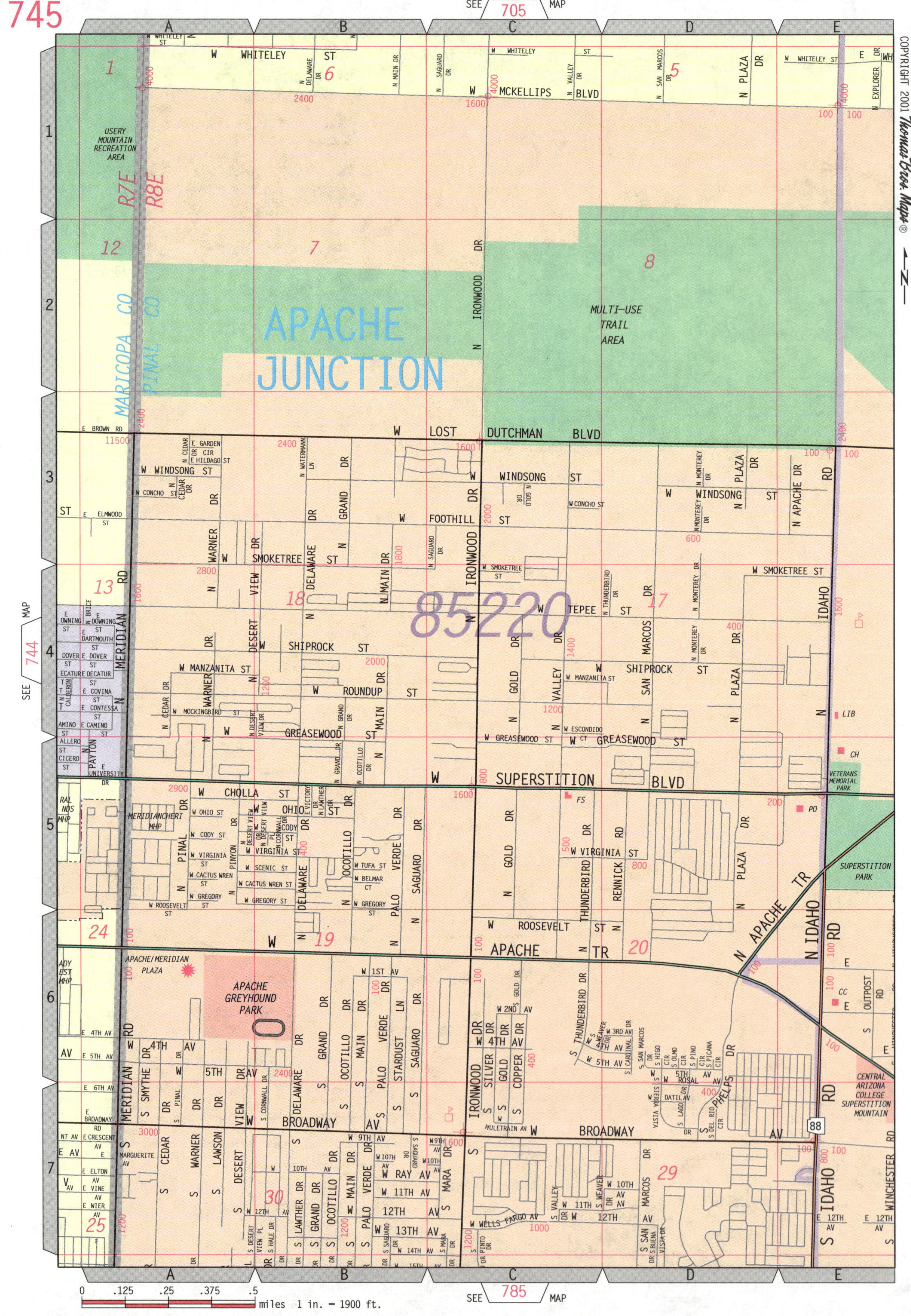

SEE 785 MAP

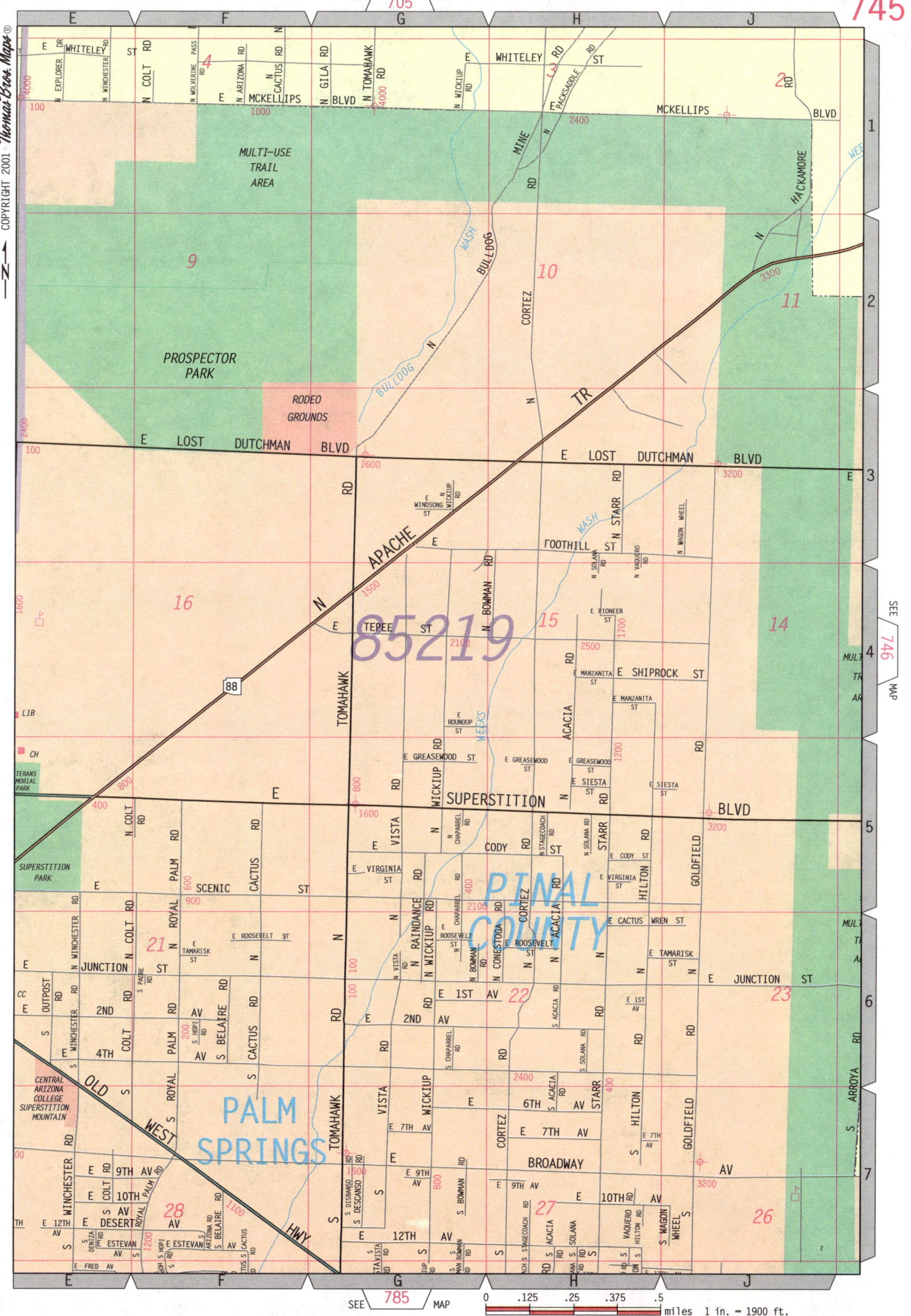

SEE 705 MAP
E MCKELLIPS BLVD
WHITELEY ST
MULTI-USE TRAIL AREA
PROSPECTOR PARK
RODEO GROUNDS
E LOST DUTCHMAN BLVD
N APACHE TR
88
85219
E SUPERSTITION BLVD
PINAL COUNTY
PALM SPRINGS
OLD WEST HWY
E JUNCTION ST
BROADWAY AV
CENTRAL ARIZONA COLLEGE SUPERSTITION MOUNTAIN
SUPERSTITION PARK
N TOMAHAWK RD
N CORTEZ RD
N GOLDFIELD RD
S ARROYA RD
SEE 746 MAP
PHOENIX
MAP
SEE 785 MAP
0 .125 .25 .375 .5 miles 1 in. = 1900 ft.

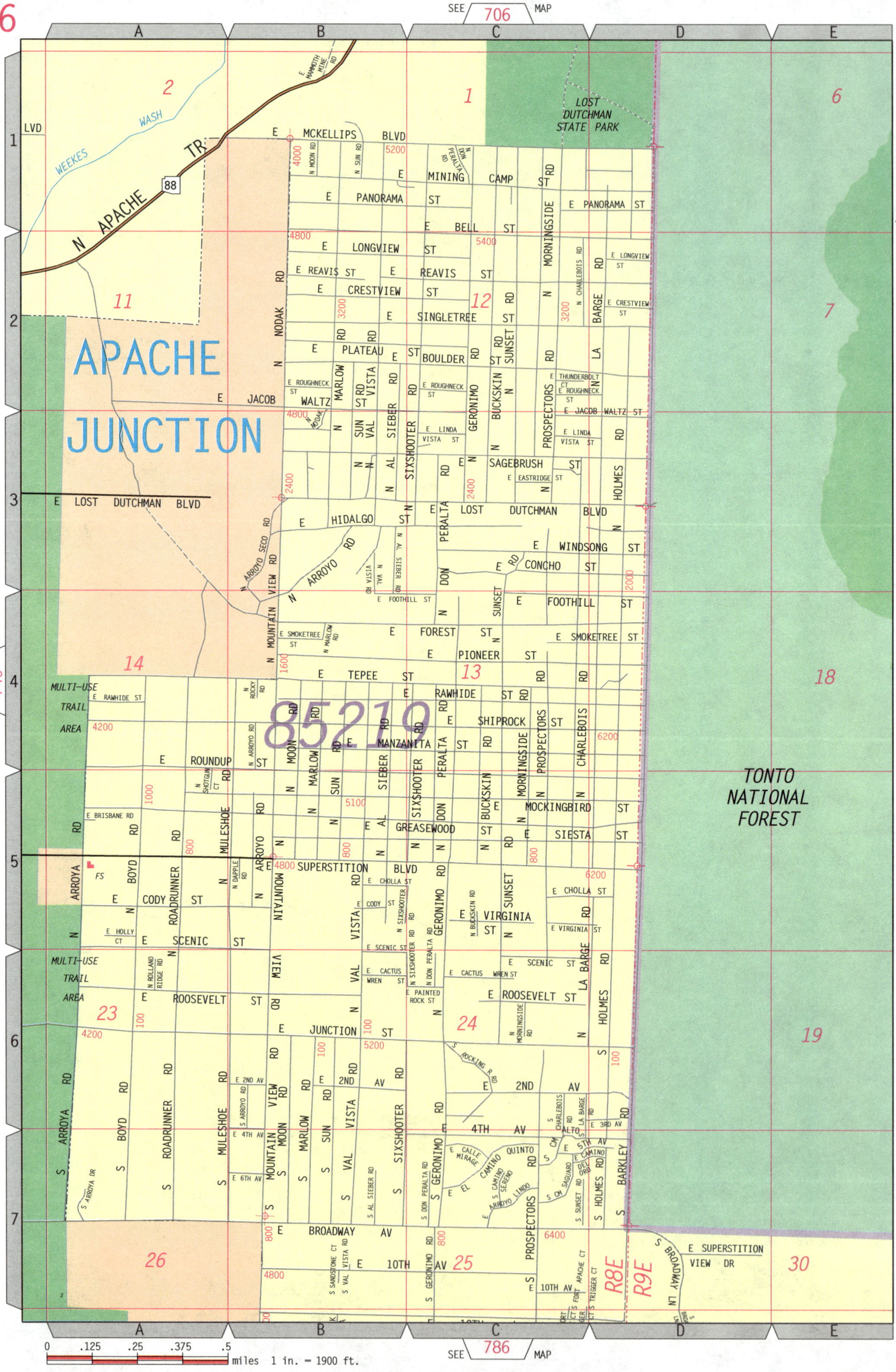
SEE 706 MAP
SEE 745 MAP
SEE 786 MAP
PHOENIX
MAP
APACHE JUNCTION
85219
LOST DUTCHMAN STATE PARK
TONTO NATIONAL FOREST
MULTI-USE TRAIL AREA
WEEKES WASH
N APACHE TR
88
E MAMMOTH MINE RD
E MCKELLIPS BLVD
E MINING CAMP ST
E PANORAMA ST
E BELL ST
E LONGVIEW ST
E REAVIS ST
E CRESTVIEW ST
E SINGLETREE ST
E PLATEAU ST
BOULDER ST
E ROUGHNECK ST
E JACOB WALTZ ST
E LINDA VISTA ST
E SAGEBRUSH ST
E EASTRIDGE ST
E LOST DUTCHMAN BLVD
E HIDALGO ST
E WINDSONG ST
E CONCHO ST
E FOOTHILL ST
E SMOKETREE ST
E FOREST ST
E PIONEER ST
E TEPEE ST
E RAWHIDE ST
E SHIPROCK ST
E MANZANITA ST
E ROUNDUP ST
E BRISBANE RD
E MOCKINGBIRD ST
E GREASEWOOD ST
E SIESTA ST
E SUPERSTITION BLVD
E CHOLLA ST
E CODY ST
E VIRGINIA ST
E HOLLY CT
E SCENIC ST
E CACTUS WREN ST
E PAINTED ROCK ST
E ROOSEVELT ST
E JUNCTION ST
E 2ND AV
E 4TH AV
E 3RD AV
E 5TH AV
E 6TH AV
E BROADWAY AV
E 10TH AV
E SUPERSTITION VIEW DR
N NODAK RD
N MOUNTAIN VIEW RD
N ARROYO SECO RD
N ARROYO RD
N MARLOW RD
N SUN VAL RD
N VISTA RD
N AL SIEBER RD
N SIXSHOOTER RD
N PERALTA RD
N DON PERALTA RD
N GERONIMO RD
N BUCKSKIN RD
N SUNSET RD
N MORNINGSIDE RD
N PROSPECTORS RD
N CHARLEBOIS RD
N LA BARGE RD
N HOLMES RD
N ROADRUNNER RD
N BOYD RD
N MULESHOE RD
N ARROYA RD
N MOON RD
S ARROYA RD
S BOYD RD
S ROADRUNNER RD
S MULESHOE RD
S MOUNTAIN VIEW RD
S MOON RD
S MARLOW RD
S SUN RD
S VISTA RD
S VAL
S SIXSHOOTER RD
S GERONIMO RD
S PROSPECTORS RD
S HOLMES RD
S BARKLEY RD
S BROADWAY LN
ROCKING R RD
E CALLE MIRAGE
E EL CAMINO QUINTO
S CAMINO SERENO
E ARROYO LINDO
S SAGUARO DEL ORO
S FORT APACHE CT
S TRIGGER CT
FS
R8E
R9E
1
2
6
7
11
12
13
14
18
19
23
24
25
26
30
A B C D E
1 2 3 4 5 6 7
0 .125 .25 .375 .5 miles 1 in. = 1900 ft.

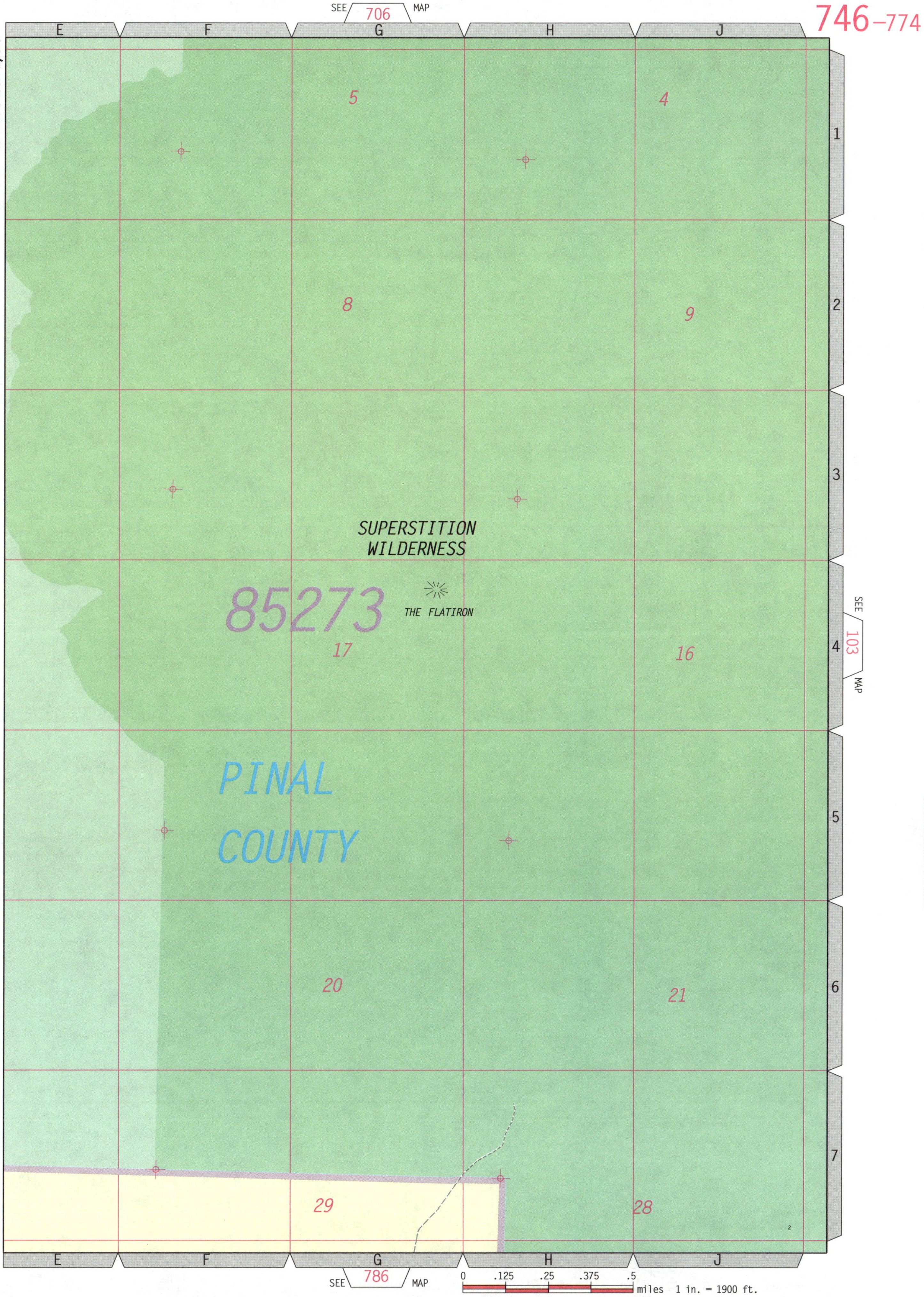

SEE 706 MAP

E F G H J

1 2 3 4 5 6 7

5 4

8 9

SUPERSTITION WILDERNESS

85273

THE FLATIRON

17 16

PINAL COUNTY

20 21

29 28

SEE 103 MAP

SEE 786 MAP

0 .125 .25 .375 .5 miles 1 in. = 1900 ft.

PHOENIX

MAP

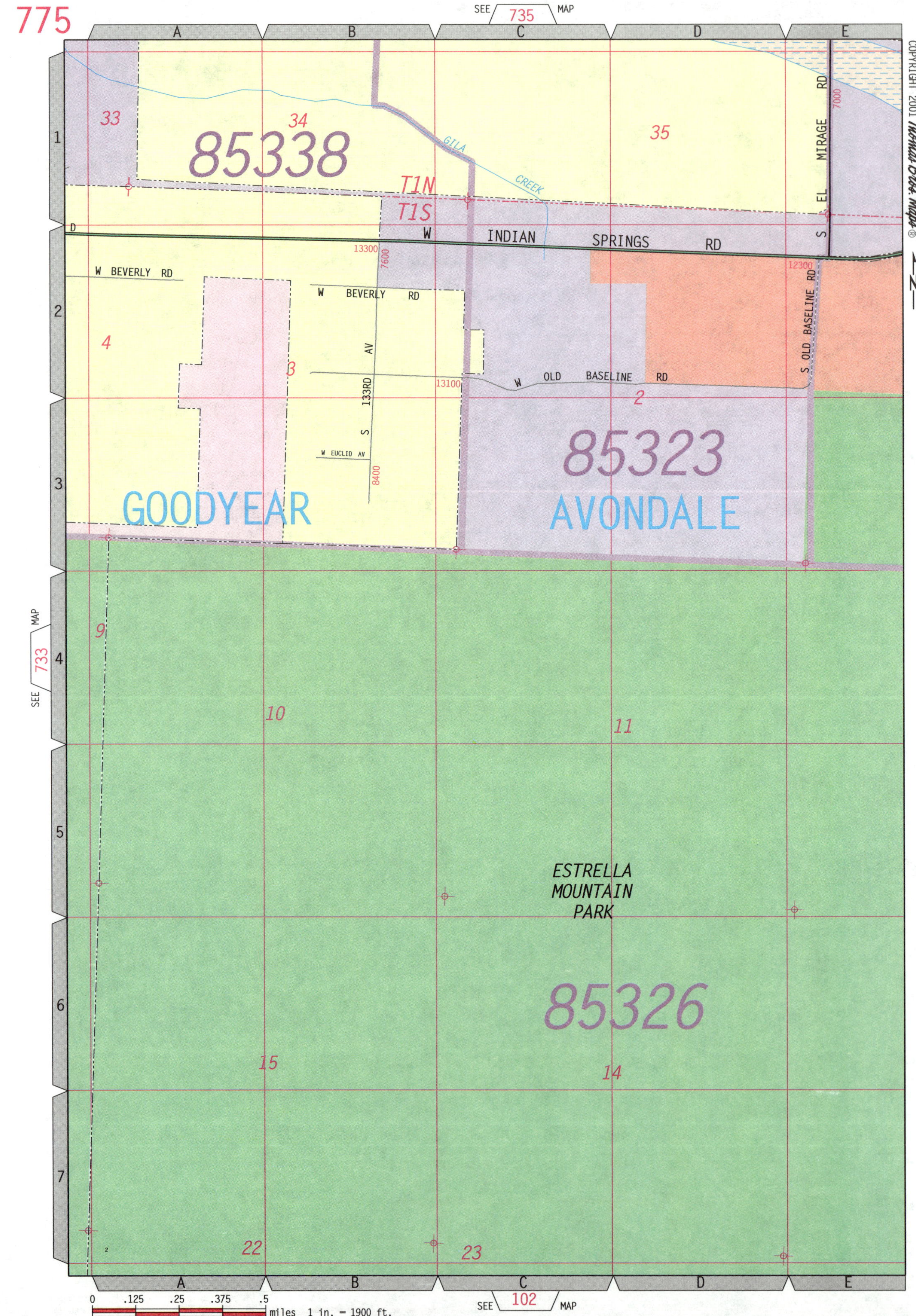
SEE 735 MAP
85338
33
34
35
GILA CREEK
T1N
T1S
W INDIAN SPRINGS RD
S EL MIRAGE RD
7000
13300
7600
12300
W BEVERLY RD
W BEVERLY RD
4
3
S 133RD AV
W OLD BASELINE RD
S OLD BASELINE RD
13100
2
W EUCLID AV
8400
85323
GOODYEAR
AVONDALE
9
SEE 733 MAP
10
11
ESTRELLA MOUNTAIN PARK
85326
15
14
22
23
SEE 102 MAP
0 .125 .25 .375 .5 miles 1 in. = 1900 ft.

PHOENIX

MAP

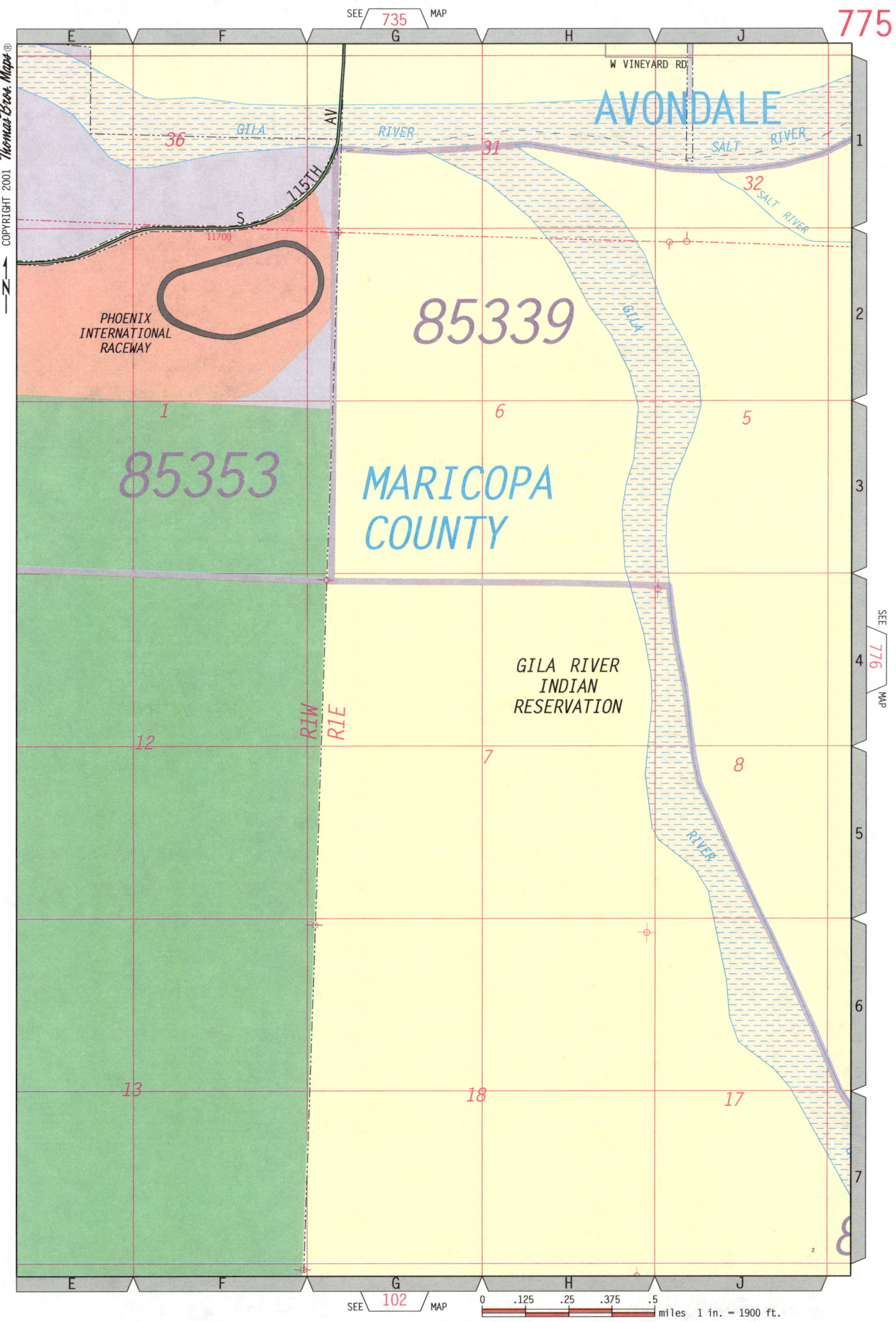

SEE 735 MAP
E
F
G
H
J
W VINEYARD RD
AVONDALE
GILA
RIVER
SALT
RIVER
36
31
32
SALT RIVER
115TH
AV
S
11700
PHOENIX
INTERNATIONAL
RACEWAY
85339
GILA
1
6
5
85353
MARICOPA
COUNTY
GILA RIVER
INDIAN
RESERVATION
R1W
R1E
12
7
8
RIVER
13
18
17
1
2
3
4
5
6
7
SEE 776 MAP
SEE 102 MAP
0 .125 .25 .375 .5
miles 1 in. = 1900 ft.

PHOENIX

MAP

SEE 736 MAP

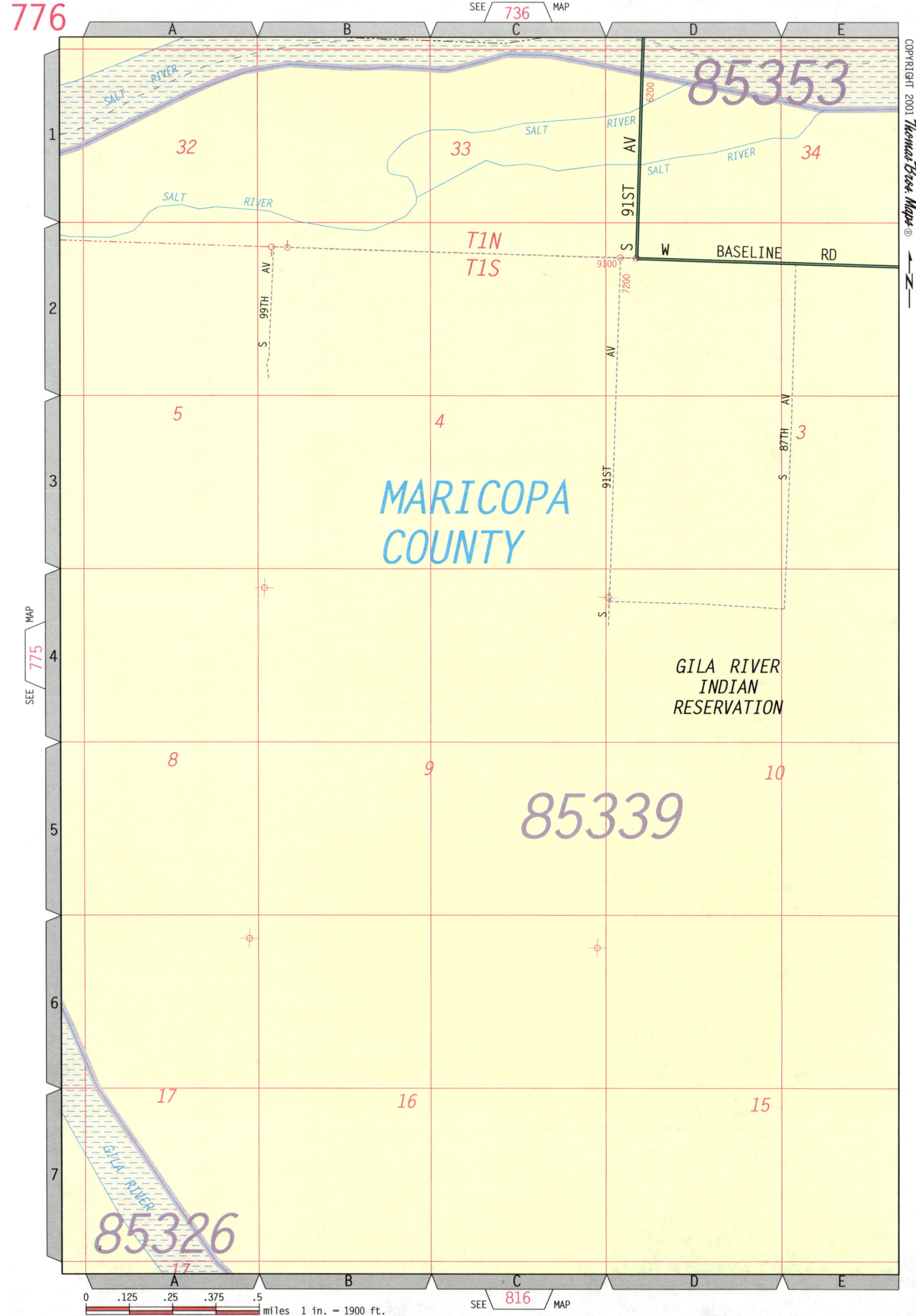

SEE 775 MAP

SEE 816 MAP

PHOENIX

MAP

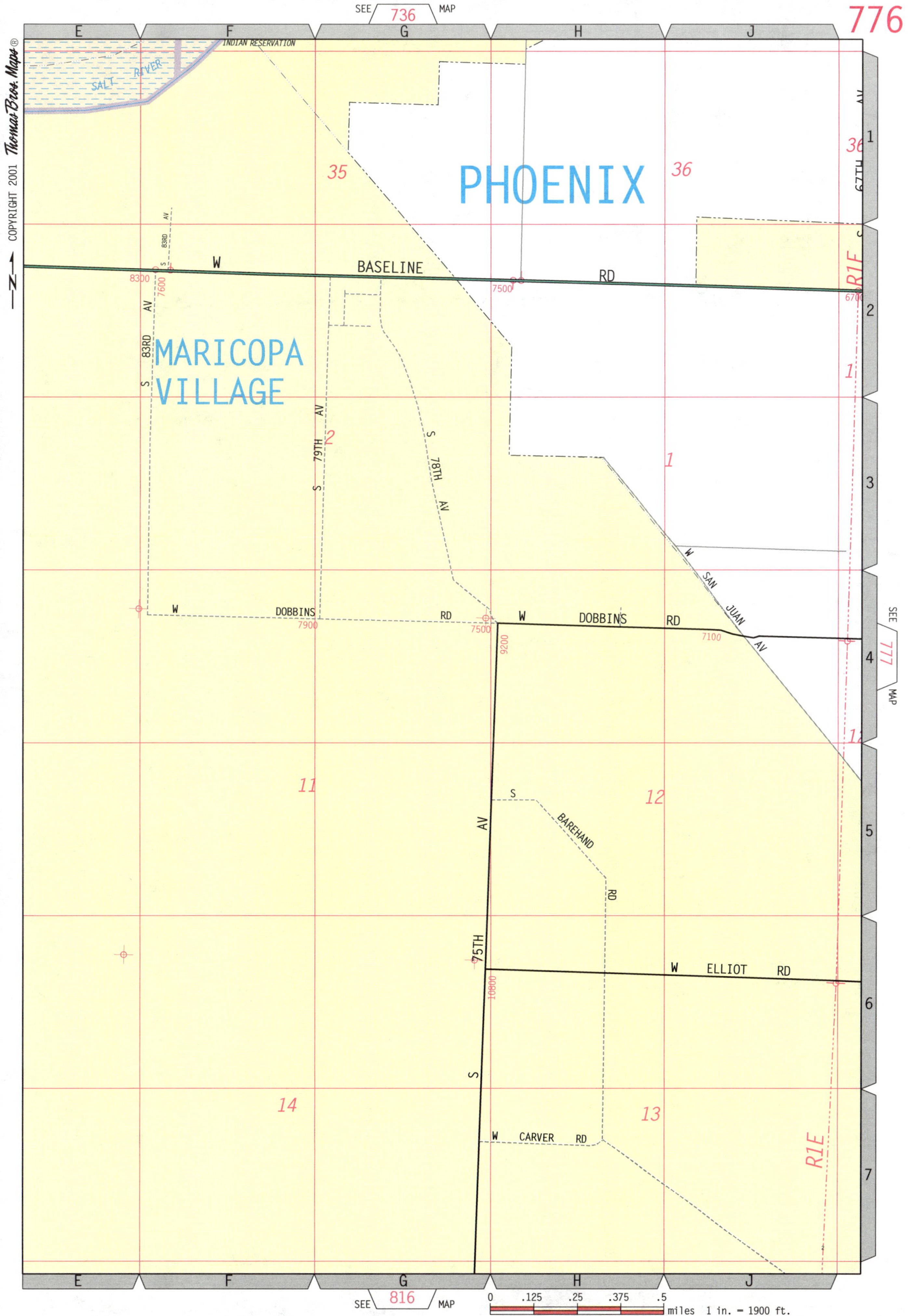

SEE 736 MAP
E
F
G
H
J
INDIAN RESERVATION
SALT RIVER
PHOENIX
35
36
MARICOPA
VILLAGE
W BASELINE RD
8300
7600
7500
6700
S 83RD AV
S 79TH AV
S 78TH AV
2
1
W DOBBINS RD
7900
7500
7100
9200
W SAN JUAN AV
S 75TH AV
10800
S BAREHAND RD
11
12
W ELLIOT RD
14
13
W CARVER RD
R1E
SEE 777 MAP
SEE 816 MAP
0 .125 .25 .375 .5 miles 1 in. = 1900 ft.
PHOENIX
MAP

SEE 737 MAP

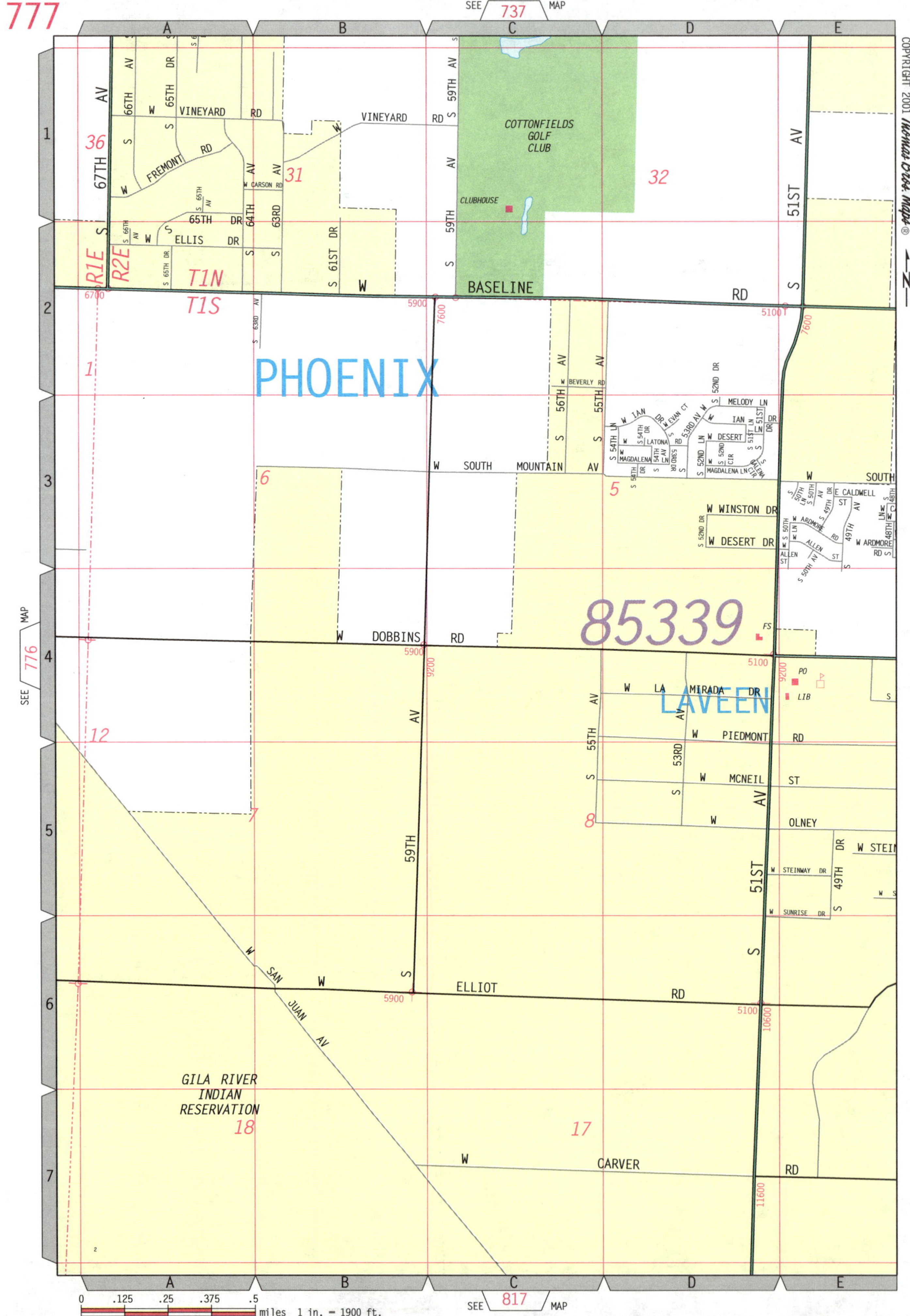

SEE 776 MAP

SEE 817 MAP

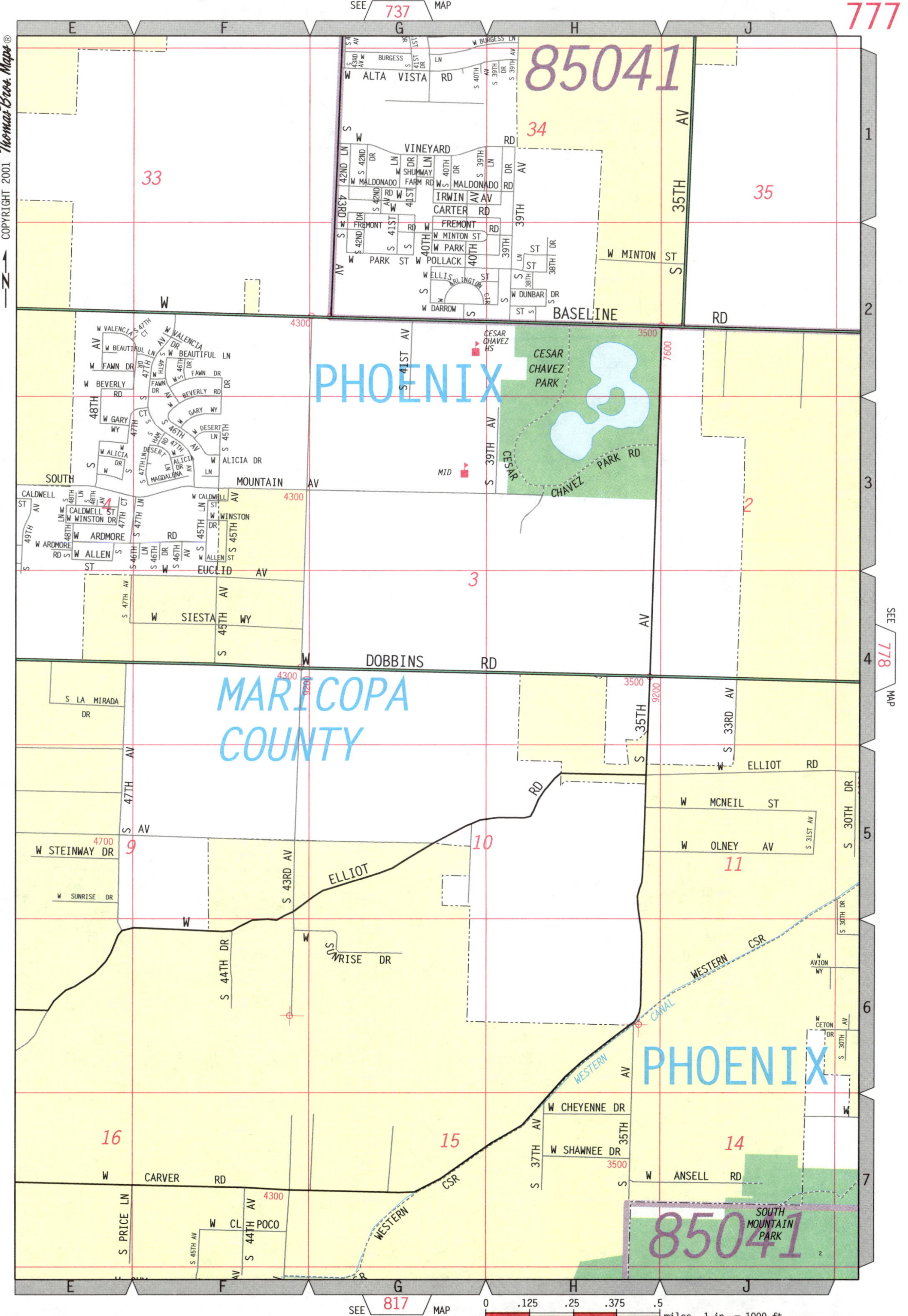

SEE 737 MAP
85041
PHOENIX
MARICOPA COUNTY
CESAR CHAVEZ PARK
SOUTH MOUNTAIN PARK
W BASELINE RD
W DOBBINS RD
W ELLIOT RD
SOUTH MOUNTAIN AV
W CARVER RD
WESTERN CANAL
W VINEYARD RD
W ALTA VISTA RD
W MINTON ST
S 35TH AV
S 43RD AV
S 47TH AV
W EUCLID AV
W SIESTA WY
W CHEYENNE DR
W SHAWNEE DR
W ANSELL RD
W MCNEIL ST
W OLNEY AV
W STEINWAY DR
W SUNRISE DR
SEE 778 MAP
SEE 817 MAP
PHOENIX
MAP

SEE 738 MAP

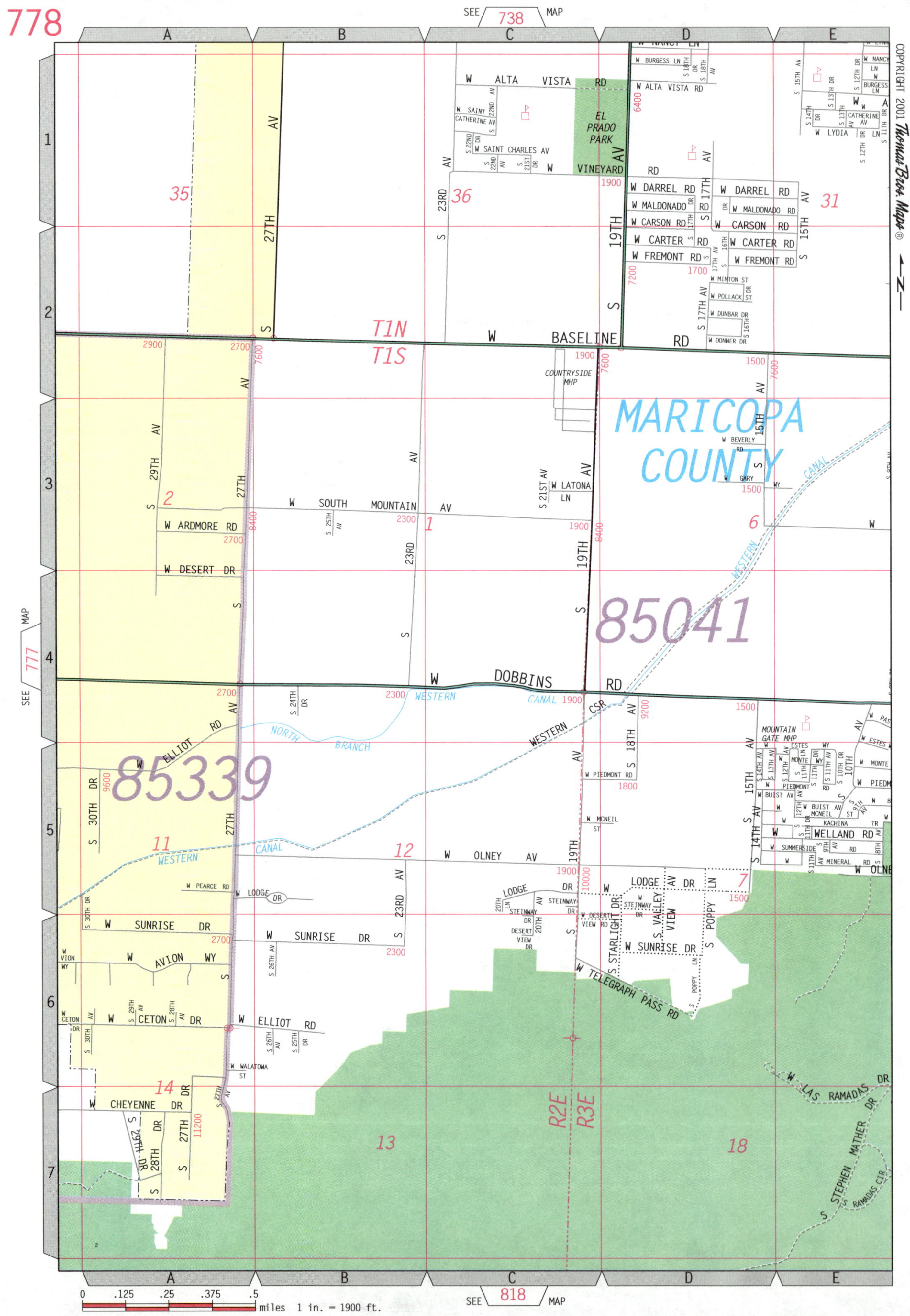

0 .125 .25 .375 .5 miles 1 in. = 1900 ft.

SEE 818 MAP

SEE 738 MAP

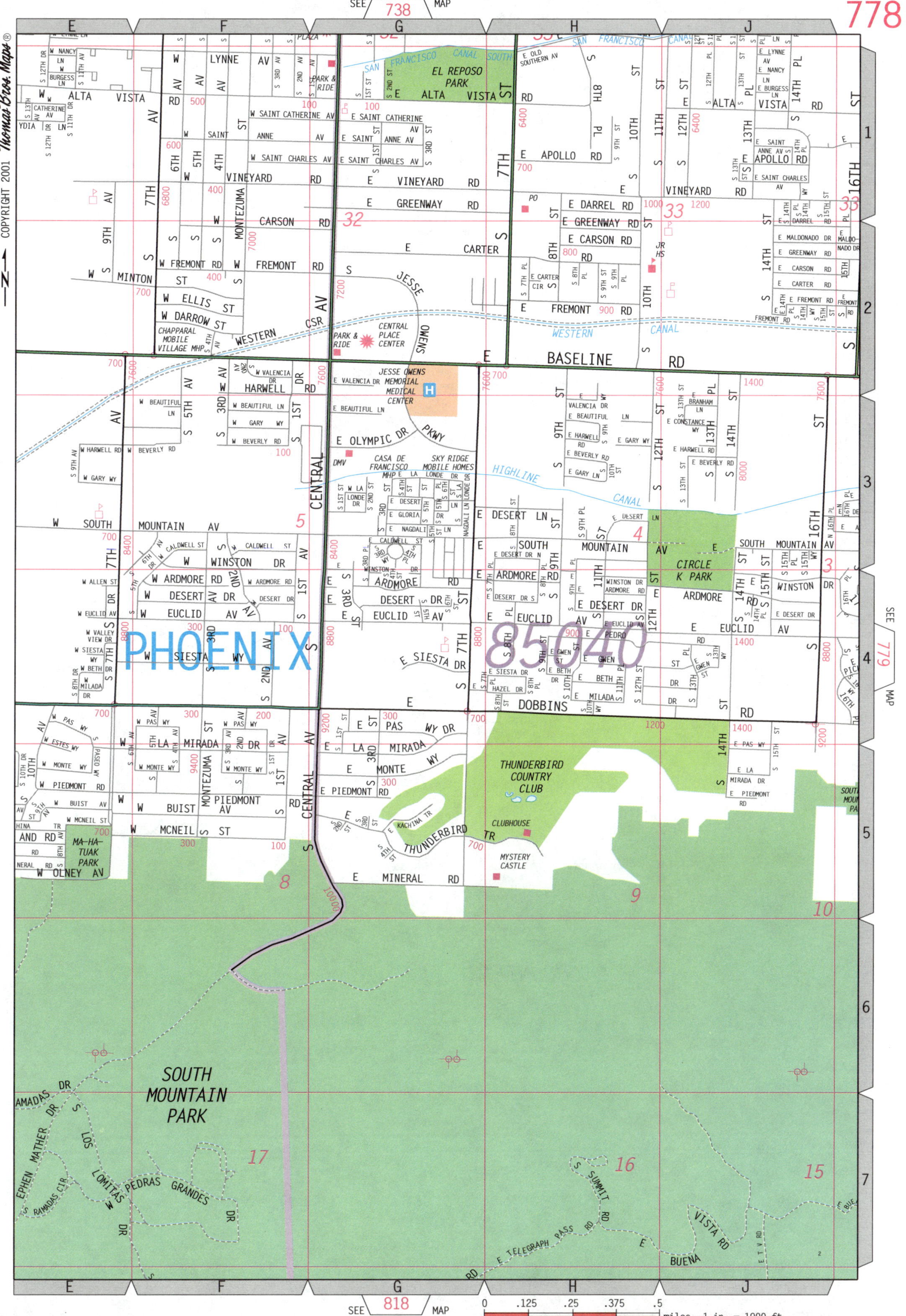

PHOENIX

MAP

SEE 779 MAP

SEE 818 MAP

0 .125 .25 .375 .5 miles 1 in. = 1900 ft.

SEE 739 MAP

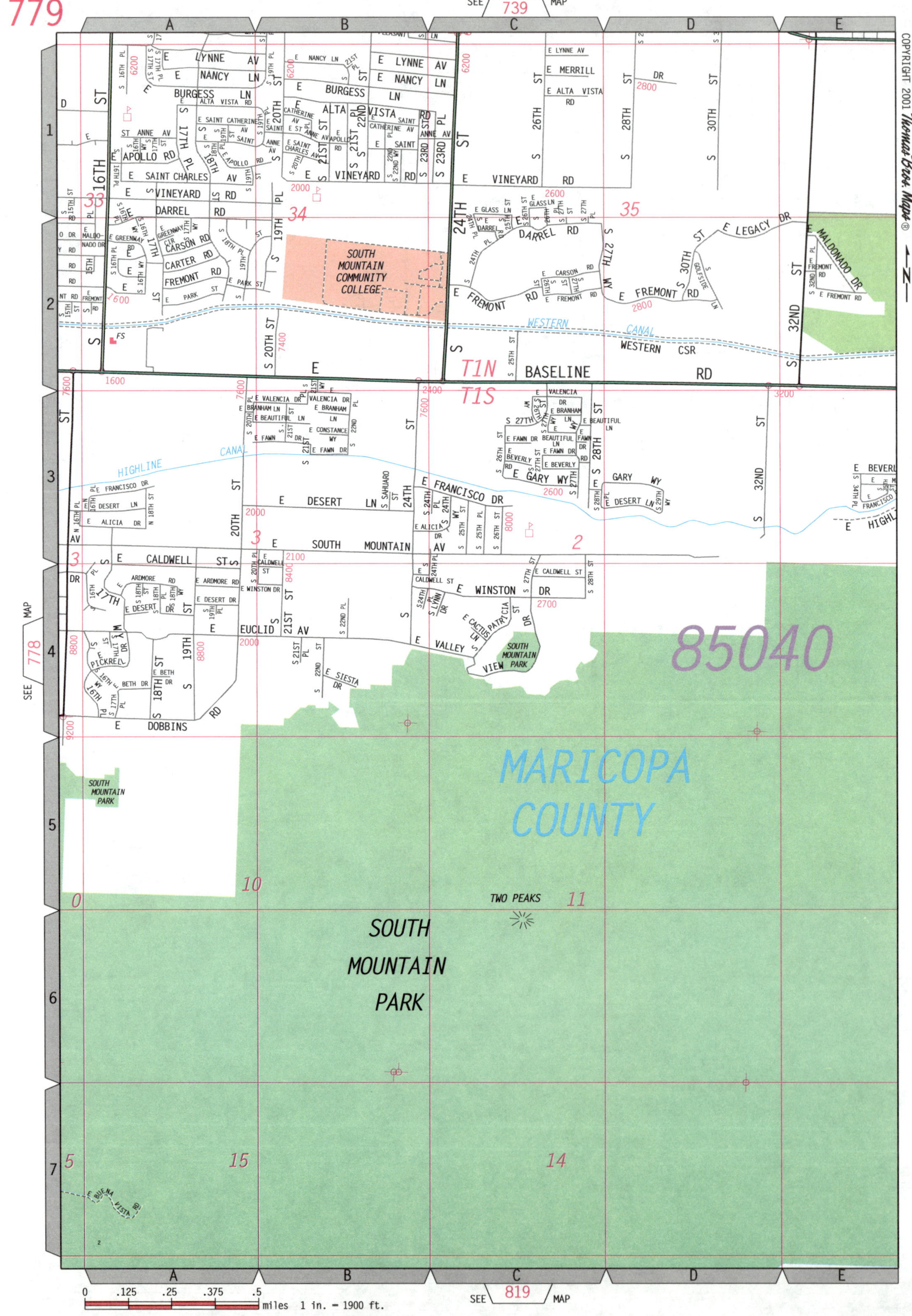

SEE 778 MAP

SEE 819 MAP

0 .125 .25 .375 .5 miles 1 in. = 1900 ft.

PHOENIX

MAP

SEE 739 MAP

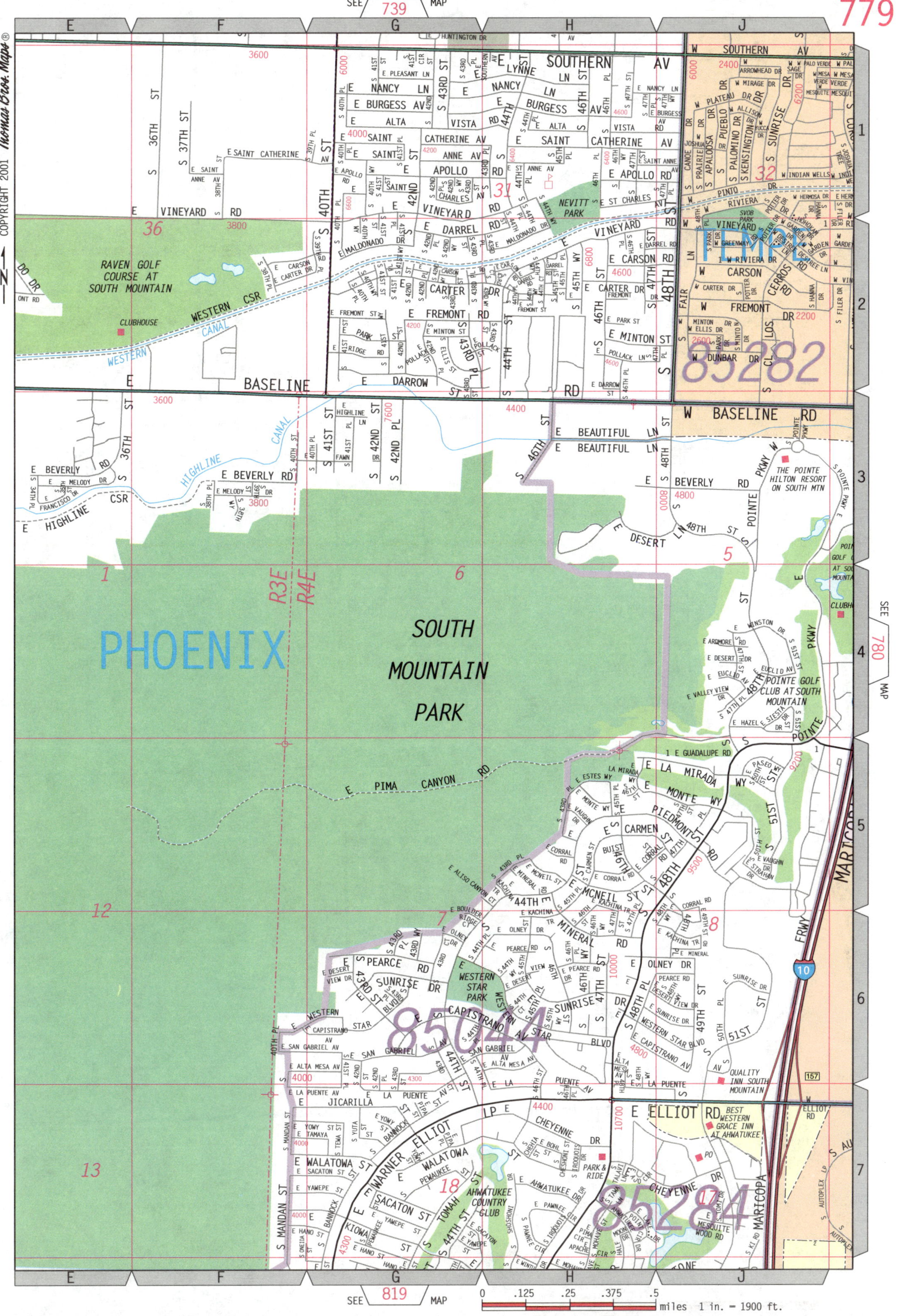

SEE 780 MAP

SEE 819 MAP

0 .125 .25 .375 .5 miles 1 in. = 1900 ft.

PHOENIX

MAP

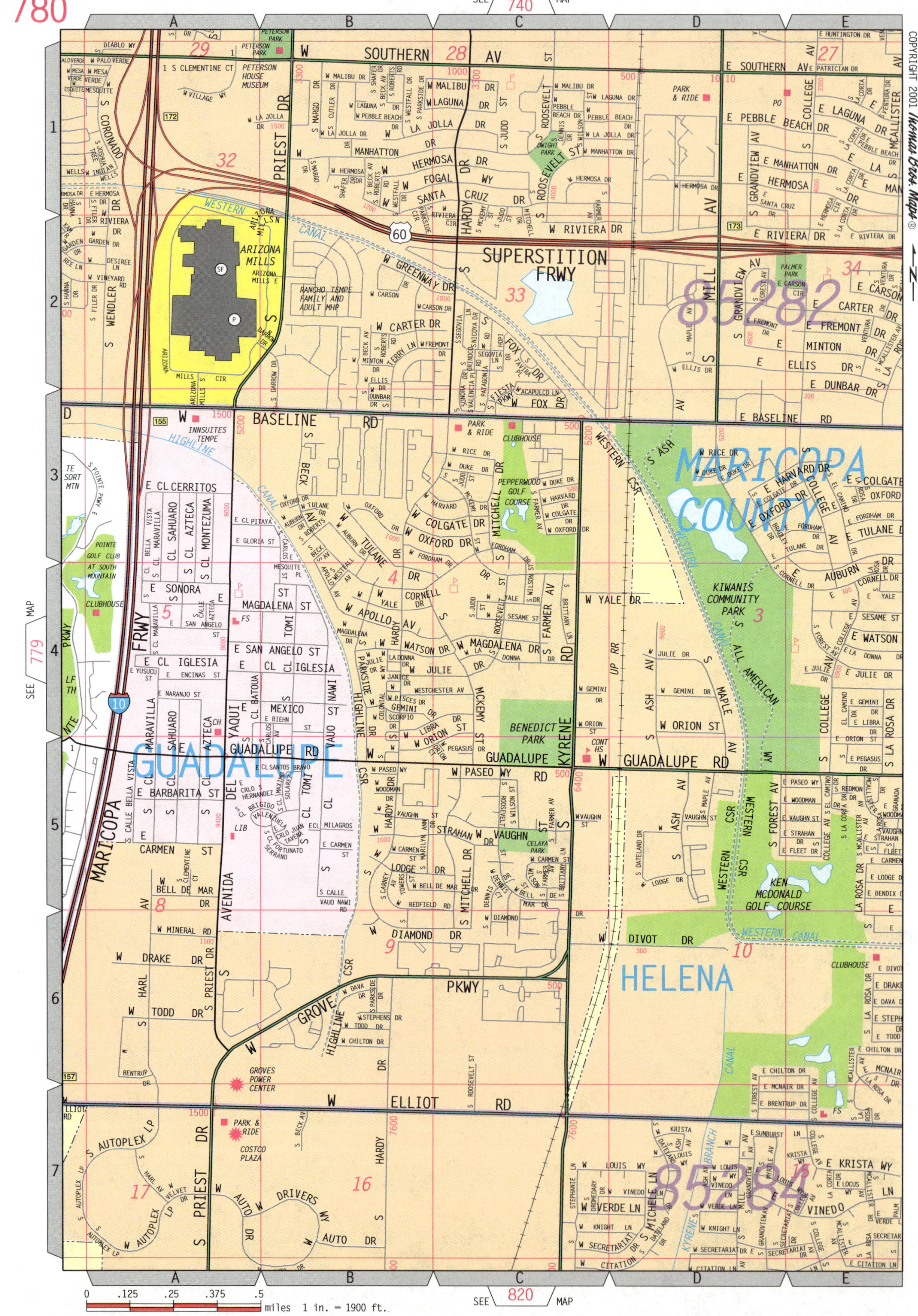
SEE 740 MAP
A
B
C
D
E
SOUTHERN AV
E SOUTHERN AV
PETERSON PARK
PETERSON HOUSE MUSEUM
PARK & RIDE
SUPERSTITION FRWY
ARIZONA MILLS
RANCHO TEMPE FAMILY AND ADULT MHP
WESTERN CANAL
85282
PALMER PARK
BASELINE RD
E BASELINE RD
INNSUITES TEMPE
HIGHLINE CANAL
PEPPERWOOD GOLF COURSE
CLUBHOUSE
MARICOPA COUNTY
KIWANIS COMMUNITY PARK
POINTE GOLF CLUB AT SOUTH MOUNTAIN
GUADALUPE
GUADALUPE RD
W GUADALUPE RD
BENEDICT PARK
MARICOPA FRWY
AVENIDA DEL YAQUI
KEN MCDONALD GOLF COURSE
HELENA
GROVE PKWY
GROVES POWER CENTER
W ELLIOT RD
COSTCO PLAZA
S PRIEST DR
AUTOPLEX LP
DRIVERS WY
AUTO DR
85284
KYRENE BRANCH CANAL
SEE 779 MAP
SEE 820 MAP
PHOENIX
MAP
COPYRIGHT 2001 Thomas Bros. Maps®
0 .125 .25 .375 .5 miles 1 in. = 1900 ft.

SEE 740 MAP

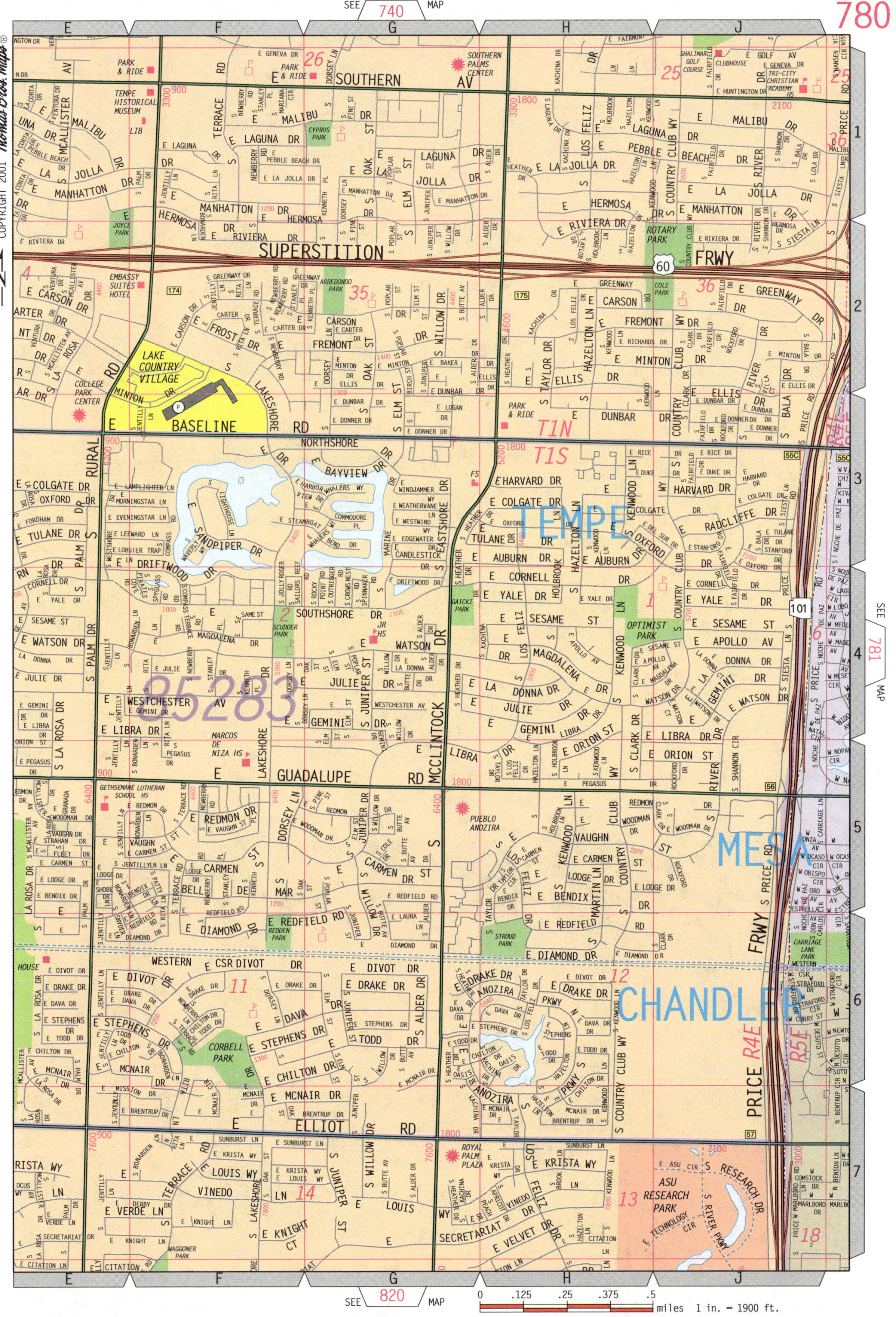

SEE 820 MAP

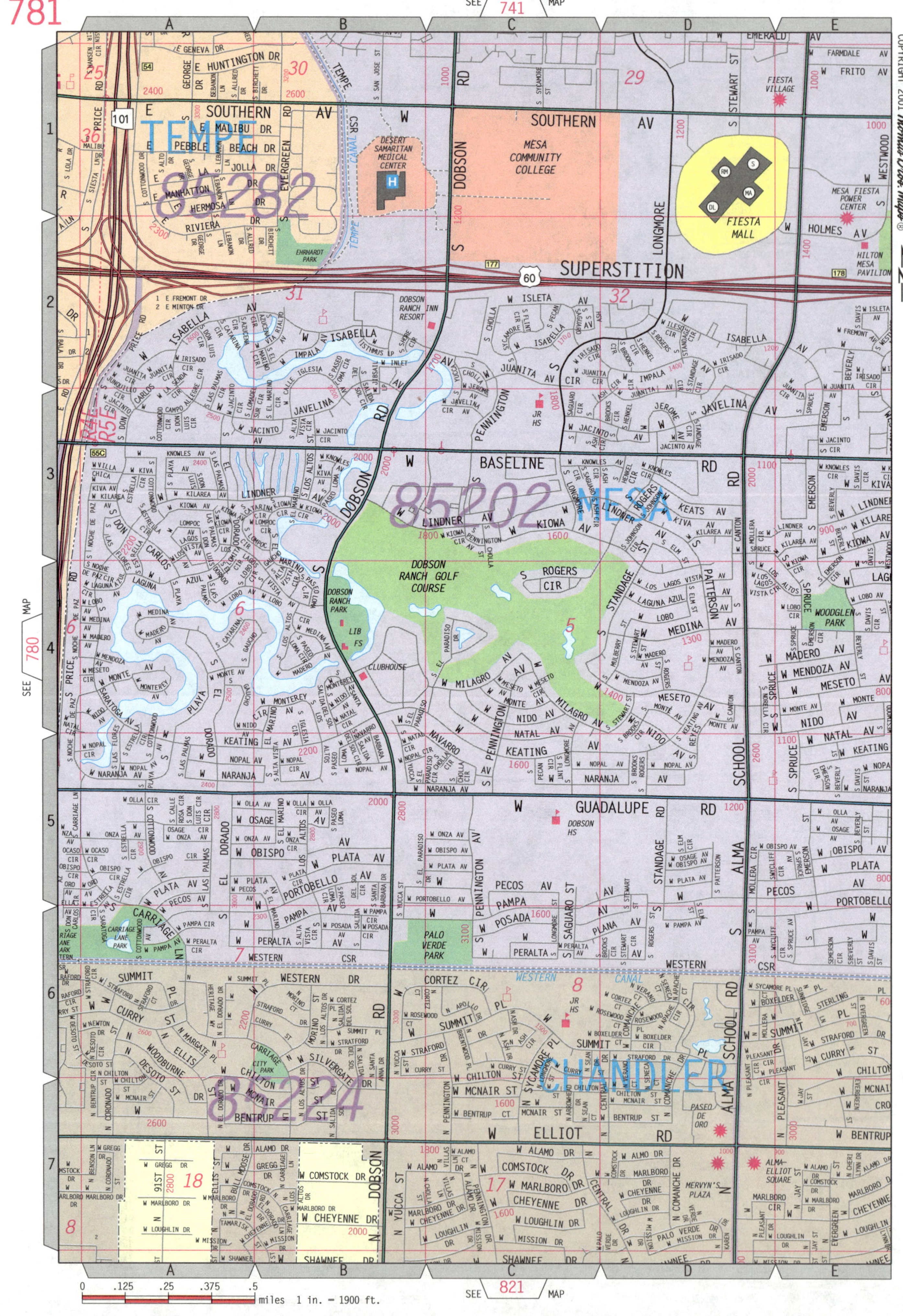

781
SEE 741 MAP
SEE 821 MAP
SEE 780 MAP
PHOENIX
MAP
COPYRIGHT 2001 Thomas Bros. Maps ®
TEMPE
85282
85202
MESA
CHANDLER
85224
SOUTHERN AV
SUPERSTITION
BASELINE RD
GUADALUPE RD
ELLIOT RD
DOBSON RD
LONGMORE
ALMA SCHOOL RD
PRICE RD
WESTERN CANAL
TEMPE CANAL
DESERT SAMARITAN MEDICAL CENTER
MESA COMMUNITY COLLEGE
FIESTA MALL
FIESTA VILLAGE
MESA FIESTA POWER CENTER
HILTON MESA PAVILION
DOBSON RANCH INN RESORT
DOBSON RANCH GOLF COURSE
DOBSON RANCH PARK
CLUBHOUSE
EHRHARDT PARK
WOODGLEN PARK
PALO VERDE PARK
CARRIAGE LANE PARK
CARRIAGE CITY PARK
DOBSON HS
PASEO DE ORO
ALMA-ELLIOT SQUARE
MERVYN'S PLAZA
0 .125 .25 .375 .5 miles 1 in. = 1900 ft.

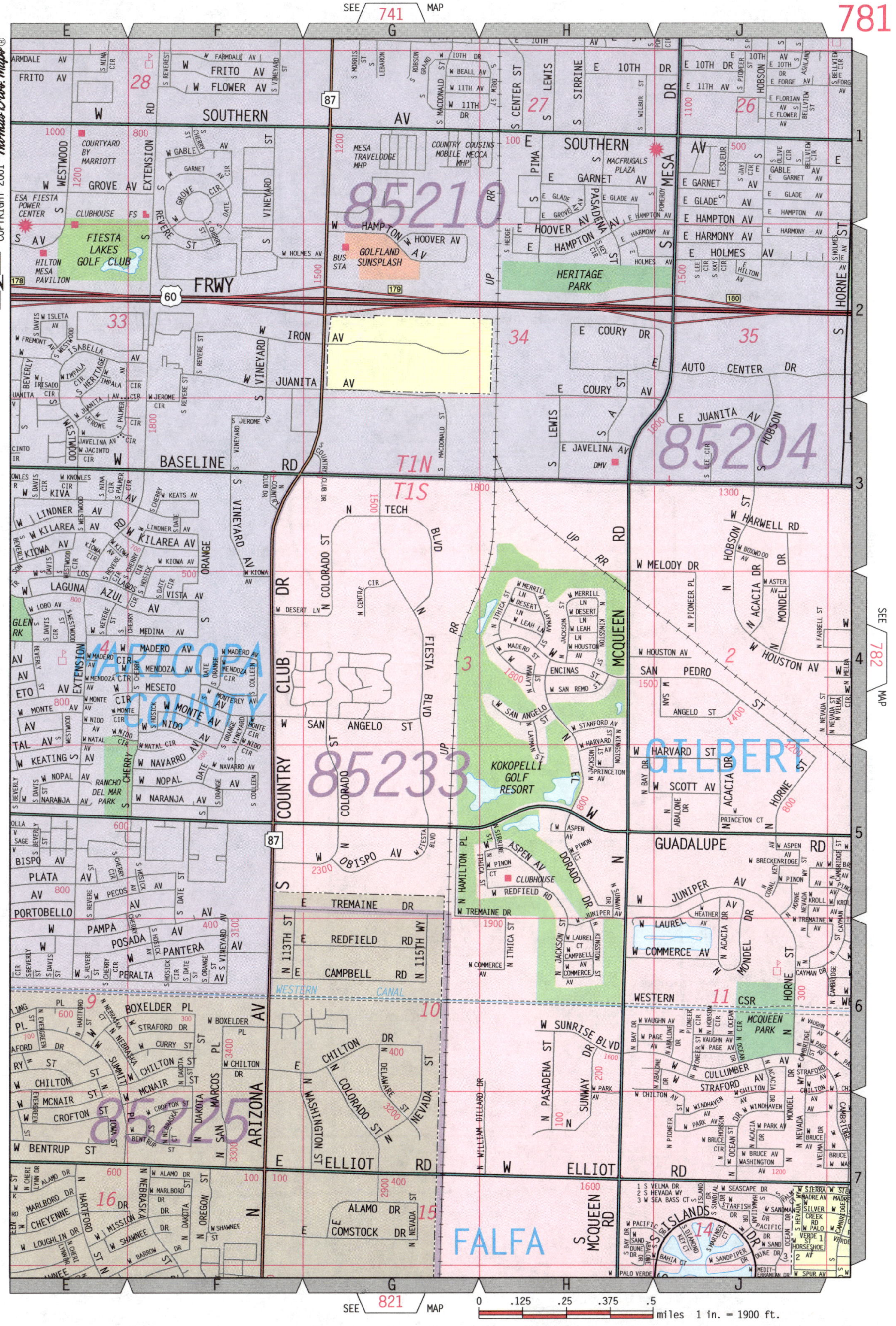

0 .125 .25 .375 .5 miles 1 in. = 1900 ft.

SEE 742 MAP

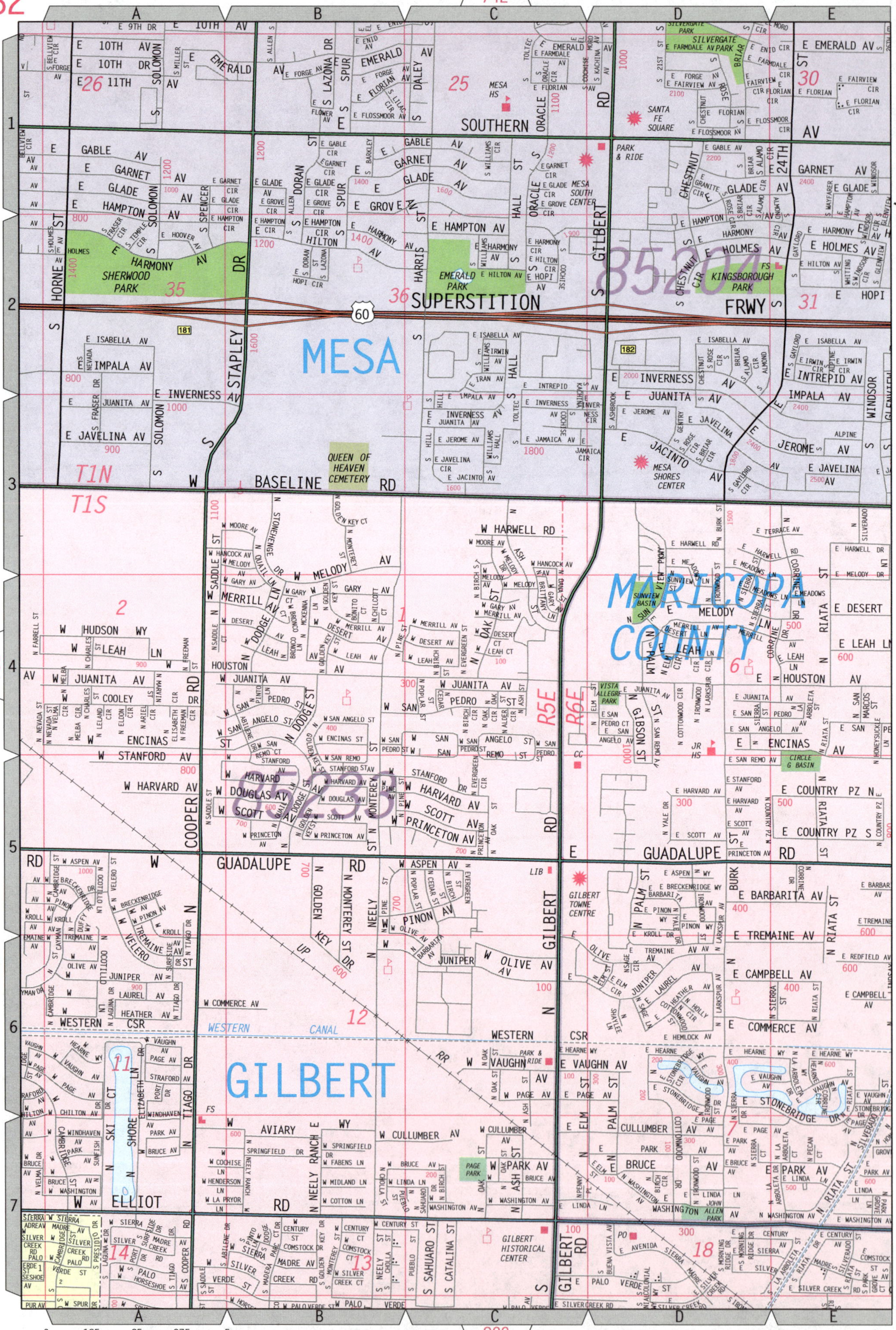
MESA
GILBERT
MARICOPA COUNTY
85204
85233
SUPERSTITION FRWY
60
BASELINE RD
GUADALUPE RD
ELLIOT RD
SOUTHERN AV
S STAPLEY DR
S GILBERT RD
N COOPER RD
N GILBERT RD
WESTERN CANAL
SHERWOOD PARK
EMERALD PARK
KINGSBOROUGH PARK
SILVERGATE PARK
QUEEN OF HEAVEN CEMETERY
MESA HS
SANTA FE SQUARE
MESA SOUTH CENTER
MESA SHORES CENTER
PARK & RIDE
SUNVIEW BASIN
VISTA ALLEGRE PARK
CIRCLE G BASIN
JR HS
GILBERT TOWNE CENTRE
PAGE PARK
JOHN ALLEN PARK
GILBERT HISTORICAL CENTER
T1N
T1S
R5E
R6E
181
182
SEE 781 MAP
A
B
C
D
E
1
2
3
4
5
6
7

SEE 822 MAP

0 .125 .25 .375 .5 miles 1 in. = 1900 ft.

PHOENIX

MAP

SEE 742 MAP

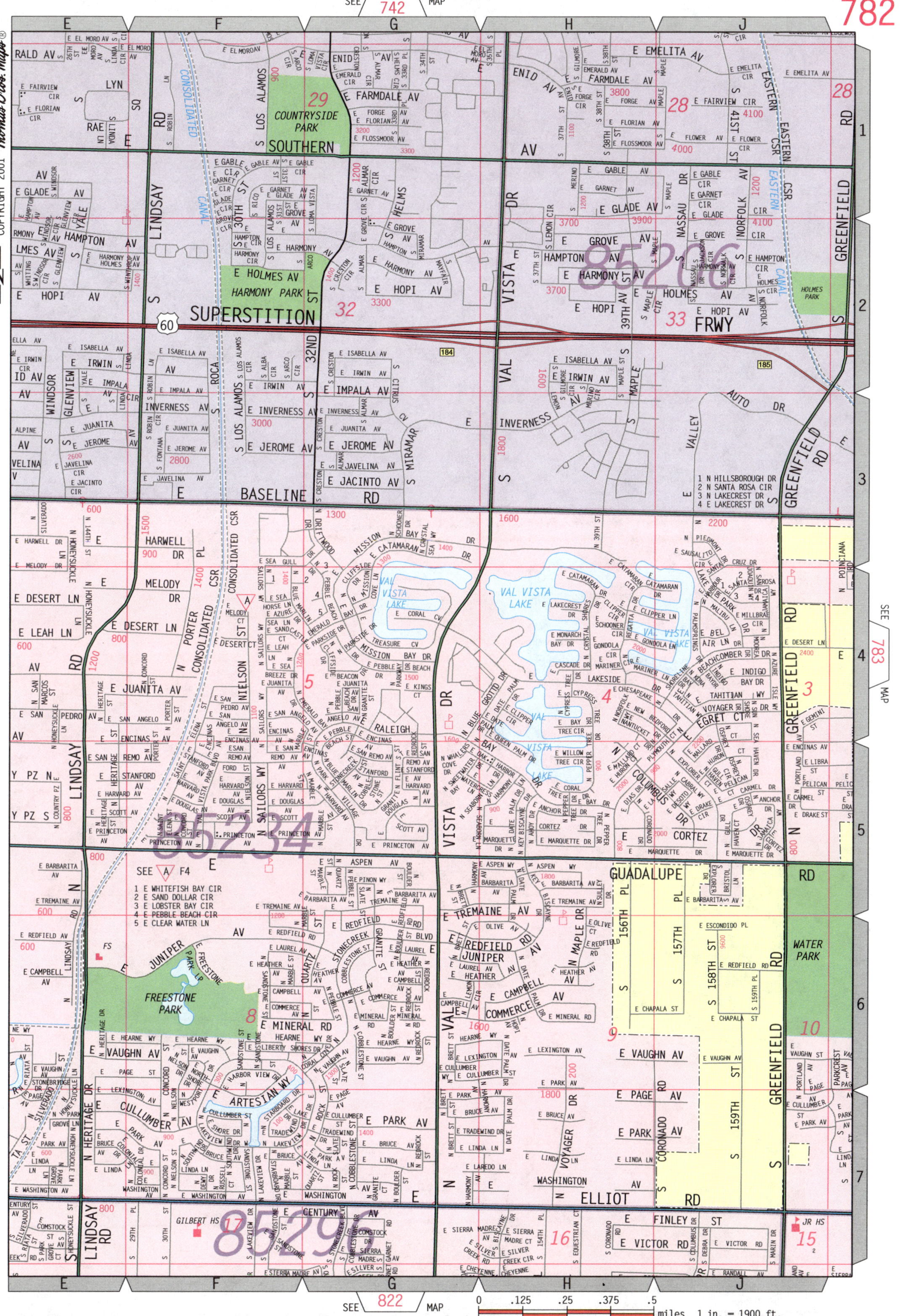

SEE 783 MAP

MAP

SEE 822 MAP

0 .125 .25 .375 .5 miles 1 in. = 1900 ft.

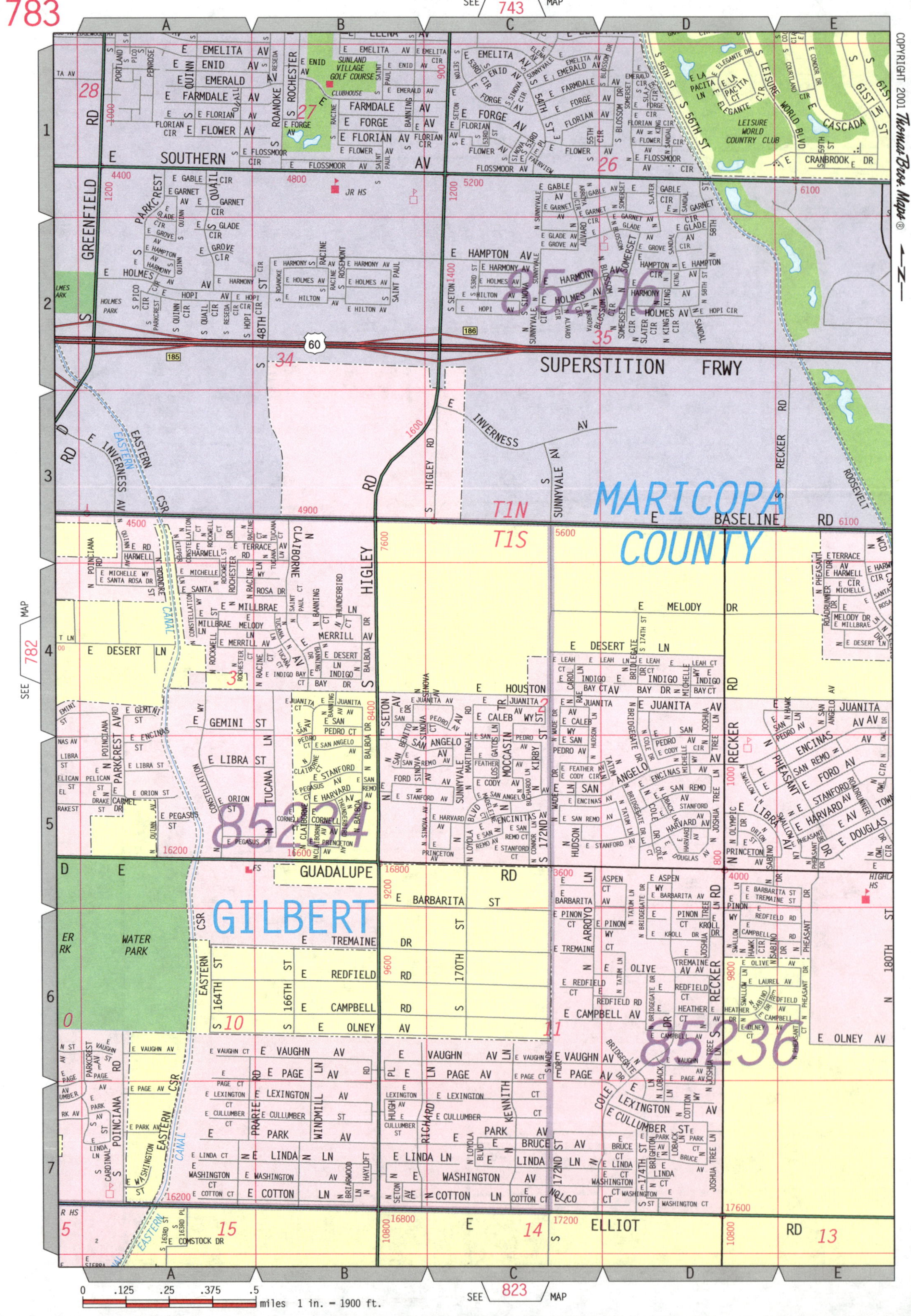

SEE 743 MAP
SEE 782 MAP
SEE 823 MAP
PHOENIX
MAP
COPYRIGHT 2001 Thomas Bros. Maps ®
A
B
C
D
E
1
2
3
4
5
6
7
E SOUTHERN AV
E EMELITA AV
E ENID AV
E EMERALD AV
E FARMDALE AV
E FLORIAN AV
E FORGE AV
E FLOWER AV
FLOSSMOOR AV
SUNLAND VILLAGE GOLF COURSE
CLUBHOUSE
LEISURE WORLD COUNTRY CLUB
LEISURE WORLD BLVD
CASCADA
E CRANBROOK DR
56TH ST
GREENFIELD RD
JR HS
E HAMPTON AV
E HARMONY AV
E HOLMES AV
E HOPI CIR
E HILTON AV
85206
85234
85236
SUPERSTITION FRWY
60
185
186
E INVERNESS AV
EASTERN CANAL
HIGLEY RD
SUNNYVALE AV
RECKER RD
ROOSEVELT
MARICOPA COUNTY
T1N
T1S
E BASELINE RD
E MELODY DR
E DESERT LN
E HOUSTON
E JUANITA AV
E SAN ANGELO AV
E ENCINAS AV
E STANFORD AV
E HARVARD AV
E DOUGLAS AV
E GUADALUPE RD
GILBERT
WATER PARK
E BARBARITA ST
E TREMAINE DR
E REDFIELD RD
E CAMPBELL RD
E OLNEY AV
E VAUGHN AV
E PAGE AV
E LEXINGTON AV
E CULLUMBER ST
E PARK AV
E LINDA LN
E WASHINGTON AV
E COTTON LN
E ELLIOT RD
164TH ST
166TH ST
170TH ST
172ND ST
174TH ST
180TH ST
27
28
26
34
35
3
2
10
11
15
14
13
5
0
miles 1 in. = 1900 ft.
0 .125 .25 .375 .5

SEE 743 MAP

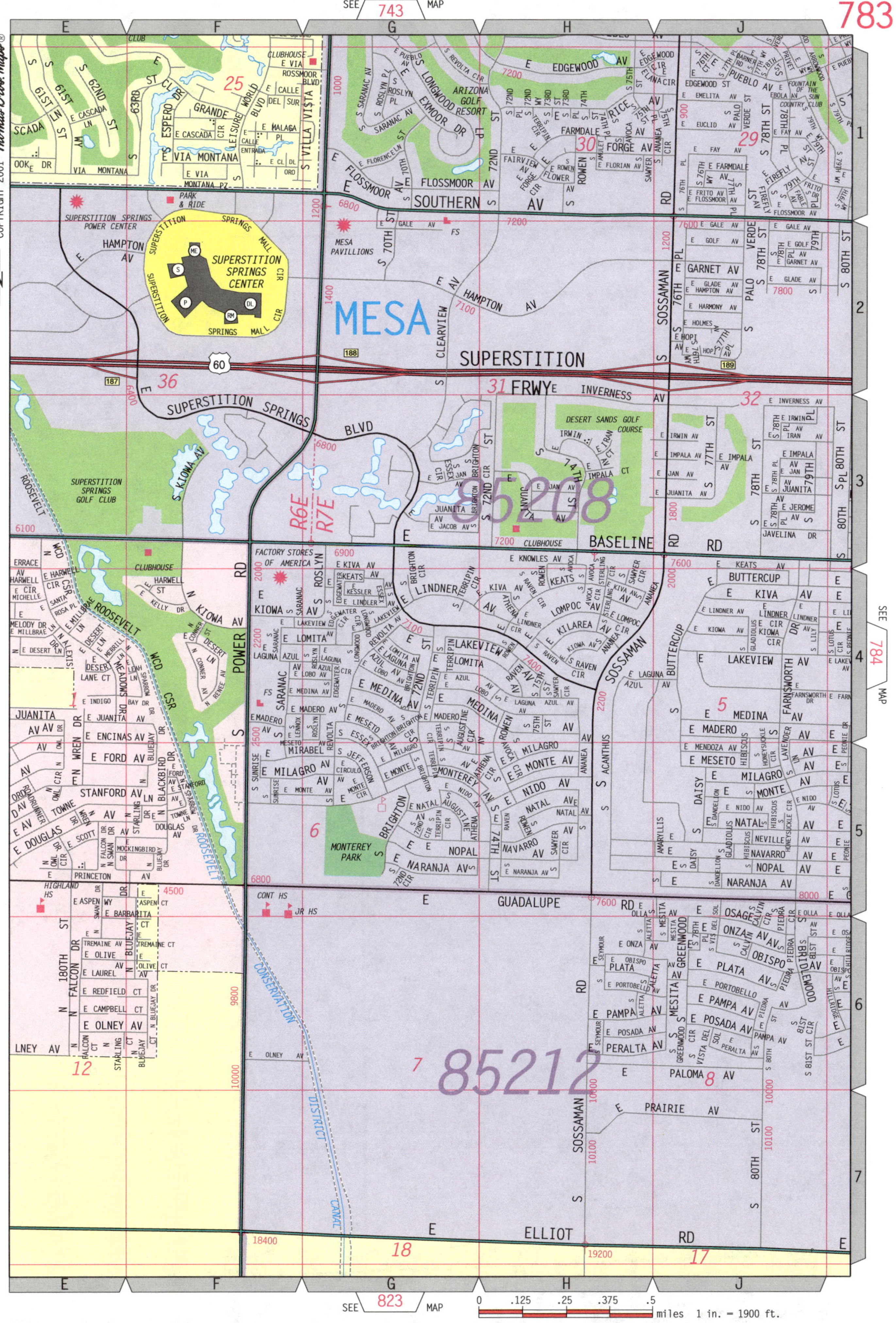

SEE 784 MAP

SEE 823 MAP

SEE 744 MAP

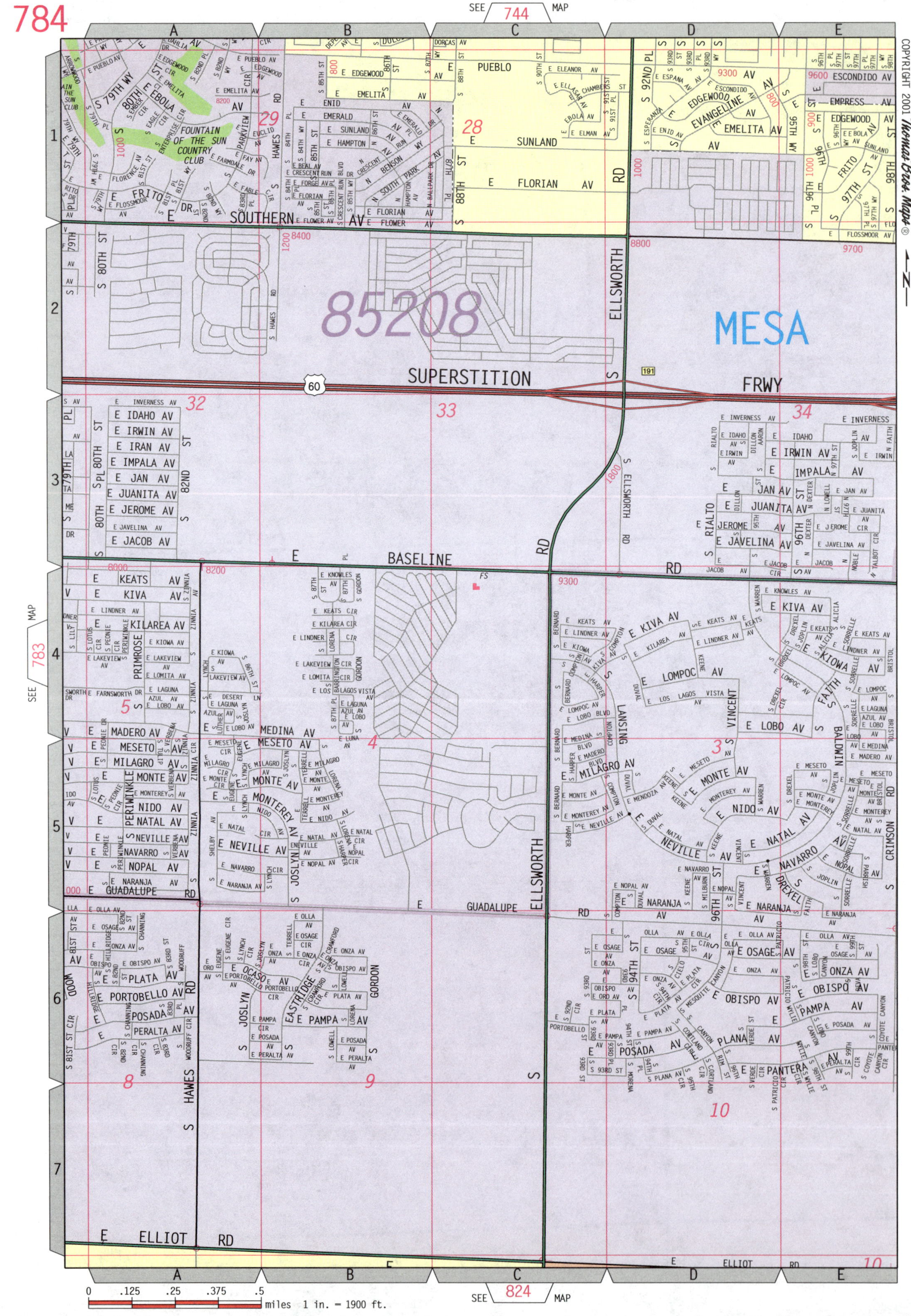

SEE 824 MAP

SEE 744 MAP

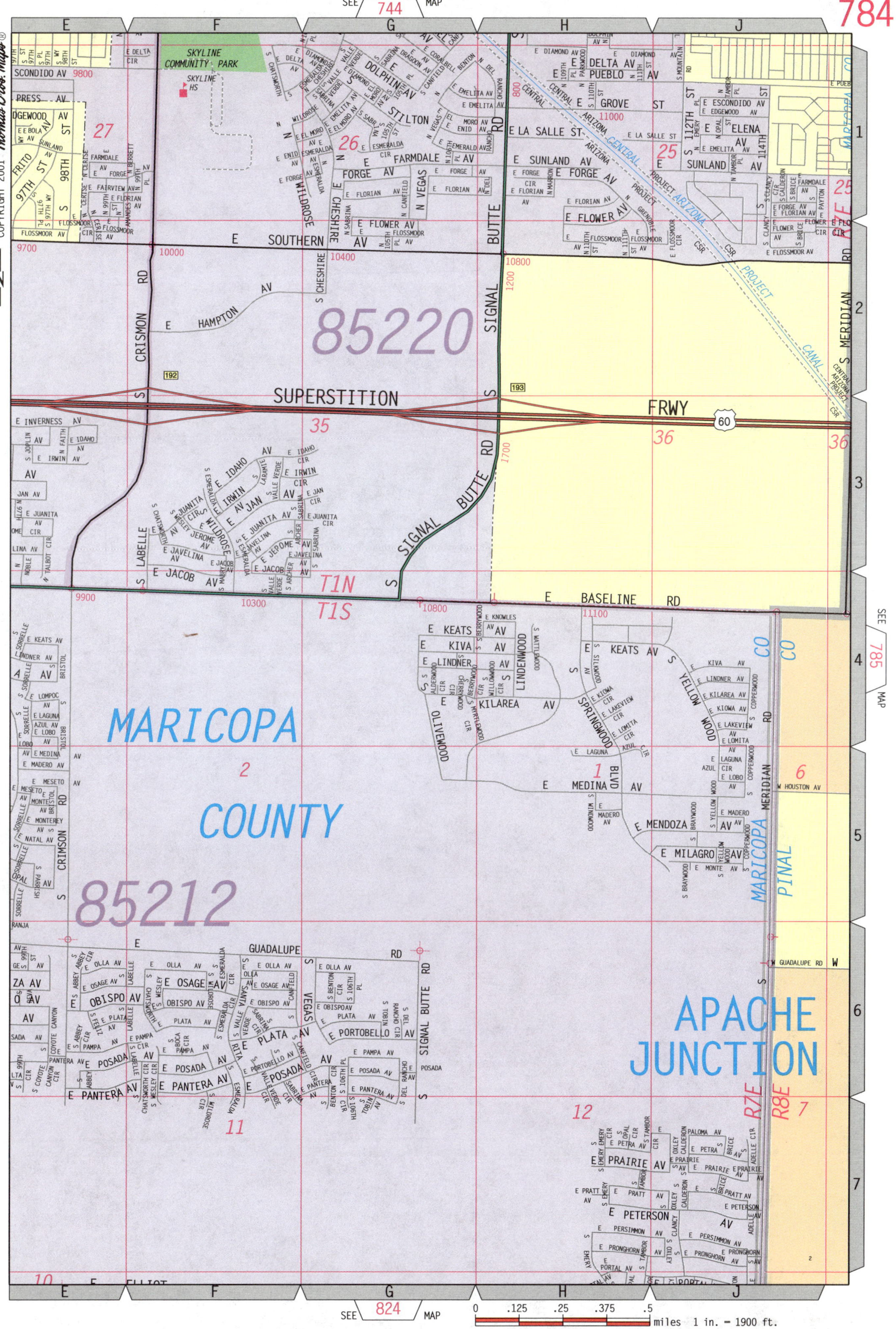

SEE 785 MAP

SEE 824 MAP

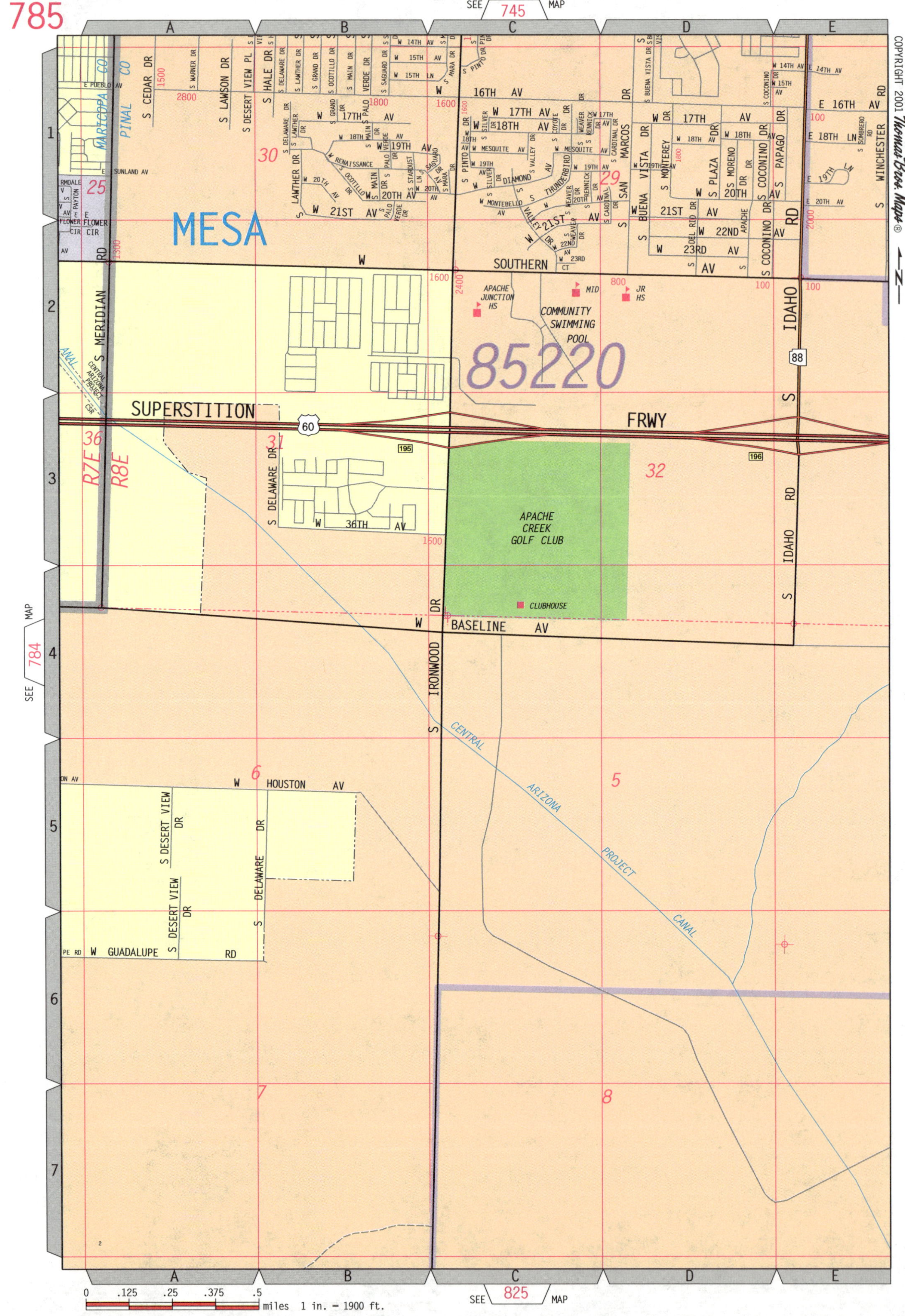
SEE 745 MAP
MESA
85220
PHOENIX
MAP
SUPERSTITION
FRWY
60
88
W SOUTHERN AV
W BASELINE AV
S IRONWOOD DR
S IDAHO RD
S MERIDIAN RD
W HOUSTON AV
W GUADALUPE RD
S DESERT VIEW DR
S DELAWARE DR
W 36TH AV
APACHE CREEK GOLF CLUB
CLUBHOUSE
APACHE JUNCTION HS
MID
JR HS
COMMUNITY SWIMMING POOL
CENTRAL ARIZONA PROJECT CANAL
MARICOPA CO
PINAL CO
R7E
R8E
SEE 784 MAP
SEE 825 MAP
COPYRIGHT 2001 Thomas Bros. Maps®
miles 1 in. = 1900 ft.

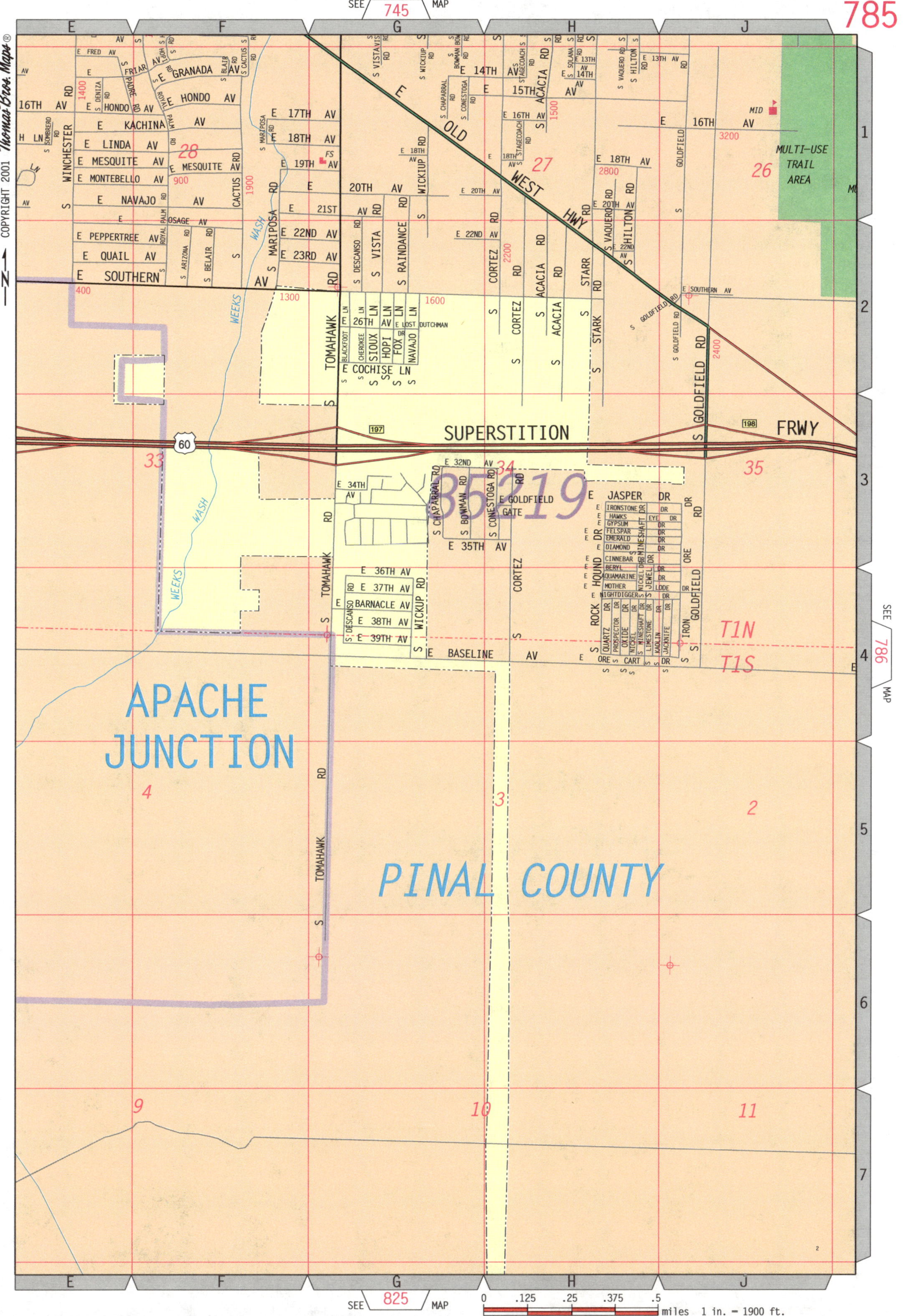
SEE 745 MAP
SEE 825 MAP
SEE 786 MAP
PHOENIX
MAP
SUPERSTITION FRWY
OLD WEST HWY
APACHE JUNCTION
PINAL COUNTY
MULTI-USE TRAIL AREA
85219
T1N
T1S
E BASELINE AV
E SOUTHERN AV
S TOMAHAWK RD
S GOLDFIELD RD
S CORTEZ RD
S ACACIA RD
WEEKS WASH
miles 1 in. = 1900 ft.

SEE 746 MAP

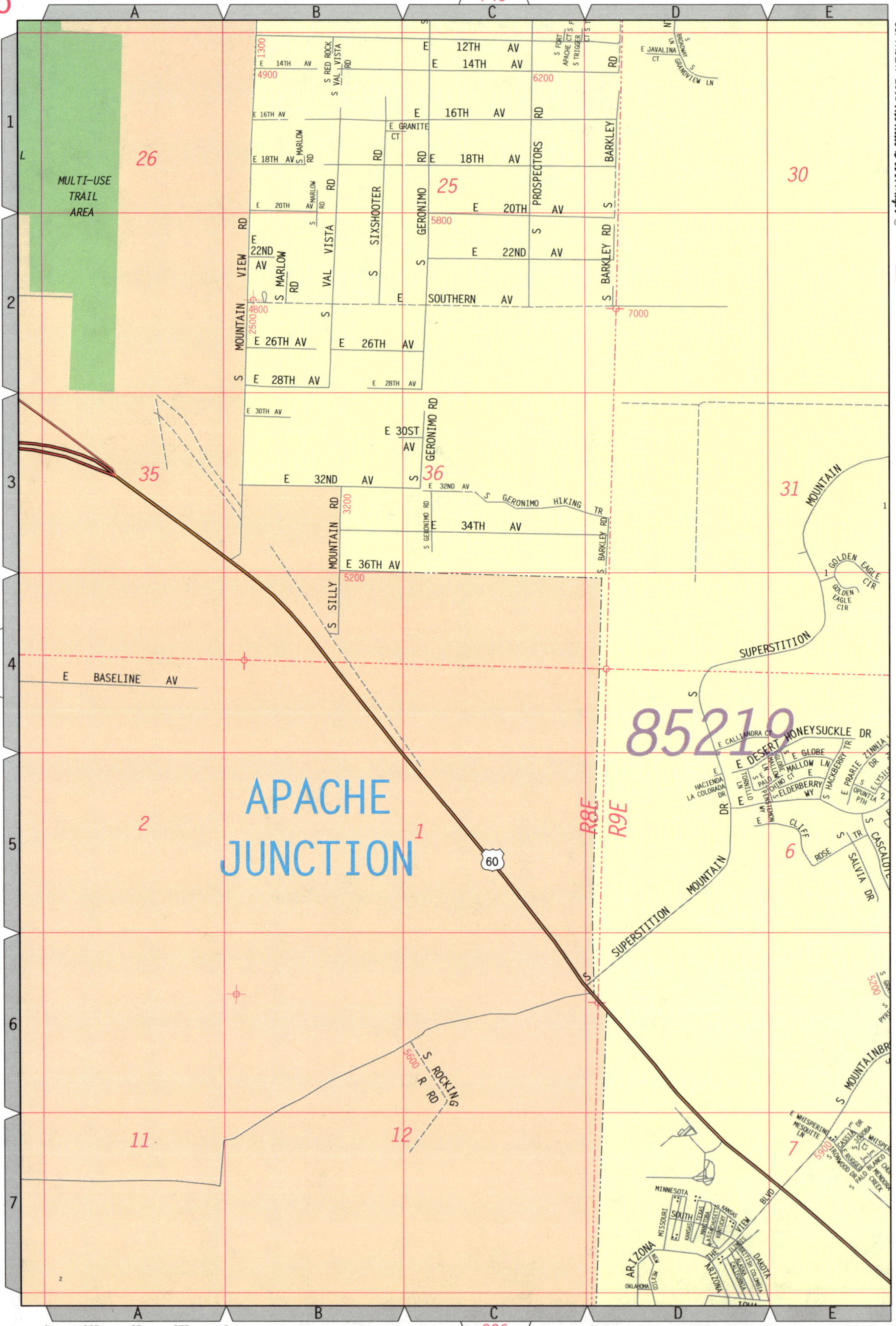

SEE 785 MAP

SEE 826 MAP

0 .125 .25 .375 .5 miles 1 in. = 1900 ft.

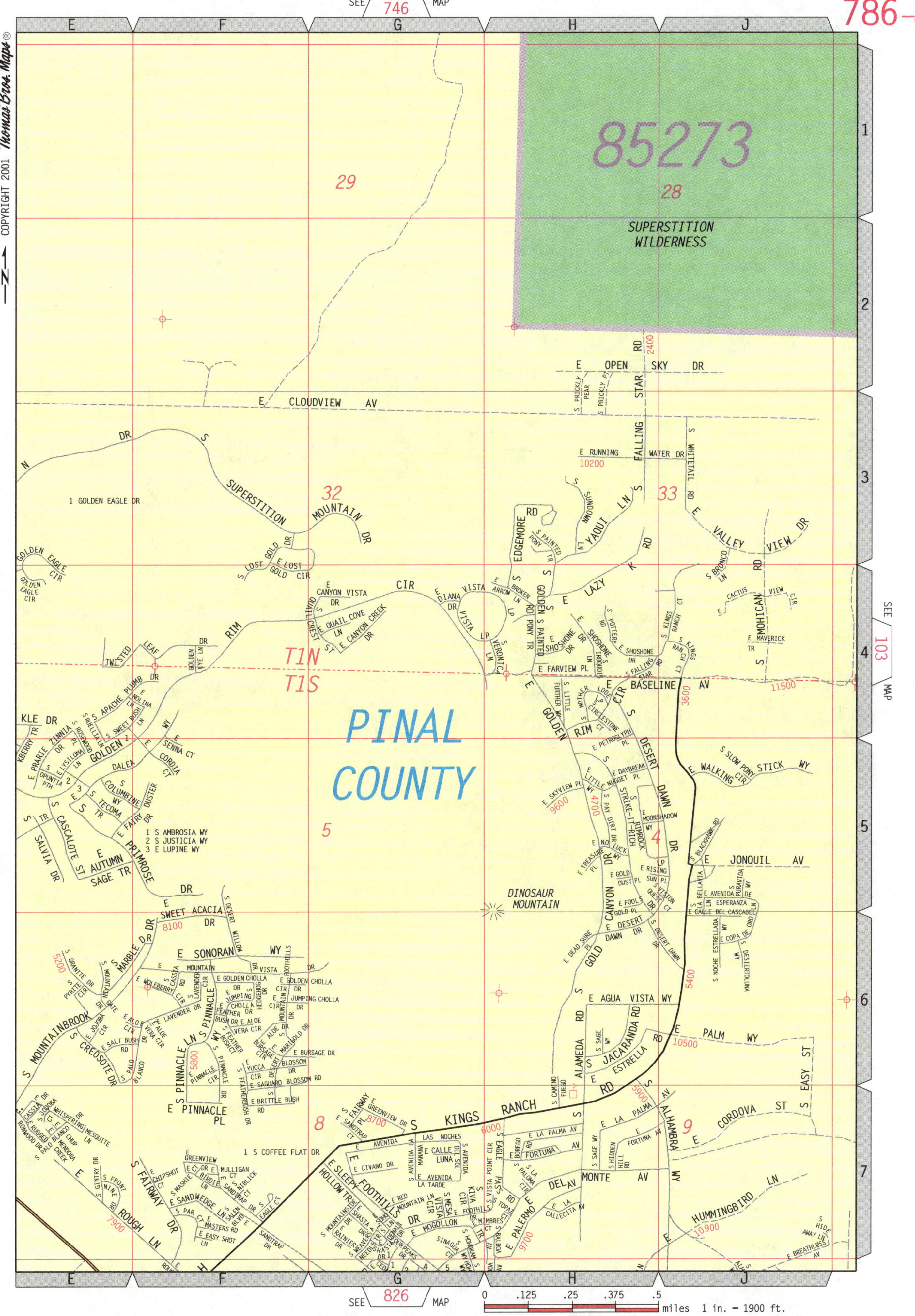
SEE 746 MAP
85273
SUPERSTITION WILDERNESS
PINAL COUNTY
T1N
T1S
DINOSAUR MOUNTAIN
E CLOUDVIEW AV
E OPEN SKY DR
S FALLING STAR RD
E RUNNING WATER DR
S SUPERSTITION MOUNTAIN DR
E VALLEY VIEW DR
E LAZY K RD
E BASELINE AV
S DESERT DAWN DR
E WALKING STICK WY
E JONQUIL AV
E AGUA VISTA WY
E PALM WY
S KINGS RANCH RD
S ALHAMBRA WY
E CORDOVA ST
S EASY ST
HUMMINGBIRD LN
E DEL MONTE AV
E SONORAN WY
S MOUNTAINBROOK DR
E PINNACLE PL
S FAIRWAY DR
E ROUGH LN
1 GOLDEN EAGLE DR
1 S AMBROSIA WY
2 S JUSTICIA WY
3 E LUPINE WY
1 S COFFEE FLAT DR
SEE 103 MAP
SEE 826 MAP
0 .125 .25 .375 .5 miles 1 in. = 1900 ft.
PHOENIX
MAP

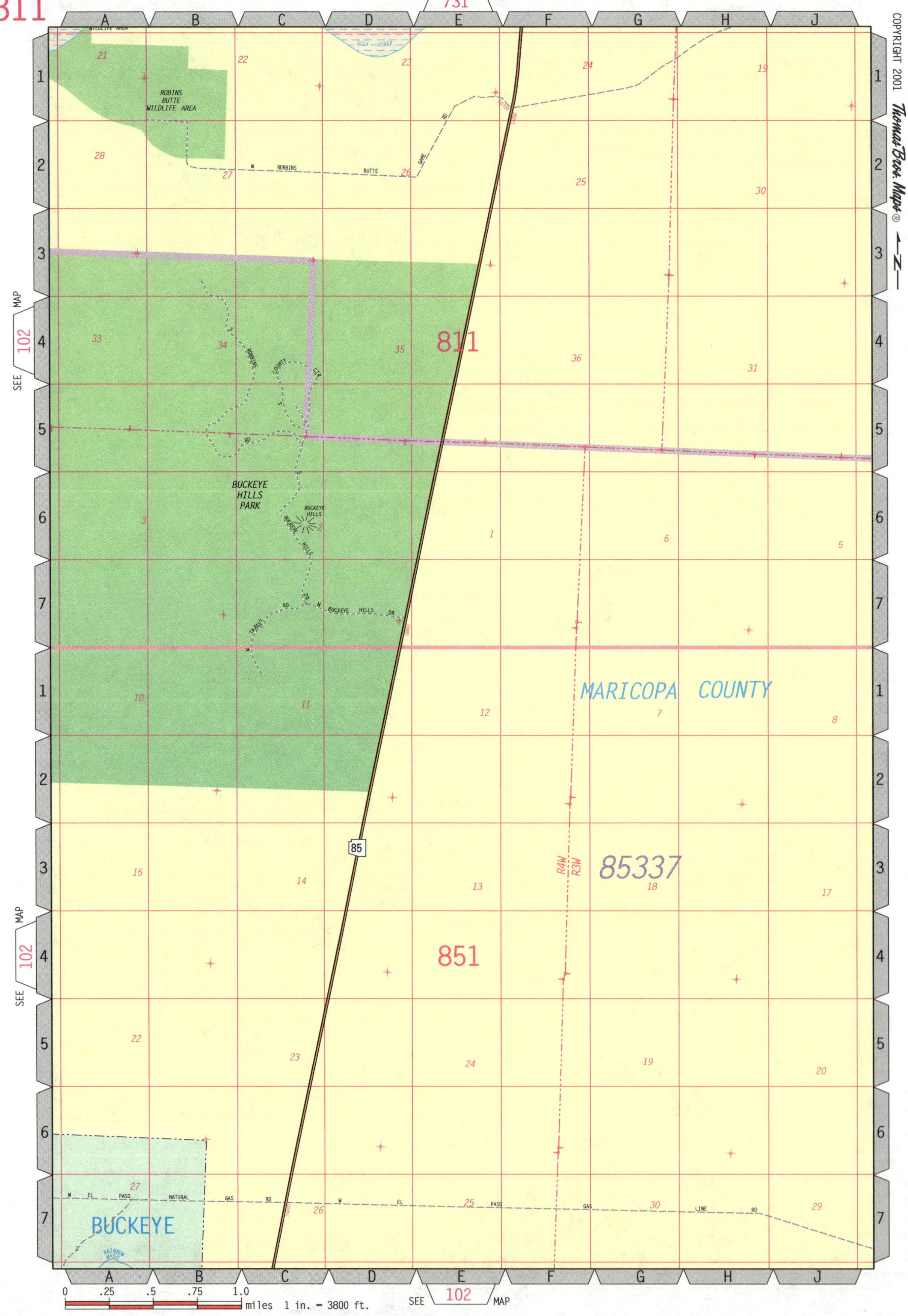
SEE 731 MAP
ROBINS BUTTE WILDLIFE AREA
W ROBBINS BUTTE
GAME RD
BUCKEYE HILLS PARK
S ROBBINS COUNTY CIR
BUCKEYE HILLS
W BUCKEYE HILLS DR
TARGET RD
811
MARICOPA COUNTY
85
R4W R3W
85337
851
W EL PASO NATURAL GAS RD
W EL PASO GAS LINE RD
BUCKEYE
SEE 102 MAP
0 .25 .5 .75 1.0
miles 1 in. = 3800 ft.

PHOENIX
MAP

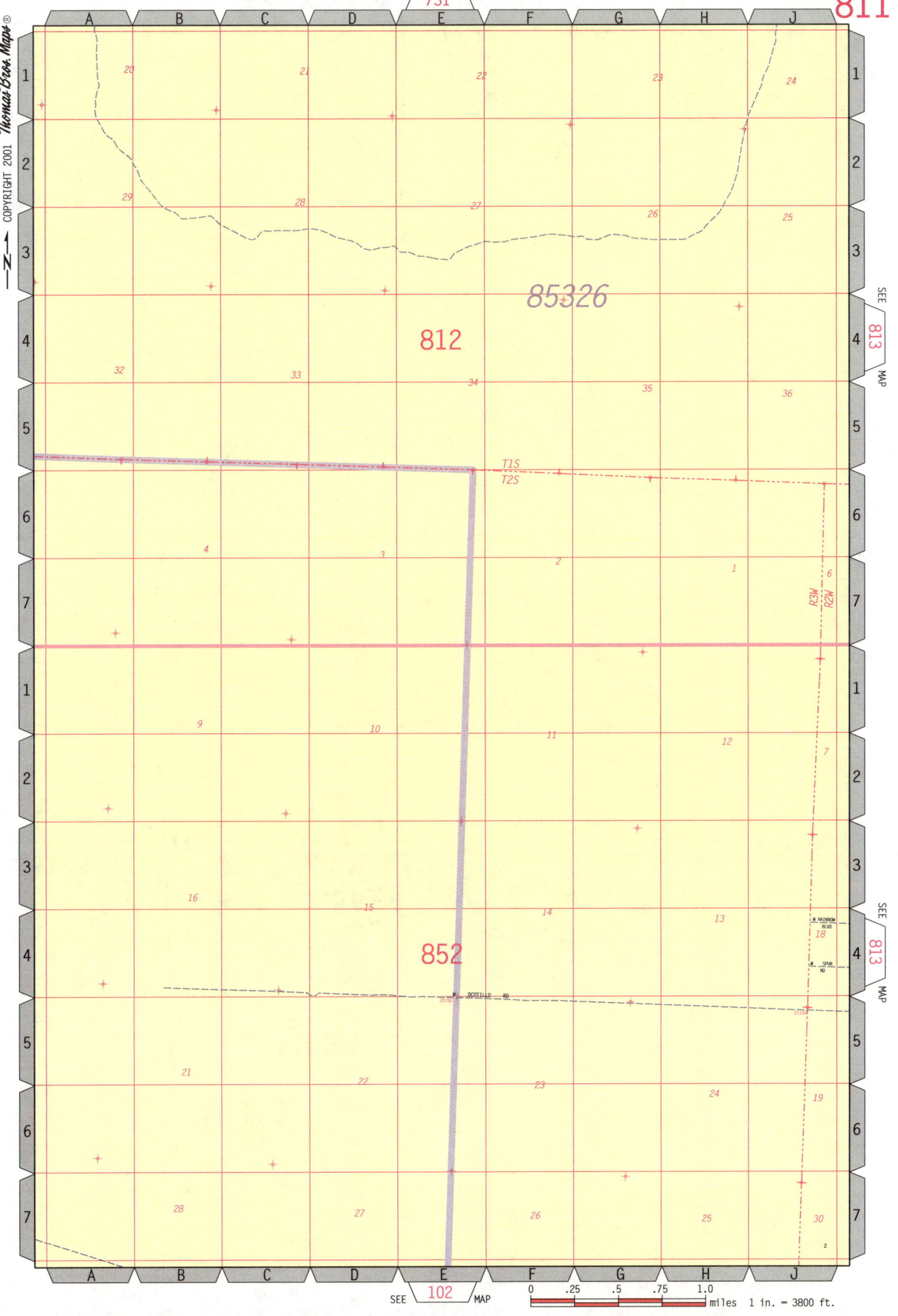

SEE 731 MAP
SEE 813 MAP
SEE 813 MAP
SEE 102 MAP
85326
812
852
T1S
T2S
R3W
R2W
W RAINBOW BLVD
W SPUR RD
W OCOTILLO RD
21100
0 .25 .5 .75 1.0 miles 1 in. = 3800 ft.

PHOENIX

MAP

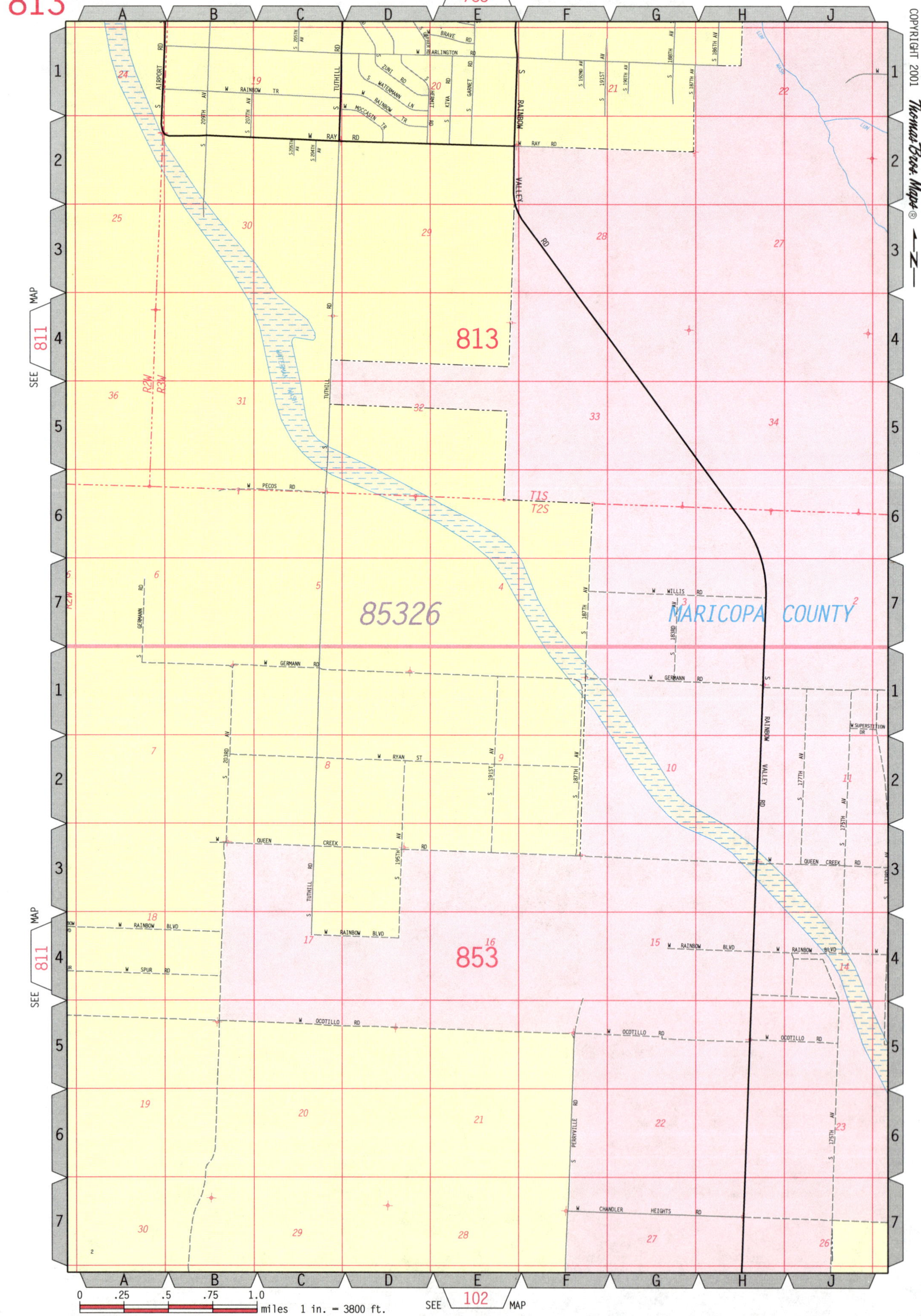
SEE 733 MAP
SEE 811 MAP
SEE 102 MAP
PHOENIX
MAP
813
85326
853
MARICOPA COUNTY
AIRPORT RD
TUTHILL RD
RAINBOW VALLEY RD
W RAY RD
W RAINBOW TR
W ARLINGTON RD
BRAVE RD
ZUNI RD
S WATERMANN LN
RAINBOW TR
W MOCCASIN TR
HERMIT RD
KIVA RD
GARNET RD
S 205TH AV
S 206TH AV
S 203RD AV
S 187TH AV
S 188TH AV
S 186TH AV
S 190TH AV
S 191ST AV
S 192ND AV
W PECOS RD
T1S
T2S
R2W
R3W
WATERMAN WASH
W WILLIS RD
GERMANN RD
W GERMANN RD
S 183RD AV
W RYAN ST
S 203RD AV
S 191ST AV
S 187TH AV
W QUEEN CREEK RD
S 195TH AV
S 177TH AV
S 175TH AV
W SUPERSTITION DR
W RAINBOW BLVD
W SPUR RD
W OCOTILLO RD
S PERRYVILLE RD
W CHANDLER HEIGHTS RD
0 .25 .5 .75 1.0 miles 1 in. = 3800 ft.

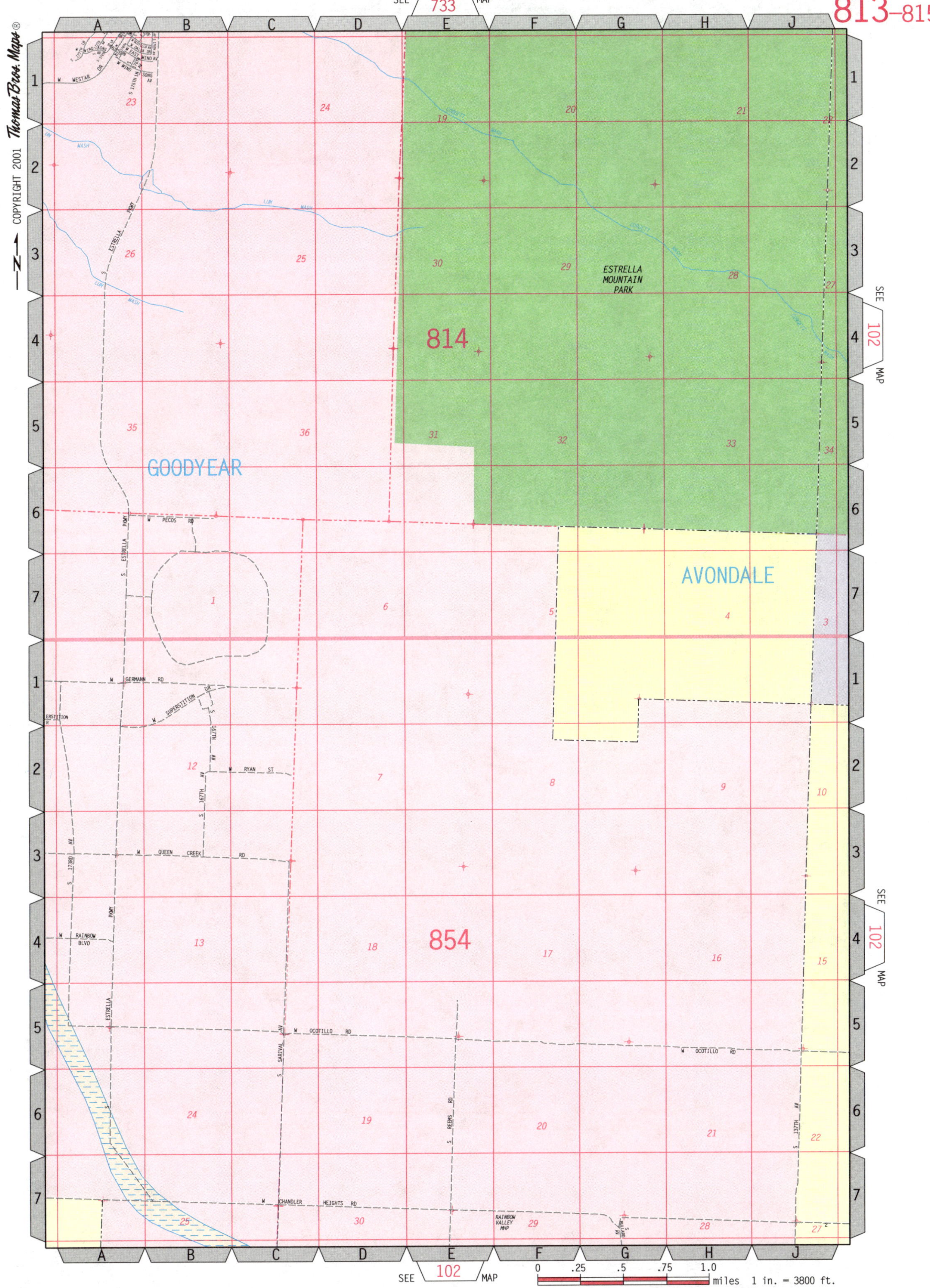
SEE 733 MAP
ESTRELLA MOUNTAIN PARK
814
GOODYEAR
AVONDALE
854
W PECOS RD
W GERMANN RD
W SUPERSTITION DR
S 167TH AV
W RYAN ST
W QUEEN CREEK RD
S 173RD AV
W RAINBOW BLVD
S ESTRELLA PKWY
W OCOTILLO RD
S SARIVAL AV
S REEMS RD
S 137TH AV
W CHANDLER HEIGHTS RD
RAINBOW VALLEY MHP
W WESTAR DR
LUM WASH
CORGETT WASH
SEE 102 MAP
PHOENIX
MAP
0 .25 .5 .75 1.0 miles 1 in. = 3800 ft.

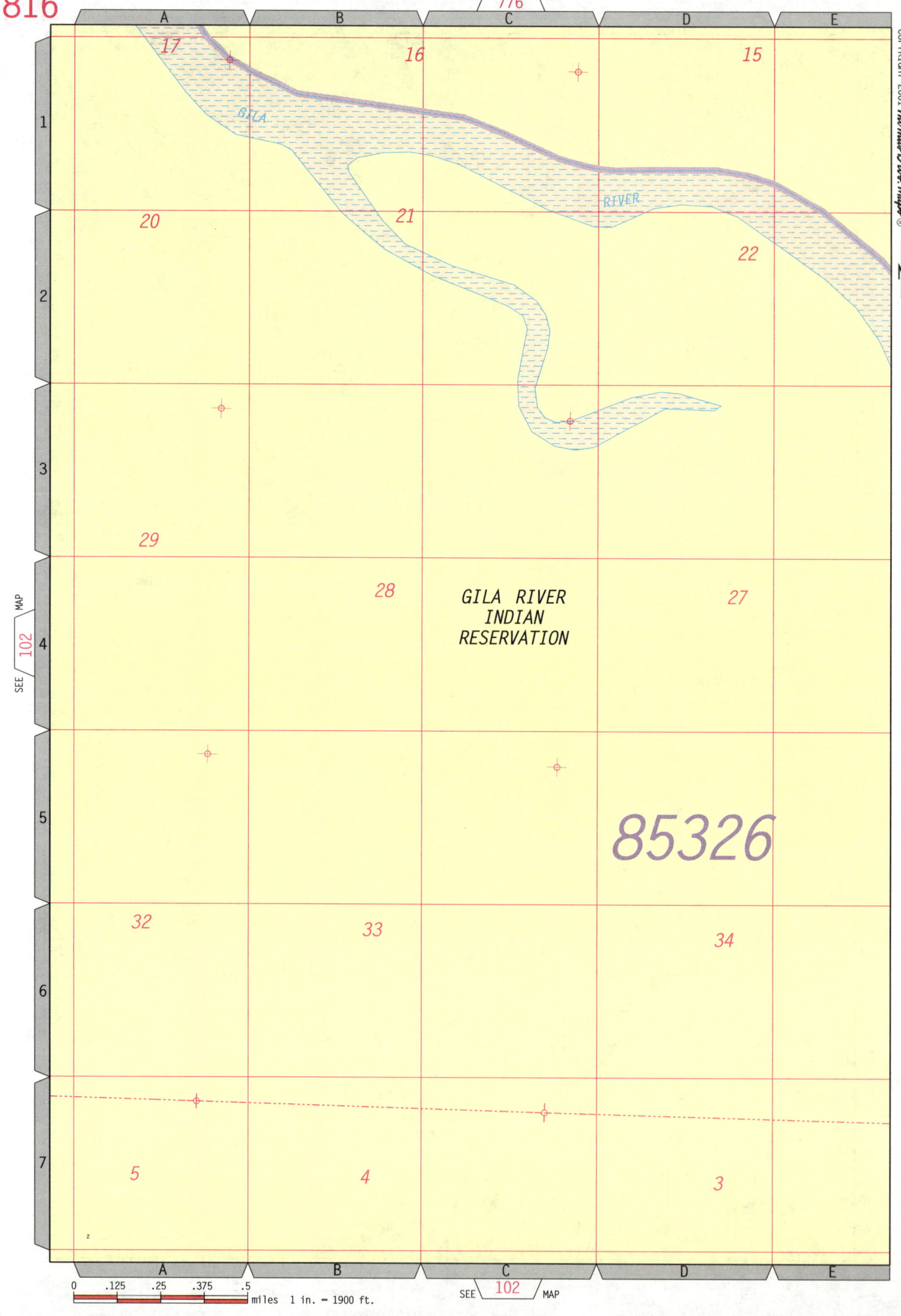
SEE 776 MAP
A
B
C
D
E
1
2
3
4
5
6
7
17
16
15
GILA
RIVER
20
21
22
29
28
27
GILA RIVER
INDIAN
RESERVATION
85326
32
33
34
5
4
3
SEE 102 MAP
0 .125 .25 .375 .5 miles 1 in. = 1900 ft.

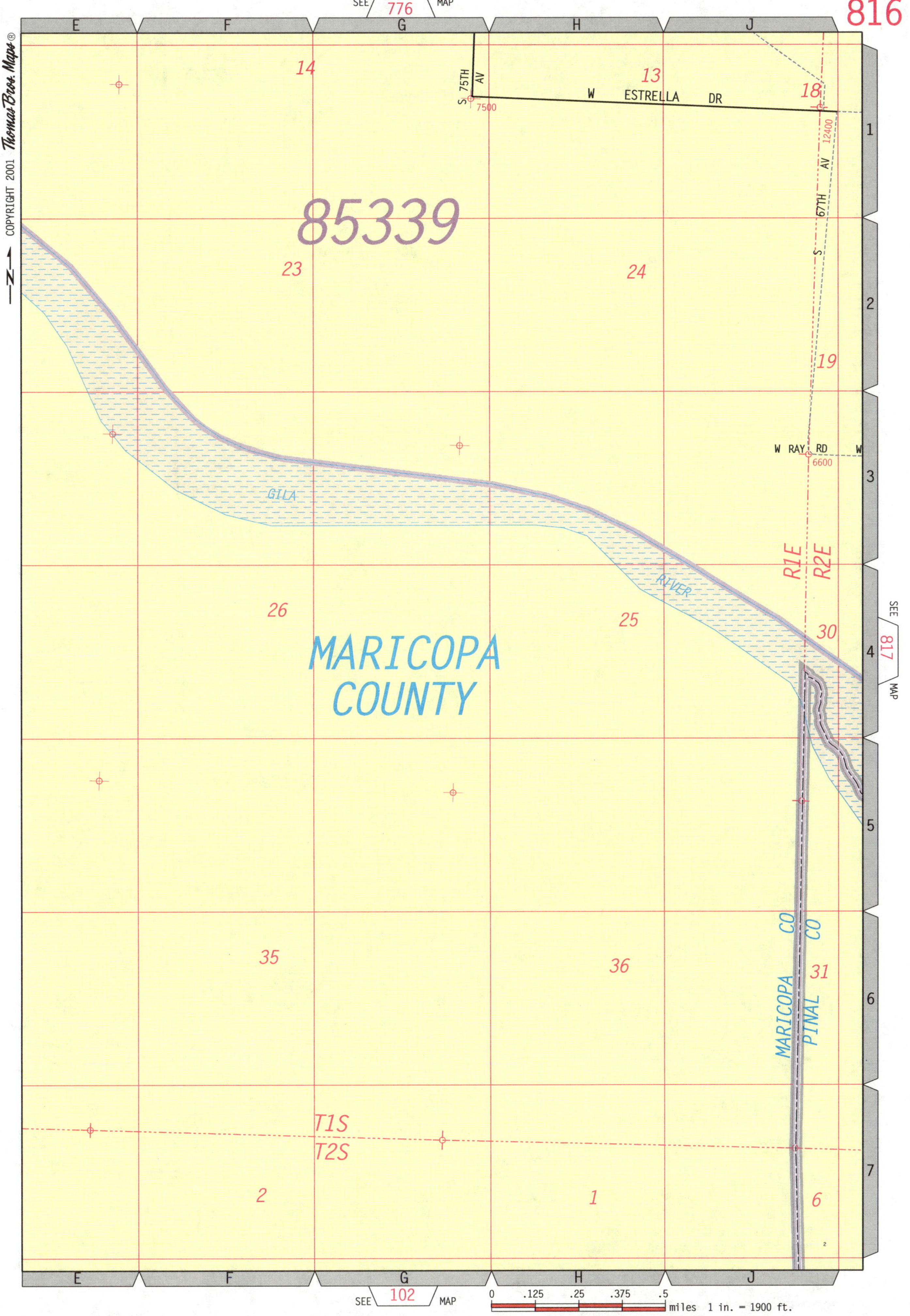

SEE 776 MAP
E
F
G
H
J
1
2
3
4
5
6
7
14
13
18
S 75TH AV
7500
W ESTRELLA DR
12400
S 67TH AV
85339
23
24
19
W RAY RD
6600
W
GILA
RIVER
R1E
R2E
26
25
30
SEE 817 MAP
MARICOPA COUNTY
35
36
31
MARICOPA CO
PINAL CO
T1S
T2S
2
1
6
SEE 102 MAP
0 .125 .25 .375 .5
miles 1 in. = 1900 ft.
PHOENIX
MAP

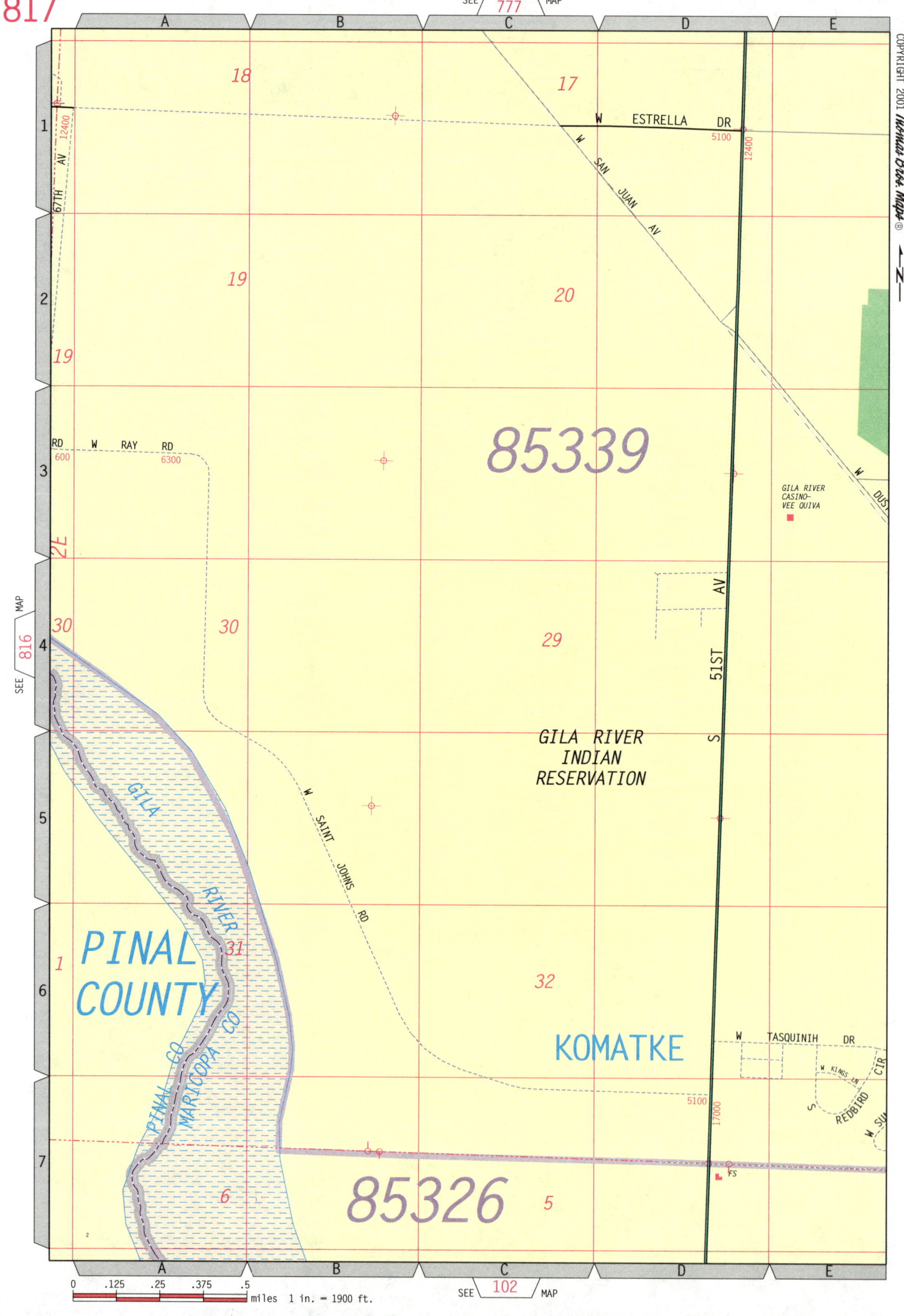

SEE 777 MAP
SEE 816 MAP
SEE 102 MAP
PHOENIX
MAP
W ESTRELLA DR
5100
12400
W SAN JUAN AV
67TH AV
12400
W RAY RD
600
6300
85339
GILA RIVER CASINO-VEE QUIVA
W DUS
S 51ST AV
GILA RIVER INDIAN RESERVATION
W SAINT JOHNS RD
GILA RIVER
PINAL COUNTY
PINAL CO
MARICOPA CO
KOMATKE
W TASQUINIH DR
W KINGS LN
CIR
S REDBIRD
W SU
5100
17000
FS
85326
2E
18
17
19
20
19
30
30
29
31
1
32
6
5
0 .125 .25 .375 .5 miles 1 in. = 1900 ft.

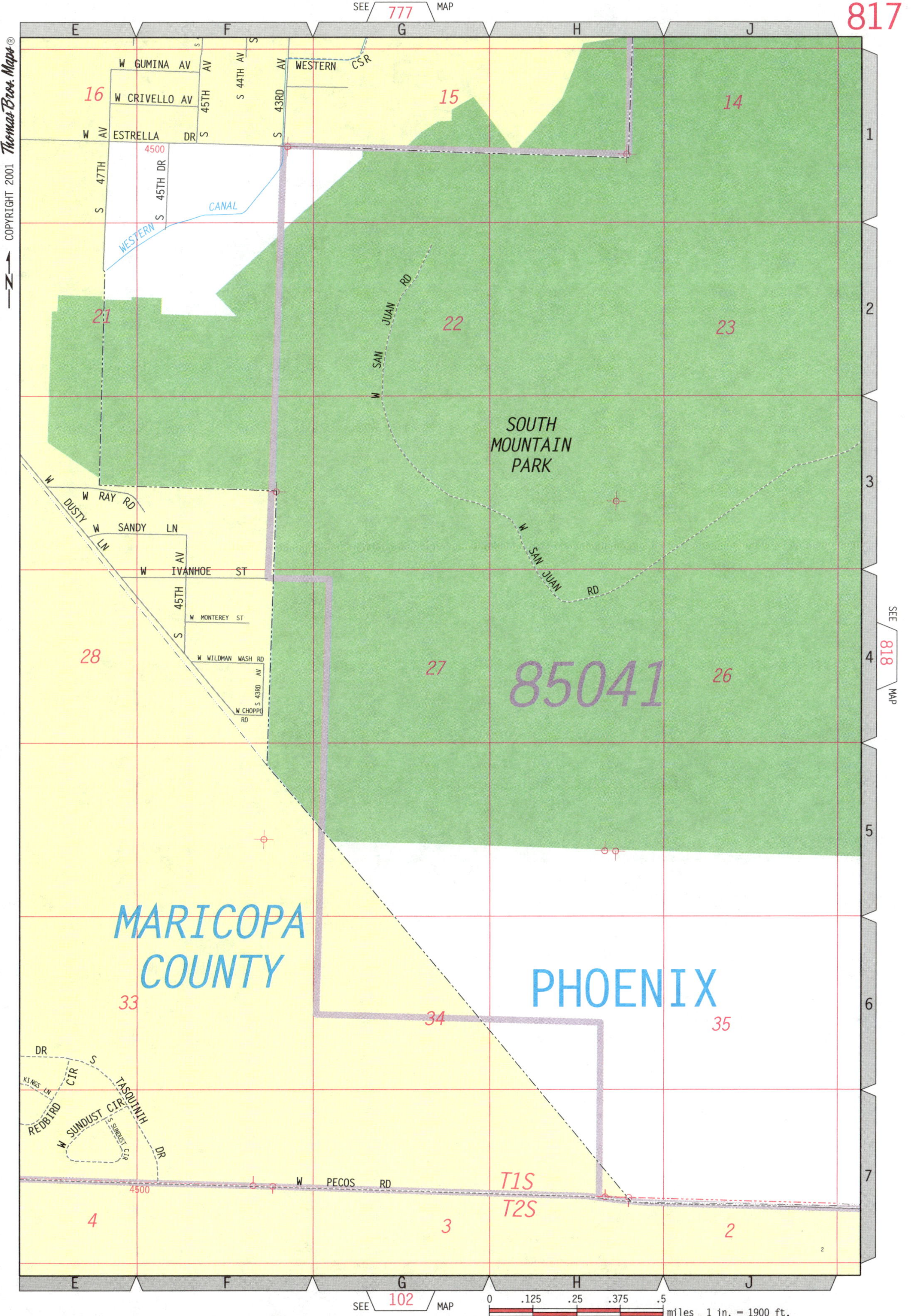
SEE 777 MAP
E
F
G
H
J
W GUMINA AV
W CRIVELLO AV
W ESTRELLA DR
S 47TH AV
S 45TH AV
S 44TH AV
S 43RD AV
WESTERN CSR
S 45TH DR
WESTERN CANAL
4500
16
15
14
21
22
23
W SAN JUAN RD
SOUTH MOUNTAIN PARK
W RAY RD
W DUSTY LN
W SANDY LN
W IVANHOE ST
S 45TH AV
W MONTEREY ST
W WILDMAN WASH RD
S 43RD AV
W CHOPPO RD
28
27
85041
26
MARICOPA COUNTY
33
34
PHOENIX
35
DR
S TASQUINTH DR
KINGS LN
CIR
REDBIRD
W SUNDUST CIR
S SUNDUST CIR
W PECOS RD
4500
T1S
T2S
4
3
2
1
2
3
4
5
6
7
SEE 818 MAP
SEE 102 MAP
0 .125 .25 .375 .5 miles 1 in. = 1900 ft.
PHOENIX
MAP

SEE 778 MAP

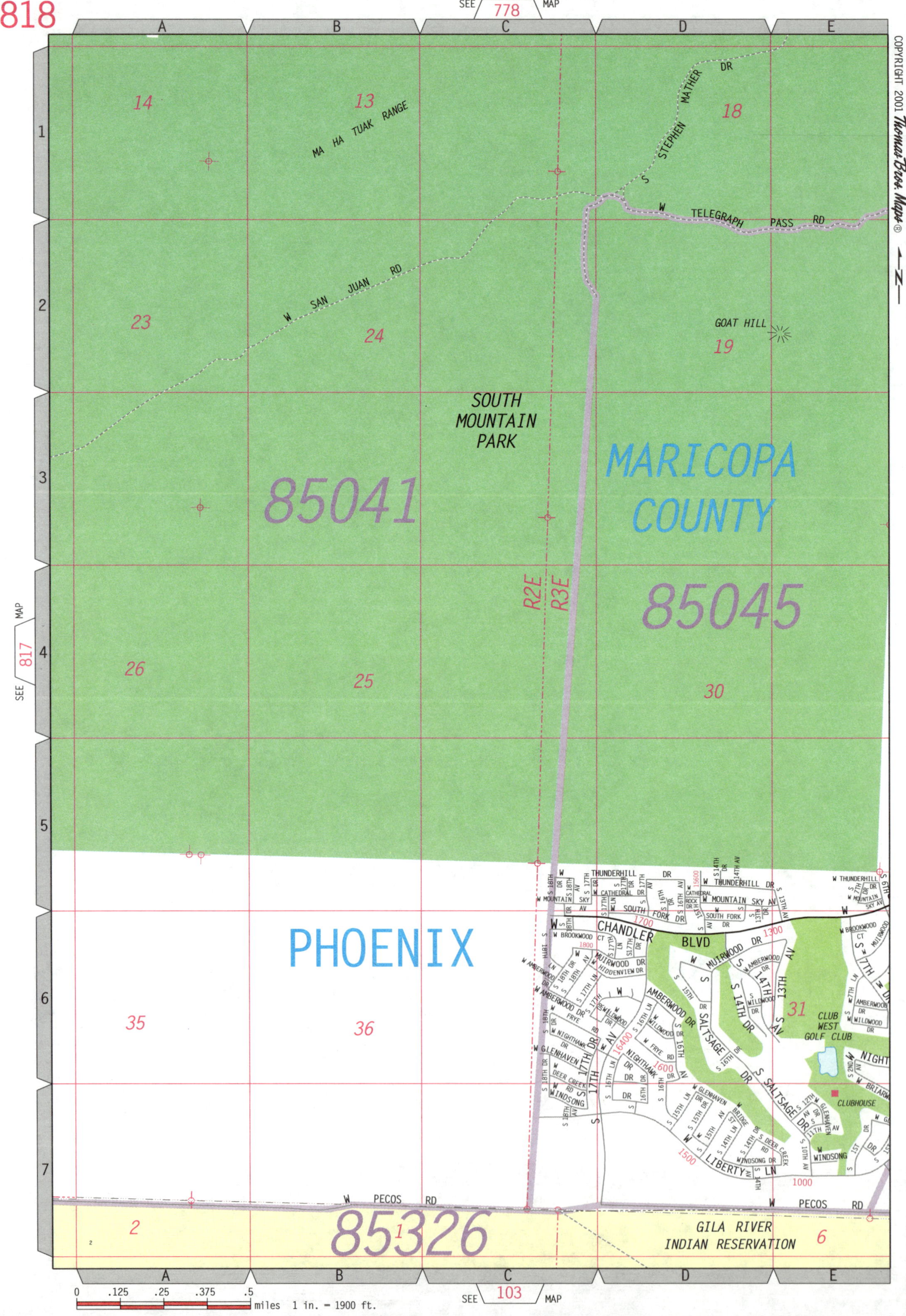

SEE 817 MAP

SEE 103 MAP

0 .125 .25 .375 .5 miles 1 in. = 1900 ft.

PHOENIX

MAP

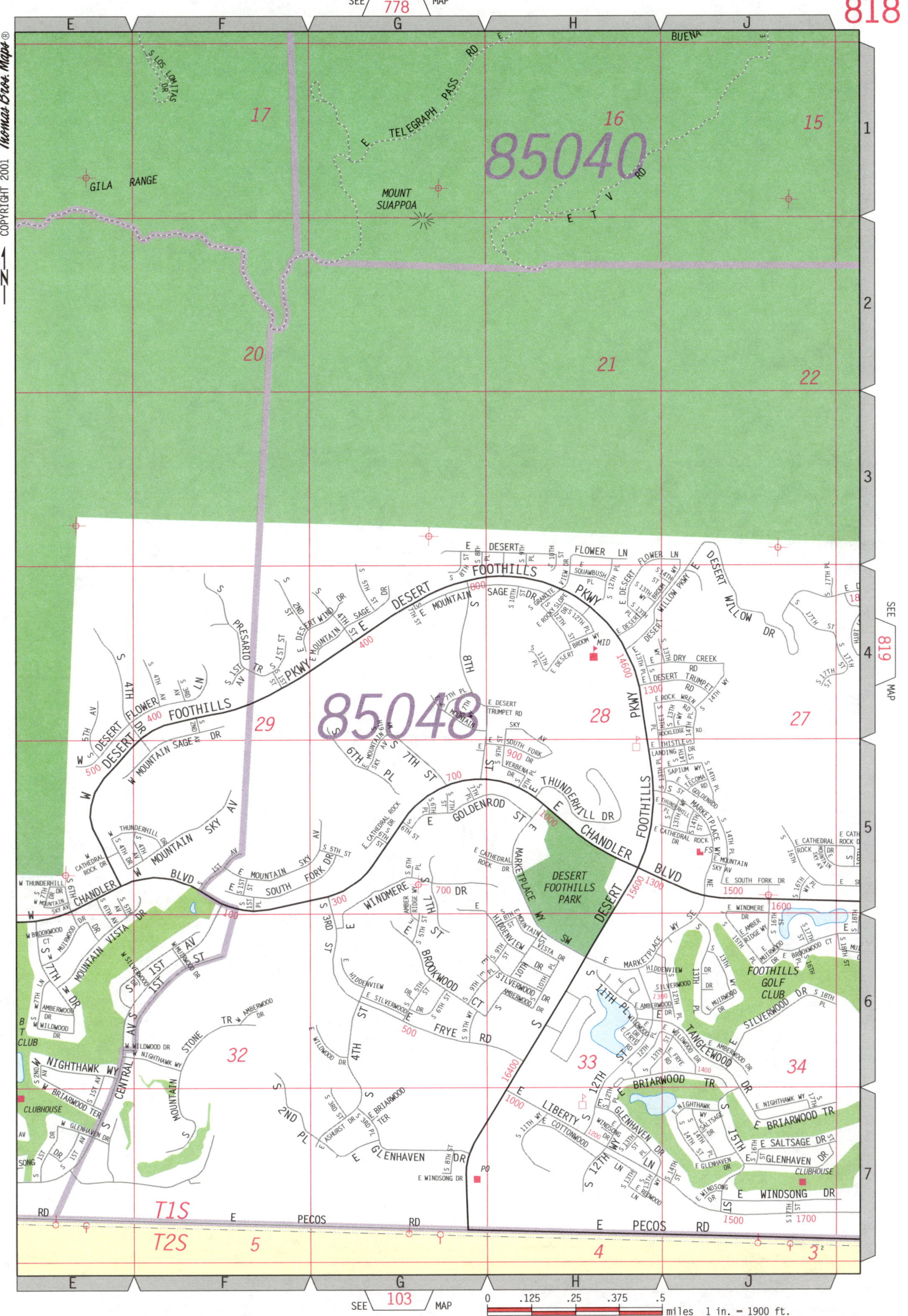
SEE 778 MAP
SEE 819 MAP
SEE 103 MAP
PHOENIX
MAP
Thomas Bros. Maps®
COPYRIGHT 2001
85040
85048
GILA RANGE
MOUNT SUAPPOA
E TELEGRAPH PASS RD
BUENA
E T V RD
S LOS LOMITAS DR
DESERT FOOTHILLS PKWY
E DESERT FLOWER LN
E DESERT WILLOW DR
S DESERT WILLOW PKWY
S PRESARIO TR
E MOUNTAIN SAGE DR
W MOUNTAIN SAGE DR
W DESERT FLOWER LN
W MOUNTAIN SKY AV
E MOUNTAIN SKY AV
E SOUTH FORK DR
W THUNDERHILL DR
E THUNDERHILL DR
E GOLDENROD ST
CHANDLER BLVD
E CATHEDRAL ROCK DR
W CATHEDRAL ROCK DR
DESERT FOOTHILLS PARK
E MARKETPLACE WY
MARKETPLACE WY SW
E WINDMERE DR
S 7TH ST
S 8TH ST
S 3RD ST
S 4TH ST
S 6TH PL
S 2ND PL
S 12TH WY
S CENTRAL AV
S 1ST ST
W MOUNTAIN VISTA DR
E MOUNTAIN VISTA DR
E SILVERWOOD DR
S BROOKWOOD CT
E HIDDENVIEW DR
E FRYE RD
S MOUNTAIN STONE TR
W AMBERWOOD DR
W NIGHTHAWK WY
W BRIARWOOD TER
E BRIARWOOD TR
E BRIARWOOD TER
CLUBHOUSE
W GLENHAVEN DR
E GLENHAVEN DR
E LIBERTY LN
E COTTONWOOD LN
S GLENHAVEN DR
E TANGLEWOOD DR
FOOTHILLS GOLF CLUB
E SILVERWOOD DR
E SALTSAGE DR
E WINDSONG DR
E DRY CREEK RD
E DESERT TRUMPET RD
E ROCK WREN RD
E THISTLE LANDING DR
E SAPIUM WY
S 14TH PL
S 15TH ST
S 17TH PL
S 18TH ST
S 11TH PL
S 13TH PL
E PECOS RD
PO
FS
MID
T1S
T2S
17 16 15 20 21 22 29 28 27 32 33 34 5 4 3
E F G H J
1 2 3 4 5 6 7
0 .125 .25 .375 .5 miles 1 in. = 1900 ft.

SEE 779 MAP

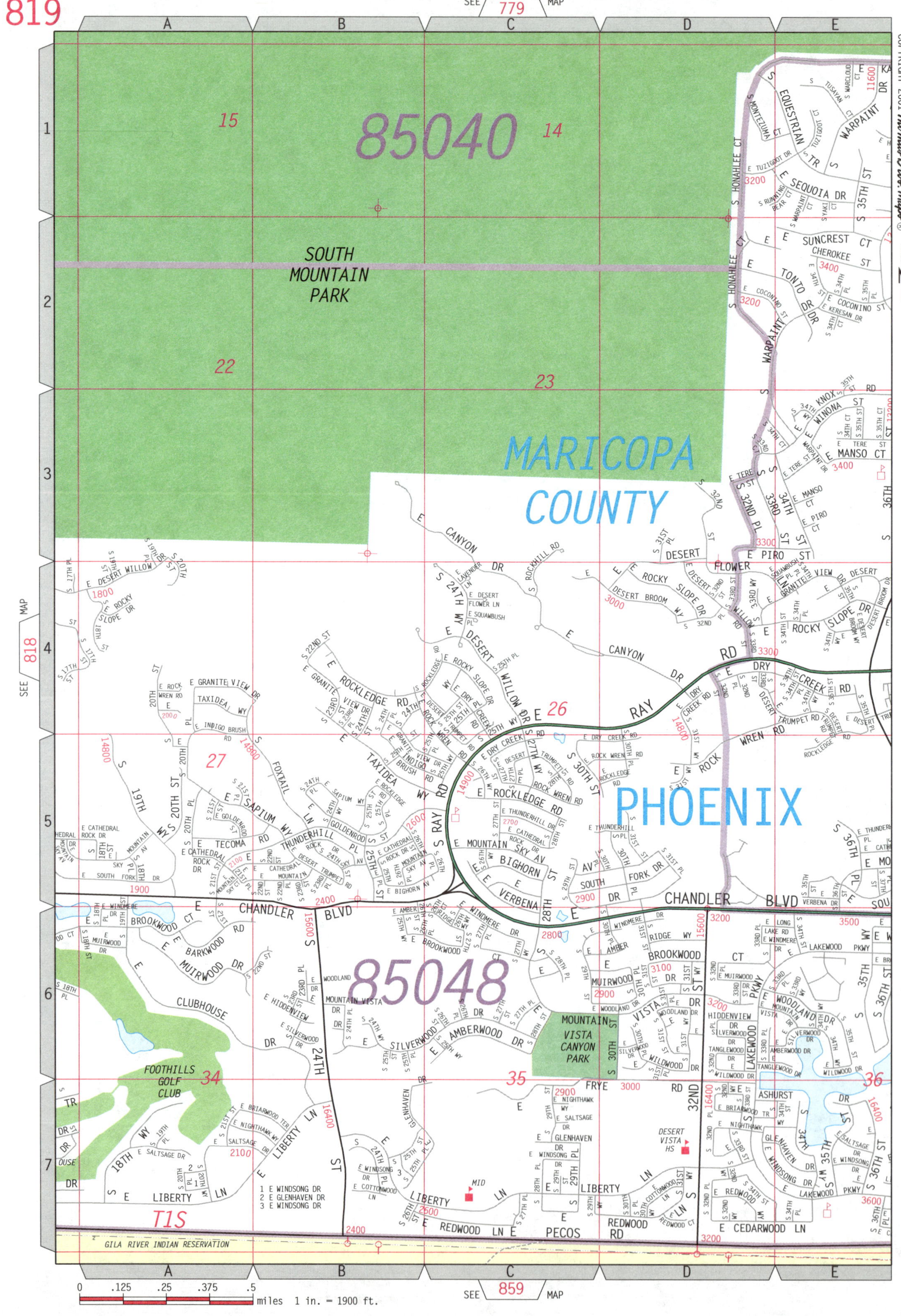

SEE 818 MAP

SEE 859 MAP

0 .125 .25 .375 .5 miles 1 in. = 1900 ft.

PHOENIX

MAP

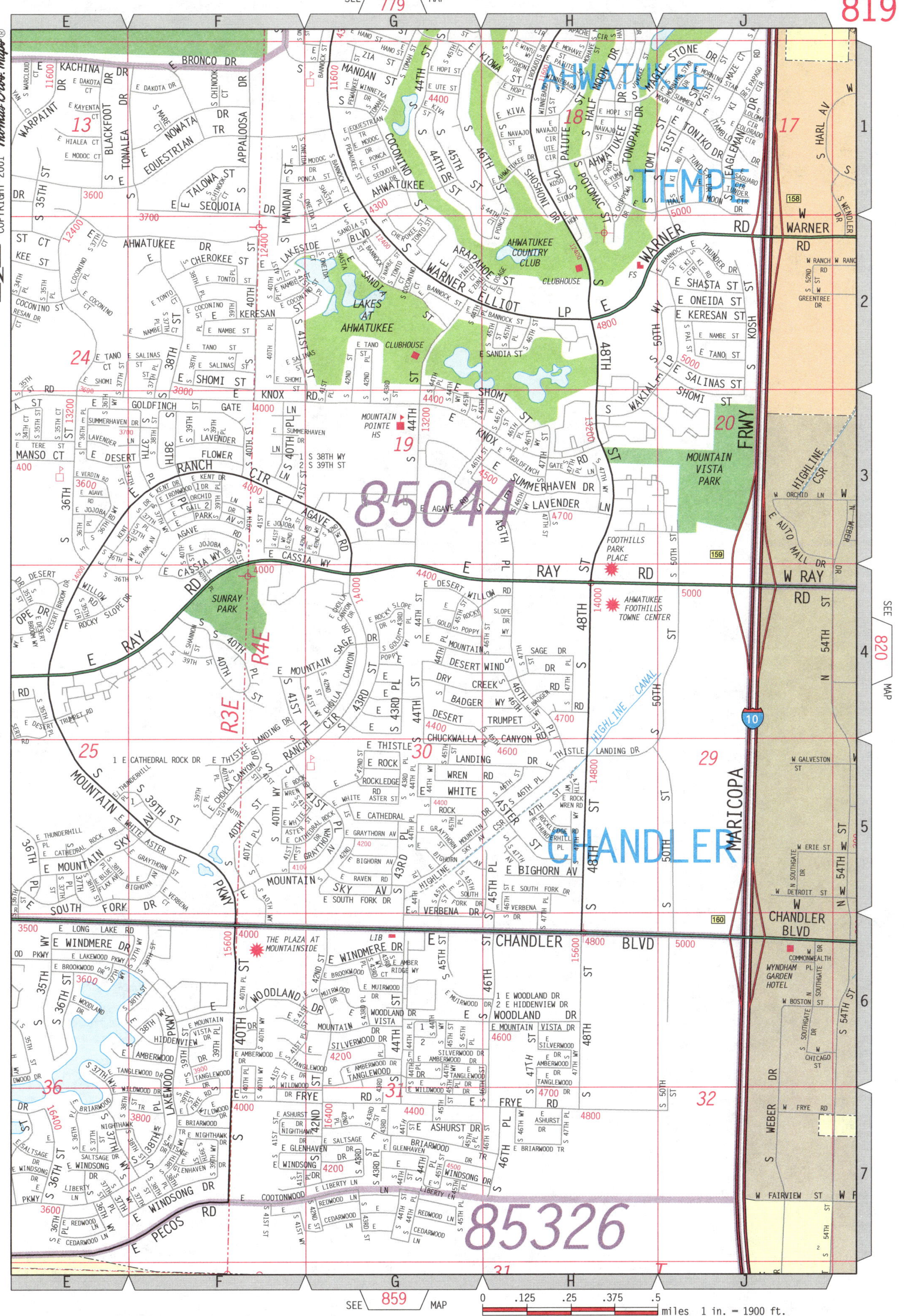
SEE 779 MAP
SEE 859 MAP
SEE 820 MAP
PHOENIX
MAP
Thomas Bros. Maps
AHWATUKEE
TEMPE
CHANDLER
85044
85326
AHWATUKEE COUNTRY CLUB
CLUBHOUSE
LAKES AT AHWATUKEE
MOUNTAIN POINTE HS
MOUNTAIN VISTA PARK
FOOTHILLS PARK PLACE
AHWATUKEE FOOTHILLS TOWNE CENTER
SUNRAY PARK
THE PLAZA AT MOUNTAINSIDE
LIB
WYNDHAM GARDEN HOTEL
FS
HIGHLINE CANAL
MARICOPA FRWY
R3E
R4E
E WARNER RD
E RAY RD
E CHANDLER BLVD
E ELLIOT RD
E KNOX RD
E FRYE RD
E PECOS RD
E COOTONWOOD LN
S 48TH ST
S 40TH ST
MOUNTAIN PKWY
RANCH CIR
W WARNER RD
W RAY RD
W CHANDLER BLVD
W FAIRVIEW ST
S 54TH ST
S WEBER DR
HIGHLINE CSR
E AUTO MALL DR
0 .125 .25 .375 .5 miles 1 in. = 1900 ft.

SEE 780 MAP

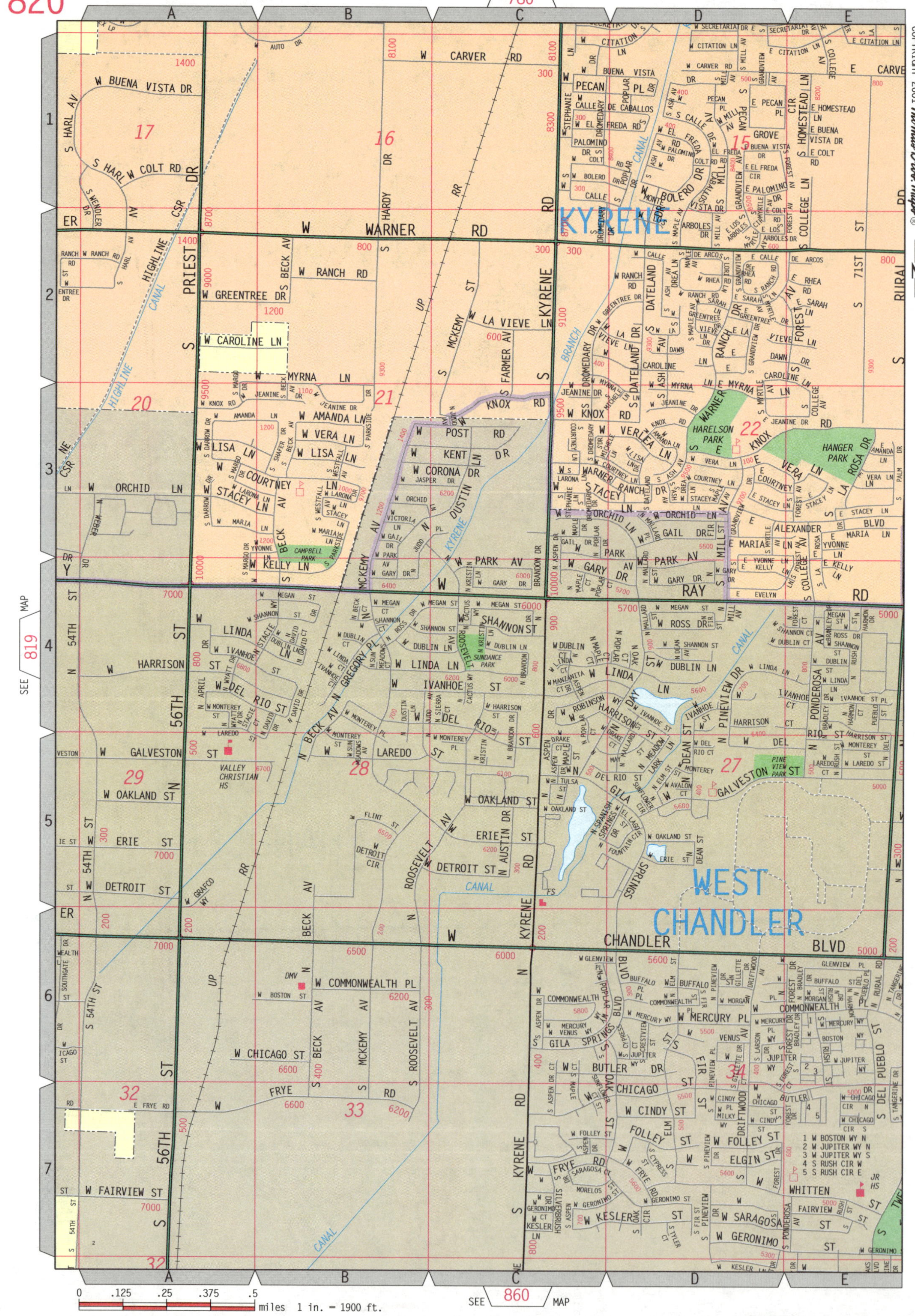

0 .125 .25 .375 .5 miles 1 in. = 1900 ft.

SEE 860 MAP

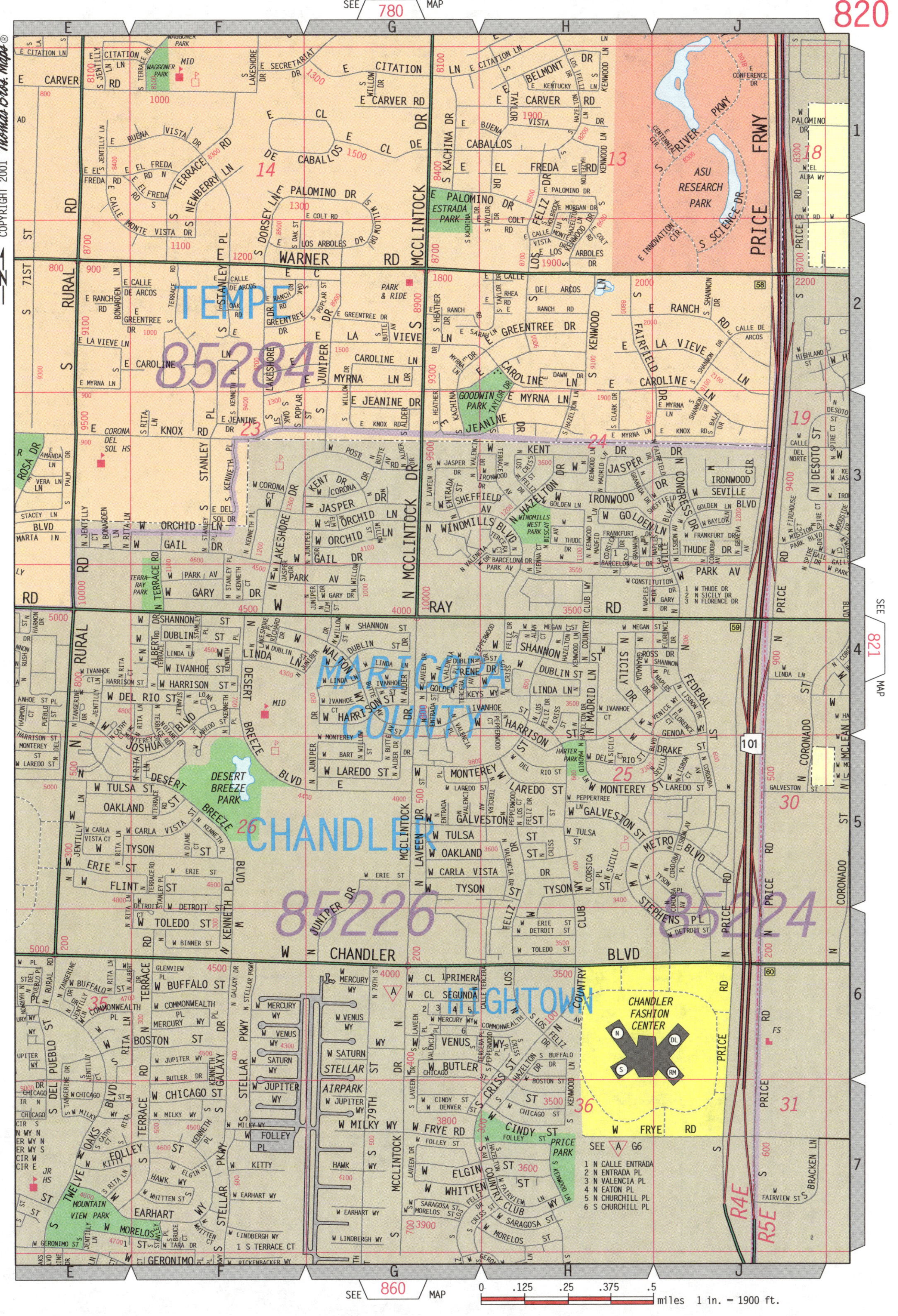

SEE 780 MAP
SEE 821 MAP
SEE 860 MAP
PHOENIX
MAP
TEMPE
85284
MARICOPA COUNTY
CHANDLER
85226
85224
HIGHTOWN
E CITATION LN
E CARVER RD
E CALLE DE ARCOS
E RANCH RD
E GREENTREE DR
E LA VIEVE LN
E CAROLINE LN
E MYRNA LN
E JEANINE DR
E KNOX RD
E SECRETARIAT DR
E EL FREDA RD
E PALOMINO DR
E CABALLOS
E BUENA VISTA DR
E LOS ARBOLES DR
WARNER RD
RAY RD
CHANDLER BLVD
RURAL RD
MCCLINTOCK DR
KENWOOD LN
PRICE FRWY
PRICE RD
RIVER PKWY
E INNOVATION CIR
S SCIENCE DR
ASU RESEARCH PARK
WAGGONER PARK
ESTRADA PARK
GOODWIN PARK
WINDMILLS WEST PARK
DESERT BREEZE PARK
HARTER PARK
FOLLEY PARK
PRICE PARK
MOUNTAIN VIEW PARK
PARK & RIDE
CORONA DEL SOL HS
JR HS
MID
CHANDLER FASHION CENTER
STELLAR AIRPARK
W ORCHID LN
W GAIL DR
W PARK AV
W GARY DR
W JASPER DR
W KENT DR
W SHEFFIELD AV
W WINDMILLS BLVD
W IRONWOOD DR
W GOLDEN LN
W THUDE DR
W SHANNON ST
W DUBLIN ST
W LINDA LN
W IVANHOE ST
W HARRISON ST
W DEL RIO ST
W JOSHUA BLVD
W LAREDO ST
W MONTEREY ST
W GALVESTON ST
W TULSA ST
W OAKLAND ST
W CARLA VISTA DR
W TYSON ST
W ERIE ST
W FLINT ST
W DETROIT ST
W TOLEDO ST
W BINNER ST
DESERT BREEZE BLVD
METRO BLVD
STEPHENS PL
N SICILY DR
FEDERAL ST
CORONADO ST
W BUFFALO ST
W COMMONWEALTH PL
W BOSTON ST
W JUPITER WY
W CHICAGO ST
W MILKY WY
W FOLLEY ST
W KITTY
W HAWK WY
W EARHART WY
W MORELOS ST
W GERONIMO ST
W MERCURY WY
W VENUS WY
W SATURN WY
W BUTLER DR
W FRYE RD
W ELGIN ST
W WHITTEN ST
W CINDY ST
W SARAGOSA ST
COUNTRY CLUB WY
STELLAR PKWY
GALAXY DR
N 79TH ST
S CRISS ST
R4E
R5E
101
13
14
18
19
23
24
25
26
30
31
35
36
1 N THUDE DR
2 N SICILY DR
3 N FLORENCE DR
SEE A G6
1 N CALLE ENTRADA
2 N ENTRADA PL
3 N VALENCIA PL
4 N EATON PL
5 N CHURCHILL PL
6 S CHURCHILL PL
0 .125 .25 .375 .5 miles 1 in. = 1900 ft.

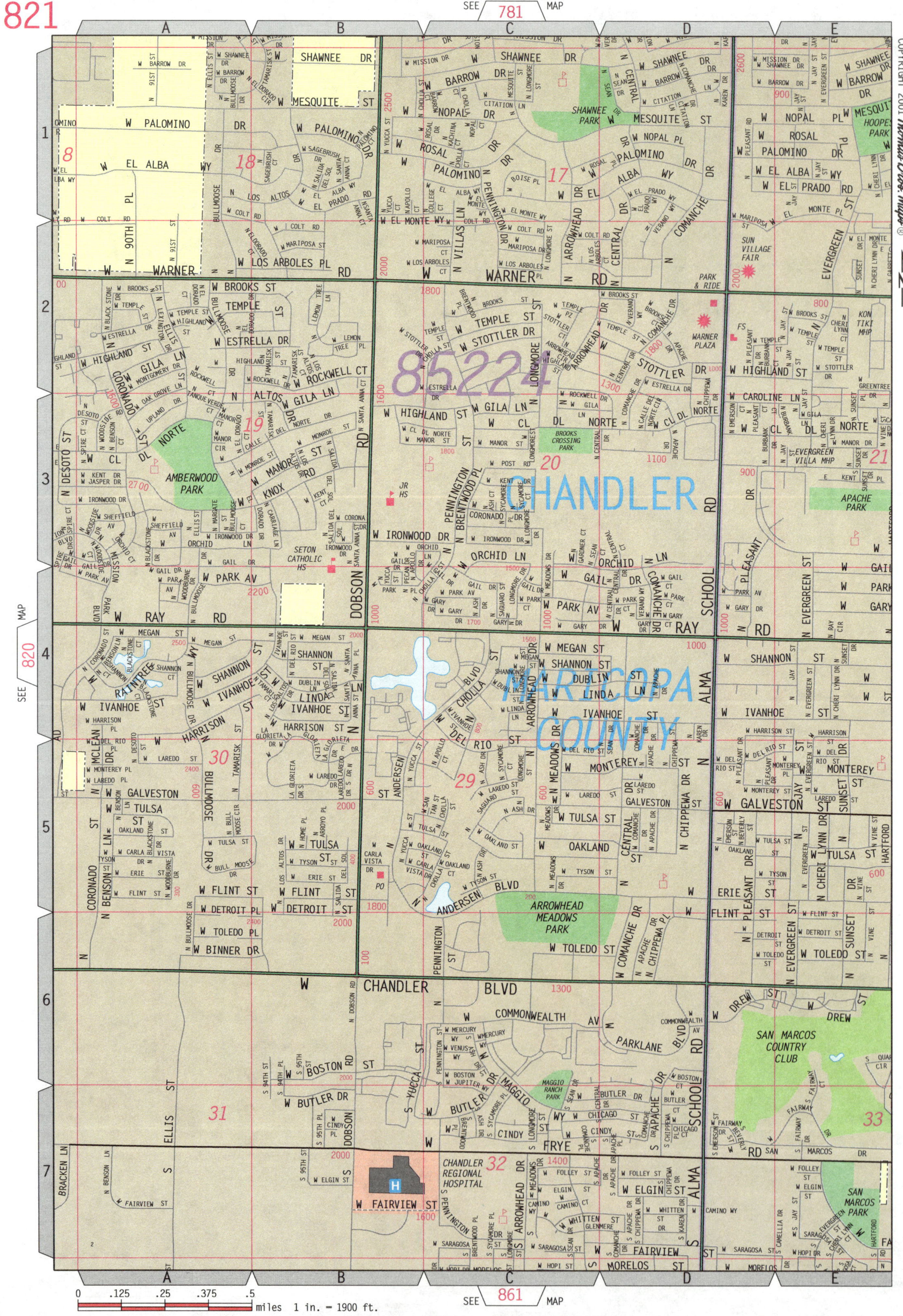

SEE 781 MAP
SEE 820 MAP
SEE 861 MAP
COPYRIGHT 2001 Thomas Bros. Maps ®
CHANDLER
MARICOPA COUNTY
85224
W WARNER RD
W RAY RD
W CHANDLER BLVD
N DOBSON RD
N ALMA SCHOOL RD
W SHAWNEE DR
W MESQUITE ST
W PALOMINO DR
W EL ALBA WY
W LOS ARBOLES PL
W BROOKS ST
W TEMPLE ST
W ESTRELLA DR
W HIGHLAND ST
W GILA LN
W NORTE DR
W IRONWOOD DR
W ORCHID LN
W GAIL DR
W PARK AV
W MEGAN ST
W SHANNON ST
W IVANHOE ST
W HARRISON ST
W GALVESTON ST
W TULSA ST
W FLINT ST
W DETROIT PL
W TOLEDO PL
W BINNER DR
W COMMONWEALTH AV
W BOSTON ST
W BUTLER DR
W FRYE RD
W FAIRVIEW ST
W MORELOS ST
SHAWNEE PARK
BROOKS CROSSING PARK
AMBERWOOD PARK
APACHE PARK
ARROWHEAD MEADOWS PARK
MAGGIO RANCH PARK
SAN MARCOS COUNTRY CLUB
SAN MARCOS PARK
HOOPES PARK
SUN VILLAGE FAIR
WARNER PLAZA
PARK & RIDE
SETON CATHOLIC HS
JR HS
CHANDLER REGIONAL HOSPITAL
EVERGREEN VILLA MHP
KON TIKI MHP
0 .125 .25 .375 .5 miles 1 in. = 1900 ft.

PHOENIX

MAP

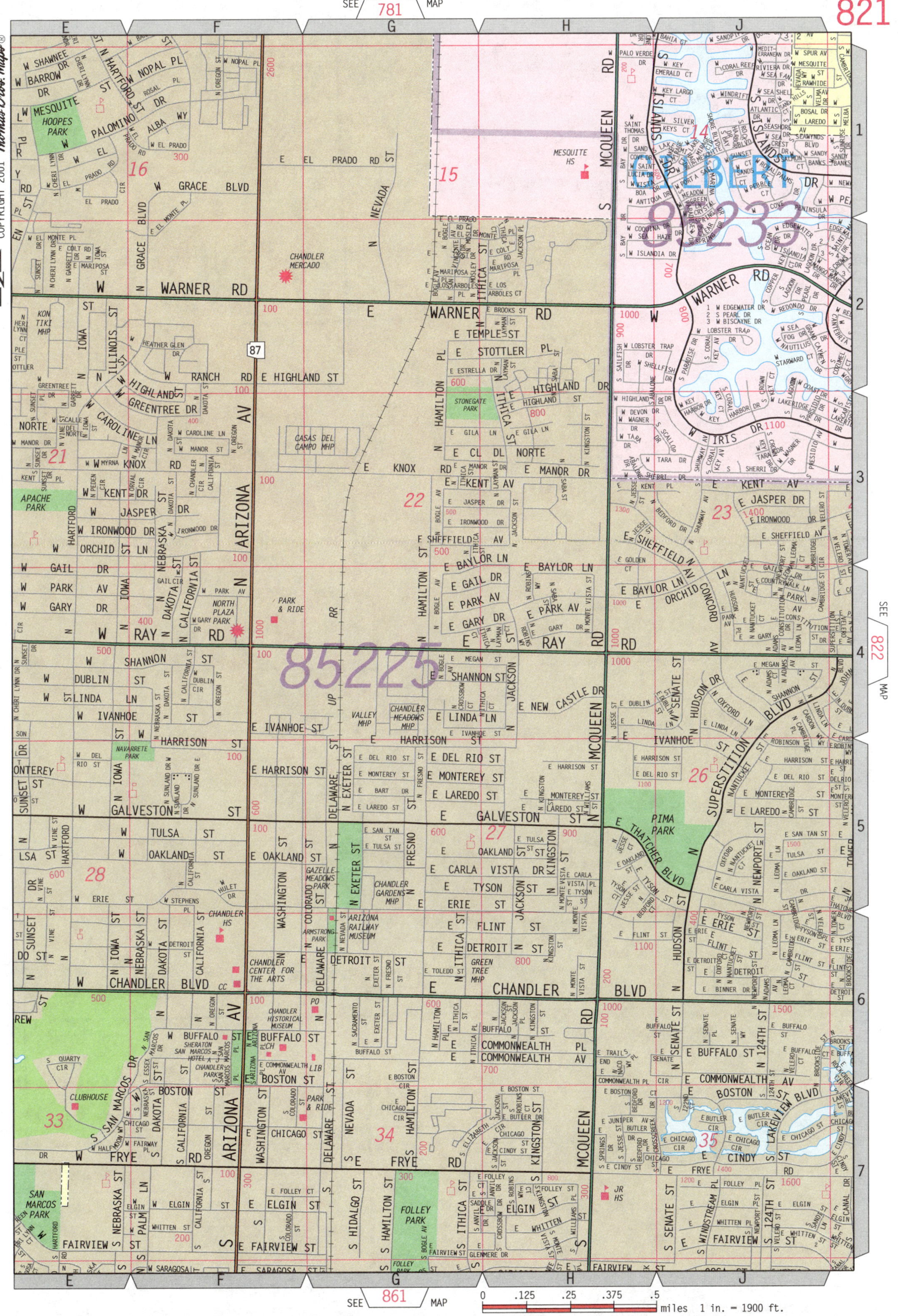
SEE 781 MAP
PHOENIX
GILBERT
85233
85225
WARNER RD
RAY RD
CHANDLER BLVD
ARIZONA AV
MCQUEEN RD
GALVESTON ST
FRYE RD
FAIRVIEW ST
FOLLEY PARK
PIMA PARK
MESQUITE HOOPES PARK
APACHE PARK
SAN MARCOS PARK
CHANDLER MERCADO
CHANDLER HS
MESQUITE HS
ARIZONA RAILWAY MUSEUM
CHANDLER HISTORICAL MUSEUM
CHANDLER CENTER FOR THE ARTS
STONEGATE PARK
SUPERSTITION BLVD
THATCHER BLVD
LAKEVIEW BLVD
SEE 822 MAP
MAP
SEE 861 MAP
0 .125 .25 .375 .5 miles 1 in. = 1900 ft.

SEE 782 MAP

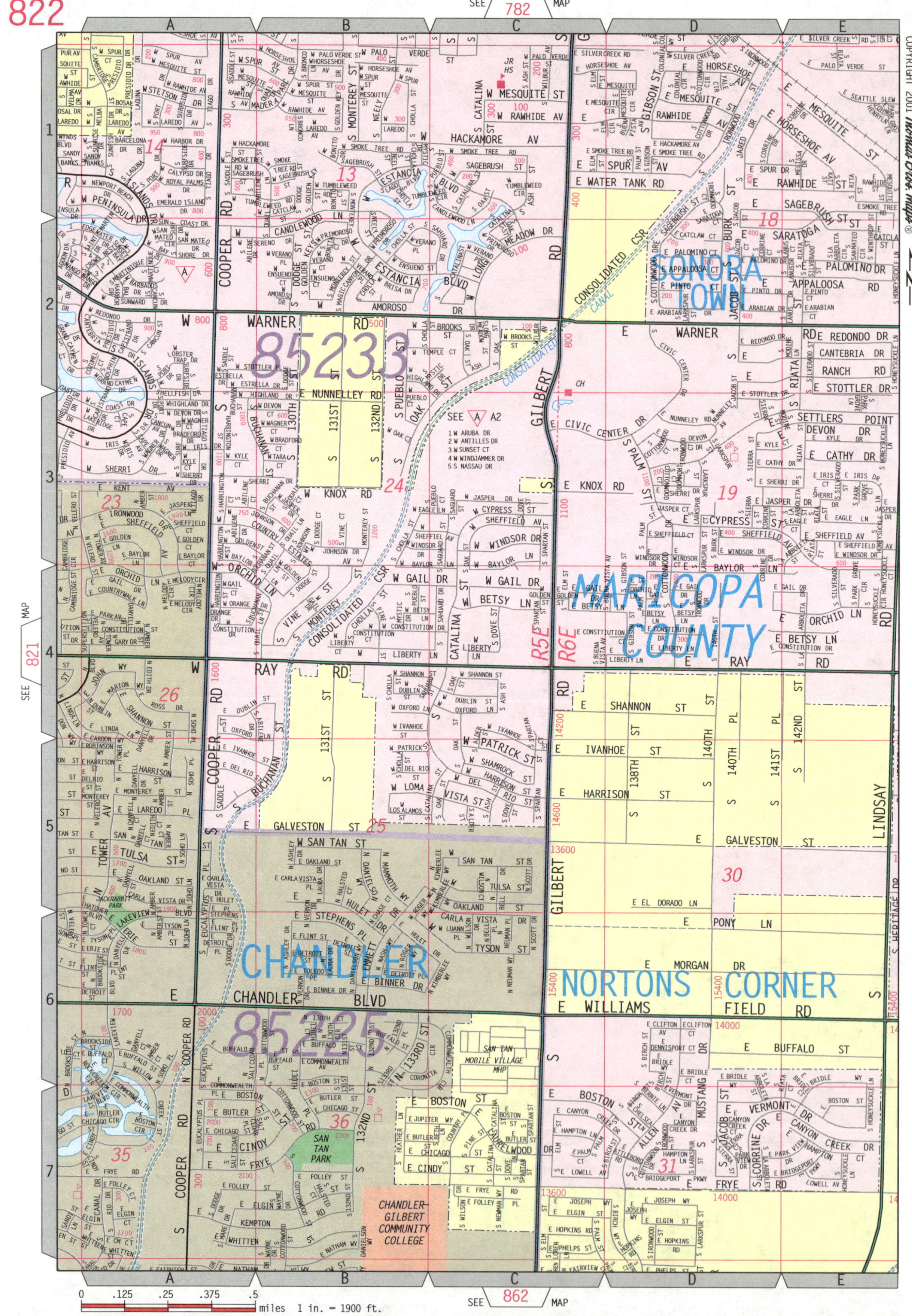

SEE 862 MAP

SEE 782 MAP

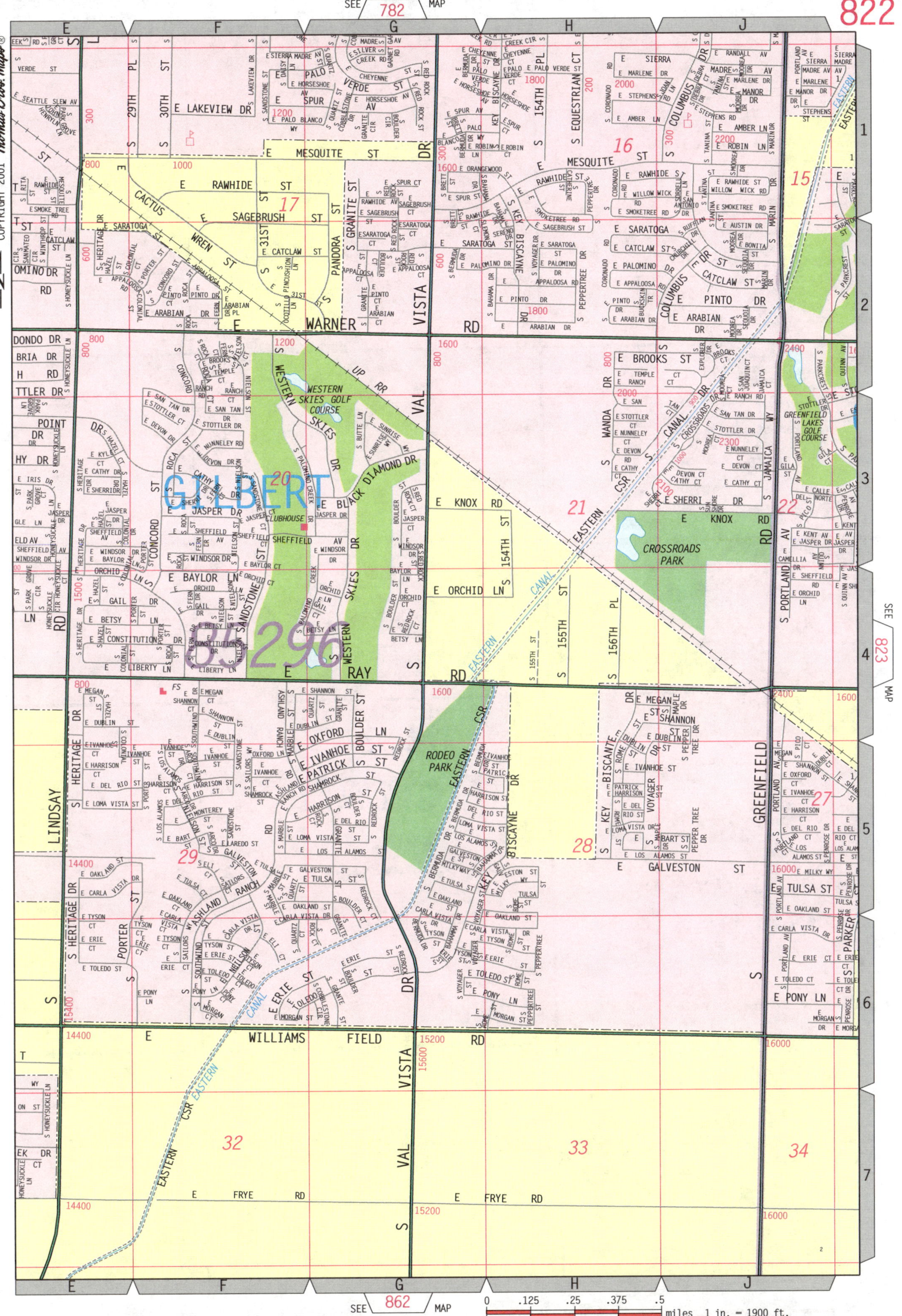

SEE 823 MAP

SEE 862 MAP

0 .125 .25 .375 .5 miles 1 in. = 1900 ft.

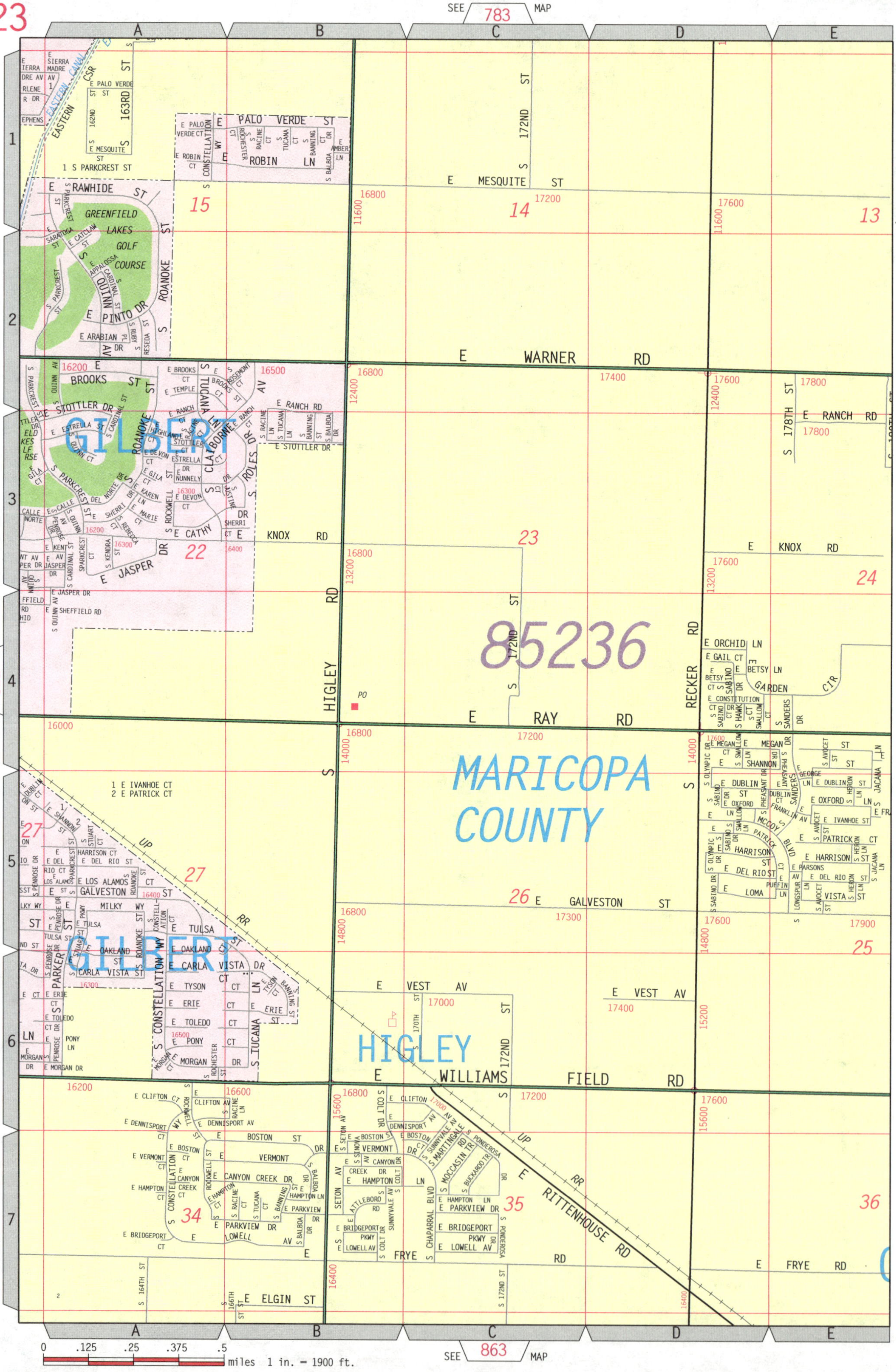

SEE 783 MAP

SEE 822 MAP

SEE 863 MAP

PHOENIX

MAP

A B C D E

1 2 3 4 5 6 7

GILBERT

HIGLEY

MARICOPA COUNTY

85236

EASTERN CANAL

GREENFIELD LAKES GOLF COURSE

E MESQUITE ST

E WARNER RD

E RANCH RD

KNOX RD

E KNOX RD

E RAY RD

E ORCHID LN

E GAIL CT

E BETSY LN

GARDEN CIR

S HIGLEY RD

S RECKER RD

S 172ND ST

S 178TH ST

E MEGAN ST

E SHANNON ST

E DUBLIN ST

E OXFORD LN

E IVANHOE ST

E PATRICK CT

E HARRISON ST

E DEL RIO ST

E LOMA

E VISTA ST

E GALVESTON ST

E VEST AV

E WILLIAMS FIELD RD

RITTENHOUSE RD

UP RR

E FRYE RD

E ELGIN ST

E RAWHIDE ST

E PINTO DR

E ARABIAN DR

E PALO VERDE ST

E ROBIN LN

E BROOKS ST

E STOTTLER DR

E JASPER DR

S ROANOKE ST

S CLAIBORNE AV

S TUCANA LN

S CONSTELLATION WY

E MILKY WY

E TULSA ST

E OAKLAND ST

E CARLA VISTA DR

E TYSON CT

E ERIE CT

E TOLEDO CT

E PONY LN

E MORGAN DR

E CLIFTON CT

E DENNISPORT AV

E BOSTON ST

E VERMONT DR

E CANYON CREEK DR

E HAMPTON LN

E PARKVIEW DR

E BRIDGEPORT PKWY

E LOWELL AV

S SETON AV

S COLT DR

S CHAPARRAL BLVD

S PONDEROSA DR

PO

13 14 15 22 23 24 25 26 27 34 35 36

16000 16200 16400 16500 16600 16800 17000 17200 17300 17400 17600 17800 17900

11600 12400 13200 14000 14800 15200 15600 16400

0 .125 .25 .375 .5 miles 1 in. = 1900 ft.

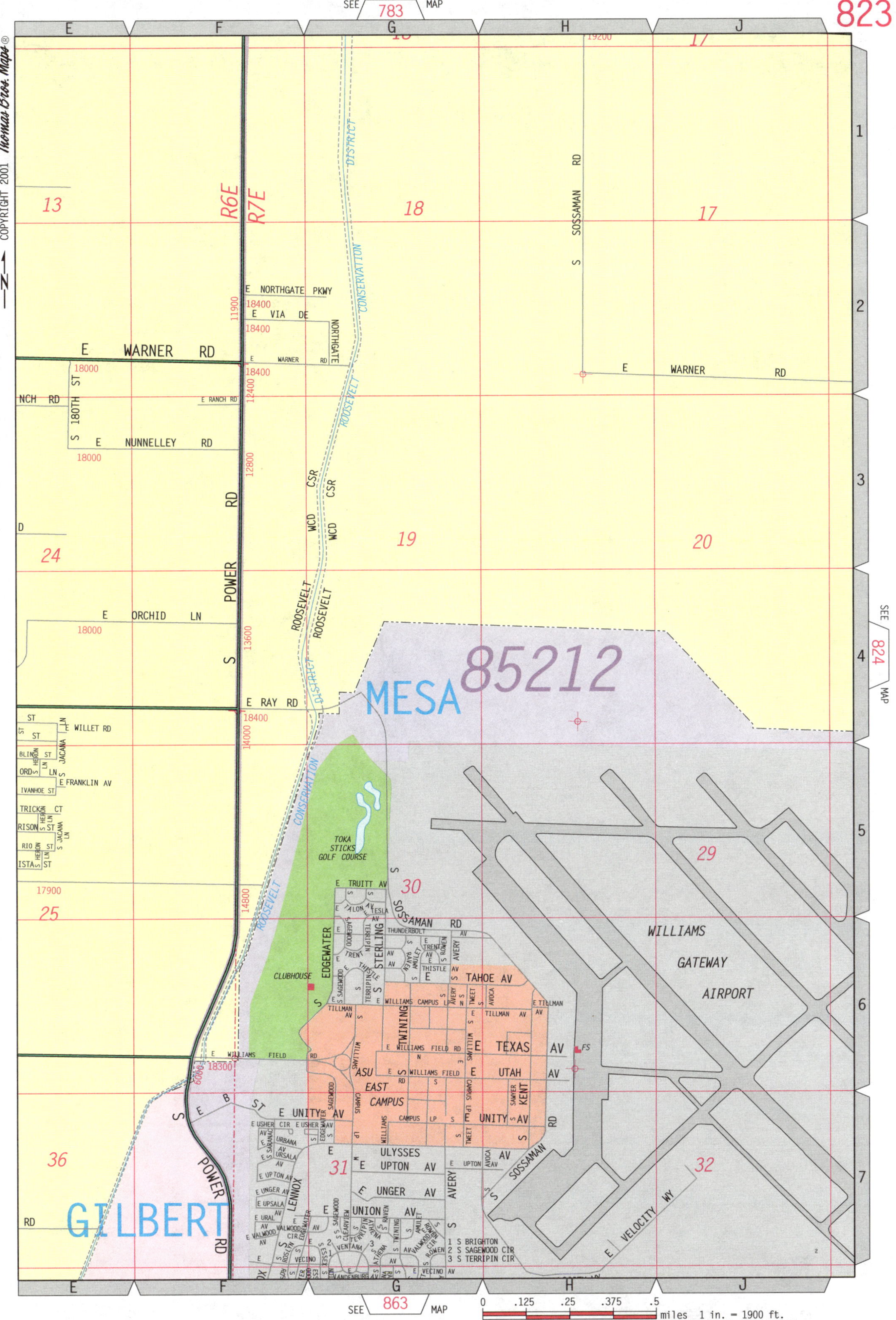
SEE 783 MAP
SEE 824 MAP
SEE 863 MAP
PHOENIX
MAP
MESA
85212
GILBERT
WILLIAMS GATEWAY AIRPORT
ASU EAST CAMPUS
TOKA STICKS GOLF COURSE
CLUBHOUSE
E WARNER RD
S POWER RD
E RAY RD
S SOSSAMAN RD
E ORCHID LN
E NUNNELLEY RD
E NORTHGATE PKWY
ROOSEVELT CONSERVATION DISTRICT
R6E
R7E
E WILLIAMS FIELD RD
E UNITY AV
E ULYSSES
E UPTON AV
E UNGER AV
E UNION AV
E TAHOE AV
E TEXAS AV
E UTAH AV
E VELOCITY WY
1 S BRIGHTON
2 S SAGEWOOD CIR
3 S TERRIPIN CIR
0 .125 .25 .375 .5 miles 1 in. = 1900 ft.

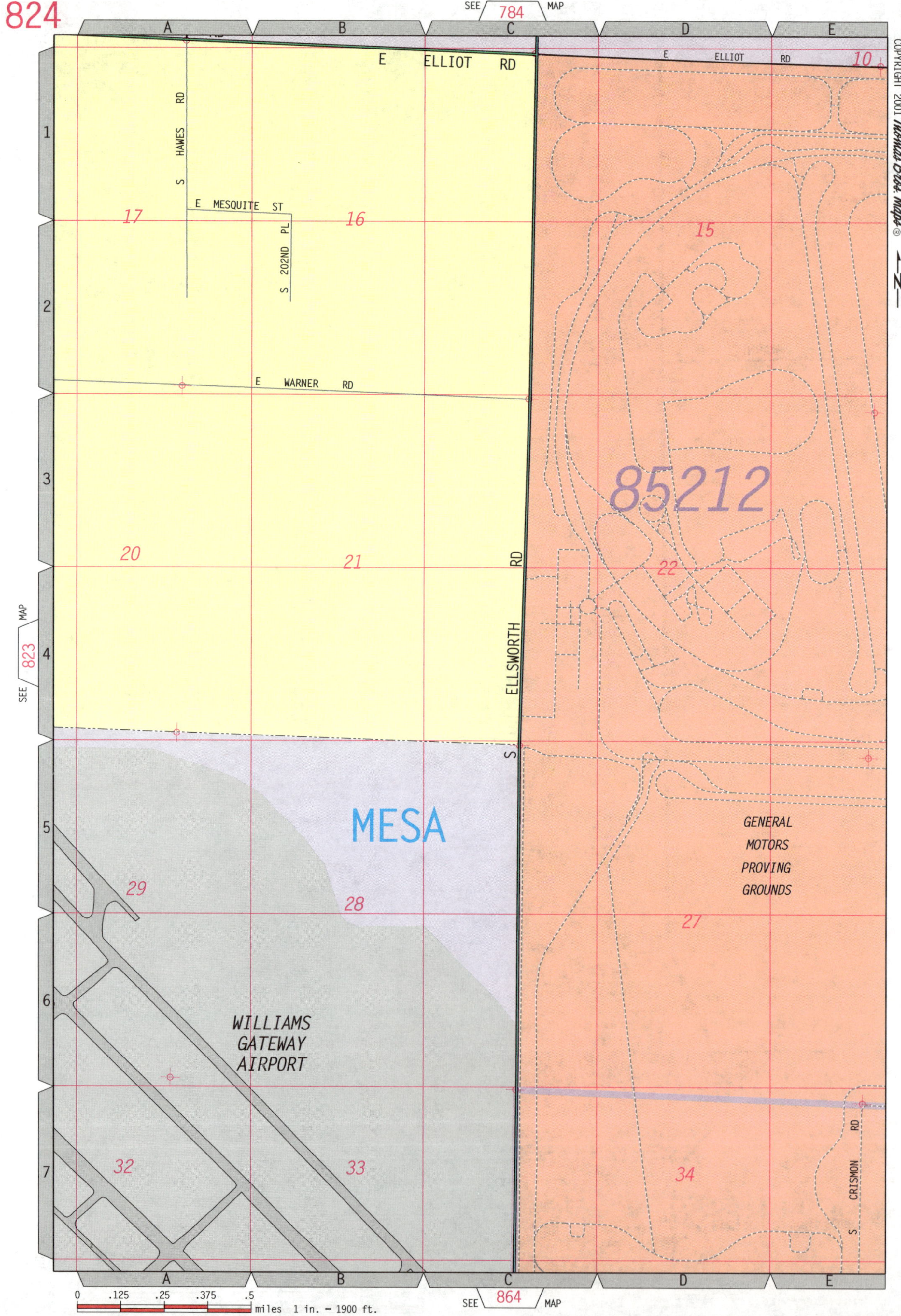

SEE 784 MAP
A
B
C
D
E
E ELLIOT RD
E ELLIOT RD
10
S HAWES RD
E MESQUITE ST
S 202ND PL
17
16
15
E WARNER RD
85212
20
21
22
S ELLSWORTH RD
SEE 823 MAP
MESA
GENERAL
MOTORS
PROVING
GROUNDS
29
28
27
WILLIAMS
GATEWAY
AIRPORT
32
33
34
S CRISMON RD
1
2
3
4
5
6
7
0 .125 .25 .375 .5 miles 1 in. = 1900 ft.
SEE 864 MAP
PHOENIX
MAP

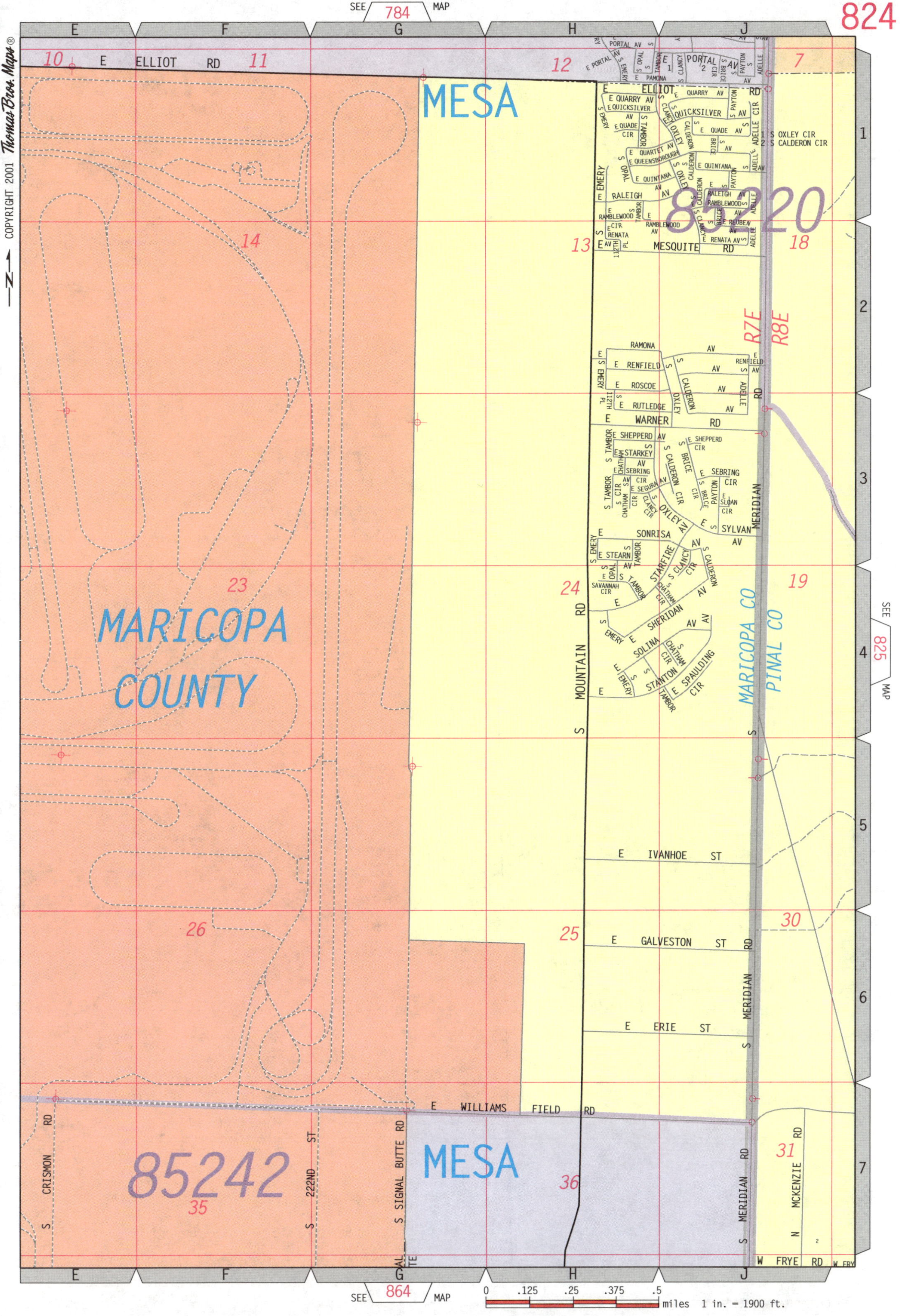

SEE 784 MAP
E
F
G
H
J
E ELLIOT RD
MESA
MARICOPA
COUNTY
85220
85242
PHOENIX
MAP
R7E
R8E
MARICOPA CO
PINAL CO
S MOUNTAIN RD
S MERIDIAN RD
E MESQUITE RD
E RAMONA AV
E WARNER RD
E IVANHOE ST
E GALVESTON ST
E ERIE ST
E WILLIAMS FIELD RD
S SIGNAL BUTTE RD
S CRISMON RD
S 222ND ST
N MCKENZIE RD
W FRYE RD
1 S OXLEY CIR
2 S CALDERON CIR
SEE 825 MAP
SEE 864 MAP
0 .125 .25 .375 .5 miles 1 in. = 1900 ft.

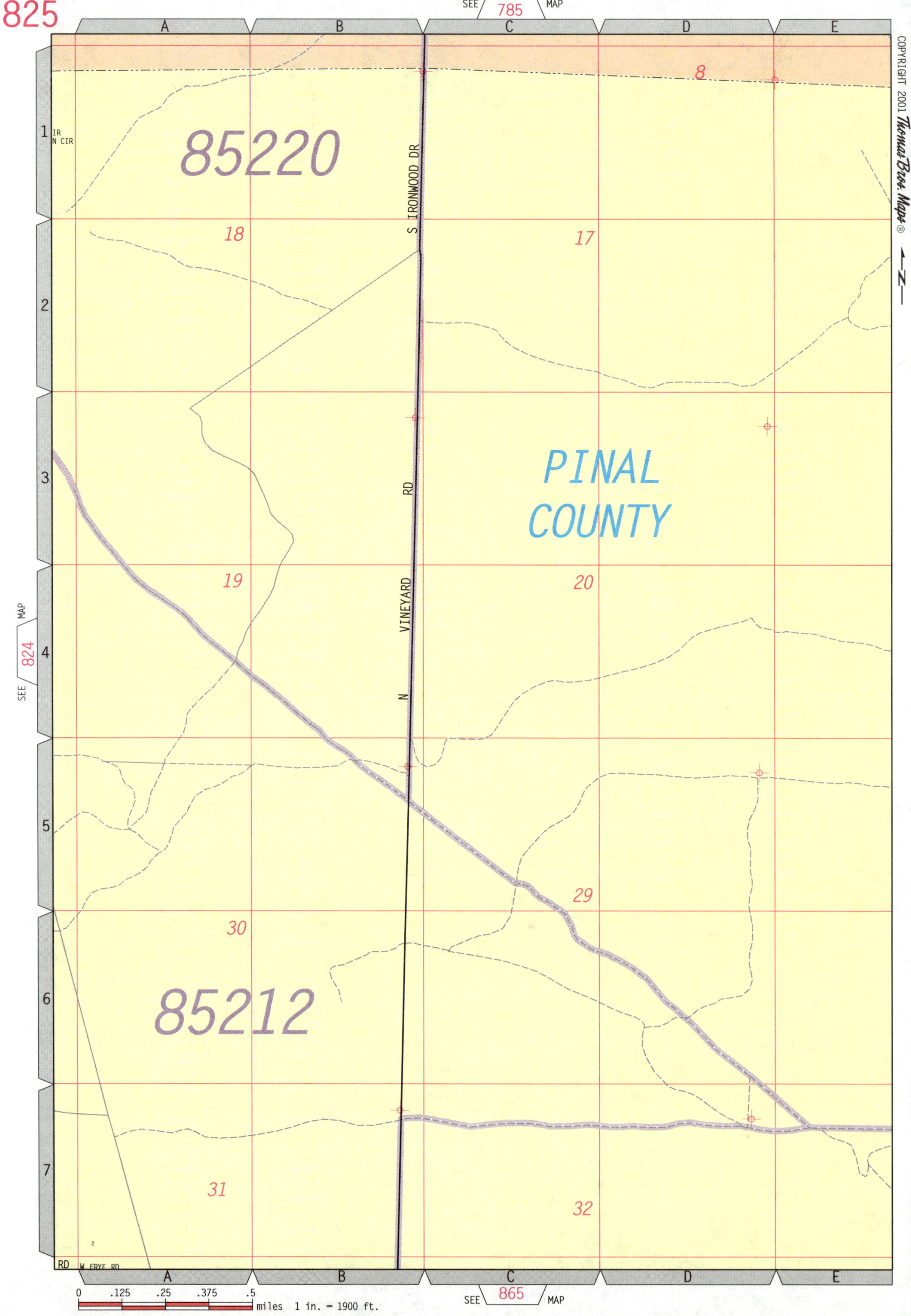
SEE 785 MAP
A
B
C
D
E
1
2
3
4
5
6
7
IR
N CIR
85220
S IRONWOOD DR
8
18
17
PINAL
COUNTY
RD
19
20
N VINEYARD
SEE 824 MAP
29
30
85212
31
32
RD
W FRYE RD
0 .125 .25 .375 .5
miles 1 in. = 1900 ft.
SEE 865 MAP

PHOENIX

MAP

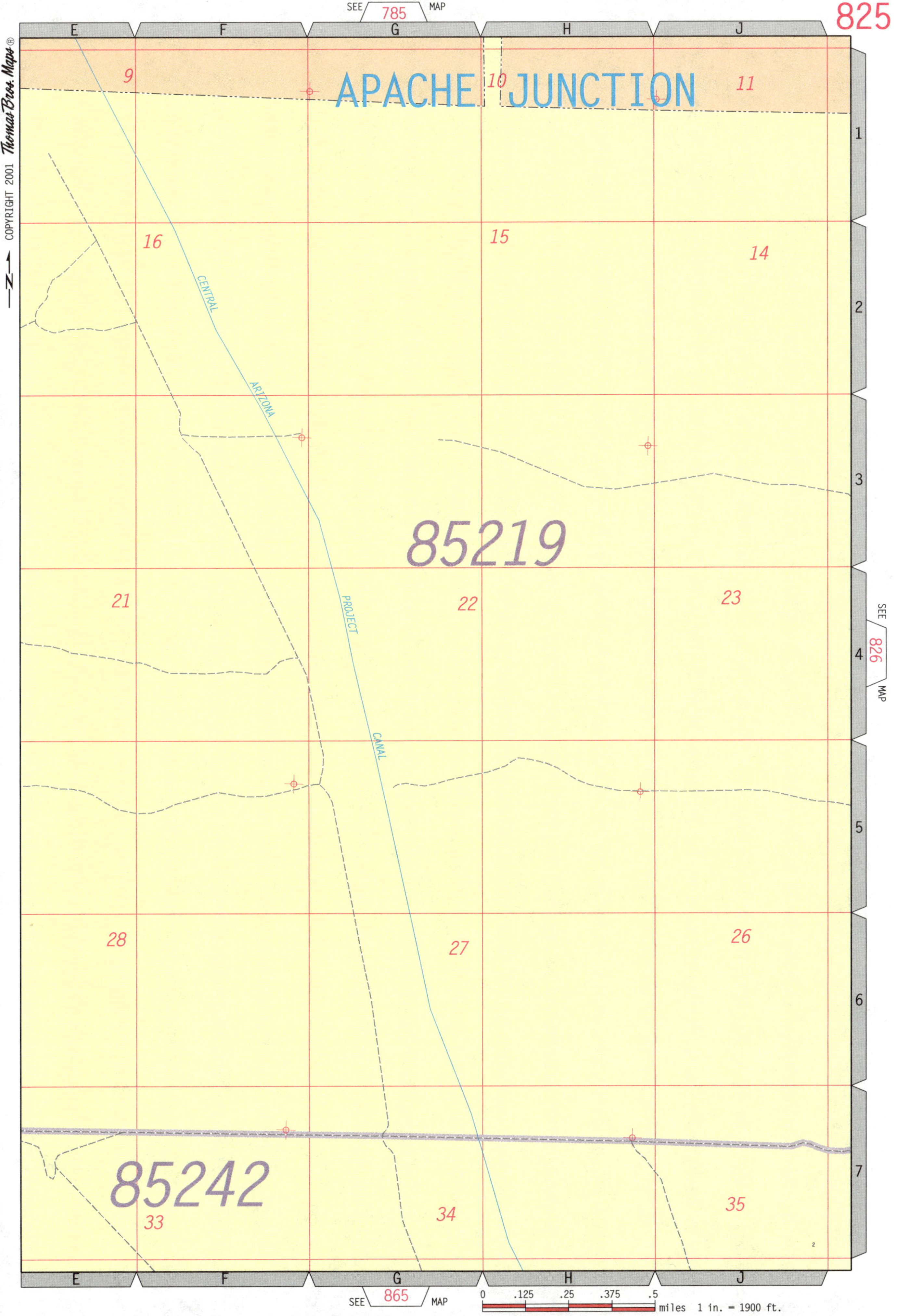
SEE 785 MAP
E
F
G
H
J
APACHE JUNCTION
9
10
11
16
15
14
CENTRAL
ARIZONA
PROJECT
CANAL
85219
21
22
23
28
27
26
85242
33
34
35
1
2
3
4
5
6
7
SEE 826 MAP
SEE 865 MAP
0
.125
.25
.375
.5
miles 1 in. = 1900 ft.
PHOENIX
MAP

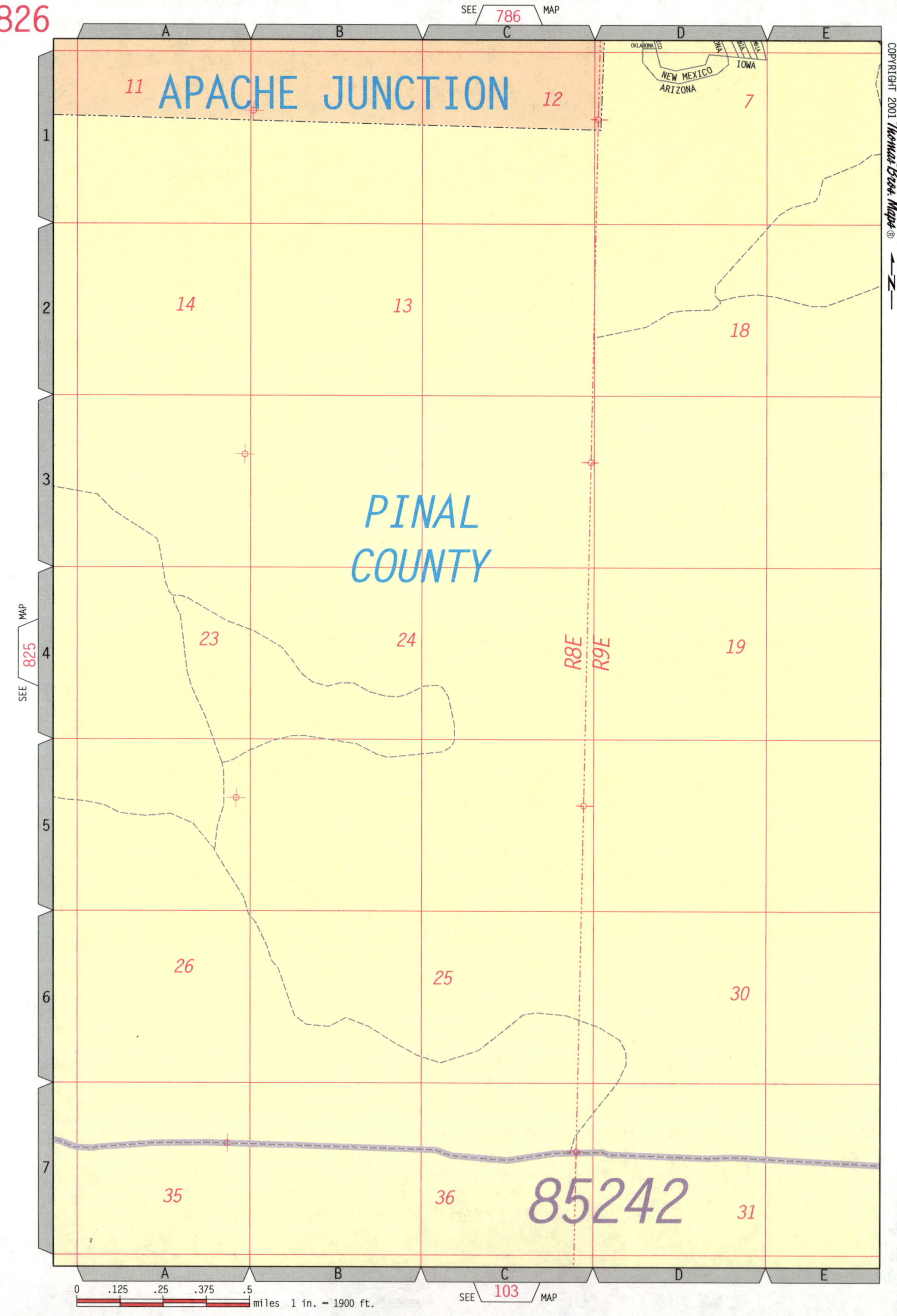
SEE 786 MAP
A
B
C
D
E
1
2
3
4
5
6
7
APACHE JUNCTION
11
12
7
OKLAHOMA
NEW MEXICO
ARIZONA
IOWA
14
13
18
PINAL
COUNTY
23
24
R8E
R9E
19
26
25
30
35
36
85242
31
SEE 825 MAP
SEE 103 MAP
0 .125 .25 .375 .5 miles 1 in. = 1900 ft.

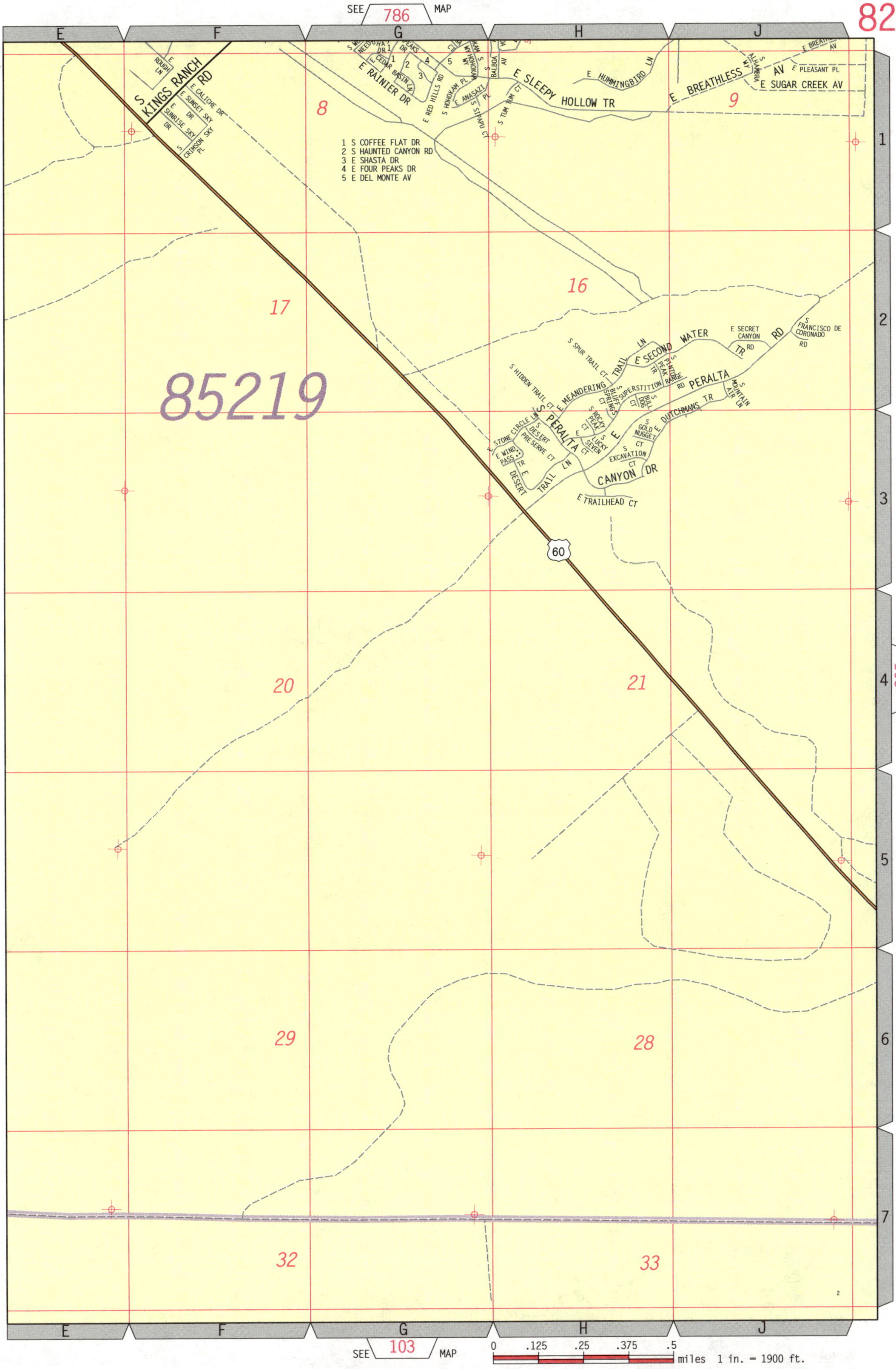

SEE 786 MAP

1 S COFFEE FLAT DR
2 S HAUNTED CANYON RD
3 E SHASTA DR
4 E FOUR PEAKS DR
5 E DEL MONTE AV

S KINGS RANCH RD
E SLEEPY HOLLOW TR
E HUMMINGBIRD LN
E BREATHLESS AV
E SUGAR CREEK AV
E PLEASANT PL
E RAINIER DR
S PERALTA TRAIL LN
E SECOND WATER TR
E SECRET CANYON RD
S FRANCISCO DE CORONADO RD
E DUTCHMANS TR
E PERALTA CANYON DR
E TRAILHEAD CT
E MEANDERING TRAIL LN
E SUPERSTITION RD
E DESERT TRAIL LN
E STONE CIRCLE LN
S DESERT PRESERVE CT
E WIND PASS TR
S MOUNTAIN AIR LN
S HIDDEN TRAIL CT
S SPUR TRAIL CT
S GOLD NUGGET CT
S EXCAVATION CT
S LUCKY SEVEN CT
S ROCKY PEAK CT
S BUFF SPRINGS CT
S BULL DOG CT
S PINTO PEAK TR
E RANGE RD
E CALICHE DR
E SUNSET SKY DR
S SUNRISE SKY DR
S CRIMSON SKY PL
E ROUGH LN

85219

60

8 9 16 17 20 21 28 29 32 33

SEE 103 MAP

PHOENIX

MAP

SEE 103 MAP

0 .125 .25 .375 .5 miles 1 in. = 1900 ft.

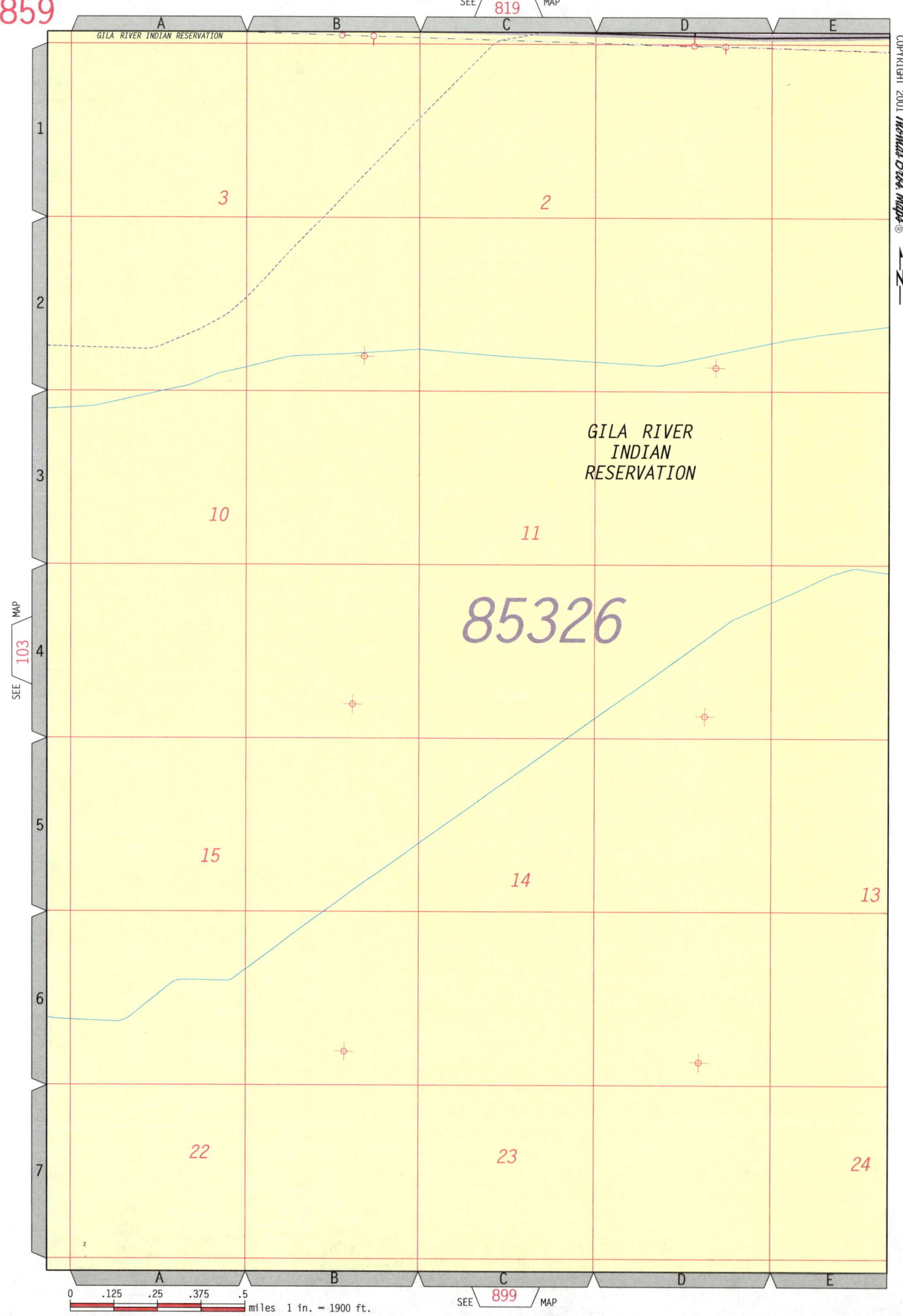
SEE 819 MAP
GILA RIVER INDIAN RESERVATION
3
2
GILA RIVER
INDIAN
RESERVATION
10
11
85326
15
14
13
22
23
24
SEE 103 MAP
SEE 899 MAP
0 .125 .25 .375 .5
miles 1 in. = 1900 ft.
COPYRIGHT 2001 Thomas Bros. Maps ®
N

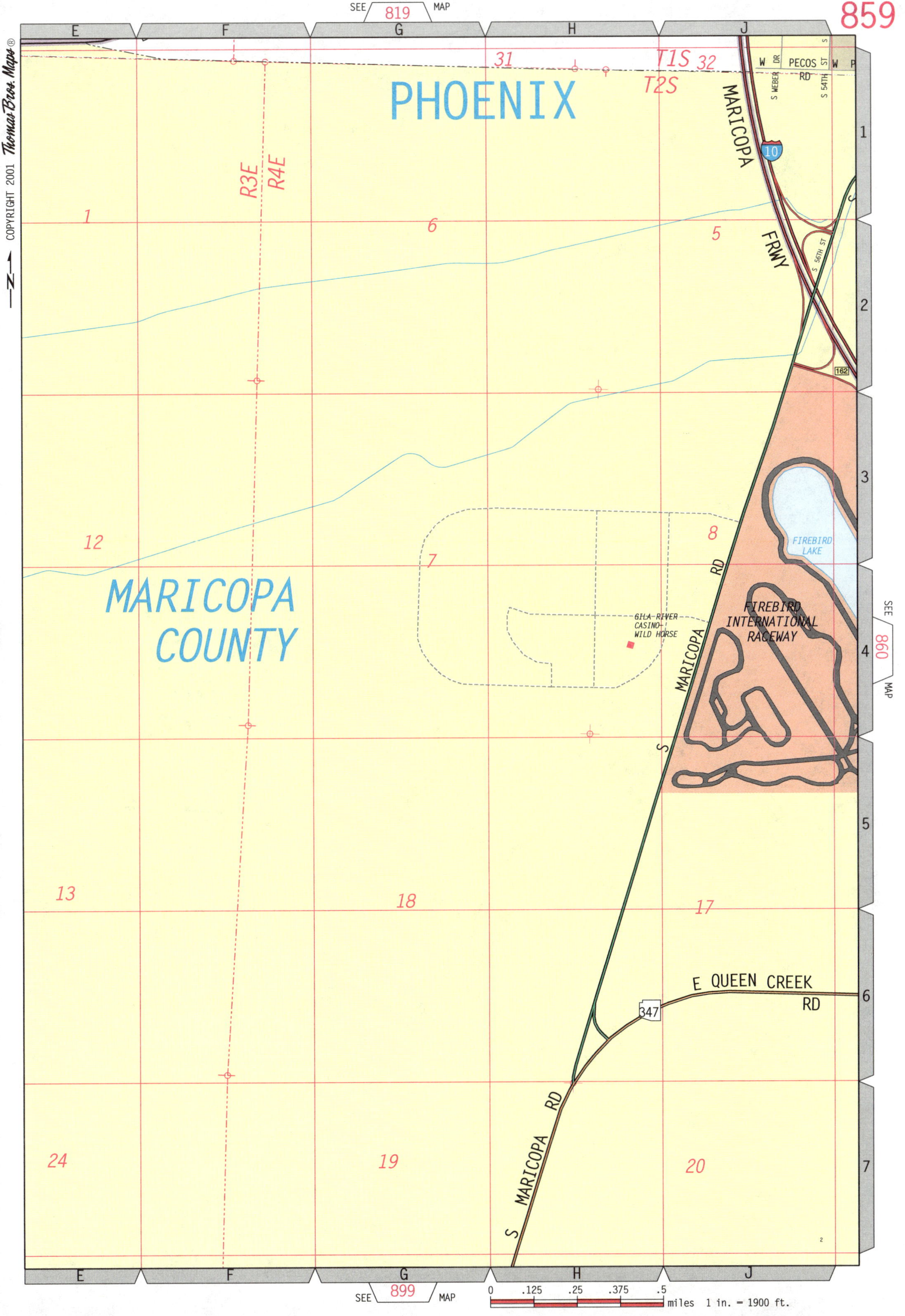
SEE 819 MAP
PHOENIX
MARICOPA FRWY
PECOS RD
S WEBER DR
S 54TH ST
S 56TH ST
10
162
R3E
R4E
T1S
T2S
FIREBIRD LAKE
FIREBIRD INTERNATIONAL RACEWAY
GILA RIVER CASINO-WILD HORSE
S MARICOPA RD
MARICOPA COUNTY
E QUEEN CREEK RD
347
SEE 860 MAP
SEE 899 MAP
0 .125 .25 .375 .5 miles 1 in. = 1900 ft.
PHOENIX
MAP

SEE 820 MAP

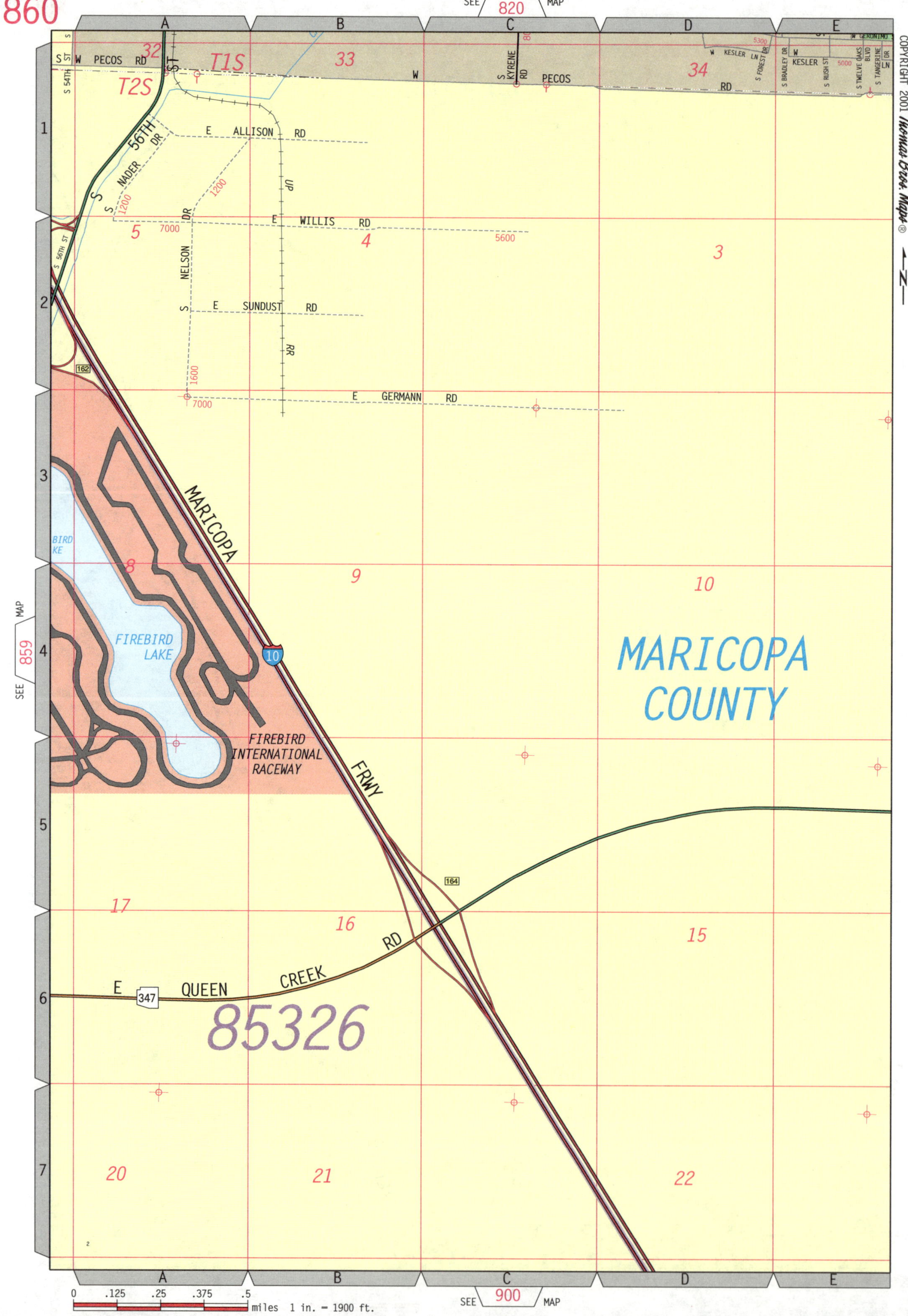

SEE 859 MAP

SEE 900 MAP

0 .125 .25 .375 .5 miles 1 in. = 1900 ft.

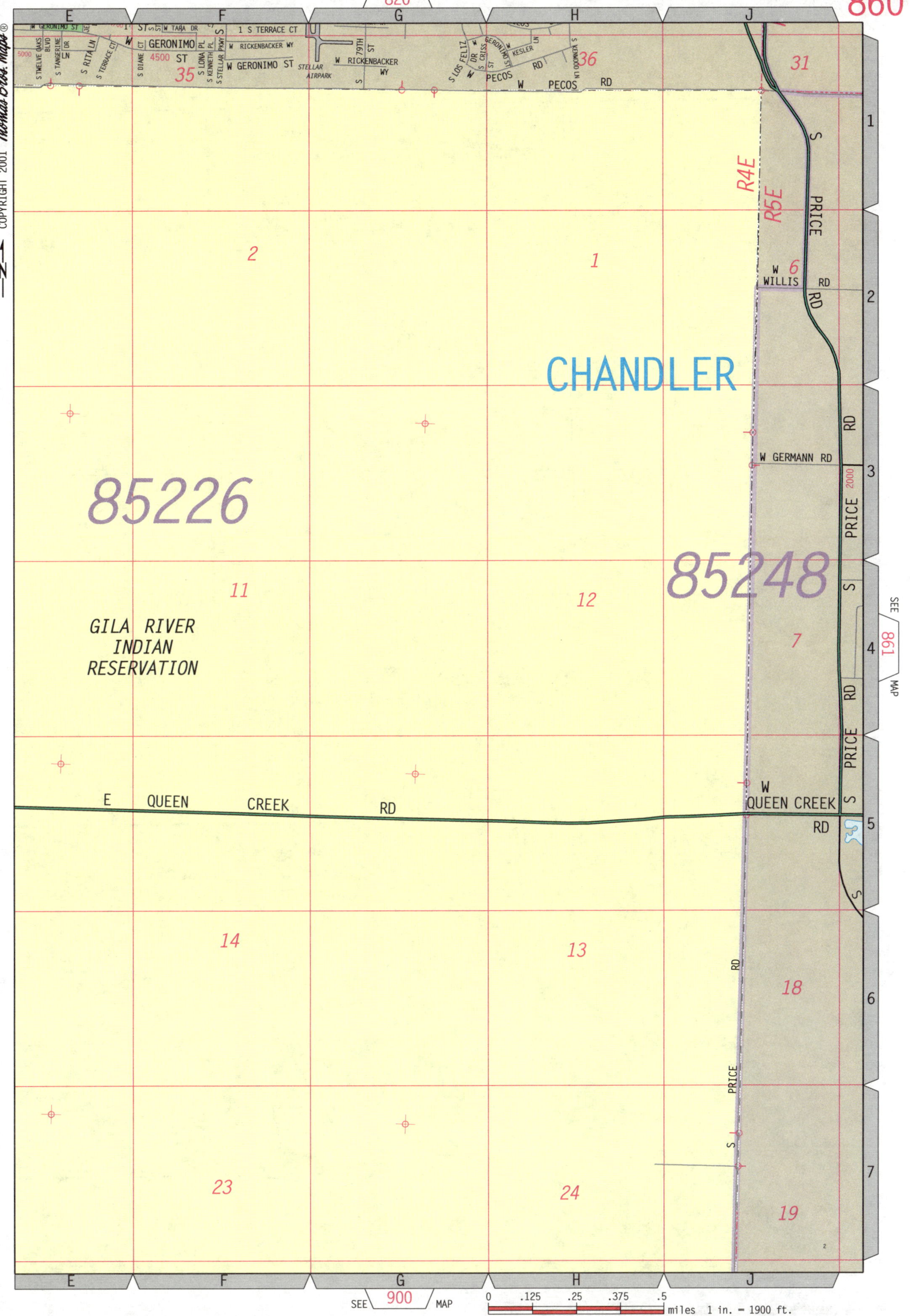
SEE 820 MAP
E
F
G
H
J
W GERONIMO ST
S TWELVE OAKS BLVD
S TANGERINE LN
S RITA LN
S TERRACE CT
W GERONIMO ST
S DIANE CT
4500
5000
35
S LONA PL
S KENNETH PL
S STELLAR PKWY
W TARA DR
1 S TERRACE CT
W RICKENBACKER WY
W GERONIMO ST
STELLAR AIRPARK
79TH ST
W RICKENBACKER WY
S LOS FELIZ DR
W CRISS ST
GERONIMO ST
W KESLER LN
W PECOS RD
W PECOS RD
36
31
R4E
R5E
S PRICE RD
W WILLIS RD
6
2
1
CHANDLER
W GERMANN RD
2000
S PRICE RD
85226
85248
11
12
7
GILA RIVER INDIAN RESERVATION
E QUEEN CREEK RD
W QUEEN CREEK RD
S PRICE RD
14
13
18
S PRICE RD
23
24
19
SEE 861 MAP
SEE 900 MAP
0 .125 .25 .375 .5 miles 1 in. = 1900 ft.
PHOENIX
MAP

SEE 821 MAP

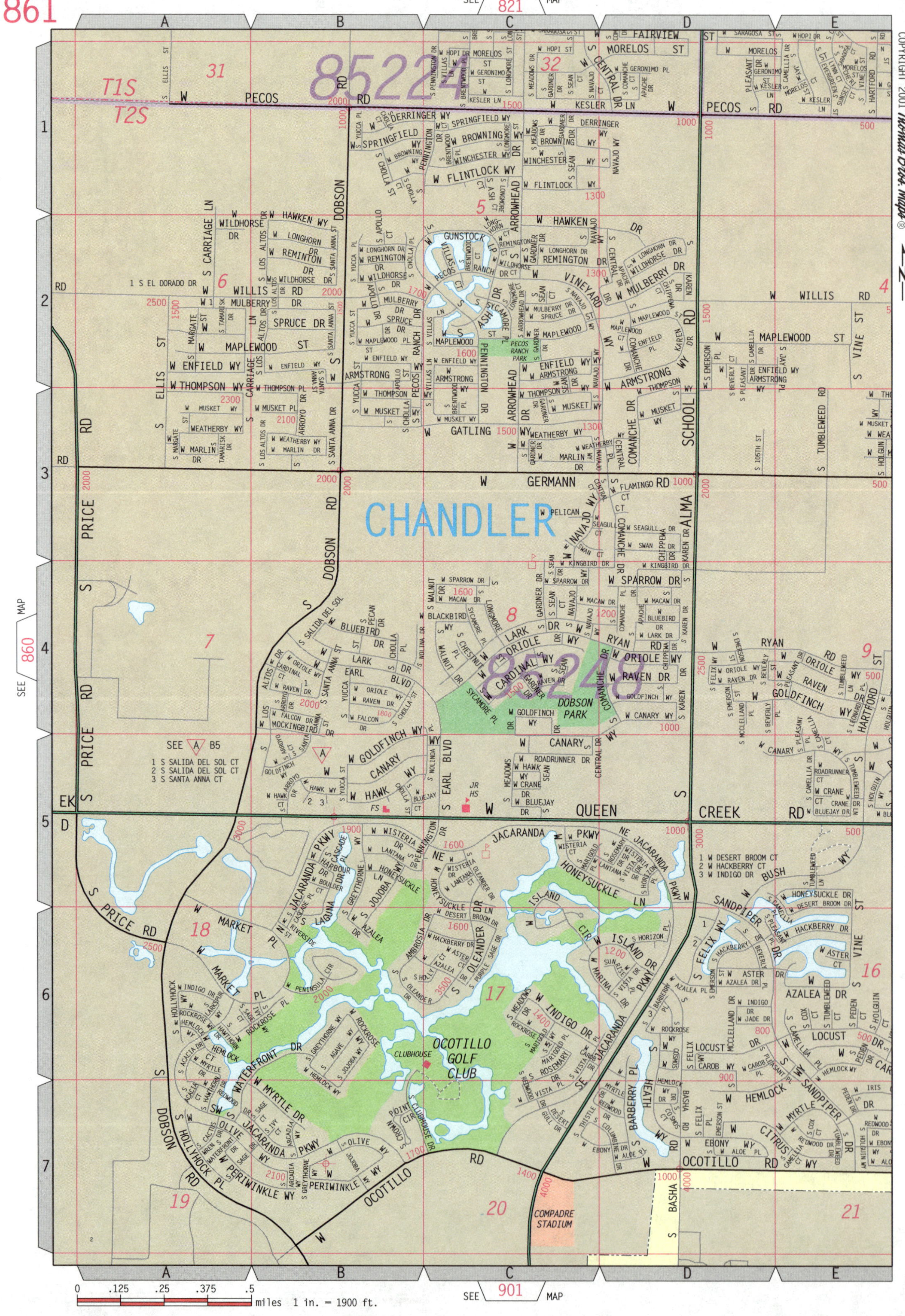

SEE 860 MAP

SEE 901 MAP

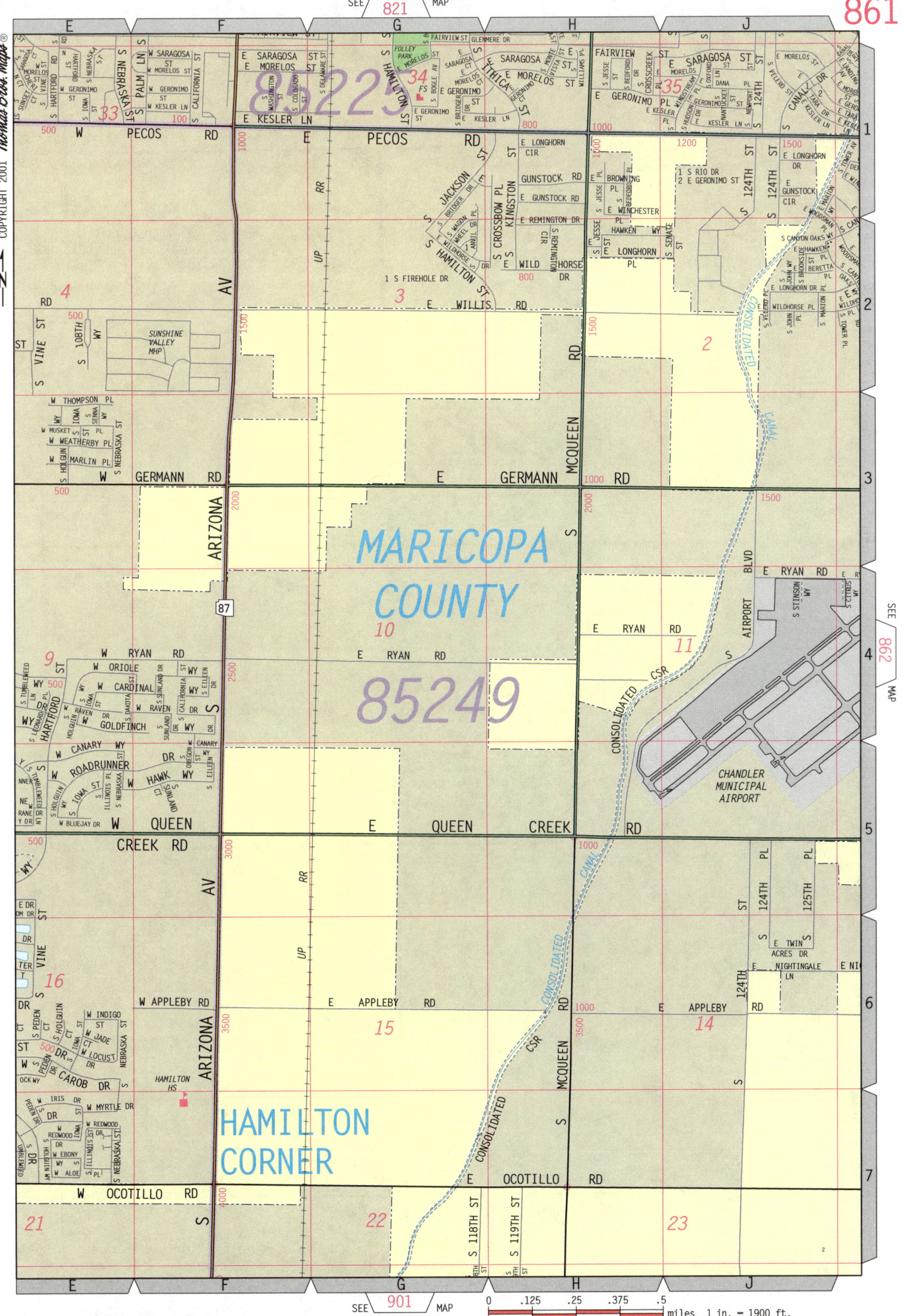

SEE 821 MAP
SEE 862 MAP
SEE 901 MAP

miles 1 in. = 1900 ft.

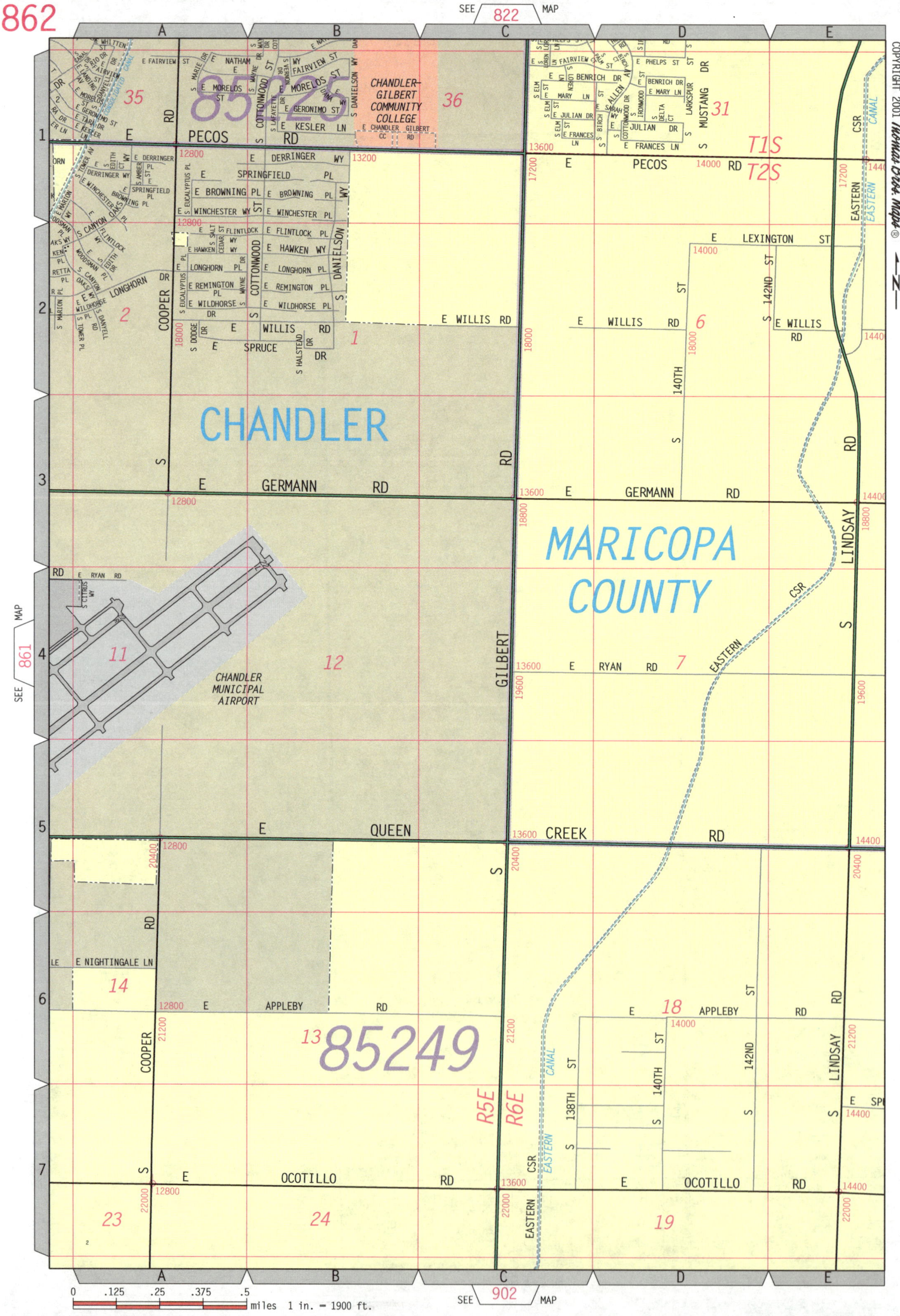
SEE 822 MAP
SEE 861 MAP
SEE 902 MAP
PHOENIX
MAP
CHANDLER
MARICOPA COUNTY
85225
85249
CHANDLER-GILBERT COMMUNITY COLLEGE
CHANDLER MUNICIPAL AIRPORT
E PECOS RD
E GERMANN RD
E QUEEN CREEK RD
E OCOTILLO RD
E WILLIS RD
E RYAN RD
E APPLEBY RD
E LEXINGTON ST
E NIGHTINGALE LN
S COOPER RD
S GILBERT RD
S LINDSAY RD
S EASTERN CSR
EASTERN CANAL
S 140TH ST
S 142ND ST
S 138TH ST
S COTTONWOOD ST
S DANIELSON WY
E DERRINGER WY
E SPRINGFIELD PL
E BROWNING PL
E WINCHESTER PL
E FLINTLOCK PL
E HAWKEN WY
E LONGHORN PL
E REMINGTON PL
E WILDHORSE PL
E SPRUCE DR
E MORELOS ST
E GERONIMO ST
E KESLER LN
E FAIRVIEW ST
E NATHAM
E BENRICH DR
E MARY LN
E JULIAN DR
E FRANCES LN
E PHELPS ST
S MUSTANG DR
S LARKSPUR
T1S
T2S
R5E
R6E
COPYRIGHT 2001 Thomas Bros. Maps®
0 .125 .25 .375 .5 miles 1 in. = 1900 ft.

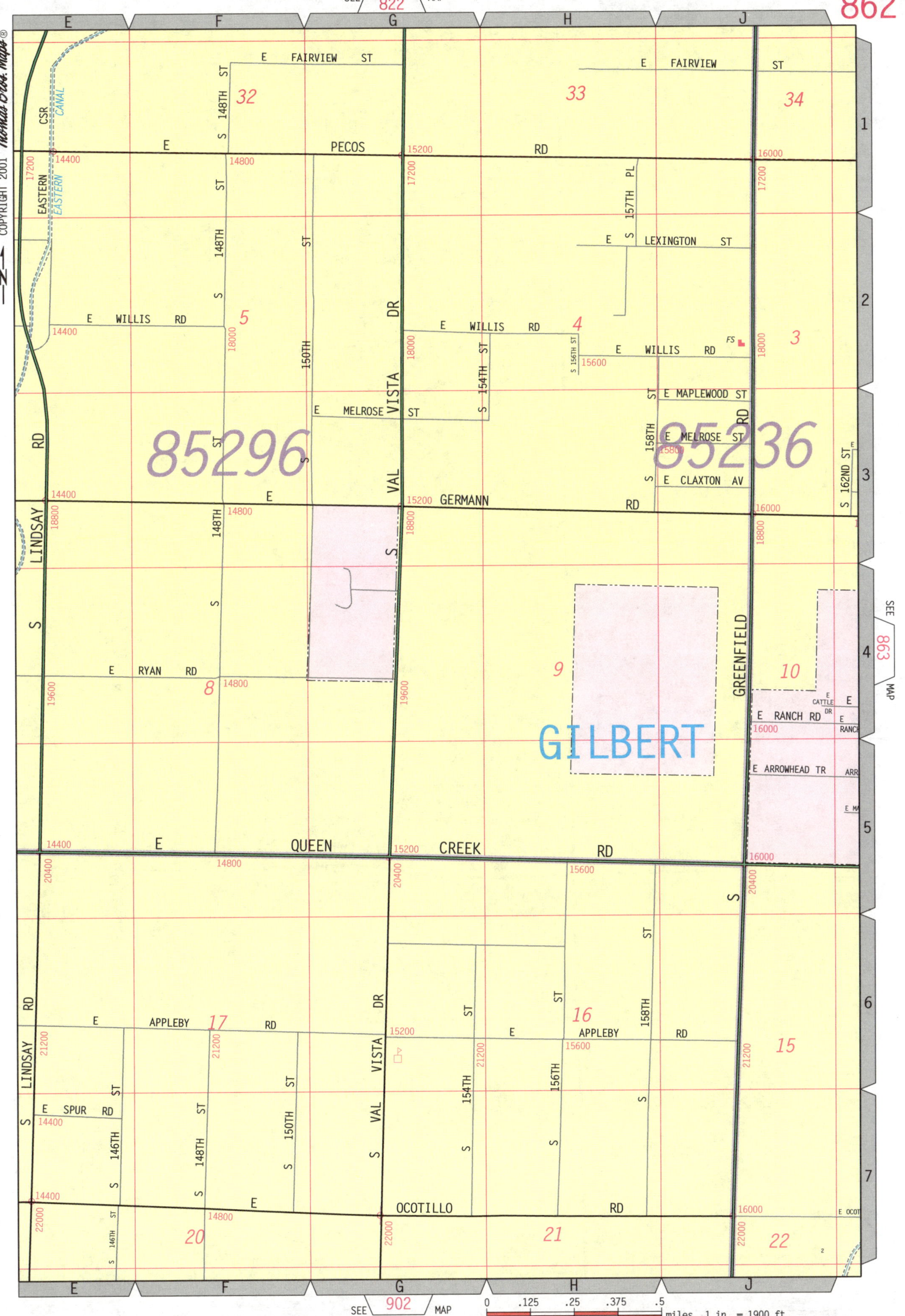
SEE 822 MAP
E
F
G
H
J
E FAIRVIEW ST
S 148TH ST
32
33
34
CSR
EASTERN CANAL
E PECOS RD
S 157TH PL
E LEXINGTON ST
S 148TH ST
S 150TH ST
E WILLIS RD
E WILLIS RD
E WILLIS RD
S 154TH ST
S 156TH ST
FS
E MAPLEWOOD ST
E MELROSE ST
E MELROSE ST
S VAL VISTA DR
S 158TH ST
E CLAXTON AV
S 162ND ST
85296
85236
S LINDSAY RD
E GERMANN RD
S 148TH ST
E RYAN RD
S GREENFIELD RD
GILBERT
E CATTLE DR
E RANCH RD
E ARROWHEAD TR
E QUEEN CREEK RD
S 158TH ST
E APPLEBY RD
E APPLEBY RD
S LINDSAY RD
E SPUR RD
S 146TH ST
S 148TH ST
S 150TH ST
S VAL VISTA DR
S 154TH ST
S 156TH ST
S 158TH ST
E OCOTILLO RD
S 146TH ST
E OCOT
1
2
3
4
5
6
7
4
5
8
9
10
15
16
17
20
21
22
3
14400
14800
15200
15600
16000
17200
18000
18800
19600
20400
21200
22000
SEE 863 MAP
PHOENIX
MAP
SEE 902 MAP
0 .125 .25 .375 .5 miles 1 in. = 1900 ft.

SEE 823 MAP

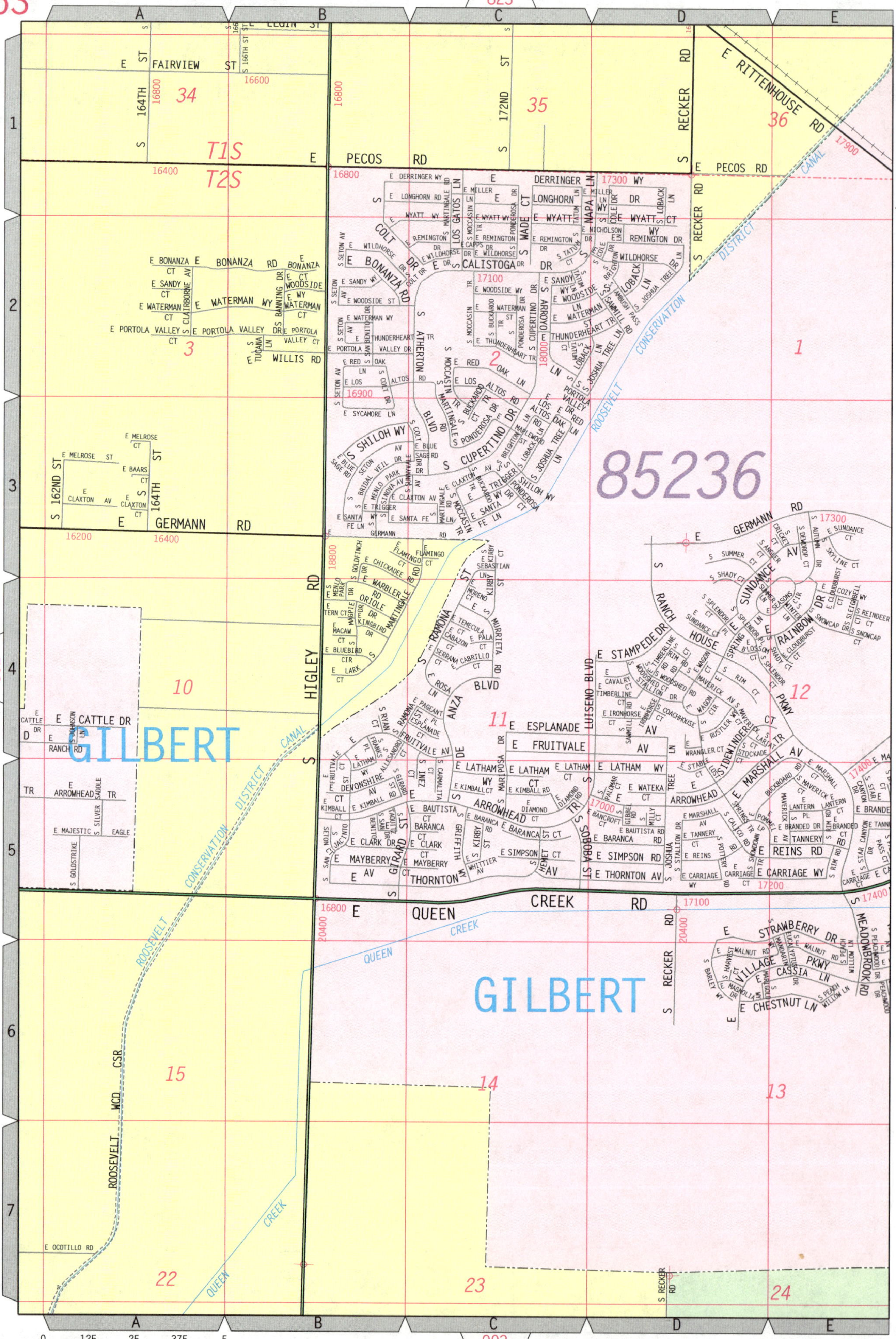

T1S
T2S

85236

GILBERT

E PECOS RD
E GERMANN RD
S HIGLEY RD
S RECKER RD
E QUEEN CREEK RD
E RITTENHOUSE RD
ROOSEVELT CONSERVATION DISTRICT CANAL
QUEEN CREEK
ROOSEVELT WCD CSR
E OCOTILLO RD

SEE 862 MAP

SEE 903 MAP

0 .125 .25 .375 .5 miles 1 in. = 1900 ft.

SEE 823 MAP

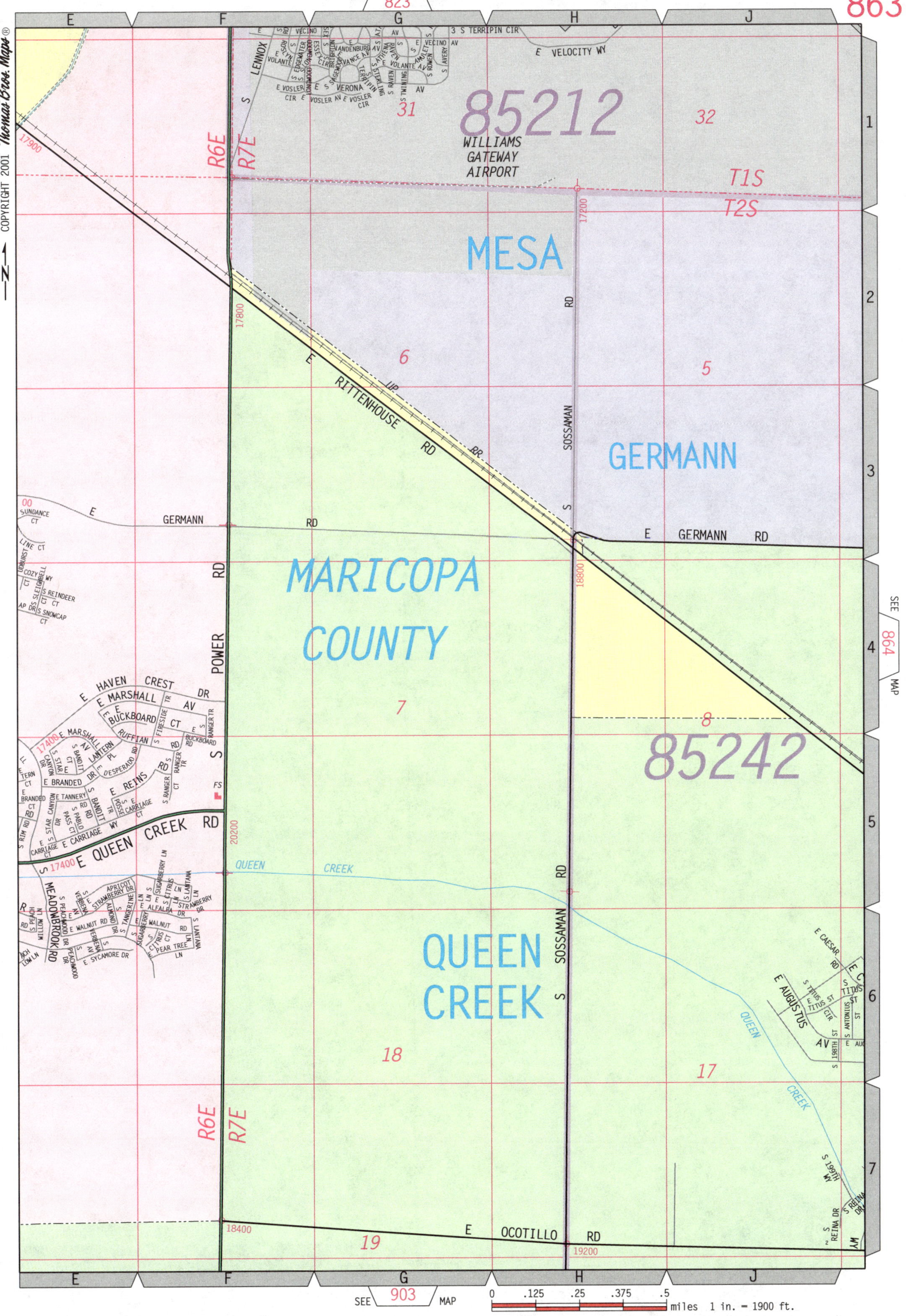

SEE 864 MAP

SEE 903 MAP

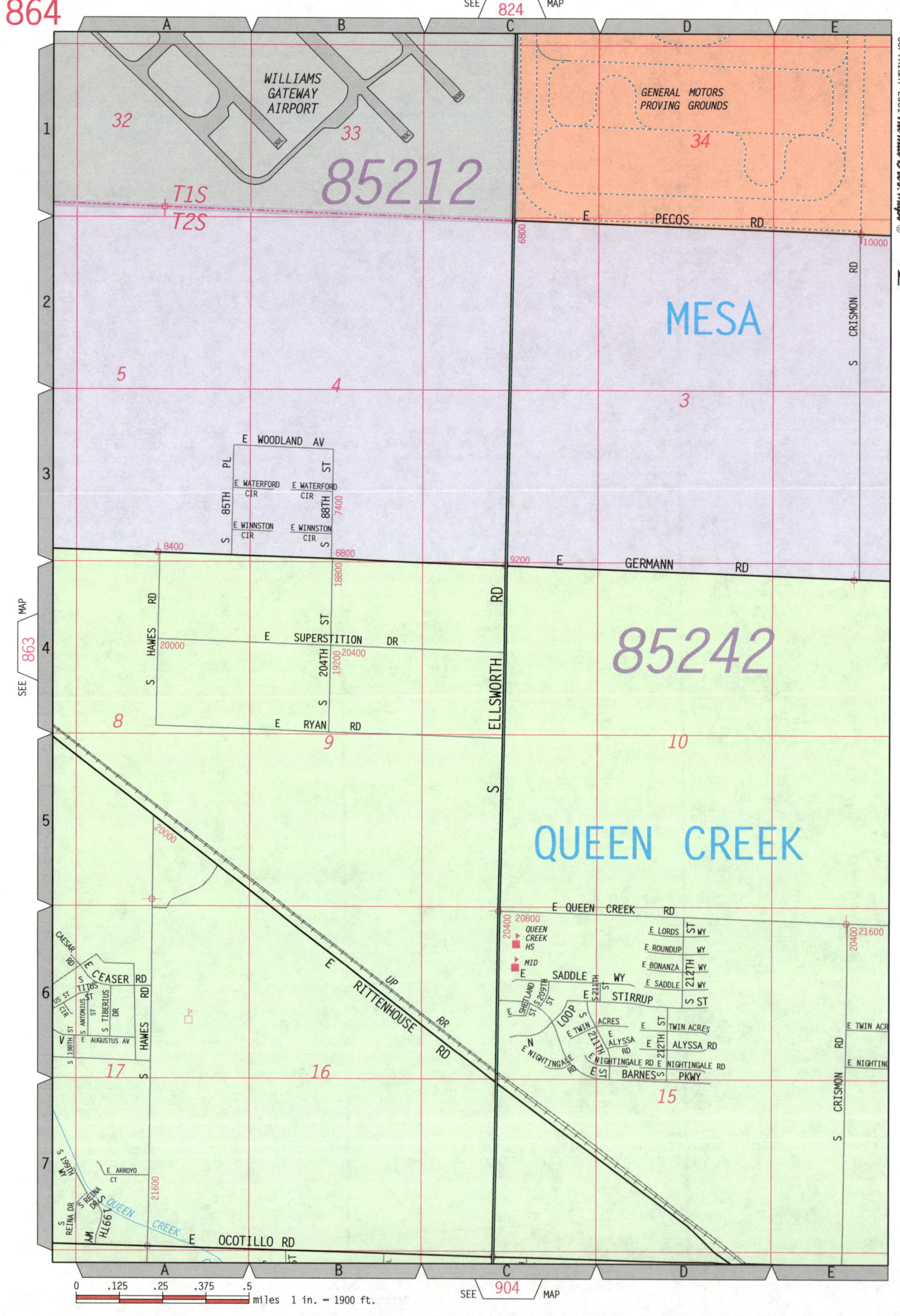

SEE 824 MAP
WILLIAMS GATEWAY AIRPORT
GENERAL MOTORS PROVING GROUNDS
85212
T1S
T2S
E PECOS RD
MESA
S CRISMON RD
E WOODLAND AV
S 85TH PL
S 88TH ST
E WATERFORD CIR
E WINNSTON CIR
E GERMANN RD
85242
S HAWES RD
E SUPERSTITION DR
S 204TH ST
E RYAN RD
S ELLSWORTH RD
QUEEN CREEK
E UP RITTENHOUSE RR RD
E QUEEN CREEK RD
QUEEN CREEK HS
MID
E SADDLE WY
E STIRRUP ST
E LORDS WY
E ROUNDUP WY
E BONANZA WY
E SADDLE WY
S 212TH ST
E TWIN ACRES
E ALYSSA RD
E NIGHTINGALE RD
E BARNES PKWY
E CEASER RD
CAESAR RD
S TIBERIUS DR
S ANTONIUS ST
E AUGUSTUS AV
E ARROYO CT
QUEEN CREEK
E OCOTILLO RD
SEE 863 MAP
SEE 904 MAP
miles 1 in. = 1900 ft.

PHOENIX
MAP

SEE 824 MAP

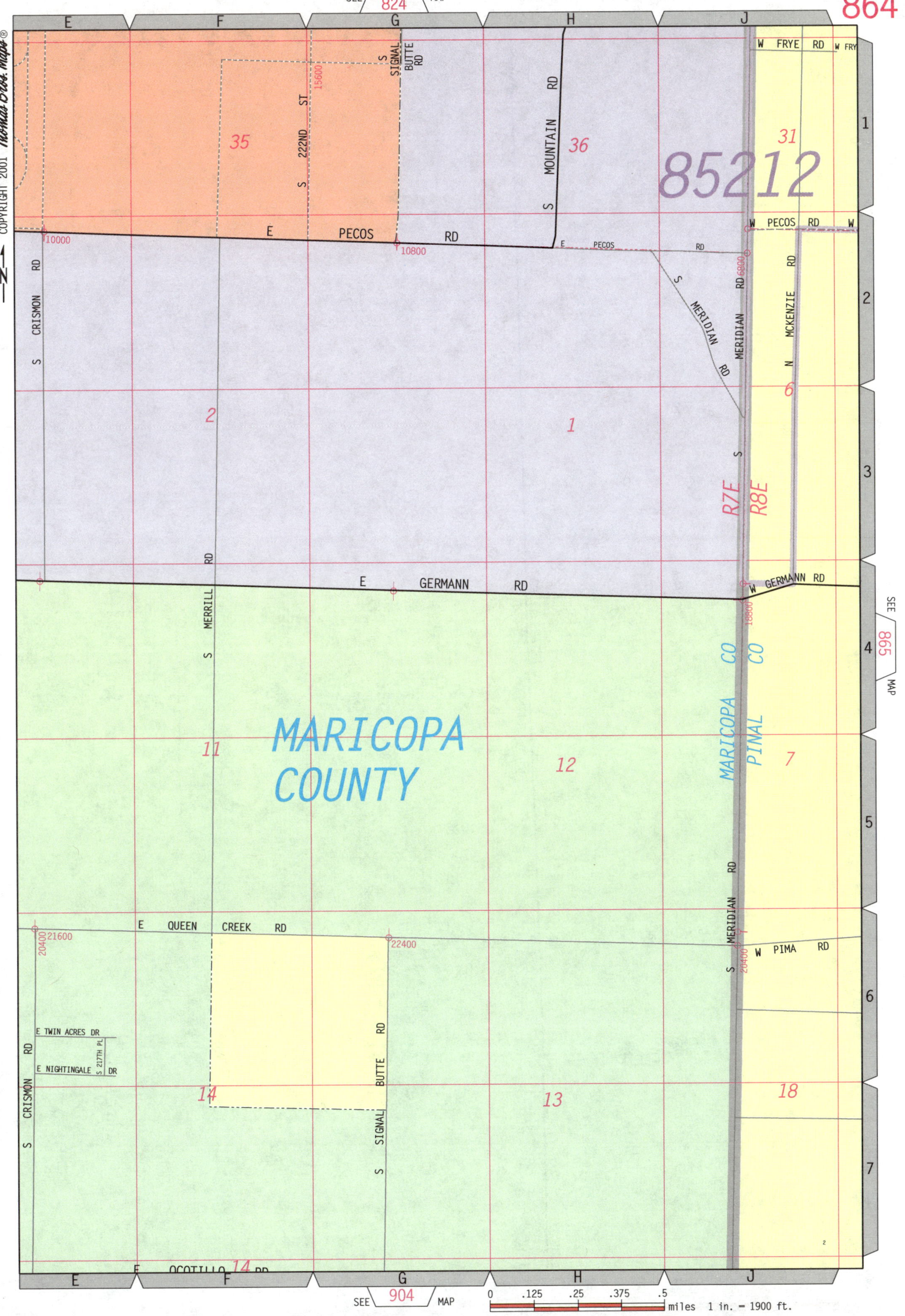

SEE 865 MAP

SEE 904 MAP

SEE 825 MAP

SEE 905 MAP

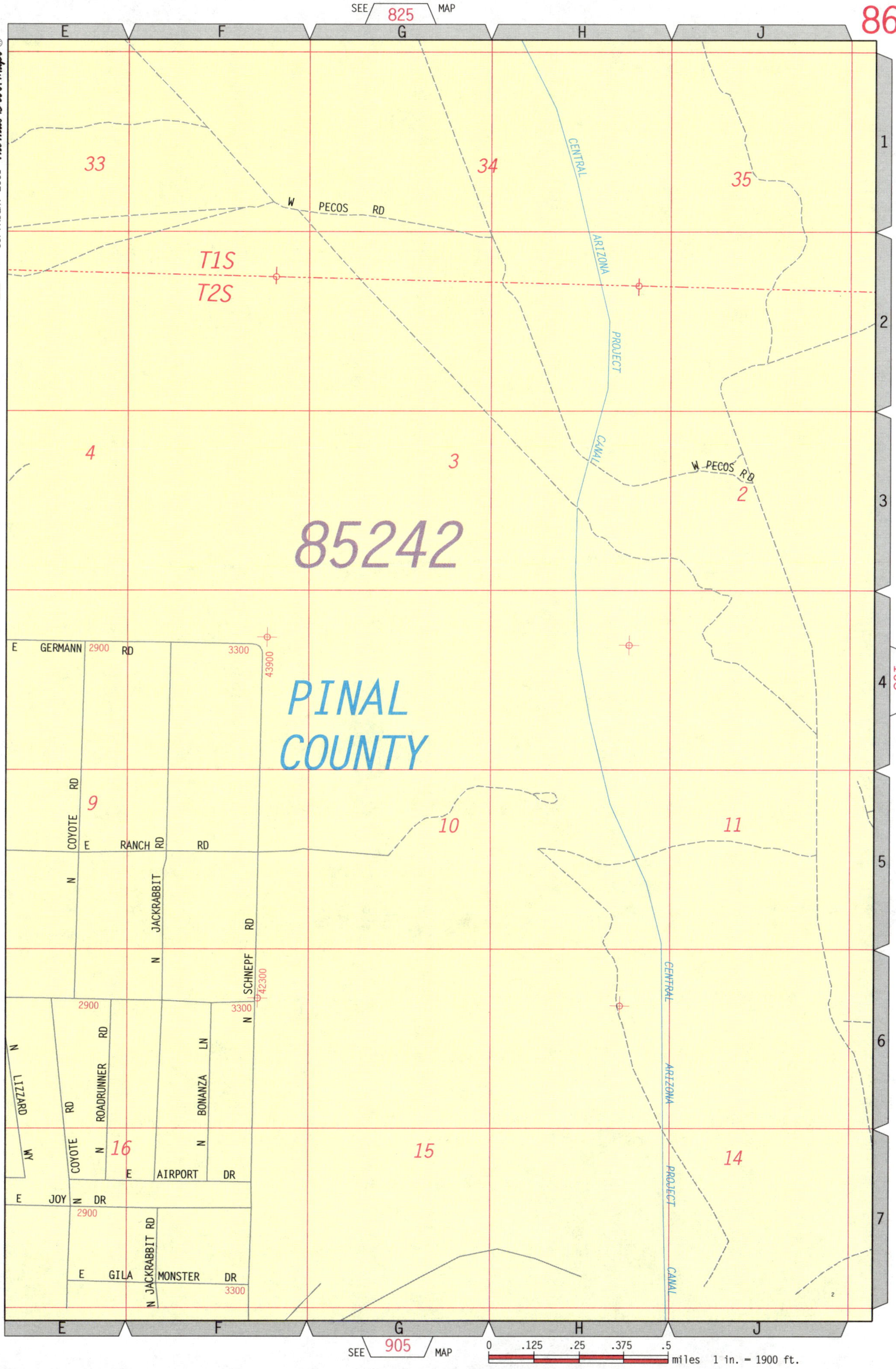

SEE 825 MAP
E
F
G
H
J
1
2
3
4
5
6
7
33
34
35
W PECOS RD
T1S
T2S
CENTRAL ARIZONA PROJECT CANAL
4
3
W PECOS RD
2
85242
SEE 103 MAP
E GERMANN 2900 RD
3300
43900
PINAL COUNTY
9
10
11
N COYOTE RD
E RANCH RD
RD
N JACKRABBIT
N SCHNEPF RD
42300
2900
3300
N LIZZARD WY
COYOTE RD
N ROADRUNNER RD
N BONANZA LN
16
15
14
E AIRPORT DR
E JOY N DR
2900
E GILA MONSTER DR
N JACKRABBIT RD
3300
SEE 905 MAP
0 .125 .25 .375 .5 miles 1 in. = 1900 ft.
PHOENIX
MAP

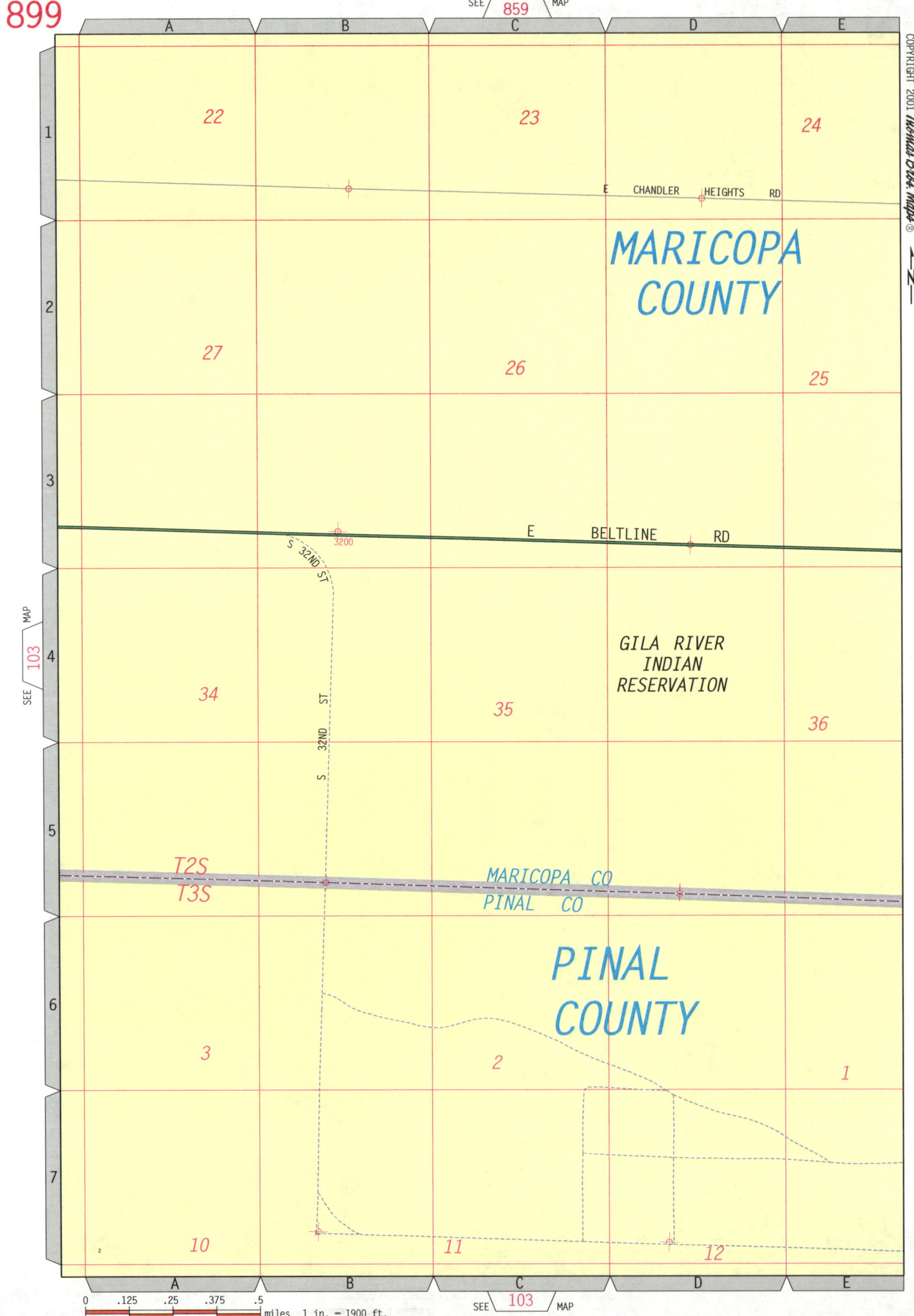

SEE 859 MAP
A
B
C
D
E
1
2
3
4
5
6
7
22
23
24
E CHANDLER HEIGHTS RD
MARICOPA
COUNTY
27
26
25
E BELTLINE RD
3200
S 32ND ST
GILA RIVER
INDIAN
RESERVATION
SEE 103 MAP
34
35
36
S 32ND ST
T2S
T3S
MARICOPA CO
PINAL CO
PINAL
COUNTY
3
2
1
10
11
12
SEE 103 MAP
0 .125 .25 .375 .5
miles 1 in. = 1900 ft.
PHOENIX
MAP

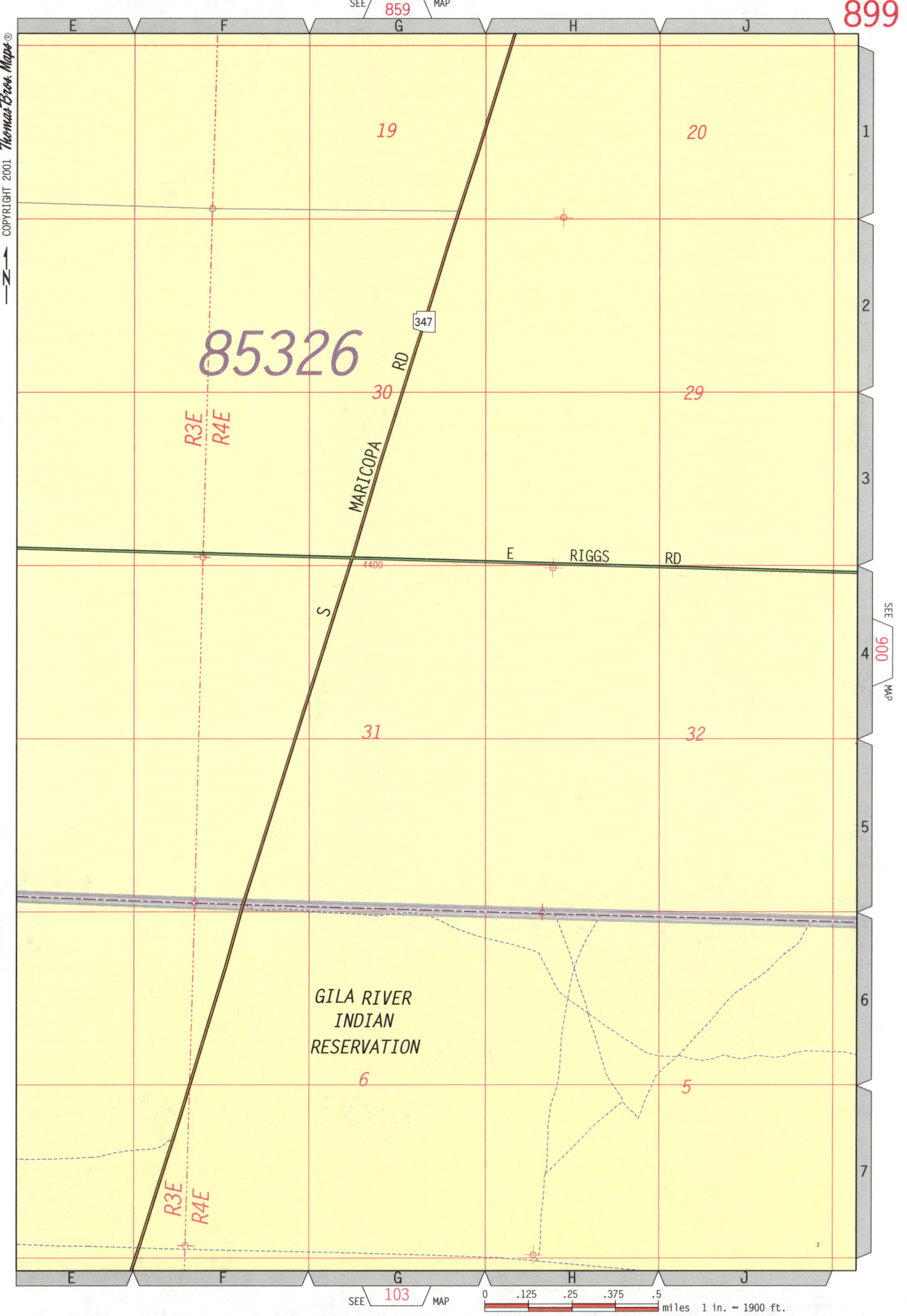
SEE 859 MAP
E
F
G
H
J
1
2
3
4
5
6
7
19
20
30
29
31
32
6
5
85326
347
MARICOPA RD
S
E RIGGS RD
4400
R3E
R4E
GILA RIVER
INDIAN
RESERVATION
SEE 900 MAP
SEE 103 MAP
0 .125 .25 .375 .5
miles 1 in. = 1900 ft.
PHOENIX
MAP

SEE 860 MAP

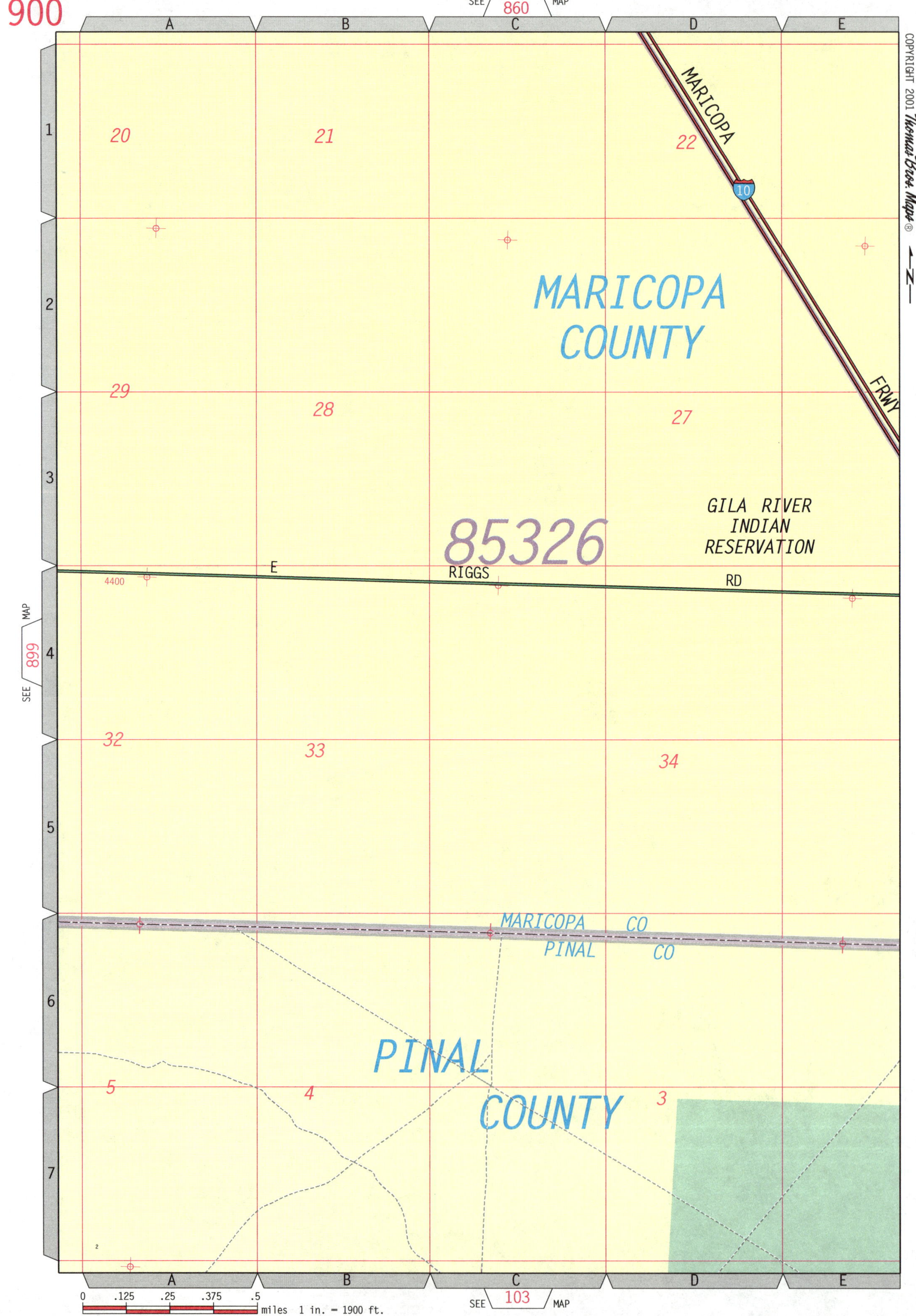

SEE 899 MAP

SEE 103 MAP

PHOENIX

MAP

SEE 860 MAP

SEE 901 MAP

PHOENIX

MAP

SEE 103 MAP

0 .125 .25 .375 .5 miles 1 in. = 1900 ft.

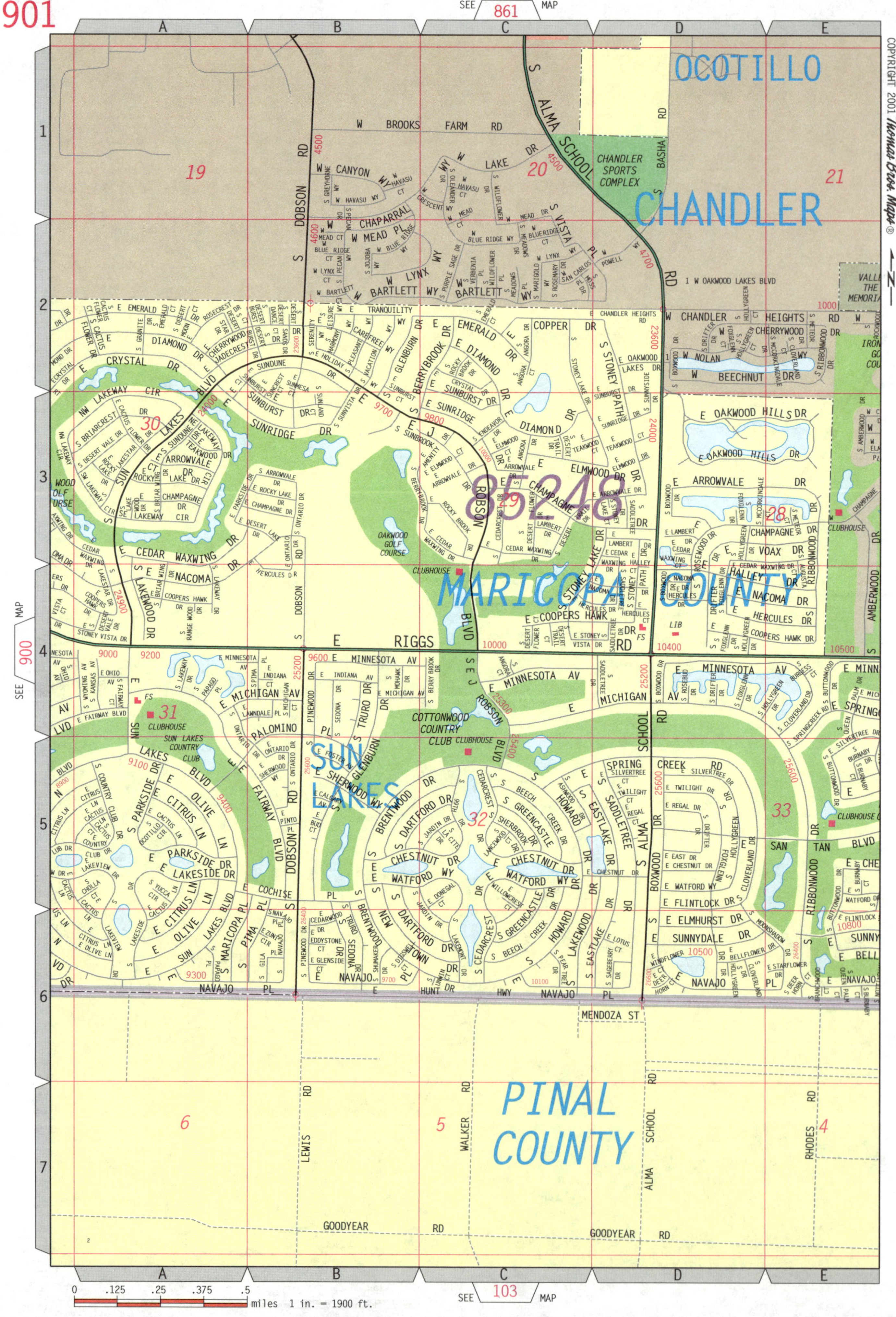
SEE 861 MAP
A
B
C
D
E
1
2
3
4
5
6
7
OCOTILLO
CHANDLER
CHANDLER SPORTS COMPLEX
W BROOKS FARM RD
S DOBSON RD
S ALMA SCHOOL RD
BASHA RD
W LAKE DR
W CANYON WY
W CHAPARRAL
W MEAD PL
W LYNX WY
W BARTLETT WY
W CHANDLER HEIGHTS RD
CHERRYWOOD DR
W NOLAN WY
W BEECHNUT DR
E OAKWOOD HILLS DR
E OAKWOOD LAKES DR
1 W OAKWOOD LAKES BLVD
VALLEY OF THE SUN MEMORIAL
19
20
21
28
29
30
31
32
33
85248
E EMERALD DR
E DIAMOND DR
E CRYSTAL DR
E COPPER DR
E SUNDUNE
E SUNBURST DR
E SUNRIDGE DR
E ARROWVALE DR
E CHAMPAGNE DR
E ELMWOOD DR
E LAMBERT DR
E CEDAR WAXWING DR
E NACOMA DR
E VOAX DR
E HALLEY DR
E HERCULES DR
E COOPERS HAWK DR
NW LAKEWAY CIR
S SUN LAKES BLVD
S LAKEWOOD DR
S STONEY LAKE DR
S STONEY PATH DR
S SADDLETREE DR
S RIBBONWOOD DR
AMBERWOOD DR
S E J ROBSON BLVD
OAKWOOD GOLF COURSE
CLUBHOUSE
MARICOPA COUNTY
LIB
FS
E RIGGS RD
E MINNESOTA AV
E MICHIGAN AV
E OHIO AV
E FAIRWAY BLVD
E PALOMINO DR
S TRURO DR
S GLENBURN DR
COTTONWOOD COUNTRY CLUB
SUN LAKES COUNTRY CLUB
SUN LAKES
E SPRING CREEK RD
E SAN TAN BLVD
E CITRUS LN
E OLIVE LN
E PARKSIDE DR
E LAKESIDE DR
E COCHISE PL
E CHESTNUT DR
E WATFORD WY
E FLINTLOCK DR
E ELMHURST DR
E SUNNYDALE DR
S DARTFORD DR
S BRENTWOOD DR
S GREENCASTLE DR
S HOWARD DR
S EASTLAKE DR
S LAKEWOOD
S BOXWOOD DR
S CLOVERLAND DR
S HOLLYGREEN DR
S FOXGLEN DR
E NAVAJO PL
E HUNT HWY
MENDOZA ST
PINAL COUNTY
LEWIS RD
WALKER RD
ALMA SCHOOL RD
RHODES RD
GOODYEAR RD
6
5
4
SEE 900 MAP
SEE 103 MAP
0 .125 .25 .375 .5
miles 1 in. = 1900 ft.
PHOENIX
MAP

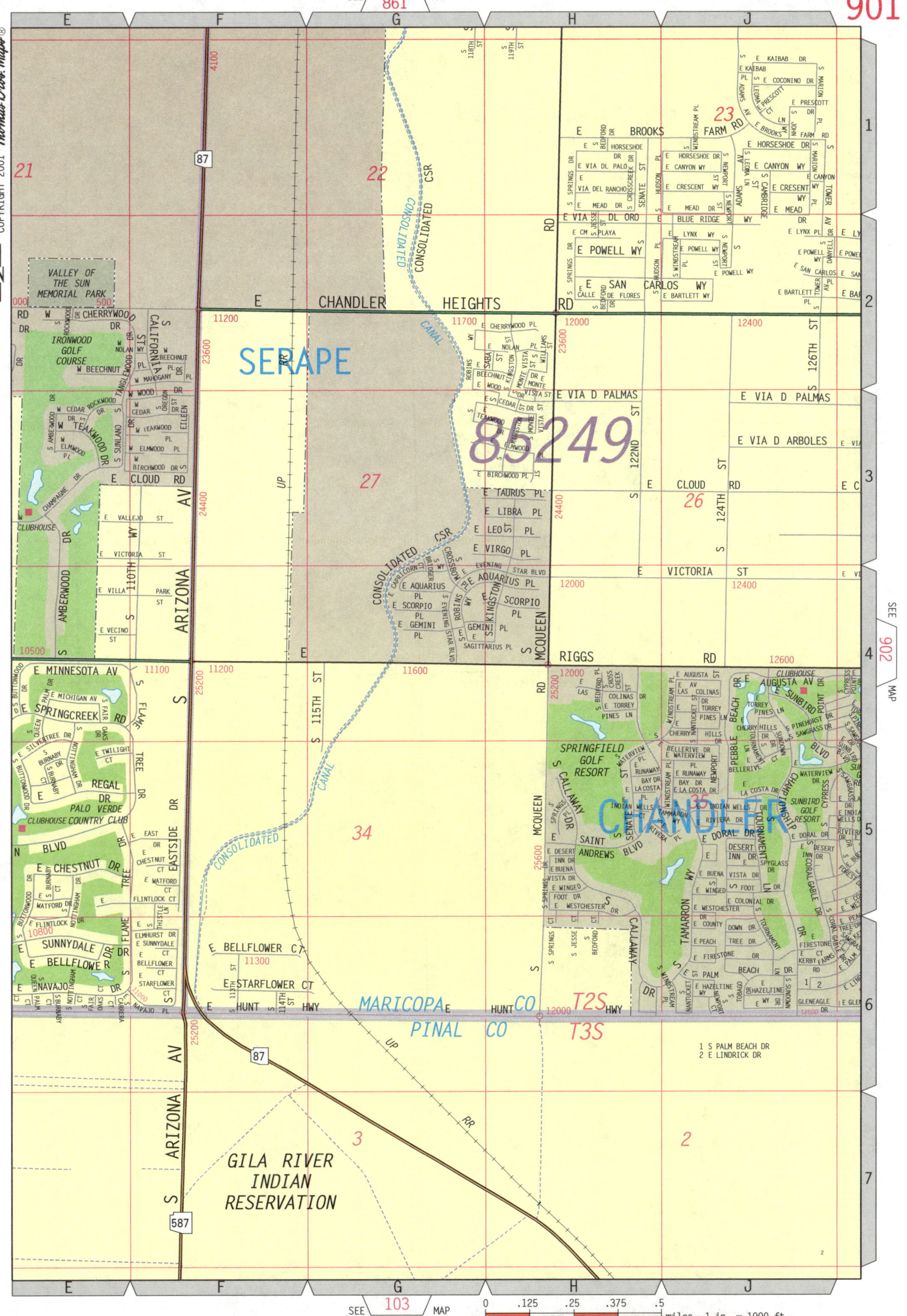
SEE 861 MAP
SERAPE
85249
CHANDLER
E CHANDLER HEIGHTS RD
E RIGGS RD
E HUNT HWY
S ARIZONA AV
S MCQUEEN RD
CONSOLIDATED CANAL
VALLEY OF THE SUN MEMORIAL PARK
IRONWOOD GOLF COURSE
SPRINGFIELD GOLF RESORT
SUNBIRD GOLF RESORT
CLUBHOUSE COUNTRY CLUB
GILA RIVER INDIAN RESERVATION
MARICOPA CO
PINAL CO
T2S
T3S
PHOENIX
SEE 902 MAP
SEE 103 MAP
1 S PALM BEACH DR
2 E LINDRICK DR
miles 1 in. = 1900 ft.

SEE 862 MAP

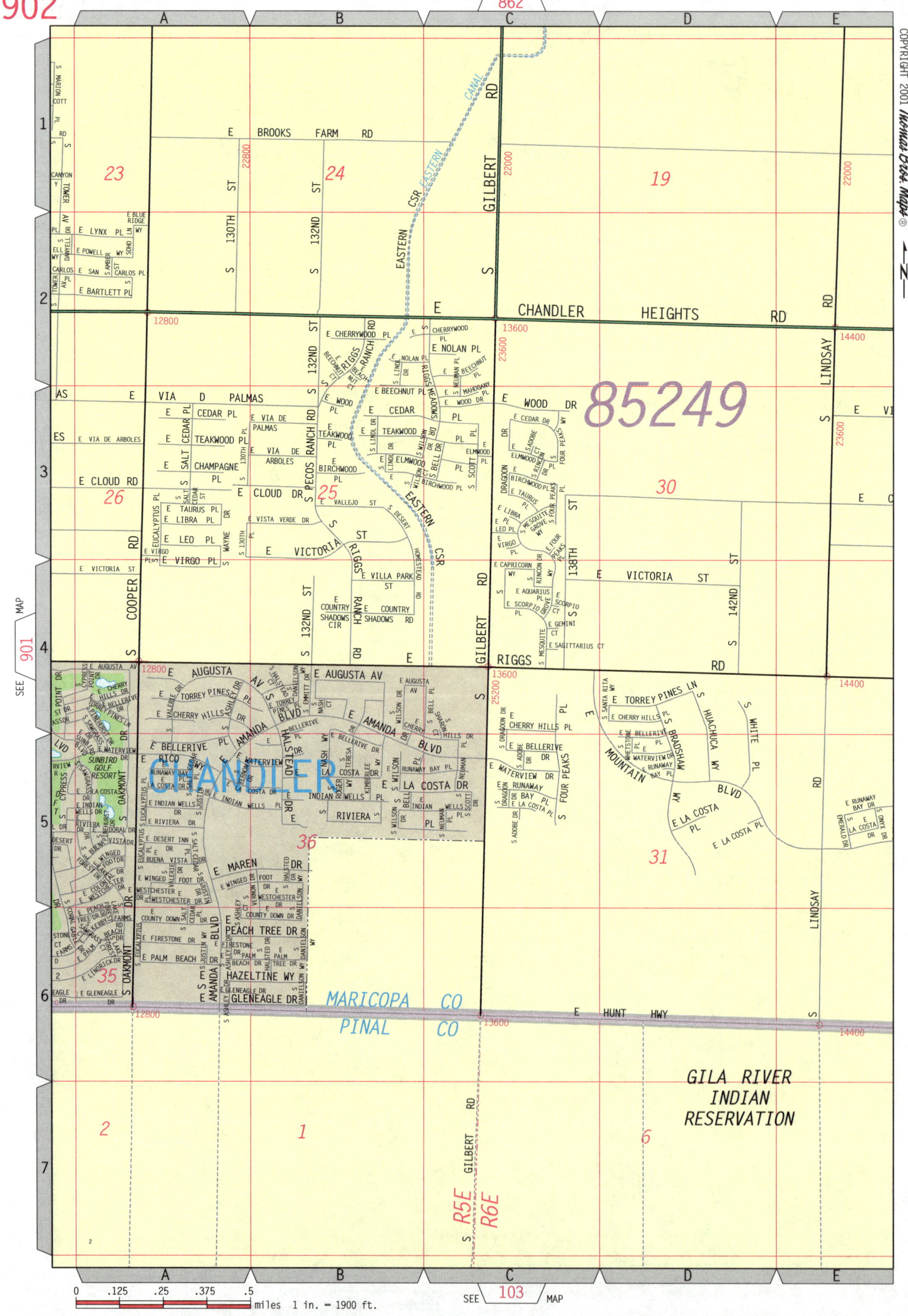

0 .125 .25 .375 .5 miles 1 in. = 1900 ft.

SEE 901 MAP

SEE 103 MAP

PHOENIX

MAP

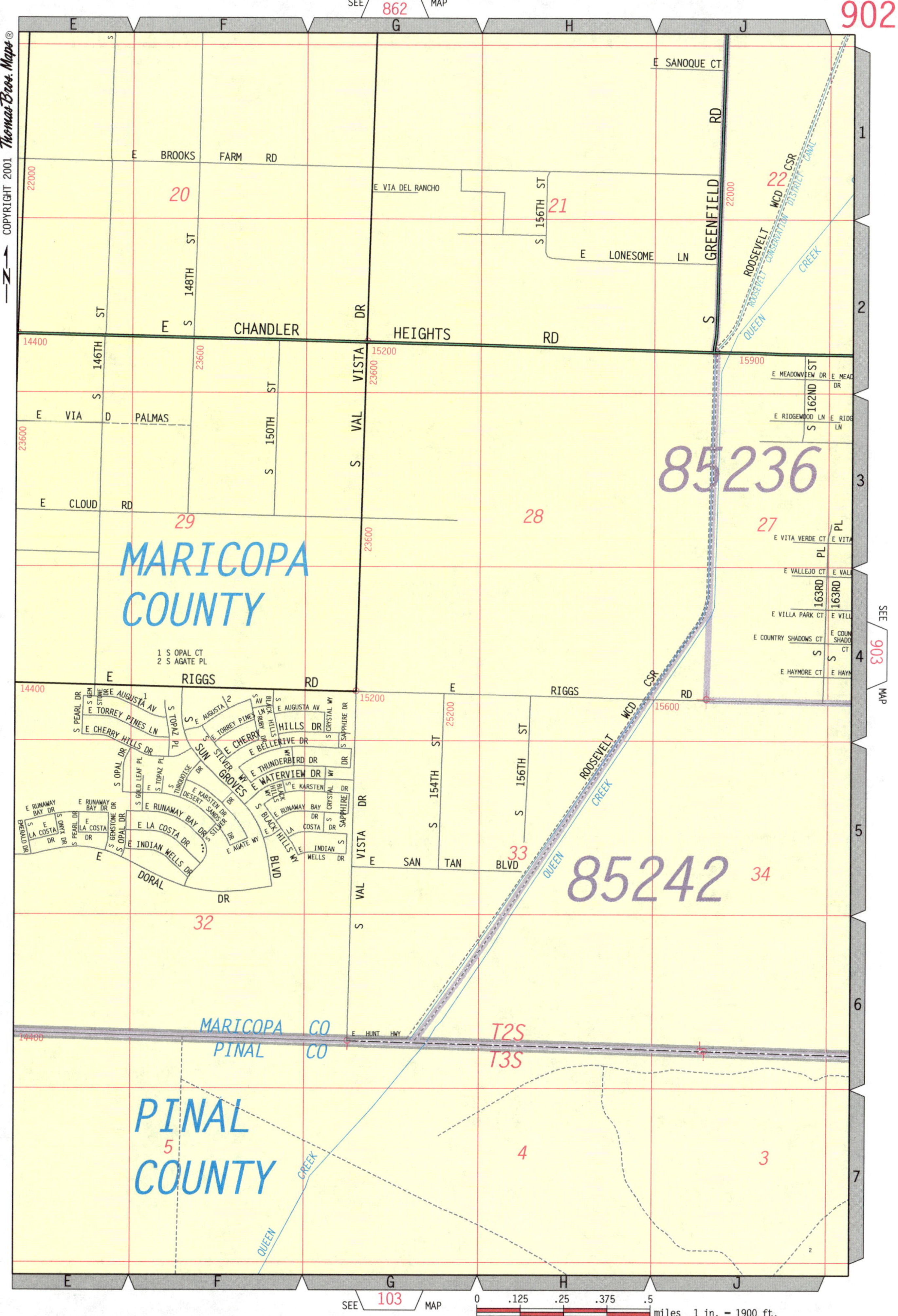
SEE 862 MAP
MARICOPA COUNTY
PINAL COUNTY
85236
85242
E BROOKS FARM RD
E CHANDLER HEIGHTS RD
S GREENFIELD RD
S VAL VISTA DR
E RIGGS RD
E SAN TAN BLVD
E HUNT HWY
ROOSEVELT WCD CSR
ROOSEVELT CONSERVATION DISTRICT CANAL
QUEEN CREEK
E VIA DEL RANCHO
E LONESOME LN
E SANOQUE CT
E VIA D PALMAS
E CLOUD RD
S 146TH ST
S 148TH ST
S 150TH ST
S 154TH ST
S 156TH ST
SUN GROVES BLVD
E DORAL DR
1 S OPAL CT
2 S AGATE PL
MARICOPA CO
PINAL CO
T2S
T3S
SEE 103 MAP
SEE 903 MAP
PHOENIX
MAP
miles 1 in. = 1900 ft.

SEE 863 MAP

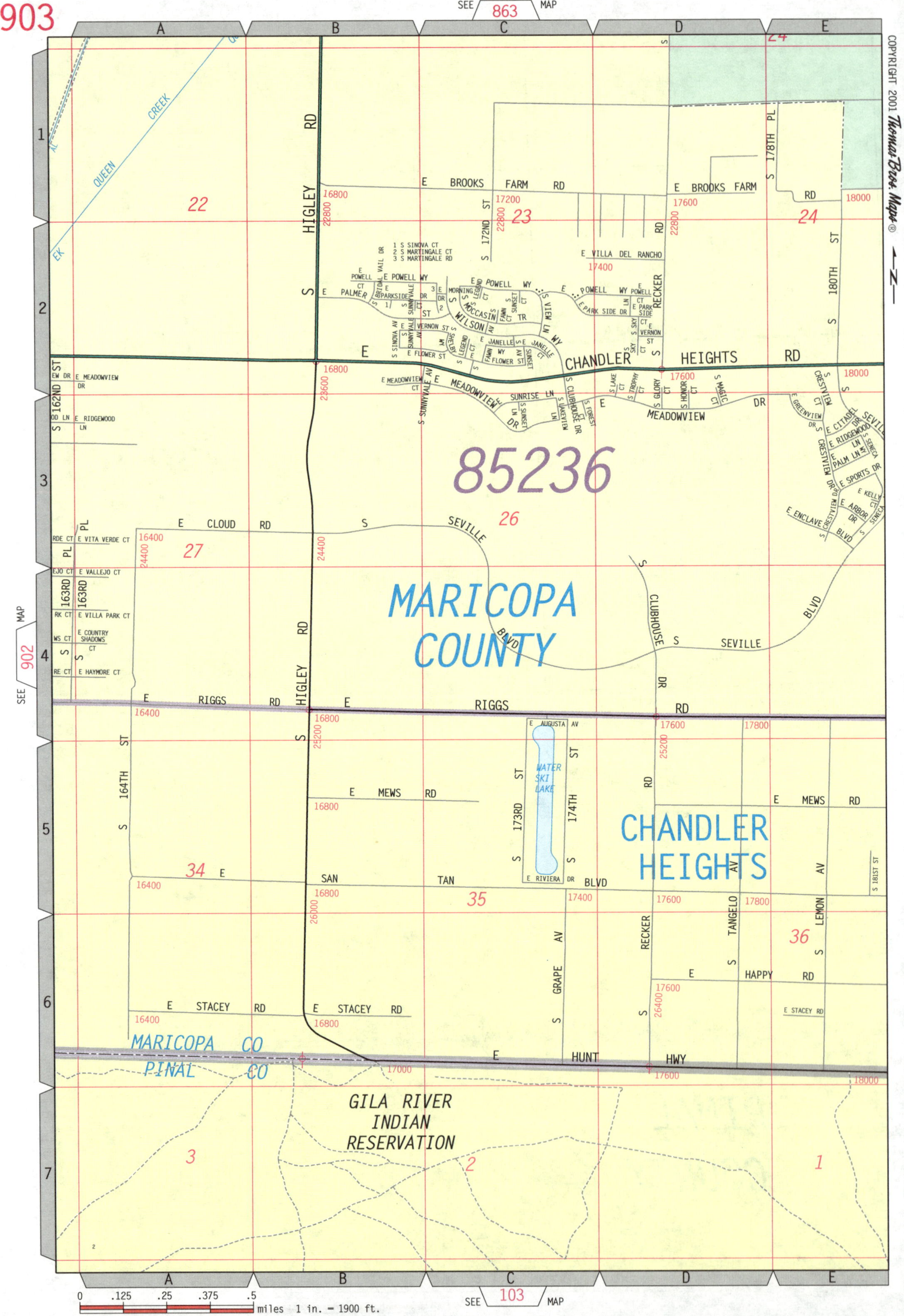

SEE 902 MAP

PHOENIX

MAP

0 .125 .25 .375 .5 miles 1 in. = 1900 ft.

SEE 103 MAP

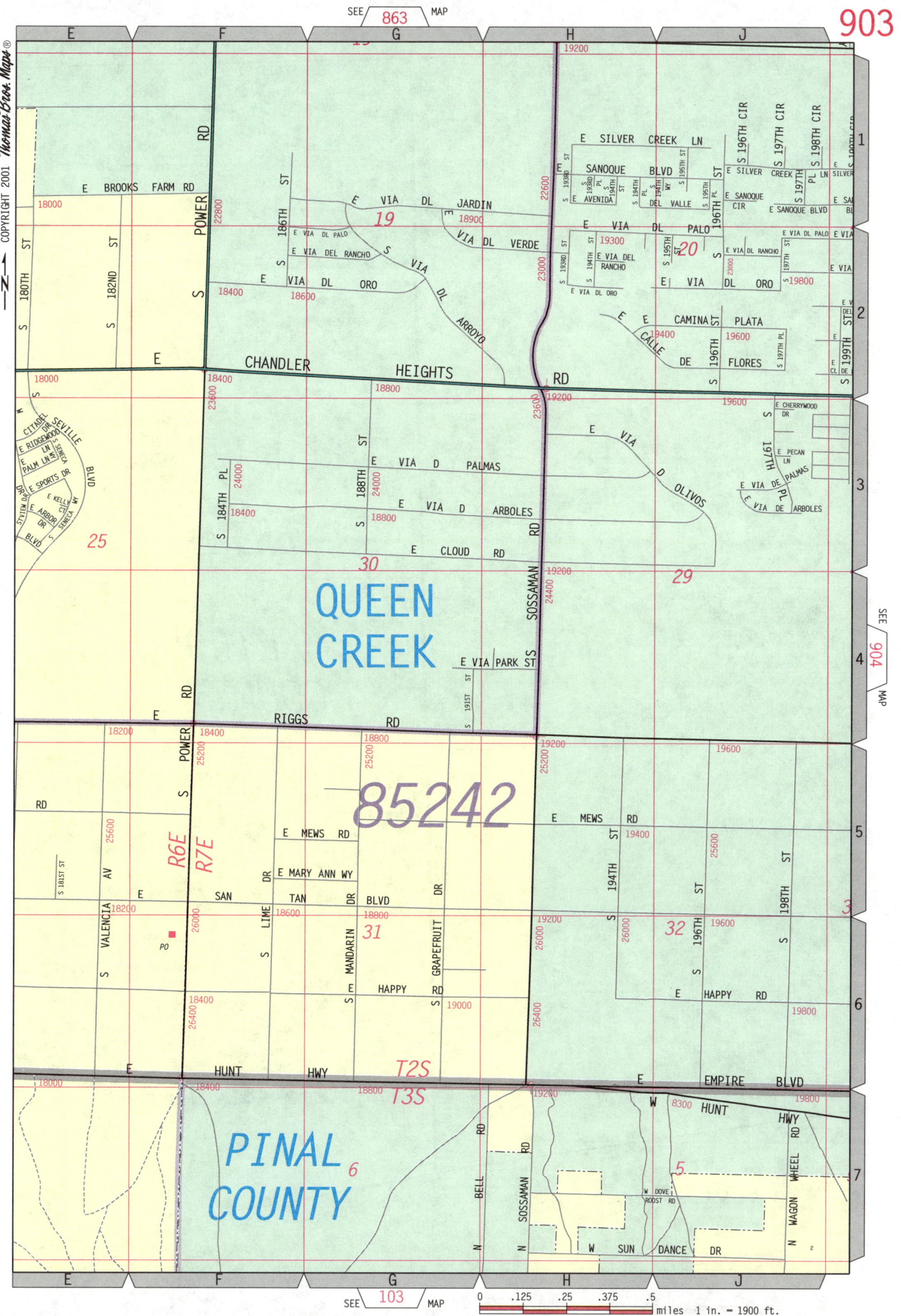
SEE 863 MAP
E
F
G
H
J
1
2
3
4
5
6
7
QUEEN CREEK
PINAL COUNTY
85242
E CHANDLER HEIGHTS RD
E RIGGS RD
E HUNT HWY
E EMPIRE BLVD
W HUNT HWY
S POWER RD
S SOSSAMAN RD
E BROOKS FARM RD
E SILVER CREEK LN
SANOQUE BLVD
E VIA DL JARDIN
E VIA DL VERDE
E VIA DL PALO
E VIA DL ORO
S VIA DL ARROYO
E CAMINA PLATA
CALLE DE FLORES
E VIA D PALMAS
E VIA D ARBOLES
E CLOUD RD
E VIA D OLIVOS
E VIA PARK ST
E MEWS RD
E MARY ANN WY
E SAN TAN BLVD
E HAPPY RD
S 180TH ST
S 182ND ST
S 184TH PL
S 186TH ST
S 188TH ST
S 191ST ST
S 194TH ST
S 196TH ST
S 197TH PL
S 198TH ST
S VALENCIA AV
S LIME DR
S MANDARIN DR
S GRAPEFRUIT DR
N BELL RD
N SOSSAMAN RD
N WAGON WHEEL RD
W DOVE ROOST RD
W SUN DANCE DR
R6E
R7E
T2S
T3S
PO
19
20
25
29
30
31
32
5
6
PHOENIX
MAP
SEE 904 MAP
SEE 103 MAP
0 .125 .25 .375 .5 miles 1 in. = 1900 ft.

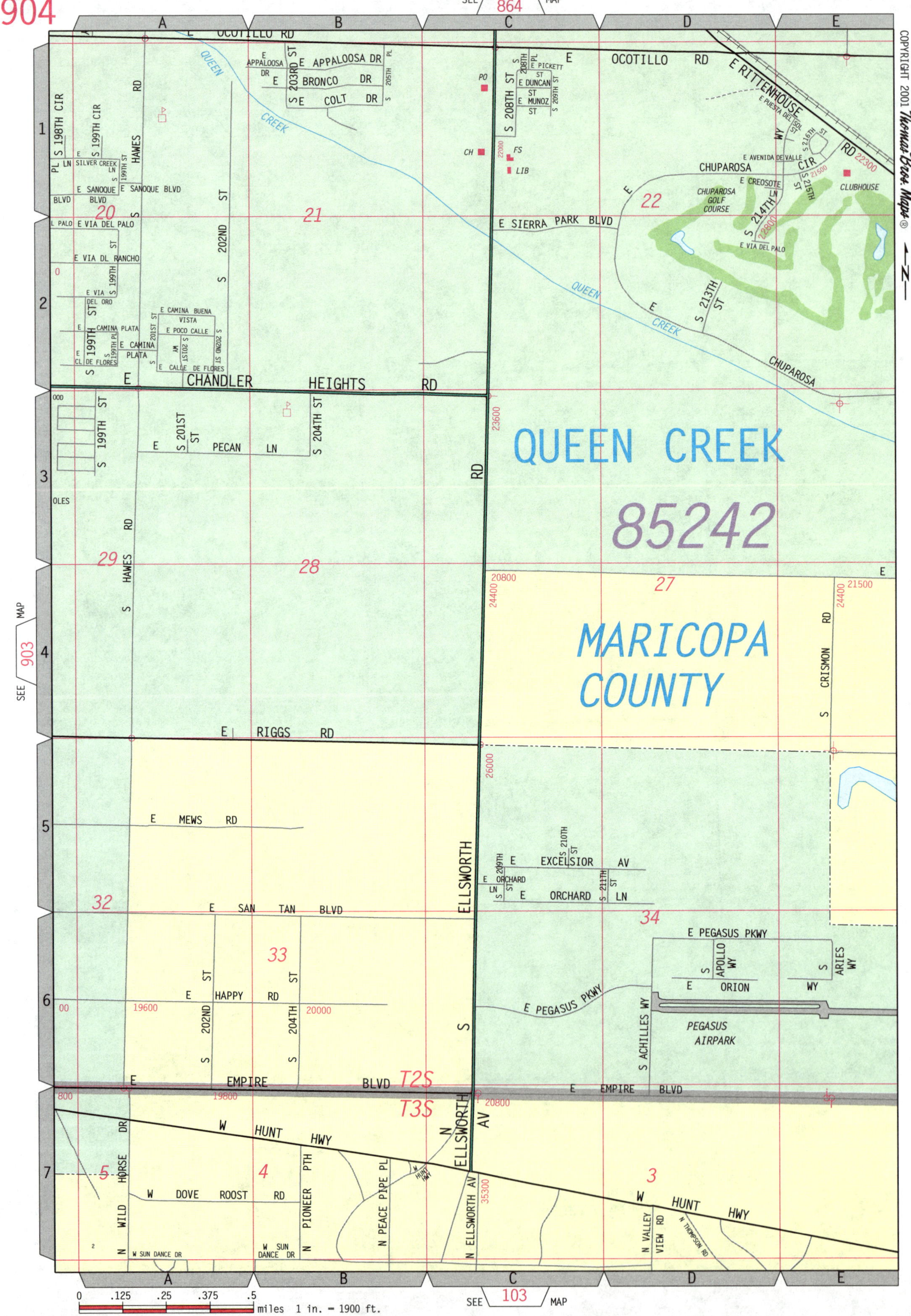
SEE 864 MAP
E OCOTILLO RD
OCOTILLO RD
E RITTENHOUSE RD
QUEEN CREEK
E APPALOOSA DR
E BRONCO DR
E COLT DR
S 203RD ST
S 205TH PL
S 198TH CIR
S 199TH CIR
S HAWES RD
E SILVER CREEK LN
E SANOQUE BLVD
E VIA DEL PALO
E VIA DL RANCHO
E VIA DEL ORO
E CAMINA BUENA VISTA
E POCO CALLE
E CAMINA PLATA
E CALLE DE FLORES
S 202ND ST
S 201ST WY
E CHANDLER HEIGHTS RD
PO
CH
FS
LIB
S 208TH ST
E PICKETT ST
E DUNCAN ST
E MUNOZ ST
S 209TH ST
E PUESTA DEL SOL
S 216TH ST
E AVENIDA DE VALLE
CHUPAROSA CIR
E CREOSOTE LN
S 214TH
S 215TH
CHUPAROSA GOLF COURSE
CLUBHOUSE
E SIERRA PARK BLVD
E VIA DEL PALO
S 213TH ST
E CHUPAROSA
20
21
22
29
28
27
32
33
34
5
4
3
E PECAN LN
S 201ST ST
S 204TH ST
S 199TH ST
QUEEN CREEK
85242
S ELLSWORTH RD
MARICOPA COUNTY
S CRISMON RD
E RIGGS RD
E MEWS RD
E EXCELSIOR AV
S 210TH ST
E ORCHARD LN
S 211TH ST
E SAN TAN BLVD
E PEGASUS PKWY
S APOLLO WY
E ORION WY
S ARIES WY
S ACHILLES WY
PEGASUS AIRPARK
E HAPPY RD
E EMPIRE BLVD
T2S
T3S
W HUNT HWY
N ELLSWORTH AV
N WILD HORSE DR
W DOVE ROOST RD
N PIONEER PTH
N PEACE PIPE PL
W SUN DANCE DR
N VALLEY VIEW RD
N THOMPSON RD
SEE 903 MAP
SEE 103 MAP
0 .125 .25 .375 .5 miles 1 in. = 1900 ft.
PHOENIX
MAP

SEE 864 MAP

SEE 905 MAP

SEE 103 MAP

0 .125 .25 .375 .5 miles 1 in. = 1900 ft.

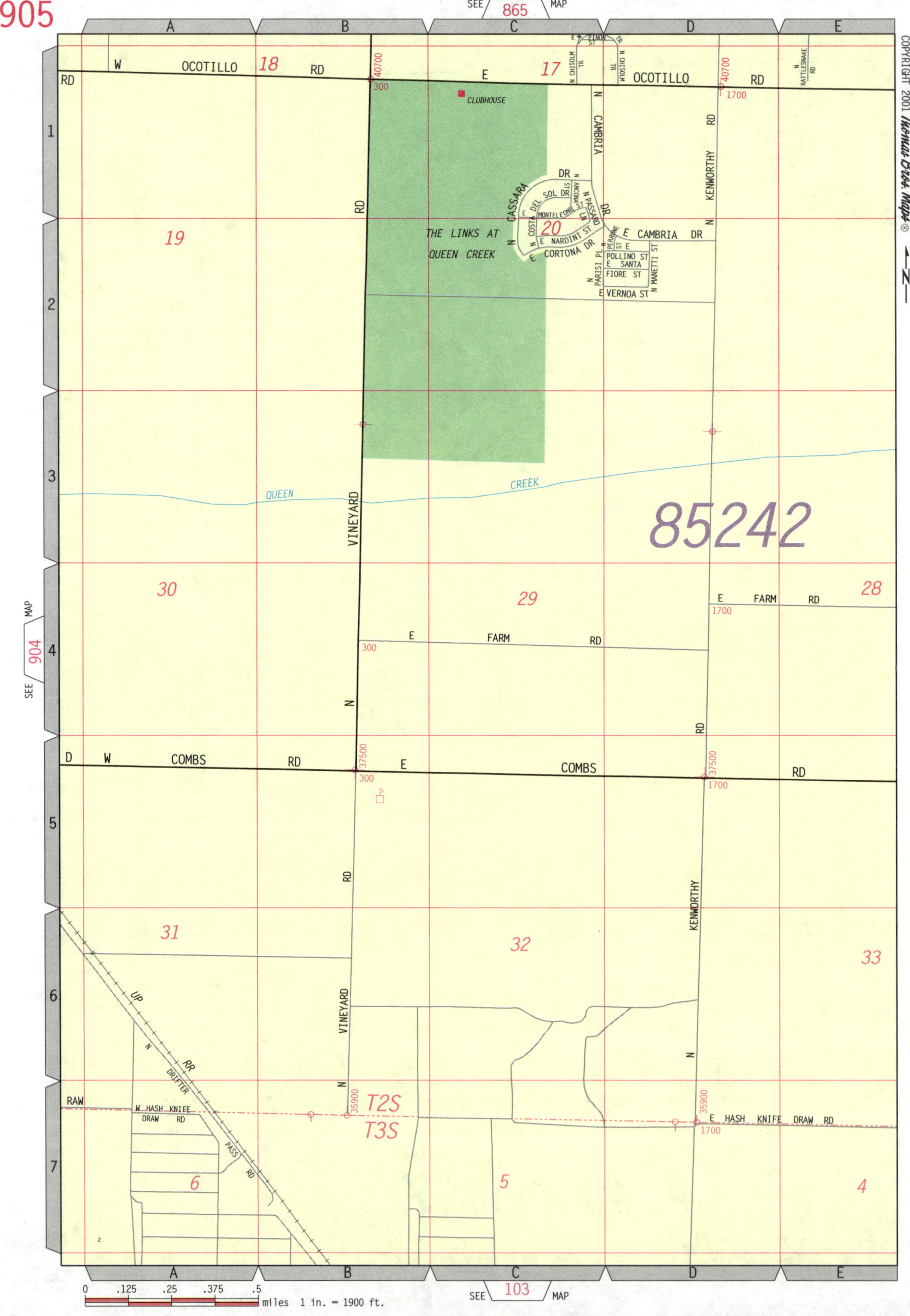

SEE 865 MAP
A
B
C
D
E
1
2
3
4
5
6
7
W OCOTILLO RD
E OCOTILLO RD
18
17
19
20
30
29
28
31
32
33
6
5
4
40700
300
1700
CLUBHOUSE
THE LINKS AT QUEEN CREEK
N CAMBRIA
N CASSARA DR
N KENWORTHY RD
E CAMBRIA DR
E CORTONA DR
E NARDINI ST
E MONTELEONE LN
N COSTA DEL SOL DR
N PASSARO DR
N PARISI PL
E POLLINO ST
E SANTA FIORE ST
N MANETTI ST
E VERNOA ST
N CHISOLM TR
E PINON ST
N RATTLESNAKE RD
N VINEYARD RD
QUEEN CREEK
85242
E FARM RD
D W COMBS RD
E COMBS RD
37500
UP RR
N DRIFTER PASS RD
RAW
W HASH KNIFE DRAW RD
E HASH KNIFE DRAW RD
35900
T2S
T3S
SEE 904 MAP
SEE 103 MAP
0 .125 .25 .375 .5 miles 1 in. = 1900 ft.
PHOENIX
MAP

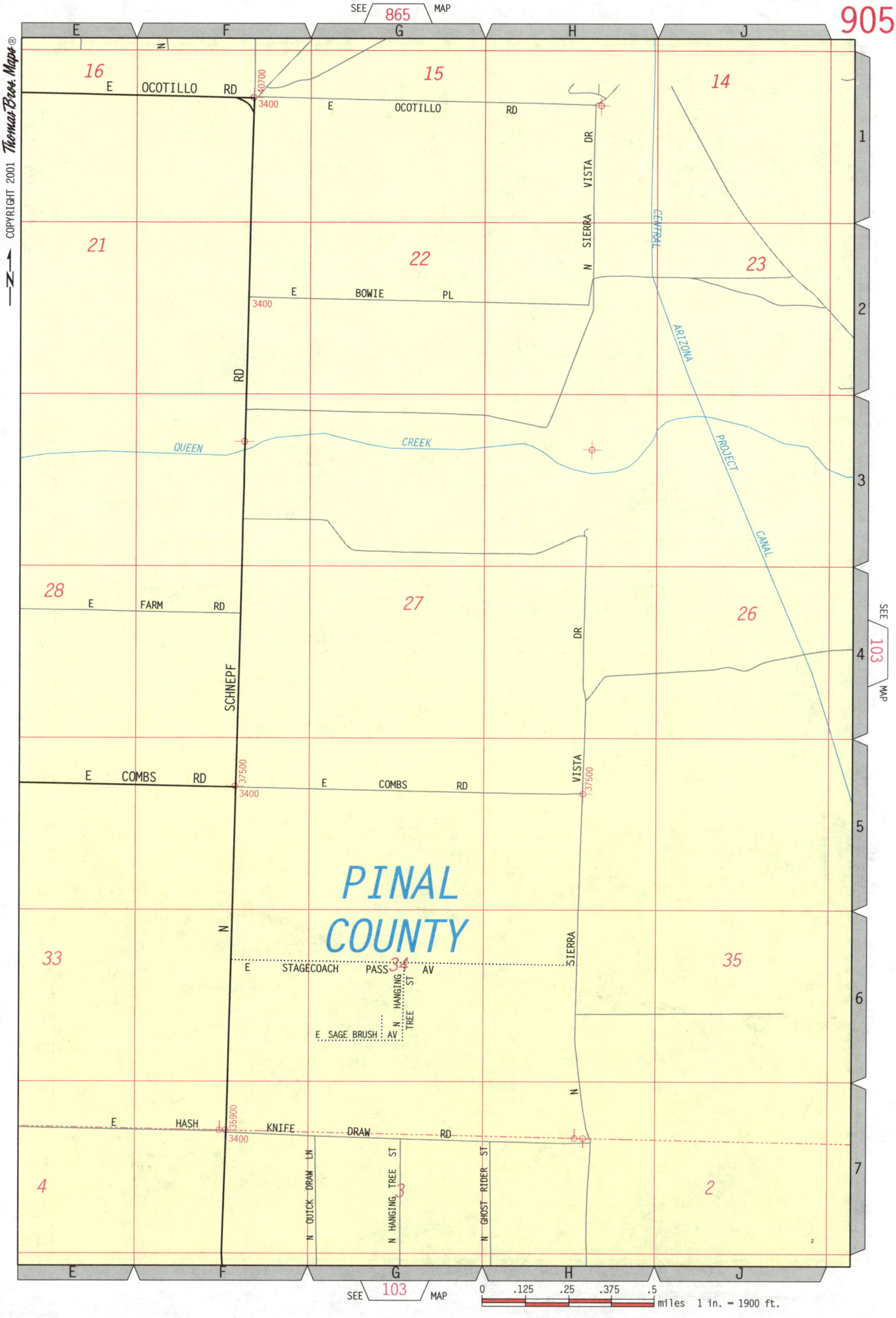
SEE 865 MAP
SEE 103 MAP
SEE 103 MAP
E
F
G
H
J
1
2
3
4
5
6
7
N
16
15
14
21
22
23
28
27
26
33
34
35
4
3
2
E OCOTILLO RD
E OCOTILLO RD
40700
3400
N SIERRA VISTA DR
CENTRAL ARIZONA PROJECT CANAL
E BOWIE PL
3400
RD
QUEEN CREEK
E FARM RD
SCHNEPF
DR
E COMBS RD
E COMBS RD
37500
3400
37500
VISTA
PINAL COUNTY
N
SIERRA
E STAGECOACH PASS AV
N HANGING TREE ST
E SAGE BRUSH AV
N
E HASH KNIFE DRAW RD
35900
3400
N QUICK DRAW LN
N HANGING TREE ST
N GHOST RIDER ST
0 .125 .25 .375 .5 miles 1 in. = 1900 ft.

PHOENIX

MAP

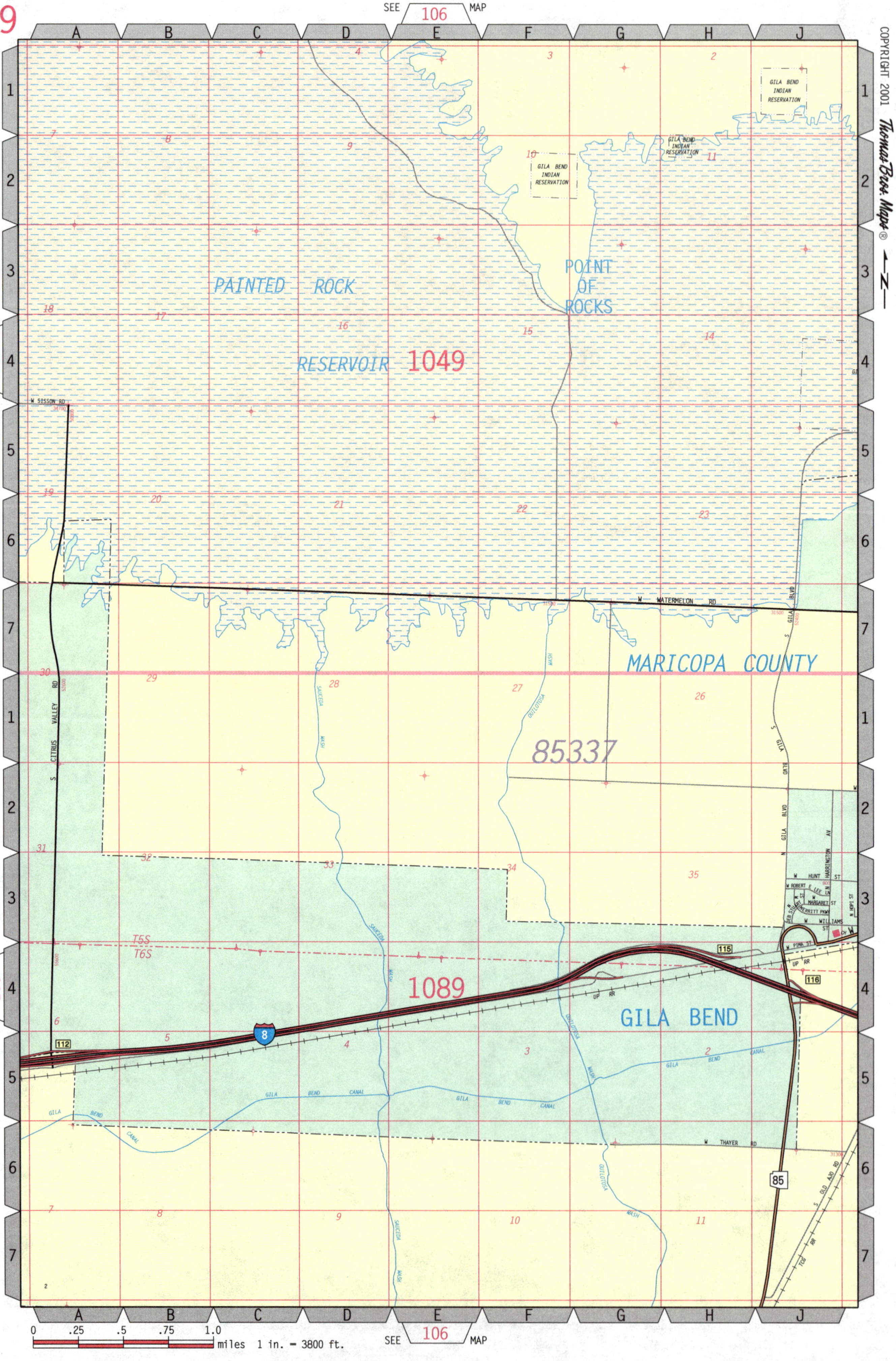
SEE 106 MAP
PAINTED ROCK
RESERVOIR
1049
POINT OF ROCKS
GILA BEND INDIAN RESERVATION
W SISSON RD
W WATERMELON RD
MARICOPA COUNTY
85337
S CITRUS VALLEY RD
S GILA BLVD
N GILA BLVD
HARRINGTON AV
HUNT ST
W ROBERT E LEE LN
MARGARET ST
MERRITT PKWY
WILLIAMS
W PIMA ST
T5S
T6S
1089
GILA BEND
UP RR
GILA BEND CANAL
SAUCEDA WASH
QUILOTOSA WASH
W THAYER RD
S OLD AJO RD
112
8
115
116
85
0 .25 .5 .75 1.0
miles 1 in. = 3800 ft.

SEE 106 MAP
GILA BEND INDIAN RESERVATION
R5W
R4W
1050
W SISSON RD
S STOUT RD
S SAN LUCY RD
W WATERMELON RD
CENTER RD
COTTON
SAN LUCY VILLAGE
GILA BEND
GILA BEND CANAL
SAND TANK WASH
W INDIAN RD
E INDIAN RD
BURLESON PARK
PIMA ST
W MARICOPA RD
GILA BEND MUNICIPAL AIRPORT
85
238
84
8
119
E MAIN ST
BUTTERFIELD TR
1090
UP RR
S CEMETERY RD
RENNER WASH
PHOENIX
MAP
miles 1 in. = 3800 ft.

PHOENIX SCHOOL DISTRICT BOUNDARY MAP

High School & Unified Districts

High School
- 201 Buckeye Union
- 205 Glendale Union
- 210 Phoenix Union
- 213 Tempe Union
- 214 Tolleson Union
- 216 Agua Fria Union

Unified
- 4 Mesa
- 11 Peoria
- 41 Gilbert
- 48 Scottsdale
- 69 Paradise Valley
- 80 Chandler
- 89 Dysart
- 97 Deer Valley

Elementary School Districts

- 1 Phoenix
- 2 Riverside
- 3 Tempe
- 4 Mesa
- 5 Isaac
- 6 Washington
- 7 Wilson
- 8 Osborn
- 11 Peoria
- 14 Creighton
- 17 Tolleson
- 21 Murphy
- 25 Liberty
- 28 Kyrene
- 31 Balsz
- 38 Madison
- 40 Glendale
- 41 Gilbert
- 44 Avondale
- 45 Fowler
- 48 Scottsdale
- 59 Laveen
- 60 Higley
- 62 Union
- 65 Littleton
- 66 Roosevelt
- 68 Alhambra
- 69 Paradise Valley
- 79 Litchfield Park
- 80 Chandler
- 81 Nadaburg
- 83 Cartwright
- 89 Dysart
- 92 Pendergast
- 93 Cave Creek
- 95 Queen Creek
- 97 Deer Valley
- 98 Fountain Hills
- 510 W.A.F.B. Accom

1 Inch to 6 Miles

0 3 6

Miles

Kilometers

LIST OF ABBREVIATIONS

PREFIXES AND SUFFIXES

AL .... ALLEY
ARC .... ARCADE
AV, AVE .... AVENUE
AVCT .... AVENUE COURT
AVD .... AVENIDA
AVD D LA .... AVENIDA DE LA
AVD D LOS .... AVENIDA DE LOS
AVD DE .... AVENIDA DE
AVD DE LAS .... AVENIDA DE LAS
AVD DEL .... AVENIDA DEL
AVDR .... AVENUE DRIVE
AVEX .... AVENUE EXTENSION
AV OF .... AVENUE OF
AV OF THE .... AVENUE OF THE
AVPL .... AVENUE PLACE
BAY .... BAY
BEND .... BEND
BL, BLVD .... BOULEVARD
BLCT .... BOULEVARD COURT
BLEX .... BOULEVARD EXTENSION
BRCH .... BRANCH
BRDG .... BRIDGE
BYPS .... BYPASS
BYWY .... BYWAY
CIDR .... CIRCLE DRIVE
CIR .... CIRCLE
CL .... CALLE
CL DE .... CALLE DE
CL DL .... CALLE DEL
CL D LA .... CALLE DE LA
CL D LAS .... CALLE DE LAS
CL D LOS .... CALLE DE LOS
CL EL .... CALLE EL
CLJ .... CALLEJON
CL LA .... CALLE LA
CL LAS .... CALLE LAS
CL LOS .... CALLE LOS
CLTR .... CLUSTER
CM .... CAMINO
CM DE .... CAMINO DE
CM DL .... CAMINO DEL
CM D LA .... CAMINO DE LA
CM D LAS .... CAMINO DE LAS
CM D LOS .... CAMINO DE LOS
CMTO .... CAMINITO
CMTO DEL .... CAMINITO DEL
CMTO D LA .... CAMINITO DE LA
CMTO D LAS .... CAMINITO DE LAS
CMTO D LOS .... CAMINITO DE LOS
CNDR .... CENTER DRIVE
COM .... COMMON
COMS .... COMMONS
CORR .... CORRIDOR
CRES .... CRESCENT
CRLO .... CIRCULO
CRSG .... CROSSING
CST .... CIRCLE STREET
CSWY .... CAUSEWAY
CT .... COURT
CTAV .... COURT AVENUE
CTE .... CORTE
CTE D .... CORTE DE
CTE DEL .... CORTE DEL
CTE D LAS .... CORTE DE LAS
CTO .... CUT OFF
CTR .... CENTER
CTST .... COURT STREET
CUR .... CURVE
CV .... COVE
DE .... DE
DIAG .... DIAGONAL
DR .... DRIVE
DRAV .... DRIVE AVENUE
DRCT .... DRIVE COURT
DRLP .... DRIVE LOOP
DVDR .... DIVISION DR
EXAV .... EXTENSION AVENUE
EXBL .... EXTENSION BOULEVARD
EXRD .... EXTENSION ROAD
EXST .... EXTENSION STREET
EXT .... EXTENSION
EXWY .... EXPRESSWAY
FOREST RT .... FOREST ROUTE
FRWY .... FREEWAY
FRY .... FERRY
GDNS .... GARDENS
GN, GLN .... GLEN
GRN .... GREEN
GRV .... GROVE
HTS .... HEIGHTS
HWY .... HIGHWAY
ISL .... ISLE
JCT .... JUNCTION
LN .... LANE
LNCR .... LANE CIRCLE
LNDG .... LANDING
LNDR .... LANE DRIVE
LNLP .... LANE LOOP
LP .... LOOP
MNR .... MANOR
MT .... MOUNT
MTWY .... MOTORWAY
MWCR .... MEWS COURT
MWLN .... MEWS LANE
NFD .... NAT'L FOREST DEV
NK .... NOOK
OH .... OUTER HIGHWAY
OVL .... OVAL
OVLK .... OVERLOOK
OVPS .... OVERPASS
PAS .... PASEO
PAS DE .... PASEO DE
PAS DE LA .... PASEO DE LA
PAS DE LAS .... PASEO DE LAS
PAS DE LOS .... PASEO DE LOS
PAS DL .... PASEO DEL
PASG .... PASSAGE
PAS LA .... PASEO LA
PAS LOS .... PASEO LOS
PASS .... PASS
PIKE .... PIKE
PK .... PARK
PKDR .... PARK DRIVE
PKWY, PKY .... PARKWAY
PL .... PLACE
PLWY .... PLACE WAY
PLZ, PZ .... PLAZA
PT .... POINT
PTAV .... POINT AVENUE
PTH .... PATH
PZ DE .... PLAZA DE
PZ DEL .... PLAZA DEL
PZ D LA .... PLAZA DE LA
PZ D LAS .... PLAZA DE LAS
PZWY .... PLAZA WAY
RAMP .... RAMP
RD .... ROAD
RDAV .... ROAD AVENUE
RDBP .... ROAD BYPASS
RDCT .... ROAD COURT
RDEX .... ROAD EXTENSION
RDG .... RIDGE
RDSP .... ROAD SPUR
RDWY .... ROAD WAY
RR .... RAILROAD
RUE .... RUE
RUE D .... RUE DE
RW .... ROW
RY .... RAILWAY
SKWY .... SKYWAY
SQ .... SQUARE
ST .... STREET
STAV .... STREET AVENUE
STCT .... STREET COURT
STDR .... STREET DRIVE
STEX .... STREET EXTENSION
STLN .... STREET LANE
STLP .... STREET LOOP
ST OF .... STREET OF
ST OF THE .... STREET OF THE
STOV .... STREET OVERPASS
STPL .... STREET PLACE
STPM .... STREET PROMENADE
STWY .... STREET WAY
STXP .... STREET EXPRESSWAY
TER .... TERRACE
TFWY .... TRAFFICWAY
THWY .... THROUGHWAY
TKTR .... TRUCK TRAIL
TPKE .... TURNPIKE
TRC .... TRACE
TRCT .... TERRACE COURT
TR, TRL .... TRAIL
TRWY .... TRAIL WAY
TTSP .... TRUCK TRAIL SPUR
TUN .... TUNNEL
UNPS .... UNDERPASS
VIA D .... VIA DE
VIA DL .... VIA DEL
VIA D LA .... VIA DE LA
VIA D LAS .... VIA DE LAS
VIA D LOS .... VIA DE LOS
VIA LA .... VIA LA
VW .... VIEW
VWY .... VIEW WAY
VIS .... VISTA
VIS D .... VISTA DE
VIS D L .... VISTA DE LA
VIS D LAS .... VISTA DE LAS
VIS DEL .... VISTA DEL
WK .... WALK
WY .... WAY
WYCR .... WAY CIRCLE
WYDR .... WAY DRIVE
WYLN .... WAY LANE
WYPL .... WAY PLACE

DIRECTIONS

E .... EAST
KPN .... KEY PENINSULA NORTH
KPS .... KEY PENINSULA SOUTH
N .... NORTH
NE .... NORTHEAST
NW .... NORTHWEST
S .... SOUTH
SE .... SOUTHEAST
SW .... SOUTHWEST
W .... WEST

DEPARTMENT STORES

BD .... BLOOMINGDALES
BN .... THE BON MARCHE
D .... DIAMONDS
DL .... DILLARDS
G .... GOLDWATERS
GT .... GOTTSCHALKS
H .... HARRIS
IM .... I MAGNIN
MA .... MACY'S
ME .... MERVYN'S
MF .... MEIER & FRANK
N .... NORDSTROM
NM .... NEIMAN-MARCUS
P .... J C PENNEY
RM .... ROBINSONS MAY
S .... SEARS
SF .... SAKS FIFTH AVENUE

BUILDINGS

CC .... CHAMBER OF COMMERCE
CH .... CITY HALL
CHP .... CALIFORNIA HIGHWAY PATROL
COMM CTR .... COMMUNITY CENTER
CON CTR .... CONVENTION CENTER
CONT HS .... CONTINUATION HIGH SCHOOL
CTH .... COURT HOUSE
DMV .... DEPT OF MOTOR VEHICLES
FAA .... FEDERAL AVIATION ADMIN
FS .... FIRE STATION
HOSP .... HOSPITAL
HS .... HIGH SCHOOL
INT .... INTERMEDIATE SCHOOL
JR HS .... JUNIOR HIGH SCHOOL
LIB .... LIBRARY
MID .... MIDDLE SCHOOL
MUS .... MUSEUM
PO .... POST OFFICE
PS .... POLICE STATION
SR CIT CTR .... SENIOR CITIZENS CENTER
STA .... STATION
THTR .... THEATER
VIS BUR .... VISITORS BUREAU

OTHER ABBREVIATIONS

BCH .... BEACH
BLDG .... BUILDING
CEM .... CEMETERY
CK .... CREEK
CO .... COUNTY
COMM .... COMMUNITY
CTR .... CENTER
EST .... ESTATE
HIST .... HISTORIC
HTS .... HEIGHTS
LK .... LAKE
MDW .... MEADOW
MED .... MEDICAL
MEM .... MEMORIAL
MHP .... MOBILE HOME PARK
MT .... MOUNT
MTN .... MOUNTAIN
NATL .... NATIONAL
PKG .... PARKING
PLGD .... PLAYGROUND
RCH .... RANCH
RCHO .... RANCHO
REC .... RECREATION
RES .... RESERVOIR
RIV .... RIVER
RR .... RAILROAD
SPG .... SPRING
STA .... SANTA
VLG .... VILLAGE
VLY .... VALLEY
VW .... VIEW

STREET
Block City ZIP Pg-Grid

A

N A PZ
4700 PHX 85031 657-E5
N A ST
4600 PHX 85031 657-E5
12600 ELMG 85335 575-G5
S A ST
- MarC 85337 (1090-B1
See Page 1049)
200 MESA 85210 781-H3
W A ST
30700 MarC 85337 (1090-B1
See Page 1049)
N AARON
9500 MarC 85207 744-E2
S AARON
1600 MESA 85208 784-D3
N AARON CIR
- MarC 85207 744-E2
N ABAJO DR
25200 MarC 85263 (504-A6
See Page 503)
N ABALONE DR
200 GIL 85233 781-J5
S ABALONE DR
100 GIL 85233 781-H7
100 GIL 85233 821-H3
S ABBEY
- MESA 85212 784-E6
S ABBEY CIR
- MESA 85212 784-E6
N ABBEY LN
11800 FTNH 85268 623-C2
W ABBOTT AV
10700 MarC 85351 615-J2
W ABERDEEN DR
- SURP 85374 534-D5
N ABERDEEN RD
10600 PHX 85254 620-C2
E ABILENE AV
- MarC 85220 744-H6
- MESA 85220 744-G6
7200 MESA 85208 743-H6
S ABILENE CT
1200 GIL 85233 822-A3
N ABILENE DR
800 GIL 85233 782-B4
S ABILENE DR
- GIL 85233 782-A7
300 GIL 85233 822-A2
S ABILENE ST
400 GIL 85233 822-B1
N ABNER
1100 MESA 85205 743-D1
S ABNER CIR
1800 MESA 85205 743-D1
E ABRAHAM LN
4300 PHX 85050 539-J2
4600 PHX 85050 540-A3
4800 PHX 85054 540-A3
W ABRAHAM LN
2900 PHX 85027 538-B2
3500 PHX 85308 538-A2
3600 PHX 85308 537-J2
5600 GLEN 85308 537-A2
7200 GLEN 85308 536-J2
E ACACIA
2000 MESA 85204 742-D7
N ACACIA
2200 MESA 85213 702-D6
S ACACIA
400 MESA 85204 742-D6
ACACIA CIR
900 LP 85340 655-B5
N ACACIA CIR
- MESA 85213 702-D7
E ACACIA CT
- GDYR 85326 (774-A7
See Page 733)
S ACACIA CT
3700 CHAN 85248 861-A7
W ACACIA CT
16100 SURP 85374 534-E2
E ACACIA DR
10000 SCTS 85260 581-F2
10300 SCTS 85259 581-F2
N ACACIA DR
- GIL 85233 781-J4
S ACACIA DR
3500 CHAN 85248 861-A6
W ACACIA DR
10800 MarC 85373 535-J6
N ACACIA RD
- APJT 85219 745-H4
S ACACIA RD
- APJT 85219 745-H6
1200 APJT 85219 785-H2
2400 PinC 85219 785-H2
S ACACIA ST
800 MESA 85213 742-D1
1800 MESA 85213 702-D7
E ACACIA WY
15300 FTNH 85268 582-J6
15500 FTNH 85268 583-A5
N ACADIA WY
- MarC 85087 (378-A3
See Page 337)
S ACANTHUS
2300 MESA 85208 783-H5
N ACAPULCO DR
21800 MarC 85375 534-H1
22500 MarC 85375 494-H7
E ACAPULCO LN
- PHX 85022 578-H3
S ACAPULCO LN
900 TEMP 85281 740-H4
W ACAPULCO LN
- SURP 85379 575-C3
600 TEMP 85282 780-C3
2300 PHX 85023 578-C3
2700 PHX 85053 578-A3
3500 PHX 85053 577-J3
5100 GLEN 85306 577-B3
7700 PEOR 85381 576-E3
15200 SURP 85379 (574-E2
See Page 573)
S ACHILLES WY
- QC 85242 904-D6
ACOMA DR
- SCTS 85259 581-G5
E ACOMA DR
- SCTS 85259 581-F5
- SCTS 85260 581-F5
700 PHX 85022 578-J4
1100 PHX 85022 579-A4
2400 PHX 85032 579-D4
4700 PHX 85032 580-A4
4800 PHX 85254 580-A4

E ACOMA DR
7200 SCTS 85254 580-F5
7200 SCTS 85260 580-H5
N ACOMA DR
14600 GLEN 85306 577-C4
W ACOMA DR
- ELMG 85335 575-D3
- ELMG 85379 575-D3
- SURP 85379 (574-G3
See Page 573)
- SURP 85379 575-C3
1600 PHX 85023 578-C4
2700 PHX 85053 578-A4
3500 PHX 85053 577-H4
4300 PHX 85306 577-F4
5100 GLEN 85306 577-C4
6700 MarC 85306 577-A4
6700 MarC 85381 577-A4
6800 PEOR 85381 577-A4
7100 MarC 85381 576-G4
7500 PEOR 85381 576-E4
17900 MarC 85379 (574-G3
See Page 573)
18000 MarC 85379 573-J3
N ACOMA RD
14400 PHX 85023 578-E4
W ACOMA RD
- SURP 85379 (574-F3
See Page 573)
1700 PHX 85023 578-E4
N ADAIR CIR
- MESA 85207 704-D6
W ADAM AV
- PEOR 85308 536-G2
- PEOR 85382 536-A2
10700 PEOR 85373 536-A2
10800 PEOR 85373 535-J2
E ADAMANDA CT
500 MarC 85086 (418-J2
See Page 417)
E ADAMANDA DR
200 MarC 85086 (418-J2
See Page 417)
N ADAMS AV
200 CHAN 85225 821-J4
S ADAMS AV
- MarC 85249 901-J1
N ADAMS CT
900 CHAN 85225 821-J4
E ADAMS ST
- PHX 85004 698-G6
1200 PHX 85034 698-J6
1400 PHX 85034 699-A6
N ADAMS ST
- WICK 85390 290-E2
S ADAMS ST
100 WICK 85390 290-E3
W ADAMS ST
- AVON 85323 695-D6
- AVON 85353 695-F6
- GDYR 85338 (694-D5
See Page 653)
- PHX 85003 698-E6
- PHX 85009 698-A6
200 PHX 85043 696-J6
600 PHX 85007 698-E6
3200 PHX 85009 697-H6
9100 TOL 85353 696-C6
E ADDAX DR
- SCTS 85262 421-F4
W ADDIE LN
- SURP 85374 534-A5
W ADELA DR
10500 PEOR 85382 496-A7
E ADELE CT
7300 SCTS 85255 500-G7
10000 SCTS 85255 501-E7
10000 SCTS 85255 541-E1
S ADELLE
- MarC 85212 824-J1
- MESA 85212 784-J7
- MESA 85212 824-J1
S ADELLE CIR
- MarC 85212 824-J1
- MESA 85212 784-J7
E ADELPHI DR
600 TEMP 85281 740-E5
N ADKINSON DR
22700 MarC 85375 494-J7
E ADOBE CIR
18600 MarC 85263 503-J3
N ADOBE CT
17800 SURP 85374 534-E6
S ADOBE CT
- MarC 85249 902-C3
W ADOBE CT
9700 MarC 85382 536-C4
E ADOBE DR
- PHX 85255 540-G2
4000 PHX 85050 539-J2
4600 PHX 85050 540-A2
8100 SCTS 85255 540-G2
8200 SCTS 85255 541-A2
S ADOBE DR
- MarC 85249 902-C5
W ADOBE DR
1900 PHX 85027 538-B1
6400 GLEN 85308 537-B4
7700 GLEN 85308 536-H4
8800 MarC 85382 536-E1
E ADOBE RD
- MarC 85220 745-A4
- MESA 85220 745-A4
3800 MESA 85205 742-J3
4200 MESA 85205 743-B3
5800 MarC 85205 743-E3
6800 MESA 85207 743-H3
7800 MESA 85207 744-A3
8900 MarC 85207 744-C4
9900 MarC 85220 744-F4
9900 MESA 85220 744-F4
E ADOBE ST
2000 MESA 85203 742-F3
2000 MESA 85213 742-F3
3600 MESA 85205 742-F3
E ADOBE WY
18200 MarC 85263 503-H3
N ADOBE WY
27700 MarC 85263 503-H3
W ADOBE DAM RD
- PHX 85027 538-A1
N ADVENTURE CT
- MarC 85086 (378-D7
See Page 337)
W ADVENTURE DR
- MarC 85086 (378-C7
See Page 337)
N ADVENTURE TR
- MarC 85087 (378-A4
See Page 337)

E AEPLI DR
200 TEMP 85282 740-E6
N AERIE CLIFF
- FTNH 85268 622-G5
N AGAPE CT
15000 FTNH 85268 583-E5
S AGATE DR
24000 MarC 85248 900-J3
S AGATE PL
- MarC 85249 902-F4
E AGATE WY
- MarC 85249 902-F5
S AGATE WY
- MarC 85249 902-F5
E AGATE KNOLL PL
16600 FTNH 85268 583-A3
E AGAVE CIR
- CARE 85377 460-D1
N AGAVE CT
- GDYR 85326 (774-A7
See Page 733)
W AGAVE CT
11600 SURP 85374 535-G6
N AGAVE DR
14400 FTNH 85268 583-A5
E AGAVE LN
- CVCK 85331 420-A7
E AGAVE PL
5800 CARE 85377 420-D7
E AGAVE RD
3600 PHX 85044 819-E3
N AGAVE RD
26000 MarC 85263 503-J5
W AGAVE ST
2700 PinC 85220 705-B6
S AGAVE WY
3600 CHAN 85248 861-B6
W AGEAN CT
14300 MarC 85375 535-A3
W AGUA CALIENTE EXRD
21000 MarC 85354 101-C3
35100 MarC 85322 102-A3
35100 MarC 85354 102-A3
S AGUA CALIENTE RD
53300 MarC 85337 105-C1
N AGUA FRIA DR
14400 MarC 85351 575-J2
AGUA FRIA FRWY Rt#-101
- GLEN - 536-G5
- GLEN - 537-A4
- GLEN - 576-E5
- MarC - 616-C6
- MarC - 656-C3
- MarC - 696-C1
- PEOR - 576-E5
- PEOR - 616-C6
- PHX - 537-G4
- PHX - 538-A4
- PHX - 656-C3
- PHX - 696-B4
- TOL - 696-B4
E AGUA FRIA LN
- AVON 85323 735-B1
W AGUA LINDA LN
15400 SURP 85374 534-G5
E AGUA VERDE DR
18400 MarC 85263 503-J4
N AGUA VERDE DR
27400 MarC 85263 503-H3
E AGUA VISTA WY
10000 PinC 85219 786-H6
W AGUILA DR
1700 WICK 85390 290-A4
N AGUILA RD
26600 MarC 85263 503-H4
40300 MarC 85320 102-A2
N AGUILAR DR
14200 FTNH 85268 583-E6
N AGUSTA LN
17000 SURP 85374 534-F7
N AHOY DR
800 GIL 85234 782-H5
E AHWATUKEE DR
3500 PHX 85044 819-G1
4700 PHX 85044 779-H7
S AHWATUKEE DR
11000 PHX 85044 779-H7
11300 PHX 85044 819-H1
E AIR LN
2400 PHX 85034 699-D7
3600 PHX 85034 739-F1
S AIRCLETA DR
- WICK 85390 290-A4
E AIRE LIBRE AV
700 PHX 85022 578-J2
1500 PHX 85022 579-A2
2500 PHX 85032 579-D2
4600 PHX 85032 580-A2
4800 PHX 85254 580-A2
W AIRE LIBRE AV
- PHX 85023 578-F2
3300 PHX 85053 578-A1
3400 PHX 85053 577-J1
4600 PHX 85306 577-F1
5200 GLEN 85306 577-D1
6700 GLEN 85382 577-A1
E AIRE LIBRE LN
6000 PHX 85254 580-E2
W AIRE LIBRE LN
2900 PHX 85053 578-B2
E AIRPORT BLVD
500 PHX 85024 538-H1
500 PHX 85027 538-H1
S AIRPORT BLVD
1900 CHAN 85249 861-J4
E AIRPORT DR
- PinC 85242 865-F7
N AIRPORT DR
14000 SCTS 85260 580-H4
S AIRPORT RD
1200 MarC 85326 (693-B7
See Page 653)
1200 MarC 85326 733-B4
4400 BUCK 85326 733-B4
4400 MarC 85326 (773-B2
See Page 733)
9200 BUCK 85326 (773-B2
See Page 733)
12800 MarC 85326 813-A1
E AJAVE DR
- SCTS 85255 501-H3
E AJO CIR
- PHX 85044 779-H7
N AJO RD
7500 SCTS 85258 660-H1
E AKRON ST
5400 MESA 85205 743-C5
6100 MESA 85205 743-E5

E AKRON ST
6700 MESA 85207 743-G5
7600 MarC 85207 743-J5
8000 MarC 85207 744-A5
10000 MarC 85220 744-F5
W ALABAMA AV
9700 MarC 85351 576-B7
10700 MarC 85351 575-J7
11100 YNTN 85335 575-H7
N ALAMANZA LN
- MarC 85340 655-B2
E ALAMEDA DR
- TEMP 85282 740-F7
100 MarC 85282 740-E7
2100 TEMP 85282 741-A7
W ALAMEDA DR
- TEMP 85282 740-A7
1800 TEMP 85282 739-J7
E ALAMEDA RD
7100 PHX 85255 500-G7
7100 SCTS 85255 500-H6
8000 SCTS 85255 501-A7
11800 SCTS 85255 502-A7
N ALAMEDA RD
6000 PHX 85310 497-D6
S ALAMEDA RD
5500 PinC 85219 786-H6
W ALAMEDA RD
3500 PHX 85027 498-A6
3500 PHX 85310 498-A6
3700 PHX 85310 497-C6
N ALAMO
2400 MESA 85213 702-E3
S ALAMO
400 MESA 85204 742-G6
N ALAMO CIR
800 MESA 85213 742-E1
2100 MESA 85213 702-E7
S ALAMO CIR
1200 MESA 85204 782-D1
W ALAMO CT
1700 CHAN 85224 781-C7
E ALAMO DR
100 CHAN 85225 781-G7
N ALAMO DR
- SURP 85374 534-A5
2800 CHAN 85224 781-C7
W ALAMO DR
300 CHAN 85225 781-E7
1300 CHAN 85224 781-B7
W ALAMO CUTOFF RD
- MarC 85320 244-F3
- YavC - 244-F3
E ALAMOSA AV
16800 FTNH 85268 583-D5
N ALAMOSA CIR
14800 FTNH 85268 583-D5
N ALAN CT
900 CHAN 85226 820-H4
E ALAN LN
4000 PHX 85028 619-H3
5400 PHX 85253 620-B3
N ALARCON BLVD
100 BUCK 85326 (732-A7
See Page 731)
ALASKA
6500 PinC 85219 786-D7
6500 PinC 85219 826-D1
N ALBA
1000 MESA 85213 742-F2
2000 MESA 85213 702-G5
N ALBA CIR
500 MESA 85213 742-F2
S ALBA CIR
600 MESA 85204 742-F7
1600 MESA 85204 782-F2
N ALBA LN
2200 MESA 85213 702-G6
E ALBANY ST
5400 MarC 85205 743-C5
6700 MESA 85205 743-F5
6700 MESA 85207 743-G5
7600 MarC 85207 743-J5
8100 MarC 85207 744-A5
10300 MarC 85220 744-G5
S ALBERT AV
500 TEMP 85281 740-B3
2900 TEMP 85282 740-B7
3200 TEMP 85282 780-A1
N ALBERT DR
- CHAN 85226 820-F4
W ALBERT LN
- PEOR 85308 536-H3
- PEOR 85382 536-D2
N ALBERTA
600 MESA 85205 742-H4
W ALBERTA
- PEOR 85345 616-C1
N ALCALA DR
600 LP 85340 655-A5
W ALCOTT ST
1600 MESA 85201 741-C5
E ALDER AV
- MESA 85206 743-F6
100 MarC 85208 744-C6
3700 MESA 85206 742-J5
6700 MESA 85208 743-F6
E ALDER CIR
2000 MESA 85204 742-D5
9500 MarC 85208 744-E6
N ALDER CIR
1100 GIL 85233 782-C4
N ALDER DR
600 CHAN 85226 820-G3
S ALDER DR
2600 TEMP 85282 740-H7
3500 TEMP 85282 780-H1
5800 TEMP 85283 780-G4
7700 TEMP 85284 780-G7
9100 TEMP 85284 820-G3
S ALDER ST
1700 GIL 85233 822-C5
S ALDERWOOD CIR
- MESA 85212 784-G4
E ALDINE ST
2300 PHX 85022 579-C7
2300 PHX 85032 579-D7
W ALEGRE DR
200 LP 85340 655-A5
W ALEGRIA CT
- SURP 85374 534-H5
W ALEPPO DR
13200 MarC 85375 535-A5
N ALETTA
- MESA 85207 743-J4
S ALETTA
- MESA 85212 783-H6
W ALEX AV
- PEOR 85308 536-G2
- PEOR 85382 536-A2

W ALEX AV
10700 PEOR 85373 535-J2
10700 PEOR 85373 536-A2
W ALEX LP
- PHX 85310 497-H4
E ALEXANDER BLVD
- TEMP 85284 820-D3
W ALEXANDRIA WY
7300 PEOR 85381 576-H5
N ALEXIS DR
1300 GIL 85236 783-E4
E ALFALFA DR
- GIL 85236 863-F5
E ALGONQUIN CT
17500 FTNH 85268 583-E5
S ALHAMBRA WY
5900 PinC 85219 786-J7
6500 PinC 85219 826-J1
E ALICE AV
- PHX 85020 618-H5
1200 PHX 85020 619-A5
N ALICE AV
8700 PHX 85051 618-A4
W ALICE AV
100 PHX 85021 618-C4
2700 PHX 85051 618-B5
3400 PHX 85051 617-J4
4300 GLEN 85302 617-C4
6900 GLEN 85345 616-J4
6900 GLEN 85345 617-A4
8300 PEOR 85345 616-A4
10500 PEOR 85345 615-H4
N ALICIA
- MarC 85207 744-E3
S ALICIA
- MESA 85212 784-E4
E ALICIA DR
- PHX 85040 778-J3
2400 PHX 85040 779-A3
W ALICIA DR
- PHX 85339 777-E3
E ALISO CANYON CT
4300 PHX 85044 779-G5
E ALISTER MCKENZIE DR
9300 SCTS 85262 421-D1
N ALISTER MCKENZIE DR
38800 SCTS 85262 421-D1
S ALL AMERICAN WY
- TEMP 85283 780-D4
E ALLEGANY ST
17700 MarC 85264 583-F6
W ALLEGRO CT
13200 MarC 85375 535-D4
W ALLEGRO DR
12300 MarC 85375 535-E4
E ALLEN
1300 MESA 85203 742-B2
N ALLEN
900 MESA 85203 742-B1
S ALLEN
- MESA 85204 742-B5
900 MESA 85204 782-B1
S ALLEN AV
- GIL 85296 822-D7
- MarC 85296 822-D7
- MarC 85296 862-D1
S ALLEN CIR
800 MESA 85204 742-B7
N ALLEN ST
- MESA 85203 702-B7
W ALLEN ST
- MarC 85339 777-F3
- PHX 85041 778-E4
- PHX 85339 777-E3
S ALLESANDRO CT
- GIL 85236 863-B5
W ALLISON DR
- TEMP 85282 779-J1
E ALLISON RD
5600 MarC 85226 860-A1
E ALLRED AV
2500 MESA 85204 742-E5
S ALLRED DR
2400 TEMP 85282 741-A7
3200 TEMP 85282 781-A1
S ALLRED ST
500 TEMP 85281 741-B4
S ALMAR
1400 MESA 85204 782-G2
E ALMAR CIR
3200 MESA 85213 742-G3
N ALMAR CIR
600 MESA 85213 742-G3
S ALMAR CIR
900 MESA 85204 782-G1
N ALMA SCHOOL PKWY
26700 SCTS 85255 501-G3
28300 SCTS 85262 501-H2
29000 SCTS 85262 (461-H7
See Page 421)
ALMA SCHOOL RD
- PinC - 901-D7
N ALMA SCHOOL RD
- MESA 85201 741-E4
- MESA 85210 741-E4
- MESA 85202 741-E4
- CHAN 85224 821-D4
- CHAN 85225 821-D4
700 MarC 85256 701-E3
1100 MESA 85201 741-E4
1600 MESA 85201 701-E6
2600 CHAN 85225 781-D7
2600 CHAN 85224 781-D7
4100 MarC 85256 661-E7
5000 MarC 85250 661-E7
7000 MarC 85258 621-E6
7000 MarC 85258 661-E7
9600 SCTS 85255 501-F5
S ALMA SCHOOL RD
- MESA 85202 741-E6
- MESA 85210 741-E6
- CHAN 85224 821-D7
- CHAN 85225 821-D7
700 CHAN 85224 861-D3
700 CHAN 85225 861-D3
1000 CHAN 85248 861-D3
1000 MESA 85202 781-D5
1000 MESA 85210 781-D5
3100 MESA 85224 781-D5
3100 MESA 85225 781-D5
4200 CHAN 85248 901-C1
23600 MarC 85248 901-D5
E ALMEDA CT
5600 MarC 85331 500-C1
W ALMERIA DR
5200 PHX 85035 697-D4
E ALMERIA RD
1100 PHX 85006 698-J4

E ALMERIA RD
1400 PHX 85006 699-A4
2200 PHX 85008 699-C4
6600 SCTS 85257 700-E4
W ALMERIA RD
- AVON 85323 695-D3
- GDYR 85338 695-B3
100 PHX 85003 698-F4
2200 PHX 85009 698-A4
3500 PHX 85009 697-G4
4700 PHX 85035 697-A4
6900 PHX 85035 696-J4
8400 PHX 85037 696-F3
W ALMO DR
1200 CHAN 85224 781-D7
N ALMOND
- MESA 85213 702-E7
1600 MESA 85213 742-E1
S ALMOND
1600 MESA 85204 782-D2
N ALMOND CIR
800 MESA 85213 742-E2
2000 MESA 85213 702-E7
S ALMOND CIR
1300 MESA 85204 782-E1
S ALMOND DR
- GIL 85236 863-E5
N ALMOND ST
2100 MESA 85213 702-E5
E ALMONT DR
16600 FTNH 85268 583-C6
E ALOE CIR
7900 PinC 85219 786-E6
N ALOE CT
19000 MarC 85375 535-A5
E ALOE DR
8600 PinC 85219 786-F6
17000 FTNH 85268 583-D6
W ALOE PL
1000 CHAN 85248 861-D7
E ALOE WY
18400 MarC 85263 503-H6
E ALOE VERA CIR
8300 PinC 85219 786-F6
E ALOE VERA DR
7100 SCTS 85262 460-G3
W ALOHA CIR
20300 MarC 85375 534-H3
W ALOHA DR
14900 MarC 85375 534-H3
E ALONDRA WY
19000 MarC 85263 503-J5
19000 MarC 85263 (504-A5
See Page 503)
N ALONDRA WY
25700 MarC 85263 503-J5
25700 MarC 85263 (504-A5
See Page 503)
W ALPACA DR
14900 MarC 85375 534-H3
S ALPHA DR
600 TEMP 85281 740-F4
S ALPINE
1600 MESA 85204 782-E2
E ALPINE AV
2200 MESA 85204 742-D5
5400 MESA 85206 743-C6
S ALPINE AV
300 MESA 85204 742-E6
W ALPINE RIDGE DR
15800 SURP 85374 534-F4
N AL SIEBER RD
500 PinC 85219 746-B3
S AL SIEBER RD
600 PinC 85219 746-B7
N ALSUP AV
1600 GDYR 85338 (694-E2
See Page 653)
4100 GDYR 85338 (654-E3
See Page 653)
5000 GLEN 85340 (654-E1
See Page 653)
5000 MarC 85340 (654-E1
See Page 653)
6300 MarC 85340 (614-E6
See Page 573)
E ALTADENA AV
2700 PHX 85028 619-D1
4800 PHX 85254 620-A1
8800 SCTS 85260 621-B1
10900 SCTS 85259 621-G2
12000 SCTS 85259 622-A1
W ALTADENA AV
2000 PHX 85029 618-A1
3100 PHX 85029 578-A7
3500 PHX 85029 617-J1
4300 PHX 85304 617-F1
4800 PHX 85304 577-D7
5200 GLEN 85304 577-B7
E ALTADENA DR
8600 SCTS 85260 621-A1
E ALTA HACIENDA DR
6200 PHX 85251 660-D6
N ALTA HACIENDA DR
4500 PHX 85018 660-B6
E ALTA LOMA CIR
17200 FTNH 85268 583-E7
N ALTA LOMA DR
19800 MarC 85375 535-B4
E ALTA MESA AV
4000 PHX 85044 779-F6
N ALTA MESA DR
800 MESA 85205 743-D1
1900 MESA 85205 703-D7
E ALTA SIERRA CIR
7800 SCTS 85262 460-J6
S ALTA VISTA
2700 MESA 85202 781-B5
S ALTA VISTA CIR
1900 MESA 85202 781-B3
E ALTA VISTA RD
- PHX 85040 778-G1
1400 PHX 85040 779-A1
W ALTA VISTA RD
- PHX 85041 778-C1
3900 PHX 85041 777-G1
4100 PHX 85339 777-G1
6500 MarC 85339 737-A7
7700 MarC 85339 736-G7
12100 MarC 85353 735-E7
12200 MarC 85353 735-E7
S ALTO DR
3600 TEMP 85282 781-A1
N ALTO ST
13800 ELMG 85335 575-F4
E ALTON RD
10400 SCTS 85255 501-G7
W ALTON ST
51000 MarC 85320 (284-J4
See Page 244)

N ALTOS DR
1500 CHAN 85224 821-B3
S ALVA ST
- BUCK 85326 (772-B2
See Page 731)
W ALVARADO CIR
13100 GDYR 85338 695-C3
N ALVARADO DR
15200 FTNH 85268 582-J4
W ALVARADO DR
- GDYR 85338 (694-J2
See Page 653)
13200 GDYR 85338 695-B2
E ALVARADO RD
100 PHX 85004 698-H3
N ALVARADO RD
1600 PHX 85004 698-G4
W ALVARADO RD
- AVON 85323 696-A3
2000 PHX 85009 698-A3
6100 PHX 85035 697-B3
7100 PHX 85035 696-H3
8600 PHX 85037 696-E3
12300 AVON 85323 695-C2
W ALVARADO ST
- PHX 85037 696-F3
N ALVARO
- MESA 85206 783-C2
900 MESA 85205 743-C3
N ALVARO CIR
- MESA 85206 783-C2
800 MESA 85205 743-C3
S ALVARO CIR
300 MESA 85206 743-D6
W ALVIN RD
50700 MarC 85320 (284-H6
See Page 244)
50700 MarC 85320 (285-A6
See Page 244)
E ALYSSA RD
- QC 85242 864-D6
N ALYSSUM DR
13000 MarC 85375 535-D6
E ALYSSUM LN
7700 MESA 85208 743-J7
N ALZORA WY
800 TOL 85353 696-E4
W ALZORA WY
8800 TOL 85353 696-D4
E AMABISCA CIR
- BUCK 85326 (772-B2
See Page 731)
E AMANDA BLVD
- CHAN 85249 902-B4
S AMANDA BLVD
- CHAN 85249 902-A6
E AMANDA LN
700 TEMP 85284 820-E3
W AMANDA LN
1000 TEMP 85284 820-A3
N AMANDES
- MESA 85208 784-F2
E AMARADO CIR
18500 MarC 85263 503-J4
W AMARANTH LN
- MarC 85390 290-E4
S AMARYLLIS
2600 MESA 85208 783-J5
E AMBASSADOR DR
200 TEMP 85281 700-E7
N AMBER
1300 MESA 85203 742-B2
N AMBER CIR
1000 MESA 85203 742-B2
N AMBER CT
- CHAN 85225 822-A5
E AMBER LN
- GIL 85236 823-B1
- MarC 85236 823-B1
2000 GIL 85236 822-H1
N AMBER ST
300 CHAN 85225 822-A3
1700 MESA 85203 742-B1
S AMBER ST
- CHAN 85249 862-A1
- MarC 85249 902-A2
W AMBER TR
9700 MarC 85351 576-A1
10700 MarC 85351 575-H1
E AMBER RIDGE WY
400 PHX 85048 818-G5
2400 PHX 85048 819-B6
E AMBER SUN DR
- PHX 85331 459-J1
6200 SCTS 85262 460-E1
E AMBERWOOD DR
800 PHX 85048 818-H6
2500 PHX 85048 819-C6
N AMBERWOOD DR
17500 SURP 85374 534-F6
S AMBERWOOD DR
5300 CHAN 85248 901-E3
W AMBERWOOD DR
- PHX 85048 818-F6
700 PHX 85045 818-D6
1800 PHX 85041 818-C6
N AMBROSIA
800 MESA 85205 743-D2
S AMBROSIA DR
3300 CHAN 85248 861-B6
S AMBROSIA WY
- PinC 85219 786-F5
S AMBUSH PASS
- GIL 85236 863-D2
E AMELIA AV
700 PHX 85012 658-H7
700 PHX 85014 658-H7
1400 PHX 85014 659-A7
1600 PHX 85016 659-A7
3400 PHX 85018 659-F7
3900 SCTS 85251 700-H1
4200 PHX 85018 699-J1
4900 PHX 85018 700-H1
8600 SCTS 85251 701-A1
W AMELIA AV
- AVON 85323 656-A7
- AVON 85340 655-D7
- GDYR 85338 (654-H6
See Page 653)
- GDYR 85338 655-D7
- MarC 85340 653-E6
100 PHX 85013 658-E7
1500 PHX 85015 658-C7
4800 PHX 85031 657-D7
6400 PHX 85033 657-A7
6900 PHX 85033 656-F7
8400 PHX 85037 656-E7
11000 AVON 85323 655-H7

STREET
Block City ZIP Pg-Grid

E ASTER DR
- PHX 85022 578-H6
2400 PHX 85032 579-D6
5600 PHX 85254 580-C7
7500 SCTS 85260 580-H7
8300 SCTS 85260 581-A7
12600 SCTS 85259 582-E7
W ASTER DR
700 CHAN 85248 861-D6
1100 PHX 85029 578-A6
3600 PHX 85029 577-H6
4200 PHX 85304 577-F6
5100 GLEN 85304 577-B6
7300 PEOR 85381 576-F6
11700 ELMG 85335 575-E5
W ASTER LN
11500 AVON 85323 655-G7
N ASTER ST
1700 TEMP 85281 700-F7
W ASTOR RD
6700 MarC 85381 577-A6
N ASTORIA WY
- MarC 85086 (378-E5 See Page 337)
E ASU CIR
2000 TEMP 85284 780-J7
N ATCHISON CIR
- WICK 85390 290-C2
N ATCHISON LN
- WICK 85390 290-C2
N ATHENA
- MESA 85207 703-H6
S ATHENA
2100 MESA 85208 783-H4
6400 MESA 85212 823-G7
6400 MESA 85212 863-G1
E ATHENA CIR
2500 MESA 85208 783-G5
W ATHENS ST
8500 PEOR 85382 536-E7
9100 PEOR 85373 536-D7
S ATHERTON BLVD
- GIL 85236 863-C2
E ATLANTA AV
700 PHX 85040 738-H6
1700 PHX 85040 739-A6
W ATLANTA AV
500 PHX 85041 738-C6
3700 PHX 85041 737-H6
E ATLANTA WY
- PHX 85040 739-E6
W ATLANTIC DR
1200 GIL 85233 821-J1
E ATREVIDO
8100 SCTS 85262 460-J7
8100 SCTS 85262 (461-A7 See Page 421)
N ATREVIDO
29800 SCTS 85262 (461-B6 See Page 421)
E ATTLEBORO RD
- GIL 85296 822-D7
- MarC 85236 823-B7
N ATWOOD
- MarC 85207 704-C6
- MESA 85207 744-C2
E AUBURN DR
200 TEMP 85283 780-H3
W AUBURN DR
1100 TEMP 85283 780-B3
E AUBURN ST
- MarC 85205 743-F5
- MESA 85205 743-F5
W AUBURN ST
1600 MESA 85201 741-C4
N AUDREY DR
10200 MarC 85351 615-J2
W AUDREY DR
- PEOR 85345 616-D2
9900 MarC 85351 616-A2
10600 MarC 85351 615-J2
E AUDREY LN
800 PHX 85022 538-J6
1200 PHX 85022 539-A6
W AUDREY LN
6000 GLEN 85308 537-C6
8300 PEOR 85382 536-F6
17900 SURP 85387 494-A5
N AUDUBON PL
15600 FTNH 85268 583-A4
E AUGUSTA AV
- MarC 85236 903-C4
- MarC 85242 903-C4
- MarC 85249 902-E4
1300 CHAN 85249 901-J4
1600 CHAN 85249 902-A4
1800 PHX 85020 619-B6
W AUGUSTA AV
200 PHX 85021 618-C6
2500 PHX 85051 618-A6
3400 PHX 85051 617-H6
4500 GLEN 85301 617-C6
7000 GLEN 85303 616-J6
7000 GLEN 85303 617-C6
7800 MarC 85307 615-J6
E AUGUSTA CIR
5900 MESA 85215 703-E6
W AUGUSTA CIR
4900 PHX 85308 537-F7
5000 PHX 85308 577-F1
E AUGUSTA CT
16900 FTNH 85268 623-D3
S AUGUSTA CT
24600 MarC 85248 901-E3
N AUGUSTA DR
100 MESA 85207 743-G5
2400 MESA 85215 703-E6
9700 MarC 85351 576-B7
10900 MarC 85351 575-J6
W AUGUSTA DR
10400 MarC 85351 576-A6
N AUGUSTINE
- MESA 85207 703-H6
S AUGUSTINE
2600 MESA 85208 783-G5
N AUGUSTINE CIR
1300 MESA 85207 743-H2
S AUGUSTINE CIR
2000 MESA 85208 783-G5
N AUGUSTINE ST
1300 MESA 85207 743-H2
E AUGUSTUS AV
- QC 85242 863-J6
- QC 85242 864-A6
E AURELIUS AV
1600 PHX 85020 659-A1
N AURORA DR
20200 MarC 85375 535-D3
W AURORA DR
5900 GLEN 85308 537-A2
7200 GLEN 85308 536-J2
12300 MarC 85375 535-E2
N AUSTIN AV
17600 SURP 85374 534-H6
E AUSTIN DR
2200 GIL 85296 822-J2
N AUSTIN DR
300 CHAN 85226 820-C5
W AUSTIN THOMAS DR
- SURP 85373 535-H6
W AUTO DR
- GDYR 85338 695-A5
- TEMP 85284 820-B1
900 TEMP 85284 780-A7
E AUTO CENTER DR
100 MESA 85210 781-J2
400 MESA 85204 781-J2
600 MESA 85204 782-A2
E AUTO MALL DR
- CHAN 85284 819-J3
- CHAN 85284 820-A3
E AUTOPLANE DR
8300 CARE 85377 421-A6
E AUTOPLANE RD
8300 CARE 85377 421-A5
S AUTOPLEX LP
7600 TEMP 85284 780-A7
7800 TEMP 85284 779-J7
W AUTOPLEX LP
1500 TEMP 85284 780-A7
W AUTUMN CIR
- SURP 85374 534-F5
N AUTUMN CT
20400 MarC 85375 535-B3
S AUTUMN DR
- GIL 85236 863-E3
E AUTUMN SAGE DR
10500 SCTS 85259 581-F4
N AUTUMN SAGE DR
- SCTS 85259 581-H4
W AUTUMN SAGE DR
15600 SURP 85374 534-F2
E AUTUMN SAGE TR
- PinC 85219 786-E5
W AVALON CIR
3000 PHX 85033 697-B2
W AVALON CT
5600 CHAN 85226 820-D5
E AVALON DR
1300 PHX 85014 698-J2
1800 PHX 85016 699-B2
4000 PHX 85018 699-G2
5100 PHX 85018 700-A2
6100 SCTS 85251 700-D2
8500 SCTS 85251 701-A2
W AVALON DR
- AVON 85340 695-C1
- GDYR 85338 (654-E7 See Page 653)
700 PHX 85013 698-F2
1500 PHX 85015 698-C2
2500 PHX 85017 698-B2
3800 PHX 85019 697-H1
4400 PHX 85031 697-C1
5900 PHX 85033 697-B1
6900 PHX 85033 696-F1
8600 PHX 85037 696-D1
10300 AVON 85323 696-A1
10500 AVON 85323 695-J1
15100 GDYR 85338 (694-E1 See Page 653)
N AVALON LN
- SURP 85374 534-G5
E AVALON ST
6300 MarC 85205 743-F5
6700 MESA 85205 743-F5
6700 MESA 85207 743-F5
8800 MarC 85207 744-C5
N AVALON ST
3100 MarC 85220 744-J5
AVENIDA ADANELLE
27700 SCTS 85255 500-H2
28100 SCTS 85262 500-H1
29000 SCTS 85262 460-H7
N AVENIDA ADANELLE
29300 SCTS 85262 460-H7
W AVENIDA CORDONIZ
10100 PHX 85037 656-A6
10600 PHX 85037 655-J6
E AVENIDA DE ESPERANZA
- PinC 85219 786-J5
E AVENIDA DEL ORO
1800 PHX 85022 579-B6
N AVENIDA DEL PUENTE
4600 PHX 85018 659-H6
E AVENIDA DEL RAY
- PEOR 85382 497-A4
18400 MarC 85263 503-J6
N AVENIDA DEL RAY
25800 MarC 85263 503-H4
W AVENIDA DEL REY
- PEOR 85382 497-A4
4700 PHX 85310 497-B4
E AVENIDA DEL SOL
- MarC 85024 499-D7
- PHX 85024 499-C7
N AVENIDA DEL SOL
8600 PVAL 85253 620-B5
S AVENIDA DEL SOL
6100 PinC 85219 786-G7
W AVENIDA DEL SOL
- PEOR 85382 497-A6
4000 PHX 85310 497-H6
7600 PEOR 85382 496-H6
8300 MarC 85382 496-D6
E AVENIDA DEL VALLE
19300 QC 85242 903-J1
S AVENIDA DEL YAQUI
5200 GUAD 85283 780-A4
5200 TEMP 85283 780-A4
E AVENIDA DE VALLE
21400 QC 85242 904-E1
E AVENIDA EL ALBA
6800 PVAL 85253 660-E1
W AVENIDA GLENROSA
10600 PHX 85037 655-J6
E AVENIDA HERMOSA AV
1200 PHX 85014 658-J4
S AVENIDA LA MANANA
6100 PinC 85219 786-G7
E AVENIDA LAS NOCHES
9100 PinC 85219 786-G7
E AVENIDA LA TARDE
9100 PinC 85219 786-G7
E AVENIDA OLIVOS WY
2800 PHX 85016 659-D7
E AVENIDA SIERRA MADRE
100 GIL 85296 782-D7
300 GIL 85296 822-D1
E AVENIDA VIDA BUENA
16200 FTNH 85268 583-B7
E A W TILLINGHAST DR
9400 SCTS 85262 421-D1
E A W TILLINGHAST RD
9500 SCTS 85262 421-E1
N AVENUE OF THE ARTS
- SURP 85373 535-H7
- SURP 85374 535-H7
E AVENUE OF THE FOUNTAINS
16300 FTNH 85268 583-D7
N AVERY
- MESA 85207 703-J3
S AVERY
5700 MESA 85212 823-G6
6400 MESA 85212 863-G1
N AVERY CIR
1800 MESA 85207 743-H1
E AVESTA CIR
7200 MESA 85208 743-H6
W AVIARY WY
400 GIL 85233 782-B7
N AVILA DR
14800 FTNH 85268 582-H4
W AVION WY
- MarC 85339 777-J6
2700 MarC 85339 778-A6
N AVISPA ST
100 WICK 85390 290-D2
N AVOCA
- MarC 85207 703-J7
- MESA 85207 703-J3
1300 MESA 85207 743-H2
S AVOCA
1000 MESA 85208 783-H1
5800 MESA 85212 823-H6
N AVOCA CIR
- MESA 85207 703-J5
1800 MESA 85207 743-J1
S AVOCA CIR
2100 MESA 85208 783-H4
N AVOCA LN
1200 MESA 85207 743-J1
S AVOCA LN
100 MESA 85208 743-H6
S AVOCET ST
- MarC 85236 823-E4
N AXIS DR
9000 FTNH 85268 623-C5
9000 MarC 85256 623-C5
E AZALEA AV
5700 MESA 85206 743-H6
7200 MESA 85208 743-H6
E AZALEA CIR
7100 MESA 85208 743-G6
W AZALEA CT
9800 MarC 85351 576-B7
S AZALEA DR
1700 TEMP 85282 740-G7
W AZALEA DR
500 CHAN 85248 861-B6
W AZALEA LN
15700 SURP 85374 534-F5
W AZALEA PL
900 CHAN 85248 861-D6
E AZALIA AV
- MarC 85220 744-H6
N AZATLAN DR
18400 MarC 85263 503-H3
W AZTEC
4100 MarC 85086 417-J4
N AZTEC CT
21800 MarC 85375 534-H1
N AZTEC DR
10400 MarC 85373 536-B5
W AZTEC DR
10300 MarC 85373 536-A5
E AZTEC PL
14900 FTNH 85268 582-H5
N AZTEC TR
- WICK 85390 290-E3
S AZUCENA CIR
1600 MESA 85202 781-A2
E AZUL AV
7200 MESA 85208 783-G4
E AZURA PL
6200 CVCK 85331 420-E1
N AZURE CT
- FTNH 85268 622-H4
17400 MarC 85373 536-C7
N AZURE LN
3100 AVON 85323 695-H1
E AZURE HILLS DR
5300 CVCK 85331 (380-C7 See Page 339)
N AZURE ISLE WY
1100 GIL 85234 782-J4
E AZURE SEA LN
1200 GIL 85234 782-F4
E AZURE VISTA TR
- FTNH 85268 622-J4
N AZURITE
- MESA 85207 704-E7
N AZURITE CIR
- MESA 85207 704-E7
N AZURITE DR
17800 MarC 85375 535-C6
W AZURITE DR
13500 MarC 85375 535-C6

B

E B ST
6600 MESA 85212 823-F7
N B ST
12300 ELMG 85335 575-G5
S B ST
- MarC 85337 (1090-B1 See Page 1049)
W B ST
5100 PHX 85031 657-E5
53000 MarC 85337 (1090-B1 See Page 1049)
E BAARS CT
- MarC 85236 863-A3
W BABBIT DR
- SURP 85374 534-B6
E BACA DR
17200 FTNH 85268 583-E4
W BACK CREEK CIR
- MarC 85086 (378-E5 See Page 337)
N BACK CREEK CT
- MarC 85086 (378-F5 See Page 337)
W BACK CREEK WY
- MarC 85086 (378-E4 See Page 337)
E BACKUS RD
2800 MESA 85213 742-F1
W BADEN AV
- GDYR 85338 (694-D4 See Page 653)
W BADEN ST
9100 TOL 85353 696-C5
9100 MarC 85353 696-D5
W BADGER CT
11500 SURP 85374 535-H7
E BADGER WY
4300 PHX 85044 819-G4
E BADGETT LN
6400 PVAL 85253 660-D4
N BAHA DR
22100 MarC 85375 534-H1
S BAHAMA DR
400 GIL 85296 822-H1
S BAHAMMA DR
- GIL 85296 822-G5
W BAHIA CT
1400 GIL 85233 781-J7
1500 GIL 85233 821-H1
E BAHIA DR
10200 SCTS 85260 581-E2
10400 SCTS 85259 581-F2
N BAHIA DR
15200 FTNH 85268 583-E4
15300 MarC 85268 583-E4
S BAHIA LN
300 LP 85340 655-B7
BAHIA LN E
100 LP 85340 655-B7
BAHIA LN W
100 LP 85340 655-A7
E BA-HON-NA ST
- MarC 85264 583-J3
N BAILEY
- MESA 85220 744-H5
N BAILEY CIR
- MESA 85220 744-H4
W BAILY
- MarC 85086 (378-D5 See Page 337)
E BAINBRIDGE AV
15800 FTNH 85268 583-B5
E BAJADA DR
10900 SCTS 85255 501-H3
W BAJADA DR
- PHX 85085 498-B2
E BAJADA RD
4500 MarC 85331 500-A3
4500 PHX 85331 500-A3
7300 SCTS 85255 500-H3
9100 SCTS 85262 421-D4
9600 SCTS 85255 501-D3
W BAJADA RD
- PHX 85085 497-C2
N BAKER CT
- MarC 85255 (462-G7 See Page 421)
E BAKER DR
1600 TEMP 85282 780-G2
5000 PHX 85331 460-A7
7500 SCTS 85262 460-H7
S BALA DR
2200 TEMP 85282 740-J6
3400 TEMP 85282 780-J1
5300 TEMP 85283 780-J3
9300 TEMP 85284 820-J3
E BALANCING ROCK RD
- SCTS 85331 500-G1
9600 SCTS 85262 501-D1
E BALAO DR
- SCTS 85262 460-H5
N BALBOA
500 MESA 85205 743-C4
S BALBOA AV
- PinC 85219 826-H1
6500 PinC 85219 786-H7
E BALBOA CIR
1000 TEMP 85282 740-F7
N BALBOA CIR
600 MESA 85205 743-C3
S BALBOA CIR
600 MESA 85206 743-C7
N BALBOA CT
- MarC 85234 783-B5
E BALBOA DR
- TEMP 85282 740-D7
2100 TEMP 85282 741-A7
2500 MESA 85202 741-A7
N BALBOA DR
- MarC 85234 783-B5
1200 GIL 85234 783-B4
9000 MarC 85351 616-B1
11400 MarC 85351 576-B6
S BALBOA DR
- GIL 85236 823-B1
- MarC 85236 823-B7
W BALBOA DR
100 TEMP 85282 740-D7
N BALCOME
13800 SURP 85379 575-D4
N BALCOME CT
- SURP 85379 575-D4
S BALDWIN
- MESA 85212 784-E4
W BALFOUR BLVD
24200 SURP 85387 494-A5
E BALFOUR RD
7000 PVAL 85253 660-F5
S BAL HARBOR DR
900 GIL 85233 822-A2
N BALLAD DR
20900 MarC 85375 534-H2
W BALLAD DR
12700 MarC 85375 535-C1
15500 MarC 85375 534-G2
N BALLPARK DR
- MESA 85208 784-C1
E BALMORAL AV
- MESA 85220 744-G6
7200 MESA 85208 743-H6
E BALSAM AV
- MESA 85220 744-G6
2000 MESA 85204 742-D6
3900 MESA 85206 742-H6
4200 MESA 85206 743-A6
8400 MarC 85208 744-B6
E BALSAM CIR
2200 MESA 85204 742-D6
7400 MESA 85208 743-H6
E BALSAM DR
16000 FTNH 85268 583-B5
E BALTIMORE CIR
- MarC 85220 744-G5
E BALTIMORE ST
- MarC 85220 744-G5
- MESA 85220 744-F5
2400 MESA 85213 742-E4
5200 MarC 85205 743-C4
5200 MESA 85205 743-C4
8100 MarC 85207 744-A5
W BALTUSROL CIR
300 PHX 85023 578-G4
E BAMBI DR
6500 MESA 85215 703-F7
E BANCROFT CT
- GIL 85236 863-D5
N BANDANA
17200 SURP 85374 534-C7
BANDERA CIR
200 LP 85340 655-B7
S BANDIT CT
- GIL 85236 863-E5
S BANDIT RD
- GIL 85236 863-E5
W BANFF LN
- SURP 85379 (574-F3 See Page 573)
- SURP 85379 575-C3
1700 PHX 85023 578-C4
2800 PHX 85053 578-A4
3500 PHX 85053 577-J4
4300 PHX 85306 577-F4
5200 GLEN 85306 577-C4
6800 MarC 85381 577-A3
6800 PEOR 85381 577-A3
7100 MarC 85381 576-J3
7300 PEOR 85381 576-E3
N BANJO DR
18000 MarC 85375 535-B6
W BANJO DR
13600 MarC 85375 535-B6
N BANNER CT
12400 MarC 85351 576-C6
N BANNING
600 MESA 85205 743-C4
S BANNING
800 MESA 85206 743-B7
900 MESA 85206 783-B1
N BANNING AV
- MarC 85234 783-B4
N BANNING CIR
700 MESA 85205 743-C3
S BANNING CIR
600 MESA 85206 743-B7
N BANNING CT
1300 GIL 85234 783-B4
S BANNING CT
- GIL 85236 823-B1
N BANNING DR
1200 GIL 85234 783-B4
S BANNING DR
- MarC 85236 863-B2
S BANNING ST
- GIL 85236 823-B3
- MarC 85236 823-B7
E BANNOCK ST
4100 PHX 85044 819-G2
S BANNOCK ST
10000 PHX 85044 779-G7
11500 PHX 85044 819-G1
W BANYAN DR
12300 MarC 85375 535-E5
E BARANCA CT
- GIL 85236 863-C5
E BARANCA RD
- GIL 85236 863-C5
W BARBADOS DR
900 GIL 85233 822-A2
N BARBADOS PL
7000 PHX 85021 658-F1
W BARBARA AV
3700 PHX 85051 617-H4
4300 GLEN 85302 617-D4
11300 PEOR 85345 615-H4
E BARBARA DR
400 TEMP 85281 700-E7
E BARBARITA AV
200 GIL 85234 782-D5
3700 GIL 85236 783-C5
N BARBARITA AV
500 GIL 85233 782-C6
E BARBARITA CT
- MarC 85236 783-E5
4500 GIL 85236 783-E5
E BARBARITA ST
4000 GIL 85236 783-D5
5400 GUAD 85283 780-A5
16800 GIL 85234 783-B5
16800 MarC 85234 783-B5
17000 MarC 85236 783-D5
N BARBER DR
2400 MESA 85215 703-E6
S BARBERRY PL
3500 CHAN 85248 861-D6
E BARBIE LN
5200 CVCK 85331 460-C1
W BARCELONA DR
400 GIL 85233 822-A1
3300 CHAN 85226 820-H3
S BAREHAND RD
- MarC 85339 776-H5
N BARKLEY
- MESA 85203 742-C1
1800 MESA 85203 702-C6
S BARKLEY
- MESA 85204 742-B6
1200 MESA 85204 782-B1
S BARKLEY RD
- PinC 85273 746-D7
- PinC 85219 746-D7
1100 PinC 85219 786-D1
E BARKWOOD RD
- PHX 85048 819-A6
S BARLEY WY
- GIL 85236 863-D6
E BARNACLE AV
- PinC 85219 785-G4
N BARNES AV
100 GBND 85337 (1090-C3 See Page 1049)
S BARNES AV
400 GBND 85337 (1090-C4 See Page 1049)
E BARNES DR
17300 FTNH 85268 623-E3
W BARNES LN
3700 PHX 85051 617-H4
E BARNES PKWY
- QC 85242 864-D6
E BARNES ST
700 PHX 85020 618-J4
N BARNUM WY
- MarC 85086 (378-B6 See Page 337)
E BARON DR
11200 FTNH 85268 623-C2
N BARREL CACTUS WY
12200 FTNH 85268 623-B1
S BARRINGTON
- MESA 85208 784-B4
N BARRON
- MESA 85207 703-J3
N BARRON CIR
- MESA 85207 703-J3
W BARROW CT
2500 CHAN 85224 821-C1
W BARROW DR
300 CHAN 85225 781-F7
400 CHAN 85225 821-D1
1000 CHAN 85224 821-A1
2500 MarC 85224 821-A1
E BARSTOW ST
6500 MarC 85205 743-F5
E BART DR
300 CHAN 85225 821-G5
W BART DR
4000 CHAN 85226 820-G5
E BART ST
1000 GIL 85296 822-F5
E BARTLETT CIR
5200 PHX 85016 659-B5
W BARTLETT CT
1900 CHAN 85248 901-B2
E BARTLETT PL
- MarC 85249 901-J2
- MarC 85249 902-A2
E BARTLETT WY
- MarC 85249 901-J2
W BARTLETT WY
1600 CHAN 85248 901-B2
1600 MarC 85248 901-B2
E BARTLETT DAM RD
11400 MarC 85262 421-J1
11400 MarC 85262 (422-A1 See Page 421)
11700 MarC 85255 (382-H7 See Page 341)
11700 MarC 85255 (422-D2 See Page 421)
15700 MarC 85255 423-J1
15700 MarC 85255 (424-A1 See Page 423)
11700 MarC 85255 103-B1
11700 MarC 85262 103-B1
N BARTLETT DAM RD N
- MarC 85255 (424-E1 See Page 423)
N BARTLETT DAM RD S
- MarC 85255 (424-D4 See Page 423)
- MarC 85263 (424-D4 See Page 423)
E BARWICK CT
- MarC 85255 (462-G7 See Page 421)
E BARWICK DR
4000 PHX 85331 459-H6
4500 PHX 85331 460-A6
6000 MarC 85331 460-D6
7000 SCTS 85331 460-G6
E BAR Z LN
5700 PVAL 85253 620-C4
E BASELINE AV
- APJT 85219 786-A4
- APJT 85220 785-G4
1600 APJT 85219 785-G4
1600 PinC 85219 785-G4
1600 PinC 85220 785-G4
9700 PinC 85219 786-H4
W BASELINE AV
- APJT 85220 785-C4
1600 PinC 85220 785-C4
E BASELINE RD
- MESA 85202 781-A3
- TEMP 85202 780-F3
- TEMP 85202 781-A3
- GIL 85234 782-F3
- PHX 85040 778-H2
- MESA 85204 782-F3
- TEMP 85283 780-D3
- TEMP 85282 780-D3
100 BUCK 85326 (732-B7 See Page 731)
200 MarC 85326 (732-B7 See Page 731)
1400 GIL 85204 782-F3
1500 PHX 85040 779-C2
1600 GIL 85206 782-F3
3600 MESA 85206 782-F3
4400 MESA 85206 783-D3
4400 GIL 85234 783-D3
4500 PHX 85044 779-F2
4900 GIL 85206 783-D3
5300 MarC 85234 783-D3
5600 MarC 85206 783-D3
5600 MarC 85236 783-D3
5600 MESA 85236 783-D3
6100 GIL 85236 783-D3
6800 MESA 85208 783-H3
7900 MESA 85208 784-B3
9300 MESA 85212 784-B3
9900 MESA 85220 784-H4
10800 MarC 85220 784-H4
11400 MarC 85220 785-A4
11400 APJT 85220 784-H4
11400 APJT 85220 785-A4
200 MarC 85326 102-B3
W BASELINE RD
- MarC 85326 (772-C1 See Page 731)
- MESA 85204 782-B3
- MESA 85233 782-B3
- GIL 85233 782-B3
- GIL 85234 782-B3
- PHX 85041 778-C2
- TEMP 85282 780-B3
- TEMP 85283 780-B3
100 BUCK 85326 (732-B7 See Page 731)
100 GIL 85204 782-B3
300 GIL 85233 781-F3
300 MESA 85210 781-F3
1300 GIL 85204 781-F3
1400 MESA 85202 781-C3
1400 GUAD 85283 780-B3
1600 MESA 85204 781-F3
1700 TEMP 85044 780-B3
1800 MESA 85233 781-F3
1900 TEMP 85044 779-J3
1900 TEMP 85282 779-J3
2000 PHX 85041 777-H2
2700 MarC 85041 778-C2
2700 MarC 85339 778-C2
2900 MarC 85339 777-C2
3300 PHX 85339 777-C2
3500 MarC 85041 777-H2
6700 MarC 85339 776-D2
6700 PHX 85339 776-G2
24200 MarC 85326 (732-B7 See Page 731)
25100 BUCK 85326 731-C7
25100 MarC 85326 731-C7
2900 MarC 85339 102-B3
3500 MarC 85041 102-B3
24200 MarC 85326 102-B3
30700 MarC 85354 102-B3
S BASHA RD
3400 CHAN 85248 861-D7
22000 MarC 85248 861-D7
22200 CHAN 85248 901-D1
22400 MarC 85248 901-D1
N BASIN RD
37700 CVCK 85331 420-E3
N BASL LN
- SURP 85374 575-B1
E BASS RD
500 WICK 85390 290-G2
E BATES DR
200 MESA 85201 701-J6
200 MESA 85203 701-J6
600 MESA 85203 702-A6
E BATES ST
1300 MESA 85203 702-C7
E BAUTISTA CT
- GIL 85236 863-C5
E BAUTISTA RD
- GIL 85236 863-D5
W BAXTER DR
8300 PHX 85037 656-F5
E BAY DR
1900 GIL 85234 782-H5
N BAY DR
300 GIL 85233 781-H5
S BAY DR
100 GIL 85233 781-H7
400 GIL 85233 821-H1
E BAYBERRY AV
2000 MESA 85204 742-D6
4300 MESA 85206 743-A6
E BAYFIELD DR
16600 FTNH 85268 583-C6
N BAY HILL WY
- MarC 85086 (378-C5 See Page 337)
E BAYLOR CT
- GIL 85296 822-F3
1900 CHAN 85225 822-A3
N BAYLOR DR
9600 FTNH 85268 623-D4
E BAYLOR LN
200 GIL 85296 822-E3
500 CHAN 85225 821-G4
1700 CHAN 85225 822-A3
W BAYLOR LN
600 GIL 85233 822-A3
3000 CHAN 85226 820-J3
S BAY SHORE BLVD
300 GIL 85233 821-J1
W BAY SHORE DR
800 GIL 85233 822-A2
W BAYSIDE RD
10300 MarC 85351 576-A4
E BAY TREE CIR
1800 GIL 85234 782-H4
E BAYVIEW DR
1300 TEMP 85283 780-G3
9900 SCTS 85258 621-D3
13500 SCTS 85259 622-D4
E BAYWOOD AV
- MarC 85220 744-G6
2200 MESA 85204 742-H6
3900 MESA 85206 742-H6
4300 MESA 85206 743-A6
7100 MESA 85208 743-H6
9100 MarC 85208 744-C6
N BAYWOOD CT
14200 MarC 85351 576-C4
E BEACHCOMBER DR
2100 GIL 85234 782-J4
W BEACON CT
20700 MarC 85361 493-B2
E BEACON DR
1300 GIL 85234 782-G4
N BEACON RD
26600 MarC 85361 493-B2
W BEACON RD
20600 MarC 85361 493-C1
W BEACON ST
- WICK 85390 289-J3
W BEACON FIELD BLVD
- SURP 85387 494-A4
E BEAL AV
8400 MESA 85208 784-B1
W BEALL AV
- MESA 85210 781-G1
N BEAR CT
4800 PinC 85220 705-D6
E BEARDSLEY RD
- PHX 85024 538-H4
2100 PHX 85024 539-C4
2400 PHX 85050 539-D4
8100 SCTS 85255 540-J5
W BEARDSLEY RD
- PEOR 85308 536-G4
- PHX 85024 538-G4
1500 PEOR 85382 536-D4
2000 PHX 85027 538-D4
9100 MarC 85382 536-D4
10100 MarC 85373 536-D4
10100 PEOR 85373 536-D4
10700 PEOR 85373 535-H4
11100 MarC 85373 535-H4
12200 MarC 85375 535-E4
14700 SURP 85374 534-H4
14700 SURP 85375 534-H4
16400 SURP 85387 534-D3
20900 SURP 85387 533-A3
BEARDSLEY CSR
- MarC - (456-B3 See Page 415)
- MarC - 494-F7
- MarC - 495-F3
- MarC - 496-A1
- MarC - 573-H2

STREET
Block City ZIP Pg-Grid

BEARDSLEY CSR
- MarC - 534-B4
- MarC - (613-G1 See Page 573)
- MarC - 653-F5
- PEOR - (416-D5 See Page 415)
- PEOR - (456-C2 See Page 415)
- SURP - 533-J7
- SURP - 534-B4
- SURP - 573-H4
E BEAR GRASS CIR
9700 SCTS 85255 501-D5
E BEATRICE ST
300 TEMP 85281 700-E6
4100 PHX 85008 699-G6
7400 SCTS 85257 700-G6
W BEATRICE ST
6100 PHX 85043 697-B5
6800 PHX 85043 696-J5
E BEAUBIEN DR
1600 PHX 85024 539-A3
W BEAUBIEN DR
- PEOR 85308 536-G3
1400 PHX 85027 538-A3
10700 PEOR 85373 535-J3
10700 PEOR 85373 536-A3
E BEAUTIFUL LN
- PHX 85040 778-G3
4600 PHX 85044 779-H3
7600 PHX 85040 779-B3
W BEAUTIFUL LN
- PHX 85339 777-E2
100 PHX 85041 778-F3
E BEAVER TAIL
1100 CARE 85377 420-H6
N BEAVER VALLEY CT
16800 MarC 85351 576-D1
N BECK AV
- CHAN 85226 820-B5
S BECK AV
- CHAN 85226 820-B6
100 TEMP 85281 740-B3
3400 TEMP 85282 780-B1
5200 TEMP 85283 780-B3
7500 TEMP 85284 780-B7
8800 TEMP 85284 820-B2
N BECK CT
900 CHAN 85226 820-B4
E BECK LN
- PHX 85022 578-H3
1800 PHX 85022 579-C3
2700 PHX 85032 579-E3
5100 PHX 85254 580-A3
7900 SCTS 85260 580-H4
10900 SCTS 85259 581-H4
W BECK LN
100 PHX 85023 578-C3
3000 PHX 85053 578-B3
5300 GLEN 85306 577-D3
N BECKE LN
- SURP 85374 534-A6
E BECKER LN
700 PHX 85020 618-J2
1200 PHX 85020 619-A2
2200 PHX 85028 619-C2
6800 SCTS 85254 620-F2
7500 SCTS 85260 620-G3
8800 SCTS 85260 621-B3
10400 SCTS 85259 621-F3
12800 SCTS 85259 622-C3
N BECKER LN
10600 PHX 85020 618-J2
W BECKER LN
900 PHX 85029 618-A2
3600 PHX 85029 617-H2
4600 GLEN 85304 617-B2
7100 PEOR 85345 616-E1
7100 PEOR 85345 617-B2
N BEDFORD CT
- CHAN 85225 821-H6
S BEDFORD CT
6600 CHAN 85249 901-H6
N BEDFORD DR
300 CHAN 85225 821-J3
S BEDFORD DR
- CHAN 85225 861-H1
- MarC 85249 901-H1
100 CHAN 85225 821-H7
S BEDFORD PL
- CHAN 85249 861-H1
- CHAN 85249 901-H4
W BEDFORD ST
1600 MESA 85201 741-C4
S BEECH CREEK DR
25600 MarC 85248 901-C5
E BEECHNUT CT
- MarC 85249 902-B2
E BEECHNUT DR
- MarC 85249 901-G2
W BEECHNUT DR
500 CHAN 85248 901-D2
E BEECHNUT PL
- MarC 85249 902-C2
W BEECHNUT PL
200 CHAN 85248 901-E2
W BEECHWOOD DR
12300 MarC 85375 535-D4
E BEEHIVE CIR
9000 SCTS 85255 501-C5
E BEEKMAN PL
2600 PHX 85016 699-D1
BEELINE HWY Rt#-87
10400 MarC 85264 103-C2
19400 MarC 85290 103-C2
21200 MarC 85263 103-C2
7800 MarC 85256 663-A4
10400 MarC 85256 623-E5
12700 MarC 85256 662-H6
12700 MarC 85256 702-A2
17200 MarC 85256 623-C7
N BEELINE HWY Rt#-87
- MarC 85256 702-A2
11000 MarC 85256 701-H4
E BEHREND DR
300 PHX 85024 538-H5
1400 PHX 85024 539-A5
2500 PHX 85050 539-D5
W BEHREND DR
- PHX 85027 538-A4
3500 PHX 85308 537-F4
3500 PHX 85308 538-A4
5800 GLEN 85308 537-A4
7500 GLEN 85308 536-H4
8300 PEOR 85382 536-C4
N BEL AIR DR
100 MESA 85207 743-G5
1400 MESA 85201 741-F1
E BEL AIR LN
2200 GIL 85234 782-J4
S BELAIR RD
2200 APJT 85219 785-F2
S BELAIRE RD
- APJT 85219 745-F6
N BELFAIR WY
- MarC 85086 (378-E5 See Page 337)
W BELFAST ST
1600 MESA 85201 741-C4
E BELGIAN TR
8400 SCTS 85258 620-J3
8400 SCTS 85258 621-A3
N BELGREEN RD
2100 MESA 85215 703-E7
E BELL CIR
7100 MESA 85208 743-G6
N BELL DR
- CHAN 85225 822-C5
S BELL DR
- MarC 85249 902-C3
N BELL PL
- CHAN 85225 822-C6
S BELL PL
- CHAN 85249 902-C4
E BELL RD
100 PHX 85022 578-H1
100 PHX 85023 578-H1
1100 PHX 85022 579-B1
2400 PHX 85032 579-H1
4400 PHX 85032 580-B2
4800 PHX 85254 580-F2
6300 PHX 85054 580-F2
7100 PHX 85260 580-F2
8000 SCTS 85255 580-J2
8000 SCTS 85255 581-D2
8000 SCTS 85260 580-J2
8000 SCTS 85260 581-D2
10300 SCTS 85259 581-F2
N BELL RD
35200 QC 85242 903-H7
35200 PinC 85242 903-H7
W BELL RD
- MarC 85351 535-F7
- MarC 85351 575-J1
- MarC 85373 535-F7
- MarC 85373 575-J1
- SURP 85373 535-F7
- SURP 85373 575-J1
- PHX 85023 578-C1
2700 PHX 85053 578-C1
3200 GLEN 85308 577-C1
3500 PHX 85308 577-H1
3500 PHX 85308 578-C1
3500 PHX 85053 577-H1
4300 PHX 85306 577-H1
5100 GLEN 85306 577-C1
6700 GLEN 85382 577-C1
7100 GLEN 85308 576-F1
7100 PEOR 85308 576-F1
7500 PEOR 85382 576-F1
7500 GLEN 85382 576-F1
9000 MarC 85351 576-B1
9000 MarC 85373 576-B1
9000 PEOR 85373 576-F1
11400 MarC 85374 535-F7
11400 SURP 85374 535-F7
12300 MarC 85375 535-C7
12700 SURP 85375 535-C7
14400 SURP 85374 534-B7
E BELL ST
4800 APJT 85219 746-C1
4800 PinC 85219 746-C1
E BELLA DR
- PHX 85254 580-A2
W BELLAROSE DR
10500 MarC 85351 576-B3
E BELLA VISTA CIR
12000 SCTS 85259 621-J5
12000 SCTS 85259 622-A5
E BELLA VISTA DR
6800 CVCK 85331 420-G4
9000 SCTS 85258 621-E5
11400 SCTS 85259 621-H5
12000 SCTS 85259 622-A5
E BELL DE MAR DR
500 TEMP 85283 780-F5
W BELL DE MAR DR
400 TEMP 85283 780-A5
E BELLERIVE CT
1500 CHAN 85249 901-J5
E BELLERIVE DR
- MarC 85249 902-C5
1300 CHAN 85249 901-J5
1900 CHAN 85249 902-A4
E BELLERIVE PL
- CHAN 85249 902-B4
- MarC 85249 902-D5
E BELLEVIEW PL
8500 SCTS 85257 700-J5
8500 SCTS 85257 701-A5
N BELLEVIEW PL
1100 SCTS 85257 701-A5
E BELLEVIEW ST
1300 SCTS 85257 700-E5
1300 TEMP 85257 700-E5
2800 PHX 85008 699-D5
8700 SCTS 85257 701-A5
W BELLEVIEW ST
2400 PHX 85009 698-A4
5200 PHX 85043 697-B4
E BELLFLOWER CT
- MarC 85249 901-F6
11000 MarC 85248 901-F6
E BELLFLOWER DR
10500 MarC 85248 901-D6
W BELLO LN
- WICK 85390 290-A3
S BELLVIEW CIR
1000 MESA 85204 782-A1
1200 MESA 85204 781-J1
W BELLVIEW ST
- MESA 85203 742-A1
2400 MESA 85203 702-A6
S BELLVIEW ST
600 MESA 85204 742-A6
1100 MESA 85204 781-J1
N BELLWOOD DR
19200 MarC 85375 535-D4
W BELMAR CT
2000 APJT 85220 745-B5
E BELMONT AV
- PHX 85020 618-H7
400 AVON 85323 695-C7
1200 PHX 85020 619-A7
2700 MESA 85204 742-E6
7000 PVAL 85253 620-F7
N BELMONT AV
7600 PHX 85051 618-A6
W BELMONT AV
- GLEN 85303 616-J6
200 PHX 85021 618-C7
2500 PHX 85051 618-A6
3400 PHX 85051 617-J6
4700 GLEN 85301 617-C6
6700 GLEN 85303 617-A6
7600 MarC 85307 615-H6
E BELMONT CT
6700 PVAL 85253 620-E7
E BELMONT DR
100 AVON 85323 695-B7
1800 TEMP 85284 820-H1
W BELMONT DR
- AVON 85353 735-F1
W BELOAT RD
19900 MarC 85326 (773-A3 See Page 733)
21100 MarC 85326 (772-E2 See Page 731)
22700 BUCK 85326 (772-E2 See Page 731)
25100 BUCK 85326 (771-J2 See Page 731)
25100 MarC 85326 (771-G2 See Page 731)
N BELOAT ST
400 BUCK 85326 (772-B1 See Page 731)
E BELTLINE RD
- MarC 85326 899-C3
E BENDIX DR
500 TEMP 85283 780-E5
E BENJAMIN DR
500 TEMP 85282 740-E6
E BENRICH DR
- MarC 85296 862-C1
N BENSON CT
1400 CHAN 85224 821-A3
N BENSON LN
800 CHAN 85224 821-A4
2900 CHAN 85224 781-A7
N BENSON WY
- MESA 85208 784-B1
N BENT BARREL
36600 CARE 85377 420-H5
W BENTLEY ST
200 MESA 85201 741-C4
E BENTLEY MINE RD
- CVCK 85331 419-E2
- MarC 85331 (379-G7 See Page 339)
- MarC 85331 419-E2
40200 CVCK 85331 (379-G7 See Page 339)
N BENTON
- MESA 85220 784-G1
S BENTON CIR
- MESA 85212 784-G6
N BENTRUP CIR
3100 CHAN 85224 781-A7
W BENTRUP CT
1600 CHAN 85224 781-C7
E BENTRUP DR
1000 TEMP 85283 780-F7
W BENTRUP DR
- TEMP 85283 780-A6
W BENTRUP ST
300 CHAN 85225 781-E7
1200 CHAN 85224 781-A7
BENT TREE CIR N
14100 LP 85340 655-A5
BENT TREE CIR S
14100 LP 85340 655-A5
BENT TREE CIR W
4500 LP 85340 655-A5
E BENT TREE DR
- PHX 85331 500-A2
6200 SCTS 85331 500-D2
7200 SCTS 85255 500-G3
W BENT TREE DR
- PHX 85085 497-D2
- PHX 85085 498-C2
E BERETTA PL
- CHAN 85249 861-J2
W BERKELEY RD
- AVON 85323 695-F3
3100 PHX 85009 698-A4
3600 PHX 85009 697-H4
4600 PHX 85035 697-A3
6800 PHX 85035 696-J3
8400 PHX 85037 696-D3
N BERMUDA CIR
600 MESA 85205 742-H3
S BERMUDA CIR
500 MESA 85206 742-H7
S BERMUDA DR
100 GIL 85296 822-G1
W BERMUDA DR
2900 AVON 85323 695-G1
N BERNARD
- MarC 85207 744-D2
S BERNARD
- MESA 85212 784-C4
N BERNARD CIR
- MarC 85207 744-D2
E BERNEIL DR
4600 PHX 85028 619-J4
4800 PVAL 85253 619-J4
4800 PVAL 85253 620-A4
E BERNEIL LN
5800 PVAL 85253 620-C4
S BERNIE LN
- GIL 85296 822-D7
N BERRETT
- MESA 85208 784-F1
W BERRIDGE CT
- MarC 85340 655-B2
E BERRIDGE LN
200 PHX 85012 658-G3
900 PHX 85014 658-J3
1200 PHX 85014 659-A3
1600 PHX 85016 659-A3
3800 PVAL 85253 659-G3
6100 SCTS 85250 660-G3
8500 SCTS 85250 661-A4
N BERRIDGE LN
3300 PVAL 85253 659-F3
6100 PHX 85016 659-E3
W BERRIDGE LN
- GLEN 85303 656-F2
- MarC 85340 655-B2
1500 PHX 85013 658-F3
1500 PHX 85015 658-D3
2500 PHX 85017 658-B3
3600 PHX 85019 657-H3
4400 GLEN 85301 657-B3
8600 GLEN 85305 656-E2
E BERRY CIR
1800 MESA 85204 742-C6
N BERRY LN
- ELMG 85335 575-E7
W BERRY LN
- ELMG 85335 575-E7
8100 PEOR 85345 616-G1
S BERRYBROOK DR
- MarC 85248 901-C2
S BERRY BROOK DR
25200 MarC 85248 901-C4
S BERRYWOOD
- MESA 85212 784-H4
S BERRYWOOD CIR
- MESA 85212 784-G4
E BERYL AV
900 PHX 85020 618-J3
2400 PHX 85028 619-D3
4800 PVAL 85253 619-H3
4800 PVAL 85253 620-A3
5400 PHX 85253 620-B3
6600 SCTS 85253 620-E3
7300 SCTS 85258 620-G3
11200 SCTS 85259 621-H3
W BERYL AV
- PHX 85020 618-H3
900 PHX 85021 618-C2
3500 PHX 85051 617-J2
4500 GLEN 85302 617-B2
6800 PEOR 85345 617-A2
7100 PEOR 85345 616-H2
17200 MarC 85355 (614-B1 See Page 573)
E BERYL DR
- APJT 85219 785-H4
E BERYL LN
4500 PHX 85028 619-J3
5900 PHX 85253 620-C3
E BETH DR
- PHX 85040 778-H4
1700 PHX 85040 779-A4
W BETH DR
- PHX 85041 778-E4
S BETH LN
16100 MarC 85225 822-C7
E BETHANY HOME RD
- PHX 85012 658-G3
700 PHX 85014 658-G3
1200 PHX 85014 659-A3
1600 PHX 85016 659-C3
3600 PVAL 85253 659-F3
3900 PVAL 85018 659-G3
W BETHANY HOME RD
- PHX 85013 658-D3
1500 PHX 85015 658-D3
2400 PHX 85017 658-A3
3300 PHX 85017 657-F3
3500 PHX 85019 657-F3
4300 GLEN 85301 657-A3
6700 GLEN 85303 657-A3
7000 GLEN 85303 656-H3
10300 PHX 85307 655-D2
10300 PHX 85307 656-A3
12300 MarC 85340 655-B2
16000 MarC 85340 (654-B2 See Page 653)
16000 GLEN 85340 (654-B2 See Page 653)
17100 MarC 85355 653-B2
17100 MarC 85355 (654-B2 See Page 653)
17100 MarC 85340 653-B2
20300 BUCK 85340 653-B2
20300 BUCK 85373 653-B2
E BETHANY HOME ST
2400 PHX 85016 659-C4
W BETHESDA CT
15600 SURP 85374 534-F7
E BETONY DR
10200 SCTS 85260 581-E3
10400 SCTS 85259 581-F3
E BETSY CT
- MarC 85236 823-D4
E BETSY LN
- MarC 85236 823-D4
200 GIL 85296 822-C4
W BETSY LN
- GIL 85233 822-B4
W BETTY DR
8300 PEOR 85345 616-F1
E BETTY ELYSE LN
- PHX 85022 578-H3
1900 PHX 85022 579-B3
3400 PHX 85032 579-F3
4800 PHX 85032 580-A3
4800 PHX 85254 580-A3
W BETTY ELYSE LN
- PHX 85023 578-C3
3000 PHX 85053 578-A3
3700 PHX 85053 577-J3
7600 PEOR 85382 576-E3
W BEVERLEY AV
- GLEN 85306 577-D2
N BEVERLY
- MESA 85201 741-E3
- MESA 85210 741-E5
S BEVERLY
- MESA 85210 741-E5
1000 MESA 85210 781-E2
N BEVERLY CIR
1300 MESA 85201 741-E2
S BEVERLY CT
- CHAN 85248 861-D3
E BEVERLY LN
1000 PHX 85022 578-J2
1100 PHX 85022 579-A2
2400 PHX 85032 579-D2
4600 PHX 85032 580-C2
5500 PHX 85254 580-C2
W BEVERLY LN
300 PHX 85023 578-F2
3000 PHX 85023 578-A2
3500 PHX 85053 577-H2
4500 PHX 85053 577-F2
5100 GLEN 85306 577-B2
S BEVERLY PL
3300 CHAN 85248 861-D4
E BEVERLY RD
1200 PHX 85040 778-H3
3400 PHX 85040 779-C3
4700 PHX 85044 779-J3
W BEVERLY RD
- PHX 85339 777-E2
100 PHX 85041 778-D3
5500 MarC 85339 777-C2
13100 AVON 85338 775-B2
13100 MarC 85338 775-A2
14100 MarC 85338 (774-J2 See Page 733)
N BEVERLY ST
500 CHAN 85225 821-D5
S BEVERLY ST
- CHAN 85248 861-D4
200 CHAN 85225 821-D7
2100 MESA 85210 781-E3
N BEVERLY WY
400 TOL 85353 696-D5
E BIEHN ST
5700 GUAD 85283 780-B4
E BIG BARREL PASS
2100 CARE 85377 420-H6
E BIGHORN AV
2400 PHX 85048 819-B5
3800 PHX 85044 819-E5
W BIGHORN CT
11500 SURP 85374 535-H6
W BIGHORN MOUNTAIN RD
20900 MarC 85361 493-B1
W BIG OAK ST
- PHX 85085 498-C2
N BIG SKY DR
- SURP 85374 534-G4
E BILLINGS CT
9800 MarC 85207 744-E5
E BILLINGS DR
10300 MarC 85220 744-G5
E BILLINGS ST
2400 MESA 85213 742-E4
5400 MarC 85205 743-C5
6700 MESA 85205 743-F5
7500 MESA 85207 743-H5
8100 MarC 85207 744-A5
9800 MarC 85220 744-G5
10300 MESA 85220 744-F5
N BILTMORE DR
10800 PHX 85029 618-B1
11400 PHX 85029 578-B7
E BILTMORE ESTATES DR
- PHX 85016 659-D4
E BINNER DR
1200 CHAN 85225 821-J6
2300 CHAN 85225 822-B6
W BINNER DR
- CHAN 85225 822-B6
2200 CHAN 85224 821-A6
W BINNER ST
4500 CHAN 85226 820-F6
N BIRCH CIR
- GIL 85234 782-D7
1100 GIL 85233 782-C4
S BIRCH CT
- MarC 85296 822-D7
- MarC 85296 862-D1
N BIRCH ST
- GIL 85233 782-C4
S BIRCH ST
- GIL 85296 822-D6
- MarC 85296 822-D7
- MarC 85296 862-D1
5000 TEMP 85282 780-G3
S BIRCH WY
- MarC 85296 822-D7
S BIRCHETT DR
2500 TEMP 85281 741-B3
3200 TEMP 85282 781-B1
E BIRCHWOOD AV
- MESA 85220 744-G6
2000 MESA 85204 742-D6
3900 MESA 85206 742-H6
7100 MESA 85208 743-H6
9100 MarC 85208 744-C6
N BIRCHWOOD AV
- MESA 85220 744-G6
W BIRCHWOOD AV
900 MESA 85210 741-E6
2500 MESA 85202 741-A6
E BIRCHWOOD CIR
- MarC 85208 744-C6
4300 MESA 85206 743-A6
W BIRCHWOOD CIR
2500 MESA 85202 741-A6
W BIRCHWOOD DR
- CHAN 85248 901-F3
E BIRCHWOOD PL
- MarC 85249 901-H3
- MarC 85249 902-B3
E BIRD LN
100 LP 85340 655-B5
E BIRDIE LN
- PinC 85219 786-F7
W BIRDSONG AV
21500 MarC 85361 (453-A1 See Page 413)
21900 MarC 85361 (452-F1 See Page 411)
22700 MarC 85342 (452-F1 See Page 411)
W BIRDSONG CT
16200 SURP 85374 534-E6
E BISBEE RD
7700 SCTS 85258 660-H1
W BISBEE VILLAGE
- SURP 85374 534-A6
N BISCAY AV
1200 CHAN 85226 820-H3
S BISCAYNE DR
- GIL 85296 782-H7
W BISCAYNE DR
1100 GIL 85233 821-J2
W BISCUIT FLAT DR
3800 PHX 85086 (418-A6 See Page 417)
3900 PHX 85086 417-J6
E BISHOP CIR
1000 TEMP 85282 740-F7
E BISHOP DR
- TEMP 85282 740-D7
2100 TEMP 85282 741-A7
S BISHOP DR
2600 TEMP 85282 740-J7
N BISHOP LN
3600 SCTS 85251 700-F1
W BISON PTH
14400 SURP 85374 534-J6
N BITTERSWEET WY
13600 FTNH 85268 583-A6
E BIVOUAC TR
36800 CARE 85377 420-G5
N BLACKBIRD DR
900 GIL 85236 783-F5
15200 FTNH 85268 583-A4
W BLACKBIRD WY
1600 CHAN 85248 861-C4
N BLACK BUTTE RD
27400 MarC 85361 (453-C7 See Page 413)
27400 MarC 85361 493-C1
N BLACK CANYON BLVD
34600 PHX 85086 417-J6
W BLACK CANYON DR
- MarC 85373 (613-C3 See Page 573)
2400 MarC 85087 (338-E3 See Page 337)
BLACK CANYON FRWY I-17
- MarC - 103-A1
- MarC - 337-J6
- MarC - (338-A4 See Page 337)
- MarC - (377-J7 See Page 337)
- MarC - (378-A7 See Page 337)
- MarC - 417-J3
- MarC - (418-A5 See Page 417)
- PHX - (377-J2 See Page 337)
- PHX - (418-A5 See Page 417)
- PHX - (458-A1 See Page 417)
- PHX - 498-C4
- PHX - 538-C5
- PHX - 578-C6
- PHX - 618-C6
- PHX - 658-C6
- PHX - 698-B3
N BLACK CANYON PKWY
- PHX 85086 (418-A6 See Page 417)
N BLACK CROSS RD
31000 SCTS 85262 (461-A5 See Page 421)
E BLACK DIAMOND DR
1300 GIL 85296 822-G3
N BLACK EAGLE RD
49400 MarC 85320 (285-A5 See Page 244)
S BLACKFOOT DR
11600 PHX 85044 819-E1
N BLACKFOOT LN
14200 FTNH 85268 583-E6
S BLACKFOOT LN
- PinC 85219 785-G2
W BLACK GOLD LN
14000 MarC 85375 495-A7
14400 MarC 85375 494-G7
W BLACKHAWK CT
16500 SURP 85374 534-D5
E BLACKHAWK DR
- PHX 85024 538-J4
1700 PHX 85024 539-A4
2800 PHX 85050 539-E4
W BLACKHAWK DR
- GLEN 85308 536-J4
- PHX 85024 538-H4
300 PHX 85027 538-A4
3700 PHX 85308 537-H4
5600 GLEN 85308 537-C3
S BLACKHAWK RD
3700 PinC 85219 786-J5
N BLACKHEATH RD
11400 PHX 85254 620-C1
S BLACK HILLS WY
- MarC 85249 902-F4
N BLACK MOUNTAIN PKWY
- PHX 85331 459-J2
- PHX 85331 460-A1
E BLACK MOUNTAIN RD
7600 SCTS 85262 460-J1
8000 SCTS 85262 (461-A1 See Page 421)
W BLACK MOUNTAIN RD
23500 MarC 85342 (412-A3 See Page 411)
25100 MarC 85342 411-G3
E BLACK ROCK RD
7200 SCTS 85255 500-G7
11200 SCTS 85255 501-H7
11300 SCTS 85255 541-H1
N BLACKROCK TR
7200 MarC 85253 619-H7
7200 MarC 85253 659-H1
N BLACKSMITH
17200 SURP 85374 534-C5
N BLACKSTONE CT
800 CHAN 85224 821-A4
N BLACKSTONE DR
1000 CHAN 85224 821-A3
N BLACK STONE DR
1900 CHAN 85224 821-A2
W BLACKWOOD DR
14400 MarC 85375 534-J2
S BLAIR RD
1300 APJT 85219 785-F1
E BLANCHE DR
- SCTS 85259 581-F4
2100 PHX 85022 579-C3
2400 PHX 85032 579-D4
4800 PHX 85254 580-A4
9000 SCTS 85260 581-B4
E BLEVINS DR
10300 MarC 85207 704-F6
N BLOODY BASIN RD
36900 CARE 85377 420-H5
N BLOOM ST
10500 PEOR 85345 616-E2
N BLOOMFIELD CT
- ELMG 85335 575-E6
E BLOOMFIELD DR
- SCTS 85259 581-J7
13400 SCTS 85259 622-D1
E BLOOMFIELD RD
2800 PHX 85032 579-E7
4900 PHX 85032 580-A7
5000 PHX 85254 580-A7
9400 SCTS 85260 581-C7
W BLOOMFIELD RD
- YNTN 85335 575-G6
2000 PHX 85029 578-A7
3600 PHX 85029 577-H7
4300 PHX 85304 577-G7
5300 GLEN 85304 577-B6
6700 PEOR 85381 577-A6
7100 PEOR 85381 576-E6
11700 ELMG 85335 575-E6
N BLOSSOM
- MESA 85206 783-D2
N BLOSSOM CIR
- MESA 85206 783-D2
E BLOSSOM CT
- GIL 85236 863-D4
S BLOSSOM DR
500 MESA 85206 743-D7
800 MESA 85206 783-D1
S BLOSSOM DR
10700 GDYR 85338 (773-J5 See Page 733)
N BLOSSOM LN
15400 SURP 85374 575-D2
E BLOSSOM RD
- MarC 85264 623-H2
W BLUE ASTER CT
16100 SURP 85374 534-E6
E BLUEBELL LN
300 TEMP 85281 700-E7
N BLUEBERRY CIR
1700 PHX 85022 539-B7
E BLUEBIRD CIR
- MarC 85236 863-B4
W BLUEBIRD DR
1000 CHAN 85248 861-B4
E BLUEBIRD LN
6300 PVAL 85253 660-E1
N BLUEBIRD LN
17400 PHX 85022 539-C7
17400 PHX 85022 579-C1
W BLUE BONNET DR
12600 MarC 85375 535-D2
E BLUE EAGLE LN
- MarC 85086 419-A3
400 MarC 85086 (418-J3 See Page 417)
E BLUE EAGLE ST
100 MarC 85086 (418-J3 See Page 417)
E BLUEFIELD AV
800 PHX 85022 538-J6
900 PHX 85022 539-A6
2500 PHX 85032 539-D6
4800 PHX 85254 540-A7
W BLUEFIELD AV
100 PHX 85023 538-D6
2700 PHX 85053 538-A6
3400 PHX 85308 538-A6
3600 PHX 85308 537-F6
5400 GLEN 85308 537-A6
7100 GLEN 85308 536-H6
8300 PEOR 85382 536-E6
W BLUEFIELD CT
11000 MarC 85351 575-J1
E BLUEFIELD DR
- PHX 85022 538-H6
W BLUEFIELD RD
1900 PHX 85023 538-D6
E BLUE FLAX AV
3800 PHX 85044 819-E5
N BLUE GROTTO DR
1000 GIL 85234 782-G4
N BLUEJAY CT
- GIL 85236 783-F6
W BLUEJAY CT
1700 CHAN 85248 861-B5
N BLUEJAY DR
600 GIL 85236 783-F5
W BLUEJAY DR
- CHAN 85248 861-C5
N BLUEJAY PL
15200 FTNH 85268 583-B4
N BLUE MARLIN DR
800 GIL 85234 782-F4
N BLUE POINT RD
7200 MarC 85290 664-F1
W BLUE RIDGE CT
1900 CHAN 85248 901-B2
E BLUE RIDGE DR
5800 CVCK 85331 420-D4
N BLUE RIDGE DR
9800 MarC 85351 576-C5
11400 MarC 85351 616-C1
E BLUE RIDGE WY
- MarC 85249 901-J2
- MarC 85249 902-A2
W BLUE RIDGE WY
1700 CHAN 85248 901-B2
E BLUE SAGE RD
- GIL 85236 863-B3
E BLUE SKY DR
- PHX 85331 499-J2
- PHX 85331 500-A2
- SCTS 85331 500-C2
9800 SCTS 85255 501-E2
W BLUE SKY DR
- PHX 85085 497-D1
- PHX 85085 498-B2
5900 GLEN 85308 537-D2
12900 MarC 85375 535-D2
W BLUESTEM DR
12300 MarC 85375 535-F2
BLUE TANK RD
- YavC - 250-G2
BLUE TANK TR
- YavC - 250-G5
W BLUE VERDE DR
14700 MarC 85375 534-H2
E BLUE WASH RD
11300 MarC 85331 (381-J4 See Page 341)
11300 MarC 85331 (382-A4 See Page 341)
S BLUFF SPRINGS CT
- PinC 85219 826-H2
W BOA VISTA DR
1400 GIL 85233 821-H1
W BOBBIE TER
4300 PHX 85306 577-G1
W BOBBY LOPEZ DR
8700 TOL 85353 696-E5
W BOBCAT CT
11500 SURP 85374 535-H6
E BOBCAT PZ
14800 FTNH 85268 582-H3
E BOBCAT TR
- SCTS 85255 501-C5
W BOB O LINK LN
600 PHX 85023 578-F4
N BOB WHITE DR
- SURP 85374 575-C2
N BOBWHITE DR
17600 MarC 85375 535-C6
W BOBWHITE DR
- MarC 85375 535-C6
E BOBWHITE WY
6800 SCTS 85331 460-G7
S BOCA CIR
- MESA 85212 784-F6
W BOCA RATON DR
4100 PHX 85053 577-H5
4500 PHX 85306 577-H5
5500 GLEN 85306 577-D5
E BOCA RATON RD
- PHX 85022 578-H5
W BOCA RATON RD
- SURP 85379 575-C4
- PHX 85023 578-G5

STREET Block City ZIP Pg-Grid

W BOCA RATON RD
7600 PEOR 85381 576-H5
W BOCA RATON ST
3000 PHX 85053 578-B5
13800 PHX 85306 577-G5
E BOGART AV
- MESA 85220 744-G7
7500 MESA 85208 743-J6
N BOGLE AV
800 CHAN 85225 821-G2
S BOGLE AV
600 CHAN 85225 821-G7
600 CHAN 85225 861-G1
E BOHL ST
4600 PHX 85044 779-H7
W BOHNE CIR
12300 AVON 85323 735-E3
W BOISE PL
1500 CHAN 85224 821-C1
E BOISE ST
1800 MESA 85203 742-C4
2500 MESA 85213 742-E4
5200 MarC 85205 743-C5
5200 MESA 85205 743-C5
6700 MESA 85207 743-H5
8100 MarC 85207 744-A5
10000 MarC 85220 744-F5
N BOKAY LN
53000 MarC 85390 290-A3
N BOLA CT
21000 MarC 85375 535-D2
W BOLA DR
12300 SURP 85374 575-B1
N BOLERO BEND
25600 MarC 85263 503-J6
25600 MarC 85263 (504-A5 See Page 503)
W BOLERO DR
100 TEMP 85284 820-C1
13200 MarC 85375 535-B6
N BOLIVAR DR
13800 MarC 85351 576-D3
W BOLIVAR DR
9900 MarC 85351 576-A4
E BONANZA CT
- MarC 85236 863-A2
N BONANZA DR
19200 MarC 85375 535-D4
W BONANZA DR
12300 MarC 85375 535-E4
N BONANZA LN
42000 PinC 85242 865-F6
E BONANZA RD
- GIL 85236 863-B2
- MarC 85236 863-A2
E BONANZA WY
- QC 85242 864-D6
N BONARDEN LN
1300 CHAN 85226 820-E3
S BONARDEN LN
1400 TEMP 85281 740-F5
2100 TEMP 85282 740-F6
3900 TEMP 85282 780-F1
5800 TEMP 85283 780-F4
7600 TEMP 85284 780-F7
8800 TEMP 85284 820-E2
N BOND DR
11600 FTNH 85268 623-D2
BONG LN
- GLEN 85309 615-A7
S BONITA CT
500 GIL 85233 822-B2
W BONITA CT
9600 MarC 85373 536-D7
E BONITA DR
6800 SCTS 85253 660-E5
7300 SCTS 85250 660-G5
8500 SCTS 85250 661-A5
N BONITA DR
- FTNH 85268 583-D6
W BONITA DR
32900 MarC 85390 290-A2
E BONITA ST
2200 GIL 85296 822-J2
17700 MarC 85264 583-F7
E BONITA WY
- TEMP 85281 740-D6
N BONITO CT
1300 GIL 85233 782-B4
S BONITO CT
500 GIL 85233 822-B1
S BONITO DR
400 GIL 85233 822-B1
N BONITOS DR
2200 PHX 85006 698-J3
E BONNELL ST
- MarC 85220 744-G5
8100 MarC 85207 744-A5
S BONNIE LN
1100 TEMP 85281 740-H5
E BONNIE ROSE AV
5400 SCTS 85250 660-G5
8500 SCTS 85250 661-A5
N BONOW DR
- SURP 85374 575-B2
S BOOJUM WY
400 MESA 85208 743-J7
W BOONE LN
- MarC 85086 (378-B6 See Page 337)
W BOOT
17200 SURP 85374 534-C7
S BOREGO RD
6000 PinC 85219 786-H7
N BORGATA DR
- SURP 85374 534-G5
E BORGHESE PL
6700 PHX 85016 659-A2
E BOSAGA WY
7400 MESA 85208 743-H6
W BOSAL DR
- MarC 85225 821-J1
- MarC 85233 822-A1
E BOSTON CIR
500 CHAN 85225 821-G6
1700 CHAN 85225 822-A7
2700 MESA 85213 742-F5
E BOSTON CT
- MarC 85236 823-A7
1000 CHAN 85225 821-H7
W BOSTON CT
1000 CHAN 85224 821-D6
E BOSTON ST
- GIL 85296 822-C7
- MarC 85236 823-B7
- CHAN 85225 821-F6
2000 CHAN 85225 822-A7
2400 MESA 85213 742-E5
5400 MarC 85205 743-C5
13200 MarC 85225 822-C7

W BOSTON ST
- CHAN 85225 821-F7
100 CHAN 85224 821-B6
3500 CHAN 85226 820-B6
7200 CHAN 85226 819-J6
W BOSTON WY
- CHAN 85226 820-E6
W BOSTON WY N
- CHAN 85226 820-E7
N BOSWELL BLVD
9800 MarC 85351 576-B1
10400 MarC 85373 536-B7
17000 MarC 85373 576-B1
W BOSWELL BLVD
10600 MarC 85373 536-A6
10700 MarC 85373 535-J7
W BOTTLE BRUSH
17100 SURP 85374 534-C6
N BOTTLEBRUSH WY
16200 FTNH 85268 583-A3
W BOTTLE TREE AV
14800 SURP 85374 534-H7
N BOTTLE TREE CT
17200 SURP 85374 534-H7
S BOULDER CIR
300 GIL 85296 822-G1
S BOULDER CT
600 GIL 85296 822-G2
W BOULDER CT
2000 CHAN 85248 861-B5
16200 SURP 85374 534-E5
E BOULDER DR
9600 MarC 85207 744-E5
9900 MarC 85220 744-G5
N BOULDER DR
1000 CARE 85377 420-H6
1000 SCTS 85377 420-H7
15200 FTNH 85268 583-B3
N BOULDER PASS
1400 CARE 85377 420-H7
1400 SCTS 85262 420-H7
1400 SCTS 85377 420-H7
E BOULDER ST
- APJT 85219 746-C2
5300 PinC 85219 746-C2
N BOULDER ST
- GIL 85234 782-G5
S BOULDER ST
- GIL 85296 822-G3
N BOULDER WY
20400 SURP 85374 534-F3
N BOULDER CANYON
- MESA 85207 703-H2
N BOULDER MOUNTAIN
- MESA 85207 704-E6
- MESA 85207 744-E1
E BOULDER RIDGE CT
4300 PHX 85044 779-G6
E BOULDERS PKWY
7300 SCTS 85262 460-H2
E BOULDER VIEW CT
11100 SCTS 85262 421-H3
N BOULDER VIEW DR
38600 SCTS 85262 421-H3
W BOULDER VISTA DR
- SURP 85374 534-D5
E BOWIE PL
4700 PinC 85242 905-G2
E BOWIE RD
7700 SCTS 85258 660-H1
E BOWKER ST
1300 PHX 85040 738-J7
1700 PHX 85040 739-A7
W BOWKER ST
- PHX 85339 737-D6
100 PHX 85041 738-C6
N BOWLING GREEN DR
15400 MarC 85351 576-D2
N BOWMAN RD
100 APJT 85219 745-H4
S BOWMAN RD
1000 APJT 85219 745-G7
1300 APJT 85219 785-G3
N BOWSTRING PZ
14800 FTNH 85268 583-E5
E BOX BAR TR
- MarC 85263 (504-A3 See Page 503)
N BOXCAR DR
16600 FTNH 85268 582-J3
W BOXELDER CIR
1200 CHAN 85224 781-D6
W BOXELDER CT
1300 CHAN 85224 781-C6
W BOXELDER PL
- CHAN 85225 781-D6
W BOXWOOD AV
1300 GIL 85233 781-J3
S BOXWOOD DR
5100 CHAN 85248 901-D2
24400 MarC 85248 901-D3
E BOXWOOD LN
14300 FTNH 85268 583-D6
N BOXWOOD LN
14400 FTNH 85268 583-D6
N BOYD RD
- PinC 85219 746-A5
S BOYD RD
- PinC 85219 746-A7
W BOYER ST
200 GBND 85337 (1090-A2 See Page 1049)
S BRACKEN LN
300 CHAN 85224 820-J7
W BRADFORD CT
600 GIL 85233 822-B3
E BRADFORD DR
16400 FTNH 85268 583-C5
W BRADFORD DR
800 GIL 85233 822-A3
W BRADFORD WY
- SURP 85374 534-D6
N BRADLEY DR
- CHAN 85226 820-E4
S BRADLEY DR
- CHAN 85226 820-E6
800 CHAN 85226 860-E1
5300 TEMP 85283 780-D3
W BRADLEY RD
20300 MarC 85361 (453-B5 See Page 413)
21700 MarC 85361 (452-D5 See Page 411)
S BRADSHAW WY
- MarC 85249 902-D5
W BRADSHAW MOUNTAIN CT
11600 SURP 85374 535-G4
E BRAEBURN DR
300 PHX 85022 578-H4

W BRAEBURN DR
100 PHX 85023 578-G4
E BRAMBLE AV
- MESA 85220 744-G6
2000 MESA 85204 742-D6
5500 MESA 85206 743-D6
7100 MESA 85208 743-G6
9100 MarC 85208 744-C6
10000 MarC 85220 744-F6
E BRAMBLE CIR
4300 MESA 85206 743-A6
E BRAMBLE BERRY LN
6900 SCTS 85262 460-G3
S BRANCHWOOD CT
26600 MarC 85248 901-E6
E BRANDED CT
- GIL 85236 863-E5
E BRANDED DR
- GIL 85236 863-E5
N BRANDING IRON
17200 SURP 85374 534-C7
N BRANDING IRON DR
9700 MarC 85351 576-C5
N BRANDON DR
600 CHAN 85226 820-C4
W BRANDYWINE DR
12500 MarC 85375 535-E6
14800 SURP 85374 534-H6
E BRANHAM LN
- PHX 85040 778-J3
- PHX 85040 779-A3
E BRANTLEY DR
17300 FTNH 85268 583-E6
W BRAVE RD
19900 MarC 85326 813-E1
E BRAVO LN
18700 MarC 85263 503-J5
N BRAVO LN
26000 MarC 85263 503-J5
S BRAYWOOD
- MESA 85212 784-J5
E BREATHLESS AV
9900 PinC 85219 826-J1
11400 PinC 85219 786-J7
E BREATHLESS DR
7700 CARE 85377 420-J5
W BRECKENRIDGE AV
600 GIL 85233 782-A5
1100 GIL 85233 781-J5
E BRECKENRIDGE WY
300 GIL 85234 782-D5
E BREEZE TREE WY
7600 SCTS 85255 540-H4
E BREMEN ST
3000 PHX 85032 539-E7
W BRENDA LYNNE LN
- SURP 85374 575-G1
E BRENTRUP DR
200 TEMP 85283 780-D7
S BRENTWOOD CT
1000 CHAN 85248 861-C2
S BRENTWOOD DR
25600 MarC 85248 901-B5
N BRENTWOOD PL
1200 CHAN 85224 821-C2
3200 CHAN 85224 781-C6
S BRENTWOOD PL
200 CHAN 85224 821-C7
700 CHAN 85224 861-C1
1100 CHAN 85248 861-C1
E BRET HILLS
6200 PVAL 85253 620-D6
N BRETT ST
500 GIL 85234 782-G5
S BRETT ST
200 GIL 85296 822-G1
S BRIAR
400 MESA 85204 742-D7
900 MESA 85204 782-D1
S BRIAR CIR
200 MESA 85204 742-D6
1300 MESA 85204 782-D1
S BRIARCREST DR
- MarC 85248 900-J4
- MarC 85248 901-A3
S BRIAR WING DR
24800 MarC 85248 901-A3
W BRIARWOOD CIR
9200 MarC 85351 576-C1
E BRIARWOOD DR
16500 FTNH 85268 583-C5
N BRIARWOOD DR
- MarC 85351 575-H1
14600 FTNH 85268 583-C5
N BRIARWOOD LN
- GIL 85234 783-B7
E BRIARWOOD TER
300 PHX 85048 818-G7
W BRIARWOOD TER
- PHX 85045 818-E7
E BRIARWOOD TR
1200 PHX 85048 818-J7
2100 PHX 85048 819-A7
N BRICE
11200 MESA 85220 745-A4
S BRICE
- MarC 85212 824-J1
- MESA 85212 784-J7
- MESA 85220 784-J1
S BRICE CIR
- MarC 85212 824-J3
- MESA 85212 824-J1
S BRIDAL VAIL DR
- MarC 85236 903-B2
S BRIDAL VEIL DR
- GIL 85236 863-B3
N BRIDALWREATH ST
1600 TEMP 85281 700-F7
W BRIDEN LN
8100 PEOR 85382 496-G6
W BRIDGE ST
1400 PHX 85045 818-D7
N BRIDGEGATE DR
300 GIL 85236 783-D4
E BRIDGEPORT CT
- MarC 85236 823-A7
E BRIDGEPORT PKWY
- GIL 85296 822-D7
- MarC 85236 823-B7
S BRIDGER CT
- CHAN 85249 901-G3
S BRIDGER DR
- CHAN 85249 861-G1
800 CHAN 85225 861-G1
W BRIDGEWATER WY
- SURP 85374 534-F4
W BRIDGEWOOD DR
15800 SURP 85374 534-F7
E BRIDLE CT
- GIL 85296 822-D6

N BRIDLE LN
17700 SURP 85374 534-D6
E BRIDLE PL
- SCTS 85255 541-C4
N BRIDLE PTH
- SCTS 85255 501-J5
E BRIDLE WY
- GIL 85296 822-D6
N BRIDLEGATE DR
- GIL 85236 783-D4
N BRIDLEWOOD
- MESA 85207 704-A7
- MESA 85207 744-A1
S BRIDLEWOOD
2700 MESA 85212 783-J6
N BRIDLEWOOD CT
- MarC 85086 (378-D6 See Page 337)
N BRIDLEWOOD WY
- MarC 85086 (378-D5 See Page 337)
W BRIDLINGTON AV
- SURP 85374 534-D5
W BRIGHT ANGEL CIR
9900 MarC 85351 576-B3
N BRIGHT ANGEL LN
18600 SURP 85374 534-F5
N BRIGHTON
- MESA 85207 703-H4
1200 MESA 85207 743-H2
S BRIGHTON
1800 MESA 85208 783-G3
6400 MESA 85212 823-G7
6400 MESA 85212 863-G1
N BRIGHTON CIR
1800 MESA 85207 743-H1
S BRIGHTON CIR
1800 MESA 85208 783-G4
N BRIGHTON LN
200 GIL 85236 783-D7
S BRIGHTON LN
- GIL 85236 863-D2
W BRIGHTON WY
- SURP 85374 534-G6
E BRILES RD
- MarC 85373 495-H3
- MarC 85024 498-H4
4000 PHX 85050 499-H4
4600 PHX 85050 500-A4
W BRILES RD
- PEOR 85382 496-J4
- PEOR 85382 497-A3
- PHX 85310 497-B3
100 MarC 85027 498-G4
15000 MarC 85375 494-H3
E BRILL ST
700 PHX 85006 698-H4
1400 PHX 85006 699-A4
2400 PHX 85008 699-D4
W BRILL ST
3900 PHX 85009 697-H4
4600 PHX 85043 697-D4
E BRILLIANT SKY DR
- PHX 85331 460-A1
6000 SCTS 85262 460-D1
N BRIMHALL ST
400 MESA 85203 741-J4
2400 MESA 85203 702-A6
E BRINKER DR
- AVON 85323 695-B7
W BRINKER DR
- AVON 85323 695-B7
E BRISA DR
- SCTS 85262 460-H5
W BRISA DR
200 GIL 85233 822-B2
E BRISBANE RD
4000 APJT 85219 746-A5
4000 PinC 85219 746-A5
S BRISTOL
- MESA 85212 784-E4
N BRISTOL BAY
15000 FTNH 85268 583-C5
S BRISTOL LN
700 GIL 85234 782-J5
W BRISTOL LN
- SURP 85374 534-D6
BRITISH COLUMBIA
6500 PinC 85219 786-D7
6500 PinC 85219 826-D1
E BRITT CT
16900 FTNH 85268 583-D6
N BRITTANY LN
1300 GIL 85233 782-C4
S BRITTANY LN
5700 TEMP 85283 780-C4
S BRITTLEBRUSH
1300 BUCK 85326 (692-C7 See Page 651)
E BRITTLE BUSH
6800 SCTS 85262 460-G4
W BRITTLE BUSH
17100 SURP 85374 534-C6
E BRITTLEBUSH LN
14200 FTNH 85268 583-A6
E BRITTLE BUSH RD
7900 PinC 85219 786-F7
W BRITTON AV
5900 PHX 85031 657-C7
5900 PHX 85033 657-A7
6400 PHX 85033 697-B1
6900 PHX 85033 656-J7
E BROADMOOR CT
300 PHX 85022 578-H4
E BROADMOR DR
- TEMP 85282 740-D6
2100 TEMP 85282 741-A6
E BROADWAY AV
- APJT 85219 745-H7
- APJT 85220 745-H7
3200 APJT 85219 746-B7
3200 PinC 85219 746-B7
W BROADWAY AV
- APJT 85220 745-B7
S BROADWAY LN
- PinC 85219 746-D7
- PinC 85219 786-D1
- PinC 85273 746-D7
E BROADWAY RD
- MESA 85210 741-H6
- PHX 85040 738-H5
- PHX 85041 738-H5
- TEMP 85282 740-F6
- TEMP 85281 740-F6
300 MESA 85204 742-D6
400 MESA 85204 741-H6
1400 PHX 85040 739-D5
2000 TEMP 85281 741-A6
2000 TEMP 85282 741-A6
3600 MESA 85206 742-G6

E BROADWAY RD
4100 MESA 85206 743-A6
6800 MESA 85208 743-F6
7900 MarC 85208 743-F6
7900 MarC 85208 744-B7
7900 MESA 85208 744-A7
10000 MarC 85220 744-F7
10000 MESA 85220 744-G7
11400 MarC 85220 745-A7
S BROADWAY RD
1700 TEMP 85281 740-A5
W BROADWAY RD
- MESA 85210 741-F6
- PHX 85041 738-B5
- TEMP 85281 740-B6
- TEMP 85282 740-B6
900 PHX 85041 737-H5
1200 MESA 85202 741-C6
1700 TEMP 85281 739-J6
2000 TEMP 85282 739-J6
2700 MarC 85041 738-B5
3100 MarC 85041 737-H5
5100 MarC 85043 737-B5
5100 PHX 85043 737-B5
6700 MarC 85043 736-F4
6700 PHX 85043 736-F4
8200 MarC 85353 736-B5
8300 PHX 85353 736-F4
10300 MarC 85353 735-F4
10700 AVON 85353 735-H5
12300 MarC 85323 735-D4
13900 GDYR 85338 735-D4
14000 GDYR 85338 (734-F4 See Page 733)
17100 GDYR 85326 (734-A3 See Page 733)
17500 GDYR 85326 733-E4
17500 MarC 85326 733-E4
17500 MarC 85326 (734-A3 See Page 733)
18700 BUCK 85326 733-E4
21100 MarC 85326 (732-G4 See Page 731)
24700 BUCK 85326 (732-G4 See Page 731)
25600 BUCK 85326 731-H3
25600 MarC 85326 731-H3
N BROCKWAY LN
15000 FTNH 85268 583-C5
E BRODIEA DR
15800 FTNH 85268 583-A7
E BROKEN ARROW DR
9200 SCTS 85262 421-C7
N BROKEN ARROW DR
20000 MarC 85375 535-B3
W BROKEN ARROW DR
- WICK 85390 290-A1
13200 MarC 85375 535-C3
E BROKEN ARROW LN
- PinC 85219 786-H4
N BROKEN BOW
9000 FTNH 85268 622-G5
W BROKEN BOW CT
18000 MarC 85373 536-D6
N BROKEN SPUR DR
- SCTS 85262 421-E3
W BROKEN SPUR TR
1100 WICK 85390 290-C2
W BROKENSTONE DR
9200 MarC 85351 576-C3
W BROMM LN
- WICK 85390 290-A1
W BRONCO CT
1300 GIL 85233 782-B4
E BRONCO DR
- QC 85242 904-B1
3800 PHX 85040 819-F1
3800 PHX 85044 819-F1
6500 PVAL 85253 620-E7
N BRONCO LN
1200 GIL 85233 782-B4
S BRONCO LN
200 GIL 85233 822-B1
3400 PinC 85219 786-J4
E BRONCO TR
8200 SCTS 85255 501-A5
N BRONCO TR
- PEOR 85382 496-J4
- PEOR 85382 497-A5
25200 SCTS 85255 500-J5
25400 SCTS 85255 501-A5
W BRONCO TR
- PEOR 85382 496-J4
- PEOR 85382 497-A4
S BRONZE DR
23700 MarC 85248 900-J2
S BROOK LN
7600 TEMP 85284 780-H7
E BROOKDALE ST
1800 MESA 85203 742-C4
W BROOK HILL CT
- MarC 85086 (378-D5 See Page 337)
E BROOK HOLLOW DR
200 PHX 85022 578-H4
S BROOKS
2700 MESA 85202 781-D5
S BROOKS CIR
1700 MESA 85202 781-D2
E BROOKS CT
- GIL 85236 823-A2
2200 GIL 85296 822-J2
W BROOKS CT
- CHAN 85224 821-D2
E BROOKS ST
700 CHAN 85225 821-H2
2000 GIL 85296 822-F2
2500 GIL 85236 823-A2
N BROOKS ST
- MESA 85201 741-D5
S BROOKS ST
200 MESA 85202 741-D6
W BROOKS ST
800 CHAN 85225 821-E2
1300 CHAN 85224 821-A2
13400 GIL 85233 822-C2
13400 MarC 85233 822-C2
E BROOKS FARM RD
- MarC 85249 901-H1
2500 MarC 85249 902-B1
16800 MarC 85236 903-C1
18000 QC 85236 903-E1
W BROOKS FARM RD
- CHAN 85248 901-B1
W BROOKSIDE DR
10000 MarC 85351 576-A1
10800 MarC 85351 575-J2
N BROOKSIDE LN
17000 SURP 85374 534-G7

N BROOKSIDE ST
- CHAN 85225 821-J6
100 CHAN 85225 822-A6
S BROOKSIDE ST
- CHAN 85249 861-J2
BROOKVIEW TR
4700 LP 85340 655-A5
N BROOKVIEW WY
7200 MarC 85253 619-H7
7200 MarC 85253 659-H1
E BROOKWOOD CT
400 PHX 85048 818-G6
1700 PHX 85048 819-A6
W BROOKWOOD CT
700 PHX 85045 818-C6
E BROOKWOOD DR
3500 PHX 85048 819-E6
N BROWN AV
3400 SCTS 85251 700-F1
4200 SCTS 85251 660-F7
W BROWN DR
- SURP 85374 534-A6
E BROWN RD
- MESA 85201 741-J2
400 MESA 85203 741-J2
600 MESA 85203 742-A2
1200 MESA 85213 742-E2
3600 MESA 85205 742-G2
4100 MESA 85205 743-B2
6800 MESA 85207 743-H2
7600 MESA 85207 744-D3
9200 MarC 85207 744-D3
10000 MarC 85220 744-J3
10800 MarC 85220 745-A3
W BROWN RD
- MESA 85201 741-G2
E BROWN ST
800 PHX 85020 618-J3
1400 PHX 85020 619-A3
2300 PHX 85028 619-C3
W BROWN ST
500 TEMP 85281 740-C3
1100 PHX 85021 618-E3
3200 PHX 85051 618-A3
3500 PHX 85051 617-J2
4400 GLEN 85302 617-B2
6700 PEOR 85345 617-A2
6900 PEOR 85345 616-C2
17500 MarC 85355 (614-A2 See Page 573)
W BROWNING DR
- SURP 85374 534-B6
E BROWNING PL
- CHAN 85249 861-H1
2200 CHAN 85249 862-A1
W BROWNING WY
1500 CHAN 85248 861-B1
E BRUCE AV
- GIL 85234 783-C7
- GIL 85236 783-D7
100 GIL 85234 783-B7
W BRUCE AV
- GIL 85233 782-A7
1200 GIL 85233 781-J7
W BRUCE CIR
1300 GIL 85233 781-J7
E BRUCE CT
- GIL 85236 783-D7
S BRUCE CT
700 CHAN 85226 820-F7
N BRUNSWICK DR
14000 FTNH 85268 583-C6
W BRYCE LN
4500 GLEN 85301 617-E6
W BUCCANEER DR
10800 MarC 85351 575-J5
N BUCCANEER WY
13600 MarC 85351 576-A5
W BUCCANEER WY
10700 MarC 85351 576-A5
E BUCHANAN ST
- PHX 85004 698-G7
S BUCHANAN ST
600 GIL 85233 822-A3
W BUCHANAN ST
- AVON 85353 695-E7
- GDYR 85338 (694-D6 See Page 653)
- PHX 85003 698-F7
800 PHX 85007 698-D7
3700 PHX 85009 697-H7
5300 PHX 85043 697-D7
N BUCHAROO LN
- GIL 85234 783-C5
W BUCK LN
- MarC 85361 (452-J6 See Page 411)
S BUCKAROO CT
- GIL 85236 863-C3
S BUCKAROO TR
- GIL 85236 863-C2
- MarC 85236 823-C7
E BUCK BASIN DR
- MarC 85263 503-J6
E BUCKBOARD CT
- GIL 85236 863-E4
E BUCKBOARD RD
- GIL 85236 863-D5
N BUCKBOARD TR
4000 SCTS 85251 700-F1
4100 SCTS 85251 660-F7
E BUCKEYE RD
- PHX 85004 738-H1
700 PHX 85034 738-H1
800 AVON 85323 695-F7
800 AVON 85323 735-C1
800 MarC 85323 695-F7
1400 PHX 85034 739-A1
11300 AVON 85353 695-F7
11300 AVON 85353 735-G1
11300 MarC 85353 695-F7
11300 MarC 85353 735-G1
S BUCKEYE RD
1600 MarC 85326 (691-B7 See Page 651)
2300 MarC 85326 731-B1
W BUCKEYE RD
- PHX 85003 738-G1
700 PHX 85007 738-E1
1900 PHX 85009 738-B1
3100 PHX 85009 737-F1
4300 PHX 85043 737-B1
5500 MarC 85043 737-B1
6700 PHX 85043 736-H1
7500 TOL 85043 736-D1
8300 TOL 85353 736-D1
8300 PHX 85353 736-D1
10300 PHX 85353 735-H1
10300 TOL 85353 735-H1
10700 AVON 85353 735-H1

W BUCKEYE RD
28500 BUCK 85326 (691-A6 See Page 651)
28500 MarC 85326 (691-A6 See Page 651)
W BUCKEYE RD Rt#-85
25100 MarC 85326 (771-H1 See Page 731)
25100 MarC 85326 (772-A1 See Page 731)
25100 BUCK 85326 (771-H1 See Page 731)
25100 BUCK 85326 (772-A1 See Page 731)
BUCKEYE CSR
- BUCK - (732-E7 See Page 731)
- BUCK - 733-H5
- BUCK - (771-J1 See Page 731)
- BUCK - (772-B1 See Page 731)
- GDYR - 733-H5
- GDYR - (734-C5 See Page 733)
- MarC - (732-E7 See Page 731)
- MarC - 733-H5
- MarC - 735-C6
- MarC - (771-B2 See Page 731)
- MarC - (772-A1 See Page 731)
S BUCKEYE HILLS DR
- MarC 85326 811-C6
- MarC 85337 811-C6
W BUCKEYE HILLS DR
- MarC 85337 811-D7
E BUCKHORN CT
- FTNH 85268 583-A5
W BUCKHORN CT
9300 MarC 85373 536-D6
E BUCKHORN DR
4600 PHX 85331 500-A3
E BUCKHORN TR
7200 SCTS 85255 500-G3
W BUCKHORN TR
- PHX 85085 497-C2
- PHX 85085 498-B2
N BUCKHORN CAMP DR
2500 MarC 85207 704-E4
N BUCKING BRONCO WY
11800 FTNH 85268 622-H2
W BUCKING HORSE TR
500 WICK 85390 290-B2
W BUCK MOUNTAIN CT
11600 SURP 85374 535-G4
N BUCKSHOT PL
- SCTS 85255 541-C3
E BUCKSKIN DR
- MarC 85263 (504-A6 See Page 503)
18600 MarC 85263 503-J6
25200 SCTS 85255 501-G6
N BUCKSKIN RD
900 PinC 85219 746-C3
E BUCKSKIN TR
8200 SCTS 85255 501-A6
S BUCKSKIN TR
600 GIL 85296 822-H2
W BUCKSKIN TR
- PEOR 85382 496-J5
- PEOR 85382 497-A5
200 WICK 85390 290-C2
2600 MarC 85087 (338-D4 See Page 337)
4600 PHX 85310 497-C5
E BUCKSKIN WY
24900 SCTS 85255 501-G6
E BUCK SPRING CT
- MarC 85263 (504-A3 See Page 503)
N BUCKTHORN
17500 SURP 85374 534-C7
E BUCKTHORN TR
- SCTS 85331 500-F3
E BUCKWHEAT CIR
26400 SCTS 85255 501-C4
E BUD CT
9600 MarC 85248 901-B5
E BUENA TERRA WY
4200 PHX 85018 659-H4
5500 SCTS 85253 660-F4
7200 SCTS 85250 660-F4
8500 SCTS 85250 661-A5
N BUENA VIDA CT
15000 FTNH 85268 583-E5
N BUENA VISTA
700 WICK 85390 290-E1
E BUENA VISTA AV
- GDYR 85338 695-A7
S BUENA VISTA AV
- GIL 85296 782-D7
300 GIL 85296 822-D1
E BUENA VISTA DR
- TEMP 85284 820-D1
1000 CHAN 85249 901-H5
1800 CHAN 85249 902-A5
S BUENA VISTA DR
1100 APJT 85220 745-D7
1100 APJT 85220 785-D1
W BUENA VISTA DR
- SURP 85374 534-A5
- TEMP 85284 820-A1
E BUENA VISTA RD
- PHX 85040 778-J7
- PHX 85040 779-A7
E BUFFALO CT
1600 CHAN 85225 821-J6
1600 CHAN 85225 822-A6
N BUFFALO DR
10800 FTNH 85268 622-J2
10800 FTNH 85268 623-A3
S BUFFALO DR
100 CHAN 85226 820-H6
W BUFFALO PL
5700 CHAN 85226 820-D6
E BUFFALO ST
- CHAN 85225 821-F6
1700 CHAN 85225 822-A6
14000 MarC 85296 822-D6
W BUFFALO ST
- CHAN 85225 821-F6
- CHAN 85226 820-D6
W BUFFALO TR
14400 SURP 85374 534-J7
W BUIST AV
100 PHX 85041 778-D5
E BUIST ST
4500 PHX 85044 779-H5

STREET
Block City ZIP Pg-Grid

N BULLARD AV
- GDYR 85338 (654-H7 See Page 653)
- GDYR 85338 (694-H2 See Page 653)
10600 SURP 85379 (574-J3 See Page 573)
10600 SURP 85379 (614-J1 See Page 573)
12200 MarC 85379 (574-J3 See Page 573)
15400 SURP 85374 534-J7
15400 SURP 85374 (574-J3 See Page 573)
25000 MarC 85375 494-J3
S BULLARD AV
- GDYR 85338 (694-H7 See Page 653)
3400 GDYR 85338 (734-H5 See Page 733)
23600 GDYR 85326 (854-G7 See Page 813)
S BULL DOG CT
- PinC 85219 826-H2
N BULLDOG MINE RD
- APJT 85219 745-G2
- PinC 85219 705-H7
- PinC 85219 745-G2
N BULLMOOSE CIR
500 CHAN 85224 821-A5
N BULLMOOSE CT
1300 CHAN 85224 821-A3
N BULLMOOSE DR
200 CHAN 85224 821-A1
N BULL MOOSE DR
2700 CHAN 85224 781-A7
W BULLMOOSE DR
2200 CHAN 85224 821-A5
N BULL RUN ST
2200 TEMP 85281 700-F6
E BUMBLEBEE LN
15500 FTNH 85268 582-J2
15500 FTNH 85268 583-A2
E BUNKER HILL DR
600 TEMP 85281 700-F6
W BUNKER PEAK RD
20300 MarC 85361 493-B1
N BUNTLINE DR
17600 MarC 85375 535-E7
N BURBANK CT
1600 CHAN 85225 821-D2
N BURBANK DR
1400 CHAN 85225 821-D3
E BURGESS AV
4000 PHX 85040 779-G1
S BURGESS CT
- MarC 85248 901-E4
E BURGESS LN
1300 PHX 85040 778-J1
1700 PHX 85040 779-A1
W BURGESS LN
1800 PHX 85041 778-D1
4000 PHX 85041 737-G7
4000 PHX 85041 777-G1
N BURK ST
- GIL 85234 782-D3
S BURK ST
400 GIL 85296 822-D2
N BURKEMO DR
9600 FTNH 85268 623-D4
N BURL CIR
300 MESA 85203 742-C4
S BURNABY CT
25600 MarC 85248 901-E5
S BURNABY DR
25600 MarC 85248 901-E5
W BURNETT RD
9700 PEOR 85382 536-A3
10700 PEOR 85373 536-A3
11000 PEOR 85373 535-J3
N BURNING TREE PL
13800 PHX 85022 578-H5
N BURNS DR
16400 MarC 85351 576-D1
17000 MarC 85373 576-D1
W BURNS DR
9500 MarC 85351 576-B2
E BURNSIDE TR
6800 SCTS 85262 460-G4
W BURNTWOOD DR
11000 MarC 85351 575-H3
E BURRO DR
15700 FTNH 85268 623-A2
S BURSAGE
1300 BUCK 85326 (692-C7 See Page 651)
W BURSAGE
17100 SURP 85374 534-C6
E BURSAGE CIR
8500 PinC 85219 786-F6
E BURSAGE DR
8900 PinC 85219 786-F6
15800 FTNH 85268 583-A6
N BURSAGE DR
14200 FTNH 85268 583-A6
N BUSH HWY
- MarC 85256 663-H6
3600 MESA 85207 703-G3
3600 MESA 85215 703-G3
4300 MarC 85215 703-G3
4300 MarC 85290 663-H6
4300 MESA 85290 663-H6
4300 MESA 85290 703-G3
4300 MarC 85290 703-G3
4400 MarC 85215 663-G7
4400 MarC 85215 663-H6
4400 MarC 85290 663-G7
5500 MarC 85290 664-G2
- MarC 85256 103-B2
N BUSH ST
- MarC 85361 (452-J6 See Page 411)
- MarC 85361 (453-A7 See Page 413)
S BUSH ST
32000 MarC 85361 (453-A2 See Page 413)
W BUSH WY
- CHAN 85248 861-D5
BUSHMASTER BLVD
- PHX 85008 700-A4
E BUTEO DR
7400 SCTS 85255 540-H4
8200 SCTS 85255 541-A5
E BUTHERUS DR
- SCTS 85259 581-F4
7200 PHX 85254 580-G4
7200 SCTS 85260 580-G4
8300 SCTS 85260 581-A4

N BUTHERUS DR
- SCTS 85259 581-G4
E BUTLER AV
100 BUCK 85326 (772-A1 See Page 731)
W BUTLER AV
8300 PEOR 85345 616-F5
E BUTLER CIR
1300 CHAN 85225 821-J7
1700 CHAN 85225 822-A7
W BUTLER CT
1000 CHAN 85224 821-D7
BUTLER DR
4800 PVAL 85253 620-A5
E BUTLER DR
- GLEN 85302 617-D5
- PHX 85020 618-G5
700 CHAN 85225 821-H7
1200 PHX 85020 619-A5
4900 PVAL 85253 620-A5
7400 SCTS 85258 620-G6
W BUTLER DR
- PHX 85021 618-E5
1100 CHAN 85224 821-B7
2700 PHX 85051 618-A5
3400 PHX 85051 617-G5
4300 GLEN 85302 617-B5
4500 CHAN 85226 820-C6
6700 GLEN 85345 617-A5
6700 GLEN 85301 617-A5
7100 PEOR 85345 616-A5
10600 PEOR 85345 615-H5
14100 MarC 85355 (614-J4 See Page 573)
14100 MarC 85355 615-A4
E BUTLER ST
2000 CHAN 85225 822-A7
13200 MarC 85225 822-B7
W BUTLER ST
100 CHAN 85226 820-G6
E BUTTE AV
1700 TEMP 85282 740-H6
N BUTTE AV
600 CHAN 85226 820-G3
S BUTTE AV
1000 TEMP 85281 740-H5
2200 TEMP 85282 740-G6
3300 TEMP 85282 780-G2
6400 TEMP 85283 780-G5
7700 TEMP 85284 780-G7
9000 TEMP 85284 820-G2
E BUTTE CIR
2600 MESA 85213 742-E4
S BUTTE DR
5900 TEMP 85283 780-G4
S BUTTE LN
900 GIL 85296 822-G3
E BUTTE ST
- MESA 85220 744-G5
2400 MESA 85213 742-E4
5200 MarC 85205 743-C4
5200 MESA 85205 743-C4
8100 MarC 85207 744-A5
10000 MarC 85220 744-F5
E BUTTE CANYON CIR
- CVCK 85331 420-C6
E BUTTE CANYON DR
- CVCK 85331 420-C6
W BUTTE CANYON RD
- PHX 85086 (418-B5 See Page 417)
W BUTTE CREEK BLVD
- MarC 85242 904-H6
E BUTTERCUP
- MESA 85208 783-J4
S BUTTERCUP
2100 MESA 85208 783-J4
N BUTTERCUP DR
14200 MarC 85351 576-C4
W BUTTERFIELD DR
12500 MarC 85375 535-D7
BUTTERFIELD TR Rt#-84
100 GBND 85337 106-B1
1300 MarC 85337 106-B1
100 GBND 85337 (1090-E4 See Page 1049)
1300 MarC 85337 (1090-E4 See Page 1049)
N BUTTERMILK
17400 SURP 85374 534-B6
E BUTTERNUT AV
9000 MarC 85208 744-E7
N BUTTERWOOD DR
- PHX 85310 497-H4
S BUTTONWOOD DR
25200 MarC 85248 901-E4
W BUTTONWOOD DR
14600 MarC 85375 534-H3

C

W C ST
5100 PHX 85031 657-E5
30700 MarC 85337 (1090-B1 See Page 1049)
E CABALLERO CIR
2200 MESA 85213 742-D4
3600 MESA 85205 742-H4
7700 MESA 85207 743-J4
W CABALLERO CIR
600 MESA 85201 741-F4
E CABALLERO DR
2600 MarC 85206 743-E7
W CABALLERO DR
13600 MarC 85375 495-A7
14600 MarC 85375 494-J7
E CABALLERO ST
- MarC 85220 744-F4
- MESA 85220 744-H5
- MarC 85220 745-A5
400 MESA 85220 742-E4
4000 MESA 85205 742-J4
4500 MESA 85205 743-A4
7800 MESA 85207 743-J4
7800 MESA 85207 744-A4
E CABALLO CIR
7000 PVAL 85253 620-F5
E CABALLO DR
5600 PVAL 85253 620-C5
N CABALLO DR
8600 PVAL 85253 620-F5
E CABALLO LN
5800 PVAL 85253 620-C5
E CABANA AV
4000 MESA 85206 742-J7
W CABANA AV
2200 MESA 85202 741-B6
N CABANA LN
22600 MarC 85375 495-A7

E CABAZON CT
- GIL 85236 863-C4
N CABOT CIR
- MESA 85207 704-D6
N CABOT ST
9200 MESA 85207 704-D6
N CABRAL WY
900 GIL 85234 782-J5
E CABRILLO CT
- GIL 85236 863-C4
E CABRILLO DR
8600 PVAL 85253 620-C5
N CABRILLO DR
15100 FTNH 85268 582-H4
CABRITO CIR
400 LP 85340 655-B7
N CACTUS
- MarC 85086 417-J4
E CACTUS CT
8100 MESA 85208 744-A7
S CACTUS CT
26000 MarC 85248 901-A5
E CACTUS DR
8200 MESA 85208 744-A7
14200 FTNH 85268 583-A6
W CACTUS DR
32600 MarC 85390 290-B2
E CACTUS LN
2500 PHX 85040 779-C4
9000 MarC 85248 900-J5
9000 MarC 85248 901-A5
N CACTUS LN
15400 SURP 85374 575-D2
W CACTUS LN
19000 SURP 85374 534-E4
E CACTUS RD
2000 PHX 85022 579-D7
2000 PHX 85028 579-D7
2300 PHX 85032 579-D7
4600 PHX 85032 580-B7
5000 PHX 85254 580-B7
6000 SCTS 85254 580-B7
6000 PHX 85254 620-D1
6000 SCTS 85254 620-D1
7200 SCTS 85260 620-G1
7300 SCTS 85260 621-D1
10400 SCTS 85259 621-F1
12400 SCTS 85259 622-B1
N CACTUS RD
- APJT 85219 745-F5
3900 PinC 85219 745-F1
4100 PinC 85219 705-F7
S CACTUS RD
- APJT 85219 745-F6
1300 APJT 85219 785-F1
W CACTUS RD
- YNTN 85335 575-G7
1900 PHX 85029 578-B7
3500 PHX 85029 577-H7
4300 PHX 85304 577-G7
5100 GLEN 85304 577-C7
6700 PEOR 85381 577-C7
6700 PEOR 85345 577-C7
7100 PEOR 85381 576-E7
7100 PEOR 85345 576-E7
11800 ELMG 85335 575-G7
13100 SURP 85379 575-C6
13500 MarC 85379 575-C6
13900 SURP 85379 (574-D6 See Page 573)
14700 MarC 85379 (574-D6 See Page 573)
17900 MarC 85379 573-H6
17900 SURP 85379 573-H6
N CACTUS WY
700 CHAN 85226 820-C4
S CACTUS FLOWER CT
23700 MarC 85248 901-A2
E CACTUS FLOWER DR
- MarC 85248 901-A3
S CACTUS FLOWER DR
23700 MarC 85248 901-A2
W CACTUS FLOWER DR
17300 GDYR 85338 (774-A5 See Page 733)
CACTUS FLOWER WY
13900 FTNH 85268 582-H6
W CACTUS RIDGE WY
- SURP 85374 534-H4
W CACTUS VALLEY LN
- SURP 85374 534-E6
E CACTUS VIEW CIR
10500 PinC 85219 786-J4
E CACTUS WREN CIR
- SCTS 85262 (461-A1 See Page 421)
E CACTUS WREN CT
15800 FTNH 85268 583-A4
W CACTUS WREN CT
11600 SURP 85374 535-G6
E CACTUS WREN DR
- PHX 85020 658-G1
- PHX 85021 658-G1
1600 PHX 85020 659-B1
S CACTUS WREN DR
3800 CHAN 85248 861-A7
W CACTUS WREN DR
- GLEN 85303 656-H1
- GLEN 85303 657-A1
700 PHX 85021 658-E1
2900 PHX 85051 658-A1
3700 PHX 85051 657-H1
E CACTUS WREN PL
6400 PVAL 85253 660-D2
E CACTUS WREN RD
5600 PVAL 85253 660-B2
5800 MarC 85253 660-B2
7200 SCTS 85250 660-F2
8400 SCTS 85250 661-A2
W CACTUS WREN RD
2100 PHX 85021 658-C1
E CACTUS WREN ST
2700 APJT 85219 745-H6
5100 PinC 85219 746-B6
14400 MarC 85296 822-F1
W CACTUS WREN ST
2400 APJT 85220 745-A5
N CADDY CT
22800 MarC 85375 494-J7
E CAHAVA RANCH RD
4000 CVCK 85331 (379-J7 See Page 339)
4000 CVCK 85331 (380-A5 See Page 339)
E CAIDA DEL SOL DR
4800 PVAL 85253 619-J5
4800 PVAL 85253 620-A5
E CAIDE DEL SOL DR
- PHX 85028 619-J5
- PHX 85253 619-J5

E CAIDE DEL SOL DR
4800 PVAL 85253 619-J5
E CAIRO CIR
2100 TEMP 85282 740-J7
2100 TEMP 85282 741-A7
E CAIRO DR
- TEMP 85282 740-D7
2100 TEMP 85282 741-A7
W CAIRO DR
1400 TEMP 85282 740-A7
W CALAVAR CIR
- SURP 85379 575-C4
E CALAVAR DR
4000 PHX 85032 579-H5
W CALAVAR LN
4400 PHX 85306 577-G5
E CALAVAR RD
- PHX 85022 578-H5
1500 PHX 85022 579-A5
2800 PHX 85032 579-A5
W CALAVAR RD
- SURP 85379 (574-H4 See Page 573)
- SURP 85379 575-C4
1600 PHX 85023 578-C5
3000 PHX 85053 578-A5
3300 PHX 85053 577-H5
5200 GLEN 85306 577-C5
6900 PEOR 85381 577-A5
7500 PEOR 85381 576-H5
W CALAVAR ST
4500 PHX 85306 577-G5
E CALAVERAS AV
17000 FTNH 85268 583-D5
E CALAVEROS DR
2800 PHX 85028 619-E4
N CALDERON
- MESA 85220 744-J4
S CALDERON
- MarC 85212 824-J1
- MESA 85212 784-J7
- MESA 85220 784-J1
S CALDERON CIR
- MarC 85212 824-J3
- MESA 85212 824-J1
E CALDWELL ST
- PHX 85339 777-E3
300 PHX 85040 778-G3
1700 PHX 85040 779-B4
W CALDWELL ST
- MarC 85339 777-F3
- PHX 85339 777-E3
100 PHX 85041 778-F3
E CALEB WY
- GIL 85234 783-C4
3600 GIL 85236 783-C4
N CALEDONIA CT
- MarC 85086 (378-D5 See Page 337)
N CALEDONIA WY
- MarC 85086 (378-E5 See Page 337)
E CALGARY AV
9600 MarC 85248 901-B5
E CALICHE DR
- PinC 85219 826-F1
E CALICO DR
17100 FTNH 85268 583-E6
N CALICO DR
17200 MarC 85373 536-D7
W CALICO DR
9500 MarC 85373 536-C7
N CALICO RD
- SCTS 85255 540-H3
S CALICO RD
- GIL 85236 863-D5
E CALIENTE DR
17300 FTNH 85268 583-E5
N CALIENTE DR
14800 FTNH 85268 583-E5
CALIFORNIA
6500 PinC 85219 786-D7
6500 PinC 85219 826-D1
W CALIFORNIA AV
11100 YNTN 85335 575-H6
N CALIFORNIA ST
100 CHAN 85225 821-F3
S CALIFORNIA ST
- CHAN 85248 861-F4
- CHAN 85248 901-F2
- CHAN 85225 821-F7
500 CHAN 85225 861-F1
E CALISTOGA CIR
7200 SCTS 85255 540-H2
N CALISTOGA CIR
- SCTS 85255 540-H2
E CALISTOGA DR
- GIL 85236 863-C2
N CALISTRO CIR
- MESA 85207 704-A3
S CALLAWAY DR
1100 CHAN 85249 901-H5
W CALLE ADOBE LN
- GDYR 85338 695-C5
E CALLE ADOBE ST
600 GDYR 85338 695-B5
E CALLE ALLEGRE
4400 PHX 85018 659-H6
S CALLE AZTECA
8000 GUAD 85283 780-A3
S CALLE BATOUA
8400 GUAD 85283 780-A4
S CALLE BELLA VISTA
8000 GUAD 85283 780-A3
E CALLE BOLO LN
600 GDYR 85338 695-B5
W CALLE BOLO LN
1500 GDYR 85338 695-C5
S CALLE BRIGIDO VALENZUELA
5600 GUAD 85283 780-A5
E CALLE BRUVIRA
6200 PVAL 85253 620-D6
E CALLE BUENA VISTA
8400 SCTS 85255 541-A1
N CALLE CABALLEROS
7700 PVAL 85253 620-E7
E CALLE CAMELIA
3700 PHX 85251 700-B1
5400 PHX 85018 700-B1
6400 SCTS 85251 700-D1
E CALLE CERRITOS
5400 GUAD 85283 780-A3
E CALLE CHULO RD
600 GDYR 85338 695-B5
E CALLE DE ALLEGRA
8300 SCTS 85255 541-A1
N CALLE DE ALLEGRA
8300 SCTS 85255 541-A1

E CALLE DE ARCOS
- TEMP 85284 820-E2
W CALLE DE ARCOS
- TEMP 85284 820-E2
E CALLE DE BACA
5200 PHX 85331 460-C4
E CALLE DE CABALLOS
1300 TEMP 85284 820-F1
S CALLE DE CABALLOS
- TEMP 85284 820-D1
W CALLE DE CABALLOS
200 TEMP 85284 820-D1
E CALLE DE CIELO CIR
10000 SCTS 85258 621-E5
W CALLE DE EDENS
10300 PHX 85037 656-A6
E CALLE DE FLORES
- MarC 85249 901-H2
- QC 85242 904-A2
19300 QC 85242 903-J2
W CALLE DE LA LUNA
- PHX 85037 656-A7
11000 PHX 85037 655-H7
E CALLE DE LAS BRISAS
- SCTS 85255 540-H1
8800 SCTS 85255 541-B2
W CALLE DE LAS CASITAS
- PHX 85037 655-J6
10400 PHX 85037 656-B6
E CALLE DE LAS ESTRELLAS
4800 MarC 85331 460-A4
5200 PHX 85331 460-B4
6900 SCTS 85331 460-G4
E CALLE DEL CASCABEL
- PinC 85219 786-J6
E CALLE DEL FLORES
17000 FTNH 85268 583-D5
E CALLE DEL MEDIO
4500 PHX 85018 659-J6
4900 PHX 85018 660-A7
6000 PHX 85251 660-D7
6400 SCTS 85251 660-D7
E CALLE DEL NORTE
600 CHAN 85225 821-H3
4400 PHX 85018 659-J6
4900 PHX 85018 660-A7
5800 PHX 85251 660-D7
W CALLE DEL NORTE
600 CHAN 85225 821-E3
800 CHAN 85224 821-A3
2800 CHAN 85224 820-J3
N CALLE DEL NORTE CIR
1600 CHAN 85224 821-D3
E CALLE DEL NORTE DR
2400 GIL 85236 822-J3
2400 GIL 85236 823-A3
W CALLE DEL NORTE DR
2000 CHAN 85224 821-B3
E CALLE DEL ORO
200 MarC 85206 783-F1
17000 FTNH 85268 583-D5
N CALLE DEL ORO
14200 FTNH 85268 583-D6
W CALLE DEL ORO
10300 PHX 85037 656-A6
E CALLE DE LOS ARBOLES
4800 MarC 85331 460-A4
5300 PHX 85331 460-C4
N CALLE DE LOS ARBOLES
31600 MarC 85331 460-A4
E CALLE DE LOS FLORES
4800 MarC 85331 460-B4
5300 PHX 85331 460-C4
N CALLE DE LOS FLORES
5000 MarC 85331 460-B4
E CALLE DEL PAISANO
5500 PHX 85018 700-B1
6000 PHX 85251 700-C1
6400 SCTS 85251 700-D1
E CALLE DEL PALO VERDE
8800 SCTS 85255 541-B2
N CALLE DEL PALO VERDE ST
8300 SCTS 85255 541-A1
N CALLE DEL PRADO
14800 FTNH 85268 583-D5
S CALLE DEL PUEBLO DR
- AVON 85323 735-A2
N CALLE DEL SANTO
5500 PHX 85018 659-H4
E CALLE DEL SOL
- PHX 85331 460-C4
5000 MarC 85331 460-B4
17000 FTNH 85268 583-D5
W CALLE DEL SOL
10500 PHX 85037 655-J6
E CALLE DEL SUD
5800 PHX 85018 660-C7
5800 PHX 85251 660-D7
E CALLE DEL SUR
- MarC 85206 783-F1
W CALLE DE PLATA
10300 PHX 85037 656-A6
E CALLE DE VALLE
23300 SCTS 85255 541-D1
E CALLE DE VALLE DR
9000 SCTS 85255 541-B1
W CALLE ENCORVADA
9900 PHX 85037 656-B5
E CALLE ENTRADA
100 MarC 85206 783-F1
N CALLE ENTRADA
100 CHAN 85226 820-H7
E CALLE FACIL
29800 SCTS 85262 (461-A7 See Page 421)
E CALLE FELIZ
4300 PHX 85018 659-H6
S CALLE FORTUNATO SERRANO
5800 GUAD 85283 780-B5
E CALLE GRANDE
- MarC 85206 743-E7
100 MarC 85206 783-F1
W CALLE HERMOSA
12300 AVON 85323 735-E2

W CALLE HERMOSA
12300 AVON 85353 735-E2
E CALLE IGLESIA
5400 GUAD 85283 780-A4
W CALLE IGLESIA AV
1800 MESA 85202 781-B2
E CALLE LA FUENDA
17000 FTNH 85268 583-D5
E CALLE LA PAZ
3400 PVAL 85253 659-F4
N CALLE LARGO
- MESA 85207 704-A7
400 MESA 85207 743-J4
N CALLE LARGO CT
- MESA 85207 704-A7
W CALLE LEJOS
3500 PHX 85310 498-A6
3700 PHX 85310 497-D6
6600 PEOR 85310 497-A6
6600 PEOR 85382 497-A6
8100 PEOR 85382 496-H6
8400 PEOR 85382 496-E6
S CALLE LOS CERROS
2100 TEMP 85282 779-J2
E CALLE LUNA
9000 PinC 85219 786-G7
E CALLE MADERAS
1800 MESA 85203 702-D7
S CALLE MARAVILLA
8000 GUAD 85283 780-A3
S CALLE MAXIMO SOLAREZ
9200 GUAD 85283 780-B5
E CALLE MILAGROS
9800 GUAD 85283 780-B5
E CALLE MIO
6000 PHX 85014 658-J3
E CALLE MIRAGE
5600 PinC 85219 746-C7
N CALLE MIRAMONTE
- SCTS 85255 542-B2
E CALLE MONTE VISTA DR
1000 TEMP 85284 820-E2
W CALLE MONTE VISTA DR
- TEMP 85284 820-D1
S CALLE MONTEZUMA
8000 GUAD 85283 780-A3
N CALLE NOVENTA
- MESA 85207 744-C2
E CALLE OCHENTA SIETE
7800 SCTS 85258 621-A7
CALLE OLIVA
8000 SCTS 85258 620-J5
E CALLE PITAYA
5600 GUAD 85283 780-A3
CALLE POCO
8000 SCTS 85258 620-J6
W CALLE POCO
4300 MarC 85339 777-F7
W CALLE PRIMERA
3800 CHAN 85226 820-G6
E CALLE REDONDA
4100 PHX 85018 659-H6
5000 PHX 85018 660-A7
5000 PHX 85018 700-A1
6200 PHX 85251 700-D1
6400 SCTS 85251 700-E1
CALLE ROCA
8400 SCTS 85258 620-J6
E CALLE ROSA
4000 PHX 85251 700-D1
6400 SCTS 85251 700-D1
S CALLE ROSA CIR
2800 MESA 85202 781-A5
N CALLE ROYALE
8500 SCTS 85255 541-A2
S CALLE SAHUARO
8000 GUAD 85283 780-A3
E CALLE SANTA CRUZ
1600 PHX 85022 579-B5
N CALLE SANTOS BRAVO
5800 GUAD 85283 780-B5
W CALLE SEGUNDA
3800 CHAN 85226 820-G6
E CALLE SERENA
- SCTS 85255 542-A2
W CALLE SILHOUETTA
4300 PHX 85086 417-H6
N CALLE TERCERA
100 CHAN 85226 820-H6
S CALLE TOMI
8400 GUAD 85283 780-B4
E CALLE TUBERIA
3800 PHX 85018 700-A1
4200 PHX 85018 659-H6
4900 PHX 85018 660-A7
6000 PHX 85251 700-C1
S CALLE VAUO NAWI RD
- GUAD 85283 780-B5
E CALLE VENTURA
4100 PHX 85018 659-H6
4100 PHX 85018 660-A7
5200 PHX 85018 700-A1
E CALLIANDRA CT
- PinC 85219 786-D4
W CALUMET DR
14600 MarC 85375 534-H4
N CALVIN
- MESA 85207 703-J7
- MESA 85207 704-A7
S CALVIN
- MESA 85212 783-J6
N CALVIN CIR
- MESA 85207 704-A7
S CALVIN CIR
2800 MESA 85212 783-J6
E CALYPSO
5400 MESA 85206 743-C6
E CALYPSO AV
400 MESA 85206 743-A6
400 MESA 85204 742-D6
400 MESA 85208 743-J7
2100 MarC 85206 743-D6
4000 MESA 85206 742-J6
8500 MESA 85208 744-B7
9300 MarC 85208 744-D7
E CALYPSO CIR
1800 MarC 85206 743-D6
7400 MESA 85208 743-H7
N CALYPSO CT
- SURP 85374 534-H6
E CALYPSO DR
1800 MarC 85206 743-E6
8100 MESA 85208 744-A7

S CALYPSO DR
400 MESA 85208 744-A7
W CALYPSO DR
800 GIL 85233 822-A1
N CALYPSO LN
10600 MarC 85373 536-A4
E CALYPSO ST
1000 MarC 85206 743-F6
1000 MESA 85206 743-F6
N CAMARGO CT
- MarC 85086 (378-E5 See Page 337)
W CAMARGO DR
- MarC 85086 (378-E5 See Page 337)
E CAMBRIA DR
- PinC 85242 905-D2
N CAMBRIA DR
- PinC 85242 905-C1
13400 FTNH 85268 583-D6
E CAMBRIDGE AV
800 PHX 85006 698-H3
1500 PHX 85006 699-A3
2400 PHX 85008 699-C3
2600 SCTS 85257 700-B3
5000 PHX 85008 700-A3
5500 SCTS 85008 700-B3
8400 SCTS 85257 701-A3
W CAMBRIDGE AV
- PHX 85003 698-F2
- PHX 85004 698-F2
700 PHX 85007 698-F2
1900 PHX 85009 698-B2
2400 GDYR 85338 695-A2
2500 PHX 85037 696-D2
2600 PHX 85035 697-A2
3300 PHX 85009 697-G2
6900 PHX 85035 696-J2
12200 AVON 85323 695-C2
N CAMBRIDGE CIR
1200 CHAN 85225 821-J4
N CAMBRIDGE PL
700 CHAN 85225 821-J4
N CAMBRIDGE ST
200 CHAN 85225 821-J4
300 GIL 85233 781-J6
400 GIL 85233 782-A5
S CAMBRIDGE ST
- GIL 85233 782-A7
- MarC 85233 782-A7
- MarC 85233 822-A1
- MarC 85249 901-J1
W CAMBRIDGE ST
- GIL 85233 782-A7
W CAMDEN AV
- PEOR 85345 616-D2
10000 MarC 85351 616-A2
10100 MarC 85351 615-J2
W CAMDEN CIR
11000 MarC 85351 615-H2
N CAMELBACK BLVD
- PHX 85016 659-D5
E CAMELBACK RD
- PHX 85012 658-H5
700 PHX 85014 658-H5
1300 PHX 85014 659-B5
1600 PHX 85016 659-B5
3200 PHX 85018 659-G5
4500 PHX 85018 660-D7
4500 PHX 85251 660-D7
4500 SCTS 85251 660-J7
4500 MarC 85256 661-A7
4500 SCTS 85251 661-A7
12000 MarC 85256 662-A7
N CAMELBACK RD
4600 PHX 85018 659-J4
W CAMELBACK RD
- MarC 85037 656-C5
- PHX 85013 658-B5
1500 PHX 85015 658-B5
2400 PHX 85017 658-A5
3300 PHX 85017 657-H5
3500 PHX 85019 657-H5
4300 GLEN 85301 657-D5
4300 PHX 85031 657-D5
5900 PHX 85033 657-D5
6200 PHX 85301 657-D5
6200 GLEN 85033 657-D5
6700 GLEN 85303 657-D5
6900 PHX 85033 656-G5
6900 GLEN 85033 656-G5
6900 GLEN 85303 656-G5
7900 PHX 85303 656-G5
8300 GLEN 85037 656-G5
8300 GLEN 85305 656-C5
8300 PHX 85037 656-C5
9400 MarC 85305 656-C5
9900 PHX 85307 656-C5
10300 PHX 85307 655-C4
10600 MarC 85307 655-C4
10600 PHX 85037 655-C4
10700 MarC 85037 655-C4
11300 MarC 85340 655-C4
13000 LP 85340 655-C4
14100 LP 85340 (654-F4 See Page 653)
14500 GDYR 85338 (654-F4 See Page 653)
14700 GDYR 85338 (654-F4 See Page 653)
15000 MarC 85340 (654-F4 See Page 653)
16300 MarC 85338 (654-F4 See Page 653)
17100 GDYR 85340 653-J4
17100 MarC 85340 653-D4
17900 GDYR 85338 653-J4
20300 BUCK 85340 653-B4
N CAMELBACK CANYON PL
5500 PHX 85018 659-J4
N CAMELBACK MANOR DR
5300 PVAL 85253 660-B3
E CAMELDALE WY
6000 PVAL 85253 660-C4
N CAMELDALE WY
5600 PVAL 85253 660-C4
E CAMELHEAD RD
4800 PHX 85018 659-J5
N CAMELHEAD RD
4800 PHX 85018 659-J5
E CAMEL HILL DR
4500 PHX 85018 660-B6
S CAMELLIA CT
- CHAN 85248 861-E5
E CAMELLIA DR
2300 GIL 85236 822-J3
S CAMELLIA DR
- CHAN 85248 861-D2

STREET
Block City ZIP Pg-Grid

S CAMELLIA DR
700 CHAN 85225 821-E7
700 CHAN 85225 861-E1
S CAMELLIA PL
700 CHAN 85248 861-D5
N CAMELLIA ST
1600 TEMP 85281 700-F7
E CAMELLO ST
4600 PHX 85018 660-B6
W CAMELOT CIR
10400 MarC 85351 575-J3
10400 MarC 85351 576-A3
W CAMELOT CT
15700 SURP 85374 534-F5
E CAMELOT DR
2700 MESA 85215 703-E5
E CAMELVIEW DR
- FTNH 85268 622-H5
N CAMEO DR
13800 FTNH 85268 583-C6
W CAMEO DR
9900 MarC 85351 576-D3
10700 MarC 85351 575-H4
N CAMEO PT
14400 MarC 85351 576-B4
N CAMEO WY
14400 MarC 85351 576-B4
W CAMERON CIR
- ELMG 85335 575-D7
N CAMERON CT
- ELMG 85335 575-E7
11200 FTNH 85268 623-D2
W CAMERON DR
- ELMG 85335 575-E7
6700 PEOR 85345 617-A1
7100 PEOR 85345 616-F1
9100 PEOR 85345 576-D7
E CAMINA BUENA VISTA
- QC 85242 904-A2
E CAMINA PLATA
- QC 85242 904-A2
19400 QC 85242 903-J2
E CAMINO CIR
- MarC 85220 744-G4
W CAMINO DR
32400 MarC 85390 290-B3
E CAMINO ST
- MESA 85220 745-A4
4500 MESA 85205 743-B4
7700 MESA 85207 743-J4
W CAMINO WY
1000 CHAN 85224 821-C7
1000 CHAN 85225 821-D7
W CAMINO ACEQUIA
3900 PHX 85051 617-H2
E CAMINO ADELE
8100 SCTS 85255 500-J7
8100 SCTS 85255 501-A7
N CAMINO ADELE
23600 SCTS 85255 501-A7
23600 SCTS 85255 541-A1
23600 SCTS 85255 500-J7
N CAMINO ALLENADA
4400 PHX 85018 660-C7
S CAMINO ALTO
400 PinC 85219 746-C7
E CAMINO CIR
2200 MESA 85213 742-D4
N CAMINO CIR
22600 MarC 85220 744-H4
W CAMINO CIR
600 MESA 85201 741-C4
E CAMINO CT
1700 CHAN 85225 822-A7
W CAMINO CT
1400 CHAN 85224 821-C7
W CAMINO DE LA CAMPANA
6600 GLEN 85308 537-B7
E CAMINO DE LAS ESTRELLAS
- PHX 85331 460-C4
N CAMINO DEL CONTENTO
5500 PVAL 85253 659-F4
E CAMINO DEL MONTE
7200 SCTS 85255 500-G7
8200 SCTS 85255 501-A7
E CAMINO DEL ORO
- PinC 85219 746-C7
W CAMINO DEL ORO
6700 PEOR 85382 497-A7
E CAMINO DE LOS RANCHOS
1700 PHX 85022 579-B6
6400 PHX 85254 580-E6
W CAMINO DEL RIO
3600 PHX 85310 497-J7
E CAMINO DEL SANTO
1600 PHX 85022 579-B6
8800 SCTS 85260 581-B6
N CAMINO DEL SANTO
13200 SCTS 85260 581-E6
N CAMINO DEL SOL
13100 MarC 85375 535-D4
W CAMINO DEL SOL
13500 MarC 85375 535-B5
W CAMINO DE ORO
7800 PEOR 85382 496-G7
8600 MarC 85382 496-C6
E CAMINO ESTRELLA
- AVON 85323 695-B6
W CAMINO ESTRELLA DR
- SURP 85374 534-G5
S CAMINO FUEGO
- PinC 85219 786-H7
S CAMINO ORO
700 GDYR 85338 695-A7
E CAMINO PLAYA
- MarC 85249 901-H2
E CAMINO REAL
7500 SCTS 85255 500-H7
8400 SCTS 85255 501-B7
W CAMINO REAL
- SURP 85374 534-A5
3600 PHX 85310 497-J6
3600 PHX 85310 498-A6
W CAMINO REAL CT
15400 SURP 85374 534-G6
E CAMINO ROCOSO
8000 SCTS 85262 460-J6
8000 SCTS 85262 (461-A6 See Page 421)
E CAMINO SAGUARO
5500 PHX 85018 660-B6
N CAMINO SAGUARO
4500 PHX 85018 660-B6

S CAMINO SAGUARO
500 PinC 85219 746-C7
E CAMINO SANTO
6400 PHX 85254 580-E6
7200 SCTS 85260 580-G6
W CAMINO SAN XAVIER
6600 GLEN 85308 577-B1
S CAMINO SERENO
600 PinC 85219 746-C7
E CAMINO SIN NOMBRE
3200 PVAL 85016 659-E4
3200 PVAL 85253 659-E4
E CAMINO ST
- MarC 85220 744-J4
- MESA 85220 744-J4
2300 MESA 85213 742-E4
4000 MESA 85205 742-J4
7800 MESA 85207 744-A4
W CAMINO ST
2100 MESA 85201 741-B4
W CAMINO VISTA
- PHX 85021 618-G3
3200 PHX 85051 618-A3
E CAMINO VISTA DR
1500 MarC 85206 743-E7
S CAMINO VISTA DR
500 MarC 85206 743-F7
N CAMINO VISTA LN
9200 PHX 85028 619-E4
E CAMINO VIVAZ
- SCTS 85255 500-J7
8400 SCTS 85255 501-B7
8400 SCTS 85255 541-B1
W CAMINO VIVAZ
4000 PHX 85310 497-H7
E CAMPANA
8500 SCTS 85262 (461-B7 See Page 421)
W CAMPANA DR
9600 MarC 85351 576-A1
10800 MarC 85351 575-H1
E CAMPBELL AV
- MarC 85234 783-D6
400 GIL 85234 782-D6
1000 PHX 85014 658-J6
1300 PHX 85014 659-A6
1500 PHX 85016 659-D6
3200 PHX 85018 659-F6
3600 GIL 85236 783-C6
W CAMPBELL AV
- MarC 85340 653-E5
- PHX 85013 658-F6
100 LP 85340 655-A5
1500 PHX 85015 658-C6
1600 GIL 85233 781-H6
2500 PHX 85017 658-A6
3300 PHX 85017 657-J6
3500 PHX 85019 657-J6
4700 PHX 85031 657-E6
5900 PHX 85033 657-A6
6900 PHX 85033 656-G5
8400 PHX 85037 656-A5
10500 PHX 85037 655-J5
E CAMPBELL CT
4400 GIL 85236 783-E6
E CAMPBELL RD
- CHAN 85225 781-G6
4000 GIL 85236 783-D6
16400 MarC 85234 783-B6
N CAMPESTRE
29900 SCTS 85262 (461-A5 See Page 421)
N CAMPGROUND RD
- CVCK 85331 419-F4
CAMPINA DR
100 LP 85340 655-B4
CAMPINA LN
800 LP 85340 655-B4
W CAMPO ALLEGRE CIR
2500 MESA 85202 781-A3
N CAMPO ALLEGRE DR
- TEMP 85281 700-D7
E CAMPO BELLO DR
100 PHX 85022 578-H1
1500 PHX 85022 579-B1
2500 PHX 85032 579-E1
5100 PHX 85254 580-B1
7600 SCTS 85255 580-H1
W CAMPO BELLO DR
300 PHX 85023 578-E1
2800 PHX 85053 538-A7
3500 PHX 85308 538-A7
3600 PHX 85308 537-H7
5600 GLEN 85308 537-B7
6900 GLEN 85308 577-E1
7800 GLEN 85308 536-G7
E CAMPUS DR
700 TEMP 85282 740-F7
4000 PHX 85018 699-G2
4900 PHX 85018 700-A2
W CAMPUS DR
800 PHX 85013 698-F2
2000 TEMP 85282 739-J7
2300 PHX 85015 698-C1
S CANAL DR
300 CHAN 85225 822-A7
500 CHAN 85225 862-A1
500 CHAN 85225 861-J1
800 GIL 85296 822-J3
E CANAL RD
- MESA 85201 741-H4
N CANARY CIR
3500 AVON 85323 655-G7
W CANARY WY
- CHAN 85249 861-F5
1000 CHAN 85248 861-D4
S CANCUN AV
1000 GIL 85233 822-A3
S CANCUN ST
700 GIL 85233 822-A2
E CANDELARIA DR
- SCTS 85255 540-H2
8200 SCTS 85255 541-A2
W CANDELARIA DR
7100 GLEN 85310 537-A1
7400 GLEN 85310 536-J1
W CANDLELIGHT DR
12300 MarC 85375 535-F3
E CANDLESTICK DR
1500 TEMP 85283 780-G3
E CANDLEWOOD CIR
9000 SCTS 85255 501-C5
E CANDLEWOOD DR
10400 SCTS 85255 501-F5
W CANDLEWOOD DR
10100 MarC 85351 576-B5
S CANDLEWOOD LN
500 GIL 85233 822-C1
W CANDLEWOOD LN
400 GIL 85233 822-B2

N CANFIELD
- MarC 85220 744-G4
- MESA 85220 744-G6
- MESA 85220 784-G1
S CANFIELD
- MESA 85212 784-F6
- MESA 85220 744-G7
- MESA 85220 784-G1
S CANFIELD CIR
- MESA 85212 784-F6
E CANNON DR
- SCTS 85259 622-C3
2600 PHX 85028 619-D2
5000 PVAL 85253 620-A2
5400 PHX 85253 620-B3
7400 SCTS 85258 620-G3
10400 SCTS 85258 621-E3
11800 SCTS 85259 621-J3
W CANNON DR
5700 GLEN 85302 617-D2
S CANOE DR
- TEMP 85282 779-J1
E CANOTIA PL
5800 CARE 85377 420-D7
W CANOTIA PL
- PHX 85086 (418-B7 See Page 417)
N CANTA BELLO
8400 PVAL 85253 620-D5
N CANTA REDONDO
8300 PVAL 85253 620-D6
N CANTATA CT
12400 MarC 85351 576-C6
E CANTEBRIA DR
400 GIL 85296 822-E2
W CANTEBRIA DR
900 GIL 85233 822-A2
W CANTEL CT
- WICK 85390 289-G3
W CANTENIA RD
- AVON 85323 695-D3
W CANTERA
- MarC 85382 536-G1
W CANTERBURY CIR
- ELMG 85335 575-D7
E CANTERBURY CT
- PHX 85022 578-H4
E CANTERBURY DR
500 PHX 85022 578-H5
1200 PHX 85022 579-A5
N CANTERBURY DR
13400 PHX 85023 578-G5
13400 PHX 85022 578-G5
W CANTERBURY DR
- ELMG 85335 575-E7
200 PHX 85023 578-G5
6800 PEOR 85345 577-A7
7100 PEOR 85345 576-F7
10700 MarC 85351 575-J7
E CANTERBURY LN
- PHX 85022 578-H4
N CANTO LN
21800 MarC 85375 535-B1
S CANTON
2100 MESA 85202 781-D3
E CANTON DR
1600 MarC 85206 743-D7
E CANYON CT
4000 MarC 85253 659-G1
W CANYON CT
17500 GDYR 85338 (773-J4 See Page 733)
E CANYON DR
- SCTS 85259 622-D3
2400 PHX 85048 819-C3
N CANYON DR
5700 PHX 85016 659-E4
16400 FTNH 85268 582-J3
W CANYON DR
9100 PEOR 85382 576-E1
W CANYON LN
- GDYR 85338 (773-J5 See Page 733)
- GDYR 85338 (774-B4 See Page 733)
E CANYON RD
6000 CVCK 85331 420-E3
E CANYON ST
100 PinC 85219 705-E7
100 PinC 85220 705-E7
W CANYON ST
- PinC 85220 705-A7
E CANYON WY
- MarC 85249 901-J1
W CANYON WY
1800 CHAN 85248 901-B1
W CANYON CREEK
- SURP 85374 575-B1
E CANYON CREEK CIR
- CARE 85377 420-D7
E CANYON CREEK CT
- GIL 85296 822-D7
- MarC 85236 823-A7
N CANYON CREEK CT
- CARE 85377 420-D7
E CANYON CREEK DR
- GIL 85296 822-C7
- MarC 85236 823-A7
- MarC 85296 822-E7
- PinC 85219 786-G4
N CANYON CREEK DR
16600 MarC 85351 575-J1
W CANYON CREEK DR
- SURP 85374 575-B1
10900 MarC 85351 575-H1
W CANYON CREST CIR
2500 PHX 85023 578-C2
E CANYONCREST CT
- SCTS 85268 582-H7
- SCTS 85268 622-H1
CANYON CROSSINGS DR
36900 CARE 85377 420-G4
N CANYON MESA WY
- SCTS 85255 541-C3
S CANYON OAKS WY
- CHAN 85249 861-J2
- CHAN 85249 862-A2
E CANYON RIDGE DR
- CARE 85377 420-D6
- CVCK 85331 420-D6
N CANYON RIDGE TR
40800 CVCK 85331 (380-D7 See Page 339)
CANYON RIDGE NORTH DR
- CVCK 85331 420-C6
S CANYON RIM
- MESA 85212 784-D6

N CANYON SPRINGS DR
41500 CVCK 85331 (380-D6 See Page 339)
E CANYON VIEW LN
- FTNH 85268 622-J4
E CANYON VISTA DR
- PinC 85219 786-G4
N CANYON WASH
- MESA 85207 704-A3
N CANYON WASH CIR
- MESA 85207 703-J4
- MESA 85207 704-A3
E CANYON WREN CIR
6900 SCTS 85262 460-G1
N CANYON WREN CIR
34000 SCTS 85262 460-G1
S CAPE AV
1000 GIL 85233 822-A3
S CAPE CT
1000 GIL 85233 822-A3
W CAPE ROYAL LN
400 PHX 85023 578-G3
CAPILLA CIR
100 LP 85340 655-B7
E CAPISTRANO AV
4000 PHX 85044 779-G6
W CAPISTRANO AV
- GDYR 85326 (773-H4 See Page 733)
- GDYR 85338 (773-H4 See Page 733)
S CAPISTRANO DR
800 GIL 85233 822-A2
N CAPITAL CT
- MarC 85086 (378-B6 See Page 337)
N CAPITOL AV
100 GBND 85337 (1090-B3 See Page 1049)
S CAPITOL AV
100 GBND 85337 (1090-B3 See Page 1049)
E CAPPS DR
- GIL 85236 863-C2
N CAPRA WY
- MarC 85086 (378-C6 See Page 337)
E CAPRI AV
- MESA 85220 744-F7
2300 MESA 85204 742-E6
3700 MESA 85206 742-J6
4200 MESA 85206 743-A6
7400 MESA 85208 743-H7
8500 MESA 85208 744-B7
W CAPRI AV
1400 MESA 85202 741-D6
E CAPRI CIR
2200 MESA 85204 742-D6
E CAPRI DR
800 MarC 85206 743-D7
N CAPRI DR
11400 MarC 85351 576-B7
E CAPRICORN WY
- CHAN 85249 901-G4
- MarC 85249 902-C4
N CAPTAIN COFFEE RD
- MarC 85264 583-H4
E CAPTAIN DREYFUS AV
1200 PHX 85022 579-A6
2500 PHX 85032 579-D6
6500 PHX 85254 580-E6
7200 SCTS 85260 580-G6
8800 SCTS 85260 581-B7
10400 SCTS 85259 581-E7
W CARAVAGGIO LN
- PHX 85086 (418-B5 See Page 417)
W CARAWAY DR
12000 MarC 85375 535-C3
W CARBINE WY
14500 MarC 85375 494-H7
CARDENO CIR
200 LP 85340 655-A7
W CARDINAL CT
2100 CHAN 85248 861-B4
11600 SURP 85374 535-G6
E CARDINAL DR
6600 PVAL 85253 660-D2
N CARDINAL DR
6600 PVAL 85253 660-C2
8600 PHX 85028 619-J5
S CARDINAL DR
- APJT 85220 785-D1
200 APJT 85220 745-D6
W CARDINAL DR
- GDYR 85338 (773-J4 See Page 733)
- GDYR 85338 (774-A4 See Page 733)
W CARDINAL LN
17500 GDYR 85338 (773-J4 See Page 733)
17500 GDYR 85338 (774-A4 See Page 733)
S CARDINAL ST
- GIL 85234 783-A7
600 GIL 85236 823-A2
W CARDINAL WY
1300 CHAN 85248 861-C4
E CARDON WY
1600 CHAN 85225 822-A5
N CARDON WY
800 CHAN 85225 821-J4
800 CHAN 85225 822-A4
E CAREFREE DR
6900 CARE 85377 420-H4
8000 CARE 85377 421-A4
8700 CARE 85262 421-B4
N CAREFREE DR
36900 CARE 85377 420-G4
CAREFREE HWY
33900 MarC 85390 102-A2
E CAREFREE HWY
- MarC 85085 (418-J7 See Page 417)
- MarC 85086 (418-J7 See Page 417)
700 MarC 85086 419-C7
1000 MarC 85085 419-C7
1600 PHX 85086 419-C7
1600 PHX 85085 419-C7
2400 CVCK 85086 419-C7
2400 CVCK 85331 419-C7
2800 PHX 85331 419-C7
4000 CVCK 85331 459-J1
4000 CVCK 85331 460-D1
4000 MarC 85331 419-C7
4000 MarC 85331 460-D1
8600 PHX 85331 459-J1
4000 PHX 85331 460-D1

E CAREFREE HWY
4900 MarC 85331 460-D1
5600 CARE 85377 460-D1
5600 SCTS 85377 460-D1
5600 SCTS 85331 460-D1
5900 CARE 85331 460-D1
6100 CARE 85262 460-D1
6100 SCTS 85262 460-E1
W CAREFREE HWY
- PEOR 85382 417-B7
- PHX 85382 417-B7
- MarC 85085 (418-C7 See Page 417)
- MarC 85086 (418-C7 See Page 417)
1500 PHX 85085 (418-C7 See Page 417)
1500 PHX 85086 (418-C7 See Page 417)
3600 PHX 85086 417-B7
3600 PHX 85085 417-B7
8500 PEOR 85382 (416-C7 See Page 415)
9800 PEOR 85373 (416-B7 See Page 415)
24200 MarC 85342 (412-B6 See Page 411)
N CAREFREE RD
- SURP 85374 533-J7
E CAREFREE WY
9500 MarC 85248 901-B2
11000 SCTS 85262 421-H2
CAREFREE ESTATES CIR
7800 CARE 85377 420-J4
N CAREFREE MOUNTAIN DR
5900 CARE 85377 420-D7
34600 CARE 85377 460-D1
W CAREY DR
17600 GDYR 85338 (773-H5 See Page 733)
N CARHILL AV
3500 SCTS 85251 700-G2
E CARIBBEAN LN
- SCTS 85259 581-F4
- PHX 85022 578-H3
8900 SCTS 85260 581-B4
W CARIBBEAN LN
- SURP 85379 (574-F2 See Page 573)
- SURP 85379 575-C3
700 PHX 85023 578-C3
2700 PHX 85053 578-A3
3500 PHX 85053 577-J3
5100 GLEN 85306 577-B3
7100 MarC 85381 577-A3
7700 PEOR 85381 576-G3
8700 PEOR 85382 576-E3
W CARIBE LN
6000 GLEN 85306 577-C3
N CARINE CT
14600 PHX 85053 578-B4
E CARLA VISTA CT
- GIL 85236 823-A6
- GIL 85296 822-F5
W CARLA VISTA CT
4800 CHAN 85226 820-E5
E CARLA VISTA DR
- GIL 85236 822-J6
- GIL 85236 823-A6
- GIL 85296 822-E5
600 CHAN 85225 821-G5
1600 CHAN 85225 822-A5
S CARLA VISTA DR
- GIL 85296 822-F6
W CARLA VISTA DR
- CHAN 85225 822-C6
600 CHAN 85225 821-B5
1300 CHAN 85224 821-A5
3500 CHAN 85226 820-G5
E CARLA VISTA PL
900 CHAN 85225 821-H5
2200 CHAN 85225 822-B5
E CARLA VISTA ST
- GIL 85236 823-A6
W CARLA VISTA ST
4500 CHAN 85226 820-F5
S CARLIN DR
2000 MESA 85206 743-D7
W CARLIN DR
- SURP 85374 535-A6
14400 SURP 85374 534-J5
E CARLISE RD
700 MarC 85086 (418-J4 See Page 417)
700 MarC 85086 419-A4
2400 MarC 85331 419-E4
W CARLISE RD
2600 MarC 85086 (418-C4 See Page 417)
2600 PHX 85086 (418-C4 See Page 417)
S CARLOS AV
9100 GUAD 85283 780-B5
S CARLOS ST
8000 GUAD 85283 780-B3
W CARLOTA LN
- PEOR 85373 535-J1
- PEOR 85373 536-A1
10500 PEOR 85382 536-A1
S CARMALITA CT
- GIL 85236 863-C5
E CARMEL AV
- MarC 85208 744-D7
- MESA 85220 744-F7
- MESA 85220 784-G1
2200 MESA 85204 742-G6
4000 MESA 85206 742-J7
4300 MESA 85206 743-A7
W CARMEL AV
1600 MESA 85202 741-C6
E CARMEL CIR
2600 MESA 85204 742-E7
E CARMEL DR
2200 GIL 85234 782-J5
2500 GIL 85234 783-A5
16100 FTNH 85268 583-B5
N CARMELITA CT
15000 FTNH 85268 582-J5
W CARMEN DR
- SURP 85374 (574-C2 See Page 573)
12700 SURP 85374 575-E2
E CARMEN ST
500 TEMP 85283 780-A5
4500 PHX 85044 779-H5
5400 GUAD 85283 780-B5
S CARMEN ST
9600 PHX 85044 779-H5

W CARMEN ST
300 TEMP 85283 780-B5
E CARNATION CIR
2900 SCTS 85018 700-C2
2900 PHX 85018 700-C2
6000 PHX 85251 700-C2
6000 SCTS 85251 700-C2
N CARNATION DR
19000 PEOR 85373 536-A5
N CARNATION LN
3000 AVON 85323 695-H1
3700 AVON 85323 655-H7
S CARNEY AV
100 TEMP 85281 740-C3
6700 TEMP 85283 780-B5
W CARO RD
7400 GLEN 85308 536-J6
W CAROB DR
1000 CHAN 85248 861-C6
10300 MarC 85373 536-A6
W CAROB PL
- CHAN 85248 861-D6
W CAROB WY
- CHAN 85248 861-D6
E CAROL AV
500 MESA 85220 744-G7
2200 MESA 85204 742-E6
2400 PHX 85028 619-C4
3600 MESA 85206 742-H6
4100 MESA 85206 743-A7
7200 MESA 85208 743-H7
8500 MESA 85208 744-B7
9300 MarC 85208 744-D7
9700 SCTS 85259 621-H4
9900 SCTS 85258 621-D4
W CAROL AV
1400 MESA 85202 741-D6
3300 PHX 85051 617-H3
3300 PHX 85051 618-A3
4300 GLEN 85302 617-B3
6700 PEOR 85345 617-A3
7100 PEOR 85345 616-C3
E CAROL CIR
3400 PHX 85028 619-F4
3800 MESA 85206 742-H6
7400 MESA 85208 743-H7
E CAROL DR
- PHX 85020 618-H3
1200 PHX 85020 619-A3
W CAROL DR
1700 PHX 85021 618-E3
E CAROL WY
7000 PHX 85254 580-F7
7300 SCTS 85260 580-G7
8300 SCTS 85260 581-B7
8600 SCTS 85260 621-A1
11400 SCTS 85259 621-H1
E CAROL ANN LN
3800 PHX 85032 579-J3
E CAROL ANN WY
200 PHX 85022 578-H3
3400 PHX 85032 579-F3
W CAROL ANN WY
1900 PHX 85023 578-D3
3700 PHX 85053 577-J3
5500 GLEN 85306 577-C2
6700 GLEN 85382 577-A2
W CAROLE LN
7300 GLEN 85303 616-H6
7500 MarC 85303 616-H6
W CAROLINA AV
13000 YNTN 85335 575-H7
E CAROLINA DR
4500 PHX 85032 579-J3
4900 PHX 85254 580-A3
E CAROLINE LN
- TEMP 85284 820-D2
W CAROLINE LN
- CHAN 85225 821-D3
- TEMP 85284 820-D2
5600 MarC 85284 820-A2
N CAROL RAE LN
1100 GIL 85236 783-C4
E CARON CIR
5800 PVAL 85253 620-C4
W CARON CIR
- PEOR 85345 616-D4
W CARON CT
11100 MarC 85351 615-H3
E CARON DR
6400 PVAL 85253 620-E4
W CARON DR
6800 PEOR 85345 617-A4
7000 PEOR 85345 616-D4
9000 MarC 85351 616-B3
10600 MarC 85351 615-J3
E CARON ST
300 PHX 85020 618-H4
4600 PHX 85028 619-J4
5500 PVAL 85253 620-B4
9600 SCTS 85258 621-D5
11400 SCTS 85259 621-H5
N CARON ST
9000 SCTS 85258 621-F5
W CARON ST
400 PHX 85021 618-G4
3600 PHX 85051 617-H4
4400 GLEN 85302 617-B4
7200 PEOR 85345 616-E4
S CARRERA CT
26600 MarC 85248 901-E6
E CARRIAGE CT
- GIL 85236 863-D5
E CARRIAGE DR
5800 CVCK 85331 420-D5
N CARRIAGE LN
200 CHAN 85224 821-B3
2600 CHAN 85224 781-A6
18800 SURP 85374 534-F5
S CARRIAGE LN
1300 CHAN 85248 861-A2
2600 MESA 85202 781-A6
2700 MESA 85202 780-J5
3100 MESA 85224 781-A6
E CARRIAGE WY
- GIL 85236 863-D5
E CARRIAGE TRAILS DR
6900 SCTS 85331 460-G7
E CARRIBEAN LN
- SCTS 85260 581-E4
N CARRIBEAN LN
- SCTS 85259 581-H4
E CARSON CIR
200 TEMP 85282 780-E2
E CARSON DR
400 TEMP 85282 780-E2
W CARSON DR
1000 TEMP 85282 780-B2

E CARSON RD
800 PHX 85040 778-H2
1400 PHX 85040 779-A2
W CARSON RD
- PHX 85041 778-D2
2200 TEMP 85282 779-J2
6300 MarC 85339 777-B1
E CARTER CIR
700 PHX 85040 778-H2
E CARTER DR
- TEMP 85282 780-E2
3600 PHX 85040 779-F2
W CARTER DR
1000 TEMP 85282 780-B2
2500 TEMP 85282 779-J2
E CARTER RD
- PHX 85040 778-G2
- PHX 85041 778-G2
1400 PHX 85040 779-A2
W CARTER RD
- PHX 85041 777-G1
1500 PHX 85041 778-D2
W CARTIER CT
- MarC 85087 (378-A3 See Page 337)
E CART PASS DR
9800 SCTS 85262 (461-E1 See Page 421)
E CARVER RD
- TEMP 85284 820-E1
1900 PHX 85040 739-B6
W CARVER RD
- MarC 85339 776-H7
- TEMP 85284 820-C1
3500 MarC 85339 777-C7
3500 PHX 85339 777-F7
19300 GDYR 85326 (773-F6 See Page 733)
19300 MarC 85326 (773-B6 See Page 733)
27900 MarC 85322 (771-A5 See Page 731)
27900 MarC 85326 (771-A5 See Page 731)
N CASA BLANCA DR
5000 PVAL 85253 660-E5
5000 SCTS 85253 660-E5
S CASA BLANCA DR
10700 GDYR 85338 (773-H5 See Page 733)
W CASA BONITA CT
16200 SURP 85374 534-E6
E CASA GRANDE RD
7600 SCTS 85258 660-G1
W CASA LINDA DR
13800 MarC 85375 535-B2
N CASA TOMAS CT
2900 PHX 85016 699-B2
N CASCABELLAS
29000 SCTS 85262 (461-A6 See Page 421)
CASCADA CIR
200 LP 85340 655-B7
E CASCADA CIR
200 MarC 85206 783-F1
E CASCADA LN
1300 MarC 85206 783-E1
CASCADA RD
400 LP 85340 655-B7
W CASCADE CT
- SURP 85374 534-G5
E CASCADE DR
1800 GIL 85234 782-H4
16900 FTNH 85268 583-D4
S CASCADE PL
3000 CHAN 85248 861-B5
E CASCALOTE DR
4000 PHX 85331 459-J6
4700 PHX 85331 460-A6
S CASCALOTE ST
- PinC 85219 786-E5
E CASEY LN
4300 PHX 85331 459-J7
4500 PHX 85331 460-A7
N CASEY ABBOTT DR
6500 GDYR 85338 (734-G7 See Page 733)
S CASEY ABBOTT DR
- GDYR 85338 (734-G7 See Page 733)
- GDYR 85338 (774-G1 See Page 733)
W CASEY ABBOTT PKWY
14300 GDYR 85338 (734-H7 See Page 733)
E CASHMAN DR
2000 PHX 85024 539-C1
4100 PHX 85050 539-J1
4100 PHX 85050 540-A1
W CASINO AV
- PHX 85085 498-B1
W CASITA CT
9800 MarC 85351 576-C7
S CASITAS DR
800 TEMP 85281 740-H4
E CASITAS DEL RIO DR
- SCTS 85255 540-H1
2100 PHX 85024 499-C7
9000 SCTS 85255 541-C1
11900 SCTS 85255 542-A1
W CASITAS DEL RIO DR
- PHX 85027 498-A7
E CASITAS LINDAS
4500 PHX 85008 699-H4
N CASITA SPRINGS CT
17100 SURP 85374 534-E7
E CASPER CIR
6600 CVCK 85331 420-F3
9500 MarC 85207 744-E4
N CASPER DR
3400 GDYR 85338 (654-F7 See Page 653)
E CASPER RD
5200 MarC 85205 743-C4
5200 MESA 85205 743-C4
E CASPER ST
500 MESA 85207 744-A4
4900 MESA 85205 743-B4
N CASSARA DR
- PinC 85242 905-C1
E CASSIA CIR
7700 SCTS 85262 420-J7
S CASSIA DR
- PinC 85219 786-E7
E CASSIA LN
- GIL 85236 863-E6
S CASSIA RD
5300 PinC 85219 786-F6

PHOENIX

INDEX

STREET — Block City ZIP Pg-Grid

E CASSIA WY
3900 PHX 85044 819-F3
E CASSIDY CT
- FTNH 85268 583-E7
S CASSIDY DR
2000 MarC 85206 743-D7
N CASSIE DR
17300 SURP 85374 534-G7
N CASTANO CT
- MarC 85340 655-B3
CASTANO DR
700 LP 85340 655-B5
N CASTANO DR
- MarC 85340 655-B2
E CASTILLO DR
900 LP 85340 655-C6
N CASTILLO DR
15000 FTNH 85268 582-H4
S CASTILLO DR
900 LP 85340 655-C6
W CASTILLO DR
900 LP 85340 655-C6
W CASTLEBAR DR
12800 MarC 85375 535-D3
N CASTLEBURY CT
15400 MarC 85351 576-C3
N CASTLE HOT SPRINGS RD
- PEOR - 335-G1
- PEOR 85342 335-G1
- YavC - 335-G1
38700 PEOR 85342 (375-F3 See Page 335)
38700 PEOR 85342 415-G1
40900 MarC 85342 (371-J3 See Page 331)
41000 MarC 85342 (372-A2 See Page 331)
41000 MarC 85342 (332-J3 See Page 331)
W CASTLE ROCK CT
12300 MarC 85375 535-F6
W CASTLE ROCK DR
12500 MarC 85375 535-C5
E CATALINA AV
- MESA 85220 744-H7
2100 MESA 85204 742-E7
4000 MESA 85206 742-J7
4300 MESA 85206 743-A7
7200 MESA 85208 743-H7
W CATALINA AV
- GDYR 85338 (694-E1 See Page 653)
2100 MESA 85202 741-B6
N CATALINA CT
- SURP 85374 534-G6
W CATALINA CT
15300 GDYR 85338 (694-F1 See Page 653)
E CATALINA DR
- PHX 85012 698-H2
- PHX 85013 698-H2
- PHX 85014 698-J2
1600 PHX 85016 699-A2
2600 MarC 85206 743-E7
3000 SCTS 85251 700-D2
4000 PHX 85018 699-G2
8500 SCTS 85251 701-A3
W CATALINA DR
- AVON 85340 695-C1
- PHX 85013 698-E2
1500 PHX 85015 698-C2
2500 PHX 85017 698-A2
3000 PHX 85019 697-G2
3000 PHX 85031 697-C1
3300 PHX 85017 697-J2
5900 PHX 85033 697-A1
6900 PHX 85033 696-F1
8200 PHX 85037 696-D1
10300 AVON 85323 696-A1
10500 AVON 85323 695-J1
15100 GDYR 85338 (694-F1 See Page 653)
19300 MarC 85340 (693-F1 See Page 653)
S CATALINA ST
- GIL 85233 782-C7
- GIL 85233 822-C1
16000 MarC 85225 822-C7
N CATALPA PL
15200 FTNH 85268 583-B4
E CATAMARAN CIR
1900 GIL 85234 782-H4
E CATAMARAN DR
1300 GIL 85234 782-G3
S CATARINA
2400 MESA 85202 781-A4
S CATARINA CIR
1700 MESA 85202 781-A2
E CATAWBA PZ
17500 FTNH 85268 583-E6
W CAT BALUE DR
3000 PHX 85027 538-B2
3600 PHX 85308 537-J2
E CATCLAW CIR
26400 SCTS 85255 501-D4
CATCLAW CT
13700 FTNH 85268 582-J6
E CATCLAW CT
200 GIL 85296 822-D2
W CATCLAW CT
11600 SURP 85374 535-G6
E CATCLAW ST
- GIL 85236 823-A2
600 GIL 85296 822-E2
1200 MarC 85296 822-F2
W CATCLAW ST
600 GIL 85233 822-B1
E CATESBY RD
6200 PVAL 85253 660-D1
W CATHEDRAL DR
1700 PHX 85045 818-D5
E CATHEDRAL ROCK DR
600 PHX 85048 818-G5
1700 PHX 85048 819-A5
3600 PHX 85044 819-E5
W CATHEDRAL ROCK DR
400 PHX 85045 818-D5
W CATHERINE AV
- PHX 85041 778-E1
N CATHERINE CT
17100 SURP 85374 534-J7
N CATHERINE DR
18100 SURP 85374 534-J6
S CATHERINE ST
400 GIL 85296 822-H1
W CATHY CIR
4300 PHX 85308 537-G7
E CATHY CT
2000 GIL 85296 822-H3

N CATHY CT
600 CHAN 85226 820-E4
S CATHY CT
300 CHAN 85226 820-E7
E CATHY DR
- GIL 85236 823-A3
400 GIL 85296 822-D3
E CATTLE DR
2500 GIL 85236 862-J4
2500 GIL 85236 863-A4
E CATTLE WY
- SCTS 85255 541-C3
E CATTLE DRIVE LN
- SCTS 85255 541-E4
N CATTLETRACK RD
6500 SCTS 85250 660-G3
E CATTLE WHIP DR
- SCTS 85255 541-B3
W CAVALCADE DR
13500 MarC 85375 535-A4
W CAVALIER CT
- MarC 85340 655-B2
E CAVALIER DR
700 TEMP 85281 700-F7
800 PHX 85014 658-J3
N CAVALIER DR
1800 TEMP 85281 700-F7
6100 GLEN 85305 656-E2
W CAVALIER DR
- GLEN 85303 657-A3
2700 PHX 85017 658-B3
3600 PHX 85019 657-G3
4300 GLEN 85301 657-C2
7100 GLEN 85303 656-G2
8300 GLEN 85305 656-E2
E CAVALRY CT
- GIL 85236 863-D4
E CAVALRY DR
9200 SCTS 85262 (461-D1 See Page 421)
9500 SCTS 85262 421-A7
W CAVALRY DR
- PHX 85086 (418-C7 See Page 417)
E CAVALRY RD
1200 MarC 85087 (379-A3 See Page 339)
W CAVALRY RD
300 MarC 85087 (378-H3 See Page 337)
E CAVANESS AV
100 WICK 85390 290-E1
W CAVANESS AV
100 WICK 85390 290-E2
E CAVE BUTTES DAM RD
700 MarC 85024 498-J6
700 MarC 85024 499-A6
N CAVE BUTTES DAM RD
- MarC 85024 499-A6
E CAVE CREEK PKWY
- CVCK 85331 419-F4
E CAVE CREEK RD
5900 CVCK 85331 420-F3
7000 CARE 85377 420-F3
7900 CARE 85377 421-B5
8800 CARE 85262 421-B5
9500 SCTS 85262 421-G3
N CAVE CREEK RD
- PHX 85020 579-D4
1600 PHX 85020 619-A2
2300 PHX 85022 539-D6
2300 PHX 85032 579-D4
9000 PHX 85020 618-J4
12200 PHX 85022 579-D4
18600 PHX 85050 539-D2
19000 PHX 85024 539-D2
22800 PHX 85050 499-F4
22800 PHX 85024 499-F4
25800 PHX 85085 499-F4
28300 MarC 85085 499-F4
28300 MarC 85331 499-F4
28700 PHX 85331 499-F4
28800 MarC 85331 459-J7
28900 PHX 85331 459-J7
30800 PHX 85331 460-A3
31400 MarC 85331 460-A3
33600 CVCK 85331 460-A3
34500 CARE 85377 420-D6
34500 CARE 85377 460-A3
34500 CVCK 85331 420-D6
38800 SCTS 85262 421-J1
39700 MarC 85262 421-J1
40300 SCTS 85262 (381-J7 See Page 341)
40300 SCTS 85331 (381-J7 See Page 341)
40300 MarC 85262 (381-J7 See Page 341)
40300 MarC 85331 (381-J7 See Page 341)
40300 MarC 85331 (382-B5 See Page 341)
41000 SCTS 85262 (382-A7 See Page 341)
41000 SCTS 85331 (382-A7 See Page 341)
42700 MarC 85262 (382-B5 See Page 341)
N CAVE CREEK DAM RD
22500 PHX 85024 539-D1
23100 PHX 85024 499-B6
23900 MarC 85024 499-B6
E CAVEDALE DR
11000 SCTS 85255 500-H4
11600 SCTS 85255 501-J4
W CAVEDALE DR
- PHX 85085 497-B3
3100 PHX 85085 498-B3
E CAVERN DR
15400 FTNH 85268 582-J7
15400 FTNH 85268 583-A7
N CAYMAN DR
400 GIL 85233 781-J6
500 GIL 85233 782-A6
E CAYUGA LN
17500 FTNH 85268 583-E5
E CAYUSE CT
12400 SCTS 85259 622-A4
E CEASER RD
- QC 85242 863-J6
- QC 85242 864-A6
W CEDAR CT
9800 MarC 85351 576-C6
E CEDAR DR
- MarC 85249 901-H3
- MarC 85249 902-C3
N CEDAR DR
1100 APJT 85220 745-A3

N CEDAR DR
4200 PinC 85220 705-A6
4200 PinC 85220 745-A3
13400 MarC 85351 576-B5
S CEDAR DR
400 APJT 85220 745-A7
1200 APJT 85220 785-A1
W CEDAR DR
300 CHAN 85248 901-E3
9700 MarC 85351 576-B5
E CEDAR PL
- MarC 85249 902-A3
E CEDAR ST
- TEMP 85281 741-A5
1400 TEMP 85281 740-G5
N CEDAR ST
700 GIL 85233 782-C4
S CEDAR ST
1300 TEMP 85281 740-G5
E CEDAR BASIN LN
- PinC 85219 826-G1
N CEDAR CHASE CT
- MarC 85086 (378-B6 See Page 337)
N CEDAR CHASE RD
- MarC 85086 (378-C6 See Page 337)
S CEDARCREST DR
25600 MarC 85248 901-C3
W CEDAR HILL CIR
9300 MarC 85351 576-D1
N CEDARHURST CT
15600 MarC 85351 576-A2
E CEDAR WAXWING CT
10400 MarC 85248 901-D3
E CEDAR WAXWING DR
9000 MarC 85248 900-J3
9000 MarC 85248 901-A3
E CEDARWOOD DR
9600 MarC 85248 901-B6
E CEDARWOOD LN
- PHX 85326 819-G7
3200 PHX 85048 819-D7
W CELESTIAL CT
- SURP 85374 534-G4
E CELESTIAL DR
9400 SCTS 85262 421-D3
E CELESTIAL ST
7600 CARE 85377 420-J3
W CELICA CIR
2900 PHX 85053 578-B1
E CELTIC DR
8700 SCTS 85260 581-D6
CEMETERY RD
- PHX 85024 539-D1
- PHX 85050 539-D1
S CEMETERY RD
100 GBND 85337 (1090-B6 See Page 1049)
100 MarC 85337 (1090-B6 See Page 1049)
W CEMETERY RD
7200 MarC 85381 576-J4
E CENTENNIAL CIR
2000 TEMP 85284 820-H1
N CENTENNIAL CIR
50300 MarC 85320 (285-H5 See Page 244)
E CENTENNIAL DR
49000 MarC 85320 (285-B5 See Page 244)
N CENTENNIAL WY
- MESA 85201 741-H5
N CENTENNIAL PEAK DR
- FTNH 85268 622-H4
W CENTER DR
- WICK 85390 290-A3
E CENTER LN
900 TEMP 85281 741-A4
1800 TEMP 85281 740-H4
N CENTER PKWY
500 TEMP 85281 740-C1
W CENTER PKWY
600 TEMP 85281 740-C1
700 TEMP 85281 700-C7
1000 PHX 85008 700-C7
1100 PHX 85008 740-C1
N CENTER RD
2100 PHX 85035 696-H3
N CENTER ST
- MESA 85201 741-H4
- MESA 85210 741-H4
1700 MESA 85201 701-H6
2600 MarC 85256 701-H2
4100 MarC 85256 661-H7
32600 MarC 85361 (453-A1 See Page 413)
S CENTER ST
- MESA 85210 741-H6
700 MarC 85337 (1090-E4 See Page 1049)
1000 MESA 85210 781-H1
32100 MarC 85361 (452-J2 See Page 411)
32200 MarC 85361 (453-A2 See Page 413)
W CENTER ST
300 WICK 85390 290-E3
N CENTERRA DR
- GDYR 85338 (694-G6 See Page 653)
W CENTERRA DR
- GDYR 85338 (694-F6 See Page 653)
E CENTIPEDE DR
15500 FTNH 85268 583-A2
E CENTRAL AV
10200 PHX 85020 618-H3
N CENTRAL AV
- MarC 85027 498-H4
- AVON 85323 695-B6
- PHX 85004 698-G2
- PHX 85003 698-G5
200 PHX 85020 618-G7
800 GDYR 85338 695-B6
2900 PHX 85013 698-G2
2900 PHX 85012 698-G2
3800 PHX 85013 658-G4
3800 PHX 85012 658-G6
7000 PHX 85021 658-G4
7200 PHX 85021 618-G7
13000 PHX 85029 578-G6
13000 PHX 85022 578-H1
15000 PHX 85023 578-H1
17400 PHX 85022 538-H6
18000 PHX 85023 538-H7
18600 PHX 85024 538-H3
19900 PHX 85027 538-H2
25800 MarC 85024 498-H4

N CENTRAL AV
33300 MarC 85085 (458-H2 See Page 417)
33300 PHX 85085 (458-H2 See Page 417)
33800 MarC 85085 (418-H7 See Page 417)
34600 MarC 85086 (418-H2 See Page 417)
39400 MarC 85086 (378-J5 See Page 337)
S CENTRAL AV
- AVON 85323 695-B7
- AVON 85323 735-B1
- PHX 85004 698-G7
- PHX 85041 778-G3
- PHX 85003 698-G7
600 PHX 85003 738-G4
600 PHX 85004 738-G4
1300 AVON 85338 735-B2
2500 PHX 85040 738-G4
2500 PHX 85041 738-G4
15600 PHX 85045 818-E7
16500 PHX 85048 818-E7
N CENTRAL BLVD
200 BUCK 85326 (732-B7 See Page 731)
400 MarC 85326 (732-B7 See Page 731)
N CENTRAL CT
1200 CHAN 85224 821-D3
S CENTRAL CT
- CHAN 85248 861-C3
N CENTRAL DR
200 CHAN 85224 821-D1
2600 CHAN 85224 781-C7
S CENTRAL DR
- CHAN 85248 861-D2
200 CHAN 85224 821-D7
700 CHAN 85224 861-C1
W CENTRAL PK
100 PHX 85013 658-G4
S CENTRAL PL
- CHAN 85248 861-D3
W CENTRAL ST
- SURP 85374 (574-C1 See Page 573)
12900 SURP 85374 575-B2
CENTRAL ARIZONA PROJECT CSR
- MarC - (453-B7 See Page 413)
- MarC - (454-B5 See Page 413)
- MarC - 493-A1
- MarC - 498-F4
- MarC - 622-C5
- MarC - 662-H1
- MarC - 663-E4
- MarC - 703-G4
- MarC - 744-B3
- MarC - 784-H1
- MarC - 785-A2
- MESA - 703-G3
- MESA - 743-J1
- MESA - 744-B3
- MESA - 784-H1
- PEOR - (454-B5 See Page 413)
- PEOR - (455-D3 See Page 415)
- PEOR - (456-F2 See Page 415)
- PEOR - (457-B5 See Page 417)
- PHX - (456-J4 See Page 415)
- PHX - (457-B6 See Page 417)
- PHX - 497-F2
- PHX - 498-A1
- PHX - 499-A7
- PHX - 539-B1
- PHX - 540-A7
- PHX - 580-D1
- SCTS - 580-H2
- SCTS - 581-A3
- SCTS - 621-G1
- SCTS - 622-C5
- SURP - (454-B5 See Page 413)
E CENTRE AV
100 BUCK 85326 (772-A2 See Page 731)
N CENTRE CIR
1200 GIL 85233 781-G4
N CENTRE CT
17200 PHX 85308 537-G7
E CENTURY AV
400 GIL 85296 782-D7
W CENTURY CT
400 GIL 85233 782-B7
E CENTURY DR
7400 SCTS 85250 660-G3
N CENTURY DR
- FTNH 85268 583-A5
N CENTURY LN
11300 PHX 85254 620-C2
W CENTURY ST
200 GIL 85233 782-B7
E CENTURY WY
1800 CARE 85377 420-J6
E CERCADO LN
400 LP 85340 655-B5
W CERCADO LN
100 LP 85340 655-B4
E CEREUS DR
2200 PHX 85022 539-C7
N CERISE
31900 MESA 85208 784-E1
N CERRITO VISTA DR
9100 SCTS 85258 621-D4
E CERRO ALTO DR
14700 FTNH 85268 582-H3
N CERRO ALTO DR
15400 FTNH 85268 582-H3
E CERVANTES CT
15700 FTNH 85268 583-A3
CERVATO CIR
- LP 85340 655-B7
N CESAR CHAVEZ DR
13200 ELMG 85335 575-F5
CESAR CHAVEZ PARK RD
- PHX 85041 777-H3
- PHX 85339 777-H3
W CETON DR
2700 MarC 85339 777-J6
2700 MarC 85339 778-A6

W CHALLENGER TR
- MarC 85087 (378-A3 See Page 337)
N CHAMA DR
12000 FTNH 85268 623-C1
W CHAMA DR
- PHX 85310 498-A5
3700 PHX 85310 497-H5
E CHAMA RD
8400 SCTS 85255 501-A6
11700 SCTS 85255 502-A6
N CHAMBERS CT
3500 SCTS 85251 700-G2
E CHAMBERS ST
1300 PHX 85040 738-J7
1600 PHX 85040 739-A7
9000 MarC 85208 784-C1
W CHAMBERS ST
- PHX 85041 738-D6
- PHX 85040 738-F7
3500 PHX 85041 737-H6
9800 MarC 85353 735-G6
9800 MarC 85353 736-A6
E CHAMPAGNE DR
9400 MarC 85248 901-A3
W CHAMPAGNE DR
200 CHAN 85248 901-E3
400 MarC 85248 901-E3
E CHAMPAGNE PL
- MarC 85249 902-A3
S CHAMPIONSHIP DR
1600 CHAN 85249 901-J5
N CHAMPLAIN AV
2400 TEMP 85281 700-F6
N CHANCE DR
17300 SURP 85374 534-G7
E CHANDLER BLVD
- CHAN 85225 821-H6
- PHX 85045 818-H5
- PHX 85048 818-H5
1200 CHAN 85225 822-A6
1700 PHX 85048 819-H6
3200 PHX 85044 819-D5
5200 CHAN 85226 819-H6
5200 PHX 85226 819-H6
W CHANDLER BLVD
- CHAN 85224 820-G6
- PHX 85041 818-D6
- CHAN 85225 821-E6
- PHX 85045 818-E5
- PHX 85048 818-E5
800 CHAN 85224 821-B6
3500 CHAN 85226 820-C6
7200 CHAN 85226 819-J6
N CHANDLER CIR
1300 CHAN 85225 821-F3
E CHANDLER GILBERT CC RD
- CHAN 85225 862-B1
E CHANDLER HEIGHTS RD
- CHAN 85249 901-G2
300 MarC 85249 901-G2
1600 MarC 85326 899-D1
8800 CHAN 85248 901-D2
8800 MarC 85248 901-D2
12600 MarC 85249 902-C2
15900 MarC 85236 902-F2
16100 MarC 85236 903-C2
18400 QC 85236 903-F2
19100 QC 85242 903-F2
19600 QC 85242 904-A2
W CHANDLER HEIGHTS RD
500 CHAN 85248 901-D2
13000 MarC 85326 (854-C7 See Page 813)
13800 GDYR 85326 (854-C7 See Page 813)
17000 GDYR 85326 (853-F7 See Page 813)
17000 MarC 85326 (853-F7 See Page 813)
W CHANDLER VILLAGE
- SURP 85374 534-A6
N CHANNING
- MESA 85207 704-A7
- MESA 85207 744-A1
S CHANNING
2800 MESA 85212 784-A6
S CHANNING CIR
2800 MESA 85212 784-A6
E CHAPALA ST
15600 MarC 85234 782-H6
E CHAPAROSA WY
4000 PHX 85331 459-H5
4600 PHX 85331 460-A5
S CHAPARRAL BLVD
- MarC 85236 823-C7
W CHAPARRAL DR
10100 MarC 85373 536-B4
W CHAPARRAL LN
16400 SURP 85374 534-D6
E CHAPARRAL RD
5000 SCTS 85251 661-A6
6400 PHX 85253 660-H6
6400 PVAL 85253 660-H6
6400 PHX 85251 660-H6
6400 SCTS 85251 660-H6
6600 PVAL 85251 660-H6
6600 SCTS 85253 660-H6
7200 SCTS 85250 660-H6
8500 SCTS 85250 661-A6
8800 MarC 85250 661-C6
8800 MarC 85256 661-A6
8800 SCTS 85256 661-A6
12000 MarC 85256 662-A6
N CHAPARRAL RD
- SCTS 85251 661-A6
S CHAPARRAL RD
1400 APJT 85219 785-G1
W CHAPARRAL RD
600 WICK 85390 290-D3
W CHAPARRAL WY
1700 CHAN 85248 901-B2
N CHAPARREL RD
- APJT 85219 745-G5
S CHAPARREL RD
300 APJT 85219 745-G6
E CHAPARRON
8000 SCTS 85262 460-J7
8100 SCTS 85262 (461-A6 See Page 421)
N CHAPARRON
8400 SCTS 85262 (461-A6 See Page 421)
N CHAPS
17100 SURP 85374 534-B7
N CHARLEBOIS RD
1500 PinC 85219 746-C2

S CHARLEBOIS RD
100 PinC 85219 746-C6
E CHARLES DR
4500 PVAL 85028 619-J5
N CHARLES DR
8100 PVAL 85028 619-H6
8200 PHX 85028 619-J6
N CHARLES ST
1100 GIL 85233 782-A4
N CHARLES BLAIR MCDONALD DR
38000 CARE 85262 421-C4
38000 CARE 85377 421-C4
38000 SCTS 85262 421-C4
E CHARLESTON AV
200 PHX 85022 538-H7
1100 PHX 85022 539-A7
2600 PHX 85032 539-D7
4700 PHX 85032 540-A7
4800 PHX 85254 540-A7
N CHARLESTON AV
17800 PHX 85022 538-H7
W CHARLESTON AV
600 PHX 85023 538-C7
2700 PHX 85053 538-A7
3500 PHX 85308 538-A7
3500 PHX 85308 537-F7
5500 GLEN 85308 537-D7
8400 PEOR 85382 536-E7
9100 PEOR 85373 536-D7
E CHARLESTON ST
1200 PHX 85022 539-A7
W CHARLOTTE DR
3500 PHX 85310 498-A6
3600 PHX 85310 497-C6
E CHARLTON CT
16200 FTNH 85268 583-B6
W CHARNWOOD CT
11000 MarC 85351 575-J3
E CHARTER OAK CIR
12400 SCTS 85259 621-J1
E CHARTER OAK DR
- SCTS 85268 622-F1
8000 SCTS 85260 580-J7
8300 SCTS 85260 581-A7
9500 SCTS 85260 621-C1
10400 SCTS 85259 581-E7
10400 SCTS 85259 621-F1
13400 SCTS 85259 622-E1
W CHARTER OAK DR
10200 MarC 85351 576-B3
E CHARTER OAK RD
3000 PHX 85032 579-E7
4900 PHX 85032 580-A7
4900 PHX 85254 580-B7
7400 SCTS 85260 580-G7
7600 SCTS 85260 620-H1
W CHARTER OAK RD
- YNTN 85335 575-G6
2200 PHX 85029 578-A1
3600 PHX 85029 577-H7
4300 PHX 85304 577-G7
5800 GLEN 85304 577-C7
6900 PEOR 85381 577-A7
7200 PEOR 85381 576-E6
11700 ELMG 85335 575-E6
N CHASE CT
300 CHAN 85225 822-B6
N CHASE OAKS WY
- MarC 85086 (378-D6 See Page 337)
E CHATEAU DR
200 GDYR 85338 695-A7
S CHATHAM
- MarC 85212 824-H3
S CHATHAM CIR
- MarC 85212 824-H3
S CHATSWORTH
- MESA 85212 784-F6
- MESA 85220 784-F1
S CHATSWORTH CIR
- MESA 85212 784-F7
W CHEERY LYNN CT
15400 GDYR 85338 (654-F7 See Page 653)
W CHEERY LYNN DR
- GDYR 85338 (694-H1 See Page 653)
3500 PHX 85019 697-J1
5400 PHX 85031 697-E1
5900 PHX 85033 697-B1
E CHEERY LYNN RD
300 PHX 85012 698-H2
1300 PHX 85014 698-J2
1300 PHX 85014 699-A2
1600 PHX 85016 699-A2
3000 PHX 85018 699-E2
3100 PHX 85018 700-A2
6600 SCTS 85251 700-E2
8700 SCTS 85251 701-A2
W CHEERY LYNN RD
- GDYR 85338 (694-H1 See Page 653)
400 PHX 85013 698-F2
2200 PHX 85015 698-C1
2500 PHX 85017 698-B1
3700 PHX 85019 697-G1
4300 PHX 85031 697-E1
6300 PHX 85033 697-A1
7500 PHX 85033 696-F1
8600 PHX 85037 696-D1
15300 GDYR 85338 (654-G7 See Page 653)
S CHEHIA ST
11000 PHX 85044 779-H7
S CHELSEA LN
- GIL 85296 822-D7
E CHENEY DR
5200 PVAL 85253 660-A1
5700 PVAL 85253 620-C7
7500 PVAL 85258 660-E1
W CHERI ANN LN
22400 MarC 85361 (412-H7 See Page 411)
N CHERI LYNN CT
600 CHAN 85225 821-E2
S CHERI LYNN CT
500 CHAN 85225 821-E7
500 CHAN 85225 861-E1
N CHERI LYNN DR
400 CHAN 85225 821-E1
2600 CHAN 85225 781-E7
N CHEROKEE LN
22800 MarC 85375 494-J7
S CHEROKEE LN
- PinC 85219 785-G2
W CHEROKEE LN
32700 MarC 85390 250-A6
E CHEROKEE ST
3200 PHX 85044 819-E2

S CHERRY
2000 MESA 85210 781-F3
S CHERRY CIR
2100 MESA 85210 781-F3
N CHERRY LN
8500 PEOR 85345 616-F2
N CHERRY ST
- MESA 85201 741-F1
1700 MESA 85201 701-F7
S CHERRY ST
900 MESA 85210 741-F7
1200 MESA 85210 781-F1
N CHERRY CREEK DR
17900 SURP 85374 534-F6
N CHERRY HILLS CT
10800 FTNH 85268 623-C3
E CHERRY HILLS DR
- MarC 85249 902-E4
1300 CHAN 85249 901-J4
1800 CHAN 85249 902-A4
N CHERRY HILLS DR
- MarC 85351 575-J6
11800 MarC 85351 576-A6
W CHERRY HILLS DR
- ELMG 85335 575-D7
6700 PEOR 85345 577-A7
7100 PEOR 85345 576-E7
10200 MarC 85351 576-A7
N CHERRY HILLS DR W
12200 MarC 85351 575-J6
W CHERRY HILLS DR W
10700 MarC 85351 575-J7
10700 MarC 85351 576-A7
E CHERRY HILLS PL
- MarC 85249 902-C4
W CHERRY LYNN DR
- GDYR 85338 (654-F7 See Page 653)
- GDYR 85338 (694-F1 See Page 653)
W CHERRY LYNN RD
- AVON 85340 695-C1
N CHERRY TREE LN
19800 MarC 85373 536-A4
W CHERRY TREE LN
10500 MarC 85373 536-A4
S CHERRYWOOD CIR
- MESA 85212 784-G4
E CHERRYWOOD DR
- QC 85242 903-J3
9400 MarC 85248 901-A2
W CHERRYWOOD DR
200 CHAN 85248 901-D2
E CHERRYWOOD PL
- MarC 85249 901-H2
- MarC 85249 902-B2
E CHERYL DR
700 PHX 85020 618-J3
1200 PHX 85020 619-A3
2300 PHX 85028 619-C3
4800 PVAL 85253 620-A3
5400 PHX 85253 620-B3
8300 SCTS 85258 620-J4
8300 SCTS 85258 621-A4
14200 SCTS 85259 622-F4
N CHERYL DR
1700 PHX 85020 619-B3
W CHERYL DR
- PHX 85020 618-F3
700 PHX 85021 618-D3
2700 PHX 85051 618-A3
3300 PHX 85051 617-J2
4500 GLEN 85302 617-B2
6700 PEOR 85345 617-A2
6900 PEOR 85345 616-J2
10100 MarC 85351 616-A2
10700 MarC 85351 615-J2
17100 MarC 85355 (614-B1 See Page 573)
17800 MarC 85355 (613-J1 See Page 573)
E CHESAPEAKE DR
2100 GIL 85234 782-H4
N CHESHIRE
- MESA 85220 744-G7
- MESA 85220 784-G1
S CHESHIRE
- MESA 85220 784-G2
S CHESHONI ST
11000 PHX 85044 779-H7
N CHESIRE
- MESA 85220 744-G6
W CHESTER RD
- PHX 85310 497-B6
N CHESTNUT
1600 MESA 85213 742-D1
3200 MESA 85213 702-D4
S CHESTNUT
- MESA 85204 742-D6
1000 MESA 85204 782-D1
S CHESTNUT AV
1800 BUCK 85326 (692-C7 See Page 651)
1900 BUCK 85326 (732-C1 See Page 731)
N CHESTNUT CIR
600 MESA 85213 742-D3
2600 MESA 85213 702-D5
S CHESTNUT CIR
1500 MESA 85204 782-D2
E CHESTNUT CT
11000 MarC 85248 901-F5
E CHESTNUT DR
9700 MarC 85248 901-B5
N CHESTNUT DR
15400 MarC 85351 576-A2
E CHESTNUT LN
- GIL 85236 863-D6
S CHESTNUT PL
2400 CHAN 85248 861-C4
N CHESTNUT ST
600 WICK 85390 290-E1
E CHEVIOT AV
8900 MarC 85208 744-C7
E CHEYENNE CT
1700 GIL 85296 822-H1
E CHEYENNE DR
4400 PHX 85044 779-H7
N CHEYENNE DR
13500 MarC 85339 535-C1
22300 MarC 85375 495-C7
W CHEYENNE DR
400 CHAN 85225 781-E7
1200 CHAN 85224 781-A7
2000 MarC 85224 781-B7
2700 MarC 85339 778-A7
2900 PHX 85339 778-A7
3000 MarC 85339 777-H7
3000 PHX 85339 777-H7
13500 MarC 85375 495-C7

STREET Block City ZIP Pg-Grid

W CHEYENNE RD
20300 MarC 85326 (773-C5
See Page 733)
E CHEYENNE ST
1400 GIL 85296 822-G1
E CHIA WY
10300 SCTS 85262 421-G2
E CHICAGO CIR
500 CHAN 85225 821-G7
W CHICAGO CIR N
200 CHAN 85226 820-E7
W CHICAGO CIR S
300 CHAN 85226 820-E7
W CHICAGO CT
1000 CHAN 85224 821-D7
E CHICAGO ST
- CHAN 85225 821-F7
1600 CHAN 85225 822-A7
13200 MarC 85225 822-B7
W CHICAGO ST
- CHAN 85225 821-E7
200 CHAN 85224 821-C7
300 CHAN 85226 820-A6
7200 CHAN 85226 819-J6
E CHICKADEE RD
- MarC 85236 863-B3
W CHICKASAW ST
- PHX 85353 736-E2
E CHICORY DR
15400 FTNH 85268 582-J7
15400 FTNH 85268 622-J1
15500 FTNH 85268 583-A7
15500 FTNH 85268 623-A1
N CHILCOTT CT
1300 GIL 85233 782-B4
CHILDRENS HOSPITAL RD
700 TEMP 85281 740-D1
W CHILTON AV
1200 GIL 85233 782-A6
1200 GIL 85233 781-J7
E CHILTON DR
- CHAN 85225 781-G6
200 TEMP 85283 780-D6
W CHILTON DR
- CHAN 85225 781-F6
1000 TEMP 85283 780-B6
N CHILTON ST
3100 CHAN 85224 781-A6
W CHILTON ST
300 CHAN 85225 781-E6
1200 CHAN 85224 781-A6
E CHINLE DR
18700 MarC 85263 503-J5
N CHINO CT
17600 MarC 85373 536-D7
E CHINO DR
8200 SCTS 85255 540-J5
8200 SCTS 85255 541-A5
W CHINO DR
- PEOR 85373 536-A4
9000 PEOR 85382 536-C4
10800 PEOR 85373 535-J4
N CHINO LN
35000 CARE 85377 420-E7
S CHINOOK CT
11800 PHX 85044 819-F1
N CHINOOK PZ
14200 FTNH 85268 583-E6
E CHIPMAN RD
800 PHX 85040 738-H6
1600 PHX 85040 739-A6
W CHIPMAN RD
500 PHX 85041 738-C6
3700 PHX 85041 737-H6
N CHIPMUNK LN
11400 FTNH 85268 623-A2
S CHIPPEWA CT
- CHAN 85248 861-D2
N CHIPPEWA DR
500 CHAN 85224 821-D3
S CHIPPEWA DR
- PHX 85044 819-H1
400 CHAN 85225 821-D7
2200 CHAN 85248 861-D4
N CHIPPEWA PL
200 CHAN 85224 821-D6
S CHIPPEWA PL
200 CHAN 85224 821-D7
N CHIPPEWA ST
600 CHAN 85224 821-D5
E CHIPSHOT CT
- PinC 85219 786-F7
E CHIQUITA DR
16200 FTNH 85268 583-B7
E CHIQUITA LN
5000 SCTS 85253 660-E6
E CHIRICAHUA PASS
- SCTS 85262 (381-E6
See Page 341)
W CHIRICAHUA RD
2600 MarC 85087 (338-D2
See Page 337)
W CHISHOLM CT
10600 MarC 85373 536-A4
N CHISOLM CT
- PinC 85220 705-C6
W CHISOLM DR
- PEOR 85373 536-A4
N CHISOLM TR
- PinC 85242 865-C7
- PinC 85242 905-D1
E CHISUM TR
4400 PHX 85050 499-J4
4500 PHX 85050 500-A4
N CHISUM TR
25800 SCTS 85255 501-B5
W CHISUM TR
- PHX 85310 497-C3
E CHOCTAW CIR
17500 FTNH 85268 583-E6
N CHOCTAW CT
5000 PinC 85220 705-C7
E CHOKEBERRY CIR
- SCTS 85255 501-D5
S CHOLLA
1600 MESA 85202 781-C2
S CHOLLA CIR
2700 MESA 85202 781-C5
N CHOLLA CT
2300 CHAN 85224 821-C1
S CHOLLA CT
1000 CHAN 85248 861-B1
26200 MarC 85248 901-A5
W CHOLLA CT
11600 SURP 85374 535-G7
E CHOLLA DR
- SCTS 85259 622-F2
6000 PVAL 85253 620-D7
8800 SCTS 85260 621-B2

E CHOLLA DR
15400 FTNH 85268 582-J7
15400 FTNH 85268 622-J1
15400 FTNH 85268 623-A1
N CHOLLA DR
- GBND 85337 (1090-C3
See Page 1049)
S CHOLLA DR
- GBND 85337 (1090-C3
See Page 1049)
E CHOLLA LN
3800 PHX 85028 619-G4
5800 PHX 85251 660-D5
7300 PVAL 85250 660-G5
7500 SCTS 85250 660-G5
10700 SCTS 85259 621-F2
N CHOLLA LN
- PinC 85242 865-D7
E CHOLLA PL
6200 PVAL 85253 620-D7
N CHOLLA PL
9300 PVAL 85253 620-D4
S CHOLLA PL
1300 CHAN 85248 861-B2
E CHOLLA RD
5800 CVCK 85331 420-D4
11000 MESA 85220 744-H4
11000 MarC 85220 744-H4
E CHOLLA ST
1200 PHX 85020 618-J1
1200 PHX 85020 619-A1
2300 PHX 85028 619-C1
4600 PHX 85028 620-A1
4900 PHX 85254 620-A1
6000 SCTS 85254 620-D1
6000 PinC 85219 746-B5
7200 SCTS 85260 620-J2
8200 SCTS 85260 621-A2
10400 SCTS 85259 621-F2
N CHOLLA ST
- GIL 85233 782-B7
200 MESA 85201 741-C4
300 CHAN 85224 821-B1
2800 CHAN 85224 781-B7
S CHOLLA ST
- GIL 85233 782-B7
- GIL 85233 822-B1
1100 CHAN 85248 861-B1
2100 MESA 85202 781-C3
W CHOLLA ST
1700 PHX 85029 618-A1
2400 APJT 85220 745-A5
3400 PHX 85029 617-H1
4300 PHX 85304 617-G1
4800 GLEN 85304 617-B1
6700 PEOR 85345 617-B1
7100 PEOR 85345 616-D1
E CHOLLA CANYON DR
3900 PHX 85044 819-G4
S CHOLLA CANYON DR
4100 PHX 85044 819-G4
E CHOLLA CREST TR
- FTNH 85268 622-H4
E CHOLULA DR
14500 FTNH 85268 582-G3
W CHOPPO RD
4300 MarC 85339 817-F4
N CHRISTA WY
800 TOL 85353 696-E5
W CHRISTA WY
8800 TOL 85353 696-D4
N CHRISTIAN CHURCH CAMP RD
38900 PEOR 85342 (375-E7
See Page 335)
38900 PEOR 85342 415-E1
W CHRISTINE CIR
4800 PHX 85308 577-F1
E CHRISTMAS CHOLLA DR
7400 SCTS 85255 500-H6
9900 SCTS 85255 501-E4
E CHRISTOPHER LN
11900 SCTS 85255 502-A7
11900 SCTS 85255 542-A1
W CHRISTOPHER MICHAEL LN
8700 PEOR 85345 616-E1
E CHRISTY DR
1200 PHX 85020 618-J2
1200 PHX 85020 619-A2
2100 PHX 85028 619-C2
W CHRISTY DR
3000 PHX 85029 618-A2
3900 PHX 85029 617-H2
4500 GLEN 85304 617-B1
CHRYSLER DR
- MarC 85375 413-E7
CHRYSLER CROSS CUT RD
- MarC 85375 413-E7
CHRYSLER FLAT TRACK RD
- MarC 85361 413-E4
- MarC 85375 413-E4
CHRYSLER LOOP RD
- MarC 85361 413-E4
- MarC 85361 (453-C1
See Page 413)
- MarC 85375 413-E4
- MarC 85375 (453-E1
See Page 413)
CHRYSLER OVAL TRACK RD
- MarC 85361 413-C6
- MarC 85375 413-C6
CHRYSLER PIT RW
- MarC 85375 413-E7
W CHUCKASAW ST
- PHX 85043 737-A2
CHUCKS TR
- SURP 85374 (454-E5
See Page 413)
E CHUCKWAGON LN
9500 SCTS 85262 (461-D1
See Page 421)
9600 SCTS 85262 421-E7
W CHUCKWALLA CT
11500 SURP 85374 535-H4
E CHUCKWALLA TR
5800 CVCK 85331 (380-D7
See Page 339)
E CHUCKWALLA CANYON RD
4200 PHX 85044 819-G5
N CHULA VISTA DR
- SURP 85374 534-B5
E CHUP
- PinC 85219 786-E7

E CHUPAROSA CIR
10200 SCTS 85255 501-F5
21400 QC 85242 904-D1
E CHUPAROSA CT
15200 FTNH 85268 582-J6
E CHUPAROSA DR
6300 SCTS 85262 460-E2
E CHUPAROSA LN
5400 CVCK 85331 420-C2
E CHUPAROSA PL
5800 CARE 85377 420-D7
W CHURCH DR
51300 MarC 85320 (284-H4
See Page 244)
N CHURCH RD
22400 SCTS 85255 541-E1
23400 SCTS 85255 501-E7
N CHURCH ST
15800 SURP 85374 575-D2
W CHURCH ST
50700 MarC 85320 (285-A4
See Page 244)
51000 MarC 85320 (284-J4
See Page 244)
S CHURCHILL DR
- GIL 85296 822-J2
N CHURCHILL PL
- CHAN 85226 820-H7
S CHURCHILL PL
- CHAN 85226 820-H7
N CIBOLA DR
40100 CARE 85377 421-A1
E CIBOLA RD
- SCTS 85259 622-C1
E CICERO CIR
- MarC 85220 744-F5
3200 MESA 85213 742-G4
E CICERO ST
- MESA 85220 744-J5
- MESA 85220 745-A5
2500 MESA 85213 742-E4
5200 MarC 85205 743-C4
5200 MESA 85205 743-C4
8000 MESA 85207 744-A4
9900 MarC 85207 744-F4
9900 MarC 85220 744-F5
S CIELO
- MESA 85212 784-D6
N CIELO CT
- SURP 85374 534-G4
E CIELO RUN
6200 CVCK 85331 (380-E6
See Page 339)
E CIELO GRANDE
- MarC 85024 499-C7
- PHX 85024 499-C7
W CIELO GRANDE
- PEOR 85382 497-A6
3600 PHX 85310 497-D6
8900 MarC 85382 496-D6
23400 PEOR 85382 496-G6
E CIELO GRANDE AV
2000 PHX 85024 539-C1
4800 PHX 85054 540-B1
E CIENEGA ST
17800 MarC 85264 583-F7
E CIMARRON AV
13400 PHX 85022 579-B6
W CIMARRON CT
10600 MarC 85373 536-A4
E CIMARRON DR
26400 SCTS 85255 501-H4
W CIMARRON DR
- PEOR 85373 535-J4
- PEOR 85373 536-A4
15600 SURP 85374 534-F2
E CINDER CONE RD
10900 SCTS 85262 (461-H7
See Page 421)
E CINDER CONE TR
9500 SCTS 85262 (461-D7
See Page 421)
9500 SCTS 85262 501-F1
W CINDY PL
2100 CHAN 85224 821-B7
5300 CHAN 85226 820-D7
E CINDY ST
700 CHAN 85225 821-H7
1600 CHAN 85225 822-A7
13200 MarC 85225 822-B7
S CINDY ST
300 CHAN 85225 822-A7
W CINDY ST
1100 CHAN 85224 821-C7
3500 CHAN 85226 820-D7
E CINNABAR AV
700 PHX 85020 618-J3
1200 PHX 85020 619-A3
2200 PHX 85028 619-C3
9600 SCTS 85258 621-D3
N CINNABAR AV
10100 SCTS 85258 621-D3
W CINNABAR AV
300 PHX 85021 618-D3
3200 PHX 85051 618-A3
3400 PHX 85051 617-H3
4500 GLEN 85302 617-B2
6700 PEOR 85345 617-A2
6900 PEOR 85345 616-C2
9700 MarC 85351 616-A3
10700 MarC 85351 615-H2
W CINNABAR DR
- PEOR 85345 616-D2
15800 SURP 85374 534-F2
E CINNEBAR DR
- APJT 85219 785-H3
E CIPALM ST
3800 MESA 85215 702-J5
W CIRCLE BLVD
32400 WICK 85390 290-A3
N CIRCLE DR
600 TEMP 85281 700-F7
8200 CARE 85377 421-B1
E CIRCLE RD
700 PHX 85020 618-H7
E CIRCLE MOUNTAIN RD
100 MarC 85087 (378-J2
See Page 337)
100 MarC 85087 (379-B2
See Page 339)
W CIRCLE MOUNTAIN RD
- MarC 85087 (378-A2
See Page 337)
3600 MarC 85087 (377-H2
See Page 337)
4100 PHX 85087 (377-H2
See Page 337)

W CIRCLE RIDGE DR
14100 MarC 85375 535-A2
S CIRCLESTONE CT
4500 PinC 85219 786-H4
E CIRCULO AV
7100 MESA 85208 783-G5
E CIRCULO JUAN TAVENA
5800 GUAD 85283 780-B5
E CIRCULO S HERNANDEZ
5700 GUAD 85283 780-B5
N CIRRUS CIR
- MESA 85207 704-A3
N CIRRUS CT
- FTNH 85268 622-G4
W CISA RIO LN
15800 SURP 85374 534-F6
E CISCO RD
9400 MarC 85207 744-E4
E CITADEL DR
- MarC 85236 903-E3
E CITATION LN
100 TEMP 85284 820-D1
1900 TEMP 85284 780-H7
W CITATION LN
- TEMP 85284 820-C1
100 TEMP 85284 780-D7
1100 CHAN 85224 821-C1
N CITRUS AV
3300 PHX 85018 700-C2
3300 PHX 85251 700-C2
S CITRUS CT
- GIL 85236 863-F6
W CITRUS CT
- MarC 85340 655-B1
E CITRUS CV
1100 MESA 85213 742-G2
N CITRUS CV
600 MESA 85213 742-G3
S CITRUS CV
1700 MESA 85204 782-G2
W CITRUS GRV
10700 AVON 85323 695-G1
E CITRUS LN
9000 MarC 85248 900-J5
9000 MarC 85248 901-A5
S CITRUS LN
- GIL 85236 863-F5
N CITRUS RD
- GDYR 85326 (693-J1
See Page 653)
- MarC 85326 (693-J3
See Page 653)
2900 GDYR 85338 653-J6
2900 GDYR 85338 (693-J1
See Page 653)
4100 GDYR 85340 653-J3
5000 MarC 85340 653-J3
6000 MarC 85355 653-J3
6500 MarC 85355 (613-J7
See Page 573)
7000 MarC 85355 (614-A5
See Page 573)
10200 MarC 85379 (614-A5
See Page 573)
10600 MarC 85379 (574-A2
See Page 573)
10600 SURP 85379 (574-A7
See Page 573)
10600 SURP 85379 (614-A5
See Page 573)
14600 MarC 85374 (574-A2
See Page 573)
15400 SURP 85374 534-A5
15400 SURP 85374 (574-A1
See Page 573)
17000 SURP 85387 534-A5
22300 SURP 85387 494-A6
S CITRUS RD
- GDYR 85326 (693-J6
See Page 653)
- MarC 85326 (693-J6
See Page 653)
1200 MarC 85326 733-J2
1200 GDYR 85326 733-J2
E CITRUS WY
1000 PHX 85014 658-J2
7300 SCTS 85250 660-G3
8500 SCTS 85250 661-A3
S CITRUS WY
2200 CHAN 85249 862-A4
W CITRUS WY
- CHAN 85248 861-D7
- MarC 85340 655-C2
- PHX 85013 658-F2
1700 PHX 85015 658-C2
2900 PHX 85017 658-A2
3400 PHX 85017 657-J2
3500 PHX 85019 657-G2
4400 GLEN 85301 657-B2
7900 GLEN 85303 656-F2
8300 GLEN 85305 656-D2
W CITRUS GROVE LN
11100 AVON 85323 695-H1
S CITRUS VALLEY RD
50800 MarC 85337 1049-A5
52400 GBND 85337 1049-A6
52600 GBND 85337 (1089-A1
See Page 1049)
56500 MarC 85337 (1089-A1
See Page 1049)
E CIVANO DR
- PinC 85219 786-G7
N CIVIC CENTER BLVD
3300 SCTS 85251 700-F2
4100 SCTS 85251 660-F7
E CIVIC CENTER DR
- GIL 85296 822-C3
S CIVIC CENTER DR
800 GIL 85296 822-D2
N CIVIC CENTER PZ
2900 SCTS 85251 700-G2
4300 SCTS 85251 660-G7
N CLAESSENS DR
400 MarC 85342 (412-D3
See Page 411)
S CLAIBORNE
700 MESA 85206 743-B7
N CLAIBORNE AV
1200 GIL 85234 783-B3
1200 MarC 85234 783-B5
S CLAIBORNE AV
- GIL 85236 823-A3
- MarC 85236 823-A3
N CLAIBORNE CT
- MarC 85234 783-B5
E CLAIR DR
3900 PHX 85032 579-G4

W CLAIR DR
- PEOR 85345 616-D2
9900 MarC 85351 616-A2
10500 MarC 85351 615-J2
S CLAIRBORNE AV
- MarC 85236 863-A2
E CLAIRE DR
1200 PHX 85022 579-A4
2300 PHX 85032 579-D4
5200 PHX 85254 580-B4
N CLANCY
- MESA 85220 744-J4
S CLANCY
- MarC 85212 824-J1
- MESA 85212 784-J7
- MESA 85212 824-J1
- MESA 85220 784-J2
S CLANCY CIR
- MarC 85212 824-H3
- MESA 85220 784-J1
N CLANDESTINE WY
- SURP 85379 (574-H3
See Page 573)
E CLANTON AV
100 BUCK 85326 (772-A2
See Page 731)
W CLARA LN
- PEOR 85308 536-G3
- PEOR 85382 536-D3
14700 SURP 85374 534-J6
E CLAREMONT AV
3000 PHX 85016 659-E3
4000 PVAL 85253 659-G3
E CLAREMONT ST
100 PHX 85012 658-H2
700 PHX 85014 658-H3
1600 PHX 85016 659-A3
3300 PVAL 85253 659-F3
7300 SCTS 85250 660-G3
W CLAREMONT ST
300 PHX 85013 658-F2
1700 PHX 85015 658-D2
2500 PHX 85017 658-A2
3400 PHX 85017 657-J2
3600 PHX 85019 657-H2
4300 GLEN 85301 657-B2
7100 GLEN 85303 656-G2
8300 GLEN 85305 656-F2
13500 MarC 85340 655-A2
15900 MarC 85340 (654-E1
See Page 653)
17300 MarC 85355 653-H1
17300 MarC 85355 (654-A1
See Page 653)
E CLARENDON AV
- PHX 85012 698-G1
1000 PHX 85014 698-J1
1300 PHX 85014 699-A1
1800 PHX 85016 699-C1
3200 PHX 85018 699-F1
4900 PHX 85018 700-A1
8000 SCTS 85251 700-J1
8500 SCTS 85251 701-A1
8700 MarC 85251 701-A1
8800 MarC 85256 701-C1
12000 MarC 85256 702-A1
N CLARENDON AV
3900 PHX 85031 657-D7
W CLARENDON AV
- AVON 85323 656-A7
- AVON 85340 655-D7
- GDYR 85338 (654-H7
See Page 653)
- GDYR 85338 655-D7
100 PHX 85013 658-A7
100 PHX 85013 698-E1
1300 PHX 85015 698-D1
2800 PHX 85017 658-A7
3400 PHX 85017 657-J7
3500 PHX 85019 657-G7
3600 PHX 85031 657-C7
3800 PHX 85033 657-A7
6900 PHX 85033 656-F7
8300 PHX 85037 656-D7
19100 MarC 85340 653-E6
E CLARK CT
- GIL 85236 863-C5
E CLARK DR
- GIL 85236 863-B5
S CLARK DR
100 TEMP 85281 740-J3
2400 TEMP 85282 740-J6
4700 TEMP 85282 780-J2
5800 TEMP 85283 780-H4
9200 TEMP 85284 820-H3
E CLARK RD
3200 PHX 85050 539-F6
N CLARK RD
19000 PHX 85024 539-C6
W CLARK ST
400 MESA 85201 741-F4
E CLAXTON AV
- GIL 85236 863-B3
- MarC 85236 863-A3
15800 MarC 85236 862-J3
15800 MarC 85296 862-J3
E CLAXTON CT
- MarC 85236 863-A3
W CLAYTON DR
7700 PHX 85033 656-G6
E CLEARBROOK DR
1600 MarC 85206 743-D7
N CLEAR CANYON DR
15500 SURP 85374 534-F4
W CLEAR CANYON DR
15900 SURP 85374 534-F4
W CLEAR CANYON DR W
- SURP 85374 534-G3
N CLEAR CREEK DR
4400 LP 85340 655-A5
N CLEAR CROSSING CT
- MarC 85086 (378-C6
See Page 337)
N CLEAR CROSSING RD
- MarC 85086 (378-C6
See Page 337)
W CLEAR SPRING DR
1300 GIL 85233 821-J2
W CLEAR STREAM DR
8300 PHX 85037 656-F5
S CLEARVIEW
6300 MESA 85212 823-G7
S CLEARVIEW AV
500 MESA 85208 743-G7
800 MESA 85208 783-G2
W CLEARVIEW BLVD
15500 SURP 85374 534-D5
W CLEARWATER CT
13500 MarC 85375 535-C1

E CLEAR WATER LN
1300 GIL 85234 782-F6
E CLEARWATER PKWY
4400 MarC 85253 619-H7
4400 MarC 85253 659-H1
4800 PVAL 85253 659-H1
4800 PVAL 85253 660-A1
W CLEAR WATER RD
10900 GDYR 85338 (773-J5
See Page 733)
W CLEARWATER WY
- SURP 85374 534-F4
N CLEMENT
400 MESA 85201 741-F4
S CLEMENTINE CT
3000 TEMP 85282 740-A7
3200 TEMP 85282 780-A1
6700 TEMP 85283 780-A5
N CLEVELAND AV
100 GBND 85337 (1090-B2
See Page 1049)
S CLEVELAND AV
100 GBND 85337 (1090-B3
See Page 1049)
N CLIFF CIR
600 MESA 85201 741-C3
E CLIFF ROSE TR
- PinC 85219 786-E5
N CLIFFSIDE DR
1200 GIL 85234 782-G4
5200 PHX 85018 660-A5
N CLIFF TOP DR
13400 FTNH 85268 583-E7
E CLIFTON AV
- GIL 85296 822-D6
- MarC 85236 823-A6
E CLIFTON CT
- GIL 85296 822-D6
- MarC 85236 823-A6
E CLINTON ST
700 PHX 85020 618-J2
2200 PHX 85028 619-C2
4700 PHX 85254 619-J2
6000 PHX 85254 620-D2
6400 SCTS 85254 620-E2
7500 SCTS 85260 620-G2
8500 SCTS 85260 621-D2
10400 SCTS 85259 621-F2
12100 SCTS 85259 622-A3
W CLINTON ST
3000 PHX 85029 618-A2
E CLIPPER CIR
1700 GIL 85234 782-H4
E CLIPPER LN
2000 GIL 85234 782-H4
E CLOISTERS DR
2400 PHX 85016 659-C5
E CLOUD DR
13000 MarC 85249 902-B3
E CLOUD RD
- MarC 85086 (418-J5
See Page 417)
800 MarC 85086 419-C5
2800 CVCK 85331 419-G5
3200 MarC 85249 902-A3
10800 MarC 85248 901-F3
12000 MarC 85249 901-J3
16400 MarC 85236 903-A3
18400 QC 85236 903-G3
19200 QC 85242 903-G3
20800 MarC 85242 904-E4
20800 QC 85242 904-E4
W CLOUD RD
- MarC 85086 (418-C5
See Page 417)
3300 PHX 85086 (418-C5
See Page 417)
18700 MarC 85342 413-E4
18700 MarC 85375 413-E4
20300 MarC 85361 413-E4
E CLOUDBURST CT
- GIL 85236 863-E4
E CLOUD CHASER LN
- SCTS 85262 (381-E6
See Page 341)
S CLOUD CREEK TR
- MarC 85242 904-F3
E CLOUDVIEW AV
9700 PinC 85219 786-F3
W CLOUSE DR
6200 PHX 85033 657-B5
E CLOVER ST
1500 MESA 85203 742-C4
W CLOVER WY
10700 AVON 85323 695-G1
S CLOVERLAND CT
5000 CHAN 85248 901-E2
S CLOVERLAND DR
25200 MarC 85248 901-E4
E CLOVIS AV
- MESA 85220 744-H7
500 MESA 85206 743-A7
2000 MESA 85204 742-D7
3700 MESA 85206 742-H7
7300 MESA 85208 743-H7
8400 MarC 85208 744-C7
8400 MESA 85208 744-B7
E CLOVIS CIR
7400 MESA 85208 743-H7
S CLUB WY
1800 TEMP 85281 740-J6
1900 TEMP 85282 740-J6
E CLUB ESTATES DR
- SCTS 85255 501-E5
N CLUBGATE DR
15300 PHX 85254 580-E3
E CLUBHOUSE CT
7500 SCTS 85262 460-H1
E CLUBHOUSE DR
1900 PHX 85048 819-A6
N CLUBHOUSE DR
- AVON 85353 695-F6
3500 GDYR 85338 (654-G7
See Page 653)
S CLUBHOUSE DR
- CHAN 85248 861-B7
- MarC 85236 903-C2
W CLUBHOUSE DR
- GDYR 85338 (694-E1
See Page 653)
15400 GDYR 85338 (654-F7
See Page 653)
E CLUBHOUSE RD
7400 SCTS 85262 420-H7
N CLUBHOUSE RD
33800 SCTS 85262 460-H1
34700 SCTS 85262 420-H7
E CLUBHOUSE WY
8600 SCTS 85255 541-B1

N CLUBHOUSE WY
8600 SCTS 85255 541-A2
E CLUB VILLA CIR
34600 SCTS 85262 420-H7
34600 SCTS 85262 460-H1
W CLUB VISTA DR
17700 SURP 85374 534-A7
E CLUFF LN
400 MESA 85203 701-J5
E CLYDESDALE TR
8500 SCTS 85258 621-A3
S COACHHOUSE CT
- GIL 85236 863-D4
N COACHWHIP WY
- CVCK 85331 420-A7
N COACHWOOD DR
15200 MarC 85351 576-A3
W COAST DR
900 GIL 85233 822-A3
1000 GIL 85233 821-J2
E COBB DR
1300 TEMP 85281 740-G1
S COBBLESTONE CIR
- GIL 85296 822-G6
N COBBLESTONE CT
- SURP 85374 534-F5
S COBBLESTONE DR
100 GIL 85296 782-G7
100 GIL 85296 822-G1
N COBBLESTONE LN
16400 FTNH 85268 583-A3
N COBBLESTONE ST
- GIL 85234 782-G5
E COBRE DR
2800 PHX 85028 619-E4
N COBRE DR
8900 PHX 85028 619-E4
E COBRE WY
18300 MarC 85263 503-H3
S COCHISE
1000 MESA 85204 782-C1
E COCHISE AV
10400 SCTS 85258 621-F3
12500 SCTS 85259 622-B3
E COCHISE DR
2400 PHX 85028 619-D3
10000 SCTS 85258 621-E3
11200 SCTS 85259 621-H3
W COCHISE DR
- PHX 85020 618-H2
700 PHX 85021 618-E2
3000 PHX 85051 618-A2
3600 PHX 85051 617-H2
4500 GLEN 85302 617-E2
6900 PEOR 85345 617-A2
7100 PEOR 85345 616-H2
18300 MarC 85355 (613-H1
See Page 573)
E COCHISE LN
- PinC 85219 785-G2
N COCHISE LN
22000 MarC 85375 535-A1
22300 MarC 85375 495-C7
W COCHISE LN
600 GIL 85233 782-A7
E COCHISE PL
9400 MarC 85248 901-B5
E COCHISE RD
- SCTS 85259 622-D3
700 PHX 85020 618-J2
4100 PHX 85028 619-H3
4900 PVAL 85253 620-A3
5800 PHX 85253 620-C3
6800 SCTS 85253 620-F3
7400 SCTS 85258 620-G3
9600 SCTS 85258 621-D3
W COCHISE ST
- WICK 85390 290-F3
E COCONINO CT
3600 PHX 85044 819-E2
S COCONINO CT
12600 PHX 85044 819-G2
E COCONINO DR
- MarC 85249 901-J1
N COCONINO DR
18100 SURP 85374 533-J6
S COCONINO DR
1400 APJT 85220 785-D1
N COCONINO LN
9200 PVAL 85253 620-D4
E COCONINO PL
3600 PHX 85044 819-E2
N COCONINO RD
8000 PVAL 85253 620-D6
E COCONINO ST
100 WICK 85390 290-F2
3200 PHX 85044 819-D2
S COCONINO ST
11800 PHX 85044 819-G1
W COCONINO ST
- WICK 85390 290-F2
COCOPAH CIR N
- AVON 85353 735-E1
E COCOPAH ST
700 PHX 85034 738-J2
1400 PHX 85034 739-A2
W COCOPAH ST
- GDYR 85326 (734-A1
See Page 733)
- GDYR 85338 (734-E1
See Page 733)
- MarC 85353 735-G1
- PHX 85043 737-A1
- PHX 85353 736-E1
- PHX 85003 738-F2
700 PHX 85007 738-D2
1900 PHX 85009 738-B2
3400 PHX 85009 737-J2
10900 AVON 85353 735-E1
W COCOPAH WY
18500 SURP 85374 534-G5
E CODY AV
- GIL 85234 783-C5
E CODY CIR
3600 GIL 85236 783-C5
E CODY DR
- PHX 85040 738-G6
W CODY DR
- PHX 85041 738-F6
- PHX 85040 738-F6
E CODY ST
1700 APJT 85219 745-H5
4300 PinC 85219 746-A5
W CODY ST
2400 APJT 85220 745-A5
E COFCO CENTER BLVD
4200 PHX 85008 699-H6
N COFCO CENTER CT
- PHX 85008 699-H6

PHOENIX
INDEX

STREET Block City ZIP Pg-Grid

N COTTONWOOD CANYON RD
43300 CVCK 85331 (380-F3 See Page 339)
W COUGAR DR
12300 MarC 85375 535-E3
N COUNCIL CT
14400 FTNH 85268 583-E5
S COUNTRY PL
16000 MarC 85225 822-C7
N COUNTRY PZ E
800 GIL 85234 782-E5
E COUNTRY PZ N
500 GIL 85234 782-E5
E COUNTRY PZ S
500 GIL 85234 782-E5
N COUNTRY PZ W
800 GIL 85234 782-D5
W COUNTRY RD
1800 MarC 85087 (338-F5 See Page 337)
W COUNTRY CLUB CT
9800 MarC 85373 536-B6
E COUNTRY CLUB DR
- PHX 85014 698-H1
8900 MarC 85248 900-J5
9000 MarC 85248 901-A5
N COUNTRY CLUB DR
- WICK 85390 290-B2
- MarC 85390 290-B2
- PHX 85014 698-H2
1500 MESA 85210 781-F3
2300 MarC 85256 701-G3
4100 MarC 85256 661-G4
17600 MarC 85373 536-D6
N COUNTRY CLUB DR Rt#-87
- MESA 85201 741-G4
- MESA 85210 741-G4
700 MarC 85201 701-G6
1500 MarC 85256 701-G6
1700 MESA 85201 701-G6
S COUNTRY CLUB DR
1900 MESA 85210 781-G3
25000 MarC 85248 901-A5
S COUNTRY CLUB DR Rt#-87
- MESA 85210 741-G7
700 GIL 85233 781-F5
700 MESA 85210 781-F5
1000 MESA 85233 781-F5
2900 CHAN 85233 781-F5
9500 MESA 85225 781-F5
9500 CHAN 85225 781-F5
W COUNTRY CLUB DR
9300 MarC 85373 536-C6
9300 MarC 85373 576-D1
N COUNTRY CLUB PKWY
18000 PEOR 85382 536-F6
W COUNTRY CLUB PKWY
8600 PEOR 85382 536-F5
W COUNTRY CLUB TER
3000 PHX 85027 538-B1
E COUNTRY CLUB TR
8400 SCTS 85255 541-A2
W COUNTRY CLUB TR
8900 PEOR 85382 536-B1
N COUNTRY CLUB WY
100 CHAN 85226 820-H4
S COUNTRY CLUB WY
- CHAN 85226 820-H7
2400 TEMP 85282 740-J7
2900 TEMP 85282 780-J1
5000 TEMP 85283 780-J4
7000 TEMP 85284 780-H7
W COUNTRY ESTATES AV
400 GIL 85233 822-A3
E COUNTRY GABLES DR
- PHX 85022 578-H4
W COUNTRY GABLES DR
- SURP 85379 (574-G3 See Page 573)
- PHX 85023 578-C3
2700 PHX 85053 578-A3
3500 PHX 85053 577-J3
4300 PHX 85306 577-G3
5100 GLEN 85306 577-C3
6800 MarC 85381 577-A3
7100 MarC 85381 576-J3
7300 PEOR 85381 576-E3
W COUNTRY GABLES RD
- SURP 85379 575-C3
W COUNTRY PLACE BLVD
- PHX 85353 736-A3
E COUNTRY SHADOWS CIR
13200 MarC 85249 902-B4
E COUNTRY SHADOWS CT
- MarC 85236 902-J4
- MarC 85236 903-A4
E COUNTRY SHADOWS RD
13200 MarC 85249 902-B4
W COUNTRYSIDE DR
13200 MarC 85375 535-B5
E COUNTRYWALK LN
1400 CHAN 85225 821-J4
1600 CHAN 85225 822-A4
S COUNTY CIR
- MarC 85326 811-C4
- MarC 85337 811-C4
N COUNTY RD
48700 MarC 85087 (338-J3 See Page 337)
E COUNTY DOWN DR
- CHAN 85249 902-A6
1400 CHAN 85249 901-J6
N COUPLES DR
- GDYR 85338 (654-H7 See Page 653)
- GDYR 85338 (694-H1 See Page 653)
N COURAGE CT
- MarC 85086 (378-A7 See Page 337)
N COURAGE TR
- MarC 85086 (378-A6 See Page 337)
- MarC 85087 (378-A4 See Page 337)
N COURAGE WY
- MarC 85086 (378-A7 See Page 337)
W COURTHOUSE RD
51000 MarC 85354 101-C2
S COURTLAND CIR
- MarC 85206 743-E7
- MarC 85206 783-E1
E COURTNEY LN
- TEMP 85284 820-D3
S COURTNEY LN
300 TEMP 85284 820-C3
W COURTNEY LN
- TEMP 85284 820-A3
E COURTSIDE DR
16800 FTNH 85268 583-D5
E COURY AV
100 MESA 85210 781-H2
E COURY DR
100 MESA 85210 781-H2
W COVE DR
500 GIL 85233 821-J1
N COVENTRY CIR
14000 FTNH 85268 583-B6
W COVEY LN
- PHX 85027 538-B3
E COVEY TR
9100 SCTS 85262 421-C3
E COVINA
- MESA 85220 744-H4
N COVINA CT
- SURP 85374 534-G6
E COVINA DR
2600 MarC 85206 743-E7
E COVINA RD
5200 MarC 85205 743-C4
5200 MESA 85205 743-C4
E COVINA ST
- MESA 85220 744-J4
- MESA 85220 745-A4
1700 MESA 85203 742-D4
2000 MESA 85213 742-D4
3600 MESA 85205 742-H4
4200 MESA 85205 743-A4
7700 MESA 85207 743-J4
7800 MESA 85207 744-A4
E COWAN CIR
2500 PHX 85050 539-D6
N COWBOY CT
- MarC 85255 (462-G7 See Page 421)
W COWDEN LN
- TOL 85353 695-J6
- TOL 85353 696-A6
E COW TRACK DR
8000 CARE 85377 420-J3
8000 CARE 85377 421-A3
E COX CT
- PHX 85331 459-J2
- PHX 85331 460-A2
S COX CT
- CHAN 85248 861-E6
E COYOTE CIR
- SCTS 85255 501-C4
W COYOTE CT
11500 SURP 85374 535-H6
S COYOTE DR
- APJT 85220 785-C1
E COYOTE PASS
1300 CARE 85377 420-H6
E COYOTE RD
13500 SCTS 85259 622-E2
N COYOTE RD
- SCTS 85259 622-F2
40800 PinC 85242 865-E5
S COYOTE CANYON
- MESA 85212 784-E6
S COYOTE CANYON CIR
- MESA 85212 784-E6
N COYOTE LAKES PKWY
17000 SURP 85374 535-G4
W COYOTE LAKES PKWY
11500 SURP 85374 535-H5
N COYOTE PASS RD
47800 MarC 85087 (338-B2 See Page 337)
S COYOTE TRAIL DR
- GDYR 85338 (774-A7 See Page 733)
E COYOTE WASH DR
- PHX 85331 459-J2
- PHX 85331 460-A2
6000 SCTS 85331 460-D2
S COZUMEL CT
900 GIL 85233 822-A2
E COZY WY
- GIL 85236 863-E4
W C P HAYES DR
8700 TOL 85353 696-E5
W CRABAPPLE DR
- PEOR 85382 496-J5
- PEOR 85382 497-A5
N CRAFTSMAN CT
4100 SCTS 85251 660-F7
E CRAGGY SPUR LN
- SCTS 85255 541-D4
E CRAIGEND DR
10400 SCTS 85255 501-F7
E CRANBROOK DR
2300 MarC 85206 783-E1
W CRANE CT
- CHAN 85248 861-E5
W CRANE DR
- CHAN 85248 861-C5
W CRATER LN
16400 SURP 85374 534-D6
S CRAVER PL
900 TEMP 85281 740-H4
S CRAWFORD
- MESA 85212 784-B6
S CRAWFORD CIR
- MESA 85212 784-B6
E CREEDANCE BLVD
- MarC 85024 499-C7
2200 PHX 85024 499-C7
W CREEDANCE BLVD
3900 PHX 85310 497-D6
E CREEK CANYON RD
4800 CVCK 85331 420-B5
N CREEK VIEW LN
- CVCK 85331 420-B6
N CREEKWOOD CT
20200 MarC 85375 535-B3
N CREIGHTON CT
3500 SCTS 85251 700-G2
N CRENSHAW CT
- GDYR 85338 (654-G7 See Page 653)
- GDYR 85338 (694-G1 See Page 653)
N CRENSHAW DR
- GDYR 85338 (654-H7 See Page 653)
W CREOSOTE
17100 SURP 85374 534-C6
CREOSOTE CT
- FTNH 85268 582-H5
E CREOSOTE DR
4000 PHX 85331 459-H5
4400 PHX 85331 460-A5
S CREOSOTE DR
5500 PinC 85219 786-E6
E CREOSOTE LN
21400 QC 85242 904-D1
E CRESCENT AV
- MESA 85210 741-H6
400 MESA 85204 741-J6
900 MESA 85204 742-A6
3700 MESA 85206 742-H6
4600 MESA 85206 743-A6
8600 MESA 85208 744-B7
9000 MarC 85208 744-C7
11000 MarC 85220 744-H7
11000 MESA 85220 744-H7
11400 MarC 85220 745-A7
W CRESCENT AV
600 MESA 85210 741-F6
1300 MESA 85202 741-D6
E CRESCENT CIR
1500 MESA 85204 742-C6
3800 MESA 85206 742-H6
7400 MESA 85208 743-H7
W CRESCENT CT
16500 SURP 85374 534-D5
E CRESCENT DR
- GDYR 85338 695-A7
1000 MarC 85206 743-D6
E CRESCENT WY
- MarC 85249 901-J1
W CRESCENT WY
1600 CHAN 85248 901-B1
S CRESCENT RUN BLVD
1000 MESA 85208 784-B1
E CRESCENT RUN DR
8400 MESA 85208 784-B1
N CRESCENT RUN DR
8500 MESA 85208 784-B1
E CRESCENT SAGUARO LN
- SCTS 85262 460-H2
E CRESENT WY
- MarC 85249 901-J1
N CRESENT WY
- SURP 85374 534-G4
E CREST LN
2100 PHX 85024 539-C2
W CREST LN
3100 PHX 85027 538-A1
5900 GLEN 85310 537-A1
6500 GLEN 85308 537-B2
7300 GLEN 85310 536-J1
W CRESTBROOK DR
10900 MarC 85351 575-H1
E CRESTED BUTTE TR
- FTNH 85268 622-J5
E CRESTED CROWN
14700 FTNH 85268 622-H5
E CRESTED QUAIL RUN
- CARE 85377 420-J2
E CRESTED SAGUARO LN
6400 SCTS 85262 460-F2
S CRESTON
400 MESA 85204 742-G6
900 MESA 85204 782-G1
S CRESTON CIR
1400 MESA 85204 782-G2
N CRESTON ST
400 MESA 85213 742-G2
E CRESTVIEW CT
- SCTS 85268 622-H1
S CRESTVIEW CT
- MarC 85236 903-E2
E CRESTVIEW DR
4900 PVAL 85253 620-A7
N CRESTVIEW DR
- FTNH 85268 622-H2
S CRESTVIEW DR
- MarC 85236 903-E3
E CRESTVIEW ST
- APJT 85219 746-B2
- PinC 85219 746-B2
S CRESTVIEW ST
- CHAN 85226 820-D6
E CRESTWOOD WY
7800 SCTS 85250 660-H5
8700 SCTS 85250 661-A5
W CRESTWOOD WY
5900 GLEN 85301 657-C4
S CRICKET CT
- GIL 85236 863-E3
N CRIMSON DR
14200 MarC 85351 576-B4
W CRIMSON LN
- AVON 85323 656-A7
11000 AVON 85323 655-G7
S CRIMSON RD
- MESA 85212 784-E5
E CRIMSON TER
4800 PHX 85331 460-A2
6800 SCTS 85262 460-F2
N CRIMSON CANYON
- FTNH 85256 622-F5
- FTNH 85268 622-F5
- MarC 85256 622-F5
- MarC 85259 622-F5
N CRIMSON RIDGE WY
19500 SURP 85374 534-E4
S CRIMSON SKY PL
- PinC 85219 826-F1
E CRIMSON SKY TR
- SCTS 85262 460-G2
E CRISMON RD
21500 MarC 85242 904-F5
N CRISMON RD
- MarC 85220 744-F3
- MarC 85207 744-F3
- MarC 85208 744-F3
600 MESA 85207 744-F3
600 MESA 85220 744-F3
S CRISMON RD
- MarC 85242 824-E7
- MESA 85208 744-F7
- MESA 85212 784-F2
- MESA 85220 744-F7
- MarC 85220 744-F7
- MarC 85208 744-F7
800 MESA 85208 784-F2
800 MESA 85220 784-F2
17200 MarC 85242 864-E2
17200 MESA 85242 864-E2
20400 QC 85242 864-E7
20400 QC 85242 904-E4
24300 MarC 85242 904-E4
S CRISS PL
- CHAN 85226 820-H6
N CRISS ST
400 CHAN 85226 820-H3
S CRISS ST
100 CHAN 85226 820-G7
600 CHAN 85226 860-G1
E CRITTENDEN AV
2500 PHX 85016 699-D1
W CRITTENDEN AV
3800 PHX 85019 697-H1
E CRITTENDEN LN
1800 PHX 85016 699-B1
W CRITTENDEN LN
- AVON 85340 655-C7
4300 PHX 85031 697-E1
5900 PHX 85033 697-A1
6700 PHX 85033 657-A7
6900 PHX 85033 656-H7
7700 PHX 85033 696-G1
W CRIVELLO AV
4500 MarC 85339 817-E1
W CRIVELLO RD
- MarC 85326 (772-G6 See Page 731)
N CROCKETT CT
- MarC 85086 (378-B6 See Page 337)
E CROCUS DR
1500 PHX 85022 579-B4
2900 PHX 85032 579-G5
4800 PHX 85254 580-A5
N CROCUS DR
14300 PEOR 85381 576-H4
W CROCUS DR
- ELMG 85335 575-D4
- SURP 85379 (574-F3 See Page 573)
- SURP 85379 575-C4
2400 PHX 85023 578-C4
3000 PHX 85053 578-A4
3500 PHX 85053 577-H4
4400 PHX 85306 577-F4
5100 GLEN 85306 577-B4
6900 PEOR 85381 577-A4
7200 PEOR 85381 576-E4
7200 MarC 85381 576-J4
W CROCUS LN
- SURP 85379 575-C4
W CROFTON ST
300 CHAN 85225 781-E7
N CROMWELL DR
11600 FTNH 85268 623-C2
N CROOKED STICK RD
41700 MarC 85086 (378-C5 See Page 337)
W CROSBY CIR N
9900 MarC 85351 616-B1
W CROSBY CIR S
9900 MarC 85351 616-B1
W CROSBY DR
10500 MarC 85351 615-J1
10500 MarC 85351 616-A1
N CROSSBOW CT
800 CHAN 85225 821-G4
S CROSSBOW DR
- CHAN 85225 821-H7
S CROSSBOW PL
- CHAN 85249 901-G3
1100 CHAN 85249 861-H2
E CROSS CANYON WY
- SCTS 85255 541-D3
N CROSS CANYON WY
- SCTS 85255 541-D3
S CROSSCREEK DR
- MarC 85249 901-H1
- CHAN 85225 821-J7
S CROSSCREEK PL
- CHAN 85225 861-H1
S CROSS CREEK ST
- CHAN 85249 901-H4
CROSSCUT CSR
- MESA - 741-G2
- MESA - 742-A2
N CROSSROADS BLVD
16800 SURP 85374 575-E1
16900 SURP 85374 535-E7
S CROSSROADS DR
900 GIL 85296 822-J3
N CROSS TIMBERS CT
- MarC 85086 (378-C4 See Page 337)
N CROSS TIMBERS TR
- MarC 85086 (378-C7 See Page 337)
W CROSS TIMBERS TR
- MarC 85086 (378-D5 See Page 337)
W CROSSWATER WY
- MarC 85086 (378-E5 See Page 337)
S CROW CT
12000 PHX 85044 819-H1
E CROWN CT
- SCTS 85268 622-H1
N CROWN RDG
9000 FTNH 85268 622-G5
E CROWN ST
1600 MESA 85203 742-C4
S CROWN KEY CT
900 GIL 85233 821-J3
S CROWN KEY DR
1000 GIL 85233 821-J3
N CROWN KING RD
- PEOR - 335-H2
W CROWN KING RD
- PHX 85043 737-A3
- PHX 85353 736-A3
S CROWN POINT CIR
- CHAN 85248 861-B7
N CROWN POINT CT
13800 MarC 85351 576-B4
N CROWN POINT DR
33900 SCTS 85262 460-H2
N CROWN RIDGE DR
20000 MarC 85375 535-C3
W CROWN RIDGE DR
12900 MarC 85375 535-C3
S CROWS NEST DR
600 GIL 85233 822-A2
S CROWS NEST RD
5500 TEMP 85283 780-G4
N CROZIER RD
15300 MarC 85374 533-F6
15300 MarC 85374 573-G1
17000 SURP 85374 533-F6
17300 SURP 85387 533-F6
17600 MarC 85387 533-C1
21800 MarC 85361 (452-J1 See Page 411)
W CRYSTAL CT
14700 SURP 85374 534-J6
E CRYSTAL DR
- MarC 85248 900-J2
9100 MarC 85248 901-A2
E CRYSTAL LN
4400 MarC 85253 659-J1
4600 PVAL 85253 619-J7
4600 PVAL 85253 659-J1
4800 PVAL 85253 620-A7
N CRYSTAL LN
3500 AVON 85323 655-G7
W CRYSTAL RD
7200 GLEN 85308 536-J3
7200 GLEN 85308 537-A3
S CRYSTAL WY
- MarC 85249 902-G4
N CRYSTAL GARDENS PKWY
- AVON 85323 695-H2
N CRYSTAL HILLS DR
12900 FTNH 85268 583-B7
W CRYSTAL LAKE DR
12600 MarC 85375 535-D3
E CRYSTAL POINT DR
16100 FTNH 85268 583-B7
E CRYSTAL RIDGE DR
16200 FTNH 85268 623-B1
N CRYSTAL SEA WY
1400 GIL 85234 782-G3
N CRYSTAL SHORES
1200 GIL 85234 782-H4
W CRYSTAL SPRING DR
1300 GIL 85233 821-J1
E CUARENTA CT
6700 PVAL 85253 620-E7
N CUCURACHA ST
- WICK 85390 290-D2
E CUDIA WY
4000 PHX 85018 659-G5
E CULLUMBER AV
- GIL 85234 782-D7
W CULLUMBER AV
100 GIL 85233 782-B7
1200 GIL 85233 781-J6
E CULLUMBER CT
- GIL 85234 783-A7
E CULLUMBER ST
- GIL 85234 783-B7
1100 GIL 85234 782-G6
3300 GIL 85236 783-D7
E CULLUMBER WY
- GIL 85234 782-G6
E CULVER ST
100 PHX 85004 698-G5
1000 PHX 85006 698-J5
1400 PHX 85006 699-A5
2500 PHX 85008 699-C5
2500 MarC 85207 703-J6
6600 SCTS 85257 700-E5
6900 MESA 85207 703-G6
7800 MarC 85207 704-A6
8700 SCTS 85257 701-A5
N CULVER ST
1100 PHX 85008 699-J5
W CULVER ST
200 PHX 85003 698-F5
700 PHX 85007 698-D4
1200 PHX 85004 698-F5
1700 PHX 85009 698-A4
3300 PHX 85009 697-G4
18000 GDYR 85326 (693-J3 See Page 653)
18700 BUCK 85326 (693-F3 See Page 653)
18700 MarC 85326 (693-F3 See Page 653)
22800 BUCK 85326 (692-F3 See Page 651)
W CUMBERLAND DR
- PEOR 85345 616-D2
9900 MarC 85351 616-B2
10600 MarC 85351 615-H2
N CUMBIE LN
16400 SURP 85374 575-E1
S CUPERTINO DR
- GIL 85236 863-C2
W CURIE CT
- MarC 85086 (378-B7 See Page 337)
E CURRY RD
600 TEMP 85281 740-E1
900 MarC 85281 740-E1
1700 MarC 85256 740-E1
W CURRY ST
300 CHAN 85225 781-E6
1400 CHAN 85224 781-A6
2800 CHAN 85224 780-J6
2900 TEMP 85283 780-J6
N CURTIS DR
2900 MarC 85207 704-F4
W CUSTER LN
8700 PEOR 85381 576-E3
11300 SURP 85379 (574-F3 See Page 573)
S CUTLER DR
1700 TEMP 85281 740-B6
1800 TEMP 85282 740-B6
3400 TEMP 85282 780-B1
N CYPERT RD
1000 MarC 85220 744-J3
E CYPRESS CIR
6500 SCTS 85257 700-D4
W CYPRESS CIR
24400 BUCK 85326 (732-C1 See Page 731)
S CYPRESS CT
- CHAN 85226 820-D6
W CYPRESS DR
11400 AVON 85323 695-G1
E CYPRESS ST
200 GIL 85296 822-D3
1400 PHX 85006 698-J3
1400 PHX 85006 699-A3
2000 SCTS 85257 700-D4
3000 PHX 85008 699-E3
6400 SCTS 85008 700-D4
8600 SCTS 85257 701-A4
S CYPRESS ST
200 CHAN 85226 820-D7
W CYPRESS ST
- GDYR 85338 (694-J2 See Page 653)
- GIL 85233 822-C3
- PHX 85003 698-F3
2000 PHX 85009 698-A3
3200 PHX 85009 697-G3
4700 PHX 85035 697-A3
6900 PHX 85035 696-H3
8600 PHX 85037 696-D3
13100 GDYR 85338 695-B2
E CYPRESS POINT CT
17100 FTNH 85268 623-D4
N CYPRESS POINT DR
- MESA 85207 743-G5
S CYPRESS POINT DR
6000 CHAN 85249 902-A4
6000 CHAN 85249 901-J5
W CYPRESS POINT DR
- SURP 85374 534-G5
E CYPRESS TREE DR
1800 GIL 85234 782-H4
N CYPRESS TREE DR
1100 GIL 85234 782-H4

D

S D ST
- MarC 85337 (1050-B7 See Page 1049)
- MarC 85337 (1090-B1 See Page 1049)
W D ST
5100 PHX 85031 657-E5
N DAFFODIL ST
1600 TEMP 85281 700-G7
E DAHLIA DR
200 PHX 85022 578-H6
1900 PHX 85022 579-D6
2400 PHX 85032 579-D6
4900 PHX 85032 580-A7
4900 PHX 85254 580-B7
8100 MESA 85208 744-A7
8600 SCTS 85260 581-A7
W DAHLIA DR
800 PHX 85029 578-A6
3600 PHX 85029 577-H6
4300 PHX 85304 577-G6
5100 GLEN 85304 577-E6
7300 PEOR 85381 576-F6
11700 ELMG 85335 575-F5
E DAILEY ST
1200 PHX 85022 579-A5
W DAILEY ST
2400 PHX 85023 578-C5
2900 PHX 85053 578-B5
3500 PHX 85053 577-H5
4300 PHX 85306 577-F5
5100 GLEN 85306 577-C4
W DAILY ST
6300 GLEN 85306 577-B4
S DAISY
2400 MESA 85208 783-J5
W DAISY CT
13500 MarC 85375 535-C6
S DAISY LN
100 GIL 85296 822-F1
W DAISY MOUNTAIN DR
- MarC 85086 (378-C7 See Page 337)
- MarC 85086 417-J1
- MarC 85086 (418-A1 See Page 417)
W DAKOTA
11000 PEOR 85345 616-C1
E DAKOTA CT
3500 PHX 85044 819-E1
E DAKOTA DR
3700 PHX 85044 819-F1
N DAKOTA ST
100 CHAN 85225 821-F3
2700 CHAN 85225 781-F6
S DAKOTA ST
- CHAN 85248 861-E4
- CHAN 85225 821-F7
W DALE CIR
1600 MESA 85201 741-D3
E DALE LN
4200 MarC 85331 499-J1
4200 PHX 85331 499-J1
4400 PHX 85331 500-A1
5700 MarC 85331 500-C1
6800 SCTS 85331 500-F1
7200 SCTS 85262 500-H1
8000 SCTS 85262 501-C1
W DALE LN
15300 MarC 85375 (454-G7 See Page 413)
16100 SURP 85375 (454-C7 See Page 413)
20900 MarC 85361 (453-B6 See Page 413)
22600 MarC 85361 (452-F6 See Page 411)
25000 MarC 85361 (451-J6 See Page 411)
E DALEA DR
5800 CARE 85377 420-D7
W DALEA DR
- GDYR 85326 (774-A7 See Page 733)
- GDYR 85326 (814-A1 See Page 813)
E DALEA WY
- PinC 85219 786-E5
W DALE EVANS
17100 SURP 85374 534-C6
E DALEY
400 MESA 85204 742-C6
N DALEY
1600 MESA 85203 742-C1
1800 MESA 85203 702-C7
S DALEY
600 MESA 85204 742-C7
900 MESA 85204 782-C1
E DALEY LN
2000 PHX 85024 539-C1
4800 PHX 85054 540-B1
W DALEY LN
3000 PHX 85027 538-A1
8100 MarC 85382 536-F1
8900 PEOR 85382 496-J7
18300 SURP 85387 493-J7
E DALLAS CIR
4800 MESA 85205 743-B4
E DALLAS ST
- MESA 85207 744-C4
4900 MESA 85205 743-C4
5200 MarC 85205 743-C4
7700 MESA 85207 743-J4
9300 MarC 85207 744-D4
W DALPHIN RD
3700 PHX 85051 617-H2
E DANA AV
700 MESA 85204 741-J5
700 MESA 85204 742-A5
W DANA AV
400 MESA 85210 741-F5
W DANA LN
- AVON 85323 656-A7
11000 AVON 85323 655-G7
E DANA PL
- CHAN 85225 861-J1
N DANA ST
1300 GIL 85233 782-C4
E DANA WY
- CHAN 85225 862-B1
E DANBURY DR
100 PHX 85022 578-H1
2400 PHX 85022 579-D1
2400 PHX 85032 579-D1
W DANBURY DR
100 PHX 85023 578-C1
2900 PHX 85053 578-B1
3500 PHX 85308 578-A1
3500 PHX 85308 577-H1
E DANBURY RD
- PHX 85022 579-C1
2800 PHX 85032 579-D1
5200 PHX 85254 580-B1
W DANBURY RD
200 PHX 85023 578-D1
E DANCING BEARS CT
- FTNH 85268 622-G2
E DANCING SKY DR
- SCTS 85262 (381-E7 See Page 341)
S DANDELION
2600 MESA 85208 783-J5
N DANIEL DR
13000 FTNH 85268 583-B7
S DANIEL RD
500 WICK 85390 290-D3
N DANIELSON WY
200 CHAN 85225 822-B5
S DANIELSON WY
- CHAN 85225 822-B7
- CHAN 85225 862-B1
- CHAN 85249 902-B4
- MarC 85249 902-B6
1100 CHAN 85249 862-B2
N DANNY LN
25300 MarC 85263 503-J6
N DANUBE CT
14800 PHX 85053 578-B4
N DANYELL CT
- CHAN 85225 822-A5
N DANYELL DR
300 CHAN 85225 822-A4
S DANYELL DR
- MarC 85249 901-J2
500 CHAN 85225 822-A7
500 CHAN 85225 862-A1
S DANYELL RD
- CHAN 85249 862-A2
N DANYELL ST
400 CHAN 85225 822-A5
N DAPPLE RD
700 PinC 85219 746-B5
W DARIEN WY
- PHX 85086 (418-C7 See Page 417)
E DARNER AV
8500 MarC 85208 744-B7
E DARNER RD
7700 MESA 85208 783-J1
E DARREL RD
800 PHX 85040 778-H1
1600 PHX 85040 779-A1
W DARREL RD
1500 PHX 85041 778-D1
N DARROW DR
- TEMP 85282 780-B2
S DARROW DR
700 TEMP 85281 740-B3
4800 TEMP 85282 780-B2
9400 TEMP 85284 820-A3
E DARROW ST
4100 PHX 85040 779-G2
W DARROW ST
- PHX 85041 777-G2
300 PHX 85041 778-F2
S DARTFORD DR
25800 MarC 85248 901-B5
E DARTMOUTH CIR
- MESA 85220 744-J4
3600 MESA 85205 742-H3
4800 MESA 85205 743-B4
E DARTMOUTH ST
- MESA 85220 744-H4
- MESA 85220 745-A4
600 MESA 85213 742-D3
700 MESA 85203 742-B3
3600 MESA 85205 742-J3
4900 MESA 85205 743-A3
7800 MESA 85207 743-J4
7800 MESA 85207 744-A4
W DARTMOUTH ST
1900 MESA 85201 741-B3
S DATE
2100 MESA 85210 781-F3
N DATE CIR
600 BUCK 85326 (772-C1 See Page 731)
600 MESA 85201 741-F3
S DATE CIR
1200 MESA 85210 781-F1
N DATE DR
1600 TEMP 85281 700-F7
N DATE ST
- MESA 85201 741-F1
- MESA 85210 741-F4
1700 MESA 85201 701-F7
S DATE ST
- MESA 85210 741-F5
3000 MESA 85210 781-F5
S DATELAND DR
100 TEMP 85284 780-D7
100 TEMP 85284 820-D2
2000 TEMP 85283 740-D6
6500 TEMP 85283 780-D5
E DATE PALM DR
1000 GIL 85234 782-H4
N DATE PALM DR
400 GIL 85234 782-H4
W DATIL AV
600 APJT 85220 745-D7
E DAVA DR
800 TEMP 85283 780-E6
W DAVA DR
1000 TEMP 85283 780-B6
E DAVENPORT DR
7600 SCTS 85260 580-H6
8200 SCTS 85260 581-A6
N DAVID CT
900 CHAN 85226 820-B4
N DAVID DR
600 CHAN 85226 820-B4

STREET
Block City ZIP Pg-Grid

E

STREET — Block City ZIP Pg-Grid

W EAGLE MOUNTAIN RD
21500 MarC 85326 (772-G6 See Page 731)
21500 MarC 85326 (773-A6 See Page 733)
E EAGLENEST DR
- MarC 85263 (504-A3 See Page 503)
N EAGLE NEST DR
15600 FTNH 85268 582-J4
S EAGLE PASS RD
6000 PinC 85219 786-H7
N EAGLE PEAK DR
27400 MarC 85361 493-C1
27400 MarC 85361 (453-B7 See Page 413)
E EAGLE RIDGE DR
- FTNH 85268 582-G7
- SCTS 85268 582-G7
- SCTS 85268 622-G1
W EAGLE RIDGE DR
16100 SURP 85374 534-E5
E EAGLE ROCK DR
15700 FTNH 85268 583-A4
E EAGLE VIEW CT
15500 FTNH 85268 583-A4
N EAGLE VIEW DR
49100 MarC 85320 (284-J5 See Page 244)
49100 MarC 85320 (285-A5 See Page 244)
W EARHART WY
4000 CHAN 85226 820-F7
S EARL BLVD
2600 CHAN 85248 861-C5
W EARL BLVD
1700 CHAN 85248 861-B4
W EARL DR
- AVON 85340 695-D1
W EARLL CT
15300 GDYR 85338 (654-G7 See Page 653)
E EARLL DR
- MarC 85256 701-F2
- PHX 85012 698-G2
- PHX 85013 698-G2
1300 PHX 85014 698-J2
1400 PHX 85014 699-A2
1600 PHX 85016 699-A2
3200 PHX 85018 699-E2
4400 MESA 85215 703-A5
4900 PHX 85018 700-A2
6200 SCTS 85251 700-D2
8500 SCTS 85251 701-A2
W EARLL DR
- AVON 85340 695-D1
300 PHX 85013 698-F2
1500 PHX 85015 698-C1
2500 PHX 85017 698-A2
3300 PHX 85017 697-H1
3300 PHX 85031 697-D1
3500 PHX 85019 697-H1
5900 PHX 85033 697-A1
6900 PHX 85033 696-F1
8500 PHX 85037 696-E1
10300 AVON 85323 696-A1
10500 AVON 85323 695-J1
15400 GDYR 85338 (654-E7 See Page 653)
15400 GDYR 85338 (694-F1 See Page 653)
19100 MarC 85340 653-F7
E EASON AV
100 BUCK 85326 (772-A1 See Page 731)
E EAST DR
10400 MarC 85248 901-D5
EASTERN CSR
- GIL - 783-A3
- GIL - 822-H3
- MarC - 783-A6
- MarC - 822-F7
- MarC - 823-A1
- MarC - 862-C7
- MarC - 902-B2
- MESA - 702-D5
- MESA - 742-G4
- MESA - 782-J1
- MESA - 783-A3
N EASTHAM PKWY
- SURP 85374 534-C6
S EASTLAKE DR
10300 MarC 85248 901-C5
W EASTMAN DR
2900 MarC 85086 (378-C6 See Page 337)
S EASTRIDGE
8400 MESA 85208 784-B6
8400 MESA 85212 784-B6
EASTRIDGE LN
12800 FTNH 85268 582-H7
E EASTRIDGE ST
5800 PinC 85219 746-C3
S EASTSHORE DR
5300 TEMP 85283 780-G3
S EASTSIDE DR
26000 MarC 85248 901-F5
W EAST WIND AV
- GDYR 85326 (814-A1 See Page 813)
E EASTWOOD LN
7200 SCTS 85253 620-G6
7200 SCTS 85258 620-G6
N EASTWOOD WY
2400 MESA 85215 703-D6
EASY ST
1200 MarC 85390 250-B7
1200 WICK 85390 250-B7
E EASY ST
- CARE 85377 420-H4
S EASY ST
5700 PinC 85219 786-J6
E EASY SHOT LN
- PinC 85219 786-F7
N EATON PL
- CHAN 85226 820-H7
E EBERLE LN
2900 PHX 85032 579-E3
E EBOLA AV
7800 MESA 85208 783-J1
8000 MESA 85208 784-A1
9000 MarC 85208 784-C1
N EBONY
2500 MESA 85215 703-G6
W EBONY DR
1100 CHAN 85248 861-C7
W EBONY WY
- CHAN 85248 861-D7
E ECHO LN
- PHX 85020 618-G5
1200 PHX 85020 619-A5
7200 SCTS 85258 620-F6
W ECHO LN
100 PHX 85021 618-C5
2700 PHX 85051 618-A5
3400 PHX 85051 617-H5
4300 GLEN 85302 617-C5
8300 PEOR 85345 616-A5
10600 PEOR 85345 615-H5
E ECHO CANYON CIR
- MESA 85207 704-B3
N ECHO CANYON CIR
- PHX 85018 659-J4
- PHX 85018 660-A4
N ECHO CANYON DR
- SURP 85374 534-G5
5600 PHX 85018 659-J4
39800 CVCK 85331 420-G1
40200 CVCK 85331 (380-G7 See Page 339)
N ECHO CANYON LN
4800 PHX 85018 659-J4
N ECHO CANYON PKWY
5700 PHX 85018 660-A4
E ECHO CANYON ST
- MESA 85207 704-A3
E ECHO HILL DR
15700 FTNH 85268 583-A7
ECHO HILL RD
- MarC 85342 331-C4
- MarC 85390 331-C4
N ECHO MESA DR
13600 MarC 85375 535-B3
W ECHOWOOD CT
15600 SURP 85374 534-F6
W ECO CIR
4900 PHX 85037 656-A5
E EDDYSTONE CT
9600 MarC 85248 901-B6
N EDEN CT
21000 MarC 85375 535-D2
E EDEN DR
4600 PHX 85331 460-A7
W EDEN MCKENZIE CIR
- SURP 85373 535-H6
W EDEN MCKENZIE DR
1400 SURP 85373 535-H6
E EDGEGROVE ST
10800 MarC 85220 744-H3
N EDGEMERE ST
2200 PHX 85006 698-J3
E EDGEMONT AV
800 PHX 85006 698-H2
1400 PHX 85006 699-A2
2400 PHX 85008 699-C2
5600 SCTS 85257 700-B3
8400 SCTS 85257 701-A3
W EDGEMONT AV
- GDYR 85338 (694-E1 See Page 653)
- PHX 85003 698-G2
- PHX 85004 698-G2
800 PHX 85007 698-E2
2000 PHX 85009 698-C2
2800 PHX 85035 697-A2
3300 PHX 85009 697-H2
7100 PHX 85035 696-J2
8500 PHX 85037 696-E2
12200 AVON 85323 695-C2
13800 GDYR 85338 695-A2
E EDGEMONT ST
- MESA 85203 741-J5
S EDGEMORE RD
3200 PinC 85219 786-H3
S EDGEWATER
2200 MESA 85208 783-G4
5500 MESA 85212 823-G6
6400 MESA 85212 863-F1
N EDGEWATER CIR
1800 MESA 85207 743-G1
S EDGEWATER CIR
2100 MESA 85208 783-G4
E EDGEWATER CT
14400 FTNH 85268 582-G3
E EDGEWATER DR
1500 TEMP 85283 780-G3
N EDGEWATER DR
16300 FTNH 85268 582-G3
S EDGEWATER DR
600 MESA 85208 743-G7
W EDGEWATER DR
1100 GIL 85233 822-A2
1100 GIL 85233 821-J2
N EDGEWATER RD
19000 PEOR 85382 536-C5
W EDGEWATER RD
9300 PEOR 85382 536-D4
W EDGEWOOD
2100 MESA 85202 741-B7
E EDGEWOOD AV
- MESA 85220 784-J1
1400 MESA 85204 742-B7
3700 MESA 85206 742-H7
4200 MESA 85206 743-A7
7200 MESA 85208 783-H1
8200 MESA 85208 784-A1
8500 MarC 85208 784-B1
W EDGEWOOD AV
500 MESA 85210 741-F7
E EDGEWOOD CIR
1900 MESA 85204 742-D7
4100 MESA 85206 742-J7
5100 MESA 85206 743-B7
7500 MESA 85208 783-H1
8000 MESA 85208 784-A1
N EDGEWOOD DR
100 MESA 85207 743-H5
W EDGEWOOD DR
10200 MarC 85351 576-A2
10900 MarC 85351 575-H2
E EDGEWOOD ST
7600 MESA 85208 783-J1
E EDGEWORTH CIR
2300 MESA 85204 742-E7
N EDGEWORTH DR
14000 FTNH 85268 583-C6
E EDISON AV
100 BUCK 85326 (772-A1 See Page 731)
W EDISON AV
25100 MarC 85326 (771-J1 See Page 731)
25100 MarC 85326 (772-A1 See Page 731)
N EDISON CIR
600 MESA 85203 742-A3
N EDITH CT
600 CHAN 85225 822-A5
S EDITH CT
- CHAN 85249 862-A1
N EDITH DR
900 CHAN 85225 822-A4
S EDITH DR
- CHAN 85249 862-A2
E EDNA AV
2300 PHX 85022 579-C2
3400 PHX 85032 579-F2
E EDWARD AV
8300 SCTS 85250 660-J3
8500 SCTS 85250 661-A3
S EDWARD DR
800 TEMP 85281 740-A4
2900 TEMP 85282 740-A7
W EDWARD DR
9700 MarC 85351 576-C7
E EDWARD LN
5900 PVAL 85253 660-C3
7400 SCTS 85250 660-G3
W EDWARDS ST
8300 PEOR 85345 616-F1
E EGRET CT
2200 GIL 85234 782-J4
E EGRET ST
5900 CVCK 85331 420-D4
E EIDER CT
16800 FTNH 85268 623-D1
S EILEEN DR
- CHAN 85248 861-F4
- CHAN 85248 901-F3
E E J ROBSON BLVD
9500 MarC 85248 901-B3
S E J ROBSON BLVD
25200 MarC 85248 901-C4
W ELAINE DR
- GDYR 85326 (694-B7 See Page 653)
W EL ALBA WY
100 CHAN 85225 821-E1
1000 CHAN 85224 821-B1
2400 MarC 85224 821-A1
2700 CHAN 85224 820-J1
2700 MarC 85224 820-J1
E ELANA CIR
7500 MESA 85208 783-H1
N EL ARROYO RD
7800 PVAL 85253 620-E7
E ELBOW BEND
7400 CARE 85377 420-H4
E EL CAMINITO DR
100 PHX 85020 618-H5
7200 SCTS 85258 620-F6
N EL CAMINITO DR
1400 TEMP 85281 700-E7
1400 TEMP 85281 740-E1
8200 PHX 85020 618-H5
W EL CAMINITO DR
- PEOR 85345 615-H5
100 PHX 85021 618-C5
2600 PHX 85051 618-A5
3400 PHX 85051 617-J5
4300 GLEN 85302 617-E5
8300 PEOR 85345 616-C5
S EL CAMINO CIR
1700 TEMP 85281 740-E6
2000 TEMP 85282 740-E6
3200 TEMP 85282 780-E1
E EL CAMINO DR
100 PHX 85020 618-H6
1400 PHX 85020 619-A6
N EL CAMINO DR
8200 PHX 85020 618-H6
S EL CAMINO DR
5300 TEMP 85283 780-E3
7700 TEMP 85284 780-E5
W EL CAMINO DR
500 PHX 85021 618-F6
3200 PHX 85051 618-A5
3400 PHX 85051 617-H5
4300 GLEN 85302 617-G5
W EL CAMINO OSO DR
- SURP 85373 535-H7
E EL CAMINO QUINTO
5600 PinC 85219 746-C7
W EL CAMINTO DR
5400 GLEN 85302 617-D5
W EL CAPITAN CIR
10400 MarC 85351 575-J4
10400 MarC 85351 576-A3
E EL CHARRO
- MarC 85206 783-G1
700 MarC 85206 743-F7
S EL CHARRO E
4900 MESA 85206 743-G7
S EL CHARRO W
4800 MarC 85206 743-F7
S EL CHARRO CIR
800 MarC 85206 743-F7
E EL CHARRO DR
800 MarC 85206 743-F7
800 MESA 85206 743-F7
E EL CHARRO DR N
800 MarC 85206 743-F7
800 MESA 85206 743-F7
E EL CHARRO DR S
700 MarC 85206 743-F7
700 MESA 85206 743-F7
E EL CHARRO LN
800 MarC 85206 743-F7
8600 SCTS 85250 661-A4
E EL CHARRO PL
700 MarC 85206 743-F7
700 MESA 85206 743-F7
E EL CHARRO PZ
18200 MarC 85206 743-F7
W EL CIELO
13900 GDYR 85338 735-A2
13900 GDYR 85338 (734-J2 See Page 733)
E EL CIRCULO DR
18700 MarC 85263 503-J4
E EL COLLADO
8700 SCTS 85262 (461-B5 See Page 421)
N EL COLLADO
8600 SCTS 85262 (461-B5 See Page 421)
W EL CORTEZ PL
- PEOR 85382 497-A4
4700 PHX 85310 497-B4
W EL CORTEZ TR
- PHX 85310 497-B4
N EL COSQUILLO
31200 SCTS 85262 (461-A5 See Page 421)
E ELDERBERRY WY
- PinC 85219 786-E5
N ELDON CIR
1100 GIL 85233 782-A4
S EL DORADO
1900 MESA 85202 781-A3
W EL DORADO AV
1100 ELMG 85335 575-F7
1100 ELMG 85335 615-F1
N EL DORADO CIR
- CHAN 85224 821-A1
S EL DORADO CIR
200 MESA 85202 741-A6
N EL DORADO CT
1500 CHAN 85224 821-A2
17600 SURP 85374 534-F6
N EL DORADO DR
600 GIL 85233 781-H5
1300 CHAN 85224 821-A2
2600 CHAN 85224 781-A6
S EL DORADO DR
- CHAN 85248 861-A2
W EL DORADO DR
9900 MarC 85351 616-B1
10700 MarC 85351 615-J1
E EL DORADO LN
13800 MarC 85296 822-D5
N EL DORADO LN
3600 SCTS 85251 700-E1
N EL DORADO PL
2600 CHAN 85224 781-A7
2600 CHAN 85224 821-A1
N EL DORADO RD
2800 CHAN 85224 781-A7
S EL DORADO RD
400 MESA 85202 741-A6
E ELEANOR AV
9000 MarC 85208 784-C1
E ELEANOR CT
1100 PHX 85020 618-J4
E ELECTRA LN
- PHX 85024 499-C7
W ELECTRA LN
- PEOR 85382 496-G7
- PEOR 85382 497-A7
3500 PHX 85310 497-D6
8900 MarC 85382 496-D7
E ELEGANTE CIR
5400 MarC 85206 783-D1
E ELEGANTE DR
17400 MarC 85206 783-D1
E ELENA AV
- MESA 85220 784-J1
4400 MESA 85206 743-A7
5400 MESA 85206 783-C1
W ELENA AV
500 MESA 85210 741-F7
W ELENA CIR
1000 MESA 85210 741-E7
N ELENA DR
15200 FTNH 85268 582-J4
E EL FREDA CIR
- TEMP 85284 820-D1
E EL FREDA RD
900 TEMP 85284 820-E1
W EL FREDA RD
- TEMP 85284 820-C1
E EL FREDA RD N
1000 TEMP 85284 820-E1
E EL FREDA RD S
1000 TEMP 85284 820-F1
N EL FRIO ST
13200 ELMG 85335 575-G4
E ELGIN CT
1700 CHAN 85225 822-A7
E ELGIN PL
- CHAN 85225 821-J7
E ELGIN ST
- MarC 85296 822-C7
- CHAN 85225 821-F7
1600 CHAN 85225 822-A7
16600 MarC 85236 823-B7
W ELGIN ST
- CHAN 85225 821-E7
500 CHAN 85226 820-D7
1000 CHAN 85224 821-B7
E ELI CT
- GIL 85296 822-F6
S ELI CT
- GIL 85296 822-F5
N EL INDIO CIR
38100 CVCK 85331 420-D3
N ELISABETH CIR
1100 GIL 85233 782-A4
N ELISEO C FELIX JR WY
500 AVON 85323 695-C6
W ELIZABETH AV
- GDYR 85326 (734-A1 See Page 733)
S ELIZABETH CIR
100 CHAN 85225 821-G7
W ELIZABETH DR
- GIL 85233 782-A6
N ELIZABETH PL
6000 PVAL 85253 659-F3
W ELK AV
11000 MarC 85351 575-J7
11100 YNTN 85335 575-H7
W ELKHORN DR
9200 MarC 85351 576-D4
N ELKO DR
14800 SURP 85374 534-H6
W ELKO DR
14900 SURP 85374 534-H6
W ELLA ST
2200 MESA 85201 741-B5
E EL LAGO
18200 MarC 85206 743-F7
E EL LAGO BLVD
15400 FTNH 85268 582-J7
15400 FTNH 85268 583-A7
16300 FTNH 85268 623-C1
W EL LAGO ST
- CHAN 85226 820-D5
E ELLASAR AV
9000 MarC 85208 784-C1
E ELLIOT RD
- CHAN 85225 781-F7
- GIL 85296 782-G7
- TEMP 85283 780-F7
- GIL 85234 782-G7
- TEMP 85284 780-F7
500 GIL 85225 781-G7
500 GIL 85233 781-G7
4600 PHX 85044 779-H7
5100 PHX 85284 779-H7
15700 MarC 85234 782-H7
15700 MarC 85296 782-H7
16000 GIL 85236 782-H7
16000 GIL 85236 783-C7
16200 GIL 85234 783-C7
16200 MarC 85236 783-C7
18400 MarC 85212 783-G7
18400 MESA 85212 783-G7
19600 MESA 85212 784-A7
19600 MarC 85212 784-A7
20000 MESA 85212 824-D1
20000 MarC 85212 824-B1
W ELLIOT RD
- CHAN 85224 780-B7
- CHAN 85284 780-B7
- GDYR 85338 (774-A4 See Page 733)
- MarC 85339 776-J6
- PHX 85041 778-B6
- TEMP 85283 779-J7
- CHAN 85225 781-C7
- GIL 85233 782-A7
- GIL 85296 782-A7
- TEMP 85284 780-B7
- GIL 85234 782-A7
- TEMP 85283 780-B7
800 GIL 85233 781-H7
900 CHAN 85224 781-C7
1900 MarC 85284 779-J7
1900 TEMP 85284 779-J7
2700 MarC 85339 778-A5
3000 MarC 85339 777-G5
3500 PHX 85339 777-G5
17500 GDYR 85338 (773-G5 See Page 733)
17700 GDYR 85326 (773-G5 See Page 733)
19300 MarC 85326 (773-A5 See Page 733)
E ELLIS CIR
- MESA 85205 742-J3
1300 MESA 85203 742-B3
4600 MESA 85205 743-A3
9600 MarC 85207 744-E3
E ELLIS DR
- TEMP 85282 780-D2
W ELLIS DR
- TEMP 85282 780-B2
2600 TEMP 85282 779-J2
6300 MarC 85339 777-A2
E ELLIS RD
- MarC 85207 744-D4
E ELLIS ST
3200 MESA 85213 742-G3
4000 MESA 85205 742-J3
4300 MESA 85205 743-A3
6000 MarC 85205 743-E3
8100 MESA 85207 744-A3
N ELLIS ST
- CHAN 85224 821-A1
2600 CHAN 85224 781-A6
S ELLIS ST
- CHAN 85224 821-A7
- CHAN 85224 861-A1
- CHAN 85248 861-A3
4300 PHX 85040 779-G2
W ELLIS ST
- PHX 85041 777-G2
300 PHX 85041 778-F2
800 MESA 85201 741-E3
N ELLSWORTH AV
35100 PinC 85242 904-C7
N ELLSWORTH RD
- MarC 85207 744-D2
900 MESA 85207 744-D2
S ELLSWORTH RD
- MarC 85208 744-D6
600 MarC 85208 784-D2
1200 MESA 85208 784-D2
1700 MESA 85212 784-D3
5100 MarC 85212 824-C4
5100 MESA 85212 824-C4
5100 MESA 85212 864-C4
6600 MarC 85242 824-C4
6600 MarC 85242 864-C4
17200 MESA 85242 864-C4
18800 QC 85242 864-C4
21100 QC 85242 904-C5
24400 MarC 85242 904-C5
N ELM
500 MESA 85201 741-E3
S ELM
600 MESA 85202 741-E7
E ELM CIR
100 GIL 85234 782-D6
N ELM CIR
1200 GIL 85234 782-D4
S ELM CIR
300 GIL 85296 822-D1
2800 MESA 85202 781-D5
E ELM DR
8000 SCTS 85257 700-J4
N ELM DR
- SURP 85374 534-A7
W ELM DR
4200 PHX 85019 657-G5
4200 PHX 85031 657-F5
E ELM LN
- AVON 85323 735-B2
S ELM LN
1600 BUCK 85326 (692-C7 See Page 651)
1800 BUCK 85326 (732-C1 See Page 731)
W ELM LN
- PHX 85043 737-A2
- AVON 85323 735-B2
E ELM ST
100 GIL 85234 782-D7
300 PHX 85012 658-H6
1000 PHX 85014 658-J6
2400 PHX 85016 659-C6
3300 PHX 85018 659-G5
N ELM ST
- CHAN 85226 820-G3
100 GIL 85234 782-D4
600 BUCK 85326 (772-C1 See Page 731)
700 BUCK 85326 (732-C7 See Page 731)
4700 PHX 85017 658-B5
S ELM ST
- MarC 85296 822-C7
- MarC 85296 862-C1
- CHAN 85226 820-D7
400 GIL 85296 822-C1
1200 TEMP 85281 740-G5
2000 TEMP 85282 740-G6
2200 MESA 85202 781-D3
3500 TEMP 85282 780-G1
5900 TEMP 85283 780-G4
W ELM ST
100 PHX 85013 658-E5
1500 PHX 85015 658-C5
2500 PHX 85017 658-A5
3300 PHX 85017 657-J5
3500 PHX 85019 657-H5
4700 PHX 85033 657-B5
5500 PHX 85031 657-C5
7500 PHX 85033 656-G5
8300 PHX 85037 656-C5
12700 SURP 85374 575-B1
15600 SURP 85374 534-F7
N EL MAJON
30000 SCTS 85262 (461-B6 See Page 421)
E ELMAN AV
9000 MarC 85208 784-C1
S EL MARINO
2100 MESA 85202 781-B3
S EL MARINO CIR
1700 MESA 85202 781-B2
E ELMARO CIR
6400 PVAL 85253 620-D6
N ELMARO CIR
6400 PVAL 85253 620-E6
W ELMBROOK DR
13700 MarC 85375 535-B3
E ELMHURST DR
10400 MarC 85248 901-D6
N EL MIRAGE RD
300 AVON 85323 695-E5
300 MarC 85323 695-E5
4100 MarC 85340 655-E4
4100 AVON 85340 655-E4
6500 MarC 85307 615-E6
6500 MarC 85307 655-E4
8000 ELMG 85335 615-E2
11300 ELMG 85335 575-F3
15100 SURP 85335 575-F3
15400 SURP 85374 575-F3
16700 SURP 85374 535-F5
17000 MarC 85374 535-F5
17000 MarC 85373 535-F5
20600 MarC 85373 535-F5
S EL MIRAGE RD
1200 AVON 85323 695-E7
1200 AVON 85323 735-E4
1200 MarC 85323 735-E4
1200 AVON 85353 695-E7
1200 AVON 85353 735-E4
2000 MarC 85353 735-E4
6800 MarC 85353 775-E1
6800 AVON 85353 775-E1
7000 MarC 85323 775-E1
7300 AVON 85323 775-E1
W EL MIRAGE RD
12100 ELMG 85335 575-F3
S ELMONT DR
- MESA 85220 744-J6
E EL MONTE PL
300 CHAN 85225 821-F2
W EL MONTE PL
600 CHAN 85225 821-E1
1400 CHAN 85224 821-E1
W EL MONTE WY
1500 CHAN 85224 821-C1
E EL MORO AV
- MESA 85220 784-F1
900 MESA 85204 742-B7
900 MESA 85204 782-C1
W EL MORO AV
2100 MESA 85202 741-B7
E EL MORO CIR
1400 MESA 85204 742-B7
W EL MORO CIR
800 MESA 85202 741-B7
E ELMWOOD CIR
1900 MESA 85203 742-D3
5200 MESA 85205 743-C3
E ELMWOOD CT
- MarC 85248 901-C3
E ELMWOOD DR
- MarC 85248 901-C3
E ELMWOOD PL
- MarC 85249 901-H3
- MarC 85249 902-B3
W ELMWOOD PL
300 CHAN 85248 901-E3
E ELMWOOD ST
900 MarC 85220 744-H3
1600 MESA 85203 742-C3
2000 MESA 85213 742-D3
4000 MESA 85205 742-J3
4200 MESA 85205 743-A3
9400 MarC 85207 744-D3
11400 MarC 85220 745-A3
W ELNA RAE ST
800 TEMP 85281 740-B4
E EL NIDO LN
8700 SCTS 85250 661-A4
W EL NINO CT
15700 SURP 85374 534-F5
W EL PAJARITO DR
600 WICK 85390 290-D2
S EL PARADISO
2700 MESA 85202 781-B4
S EL PARADISO CIR
2700 MESA 85202 781-B5
S EL PARADISO DR
1800 MESA 85202 781-C4
E EL PARQUE DR
- TEMP 85282 740-D6
2300 TEMP 85282 741-A6
E EL PASO
- MarC 85207 744-D3
E EL PASO ST
6000 MarC 85205 743-E3
9600 MarC 85207 744-E3
21700 MarC 85207 744-F3
N EL PASO ST
900 MarC 85220 744-H4
W EL PASO GAS LINE RD
22600 MarC 85337 (851-D7 See Page 811)
22600 MarC 85337 (852-A7 See Page 811)
EL PASO NATURAL GAS RD
27800 BUCK 85337 (851-A7 See Page 811)
W EL PASO NATURAL GAS RD
27100 BUCK 85337 (851-A7 See Page 811)
27100 MarC 85337 (851-A7 See Page 811)
N EL PEDREGAL
- MarC 85242 904-H6
N EL PEDREGAL CIR
- MarC 85242 904-H6
N EL PRADO
26200 MarC 85263 503-J5
W EL PRADO
300 CHAN 85225 821-F1
W EL PRADO CIR
500 CHAN 85225 821-E1
E EL PRADO RD
- CHAN 85225 821-F1
W EL PRADO RD
400 CHAN 85225 821-E1
1900 CHAN 85224 821-B1
W EL PRADO WY
1100 CHAN 85224 821-D1
E EL PUEBLO BLVD
16700 FTNH 85268 583-D4
N EL PUEBLO BLVD
13400 FTNH 85264 583-E6
13400 FTNH 85268 583-E6
E EL RANCHO DR
7600 SCTS 85260 620-H1
10800 SCTS 85259 621-G2
W EL RANCHO DR
10300 MarC 85351 576-A7
10300 MarC 85351 616-A1
10600 MarC 85351 575-J7
E EL RECREO CT
400 WICK 85390 290-G2
N EL RECREO DR
600 WICK 85390 290-F2
N EL RIO CT
20200 MarC 85375 534-H3
E EL SENDERO CIR
7700 SCTS 85262 460-J1
E EL SENDERO DR
5000 CVCK 85331 420-C7
5400 CARE 85377 420-C7
E EL SENDERO RD
- CVCK 85331 419-G7
6400 CARE 85377 420-F7
N EL SENDERO RD
35000 CARE 85377 420-E7
N EL SERENO
- MESA 85207 704-A2
N EL SERENO CIR
- MarC 85290 703-J1
- MESA 85207 704-A2
N ELSIE AV
4500 PHX 85251 660-C6
N EL SOBRANTE AV
14600 FTNH 85268 583-E5
15200 MarC 85268 583-E5
W EL SOL
14400 GDYR 85338 (734-H3 See Page 733)
W EL TECALOTE DR
700 WICK 85390 290-D2
E ELTON AV
1200 MESA 85204 742-B6
11000 MarC 85220 744-H7
11400 MarC 85220 745-A7
E ELWOOD ST
- PHX 85040 738-G4
- PHX 85041 738-G4
1200 PHX 85040 739-A4
3100 PHX 85034 739-E4
W ELWOOD ST
- PHX 85043 736-H4
- PHX 85041 738-F4
700 PHX 85007 738-F4
3600 PHX 85009 737-J3
4300 PHX 85043 737-A3
12300 AVON 85323 735-D3
12300 AVON 85353 735-D3
W ELY DR
14300 SURP 85374 535-A6
14400 SURP 85374 534-J6
W ELY LN
- AVON 85323 735-B1
E EMBASSY ST
300 TEMP 85281 700-E6
S EMBER CIR
900 MESA 85208 784-A1
N EMBERWOOD DR
9700 MarC 85351 576-B5
E EMELITA AV
800 MESA 85204 742-B7
900 MESA 85206 783-A1
900 MESA 85206 782-H1
7600 MESA 85208 783-J1
8200 MESA 85208 784-A1
8500 MarC 85208 784-B1
10800 MESA 85220 784-G1
S EMELITA AV
2100 MESA 85204 742-D7
W EMELITA AV
500 MESA 85210 741-E7
1000 MESA 85202 741-B7
E EMELITA CIR
2300 MESA 85204 742-E7
4100 MESA 85206 782-J1
5100 MESA 85206 783-B1
W EMELITA CIR
900 MESA 85210 741-E7
E EMELITA CT
8000 MESA 85208 784-A1
N EMELITA CT
- SURP 85374 534-G6
E EMERALD AV
- MESA 85220 784-G1
1000 MESA 85204 782-A1
3700 MESA 85206 782-H1
4500 MESA 85206 783-A1
8400 MESA 85208 784-B1
W EMERALD AV
400 MESA 85210 741-F7
1200 MESA 85202 741-B7
E EMERALD CIR
- MESA 85206 783-D1
3200 MESA 85204 782-G1
W EMERALD CIR
900 MESA 85210 741-E7
2200 MESA 85202 741-B7
S EMERALD CT
23600 MarC 85248 901-A2
E EMERALD DR
- APJT 85219 785-H3
8900 MarC 85248 900-J2
9000 MarC 85248 901-A2
16100 FTNH 85268 623-B2
S EMERALD DR
- MarC 85249 902-E5
100 MarC 85220 744-J6
3800 MarC 85326 (732-A3 See Page 731)
W EMERALD DR
10700 MarC 85351 576-A4
10800 MarC 85351 575-H4
W EMERALD LN
- AVON 85323 656-A7
11300 AVON 85323 655-G7
E EMERALD PL
- MESA 85208 784-B1

PHOENIX INDEX

STREET
Block City ZIP Pg-Grid

W EMERALD PT
10600 MarC 85351 576-A5
N EMERALD BAY DR
1000 GIL 85234 782-F4
W EMERALD ISLAND DR
800 GIL 85233 822-A1
W EMERALD KEY CT
1400 GIL 85233 821-J1
N EMERALD LAKE DR
3100 MarC 85086 (378-B5 See Page 337)
N EMERSON
400 MESA 85201 741-E2
S EMERSON
1700 MESA 85210 781-E3
S EMERSON CIR
2200 MESA 85210 781-E4
N EMERSON CT
1600 CHAN 85225 821-D3
S EMERSON PL
- CHAN 85248 861-D2
N EMERSON ST
500 CHAN 85225 821-D5
S EMERSON ST
200 CHAN 85225 821-D7
700 CHAN 85225 861-D4
800 MESA 85210 781-E5
3400 CHAN 85248 861-D4
N EMERY
- MESA 85220 744-J4
S EMERY
- MarC 85212 824-H1
- MESA 85212 784-H7
- MESA 85212 824-H1
S EMERY CIR
- MESA 85212 784-H7
N EMERY PL
- MESA 85220 784-J1
W EMIG RD
3500 PHX 85053 577-J2
3500 PHX 85053 578-A2
E EMILE ZOLA AV
1200 PHX 85022 579-A6
2600 PHX 85032 579-D6
4700 PHX 85032 580-A6
4800 PHX 85254 580-A6
W EMILE ZOLA AV
2400 PHX 85029 578-C5
6800 PEOR 85381 577-A5
7100 PEOR 85381 576-F5
N EMMETT DR
- CHAN 85225 822-B6
S EMMITT DR
- CHAN 85249 902-B4
W EMORY LN
- PEOR 85382 496-H5
E EMPIRE BLVD
19300 QC 85242 903-H6
19300 QC 85242 903-H6
19600 QC 85242 904-C7
19600 QC 85242 904-A7
20000 MarC 85242 904-A7
20000 PinC 85242 904-A7
E EMPRESS AV
- MESA 85208 784-E1
9500 MarC 85208 784-E1
W ENCANTADA DR
- SURP 85374 534-G6
E ENCANTADA PL
1200 PHX 85014 658-J2
W ENCANTO BLVD
- PHX 85003 698-F3
500 PHX 85007 698-F3
1500 PHX 85009 698-A3
1700 PHX 85009 698-A3
3200 PHX 85009 697-F3
4300 PHX 85035 697-B3
6700 PHX 85035 696-F3
7900 PHX 85037 696-D3
9900 AVON 85037 696-A3
9900 AVON 85323 696-A3
9900 MarC 85323 696-A3
10500 AVON 85323 695-C2
10500 MarC 85323 695-G3
13100 GDYR 85323 695-C2
13100 GDYR 85338 695-C2
14300 GDYR 85338 (694-E2 See Page 653)
19500 MarC 85326 (693-D2 See Page 653)
E ENCANTO DR
100 TEMP 85281 740-D5
N ENCANTO DR
- SURP 85374 534-A6
S ENCANTO DR
1700 TEMP 85281 740-E5
ENCANTO DR NE
2200 PHX 85007 698-F3
ENCANTO DR NW
2200 PHX 85007 698-F3
ENCANTO DR SE
700 PHX 85007 698-F3
ENCANTO DR SW
900 PHX 85007 698-F3
E ENCANTO ST
1000 MESA 85203 742-B2
2000 MESA 85213 742-D3
4000 MESA 85205 742-J3
4200 MESA 85205 743-A3
8000 MESA 85207 744-A3
E ENCHANTMENT LEDGE PL
- SCTS 85262 (381-F5 See Page 341)
E ENCINAS AV
400 GIL 85234 782-D4
2400 GIL 85234 783-C5
3600 GIL 85236 783-E4
E ENCINAS LN
1700 PHX 85040 739-A5
W ENCINAS LN
- PHX 85043 736-G4
- PHX 85043 737-B4
E ENCINAS ST
2600 GIL 85234 783-A5
5400 GUAD 85283 780-A4
W ENCINAS ST
400 GIL 85233 782-A4
800 GIL 85233 781-H4
E ENCINITAS AV
- GIL 85234 783-C5
E ENCLAVE BLVD
- MarC 85236 903-E3
W END ST
12200 ELMG 85335 575-F3
S ENDEAVOR DR
- MarC 85248 901-C3
W ENFIELD PL
- CHAN 85248 861-D2
W ENFIELD WY
1200 CHAN 85248 861-A2

N ENGLISH WELLS RD
33400 MarC 85361 413-B7
W ENGLISH WELLS RD
21000 MarC 85361 413-B5
E ENID AV
- MESA 85208 784-B1
- MESA 85220 784-F1
900 MESA 85204 782-B1
1400 MESA 85204 782-B7
3600 MESA 85206 782-H1
4500 MESA 85206 783-A1
9200 MarC 85208 784-D1
S ENID AV
1000 MESA 85206 782-H1
W ENID AV
500 MESA 85210 741-E7
2100 MESA 85202 741-B7
E ENID CIR
1900 MESA 85204 742-D7
2300 MESA 85204 782-D1
3700 MESA 85206 782-D1
W ENID CIR
900 MESA 85210 741-E7
W ENOCH DR
17900 SURP 85387 494-A4
18100 SURP 85387 493-J4
E ENROSE CIR
1300 MESA 85203 742-B3
5300 MESA 85205 743-C3
8000 MESA 85207 744-A3
E ENROSE ST
800 MESA 85203 742-C3
2000 MESA 85213 742-D3
4000 MESA 85205 742-J3
4200 MESA 85205 743-A3
8100 MESA 85207 744-A3
N ENROSE ST
800 MESA 85203 742-C3
N ENSENADA CT
14600 PHX 85053 578-B4
E ENSENADA ST
6000 MarC 85205 743-E3
6500 MESA 85205 743-F3
8000 MESA 85207 744-A3
9500 MarC 85207 744-E3
N ENSUENO
29800 SCTS 85262 (461-A6 See Page 421)
W ENSUENO CT
400 GIL 85233 822-B2
W ENSUENO ST
200 GIL 85233 822-B2
S ENTERPRISE CIR
900 MESA 85208 784-A1
E ENTERPRISE DR
16900 FTNH 85268 623-D1
S ENTERPRISE RD
25400 MarC 85322 102-A3
25400 MarC 85337 102-A3
N ENTRADA PL
- CHAN 85226 820-H7
N ENTRADA ST
500 CHAN 85226 820-G3
S EQUESTRIAN CT
- GIL 85296 782-H7
- GIL 85296 822-H1
E EQUESTRIAN TR
3400 PHX 85044 819-E1
S EQUESTRIAN TR
11600 PHX 85044 819-E1
E EQUINOX CIR
- SCTS 85262 (461-A3 See Page 421)
N ERICSON CT
- MarC 85087 (378-A4 See Page 337)
W ERICSON LN
- MarC 85087 (378-A4 See Page 337)
E ERIE CT
- GIL 85236 822-J6
- GIL 85236 823-A6
- GIL 85296 822-E6
- MarC 85236 823-A6
E ERIE DR
- TEMP 85282 740-D7
W ERIE DR
100 TEMP 85282 740-D7
2400 TEMP 85282 739-J7
E ERIE ST
- GIL 85236 823-B6
- GIL 85296 822-F6
- CHAN 85225 821-G5
1500 CHAN 85225 822-A6
22800 MarC 85212 824-H6
W ERIE ST
- CHAN 85225 821-D5
1000 CHAN 85224 821-A5
3500 CHAN 85226 820-A5
7200 CHAN 85226 819-J5
N ERIN LN
- SURP 85374 533-J7
S ERNIE PL
500 TEMP 85281 740-B3
N ESCALANTE DR
15000 FTNH 85268 583-F5
16200 SURP 85374 534-E6
W ESCALANTE ST
100 BUCK 85326 (732-A7 See Page 731)
W ESCARPA
1300 MESA 85201 741-D3
N ESCOBAR WY
12200 PHX 85022 579-C7
E ESCONDIDO AV
- MESA 85208 784-E1
- MESA 85220 784-J1
800 MESA 85206 743-A7
2800 MESA 85204 742-F7
9400 MarC 85208 784-D1
E ESCONDIDO CIR
3700 MESA 85206 742-H7
5100 MESA 85206 743-B7
W ESCONDIDO CT
1000 APJT 85220 745-C4
16300 SURP 85374 534-E7
E ESCONDIDO DR
1200 PHX 85014 658-J4
N ESCONDIDO DR
15000 FTNH 85268 583-D5
E ESCONDIDO PL
15800 MarC 85234 782-J6
E ESCUDA DR
900 PHX 85024 538-J4
1000 PHX 85024 539-A4
W ESCUDA DR
1500 PHX 85027 538-D4
3600 PHX 85308 537-G4
6900 GLEN 85308 537-A4
7600 GLEN 85308 536-J4

W ESCUDA DR
8300 PEOR 85382 536-C4
E ESCUDA RD
2000 PHX 85024 539-C4
2500 PHX 85050 539-D4
W ESCUDA RD
1200 PHX 85027 538-F4
5100 GLEN 85308 537-A4
10900 PEOR 85373 535-J4
E ESMERALDA
- MarC 85220 744-G5
- MESA 85220 744-G7
N ESMERALDA
- MESA 85220 784-G1
S ESMERALDA
- MESA 85212 784-F6
- MESA 85220 784-G1
E ESMERALDA AV
- MESA 85220 784-G1
E ESMERALDA CIR
- MESA 85220 784-G1
S ESMERALDA CIR
- MESA 85212 784-F6
E ESPANA AV
9200 MarC 85208 784-D1
W ESPARTERO WY
- PHX 85086 (418-C6 See Page 417)
S ESPERANZA AV
800 MarC 85208 784-D1
ESPERANZA DR
- LP 85340 655-A7
S ESPERO DR
300 MarC 85206 783-F1
E ESPLANADE AV
- GIL 85236 863-C4
E ESPLANADE CT
- GIL 85236 863-C4
E ESPLANADE LN
2700 PHX 85016 659-C6
N ESPLANADE ST
800 MESA 85201 741-D3
W ESPLANADE ST
800 MESA 85201 741-E3
S ESQUIRE WY
400 MESA 85202 741-B6
S ESSEX
2400 MESA 85208 783-G4
6400 MESA 85212 823-G7
6400 MESA 85212 863-G1
N ESSEX CIR
1800 MESA 85207 743-H1
S ESSEX CIR
1800 MESA 85208 783-G3
S ESSEX LN
500 MESA 85208 743-G7
E ESSEX ST
- CHAN 85225 821-F6
W ESTANCIA BLVD
- GIL 85233 822-B1
E ESTANCIA WY
9600 SCTS 85255 501-D3
W ESTER DR
11800 ELMG 85335 575-G6
E ESTERO LN
400 LP 85340 655-B5
W ESTERO LN
100 LP 85340 655-B5
E ESTES WY
4300 PHX 85044 779-H5
W ESTES WY
800 PHX 85041 778-E4
E ESTEVAN AV
500 APJT 85219 745-E7
E ESTEVAN RD
4800 PHX 85054 540-B1
N ESTHER ST
1100 TEMP 85281 740-F1
N ESTRADA
- MarC 85207 704-B6
N ESTRADA CIR
- MESA 85207 744-B2
E ESTRELA DR
- SCTS 85262 460-H5
S ESTRELLA
2200 MESA 85202 781-A4
E ESTRELLA AV
11600 SCTS 85259 621-H4
13400 SCTS 85259 622-D4
W ESTRELLA AV
2700 MESA 85202 781-A6
2700 MESA 85202 780-J5
S ESTRELLA CIR
2000 MESA 85202 781-A3
E ESTRELLA CT
- GIL 85236 823-A3
N ESTRELLA CT
- MarC 85255 (462-F6 See Page 421)
E ESTRELLA DR
- GIL 85236 823-A3
600 CHAN 85225 821-G2
W ESTRELLA DR
600 GIL 85233 822-A2
1000 CHAN 85224 821-A2
4100 MarC 85041 817-E1
4100 MarC 85339 817-D1
4100 PHX 85041 817-E1
4300 PHX 85339 817-E1
5500 MarC 85339 816-H1
ESTRELLA FRWY Rt#-303
- GDYR - (654-C5 See Page 653)
- GDYR - (694-C1 See Page 653)
- MarC - (654-C5 See Page 653)
- MarC - (654-C5 See Page 653)
- MarC - (614-C5 See Page 573)
- MarC - (614-C5 See Page 573)
- MarC - (614-C5 See Page 573)
- MarC - (574-D5 See Page 573)
- SURP - (614-C5 See Page 573)
- SURP - 534-D6
- SURP - (574-D5 See Page 573)
- SURP - 534-E2
N ESTRELLA PKWY
- GDYR 85338 (694-F3 See Page 653)
S ESTRELLA PKWY
- GDYR 85326 (774-B6 See Page 733)

S ESTRELLA PKWY
- GDYR 85326 (814-A3 See Page 813)
200 GDYR 85338 (694-F6 See Page 653)
1200 GDYR 85338 (734-F4 See Page 733)
6400 GDYR 85338 (774-D3 See Page 733)
18700 GDYR 85326 (854-A5 See Page 813)
E ESTRELLA RD
5500 PinC 85219 786-H6
W ESTRELLA RD
2100 MarC 85087 (338-E2 See Page 337)
E ESTRELLA ST
2500 GIL 85236 822-J3
2500 GIL 85236 823-A3
17800 MarC 85264 623-F1
N ESTRELLA VISTA DR
17100 SURP 85374 534-D6
E ESTRID AV
1400 PHX 85022 579-A5
5600 PHX 85254 580-B5
E ESTRID CIR
5700 PHX 85254 580-C5
W EUCALYPTUS AV
- GDYR 85326 (814-A1 See Page 813)
W EUCALYPTUS CT
15700 SURP 85374 534-F5
N EUCALYPTUS DR
- LP 85340 655-B6
7300 PVAL 85253 620-A7
7300 PVAL 85253 660-A1
S EUCALYPTUS DR
- GIL 85236 863-E5
W EUCALYPTUS DR
32200 MarC 85390 290-B1
S EUCALYPTUS PL
- CHAN 85249 862-A1
- CHAN 85249 902-A5
- MarC 85249 902-A3
- CHAN 85225 822-A6
E EUCLID AV
- PHX 85040 778-G4
1600 PHX 85040 779-A4
4600 PHX 85044 779-J4
7600 MESA 85208 783-J1
8000 MESA 85208 784-A1
N EUCLID AV
100 GBND 85337 (1090-B3 See Page 1049)
S EUCLID AV
300 GBND 85337 (1090-B4 See Page 1049)
W EUCLID AV
- PHX 85041 778-E4
4300 MarC 85339 777-F4
4500 PHX 85339 777-F4
13300 MarC 85338 775-B3
W EUCLID ST
- WICK 85390 289-J3
S EUGENE
- MESA 85208 784-A5
- MESA 85212 784-A6
S EUGENE CIR
- MESA 85212 784-A6
E EUGIE AV
100 PHX 85022 578-H5
1200 PHX 85022 579-A5
3600 PHX 85032 579-G6
W EUGIE AV
1600 PHX 85029 578-A5
3500 PHX 85029 577-J5
5100 GLEN 85304 577-B5
6900 PEOR 85381 577-A5
7100 PEOR 85381 576-G5
E EUGIE TR
2000 PHX 85022 579-C5
2200 PHX 85032 579-C6
6400 PHX 85254 580-E6
N EUREKA CT
- SURP 85374 534-G7
W EUREKA TR
14900 SURP 85374 534-G6
E EVA ST
- PHX 85020 618-G4
1200 PHX 85020 619-A4
3200 PHX 85028 619-E4
W EVA ST
- PHX 85021 618-E4
3500 PHX 85051 617-H3
4200 PHX 85302 617-G4
4400 GLEN 85302 617-B3
6800 PEOR 85345 617-B4
7000 PEOR 85345 616-F4
W EVAN CT
- PHX 85339 777-D3
S EVANGELINE AV
800 MarC 85208 784-D1
E EVANS DR
1700 PHX 85022 579-C4
2800 PHX 85032 579-D4
4800 PHX 85254 580-C4
9800 SCTS 85260 581-D5
N EVANS DR
6100 PHX 85251 660-C6
W EVANS DR
- ELMG 85335 575-D4
- SURP 85379 (574-F3 See Page 573)
- SURP 85379 575-C3
1600 PHX 85023 578-C4
2700 PHX 85053 578-A4
3500 PHX 85053 577-H4
4400 PHX 85306 577-F4
5100 GLEN 85306 577-B4
6700 MarC 85381 577-A4
6900 PEOR 85381 577-A4
9100 PEOR 85381 576-E4
E EVANS RD
- SCTS 85259 581-G5
7200 PHX 85254 580-G5
7200 SCTS 85254 580-G5
7200 SCTS 85260 580-G5
8200 SCTS 85260 581-A5
E EVELYN LN
- TEMP 85284 820-D4
E EVENING GLO DR
7500 SCTS 85262 460-H2
E EVENING GLOW DR
- SCTS 85331 460-D2
6000 SCTS 85262 460-E2
N EVENINGSIDE DR
21600 MarC 85375 535-D1
W EVENINGSIDE DR
12300 MarC 85375 535-E2

E EVENING STAR BLVD
- CHAN 85249 901-G4
S EVENING STAR BLVD
- CHAN 85249 901-G4
W EVENING STAR CT
20600 MarC 85361 (453-C7 See Page 413)
20600 MarC 85361 493-C1
E EVENINGSTAR LN
900 TEMP 85283 780-E3
W EVENING STAR TR
14800 SURP 85374 534-H6
N EVEREST
4100 MESA 85215 703-G2
N EVEREST CIR
4300 MESA 85215 703-G2
E EVERETT DR
1900 PHX 85022 579-B4
3300 PHX 85032 579-F4
4800 PHX 85254 580-A4
E EVERGREEN CIR
- MESA 85203 742-C3
N EVERGREEN CIR
1000 GIL 85233 782-C5
W EVERGREEN DR
9800 MarC 85373 536-C6
S EVERGREEN RD
400 TEMP 85281 741-B4
400 MESA 85201 741-B4
2200 TEMP 85282 741-A6
3100 TEMP 85282 781-B1
W EVERGREEN RD
5500 GLEN 85302 617-C5
E EVERGREEN ST
1200 MESA 85203 742-B3
2000 MESA 85213 742-D3
4700 MESA 85205 743-B3
6000 MarC 85205 743-E3
8000 MESA 85207 744-A3
9500 MESA 85207 744-D3
21800 MarC 85220 744-F3
N EVERGREEN ST
100 CHAN 85225 821-E1
500 GIL 85233 782-C4
2200 PHX 85006 698-J3
2700 CHAN 85225 781-E6
2900 PHX 85014 698-J2
S EVERGREEN ST
300 CHAN 85225 821-E7
500 CHAN 85225 861-E1
N EVERSON DR
17800 GLEN 85308 537-A7
W EWERS DR
- SURP 85374 533-J6
S EXCAVATION CT
- PinC 85219 826-H3
E EXCELSIOR AV
- QC 85242 904-C5
N EXECUTIVE WY
21800 MarC 85375 534-G1
22300 MarC 85375 494-H7
E EXETER BLVD
4300 SCTS 85251 660-D7
4400 PHX 85018 659-J6
4900 PHX 85018 660-C7
5800 PHX 85251 660-D7
6600 MarC 85251 660-D7
N EXETER ST
- CHAN 85225 821-G5
E EXMOOR DR
6900 MESA 85208 783-G1
W EXPERT LN
- PHX 85086 417-J6
N EXPLORATION TR
- MarC 85086 (378-B7 See Page 337)
N EXPLORER DR
800 GIL 85234 782-J5
3900 PinC 85219 745-E1
S EXPLORER DR
700 GIL 85234 782-J5
800 GIL 85296 822-J2
N EXTENSION RD
- MESA 85201 741-F4
- MESA 85210 741-F4
1600 MarC 85256 701-F3
4100 MarC 85256 661-F6
S EXTENSION RD
- MESA 85210 741-F6
900 MESA 85210 781-F1
EXTENSION CSR
- BUCK 85326 (773-E1 See Page 733)
- GDYR 85326 733-H7
- GDYR 85326 (773-E1 See Page 733)
- MarC 85326 733-H7
- MarC 85326 (773-E1 See Page 733)

F

W F CIR
4600 PHX 85031 657-E5
N F PZ
4700 PHX 85031 657-E5
N F ST
4600 PHX 85031 657-E5
W F ST
30600 MarC 85337 (1050-B7 See Page 1049)
W FABENS LN
500 GIL 85233 782-B7
S FABLE AV
1100 MESA 85208 783-J1
E FABLE CIR
8200 MESA 85208 784-A1
N FACTORY ST
- ELMG 85335 575-E3
- SURP 85335 575-E2
15400 SURP 85374 575-E2
S FAIR LN
2700 TEMP 85282 739-J7
3200 TEMP 85282 779-J2
E FAIRBROOK
1000 MESA 85203 742-A2
E FAIRBROOK CIR
1100 MESA 85203 742-J2
3900 MESA 85205 742-J2
4600 MESA 85205 743-A2
E FAIRBROOK ST
- MESA 85207 744-C3
1200 MESA 85203 742-B2
2200 MESA 85213 742-D2
4000 MESA 85205 742-J2
4900 MESA 85205 743-B2
9400 MarC 85207 744-D3
E FAIRFAX DR
16500 FTNH 85268 583-C6

E FAIRFIELD CIR
- MESA 85205 742-J3
1000 MESA 85203 742-A2
5200 MESA 85205 743-C3
9500 MarC 85207 744-E3
E FAIRFIELD DR
2100 TEMP 85283 780-J3
N FAIRFIELD DR
1400 CHAN 85226 820-J3
S FAIRFIELD DR
2500 TEMP 85282 740-J6
3200 TEMP 85282 780-J1
5300 TEMP 85283 780-J3
8800 TEMP 85284 820-H2
9300 CHAN 85284 820-H2
E FAIRFIELD ST
- MarC 85207 744-D3
- MESA 85205 742-J3
400 MESA 85203 741-J2
900 MESA 85203 742-A2
2000 MESA 85213 742-D2
4400 MESA 85205 743-A3
8000 MESA 85207 744-A3
N FAIRFIELD ST
1000 MESA 85203 741-J2
N FAIRGREEN CT
42000 MarC 85086 (378-C5 See Page 337)
N FAIRGREEN WY
- MarC 85086 (378-C5 See Page 337)
E FAIRLYNN DR
16300 FTNH 85268 583-C5
N FAIRLYNN DR
14400 FTNH 85268 583-C5
W FAIRMONT AV
- AVON 85340 655-D7
E FAIRMONT DR
- TEMP 85282 740-D7
2400 TEMP 85282 741-A7
W FAIRMONT DR
- TEMP 85282 740-A7
2200 TEMP 85282 739-J7
E FAIRMOUNT AV
300 PHX 85012 658-H7
700 PHX 85014 658-H7
1200 PHX 85014 698-J1
1800 PHX 85016 699-C1
3200 PHX 85018 699-F1
4800 PHX 85018 700-H1
8000 SCTS 85251 700-H1
8500 SCTS 85251 701-A1
W FAIRMOUNT AV
- GDYR 85338 655-A7
800 PHX 85013 658-E7
1500 PHX 85015 658-C7
2800 PHX 85017 658-A7
4000 PHX 85019 657-H7
4500 PHX 85031 657-C7
5900 PHX 85033 657-B7
6900 PHX 85033 656-F7
8300 PHX 85037 656-D7
14800 GDYR 85338 (654-J6 See Page 653)
S FAIR OAKS CT
26600 MarC 85248 901-E6
S FAIR OAKS DR
25200 MarC 85248 901-E4
E FAIRVIEW
1100 MESA 85206 783-C1
E FAIRVIEW AV
- MESA 85208 784-E1
2100 MESA 85204 782-D1
7200 MESA 85208 783-H1
W FAIRVIEW AV
18200 SURP 85387 493-J7
E FAIRVIEW CIR
2200 MESA 85204 782-D1
4000 MESA 85206 782-J1
N FAIRVIEW CT
40300 CVCK 85331 (380-D7 See Page 339)
N FAIRVIEW DR
8500 SCTS 85258 620-G5
N FAIRVIEW LN
600 CHAN 85226 820-H7
E FAIRVIEW ST
- CHAN 85225 821-F7
1000 CHAN 85225 861-H1
1600 CHAN 85225 862-A1
14800 MarC 85296 862-C1
16000 MarC 85236 862-J1
16000 MarC 85236 863-A1
W FAIRVIEW ST
- CHAN 85225 821-E7
900 CHAN 85224 821-A7
2900 CHAN 85224 820-J7
5000 CHAN 85226 820-A7
5200 CHAN 85226 819-J7
5200 MarC 85226 819-J7
E FAIRWAY BLVD
8800 MarC 85248 900-J5
8900 MarC 85248 901-A4
N FAIRWAY CIR
100 LP 85340 655-C6
33800 SCTS 85262 460-J1
W FAIRWAY CIR
400 MESA 85201 741-G1
E FAIRWAY CT
17100 FTNH 85268 623-D4
N FAIRWAY CT
17200 PHX 85308 537-G7
S FAIRWAY CT
- CHAN 85225 821-E7
25600 MarC 85248 901-A4
FAIRWAY DR
- LP 85340 655-A6
E FAIRWAY DR
600 LP 85340 655-C6
9400 MarC 85207 744-D3
N FAIRWAY DR
- AVON 85323 695-E6
- AVON 85353 695-E6
S FAIRWAY DR
- PinC 85219 786-F7
- PinC 85219 826-F1
300 CHAN 85225 821-E7
2800 TEMP 85282 740-J7
2900 TEMP 85282 741-A7
3100 TEMP 85282 780-J1
W FAIRWAY DR
- SURP 85374 534-A6
100 LP 85340 655-A6
400 MESA 85201 741-E2
800 CHAN 85225 821-D7
17200 SURP 85374 533-J7
FAIRWAY LP N
2400 GDYR 85338 695-B2
FAIRWAY LP S
13400 GDYR 85338 695-B2

S FAIRWAY PL
6100 PinC 85219 786-G7
W FAIRWAY PL
200 CHAN 85225 821-F7
E FAIRWAY TR
- CVCK 85331 420-C3
W FAIRWOOD WY
16000 SURP 85374 534-E6
FAIRY DUSTER CT
15200 FTNH 85268 582-J6
S FAIRY DUSTER DR
- PinC 85219 786-E5
E FAITH
- MarC 85207 744-E3
N FAITH
- MarC 85207 744-E2
- MESA 85208 784-E3
S FAITH
- MESA 85212 784-E4
N FAITH LN
- MarC 85086 (378-B7 See Page 337)
E FALCON CIR
19100 MarC 85263 (504-A5 See Page 503)
N FALCON CT
400 GIL 85236 783-E6
E FALCON DR
4700 MESA 85215 703-B6
17100 FTNH 85268 623-D2
N FALCON DR
400 GIL 85236 783-E5
12000 FTNH 85268 623-D1
W FALCON DR
1800 CHAN 85248 861-B4
FALCON ST
- GLEN 85309 615-A7
W FALCON RIDGE DR
15800 MarC 85375 534-G1
N FALLBROOK CT
14600 MarC 85351 576-D3
W FALLEN LEAF
- PHX 85310 497-J5
W FALLEN LEAF AV
- PHX 85310 498-A5
W FALLEN LEAF LN
3700 PHX 85310 497-C5
E FALLING STAR DR
11000 SCTS 85262 (381-H6 See Page 341)
S FALLING STAR RD
2400 PinC 85219 786-H3
FAN BELT TRACK
- MarC 85375 413-E6
E FANFOL DR
4000 PHX 85028 619-H4
4800 PVAL 85253 619-J4
4800 PVAL 85253 620-A4
9900 SCTS 85258 621-D4
E FANFOL LN
10400 SCTS 85258 621-F4
E FARGO CIR
3100 MESA 85213 742-G2
W FARGO DR
- SURP 85374 575-B2
8700 PEOR 85382 576-E2
11000 MarC 85351 575-J2
E FARM RD
- PinC 85242 905-C4
E FARMDALE AV
- MESA 85208 784-E1
- MESA 85220 784-G1
1800 MESA 85204 782-C1
3700 MESA 85206 782-H1
4500 MESA 85206 783-A1
7200 MESA 85208 783-H1
W FARMDALE AV
500 MESA 85210 781-E1
2100 MESA 85202 741-B7
E FARMDALE CIR
2300 MESA 85204 782-D1
E FARMDALE DR
8000 MESA 85208 784-A1
S FARMER AV
- TEMP 85281 740-D3
1900 TEMP 85282 740-D3
3900 TEMP 85282 780-C1
5300 TEMP 85283 780-C3
9000 TEMP 85284 820-C2
S FARMER RD
- PHX 85043 696-J6
- PHX 85043 697-A6
W FARMERS LN
100 MarC 85320 (284-H3 See Page 244)
E FARNSWORTH DR
8000 MESA 85208 783-J4
8000 MESA 85208 784-A4
S FARNSWORTH DR
2000 MESA 85208 783-J4
N FARRELL ST
1200 GIL 85233 781-J4
N FARRIS DR
- SURP 85374 534-B5
E FARVIEW PL
9500 PinC 85219 786-H4
N FATHER KINO TR
39500 CARE 85377 421-A1
S FAWN AV
- MarC 85236 903-C2
E FAWN CIR
1000 MESA 85203 742-A3
S FAWN CT
- MarC 85236 903-C2
E FAWN DR
4000 PHX 85040 779-B3
W FAWN DR
- PHX 85339 777-E2
W FAWN LN
11100 AVON 85323 695-H1
E FAY AV
7600 MESA 85208 783-J1
8000 MESA 85208 784-A1
W FAYE WY
17900 SURP 85387 494-A4
E FAYETTE DR
16300 FTNH 85268 583-C5
N FAYETTE DR
14600 FTNH 85268 583-B5
W F BOND RD
4100 MarC 85087 337-J6
E FEATHER AV
- GIL 85234 783-C5
3600 GIL 85236 783-C5
S FEATHER BUSH CT
5400 PinC 85219 786-F6
E FEATHER BUSH DR
8100 PinC 85219 786-F6
S FEATHERBUSH DR
5600 PinC 85219 786-F6

STREET
Block City ZIP Pg-Grid

E GAIL RD
- SCTS 85259 621-J2
6700 SCTS 85254 620-E2
7800 SCTS 85260 620-J2
8500 SCTS 85260 621-A2
12000 SCTS 85259 622-E2
W GAIL RD
3000 PHX 85029 618-B1
N GAINEY CENTER DR
8700 SCTS 85258 620-H5
E GAINEY CLUB DR
7400 SCTS 85258 620-G5
E GAINEY RANCH RD
7100 SCTS 85258 620-G4
E GAINEY SUITES DR
- SCTS 85258 620-F5
N GALATEA DR
14200 FTNH 85268 583-C6
N GALAXY DR
- CHAN 85226 820-F6
S GALAXY DR
- CHAN 85226 820-F6
W GALAXY DR
12300 MarC 85375 535-E5
E GALE AV
6900 MESA 85208 783-G2
7900 MESA 85208 784-A2
S GALENA CIR
- PHX 85339 777-D3
N GALILEO LN
- SURP 85374 534-E7
N GALLATIN
3800 MESA 85215 703-F3
N GALLATIN CIR
3600 MESA 85215 703-F3
E GALLEGO LN
7200 SCTS 85255 540-G3
W GALLERIA LN
16100 SURP 85374 534-E4
N GALLOWAY DR
- CVCK 85331 420-G3
E GALVESTON ST
- CHAN 85225 821-H5
1900 GIL 85296 822-F5
1900 MarC 85296 822-D5
2300 CHAN 85225 822-B5
13000 GIL 85233 822-B5
16000 GIL 85236 822-H5
16100 GIL 85236 823-A5
16800 MarC 85236 823-C5
18400 MarC 85212 823-C5
22800 MarC 85212 824-H6
S GALVESTON ST
- GIL 85296 822-F5
W GALVESTON ST
- CHAN 85224 820-J5
- CHAN 85225 821-D5
1000 CHAN 85224 821-A5
3000 CHAN 85226 820-A5
7200 CHAN 85226 819-J5
N GALVIN PKWY
1200 PHX 85008 700-C6
GALVIN ST
28800 MarC 85342 411-A4
E GALVIN ST
- CVCK 85331 419-H7
- MarC 85086 (418-J6 See Page 417)
700 MarC 85086 419-A6
N GALVIN ST
- PHX 85086 (418-D6 See Page 417)
W GALVIN ST
- MarC 85086 (418-G6 See Page 417)
1100 PHX 85086 (418-B6 See Page 417)
N GAMBEL DR
12200 FTNH 85268 623-E1
W GAMBIT TR
- PHX 85085 497-C2
- PHX 85085 498-C2
E GAMBLE LN
9400 SCTS 85262 501-D2
W GAMEN TR
- PHX 85085 498-D2
N GAMEZNO CIR
44600 MarC 85087 (378-H2 See Page 337)
N GANADO DR
22300 MarC 85375 494-G7
22300 MarC 85375 534-G1
W GANADO DR
14600 MarC 85375 494-G7
E GARCES ST
100 MarC 85326 (732-B7 See Page 731)
N GARCIA ST
100 WICK 85390 290-F2
E GARDEN CIR
- APJT 85220 745-A3
- MarC 85236 823-D4
W GARDEN CIR
1300 MESA 85201 741-D4
N GARDEN CT
20800 SURP 85374 534-F2
E GARDEN DR
- SCTS 85260 621-B2
3600 PHX 85028 619-G2
W GARDEN DR
2000 TEMP 85282 779-J2
2000 TEMP 85282 780-A2
3800 PHX 85029 617-H1
4300 PHX 85304 617-G1
5100 GLEN 85304 617-B1
N GARDEN LN
3300 AVON 85323 695-G1
W GARDEN ST
1500 MESA 85201 741-D4
E GARDEN CHOLLA DR
26000 SCTS 85255 501-E4
GARDEN CITY RD
- MarC 85342 331-D7
- MarC 85342 (371-E1 See Page 331)
N GARDEN COURT DR
13600 MarC 85351 575-H5
N GARDEN HOME RD
800 AVON 85323 695-C5
N GARDENIA AV
7400 GLEN 85303 617-A7
W GARDENIA AV
- GLEN 85303 616-G7
1300 PHX 85021 618-E7
4500 GLEN 85301 617-C7
6800 GLEN 85303 617-A7
E GARDENIA CIR
1600 PHX 85020 619-A7
E GARDENIA DR
100 AVON 85323 695-B6
300 PHX 85020 618-H7
1200 PHX 85020 658-J1
1200 PHX 85020 659-A1
1800 PHX 85020 619-B7
W GARDENIA DR
100 PHX 85021 618-C7
2800 PHX 85051 618-B7
3500 PHX 85051 617-G7
4300 GLEN 85301 617-E7
N GARDEN LAKES PKWY
2900 AVON 85323 695-G1
3400 AVON 85323 655-H7
W GARDEN LAKES PKWY
3700 AVON 85323 655-H7
N GARDENVIEW DR
18200 MarC 85375 535-A6
W GARDENVIEW DR
13600 MarC 85375 535-B6
N GARDNER CT
1200 CHAN 85224 821-C3
S GARDNER DR
800 CHAN 85224 861-C1
1600 CHAN 85248 861-C1
E GARFIELD ST
- PHX 85004 698-G5
- TEMP 85281 700-E6
700 PHX 85006 698-J5
1400 PHX 85006 699-A5
2800 PHX 85008 699-D5
7200 SCTS 85257 700-F6
8600 SCTS 85257 701-A6
W GARFIELD ST
- GDYR 85338 (694-C4 See Page 653)
1500 PHX 85007 698-D5
2700 PHX 85009 698-A5
3200 PHX 85009 697-J5
5900 PHX 85043 697-A5
6800 PHX 85043 696-J5
9100 TOL 85353 696-C5
N GARLAND CIR
11000 FTNH 85268 622-J2
E GARNET AV
100 MESA 85210 781-H1
400 MESA 85204 781-J1
600 MESA 85204 782-A1
3800 MESA 85206 782-H1
4500 MESA 85206 783-A1
7600 MESA 85208 783-J2
W GARNET AV
600 MESA 85210 781-F1
E GARNET CIR
1100 MESA 85204 782-A1
4000 MESA 85206 782-J1
4600 MESA 85206 783-A1
S GARNET RD
- GIL 85296 782-G7
100 GIL 85296 822-G1
12400 MarC 85326 (773-E7 See Page 733)
12900 MarC 85326 813-E1
W GARNETTE DR
9300 MarC 85373 536-A6
N GARRETT DR
1600 CHAN 85225 821-E2
N GARRISON
- MESA 85220 744-H4
N GARRISON ST
- MESA 85220 744-H4
W GARY AV
- GIL 85233 782-B4
E GARY CIR
200 MESA 85201 741-J2
1200 MESA 85203 742-B2
2000 MESA 85213 742-D2
6200 MESA 85205 743-F2
6900 MESA 85207 743-G2
W GARY CT
600 GIL 85233 782-B4
1100 CHAN 85224 821-D4
E GARY DR
500 CHAN 85225 821-G4
1500 CHAN 85225 822-A4
N GARY DR
1000 CHAN 85224 821-C4
S GARY DR
900 TEMP 85281 740-G4
2300 TEMP 85282 740-G6
W GARY DR
100 CHAN 85225 821-D4
1200 CHAN 85224 821-C4
3200 CHAN 85226 820-B4
E GARY LN
- PHX 85040 778-H3
E GARY RD
6400 SCTS 85254 620-E2
8000 SCTS 85260 620-J2
8400 SCTS 85260 621-A2
10900 SCTS 85259 621-G2
12200 SCTS 85259 622-A2
N GARY RD
- PinC 85242 904-J7
W GARY RD
3300 PHX 85029 618-A1
9100 PEOR 85345 616-D1
E GARY ST
1300 MESA 85207 743-H2
1400 MESA 85203 742-C2
1800 MESA 85213 742-F2
4600 MESA 85205 743-B2
8500 MESA 85207 744-B2
9000 MarC 85207 744-D2
N GARY ST
2600 MESA 85213 742-E2
W GARY ST
1100 MESA 85201 741-E2
1100 MarC 85201 741-E2
E GARY WY
- PHX 85040 779-C3
1000 PHX 85040 778-H3
W GARY WY
- PHX 85339 777-E3
100 PHX 85041 778-D3
N GASLINE RD
4200 MarC 85087 337-H5
W GATES RD
25600 MarC 85342 (371-E5 See Page 331)
E GATEWAY BLVD
500 PHX 85008 699-G6
N GATEWAY BLVD
- PHX 85034 699-H6
500 PHX 85008 699-G6
N GATEWAY CC CIR
400 PHX 85008 699-H6
GATEWAY COMMERCE PARK BLVD
500 PHX 85008 699-G6
W GATEWOOD CT
9700 MarC 85351 576-C6
E GATEWOOD RD
4300 PHX 85050 539-J2
4500 PHX 85050 540-A3
W GATLIN ST
200 GBND 85337 (1090-A2 See Page 1049)
W GATLING WY
1200 CHAN 85248 861-C3
S GAUCHO
2200 MESA 85202 781-A4
W GAUCHO DR
13200 MarC 85375 535-D5
N GAVILAN PEAK PKWY
- MarC 85086 (378-A6 See Page 337)
- MarC 85086 (418-A1 See Page 417)
- MarC 85087 (377-J3 See Page 337)
- MarC 85087 (378-A4 See Page 337)
E GAYLON DR
1600 TEMP 85282 740-G7
N GAYLORD
1100 MESA 85213 742-E2
2200 MESA 85213 702-E6
S GAYLORD
400 MESA 85204 742-E6
1400 MESA 85204 782-E2
N GAYLORD CIR
200 MESA 85213 742-E1
S GAYLORD CIR
1900 MESA 85204 782-D3
N GAYRIDGE RD
2100 MESA 85215 703-D7
W GAYTIME CT
11100 MarC 85351 575-H4
E GAZER TR
- SCTS 85262 (381-D7 See Page 341)
GECKO CT
- FTNH 85268 582-G5
W GECKO CT
11500 SURP 85374 535-H4
W GELDING CIR
- SURP 85379 575-C4
E GELDING DR
- SCTS 85259 581-G5
1700 PHX 85022 579-C4
2800 PHX 85032 579-D4
5000 PHX 85254 580-A5
7600 SCTS 85260 580-H5
8200 SCTS 85260 581-B5
W GELDING DR
- ELMG 85335 575-D4
- SURP 85379 (574-F3 See Page 573)
- SURP 85379 575-D4
2400 PHX 85023 578-C4
2800 PHX 85053 578-A4
3500 PHX 85053 577-H4
4300 PHX 85306 577-F4
5700 GLEN 85306 577-B4
6700 MarC 85381 577-A4
9100 PEOR 85381 576-D4
18500 MarC 85379 573-H3
W GELDING LN
5100 GLEN 85306 577-E4
E GEMINI CT
- MarC 85249 902-C4
E GEMINI DR
400 TEMP 85283 780-E4
S GEMINI DR
6100 TEMP 85283 780-G4
W GEMINI DR
100 TEMP 85283 780-B4
E GEMINI PL
- CHAN 85249 901-G4
E GEMINI ST
2400 GIL 85234 782-J4
2500 GIL 85234 783-A4
E GEMMILL DR
18600 MarC 85263 503-J4
N GEMSTONE DR
17800 MarC 85375 535-B6
S GEM STONE DR
- MarC 85249 902-E4
S GEMSTONE DR
- MarC 85249 902-E5
W GEMSTONE DR
13200 MarC 85375 535-B6
N GENE AV
1400 TEMP 85281 740-E1
N GENEVA AV
1100 CHAN 85226 820-J3
W GENEVA CIR
100 TEMP 85282 740-D7
E GENEVA DR
- TEMP 85282 740-D7
1100 TEMP 85282 780-F1
2200 TEMP 85282 781-A1
2600 TEMP 85282 741-B7
W GENEVA DR
- TEMP 85282 740-B7
2400 TEMP 85282 739-J7
E GENISTA WY
7800 MESA 85208 743-J7
7800 MESA 85208 783-J1
E GENOA WY
15800 FTNH 85268 623-A3
W GENOA WY
3100 CHAN 85226 820-J5
W GENTLE BREEZE WY
- SURP 85374 534-H5
E GENTRY
2200 MESA 85213 702-E7
N GENTRY
2000 MESA 85213 702-D6
S GENTRY
700 MESA 85204 742-D7
1800 MESA 85204 782-D3
E GENTRY CIR
2000 MESA 85213 742-D3
N GENTRY CIR
600 MESA 85213 742-D1
S GENTRY CIR
900 MESA 85204 742-D7
E GENUNG AV
100 WICK 85390 290-E1
200 MarC 85390 290-E1
S GEORGE DR
800 TEMP 85281 741-A4
2700 TEMP 85282 741-A7
3100 TEMP 85282 781-A1
E GEORGE LN
- MarC 85236 823-E5
E GEORGIA AV
200 PHX 85012 658-H4
900 PHX 85014 658-J5
1300 PHX 85014 659-A4
1600 PHX 85016 659-A5
3200 PHX 85018 659-E4
W GEORGIA AV
- MarC 85340 655-D4
- PHX 85013 658-F4
1900 PHX 85015 658-C4
2500 PHX 85017 658-B4
3500 PHX 85017 657-J4
3500 PHX 85019 657-J4
5200 GLEN 85303 656-F4
5400 PHX 85307 656-A4
6100 GLEN 85301 657-B4
6700 GLEN 85303 657-A4
8500 GLEN 85305 656-E4
10600 MarC 85307 655-J4
11100 YNTN 85335 575-H7
19600 MarC 85340 653-E3
N GEORGIA WY
500 TOL 85353 696-D5
E GERMANN RD
- GIL 85236 863-D3
- QC 85236 863-F3
- CHAN 85249 861-H3
- MarC 85249 861-H3
- PinC 85242 865-C4
1500 CHAN 85249 862-B3
5600 MarC 85226 860-B3
7600 MarC 85242 863-J3
7600 MESA 85242 863-J3
7600 MESA 85242 864-D4
7600 QC 85242 863-J3
8800 QC 85242 864-D4
13600 MarC 85296 862-D3
15000 GIL 85296 862-G3
16000 MarC 85296 862-G3
16000 MarC 85236 863-A3
S GERMANN RD
18000 MarC 85326 813-A7
18000 MarC 85326 (853-A1 See Page 813)
W GERMANN RD
- CHAN 85248 861-C3
- PinC 85242 865-A4
100 PinC 85242 864-J4
3000 CHAN 85248 860-J3
16500 GDYR 85326 (854-A1 See Page 813)
17300 GDYR 85326 (853-G1 See Page 813)
18700 MarC 85326 (853-C1 See Page 813)
E GERONIMO CT
700 CHAN 85225 861-H1
W GERONIMO CT
5900 CHAN 85226 820-C7
E GERONIMO PL
- CHAN 85225 861-H1
W GERONIMO PL
1100 CHAN 85224 861-D1
E GERONIMO RD
13600 SCTS 85259 622-E2
N GERONIMO RD
200 PinC 85219 746-C3
S GERONIMO RD
- PinC 85219 746-C7
1000 PinC 85219 786-C2
E GERONIMO ST
600 CHAN 85225 861-G1
1700 CHAN 85225 862-A1
W GERONIMO ST
100 CHAN 85225 861-D1
700 CHAN 85226 820-C7
1500 CHAN 85224 861-C1
3700 CHAN 85226 860-F1
S GERONIMO HIKING TR
5800 PinC 85219 786-C3
W GERSHWIN DR
- MarC 85086 (378-B7 See Page 337)
N GHOST RIDER ST
35300 PinC 85242 905-H7
N GHOST RIDERS
18200 SURP 85374 534-B5
S GIBBEL RD
- GIL 85236 863-D5
W GIBBONS RD
1100 MarC 85087 (338-G6 See Page 337)
W GIBRALTAR LN
500 PHX 85023 578-G3
E GIBSON LN
1100 PHX 85034 738-J3
1600 PHX 85034 739-A3
W GIBSON LN
- PHX 85043 736-F2
200 PHX 85003 738-F2
3200 PHX 85009 737-G2
22400 BUCK 85326 (732-G1 See Page 731)
22600 MarC 85326 (732-F1 See Page 731)
N GIBSON ST
1000 GIL 85234 782-D4
S GIBSON ST
200 GIL 85296 822-D1
E GILA BEND
- SCTS 85258 660-G1
N GILA BLVD
200 MarC 85337 (1089-J2 See Page 1049)
200 GBND 85337 (1089-J2 See Page 1049)
S GILA BLVD
50900 MarC 85337 1049-J7
50900 GBND 85337 1049-J7
52500 MarC 85337 (1089-J1 See Page 1049)
E GILA CT
2500 GIL 85236 822-J3
2500 GIL 85236 823-A3
E GILA LN
600 CHAN 85225 821-G3
W GILA LN
700 CHAN 85225 821-E3
1300 CHAN 85224 821-A2
S GILA PL
26600 MarC 85248 901-B6
N GILA RD
3900 PinC 85219 745-G1
4500 PinC 85219 705-G7
E GILA ST
- GIL 85236 822-J3
S GILA BEND AIRPORT RD
- GBND 85337 (1090-F1 See Page 1049)
W GILA MONSTER CT
11500 SURP 85374 535-H4
E GILA MONSTER DR
2900 PinC 85242 865-E7
N GILA SPRINGS BLVD
- CHAN 85226 820-D5
S GILA SPRINGS BLVD
- CHAN 85226 820-C6
N GILA SPRINGS DR
- SURP 85374 534-G5
N GILA VERDE
800 MESA 85207 744-A3
N GIL BALCOME
- SURP 85379 575-C3
N GIL BALCOME CT
- SURP 85379 575-D2
E GILBERT DR
700 TEMP 85281 740-F2
900 MarC 85281 740-F2
N GILBERT RD
- GIL 85233 782-C6
- GIL 85234 782-C6
- MESA 85213 742-D4
- MESA 85203 742-D4
1600 MarC 85203 702-D4
1600 MarC 85213 702-D4
1600 MESA 85213 702-D4
1800 MESA 85203 702-D4
3900 MarC 85256 662-D7
3900 MarC 85256 702-D4
S GILBERT RD
- PinC - 902-C7
- GIL 85233 782-C7
- MESA 85204 742-D6
- GIL 85296 782-C7
100 GIL 85233 822-C3
100 GIL 85296 822-C3
400 MarC 85296 822-C6
600 MarC 85233 822-C3
900 MESA 85204 782-D2
4800 MarC 85249 902-C1
14600 CHAN 85233 822-C6
15200 CHAN 85225 822-C6
15600 GIL 85225 822-C6
15600 MarC 85225 822-C6
16800 CHAN 85296 862-C4
16800 MarC 85296 862-C4
18800 CHAN 85249 862-C4
20400 MarC 85249 862-C4
25200 CHAN 85249 902-C4
E GILDED PERCH DR
8100 SCTS 85255 540-J4
8100 SCTS 85255 541-A4
E GILDED PERCH LN
- SCTS 85255 541-A5
S GILLETTE CT
200 CHAN 85226 820-D7
N GILLETTE DR
- CHAN 85226 820-D6
S GILLETTE DR
100 CHAN 85226 820-D6
N GILLON
- MarC 85207 744-E2
S GILMORE
800 MESA 85206 742-H7
900 MESA 85206 782-H1
S GILMORE CIR
1700 MESA 85206 782-H3
N GINA AV
1500 PHX 85020 619-A6
W GINGER CT
12300 MarC 85375 535-F5
N GINGER DR
18800 MarC 85375 535-E5
W GINGER DR
12400 MarC 85375 535-E5
S GINTRY DR
- PinC 85219 786-E7
S GIRARD ST
- GIL 85236 863-B5
W GLACIER CT
- MarC 85087 (378-A3 See Page 337)
E GLADE AV
- MESA 85206 783-C2
100 MESA 85210 781-H1
400 MESA 85204 781-J1
600 MESA 85204 782-A1
3700 MESA 85206 782-H1
7600 MESA 85208 783-J2
7900 MESA 85208 784-A2
E GLADE CIR
1100 MESA 85204 782-B1
4000 MESA 85206 782-J1
4500 MESA 85206 783-A1
S GLADIOLUS
2100 MESA 85208 783-J4
E GLASS LN
- PHX 85040 779-C1
E GLEN DR
5700 PVAL 85253 660-C1
W GLENAIRE DR
3900 PHX 85053 577-H4
E GLENBROOK BLVD
16000 FTNH 85268 583-C4
S GLENBURN DR
9600 MarC 85248 901-B2
N GLEN CANYON CT
9100 MarC 85351 576-E1
E GLENCOVE AV
8500 MESA 85207 744-B2
9000 MarC 85207 744-C2
E GLENCOVE CIR
- MarC 85207 744-E2
1200 MESA 85203 742-B2
2300 MESA 85213 742-E2
5200 MESA 85205 743-C2
7500 MESA 85207 743-J2
E GLENCOVE ST
- MarC 85207 744-E2
- MESA 85207 744-E2
200 MESA 85201 741-J2
400 MESA 85203 741-J2
900 MESA 85203 742-A2
1800 MESA 85213 742-D2
4000 MESA 85205 742-J2
4200 MESA 85205 743-A2
7200 MESA 85207 743-H2
E GLENDALE AV
- PHX 85012 658-H1
- PHX 85020 658-H1
700 PHX 85014 658-H1
1200 PHX 85020 659-A1
1200 PHX 85014 659-A1
1600 PHX 85016 659-B1
W GLENDALE AV
- PHX 85013 658-B1
- PHX 85021 658-B1
1500 PHX 85015 658-B1
2400 PHX 85051 658-B1
2400 PHX 85017 658-B1
3400 PHX 85017 657-F1
3500 PHX 85051 657-F1
3500 PHX 85019 657-F1
4300 GLEN 85301 657-A1
6700 GLEN 85303 657-A1
7100 GLEN 85303 656-G1
8200 GLEN 85305 656-C1
9100 MarC 85305 656-C1
9900 GLEN 85307 656-C1
10600 GLEN 85307 655-H1
10900 MarC 85307 655-H1
12200 MarC 85307 615-D7
13100 GLEN 85307 615-D7
15500 MarC 85309 (614-E7 See Page 573)
15500 MarC 85340 (614-E7 See Page 573)
17100 MarC 85355 (614-B7 See Page 573)
17700 MarC 85355 (613-G7 See Page 573)
W GLENDORA CT
16100 SURP 85374 534-E7
E GLENDORA DR
16000 FTNH 85268 583-B5
E GLENEAGLE DR
1300 CHAN 85249 901-J6
1700 CHAN 85249 902-A6
16000 FTNH 85268 583-B5
W GLENEAGLES DR
300 PHX 85023 578-F4
N GLEN HARBOR BLVD
6100 GLEN 85307 655-H2
7000 GLEN 85307 615-J7
7300 GLEN 85307 616-A6
E GLENHAVEN DR
200 PHX 85048 818-G7
2000 PHX 85048 819-B7
W GLENHAVEN DR
- PHX 85045 818-C6
- PHX 85048 818-E7
1800 PHX 85041 818-C6
S GLENMAR RD
- MarC 85208 744-C6
E GLENMERE DR
700 CHAN 85225 821-G7
W GLENMERE DR
600 CHAN 85224 821-C7
E GLENN DR
- PHX 85020 658-G1
1300 PHX 85020 659-A1
W GLENN DR
- GLEN 85303 617-A7
- PHX 85021 658-D1
2800 PHX 85051 658-A1
3300 PHX 85051 657-H1
4800 GLEN 85301 657-C1
6700 GLEN 85303 657-A1
7500 GLEN 85303 616-H7
8100 GLEN 85303 656-G1
10900 GLEN 85307 615-J7
E GLENN MOOR RD
10700 SCTS 85255 501-G7
E GLENN MOORE RD
7400 SCTS 85255 500-H6
W GLEN OAKS CIR
9200 MarC 85351 576-C1
E GLENPOINT DR
16100 FTNH 85268 583-B5
E GLENROSA AV
1000 PHX 85014 658-J7
1300 PHX 85014 659-A7
1600 PHX 85016 659-B7
3200 PHX 85018 659-E7
6900 SCTS 85251 660-E7
W GLENROSA AV
- MarC 85037 655-H6
- PHX 85013 658-F7
1500 PHX 85015 658-C6
2500 PHX 85017 658-A6
3300 PHX 85017 657-J6
4000 PHX 85019 657-G6
4300 PHX 85031 657-D6
6300 PHX 85033 657-B6
7100 PHX 85033 656-F6
8300 PHX 85037 656-A6
10700 PHX 85037 655-H6
E GLENROSA DR
- MarC 85256 661-H7
- MarC 85256 701-H1
E GLENSIDE CT
9600 MarC 85248 901-B6
N GLENVIEW
100 MESA 85213 742-E4
2100 MESA 85213 702-E6
S GLENVIEW
1400 MESA 85204 782-E2
N GLENVIEW CIR
400 MESA 85213 742-E4
S GLENVIEW CIR
600 MESA 85204 742-E7
1300 MESA 85204 782-E2
E GLENVIEW DR
16000 FTNH 85268 583-B5
E GLENVIEW PL
16000 FTNH 85268 583-B5
W GLENVIEW PL
4600 CHAN 85226 820-C6
S GLENWOOD CIR
500 MESA 85204 742-G7
W GLOBE
- MarC 85086 417-J4
E GLOBE MALLOW LN
- PinC 85219 786-E5
S GLOBE MALLOW LN
- PinC 85219 786-E5
E GLORIA DR
8100 PHX 85040 778-G3
E GLORIA LN
5200 PHX 85331 460-B4
6400 MarC 85331 460-E4
E GLORIA ST
5600 GUAD 85283 780-A3
S GLORY CT
- MarC 85236 903-D3
N GLORY DR
- MarC 85086 (378-C7 See Page 337)
N GNATCATCHER LN
17700 SURP 85374 535-H6
W GNATCATCHER LN
11500 SURP 85374 535-H6
N GOLD CT
16200 FTNH 85268 583-A3
N GOLD DR
200 APJT 85220 745-C3
4400 PinC 85220 705-C6
S GOLD DR
- APJT 85220 745-C6
E GOLD BLUFF RD
- SCTS 85262 421-E7
S GOLD CANYON DR
4500 PinC 85219 786-H6
N GOLDCLIFF CIR
- MESA 85207 704-A3
E GOLD CREEK CT
- MarC 85263 (504-A3 See Page 503)
E GOLD DUST AV
3300 PHX 85028 619-F3
4600 PHX 85253 619-J3
5000 PVAL 85253 620-A3
5200 PHX 85253 620-C3
6400 SCTS 85253 620-E3
7200 SCTS 85258 620-H3
9400 SCTS 85258 621-C3
11700 SCTS 85259 621-J3
12000 SCTS 85259 622-A3
N GOLD DUST AV
10300 SCTS 85258 621-D3
W GOLD DUST AV
8900 PEOR 85345 616-E2
N GOLD DUST CT
17000 MarC 85373 576-D1
W GOLD DUST LN
- WICK 85390 290-A1
E GOLD DUST PL
9900 PinC 85219 786-H5
E GOLD DUST ST
1700 PHX 85020 619-B3
N GOLD DUST ST
7900 PEOR 85345 616-G2
W GOLD DUST ST
7900 PEOR 85345 616-G2
W GOLDEN AV
- GLEN 85302 617-B4
E GOLDEN CT
1000 CHAN 85225 821-H3
1900 CHAN 85225 822-A3
E GOLDEN LN
1300 PHX 85020 619-A4
1700 CHAN 85225 822-A3
W GOLDEN LN
1000 PHX 85021 618-E4
2900 PHX 85051 618-A4
3100 CHAN 85226 820-H3
3700 PHX 85051 617-H4
4300 GLEN 85302 617-B4
7700 PEOR 85345 616-A4
8800 GLEN 85345 617-A4
10900 PEOR 85345 615-H4
S GOLDEN RD
3700 PinC 85219 786-H4
E GOLDEN ST
- GIL 85296 822-C4
2500 MESA 85213 742-E2
4900 MESA 85205 743-B2
N GOLDEN ST
- MarC 85207 744-E2
W GOLDEN ST
500 GIL 85233 822-A3
E GOLDEN CHOLLA CIR
8500 PinC 85219 786-F6
E GOLDEN CHOLLA DR
8200 PinC 85219 786-F6
E GOLDEN EAGLE BLVD
14400 FTNH 85268 582-H3
14700 FTNH 85268 583-A5
GOLDEN EAGLE CIR
- PinC 85219 786-E3
GOLDEN EAGLE DR
- PinC 85219 786-E3
N GOLDEN ECHO DR
47700 MarC 85087 (338-F5 See Page 337)
GOLDEN EYE LN
- PinC 85219 786-F4
E GOLDEN HILLS WY
6800 MESA 85208 743-G6
N GOLDEN KEY CT
1100 GIL 85233 782-B3
N GOLDEN KEY DR
600 GIL 85233 782-B5
S GOLDEN KEY DR
- GIL 85233 782-B7
100 GIL 85233 822-B1
N GOLDEN KEY ST
800 GIL 85233 782-B4
S GOLDEN KEY ST
400 GIL 85233 822-B1
S GOLDEN KEYS ST
500 GIL 85233 822-B2
W GOLDEN KEYS WY
800 CHAN 85226 820-G4
W GOLDEN PRINCE PL
- SURP 85374 575-G1
E GOLDEN RIM CIR
3900 PinC 85219 786-H4
W GOLDENROD DR
15700 SURP 85374 534-F6
E GOLDENROD ST
600 PHX 85048 818-G5
2300 PHX 85048 819-A5
E GOLDEN SPUR LN
8000 CARE 85377 420-J3
8000 CARE 85377 421-A2
N GOLDEN SPUR LN
38800 CARE 85377 421-B2
E GOLDEN VISTA LN
3000 PHX 85028 619-E4
N GOLDFIELD RD
- APJT 85219 745-J5
S GOLDFIELD RD
- APJT 85219 745-J7
700 APJT 85219 785-J1
E GOLDFIELD GATE
- APJT 85219 785-H3
S GOLDFINCH DR
- MarC 85236 863-B3
W GOLDFINCH WY
1000 CHAN 85248 861-C4
E GOLDFINCH GATE LN
3600 PHX 85044 819-F3
S GOLD LEAF PL
- MarC 85249 902-F5
S GOLD NUGGET CT
- PinC 85219 826-H3
W GOLDPOPPY ST
600 PHX 85220 705-D6
E GOLD POPPY WY
4400 PHX 85044 819-G4
S GOLD POPPY WY
4300 PHX 85044 819-G4
S GOLDSTRIKE
20100 GIL 85236 863-A5
20100 MarC 85236 863-A5

STREET
Block City ZIP Pg-Grid

N GOLDWATER BLVD
3500 SCTS 85251 700-F1
4100 SCTS 85251 660-F6
N GOLDWATER DR
18000 SURP 85374 533-J6
18000 SURP 85374 534-A6
N GOLDWATER CANYON DR
16100 SURP 85374 534-E5
N GOLDWATER RIDGE DR
15700 SURP 85374 534-F6
E GOLF AV
2000 TEMP 85282 780-J1
2100 TEMP 85282 740-J7
2100 TEMP 85282 741-A7
7600 MESA 85208 783-J2
E GOLF DR
6900 PVAL 85253 620-F5
N GOLF DR
8000 PVAL 85253 620-F6
S GOLF DR
3100 TEMP 85282 740-J7
3100 TEMP 85282 780-J1
E GOLF TR
10000 SCTS 85262 421-F4
N GOLF CLUB DR
9900 SCTS 85255 501-E6
22000 MarC 85375 535-B1
S GOLF CLUB DR
- GDYR 85326 (774-A7
See Page 733)
11500 GDYR 85338 (774-A7
See Page 733)
S GOLF COURSE RD
- GDYR 85338 (734-F7
See Page 733)
- GDYR 85338 (774-G1
See Page 733)
W GOLF CREST CT
3100 MarC 85086 (378-B5
See Page 337)
S GOLFSIDE LN
- PHX 85040 779-D2
E GOMPERS CIR
100 MarC 85342 (412-D3
See Page 411)
W GOMPERS CIR
100 MarC 85342 (412-D3
See Page 411)
E GONDOLA CIR
1900 GIL 85234 782-H4
E GONDOLA LN
2000 GIL 85234 782-H4
GOODYEAR BLVD E
- GDYR 85338 (694-F7
See Page 653)
GOODYEAR BLVD N
- GDYR 85338 (694-F7
See Page 653)
GOODYEAR BLVD W
- GDYR 85338 (694-F7
See Page 653)
- GDYR 85338 (734-E1
See Page 733)
GOODYEAR RD
- PinC - 901-B7
E GOODYEAR RD
- LP 85340 655-A6
W GOOLD BLVD
- AVON 85323 695-B7
S GOPHER RD
12400 MarC 85326 (773-D7
See Page 733)
12900 MarC 85326 813-D1
N GORDEN DR
9600 FTNH 85264 623-E4
9600 FTNH 85268 623-E4
S GORDON
- MESA 85208 784-B4
- MESA 85212 784-B6
N GRACE BLVD
2000 CHAN 85225 821-F2
W GRACE BLVD
- CHAN 85225 821-F1
E GRACE DR
600 TEMP 85281 700-E7
N GRACE DR
1300 SCTS 85257 701-A5
N GRACE ST
800 SCTS 85257 700-J6
W GRAFCO WY
- CHAN 85226 820-A5
E GRANADA AV
800 APJT 85219 785-F1
E GRANADA CIR
1400 MESA 85203 742-C2
E GRANADA DR
700 TEMP 85281 740-F5
2200 TEMP 85281 741-A6
N GRANADA DR
700 CHAN 85226 820-H3
S GRANADA DR
1700 TEMP 85281 740-E5
2000 TEMP 85282 740-F6
6500 TEMP 85283 780-E5
W GRANADA DR
9500 MarC 85373 576-A1
10800 MarC 85373 535-H7
10800 MarC 85373 575-J1
E GRANADA RD
700 PHX 85006 698-H4
1400 PHX 85006 699-A4
2400 PHX 85008 699-C4
6600 SCTS 85257 700-E4
N GRANADA RD
5400 PVAL 85253 620-B7
W GRANADA RD
- AVON 85323 695-C3
- AVON 85323 696-A3
100 PHX 85003 698-F4
500 PHX 85007 698-D4
1800 PHX 85037 696-D3
1900 PHX 85009 698-A4
3200 PHX 85009 697-G4
4500 PHX 85035 697-A3
7100 PHX 85035 696-H3
13100 GDYR 85338 695-C3
E GRANADA ST
- MESA 85207 743-G2
1200 MESA 85203 742-B2
E GRANADA PARK DR
- PHX 85016 659-B2
W GRANBURY CT
- SURP 85374 534-G5
N GRAND
400 MESA 85201 741-G1
1700 MESA 85201 701-G7
37300 MarC 85086 417-J3

S GRAND
400 MESA 85210 741-G7
1000 MESA 85210 781-G1
GRAND AV
700 PHX 85007 698-E5
GRAND AV U.S.-60
- MarC 85374 575-C1
- PEOR 85351 576-E7
- PHX 85017 657-H6
- SURP 85374 575-C1
1900 PHX 85009 698-B2
3100 PHX 85017 698-B2
3600 PHX 85019 657-H6
3600 PHX 85017 658-A7
8700 PEOR 85345 576-E7
8700 PEOR 85345 616-G3
9300 PEOR 85381 576-E7
9900 MarC 85351 576-A6
13500 MarC 85374 535-A6
13500 MarC 85375 535-A6
13500 SURP 85374 535-A6
13900 SURP 85375 535-A6
14300 MarC 85374 534-G3
14300 MarC 85375 534-G3
14300 SURP 85374 534-G3
14500 SURP 85375 534-G3
15800 SURP 85387 534-G3
16000 MarC 85375 494-C5
16000 MarC 85387 534-G3
16000 SURP 85375 494-C5
16300 SURP 85387 494-C5
17500 MarC 85387 494-C5
17900 MarC 85361 494-C5
17900 MarC 85375 493-G1
17900 MarC 85361 493-G1
19100 MarC 85361 (453-F7
See Page 413)
19300 MarC 85375 (453-F7
See Page 413)
NW GRAND AV
12700 SURP 85374 575-D2
14600 ELMG 85335 575-E3
15400 SURP 85374 575-D2
NW GRAND AV U.S.-60
- SURP 85374 575-J5
10700 MarC 85351 575-J5
10700 MarC 85351 576-A5
11100 YNTN 85335 575-J5
11300 MarC 85335 575-J5
11300 ELMG 85335 575-J5
13400 SURP 85335 575-J5
W GRAND AV
3000 PHX 85017 698-A1
8100 PEOR 85345 616-G2
11700 ELMG 85335 575-F4
W GRAND AV U.S.-60
3900 PHX 85019 657-F3
4300 GLEN 85301 657-D1
5900 GLEN 85301 617-B6
6700 GLEN 85301 616-J5
6700 GLEN 85345 616-J5
7100 PEOR 85345 616-E1
N GRAND DR
800 APJT 85220 745-B3
4200 PinC 85220 705-B7
4200 PinC 85220 745-B3
S GRAND DR
- APJT 85220 745-B6
1300 APJT 85220 785-B1
N GRAND ST
- MarC 85256 701-H1
W GRAND CANYON UNIV
3400 PHX 85017 657-J5
W GRAND CAYMEN DR
900 GIL 85233 822-A2
1000 GIL 85233 821-J2
W GRAND CREEK LN
15600 SURP 85374 534-G3
GRAND CSR
- GLEN - 656-G3
- MarC - 656-E3
- PHX - 656-H5
- PHX - 657-A6
- PHX - 658-G6
- PHX - 659-A7
- PHX - 697-H1
- PHX - 698-A1
- PHX - 699-A1
- PHX - 739-H1
- PHX - 740-A1
- TEMP - 740-B1
E GRANDE BLVD
16800 FTNH 85268 583-E6
17400 MarC 85268 583-E6
17400 FTNH 85264 583-E6
17400 MarC 85264 583-F7
17900 MarC 85264 623-F1
W GRAND ISLE WY
15800 SURP 85374 534-F4
W GRAND POINT LN
15700 SURP 85374 534-F3
S GRANDVIEW AV
- TEMP 85284 820-D1
3700 TEMP 85282 780-D1
7900 TEMP 85284 780-D7
E GRANDVIEW CIR
- MarC 85207 744-D2
2300 MESA 85213 742-E2
4100 MESA 85205 742-J2
6200 MESA 85205 743-E2
7500 MESA 85207 743-J2
GRANDVIEW DR
- FTNH 85268 582-H7
E GRANDVIEW DR
1800 PHX 85022 579-B2
8500 MESA 85207 744-B2
9000 MarC 85207 744-B2
N GRANDVIEW DR
18800 MarC 85375 535-A5
S GRANDVIEW DR
1400 TEMP 85281 740-D5
2500 TEMP 85282 740-D7
8800 TEMP 85284 820-D2
W GRANDVIEW DR
1900 PHX 85023 578-D2
E GRANDVIEW LN
4900 PHX 85018 660-A5
S GRANDVIEW LN
- PinC 85219 786-D1
E GRANDVIEW RD
300 PHX 85022 578-H2
1100 PHX 85022 579-A2
2400 PHX 85032 579-D2
4600 PHX 85032 580-A2
4900 PHX 85254 580-A2
N GRANDVIEW RD
16400 PHX 85053 577-H2
W GRANDVIEW RD
- GLEN 85308 577-A1
- GLEN 85382 576-J1

W GRANDVIEW RD
- GLEN 85382 577-A1
- PHX 85023 578-C2
2600 PHX 85053 578-A2
3600 PHX 85053 577-H2
4700 PHX 85306 577-F2
6000 GLEN 85306 577-B1
E GRANDVIEW ST
- MarC 85207 744-D2
200 MESA 85201 741-J2
500 MESA 85203 741-J2
700 MESA 85203 742-A2
1200 MESA 85213 742-D2
1300 MESA 85205 743-A2
4000 MESA 85205 742-J2
7200 MESA 85207 743-G2
W GRANDVIEW ST
900 MESA 85201 741-E2
N GRAND VISTA RD
24400 SCTS 85255 501-D6
E GRANITE CIR
2200 MESA 85204 782-D1
S GRANITE CIR
300 GIL 85296 822-G1
E GRANITE CT
5400 PinC 85219 786-B1
N GRANITE CT
- GIL 85234 782-G7
S GRANITE CT
- GIL 85296 822-G5
N GRANITE DR
3600 GDYR 85338 (654-F7
See Page 653)
S GRANITE DR
5200 PinC 85219 786-E6
23600 MarC 85248 901-A2
N GRANITE ST
400 GIL 85234 782-G4
S GRANITE ST
400 GIL 85296 822-G2
GRANITE WY
- FTNH 85268 582-J7
N GRANITE MOUNTAIN RD
- MarC 85263 503-J3
- MarC 85263 (504-A3
See Page 503)
E GRANITE PASS RD
- SCTS 85262 460-J2
- SCTS 85262 (461-A2
See Page 421)
N GRANITE REEF RD
800 SCTS 85257 700-J4
2900 SCTS 85251 700-J1
4200 SCTS 85251 660-J6
5000 SCTS 85250 660-J2
31100 SCTS 85262 (461-A5
See Page 421)
W GRANITE VALLEY DR
14300 MarC 85375 534-J3
14300 MarC 85375 535-A4
E GRANITE VIEW DR
2000 PHX 85048 819-A4
3300 PHX 85044 819-E4
S GRANITE VIEW DR
1200 PHX 85048 818-H4
W GRAN PARADISO DR
- PHX 85086 (418-B6
See Page 417)
E GRANT ST
- PHX 85004 738-G1
1500 PHX 85034 739-A1
N GRANT ST
- WICK 85390 290-E3
S GRANT ST
700 MarC 85337 (1090-E4
See Page 1049)
W GRANT ST
- GDYR 85338 (694-D6
See Page 653)
- PHX 85003 738-F1
600 PHX 85007 738-E1
1500 PHX 85007 698-D7
1900 PHX 85009 698-B7
3500 PHX 85009 697-G7
6500 PHX 85043 697-A7
8000 PEOR 85345 616-G1
S GRANTE ST
- GIL 85296 822-G6
- MarC 85296 822-G6
W GRANT MINE RD
20400 MarC 85361 493-C1
S GRAPE AV
- MarC 85242 903-C6
W GRAPEFRUIT CT
11600 SURP 85374 535-G5
S GRAPEFRUIT DR
25200 MarC 85242 903-G6
E GRAPEVINE RD
5800 CVCK 85331 420-E3
7200 CARE 85377 420-H3
N GRAPEVINE RD
38200 CVCK 85331 420-G3
E GRAPEVINE RD N
6700 CVCK 85331 420-G2
6900 CARE 85377 420-G2
7800 CARE 85377 421-A1
7800 CVCK 85331 421-A1
E GRASSLAND DR
15500 FTNH 85268 583-A3
E GRAVEL PIT RD
4800 MESA 85215 703-B2
16400 MarC 85215 703-B2
E GRAY RD
7500 SCTS 85260 580-H5
8800 SCTS 85260 581-B5
W GRAY WY
5000 GLEN 85301 617-E7
E GRAYHAWK DR
7200 PHX 85255 540-H4
7200 SCTS 85255 540-H4
N GRAYHAWK DR
8200 SCTS 85255 541-A5
20800 SCTS 85255 540-J3
E GRAYTHORN AV
4200 PHX 85044 819-F5
E GRAYTHORN DR
10500 SCTS 85262 421-E2
E GRAYTHORN ST
3900 PHX 85044 819-F5
N GRAYTHORN WY
17800 FTNH 85268 583-A6
E GREASEWOOD ST
1900 APJT 85219 745-J6
4300 PinC 85219 746-B5
N GREASEWOOD ST
15400 SURP 85374 575-E1
16800 SURP 85374 535-E7
W GREASEWOOD ST
600 APJT 85220 745-C5

W GREAT BASIN CT
11500 SURP 85374 535-H5
N GREEN RD
100 MarC 85342 (412-D3
See Page 411)
N GREENAN RD
24000 SCTS 85255 501-F6
W GREENBRIAN DR
8600 PEOR 85382 536-E7
W GREENBRIAR CIR
900 MESA 85201 741-E1
W GREENBRIAR DR
1900 PHX 85023 538-D7
5000 PHX 85308 537-E7
6700 GLEN 85308 537-A7
E GREENBRIAR LN
16600 FTNH 85268 623-C4
W GREENBRIER DR
5500 GLEN 85308 537-C7
S GREENCASTLE DR
25800 MarC 85248 901-C5
E GREENE VALLEY DR
15000 FTNH 85268 582-H2
N GREENFIELD RD
- MarC 85215 703-A1
- MarC 85256 663-A7
- MarC 85256 703-A1
- MESA 85205 743-A1
800 GIL 85234 782-J4
1600 MESA 85205 703-A7
2000 MESA 85215 703-A7
2000 MarC 85234 782-J4
2700 PHX 85006 699-C1
2900 PHX 85016 699-B2
S GREENFIELD RD
- MESA 85206 743-A6
100 GIL 85234 782-J3
100 MarC 85234 782-J7
900 MESA 85206 783-A2
1600 MESA 85206 782-J3
10800 GIL 85296 782-J7
10800 GIL 85296 822-J5
10800 GIL 85236 782-J7
10800 GIL 85236 822-J5
12100 MarC 85236 822-J5
12100 MarC 85296 822-J5
16400 MarC 85236 862-J4
17200 MarC 85236 862-J4
20400 MarC 85249 862-J4
22000 MarC 85249 902-J2
22000 MarC 85236 902-J2
GREEN HOLLOW TER
14100 LP 85340 655-A5
W GREENHURST AV
14400 FTNH 85268 583-C5
W GREENHURST DR
9500 MarC 85351 576-C2
S GREENLEAF
800 AVON 85323 735-A2
800 AVON 85338 735-A2
E GREEN RIVER LN
- MarC 85263 503-J6
E GREENTREE DR
- TEMP 85284 820-D2
4700 LP 85340 655-A4
W GREENTREE DR
- TEMP 85284 819-J2
- TEMP 85284 820-A2
400 CHAN 85225 821-E2
W GREENTREE DR S
4900 LP 85340 655-A4
14100 LP 85340 (654-J5
See Page 653)
N GREENTREE DR W
4800 LP 85340 (654-J4
See Page 653)
N GREENVIEW CIR
4600 LP 85340 (654-J5
See Page 653)
4600 LP 85340 655-A5
W GREENVIEW CIR
4700 LP 85340 (654-J5
See Page 653)
4700 LP 85340 655-A5
E GREENVIEW DR
- MarC 85236 903-E3
8700 PinC 85219 786-G7
N GREENVIEW DR
19800 MarC 85375 535-B4
W GREENVIEW DR
13500 MarC 85375 535-B3
E GREENWAY
4200 MESA 85205 742-J2
4200 MESA 85205 743-A2
E GREENWAY CIR
1200 MESA 85203 742-B2
1700 PHX 85040 779-A2
4000 MESA 85205 742-J2
5200 MESA 85205 743-C2
7500 MESA 85207 743-J2
E GREENWAY DR
400 TEMP 85282 780-F2
W GREENWAY DR
1000 TEMP 85282 780-B2
E GREENWAY LN
3200 PHX 85032 579-F3
5900 PHX 85254 580-D4
E GREENWAY PKWY
- PHX 85022 578-H2
600 PHX 85022 579-C2
2400 PHX 85032 579-C2
6400 PHX 85254 580-F4
W GREENWAY PKWY
- PHX 85022 578-F3
- PHX 85023 578-F3
E GREENWAY RD
- SCTS 85259 581-G4
- PHX 85040 778-G1
1400 PHX 85040 779-A2
1900 PHX 85022 579-C3
2400 PHX 85032 579-H3
4900 PHX 85254 580-C4
7300 SCTS 85260 580-H4
9100 SCTS 85260 580-C4
N GREENWAY RD
- SCTS 85259 581-G4
W GREENWAY RD
- GLEN 85382 576-J2
1900 PHX 85023 578-B3
2400 TEMP 85282 779-J2
2600 PHX 85053 578-B3
3400 SURP 85374 (574-B2
See Page 573)
3400 SURP 85379 (574-B2
See Page 573)
3500 PHX 85053 577-G3
4300 PHX 85306 577-G3
5100 GLEN 85306 577-B3
6700 GLEN 85382 577-B3
6700 GLEN 85381 577-B3

W GREENWAY RD
7100 MarC 85382 576-J2
7100 MarC 85382 577-B3
7100 MarC 85381 576-J2
7100 MarC 85381 577-B3
7700 PEOR 85382 576-G3
7700 PEOR 85381 576-J2
9000 PEOR 85351 576-D3
9100 MarC 85351 576-D3
12300 SURP 85374 575-C2
12300 SURP 85335 575-E2
12600 ELMG 85335 575-C2
13100 SURP 85379 575-C2
13900 MarC 85374 575-C2
13900 MarC 85379 575-C2
16600 MarC 85374 (574-B2
See Page 573)
16600 MarC 85379 (574-B2
See Page 573)
17900 MarC 85374 573-G2
17900 SURP 85374 573-G2
17900 MarC 85379 573-G2
18500 MarC 85373 573-G2
18500 SURP 85373 573-G2
E GREENWAY ST
- MarC 85207 744-E3
800 MESA 85203 742-A2
1200 MESA 85205 743-A2
2000 MESA 85213 742-D2
7000 MESA 85207 743-H2
W GREENWAY ST
900 MESA 85201 741-E2
N GREENWAY HAYDEN LP
8000 SCTS 85260 580-G3
N GREENWOOD
400 MESA 85207 743-J4
S GREENWOOD
2800 MESA 85212 783-J6
S GREENWOOD CIR
3000 MESA 85212 783-J6
W GREER AV
7900 PEOR 85345 616-E1
10900 MarC 85351 615-J1
11100 YNTN 85335 615-H1
W GREGG DR
2300 CHAN 85224 781-A7
2500 MarC 85224 781-A7
N GREGORY PL
600 CHAN 85226 820-B4
W GREGORY ST
1900 APJT 85220 745-A5
W GRENADINE RD
- PHX 85339 737-D6
N GRENOBLE
- MESA 85220 784-H1
E GRETTA PL
2100 PHX 85022 579-C3
S GREYHORNE WY
4600 CHAN 85248 901-B1
N GREYLOCK CIR
3600 MESA 85215 703-F3
E GREYSTONE DR
15400 FTNH 85268 622-J1
15500 FTNH 85268 623-A1
W GREYSTONE DR
14400 MarC 85375 534-F1
E GREYTHORN DR
- SCTS 85331 500-C2
10700 SCTS 85255 501-G2
S GREYTHORNE WY
1900 CHAN 85248 861-B5
W GRIFFIN AV
7300 GLEN 85303 656-H2
8300 GLEN 85305 656-F2
21700 MarC 85361 (453-A1
See Page 413)
33000 MarC 85361 (452-J1
See Page 411)
S GRIFFITH WY
- GIL 85236 863-C5
E GRISWOLD RD
- PHX 85020 618-H6
1400 PHX 85020 619-A6
7200 SCTS 85258 620-G6
W GRISWOLD RD
- PHX 85021 618-E6
2700 PHX 85051 618-A6
3500 PHX 85051 617-H5
4300 GLEN 85302 617-G5
8900 PEOR 85345 616-A5
10600 PEOR 85345 615-H5
W GROSS AV
- PHX 85353 736-E2
E GROUNDCHERRY LN
9900 SCTS 85262 421-F1
E GROVE AV
100 MESA 85210 781-H1
1300 MESA 85204 782-B1
3700 MESA 85206 782-H2
4500 MESA 85206 783-A2
W GROVE AV
800 MESA 85210 781-E1
1000 MESA 85202 781-E1
E GROVE CIR
1200 MESA 85204 782-B1
4000 MESA 85206 782-J2
4600 MESA 85206 783-A2
W GROVE CIR
600 MESA 85210 781-F1
W GROVE PKWY
300 TEMP 85283 780-B6
E GROVE ST
1300 PHX 85040 738-J6
3700 PHX 85040 739-F7
10800 MESA 85220 784-H1
W GROVE ST
- PHX 85339 737-D6
100 PHX 85041 738-D6
3500 PHX 85041 737-H6
E GROVERS AV
- PHX 85022 538-H7
900 PHX 85022 539-C7
2300 PHX 85032 539-E7
4600 PHX 85032 540-A7
4800 PHX 85254 540-A7
W GROVERS AV
- PHX 85022 538-F7
- PHX 85023 538-F7
2600 PHX 85053 538-A7
3500 PHX 85308 537-H7
3500 PHX 85308 538-A7
5100 GLEN 85308 537-A7
7100 GLEN 85308 536-J7
8400 PEOR 85382 536-E7
9100 PEOR 85373 536-D7
N GUADAL DR
4600 PHX 85037 656-B5
E GUADALUPE RD
- MESA 85202 780-F5

E GUADALUPE RD
- TEMP 85202 780-F5
- TEMP 85283 780-F5
- GIL 85234 782-D5
2400 GIL 85234 783-B5
2800 MarC 85234 783-B5
3600 GIL 85236 783-B5
4800 PHX 85044 779-J5
4800 PHX 85044 780-A5
5300 PHX 85283 780-A5
5400 GUAD 85283 780-A5
6800 MESA 85208 783-H5
6800 MESA 85212 783-H5
8000 MESA 85208 784-A5
8000 MESA 85212 784-F6
W GUADALUPE RD
- APJT 85220 784-J6
- APJT 85220 785-A6
- PinC 85220 784-J6
- PinC 85220 785-A6
- GIL 85233 782-A5
- TEMP 85283 780-C5
400 MESA 85210 781-C5
1100 GIL 85233 781-J5
1200 MESA 85202 781-C5
2500 MESA 85202 780-D5
N GULF HILLS CT
15600 MarC 85351 576-B2
W GULF HILLS DR
9700 MarC 85351 576-B2
11000 MarC 85351 575-J2
N GULL HAVEN CT
800 GIL 85234 782-J5
W GUMINA AV
4500 MarC 85339 817-F1
N GUNPOWDER
17900 SURP 85374 534-B6
W GUNPOWDER LN
3800 PHX 85086 417-J7
3800 PHX 85086 (418-A7
See Page 417)
E GUN RANGE RD
- MarC 85207 704-E2
E GUNSIGHT DR
16500 FTNH 85268 623-C1
W GUNSIGHT DR
13600 MarC 85375 495-A7
14400 MarC 85375 494-H7
14600 MarC 85375 534-G1
E GUNSIGHT RD
5800 CVCK 85331 420-D2
N GUNSMOKE CT
33400 MarC 85331 460-B2
E GUNSTOCK CIR
1500 CHAN 85249 861-J1
W GUNSTOCK LP
1500 CHAN 85248 861-C2
E GUNSTOCK RD
600 CHAN 85249 861-H1
N GUNSTONE DR
13800 MarC 85351 576-D4
W GUSKIN RD
100 MarC 85342 (412-D3
See Page 411)
N GUTHRIE ST
- MESA 85203 742-C5
E GWEN ST
- PHX 85040 778-H4
E GYAWS RD
10400 SCTS 85255 501-F7
E GYPSUM DR
- APJT 85219 785-H3

H

H ST
- GLEN 85309 615-A7
W H ST
5100 PHX 85031 657-E5
N HABITAT CIR
- CVCK 85331 420-D3
HACIENDA CIR
200 LP 85340 655-B7
W HACIENDA CT
15900 SURP 85374 534-F6
E HACIENDA DR
2600 MarC 85206 743-E7
N HACIENDA DR
11400 MarC 85351 576-A6
S HACIENDA DR
600 TEMP 85281 740-H4
10700 GDYR 85338 (773-J4
See Page 733)
E HACIENDA WY
7300 SCTS 85255 580-G1
E HACIENDA LA COLORADA DR
- PinC 85219 786-D5
E HACKAMORE AV
200 GIL 85296 822-D1
W HACKAMORE AV
- GIL 85233 822-C1
E HACKAMORE CIR
2800 MESA 85213 742-F1
4000 MESA 85205 742-J2
7500 MESA 85207 743-J2
E HACKAMORE DR
8400 SCTS 85255 501-A5
W HACKAMORE DR
5000 PHX 85310 497-C5
N HACKAMORE RD
- APJT 85219 745-J1
- PinC 85219 705-J7
- PinC 85219 745-J1
E HACKAMORE ST
200 MESA 85201 741-J1
400 MESA 85203 741-J1
700 MESA 85203 742-B1
2000 MESA 85213 742-D1
4200 MESA 85205 742-J2
4200 MESA 85205 743-A2
7500 MESA 85207 743-D2
W HACKAMORE ST
700 GIL 85233 822-A1
900 MESA 85201 741-E1
1100 MarC 85201 741-E1
W HACKBERRY CT
900 CHAN 85248 861-D5
N HACKBERRY DR
- PHX 85310 497-J4
S HACKBERRY DR
700 CHAN 85248 861-D6
W HACKBERRY DR
500 CHAN 85248 861-C6
S HACKBERRY TR
- PinC 85219 786-E5
W HACKBERRY MOUNTAIN CT
11600 SURP 85374 535-G4

W HACKBERRY TREE WY
24300 BUCK 85326 (692-C7
See Page 651)
W HACKMORE DR
4900 PHX 85310 497-F5
E HADLEY ST
- PHX 85004 738-G1
800 PHX 85034 738-H1
1400 PHX 85034 739-A1
W HADLEY ST
- GDYR 85338 (694-D7
See Page 653)
- PHX 85003 738-F1
600 PHX 85007 738-D1
900 PHX 85043 696-J7
900 PHX 85043 736-J1
1900 PHX 85009 738-B1
3300 PHX 85009 737-J1
3500 PHX 85009 697-G7
4300 PHX 85043 697-D7
N HAGEN DR
10000 MarC 85351 576-B7
11400 MarC 85351 616-B1
E HAGEN LN
17100 FTNH 85268 623-D3
E HALE CIR
4000 MESA 85205 742-J1
S HALE DR
1400 APJT 85220 745-B7
1400 APJT 85220 785-B1
E HALE ST
400 MESA 85203 741-J1
700 MESA 85203 742-A1
2000 MESA 85213 742-E1
4200 MESA 85205 742-J1
4200 MESA 85205 743-A1
S HALE BOP CT
- GDYR 85338 (774-A6
See Page 733)
W HALE IRWIN BLVD
- GDYR 85338 (654-J7
See Page 653)
N HALEY DR
- MarC 85086 (378-C7
See Page 337)
E HALF MOON DR
- PHX 85044 819-J1
N HALF MOON DR
- SURP 85374 534-G4
S HALF MOON DR
- PHX 85044 779-H7
11700 PHX 85044 819-H1
W HALF MOON WY
200 CHAN 85225 821-E7
E HALIFAX CIR
- MESA 85205 742-H1
- MESA 85207 744-B2
7400 MESA 85207 743-H2
E HALIFAX DR
4400 MESA 85205 743-A2
6800 MESA 85207 743-G2
E HALIFAX ST
- MarC 85207 744-D2
- MESA 85207 744-C2
200 MESA 85201 741-J1
400 MESA 85203 741-J1
700 MESA 85203 742-B1
7200 MESA 85207 743-H2
W HALIFAX ST
- SURP 85374 534-D5
N HALL
- MESA 85203 702-C7
200 MESA 85203 742-C3
S HALL
100 MESA 85204 742-C5
1600 MESA 85204 782-C2
N HALL CIR
2300 MESA 85203 702-C6
E HALL ST
1200 TEMP 85281 740-G5
S HALL ST
1200 MESA 85204 782-C1
E HALLEY CT
10300 MarC 85248 901-D3
E HALLEY DR
10400 MarC 85248 901-D4
E HALLIHAN DR
4100 PHX 85331 459-J6
S HALSTEAD CT
- CHAN 85249 902-B4
S HALSTEAD DR
- CHAN 85249 862-B2
- CHAN 85249 902-B5
W HALSTEAD DR
1000 PHX 85023 538-F7
N HALSTED CT
400 CHAN 85225 822-B5
S HALSTED CT
- CHAN 85225 822-B7
S HALSTED DR
- CHAN 85249 902-B5
S HAM RD
- PHX 85339 777-F3
E HAMBLIN DR
4200 PHX 85050 539-J1
4200 PHX 85050 540-A1
4800 PHX 85054 540-B1
E HAMEL WY
- PHX 85022 579-B2
N HAMILTON DR
13400 FTNH 85268 583-D6
N HAMILTON PL
- CHAN 85225 821-G3
600 GIL 85233 781-G5
N HAMILTON ST
- CHAN 85225 821-G4
S HAMILTON ST
- CHAN 85225 821-G7
600 CHAN 85225 861-G1
17800 CHAN 85249 861-G2
17800 MarC 85249 861-G2
S HAMMOND AV
- TEMP 85282 740-E6
W HAMMOND DR
- MarC 85326 733-D1
15600 GDYR 85338 (734-F2
See Page 733)
E HAMMOND LN
800 PHX 85034 738-H3
1400 PHX 85034 739-H3
9900 MarC 85207 744-F4
9900 MarC 85220 744-F4
W HAMMOND LN
- PHX 85043 736-F2
- PHX 85353 736-F2
500 PHX 85003 738-F3
22300 BUCK 85326 (732-G1
See Page 731)
22800 MarC 85326 (732-F1
See Page 731)

PHOENIX
INDEX

STREET Block City ZIP Pg-Grid

N HAMPSTEAD DR
13800 FTNH 85268 583-B6
E HAMPTON AV
- MESA 85204 784-B1
- MESA 85220 784-F2
- MESA 85210 781-H1
300 MESA 85204 781-J1
600 MESA 85204 782-A1
1400 MESA 85206 783-A2
3500 MESA 85206 782-H2
6800 MESA 85208 783-G2
N HAMPTON AV
- MESA 85208 784-B1
W HAMPTON AV
- MESA 85210 781-G2
E HAMPTON CIR
- MESA 85206 783-D2
1100 MESA 85204 782-A2
3900 MESA 85206 782-J2
E HAMPTON CT
- GIL 85296 822-E7
- MarC 85236 823-A7
E HAMPTON LN
- GIL 85296 822-C7
- MarC 85236 823-B7
W HAMSTER LN
- PHX 85353 736-E2
N HANA MAUI DR
14600 PHX 85022 578-H3
14600 PHX 85023 578-H4
N HANCE BLVD
- PHX 85027 498-A7
- PHX 85027 538-A1
W HANCE BLVD
- PHX 85027 538-A1
E HANCOCK AV
600 TEMP 85281 700-F7
W HANCOCK AV
- GIL 85233 782-A3
E HANCOCK DR
4000 PHX 85028 619-H2
N HANGING TREE ST
- PinC 85242 905-G6
S HANNA DR
4000 TEMP 85282 779-J1
E HANNIBAL CIR
- MarC 85207 744-E2
7300 MESA 85207 743-H2
E HANNIBAL PL
4400 MESA 85205 743-A1
E HANNIBAL ST
- MESA 85207 744-B2
5200 MESA 85205 743-C1
7300 MESA 85207 743-H2
E HANO ST
4000 PHX 85044 779-F7
4200 PHX 85044 819-G1
E HANOVER WY
7300 SCTS 85255 500-G7
S HANSEN CIR
3100 TEMP 85282 741-A7
3100 TEMP 85282 781-A1
W HAPPY LN
22200 MarC 85361 (412-H7 See Page 411)
E HAPPY RD
17600 MarC 85242 903-D6
19400 QC 85242 903-J6
19600 MarC 85242 904-A6
19600 QC 85242 904-A6
E HAPPY COYOTE TR
- PHX 85331 459-J1
- PHX 85331 460-A1
E HAPPY HOLLOW
7400 CARE 85377 420-H4
E HAPPY HOLLOW DR
9000 SCTS 85262 421-C4
N HAPPY HOLLOW LN
9200 SCTS 85255 541-C3
N HAPPY TRAILS
16900 SURP 85374 534-B7
18500 SURP 85387 534-B5
E HAPPY VALLEY RD
- MarC 85024 499-B6
- MarC 85024 498-H5
2800 PHX 85024 499-G6
2900 PHX 85050 499-G6
2900 PHX 85050 500-H6
7200 PHX 85255 500-H6
7200 SCTS 85255 500-H6
8000 SCTS 85255 501-A6
W HAPPY VALLEY RD
- MarC 85024 498-F5
- MarC 85027 498-F5
1500 PHX 85027 498-D5
3500 PHX 85310 497-C5
3500 PHX 85310 498-D5
7400 PEOR 85382 496-D5
7400 PEOR 85382 497-A5
10700 MarC 85373 496-A5
10700 MarC 85382 496-A5
17800 MarC 85387 494-A4
17800 SURP 85387 494-A4
17800 MarC 85361 494-A4
17800 SURP 85361 494-A4
18100 MarC 85361 493-H4
18100 SURP 85361 493-H4
18100 SURP 85387 493-H4
18300 MarC 85387 493-H4
W HARBOR DR
800 GIL 85233 822-A1
W HARBOR HILLS DR
9100 MarC 85351 576-D2
HARBOR SHORES BLVD
- AVON 85323 695-J3
E HARBOR VIEW DR
1000 GIL 85234 782-F6
1200 TEMP 85283 780-F3
E HARBOUR DR
1400 GIL 85234 782-J4
3200 PHX 85034 739-E4
W HARBOUR DR
2000 CHAN 85248 861-B5
N HARBOUR TOWN CT
- MarC 85086 (378-E5 See Page 337)
N HARBOUR TOWN WY
- MarC 85086 (378-E6 See Page 337)
W HARCUVAR ST
51000 MarC 85320 (284-H3 See Page 244)
E HARDING DR
5700 PVAL 85253 659-F4
E HARDING ST
21500 MarC 85361 (453-A2 See Page 413)
W HARDING ST
20300 MarC 85361 (453-A1 See Page 413)
21800 MarC 85361 (452-J1 See Page 411)
W HARDWOOD DR
13200 MarC 85375 535-C6
S HARDY DR
- TEMP 85281 740-C3
1900 TEMP 85282 740-C6
3100 TEMP 85282 780-C2
4800 TEMP 85283 780-B4
7400 TEMP 85283 780-B7
7600 TEMP 85284 820-B2
S HARL AV
- TEMP 85284 819-J1
- TEMP 85284 820-A1
2900 TEMP 85282 740-A7
6700 TEMP 85283 780-A6
7500 TEMP 85284 780-A7
E HARMON CIR
5500 MESA 85215 703-D6
N HARMON CT
700 CHAN 85226 820-E4
N HARMON DR
- CHAN 85226 820-E4
S HARMON PKWY
1200 PHX 85003 738-F1
E HARMONT DR
- PHX 85020 618-H6
1200 PHX 85020 619-A6
7200 SCTS 85258 620-G6
W HARMONT DR
- PEOR 85345 615-H5
- PHX 85021 618-E6
2900 PHX 85051 618-A6
3500 PHX 85051 617-G6
4200 PHX 85302 617-G6
4500 GLEN 85302 617-C5
7500 MarC 85345 616-H5
7500 PEOR 85345 616-A5
E HARMONY AV
200 MESA 85210 781-H2
400 MESA 85204 781-J2
600 MESA 85204 782-A2
3700 MESA 85206 782-H2
4500 MESA 85206 783-A2
7600 MESA 85208 783-J2
N HARMONY AV
400 GIL 85234 782-G5
E HARMONY CIR
1400 MESA 85206 783-A2
1800 MESA 85204 782-C2
N HARMONY LN
900 GIL 85234 782-H5
W HARMONY LN
- PEOR 85308 536-G3
- PEOR 85373 535-J2
- PEOR 85373 536-A2
- PEOR 85382 536-A3
11500 MarC 85373 535-G2
W HARMONY ST
22300 MarC 85361 (452-H1 See Page 411)
S HARMONY WY
23600 MarC 85248 901-B2
N HAROLD ST
1000 MarC 85281 740-F1
1000 TEMP 85281 740-F1
S HARPER
- MESA 85208 784-B5
- MESA 85212 784-C4
N HARPER CIR
- MarC 85207 744-D2
W HARQUAHALA ST
51300 MarC 85320 (284-H4 See Page 244)
N HARQUAHALA VALLEY RD
1600 MarC 85354 101-C2
S HARQUAHALA VALLEY RD
6700 MarC 85354 101-C3
E HARQUE-DA TR
- MarC 85264 583-H3
N HARRINGTON AV
100 GBND 85337 (1089-J3 See Page 1049)
S HARRINGTON CT
1200 GIL 85233 822-A3
S HARRINGTON ST
1000 GIL 85233 822-A3
HARRIS LN
- GLEN 85309 615-A7
- GLEN 85309 655-A1
N HARRIS ST
- MESA 85203 742-C3
1600 MESA 85203 702-C4
1600 MESA 85203 702-C7
S HARRIS ST
200 MESA 85204 742-C6
900 MESA 85204 782-C2
E HARRIS HAWK TR
- SCTS 85262 (461-H7 See Page 421)
E HARRISON CT
- GIL 85236 822-J5
- GIL 85236 823-A5
1000 GIL 85296 822-E5
W HARRISON CT
5200 CHAN 85226 820-D4
E HARRISON DR
- AVON 85323 735-B1
W HARRISON PL
- CHAN 85224 821-A4
E HARRISON ST
- MarC 85236 823-D5
- CHAN 85225 821-F5
400 PHX 85034 699-B7
1000 GIL 85296 822-F5
1400 CHAN 85225 822-A5
13600 MarC 85296 822-C5
W HARRISON ST
- AVON 85323 695-E7
- AVON 85353 695-E7
- CHAN 85226 819-J4
- GDYR 85338 (694-D6 See Page 653)
- CHAN 85225 821-D4
- GIL 85233 822-C5
400 PHX 85003 698-F7
1200 PHX 85007 698-E7
2000 CHAN 85224 821-B4
2100 PHX 85009 698-A7
3100 PHX 85009 697-J7
3200 CHAN 85226 820-A4
8100 TOL 85043 696-F6
8100 TOL 85353 696-B6
17900 MarC 85326 (693-J6 See Page 653)
E HARRY ST
900 TEMP 85281 740-F1
W HART DR
11000 MarC 85351 575-J6
E HARTFORD AV
100 PHX 85022 578-H1
1000 PHX 85022 579-A1
2500 PHX 85032 579-D1
5100 PHX 85254 580-B1
W HARTFORD AV
- PHX 85023 578-D1
3100 PHX 85053 538-B7
3100 PHX 85053 578-B1
3600 PHX 85308 577-H1
5500 GLEN 85308 577-D1
E HARTFORD DR
5600 PHX 85254 580-C1
7600 SCTS 85255 580-H1
8300 SCTS 85255 581-A2
N HARTFORD DR
- SURP 85374 534-G6
17200 SCTS 85255 581-A1
W HARTFORD DR
2900 PHX 85053 538-B7
S HARTFORD RD
600 CHAN 85225 821-E7
600 CHAN 85225 861-E1
N HARTFORD ST
200 CHAN 85225 821-E1
700 CHAN 85225 861-E1
2600 CHAN 85225 781-E6
S HARTFORD ST
- CHAN 85248 861-E4
E HARVARD AV
- GIL 85234 783-C5
- MarC 85234 783-B5
300 GIL 85234 782-D5
3800 GIL 85236 783-D5
N HARVARD AV
800 GIL 85234 782-G5
W HARVARD AV
200 GIL 85233 782-A5
1600 GIL 85233 781-H5
E HARVARD DR
100 TEMP 85283 780-D3
W HARVARD DR
500 TEMP 85283 780-B3
E HARVARD ST
1500 PHX 85006 699-A3
2300 PHX 85008 699-D3
6000 SCTS 85257 700-C4
W HARVARD ST
- GIL 85233 781-J5
S HARVEST CT
- GIL 85236 863-D6
E HARVEST ST
1200 MESA 85203 742-B1
W HARVEST ST
1000 MESA 85201 741-E1
1000 MarC 85201 741-E1
E HARWELL CIR
4200 GIL 85236 783-E4
E HARWELL DR
600 GIL 85234 782-E3
E HARWELL RD
- GIL 85234 783-A3
- MarC 85234 783-A3
- PHX 85040 778-H3
300 GIL 85234 782-D3
W HARWELL RD
- GIL 85233 782-C3
100 PHX 85041 778-F2
1200 GIL 85233 781-J3
E HARWELL ST
4500 GIL 85236 783-F4
E HASHKNIFE RD
4800 PHX 85054 540-B1
E HASH KNIFE DRAW RD
1800 PinC 85242 905-D7
W HASH KNIFE DRAW RD
- PinC 85242 904-J7
600 PinC 85242 905-A7
W HASSAYAMPA DR
9700 MarC 85382 536-C4
S HASSETT
- MarC 85220 744-H6
- MESA 85220 744-H7
S HASSETT CIR
- MarC 85220 744-H6
N HASSETT ST
- MESA 85220 744-H4
N HASTINGS
- MESA 85220 744-G7
E HATCHER DR
1600 PHX 85020 619-B4
E HATCHER RD
- PHX 85020 618-H4
1200 PHX 85020 619-A4
2300 PHX 85028 619-C4
5200 PVAL 85253 620-A4
W HATCHER RD
- PHX 85021 618-E3
1400 PEOR 85345 616-C3
3700 PHX 85051 617-H3
4100 PHX 85302 617-G3
4400 GLEN 85302 617-B3
10700 MarC 85351 615-H3
17800 MarC 85355 (613-J2 See Page 573)
17800 MarC 85355 (614-A2 See Page 573)
W HATFIELD DR
9000 PEOR 85382 496-E5
W HATFIELD RD
700 MarC 85027 498-F5
1500 PHX 85027 498-D5
6600 PEOR 85310 497-A5
6600 PEOR 85382 497-A5
8100 PEOR 85382 496-E5
10700 MarC 85373 496-A5
10700 MarC 85382 496-A5
10900 MarC 85373 495-H5
S HAUNTED CANYON RD
- PinC 85219 786-G7
- PinC 85219 826-G1
W HAVASU CT
1500 CHAN 85248 901-B1
W HAVASU WY
1700 CHAN 85248 901-B1
E HAVASUPAI DR
8800 SCTS 85255 541-B5
N HAVASUPAI DR
15500 SURP 85374 534-F6
19600 PHX 85308 537-F4
W HAVASUPAI DR
4600 PHX 85308 537-F4
W HAVEN AV
6900 PHX 85035 696-J2
E HAVEN CREST DR
- GIL 85236 863-E4
S HAWAIIAN DR
- GIL 85233 781-J7
N HAWES RD
100 MarC 85207 744-B5
400 MESA 85207 744-B5
2000 MESA 85207 704-B4
2400 MESA 85207 704-B4
S HAWES RD
- MarC 85208 744-B6
400 MESA 85208 744-B6
600 MarC 85208 784-B1
600 MESA 85208 784-B1
2400 MESA 85212 784-A7
9200 MarC 85212 784-A7
10800 MESA 85212 824-A1
18800 QC 85242 864-A4
23500 QC 85242 904-A1
25200 MarC 85242 904-A4
N HAWK CIR
600 GIL 85236 783-D6
S HAWK CT
- MarC 85236 823-D4
W HAWK CT
2100 CHAN 85248 861-B5
11600 SURP 85374 535-G6
E HAWK DR
16600 FTNH 85268 623-C2
N HAWK LN
1100 GIL 85236 783-E4
W HAWK WY
1700 CHAN 85248 861-B5
W HAWKEN DR
- CHAN 85248 861-C2
E HAWKEN PL
- CHAN 85249 861-J2
E HAWKEN WY
- CHAN 85249 861-H2
2200 CHAN 85249 862-A2
W HAWKEN WY
- CHAN 85248 861-B2
E HAWKNEST RD
8000 SCTS 85262 420-J7
8000 SCTS 85262 421-A7
E HAWKS EYE DR
- APJT 85219 785-H3
E HAWKSNEST RD
6900 CARE 85377 420-F5
E HAWLEY DR
17500 FTNH 85268 583-E4
N HAWTHORN CT
14200 FTNH 85268 583-C6
W HAWTHORN CT
9700 MarC 85351 576-C5
N HAWTHORN DR
13600 MarC 85351 576-B5
S HAWTHORN DR
3600 CHAN 85248 861-A6
W HAWTHORN DR
9700 MarC 85351 576-C5
W HAYDEN DR
- SURP 85374 534-B6
E HAYDEN LN
1800 TEMP 85281 740-H4
N HAYDEN RD
300 SCTS 85257 700-H7
500 MarC 85256 740-H1
500 TEMP 85281 740-H1
500 MarC 85281 740-H1
1400 TEMP 85256 700-H7
1400 TEMP 85281 700-H7
1400 MarC 85256 700-H7
1900 TEMP 85257 700-H7
1900 MarC 85257 700-H7
2900 SCTS 85251 700-H3
4200 SCTS 85251 660-H6
5000 SCTS 85250 660-H6
7000 SCTS 85258 660-H1
7500 SCTS 85258 620-J4
8100 SCTS 85258 621-A7
10600 SCTS 85260 620-H1
12200 SCTS 85260 580-J2
15200 SCTS 85260 581-A4
17000 SCTS 85255 580-J1
20100 SCTS 85255 540-J2
23800 SCTS 85255 500-J2
28200 SCTS 85262 500-J2
29000 SCTS 85262 460-J1
N HAYDEN RANCH RD
53900 MarC 85320 244-H4
N HAYLOFT RD
- GIL 85234 783-B7
E HAYMORE CT
- MarC 85236 902-J4
- MarC 85236 903-A4
E HAYWARD AV
- PHX 85020 618-H7
- PHX 85021 618-H7
1200 PHX 85020 619-B7
W HAYWARD AV
- PHX 85021 618-C6
2500 PHX 85051 618-A6
3500 PHX 85051 617-H6
4500 GLEN 85301 617-D6
7800 MarC 85307 615-H6
S HAZEL CT
- GIL 85296 822-E3
E HAZEL DR
700 PHX 85040 778-H4
4800 PHX 85044 779-J4
8700 MarC 85208 744-B6
S HAZEL DR
- GIL 85296 822-E3
S HAZEL ST
1200 GIL 85296 822-E2
W HAZELHURST CT
- MarC 85086 (378-E5 See Page 337)
W HAZELHURST DR
3200 MarC 85086 (378-B5 See Page 337)
E HAZELTINE WY
- CHAN 85249 902-A6
1400 CHAN 85249 901-J6
S HAZELTON AV
3600 CHAN 85226 820-H7
N HAZELTON CT
900 CHAN 85226 820-H4
N HAZELTON DR
700 CHAN 85226 820-H3
S HAZELTON DR
100 CHAN 85226 820-H7
S HAZELTON LN
1100 TEMP 85281 740-J5
1800 TEMP 85283 780-H3
3200 TEMP 85282 780-H1
7900 TEMP 85284 780-H7
8200 TEMP 85284 820-H1
W HAZELWOOD AV
5500 PHX 85031 657-D6
10200 PHX 85037 656-A5
N HAZELWOOD CIR
38300 CVCK 85331 420-E3
W HAZELWOOD CT
10600 MarC 85373 536-A5
E HAZELWOOD ST
1800 PHX 85016 659-B6
3200 PHX 85018 659-F6
7500 SCTS 85251 660-G6
8500 SCTS 85251 661-A6
W HAZELWOOD ST
300 PHX 85013 658-E6
1500 PHX 85015 658-C6
2500 PHX 85017 658-A6
3500 PHX 85019 657-H6
4700 PHX 85031 657-D6
5900 PHX 85033 657-A5
7100 PHX 85033 656-F5
8500 PHX 85037 656-C5
W HAZEN RD
24600 BUCK 85326 (771-D3 See Page 731)
24600 BUCK 85326 (772-A3 See Page 731)
24600 MarC 85326 (771-D3 See Page 731)
25900 MarC 85322 (771-B3 See Page 731)
E HEADAWAY LN
- SCTS 85255 541-D3
W HEARN CIR
- SURP 85379 (574-H4 See Page 573)
E HEARN RD
600 PHX 85022 578-J5
1100 PHX 85022 579-A5
3200 PHX 85032 579-F5
4600 PHX 85032 580-A5
4800 PHX 85254 580-A5
W HEARN RD
- ELMG 85335 575-D4
- SURP 85379 (574-F4 See Page 573)
- SURP 85379 575-C4
2400 PHX 85023 578-C5
2700 PHX 85053 578-B4
3500 PHX 85053 577-H4
4400 PHX 85306 577-G4
5100 GLEN 85306 577-C4
6900 PEOR 85381 577-A4
7100 MarC 85381 576-J4
7100 MarC 85381 577-A4
7100 PEOR 85381 576-E4
18000 MarC 85379 573-J3
18000 MarC 85379 (574-F4 See Page 573)
E HEARNE WY
- GIL 85234 782-C6
N HEARNE WY
200 GIL 85234 782-E6
W HEARNE WY
100 GIL 85233 782-A6
W HEARST DR
- MarC 85086 (378-A6 See Page 337)
N HEARTHSTONE DR
19600 SURP 85374 534-E4
W HEARTHSTONE DR
16200 SURP 85374 534-E3
S HEATH WY
3500 CHAN 85248 861-D7
E HEATHER AV
100 GIL 85234 782-D6
3900 GIL 85236 783-D6
W HEATHER AV
800 GIL 85233 782-A6
1400 GIL 85233 781-J5
E HEATHER CT
3800 GIL 85236 783-D6
E HEATHER DR
- MarC 85236 783-D6
1800 TEMP 85282 780-H1
6400 MESA 85215 703-F6
6700 MESA 85207 703-F6
16400 FTNH 85268 583-C5
S HEATHER DR
3800 TEMP 85282 780-H2
5300 TEMP 85283 780-G3
7700 TEMP 85284 780-G7
8800 TEMP 85284 820-G2
W HEATHER DR
800 MESA 85201 741-E1
1100 MarC 85201 741-E1
N HEATHER LN
3500 AVON 85323 655-G7
20500 SURP 85374 534-F3
S HEATHER LN
15900 CHAN 85225 822-B7
15900 MarC 85225 822-B7
E HEATHERBRAE AV
7700 SCTS 85251 660-G7
8500 SCTS 85251 661-A7
E HEATHERBRAE DR
1400 PHX 85014 659-A7
2200 PHX 85016 659-C7
3800 PHX 85018 659-G7
8100 SCTS 85251 660-J7
W HEATHERBRAE DR
700 PHX 85013 658-E7
1700 PHX 85015 658-C7
2700 PHX 85017 658-A7
4800 PHX 85031 657-D6
6400 PHX 85033 657-A6
6900 PHX 85033 656-F6
8300 PHX 85037 656-D6
10500 PHX 85037 655-H6
W HEATHER GLEN DR
100 CHAN 85225 821-F2
E HEAVENLY VISTA TR
- FTNH 85268 622-J5
W HECTOR RD
50700 MarC 85320 (285-A5 See Page 244)
51000 MarC 85320 (284-J5 See Page 244)
W HECTOR ST
51500 MarC 85320 (284-G5 See Page 244)
S HEDGE
1400 MESA 85210 781-H2
E HEDGEHOG CT
15600 FTNH 85268 583-A5
W HEDGEHOG CT
11600 SURP 85374 535-G6
S HEDGEHOG DR
5400 PinC 85219 786-F6
W HEDGEHOG LN
- PHX 85085 497-C2
E HEDGEHOG PL
- PHX 85331 500-A2
- SCTS 85331 500-C2
10800 SCTS 85255 501-G2
W HEDGEHOG PL
- PHX 85085 497-D2
- PHX 85085 498-C2
E HEDGES RD
9100 MarC 85207 744-D3
S HEIGHTS RD
600 WICK 85390 290-D3
E HEILD ST
- PHX 85020 618-H3
N HEILD ST
9400 PHX 85020 618-H4
E HELEN DR
5800 PHX 85251 660-C6
E HELENA DR
- PHX 85022 578-H1
1200 PHX 85022 579-A1
2600 PHX 85032 579-D1
3300 PHX 85032 539-F7
5200 PHX 85254 580-B1
W HELENA DR
100 PHX 85023 578-F1
900 PHX 85023 538-E7
3200 PHX 85053 538-A7
3500 PHX 85308 538-A7
3700 PHX 85308 537-H7
E HELM DR
- SCTS 85259 581-F5
6200 PHX 85254 580-D4
7300 SCTS 85260 580-G4
9000 SCTS 85260 581-B4
N HELM DR
- SCTS 85259 581-H5
N HELMS
700 MESA 85213 742-G3
S HELMS
400 MESA 85204 742-G6
1200 MESA 85204 782-G1
S HELMS CIR
900 MESA 85204 782-G1
S HEMET ST
- GIL 85236 863-C5
W HEMINGWAY LN
- MarC 85086 (418-B1 See Page 417)
E HEMLOCK AV
200 GIL 85234 782-D6
W HEMLOCK CT
2200 CHAN 85248 861-A6
W HEMLOCK WY
1000 CHAN 85248 861-A6
W HENDERSON LN
600 GIL 85233 782-A7
W HENDERSON ST
100 WICK 85390 290-E3
N HENKEL CIR
300 MESA 85201 741-D4
S HENKEL CIR
1700 MESA 85202 781-D2
E HENRY ST
900 TEMP 85281 740-F1
E HERCULES CT
- MarC 85248 900-J3
10300 MarC 85248 901-D4
E HERCULES DR
9400 MarC 85248 901-B4
E HERDON RD
29900 MarC 85390 290-H5
N HEREFORD
17000 SURP 85374 534-C7
E HERE TO THERE DR
9400 CARE 85377 421-D5
N HERITAGE
800 MESA 85201 741-F3
S HERITAGE
1700 MESA 85210 781-E2
N HERITAGE DR
- GIL 85234 782-E6
S HERITAGE DR
1200 GIL 85296 822-E2
W HERITAGE DR
14000 MarC 85375 535-A1
14400 MarC 85375 534-F1
N HERITAGE ST
800 GIL 85234 782-E4
N HERITAGE WY
2500 CHAN 85224 781-A6
W HERITAGE OAK WY
14900 SURP 85374 534-H7
S HERMIT RD
12500 MarC 85326 (773-D7 See Page 733)
12500 MarC 85326 813-E1
S HERMOSA
2600 MarC 85206 743-E7
E HERMOSA CIR
3900 TEMP 85282 780-E2
E HERMOSA DR
- TEMP 85282 780-A1
2300 TEMP 85282 781-A1
W HERMOSA DR
- TEMP 85282 780-B1
700 WICK 85390 290-D2
2100 TEMP 85282 779-J1
E HERMOSA VISTA DR
1500 MESA 85203 702-C6
2000 MESA 85213 702-E6
3600 MESA 85215 702-H6
5200 MESA 85215 703-C6
6700 MESA 85207 703-G6
7100 MarC 85207 703-J6
7800 MarC 85207 704-C7
7800 MESA 85207 704-D7
N HERMOSILLO DR
22400 MarC 85375 494-H7
N HERON DR
26500 MarC 85263 503-J4
S HERON LN
- MarC 85236 823-E5
E HERRERA DR
5200 PHX 85054 540-C1
E HESS AV
1200 PHX 85034 738-J2
W HESS AV
- PHX 85043 736-F2
W HESS LN
24900 MarC 85326 (732-A1 See Page 731)
25000 BUCK 85326 (732-A1 See Page 731)
E HESTON DR
- PHX 85024 499-D7
S HEVADA WY
- MarC 85233 781-J7
- MarC 85233 821-J1
W HEYERDAHL DR
- MarC 85087 (378-A4 See Page 337)
E HIALEA CT
3500 PHX 85044 819-E1
N HIBBERT
- MESA 85201 741-H4
- MESA 85210 741-H5
1800 MESA 85201 701-J7
S HIBBERT
- MESA 85210 741-H5
N HIBBERT CIR
- MESA 85201 701-H6
S HIBISCUS
2400 MESA 85208 783-J5
W HIBISCUS DR
10700 MarC 85373 535-J7
10700 MarC 85373 536-A7
N HIBISCUS LN
- SURP 85374 534-H5
E HIBISCUS WY
6900 SCTS 85262 460-G3
W HICKORY ST
1000 MESA 85201 741-E1
E HIDALGO AV
- PHX 85040 738-G7
1600 PHX 85040 739-A7
S HIDALGO AV
2100 PHX 85041 738-C7
W HIDALGO AV
1300 PHX 85041 738-C7
3700 PHX 85041 737-H7
3900 MarC 85041 737-G7
10900 MarC 85353 735-G6
12300 MarC 85323 735-C6
E HIDALGO ST
- APJT 85219 746-B3
4800 PinC 85219 746-B3
S HIDALGO ST
300 CHAN 85225 821-G7
HIDDEN TER
4800 LP 85340 655-A5
N HIDDEN CANYON CT
- FTNH 85268 623-A4
N HIDDEN CANYON DR
18500 SURP 85374 534-E5
E HIDDEN CANYON RD
6200 CARE 85377 420-E7
W HIDDEN CREEK LN
- SURP 85374 534-G3
E HIDDEN GREEN DR
9300 SCTS 85262 501-D1
S HIDDEN HILL RD
6100 PinC 85219 786-H7
N HIDDEN RIDGE DR
- SURP 85374 534-F4
E HIDDEN ROCK LN
6600 CVCK 85331 420-F3
E HIDDEN SPRINGS RD
5700 CVCK 85331 (380-D6 See Page 339)
E HIDDEN SPRINGS TR
- FTNH 85268 622-J3
E HIDDEN STAR DR
- SCTS 85262 (381-D7 See Page 341)
S HIDDEN TRAIL CT
- PinC 85219 826-H2
W HIDDEN VALLEY CIR
9300 MarC 85351 576-C1
E HIDDEN VALLEY DR
6000 CVCK 85331 420-E3
N HIDDEN VALLEY DR
6000 CVCK 85331 420-E3
W HIDDEN VALLEY LN
9100 MarC 85351 576-D2
E HIDDEN VALLEY RD
9700 SCTS 85262 421-E4
E HIDDENVIEW DR
300 PHX 85048 818-G6
2300 PHX 85048 819-B6
W HIDDENVIEW DR
1700 PHX 85045 818-D6
E HIDE TR
4000 PHX 85050 499-H4
W HIDE TR
- PHX 85310 497-H4
S HIDE AWAY LN
6300 PinC 85219 786-J7
E HIERRO CIR
18500 MarC 85263 503-H3
N HIGHCLIFF DR
7300 MarC 85253 659-H1
7400 MarC 85253 619-G7
E HIGHLAND AV
- MarC 85256 661-D6
300 PHX 85012 658-H6
700 PHX 85014 658-J6
1300 PHX 85014 659-B6
1600 PHX 85016 659-B6
3200 PHX 85018 659-E6
6600 SCTS 85251 660-E6
8500 SCTS 85251 661-A6
W HIGHLAND AV
- PHX 85013 658-F6
1400 PHX 85015 658-D6
2500 PHX 85017 658-B6
4200 PHX 85019 657-G5
4300 PHX 85031 657-D5
4600 PHX 85033 656-G5
4800 PHX 85033 657-A5
8300 PHX 85037 656-A5
E HIGHLAND CT
2700 GIL 85236 823-A3
E HIGHLAND DR
800 CHAN 85225 821-H3
W HIGHLAND DR
600 GIL 85233 822-B2
600 MarC 85233 822-B2
1400 GIL 85233 821-H3
E HIGHLAND RD
5000 CVCK 85331 420-B1
7300 CVCK 85331 (380-J7 See Page 339)
E HIGHLAND ST
800 CHAN 85225 821-H3
2400 MESA 85213 742-E2
W HIGHLAND ST
- CHAN 85224 820-J2
- CHAN 85225 821-D2
1100 CHAN 85224 821-A2
E HIGHLANDS DR
4200 PVAL 85253 659-H2
E HIGHLINE LN
4100 PHX 85040 779-G3
HIGHLINE CSR
- CHAN - 819-J3
- CHAN - 820-A2
- GUAD - 780-B4
- PHX - 819-G5
- TEMP - 780-B4
- TEMP - 820-A2
3300 PHX 85040 779-E3

PHOENIX
INDEX

STREET
Block City ZIP Pg-Grid

E HIGHPOINT DR
- SCTS 85262 460-J1
E HIGH POINT DR
- SCTS 85262 (461-A1
See Page 421)
E HIGHPOINT DR
- SCTS 85262 (461-A1
See Page 421)
E HIGH POINT DR
7300 SCTS 85262 460-H1
N HIGH POINT DR
33800 SCTS 85262 460-H1
W HIGHRIDGE RD
- WICK 85390 289-J2
- WICK 85390 290-A2
W HIGHRIDGE ST
100 MESA 85201 741-G1
N HIGHVIEW
- MESA 85207 704-A3
N HIGHVIEW CIR
- MESA 85207 704-A2
HIGHWAY Rt#-71
- MarC 85320 101-C1
- MarC 85320 (245-F3
See Page 244)
- MarC 85320 (285-C1
See Page 244)
- YavC - (245-J1
See Page 244)
HIGHWAY Rt#-85
- BUCK 85337 102-B3
- BUCK 85326 102-B3
- MarC 85337 102-B3
- MarC 85337 106-B1
- MarC 85326 (734-A5
See Page 733)
- MarC 85337 811-D7
- MarC 85337 (851-D1
See Page 811)
200 BUCK 85326 (772-C1
See Page 731)
900 MarC 85326 (772-E1
See Page 731)
6000 MarC 85326 733-J5
7200 MarC 85326 (732-C7
See Page 731)
12100 GBND 85337 (1090-G1
See Page 1049)
12100 MarC 85337 (1090-F2
See Page 1049)
12100 GBND 85337 106-B1
12200 MarC 85326 106-B1
12200 GBND 85337 (1050-G7
See Page 1049)
12200 MarC 85337 (1050-J2
See Page 1049)
17000 GDYR 85326 (773-G1
See Page 733)
17000 MarC 85326 (773-A1
See Page 733)
17200 GDYR 85326 733-J5
17400 GDYR 85326 (734-B4
See Page 733)
17400 GDYR 85338 (734-J2
See Page 733)
17700 GDYR 85338 735-A2
19100 BUCK 85326 (773-G1
See Page 733)
23700 BUCK 85326 (732-D7
See Page 731)
55800 GBND 85337 (1089-J3
See Page 1049)
57200 MarC 85337 (1089-J4
See Page 1049)
HIGHWAY Rt#-87
- PinC - 901-F6
- MarC 85249 901-F6
HIGHWAY Rt#-88
20500 MarC 85290 103-C2
HIGHWAY Rt#-188
- MarC 85290 104-A2
HIGHWAY U.S.-60
- MarC 85320 102-A1
- MarC 85342 102-B1
- MarC 85390 102-A1
- WICK 85390 102-A1
19500 MarC 85361 102-B2
19500 MarC 85375 102-B2
- APJT 85219 786-A3
- MarC 85320 101-C1
- MarC 85320 (284-J4
See Page 244)
- MarC 85320 (285-A4
See Page 244)
- MarC 85342 331-C4
- MarC 85342 (371-E1
See Page 331)
- MarC 85342 (372-A5
See Page 331)
- MarC 85342 (412-B1
See Page 411)
- MarC 85361 (412-G6
See Page 411)
- MarC 85361 (452-J1
See Page 411)
- MarC 85390 289-E2
- MarC 85390 290-G3
- MarC 85390 331-A1
- PinC 85219 786-D6
- WICK 85390 289-F2
- WICK 85390 290-G3
6500 PinC 85219 826-E1
19500 MarC 85361 (453-A1
See Page 413)
19500 MarC 85375 (453-D5
See Page 413)
HIGHWAY U.S.-93
- MarC 85390 102-B1
- MarC 85390 250-B5
- YavC - 250-A4
N HIGHWOOD CT
18000 MarC 85373 536-B6
W HIGHWOOD CT
9800 MarC 85373 536-B6
W HIGHWOOD LN
9900 MarC 85373 536-B7
N HIGLEY RD
- MESA 85205 743-C3
1800 MESA 85205 703-C7
2000 MESA 85215 703-C4
S HIGLEY RD
- GIL 85236 783-B4
- GIL 85236 863-B4
- MarC 85236 783-B4
- MESA 85206 743-C7
900 MESA 85206 783-C3
1600 GIL 85206 783-C3
7600 GIL 85234 783-B4
7600 MarC 85234 783-B3
9300 MarC 85236 823-B4

S HIGLEY RD
12400 GIL 85236 823-B4
16600 MarC 85236 863-B4
22000 MarC 85236 903-B2
25200 MarC 85242 903-B4
S HIGO CIR
400 APJT 85220 745-D6
E HILDAGO ST
- APJT 85220 745-A3
N HILL
- MESA 85203 702-C7
200 MESA 85203 742-C4
S HILL
100 MESA 85204 742-C5
1700 MESA 85204 782-C3
N HILL CIR
800 MESA 85203 742-C3
E HILL DR
- AVON 85323 695-B7
W HILL DR
- AVON 85323 695-B7
W HILL LN
6500 GLEN 85310 537-A1
7300 GLEN 85310 536-J1
N HILL ST
2400 MESA 85203 702-C6
N HILLCREST
1200 MESA 85201 741-F2
E HILLCREST BLVD
6200 PHX 85251 660-D6
W HILLCREST BLVD
- PEOR 85308 536-J1
- PEOR 85382 536-G1
6600 GLEN 85310 537-A1
7200 GLEN 85310 536-J1
N HILLCREST CIR
1300 MESA 85201 741-E1
E HILLCREST DR
17100 FTNH 85268 623-D4
N HILLCREST DR
10700 MarC 85351 575-J7
E HILLERY DR
- SCTS 85259 581-F4
1900 PHX 85022 579-B4
2500 PHX 85032 579-D4
4800 PHX 85254 580-A4
9000 SCTS 85260 581-B4
E HILLERY WY
9200 SCTS 85260 581-C4
N HILLRIDGE
- MESA 85207 704-A7
S HILLRIDGE
2900 MESA 85212 784-A6
N HILLRIDGE CIR
- MESA 85207 704-A7
N HILLRIDGE ST
800 MESA 85207 744-A3
HILLS RD
- YavC - 250-A2
N HILLSBOROUGH DR
1400 GIL 85233 782-J3
E HILLSIDE DR
- FTNH 85268 622-J3
N HILLSIDE DR
4200 MarC 85253 659-H2
4200 PVAL 85253 659-H2
E HILLSIDE RD
- MarC 85268 583-F6
17900 MarC 85264 583-F6
E HILLSIDE ST
- MESA 85201 741-H1
W HILLSIDE ST
- GDYR 85338 (654-H6
See Page 653)
- MESA 85201 741-G1
N HILLTOP DR
4500 PHX 85018 660-C6
4500 PHX 85251 660-C6
N HILLTOP LN
- CVCK 85331 420-F3
E HILLVIEW
7200 MESA 85207 743-H2
E HILLVIEW CIR
- MarC 85207 744-D2
- MESA 85207 744-B2
700 MESA 85203 742-A1
W HILLVIEW CIR
400 MESA 85201 741-G1
E HILLVIEW ST
- MESA 85207 744-C2
1400 MESA 85207 743-F2
6000 MESA 85205 743-E2
W HILLVIEW ST
- MESA 85201 741-E1
N HILQUIT DR
400 MarC 85342 (412-D3
See Page 411)
E HILTON AV
500 MESA 85204 781-J2
1100 PHX 85034 738-J3
1200 MESA 85204 782-B2
4600 PHX 85034 739-H3
4800 MESA 85206 783-B2
S HILTON AV
- BUCK 85326 (692-E7
See Page 651)
W HILTON AV
- GDYR 85326 (734-A1
See Page 733)
- PHX 85043 736-F2
- PHX 85353 736-E2
200 PHX 85003 738-F2
1100 PHX 85007 738-E2
1900 PHX 85009 738-C2
15600 GDYR 85338 (734-E2
See Page 733)
16600 MarC 85338 (734-C1
See Page 733)
19500 MarC 85326 733-D1
21900 BUCK 85326 (732-G1
See Page 731)
22800 MarC 85326 (732-F1
See Page 731)
23300 MarC 85326 (692-E7
See Page 651)
E HILTON CIR
1800 MESA 85204 782-C2
N HILTON RD
- APJT 85219 745-H5
S HILTON RD
- APJT 85219 745-H7
1200 APJT 85219 785-H1
N HITCHING POST DR
17400 MarC 85373 536-C7
W HITCHING POST DR
9500 MarC 85373 536-D7
E HO RD
7200 CARE 85377 420-H4
E HOBAR CIR
- MarC 85207 744-E2

E HOBART CIR
7200 MESA 85207 743-H2
E HOBART ST
- MarC 85207 744-D2
- MESA 85207 744-C2
4400 MESA 85205 743-A1
6800 MESA 85207 743-G2
N HOBSON
- MESA 85203 741-J1
- MESA 85204 741-J4
S HOBSON
- MESA 85204 741-J5
900 MESA 85204 781-J1
N HOBSON CIR
300 GIL 85233 781-J6
800 MESA 85203 741-J3
N HOBSON PZ
500 MESA 85203 741-J4
N HOBSON ST
- GIL 85233 781-J3
N HOGAN AV
2400 MESA 85215 703-C6
N HOGAN CIR
6200 PVAL 85253 659-H3
N HOGAN DR
3200 GDYR 85338 (654-F7
See Page 653)
3200 GDYR 85338 (694-F1
See Page 653)
6100 PVAL 85018 659-H3
6100 PVAL 85253 659-H3
S HOGAN DR
26400 MarC 85248 900-J6
W HOGAN DR
10600 MarC 85351 576-A6
E HOH
4700 PHX 85044 819-H2
S HOHOKAM DR
- TEMP 85281 739-J5
800 TEMP 85281 740-A4
2200 TEMP 85282 779-J2
W HOHOKAM DR
11100 MarC 85373 535-J7
HOHOKAM EXWY Rt#-143
- PHX - 699-J7
- PHX - 739-J1
- TEMP - 739-J1
E HOHOKAM LN
11200 MarC 85331 (381-J4
See Page 341)
E HOHOKAM PL
5800 CVCK 85331 420-D4
S HOHOKAM PL
6800 PinC 85219 826-G1
N HOHOKAM RD
42800 MarC 85331 (381-J5
See Page 341)
S HOHOKAM WY
6700 PinC 85219 786-G7
6700 PinC 85219 826-G1
S HOLBEN PL
1100 AVON 85323 735-B2
S HOLBROOK LN
1100 TEMP 85281 740-H5
1900 TEMP 85283 780-H4
2600 TEMP 85282 740-H7
3200 TEMP 85282 780-H1
8600 TEMP 85284 820-H2
S HOLGUIN CT
- CHAN 85248 861-E6
S HOLGUIN WY
- CHAN 85248 861-E4
S HOLGUN WY
- CHAN 85248 861-E3
E HOLIDAY DR
6400 MESA 85215 703-F7
N HOLIDAY LN
37000 CARE 85377 420-G4
E HOLIDAY WY
9600 MarC 85248 901-B2
N HOLLY CIR
400 GIL 85234 782-D6
E HOLLY CT
4000 PinC 85219 746-A5
S HOLLY CT
3400 CHAN 85248 861-B6
E HOLLY DR
6400 MESA 85215 703-F7
W HOLLY DR
- SURP 85374 534-A6
W HOLLY LN
- AVON 85323 735-B1
E HOLLY ST
3200 PHX 85008 699-E4
5000 PHX 85008 700-A4
6400 SCTS 85257 700-D4
8400 SCTS 85257 701-A4
W HOLLY ST
- AVON 85323 695-C3
- AVON 85323 696-A3
- PHX 85003 698-F4
- PHX 85007 698-E4
1100 PHX 85007 698-E4
1900 PHX 85009 698-A3
3200 PHX 85009 697-G3
4600 PHX 85035 697-A3
6700 PHX 85035 696-H3
8300 PHX 85037 696-D3
13100 GDYR 85338 695-B3
S HOLLYGREEN CT
4900 CHAN 85248 901-D2
S HOLLYGREEN DR
24400 MarC 85248 901-D3
W HOLLYHOCK DR
- AVON 85340 655-D7
- AVON 85340 695-D1
3300 PHX 85033 697-B1
6900 PHX 85033 696-G1
S HOLLYHOCK PL
3800 CHAN 85248 861-A7
E HOLLYHOCK ST
5900 PHX 85018 700-C2
N HOLLYHOCK ST
15500 SURP 85374 575-E1
S HOLLYHOCK WY
3500 CHAN 85248 861-A6
W HOLLYWOOD AV
9200 PEOR 85345 616-D1
11100 YNTN 85335 575-H7
11100 YNTN 85335 615-H1
E HOLMES AV
300 MESA 85210 781-H2
400 MESA 85204 781-J2
600 MESA 85204 782-A2
3700 MESA 85206 782-J2
4400 MESA 85206 783-A2
7600 MESA 85208 783-J2
S HOLMES AV
700 MESA 85204 782-A2

W HOLMES AV
400 MESA 85210 781-E2
5500 MESA 85202 781-E2
N HOLMES BLVD
17000 PHX 85053 578-B1
17200 PHX 85053 538-C7
E HOLMES CIR
4100 MESA 85206 782-J2
N HOLMES RD
700 PinC 85219 746-D3
S HOLMES RD
500 PinC 85219 746-D6
N HOME PL
500 CHAN 85224 821-B5
HOMER DR
- GLEN 85309 615-A7
E HOMESTEAD CIR
- SCTS 85262 (461-B2
See Page 421)
W HOMESTEAD DR
32600 MarC 85390 290-A5
E HOMESTEAD LN
400 TEMP 85284 820-E1
N HOMESTEAD LN
5500 PVAL 85253 659-F4
22400 MarC 85375 495-B7
S HOMESTEAD LN
400 TEMP 85284 820-E1
S HONAHLEE CT
12000 PHX 85040 819-D1
12500 PHX 85044 819-D2
12600 PHX 85048 819-D2
N HONCHO RD
13800 ELMG 85335 575-G4
E HONDA BOW RD
- SCTS 85262 (381-J5
See Page 341)
- MarC 85086 (378-J4
See Page 337)
- MarC 85087 (378-J4
See Page 337)
300 MarC 85087 (379-A4
See Page 339)
300 MarC 85086 (379-A4
See Page 339)
5400 CVCK 85331 (380-C5
See Page 339)
5400 MarC 85331 (380-C5
See Page 339)
W HONDA BOW RD
- PHX 85086 (377-H4
See Page 337)
- PHX 85087 (377-H4
See Page 337)
- MarC 85086 (378-G4
See Page 337)
- MarC 85087 (378-G4
See Page 337)
E HONDO AV
400 APJT 85219 785-E1
E HONDO DR
8300 SCTS 85262 421-A7
E HONEY MESQUITE DR
10400 SCTS 85262 (381-H6
See Page 341)
S HONEYSUCKLE CIR
1400 GIL 85296 822-E4
2400 MESA 85208 783-J5
S HONEYSUCKLE CT
1300 GIL 85296 822-E4
HONEYSUCKLE DR
- FTNH 85268 582-H5
W HONEYSUCKLE DR
- CHAN 85248 861-E5
- PEOR 85382 497-A4
4500 PHX 85310 497-C4
N HONEYSUCKLE LN
100 GIL 85234 782-E3
S HONEYSUCKLE LN
500 GIL 85296 822-E2
W HONEYSUCKLE LN
1100 CHAN 85248 861-B5
14700 SURP 85374 534-G6
S HONEYSUCKLE ST
- GIL 85296 782-E7
W HONEYSUCKLE ST
100 LP 85340 655-A6
E HONONEGH DR
2800 PHX 85050 539-E4
W HONONEGH DR
- PHX 85024 538-J4
300 PHX 85027 538-E4
S HONOR CT
- MarC 85236 903-D3
W HONOR CT
- MarC 85086 (378-B7
See Page 337)
E HOOVER AV
- MESA 85210 781-H2
1000 MESA 85204 782-A2
W HOOVER AV
- MESA 85210 781-G2
E HOOVER ST
- PHX 85003 698-G3
- PHX 85004 698-G3
1400 PHX 85006 698-G3
1400 PHX 85006 699-A3
N HOPBUSH WY
14100 FTNH 85268 582-J6
E HOPE CIR
500 MESA 85203 741-J1
2200 MESA 85213 742-E1
4100 MESA 85205 742-J1
W HOPE CIR N
9900 MarC 85351 616-B1
W HOPE CIR S
9900 MarC 85351 616-B1
E HOPE DR
10600 SCTS 85259 621-F2
W HOPE DR
- GDYR 85338 (774-B5
See Page 733)
7600 PEOR 85345 616-H1
10500 MarC 85351 616-A1
10500 MarC 85351 615-J1
10700 MarC 85351 575-J7
E HOPE ST
300 MESA 85201 741-J1
700 MESA 85203 742-A1
1500 MESA 85213 742-E1
4000 MESA 85205 742-J1
4200 MESA 85205 743-A1
E HOPI AV
1300 MESA 85204 782-C2
3700 MESA 85206 782-H2
4500 MESA 85206 783-A2
7600 MESA 85208 783-J2
N HOPI AV
400 GIL 85234 782-H6

S HOPI AV
900 WICK 85390 290-B4
E HOPI CIR
1300 MESA 85204 782-B2
4200 MESA 85206 782-B2
4700 MESA 85206 783-A2
S HOPI CIR
1500 MESA 85206 783-A2
S HOPI DR
- GDYR 85338 (773-J6
See Page 733)
800 TEMP 85282 780-C2
W HOPI DR
700 CHAN 85225 821-E7
1600 CHAN 85224 861-C1
S HOPI LN
- GDYR 85338 (774-A4
See Page 733)
- PinC 85219 785-G2
10700 GDYR 85338 (773-J4
See Page 733)
HOPI RD
3100 GLEN 85307 615-C7
S HOPI RD
300 APJT 85219 745-F6
1200 APJT 85219 785-F1
E HOPI ST
4400 PHX 85044 819-G1
N HOPI ST
200 GBND 85337 (1090-A3
See Page 1049)
S HOPI ST
- GDYR 85338 (773-J6
See Page 733)
W HOPI ST
- MarC 85353 735-G1
1300 CHAN 85224 861-C1
10700 AVON 85353 735-E1
N HOPI TR
17600 SURP 85374 534-J6
N HOPI WY
3500 SCTS 85251 700-E1
E HOPKINS RD
- MarC 85296 822-C7
E HORIZON DR
- CVCK 85331 420-G3
7300 CARE 85377 420-H3
9200 SCTS 85262 421-D3
N HORIZON DR
23000 MarC 85375 494-J7
W HORIZON DR
14000 MarC 85375 495-A7
14400 MarC 85375 494-J7
S HORIZON PL
1000 CHAN 85248 861-D5
N HORIZON TR
- FTNH 85268 623-A5
N HORNE ST
- MESA 85203 742-A3
300 GIL 85233 781-J5
1600 MarC 85203 702-A4
1600 MESA 85203 702-A6
4100 MarC 85256 662-A7
4100 MarC 85256 702-A4
S HORNE ST
- MESA 85204 742-A6
900 MESA 85204 782-A2
1500 MESA 85203 742-A1
E HORNED OWL TR
- SCTS 85262 (461-E7
See Page 421)
6600 SCTS 85331 460-F7
W HORSEMAN LN
14700 MarC 85375 534-H1
E HORSESHOE AV
200 GIL 85296 822-C1
W HORSESHOE AV
- MarC 85233 781-J7
- MarC 85233 782-A7
300 GIL 85233 822-B1
800 GIL 85233 782-A7
E HORSESHOE BEND
18400 MarC 85263 503-H4
N HORSESHOE CIR
- MarC 85264 583-G7
E HORSESHOE CT
1700 GIL 85296 822-H1
E HORSESHOE DR
- MarC 85249 901-H1
E HORSESHOE LN
6600 PVAL 85253 660-E2
7800 SCTS 85250 660-H3
N HORSESHOE LN
17400 MarC 85373 536-C7
E HORSESHOE RD
4400 PHX 85028 619-J5
5000 PHX 85028 619-J5
5000 PVAL 85253 620-A5
N HORSESHOE TR
- WICK 85390 290-C2
25000 SCTS 85255 501-B4
HORSESHOE DAM RD
42700 MarC 85255 103-B1
W HORSHAM DR
2900 PHX 85027 538-B2
N HOSICK
200 MESA 85201 741-F4
S HOSICK
2200 MESA 85210 781-F4
S HOSICK AV
3000 MESA 85210 781-F5
N HOSICK CIR
600 MESA 85201 741-F3
S HOSICK CIR
2000 MESA 85210 781-F6
HOSPITAL DR
- PHX 85008 699-C6
E HOUSTON AV
- GIL 85234 782-E4
2700 GIL 85234 783-C4
3000 MarC 85234 783-C4
4000 MarC 85236 783-C4
4000 GIL 85236 783-C4
W HOUSTON AV
- GIL 85233 782-A4
1100 GIL 85233 781-H4
1600 APJT 85220 785-B5
1600 PinC 85220 785-B5
2600 APJT 85220 784-J5
2600 PinC 85220 784-J5
E HOVERLAND RD
8100 SCTS 85255 540-J4
20600 SCTS 85255 541-A4
E HOVEY AV
21600 MarC 85361 (453-A1
See Page 413)
W HOVEY AV
21700 MarC 85361 (453-A1
See Page 413)

S HOWARD CT
- WICK 85390 290-F3
S HOWARD DR
25600 MarC 85248 901-C5
E HOWE ST
2000 TEMP 85281 740-J5
2100 TEMP 85281 741-A5
W HOWE ST
400 TEMP 85281 740-B4
S HUACHUCA WY
- MarC 85249 902-D4
E HUALAPAI DR
8800 SCTS 85255 541-C6
W HUBBARD DR
17400 GDYR 85338 (774-A6
See Page 733)
18100 GDYR 85338 (773-H6
See Page 733)
W HUBBEL ST
- AVON 85323 695-H3
E HUBBELL ST
1200 PHX 85006 698-J4
1400 PHX 85006 699-A4
2000 SCTS 85257 700-D4
2400 PHX 85008 699-C4
5100 PHX 85008 700-A4
8700 SCTS 85257 701-A4
8700 MarC 85256 701-A4
8700 MarC 85257 701-A4
W HUBBELL ST
- AVON 85323 695-G3
3500 PHX 85009 697-G3
4300 PHX 85035 697-A3
6900 PHX 85035 696-J3
8300 PHX 85037 696-D3
E HUBER CIR
4100 MESA 85205 742-J2
E HUBER ST
200 MESA 85201 741-J2
400 MESA 85203 741-J2
700 MESA 85203 742-A2
1800 MESA 85213 742-D2
3600 MESA 85205 742-H2
5600 MESA 85205 743-D2
N HUDSON CT
- MarC 85087 (378-A4
See Page 337)
W HUDSON CT
- MarC 85087 (378-A3
See Page 337)
E HUDSON DR
1400 TEMP 85281 740-G5
N HUDSON DR
800 CHAN 85225 821-J4
S HUDSON DR
- CHAN 85225 861-J1
N HUDSON LN
800 GIL 85236 783-C5
W HUDSON LN
- TEMP 85281 740-D5
N HUDSON PL
1000 CHAN 85225 821-J4
S HUDSON PL
- MarC 85249 901-H2
N HUDSON ST
200 CHAN 85225 821-J6
W HUDSON WY
900 GIL 85233 782-A4
1100 GIL 85233 781-J4
W HU ESTA DR
- TEMP 85282 740-D6
N HUFF N PUFF PL
36400 CARE 85377 420-J6
N HUGH PL
- GIL 85234 783-B7
W HUGHES DR
- PHX 85043 736-H2
- PHX 85353 736-E2
E HULET DR
2200 CHAN 85225 822-B5
W HULET DR
- CHAN 85225 822-B6
- CHAN 85225 821-F5
E HULET PL
- CHAN 85225 822-A5
E HUM RD
7400 CARE 85377 420-H4
N HUM RD
7300 CARE 85377 420-H4
E HUMMINGBIRD LN
4800 PVAL 85253 659-J1
4800 PVAL 85253 660-A1
5800 PVAL 85253 620-C7
10100 PinC 85219 786-J7
10100 PinC 85219 826-H1
N HUMMINGBIRD LN
7600 PVAL 85253 620-D7
N HUMMINGBIRD TR
900 FTNH 85268 623-B5
N HUNT CIR
2000 MESA 85203 702-C6
N HUNT DR
- MESA 85203 742-C1
2100 MESA 85203 702-C6
S HUNT DR
100 MESA 85204 742-C6
N HUNT DR E
- MESA 85203 742-C5
N HUNT DR W
- MESA 85203 742-C5
E HUNT HWY
9600 MarC 85248 901-C6
9600 PinC - 901-C6
11200 MarC 85249 901-F6
12000 CHAN 85249 901-H6
12500 CHAN 85249 902-D6
12500 PinC - 902-D6
12800 MarC 85249 902-D6
17000 MarC 85242 903-C6
17000 PinC - 903-C6
18400 QC 85242 903-F6
19000 PinC 85242 903-F6
19200 QC 85242 903-F6
W HUNT HWY
- PinC - 903-J7
4100 PinC 85242 904-B7
8100 QC 85242 903-J7
8100 QC 85242 904-B7
W HUNT ST
200 GBND 85337 (1090-A3
See Page 1049)
500 GBND 85337 (1089-J3
See Page 1049)
E HUNTER CT
9400 SCTS 85262 501-D1
W HUNTER ST
- MESA 85201 741-G1
E HUNTINGTON DR
200 TEMP 85282 740-E7
200 TEMP 85282 780-J1

E HUNTINGTON DR
1200 PHX 85040 738-J7
2400 TEMP 85282 781-A1
4100 PHX 85040 739-G7
S HUNTINGTON DR
3100 TEMP 85282 739-J7
3100 TEMP 85282 740-A7
W HUNTINGTON DR
- PHX 85339 737-D7
1400 TEMP 85282 740-A7
2200 TEMP 85282 739-J7
3700 PHX 85041 737-G7
3900 MarC 85041 737-G7
W HUNTLY CT
15700 SURP 85374 534-F6
E HUNTRESS DR
6000 PVAL 85253 660-D3
E HURON CT
2000 GIL 85234 782-H5
W HURON DR
14400 MarC 85375 534-G2
14400 MarC 85375 535-A2
E HURON LN
17500 FTNH 85268 583-E5
W HURON LN
19300 MarC 85326 (773-F6
See Page 733)
W HUTTON DR
9100 MarC 85351 576-A1
10700 MarC 85351 575-H1
N HYACINTH DR
17900 MarC 85375 535-B6
W HYACINTH DR
13200 MarC 85375 535-C6
E HYDE PARK PL
16200 FTNH 85268 583-B5
W HYDER RD
- MarC 85354 105-C1

I

I-8 FRONT
34700 MarC 85337 (1089-A5
See Page 1049)
I-10 FRONT
- PHX 85034 739-B1
- PHX 85034 699-B7
W IAN DR
- PHX 85339 777-D3
N IBIS CT
20000 MarC 85375 534-H3
E IBSEN DR
16800 FTNH 85268 583-D6
N IBSEN DR
14200 FTNH 85268 583-D5
W IDA LN
17500 SURP 85387 534-A1
E IDAHO AV
- MESA 85220 784-F3
8000 MESA 85208 784-A3
E IDAHO CIR
- MESA 85220 784-F3
S IDAHO CT
25600 MarC 85248 900-J4
N IDAHO RD
500 APJT 85219 745-E4
800 APJT 85220 745-E4
4000 PinC 85220 745-E4
4200 PinC 85220 705-E7
N IDAHO RD Rt#-88
- APJT 85219 745-E6
S IDAHO RD
- APJT 85220 785-E3
S IDAHO RD Rt#-88
- APJT 85219 745-E7
600 APJT 85220 745-E7
1100 APJT 85220 785-E2
S IGLESIA CIR
2600 MESA 85202 781-B4
W ILESO CIR
1500 MESA 85202 781-D2
ILINOIS
6800 PinC 85219 786-D7
6800 PinC 85219 826-D1
E ILLINI ST
- PHX 85040 738-G5
1500 PHX 85040 739-A5
10000 MarC 85220 744-F6
W ILLINI ST
- BUCK 85326 731-J3
- PHX 85043 736-H4
- PHX 85043 737-B4
- PHX 85041 738-F5
6500 MarC 85043 737-A4
12300 AVON 85323 735-D4
12300 AVON 85353 735-D4
12300 MarC 85323 735-D4
12300 MarC 85353 735-D4
25100 BUCK 85326 (732-A3
See Page 731)
E ILLINOIS AV
8800 MarC 85248 900-J5
S ILLINOIS AV
25400 MarC 85248 900-J4
W ILLINOIS AV
11400 YNTN 85335 615-H1
S ILLINOIS PL
- CHAN 85248 861-E5
N ILLINOIS ST
1900 CHAN 85225 821-E2
S ILLINOIS ST
- CHAN 85248 861-E7
E IMPALA AV
800 MESA 85204 782-A2
7500 MESA 85208 783-J3
8000 MESA 85208 784-A3
W IMPALA AV
1400 MESA 85202 781-B2
E IMPALA CIR
2700 MESA 85204 782-F3
W IMPALA CIR
800 MESA 85210 781-E2
E IMPALA CT
7400 MESA 85208 783-H3
E INCA AV
16200 FTNH 85268 623-C2
N INCA AV
11000 FTNH 85268 623-D2
E INCA CIR
1600 MESA 85203 742-D1
N INCA CT
21800 MarC 85375 534-G1
N INCA PL
17200 SURP 85374 535-B7
S INCA RD
- LP 85340 655-A6
E INCA ST
800 MESA 85203 742-A1
2000 MESA 85213 742-D1
5700 MESA 85205 743-E1

STREET
Block City ZIP Pg-Grid

N INDEPENDENCE WY
40500 MarC 85086 (378-C6
See Page 337)
N INDIAN LN
4100 PHX 85013 658-F7
E INDIAN PZ
7300 SCTS 85251 660-F7
E INDIAN RD
300 GBND 85337 (1090-C2
See Page 1049)
W INDIAN RD
200 MarC 85337 (1090-A2
See Page 1049)
200 GBND 85337 (1090-A2
See Page 1049)
500 MarC 85337 (1089-J2
See Page 1049)
500 GBND 85337 (1089-J2
See Page 1049)
N INDIAN TR
800 PHX 85008 699-E5
E INDIANA AV
8800 MarC 85248 900-J4
9600 MarC 85248 901-B4
W INDIANA AV
11100 YNTN 85335 615-H1
E INDIANA CT
9400 MarC 85248 901-B4
E INDIAN BASKET RD
1200 CARE 85377 420-H6
E INDIAN BEND RD
- MarC 85256 662-A2
- MarC 85256 663-A4
4500 PVAL 85253 659-J1
4800 PVAL 85253 660-C2
7100 SCTS 85253 660-E2
7200 SCTS 85258 660-G2
7200 SCTS 85250 660-J2
8400 SCTS 85258 661-A2
8400 SCTS 85250 661-A2
8800 MarC 85250 661-A2
8800 MarC 85258 661-A2
10400 MarC 85256 661-A2
S INDIAN BEND FRONT
1500 TEMP 85281 741-A6
N INDIAN CAMP TR
34700 SCTS 85262 420-J7
34700 SCTS 85262 460-J1
35100 CARE 85377 420-J7
35100 SCTS 85377 420-J7
W INDIAN HILLS DR
9200 MarC 85351 576-C3
W INDIAN HILLS PL
1000 PHX 85023 578-F5
N INDIAN KNOLL
26500 MarC 85263 503-J4
E INDIANOLA AV
- PHX 85012 658-G7
- PHX 85012 698-G1
1000 PHX 85014 698-J1
1300 PHX 85014 699-A1
1600 PHX 85016 699-A1
3400 PHX 85018 699-G1
4300 PHX 85018 659-J7
4800 PHX 85018 700-J1
8000 SCTS 85251 700-J1
8500 SCTS 85251 701-A1
W INDIANOLA AV
- AVON 85323 655-D7
- GDYR 85338 655-D7
100 PHX 85013 658-E7
600 PHX 85013 698-F1
1500 PHX 85015 658-C7
3700 GDYR 85338 (654-E7
See Page 653)
3800 PHX 85033 657-C7
4200 PHX 85031 657-C7
7000 PHX 85033 656-F7
8300 PHX 85037 656-D7
W INDIANOLA CT
- MarC 85340 653-E6
N INDIAN PONY WY
11200 FTNH 85268 623-A3
E INDIAN ROCK RD
1500 CARE 85377 420-H7
E INDIAN SCHOOL RD
- PHX 85012 658-H7
700 PHX 85014 658-H7
1300 PHX 85014 659-D7
1600 PHX 85016 659-D7
3200 PHX 85018 659-D7
4700 PHX 85018 699-J1
4900 PHX 85018 700-B1
6000 SCTS 85251 700-F1
8500 SCTS 85251 701-B1
8800 MarC 85256 701-B1
12000 MarC 85256 702-A1
W INDIAN SCHOOL RD
- GDYR 85338 655-A6
- PHX 85012 658-B7
- PHX 85013 658-B7
1000 MarC 85037 656-C7
1500 PHX 85015 658-B7
2500 PHX 85017 658-A7
3200 PHX 85017 657-G7
3400 PHX 85019 657-G7
4000 PHX 85031 657-G7
5900 PHX 85033 657-A7
6900 PHX 85033 656-G7
8300 PHX 85037 656-E7
9900 AVON 85323 656-C7
10400 PHX 85037 655-F6
10400 AVON 85323 655-F6
10400 AVON 85037 655-F6
11000 MarC 85037 655-F6
11700 MarC 85340 655-D6
11700 AVON 85340 655-F6
13100 LP 85340 655-A6
14100 GDYR 85340 (654-H6
See Page 653)
14100 LP 85338 655-A6
14100 LP 85340 (654-H6
See Page 653)
14300 GDYR 85338 (654-D6
See Page 653)
14300 LP 85338 (654-H6
See Page 653)
17100 GDYR 85338 653-H6
18700 MarC 85338 653-H6
18700 MarC 85340 653-E6
20300 BUCK 85340 653-B6
21100 BUCK 85340 (652-H6
See Page 651)
27500 BUCK 85373 651-B5
1000 MarC 85037 102-A2
W INDIAN SCHOOL RD BYPS
13300 LP 85340 655-A7
13300 AVON 85340 655-A7
13900 LP 85338 655-A7

STREET
Block City ZIP Pg-Grid

W INDIAN SCHOOL RD BYPS
13900 GDYR 85338 655-A7
14800 GDYR 85338 (654-H7
See Page 653)
W INDIAN SPRINGS RD
- MarC 85353 775-C2
12300 AVON 85323 775-C2
12300 AVON 85338 775-C2
12300 MarC 85323 775-C2
13300 MarC 85338 775-C2
13900 MarC 85338 (774-J2
See Page 733)
W INDIAN WELLS
- TEMP 85282 779-J1
- TEMP 85282 780-A1
E INDIAN WELLS CT
1200 CHAN 85249 901-H5
E INDIAN WELLS DR
- MarC 85249 902-E5
1400 MarC 85249 901-J5
1800 CHAN 85249 902-A5
N INDIAN WELLS DR
10400 FTNH 85268 623-D3
S INDIAN WELLS DR
10700 GDYR 85338 (774-A5
See Page 733)
W INDIAN WELLS DR
10400 MarC 85373 536-A4
E INDIAN WELLS PL
- CHAN 85249 902-A5
- CHAN 85249 902-B5
E INDIGO CIR
1300 MESA 85203 742-B1
3600 MESA 85205 742-H1
3600 MESA 85213 742-G1
N INDIGO CIR
1600 MESA 85201 741-F1
E INDIGO DR
10200 SCTS 85260 581-E2
N INDIGO DR
11000 FTNH 85268 623-B3
W INDIGO DR
1000 CHAN 85248 861-A6
W INDIGO LN
- SURP 85374 534-F2
E INDIGO ST
- MESA 85213 742-F1
- MESA 85201 741-H1
1000 MESA 85203 742-B1
5700 MESA 85205 743-B1
6800 MESA 85207 743-G1
W INDIGO ST
- CHAN 85248 861-E6
100 MESA 85201 741-F1
E INDIGO BAY CT
- GIL 85236 783-C4
3000 GIL 85234 783-B4
E INDIGO BAY DR
2200 GIL 85234 782-J4
3000 GIL 85234 783-B4
4400 GIL 85236 783-D4
N INDIGO BAY DR
1200 GIL 85234 782-J4
E INDIGO BRUSH RD
2000 PHX 85048 819-A4
N INDIGO HILL DR
- FTNH 85268 622-H4
N INDUSTRIAL DR
- WICK 85390 289-F2
S INDUSTRIAL DR
100 TEMP 85281 740-H3
W INDUSTRIAL RD
3400 MarC 85390 289-E2
3400 WICK 85390 289-E2
W INDUSTRIAL ST
25000 MarC 85326 (771-J1
See Page 731)
25000 MarC 85326 (772-A1
See Page 731)
S INDUSTRIAL PARK AV
1000 TEMP 85281 740-B6
1000 TEMP 85282 740-B6
S INEZ CT
- GIL 85236 863-C5
W INGLESIDE DR
- SURP 85374 534-B6
E INGLEWOOD CIR
- MESA 85213 742-G1
E INGLEWOOD ST
- MESA 85201 741-H1
1600 MESA 85203 742-D1
2100 MESA 85213 742-D1
5600 MESA 85205 743-D1
7000 MESA 85207 743-G1
W INGLEWOOD ST
- MESA 85201 741-F1
600 MESA 85201 701-F7
900 MarC 85201 701-F7
E INGRAM CIR
7200 MESA 85207 743-H1
E INGRAM ST
- MESA 85201 741-H1
400 MESA 85203 741-J1
1000 MESA 85203 742-B1
4600 MESA 85205 743-B1
W INGRAM ST
600 MESA 85201 741-F1
W INLET LP
1800 MESA 85202 781-B2
E INNER CIR
- SCTS 85258 661-A1
E INNOVATION CIR
- TEMP 85284 820-H2
INNOVATIVE DR
- PHX 85086 (377-J5
See Page 337)
N INTEGRITY CT
- MarC 85086 (418-A1
See Page 417)
N INTEGRITY TR
- MarC 85086 (378-B7
See Page 337)
- MarC 85086 (418-A1
See Page 417)
E INTERLACKEN DR
- PHX 85022 578-H4
W INTERLACKEN DR
- PHX 85023 578-G4
E INTREPID AV
1800 MESA 85204 782-C2
N INVERGORDON PL
7800 PVAL 85253 620-D7
N INVERGORDON RD
3800 PHX 85251 700-D1
3800 SCTS 85251 700-D1
4000 PHX 85251 660-D7
4000 SCTS 85251 660-D5
5000 PVAL 85251 660-D5

STREET
Block City ZIP Pg-Grid

N INVERGORDON RD
5000 PVAL 85253 660-D1
7500 PVAL 85253 620-D4
E INVERNESS AV
- GIL 85206 783-C3
1000 MESA 85204 782-D2
1800 MESA 85206 783-A3
3600 MESA 85206 782-H3
7200 MESA 85208 783-H2
7900 MESA 85208 784-A3
E INVERNESS CIR
1900 MESA 85204 782-C3
W INVERNESS DR
1600 TEMP 85282 740-A7
W INWOOD CT
10200 MarC 85351 576-B7
N IONA CT
18600 MarC 85375 535-A5
E IONA PL
- SCTS 85331 500-D3
IOWA
- PinC 85219 826-D1
W IOWA
11200 PEOR 85345 616-C1
W IOWA AV
11100 YNTN 85335 615-H1
N IOWA ST
200 CHAN 85225 821-E2
600 CHAN 85225 781-E7
S IOWA ST
- CHAN 85225 861-E1
- CHAN 85248 861-E3
W IPSWITCH WY
- SURP 85374 534-D6
E IRAN AV
1600 MESA 85204 782-C2
7800 MESA 85208 783-J3
7900 MESA 85208 784-A3
E IRAN CT
7400 MESA 85208 783-H3
W IRENE LN
8700 TOL 85353 696-D5
E IRIS CT
- GIL 85296 822-E3
E IRIS DR
- GIL 85296 822-E3
W IRIS DR
- CHAN 85248 861-E7
700 GIL 85233 822-A3
800 GIL 85233 821-J3
E IRIS RD
10100 MarC 85207 744-F1
E IRIS ST
3000 MESA 85213 742-F1
W IRISADO CIR
1000 MESA 85210 781-E2
1300 MESA 85202 781-A2
W IRISH GOLD DR
- SURP 85374 575-G1
E IRISH HUNTER TR
8500 SCTS 85258 621-A3
E IRMA LN
- PHX 85050 579-G4
1000 PHX 85024 538-J4
1000 PHX 85024 539-A4
W IRMA LN
- GLEN 85308 536-J3
700 PHX 85024 538-J4
2200 PHX 85027 538-A3
3600 PHX 85308 537-H3
3600 PHX 85308 538-A3
5500 GLEN 85308 537-A3
9800 PEOR 85382 536-A3
10700 PEOR 85373 536-A3
10800 PEOR 85373 535-J3
W IRON AV
- MarC 85210 781-F2
300 MESA 85210 781-F2
E IRONHORSE CT
- GIL 85236 863-D4
N IRON HORSE CT
- MarC 85086 (378-D5
See Page 337)
N IRON HORSE DR
- MarC 85086 (378-D5
See Page 337)
N IRONHORSE DR
16400 SURP 85374 534-D6
E IRONHORSE RD
- GIL 85236 863-D4
N IRON HORSE WY
- MarC 85086 (378-D6
See Page 337)
W IRON MOUNTAIN CT
11500 SURP 85374 535-G5
S IRON ORE DR
- APJT 85219 785-J4
E IRON RINGS DR
- SCTS 85255 541-D3
E IRONSTONE DR
- APJT 85219 785-H3
N IRONWOOD
200 MESA 85201 741-C4
S IRONWOOD
1300 BUCK 85326 (692-C7
See Page 651)
W IRONWOOD
17100 SURP 85374 534-B5
E IRONWOOD CIR
- CVCK 85331 (380-D6
See Page 339)
- MarC 85263 503-J3
N IRONWOOD CIR
1100 GIL 85234 782-D4
W IRONWOOD CIR
1300 CHAN 85226 820-J3
E IRONWOOD CT
7300 SCTS 85258 620-G3
S IRONWOOD CT
500 GIL 85296 822-D1
E IRONWOOD DR
400 PHX 85020 618-J3
500 CHAN 85225 821-G3
1500 PHX 85020 619-A3
1600 CHAN 85225 822-A3
2700 PHX 85028 619-D3
3600 PHX 85044 819-F3
5900 PVAL 85253 620-C6
6200 SCTS 85331 500-E3
6300 PVAL 85253 660-D2
7600 SCTS 85258 620-G3
9600 SCTS 85258 621-D4
11700 SCTS 85259 621-J4
12000 SCTS 85259 622-A4
16000 FTNH 85268 623-B1
N IRONWOOD DR
- SCTS 85331 500-D2
- APJT 85220 745-C2
600 BUCK 85326 (772-C1
See Page 731)

STREET
Block City ZIP Pg-Grid

N IRONWOOD DR
4000 PinC 85220 745-C2
4200 PinC 85220 705-C7
7500 PVAL 85253 620-D4
7500 PVAL 85253 660-D1
7500 SCTS 85262 460-J1
9800 PHX 85020 618-H3
S IRONWOOD DR
- APJT 85220 745-C7
- APJT 85220 785-C4
1200 APJT 85220 785-C4
1400 GIL 85296 822-D4
2300 PinC 85220 785-C4
5300 APJT 85219 785-C4
6900 APJT 85219 825-B2
6900 PinC 85219 825-B2
6900 APJT 85220 825-B2
6900 PinC 85220 825-B2
W IRONWOOD DR
100 CHAN 85225 821-E3
900 PHX 85021 618-D3
1500 CHAN 85224 821-A3
2700 CHAN 85224 820-H3
3200 CHAN 85226 820-H3
3200 PHX 85051 618-A3
3400 PHX 85051 617-G3
4300 GLEN 85302 617-D2
6700 PEOR 85302 617-B3
6700 PEOR 85345 617-B3
6900 PEOR 85345 616-C3
9400 MarC 85351 616-B3
E IRONWOOD LN
10600 MarC 85220 744-G7
10600 MESA 85220 744-G7
E IRONWOOD RD
- MarC 85264 623-H3
N IRONWOOD RD
3000 CARE 85377 420-J7
3000 SCTS 85377 420-J7
3000 CARE 85262 420-J7
3000 SCTS 85262 420-J7
N IRONWOOD ST
- GIL 85234 782-D4
S IRONWOOD ST
- MarC 85296 822-D7
- MarC 85296 862-D1
100 GIL 85296 822-D1
W IRONWOOD ST
- SURP 85374 (574-D1
See Page 573)
12400 SURP 85374 575-B2
E IRONWOOD BLUFF
41500 CVCK 85331 (380-D6
See Page 339)
S IROQUOIS DR
11000 PHX 85044 779-H7
11400 PHX 85044 819-H1
S IROQUOIS LN
3800 PinC 85219 786-H4
E IRVINE RD
- MarC 85086 (418-J2
See Page 417)
700 MarC 85086 419-A2
W IRVINE RD
- MarC 85086 (418-C2
See Page 417)
E IRWIN AV
- MESA 85220 784-F3
100 BUCK 85326 (772-A2
See Page 731)
1700 MESA 85204 782-C2
3700 MESA 85206 782-H2
7400 MESA 85208 783-H3
8000 MESA 85208 784-A3
W IRWIN AV
- PHX 85041 777-G1
E IRWIN CIR
- MESA 85220 784-F3
2400 MESA 85204 782-E2
E ISABELLA AV
800 MESA 85204 782-A2
3700 MESA 85206 782-H2
W ISABELLA AV
800 MESA 85210 781-E2
1200 MESA 85202 781-A2
E ISLAND CIR
9900 SCTS 85258 621-D3
N ISLAND CIR
10500 SCTS 85258 621-D3
W ISLAND CIR
1200 CHAN 85248 861-C5
S ISLAND DR
- GIL 85233 781-J7
W ISLAND DR
1200 CHAN 85248 861-D6
W ISLANDIA DR
1100 GIL 85233 821-H2
S ISLANDS DR
100 GIL 85233 781-J7
100 GIL 85233 821-J1
400 GIL 85233 822-A1
W ISLETA AV
1000 MESA 85210 781-E2
1700 MESA 85202 781-C2
W ISTHMUS LP
1700 MESA 85202 781-B2
N ITHICA CT
800 CHAN 85225 821-H2
N ITHICA PL
- CHAN 85225 821-G6
N ITHICA ST
100 CHAN 85225 821-H2
500 GIL 85233 781-H4
S ITHICA ST
600 CHAN 85225 821-G7
700 CHAN 85225 861-G1
900 CHAN 85249 861-G1
E IVANHOE CT
- GIL 85236 822-J5
- GIL 85236 823-A5
- GIL 85236 822-E5
W IVANHOE CT
3400 CHAN 85226 820-B4
W IVANHOE PL
5000 CHAN 85226 820-E4
E IVANHOE ST
- MarC 85236 823-E5
- CHAN 85225 821-F4
600 GIL 85233 822-A5
1000 GIL 85296 822-A5
1900 CHAN 85225 822-A5
1900 CHAN 85233 822-A5
13600 MarC 85296 822-C5
22800 MarC 85212 824-H5
N IVANHOE ST
900 CHAN 85224 821-B4
W IVANHOE ST
- CHAN 85225 821-B4
- GIL 85233 822-B4
- MarC 85233 822-C4
700 CHAN 85226 820-A4

STREET
Block City ZIP Pg-Grid

W IVANHOE ST
1000 CHAN 85224 821-A4
2700 CHAN 85224 820-G4
4300 MarC 85339 817-F4
W IVER RD
50700 MarC 85320 (285-A6
See Page 244)
50800 MarC 85320 (284-J6
See Page 244)
N IVORY DR
15000 FTNH 85268 583-D5
N IVORY LN
3100 AVON 85323 695-H1
W IVORY LN
10700 AVON 85323 695-H1
W IVORY FASHION LN
- SURP 85374 575-G1
E IVY CIR
3800 MESA 85205 742-H1
W IVY CIR
600 MESA 85201 741-F1
S IVY CT
3700 CHAN 85248 861-B7
E IVY ST
- MESA 85201 741-H1
400 MESA 85203 741-J1
1000 MESA 85203 742-B1
1600 MESA 85205 743-A1
1900 MESA 85203 742-D1
1900 MESA 85213 742-D1
3800 MESA 85205 742-J1
7300 MESA 85207 743-H1
S IVY WY
3500 CHAN 85248 861-B6
E IVYGLEN CIR
- MESA 85213 742-G1
3800 MESA 85205 742-J1
E IVYGLEN ST
1200 MESA 85203 742-B1
2400 MESA 85213 742-E1
3800 MESA 85205 742-H1
6000 MESA 85205 743-C1
7200 MESA 85207 743-H1
W IVYGLEN ST
- MESA 85201 741-G1

J

S JACANA LN
- MarC 85236 823-E5
E JACARANDA
- MESA 85201 701-H7
2200 MESA 85213 702-E7
E JACARANDA CIR
- MESA 85213 742-E1
1900 MESA 85203 702-D7
W JACARANDA DR
10900 MarC 85373 535-J7
N JACARANDA PKWY
1700 CHAN 85248 861-B5
NE JACARANDA PKWY
1100 CHAN 85248 861-C5
SE JACARANDA PKWY
1300 CHAN 85248 861-D6
SW JACARANDA PKWY
1700 CHAN 85248 861-A7
S JACARANDA RD
5500 PinC 85219 786-H6
E JACARANDA ST
5600 MESA 85205 743-D1
E JACINTO AV
1600 MESA 85204 782-C3
W JACINTO AV
1400 MESA 85202 781-A3
E JACINTO CIR
2600 MESA 85204 782-E3
W JACINTO CIR
900 MESA 85210 781-E3
2200 MESA 85202 781-A3
N JACK BURDEN RD
- WICK 85390 290-F1
- MarC 85390 290-F1
1200 MarC 85390 250-E6
E JACKLIN DR
16300 FTNH 85268 623-C3
E JACK NEVILLE DR
8800 SCTS 85262 421-C3
S JACKNIFE DR
- APJT 85219 785-J4
W JACKPOT WY
15000 SURP 85374 534-H6
E JACKRABBIT LN
- FTNH 85268 583-A6
W JACKRABBIT LN
- PEOR 85382 497-A4
E JACKRABBIT RD
- MarC 85256 661-C5
- MarC 85256 662-A5
6300 PVAL 85251 660-D5
6300 PHX 85251 660-D5
6400 PVAL 85253 660-D5
7100 SCTS 85253 660-F5
7200 SCTS 85250 660-H5
7200 PVAL 85250 660-G5
8400 SCTS 85250 661-C5
8600 MarC 85250 661-C5
N JACKRABBIT RD
40800 PinC 85242 865-F5
N JACKRABBIT TR
- BUCK 85326 (693-E2
See Page 653)
300 MarC 85326 (693-E2
See Page 653)
2900 MarC 85340 653-E3
2900 MarC 85340 (693-E2
See Page 653)
S JACKRABBIT TR
- BUCK 85326 (693-E7
See Page 653)
900 MarC 85326 (693-E7
See Page 653)
1200 MarC 85326 733-E5
2800 BUCK 85326 733-E5
7100 MarC 85326 (773-E1
See Page 733)
7600 BUCK 85326 (773-E1
See Page 733)
E JACKSON AV
100 BUCK 85326 (772-A1
See Page 731)
N JACKSON CIR
600 MESA 85205 742-J3
S JACKSON CIR
1400 MESA 85206 782-J2
E JACKSON PL
2100 CHAN 85225 821-H2
N JACKSON PL
- CHAN 85225 821-H6
E JACKSON ST
- PHX 85004 698-G7
700 PHX 85034 698-J7

STREET
Block City ZIP Pg-Grid

E JACKSON ST
800 AVON 85323 695-C6
1400 PHX 85034 699-A7
N JACKSON ST
- WICK 85390 290-E2
100 CHAN 85225 821-H3
400 GIL 85233 781-H4
S JACKSON ST
- WICK 85390 290-E3
100 CHAN 85225 821-H7
900 CHAN 85249 861-G1
W JACKSON ST
- AVON 85323 695-E6
- AVON 85353 695-E6
- GDYR 85338 (694-D6
See Page 653)
- PHX 85003 698-F7
700 PHX 85007 698-E7
1900 PHX 85009 698-A7
3100 PHX 85009 697-J7
6400 PHX 85043 697-B7
9200 TOL 85353 696-C6
E JACOB AV
- MESA 85220 784-F3
7000 MESA 85208 783-G3
8000 MESA 85208 784-A3
E JACOB CIR
9500 MESA 85208 784-D3
S JACOB CT
600 GIL 85296 822-D2
S JACOB ST
500 GIL 85296 822-D2
W JACOBSON DR
- MarC 85340 655-C1
E JACOB WALTZ ST
- APJT 85219 746-B2
4800 PinC 85219 746-C3
N JACQUELINE DR
6100 CVCK 85331 420-E3
N JADE CIR
100 MESA 85201 741-C4
W JADE CT
- CHAN 85248 861-E6
W JADE DR
- CHAN 85248 861-D6
E JADECREST DR
9300 MarC 85248 901-A2
W JADESTONE DR
12300 MarC 85375 535-D4
E JAEGER CIR
- MESA 85213 702-G7
E JAEGER RD
4400 PHX 85050 540-A2
E JAEGER ST
2200 MESA 85213 702-E7
5600 MESA 85205 743-D1
N JAGGED CIR
- FTNH 85268 622-G4
W JAGUAR DR
13900 MarC 85375 535-B3
E JAMAICA AV
1800 MESA 85204 782-C3
E JAMAICA CIR
1900 MESA 85204 782-C3
S JAMAICA CT
900 GIL 85296 822-J3
E JAMAICA LN
15500 FTNH 85268 583-A4
N JAMAICA WY
800 GIL 85234 782-J4
S JAMAICA WY
900 GIL 85296 822-J3
N JAMES SHERWOOD ST
300 TOL 85353 696-D5
E JAMIE CT
5600 MarC 85331 500-C1
E JAN AV
- MESA 85220 784-F3
7000 MESA 85208 783-G3
7800 MESA 85208 784-A3
E JAN CIR
- MESA 85220 784-G3
E JANELLE CT
- MarC 85236 903-C2
E JANELLE WY
- MarC 85236 903-C2
W JANICE DR
1000 TEMP 85283 780-B4
E JANICE WY
1900 PHX 85022 579-C3
2800 PHX 85032 579-D3
5000 PHX 85254 580-A4
9000 SCTS 85260 581-B4
N JANICE WY
15000 PHX 85254 580-A4
S JARDIN DR
25800 MarC 85248 901-B5
S JARED DR
300 GIL 85296 822-D1
E JARVIS AV
1000 MESA 85204 742-A6
N JARVIS ST
200 MarC 85207 744-E5
E JASMINE CIR
- MESA 85203 702-A7
E JASMINE DR
10200 SCTS 85260 581-E2
10800 SCTS 85259 581-G2
W JASMINE DR
17200 MarC 85373 536-D7
E JASMINE ST
- MESA 85201 701-H7
800 MESA 85203 702-A7
2200 MESA 85213 702-E7
4700 MESA 85205 743-B1
6600 MESA 85205 703-G7
7200 MESA 85207 743-H1
N JASMINE ST
1900 MarC 85207 744-G1
W JASMINE ST
200 MESA 85201 701-G7
E JASON DR
2500 PHX 85050 539-D6
W JASON DR
4200 PHX 85308 537-H6
9200 PEOR 85382 536-D6
E JASPER CT
100 GIL 85296 822-D3
E JASPER DR
- APJT 85219 785-H3
400 GIL 85296 822-D3
500 CHAN 85225 821-G3
2400 GIL 85236 822-J3
2400 GIL 85236 823-A3
W JASPER DR
- GIL 85233 822-B3
100 CHAN 85225 821-E3
1200 CHAN 85224 820-B3
1500 CHAN 85224 821-A3
2700 CHAN 85224 820-H3

STREET
Block City ZIP Pg-Grid

E JASPER LN
1900 CHAN 85225 822-A3
W JASPER WY
15600 SURP 85374 534-F3
E JAVALINA CT
- PinC 85219 786-D1
E JAVALINA TER
- MarC 85263 (504-A4
See Page 503)
N JAVALINA TER
- MarC 85263 (504-A4
See Page 503)
E JAVELINA AV
- MESA 85220 784-F3
100 MESA 85210 781-H3
800 MESA 85204 782-A3
8000 MESA 85208 784-A3
W JAVELINA AV
800 MESA 85210 781-E3
1100 MESA 85202 781-B3
E JAVELINA CIR
1600 MESA 85204 782-C3
W JAVELINA CIR
800 MESA 85210 781-E3
1900 MESA 85202 781-C3
W JAVELINA CT
11500 SURP 85374 535-H7
E JAVELINA DR
7800 MESA 85208 783-J3
7800 MESA 85208 784-A3
N JAVELINA DR
- SURP 85374 533-J7
S JAY CIR
1200 MESA 85204 781-J1
S JAY PL
- CHAN 85248 861-E2
N JAY ST
400 CHAN 85225 821-E1
2600 CHAN 85225 781-E6
S JAY ST
300 CHAN 85225 821-E7
600 CHAN 85225 861-E1
W JAY ST
700 CHAN 85225 781-E7
E JEAN AV
5800 PHX 85251 660-C6
E JEAN DR
6400 PHX 85254 580-E6
S JEAN ELIZABETH PL
1200 AVON 85353 735-H1
E JEANINE DR
100 TEMP 85284 820-D3
1800 TEMP 85226 820-G3
W JEANINE DR
100 TEMP 85284 820-B3
N JEB STUART ST
200 GBND 85337 (1089-J3
See Page 1049)
W JEDIONDIA DR
1100 WICK 85390 290-C3
S JEFFERSON
2500 MESA 85208 783-G5
S JEFFERSON AV
- MESA 85208 743-G6
E JEFFERSON ST
- PHX 85004 698-G7
700 PHX 85034 698-G7
1400 PHX 85034 699-A7
N JEFFERSON ST
- WICK 85390 290-E2
S JEFFERSON ST
- WICK 85390 290-F3
W JEFFERSON ST
- GDYR 85338 (694-D6
See Page 653)
- PHX 85003 698-F7
700 PHX 85007 698-C7
1900 PHX 85009 698-A7
3100 PHX 85009 697-J7
4300 PHX 85043 697-C6
8200 PEOR 85345 616-E2
9100 TOL 85353 696-C6
17900 MarC 85326 (693-H5
See Page 653)
E JEFFREY AV
600 PHX 85020 618-H7
JEMEZ RD
5400 GLEN 85307 615-B7
5400 GLEN 85307 655-C1
E JENAN DR
6000 SCTS 85254 620-D1
7200 SCTS 85260 620-G1
8400 SCTS 85260 621-A1
11200 SCTS 85259 621-H1
12500 SCTS 85259 622-B1
W JENAN DR
6700 PEOR 85345 577-A7
7100 PEOR 85345 576-F7
E JENAN ST
11800 SCTS 85259 621-G1
W JENNIFER ROSE CT
8800 PEOR 85345 616-E1
W JENNY LIN RD
3400 MarC 85087 (338-B6
See Page 337)
3700 MarC 85087 337-J7
E JENSEN ST
400 MESA 85203 701-J7
500 MESA 85203 741-J1
600 MESA 85203 742-B1
600 MESA 85203 702-A7
1800 MESA 85207 743-G1
2000 MESA 85213 742-E1
4500 MESA 85205 743-A1
10000 MarC 85207 744-E1
10500 MarC 85220 744-F1
N JENTILLY CT
1300 CHAN 85226 820-E3
S JENTILLY CT
100 CHAN 85226 820-E6
E JENTILLY LN
900 TEMP 85283 780-E4
N JENTILLY LN
- CHAN 85226 820-E4
S JENTILLY LN
700 CHAN 85226 820-E7
900 TEMP 85283 780-E4
1400 TEMP 85281 740-F5
2500 TEMP 85282 740-F6
3700 TEMP 85282 780-F1
7800 TEMP 85284 780-E7
8100 TEMP 85284 820-E1
E JERICHO DR
15700 FTNH 85268 583-A7
E JEROME AV
- MESA 85220 784-F3
1600 MESA 85204 782-C3
7800 MESA 85208 783-J3
8000 MESA 85208 784-A3

STREET
Block City ZIP Pg-Grid

S JEROME AV
500 MESA 85210 781-F3
W JEROME AV
1400 MESA 85202 781-D3
4000 MarC 85086 417-J3
E JEROME CIR
- MESA 85208 784-E3
W JEROME CIR
700 MESA 85210 781-E3
N JERRY ST
15400 SURP 85374 575-E2
W JERSEY AV
11100 YNTN 85335 575-H6
JERSTAD LN
- GLEN 85309 615-A7
N JESSE CT
500 CHAN 85225 821-H5
S JESSE CT
6600 CHAN 85249 901-H6
S JESSE PL
- CHAN 85249 861-H1
N JESSE ST
400 CHAN 85225 821-H3
S JESSE ST
- CHAN 85225 861-H1
- CHAN 85249 861-H2
- MarC 85249 901-H2
100 CHAN 85225 821-H7
S JESSE OWENS PKWY
- PHX 85040 778-G2
- PHX 85041 778-G2
W JESSICA LN
- PHX 85339 737-D7
3500 PHX 85310 498-A6
W JESSIE LN
10500 PEOR 85382 496-A7
S JEWEL DR
- APJT 85219 785-H4
W JEZEBEL DR
10900 MarC 85373 535-J7
W JIBSAIL LP
2000 MESA 85202 781-B2
E JICARILLA ST
4000 PHX 85044 779-G7
W JILL LN
15300 SURP 85374 534-G7
N JIMMY D MESSER ST
300 TOL 85353 696-E5
E JIMSON LOCO LN
11100 SCTS 85262 421-H3
N JIMSON LOCO LN
- SCTS 85262 421-H3
S JOAN LN
200 GIL 85296 822-J1
E JOAN DE ARC AV
100 PHX 85022 578-J5
1200 PHX 85022 579-A5
2600 PHX 85032 579-D6
6000 PHX 85254 580-D6
7000 SCTS 85254 580-F6
7000 SCTS 85260 580-F6
W JOAN DE ARC AV
- PHX 85304 577-G5
1300 PHX 85029 578-A5
3500 PHX 85029 577-H5
5100 GLEN 85304 577-D5
8500 PEOR 85381 576-F5
W JOANNE CIR
5000 PHX 85308 577-F1
W JOBLANCA RD
11100 AVON 85353 735-F1
W JOEDAD TER
- PEOR 85308 536-G2
S JOHN PL
- CHAN 85249 861-J2
E JOHN WY
1600 CHAN 85225 822-A4
N JOHN WY
1600 CHAN 85225 821-J4
1600 CHAN 85225 822-A4
S JOHN WY
- CHAN 85249 861-J2
- MarC 85249 901-J1
N JOHN BURDEN LN
34200 MarC 85390 290-F1
E JOHN CABOT RD
1600 PHX 85022 539-C7
2400 PHX 85032 539-D7
W JOHN CABOT RD
5400 GLEN 85308 537-C6
7100 GLEN 85308 536-H7
8400 PEOR 85382 536-F6
9200 PEOR 85373 536-D6
E JOHN HENRY LN
- GIL 85296 822-E1
N JOHNNY ST
100 GBND 85337 (1090-A3
See Page 1049)
S JOHNSON
400 MESA 85202 741-D6
2100 MESA 85202 781-D3
S JOHNSON CIR
2200 MESA 85202 781-D3
W JOHNSON DR
400 GIL 85233 822-A3
JOHNSON LN
- GLEN 85309 655-A1
S JOHNSON LN
4400 GIL 85236 863-A4
E JOHNSON RD
1000 MarC 85087 (379-A1
See Page 339)
S JOHNSON WY
1300 GIL 85233 822-B3
E JOJOBA CIR
7800 PinC 85219 786-E6
26400 SCTS 85255 501-C4
N JOJOBA CT
- SURP 85374 534-H4
S JOJOBA CT
- PinC 85219 786-E7
E JOJOBA LN
- FTNH 85268 582-J6
- FTNH 85268 583-A6
E JOJOBA RD
3600 PHX 85044 819-E3
S JOJOBA WY
3100 CHAN 85248 861-B6
4800 CHAN 85248 901-B2
N JOKAKE RD
3800 PHX 85018 700-C1
3800 PHX 85251 700-C1
4100 PHX 85251 660-C7
4300 PHX 85018 660-C7
S JOKAKE ST
11600 PHX 85044 819-H1
S JOLLY ROGER RD
5500 TEMP 85283 780-F4
E JOMAX DR
4800 PHX 85054 500-B4

STREET
Block City ZIP Pg-Grid

E JOMAX DR
4800 PHX 85331 500-B4
4800 SCTS 85331 500-B4
4800 SCTS 85054 500-B4
E JOMAX RD
2000 MarC 85024 499-D4
2000 MarC 85085 499-D4
2000 PHX 85024 499-H3
2700 PHX 85085 499-H3
4000 PHX 85331 499-H3
4000 PHX 85050 499-H3
4500 PHX 85331 500-A4
4500 PHX 85050 500-A4
5600 SCTS 85331 500-E4
5600 PHX 85054 500-A4
5600 SCTS 85054 500-A4
7200 PHX 85255 500-E4
7200 SCTS 85255 500-E4
8000 SCTS 85255 501-B4
12800 SCTS 85255 502-C4
14800 MarC 85255 502-H4
15800 MarC 85255 503-B4
17700 MarC 85263 503-G4
W JOMAX RD
- PHX 85027 498-B3
- PHX 85085 498-B3
- PHX 85310 497-B3
5300 PEOR 85382 496-C3
5300 PEOR 85382 497-B3
7400 PHX 85085 497-B3
9800 MarC 85382 496-C3
12400 MarC 85375 494-E2
12400 MarC 85375 495-A2
15500 SURP 85375 494-E2
18600 MarC 85361 493-C2
20800 SURP 85361 493-C2
S JONES
700 MESA 85204 742-B7
E JONES AV
700 PHX 85040 738-J5
1600 PHX 85040 739-A5
10000 MarC 85220 744-F6
10200 MESA 85220 744-F6
W JONES AV
- PHX 85043 736-H4
- PHX 85043 737-B4
- PHX 85041 738-F5
- PHX 85040 738-G5
N JONES CIR
1600 MESA 85203 742-B1
S JONES CIR
800 MESA 85204 742-B7
W JONES RD
32300 MarC 85390 290-C4
E JONQUIL AV
10500 PinC 85219 786-H3
E JOPEDA LN
10000 SCTS 85255 501-E7
N JOPLIN
- MarC 85207 744-E2
S JOPLIN
- MESA 85208 784-E3
- MESA 85212 784-E4
N JOPLIN CIR
- MarC 85207 744-E2
E JORDON LN
100 MarC 85086 (418-J2
See Page 417)
W JOSAC ST
6900 GLEN 85308 537-A7
E JOSEPH WY
- MarC 85296 822-C7
S JOSHUA
1300 BUCK 85326 (692-C7
See Page 651)
W JOSHUA BLVD
4500 CHAN 85226 820-E5
W JOSHUA DR
- TEMP 85282 779-J1
N JOSHUA PTH
17000 SURP 85374 534-J7
S JOSHUA TREE
- TEMP 85282 780-A1
N JOSHUA TREE CT
17000 MarC 85373 535-J7
W JOSHUA TREE DR
15700 SURP 85374 534-F3
E JOSHUA TREE LN
4500 PVAL 85253 659-H2
5600 PVAL 85253 660-C2
7200 SCTS 85250 660-F2
8600 SCTS 85250 661-A2
N JOSHUA TREE LN
100 GIL 85236 783-D4
4800 PVAL 85253 660-A2
6700 PVAL 85253 659-J2
S JOSHUA TREE LN
- GIL 85236 863-D2
7700 MESA 85208 743-J7
W JOSIE DR
10800 PEOR 85373 535-J5
S JOSLYN
- MESA 85208 784-A4
20100 MESA 85212 784-A6
E JOURNEY LN
7400 SCTS 85255 540-G4
E JOY DR
2000 PinC 85242 865-E7
W JOYCE CIR
4900 PHX 85308 577-F1
E JOY RANCH RD
- MarC 85086 (418-J3
See Page 417)
700 MarC 85086 419-B3
10100 SCTS 85262 421-F4
37800 MarC 85331 419-E3
W JOY RANCH RD
- MarC 85342 (412-E2
See Page 411)
500 MarC 85086 (418-C3
See Page 417)
1900 PHX 85086 (418-C3
See Page 417)
21000 MarC 85342 413-B2
E JUANA CT
4600 PHX 85331 500-A1
5700 MarC 85331 500-C1
W JUANA CT
- PHX 85085 498-B1
E JUANITA AV
- MarC 85234 783-B4
- MESA 85220 784-F3
100 GIL 85234 782-D4
400 MESA 85204 781-J3
700 MESA 85204 782-A3
3600 GIL 85234 783-B4
3600 GIL 85234 783-C4
7000 MESA 85208 783-G3
7900 MESA 85208 784-A3

STREET
Block City ZIP Pg-Grid

W JUANITA AV
- GIL 85233 782-A4
100 MarC 85210 781-F2
100 MESA 85210 781-E2
1100 GIL 85233 781-F2
1300 MESA 85202 781-C2
E JUANITA CIR
- MESA 85220 784-G3
W JUANITA CIR
800 MESA 85210 781-E2
1500 MESA 85202 781-A2
E JUANITA CT
- MarC 85234 783-B4
E JUAN TABO RD
7100 PHX 85255 500-G6
7100 SCTS 85255 500-G6
8100 SCTS 85255 501-A6
11800 SCTS 85255 502-A7
W JUBILEE DR
13200 MarC 85375 535-D7
N JUDD AV
600 CHAN 85226 820-C4
1400 TEMP 85226 820-C3
1400 CHAN 85284 820-C3
1400 TEMP 85284 820-C3
N JUDD PL
1000 CHAN 85226 820-B3
S JUDD ST
1000 TEMP 85281 740-C4
3300 TEMP 85282 780-C1
5400 TEMP 85283 780-C3
E JUDSON RD
- PVAL 85253 660-E2
W JUDY LYNN LN
- GLEN 85382 576-J1
6900 GLEN 85382 577-A1
E JULEP CIR
1500 MESA 85203 702-C7
E JULEP ST
- MESA 85203 702-C7
400 MESA 85201 701-J7
400 MESA 85203 701-J7
4700 MESA 85205 703-B7
5600 MESA 85205 743-D1
E JULIAN DR
- MarC 85296 862-C1
W JULIE CIR
2000 PHX 85027 538-D6
E JULIE DR
200 TEMP 85283 780-E4
W JULIE DR
100 TEMP 85283 780-B4
2900 PHX 85027 538-A6
4300 PHX 85308 537-F6
6100 GLEN 85308 537-A6
7200 GLEN 85308 536-H6
N JULY CIR
1000 MESA 85203 741-J2
2200 MESA 85203 701-J6
S JUMPING CHOLLA
1300 BUCK 85326 (692-C7
See Page 651)
E JUMPING CHOLLA CIR
8500 PinC 85219 786-F6
E JUMPING CHOLLA DR
8500 PinC 85219 786-F6
E JUNCTION ST
- APJT 85219 746-B6
- APJT 85219 745-E6
4200 PinC 85219 746-B6
E JUNE CIR
- MESA 85213 702-G7
900 MESA 85203 702-G7
3800 MESA 85205 702-G7
E JUNE ST
- MESA 85201 701-H7
800 MESA 85203 702-A7
1800 MESA 85205 743-F1
2200 MESA 85213 702-E7
3900 MESA 85205 702-E7
5600 MESA 85205 703-D7
7200 MESA 85207 743-H1
W JUNE ST
- MESA 85201 701-H7
W JUNEBERRY WY
14700 SURP 85374 534-H6
E JUNIPER AV
- GIL 85233 782-D6
- GIL 85234 782-D6
1000 CHAN 85225 821-H7
1600 PHX 85022 579-B1
2600 PHX 85032 579-D1
5300 PHX 85254 580-B2
W JUNIPER AV
- GLEN 85382 577-A1
- GIL 85233 782-A6
1300 GIL 85233 781-H5
2900 PHX 85053 578-A1
3600 PHX 85053 577-H1
4600 PHX 85306 577-F1
6000 GLEN 85306 577-C1
E JUNIPER CIR
1900 MESA 85203 702-D7
3900 MESA 85205 742-J1
E JUNIPER DR
- GDYR 85326 (774-A7
See Page 733)
N JUNIPER DR
200 CHAN 85226 820-G3
S JUNIPER DR
1400 CHAN 85226 820-G2
1400 TEMP 85226 820-G2
6400 TEMP 85283 780-G5
8500 TEMP 85284 820-G2
S JUNIPER LN
300 WICK 85390 290-A3
E JUNIPER ST
- MESA 85201 701-H7
2100 MESA 85203 702-C7
3800 MESA 85205 742-H1
6600 MESA 85205 743-G1
S JUNIPER ST
2400 TEMP 85282 740-G7
3500 TEMP 85282 780-G1
5900 TEMP 85283 780-G4
7500 TEMP 85284 780-G7
W JUNIPER ST
- MESA 85201 701-G7
W JUNQUILLO CIR
2700 MESA 85202 781-A2
E JUPITER DR
11200 MarC 85220 744-J5
E JUPITER WY
13200 MarC 85225 822-B7
W JUPITER WY
100 CHAN 85226 820-D6
1600 CHAN 85226 821-C6
W JUPITER WY N
100 CHAN 85226 820-E7

STREET
Block City ZIP Pg-Grid

W JUPITER WY S
200 CHAN 85226 820-E7
E JUSTICA ST
4000 PHX 85331 459-H6
4900 PHX 85331 460-B6
N JUSTICE WY
- MarC 85086 (378-B7
See Page 337)
S JUSTICIA WY
- PinC 85219 786-F5
S JUSTIN DR
- CHAN 85249 902-A5
S JUSTIN WY
- CHAN 85249 902-A6
S JUSTINE CT
- GIL 85236 823-A3
E JUSTINE RD
5400 PHX 85254 580-C3

K

N KAANAPALI DR
13800 MarC 85351 576-A4
N KAANAPALI PT
13600 MarC 85351 576-A5
KACHINA
1300 GLEN 85307 615-B7
N KACHINA
800 MESA 85203 742-C3
1800 MESA 85203 702-D6
S KACHINA
500 MESA 85204 742-C6
1700 MESA 85204 782-C2
E KACHINA AV
500 APJT 85219 785-E1
N KACHINA AV
400 MESA 85203 742-D1
1800 MESA 85203 702-D7
S KACHINA AV
800 MESA 85204 742-D7
900 MESA 85204 782-D1
N KACHINA CIR
1600 MESA 85203 742-D1
N KACHINA CT
2300 CHAN 85224 821-C1
E KACHINA DR
3200 PHX 85040 819-E1
3200 PHX 85044 819-E1
S KACHINA DR
800 WICK 85390 290-A3
1700 TEMP 85281 740-H6
1800 TEMP 85282 740-H6
3100 TEMP 85282 780-H1
5600 TEMP 85283 780-H4
7500 TEMP 85284 780-G7
8100 TEMP 85284 820-G1
W KACHINA DR
- SURP 85374 534-A5
N KACHINA LN
3400 SCTS 85251 700-D1
6000 PVAL 85253 660-E3
N KACHINA RD
41200 MarC 85331 (381-J6
See Page 341)
41400 MarC 85331 (382-A6
See Page 341)
N KACHINA ST
100 MESA 85203 742-C5
2400 MESA 85203 702-D5
E KACHINA TR
400 PHX 85040 778-G5
4300 PHX 85044 779-H5
W KACHINA TR
800 PHX 85041 778-E5
E KAEL CIR
- MarC 85207 703-J7
2000 MESA 85213 702-D7
3900 MESA 85215 702-E7
E KAEL ST
- MESA 85207 703-J7
- MESA 85207 704-A7
600 MESA 85203 701-J7
600 MESA 85203 702-A7
2600 MESA 85213 702-F7
N KAEL ST
- MESA 85207 704-A7
E KAIBAB DR
- MarC 85249 901-J1
W KAIBAB DR
10700 MarC 85373 536-A6
10800 MarC 85373 535-J7
E KAIBAB PL
- MarC 85249 901-J1
W KAIBAB RD
19800 MarC 85326 (773-E7
See Page 733)
N KALARAMA AV
3400 SCTS 85251 700-G1
W KALER AV
- GLEN 85303 616-J6
4400 GLEN 85301 617-G6
W KALER CIR
4600 GLEN 85301 617-E6
E KALER DR
- PHX 85020 618-H7
- PHX 85021 618-H7
1200 PHX 85020 619-A7
N KALER DR
7600 PHX 85020 619-C7
W KALER DR
- PHX 85021 618-F7
3400 PHX 85051 617-H6
4900 GLEN 85301 617-F6
7500 MarC 85307 615-J6
E KALIL CIR
7400 SCTS 85260 620-F1
E KALIL DR
7100 SCTS 85254 620-F1
8000 SCTS 85260 620-G1
8400 SCTS 85260 621-B1
10800 SCTS 85259 621-G2
12200 SCTS 85259 622-A2
E KANIKSU ST
100 PinC 85219 705-E7
100 PinC 85220 705-E7
W KANIKSU ST
- PinC 85220 705-A7
KANSAS
5900 PinC 85219 786-D7
S KANSAS AV
25200 MarC 85248 901-A4
W KANSAS AV
11100 YNTN 85335 615-H1
S KAOLIN DR
- APJT 85219 785-J4
E KAREN DR
1900 PHX 85022 579-B3
2400 PHX 85032 579-E3
4900 PHX 85254 580-A3
7400 SCTS 85260 580-H4

STREET
Block City ZIP Pg-Grid

E KAREN DR
9000 SCTS 85260 581-B4
10400 SCTS 85259 581-F4
N KAREN DR
700 CHAN 85224 821-D4
2700 CHAN 85224 781-D7
S KAREN DR
400 CHAN 85224 821-D7
700 CHAN 85224 861-D2
2100 CHAN 85248 861-D2
W KAREN DR
1000 CHAN 85224 821-D1
6600 GLEN 85308 537-B7
E KAREN LN
2700 GIL 85236 823-A3
W KAREN LEE LN
6000 GLEN 85306 577-B3
6700 GLEN 85382 577-A3
7600 PEOR 85382 576-E2
W KARIBA DR
3700 PHX 85051 617-J3
N KARINA CT
- MarC 85340 655-B2
E KARSTEN DR
- MarC 85249 902-F5
N KASBA CIR E
5300 PVAL 85253 660-E5
E KASBA CIR S
5300 PVAL 85253 660-E5
N KASBA CIR W
5200 PVAL 85253 660-E5
N KASHMIR
2800 MESA 85215 703-F3
N KASHMIR CIR
3400 MESA 85215 703-F4
E KATHLEEN DR
2000 PHX 85022 579-C3
6800 PHX 85254 580-F2
E KATHLEEN RD
- PHX 85022 578-H3
1800 PHX 85022 579-J3
2800 PHX 85032 579-J3
4700 PHX 85032 580-A3
4700 PHX 85254 580-A3
N KATHLEEN RD
15800 PHX 85254 580-D3
W KATHLEEN RD
- PHX 85023 578-C2
2700 PHX 85053 578-B2
5900 GLEN 85306 577-D2
8700 PEOR 85382 576-E2
S KATI ST
400 GIL 85296 822-E1
N KATMAI
3600 MESA 85215 703-F3
N KATMAI CIR
3700 MESA 85215 703-G3
W KATMAI DR
- MarC 85087 (378-B4
See Page 337)
S KAY CIR
1500 MESA 85204 781-J2
N KAY DR
14800 PHX 85032 579-E4
W KAY LN
8900 TOL 85353 696-D5
E KAYENTA CT
3500 PHX 85044 819-E1
S KEATING AV
2500 MESA 85202 781-D4
W KEATING AV
700 MESA 85210 781-E5
1300 MESA 85202 781-A5
W KEATING CIR
4400 PHX 85308 577-G1
4400 PHX 85308 537-G7
E KEATS AV
- MESA 85212 784-C4
2000 MESA 85208 783-J3
8000 MESA 85208 784-A4
W KEATS AV
500 MESA 85210 781-F3
1200 MESA 85202 781-D3
E KEATS CIR
- MESA 85208 784-B4
S KEENE
- MESA 85212 784-D4
N KEESHA
- MarC 85207 704-C6
W KEIM CT
- MarC 85340 655-B2
E KEIM DR
200 PHX 85012 658-G3
800 PHX 85014 658-H3
1400 PHX 85014 659-A3
1700 PHX 85016 659-B3
4000 PVAL 85018 659-H3
4000 PVAL 85253 659-H3
6200 PVAL 85253 660-D3
7300 SCTS 85250 660-G3
8400 SCTS 85250 661-A3
W KEIM DR
- GLEN 85303 657-A2
- MarC 85340 655-B2
- PHX 85013 658-E3
1500 PHX 85015 658-C3
2700 PHX 85017 658-A3
3600 PHX 85019 657-H2
4300 GLEN 85301 657-F2
7100 GLEN 85303 656-J2
8700 GLEN 85305 656-E2
N KEITH ST
300 MarC 85220 744-H5
N KELL ST
400 BUCK 85326 (772-B1
See Page 731)
W KELLER CT
- MarC 85086 (378-A6
See Page 337)
W KELLER DR
3000 MarC 85086 (378-C6
See Page 337)
N KELLEY RD
47000 MarC 85087 (338-B4
See Page 337)
S KELLIS RD
- MarC 85390 290-E4
300 WICK 85390 290-E4
E KELLY CT
- MarC 85236 903-E3
W KELLY CT
14700 SURP 85374 534-J6
E KELLY DR
4500 GIL 85236 783-F4
E KELLY LN
- TEMP 85284 820-D4
W KELLY LN
1100 TEMP 85284 820-B4
W KELSO DR
9900 MarC 85351 616-A3

STREET
Block City ZIP Pg-Grid

W KELSO DR
10600 MarC 85351 615-J3
W KELTON AV
3900 PHX 85053 577-H1
E KELTON LN
1600 PHX 85022 579-B2
2400 PHX 85032 579-D2
4500 PHX 85032 580-A2
4800 PHX 85254 580-A2
N KELTON LN
16800 PHX 85254 580-A2
W KELTON LN
300 PHX 85023 578-F1
2800 PHX 85053 578-A1
3500 PHX 85053 577-J1
4700 PHX 85306 577-F1
8500 PEOR 85382 576-E1
E KEMPTON RD
- CHAN 85225 822-A7
W KENAI DR
- MarC 85087 (378-A3
See Page 337)
N KENDALL DR
13800 FTNH 85268 583-C6
E KENDRA LN
11400 MarC 85331 (381-J6
See Page 341)
S KENDRA ST
- GIL 85236 823-A3
N KENNETH CT
1100 CHAN 85226 820-F4
N KENNETH PL
200 CHAN 85226 820-F3
S KENNETH PL
- CHAN 85226 820-F7
800 CHAN 85226 860-F1
1200 TEMP 85282 780-G1
1400 TEMP 85281 740-G5
2600 TEMP 85282 740-G7
5900 TEMP 85283 780-F4
7800 TEMP 85284 780-F5
9100 TEMP 85284 820-F3
9400 TEMP 85226 820-F3
N KENNITH LN
17100 GIL 85234 783-C7
S KENSINGTON DR
- TEMP 85282 779-J1
E KENSINGTON PL
17100 FTNH 85268 623-D5
17200 FTNH 85264 623-D5
S KENT
5800 MESA 85212 823-H7
E KENT AV
500 CHAN 85225 821-G3
1400 CHAN 85225 822-A3
2400 GIL 85236 822-J3
2400 GIL 85236 823-A3
W KENT CT
2100 CHAN 85224 821-B3
E KENT DR
3600 PHX 85044 819-E3
W KENT DR
100 CHAN 85225 821-E3
1500 CHAN 85224 821-A3
2700 CHAN 85224 820-H3
3400 CHAN 85226 820-C3
E KENT PL
1000 CHAN 85225 821-E3
N KENTON
- MESA 85215 703-E5
KENTUCKY
6300 PinC 85219 786-D7
E KENTUCKY LN
1900 TEMP 85284 820-H1
E KENWOOD CIR
- MESA 85207 704-E7
1300 MESA 85203 702-D7
2000 MESA 85213 702-D7
S KENWOOD CIR
900 TEMP 85281 740-J4
S KENWOOD DR
8600 TEMP 85284 820-H2
N KENWOOD LN
800 CHAN 85226 820-H3
S KENWOOD LN
100 CHAN 85226 820-H7
600 CHAN 85226 860-H1
1900 TEMP 85283 780-H3
2800 TEMP 85282 740-J7
3200 TEMP 85282 780-H1
7600 TEMP 85284 780-H7
8000 TEMP 85284 820-H1
E KENWOOD RD
5900 MESA 85215 703-E7
E KENWOOD ST
- MarC 85207 703-J7
- MESA 85207 704-A7
400 MESA 85203 701-J7
600 MESA 85203 702-A7
2300 MESA 85213 702-D7
6300 MESA 85215 703-J7
KENWORTHY RD
- PinC 85242 905-D2
N KENWORTHY RD
36000 PinC 85242 905-D1
41400 PinC 85242 865-D6
E KEOGH DR
200 PHX 85022 538-H7
E KEOTA DR
16100 FTNH 85268 623-B3
E KERBY AV
3400 PHX 85040 739-F4
E KERBY FARMS RD
1700 CHAN 85249 901-J6
1700 CHAN 85249 902-A6
E KERESAN DR
3400 PHX 85044 819-E2
E KERESAN ST
3800 PHX 85044 819-F2
N KERKES ST
- WICK 85390 290-F2
S KERKES ST
- WICK 85390 290-F2
E KERN CT
- FTNH 85268 622-F5
E KERRY LN
400 PHX 85024 538-H5
1000 PHX 85024 539-A5
3000 PHX 85050 539-E5
W KERRY LN
- PHX 85024 538-H5
- PHX 85027 538-B5
4800 PHX 85308 537-F5
5000 GLEN 85308 537-A5
7900 GLEN 85308 536-H5
8900 PEOR 85382 536-C5
W KERRY WY
7300 GLEN 85308 536-H5
E KESLER LN
- CHAN 85225 861-F1

STREET
Block City ZIP Pg-Grid

E KESLER LN
1700 CHAN 85225 862-A1
W KESLER LN
100 CHAN 85225 861-D1
1100 CHAN 85224 861-C1
3600 CHAN 85226 820-C7
3600 CHAN 85226 860-D1
E KESLER PL
- CHAN 85225 861-H1
W KESLER ST
700 CHAN 85226 820-C7
E KESSLER AV
6900 MESA 85208 783-G4
S KEY CIR
1400 MESA 85210 781-H2
W KEY LN
- MarC 85086 (378-B6
See Page 337)
8500 GLEN 85305 656-E1
S KEY BISCANTE DR
- GIL 85296 822-H5
N KEY BISCAYNE DR
600 GIL 85234 782-H5
S KEY BISCAYNE DR
100 GIL 85296 782-H7
100 GIL 85296 822-H1
N KEY ESTRELLA DR
16300 SURP 85374 534-E6
W KEY HARBOR DR
1200 GIL 85233 821-J3
W KEY LARGO CT
1400 GIL 85233 821-J1
E KEYMAR DR
16200 FTNH 85268 583-B6
N KEYSTONE DR
19200 MarC 85375 535-E4
W KEYSTONE DR
12300 MarC 85375 535-D4
N KHALIL CIR
- MESA 85201 701-J6
E KI CIR
- PHX 85044 819-J2
S KI RD
11600 PHX 85044 779-J7
11600 PHX 85044 819-J1
W KIEM DR
- MarC 85340 655-B2
N KIERLAND BLVD
7100 PHX 85254 580-F4
E KIISA DR
- SCTS 85262 (461-D1
See Page 421)
E KILAREA AV
- MESA 85212 784-D4
7400 MESA 85208 783-H4
8000 MESA 85208 784-A4
W KILAREA AV
500 MESA 85210 781-E3
1200 MESA 85202 781-A3
E KILAREA CIR
- MESA 85208 784-B4
N KILLDEER RD
- MarC 85390 289-J6
- MarC 85390 290-A6
W KILLDEER RD
33100 MarC 85390 290-A6
N KILMER CT
16200 FTNH 85268 583-A3
E KIM DR
15700 FTNH 85268 583-A3
N KIM DR
16400 FTNH 85268 583-A3
E KIMBALL AV
400 MESA 85204 741-J5
E KIMBALL CT
- GIL 85236 863-B5
E KIMBALL RD
- GIL 85236 863-B5
N KIMBERLEE WY
- CHAN 85225 822-C5
S KIMBERLEE WY
- CHAN 85249 902-B5
W KIMBERLY DR
1900 PHX 85027 538-D6
E KIMBERLY WY
3900 PHX 85050 539-G6
9100 SCTS 85255 541-C6
N KIMBERLY WY
17200 SURP 85374 534-J7
W KIMBERLY WY
3100 PHX 85027 538-A5
4100 PHX 85308 537-F5
5900 GLEN 85308 537-A5
7100 GLEN 85308 536-J5
8400 PEOR 85382 536-C5
E KIMSEY LN
7400 SCTS 85257 700-G6
E KINDERMAN DR
- AVON 85323 695-B7
W KINDERMAN DR
100 AVON 85323 695-B7
N KING
- MESA 85206 783-D1
N KING CIR
- MESA 85206 783-D2
W KING DR
- MarC 85086 (378-B7
See Page 337)
- MarC 85086 (418-B1
See Page 417)
E KINGBIRD DR
- MarC 85236 863-B4
W KINGBIRD DR
1000 CHAN 85248 861-C4
E KINGS AV
300 PHX 85022 578-H2
1100 PHX 85022 579-A2
2500 PHX 85032 579-D2
4600 PHX 85032 580-A2
4800 PHX 85254 580-A2
W KINGS AV
- GLEN 85382 576-J1
- PHX 85023 578-F2
3100 PHX 85053 578-A1
3600 PHX 85053 577-J2
4600 PHX 85306 577-G1
5100 GLEN 85306 577-C1
6700 GLEN 85382 577-A1
8700 PEOR 85382 576-E1
E KINGS CT
- GIL 85234 782-G4
N KINGS DR
16400 SURP 85374 575-D1
W KINGS DR
14900 SURP 85374 534-H6
W KINGS LN
100 MESA 85339 817-E6
N KINGS WY
14400 FTNH 85268 583-D5

STREET Block City ZIP Pg-Grid

PHOENIX

INDEX

STREET
Block City ZIP Pg-Grid

PHOENIX INDEX

STREET
Block City ZIP Pg-Grid

E MAIN ST
400 MESA 85203 741-H5
400 MESA 85203 741-H5
700 MESA 85204 742-C5
700 MESA 85203 742-C5
1200 MarC 85337 (1090-D4
See Page 1049)
1900 MESA 85213 742-G5
2500 MESA 85202 741-H5
3600 MESA 85205 742-G5
3800 MESA 85206 742-G5
4200 MESA 85205 743-C5
4200 MESA 85206 743-C5
6800 MESA 85207 743-G5
6800 SCTS 85251 700-F1
6800 MESA 85208 743-G5
7600 MarC 85207 743-G5
7700 MESA 85208 744-A5
7700 MarC 85207 744-A5
E MAIN ST Rt#-85
- AVON 85323 735-B1
N MAIN ST
100 BUCK 85326 (772-B1
See Page 731)
11700 ELMG 85335 575-G5
S MAIN ST
100 BUCK 85326 (772-B2
See Page 731)
W MAIN ST
100 MESA 85210 741-F5
100 MESA 85201 741-F5
1200 MESA 85202 741-D5
W MAIN ST Rt#-85
- AVON 85323 735-A2
100 GDYR 85323 735-A2
500 GDYR 85338 735-A2
500 AVON 85338 735-A2
E MAJESTIC EAGLE
2600 GIL 85236 863-A5
N MAJESTY CT
- MarC 85086 (378-C7
See Page 337)
- MarC 85086 (418-B1
See Page 417)
N MAJESTY TR
- MarC 85086 (378-C7
See Page 337)
- MarC 85086 (418-A1
See Page 417)
N MAJESTY WY
- MarC 85086 (378-C6
See Page 337)
E MAJORCA LN
6700 PHX 85016 659-A2
E MAJORCA WY
1600 PHX 85016 659-A2
N MALACHITE
- MESA 85207 704-D7
N MALACHITE CIR
- MESA 85207 704-D7
E MALAGA PL
- MarC 85206 783-F1
E MALAPAI DR
1400 PHX 85020 619-A3
2800 PHX 85028 619-G3
W MALAPAI DR
3200 PHX 85051 618-A3
3400 PHX 85051 617-H2
8200 PEOR 85345 616-E2
S MALCOLM DR
- MarC 85220 744-J6
E MALCOMB DR
6300 SCTS 85253 660-F3
6400 PVAL 85253 660-D3
7200 SCTS 85250 660-G3
8500 SCTS 85250 661-A3
E MALDONADO DR
- PHX 85040 778-J2
4000 PHX 85040 779-A2
W MALDONADO RD
- PHX 85041 777-G1
- PHX 85040 778-D1
- PHX 85041 778-D1
E MALIBU DR
300 TEMP 85282 780-E1
2100 TEMP 85282 781-A1
W MALIBU DR
500 TEMP 85282 780-B1
N MALIBU LN
1300 GIL 85234 782-J4
W MALL PL
- WICK 85390 290-A3
E MALLARD CT
2000 GIL 85234 782-H5
16800 FTNH 85268 623-D1
N MALLARD PL
1100 CHAN 85226 820-D3
N MALLARD ST
700 CHAN 85226 820-D4
E MALLORY CIR
- MESA 85207 703-H6
- MESA 85215 702-J6
2200 MESA 85213 702-E6
4400 MESA 85215 703-A6
E MALLORY ST
- MESA 85207 704-D6
1600 MESA 85203 702-C6
2000 MESA 85213 702-D6
3600 MESA 85215 702-H6
6200 MESA 85215 703-F6
6800 MESA 85207 703-G6
7400 MarC 85207 703-J6
8500 MarC 85207 704-B6
E MALLOW CIR
- SCTS 85260 581-E5
E MALTA DR
16800 FTNH 85268 623-D2
N MAMIE MAUDE DR
35600 CARE 85377 420-D6
N MAMMOTH WY
- CHAN 85225 822-B5
E MAMMOTH MINE RD
- PinC 85219 706-B7
- PinC 85219 746-B1
- PinC 85290 706-B7
E MANANA DR
- SCTS 85255 540-H2
E MANANA RD
11300 MarC 85331 (381-J4
See Page 341)
11300 MarC 85331 (382-A5
See Page 341)
W MANCHESTER DR
- SURP 85374 534-D7
W MANDALAY LN
1600 PHX 85023 578-C4
2900 PHX 85053 578-A4
3500 PHX 85053 577-J4
S MANDAN ST
10800 PHX 85040 779-F7

S MANDAN ST
10800 PHX 85044 779-F7
11500 PHX 85044 819-G1
11500 PHX 85044 819-G1
S MANDARIN DR
25200 MarC 85242 903-G6
S MANDARIN WY
- GIL 85236 863-E5
W MANDERAS LN
17800 SURP 85387 494-A7
N MANETTI ST
- PinC 85242 905-D2
W MANGO CT
12300 MarC 85375 535-F5
W MANGO DR
1100 GIL 85233 822-A2
1100 GIL 85233 821-J2
N MANGRUM CT
10800 FTNH 85268 623-D3
E MANGUN RD
7700 MarC 85207 703-J6
8400 MarC 85207 704-B6
E MANHATTON DR
100 TEMP 85282 780-D1
2200 TEMP 85282 781-A1
W MANHATTON DR
300 TEMP 85282 780-B1
MANITOBA
6300 PinC 85219 786-D7
N MANITOU DR
11600 FTNH 85268 623-C2
E MANNING ST
- MESA 85207 703-H6
6700 MESA 85215 703-G6
E MANO DR
100 MarC 85087 (378-J1
See Page 337)
N MANOR CIR
1400 CHAN 85225 821-F3
W MANOR CIR
2300 CHAN 85224 821-A3
W MANOR CT
2400 CHAN 85224 821-A3
E MANOR DR
- GIL 85236 822-J1
600 CHAN 85225 821-G3
2100 GIL 85296 822-J1
W MANOR DR
600 CHAN 85225 821-E3
N MANOR DR E
2900 PHX 85014 698-J2
N MANOR DR W
2900 PHX 85014 698-J2
W MANOR ST
- CHAN 85225 821-F3
1100 CHAN 85224 821-B3
W MANRAD DR
32700 MarC 85390 290-B5
E MANSO CT
3300 PHX 85044 819-E3
N MANTLE CT
- MarC 85086 (378-B6
See Page 337)
W MANZANITA CT
5900 CHAN 85226 820-C4
E MANZANITA DR
1800 PHX 85020 619-B6
7200 SCTS 85258 620-G7
8700 SCTS 85258 621-A7
N MANZANITA DR
1400 GDYR 85338 695-C5
W MANZANITA DR
5900 GLEN 85302 617-C5
8900 PEOR 85345 616-E5
9300 MarC 85373 536-A6
10800 MarC 85373 535-J6
10800 PEOR 85345 615-H5
16200 SURP 85374 534-E4
N MANZANITA LN
- FTNH 85268 582-H7
E MANZANITA ST
2400 APJT 85219 745-H4
4700 PinC 85219 746-B4
W MANZANITA ST
1000 APJT 85220 745-A4
N MAPLE
- MESA 85205 742-H1
2000 MESA 85215 702-J5
S MAPLE
400 MESA 85206 742-H7
900 MESA 85206 782-J1
1600 BUCK 85326 (692-C7
See Page 651)
S MAPLE AV
- TEMP 85281 740-D3
2500 TEMP 85282 740-D7
4500 TEMP 85282 780-D2
6000 TEMP 85283 780-D4
8100 TEMP 85284 780-D5
8100 TEMP 85284 820-D2
N MAPLE CIR
600 MESA 85205 742-H3
S MAPLE CIR
2400 MESA 85206 782-H2
N MAPLE CT
800 CHAN 85226 820-C4
S MAPLE CT
- CHAN 85226 820-C6
E MAPLE DR
8800 SCTS 85255 541-B6
N MAPLE DR
500 GIL 85234 782-H6
1100 CHAN 85226 820-C3
15000 FTNH 85268 583-B5
S MAPLE DR
- GIL 85296 822-J4
W MAPLE DR
2100 PHX 85027 538-D5
E MAPLE LN
9100 SCTS 85255 541-C6
N MAPLE ST
500 CHAN 85226 820-C5
S MAPLE ST
100 CHAN 85226 820-C7
1600 MESA 85206 782-H2
32300 MarC 85361 (452-J2
See Page 411)
32300 MarC 85361 (453-A1
See Page 413)
W MAPLEWOOD CT
- CHAN 85248 861-D2
N MAPLEWOOD DR
18600 MarC 85375 535-D5
W MAPLEWOOD DR
12700 MarC 85375 535-C5
W MAPLEWOOD PL
- CHAN 85248 861-B2
E MAPLEWOOD ST
- GIL 85236 863-C3
15800 MarC 85296 862-J3

W MAPLEWOOD ST
600 CHAN 85248 861-A2
S MARA DR
500 APJT 85220 745-C7
1200 APJT 85220 785-C1
E MARATHON DR
14900 FTNH 85268 582-H3
MARAUDER ST
- GLEN 85309 615-A6
N MARAVILLA DR
23100 MarC 85375 495-B7
N MARBLE DR
19200 MarC 85375 535-E5
S MARBLE DR
5500 PinC 85219 786-E6
W MARBLE DR
12300 MarC 85375 535-D4
N MARBLE ST
- GIL 85234 782-F5
S MARBLE ST
- GIL 85296 822-F5
S MARBLE CANYON CT
18700 SURP 85374 534-E5
N MARCH
1000 MESA 85203 741-J2
N MARCH CIR
1100 MESA 85203 741-J2
E MARCONI AV
200 PHX 85022 578-H2
1100 PHX 85022 579-A2
2600 PHX 85032 579-D3
4800 PHX 85254 580-A3
W MARCONI AV
- SURP 85374 (574-C1
See Page 573)
- PHX 85023 578-C2
2900 PHX 85053 578-A2
3700 PHX 85053 577-J2
4700 PHX 85306 577-F2
5500 GLEN 85306 577-B2
7600 PEOR 85382 576-E2
W MARCO POLO DR
6900 GLEN 85308 537-A4
7700 GLEN 85308 536-J4
9800 PEOR 85382 536-C4
E MARCO POLO RD
400 PHX 85024 538-H5
1000 PHX 85024 539-A5
2400 PHX 85050 539-D5
W MARCO POLO RD
- PEOR 85373 535-J4
- PHX 85027 538-A4
3600 PHX 85308 537-F4
6700 GLEN 85308 537-A4
7500 GLEN 85308 536-J4
8300 PEOR 85382 536-C4
W MARCUS DR
- PHX 85310 497-G3
- SURP 85374 534-J6
- SURP 85374 535-A6
S MARE CT
11900 PHX 85044 819-F1
S MARE DR
- CHAN 85225 822-A7
E MAREN DR
- CHAN 85249 902-A5
- CHAN 85249 902-A5
W MARGARET ST
800 GBND 85337 (1089-J3
See Page 1049)
E MARGARITA WY
- CARE 85377 420-J5
- CARE 85377 421-A5
N MARGATE PL
3200 CHAN 85224 781-A6
N MARGATE ST
1300 CHAN 85224 821-A3
S MARGATE ST
- CHAN 85248 861-A2
S MARGO DR
500 TEMP 85281 740-B3
3100 TEMP 85282 740-B7
3300 TEMP 85282 780-B1
9300 TEMP 85284 820-A3
E MARGUERITE AV
200 PHX 85040 738-G6
1500 PHX 85040 739-A6
9000 MarC 85208 744-C7
11300 MarC 85220 744-J7
11400 MarC 85220 745-A7
W MARGUERITE AV
- PHX 85041 738-G6
- PHX 85040 738-G6
W MARGUERITE ST
3700 PHX 85041 737-H5
E MARIA
6400 MarC 85331 460-F3
N MARIA CT
16200 FTNH 85268 582-H3
E MARIA LN
- TEMP 85284 820-D3
W MARIA LN
1000 TEMP 85284 820-A3
E MARIA WY
8000 SCTS 85255 580-J1
S MARIANA CIR
3300 TEMP 85282 780-F1
S MARIANA ST
900 TEMP 85281 740-G4
MARICOPA FRWY I-10
- CHAN - 819-J5
- GUAD - 780-A5
- MarC - 819-J5
- MarC - 859-J1
- MarC - 860-A3
- MarC - 900-D1
- PHX - 739-D4
- PHX - 779-J7
- PHX - 780-A5
- PHX - 819-J5
- PHX - 859-J1
- TEMP - 739-G5
- TEMP - 740-A6
- TEMP - 779-J7
- TEMP - 780-A5
- TEMP - 819-J5
MARICOPA FRWY I-17
- PHX - 738-C2
- PHX - 739-A3
S MARICOPA PL
26400 MarC 85248 901-A6
E MARICOPA RD
100 MarC 85326 (732-B6
See Page 731)
S MARICOPA RD
- MarC 85326 859-J4
S MARICOPA RD Rt#-347
- PinC - 899-G3
21900 MarC 85326 859-H7

S MARICOPA RD Rt#-347
21900 MarC 85326 899-G3
W MARICOPA RD
100 MarC 85326 (732-B6
See Page 731)
100 BUCK 85326 (732-A6
See Page 731)
W MARICOPA RD Rt#-238
- GBND 85337 106-B1
7800 MarC 85239 106-C1
9700 MarC 85337 106-B1
- GBND 85337 (1090-G2
See Page 1049)
E MARICOPA ST
100 GBND 85337 (1090-B4
See Page 1049)
W MARICOPA ST
- GDYR 85338 (694-D7
See Page 653)
1500 PHX 85007 738-D1
1900 PHX 85009 738-A1
3300 PHX 85009 737-G1
5500 PHX 85043 737-D1
E MARICOPA MESA
10700 SCTS 85259 621-F1
12500 SCTS 85259 581-F7
E MARIE CT
2700 GIL 85236 823-A3
S MARIE DR
- CHAN 85225 862-A1
S MARIGOLD
1300 BUCK 85326 (692-C7
See Page 651)
E MARIGOLD CIR
9300 SCTS 85255 501-D4
E MARIGOLD CT
15200 FTNH 85268 582-J6
N MARIGOLD DR
3000 PHX 85018 700-C2
3000 SCTS 85018 700-C2
E MARIGOLD LN
400 TEMP 85281 700-E7
N MARIGOLD LN
1600 TEMP 85281 700-F7
S MARIGOLD PL
3000 CHAN 85248 861-C5
S MARIGOLD WY
- CHAN 85248 901-C2
- GIL 85236 863-D6
3500 CHAN 85248 861-C6
E MARILYN AV
- MESA 85210 741-H7
500 MESA 85204 741-J7
600 MESA 85204 742-A7
E MARILYN RD
1800 PHX 85022 579-C4
2400 PHX 85032 579-D4
4700 PHX 85032 580-A4
4800 PHX 85254 580-A4
S MARILYN ANN DR
800 TEMP 85281 740-C5
6500 TEMP 85283 780-B5
S MARIN DR
- GIL 85296 782-J7
100 GIL 85296 822-J1
S MARINA DR
400 GIL 85233 821-J1
W MARINA DR
1200 CHAN 85248 861-C6
S MARINE DR
5100 TEMP 85282 780-G3
5100 TEMP 85283 780-G3
E MARINER CIR
1900 GIL 85234 782-H4
S MARINER CT
100 GIL 85233 781-J7
E MARINER LN
2000 GIL 85234 782-H4
W MARINERS WY
8100 PEOR 85382 576-G2
E MARINO DR
4200 PHX 85032 539-H7
4900 PHX 85254 540-A7
E MARIOCA CIR
6300 SCTS 85262 460-E2
E MARIOLA WY
11000 SCTS 85262 (381-G6
See Page 341)
S MARION PL
- CHAN 85249 861-J2
- MarC 85249 901-J1
E MARION WY
- CHAN 85249 861-J1
800 CHAN 85225 822-A4
4200 PHX 85018 659-H4
N MARION WY
5500 PHX 85018 659-H4
E MARIPOSA
1300 MESA 85203 742-B2
MARIPOSA CT
- FTNH 85268 582-G5
W MARIPOSA CT
1700 CHAN 85224 821-B2
E MARIPOSA DR
6900 SCTS 85251 660-E6
8500 SCTS 85251 661-A6
N MARIPOSA DR
- WICK 85390 290-D2
17800 SURP 85374 534-A6
S MARIPOSA DR
- GIL 85236 863-C5
100 WICK 85390 290-D4
W MARIPOSA DR
1100 CHAN 85224 821-C2
6200 PHX 85033 657-B5
7700 PHX 85033 656-G5
8500 PHX 85037 656-C5
E MARIPOSA PL
700 CHAN 85225 821-G2
S MARIPOSA RD
1600 APJT 85219 785-F1
2200 PinC 85219 785-F2
E MARIPOSA ST
- CHAN 85225 821-E2
- PHX 85012 658-G5
1000 PHX 85014 658-J5
2900 PHX 85016 659-D5
3200 PHX 85018 659-F5
5300 PHX 85018 660-B7
6000 PHX 85251 660-C7
W MARIPOSA ST
- PHX 85013 658-E5
900 CHAN 85225 821-D1
2100 PHX 85015 658-C5
2200 CHAN 85224 821-B2
2500 PHX 85017 658-A5
3300 PHX 85017 657-J5
3400 PHX 85019 657-H5

W MARIPOSA ST
5600 PHX 85031 657-C5
6400 PHX 85033 657-A5
7000 PHX 85033 656-J5
8700 PHX 85037 656-A5
10500 PHX 85037 655-J5
E MARIPOSA WY
700 MESA 85208 743-J7
N MARIPOSA WY
20100 SURP 85374 534-E3
E MARIPOSA GRANDE
- MarC 85024 499-C6
- PHX 85024 499-C6
7400 SCTS 85255 500-H7
W MARIPOSA GRANDE
3500 PHX 85310 498-A6
3700 PHX 85310 497-D6
6800 PEOR 85382 497-A6
8600 MarC 85382 496-B6
9900 PEOR 85382 496-G6
E MARIPOSA GRANDE DR
8000 SCTS 85255 500-H7
9400 SCTS 85255 501-C7
11800 SCTS 85255 502-A7
N MARIPOSA GRANDE DR
23600 SCTS 85255 500-H7
W MARIPOSA GRANDE LN
- PEOR 85382 497-A6
4500 PHX 85310 497-G6
W MARISSA DR
- MarC 85340 655-B2
E MARK LN
4200 PHX 85331 499-J1
4200 MarC 85331 499-J1
4900 PHX 85331 500-A1
6400 MarC 85331 500-E1
6800 SCTS 85331 500-F1
7300 SCTS 85262 500-G1
9300 SCTS 85262 501-D2
10200 SCTS 85255 501-F2
11500 SCTS 85262 502-A2
N MARK LN
19000 PEOR 85373 536-A5
W MARK LN
- PHX 85085 498-B1
10700 PEOR 85373 535-J5
10700 PEOR 85373 536-A5
17700 SURP 85387 494-A7
22400 MarC 85361 (452-H6
See Page 411)
E MARK WY
6200 CVCK 85331 420-E3
N MARKDALE
1300 MESA 85201 741-F1
1700 MESA 85201 701-F7
W MARKET PL
2100 CHAN 85248 861-A6
N MARKET ST
4300 PHX 85019 657-H6
8100 PEOR 85345 616-G2
15400 SURP 85374 575-C1
W MARKET ST
- WICK 85390 289-J3
5700 GLEN 85301 657-C1
7800 GLEN 85303 656-G1
S MARKETPLACE WY NE
1200 PHX 85048 818-J5
E MARKETPLACE WY SE
1100 PHX 85048 818-H6
E MARKETPLACE WY SW
900 PHX 85048 818-H5
W MARLBORO CIR
900 CHAN 85225 781-D7
W MARLBORO DR
300 CHAN 85225 781-E7
1200 CHAN 85224 781-A7
2500 MarC 85224 781-A7
2900 CHAN 85224 780-J7
W MARLBORO LN
2900 CHAN 85224 780-J7
E MARLENE DR
- GIL 85236 822-J1
- GIL 85236 823-A1
2000 GIL 85296 822-H1
E MARLETTE AV
- PHX 85012 658-G2
700 PHX 85014 658-H2
1300 PHX 85014 659-A2
1800 PHX 85016 659-B3
3400 PVAL 85253 659-F3
7300 SCTS 85250 660-G3
N MARLETTE AV
6200 PHX 85016 659-E3
6300 PVAL 85253 659-E3
W MARLETTE AV
- GLEN 85303 656-G2
- PHX 85013 658-F2
1500 PHX 85015 658-C2
2700 PHX 85017 658-A2
3400 PHX 85017 657-J2
3500 PHX 85019 657-G2
4400 GLEN 85301 657-B2
8300 GLEN 85305 656-F2
13500 MarC 85340 655-B2
W MARLETTE CT
- MarC 85340 655-B2
W MARLIN DR
- CHAN 85248 861-A3
E MARLIN PL
5700 MESA 85215 703-D6
W MARLIN PL
- CHAN 85248 861-E3
N MARLOW RD
1400 PinC 85219 746-B2
S MARLOW RD
100 PinC 85219 746-B7
1800 PinC 85219 786-B1
E MARMORA ST
2200 PHX 85022 579-C7
2300 PHX 85032 579-F7
E MARNY RD
400 TEMP 85281 740-E1
E MARQUETTE DR
1600 GIL 85234 782-H5
E MARQUIS LN
26200 MarC 85263 503-H5
N MARRON
- MESA 85220 784-H1
E MARSHALL AV
- GIL 85236 863-E4
- PHX 85012 658-G4
1200 PHX 85014 658-J4
1300 PHX 85014 659-A4
1700 PHX 85016 659-B4
W MARSHALL AV
- GLEN 85303 657-A4
- PHX 85013 658-F4

W MARSHALL AV
1900 PHX 85015 658-C4
2500 PHX 85017 658-A4
3300 PHX 85017 657-J4
3500 PHX 85019 657-G4
4500 GLEN 85301 657-B4
9100 MarC 85305 656-C3
E MARSHALL CT
- GIL 85236 863-E5
W MARSHALL DR
- MarC 85340 655-A3
W MARSHALL LN
- SURP 85374 (574-D1
See Page 573)
12300 SURP 85374 575-E2
N MARSHALL WY
3500 SCTS 85251 700-F1
4100 SCTS 85251 660-F7
N MARSHALL RANCH DR
5700 GLEN 85304 577-D6
E MARSTON DR
4700 PVAL 85253 659-J3
4700 PVAL 85253 660-A3
N MARTIN AV
100 GBND 85337 (1090-B3
See Page 1049)
S MARTIN AV
- MarC 85337 (1090-B4
See Page 1049)
100 GBND 85337 (1090-B3
See Page 1049)
S MARTIN LN
1300 TEMP 85281 740-J5
6700 TEMP 85283 780-H5
S MARTINGALE CT
- MarC 85236 903-B2
N MARTINGALE RD
- GIL 85234 783-C5
8800 PVAL 85253 620-A4
S MARTINGALE RD
- GIL 85236 863-C2
- MarC 85236 823-C7
- MarC 85236 863-B4
- MarC 85236 903-B2
S MARTINIQUE DR
700 GIL 85233 822-A2
E MARTIN LUTHER KING CIR
200 PHX 85034 698-J6
S MARTINQUE CT
600 GIL 85233 822-A2
N MARVELLA DR
22200 MarC 85375 535-A1
N MARVIN ST
1100 GIL 85233 782-A4
W MARY CIR
- PHX 85308 537-H7
W MARY CT
14700 SURP 85374 534-J6
E MARY LN
- MarC 85296 862-C1
N MARY ST
600 MarC 85281 740-F1
1000 TEMP 85281 740-F1
W MARY ANN DR
- PEOR 85308 536-G3
- PEOR 85382 536-D3
E MARY ANN WY
18500 MarC 85242 903-F5
W MARY JANE LN
5800 GLEN 85306 577-C2
6700 GLEN 85382 577-B2
7600 PEOR 85382 576-H2
E MARY KATHERINE DR
10400 SCTS 85259 621-F2
E MARY KATHERING DR
12200 SCTS 85259 622-A2
E MARYLAND AV
- PHX 85012 658-H2
700 PHX 85014 658-H2
1200 PHX 85014 659-A2
1600 PHX 85016 659-B2
8800 MarC 85248 900-J5
N MARYLAND AV
16400 SURP 85374 575-D1
W MARYLAND AV
- PHX 85013 658-F2
1500 PHX 85015 658-C2
2500 PHX 85017 658-B2
3300 PHX 85017 657-H2
3500 PHX 85019 657-H2
4300 GLEN 85301 657-A2
6700 GLEN 85303 657-A2
6900 GLEN 85303 656-G2
8300 GLEN 85305 656-D2
9800 GLEN 85307 656-B1
12300 MarC 85307 655-B1
12300 MarC 85340 655-B1
15600 MarC 85340 (654-E1
See Page 653)
17100 MarC 85355 (654-A1
See Page 653)
17500 MarC 85355 653-H1
N MARYLAND CIR
6500 PHX 85013 658-F2
E MARYLAND DR
2200 TEMP 85281 741-A4
N MARY MUNDE DR
- FTNH 85268 583-B7
E MARY SHARON DR
7200 SCTS 85262 460-G6
8200 SCTS 85262 (461-A6
See Page 421)
N MARYVALE PKWY
3800 PHX 85031 657-E5
W MARYVALE PKWY
- PHX 85031 657-E7
S MASHIE CT
- PinC 85219 786-F7
MASSACHUSETTS
6300 PinC 85219 786-D7
E MASTERS RD
- PinC 85219 786-F7
N MATADOR CT
20000 MarC 85373 536-B4
20000 MarC 85382 536-B4
E MATEO CIR
1700 MESA 85204 742-C6
N MATILDA LN
19900 GLEN 85308 536-J4
W MATILDA LN
6300 GLEN 85308 537-B4
7400 GLEN 85308 536-J4
N MATLOCK
- MESA 85203 742-A1
S MATLOCK
- MESA 85204 742-A5
N MATLOCK CIR
1200 MESA 85203 742-B2

S MATLOCK CIR
800 MESA 85204 742-A7
E MATT DILLON TR
- PHX 85331 460-A2
W MATTHEW DR
- PHX 85027 538-B3
E MATTIE AV
10800 MarC 85220 744-H5
W MAUI LN
- SURP 85379 (574-F2
See Page 573)
- SURP 85379 575-C3
5100 GLEN 85306 577-C3
7500 PEOR 85381 576-E3
N MAUNA LOA LN
14800 PHX 85053 578-B4
W MAUNA LOA LN
- SURP 85379 (574-F3
See Page 573)
- SURP 85379 575-C3
2800 PHX 85053 578-A3
3500 PHX 85053 577-J4
5100 GLEN 85306 577-C3
7500 PEOR 85381 576-E3
W MAURA LN
6500 GLEN 85306 577-B2
W MAURO LN
- PEOR 85382 576-F2
N MAVERICK
17000 SURP 85374 534-C7
S MAVERICK AV
- GIL 85236 863-D4
E MAVERICK CIR
8600 CARE 85377 421-B3
S MAVERICK CT
- GIL 85236 863-D4
E MAVERICK RD
6200 PVAL 85253 620-D6
7200 SCTS 85258 620-G6
E MAVERICK TR
10400 PinC 85219 786-J4
E MAWSON RD
7600 MarC 85207 703-J6
7800 MarC 85207 704-B6
N MAY ST
- MESA 85201 741-B3
600 CHAN 85226 820-D5
N MAYA CT
21800 MarC 85375 534-G1
MAYA DR
200 LP 85340 655-A6
W MAYA DR
- PHX 85085 497-C3
E MAYA WY
4000 PHX 85331 499-H3
4500 PHX 85331 500-A3
W MAYA WY
- PHX 85085 497-B2
- PHX 85085 498-B3
E MAYAN DR
14900 FTNH 85268 582-H5
N MAYAN DR
18800 MarC 85373 536-B5
E MAYBERRY AV
- GIL 85236 863-B5
E MAYBERRY CT
- GIL 85236 863-C5
N MAYFAIR
- MESA 85213 702-H6
500 MESA 85213 742-H2
S MAYFAIR
1400 MESA 85204 782-G2
N MAYFLOWER DR
14800 FTNH 85268 583-C5
E MAYO BLVD
- MarC 85054 540-D6
4800 PHX 85054 540-B5
MAYO CLINIC ENTR
10600 SCTS 85259 622-D3
N MAZATLAN DR
22600 MarC 85375 494-H7
E MAZATZAL CIR
15100 FTNH 85268 582-J4
18500 MarC 85263 503-H5
E MAZATZAL DR
4400 PHX 85331 499-J1
4400 PHX 85331 500-A1
4900 PHX 85331 460-B7
S MAZE CT
11400 PHX 85044 819-J1
N MCALLISTER AV
600 TEMP 85281 740-F1
1400 TEMP 85281 700-E6
S MCALLISTER AV
400 TEMP 85281 740-E4
3200 TEMP 85282 780-E1
6400 TEMP 85283 780-E5
7700 TEMP 85284 780-E7
8400 TEMP 85284 820-E1
E MCARTHUR DR
2200 TEMP 85281 741-A5
W MCARTHUR RD
3500 PHX 85085 498-A2
3600 PHX 85085 497-J2
MCCARROLL RD
27600 MarC 85342 (371-E1
See Page 331)
W MCCASLIN ROSE LN
- SURP 85373 535-H6
E MCCLAIN DR
7800 SCTS 85260 580-H3
W MCCLELLAN BLVD
7400 PHX 85013 658-E2
S MCCLELLAND DR
- CHAN 85248 861-D6
S MCCLELLAND PL
- CHAN 85248 861-D5
N MCCLINTOCK DR
- CHAN 85226 820-G4
- MarC 85281 740-H2
- TEMP 85281 740-H2
500 TEMP 85256 740-H2
S MCCLINTOCK DR
- TEMP 85226 820-G2
100 TEMP 85281 740-H5
300 CHAN 85226 820-G7
700 CHAN 85226 860-G1
1500 TEMP 85282 740-H5
3000 TEMP 85282 780-G5
4900 TEMP 85283 780-G5
7600 TEMP 85284 780-G5
7900 TEMP 85284 820-G2
S MCCORKINDALE CT
24400 MarC 85248 901-D3
S MCCORKINGDALE DR
5000 CHAN 85248 901-E2
E MCCORMICK DR
7400 SCTS 85258 620-G7
E MCCORMICK PKWY
- SCTS 85258 620-G7

STREET
Block City ZIP Pg-Grid

E MCCORMICK PKWY
7700 SCTS 85258 660-H1
E MCCOWAN LN
- QC 85242 904-E1
E MCCOY BLVD
- MarC 85236 823-D5
MCDONALD DR
- MarC 85250 661-A4
E MCDONALD DR
4000 PVAL 85018 659-H3
4000 PHX 85018 659-H3
4400 PVAL 85253 659-J3
4400 PHX 85253 659-J3
4800 PVAL 85018 660-C4
4800 PHX 85018 660-C4
5000 PVAL 85253 660-C4
7100 SCTS 85253 660-G4
7200 SCTS 85250 660-G4
8400 SCTS 85250 661-A4
8700 MarC 85250 661-C4
10400 MarC 85256 661-H4
12000 MarC 85256 662-A4
N MCDONALD DR
- MarC 85256 701-H1
1900 MESA 85201 701-H7
S MCDOT DR
- PHX 85009 738-A2
W MCDOT DR
- PHX 85009 738-B2
E MCDOWELL BLVD
- PinC 85219 705-E6
- MarC 85290 705-E6
W MCDOWELL BLVD
- PinC 85220 705-A6
- MarC 85220 705-A6
E MCDOWELL RD
- MarC 85207 744-F1
- PHX 85004 698-H4
400 MarC 85203 702-B5
400 MESA 85203 701-E5
400 MESA 85203 702-B5
700 PHX 85006 698-H4
1400 PHX 85006 699-D4
1500 MarC 85256 701-B5
1600 MESA 85213 702-G5
2400 PHX 85008 699-D4
3500 MESA 85215 702-G5
4100 MESA 85215 703-D5
5000 PHX 85008 700-D5
6400 PHX 85257 700-D5
6400 SCTS 85008 700-D5
6400 SCTS 85257 700-D5
6800 MESA 85207 703-H5
7400 MarC 85207 703-H5
7800 MarC 85207 704-B5
8700 SCTS 85257 701-B5
8800 SCTS 85256 701-B5
9000 MESA 85207 704-D6
W MCDOWELL RD
- PHX 85003 698-C4
- PHX 85004 698-C4
700 PHX 85007 698-C4
1600 GDYR 85338 695-C3
1800 PHX 85009 698-C4
2300 PHX 85037 696-C4
2300 PHX 85353 696-C4
3300 PHX 85009 697-F4
4300 PHX 85035 697-B4
4300 PHX 85043 697-F4
6700 PHX 85035 696-C4
6700 PHX 85043 696-C4
7900 TOL 85353 696-C4
9800 TOL 85037 696-C4
9900 AVON 85323 696-C4
10600 AVON 85323 695-C3
10700 MarC 85323 695-G4
14100 GDYR 85338 (694-E3
See Page 653)
17100 GDYR 85326 (693-H3
See Page 653)
17100 GDYR 85326 (694-E3
See Page 653)
18300 MarC 85326 (693-B3
See Page 653)
18900 BUCK 85326 (693-B3
See Page 653)
22100 BUCK 85326 (692-G3
See Page 651)
22100 MarC 85326 (692-G3
See Page 651)
26700 BUCK 85373 (691-C2
See Page 651)
26700 MarC 85326 (691-C2
See Page 651)
26700 MarC 85373 (691-C2
See Page 651)
27400 BUCK 85326 (691-C2
See Page 651)
E MCDOWELL MOUNTAIN DR
18600 MarC 85263 503-J7
N MCDOWELL MOUNTAIN DR
24800 MarC 85263 503-J7
E MCDOWELL MOUNTAIN RD
- MarC 85264 (504-A7
See Page 503)
N MCDOWELL MOUNTAIN RD
15400 MarC 85255 (543-G4
See Page 503)
15400 MarC 85255 583-F4
15400 MarC 85264 583-F4
15400 MarC 85268 583-D4
15400 MarC 85264 (543-G4
See Page 503)
19800 MarC 85255 503-H7
19800 MarC 85263 503-H7
19800 MarC 85263 (504-A7
See Page 503)
19800 MarC 85264 503-H7
19800 MarC 85264 (504-A7
See Page 503)
15400 MarC 85255 103-B2
15400 MarC 85264 103-B2
15400 MarC 85268 103-B2
19800 MarC 85263 103-B2
N MCDOWELL MOUNTAIN PARK DR
- MarC 85255 503-D7
- MarC 85255 (543-D3
See Page 503)
- MarC 85263 503-D7
E MCDOWELL MOUNTAIN RANCH RD
10000 SCTS 85260 581-E3
10300 SCTS 85259 581-F3

N MCDOWELL MOUNTAIN RANCH RD
16500 SCTS 85259 581-G2
E MCDOWELL VIEW TR
- FTNH 85268 622-J4
N MCGILL DR
2700 MarC 85207 704-F4
N MCKEIGHAN DR
2300 MarC 85207 704-E4
E MCKELLIPS BLVD
- APJT 85219 746-B1
- APJT 85219 745-F1
- APJT 85220 745-F1
- PinC 85219 745-F1
- PinC 85220 745-F1
4900 PinC 85219 746-B1
W MCKELLIPS BLVD
- APJT 85220 745-C1
- PinC 85220 745-C1
E MCKELLIPS RD
- MESA 85201 701-H7
100 TEMP 85281 700-E7
400 MESA 85203 701-H7
600 MESA 85203 702-B7
1400 TEMP 85257 700-F7
2000 MESA 85213 702-G7
3600 MESA 85215 702-G7
3600 MESA 85205 702-G7
4200 MESA 85215 703-B7
4200 MESA 85205 703-B7
6800 MESA 85207 703-H7
7200 MarC 85207 703-H7
7200 SCTS 85257 700-F7
7600 SCTS 85281 700-F7
7700 MESA 85207 704-A7
7700 MESA 85207 744-C1
8000 MarC 85257 700-H7
8000 SCTS 85256 700-H7
8000 MarC 85256 701-B7
8400 MarC 85257 701-B7
8400 MarC 85256 700-H7
9000 MarC 85207 744-E1
10400 MarC 85201 701-E6
W MCKELLIPS RD
- MESA 85201 701-G7
700 MarC 85201 701-G7
N MCKEMY AV
- CHAN 85226 820-B4
1000 CHAN 85284 820-B4
S MCKEMY AV
- CHAN 85226 820-B6
S MCKEMY ST
100 TEMP 85281 740-C3
700 TEMP 85283 780-C3
4000 TEMP 85282 780-C2
8800 TEMP 85284 820-C2
N MCKENNA LN
1200 GIL 85233 782-B4
N MCKENZIE RD
- PinC 85212 824-J7
- PinC 85212 864-J2
- PinC 85242 864-J2
E MCKINLEY ST
- PHX 85004 698-G5
- TEMP 85281 700-E6
600 PHX 85008 699-D6
700 PHX 85006 698-J5
1400 PHX 85006 699-B6
7200 SCTS 85257 700-F6
8600 SCTS 85257 701-A6
W MCKINLEY ST
- GDYR 85338 (694-C4
See Page 653)
- PHX 85003 698-F5
600 PHX 85007 698-E5
2700 PHX 85009 698-A5
3200 PHX 85009 697-H5
4400 PHX 85043 697-A5
6900 PHX 85043 696-J5
9100 TOL 85353 696-D5
E MCKNIGHT AV
7500 SCTS 85251 700-G1
N MCKNIGHT LP
17800 GLEN 85308 537-B7
W MCKNIGHT LP
6800 GLEN 85308 537-A7
N MCLEAN DR
- CHAN 85224 821-A5
600 WICK 85390 290-D2
W MCLEAN DR
- WICK 85390 290-D1
E MCLELLAN AV
7400 SCTS 85250 660-G2
E MCLELLAN BLVD
100 PHX 85012 658-H2
700 PHX 85014 658-H2
1400 PHX 85014 659-A2
1600 PHX 85016 659-A2
7300 SCTS 85250 660-G2
W MCLELLAN BLVD
- PHX 85013 658-F2
1500 PHX 85015 658-C2
2600 PHX 85017 658-A2
3300 PHX 85017 657-J2
3500 PHX 85019 657-G2
4500 GLEN 85301 657-E2
E MCLELLAN LN
7500 SCTS 85250 660-G2
E MCLELLAN RD
- MESA 85201 741-H1
1200 MESA 85203 742-B1
1800 MESA 85213 742-F1
3600 MESA 85205 742-H1
4200 MESA 85205 743-A1
7300 MESA 85207 743-H1
8000 MESA 85207 744-C2
9200 MarC 85207 744-G2
W MCLELLAN RD
- MESA 85201 741-F1
1000 MESA 85201 741-F1
5700 GLEN 85301 657-B1
6600 GLEN 85303 656-D1
6900 GLEN 85303 656-G1
6900 GLEN 85303 657-A1
13100 MarC 85307 655-C1
E MCNAIR CIR
1000 TEMP 85283 780-F7
E MCNAIR DR
200 TEMP 85283 780-E6
W MCNAIR ST
300 CHAN 85225 781-E7
1200 CHAN 85224 781-A7
E MCNEIL ST
4300 PHX 85044 779-H5
W MCNEIL ST
- GDYR 85326 (773-H4
See Page 733)
- GDYR 85338 (773-H4
See Page 733)
100 PHX 85041 778-C5

W MCNEIL ST
3100 MarC 85339 777-D5
N MCPHEE DR
14200 MarC 85351 576-B4
N MCQUEEN RD
- CHAN 85225 821-H5
- GIL 85233 781-H4
1500 GIL 85233 821-H5
S MCQUEEN RD
- GIL 85233 781-H7
- GIL 85233 821-H1
- CHAN 85225 821-H7
500 CHAN 85225 861-H3
1000 CHAN 85249 861-H3
1300 MarC 85249 861-H3
2200 GIL 85225 821-H1
23600 MarC 85249 901-H5
24400 CHAN 85249 901-H4
W MCRAE DR
- PHX 85027 538-G6
W MCRAE WY
2000 PHX 85027 538-A6
4400 PHX 85308 537-F6
6100 GLEN 85308 537-A6
7200 GLEN 85308 536-H6
8400 PEOR 85382 536-C6
W MEAD CT
- CHAN 85248 901-C1
E MEAD DR
- MarC 85249 901-H1
W MEAD DR
- CHAN 85248 901-C1
W MEAD PL
- CHAN 85248 901-B2
W MEADE DR
10300 MarC 85351 576-A2
10700 MarC 85351 575-J2
W MEADE LN
- GDYR 85326 (734-A1
See Page 733)
15700 GDYR 85338 (734-E2
See Page 733)
22100 BUCK 85326 (732-H1
See Page 731)
E MEADOW DR
- PHX 85022 578-H1
1900 TEMP 85282 740-H7
3400 PHX 85032 579-F1
6000 PHX 85254 580-D1
10000 SCTS 85260 581-E6
N MEADOW DR
3000 AVON 85323 695-H1
W MEADOW DR
100 PHX 85023 578-D1
1900 PHX 85023 538-D7
2900 PHX 85053 578-B1
3600 PHX 85308 577-H1
8300 PEOR 85382 536-E7
E MEADOW LN
500 PHX 85022 578-H4
1200 PHX 85022 579-A4
N MEADOW LN
- MESA 85201 741-G5
2900 AVON 85323 695-J1
E MEADOWBROOK AV
300 PHX 85012 658-H6
700 PHX 85014 658-H6
1300 PHX 85014 659-A6
1500 PHX 85016 659-B6
3200 PHX 85018 659-E6
7600 SCTS 85251 660-G6
8600 SCTS 85251 661-A7
W MEADOWBROOK AV
- MarC 85340 653-E4
1000 PHX 85037 656-A5
1200 PHX 85013 658-E6
2700 PHX 85017 658-B6
3500 PHX 85019 657-H6
4500 PHX 85033 656-G5
5300 PHX 85031 657-D6
5900 PHX 85033 657-A5
S MEADOWBROOK RD
- GIL 85296 863-E5
W MEADOW GREEN LN
1300 GIL 85233 821-J1
E MEADOW HILL DR
- SCTS 85259 581-F5
E MEADOWHILL DR
- SCTS 85259 581-F5
- SCTS 85260 581-F5
E MEADOW HILLS DR
8800 SCTS 85260 581-B5
W MEADOW HILLS DR
9200 MarC 85351 576-D4
E MEADOWLARK LN
6500 PVAL 85253 660-E1
N MEADOW LARK LN
700 CHAN 85226 820-D5
N MEADOWOOD DR
20200 MarC 85375 535-A3
W MEADOWOOD DR
14200 MarC 85375 535-A3
N MEADOW PARK DR
9100 MarC 85351 576-D1
N MEADOWS DR
400 CHAN 85224 821-C4
1100 GIL 85236 783-E4
S MEADOWS DR
- CHAN 85248 901-C2
300 CHAN 85224 821-C7
800 CHAN 85248 861-C1
2700 CHAN 85248 861-C1
E MEADOWS LN
300 GIL 85234 782-D3
S MEADOWS PL
- CHAN 85248 901-C2
E MEADOWVIEW CT
- MarC 85236 903-B2
E MEADOWVIEW DR
- MarC 85236 902-J2
- MarC 85236 903-A2
N MEANDER RD
47000 MarC 85087 (338-B5
See Page 337)
W MEANDER RD
3500 MarC 85087 (338-A6
See Page 337)
E MEANDER WY
35600 CARE 85377 420-G6
E MEANDERING TRAIL LN
- PinC 85219 826-H2
N MEDALLION CT
20200 MarC 85375 535-B3
N MEDELICE LN
26000 MarC 85263 503-J5
E MEDINA AV
- MESA 85212 784-E5
6900 MESA 85208 783-F4
8000 MESA 85208 784-B4

W MEDINA AV
500 MESA 85210 781-F4
1200 MESA 85202 781-A4
2700 MESA 85202 780-J4
E MEDINA BLVD
- MESA 85212 784-C5
W MEDINAH CT
- SURP 85374 534-H5
W MEDINAH WY
- SURP 85374 534-H5
N MEDINAN DR
13800 PHX 85022 578-H4
W MEDITERRANEAN DR
1200 GIL 85233 781-J7
1200 GIL 85233 821-J1
4700 GLEN 85301 617-F7
W MEDLOCK AV
10100 PHX 85307 656-A4
E MEDLOCK DR
- PHX 85012 658-G5
- PHX 85013 658-G5
900 PHX 85014 658-J5
1600 PHX 85016 659-A5
3200 PHX 85018 659-E5
7600 SCTS 85250 660-G5
W MEDLOCK DR
- MarC 85340 655-B4
- PHX 85013 658-E5
2000 PHX 85015 658-C5
2700 PHX 85017 658-B5
3500 PHX 85019 657-G4
5900 GLEN 85301 657-B4
6700 GLEN 85303 657-A4
6900 GLEN 85303 656-G4
8500 GLEN 85305 656-E4
19500 MarC 85340 653-D3
W MEEKER BLVD
12800 MarC 85375 535-B3
14300 MarC 85375 534-J5
14600 MarC 85374 534-J5
E MEGAN CT
- MarC 85236 823-D4
1000 GIL 85296 822-F4
W MEGAN CT
6400 CHAN 85226 820-B4
E MEGAN ST
- GIL 85236 822-J5
- GIL 85296 822-E4
- MarC 85236 823-D4
500 CHAN 85225 821-G4
W MEGAN ST
1400 CHAN 85224 821-A4
3200 CHAN 85226 820-B4
W MEGHAN DR
- GDYR 85326 (734-A1
See Page 733)
E MELANIE DR
4400 PHX 85331 459-J7
4500 PHX 85331 460-A6
N MELBA
1100 GIL 85233 782-A4
N MELBA CIR
1100 GIL 85233 782-A4
S MELBA ST
- MarC 85233 822-A1
W MELINDA AV
- PEOR 85382 536-G2
W MELINDA DR
6900 GLEN 85308 537-A2
E MELINDA LN
4300 PHX 85050 539-J2
4500 PHX 85050 540-A2
21600 PHX 85054 540-A3
N MELINDA LN
- PEOR 85382 536-E2
W MELINDA LN
- PEOR 85308 536-G2
- PEOR 85382 536-A2
300 PHX 85027 538-A2
3600 PHX 85308 537-J2
5200 GLEN 85308 537-A2
5500 GLEN 85310 537-D2
7100 GLEN 85308 536-J2
10700 PEOR 85373 536-A2
10800 PEOR 85373 535-J2
S MELISSA DR
300 GIL 85296 822-E1
N MELISSA LN
15100 SURP 85374 534-G6
W MELLOW ST
22300 MarC 85361 (412-H7
See Page 411)
W MELODY AV
- GIL 85233 782-B3
E MELODY CIR
1800 CHAN 85225 822-A4
N MELODY CIR
1100 CHAN 85225 822-A4
E MELODY CT
- GIL 85234 782-F4
E MELODY DR
600 GIL 85234 782-E4
3400 PHX 85040 779-E3
4200 GIL 85236 783-E4
17200 MarC 85236 783-D4
W MELODY DR
- GIL 85233 782-C3
1400 GIL 85233 781-H3
E MELODY LN
200 GIL 85234 782-D4
2900 GIL 85234 783-A4
S MELODY LN
800 TEMP 85281 740-H4
W MELODY LN
- PHX 85339 777-D3
S MELON LN
- PHX 85353 736-A3
E MELROSE CT
- MarC 85236 863-A3
E MELROSE ST
- MarC 85207 703-H6
- MarC 85236 863-A3
- MESA 85213 702-E6
1400 MarC 85296 862-G3
6400 MESA 85215 703-F6
6700 MESA 85207 703-H6
15800 MarC 85236 862-J3
E MELVIN ST
3400 PHX 85008 699-F6
W MELVIN ST
- GDYR 85338 (694-C5
See Page 653)
2600 PHX 85009 698-A6
3200 PHX 85009 697-H6
6900 PHX 85043 696-J6
19100 MarC 85326 (693-E5
See Page 653)
W MEMORIAL DR
- MarC 85086 (378-C7
See Page 337)

W MEMORY LN
15300 SURP 85374 534-G7
E MENADOTA DR
2100 PHX 85024 539-C4
3200 PHX 85050 539-F4
W MENADOTA DR
1300 PHX 85027 538-E4
4700 PHX 85308 537-F4
7500 GLEN 85308 536-J4
9100 PEOR 85382 536-C4
E MENDORA CREEK
- PinC 85219 786-E7
E MENDOZA AV
- MESA 85212 784-D5
7800 MESA 85208 783-J5
W MENDOZA AV
500 MESA 85210 781-E4
1200 MESA 85202 781-A4
2700 MESA 85202 780-J4
W MENDOZA CIR
400 MESA 85210 781-F4
MENDOZA ST
- PinC - 901-C6
E MENLO CIR
- MarC 85207 704-E6
- MESA 85207 704-E6
- MESA 85215 702-J6
2800 MESA 85213 702-H6
E MENLO ST
- MarC 85207 704-C6
- MESA 85207 704-D6
1600 MESA 85203 702-C6
2400 MESA 85213 702-E6
3600 MESA 85215 702-H6
6400 MESA 85215 703-F6
6800 MESA 85207 703-G6
S MENLO PARK DR
- GIL 85236 863-B3
- MarC 85236 863-B4
E MERCER LN
1200 PHX 85020 618-J2
1200 PHX 85020 619-A2
2200 PHX 85028 619-C2
5300 PHX 85254 620-B2
7100 SCTS 85254 620-F2
7200 SCTS 85260 620-G2
8500 SCTS 85260 621-A2
10400 SCTS 85259 621-F2
12000 SCTS 85259 622-B3
W MERCER LN
900 PHX 85029 618-A1
3500 PHX 85029 617-H1
4300 PHX 85304 617-G2
4700 GLEN 85304 617-B1
7100 PEOR 85345 616-E1
7100 PEOR 85345 617-B1
E MERCURY DR
10400 MarC 85220 744-G5
W MERCURY PL
5200 CHAN 85226 820-D6
W MERCURY WY
- CHAN 85226 820-C6
1600 CHAN 85224 821-C6
N MERIDIAN RD
- APJT 85220 745-A4
- APJT 85220 745-A4
- MarC 85220 745-A4
800 MESA 85220 745-A4
4000 MarC 85220 705-A7
4000 PinC 85220 705-A7
4000 PinC 85220 745-A4
S MERIDIAN RD
- APJT 85220 784-J5
- APJT 85220 824-J3
- MarC 85212 824-J3
- MESA 85212 784-J5
- MESA 85212 824-J3
- MESA 85220 784-J5
- MESA 85242 824-J7
- MESA 85242 864-J2
- PinC 85212 824-J3
- PinC 85212 864-J2
- PinC 85220 784-J5
- PinC 85220 824-J3
- QC 85242 904-J4
1200 PinC 85220 745-A7
- MarC 85220 745-A7
1200 MarC 85220 785-A2
1200 PinC 85220 785-A2
1300 MESA 85220 785-A2
1300 APJT 85220 785-A2
18800 QC 85242 864-J6
18800 PinC 85242 864-J2
22000 MarC 85242 904-J4
22000 PinC 85242 904-J4
N MERINO
- MESA 85205 742-H4
S MERINO
1200 MESA 85206 782-H1
S MERINO CIR
1700 MESA 85206 782-H3
N MERION WY
8200 PVAL 85253 620-F6
W MERRELL ST
- AVON 85340 695-C1
- PHX 85037 696-D1
- PHX 85013 698-G2
4900 PHX 85031 697-E2
6700 PHX 85033 697-A1
6900 PHX 85033 696-J1
15100 GDYR 85338 (694-F1
See Page 653)
E MERRILL AV
200 GIL 85234 782-D4
2800 GIL 85234 783-A4
W MERRILL AV
100 GIL 85233 782-B4
E MERRILL DR
2600 PHX 85040 779-C1
E MERRILL LN
4400 GIL 85236 783-E4
W MERRILL LN
1600 GIL 85233 781-H4
N MERRILL RD
- MarC 85220 744-G4
300 MESA 85220 744-G4
S MERRILL RD
6800 MESA 85242 864-F4
18700 QC 85242 864-F4
W MERRILL ST
- GDYR 85338 (694-E1
See Page 653)
W MERRITT PKWY
800 GBND 85337 (1089-J3
See Page 1049)
N MESA DR
- MarC 85256 621-J7
- MESA 85203 741-J3
- MESA 85204 741-J3
- MESA 85201 741-J3

N MESA DR
- MESA 85210 741-J3
1700 MESA 85201 701-J7
1700 MESA 85203 701-J6
3200 MarC 85256 701-J1
4100 MarC 85256 661-J3
S MESA DR
- MESA 85204 741-J6
- MESA 85210 741-J6
1000 MESA 85204 781-J1
1000 MESA 85210 781-J1
E MESA LUTHERAN HOSP
- MESA 85201 741-F2
W MESA VERDE
- TEMP 85282 779-J1
- TEMP 85282 780-A1
N MESA VERDE DR
- WICK 85390 289-J2
W MESA VERDE DR
12300 MarC 85375 535-D4
S MESA VISTA CIR
- PinC 85219 786-G7
E MESA VISTA LN
400 MESA 85203 741-J1
W MESCAL DR
8700 PEOR 85345 616-E1
W MESCAL RD
7700 PEOR 85345 616-G1
E MESCAL ST
- SCTS 85259 622-A2
900 PHX 85020 618-J1
1200 PHX 85020 619-A2
2300 PHX 85028 619-D2
6000 PHX 85254 620-D2
6200 SCTS 85254 620-E2
8600 SCTS 85260 621-A2
10600 SCTS 85259 621-F2
W MESCAL ST
2300 PHX 85029 618-A1
3400 PHX 85029 617-H1
4300 PHX 85304 617-G1
4500 GLEN 85304 617-B1
7100 PEOR 85345 616-D1
7100 PEOR 85345 617-B1
W MESCALERO CT
9900 MarC 85382 536-C4
E MESCALERO DR
18700 MarC 85263 503-J6
E MESETO AV
- MESA 85212 784-D5
6800 MESA 85208 783-G4
8000 MESA 85208 784-A5
W MESETO AV
400 MESA 85210 781-E4
1100 MESA 85202 781-C4
E MESETO CIR
- MESA 85208 784-A5
W MESETO CIR
700 MESA 85210 781-C4
1600 MESA 85202 781-A4
2700 MESA 85202 780-J4
S MESITA
7600 MESA 85212 783-J6
N MESQUITE
18200 SURP 85374 534-C5
W MESQUITE
- TEMP 85282 779-J1
- TEMP 85282 780-A1
E MESQUITE AV
500 APJT 85219 785-E1
W MESQUITE AV
- APJT 85220 785-C1
W MESQUITE BLVD
1300 GIL 85233 821-J1
E MESQUITE CIR
- MarC 85263 503-J3
- GIL 85296 822-D1
700 TEMP 85281 740-E1
W MESQUITE CT
- SURP 85374 534-F4
E MESQUITE DR
- SCTS 85262 (381-J7
See Page 341)
1200 CARE 85377 420-H6
W MESQUITE DR
- GDYR 85338 (694-D6
See Page 653)
E MESQUITE LN
5600 PHX 85018 660-B6
N MESQUITE LN
13600 FTNH 85268 582-J6
W MESQUITE LN
4000 PHX 85019 657-H5
E MESQUITE PL
5700 GUAD 85283 780-B4
E MESQUITE RD
- MarC 85212 824-J2
6000 CVCK 85331 420-E2
E MESQUITE ST
200 GIL 85296 822-D1
700 MarC 85086 419-A1
800 MarC 85296 822-F1
16200 MarC 85236 823-A1
16300 GIL 85236 823-A1
20000 MarC 85212 824-A1
N MESQUITE ST
2500 CHAN 85224 821-C1
S MESQUITE ST
- WICK 85390 290-E3
400 GIL 85296 822-E1
W MESQUITE ST
- MarC 85233 821-J1
- MarC 85233 822-A1
- GIL 85233 822-A1
400 CHAN 85225 781-F7
400 CHAN 85225 821-E1
1000 CHAN 85224 821-B1
2500 MarC 85224 821-B1
S MESQUITE CANYON
- MESA 85212 784-D6
S MESQUITE GROVE WY
- MarC 85249 902-C3
E MESQUITE WOOD RD
5000 PHX 85044 779-J7
S METEOR CT
24400 MarC 85248 901-E3
S METEOR DR
4900 CHAN 85248 901-E2
N METRO BLVD
200 CHAN 85226 820-H5
N METRO PKWY E
9400 PHX 85051 618-B3
N METRO PKWY W
9400 PHX 85051 618-A3
METROCENTER LP
2800 PHX 85051 618-B3
METROCENTER ACCESS
2900 PHX 85051 618-A3

E MEWS RD
16800 MarC 85242 903-B5
19200 QC 85242 903-H5
19600 QC 85242 904-A5
20000 MarC 85242 904-A5
E MEXICO ST
5600 GUAD 85283 780-B4
W MIAMI AV
10700 AVON 85353 735-G3
10700 MarC 85353 735-G3
12400 AVON 85323 735-D3
E MIAMI RD
- SCTS 85258 660-H1
E MIAMI ST
3600 PHX 85040 739-F4
W MIAMI ST
- GDYR 85338 (734-D2
See Page 733)
- PHX 85353 735-J3
- PHX 85353 736-A3
4900 PHX 85043 737-A3
N MICA DR
18400 MarC 85375 535-C5
E MICHAEL DR
2800 PHX 85032 579-E3
W MICHAEL DR
10800 PEOR 85373 535-J5
10800 PEOR 85373 536-A5
S MICHELE LN
7800 TEMP 85284 780-D7
9400 TEMP 85284 820-C3
E MICHELLE
4200 GIL 85236 783-E4
W MICHELLE AV
- PHX 85022 538-G7
- PHX 85023 538-F7
E MICHELLE DR
- PHX 85022 538-H7
900 PHX 85022 539-A7
2600 PHX 85032 539-D7
4600 PHX 85032 540-A7
4900 PHX 85254 540-A7
8000 SCTS 85255 580-J1
W MICHELLE DR
600 PHX 85023 538-D7
2700 PHX 85053 538-B7
3500 PHX 85308 538-A7
3500 PHX 85308 537-F6
5300 GLEN 85308 537-C6
8300 PEOR 85382 536-E6
9200 PEOR 85373 536-D7
W MICHELLE ST
- GBND 85337 (1090-A3
See Page 1049)
E MICHELLE WY
- GIL 85234 783-A4
- MarC 85234 783-A4
N MICHELLE WY
1000 GIL 85236 783-D4
W MICHIGAN
11000 PEOR 85345 616-C1
E MICHIGAN AV
100 PHX 85022 538-H6
900 PHX 85022 539-A7
2400 PHX 85032 539-D7
4600 PHX 85032 540-A7
4800 PHX 85254 540-A7
8900 MarC 85248 900-J5
8900 MarC 85248 901-A4
N MICHIGAN AV
18000 PHX 85032 539-D7
18200 PHX 85022 538-H7
W MICHIGAN AV
100 PHX 85023 538-D6
2700 PHX 85053 538-A6
3400 PHX 85308 538-A6
3600 PHX 85308 537-F6
5300 GLEN 85308 537-C6
7500 GLEN 85308 536-H6
11100 YNTN 85335 575-H5
S MICHIGAN CT
25400 MarC 85248 901-B4
N MICHNER WY
- MarC 85086 (378-B7
See Page 337)
S MICROAGE WY
2300 TEMP 85282 740-A6
E MICROTOWER RD
- MarC 85207 704-D2
- MarC 85290 704-D2
- MESA 85207 704-D2
N MIDDLECOFF DR
2000 MESA 85215 703-C7
10800 FTNH 85268 623-C3
N MIDLAND DR
14000 FTNH 85268 583-B6
W MIDLAND LN
500 GIL 85233 782-B7
W MIDWAY AV
- GLEN 85303 617-A7
4600 GLEN 85301 617-F7
7700 GLEN 85303 616-G7
E MIGHTY SAGUARO WY
6800 SCTS 85262 460-G3
E MILADA DR
- PHX 85040 778-H4
W MILADA DR
- PHX 85041 778-E4
E MILAGRO AV
- MESA 85212 784-C5
6800 MESA 85208 783-F5
8000 MESA 85208 784-A5
W MILAGRO AV
1500 MESA 85202 781-C4
E MILAGRO CIR
- MESA 85208 784-A5
N MILANO CT
- MarC 85340 655-B2
N MILANO DR
- MarC 85340 655-B3
S MILBURN
- MESA 85212 784-D5
E MILITARY RD
- CARE 85377 420-F4
6400 CVCK 85331 420-F4
E MILKWOOD CIR
- SCTS 85255 501-C4
E MILKY WY
- GIL 85236 822-J5
- GIL 85236 823-A5
- GIL 85296 822-H5
W MILKY WY
4000 CHAN 85226 820-D7
E MILKY WAY ST
- GIL 85296 822-G5
N MILL AV
- TEMP 85281 740-C1
700 TEMP 85281 700-C7
900 CHAN 85226 820-D4

STREET Block City ZIP Pg-Grid

S MILL AV
100 TEMP 85281 740-D4
1700 TEMP 85282 740-D6
3100 TEMP 85282 780-D2
4900 TEMP 85283 780-D2
7500 TEMP 85284 780-D7
8000 TEMP 85284 820-D1
9600 CHAN 85226 820-D3
W MILL AV
- TEMP 85284 820-D1
E MILLBRAE CIR
2200 GIL 85234 782-J4
E MILLBRAE LN
2800 GIL 85234 783-A4
4200 GIL 85236 783-E4
N MILL CREEK WY
- MarC 85086 (378-D5 See Page 337)
N MILLER
- MESA 85203 742-A2
S MILLER
- MESA 85204 742-A5
N MILLER CIR
1200 MESA 85203 742-A2
S MILLER CIR
800 MESA 85204 742-A7
E MILLER LN
- GIL 85236 863-C1
MILLER RD
26600 SCTS 85255 500-H2
28200 SCTS 85262 500-H2
29000 SCTS 85262 460-H7
N MILLER RD
100 BUCK 85326 (772-A1 See Page 731)
100 MarC 85326 (772-A1 See Page 731)
300 SCTS 85257 700-G4
500 BUCK 85326 (732-A7 See Page 731)
1000 TEMP 85281 740-G1
1400 TEMP 85281 700-G7
1500 SCTS 85281 700-G7
3400 SCTS 85251 700-G1
4100 SCTS 85251 660-G6
5000 SCTS 85250 660-G3
5500 PVAL 85250 660-G5
6200 MarC 85250 660-G3
9800 SCTS 85258 620-G2
10600 SCTS 85260 620-G2
22200 SCTS 85255 540-H2
23500 SCTS 85255 500-H6
29000 SCTS 85262 460-H6
S MILLER RD
- MarC 85326 (692-A5 See Page 651)
- BUCK 85326 (692-A5 See Page 651)
100 BUCK 85326 (772-A2 See Page 731)
2000 MarC 85326 (732-A4 See Page 731)
2000 BUCK 85326 (732-A4 See Page 731)
10300 MarC 85326 (772-A3 See Page 731)
N MILLER ST
1300 MESA 85203 742-A1
S MILLER ST
1000 MESA 85204 782-A1
E MILLETT AV
- MESA 85210 741-H7
400 MESA 85204 741-J7
600 MESA 85204 742-A7
E MILLS CT
5200 MESA 85215 703-C6
E MILLS ST
- MESA 85207 703-H6
2400 MESA 85215 703-F6
W MILL VALLEY LN
15700 SURP 85374 534-F6
S MILLY CT
- GIL 85236 863-D5
E MILTON CT
- MarC 85255 (462-F6 See Page 421)
E MILTON DR
4000 PHX 85331 459-H6
4700 PHX 85331 460-A6
5600 MarC 85331 460-C6
6900 SCTS 85331 460-F6
7300 SCTS 85262 460-H6
E MIMBRES CT
9500 PinC 85219 786-G7
E MIMOSA DR
11400 SCTS 85255 501-H4
N MIMOSA DR
12600 FTNH 85268 583-B7
12600 FTNH 85268 623-B1
W MIMOSA DR
10600 MarC 85373 536-A6
10700 MarC 85373 535-J6
N MINE 1 RD
45000 MarC 85342 (332-C5 See Page 331)
N MINE 2 RD
- MarC 85342 (332-E3 See Page 331)
W MINER RD
33200 MarC 85390 289-J4
E MINERAL RD
- PHX 85040 778-G5
1200 GIL 85234 782-F6
4300 PHX 85044 779-H5
W MINERAL RD
800 PHX 85041 778-E5
1500 TEMP 85283 780-A6
S MINESHAFT DR
- APJT 85219 785-H3
N MINGUS
37300 MarC 85086 417-J4
W MINGUS RD
2300 MarC 85087 (338-D3 See Page 337)
W MINGUS MOUNTAIN CT
11600 SURP 85374 535-G4
E MINING CAMP ST
- APJT 85219 746-C1
5200 PinC 85219 746-C1
MINNESOTA
6100 PinC 85219 786-D7
W MINNESOTA
- PEOR 85351 616-C1
10900 PEOR 85345 616-C1
E MINNESOTA AV
9000 MarC 85248 900-J4
9000 MarC 85248 901-A4
E MINNEZONA AV
700 PHX 85014 658-H6
1800 PHX 85016 659-B6
3400 PHX 85018 659-F6
7300 SCTS 85251 660-G6
8700 SCTS 85251 661-A7
W MINNEZONA AV
- PHX 85013 658-F6
2000 PHX 85015 658-C6
2700 PHX 85017 658-B6
3500 PHX 85019 657-J6
4500 PHX 85033 657-A6
4600 PHX 85037 656-A5
5000 PHX 85031 657-C6
7100 PHX 85033 656-J5
E MINNEZONA CIR
3200 PHX 85018 659-E6
E MINTON CIR
- MESA 85207 703-H6
- MESA 85215 702-J6
1700 MESA 85203 702-H6
3100 MESA 85213 702-H6
E MINTON DR
100 TEMP 85282 780-E2
2100 TEMP 85282 781-A2
S MINTON DR
4800 TEMP 85282 779-J2
W MINTON DR
1100 TEMP 85282 780-B2
2500 TEMP 85282 779-J2
7000 PHX 85282 779-J2
E MINTON PL
3600 MESA 85215 702-H6
6100 MESA 85215 703-E6
7600 MarC 85207 703-J6
E MINTON ST
- MarC 85207 704-C6
- MESA 85203 702-D6
- MESA 85207 703-G6
- MESA 85207 704-E6
- TEMP 85040 779-H2
- TEMP 85282 779-H2
2100 MESA 85213 702-D6
4200 PHX 85040 779-G2
6700 MESA 85215 703-G6
W MINTON ST
- PHX 85041 777-G2
300 PHX 85041 778-D2
3500 MarC 85041 777-H2
E MIRABEL AV
6800 MESA 85208 783-F5
N MIRADA CIR
- MESA 85207 704-A3
N MIRADAR
29000 SCTS 85262 (461-A6 See Page 421)
N MIRADAR CT
- MarC 85255 (462-F7 See Page 421)
W MIRAGE DR
- TEMP 85282 779-J1
N MIRAGE LN
22000 MarC 85375 535-A1
22300 MarC 85375 495-A6
E MIRAGE CROSSING CT
16800 FTNH 85268 583-D5
N MIRAGE CROSSING CT
15000 FTNH 85268 583-D5
N MIRAMAR
400 MESA 85213 742-G1
3300 MESA 85213 702-G7
S MIRAMAR
1400 MESA 85204 782-G2
N MIRA MAR CIR
25400 SCTS 85255 501-A5
N MIRAMONTE CT
9900 SCTS 85262 421-E3
W MIRAMONTE CT
- SURP 85374 534-G4
E MIRAMONTE DR
5300 CVCK 85331 420-C3
9700 SCTS 85262 421-E3
N MIRAMONTE DR
38000 CVCK 85331 420-D3
E MIRAMONTE WY
9500 FTNH 85268 622-G5
W MIRANDY CT
11100 MarC 85351 575-H3
N MIRANDY LN
- SURP 85374 575-H1
E MIRASOL CIR
10600 SCTS 85259 581-F3
E MIRAVISTA
- FTNH 85268 622-H5
E MIRISOL CIR
10900 SCTS 85259 581-G3
E MISSION DR
900 TEMP 85283 780-E7
N MISSION DR
11800 MarC 85351 576-B6
W MISSION DR
300 CHAN 85225 781-E7
600 CHAN 85225 821-D1
1200 CHAN 85224 781-B7
1200 CHAN 85224 821-B1
E MISSION LN
- PHX 85020 618-G4
1200 PHX 85020 619-A4
2800 PHX 85028 619-E4
9100 SCTS 85258 621-C4
9300 SCTS 85259 622-A5
11400 SCTS 85259 621-H5
N MISSION LN
9400 PHX 85051 617-H3
W MISSION LN
- PHX 85021 618-C4
3000 PHX 85051 618-A3
3500 PHX 85051 617-H3
4100 PHX 85302 617-H3
4400 GLEN 85302 617-B3
6800 PEOR 85345 617-A3
6900 PEOR 85345 616-C3
9200 MarC 85351 616-A3
10600 MarC 85351 615-J3
E MISSION BAY DR
1100 GIL 85234 782-G3
N MISSION BELL CT
11600 FTNH 85268 623-D2
N MISSION COVE LN
1300 GIL 85234 782-G4
W MISSION COVE LN
16300 SURP 85374 534-E5
E MISSION LANE CIR
12000 SCTS 85259 621-J5
12000 SCTS 85259 622-A5
N MISSION PARK BLVD
1000 CHAN 85224 821-A3
W MISSION PARK BLVD
2700 CHAN 85224 821-A4
2800 CHAN 85224 820-J3
MISSOURI
6200 PinC 85219 786-D7
E MISSOURI AV
- PHX 85012 658-H4
700 PHX 85014 658-H4
1300 PHX 85014 659-B4
1400 PHX 85016 659-B4
3200 PHX 85018 659-E4
W MISSOURI AV
- PHX 85013 658-E4
1100 PHX 85015 658-B4
2500 PHX 85017 658-B4
3300 PHX 85017 657-H4
3500 PHX 85019 657-G4
4300 GLEN 85301 657-C4
5500 GLEN 85303 656-G4
6700 GLEN 85303 657-A4
8700 GLEN 85305 656-E4
9100 MarC 85305 656-C4
10100 PHX 85307 656-A4
10600 MarC 85307 655-J4
10600 MarC 85307 656-A4
11100 YNTN 85335 615-H1
12800 MarC 85340 655-A3
19900 MarC 85340 653-D3
E MISTY CT
- MarC 85242 904-F3
- QC 85242 904-F3
W MISTY WILLOW LN
3500 PHX 85310 498-A6
3700 PHX 85310 497-B6
E MITCHELL DR
- PHX 85012 698-G1
700 PHX 85014 698-H1
1300 PHX 85014 699-A1
1600 PHX 85016 699-A1
3200 PHX 85018 699-E1
4900 PHX 85018 700-A1
6300 SCTS 85251 700-D2
8500 SCTS 85251 701-A2
N MITCHELL DR
3400 PHX 85018 699-J1
S MITCHELL DR
400 TEMP 85281 740-C3
3800 TEMP 85282 780-C1
5300 TEMP 85283 780-C3
W MITCHELL DR
- GDYR 85338 (654-J7 See Page 653)
600 TEMP 85281 740-C4
800 PHX 85013 698-F1
1500 PHX 85015 698-C1
3500 PHX 85019 697-H1
3500 PHX 85033 697-B1
4400 PHX 85031 657-F7
4400 PHX 85031 697-E1
7000 PHX 85033 656-G7
8500 PHX 85037 696-E1
MITCHELL ST
- GLEN 85309 615-A7
N MITCHELL ST
1800 PHX 85006 698-J3
4100 PHX 85014 658-J7
W MITCHELL ST
14100 GLEN 85309 (614-J7 See Page 573)
N MITCHNER WY
- MarC 85086 (378-B6 See Page 337)
W MOBILE AV
3700 PHX 85041 737-H6
7000 PHX 85043 736-J5
9200 PEOR 85345 576-D7
E MOBILE LN
700 PHX 85040 738-H6
1700 PHX 85040 739-A6
W MOBILE LN
500 PHX 85041 738-C6
8300 PHX 85353 736-E5
8300 MarC 85353 736-E5
N MOCCASIN TR
- GIL 85234 783-C5
17000 SURP 85374 534-J7
S MOCCASIN TR
- GIL 85236 863-C2
- MarC 85236 823-C7
- MarC 85236 903-C2
W MOCCASIN TR
14400 SURP 85374 534-J7
20100 MarC 85326 813-D1
E MOCKINGBIRD DR
4500 GIL 85236 783-E5
W MOCKINGBIRD DR
1800 CHAN 85248 861-B4
9700 MarC 85373 536-C7
E MOCKINGBIRD LN
4400 PHX 85028 619-J5
4500 PVAL 85028 619-J5
4900 PVAL 85253 620-B5
N MOCKINGBIRD LN
- PVAL 85253 660-E2
7500 PVAL 85253 620-A6
N MOCKINGBIRD RD
51100 MarC 85390 290-J5
E MOCKINGBIRD ST
4700 PinC 85219 746-C5
W MOCKINGBIRD ST
2600 APJT 85220 745-A4
W MODEL WY
- PHX 85310 537-H2
E MODESTO DR
- MarC 85340 655-C6
W MODESTO DR
300 LP 85340 655-A6
S MODINE LN
800 GIL 85296 822-E2
S MODINE ST
900 GIL 85296 822-D3
E MODOC CT
3500 PHX 85044 819-E1
E MODOC DR
4100 PHX 85044 819-G1
MOEUR PARK RD
700 TEMP 85281 740-D2
E MOGOLLON TR
9200 PinC 85219 786-G7
MOHAVE CIR
1600 GLEN 85307 615-B7
W MOHAVE CT
11500 SURP 85374 535-H6
E MOHAVE PL
4700 PVAL 85253 619-J6
4700 PVAL 85253 620-A6
E MOHAVE RD
17600 MarC 85264 583-F7
18000 MarC 85264 623-H1
N MOHAVE RD
7800 PVAL 85253 620-C6
E MOHAVE ST
- PHX 85004 738-H2
700 PHX 85034 738-H2
1400 PHX 85034 739-A2
4800 PHX 85044 819-H1
S MOHAVE ST
11400 PHX 85044 779-H7
11600 PHX 85044 819-H1
W MOHAVE ST
- GDYR 85326 (734-A1 See Page 733)
- GDYR 85338 (734-E1 See Page 733)
- MarC 85353 735-G1
- PHX 85353 736-E1
- PHX 85003 738-F2
100 WICK 85390 290-E2
700 PHX 85007 738-D2
2300 PHX 85009 738-A2
3100 PHX 85009 737-H2
5400 PHX 85043 737-A1
5500 MarC 85043 737-D2
10900 AVON 85353 735-E1
N MOHAVE WY
3600 SCTS 85251 700-E1
S MOHAWK DR
25200 MarC 85248 901-B4
W MOHAWK DR
900 PHX 85024 538-J4
3300 PHX 85027 538-A3
E MOHAWK LN
1600 PHX 85024 539-B4
2400 PHX 85050 539-D4
8100 SCTS 85255 540-J4
8100 SCTS 85255 541-A4
W MOHAWK LN
- GLEN 85308 536-J3
- PHX 85027 538-A3
3500 PHX 85308 538-A3
3600 PHX 85308 537-J3
5200 GLEN 85308 537-A3
9700 PEOR 85382 536-A3
10700 PEOR 85373 536-A3
10900 PEOR 85373 535-J3
S MOHICAN RD
3200 PinC 85219 786-J4
N MOLLERA
1300 MESA 85201 741-E2
S MOLLERA CIR
2100 MESA 85210 781-D3
N MOLLERA CT
3300 CHAN 85225 781-D6
W MOLLY DR
- PHX 85085 497-C3
E MOLLY LN
4000 PHX 85331 499-H3
4500 PHX 85331 500-A3
W MOLLY LN
- PHX 85085 497-B3
- PHX 85085 498-B3
E MONACO DR
16400 FTNH 85268 623-C1
E MONARCH BAY DR
1800 GIL 85234 782-H4
N MONDEL DR
- GIL 85233 781-J4
W MONDELL RD
14800 SURP 85374 534-H7
E MONICA AV
3300 PHX 85032 579-F1
E MONICA DR
7700 SCTS 85255 580-H1
W MONOMA DR
7000 GLEN 85308 536-J3
E MONONA DR
- PHX 85050 539-G3
1100 PHX 85024 538-J3
1100 PHX 85024 539-A3
W MONONA DR
- PHX 85027 538-A3
700 PHX 85024 538-J3
3400 PHX 85308 538-A3
3500 PHX 85308 537-H3
5500 GLEN 85308 537-A3
E MONROE AV
900 BUCK 85326 (772-B1 See Page 731)
E MONROE AV Rt#-85
100 BUCK 85326 (772-A1 See Page 731)
E MONROE ST
- PHX 85004 698-H6
900 PHX 85034 698-H6
1400 PHX 85034 699-A6
W MONROE ST
- AVON 85323 695-D6
- AVON 85353 695-E6
- GDYR 85338 (694-D5 See Page 653)
- PHX 85003 698-F6
1200 PHX 85007 698-D6
1900 PHX 85009 698-B6
2000 CHAN 85224 821-A3
3200 PHX 85009 697-J6
5200 PHX 85043 697-C6
8000 PEOR 85345 616-F2
9100 TOL 85353 696-C6
W MONTANA
11000 PEOR 85345 616-C1
E MONTANA AV
8800 MarC 85248 900-J5
S MONTANA AV
25400 MarC 85248 900-J4
W MONTANA AV
11000 MarC 85351 615-H1
11100 YNTN 85335 615-H1
N MONTANA DR
18500 MarC 85263 503-J3
N MONTANOSO
30000 SCTS 85262 (461-B5 See Page 421)
E MONTANOSO DR
8200 SCTS 85262 (461-A6 See Page 421)
E MONTARA PL
5700 MESA 85215 703-D6
E MONTE AV
- MESA 85212 784-C5
7000 MESA 85208 783-F5
8000 MESA 85208 784-A5
S MONTE AV
1300 MESA 85202 781-D4
W MONTE AV
500 MESA 85210 781-E4
1200 MESA 85202 781-A4
2700 MESA 85202 780-J4
E MONTE CIR
- MESA 85208 784-A5
7000 MESA 85208 783-G5
W MONTE CIR
400 MESA 85210 781-E4
E MONTE WY
- PHX 85040 778-G5
4300 PHX 85044 779-H5
W MONTE WY
100 PHX 85041 778-E5
E MONTEBELLO AV
- PHX 85012 658-G4
600 APJT 85219 785-E1
700 PHX 85014 658-G4
1300 PHX 85014 659-A4
1600 PHX 85016 659-A4
4000 PHX 85018 659-G4
5700 SCTS 85250 660-F4
6800 PVAL 85253 660-E4
8400 SCTS 85250 661-A4
W MONTEBELLO AV
- APJT 85220 785-C1
- MarC 85340 655-A3
- PHX 85013 658-F4
1500 PHX 85015 658-C4
2500 PHX 85017 658-A3
3300 PHX 85017 657-J3
3500 PHX 85019 657-G3
4300 GLEN 85301 657-A3
5800 GLEN 85303 656-F3
6700 GLEN 85303 657-A3
10300 PHX 85307 656-F3
E MONTEBELLO CIR
1100 PHX 85014 658-J4
E MONTECITO AV
- MarC 85256 661-D7
700 PHX 85014 658-H7
1600 PHX 85014 659-A7
1600 PHX 85016 659-A7
3200 PHX 85018 659-E7
5400 PHX 85018 660-B7
6000 PHX 85251 660-C7
6700 SCTS 85251 660-E7
8400 SCTS 85251 661-A7
W MONTECITO AV
200 PHX 85013 658-F6
1700 PHX 85015 658-D6
2700 PHX 85017 658-A6
3300 PHX 85017 657-J6
3900 PHX 85019 657-H6
4800 PHX 85031 657-C6
7100 PHX 85033 656-F6
8300 PHX 85037 656-A6
10600 PHX 85037 655-H6
W MONTECITO CIR
11100 PHX 85037 655-H6
E MONTE CRISTO AV
- SCTS 85260 580-G3
100 PHX 85022 578-H2
1000 PHX 85022 579-A2
2600 PHX 85032 579-D2
4600 PHX 85032 580-A3
4800 PHX 85254 580-A3
W MONTE CRISTO AV
- GLEN 85382 576-J2
- GLEN 85382 577-A2
- SURP 85374 (574-E1 See Page 573)
- PHX 85023 578-C2
2900 PHX 85053 578-A2
3600 PHX 85053 577-H2
4300 PHX 85306 577-E2
5100 GLEN 85306 577-B2
W MONTE CRISTO CIR
2400 PHX 85023 578-C2
W MONTE CRISTO DR
- WICK 85390 290-E3
N MONTEGO CT
14600 PHX 85053 578-B4
W MONTEGO DR
15100 MarC 85375 534-H1
W MONTEGO LN
6300 GLEN 85306 577-B3
E MONTELEONE ST
- PinC 85242 905-C1
W MONTE LINDO
6900 GLEN 85310 497-A7
7300 GLEN 85310 496-J7
8100 MarC 85382 496-G7
8800 PEOR 85382 496-E7
E MONTELLO RD
8200 SCTS 85262 421-A6
E MONTEREY
- MESA 85212 784-E5
E MONTEREY AV
- MESA 85212 784-C5
6800 MESA 85208 783-G5
8200 MESA 85208 784-A5
W MONTEREY AV
400 MESA 85210 781-F4
2000 MESA 85202 781-A4
W MONTEREY CIR
2300 MESA 85202 781-B4
W MONTEREY CT
- GDYR 85338 (654-H7 See Page 653)
E MONTEREY DR
16800 FTNH 85268 623-D4
N MONTEREY DR
700 APJT 85220 745-D3
4800 PinC 85220 705-D6
9400 FTNH 85268 623-D5
S MONTEREY DR
1600 APJT 85220 785-D1
W MONTEREY PL
- CHAN 85224 821-A5
800 CHAN 85225 821-E5
6200 CHAN 85226 820-B4
E MONTEREY ST
300 CHAN 85225 821-G5
1000 GIL 85296 822-F5
1500 CHAN 85225 822-A5
N MONTEREY ST
600 GIL 85233 782-B3
S MONTEREY ST
- GIL 85233 782-B7
100 GIL 85233 822-B1
W MONTEREY ST
500 CHAN 85225 821-D5
1000 CHAN 85225 821-C5
3200 CHAN 85226 820-J5
4300 MarC 85339 817-F4
E MONTEREY WY
- PHX 85012 698-G1
- PHX 85013 698-G1
1800 PHX 85016 699-B2
3200 SCTS 85251 701-A2
6100 SCTS 85018 700-C2
6200 SCTS 85251 700-E2
W MONTEREY WY
- AVON 85340 695-C1
- GDYR 85338 (694-J1 See Page 653)
2500 PHX 85017 698-B1
3100 PHX 85033 696-F1
3100 PHX 85019 697-G1
4300 PHX 85031 697-G1
6100 PHX 85033 697-A1
8500 PHX 85037 696-D1
15400 GDYR 85338 (654-F7 See Page 653)
E MONTEROSA AV
6200 PHX 85251 660-D7
W MONTEROSA AV
6700 PHX 85033 657-A6
9900 PHX 85037 656-A6
N MONTEROSA CIR
4100 PHX 85033 656-J6
W MONTEROSA CIR
6900 PHX 85033 656-J6
E MONTEROSA DR
- MarC 85256 701-H1
W MONTEROSA DR
10300 MarC 85351 616-A1
E MONTEROSA LN
5500 PHX 85018 660-B7
E MONTEROSA ST
1300 PHX 85014 658-J7
1300 PHX 85014 659-A7
2200 PHX 85016 659-C7
3400 PHX 85018 659-F7
4100 SCTS 85251 701-A1
6400 SCTS 85251 660-D7
7800 SCTS 85251 700-H1
W MONTEROSA ST
- PHX 85013 658-E7
1600 PHX 85015 658-D7
2800 PHX 85017 658-A7
3300 PHX 85017 657-J7
3500 PHX 85019 657-J7
4100 PHX 85033 656-G7
4400 PHX 85031 657-C6
6300 PHX 85033 657-A7
8400 PHX 85037 656-A6
10400 PHX 85037 655-H6
E MONTERRA WY
- SCTS 85331 500-F4
7300 SCTS 85255 500-H4
W MONTEVERDE LN
16400 SURP 85374 534-D7
N MONTE VISTA
300 CHAN 85225 821-H6
W MONTE VISTA CIR
- GDYR 85338 695-B3
N MONTE VISTA CT
17800 MarC 85373 535-J7
N MONTE VISTA DR
5700 PVAL 85253 660-E4
W MONTE VISTA DR
12300 AVON 85323 695-D3
13100 GDYR 85338 695-C3
E MONTE VISTA RD
- PHX 85003 698-H3
- PHX 85004 698-H3
700 PHX 85006 698-H3
1400 PHX 85006 699-A3
2400 PHX 85008 699-D4
5100 PHX 85008 700-A4
6600 SCTS 85257 700-E4
8700 SCTS 85257 701-A4
W MONTE VISTA RD
- AVON 85323 696-A3
- GDYR 85338 (694-J2 See Page 653)
- GDYR 85338 695-B3
300 PHX 85003 698-F3
700 PHX 85007 698-E3
1900 PHX 85009 698-A3
2100 PHX 85009 696-H3
3200 PHX 85009 697-G3
4700 PHX 85035 697-A3
8300 PHX 85037 696-D3
12300 AVON 85323 695-C3
19100 MarC 85326 (693-E2 See Page 653)
E MONTE VISTA ST
- MarC 85249 901-H2
N MONTE VISTA ST
200 CHAN 85225 821-H4
S MONTE VISTA ST
- MarC 85249 901-H2
600 CHAN 85225 821-H7
600 CHAN 85225 861-H1
S MONTEZUMA CT
11800 PHX 85044 819-D1
N MONTEZUMA RD
8200 CARE 85377 421-A1
S MONTEZUMA ST
5200 PHX 85041 738-F7
6000 PHX 85041 778-F2
E MONTGOMERY CT
- MarC 85255 (462-G6 See Page 421)
W MONTGOMERY DR
2600 CHAN 85224 821-A2
E MONTGOMERY RD
4000 PHX 85331 459-J5
4500 PHX 85331 460-A5
5600 MarC 85331 460-C6
6900 SCTS 85331 460-E6
W MONTGOMERY RD
16300 MarC 85375 (454-D4 See Page 413)
21900 MarC 85361 (452-J4 See Page 411)
W MONTOYA DR
16100 SURP 85374 534-E6
E MONTOYA LN
- PHX 85024 538-J4
1600 PHX 85024 539-A4
W MONTOYA LN
- PHX 85024 538-J4
- PHX 85027 538-F4
E MONTREAL PL
2700 PHX 85032 579-D2
6300 PHX 85254 580-E3
E MONTROSE DR
16100 FTNH 85268 583-B5
N MONTROSE WY
5800 PHX 85253 620-C2
5800 PHX 85254 620-C2
E MONUMENT DR
9300 SCTS 85262 501-C1
10700 SCTS 85255 501-G2
W MOON DR
1400 PHX 85023 578-F5
N MOON RD
1400 PinC 85219 746-B1
S MOON RD
- PinC 85219 746-B7
W MOON BLOSSOM LN
- PHX 85310 497-G4
S MOONCREST DR
- MarC 85248 900-J4
N MOONLIGHT LN
7600 PVAL 85253 619-J7
E MOONLIGHT PASS
- SCTS 85262 (461-B3 See Page 421)
E MOONLIGHT WY
4600 MarC 85253 619-J7
4600 PVAL 85253 619-J7
4800 PVAL 85253 620-A7
N MOONLIGHT WY
7500 MarC 85253 619-J7
7500 PVAL 85253 619-J7
W MOONLIGHT WY
- SURP 85374 534-G4
E MOONLIGHT CANYON
- SCTS 85255 541-D4
MOONLIGHT MESA RD
- YavC - 250-A3
W MOON MOUNTAIN TR
- PHX 85023 578-F4
MOONSET CLOSE
10600 SCTS 85259 621-F1
S MOONSHADOW DR
26400 MarC 85248 901-D6
E MOONSHADOW WY
10100 PinC 85219 786-H5
E MOON VALLEY DR
100 PHX 85022 578-H4
N MOON VALLEY DR
- PHX 85022 578-H4
600 PHX 85023 578-F5
W MOON VALLEY DR
- PHX 85023 578-G4
- PHX 85022 578-G4
E MOON VISTA ST
100 PinC 85219 705-E7
W MOON VISTA ST
200 PinC 85220 705-B7
W MOORE AV
100 GIL 85233 782-B3
S MOOREA CT
900 GIL 85296 822-J3
N MOOREA DR
1200 GIL 85234 782-J4
S MOOREA DR
100 GIL 85296 822-J1
N MOQUI CT
17800 MarC 85373 536-C6
E MORELAND ST
100 PHX 85004 698-G5
700 PHX 85006 698-H5
1400 PHX 85006 699-A5
2400 PHX 85008 699-D5
5200 PHX 85008 700-A5
6600 SCTS 85257 700-E5
8500 SCTS 85257 701-A5
W MORELAND ST
- GDYR 85338 (694-C4 See Page 653)
700 PHX 85007 698-E5
1200 PHX 85009 697-H5
2900 PHX 85009 698-A5
6100 PHX 85043 697-B4
18300 GDYR 85326 (693-G3 See Page 653)
18300 MarC 85326 (693-G3 See Page 653)
22700 BUCK 85326 (692-G3 See Page 651)
E MORELOS CT
600 CHAN 85225 861-G1
W MORELOS CT
700 CHAN 85225 861-E1
E MORELOS ST
- CHAN 85225 861-F1
1700 CHAN 85225 862-A1
W MORELOS ST
100 CHAN 85225 861-D1
700 CHAN 85225 820-C7
1000 CHAN 85224 861-C1
S MORENA
- MESA 85212 784-D6
W MORENO BLVD
11700 ELMG 85335 575-F6
S MORENO CIR
300 LP 85340 655-A7
E MORENO CT
- GIL 85236 863-C4
S MORENO DR
1800 APJT 85220 785-D1
E MORGAN CT
- GIL 85236 823-A6
- GIL 85296 822-F6
E MORGAN DR
- GIL 85236 822-J6
- GIL 85236 823-A6
- MarC 85236 823-A6
1900 TEMP 85284 820-H1
13600 MarC 85296 822-D6
W MORGAN DR
4900 CHAN 85226 820-E6
W MORGAN PL
5200 CHAN 85226 820-D6
E MORGAN ST
- GIL 85296 822-F6
E MORGAN TR
8000 SCTS 85258 620-J3
N MORINO CT
2200 CHAN 85224 781-B6
N MORINO ST
3100 CHAN 85224 781-B6
E MORNING DR
- MarC 85236 903-C2
N MORNING BREEZE DR
- SCTS 85262 (381-F6 See Page 341)
N MORNING DOVE
- MESA 85207 703-J3
N MORNING DOVE CIR
- MESA 85207 703-J2
N MORNING DOVE DR
21400 MarC 85375 535-F2
W MORNING DOVE DR
5900 GLEN 85308 537-A2
12300 MarC 85375 535-E2
W MORNING GLORY CT
14900 SURP 85374 534-H7
N MORNING GLORY RD
6000 PVAL 85253 620-D4
W MORNING GLORY ST
- GDYR 85338 (694-D6 See Page 653)
N MORNING GLORY WY
- FTNH 85268 583-A6
S MORNING RIDGE DR
- GIL 85296 782-D7
E MORNINGSIDE DR
700 PHX 85022 538-J7

PHOENIX

INDEX

STREET Block City ZIP Pg-Grid

W NOCTURNE CT
11100 MarC 85351 575-H3
N NODAK
- PinC 85219 746-B3
N NODAK RD
2600 PinC 85219 746-B2
2600 APJT 85219 746-B2
E NOGALES RD
- SCTS 85258 660-G1
E NOLAN PL
- MarC 85249 901-H2
- MarC 85249 902-B2
W NOLAN WY
500 CHAN 85248 901-D2
S NOLINA DR
2400 CHAN 85248 861-C4
E NOLINA LN
- PinC 85219 786-E4
E NOLINA TR
9500 SCTS 85262 421-F2
S NOLINDA PL
2700 CHAN 85248 861-C5
E NO LUCK WY
9800 PinC 85219 786-H5
E NO MORE RD
8700 CARE 85377 421-B4
E NONCHALANT AV
7400 CARE 85377 420-H5
E NOPAL AV
- MESA 85212 784-D5
7200 MESA 85208 783-G5
8000 MESA 85208 784-A5
W NOPAL AV
400 MESA 85210 781-E5
1300 MESA 85202 781-A5
E NOPAL CIR
- MESA 85208 784-B5
W NOPAL CIR
1900 MESA 85202 781-A5
2700 MESA 85202 780-J5
W NOPAL CT
2400 CHAN 85224 821-C1
W NOPAL DR
1600 CHAN 85224 821-C1
W NOPAL PL
- CHAN 85225 821-E1
1000 CHAN 85224 821-D1
E NORA CIR
- MarC 85207 704-C6
- MESA 85215 702-J5
3100 MESA 85213 702-J5
6500 MESA 85215 703-F5
E NORA ST
- MarC 85207 704-C6
- MESA 85207 703-H5
- MESA 85207 704-E6
2200 MESA 85213 702-E5
5600 MESA 85215 703-E5
E NORCROFT CIR
- MarC 85207 704-C6
- MESA 85213 702-H5
- MESA 85215 702-J6
E NORCROFT ST
2000 MESA 85203 702-D5
2000 MESA 85213 702-D5
S NORELLA CIR
2500 MESA 85210 781-D4
N NORFOLK
400 MESA 85205 742-J3
3000 MESA 85215 702-J4
S NORFOLK
- MESA 85206 742-J5
S NORFOLK AV
1200 MESA 85206 782-J2
N NORFOLK CIR
600 MESA 85205 742-J2
S NORFOLK CIR
100 MESA 85206 742-J6
N NORFOLK WY
1000 GIL 85234 782-H4
E NORLAND ST
5900 MESA 85215 703-E5
W NORMA ST
400 GBND 85337 (1090-A3 See Page 1049)
N NORMAL AV
2000 TEMP 85281 700-E6
S NORMAL AV
1300 TEMP 85281 740-E5
N NORTERRA PKWY
- PHX 85027 498-C4
2300 PHX 85085 498-D2
N NORTE VISTA
15600 FTNH 85268 582-H3
W NORTH DR
- WICK 85390 290-A3
E NORTH LN
- GLEN 85302 617-D2
700 PHX 85020 618-J2
2200 PHX 85028 619-C2
5900 PHX 85253 620-C3
6600 SCTS 85253 620-E3
7400 SCTS 85258 620-G3
11100 SCTS 85258 621-G3
11200 SCTS 85259 621-H3
W NORTH LN
- PHX 85020 618-H2
900 PHX 85021 618-D2
2700 PHX 85051 618-B2
2700 PHX 85051 617-H2
4500 GLEN 85302 617-B2
6900 PEOR 85345 617-A2
7100 PEOR 85345 616-C2
W NORTHAMPTON RD
- SURP 85374 534-D5
E NORTHERN AV
- PHX 85020 618-H6
1200 PHX 85020 619-A6
2900 PHX 85028 619-D4
6200 PVAL 85253 620-D7
7400 SCTS 85258 620-G7
W NORTHERN AV
- PHX 85021 618-D6
2500 PHX 85051 618-D6
3400 PHX 85051 617-F6
4300 GLEN 85302 617-D6
4300 GLEN 85301 617-D6
6700 GLEN 85303 617-D6
7000 GLEN 85301 616-E6
7000 GLEN 85303 616-E6
7100 GLEN 85303 616-E6
7500 MarC 85345 616-E6
7500 MarC 85305 616-E6
8300 MarC 85305 616-A6
9300 PEOR 85305 616-A6
9900 GLEN 85307 616-A6
10000 PEOR 85307 616-A6
10600 PEOR 85345 615-G6
10600 GLEN 85307 615-G6
10700 MarC 85307 615-B5

W NORTHERN AV
11200 PEOR 85307 615-G6
11600 MarC 85345 615-G6
11700 ELMG 85335 615-B5
11700 MarC 85335 615-B5
13900 MarC 85355 615-B5
13900 GLEN 85309 615-B5
13900 GLEN 85335 615-B5
13900 GLEN 85355 615-B5
14100 MarC 85309 (614-E5 See Page 573)
14100 MarC 85355 (614-E5 See Page 573)
14100 GLEN 85309 (614-E5 See Page 573)
15500 MarC 85340 (614-E5 See Page 573)
17900 MarC 85355 (613-G5 See Page 573)
18700 MarC 85373 (613-G5 See Page 573)
E NORTHGATE PKWY
18400 MarC 85212 823-F2
E NORTHLAND DR
7300 SCTS 85251 660-G6
8500 SCTS 85251 661-A6
NORTH MOUNTAIN REC AREA LP
600 PHX 85020 618-H2
NORTH MOUNTAIN REC AREA ACCESS
- PHX 85020 618-H2
- PHX 85022 578-H7
W NORTH PARK RD
- PEOR 85342 (375-J4 See Page 335)
E NORTH RANCH GATE RD
10300 SCTS 85255 501-F6
E NORTHRIDGE CIR
- MESA 85207 703-H6
- MESA 85207 704-E6
- MESA 85213 702-H5
2600 MESA 85213 702-F5
E NORTHRIDGE ST
- MarC 85207 704-E6
- MESA 85207 703-H6
- MESA 85207 704-E6
1900 MESA 85203 702-D6
2200 MESA 85213 702-F5
2600 MESA 85215 703-F6
N NORTHRIDGE ST
2500 MESA 85203 702-D6
N NORTH RIM DR
18600 SURP 85374 534-F4
E NORTHSHORE DR
1000 GIL 85234 782-F6
1200 TEMP 85283 780-G3
W NORTHSHORE DR
- WICK 85390 289-H3
N NORTHSIGHT BLVD
14400 SCTS 85260 581-A3
N NORTHSTAR CIR
- SCTS 85262 (461-A3 See Page 421)
NORTH VALLEY PKWY
- PHX 85085 (418-B7 See Page 417)
- PHX 85085 (458-B1 See Page 417)
- PHX 85085 498-E1
- PHX 85086 (418-B7 See Page 417)
E NORTHVIEW AV
- PHX 85020 618-G7
- PHX 85021 618-G7
600 PHX 85020 658-H1
1800 PHX 85020 659-B1
1800 PHX 85020 619-B7
W NORTHVIEW AV
- PHX 85021 618-D7
- PHX 85021 658-G1
2500 PHX 85051 618-A7
3300 PHX 85051 617-G7
4300 GLEN 85301 617-A7
7000 GLEN 85303 616-F7
7000 GLEN 85303 617-A7
10800 GLEN 85307 615-J7
E NORTHVIEW LN
8900 CARE 85262 421-C5
W NORTHWEST RANCH PKWY
- SURP 85374 (574-D1 See Page 573)
W NORTHWOOD DR
5500 PHX 85310 497-E5
S NORTON DR
9100 BUCK 85326 (772-B3 See Page 731)
9100 MarC 85326 (772-B4 See Page 731)
W NORTON ST
- AVON 85323 735-A1
- GDYR 85323 735-A1
N NORWALK
400 MESA 85205 742-J2
2800 MESA 85215 702-J5
S NORWALK
100 MESA 85206 742-J7
N NORWALK CIR
600 MESA 85205 742-J3
S NORWALK CIR
100 MESA 85206 742-J6
1400 MESA 85206 782-J2
W NORWICH DR
17600 SURP 85387 494-B5
19100 MarC 85387 493-G5
E NORWOOD CIR
- MarC 85207 704-C6
- MESA 85213 702-H6
6400 MESA 85215 703-F6
E NORWOOD ST
- MarC 85207 704-C6
- MESA 85207 703-H6
1000 MESA 85203 702-A5
2000 MESA 85213 702-E5
5800 MESA 85215 703-E6
S NOTTINGHAM CT
26600 MarC 85248 901-E6
S NOTTINGHAM DR
25400 MarC 85248 901-E5
W NOTTINGHAM WY
- SURP 85374 534-D6
E NOWATA DR
3700 PHX 85044 819-F1
W NUGGET CT
12400 MarC 85375 535-F3
E NUGGET DR
10900 SCTS 85262 (381-H7 See Page 341)

W NUNNELEY AV
- GIL 85296 822-D3
E NUNNELEY CT
2000 GIL 85296 822-H3
E NUNNELEY RD
200 GIL 85296 822-D3
E NUNNELLEY RD
13000 MarC 85233 822-B3
18000 MarC 85236 823-E3
E NUNNELY DR
- GIL 85236 823-A3
E NUTTAL DR
800 AVON 85323 695-C5
E NU VISTA LN
- TEMP 85282 740-D7
N NYACK DR
15800 FTNH 85268 582-J3

O

N OACHS DR
- SURP 85374 575-B1
N OAK CIR
1100 GIL 85233 782-C4
S OAK CIR
600 CHAN 85226 820-D7
N OAK CT
800 CHAN 85226 820-D4
W OAK CT
- GIL 85233 822-B3
E OAK RD
1200 TEMP 85284 820-F2
S OAK RD
8800 TEMP 85284 820-F2
E OAK ST
300 PHX 85004 698-J3
700 PHX 85006 698-J3
1400 PHX 85006 699-A3
2200 SCTS 85257 700-D4
2300 PHX 85008 699-C3
4800 PHX 85008 700-D4
5600 SCTS 85008 700-D4
8600 SCTS 85257 701-A4
8700 MarC 85257 701-A4
8800 MarC 85256 701-D4
8900 MarC 85207 704-C5
12100 MarC 85203 701-D4
12100 MarC 85203 702-B4
13200 MESA 85203 702-B4
N OAK ST
- GIL 85233 782-C4
1400 TEMP 85281 740-G1
1400 TEMP 85281 700-G7
32700 MarC 85361 (453-A1 See Page 413)
S OAK ST
- CHAN 85226 820-C6
400 GIL 85233 822-C1
1300 TEMP 85281 740-G5
2300 TEMP 85281 740-G6
3300 TEMP 85282 780-G1
5900 TEMP 85283 780-G4
7600 TEMP 85283 780-F7
8600 TEMP 85284 820-F2
12500 MarC 85233 822-C2
32300 MarC 85361 (452-J1 See Page 411)
32400 MarC 85361 (453-A1 See Page 413)
W OAK GLEN DR
13700 MarC 85375 535-B3
W OAK GROVE LN
2600 CHAN 85224 821-A3
E OAK HARBOR DR
1700 GIL 85234 782-G5
N OAK HARBOR DR
900 GIL 85234 782-H5
N OAKHURST CT
- MarC 85086 (378-B7 See Page 337)
E OAKHURST WY
5000 PHX 85254 620-A1
N OAKHURST WY
11600 PHX 85254 620-C1
N OAKLAND
500 MESA 85205 743-A2
2900 MESA 85215 703-A5
S OAKLAND
100 MESA 85206 743-A6
600 MESA 85206 742-J7
N OAKLAND CIR
1400 MESA 85205 743-A2
E OAKLAND CT
- GIL 85236 823-A6
- GIL 85296 822-F5
N OAKLAND CT
- MarC 85086 (378-B5 See Page 337)
W OAKLAND CT
1700 CHAN 85224 821-C5
E OAKLAND ST
- GIL 85236 822-J5
- GIL 85236 823-A6
- GIL 85296 822-E5
- CHAN 85225 821-F5
1500 CHAN 85225 822-A5
W OAKLAND ST
- CHAN 85225 822-C5
- CHAN 85225 821-D5
1000 CHAN 85224 821-A5
3400 CHAN 85226 820-A5
E OAKLEAF DR
1100 PHX 85008 699-E5
S OAKLEY PL
1400 TEMP 85281 740-E5
N OAKMONT CT
17600 SURP 85374 534-G6
E OAKMONT DR
7100 PVAL 85253 620-F6
N OAKMONT DR
12200 MarC 85351 576-B6
S OAKMONT DR
6000 CHAN 85249 902-A5
W OAKMONT DR
10000 MarC 85351 576-A6
10700 MarC 85351 575-J6
W OAKRIDGE CT
15500 SURP 85374 534-G7
W OAK RIDGE DR
9500 MarC 85351 576-B2
11000 MarC 85351 575-H2
W OAK RIDGE RD
- SURP 85374 575-B2
E OAK SHORE DR
7700 SCTS 85258 620-H7
E OAK SPRING RD
- MarC 85263 (504-A3 See Page 503)
W OAKSTONE DR
9500 MarC 85351 576-C4

S OAKWOOD DR
10900 GDYR 85338 (774-A5 See Page 733)
E OAKWOOD LN
14200 FTNH 85268 583-D6
N OAKWOOD LN
14200 FTNH 85268 583-D6
E OAKWOOD HILLS DR
- CHAN 85248 901-D3
- MarC 85248 901-D3
W OAKWOOD LAKES BLVD
10400 CHAN 85248 901-D2
E OAKWOOD LAKES DR
- MarC 85248 901-D2
E OASIS CIR
- MESA 85207 703-J5
3600 MESA 85215 702-H5
E OASIS DR
1800 TEMP 85283 780-G6
10600 MarC 85220 744-G7
10700 MESA 85220 744-G7
N OASIS DR
11800 FTNH 85268 623-D2
S OASIS DR
7300 TEMP 85283 780-H6
W OASIS DR
800 WICK 85390 290-D3
E OASIS ST
- MESA 85207 703-H5
2000 MarC 85203 702-D5
2000 MarC 85213 702-D5
2000 MESA 85213 702-D5
6200 MESA 85215 703-F5
N OASIS VERDE WY
20700 SURP 85374 534-E2
E OATMAN DR
10800 SCTS 85262 (381-H6 See Page 341)
E OBERLIN DR
- SCTS 85331 500-F2
E OBERLIN WY
- PHX 85331 500-A2
- SCTS 85331 500-D2
7200 SCTS 85255 500-H2
9600 SCTS 85255 501-D2
12800 SCTS 85255 502-C3
W OBERLIN WY
- PHX 85085 497-D1
2800 PHX 85085 498-A2
23400 MarC 85361 (452-D7 See Page 411)
E OBISPO AV
7800 MESA 85212 783-H6
8000 MESA 85212 784-A6
S OBISPO AV
- MESA 85212 784-B6
W OBISPO AV
800 MESA 85210 781-D5
1300 MESA 85202 781-A5
2000 GIL 85233 781-G5
W OBISPO CIR
2400 MESA 85202 781-A5
2700 MESA 85202 780-J5
S OBISPO DR
10900 GDYR 85338 (773-J5 See Page 733)
10900 GDYR 85338 (774-A6 See Page 733)
E OCASO AV
- MESA 85212 784-A6
W OCASO CIR
2600 MESA 85202 781-A5
2700 MESA 85202 780-J5
E OCATILLA RD
9000 MESA 85207 744-C3
N OCEAN CIR
300 GIL 85233 781-J6
N OCEAN DR
- GIL 85233 781-J6
S OCEAN DR
- GIL 85233 781-J7
100 GIL 85233 821-J2
W OCOTILLA DR
- MarC 85390 290-B2
E OCOTILLA LN
3000 PHX 85028 619-G3
S OCOTILLO
1300 BUCK 85326 (692-C7 See Page 651)
E OCOTILLO AV
7800 MESA 85208 743-J7
7800 MESA 85208 744-A7
W OCOTILLO AV
- GDYR 85326 (774-A7 See Page 733)
- GDYR 85326 (814-A1 See Page 813)
E OCOTILLO CIR
1100 CARE 85377 420-H6
S OCOTILLO CIR
26000 MarC 85248 901-A5
E OCOTILLO DR
15600 FTNH 85268 623-A2
N OCOTILLO DR
- APJT 85220 745-B5
17300 MarC 85373 536-A7
51400 MarC 85390 290-C4
51400 WICK 85390 290-C4
S OCOTILLO DR
- WICK 85390 290-C3
100 APJT 85220 745-B6
1300 APJT 85220 785-B1
N OCOTILLO LN
400 GIL 85233 782-A5
S OCOTILLO LN
12200 MarC 85296 822-F2
W OCOTILLO LN
- SURP 85374 575-B2
E OCOTILLO RD
- SCTS 85268 622-G1
- PHX 85012 658-G2
- PinC 85242 905-D1
600 CHAN 85249 861-H7
600 MarC 85249 861-H7
700 PHX 85014 658-J2
1200 PHX 85014 659-A2
1600 PHX 85016 659-B2
4600 PVAL 85253 659-J2
5500 CVCK 85331 420-D2
6600 PVAL 85253 660-E2
7800 SCTS 85250 660-H2
12000 MarC 85249 862-B7
13400 SCTS 85259 582-D7
13500 SCTS 85259 622-G1
16000 MarC 85236 862-G7
16000 MarC 85236 863-A7
18400 QC 85236 863-H7
19200 QC 85236 863-H7
19400 QC 85242 864-A7

E OCOTILLO RD
20300 QC 85242 904-D1
22400 MarC 85242 904-F1
W OCOTILLO RD
- MarC 85248 861-E7
- MarC 85326 (852-E4 See Page 811)
- MarC 85337 (852-E4 See Page 811)
- CHAN 85248 861-B7
- PHX 85013 658-F2
1100 PinC 85242 904-J1
1100 PinC 85242 905-A1
1500 PHX 85015 658-D1
2500 PHX 85017 658-A1
3300 PHX 85017 657-H1
3500 PHX 85019 657-H1
4300 GLEN 85301 657-D1
6700 GLEN 85303 657-A1
6700 GLEN 85305 656-H1
6900 GLEN 85303 656-G1
11500 MarC 85326 (854-H5 See Page 813)
13100 MarC 85307 655-H1
14900 GDYR 85326 (854-C5 See Page 813)
15400 MarC 85309 (654-E1 See Page 653)
15400 MarC 85340 (654-E1 See Page 653)
17400 GDYR 85326 (853-C5 See Page 813)
17500 MarC 85355 (613-J7 See Page 573)
17500 MarC 85355 (614-A7 See Page 573)
18600 MarC 85326 (853-C5 See Page 813)
W OCOTILLO ST
- SURP 85374 (574-D2 See Page 573)
12400 SURP 85374 575-E2
E OCOTILLO HERMOSA CIR
6700 PHX 85016 659-B2
N OCOTILLO HERMOSO DR
6700 PHX 85016 659-B2
N OCOTILLO RIDGE DR
- CARE 85377 420-J2
E OCUPADO DR
4800 PHX 85331 460-A3
4800 MarC 85331 460-A3
W OCUPADO DR
22000 MarC 85361 (452-H1 See Page 411)
E ODESSA CIR
- MESA 85207 703-J5
E ODESSA ST
- MESA 85207 703-H5
6600 MESA 85215 703-F5
OESTE LN
100 LP 85340 655-A7
N OGDEN
500 MESA 85205 742-J1
1600 MESA 85205 743-A1
S OGDEN
500 MESA 85206 742-J7
N OGDEN CIR
700 MESA 85205 742-J3
S OGDEN CIR
100 MESA 85206 742-J6
S OGLESBY RD Rt#-85
- BUCK 85326 (771-F1 See Page 731)
2800 MarC 85326 731-F5
4300 BUCK 85326 731-F5
8300 MarC 85326 (771-F1 See Page 731)
9400 MarC 85322 (771-F1 See Page 731)
12600 MarC 85326 811-F1
12600 MarC 85337 811-E5
W OHIO
9600 PEOR 85345 616-C1
9600 PEOR 85351 616-C1
E OHIO AV
8800 MarC 85248 900-J4
9000 MarC 85248 901-A4
S OHIO AV
25400 MarC 85248 900-J4
W OHIO AV
11100 YNTN 85335 615-H1
W OHIO ST
2100 APJT 85220 745-A5
OKLAHOMA
- PinC 85219 786-D7
S OKLAHOMA AV
25400 MarC 85248 900-J4
E OLD ADOBE LN
3600 PVAL 85253 659-F4
S OLD AJO RD
56200 MarC 85337 (1090-A5 See Page 1049)
57100 MarC 85337 (1089-J6 See Page 1049)
S OLD BASELINE RD
- AVON 85323 775-E2
- AVON 85353 775-E2
- MarC 85353 775-E2
W OLD BASELINE RD
13100 AVON 85323 775-C2
13100 AVON 85338 775-C2
13100 MarC 85338 775-C2
N OLD COLONY
1600 MESA 85201 741-F1
1700 MESA 85201 701-F7
E OLD FIELD RD
- SCTS 85262 (461-A4 See Page 421)
N OLD GILBERT RD
- MESA 85203 702-D6
- MESA 85213 702-D6
OLD HIGHWAY 80
27300 MarC 85322 (771-B4 See Page 731)
27300 MarC 85322 102-B3
N OLD LAKE PLEASANT RD
21000 PEOR 85382 536-A2
N OLD LAKE PLEASANT ACCESS RD
- PEOR 85342 (376-B7 See Page 335)
37900 PEOR 85342 (416-B2 See Page 415)
N OLD MINE RD
22100 MarC 85375 535-B1
42000 MarC 85331 (382-A5 See Page 341)

N OLD MINE RD
42000 MarC 85331 (381-J5 See Page 341)
E OLD NEW RIVER RD
2500 MarC 85086 419-E5
2700 CVCK 85086 419-E5
2700 CVCK 85331 419-E5
W OLD PAINT
17200 SURP 85374 534-B6
E OLD PAINT TR
6200 CARE 85377 420-E7
6200 CARE 85377 460-F1
7600 SCTS 85262 420-J7
7700 SCTS 85262 460-J1
W OLD PAINT TR
- PHX 85086 (418-D7 See Page 417)
E OLD SOUTHERN AV
700 PHX 85040 738-H7
700 PHX 85040 778-H1
3000 PHX 85040 739-D7
N OLD STAGE RD
39100 CVCK 85331 420-C2
41100 CVCK 85331 (380-C6 See Page 339)
47800 MarC 85087 (338-B2 See Page 337)
E OLD TOWER RD
2400 PHX 85034 739-C2
S OLD TOWER RD
2100 PHX 85034 739-C3
N OLD TRAIL CT
11600 FTNH 85268 623-B2
E OLD TRAIL RD
9500 SCTS 85262 421-F2
E OLD TRAILS RD
10900 SCTS 85262 (381-H7 See Page 341)
OLD WEST HWY
- APJT 85219 745-E7
- APJT 85220 745-E7
1000 APJT 85219 785-G1
E OLD WEST HWY
1700 APJT 85219 785-G1
W OLD WEST TR
- MarC 85087 (377-J3 See Page 337)
- PHX 85087 (377-J3 See Page 337)
E OLD WEST WY
5800 SCTS 85331 460-D3
S OLEANDER DR
1600 CHAN 85248 861-C5
4500 CHAN 85248 901-C1
N OLEANDER ST
- WICK 85390 290-D1
1100 TEMP 85281 740-G1
1500 TEMP 85281 700-G7
E OLESEN RD
5100 MarC 85331 460-B1
5200 CVCK 85331 460-B1
5600 SCTS 85331 460-C1
W OLIA WY
15500 SURP 85375 (454-B7 See Page 413)
N OLIVE
400 MESA 85203 741-J3
2000 MESA 85203 701-J7
S OLIVE
- MESA 85204 741-J5
900 MESA 85204 781-J1
E OLIVE AV
- MarC 85236 783-D6
- GIL 85233 782-D6
- GIL 85234 782-D6
3700 GIL 85236 783-D6
8700 MarC 85251 701-A1
8700 MarC 85256 701-A1
8700 SCTS 85251 701-A1
W OLIVE AV
- GIL 85233 782-B5
4300 GLEN 85302 617-B4
6700 PEOR 85345 617-B4
6700 GLEN 85345 617-B4
6900 PEOR 85345 616-F4
6900 GLEN 85345 616-F4
9500 MarC 85345 616-C4
9800 MarC 85351 616-C4
10600 MarC 85351 615-H4
10600 MarC 85345 615-H4
10900 PEOR 85345 615-H4
11100 YNTN 85351 615-H4
11100 PEOR 85351 615-H4
11700 MarC 85335 615-C3
12000 ELMG 85335 615-C3
13500 MarC 85355 615-C3
13900 MarC 85355 (614-F3 See Page 573)
17900 MarC 85355 (613-J3 See Page 573)
S OLIVE CIR
1200 MESA 85204 781-J1
E OLIVE CT
- GIL 85236 783-F6
- MarC 85236 783-F6
1900 GIL 85234 782-H6
W OLIVE DR
11100 AVON 85323 695-G1
E OLIVE LN
8900 MarC 85248 900-J5
9000 MarC 85248 901-A5
N OLIVE ST
13500 ELMG 85335 575-G5
W OLIVE WY
2100 CHAN 85248 861-A7
S OLIVEWOOD
- MESA 85212 784-G4
N OLIVIDAD WY
18200 SURP 85374 534-D5
E OLIVINE AV
- CVCK 85331 419-F4
E OLIVOS AV
2800 PHX 85016 659-D7
E OLLA AV
8000 MESA 85212 783-H5
8000 MESA 85212 784-A6
W OLLA AV
900 MESA 85210 781-E5
2100 MESA 85202 781-A5
E OLLA CIR
- MESA 85212 784-D6
W OLLA CIR
2200 MESA 85202 781-A5
S OLMO CIR
400 APJT 85220 745-D6
E OLNEY AV
4200 MESA 85236 783-E6
4200 GIL 85236 783-E6
16400 MarC 85234 783-B6
18400 MESA 85212 783-F6

W OLNEY AV
600 PHX 85041 778-C5
2500 PHX 85339 778-C5
3900 MarC 85339 777-E5
3900 PHX 85339 777-E5
E OLNEY CT
- MarC 85236 783-D6
E OLNEY DR
4300 PHX 85044 779-G6
N OLYMPIC
900 MESA 85205 743-E1
3000 MESA 85215 703-E4
N OLYMPIC CIR
1300 MESA 85205 743-E2
2600 MESA 85215 703-E2
E OLYMPIC DR
- PHX 85040 778-G3
N OLYMPIC DR
800 GIL 85236 783-D5
N OLYMPIC WY
14600 FTNH 85268 583-D5
S OLYNPIC DR
- MarC 85236 823-D5
N OMAHA
500 MESA 85205 742-J3
2900 MESA 85215 703-A5
S OMAHA
- MESA 85206 742-J5
E OMAHA CIR
- MESA 85205 742-J2
N OMAHA CIR
1400 MESA 85205 743-A2
S OMAHA ST
400 MESA 85206 742-J6
E OMEGA CIR
2500 MESA 85213 702-E5
3600 MESA 85215 702-H5
W OMEGA DR
12700 MarC 85375 535-E5
E OMEGA ST
4200 MESA 85215 703-A5
S ONEIDA CT
12400 PHX 85044 819-G2
E ONEIDA ST
5000 PHX 85044 819-J2
S ONEIDA ST
11400 PHX 85044 779-F7
11400 PHX 85044 819-F1
W O NEIL DR
11000 MarC 85351 575-J6
E ONTARIO DR
9400 MarC 85248 901-B3
S ONTARIO DR
9500 MarC 85248 901-B3
E ONYX AV
3000 PHX 85028 619-E3
4800 PVAL 85028 619-J3
4800 PVAL 85253 619-J3
4800 PVAL 85253 620-A3
5300 PHX 85253 620-B3
6600 SCTS 85253 620-E3
8600 SCTS 85258 621-A4
11600 SCTS 85259 621-J3
N ONYX AV
9800 PHX 85028 619-J3
W ONYX AV
4300 GLEN 85302 617-B2
E ONYX CT
7300 SCTS 85258 620-G3
13500 SCTS 85259 622-D3
S ONYX DR
- MarC 85249 902-E5
E ONZA AV
7800 MESA 85212 783-H6
8100 MESA 85212 784-A6
W ONZA AV
1800 MESA 85202 781-A5
2600 MESA 85202 780-J5
E ONZA CIR
- MESA 85212 784-B6
W ONZA CIR
2200 MESA 85202 781-B5
N OOTAM RD
37400 CVCK 85331 420-D4
N OPAL
11200 MESA 85220 744-J4
S OPAL
- MarC 85212 824-H1
- MESA 85212 784-H7
- MESA 85212 824-H1
S OPAL CIR
- MESA 85212 784-H7
S OPAL CT
- MarC 85249 902-F4
S OPAL DR
- MarC 85249 902-E5
W OPAL DR
13200 MarC 86376 536-C6
N OPAL ST
- MESA 85220 784-J1
E OPEN SKY DR
10100 PinC 85219 786-H2
OPERATIONS DR
700 TEMP 85281 740-D1
OPPORTUNITY WY
- PHX 85086 (377-H5 See Page 337)
N OPPORTUNITY WY
- MarC 85086 (378-B7 See Page 337)
S OPUNTIA PTH
- PinC 85219 786-E5
E ORACLE
1800 MESA 85203 702-C7
N ORACLE
500 MESA 85203 742-C3
S ORACLE
600 MESA 85204 742-C7
1100 MESA 85204 782-C1
S ORACLE CIR
1000 MESA 85204 782-C1
E ORAIBI DR
300 PHX 85024 538-H5
900 PHX 85024 539-D5
2500 PHX 85050 539-D5
W ORAIBI DR
- PEOR 85308 536-G4
- PEOR 85373 536-J4
- PEOR 85373 536-C4
- PHX 85027 538-A5
1900 PEOR 85382 536-C4
3600 PHX 85308 537-F4
5100 GLEN 85308 537-C4
7200 GLEN 85308 536-H5
W ORAIBI RD
9100 PEOR 85382 536-D5
E ORANGE
1500 BUCK 85326 (772-C1 See Page 731)

PHOENIX
INDEX

PHOENIX
INDEX

STREET
Block City ZIP Pg-Grid

STREET Block City ZIP Pg-Grid

W ROANOKE AV
13800 GDYR 85338 695-A2
N ROANOKE CIR
- MESA 85205 743-B4
N ROANOKE ST
- GIL 85234 783-A4
S ROANOKE ST
400 GIL 85236 823-A2
S ROBBINS RD
- MarC 85337 811-C4
W ROBBINS BUTTE GAME RD
- MarC 85326 811-C2
E ROBERTA DR
- PHX 85331 500-B1
W ROBERTA DR
- PHX 85085 498-B1
W ROBERT E LEE LN
300 GBND 85337 (1089-J3 See Page 1049)
E ROBERT E LEE ST
2400 PHX 85032 539-D7
4600 PHX 85032 540-A7
4800 PHX 85254 540-A7
W ROBERT E LEE ST
6500 GLEN 85308 537-A6
E ROBERT HUNTER DR
8800 SCTS 85262 421-C3
S ROBERTS
5600 TEMP 85283 780-B3
E ROBERTS RD
700 PHX 85022 578-J5
1100 PHX 85022 579-A5
S ROBERTS RD
300 TEMP 85281 740-B3
3300 TEMP 85282 780-B1
7200 TEMP 85283 780-B2
W ROBERTSON CT
15200 MarC 85375 534-H1
N ROBERTSON DR
22400 MarC 85375 494-J7
22400 MarC 85375 495-B7
W ROBERTSON DR
13600 MarC 85375 495-A7
14400 MarC 85375 494-G7
15300 MarC 85375 534-G1
N ROBIN CIR
2600 MESA 85213 702-F6
S ROBIN CIR
1800 MESA 85204 782-F3
E ROBIN CT
- GIL 85236 823-A1
1700 GIL 85296 822-H1
E ROBIN DR
- FTNH 85268 582-J4
- FTNH 85268 583-A5
E ROBIN LN
- GIL 85236 823-B1
1600 GIL 85296 822-G1
2000 PHX 85024 539-C1
4100 PHX 85050 539-J1
4100 PHX 85050 540-A2
4800 PHX 85054 540-B2
N ROBIN LN
1000 MESA 85213 742-F1
2300 MESA 85213 702-F5
6000 GLEN 85310 537-C1
S ROBIN LN
500 MESA 85204 742-F7
800 MESA 85204 782-F1
W ROBIN LN
- PEOR 85373 536-A1
2700 PHX 85027 538-B1
5900 GLEN 85310 537-A1
7300 GLEN 85310 536-J1
10500 PEOR 85382 536-A1
13500 MarC 85375 495-C7
S ROBINS CT
100 CHAN 85225 821-H7
N ROBINS WY
1000 CHAN 85225 821-H4
S ROBINS WY
- CHAN 85249 901-G4
- MarC 85249 901-G2
300 CHAN 85225 821-H7
W ROBINSON DR
- MarC 85086 (378-B6 See Page 337)
E ROBINSON WY
1400 CHAN 85225 821-J5
1600 CHAN 85225 822-A5
W ROBINSON WY
5700 CHAN 85226 820-C4
ROBLES DR
700 LP 85340 655-B5
N ROBLES DR
- MarC 85340 655-B2
N ROBSON
- MESA 85201 741-G3
- MESA 85210 741-G4
1800 MESA 85201 701-G7
S ROBSON
- MESA 85210 741-G5
1000 MESA 85210 781-G1
N ROBSON CIR
3100 GDYR 85338 (694-G1 See Page 653)
3200 GDYR 85338 (654-F7 See Page 653)
W ROBSON CIR
- GDYR 85338 (654-G7 See Page 653)
W ROBSON CIR N
14600 GDYR 85338 (654-G7 See Page 653)
14600 GDYR 85338 (694-H1 See Page 653)
W ROBSON CIR S
6100 GDYR 85338 (694-G1 See Page 653)
N ROCA
1300 MESA 85213 742-F2
2200 MESA 85213 702-F5
S ROCA
700 MESA 85204 742-F7
1600 MESA 85204 782-F2
N ROCA CIR
400 MESA 85213 742-F1
S ROCA CT
- GIL 85296 822-F2
N ROCA ST
600 MESA 85213 742-F3
S ROCA ST
1200 GIL 85296 822-F2
E ROCHELLE CIR
- MESA 85207 703-H3
6500 MESA 85215 703-F3
E ROCHELLE ST
6000 MESA 85215 703-F3

N ROCHESTER
400 MESA 85205 743-B1
1800 MESA 85205 703-B7
S ROCHESTER
400 MESA 85206 743-B7
800 MESA 85206 783-B1
N ROCHESTER CIR
1500 MESA 85205 743-B1
N ROCHESTER CT
1200 GIL 85234 783-A4
S ROCHESTER CT
- GIL 85236 823-B1
N ROCHESTER DR
- GIL 85234 783-A4
S ROCHESTER ST
- GIL 85236 823-A6
- MarC 85236 823-A6
S ROCK CT
- GIL 85296 822-G5
N ROCK ST
- GIL 85234 782-G7
E ROCKAWAY HILLS DR
5100 CVCK 85331 (380-F7 See Page 339)
N ROCKAWAY HILLS DR
- SCTS 85262 (381-F7 See Page 341)
W ROCKAWAY HILLS DR
23400 MarC 85342 (372-B5 See Page 331)
25700 MarC 85342 (371-H4 See Page 331)
E ROCKAWAY HILLS RD
6400 CVCK 85331 (380-F7 See Page 339)
W ROCKAWAY HILLS RD
- MarC 85086 (378-H6 See Page 337)
4100 MarC 85086 (377-G6 See Page 337)
4100 PHX 85086 (377-G6 See Page 337)
E ROCK CREEK CIR
- CHAN 85225 822-A6
S ROCKFORD DR
100 TEMP 85281 740-J4
4700 TEMP 85282 780-J2
6300 TEMP 85283 780-J5
S ROCK HARBOR DR
300 GIL 85233 821-J1
S ROCKHILL RD
2700 PHX 85048 819-C4
S ROCK HOUND DR
- APJT 85219 785-H4
N ROCKING RD
6700 SCTS 85250 660-G2
E ROCKING CHAIR RD
7600 CARE 85377 420-J4
S ROCKING R RD
- PinC 85219 746-C6
5500 APJT 85219 786-C6
E ROCKLEDGE RD
1300 PHX 85048 818-H4
2300 PHX 85048 819-B4
3400 PHX 85044 819-E5
S ROCKLEDGE RD
14400 PHX 85048 819-B4
W ROCK LEDGE RD
- GDYR 85338 (774-B6 See Page 733)
N ROCKNE RD
9100 SCTS 85258 621-E5
E ROCKRIDGE RD
4500 PHX 85018 659-J5
4800 PHX 85018 660-A5
N ROCK RIDGE TR
- FTNH 85268 623-A4
E ROCKROSE DR
- CVCK 85331 420-A7
N ROCKROSE DR
- CVCK 85331 420-A7
W ROCKROSE PL
2200 CHAN 85248 861-B6
W ROCKROSE WY
900 CHAN 85248 861-A6
14900 SURP 85374 534-H7
W ROCK SPRING DR
12300 MarC 85375 535-E3
W ROCK SPRINGS LN
- SURP 85374 534-D7
ROCKVIEW CT
- FTNH 85268 582-J7
N ROCK VIEW DR
34000 SCTS 85262 460-H1
E ROCK VIEW RD
7300 SCTS 85262 460-H1
N ROCKWELL CT
- GIL 85234 783-A3
W ROCKWELL CT
1900 CHAN 85224 821-A2
W ROCKWELL DR
1300 CHAN 85224 821-B2
N ROCKWELL ST
1300 GIL 85234 783-A4
S ROCKWELL ST
- GIL 85236 823-A3
- MarC 85236 823-A6
W ROCKWOOD CIR
1100 PHX 85027 538-F6
E ROCKWOOD DR
400 PHX 85024 538-H6
1000 PHX 85024 539-A6
3000 PHX 85050 539-E6
9000 SCTS 85255 541-B7
17100 FTNH 85268 623-D5
S ROCKWOOD DR
5000 CHAN 85248 901-E2
W ROCKWOOD DR
100 PHX 85027 538-F6
4200 PHX 85308 537-H6
8300 PEOR 85382 536-D6
W ROCKWOOD WY
- SURP 85374 534-G6
W ROCK WREN CT
- GDYR 85338 (774-B7 See Page 733)
E ROCK WREN RD
1300 PHX 85048 818-H4
2000 PHX 85048 819-A4
3200 PHX 85044 819-F5
W ROCK WREN RD
- GDYR 85338 (774-B6 See Page 733)
N ROCKY RD
1400 PinC 85219 746-B4
E ROCKY BROOK DR
- MarC 85248 901-C3
S ROCKY BROOK DR
- MarC 85248 901-C2

E ROCKY LAKE DR
9400 MarC 85248 901-A3
E ROCKY MOUNTAIN PL
15900 FTNH 85268 583-A3
S ROCKY PEAK CT
- PinC 85219 826-H3
S ROCKY POINT RD
5500 TEMP 85283 780-G4
W ROCKY POINT RD
40500 MarC 85354 105-C1
E ROCKY SLOPE DR
1200 PHX 85048 818-H4
1700 PHX 85048 819-A4
3300 PHX 85044 819-E4
W RODEO CT
9700 MarC 85382 536-C4
W RODERICK LN
33000 MarC 85390 290-A3
E ROESER RD
- PHX 85040 738-H6
- PHX 85041 738-H6
1400 PHX 85040 739-D6
W ROESER RD
- AVON 85353 735-H6
- MarC 85326 (732-F4 See Page 731)
- MarC 85339 737-D6
- PHX 85339 737-D6
- PHX 85041 738-C6
3500 PHX 85041 737-H6
3900 MarC 85041 737-H6
6700 MarC 85043 736-J6
8700 MarC 85353 736-D6
8700 PHX 85353 736-D6
11300 MarC 85353 735-G6
N ROGER WY
- CHAN 85225 822-B6
S ROGER WY
- CHAN 85249 902-B5
W ROGER WY
- CHAN 85225 822-B5
N ROGERS
- MESA 85201 741-D3
S ROGERS
400 MESA 85202 741-D6
1900 MESA 85202 781-D3
S ROGERS CIR
1700 MESA 85202 781-D2
W ROGERS CIR
10300 MarC 85351 616-A3
N ROGERS LN
4000 SCTS 85251 700-H1
S ROGERS ST
2400 MESA 85202 781-D4
E ROLAND CIR
- MESA 85207 703-J4
E ROLAND ST
6000 MESA 85215 703-E4
S ROLES DR
- GIL 85236 823-B3
N ROLLAND RIDGE RD
- PinC 85219 746-A6
E ROLLING CREEK DR
5200 CVCK 85331 420-C6
N ROLLING GREEN WY
- MarC 85086 (378-E5 See Page 337)
W ROLLING HILLS DR
9200 MarC 85351 576-C3
E ROLLING ROCK DR
- SCTS 85262 (381-H5 See Page 341)
E ROLLINS ST
- MESA 85215 703-G4
E ROMA AV
700 PHX 85014 658-H6
1600 PHX 85014 659-A6
1600 PHX 85016 659-A6
3200 PHX 85018 659-E6
4400 SCTS 85251 660-E7
5000 PHX 85018 660-A7
5200 PHX 85018 700-A1
8500 SCTS 85251 661-A7
W ROMA AV
100 PHX 85013 658-E6
1500 PHX 85015 658-D6
2700 PHX 85017 658-A6
3300 PHX 85017 657-J6
3600 PHX 85019 657-J6
4400 PHX 85037 656-A6
4700 PHX 85031 657-C6
6400 PHX 85033 657-A6
7100 PHX 85033 656-F6
10600 PHX 85037 655-H6
N ROMAIN CT
- MarC 85340 655-C2
S ROME ST
- GIL 85296 822-H5
- MarC 85296 822-H6
E ROMLEY AV
1000 PHX 85040 738-H6
W ROMLEY AV
500 PHX 85041 738-C6
3700 PHX 85041 737-H6
6800 PHX 85043 736-J5
N ROMO LP
- PHX 85027 498-A7
- PHX 85027 538-A1
E ROMPING RD
9200 CARE 85377 421-D5
N ROMPING RD
36200 CARE 85377 421-D5
E RONALD RD
1800 PHX 85022 579-B7
W RONALD RD
2000 PHX 85029 578-D7
E RON RICO RD
4600 MarC 85331 460-A3
5400 PHX 85331 460-C3
S ROOKS RD
2800 MarC 85326 771-H4
7600 BUCK 85326 (771-H2 See Page 731)
7600 MarC 85326 (771-H2 See Page 731)
E ROOSEVELT AV
100 BUCK 85326 (772-A1 See Page 731)
N ROOSEVELT AV
- CHAN 85225 820-C4
S ROOSEVELT AV
- CHAN 85226 820-B6
E ROOSEVELT CIR
900 SCTS 85257 700-J6
8600 SCTS 85257 701-A6
N ROOSEVELT CIR
800 SCTS 85257 701-A6
900 SCTS 85257 700-J6
N ROOSEVELT RD
- MESA 85201 741-B5

N ROOSEVELT RD
300 MarC 85256 701-B6
S ROOSEVELT RD
- MarC 85256 701-B7
- MESA 85202 741-B5
E ROOSEVELT ST
- PHX 85004 698-J5
600 PHX 85006 698-J5
900 APJT 85219 745-F6
1400 PHX 85006 699-A5
2200 PHX 85008 699-C5
4300 PinC 85219 746-A6
5000 PHX 85008 700-A6
7200 SCTS 85257 700-F6
9600 MarC 85256 701-D6
21600 MarC 85361 (453-A2 See Page 413)
S ROOSEVELT ST
100 TEMP 85281 740-C4
600 TEMP 85283 780-C4
2000 TEMP 85282 740-C7
3100 TEMP 85282 780-C1
W ROOSEVELT ST
- GDYR 85338 (694-C4 See Page 653)
- PHX 85003 698-E5
700 PHX 85007 698-E5
900 APJT 85220 745-A5
900 PHX 85043 697-A5
2100 PHX 85009 698-A5
3300 PHX 85009 697-H5
6800 PHX 85043 696-H5
8100 PEOR 85345 576-G7
9100 MarC 85353 696-D5
9100 TOL 85353 696-B4
17600 GDYR 85326 (693-J4 See Page 653)
17600 GDYR 85326 (694-A4 See Page 653)
17900 MarC 85326 (693-G4 See Page 653)
18700 BUCK 85326 (693-G4 See Page 653)
21700 MarC 85361 (452-J1 See Page 411)
21700 MarC 85361 (453-A2 See Page 413)
22700 BUCK 85326 (692-F3 See Page 651)
23100 MarC 85326 (692-F3 See Page 651)
ROOSEVELT IRRIGATION DISTRICT
- AVON - 655-A7
- AVON - 695-C1
- AVON - 696-A1
- BUCK - (693-E6 See Page 653)
- BUCK - 731-F3
- BUCK - (732-A2 See Page 731)
- BUCK - 733-A1
- GDYR - 655-A7
- GDYR - (693-E6 See Page 653)
- GDYR - (694-A4 See Page 653)
- GDYR - 695-C1
- MarC - 696-B2
- MarC - (693-E6 See Page 653)
- MarC - 731-F3
- MarC - (732-A2 See Page 731)
- MarC - 733-A1
- MarC - 737-C2
- PHX - 696-B2
- PHX - 697-A7
- PHX - 737-F2
- TOL - 696-E5
ROOSEVELT WCD CSR
- GIL - 783-E4
- GIL - 823-F4
- GIL - 863-A7
- MarC - 743-B4
- MarC - 783-E3
- MarC - 823-F4
- MarC - 863-A7
- MarC - 902-H2
- MarC - 903-A1
- MESA - 702-J5
- MESA - 703-A7
- MESA - 743-A2
- MESA - 783-E4
- MESA - 823-F4
N ROPING RD
24600 SCTS 85255 501-A5
E ROSA LN
- GIL 85236 863-C4
W ROSAL AV
400 APJT 85220 745-D6
W ROSAL DR
1700 CHAN 85224 821-C1
W ROSAL PL
300 CHAN 85225 821-E1
1400 CHAN 85224 821-C1
W ROSALIE RANCH RD
32200 MarC 85390 290-B5
E ROSARITA DR
2100 TEMP 85281 740-J5
N ROSBURG DR
2000 MESA 85215 703-C7
E ROSCOE AV
- MarC 85212 824-H2
N ROSE
2100 MESA 85213 702-D6
S ROSE
700 MESA 85204 742-D7
1000 MESA 85204 782-D1
E ROSE CIDR
6000 PHX 85018 700-C2
6000 PHX 85251 700-C2
6100 SCTS 85018 700-C2
6100 SCTS 85251 700-D2
N ROSE CIDR
3100 PHX 85018 700-C2
3400 SCTS 85251 700-D1
E ROSE CIR
1800 PHX 85016 659-B3
N ROSE CIR
1400 MESA 85213 742-D1
S ROSE CIR
1300 MESA 85204 782-D1
W ROSE CIR
6100 PHX 85033 697-B1
E ROSE LN
- PHX 85012 658-H3
- PHX 85016 659-B3
100 AVON 85323 735-B1
700 PHX 85014 658-H3

E ROSE LN
1200 PHX 85014 659-A3
3500 PVAL 85253 659-F3
6100 SCTS 85250 660-G3
7000 PVAL 85253 660-F3
7000 SCTS 85253 660-F3
8400 SCTS 85250 661-A3
N ROSE LN
6200 PHX 85016 659-D3
W ROSE LN
- PHX 85013 658-E3
400 WICK 85390 290-D1
1500 PHX 85015 658-C2
2500 PHX 85017 658-B2
3300 PHX 85017 657-H2
3500 PHX 85019 657-H2
4300 GLEN 85301 657-B2
6000 GLEN 85303 656-G2
6700 GLEN 85303 657-A2
8300 GLEN 85305 656-D2
12700 MarC 85340 655-B2
E ROSE ST
8700 MarC 85208 744-B6
N ROSE ST
1100 TEMP 85281 740-F1
S ROSEBUD DR
25200 MarC 85248 901-D4
E ROSECREST DR
23600 MarC 85248 901-A2
E ROSEDALE ST
- MESA 85215 703-G4
E ROSE GARDEN LN
2000 PHX 85024 539-B3
2400 PHX 85050 539-D3
7400 SCTS 85255 540-H4
N ROSE GARDEN LN
2000 AVON 85323 695-C5
W ROSE GARDEN LN
- PEOR 85308 536-G3
- PHX 85027 538-A3
700 PHX 85024 538-J3
3400 PHX 85308 538-A3
3500 PHX 85308 537-H3
5200 GLEN 85308 537-A3
7100 GLEN 85308 536-J3
10200 PEOR 85382 536-A3
10700 PEOR 85373 535-H3
10700 PEOR 85373 536-A3
10900 MarC 85373 535-H2
20600 MarC 85387 533-B2
20600 SURP 85387 533-B2
E ROSE GARDEN LP
2200 PHX 85024 539-C3
E ROSE MARIE LN
800 PHX 85022 538-J6
4200 PHX 85032 539-H7
W ROSE MARIE LN
1100 PHX 85023 538-F6
S ROSEMARY DR
- CHAN 85248 901-C2
3000 CHAN 85248 861-D5
E ROSEMARY LN
10300 SCTS 85260 581-F3
10600 SCTS 85259 581-G3
N ROSEMONT
500 MESA 85205 743-B1
1800 MESA 85205 703-B7
S ROSEMONT
400 MESA 85206 743-B7
1400 MESA 85206 783-B2
N ROSEMONT CIR
600 MESA 85205 743-B4
N ROSEMONT CT
- FTNH 85268 622-J3
S ROSEMONT CT
- GIL 85236 823-B2
E ROSEMONTE DR
400 PHX 85024 538-H6
1000 PHX 85024 539-A6
3200 PHX 85050 539-D6
9000 SCTS 85255 541-C7
N ROSEMONTE DR
8700 PEOR 85382 536-F6
W ROSEMONTE DR
300 PHX 85027 538-F6
4100 PHX 85308 537-H5
8300 PEOR 85382 536-C5
ROSEN DR
600 TEMP 85281 740-C4
W ROSE PILAR CT
8400 PEOR 85382 536-F6
E ROSETTA DR
16200 FTNH 85268 583-B7
N ROSEWOOD AV
12600 PHX 85029 577-J6
W ROSEWOOD AV
3300 PHX 85029 578-A6
3700 PHX 85029 577-J6
W ROSEWOOD CT
1300 CHAN 85224 781-B6
E ROSEWOOD DR
9400 SCTS 85255 501-C4
N ROSEWOOD DR
3700 AVON 85323 655-H7
15200 MarC 85351 576-B3
S ROSEWOOD DR
24600 MarC 85248 901-D4
W ROSEWOOD DR
- AVON 85323 656-A7
4700 PHX 85304 577-F6
11300 AVON 85323 655-G7
11800 ELMG 85335 575-E6
E ROSEWOOD LN
8400 SCTS 85251 660-J6
W ROSEWOOD LN
- ELMG 85335 575-E6
4600 PHX 85031 657-C5
S ROSEWOOD PL
- PinC 85219 786-E4
W ROSEWOOD PL
1200 CHAN 85224 781-D6
W ROSEWOOD WY
15800 SURP 85374 534-F3
E ROSITA DR
17100 FTNH 85268 583-E6
N ROSITA DR
14000 FTNH 85268 583-E6
S ROSLYN
2200 MESA 85208 783-G4
6400 MESA 85212 823-F7
6400 MESA 85212 863-F1
S ROSLYN PL
900 MESA 85208 783-G1
E ROSS AV
1000 PHX 85024 539-A3
W ROSS AV
- PEOR 85308 536-G3
- PHX 85353 736-E4
- PHX 85027 538-A3
800 PHX 85024 538-J3

W ROSS AV
3500 PHX 85308 537-H3
3500 PHX 85308 538-A3
9700 PEOR 85382 536-A3
E ROSS DR
1800 CHAN 85225 822-A4
N ROSS DR
800 CHAN 85226 820-B4
W ROSS DR
- PEOR 85308 536-H3
2500 PHX 85027 538-C3
3200 CHAN 85226 820-D4
E ROUGH CIR
9800 FTNH 85268 623-D4
E ROUGH LN
- PinC 85219 786-E7
- PinC 85219 826-F1
E ROUGHNECK ST
- PinC 85219 746-B2
W ROUGH RIDER RD
2300 MarC 85087 (338-D3 See Page 337)
W ROUNDELAY CIR
10400 MarC 85351 575-J4
10400 MarC 85351 576-A3
E ROUND HILL DR
4000 PHX 85028 619-H1
N ROUND ROBIN CT
37600 CARE 85377 421-A4
E ROUND UP CIR
15400 FTNH 85268 582-J4
W ROUNDUP CT
9800 MarC 85373 536-B7
E ROUNDUP PL
- SCTS 85255 541-B3
E ROUNDUP ST
- APJT 85219 746-A4
2000 APJT 85219 745-G4
4100 PinC 85219 746-A4
W ROUNDUP ST
800 APJT 85220 745-B4
E ROUNDUP WY
- QC 85242 864-D6
E ROVEEN AV
3200 PHX 85032 579-E6
W ROVEEN AV
2500 PHX 85029 578-C6
E ROVEY AV
300 PHX 85012 658-H3
800 PHX 85014 658-H3
1500 PHX 85014 659-A3
1600 PHX 85016 659-A3
4800 PVAL 85253 660-A3
6000 SCTS 85250 660-G4
8500 SCTS 85250 661-A4
W ROVEY AV
- MarC 85340 655-B2
900 PHX 85013 658-F3
1500 PHX 85015 658-D3
2700 PHX 85017 658-A3
3500 PHX 85017 657-J3
3500 PHX 85019 657-H3
4400 GLEN 85301 657-F3
8700 GLEN 85305 656-E3
E ROVEY CIR
1900 PHX 85016 659-B3
W ROVEY CT
- MarC 85340 655-B2
E ROVEY DR
5300 PVAL 85253 660-B3
E ROVEY LN
3300 PVAL 85253 659-F3
N ROWDEN ST
- MESA 85207 703-H6
E ROWEL RD
4000 PHX 85050 499-H4
4500 PHX 85050 500-A4
8200 SCTS 85255 501-A4
W ROWEL RD
- PEOR 85382 496-J3
- PEOR 85382 497-A3
- PHX 85310 497-B3
900 MarC 85085 498-F3
900 MarC 85027 498-F3
N ROWEN
- MESA 85207 703-J3
1200 MESA 85207 743-H2
S ROWEN
- MESA 85212 863-G1
400 MESA 85208 743-H7
1000 MESA 85208 783-H1
5700 MESA 85212 823-G6
N ROWEN CIR
- MESA 85207 703-H5
1600 MESA 85207 743-H1
E ROWLAND CIR
3400 MESA 85207 703-J3
E ROWLANDS LN
700 PHX 85022 578-J4
1100 PHX 85022 579-A4
N ROXY CIR
- MESA 85205 743-B4
N ROYAL CIR
5600 PVAL 85253 659-G4
N ROYAL CT
11000 FTNH 85268 623-D3
21600 MarC 85375 535-A1
W ROYAL OAK RD
9700 MarC 85351 576-B5
W ROYAL PALM AV
2200 PHX 85021 618-C6
E ROYAL PALM CIR
1200 PHX 85020 618-J6
N ROYAL PALM CIR
4500 PHX 85018 660-A6
8100 PHX 85020 618-J6
N ROYAL PALM CT
- SURP 85374 534-G3
E ROYAL PALM DR
400 MESA 85203 741-J3
E ROYAL PALM RD
- PHX 85020 618-H6
1400 PHX 85020 619-A6
5300 PVAL 85253 620-B6
7200 SCTS 85258 620-G6
8400 SCTS 85258 621-A6
N ROYAL PALM RD
- PVAL 85253 620-D7
- APJT 85219 745-F6
S ROYAL PALM RD
- APJT 85219 745-F7
1200 APJT 85219 785-F1
W ROYAL PALM RD
- PHX 85021 618-E5
2700 PHX 85051 618-A6
3500 PHX 85051 617-H5
4300 GLEN 85302 617-C5
8100 PEOR 85345 616-A5
10800 PEOR 85345 615-H5

E ROYAL PALM SQ
600 PHX 85020 618-H6
N ROYAL PALM SQ
600 PHX 85020 618-H6
W ROYAL PALMS CT
1200 GIL 85233 821-J1
W ROYAL PALMS DR
800 GIL 85233 822-A1
W ROYAL RIDGE DR
9700 MarC 85351 576-C5
N ROYAL VIEW DR
4500 PHX 85018 660-A6
W ROY ROGERS
17100 SURP 85374 534-B6
E ROY ROGERS RD
4000 MarC 85331 499-H1
4500 PHX 85331 499-J1
4600 PHX 85331 500-A1
6000 MarC 85331 500-D1
N RUBEL CT
- BUCK 85326 (772-B1 See Page 731)
N RUBICON AV
4300 PHX 85018 660-A7
S RUBY DR
- MarC 85249 902-F4
S RUBY PL
700 GIL 85236 823-A2
E RUBY WY
- PHX 85024 499-C7
W RUE DE LAMOUR
7000 PEOR 85381 577-A5
7100 PEOR 85381 576-F5
W RUE DE LAMOUR AV
2300 PHX 85029 578-A5
3600 PHX 85029 577-J5
S RUELLIA LN
- PinC 85219 786-E4
S RUFFIAN DR
2100 GIL 85296 822-J2
E RUFFIAN RD
- GIL 85236 863-E4
N RUGBY
2400 MESA 85215 703-F6
N RUGBY CIR
2700 MESA 85215 703-F5
E RUGGED IRONWOOD DR
- PinC 85219 786-E7
E RUNAWAY BAY DR
- MarC 85249 902-E5
1300 CHAN 85249 901-H5
E RUNAWAY BAY PL
- CHAN 85249 902-A5
- MarC 85249 902-C5
E RUNION DR
1600 PHX 85024 539-B4
W RUNION DR
- PHX 85027 538-A3
3700 PHX 85308 537-H3
9600 PEOR 85382 536-A3
10700 PEOR 85373 536-A3
11000 PEOR 85373 535-J3
S RUNNING BEAR CT
- PHX 85044 819-D1
E RUNNING BEAR TR
- PHX 85331 500-A2
E RUNNING DEER TR
- SCTS 85331 500-E2
9700 SCTS 85255 501-F2
W RUNNING DEER TR
- PHX 85085 497-D1
- PHX 85085 498-B1
E RUNNING WATER DR
10200 PinC 85219 786-H3
N RUNYON PL
16200 FTNH 85268 583-A3
N RURAL RD
- CHAN 85226 820-E4
1000 CHAN 85284 820-E4
1000 TEMP 85284 820-E4
S RURAL RD
100 TEMP 85281 740-F5
1700 TEMP 85282 740-F5
3100 TEMP 85282 780-E3
4800 TEMP 85283 780-E3
7500 TEMP 85284 780-E3
8100 TEMP 85284 820-E2
S RUSH CIR E
200 CHAN 85226 820-E7
S RUSH CIR W
200 CHAN 85226 820-E7
N RUSH ST
- CHAN 85226 820-E4
S RUSH ST
- CHAN 85226 820-E6
800 CHAN 85226 860-E1
W RUSHMORE DR
- MarC 85087 (378-A4 See Page 337)
E RUSKIN LN
15800 FTNH 85268 583-A3
E RUSSELL CIR
- MESA 85207 703-J4
N RUSSELL CT
- GIL 85234 782-F7
E RUSSELL ST
3300 MESA 85215 703-F4
E RUSSET SKY DR
6800 SCTS 85262 460-F2
E RUSTIC DR
6400 MESA 85215 703-F7
W RUSTLER RD
18500 MarC 85326 (773-E7 See Page 733)
E RUSTLER WY
- GIL 85236 863-D4
E RUSTLING PASS
7200 SCTS 85255 540-G3
N RUSTY LN
17100 SURP 85374 534-G6
E RUSTY NAIL CT
15200 FTNH 85268 582-J3
E RUSTY SPUR LN
- SCTS 85255 541-C4
E RUSTY SPUR PL
- SCTS 85255 541-B4
E RUTH AV
- PHX 85020 618-H5
- PHX 85021 618-H5
1200 PHX 85020 619-A5
W RUTH AV
100 PHX 85021 618-E5
2700 PHX 85051 618-A5
3600 PHX 85051 617-H5
4300 GLEN 85302 617-C5
6700 GLEN 85345 617-A4
8300 PEOR 85345 616-A4
10400 PEOR 85345 615-H4

STREET Block City ZIP Pg-Grid

E RUTLEDGE AV
- MarC 85212 824-H3
S RYAN CT
- GIL 85236 863-B4
E RYAN RD
- CHAN 85249 861-G4
300 MarC 85249 861-H4
1500 GIL 85296 862-F4
1500 MarC 85296 862-D4
1700 CHAN 85249 862-A4
20000 QC 85242 864-B4
W RYAN RD
1000 CHAN 85248 861-D4
W RYAN ST
16200 GDYR 85326 (854-C2 See Page 813)
18700 MarC 85326 (853-D2 See Page 813)
N RYAN WY
12600 FTNH 85268 623-B1
12700 FTNH 85268 583-B7
W RYANS WY
18000 SURP 85374 533-J7
18000 SURP 85374 534-A7

S

N SABA ST
1100 CHAN 85225 821-H2
S SABA ST
- MarC 85249 901-H2
E SABER RD
6600 CVCK 85331 420-F2
E SABINAS DR
16900 FTNH 85268 583-D5
SABIN BROWN RD
3800 WICK 85390 289-F2
S SABINO CT
- MarC 85236 823-D4
N SABINO DR
- MarC 85236 783-D6
600 GIL 85236 783-D5
S SABINO DR
- MarC 85236 823-D4
W SABLE CT
14200 MarC 85375 535-A4
N SABRINA
- MESA 85220 784-G2
S SABRINA
- MESA 85220 744-G7
- MESA 85220 784-G1
S SABRINA CIR
- MESA 85212 784-F6
W SABRINA DR
- SURP 85374 534-A5
E SABROSA DR
- MarC 85087 (378-J1 See Page 337)
W SABROSA DR
- MarC 85087 (378-H1 See Page 337)
N SACATON RD
7500 SCTS 85258 660-G1
7500 SCTS 85258 620-G7
E SACATON ST
4000 PHX 85044 779-G7
E SACK DR
400 PHX 85024 538-H6
W SACK DR
1300 PHX 85027 538-F6
5900 GLEN 85308 537-A5
7200 GLEN 85308 536-J5
10700 PEOR 85373 536-A5
10700 PEOR 85373 535-J5
N SACRAMENTO ST
- CHAN 85225 821-G6
N SADDLE CT
1200 GIL 85233 782-A4
E SADDLE DR
- CHAN 85225 821-G7
E SADDLE LN
100 PHX 85020 618-H3
W SADDLE RD
47400 MarC 85354 101-C3
N SADDLE ST
800 GIL 85233 782-A4
S SADDLE ST
100 GIL 85233 782-A7
100 GIL 85233 822-A1
N SADDLE TR
10100 PHX 85020 618-H3
E SADDLE WY
- QC 85242 864-C6
E SADDLEBACK
3800 MESA 85215 703-F3
N SADDLEBACK
3800 MESA 85215 703-E3
E SADDLEBACK CIR
- MESA 85207 703-G3
- MESA 85207 704-A3
6600 MESA 85215 703-G3
N SADDLEBACK LN
- SCTS 85255 501-J5
E SADDLEBACK ST
7100 MESA 85207 703-H3
N SADDLEBACK TR
- WICK 85390 290-A1
N SADDLEBAG TR
4400 SCTS 85251 660-G7
E SADDLE BUTTE ST
100 PinC 85219 705-E6
W SADDLE BUTTE ST
500 PinC 85220 705-A6
E SADDLE CLUB DR
30800 MarC 85390 290-F1
W SADDLEHORN
17200 SURP 85374 534-B6
E SADDLEHORN DR
10500 SCTS 85258 621-F4
E SADDLEHORN RD
8000 SCTS 85255 500-J5
W SADDLEHORN RD
- PEOR 85382 497-A4
1300 MarC 85027 498-F5
4600 PHX 85310 497-B4
9100 PEOR 85382 496-E4
E SADDLE HORN TR
- SCTS 85259 622-C4
E SADDLEHORN TR
9400 SCTS 85259 622-B4
9900 SCTS 85258 621-D4
10000 SCTS 85255 501-E6
N SADDLE HORSE LN
- SCTS 85255 541-C4
W SADDLE MOUNTAIN CT
20600 MarC 85361 (453-C7 See Page 413)
E SADDLE MOUNTAIN RD
700 MarC 85086 (379-A7 See Page 339)
2600 CVCK 85331 (379-E7 See Page 339)
2600 MarC 85331 (379-E7 See Page 339)
W SADDLE MOUNTAIN RD
200 MarC 85086 (378-H7 See Page 337)
6900 MarC 85086 (376-F6 See Page 335)
6900 MarC 85086 (377-A7 See Page 337)
8600 PEOR 85086 (376-F6 See Page 335)
N SADDLE RIDGE DR
17200 SURP 85374 534-E6
W SADDLE RIDGE DR
10000 MarC 85373 536-B5
10000 MarC 85382 536-B5
16100 SURP 85374 534-E6
W SADDLE RIDGE WY
- WICK 85390 289-G2
SADDLE RIDGE RANCH RD
- YavC - 250-G5
N SADDLEROCK DR
5100 PHX 85018 660-A5
5200 PHX 85253 660-A5
S SADDLETREE DR
10300 MarC 85248 901-D3
S SAFFORD
- MESA 85220 744-G7
N SAFFRON
- MarC 85205 743-F4
900 MESA 85205 743-G1
3000 MESA 85215 703-G4
N SAFFRON CIR
- MarC 85205 743-F4
2600 MESA 85215 703-G6
N SAFFRON ST
2400 MESA 85215 703-F6
E SAFI WY
5100 PVAL 85253 660-E5
N SAGE CIR
500 GIL 85234 782-D6
3100 AVON 85323 695-H1
S SAGE CT
3700 CHAN 85248 861-A6
W SAGE CT
11400 AVON 85323 695-G1
E SAGE DR
5300 PVAL 85250 660-G5
6000 PHX 85251 660-D5
7400 SCTS 85250 660-H5
8500 SCTS 85250 661-A5
15200 FTNH 85268 582-H7
15200 FTNH 85268 622-J1
S SAGE DR
- CHAN 85248 861-A7
W SAGE DR
- TEMP 85282 779-J1
11500 AVON 85323 695-G1
N SAGE LN
400 GIL 85234 782-D6
W SAGE LN
- AVON 85340 695-C1
W SAGE TR
- SURP 85374 534-F7
S SAGE WY
5600 PinC 85219 786-H6
S SAGEBERRY DR
26600 MarC 85248 901-D6
N SAGE BRUSH
17700 SURP 85374 534-C6
S SAGE BRUSH
1300 BUCK 85326 (692-C7 See Page 651)
E SAGE BRUSH AV
- PinC 85242 905-G6
E SAGEBRUSH CIR
100 LP 85340 655-B7
4900 MarC 85331 460-B1
9000 SCTS 85255 501-C5
E SAGEBRUSH CT
1500 GIL 85296 822-G1
N SAGEBRUSH CT
2300 CHAN 85224 821-B1
E SAGEBRUSH DR
- MarC 85085 (458-H1 See Page 417)
W SAGEBRUSH DR
2100 CHAN 85224 821-B1
SAGEBRUSH LN
- FTNH 85268 582-H5
E SAGEBRUSH LN
2200 CARE 85377 420-G7
E SAGEBRUSH ST
200 GIL 85296 822-E1
400 LP 85340 655-B7
2400 GIL 85236 822-H2
2400 GIL 85236 823-A1
4800 PinC 85219 746-C3
14600 MarC 85296 822-F1
W SAGEBRUSH ST
100 GIL 85233 822-A1
100 LP 85340 655-A7
N SAGEBRUSH TR
- WICK 85390 290-A2
N SAGE CREEK CIR
- MarC 85290 704-A1
- MESA 85207 704-A2
N SAGEWOOD
- MESA 85207 703-H2
S SAGEWOOD
5500 MESA 85212 823-G5
6400 MESA 85212 863-G1
N SAGEWOOD CIR
- MESA 85207 703-H4
S SAGEWOOD CIR
6400 MESA 85212 823-G7
E SAGITTARIUS CT
- MarC 85249 902-C4
E SAGITTARIUS PL
- CHAN 85249 901-G4
E SAGO DR
- MarC 85263 503-J6
N SAGUARO
400 MESA 85201 741-D4
S SAGUARO
400 MESA 85202 741-C6
1300 BUCK 85326 (692-C7 See Page 651)
1600 MESA 85202 781-C2
W SAGUARO
1600 MESA 85201 741-D3
N SAGUARO BLVD
9500 FTNH 85268 623-D4
12700 FTNH 85268 583-D6
E SAGUARO CIR
- PHX 85044 819-J1
S SAGUARO CIR
1800 MESA 85202 781-C3
N SAGUARO CT
20100 SURP 85374 534-F3
E SAGUARO DR
600 TEMP 85281 700-F7
5200 PVAL 85253 620-B6
N SAGUARO DR
- APJT 85220 745-C3
1500 TEMP 85281 700-E7
4200 PinC 85220 705-C7
4200 PinC 85220 745-C1
5900 PVAL 85253 620-C7
S SAGUARO DR
- APJT 85220 745-B6
- WICK 85390 290-B4
700 MarC 85390 290-B4
1300 APJT 85220 785-B1
W SAGUARO DR
4500 GLEN 85304 617-B2
7900 PEOR 85345 616-G2
E SAGUARO LN
18400 MarC 85263 503-H5
W SAGUARO LN
- SURP 85374 (574-C2 See Page 573)
5500 PHX 85310 497-E5
E SAGUARO PL
4700 PVAL 85253 619-J6
4700 PVAL 85253 620-A6
E SAGUARO RD
5700 CVCK 85331 420-D1
N SAGUARO RD
5500 PVAL 85253 660-D4
N SAGUARO ST
500 CHAN 85224 821-C4
S SAGUARO ST
- GIL 85233 822-C3
3000 MESA 85202 781-C6
E SAGUARO WY
500 MESA 85208 743-J7
S SAGUARO WY
500 MESA 85208 743-J7
N SAGUARO BLOSSOM LN
43800 MarC 85342 331-D7
E SAGUARO BLOSSOM RD
8500 PinC 85219 786-F7
N SAGUARO FOREST DR
10800 SCTS 85262 (381-F6 See Page 341)
N SAGUARO LAKE RD
8500 MarC 85290 103-B2
W SAGUARO PARK LN
3500 PHX 85310 498-A5
3700 PHX 85310 497-C5
E SAGUARO VISTA CT
6000 MarC 85331 500-D1
N SAHARA DR
9200 MarC 85351 576-D4
W SAHARA DR
9900 MarC 85351 576-B7
E SAHUARO BLVD
3800 PHX 85028 619-G4
E SAHUARO DR
900 PHX 85020 618-J2
1200 PHX 85020 619-A2
2100 PHX 85028 619-C2
5200 PHX 85254 620-F2
6800 SCTS 85254 620-F2
8400 SCTS 85260 581-A7
10000 SCTS 85260 621-E2
10400 SCTS 85259 621-F2
10700 SCTS 85259 622-A3
N SAHUARO DR
- GIL 85233 782-C7
S SAHUARO DR
500 GIL 85233 822-B2
W SAHUARO DR
700 PHX 85029 618-A2
3500 PHX 85029 617-H2
7100 PEOR 85345 616-C1
7100 PEOR 85345 617-H2
12700 ELMG 85335 615-D1
E SAHUARO LN
5400 PHX 85254 620-B2
W SAHUARO LN
12900 SURP 85374 575-B2
E SAHUARO RD
2100 PHX 85022 579-C7
N SAHUARO RD
- LP 85340 655-B6
S SAHUARO ST
- GIL 85233 782-C7
- GIL 85233 822-B4
8000 PHX 85040 779-B3
W SAHUARO ST
25500 MarC 85326 (691-J5 See Page 651)
N SAILBOAT LN
3500 AVON 85323 655-H7
S SAILFISH DR
900 GIL 85233 821-H2
S SAILORS CT
- GIL 85296 822-F5
N SAILORS WY
800 GIL 85234 782-F3
S SAILORS WY
- GIL 85296 822-F5
S SAILORS REEF RD
5600 TEMP 85283 780-F4
N SAINT ANDREW DR
12200 MarC 85351 576-A6
12400 MarC 85351 575-J6
N SAINT ANDREW WY
5700 PHX 85254 620-C1
E SAINT ANDREWS BLVD
1000 CHAN 85249 901-H5
W SAINT ANDREWS WY
- SURP 85374 534-G5
E SAINT ANNE AV
- PHX 85040 778-G1
1400 PHX 85040 779-A1
W SAINT ANNE AV
- PHX 85041 778-F1
N SAINT ANNES DR
12000 MarC 85351 575-J7
E SAINT CATHERINE AV
- PHX 85040 778-G1
1800 PHX 85040 779-A1
W SAINT CATHERINE AV
- PHX 85041 778-C1
E SAINT CHARLES AV
- PHX 85040 778-G1
- PHX 85041 778-G1
1600 PHX 85040 779-A1
W SAINT CHARLES AV
- PHX 85041 778-C1
N SAINT CLAIR CIR
- MESA 85220 744-H5
N SAINT CLAIR ST
- MESA 85220 744-H4
S SAINT CLARIE
- MESA 85220 744-H7
N SAINT ELENA ST
800 GIL 85234 782-F5
N SAINT ELIAS
4100 MESA 85215 703-G2
N SAINT ELIAS CIR
3800 MESA 85215 703-G3
W SAINT JOHN AV
5500 GLEN 85308 537-B7
E SAINT JOHN RD
- PHX 85022 538-H7
1000 PHX 85022 539-A7
2700 PHX 85032 539-D7
3200 PHX 85032 579-F1
3400 PHX 85032 579-G1
4700 PHX 85032 540-A7
5400 PHX 85254 540-B7
5600 PHX 85254 580-B1
8400 SCTS 85255 581-A1
W SAINT JOHN RD
200 PHX 85023 538-C7
3400 PHX 85053 538-A7
3600 PHX 85308 537-F7
5700 GLEN 85308 537-A7
7200 GLEN 85308 536-H7
8400 PEOR 85382 536-F7
9100 PEOR 85373 536-F7
W SAINT JOHNS RD
5100 MarC 85339 817-B5
E SAINT JOSEPH WY
4000 PHX 85018 659-G4
N SAINT LOUIS AV
100 GBND 85337 (1090-B2 See Page 1049)
S SAINT LOUIS AV
400 GBND 85337 (1090-B3 See Page 1049)
W SAINT LUCIA DR
1500 GIL 85233 821-H1
S SAINT MARTIN DR
700 GIL 85233 822-A2
N SAINT MORITZ LN
14600 PHX 85053 578-B4
W SAINT MORITZ LN
1800 PHX 85023 578-C4
2700 PHX 85053 578-A4
3500 PHX 85053 577-J4
5100 GLEN 85306 577-C4
N SAINT PAUL
400 MESA 85205 743-B4
S SAINT PAUL
600 MESA 85206 743-B7
900 MESA 85206 783-B1
S SAINT PAUL CIR
700 MESA 85206 743-B7
N SAINT PAUL CT
1300 GIL 85234 783-B4
W SAINT THOMAS DR
1500 GIL 85233 821-H1
N SAKI DR
16200 FTNH 85268 583-A3
SALADO RD
5900 GLEN 85307 615-B7
5900 GLEN 85307 655-B1
E SALADO ST
1200 MESA 85203 702-B6
N SALEM
800 MESA 85205 743-E3
N SALEM CIR
900 MESA 85205 743-E1
W SALEM DR
10300 MarC 85351 616-A3
10700 MarC 85351 615-J3
N SALEM ST
1800 MESA 85205 743-E1
2300 MESA 85215 703-E6
S SALEN BLVD
- PinC 85219 786-F7
E SALERO DR
10700 SCTS 85262 (381-H7 See Page 341)
E SALIDA DR
16900 FTNH 85268 623-D2
N SALIDA DEL SOL
300 CHAN 85224 821-B1
3000 CHAN 85224 781-B6
S SALIDA DEL SOL
- CHAN 85248 861-B4
2500 MESA 85202 781-B4
S SALIDA DEL SOL CIR
1800 MESA 85202 781-B2
N SALIDA DEL SOL CT
900 CHAN 85224 821-B4
S SALIDA DEL SOL CT
2600 CHAN 85248 861-A5
E SALINAS ST
3700 PHX 85044 819-F2
N SALIOA DEL SOL
- CHAN 85224 821-B3
W SALMON CT
1100 GIL 85233 821-J1
W SALOME HWY
6800 MarC 85354 101-C2
57900 MarC 85348 101-C2
31300 MarC 85322 102-A3
31300 MarC 85326 102-A3
31700 MarC 85354 102-A3
W SALSA LN
8200 MarC 85382 496-G7
W SALTBUSH
17100 SURP 85374 534-C6
E SALT BUSH DR
10300 SCTS 85260 581-F3
10400 SCTS 85259 581-F3
E SALT BUSH RD
7900 PinC 85219 786-E6
N SALT CEDAR PL
- CHAN 85225 822-A6
S SALT CEDAR PL
- CHAN 85249 902-A5
- MarC 85249 902-A3
100 CHAN 85225 822-B7
S SALT CEDAR ST
- CHAN 85249 862-A2
- MarC 85249 902-A3
S SALT CEDAR ST
200 CHAN 85225 822-A7
W SALTER DR
- PEOR 85308 536-G2
- PEOR 85382 536-A2
2900 PHX 85027 538-A2
3500 PHX 85308 538-A2
3600 PHX 85308 537-H2
10700 PEOR 85373 535-J2
10700 PEOR 85373 536-A2
E SALTILLO DR
10300 SCTS 85259 581-F2
10300 SCTS 85260 581-E3
N SALTON CIR
4300 PHX 85037 656-A6
E SALT RIVER DR
- PHX 85008 700-B7
- PHX 85281 700-B7
- TEMP 85008 700-B7
- TEMP 85281 700-B7
E SALT RIVER RD
2700 PHX 85034 739-D3
N SALT RIVER REC CIR
- MarC 85290 664-F2
E SALTSAGE DR
1400 PHX 85048 818-J7
1800 PHX 85048 819-A7
S SALTSAGE DR
1000 PHX 85045 818-D6
S SALVIA DR
- PinC 85219 786-E5
W SAMMY WY
- SURP 85374 534-A5
E SAMUEL DR
1700 PHX 85024 539-B3
S SAN ADRIAN LN
11400 GDYR 85338 (773-J6 See Page 733)
E SAN ALBERTO
8400 SCTS 85258 621-A6
W SAN ALEJANDRO DR
17200 GDYR 85338 (774-A5 See Page 733)
17500 GDYR 85338 (773-J5 See Page 733)
E SAN ALFREDO DR
- SCTS 85258 620-F5
8600 SCTS 85258 621-A6
E SAN ANDRES LN
14800 FTNH 85268 582-H3
N SAN ANDRES LN
16000 FTNH 85268 582-H3
E SAN ANGELO AV
- GIL 85234 783-B5
- MarC 85234 783-B5
100 GIL 85234 782-D4
1100 GIL 85236 783-C5
N SAN ANGELO AV
1100 GIL 85236 783-E4
E SAN ANGELO ST
5400 GUAD 85283 780-A4
W SAN ANGELO ST
- GIL 85233 782-B4
1000 GIL 85233 781-G4
E SAN ANTONIO DR
2100 GIL 85296 822-J1
E SAN ARDO DR
8700 SCTS 85258 621-A6
N SAN ARDO DR
8400 SCTS 85258 621-A6
S SAN BENITO
- GIL 85236 863-B5
E SAN BENITO DR
8300 SCTS 85258 620-J5
8400 SCTS 85258 621-A5
N SAN BENITO DR
- GIL 85234 783-B5
S SAN BENITO DR
- GIL 85236 863-B2
E SAN BERNARDO DR
8300 SCTS 85258 620-J5
8400 SCTS 85258 621-D4
E SAN BLAS CIR
15000 FTNH 85268 582-H5
W SANBORN RD
- WICK 85390 250-C6
32300 MarC 85390 250-C6
E SAN BRUNO DR
8400 SCTS 85258 621-A6
E SAN CANDIDO DR
8400 SCTS 85258 620-J5
8400 SCTS 85258 621-A5
W SAN CARLOS
- SURP 85374 534-A6
W SAN CARLOS CIR
16400 GDYR 85338 (774-D4 See Page 733)
E SAN CARLOS DR
17500 FTNH 85268 583-E5
N SAN CARLOS DR
14200 FTNH 85268 583-E6
E SAN CARLOS PL
- MarC 85249 901-J2
- MarC 85249 902-A2
W SAN CARLOS PL
- CHAN 85248 901-C2
E SAN CARLOS RD
7800 SCTS 85258 660-H1
E SAN CARLOS WY
- MarC 85249 901-H2
N SANDAL
- MESA 85206 783-D1
1000 MESA 85205 743-D1
N SANDAL CIR
900 MESA 85205 743-D3
E SANDALWOOD DR
7600 SCTS 85250 660-H5
8500 SCTS 85250 661-A5
E SAN DANIEL DR
8400 SCTS 85258 621-A6
E SANDCASTLE CT
1200 GIL 85234 782-F4
W SAND COVE DR
1500 GIL 85233 821-H1
W SANDCREEK TR
14500 SURP 85374 534-J7
E SAND DOLLAR CIR
1300 GIL 85234 782-F5
W SAND DUNE DR
1200 GIL 85233 781-H7
S SANDERS DR
- MarC 85236 823-E4
E SAND FLOWER DR
8000 SCTS 85262 460-J1
8000 SCTS 85262 (461-A1 See Page 421)
E SAND HILL RD
11900 SCTS 85255 502-A7
E SAND HILLS CT
10300 SCTS 85255 501-F7
W SAND HILLS CT
1200 GIL 85233 821-J1
E SAND HILLS RD
- SCTS 85255 502-A7
7200 SCTS 85255 500-G7
11000 SCTS 85255 501-G7
S SANDI LN
400 CHAN 85225 821-J7
E SANDIA CIR
- MESA 85207 703-J3
- MESA 85207 704-A3
E SANDIA ST
4100 PHX 85044 819-G2
S SANDIA ST
12600 PHX 85044 819-G2
W SANDIA PARK DR
16100 SURP 85374 534-D7
N SAN DIEGO CIR
15000 FTNH 85268 582-J4
W SANDMAN DR
1200 GIL 85233 781-J7
SAN DOMINGO PEAK TR
- MarC 85342 331-C2
- MarC 85390 331-C2
SANDPIPER DR
- SCTS 85258 620-H7
- SCTS 85258 660-H1
E SANDPIPER DR
1000 TEMP 85283 780-F3
S SANDPIPER DR
- CHAN 85248 861-E6
W SANDPIPER DR
900 CHAN 85248 861-D5
1300 GIL 85233 781-J7
N SANDRA AV
16200 GLEN 85306 577-E2
W SANDRA AV
5100 GLEN 85306 577-E2
N SANDRA CIR
4300 PHX 85308 537-G7
W SANDRA CIR
4300 PHX 85308 537-G7
W SANDRA LN
- SURP 85374 (574-D1 See Page 573)
E SANDRA TER
700 PHX 85022 578-J2
1100 PHX 85022 579-A2
2600 PHX 85032 579-D2
4600 PHX 85032 580-A2
4700 PHX 85254 580-B2
N SANDRA TER
16200 PHX 85254 580-E2
W SANDRA TER
- GLEN 85382 576-J1
- GLEN 85382 577-A1
300 PHX 85023 578-F2
2900 PHX 85053 578-A2
3600 PHX 85053 577-H2
4300 PHX 85306 577-F2
6000 GLEN 85306 577-B2
8800 PEOR 85382 576-E2
W SANDRIDGE DR
13400 MarC 85375 535-B5
W SANDS CT
1300 GIL 85233 821-J1
E SANDS DR
4500 PHX 85050 540-A2
8000 SCTS 85255 540-H2
8200 SCTS 85255 541-A2
22100 PHX 85050 539-J2
W SANDS DR
- PEOR 85373 535-J1
- PEOR 85373 536-A1
2400 PHX 85027 538-B1
3500 PHX 85310 538-A2
10500 PEOR 85382 536-A1
W SANDS RD
5000 GLEN 85301 617-E6
7900 GLEN 85302 617-E6
W SANDSNAKE CT
11500 SURP 85374 535-H5
E SANDSTONE CT
9500 FTNH 85268 622-H5
S SANDSTONE CT
- GIL 85296 822-F3
1000 PinC 85219 746-B7
W SAND STONE DR
- SURP 85374 534-A6
W SANDSTONE DR
9400 MarC 85351 576-B3
E SANDSTONE ST
1200 GIL 85296 782-F7
N SANDSTONE ST
- GIL 85234 782-F6
S SANDSTONE ST
- GIL 85296 782-F7
100 GIL 85296 822-F1
N SANDSTONE SPRINGS RD
- MarC 85263 (504-A4 See Page 503)
E SANDTRAP CT
8700 PinC 85219 786-G7
N SANDTRAP CT
17200 PHX 85308 537-G7
E SANDTRAP DR
- PinC 85219 786-F7
N SANDTRAP RD
- MarC 85264 623-J3
W SAND TROUT CT
11500 SURP 85374 535-H5
E SANDWEDGE LN
- PinC 85219 786-F7
E SANDY CT
- MarC 85236 863-A2
N SANDY DR
2200 MESA 85215 703-G7
E SANDY LN
5600 PHX 85254 580-C7
W SANDY LN
4500 MarC 85339 817-E3
E SANDY WY
- GIL 85236 863-B2
W SANDY BANKS
1000 GIL 85233 822-A1
1100 GIL 85233 821-J1
E SANDY MOUNTAIN RD
4100 MarC 85253 659-H1
E SANDY VISTA DR
9300 SCTS 85262 421-D7
E SAN ESTEBAN DR
8600 SCTS 85258 621-A6
S SAN ESTEBAN DR
11000 GDYR 85338 (773-J5 See Page 733)
W SAN ESTEBAN DR
17700 GDYR 85338 (773-J6 See Page 733)
E SAN FELIPE DR
8500 SCTS 85258 621-A6
S SAN FELIPE DR
- GDYR 85338 (774-D3 See Page 733)
E SAN FERNANDO DR
- SCTS 85255 540-H2
E SANFORD CIR
6000 MESA 85215 703-E3
E SAN FRANCISCO DR
3400 PHX 85040 739-E7
N SAN GABRIEL
3600 MESA 85215 703-E3
E SAN GABRIEL AV
4000 PHX 85044 779-F6
4000 PHX 85040 779-F6
N SAN GABRIEL CIR
3500 MESA 85215 703-E2
S SAN GABRIEL DR E
- GDYR 85338 (773-J3 See Page 733)
- GDYR 85338 (774-A3 See Page 733)
S SAN GABRIEL DR W
- GDYR 85338 (773-H3 See Page 733)
S SAN GABRIEL ST
- GDYR 85326 (773-H4 See Page 733)
- GDYR 85338 (773-H4 See Page 733)
E SAN JACINTO DR
- SCTS 85258 620-G5
8500 SCTS 85258 621-A6
S SAN JACINTO ST
- GIL 85236 863-B5
S SAN JOAQUIN CT
900 GIL 85296 822-J2
N SAN JOAQUIN WY
1400 GIL 85234 782-J4
N SAN JOSE CIR
400 MESA 85201 741-B3
N SAN JOSE ST
- MESA 85201 741-B4
S SAN JOSE ST
600 MESA 85202 741-B7
1000 MESA 85202 781-B1
E SAN JUAN AV
500 PHX 85012 658-H4
900 PHX 85014 658-J4
1400 PHX 85014 659-A4
1700 PHX 85016 659-B4
4000 PHX 85018 659-G4
6700 PVAL 85253 660-E4
W SAN JUAN AV
- MarC 85339 776-J4
- MarC 85339 777-B6
- PHX 85339 776-J4
- PHX 85339 777-B6
- PHX 85013 658-F4
1900 PHX 85015 658-C4
2700 PHX 85017 658-A4
3500 PHX 85017 657-H4
3500 PHX 85019 657-H4
4500 GLEN 85301 657-B3
5000 MarC 85339 817-C1
5600 GLEN 85303 656-G3
6700 GLEN 85303 657-A3
9100 MarC 85305 656-D3
10300 PHX 85307 656-A3
12800 MarC 85340 655-D3
W SAN JUAN CT
- MarC 85340 655-B3
W SAN JUAN RD
- PHX 85041 817-G2
- PHX 85041 818-B2
- PHX 85045 818-B2
E SAN LORENZO DR
8400 SCTS 85258 620-J6
8400 SCTS 85258 621-A5
S SAN LORETTA DR
16100 GDYR 85338 (774-D4 See Page 733)
E SAN LUCAS DR
8500 SCTS 85258 621-A5
N SAN LUCY RD
52400 MarC 85337 (1050-B7 See Page 1049)
52400 MarC 85337 (1090-B1 See Page 1049)
52400 GBND 85337 (1050-B7 See Page 1049)
52400 GBND 85337 (1090-B1 See Page 1049)
S SAN LUCY RD
- GBND 85337 (1050-B6 See Page 1049)
- MarC 85337 (1050-B6 See Page 1049)
N SAN MANUEL RD
7400 SCTS 85258 660-H1
S SAN MARCOS CIR
9800 GDYR 85338 (774-D4 See Page 733)
E SAN MARCOS DR
8500 SCTS 85258 621-A5
N SAN MARCOS DR
- CHAN 85225 821-F6
500 APJT 85220 745-D4
4000 PinC 85220 745-D1
4200 PinC 85220 705-D7
S SAN MARCOS DR
- CHAN 85225 821-E7
300 APJT 85220 745-D6
1200 APJT 85220 785-D1
9500 GDYR 85338 (774-D4 See Page 733)
W SAN MARCOS DR
600 CHAN 85225 821-D7
N SAN MARCOS PL
- CHAN 85225 821-F6
3300 CHAN 85225 781-F7
S SAN MARCOS PL
- CHAN 85225 821-F6
N SAN MARCOS ST
1100 GIL 85234 782-E4
E SAN MARCUS DR
17300 FTNH 85268 583-E5
E SAN MARINO DR
8000 SCTS 85258 620-J5
8400 SCTS 85258 621-A5
E SAN MARTIN DR
8700 SCTS 85258 621-A5
S SAN MATEO CIR
600 GIL 85296 822-E2
W SAN MATEO CIR
900 GIL 85233 822-A2

PHOENIX INDEX

STREET
Block City ZIP Pg-Grid

W SAN MATEO DR
800 GIL 85233 822-A2
E SAN MIGUEL AV
- PHX 85012 658-G4
900 PHX 85014 658-J4
1300 PHX 85014 659-A4
1700 PHX 85016 659-B4
3200 PVAL 85253 659-G4
4000 PHX 85018 659-H4
5200 PVAL 85253 660-A4
7200 SCTS 85250 660-G4
8500 SCTS 85250 661-A5
W SAN MIGUEL AV
- PHX 85307 655-J3
700 PHX 85013 658-E4
1900 PHX 85015 658-C4
2500 PHX 85017 658-A4
3500 PHX 85019 657-G3
4500 GLEN 85301 657-B3
5500 GLEN 85303 656-G3
6700 GLEN 85303 657-A3
9200 MarC 85305 656-C3
10300 PHX 85307 656-A3
12600 MarC 85340 655-B3
S SAN MIGUEL DR
10800 GDYR 85338 (773-J5 See Page 733)
17100 GDYR 85338 (774-A6 See Page 733)
W SANNA CIR
- PEOR 85345 616-D3
E SANNA ST
4600 PHX 85028 619-J4
5000 PVAL 85253 620-A4
W SANNA ST
4400 GLEN 85302 617-E3
6800 PEOR 85345 617-E3
7000 PEOR 85345 616-D3
E SANOQUE BLVD
- QC 85242 904-A1
19200 QC 85242 903-H1
E SANOQUE CIR
- QC 85242 903-J1
E SANOQUE CT
- MarC 85249 902-J1
S SAN PABLO CIR
9100 GDYR 85338 (774-D3 See Page 733)
E SAN PABLO DR
8700 SCTS 85258 621-A5
S SAN PABLO DR
8900 GDYR 85338 (774-E3 See Page 733)
S SAN PABLO LN
9000 GDYR 85338 (774-D2 See Page 733)
E SAN PAULO PL
17500 FTNH 85268 583-E6
E SAN PEDRO AV
400 GIL 85234 782-D4
1100 GIL 85236 783-D4
3600 GIL 85234 783-B4
W SAN PEDRO CIR
16000 GDYR 85338 (774-D3 See Page 733)
E SAN PEDRO CT
- MarC 85234 783-B4
100 GIL 85234 782-D4
E SAN PEDRO DR
8400 SCTS 85258 620-J5
8700 SCTS 85258 621-A5
W SAN PEDRO ST
- GIL 85233 782-B4
1200 GIL 85233 781-H4
E SAN RAFAEL DR
8300 SCTS 85258 620-J5
8600 SCTS 85258 621-A5
E SAN RAMON DR
8300 SCTS 85258 620-J5
E SAN REMO AV
- MarC 85234 783-B5
400 GIL 85234 782-D5
3600 GIL 85234 783-B5
3600 GIL 85236 783-C5
N SAN REMO AV
100 GIL 85234 782-D4
E SAN REMO CT
- GIL 85234 783-C5
W SAN REMO CT
600 GIL 85233 782-B4
W SAN REMO ST
- GIL 85233 782-C4
1600 GIL 85233 781-H4
E SAN RICARDO DR
8300 SCTS 85258 620-J4
S SAN RICARDO DR
10800 GDYR 85338 (773-H5 See Page 733)
S SAN ROBERTO DR
11200 GDYR 85338 (773-H6 See Page 733)
N SAN ROSENDO CT
9200 SCTS 85258 620-J4
E SAN ROSENDO DR
8300 SCTS 85258 620-J4
N SAN SALVADOR CT
- SURP 85374 534-G6
E SAN SALVADOR DR
8300 SCTS 85258 620-J4
9100 SCTS 85258 621-C4
N SAN SALVADOR DR
9300 SCTS 85258 621-D4
E SAN SEBASTIAN DR
8300 SCTS 85258 620-J4
E SAN SIMEON DR
9300 SCTS 85259 622-A4
E SAN SIMON DR
8300 SCTS 85258 620-J4
W SANTA ALBERTA LN
11200 GDYR 85338 (773-J6 See Page 733)
17400 GDYR 85338 (774-A5 See Page 733)
N SANTA ANNA
- MESA 85201 741-C3
N SANTA ANNA CT
1300 CHAN 85224 821-B1
S SANTA ANNA CT
2900 CHAN 85248 861-A5
N SANTA ANNA DR
3200 CHAN 85224 781-B6
S SANTA ANNA DR
- CHAN 85248 861-B3
N SANTA ANNA PL
900 CHAN 85224 821-B4
N SANTA ANNA ST
800 CHAN 85224 821-B4
S SANTA ANNA ST
2400 CHAN 85248 861-B2
S SANTA BARBARA
2500 MESA 85202 781-B4
S SANTA BARBARA DR
3000 MESA 85202 781-B5
N SANTA BARBARA ST
- MESA 85201 741-C3
S SANTA BARBARA ST
800 MESA 85202 741-B7
E SANTA CATALINA DR
7400 SCTS 85255 500-H6
10000 SCTS 85255 501-E7
E SANTA CATALINA RD
8500 SCTS 85255 501-B6
S SANTA COLUMBIA DR
10900 GDYR 85338 (773-H5 See Page 733)
E SANTA CRUZ DR
- GDYR 85338 695-A7
100 TEMP 85282 780-D1
2200 GIL 85234 782-J4
W SANTA CRUZ DR
300 TEMP 85282 780-B1
W SANTA CRUZ ST
- WICK 85390 290-E2
S SANTA ELIZABETH DR
9000 GDYR 85338 (774-D3 See Page 733)
N SANTA FE CIR
- WICK 85390 290-D2
W SANTA FE DR
600 WICK 85390 290-C2
9800 MarC 85351 576-A5
10700 MarC 85351 575-J5
12300 ELMG 85335 575-E4
12500 SURP 85374 575-D1
16300 GDYR 85338 (774-D3 See Page 733)
E SANTA FE LN
- GIL 85236 863-B3
S SANTA FE LN
10200 GDYR 85338 (773-J5 See Page 733)
10200 GDYR 85338 (774-A6 See Page 733)
E SANTA FE TR
10600 SCTS 85262 421-H3
N SANTA FE TR
- AVON 85323 695-D2
- AVON 85340 655-D7
- AVON 85340 695-D1
W SANTA FE TR
- AVON 85323 695-C3
E SANTA FIORE ST
- PinC 85242 905-D2
W SANTA IRENE DR
17900 GDYR 85338 (773-H5 See Page 733)
S SANTA MARGARITA LN
10700 GDYR 85338 (773-H5 See Page 733)
W SANTA MARIA CIR
9800 GDYR 85338 (774-D3 See Page 733)
W SANTA MARIA DR
10000 GDYR 85338 (774-D3 See Page 733)
E SANTA MARIA PL
14900 FTNH 85268 582-H4
N SANTA MARTA CIR
15000 FTNH 85268 582-J5
E SAN TAN BLVD
10300 MarC 85248 901-E5
15200 MarC 85249 902-G5
16400 MarC 85242 903-B5
19200 QC 85242 903-F5
19600 QC 85242 904-A6
20000 MarC 85242 904-A6
E SAN TAN CT
2000 GIL 85296 822-H3
E SAN TAN DR
2200 GIL 85296 822-F3
E SAN TAN ST
400 CHAN 85225 821-G5
1500 CHAN 85225 822-A5
W SAN TAN ST
- CHAN 85225 822-B5
500 CHAN 85224 821-C5
S SANTA RITA
- MESA 85212 784-F6
S SANTA RITA WY
- MarC 85249 902-D4
N SANTA ROSA CIR
1400 GIL 85234 782-J3
E SANTA ROSA DR
- GIL 85234 783-A4
- MarC 85234 783-A4
2200 GIL 85234 782-J4
E SANTA ROSA LN
17400 FTNH 85268 583-E6
E SANTA ROSA PL
4300 GIL 85236 783-E4
W SANTEE WY
13900 SURP 85374 535-A7
S SAN THOMAS CIR
9000 GDYR 85338 (774-D3 See Page 733)
S SAN THOMAS DR
9800 GDYR 85338 (774-D4 See Page 733)
N SANTIAGO
3700 MESA 85215 703-F3
N SANTIAGO CIR
3600 MESA 85215 703-F1
N SANTIAGO PL
15000 FTNH 85268 582-H5
N SANTIAGO ST
3600 MESA 85215 703-F3
W SANTOLINA
17100 SURP 85374 534-C6
N SAN TOMAS PL
15000 FTNH 85268 582-J4
E SAN VERBENA WY
500 MESA 85208 743-J7
E SAN VICENTE DR
8700 SCTS 85258 621-A4
E SAN VICTOR DR
- SCTS 85259 622-A4
8700 SCTS 85258 621-A4
N SAN VINCENTE DR
- CHAN 85225 821-G2
W SAN YSIDRO
15700 MarC 85375 494-F5
E SAPIUM WY
1300 PHX 85048 818-J5
2000 PHX 85048 819-A5
N SAPPHIRE
3600 MESA 85215 703-E3
N SAPPHIRE CIR
3400 MESA 85215 703-E4
S SAPPHIRE DR
- MarC 85249 902-G5
E SAPPHIRE LN
5300 PVAL 85253 620-B6
W SARABANDE CIR
10800 MarC 85351 575-J3
N SARABANDE WY
14200 MarC 85351 575-J4
E SARAGOSA CT
600 CHAN 85225 861-G1
S SARAGOSA CT
600 CHAN 85225 821-E7
600 CHAN 85225 861-E1
W SARAGOSA CT
5900 CHAN 85226 820-C7
E SARAGOSA ST
- CHAN 85225 861-F1
W SARAGOSA ST
100 CHAN 85225 861-F1
600 CHAN 85225 821-D7
1000 CHAN 85224 821-C7
3500 CHAN 85226 820-D7
E SARAH LN
- TEMP 85284 820-D2
W SARAH LN
- TEMP 85284 820-D2
E SARAH WY
- MarC 85296 862-D1
S SARANAC
2100 MESA 85208 783-F4
6100 MESA 85212 823-F7
S SARANAC AV
700 MESA 85208 743-G7
800 MESA 85208 783-G1
N SARANAC CIR
1800 MESA 85207 743-G1
S SARATOGA AV
2200 MESA 85202 781-A4
S SARATOGA CIR
3100 MESA 85202 781-A6
W SARATOGA CIR
10400 MarC 85351 576-A3
10600 MarC 85351 575-J3
E SARATOGA CT
300 GIL 85296 822-D2
E SARATOGA ST
400 GIL 85296 822-D2
2400 GIL 85236 822-H2
2400 GIL 85236 823-A2
N SARATOGA ST
2500 TEMP 85281 700-F6
N SARATOGA WY
20700 SURP 85374 534-F2
N SARAZEN CIR
10400 FTNH 85268 623-D3
E SARGENT DR
3600 MESA 85215 702-H4
N SARIVAL AV
- GDYR 85338 (694-D1 See Page 653)
2900 GDYR 85338 (654-D3 See Page 653)
5000 MarC 85340 (654-D3 See Page 653)
6000 MarC 85340 (614-D7 See Page 573)
7500 MarC 85355 (614-E4 See Page 573)
9000 MarC 85379 (614-E1 See Page 573)
10600 MarC 85379 (574-E2 See Page 573)
10600 SURP 85379 (614-E1 See Page 573)
13800 MarC 85374 (574-E2 See Page 573)
13800 SURP 85374 (574-E1 See Page 573)
13800 SURP 85379 (574-E2 See Page 573)
16400 SURP 85374 534-E7
22200 MarC 85375 494-E5
22200 SURP 85375 494-E5
S SARIVAL AV
600 GDYR 85338 (694-D7 See Page 653)
1500 GDYR 85338 (734-D2 See Page 733)
2400 MarC 85338 (734-D2 See Page 733)
20300 GDYR 85326 (854-C5 See Page 813)
E SAT NAM WY
- CVCK 85331 419-G7
5000 CVCK 85331 420-B7
W SATURN WY
4000 CHAN 85226 820-F6
E SAUSALITO CIR
2200 GIL 85234 782-J3
W SAVAGE ST
300 WICK 85390 290-E3
E SAVANNAH CIR
- MarC 85212 824-H4
S SAWGRASS CT
- CHAN 85249 902-A6
S SAWGRASS DR
- CHAN 85249 901-J4
6100 CHAN 85249 902-A4
E SAWIK CIR
16200 FTNH 85268 623-B2
E SAWMILL CIR
4900 CVCK 85331 460-B1
S SAWMILL RD
- GIL 85236 863-D2
N SAWTOOTH CIR
3700 MESA 85215 703-F3
N SAWYER
1400 MESA 85207 743-J2
S SAWYER
1000 MESA 85208 783-H1
6000 MESA 85212 823-H7
N SAWYER CIR
- MESA 85207 703-J5
S SAWYER CIR
2000 MESA 85208 783-H4
E SAXON DR
17300 FTNH 85268 623-E2
E SAYAN CIR
6000 MESA 85215 703-E3
E SAYAN ST
- MESA 85207 703-H3
- MESA 85207 704-A3
E SCAFELL CIR
6000 MESA 85215 703-E3
S SCALLOP DR
600 GIL 85233 821-J3
E SCARLET RD
- MarC 85207 704-D3
8300 MESA 85207 704-B3
N SCARLET CANYON DR
16300 SURP 85374 534-E5
W SCARLET KNIGHT LN
- SURP 85374 575-G1
E SCARLET SKY LN
- FTNH 85268 622-H4
N SCENIC CT
18400 MarC 85373 536-D6
SCENIC LP
- YavC - 250-A1
E SCENIC ST
600 APJT 85219 745-F5
4000 PinC 85219 746-A5
W SCENIC ST
2400 APJT 85220 745-B5
W SCHELL DR
2000 PHX 85023 538-D7
8600 PEOR 85382 536-F7
W SCHMIDT ST
6500 GLEN 85308 537-A7
S SCHNELL ST
- MarC 85337 (1090-E4 See Page 1049)
N SCHNEPF RD
38200 PinC 85242 905-F4
40700 PinC 85242 865-F6
N SCHOOL AV
50200 MarC 85320 (284-H4 See Page 244)
E SCHOOL DR
2200 PHX 85040 739-B6
N SCHOOL HOUSE RD
6400 CVCK 85331 420-E3
40200 CVCK 85331 (380-E6 See Page 339)
E SCHOONER CIR
1900 GIL 85234 782-H4
N SCHOONER DR
1500 GIL 85234 782-G3
N SCIARRO TR
- CVCK 85331 420-C6
S SCIENCE DR
2100 TEMP 85284 820-J2
E SCOPA TR
7200 CARE 85377 420-H3
10000 SCTS 85262 421-F3
N SCOPA TR
37800 CARE 85377 420-G4
E SCORPIO CT
- MarC 85249 902-C4
W SCORPIO DR
1000 TEMP 85283 780-B4
E SCORPIO PL
- CHAN 85249 901-G4
- MarC 85249 902-C4
E SCORPION DR
15500 FTNH 85268 583-A2
N SCORPION DR
16400 FTNH 85268 583-A3
W SCOTLAND AV
9100 PEOR 85345 576-D7
S SCOTLAND CT
- QC 85242 904-E1
E SCOTT AV
300 GIL 85234 782-D5
4400 GIL 85236 783-E5
N SCOTT AV
100 GBND 85337 (1090-A3 See Page 1049)
S SCOTT AV
- GBND 85337 (1090-B3 See Page 1049)
W SCOTT AV
- GIL 85233 781-J5
200 GIL 85233 782-B5
N SCOTT DR
- CHAN 85225 822-C5
S SCOTT DR
- CHAN 85249 902-C5
S SCOTT PL
- MarC 85249 902-C3
W SCOTTS DR
11800 ELMG 85335 575-E6
N SCOTTSDALE RD
- TEMP 85281 740-F1
300 TEMP 85281 700-F4
1000 SCTS 85257 700-F4
2300 SCTS 85281 700-F4
2900 SCTS 85251 700-F2
4100 SCTS 85251 660-F5
5000 SCTS 85250 660-F5
5000 SCTS 85253 660-F5
5100 PVAL 85253 660-F5
5200 PVAL 85250 660-F2
7000 SCTS 85258 660-F2
7400 SCTS 85258 620-F3
7800 PVAL 85253 620-F6
7800 SCTS 85253 620-F3
10400 SCTS 85254 620-F3
10400 SCTS 85260 620-F3
12200 SCTS 85260 580-F6
12500 PHX 85254 580-G6
12500 SCTS 85254 580-G6
15400 PHX 85260 580-G3
16900 PHX 85054 580-G3
17700 MarC 85054 540-G4
17700 PHX 85054 580-G3
17700 PHX 85255 540-G4
17700 PHX 85255 580-G3
18100 PHX 85054 540-G4
21000 SCTS 85255 540-G4
23400 PHX 85054 500-G4
23400 PHX 85255 500-G4
26600 PHX 85331 500-G4
26600 SCTS 85331 500-G4
26600 SCTS 85255 500-G4
28200 SCTS 85262 500-G4
29000 SCTS 85331 460-G4
29000 SCTS 85262 460-G4
E SCOTTSDALE MEMORIAL DR
- SCTS 85255 540-G4
W SCOTTY LN
22300 MarC 85361 (412-H7 See Page 411)
E SCOUT CAMP DR
- MarC 85263 503-G5
N SCOVEL ST
900 MarC 85281 740-G2
1000 TEMP 85281 740-G1
1400 TEMP 85281 700-G7
W SEA BASS CT
1200 GIL 85233 781-H7
N SEABORN LN
800 GIL 85234 782-G5
N SEA BREEZE AV
- SURP 85374 575-H1
E SEA BREEZE DR
1200 GIL 85234 782-F4
W SEA CREST DR
1200 GIL 85233 821-J1
W SEA FAN DR
1200 GIL 85233 821-J1
W SEA FOG DR
1100 GIL 85233 821-J2
W SEAGULL CT
- CHAN 85248 861-C3
E SEA GULL DR
1200 GIL 85234 782-F3
W SEAGULL DR
1000 CHAN 85248 861-D3
N SEA HAVEN DR
1000 GIL 85234 782-J4
W SEA HAZE DR
1400 GIL 85233 821-H2
E SEA HORSE LN
1200 GIL 85234 782-F4
N SEAN CT
1200 CHAN 85224 821-C3
3000 CHAN 85224 781-C7
S SEAN CT
800 CHAN 85224 861-C1
1400 CHAN 85248 861-C2
N SEAN DR
700 CHAN 85224 821-D1
3200 CHAN 85224 781-C6
S SEAN DR
100 CHAN 85224 821-C7
700 CHAN 85224 861-C1
2200 CHAN 85248 861-C1
W SEAN DR
1700 CHAN 85248 861-C3
N SEA PINES
1700 MESA 85205 743-F1
2500 MESA 85215 703-F4
N SEA PINES CIR
3300 MESA 85215 703-F4
W SEASCAPE DR
1200 GIL 85233 781-J7
W SEA SHELL DR
1200 GIL 85233 821-J1
W SEASHORE DR
1200 GIL 85233 821-J1
E SEASONS CIR
- GIL 85236 863-E4
E SEATTLE SLEW AV
600 GIL 85296 822-E1
S SEAWYNDS BLVD
400 GIL 85233 821-J1
E SEBASTIAN LN
- GIL 85236 863-C3
E SEBRING AV
- MarC 85212 824-H3
E SEBRING CIR
- MarC 85212 824-J3
E SECO PL
6200 CVCK 85331 420-E1
E SECOND WATER TR
- PinC 85219 826-H3
E SECRETARIAT DR
- TEMP 85284 780-D7
300 TEMP 85284 820-F1
S SECRETARIAT DR
7900 TEMP 85284 780-D7
W SECRETARIAT DR
- TEMP 85284 780-C7
E SECRET CANYON RD
- PinC 85219 826-J2
S SEDONA DR
25200 MarC 85248 901-B4
S SEELY ST
- PHX 85339 737-D6
E SEGOVIA DR
1000 LP 85340 655-C5
N SEGOVIA DR
900 LP 85340 655-C5
S SEGOVIA LN
4500 TEMP 85282 780-C2
W SEGOVIA LN
800 TEMP 85282 780-C2
E SEGUNDO DR
16300 FTNH 85268 623-B1
N SEGUNDO DR
34000 SCTS 85262 (461-D1 See Page 421)
E SEGURA AV
- MarC 85212 824-H3
E SELDON LN
800 PHX 85020 618-J5
1200 PHX 85020 619-A5
W SELDON LN
- PHX 85021 618-C5
2800 PHX 85051 618-B5
3400 PHX 85051 617-H5
4300 GLEN 85302 617-C5
6800 GLEN 85345 617-A5
7700 PEOR 85345 616-A4
10500 PEOR 85345 615-H5
W SELDON WY
1500 PHX 85021 618-D5
E SELKIRK CIR
6000 MESA 85215 703-E3
E SELLERS ST
- PHX 85040 739-D7
W SELLS CIR
5600 PHX 85031 657-D6
E SELLS DR
2200 PHX 85016 659-C6
3200 PHX 85018 659-F6
6600 SCTS 85251 660-E7
8500 SCTS 85251 661-A7
W SELLS DR
1300 PHX 85013 658-E6
3100 PHX 85017 658-A6
3300 PHX 85017 657-J6
5600 PHX 85031 657-C6
6900 PHX 85033 657-B6
8300 PHX 85037 656-F6
10700 PHX 85037 655-H6
W SELLS RD
4100 MarC 85340 653-F5
W SEMINOLE CT
2300 MarC 85087 (338-E3 See Page 337)
E SEMINOLE DR
- PHX 85022 578-H4
1000 PHX 85022 579-A4
W SEMINOLE DR
100 PHX 85023 578-G4
E SEMINOLE LN
16000 FTNH 85268 583-B6
E SENATE CIR
1200 CHAN 85225 821-H6
N SENATE PL
100 CHAN 85225 821-J6
N SENATE ST
- CHAN 85225 821-J4
S SENATE ST
- CHAN 85249 861-J2
- MarC 85249 901-H1
- CHAN 85225 821-J7
300 CHAN 85225 861-J2
6200 CHAN 85249 901-H5
N SENATE WY
100 CHAN 85225 821-J6
N SENDERO TRES
8300 PVAL 85253 620-D6
N SENECA CT
3100 CHAN 85224 781-D6
W SENECA DR
12500 MarC 85375 535-E6
W SENECA LN
15500 SURP 85374 534-G3
S SENECA WY
- MarC 85236 903-E3
E SENITA AV
7800 MESA 85208 743-J7
E SENITA CIR
6300 SCTS 85262 460-E2
N SENITA WY
- CVCK 85331 419-H7
E SENNA CT
- PinC 85219 786-F5
S SENNA WY
- CHAN 85248 861-E3
W SENTINAL DR
14400 MarC 85375 534-G1
E SENTINEL ROCK RD
5700 CARE 85377 420-D6
W SENTINEL ROCK RD
- PHX 85086 (418-C6 See Page 417)
E SEQUOIA DR
300 PHX 85024 538-J5
1000 PHX 85024 539-A5
2900 PHX 85050 539-E5
3200 PHX 85044 819-E1
S SEQUOIA DR
500 GIL 85296 822-J2
W SEQUOIA DR
- PEOR 85373 535-J4
- PEOR 85373 536-A4
- PHX 85027 538-D5
6000 GLEN 85308 537-C5
7500 GLEN 85308 536-F4
8600 PEOR 85382 536-E4
10600 MarC 85373 536-A7
10700 MarC 85373 535-J7
N SERENADE CIR
13300 MarC 85375 535-C2
W SERENADE CIR
13200 MarC 85375 535-C2
E SERENE ST
7800 CARE 85377 420-J4
8000 CARE 85377 421-A4
S SERENITY WY
23700 MarC 85248 901-B2
E SERENO DR
1700 GIL 85296 822-H2
W SERENO DR
400 GIL 85233 822-B2
N SERICIN
1000 MESA 85205 743-F3
2800 MESA 85215 703-G5
N SERICIN CIR
900 MESA 85205 743-G1
2600 MESA 85215 703-G6
N SERINA
- MESA 85205 743-C1
N SERINA CIR
1400 MESA 85205 743-C1
E SERRANA CT
- GIL 85236 863-C4
S SERRANO DR
200 LP 85340 655-A7
W SERRANO ST
- PHX 85037 656-D6
E SESAME ST
200 TEMP 85283 780-E4
W SESAME ST
500 TEMP 85283 780-C4
N SETON
800 MESA 85205 743-C1
S SETON
600 MESA 85206 743-C7
900 MESA 85206 783-C1
N SETON AV
- GIL 85234 783-B4
S SETON AV
- GIL 85236 863-B2
- MarC 85236 823-B7
S SETON CT
- GIL 85236 863-B5
E SETTLERS POINT DR
200 GIL 85296 822-E3
E SEVEN PALMS DR
- MarC 85331 460-C2
5200 CVCK 85331 460-C2
5200 PHX 85331 460-C2
5700 SCTS 85331 460-C2
E SEVEN PALMS WY
- SCTS 85262 (461-E2 See Page 421)
N SEVEN SPRINGS RD
- MarC 85331 (342-B3 See Page 341)
- MarC 85331 (382-B2 See Page 341)
43300 MarC 85262 (382-B2 See Page 341)
- MarC 85331 103-A1
N SEVILLA LN
25400 MarC 85263 503-J6
N SEVILLE BLVD
600 CHAN 85226 820-J4
S SEVILLE BLVD
- MarC 85236 903-E2
W SEVILLE BLVD
3100 CHAN 85226 820-J3
W SEVILLE DR
12800 MarC 85375 535-D3
N SEYMOUR
- MESA 85207 743-J4
S SEYMOUR
- MESA 85212 783-H6
N SHADOW CT
- SURP 85374 534-G6
N SHADOW LN
8600 GLEN 85345 617-A4
W SHADOW LN
2000 MESA 85201 741-C4
SHADOW CANYON DR
- FTNH 85268 582-G5
E SHADOW CASTER TR
- SCTS 85262 (381-F6 See Page 341)
N SHADOW CREEK CT
- MarC 85086 (378-D6 See Page 337)
N SHADOW CREEK WY
- MarC 85086 (378-E5 See Page 337)
W SHADOW GLEN CT
- MarC 85086 (378-D5 See Page 337)
N SHADOW GLEN WY
- MarC 85086 (378-E6 See Page 337)
W SHADOW GLEN WY
- MarC 85086 (378-E5 See Page 337)
W SHADOW HILLS DR
12500 MarC 85375 535-D5
N SHADOW MOUNTAIN DR
16000 SURP 85374 534-E3
E SHADOW MOUNTAIN RD
7300 PVAL 85253 660-A1
7500 PVAL 85253 620-A7
N SHADOW RIDGE TR
- FTNH 85268 622-J5
E SHADOW ROCK RD
4400 PHX 85028 619-J5
S SHADY CT
- GIL 85236 863-D3
E SHADY GLEN AV
7700 SCTS 85255 580-H1
W SHADY GLEN AV
1900 PHX 85023 538-D7
S SHAFER DR
1300 TEMP 85281 740-B5
3300 TEMP 85282 780-B1
9400 TEMP 85284 820-B3
SHAFFER LN
26600 SCTS 85255 500-J2
28200 SCTS 85262 500-J2
29000 SCTS 85262 460-J7
N SHAFFER LN
29000 SCTS 85262 460-J7
N SHAGBARK CT
15200 FTNH 85268 583-B4
E SHALLMO DR
- MarC 85255 (543-C2 See Page 503)
N SHAMROCK DR
21200 MarC 85375 535-B2
E SHAMROCK ST
- GIL 85296 822-F5
W SHAMROCK ST
- GIL 85233 822-C5
E SHANE AV
- PinC 85242 865-D5
N SHANGRI LA LN
44600 MarC 85087 (378-H2 See Page 337)
E SHANGRI LA RD
1000 PHX 85020 618-J1
1200 PHX 85020 619-A1
2300 PHX 85028 619-C1
4600 PHX 85028 620-B2
5200 PHX 85254 620-B2
9400 SCTS 85260 621-B2
10400 SCTS 85259 621-F2
12000 SCTS 85259 622-A2
W SHANGRI LA RD
1300 PHX 85029 618-A1
3400 PHX 85029 617-H1
4300 PHX 85304 617-G1
4700 GLEN 85304 617-B1
6700 PEOR 85345 617-A1
7100 PEOR 85345 616-G1
N SHANNON
900 MESA 85205 743-E3
N SHANNON CIR
900 MESA 85205 743-E3
S SHANNON CIR
6200 TEMP 85283 780-J5
E SHANNON CT
1000 GIL 85296 822-F4
W SHANNON CT
2500 CHAN 85224 821-A4
4700 CHAN 85226 820-B4
S SHANNON DR
1700 TEMP 85281 740-J6
2100 TEMP 85282 740-J6
3400 TEMP 85282 780-J1
8800 TEMP 85284 820-J2
W SHANNON PL
3200 CHAN 85226 820-J4
E SHANNON ST
- GIL 85236 822-J5
- GIL 85236 823-A5
- MarC 85236 823-D4
500 CHAN 85225 821-G4
1000 GIL 85296 822-F4
1800 CHAN 85225 822-A4
3900 PHX 85044 819-F4
13600 MarC 85296 822-D4
W SHANNON ST
100 CHAN 85225 821-D4
100 GIL 85233 822-B4
1400 CHAN 85224 821-A4
3400 CHAN 85226 820-A4
N SHANNON WY
2100 MESA 85215 703-E7
E SHARON AV
100 PHX 85022 578-H5
W SHARON AV
1600 PHX 85029 578-A5
3600 PHX 85029 577-H5
S SHARON CT
- CHAN 85249 902-C4
E SHARON DR
1400 PHX 85022 579-B5
3300 PHX 85032 579-J5
4800 PHX 85254 580-A5
8000 SCTS 85260 580-J6
8200 SCTS 85260 581-A6
W SHARON DR
- ELMG 85335 575-D5
- SURP 85374 (574-D2 See Page 573)
W SHARPSHOOTER LN
- PHX 85086 417-J7
N SHARPSHOOTER WY
- PHX 85086 417-J7
S SHASTA CT
12400 PHX 85044 819-G2
E SHASTA DR
- PinC 85219 826-G1
8800 PinC 85219 786-G7

PHOENIX

INDEX

STREET
Block City ZIP Pg-Grid

W SONNET DR
6800 GLEN 85308 537-B3
12300 MarC 85375 535-E3
W SONOMA DR
200 LP 85340 655-A5
E SONORA CIR
17300 MarC 85206 743-D7
S SONORA DR
4900 TEMP 85282 780-C3
E SONORA LN
10000 SCTS 85255 501-E7
N SONORA LN
21900 MarC 85375 534-G1
22400 MarC 85375 494-G7
E SONORA ST
5400 GUAD 85283 780-A4
S SONORA ST
1600 PHX 85007 738-D2
W SONORA ST
- GDYR 85338 (734-E1 See Page 733)
- PHX 85353 736-E1
1600 PHX 85007 738-D2
6300 PHX 85043 737-A1
N SONORA HILLS
- MESA 85207 703-G3
N SONORAN CT
20100 SURP 85374 534-E3
W SONORAN CT
11500 SURP 85374 535-H5
N SONORAN HTS
- MESA 85207 703-J3
E SONORAN TR
- SCTS 85262 460-G4
5900 SCTS 85331 460-D2
E SONORAN WY
8200 PinC 85219 786-F6
17100 FTNH 85268 623-D5
E SONORAN HIGHLANDS DR
10300 SCTS 85255 501-F7
E SONRISA AV
- MarC 85212 824-H3
N SOPHIE BURDEN DR
300 MarC 85390 290-F1
N SOPHORA DR
34900 CARE 85377 420-D7
E SORENSEN ST
800 MESA 85203 702-A6
E SORREL LN
9400 SCTS 85259 622-A4
11000 SCTS 85258 621-G4
11200 SCTS 85259 621-H4
E SORREL TR
8400 SCTS 85255 501-A5
S SORRELL LN
400 GIL 85296 822-J1
S SORRELLE
- MESA 85212 784-E4
E SORRELWOOD CT
7700 SCTS 85258 620-H7
N SOSSAMAN RD
- MarC 85207 743-J4
- MESA 85207 743-J4
1500 MarC 85207 703-J7
35000 PinC 85242 903-H7
35000 QC 85242 903-H7
S SOSSAMAN RD
- MESA 85207 743-J7
- MESA 85208 743-J7
800 MESA 85208 783-J2
2500 MESA 85212 783-H7
5800 MESA 85212 823-G5
10000 MarC 85212 783-H7
10800 MESA 85212 823-H2
17200 MarC 85236 863-H3
17200 MESA 85236 863-H3
17200 MarC 85242 863-H3
17200 MESA 85242 863-H3
18800 QC 85236 863-H6
18800 QC 85242 863-H3
22800 QC 85236 903-H4
22800 QC 85242 903-H4
25200 MarC 85242 903-H4
N SOURDOUGH PL
16800 FTNH 85268 582-J2
W SOUSA CT
- MarC 85086 (378-A7 See Page 337)
W SOUSA DR
- MarC 85086 (378-B7 See Page 337)
E SOUTH AV
400 BUCK 85326 (772-A2 See Page 731)
W SOUTH RD
500 WICK 85390 290-D3
W SOUTHAMPTON RD
- SURP 85374 534-D7
SOUTH DAKOTA
5900 PinC 85219 786-D7
7000 PinC 85219 826-D1
E SOUTHERN AV
- APJT 85220 785-E2
- MESA 85210 781-H1
- PHX 85040 738-H7
- PHX 85041 738-H7
- TEMP 85282 780-D1
300 APJT 85219 785-E2
400 MESA 85204 781-H1
600 MESA 85204 782-C1
1100 PinC 85219 785-E2
1400 PHX 85040 739-A7
2100 TEMP 85282 781-A1
2600 MESA 85202 781-A1
3200 APJT 85219 786-C2
3600 MESA 85206 782-F1
3600 PHX 85040 779-H1
4200 MESA 85206 783-A1
4800 PinC 85219 786-C2
6800 MESA 85208 783-G1
7800 MESA 85208 784-A2
8500 MarC 85208 784-F2
10000 MESA 85208 784-F2
10800 MarC 85220 784-F2
22900 MarC 85220 785-E2
22900 MESA 85220 785-E2
W SOUTHERN AV
- APJT 85220 785-C2
- PHX 85041 738-C7
- TEMP 85282 780-B1
- MESA 85210 781-F1
300 MarC 85339 737-B7
300 PHX 85339 737-B7
1200 MESA 85202 781-C1
1500 PinC 85220 785-C2
1800 TEMP 85282 779-J1
2600 PHX 85040 779-J1
2700 MarC 85041 737-G7
2700 MarC 85041 738-C7

STREET
Block City ZIP Pg-Grid

W SOUTHERN AV
2700 PHX 85041 737-G7
6700 MarC 85339 736-H7
6700 PHX 85339 736-H7
9700 MarC 85353 736-A7
10300 MarC 85353 735-F6
10700 AVON 85353 735-F6
12200 MarC 85323 735-F6
13000 MarC 85338 735-F6
17700 GDYR 85326 733-G6
17700 MarC 85326 733-G6
18700 BUCK 85326 733-G6
21900 BUCK 85326 (732-H6 See Page 731)
21900 MarC 85326 (732-H6 See Page 731)
25100 MarC 85326 731-A5
25100 BUCK 85326 731-H5
E SOUTHERN LN
- AVON - 735-B1
SOUTHERN CSR
- MarC - 663-D7
- MarC - 702-G4
- MarC - 703-C1
- MESA - 702-G4
- MESA - 703-C1
W SOUTHERN HILLS RD
- PHX 85023 578-G5
E SOUTHERN PACIFIC DR
800 PHX 85034 698-H7
E SOUTH FORK DR
- PHX 85048 818-F5
1700 PHX 85048 819-A5
3500 PHX 85044 819-G5
W SOUTH FORK DR
1400 PHX 85045 818-D6
E SOUTHGATE AV
- PHX 85040 738-G5
- PHX 85041 738-G5
2500 PHX 85040 739-C5
W SOUTHGATE AV
- PHX 85043 736-G4
- PHX 85041 738-E5
N SOUTHGATE DR
- CHAN 85226 819-J5
S SOUTHGATE DR
100 CHAN 85226 819-J6
W SOUTHGATE ST
- PHX 85043 737-B4
SOUTH MOUNTAIN AV
8300 PHX 85040 779-C3
E SOUTH MOUNTAIN AV
- PHX 85040 778-H3
1600 PHX 85040 779-B3
W SOUTH MOUNTAIN AV
- PHX 85041 778-B3
1200 PHX 85339 777-C3
2700 MarC 85041 778-B3
2700 MarC 85339 778-B3
4500 MarC 85339 777-E3
N SOUTH PARK AV
- MESA 85208 784-B1
N SOUTH PARK RD
- PEOR 85342 (375-J5 See Page 335)
- PEOR 85342 (376-A6 See Page 335)
E SOUTHSHORE DR
900 TEMP 85283 780-F4
W SOUTHSHORE DR
- WICK 85390 289-H3
S SOUTHWIND CT
1700 GIL 85296 822-F5
N SOUTHWIND DR
100 GIL 85234 782-F7
S SOUTHWIND DR
1500 GIL 85296 822-F4
E SOUTHWIND LN
9300 SCTS 85262 501-D1
S SOUTHWIND ST
- GIL 85296 822-F6
SPAD ST
- GLEN 85309 655-A1
W SPAD ST
14100 GLEN 85309 (654-J1 See Page 653)
E SPANISH BARB TR
8600 SCTS 85258 621-A3
E SPANISH BOOT LN
8100 CARE 85377 421-A2
E SPANISH BOOT RD
8100 CARE 85377 421-A2
N SPANISH BOOT RD
37800 CARE 85377 421-B1
N SPANISH GARDEN DR
18400 MarC 85375 535-B5
W SPANISH GARDEN DR
12900 MarC 85375 535-C6
W SPANISH MOSS CT
9800 MarC 85373 536-B6
E SPANISH MOSS LN
800 PHX 85022 538-J6
W SPANISH MOSS LN
9300 MarC 85373 536-B6
E SPANISH OAKS DR
7700 SCTS 85258 620-H7
N SPANISH SPRINGS DR
400 CHAN 85226 820-C5
E SPARKLING LN
4300 MarC 85253 659-H1
4600 PVAL 85253 619-J7
4600 PVAL 85253 659-J1
N SPARROW DR
1000 GIL 85236 783-F4
W SPARROW DR
1000 CHAN 85248 861-C4
N SPARROW LN
11600 FTNH 85268 623-D2
S SPARTAN CT
1700 GIL 85233 822-C5
W SPARTAN CT
11100 MarC 85351 575-H3
S SPARTAN ST
1200 GIL 85233 822-C3
16000 MarC 85225 822-C7
E SPAULDING CIR
- MarC 85212 824-J4
E SPEER TR
800 MarC 85086 419-A2
E SPENCE AV
900 TEMP 85281 740-F5
N SPENCER
- MESA 85203 742-B1
S SPENCER
100 MESA 85204 742-B5
1300 MESA 85204 782-A2
N SPENCER CIR
500 MESA 85203 742-B4

STREET
Block City ZIP Pg-Grid

W SPENCER DR
- SURP 85374 534-A5
N SPENCER ST
1600 MESA 85203 742-B1
S SPINNAKER RD
5600 TEMP 85283 780-G4
N SPIRE CT
1200 CHAN 85224 820-J3
1400 CHAN 85224 821-A3
N SPIRE DR
1100 CHAN 85224 820-J4
W SPIRIT DR
- MarC 85086 (378-B6 See Page 337)
W SPIRIT LN
- MarC 85086 (378-A6 See Page 337)
S SPLENDOR CT
- GIL 85236 863-D4
S SPLENDOR PL
- GIL 85236 863-D4
E SPORTS DR
- MarC 85236 903-E3
N SPOTTED HORSE LN
11600 FTNH 85268 622-H2
N SPRING
400 MESA 85203 741-J1
N SPRING CIR
1700 MESA 85203 701-J7
1700 MESA 85203 741-J1
W SPRING DR
10700 GDYR 85338 (773-H5 See Page 733)
E SPRING LN
- GIL 85236 863-D4
4300 MarC 85253 619-H7
4300 MarC 85253 659-H1
E SPRING RD
- PHX 85032 579-D4
5700 PHX 85254 580-C5
N SPRING ST
1500 MESA 85203 741-J1
2000 MESA 85203 701-J7
W SPRING CANYON WY
16300 SURP 85374 534-E4
E SPRING CREEK RD
10200 MarC 85248 901-D5
E SPRINGCREEK RD
10800 MarC 85248 901-E4
S SPRINGCREEK RD
25400 MarC 85248 901-E5
W SPRINGDALE DR
13600 MarC 85375 535-B2
N SPRINGFIELD DR
14200 FTNH 85268 583-B6
19800 MarC 85373 536-A4
W SPRINGFIELD DR
400 GIL 85233 782-B7
E SPRINGFIELD PL
2200 CHAN 85249 862-A1
N SPRINGFIELD WY
14400 FTNH 85268 583-B5
W SPRINGFIELD WY
1500 CHAN 85248 861-B1
N SPRING MEADOW DR
13500 MarC 85375 535-C3
W SPRING RIDGE DR
12400 MarC 85375 535-E2
S SPRINGS CT
6600 CHAN 85249 901-H6
S SPRINGS DR
- MarC 85249 901-H1
200 CHAN 85225 821-H7
6500 CHAN 85249 901-H5
S SPRINGS PL
- CHAN 85249 901-H5
W SPRING TREE WY
15700 SURP 85374 534-F5
S SPRINGWOOD BLVD
- MESA 85212 784-H4
S SPRUCE
1800 MESA 85210 781-E3
S SPRUCE AV
2200 MESA 85210 781-E3
W SPRUCE AV
1100 MESA 85210 781-D3
1200 MESA 85202 781-D3
N SPRUCE CIR
1300 MESA 85203 741-J2
1500 MESA 85201 741-E1
E SPRUCE DR
- CHAN 85249 862-A2
W SPRUCE DR
1300 CHAN 85248 861-B2
9900 MarC 85351 576-C3
S SPRUCE ST
32500 MarC 85361 (452-J1 See Page 411)
W SPRUCE ST
1700 PHX 85007 698-D5
22700 BUCK 85326 (692-E3 See Page 651)
23100 MarC 85326 (692-F3 See Page 651)
N SPUR
17100 SURP 85374 534-B7
S SPUR
400 MESA 85204 742-B6
900 MESA 85204 782-B1
W SPUR
- SURP 85374 534-B7
300 GIL 85233 822-B1
E SPUR AV
- GIL 85296 822-D1
W SPUR AV
- MarC 85233 821-J1
- MarC 85233 822-A1
800 GIL 85233 822-A1
N SPUR CIR
- SCTS 85251 700-C1
800 MESA 85203 742-B3
S SPUR CIR
600 MESA 85204 742-B7
E SPUR CT
1500 GIL 85296 822-G1
W SPUR CT
- MarC 85233 822-A1
E SPUR DR
400 GIL 85296 822-D1
3900 PHX 85085 499-H3
3900 PHX 85331 499-H3
4700 PHX 85331 500-A3
W SPUR DR
- PHX 85085 497-C3
- PHX 85085 498-B3
E SPUR RD
14400 MarC 85249 862-E7
W SPUR RD
20200 MarC 85326 (852-J4 See Page 811)

STREET
Block City ZIP Pg-Grid

W SPUR RD
20200 MarC 85326 (853-A4 See Page 813)
E SPUR ST
1600 GIL 85296 822-G1
W SPUR ST
400 GIL 85233 822-A1
N SPUR CROSS RD
- MarC 85331 (340-E5 See Page 339)
38400 CVCK 85331 420-D1
40200 CVCK 85331 (380-D6 See Page 339)
42200 MarC 85331 (380-D3 See Page 339)
S SPUR TRAIL CT
- PinC 85219 826-H2
E SPYGLASS DR
1500 CHAN 85249 901-J5
S SPYGLASS RD
5600 TEMP 85283 780-F4
E SQUAWBUSH PL
1100 PHX 85048 818-H4
2600 PHX 85048 819-C4
3400 PHX 85044 819-E4
E SQUAW PEAK CIR
3000 PHX 85016 659-E2
E SQUAW PEAK DR
2200 PHX 85020 659-D1
2200 PHX 85016 659-D2
SQUAW PEAK FRWY Rt#-51
- PHX - 659-B7
- PHX - 699-B3
SQUAW PEAK HWY Rt#-51
- PHX 85020 619-C5
- PHX 85020 659-A6
- PHX 85028 579-F4
- PHX 85028 619-F2
- PHX 85032 539-G6
- PHX 85032 579-F4
- PHX 85050 539-G6
4300 PHX 85016 659-A6
N SQUIRE AV
2000 TEMP 85281 700-E7
SR 101 FRONT
1800 PHX 85308 537-F4
2700 PHX 85027 538-A4
3600 PHX 85308 538-A4
5100 GLEN 85308 537-A4
6900 GLEN 85308 536-J4
SR 202 ACCESS
- TEMP 85281 740-C2
SR 202 FRONT
- PHX 85034 740-C2
- TEMP 85034 740-C2
600 TEMP 85281 740-C2
E STABLE CT
- GIL 85236 863-D5
E STACEY LN
100 TEMP 85284 820-D3
W STACEY LN
- TEMP 85284 820-A3
E STACEY RD
16400 MarC 85242 903-A6
N STACIE CT
600 CHAN 85226 820-A4
N STACIE WY
800 CHAN 85226 820-B4
N STACY LYNN LN
- PHX 85331 499-J2
N STADEM DR
900 TEMP 85281 740-G1
S STADIUM DR
300 TEMP 85281 740-E3
W STADIUM WY
- PEOR 85382 576-G2
W STAGECOACH CT
9700 MarC 85382 536-C4
E STAGECOACH PASS
5000 CVCK 85331 420-B6
5900 CARE 85377 420-D6
6800 CARE 85377 460-F1
8000 CARE 85262 420-H6
8000 SCTS 85262 420-H6
8000 SCTS 85262 421-E6
8000 SCTS 85377 421-B6
8900 CARE 85377 421-B6
8900 CARE 85262 421-A6
10300 MarC 85262 421-E6
N STAGECOACH RD
700 APJT 85219 745-H5
S STAGECOACH RD
1000 APJT 85219 745-H7
1200 APJT 85219 785-H1
N STAGECOACH RUN
- WICK 85390 290-A2
E STAGECOACH PASS AV
- PinC 85242 905-F6
E STAGHORN CIR
9500 SCTS 85255 501-D4
STAGHORN DR
- FTNH 85268 582-H6
E STAGHORN LN
- SCTS 85262 421-B7
1700 CARE 85377 420-J7
E STAGHORN RD
6200 PHX 85251 660-D6
N STALLION
17200 SURP 85374 534-C6
S STALLION DR
- GIL 85236 863-D4
E STALLION RD
6400 PVAL 85253 620-E7
E STAMPEDE DR
- GIL 85236 863-D4
E STANCREST DR
16200 FTNH 85268 583-B6
N STANDAGE
- MESA 85201 741-D3
S STANDAGE
400 MESA 85202 741-D6
S STANDAGE CIR
1700 MESA 85202 781-D2
S STANDAGE RD
2800 MESA 85202 781-D5
S STANDAGE ST
2200 MESA 85202 781-D3
E STANDING STONES RD
- SCTS 85262 421-G5
E STANFORD AV
- GIL 85234 783-B5
- MarC 85234 783-B5
400 GIL 85234 782-D5
3600 GIL 85236 783-C5
W STANFORD AV
400 GIL 85233 782-A5

STREET
Block City ZIP Pg-Grid

W STANFORD AV
1600 GIL 85233 781-H4
E STANFORD CT
- GIL 85234 783-C5
E STANFORD DR
2000 TEMP 85283 780-J3
3200 PVAL 85253 659-G4
4000 PHX 85018 659-G4
W STANFORD DR
200 GIL 85233 782-C5
N STANLEY PL
200 CHAN 85226 820-F3
1200 CHAN 85284 820-F3
9600 TEMP 85284 820-F3
S STANLEY PL
700 CHAN 85226 820-F7
1000 TEMP 85281 740-F4
2100 TEMP 85282 740-F6
3100 TEMP 85282 780-F1
5800 TEMP 85283 780-F4
7800 TEMP 85284 780-F5
8500 TEMP 85284 820-F2
W STANLEY A GOFF DR
8700 TOL 85353 696-E5
E STANLEY THOMPSON LN
8800 SCTS 85262 421-C2
E STANTON AV
- MarC 85212 824-H4
N STAPLEY DR
- MESA 85203 742-B3
1800 MESA 85203 702-B7
2300 MarC 85203 702-B5
4700 MarC 85256 662-B4
S STAPLEY DR
- MESA 85204 742-B7
900 MESA 85204 782-B2
S STAR CT
- GDYR 85338 (774-A5 See Page 733)
N STARBOARD DR
- GIL 85234 782-F7
S STAR CANYON DR
- GIL 85236 863-E5
E STARCREST CT
- MarC 85248 900-J2
S STARCREST DR
24000 MarC 85248 900-J3
N STARDUST BLVD
19600 MarC 85375 534-J4
20600 MarC 85375 535-A3
W STARDUST BLVD
12700 MarC 85375 535-C2
N STARDUST CIR
9400 FTNH 85268 623-D5
E STARDUST DR
- FTNH 85268 622-J1
N STARDUST LN
36200 CARE 85377 421-D5
S STARDUST LN
200 APJT 85220 745-B6
1800 APJT 85220 785-B1
STARFIGHTER ST
- GLEN 85309 655-A1
E STARFIRE AV
- MarC 85212 824-H4
W STARFISH DR
1300 GIL 85233 781-J7
E STARFLOWER CT
- MarC 85249 901-F6
11000 MarC 85248 901-F6
E STARFLOWER DR
10700 MarC 85248 901-E6
N STAR GAZE TR
- FTNH 85268 623-B4
S STARK RD
- APJT 85219 785-H2
E STARKEY AV
- MarC 85212 824-H3
E STARLA DR
7200 SCTS 85255 500-G7
S STARLEY DR
700 TEMP 85281 740-B4
S STARLIGHT DR
10000 PHX 85041 778-D6
W STARLIGHT DR
15900 SURP 85374 534-E3
N STARLIGHT LN
- WICK 85390 289-J2
- WICK 85390 290-A2
E STARLIGHT WY
5700 PVAL 85253 660-C4
7800 SCTS 85250 660-H4
8600 SCTS 85250 661-A4
E STARLING CIR
- SCTS 85255 501-D5
N STARLING CT
- GIL 85236 783-E6
N STARLING DR
900 GIL 85236 783-F5
N STARLING LN
8500 PHX 85028 619-J5
E STAR OF THE DESERT DR
10300 SCTS 85259 581-E3
10300 SCTS 85260 581-E3
N STARR RD
100 APJT 85219 745-H3
S STARR RD
- APJT 85219 745-H7
1200 APJT 85219 785-H2
2400 PinC 85219 785-H2
N STAR RIDGE DR
19000 MarC 85375 535-C4
W STAR RIDGE DR
13000 MarC 85375 535-D3
N STARRY PASS CIR
- MESA 85207 703-J2
W STARRY SKY DR
16200 SURP 85374 534-E5
E STAR VALLEY ST
5900 MESA 85215 703-E3
W STAR VIEW LN
15700 SURP 85374 534-F7
W STARWARD CT
1000 GIL 85233 821-J2
E STATE AV
- PHX 85020 618-H7
1300 PHX 85020 619-A7
2100 PHX 85020 659-C1
W STATE AV
- GLEN 85303 616-F7
- MarC 85303 616-G7
- PHX 85021 618-D7
2500 PHX 85051 618-A7
3300 PHX 85051 617-G7
4300 GLEN 85301 617-A7
6700 GLEN 85303 617-A7
15900 MarC 85340 (614-E6 See Page 573)

STREET
Block City ZIP Pg-Grid

W STATLER BLVD
- SURP 85374 575-C1
W STATLER ST
- SURP 85374 (574-C1 See Page 573)
12500 SURP 85374 575-E1
E STEAMBOAT BEND DR
1200 TEMP 85283 780-F3
E STEARN AV
- MarC 85212 824-H3
N STEELE
- MESA 85207 744-C2
W STEINBECK CT
- MarC 85086 (378-A6 See Page 337)
W STEINBECK DR
- MarC 85086 (378-B6 See Page 337)
STEINWAY DR
- PHX 85041 778-C5
N STEINWAY DR
50600 MarC 85390 290-A5
50700 WICK 85390 290-A5
W STEINWAY DR
1700 PHX 85041 778-D5
4600 MarC 85339 777-E5
W STELLA AV
4900 GLEN 85301 657-E2
6200 GLEN 85305 656-E2
7900 GLEN 85303 656-F2
E STELLA LN
400 PHX 85012 658-H2
700 PHX 85014 658-H2
1800 PHX 85016 659-B2
3800 PVAL 85253 659-G2
5900 PVAL 85253 660-C3
8300 SCTS 85250 660-J3
W STELLA LN
- PHX 85013 658-E2
1600 PHX 85015 658-C2
2900 PHX 85017 658-A2
3400 PHX 85017 657-J2
3500 PHX 85019 657-G2
5900 GLEN 85301 657-B2
13500 MarC 85340 655-A1
N STELLAR PKWY
- CHAN 85226 820-F6
S STELLAR PKWY
- CHAN 85226 860-F1
- CHAN 85226 820-F7
S STEPHANIE LN
7800 TEMP 85284 780-C7
8000 TEMP 85284 820-C1
S STEPHEN MATHER DR
- PHX 85041 818-D1
10200 PHX 85041 778-E7
E STEPHENS DR
800 TEMP 85283 780-E6
W STEPHENS DR
1000 TEMP 85283 780-B6
E STEPHENS PL
2200 CHAN 85225 822-A6
W STEPHENS PL
100 CHAN 85225 821-F5
3100 CHAN 85226 820-H5
E STEPHENS RD
2000 GIL 85296 822-H1
E STEPHENS ST
- GIL 85236 822-J1
N STERLING
1200 MESA 85207 743-H1
S STERLING
2000 MESA 85208 783-H4
5500 MESA 85212 823-G6
6400 MESA 85212 863-G1
S STERLING CIR
2000 MESA 85208 783-H3
N STERLING DR
15600 SURP 85374 534-F5
W STERLING PL
600 CHAN 85225 781-E6
N STERLING ST
- MESA 85207 703-J6
E STERLING WY
16800 FTNH 85268 583-D5
E STERLING RIDGE RD
- SCTS 85262 (381-E6 See Page 341)
E STETSON DR
7100 SCTS 85251 660-F7
W STETSON DR
800 GIL 85233 822-A1
W STETSON HILLS LP
- PHX 85310 497-H4
W STEVENAGE ST
- SURP 85374 534-D6
N STEVENS CIR
1900 MESA 85205 702-J7
E STEVENS RD
6900 CVCK 85331 420-G2
7000 CARE 85377 420-H3
S STEWART CIR
3100 MESA 85202 781-D6
N STEWART ST
- MESA 85201 741-D3
S STEWART ST
400 MESA 85202 741-D6
1000 MESA 85202 781-D1
E STEWART VISTA AV
16600 FTNH 85268 583-C7
16700 FTNH 85268 623-D1
N STILLWATER DR
21100 MarC 85375 535-B2
N STILTON
- MarC 85220 744-G5
S STILTON
- MESA 85220 784-G1
W STINSON DR
- SURP 85374 534-B6
S STINSON WY
2200 CHAN 85249 861-J4
N STIRRUP DR
- WICK 85390 289-H2
N STIRRUP LN
37800 CARE 85377 421-B4
E STIRRUP ST
- QC 85242 864-D6
S STOCKADE CT
- GIL 85236 863-D4
W STOCKMAN RD
6900 GLEN 85308 537-A6
N STOCKTON PL
2100 MESA 85215 703-D7
W STONE ST
8300 PEOR 85345 616-F1
E STONEBRIDGE CIR
200 GIL 85234 782-D6
E STONEBRIDGE DR
200 GIL 85234 782-D6

STREET
Block City ZIP Pg-Grid

N STONEBROOK DR
18200 MarC 85375 535-C6
W STONEBROOK DR
13300 MarC 85375 535-C6
E STONE CIRCLE LN
- PinC 85219 826-H3
E STONECLIFF CIR
- MESA 85207 704-A2
E STONECLIFF ST
- MESA 85207 704-A2
N STONECREEK BLVD
300 GIL 85234 782-G6
S STONECREEK BLVD
- GIL 85296 782-G7
100 GIL 85296 822-G1
N STONECREEK ST
800 GIL 85234 782-G5
E STONE CUTTER DR
- SCTS 85262 (381-F6 See Page 341)
E STONEGATE CIR
9800 SCTS 85259 621-H4
N STONEGATE DR
13800 MarC 85375 535-B3
N STONE GULLY
- MESA 85207 703-J4
- MESA 85207 704-A4
N STONE GULLY CIR
- MESA 85207 704-A3
N STONEHAVEN DR
- SCTS 85262 421-G4
N STONE HAVEN DR
15500 SURP 85374 534-F7
E STONEHEDGE RANCH RD
55600 MarC 85390 250-F7
55600 MarC 85390 290-F1
N STONEHENGE DR
1400 GIL 85233 782-B3
N STONEMARK DR
3000 MarC 85086 (378-B4 See Page 337)
N STONE PEAK CIR
- MESA 85207 704-A3
N STONE POINT CIR
- MESA 85207 704-B3
E STONE RAVEN TR
34200 SCTS 85262 460-G1
N STONERIDGE CT
16800 FTNH 85268 583-A2
W STONEWALL CT
- MarC 85086 (378-E5 See Page 337)
W STONEWALL DR
- MarC 85086 (378-E5 See Page 337)
E STONEY LN
10700 SCTS 85262 (381-G7 See Page 341)
10700 SCTS 85262 421-G1
S STONEY LAKE CT
- MarC 85248 901-D3
S STONEY LAKE DR
24600 MarC 85248 901-C2
S STONEY PATH DR
24600 MarC 85248 901-D2
S STONEY VISTA CT
- MarC 85248 900-J4
E STONEY VISTA DR
- MarC 85248 900-J4
10200 MarC 85248 901-A4
E STOTTLER CT
- GIL 85236 823-A3
2000 GIL 85296 822-F3
W STOTTLER CT
1400 CHAN 85224 821-C2
E STOTTLER DR
400 GIL 85296 822-D3
2500 GIL 85236 822-J3
2500 GIL 85236 823-A3
W STOTTLER DR
700 CHAN 85225 821-E2
1000 CHAN 85224 821-B2
E STOTTLER PL
600 CHAN 85225 821-H2
W STOTTLER PL
600 GIL 85233 822-A2
N STOUT RD
100 GBND 85337 (1090-D1 See Page 1049)
52400 GBND 85337 (1050-D7 See Page 1049)
S STOUT RD
49200 GBND 85337 (1050-D5 See Page 1049)
49200 MarC 85337 (1050-D5 See Page 1049)
E STOUT ST
100 GBND 85337 (1090-B2 See Page 1049)
W STOUT ST
200 GBND 85337 (1090-A2 See Page 1049)
W STOWE CT
- MarC 85086 (378-C6 See Page 337)
W STRAFORD AV
- GIL 85233 782-A6
1200 GIL 85233 781-J6
W STRAFORD CIR
2800 CHAN 85224 781-A6
2800 CHAN 85224 780-J6
N STRAFORD CT
3400 CHAN 85224 781-A6
W STRAFORD DR
400 CHAN 85225 781-E6
1200 CHAN 85224 781-A6
2900 CHAN 85224 780-J6
E STRAHAN DR
200 TEMP 85283 780-E5
5000 PHX 85044 779-J5
W STRAHAN DR
600 TEMP 85283 780-C5
W STRAIGHT ARROW LN
- PHX 85085 497-D2
- PHX 85085 498-C2
N STRAIGHT BAR DR
- SCTS 85255 541-D4
N STRATFORD CIR
15000 FTNH 85268 583-C5
W STRATFORD DR
2000 CHAN 85224 781-B6
S STRATTON LN
1100 TEMP 85281 740-H5
N STRATUS LN
- SURP 85374 534-G4
E STRAWBERRY DR
- GIL 85236 863-D5

STREET
Block City ZIP Pg-Grid

STREET A
- SCTS 85262 (381-F6
See Page 341)
STREET B
- SCTS 85262 (381-F7
See Page 341)
STREET C
- SCTS 85262 (381-F7
See Page 341)
STREET D
- SCTS 85262 (381-F7
See Page 341)
STREET E
- SCTS 85262 (381-F6
See Page 341)
STREET F
- SCTS 85262 (381-F7
See Page 341)
W STRIKE EAGLE ST
14300 MarC 85340 (654-H2
See Page 653)
S STRIKE-IT-RICH DR
4600 PinC 85219 786-H5
S STUART CT
- GIL 85236 823-A5
S STUART PKWY
- GIL 85236 823-A6
E STURRIP LN
18400 MarC 85263 503-H5
N SUBURBAN AV
41800 PinC 85242 865-C5
S SUGARBERRY LN
- GIL 85236 863-F5
W SUGAR BUSH WY
15700 SURP 85374 534-F3
E SUGAR CREEK AV
11000 PinC 85219 826-J1
E SUGARLOAF CIR
- MESA 85207 703-G3
- MESA 85207 704-A3
6700 MESA 85215 703-G3
E SUGARLOAF ST
- MESA 85207 703-J3
- MESA 85207 704-A3
6400 MESA 85215 703-F3
E SUGARLOAF TR
5500 CVCK 85331 420-D3
E SULKY CIR
8200 SCTS 85255 501-A5
N SULLEY DR
400 GIL 85234 782-H5
N SULLEYS CIR
700 MESA 85205 742-J3
N SULLEYS DR
- MESA 85205 742-J4
E SULLIVAN DR
16300 FTNH 85268 623-C2
S SULLIVAN ST
- WICK 85390 290-F2
S SUMAC AV
1800 BUCK 85326 (692-C7
See Page 651)
1800 BUCK 85326 (732-C1
See Page 731)
N SUMAC DR
12400 FTNH 85268 623-A1
12600 FTNH 85268 583-A7
N SUMMER CIR
1700 MESA 85203 701-J7
1700 MESA 85203 741-J1
S SUMMER CT
- GIL 85236 863-D3
W SUMMER DR
10700 GDYR 85338 (773-H5
See Page 733)
S SUMMER LN
- GIL 85236 863-D3
N SUMMER ST
2000 MESA 85203 701-J7
N SUMMERBREEZE WY
- SURP 85374 534-H5
E SUMMERHAVEN DR
3600 PHX 85044 819-E3
N SUMMER HILL BLVD
- FTNH 85256 622-G4
- FTNH 85268 622-G4
- MarC 85256 622-G4
- MarC 85268 622-G4
E SUMMER MOON LN
5000 PHX 85044 819-J1
W SUMMER RAINBOW LN
- SURP 85374 575-G1
E SUMMERSET CIR
5000 CVCK 85331 460-B1
W SUMMERSET CIR
300 PHX 85023 578-G2
11000 MarC 85351 575-J2
W SUMMERSIDE RD
800 PHX 85041 778-E5
N SUMMERSTAR DR
18400 MarC 85375 535-A5
W SUMMERSTAR DR
13700 MarC 85375 535-A5
14400 MarC 85375 534-J5
N SUMMER SUNSHINE AV
- MarC 85335 575-H1
- SURP 85335 575-H1
- SURP 85374 575-H1
W SUMMERWALK DR
21000 SURP 85374 534-F2
W SUMMERWIND LN
- SURP 85374 534-G4
E SUMMIT CV
- CVCK 85331 420-D6
E SUMMIT DR
- SCTS 85255 501-E3
- SCTS 85268 582-G7
- SCTS 85268 622-H1
11800 SCTS 85259 622-A1
N SUMMIT DR
- CVCK 85331 420-D6
- SCTS 85268 622-H1
S SUMMIT DR
- SCTS 85268 622-H2
W SUMMIT DR
17100 GDYR 85338 (774-A5
See Page 733)
W SUMMIT PL
500 CHAN 85225 781-E6
1000 CHAN 85248 781-A6
S SUMMIT RD
- PHX 85040 778-H7
E SUMMIT VIEW TR
38700 CARE 85377 420-H2
SUMMIT WALK CT
- PHX 85086 (377-J4
See Page 337)
W SUMMIT WALK CT
- MarC 85086 (378-B4
See Page 337)
- MarC 85087 (378-B4
See Page 337)
N SUN RD
900 PinC 85219 746-B1
S SUN RD
- PinC 85219 746-B7
N SUNAIRE
2500 MESA 85215 703-G4
N SUNAIRE CIR
1800 MESA 85205 743-G1
3000 MESA 85215 703-G5
N SUNAIRE DR
- MarC 85205 743-G5
- MESA 85205 743-G5
S SUNAIRE DR
- MESA 85206 743-G6
W SUNBELT DR
- SURP 85374 534-A6
E SUNBIRD BLVD
1600 CHAN 85249 901-J4
1800 CHAN 85249 902-A5
S SUNBROOK DR
- MarC 85248 901-B3
N SUNBURST
10900 SURP 85374 534-D4
N SUNBURST CIR
12400 FTNH 85268 622-H1
E SUNBURST CT
- MarC 85248 901-A2
E SUNBURST DR
9400 MarC 85248 901-B3
13600 SCTS 85259 622-H1
15200 FTNH 85268 622-H1
15500 FTNH 85268 623-A2
E SUNBURST LN
400 TEMP 85284 780-D7
W SUN CITY BLVD
9800 MarC 85351 616-A1
10600 MarC 85351 615-J1
10700 MarC 85351 575-J7
W SUN COAST DR
800 GIL 85233 822-A2
E SUNCREST CT
3300 PHX 85044 819-E2
23900 MarC 85248 901-B3
N SUNCREST CT
18800 MarC 85375 535-A5
E SUNDANCE AV
- GIL 85236 863-D4
E SUNDANCE CT
- GIL 85236 863-E3
E SUNDANCE DR
9100 SCTS 85262 421-C4
W SUNDANCE DR
7300 PEOR 85345 616-J1
W SUN DANCE DR
7700 PinC 85242 904-A7
8600 PinC 85242 903-H7
8800 QC 85242 903-H7
E SUNDANCE TR
900 CARE 85377 420-H4
9400 SCTS 85262 421-E4
E SUNDANCE WY
15500 FTNH 85268 622-J2
15500 FTNH 85268 623-A2
N SUNDANCE WY
20200 SURP 85374 534-E3
W SUNDERLAND AV
- PHX 85033 656-J7
N SUNDIAL
1600 MESA 85205 743-E1
SUNDIAL CIR
- CARE 85377 420-H4
S SUNDIAL DR
- GIL 85233 781-J7
E SUNDOWN CIR
5800 SCTS 85250 660-G4
N SUNDOWN CT
17600 SURP 85374 534-F6
E SUNDOWN DR
- FTNH 85268 582-J5
- FTNH 85268 583-A5
N SUNDOWN DR
5800 SCTS 85250 660-G4
10600 SCTS 85260 620-H2
S SUNDOWN DR
6200 CHAN 85249 901-J4
S SUNDOWN LN
3100 PinC 85219 786-H3
N SUNDRIFT CT
- SURP 85374 534-G5
E SUNDUNE DR
9400 MarC 85248 901-B2
S SUNDUNE DR
- MarC 85248 901-A3
S SUNDUST CIR
100 MarC 85339 817-E7
W SUNDUST CIR
100 MarC 85339 817-E7
E SUNDUST RD
5600 MarC 85226 860-A2
N SUNFISH DR
- GIL 85233 782-A7
S SUNFISH DR
300 GIL 85233 822-A1
300 MarC 85233 822-A1
W SUNFLOWER AV
600 WICK 85390 290-D1
N SUNFLOWER CIR
600 CHAN 85226 820-D5
E SUNFLOWER CT
7400 SCTS 85262 460-H1
S SUNFLOWER CT
- CHAN 85226 820-C6
E SUNFLOWER DR
15600 FTNH 85268 583-A6
W SUNFLOWER PL
- AVON 85323 656-A7
3500 AVON 85323 655-H7
N SUNGLOW DR
20800 MarC 85375 535-D2
S SUN GROVES BLVD
- MarC 85249 902-F4
E SUN LAKES BLVD
8900 MarC 85248 900-J5
9000 MarC 85248 901-A4
S SUN LAKES BLVD
7400 MarC 85248 901-A3
E SUNLAND AV
- MarC 85220 784-J1
- MarC 85220 785-A1
- MESA 85220 785-A1
- PHX 85040 738-G7
- PHX 85041 738-G7
1600 PHX 85040 739-A7
8800 MarC 85208 784-C1
9300 MESA 85208 784-B1
E SUNLAND AV
10800 MESA 85220 784-H1
W SUNLAND AV
- MarC 85043 736-F6
- PHX 85039 737-D6
- PHX 85041 738-C7
3600 PHX 85041 737-H7
8300 PHX 85353 736-D6
11300 MarC 85353 735-G6
11500 MarC 85323 735-C6
13100 MarC 85338 735-C6
S SUNLAND CT
- CHAN 85248 861-F5
24000 MarC 85248 901-B3
N SUNLAND DR
600 CHAN 85225 821-F5
S SUNLAND DR
- CHAN 85248 861-F4
- CHAN 85248 901-E3
W SUNLAND DR
- MarC 85351 576-A2
11000 MarC 85351 575-J2
N SUNLAND DR E
600 CHAN 85225 821-F5
N SUNLAND DR W
600 CHAN 85225 821-F5
W SUN MEADOWS AV
6400 CHAN 85226 820-B5
N SUN MEADOWS CT
800 CHAN 85226 820-B4
E SUNMESA CT
9500 MarC 85248 901-B2
N SUNNY LN
15400 SURP 85374 575-D2
W SUNNY COVE
HEIGHTS RD
500 WICK 85390 290-D3
E SUNNYDALE CT
11000 MarC 85248 901-F6
E SUNNYDALE DR
10400 MarC 85248 901-D6
W SUNNYSIDE CIR
- ELMG 85335 575-D7
E SUNNYSIDE DR
1400 PHX 85020 619-A1
2200 PHX 85028 619-C1
4800 PHX 85032 620-A1
4800 PHX 85254 620-A1
6000 SCTS 85254 620-D1
7200 SCTS 85260 620-G1
8500 SCTS 85260 621-A1
10400 SCTS 85259 621-F1
12700 SCTS 85259 622-B1
N SUNNYSIDE DR
11600 PHX 85028 619-H1
S SUNNYSIDE DR
- MarC 85248 901-D3
W SUNNYSIDE DR
- ELMG 85335 575-E7
1600 PHX 85029 618-D1
2100 PHX 85029 578-A7
3600 PHX 85029 577-H7
3800 PHX 85029 617-J1
4300 PHX 85304 577-F7
5000 GLEN 85304 577-B7
6700 PEOR 85345 577-A7
7100 PEOR 85345 576-J7
E SUNNYSIDE LN
3200 PHX 85032 579-F4
E SUNNYSIDE PL
11100 SCTS 85259 621-H1
E SUNNYSLOPE LN
- PHX 85020 618-G4
1200 PHX 85020 619-A4
9900 SCTS 85258 621-D4
N SUNNYSLOPE LN
9600 PEOR 85345 617-A3
W SUNNYSLOPE LN
- PHX 85021 618-E4
4400 GLEN 85302 617-B3
6900 PEOR 85345 617-A3
7000 PEOR 85345 616-C3
N SUNNYVALE
- MESA 85206 783-C2
900 MESA 85205 743-C2
S SUNNYVALE
400 MESA 85206 743-C7
900 MESA 85206 783-C1
N SUNNYVALE AV
- GIL 85234 783-C5
S SUNNYVALE AV
- GIL 85236 863-C3
- MarC 85236 823-B7
- MarC 85236 903-B2
- MESA 85206 783-C3
N SUNNYVALE CIR
- MESA 85206 783-C2
S SUNNYVALE CT
- MarC 85236 903-B2
E SUNNYVALE DR
- SCTS 85258 620-G5
E SUNNYVALE RD
6600 PVAL 85253 620-F5
N SUNNYVALE ST
1200 MESA 85205 743-D2
W SUN PRAIRIE CT
16100 SURP 85374 534-E7
W SUN PRAIRIE LN
17200 SURP 85374 534-E7
N SUNRAY CT
18400 SURP 85374 534-F5
E SUNRIDGE DR
9400 MarC 85248 901-B3
N SUNRIDGE DR
12800 FTNH 85268 582-H6
N SUNRIDGE LN
3300 CHAN 85225 781-E6
N SUNRISE
- MESA 85207 703-G6
- MESA 85207 743-G5
S SUNRISE
2500 MESA 85208 783-F5
N SUNRISE BLVD
17000 SURP 85374 534-F4
W SUNRISE BLVD
300 GIL 85233 781-H6
E SUNRISE CIR
9400 CARE 85377 421-D5
N SUNRISE CIR
1800 MESA 85207 743-G1
9800 FTNH 85268 623-D4
E SUNRISE DR
- MarC 85263 (504-A4
See Page 503)
4200 PHX 85044 779-G6
S SUNRISE DR
- TEMP 85282 779-J1
500 GIL 85233 822-A1
W SUNRISE DR
- GDYR 85326 (773-H4
See Page 733)
- GDYR 85338 (773-H4
See Page 733)
1500 PHX 85041 778-B6
2700 MarC 85041 778-A6
2700 MarC 85339 778-A6
4000 MarC 85339 777-E5
24300 MarC 85326 (772-A4
See Page 731)
E SUNRISE LN
- MarC 85236 903-C3
W SUNRISE PL
1100 CHAN 85248 861-D6
W SUNRISE TR
1000 WICK 85390 290-C3
E SUNRISE WY
1000 GIL 85296 822-G3
E SUNRISE SKY DR
- PinC 85219 826-F1
N SUNRISE SPRINGS
WY
- SCTS 85255 541-D4
E SUNSCAPE DR
- FTNH 85268 583-E7
- FTNH 85268 623-E1
N SUNSCAPE DR
- FTNH 85268 583-E7
S SUNSET AV
- MarC 85236 903-C2
W SUNSET BAY
1000 GIL 85233 822-A2
W SUNSET CIR
400 MESA 85201 741-G1
S SUNSET CT
- MarC 85236 903-C2
800 CHAN 85225 861-E1
W SUNSET CT
1000 GIL 85233 822-C3
1300 GIL 85233 821-J1
E SUNSET DR
4400 PHX 85028 619-J5
6400 MESA 85205 743-F1
N SUNSET DR
200 CHAN 85225 821-E2
700 TEMP 85281 740-F1
700 TEMP 85281 700-F6
2200 MESA 85215 703-G7
14100 FTNH 85268 582-J6
S SUNSET DR
- CHAN 85248 821-E3
- MESA 85206 743-F5
1300 TEMP 85281 740-F5
10600 GDYR 85338 (773-H5
See Page 733)
W SUNSET DR
300 WICK 85390 290-E3
2500 MarC 85087 (338-D4
See Page 337)
W SUNSET DR W
4000 PHX 85033 657-B7
S SUNSET LN
- MarC 85236 903-C3
N SUNSET PL
1500 CHAN 85225 821-E3
N SUNSET RD
- PinC 85219 746-C2
S SUNSET RD
- PinC 85219 746-C7
N SUNSET TR
17400 SURP 85374 535-B7
34600 CARE 85377 420-E7
34600 CARE 85377 460-E1
36600 CVCK 85331 420-E4
W SUNSET TR
1200 WICK 85390 290-B2
N SUNSET CLOSE
12500 SCTS 85259 581-F7
E SUNSET RIDGE CIR
6800 SCTS 85262 460-F3
N SUNSET RIDGE WY
9300 FTNH 85268 622-H5
E SUNSET SKY CIR
6800 SCTS 85262 460-F2
E SUNSET SKY DR
- PinC 85219 826-F1
W SUNSHINE DR
22300 MarC 85361 (412-H7
See Page 411)
E SUNSHINE WY
- CARE 85377 420-H4
N SUN SHORE DR
1200 GIL 85234 782-J4
S SUN SHORE DR
1100 GIL 85296 822-J3
N SUNSTONE DR
13800 MarC 85351 576-D5
W SUNSTONE LN
- SURP 85374 534-F5
N SUNVALLEY BLVD
100 MESA 85207 743-H3
N SUN VALLEY DR
9800 MarC 85351 576-C4
11400 MarC 85351 616-C1
W SUN VALLEY LN
11700 MarC 85373 535-G3
N SUN VALLEY PKWY
300 MarC 85326 102-B2
300 BUCK 85326 102-B2
700 BUCK 85373 102-B2
1400 MarC 85373 102-B2
17000 BUCK 85390 102-B2
W SUN VALLEY PKWY
17800 SURP 85374 534-A7
18300 SURP 85374 533-D5
19100 MarC 85374 533-C5
21100 MarC 85387 533-A4
21100 SURP 85387 533-A4
17800 SURP 85374 102-B2
19100 MarC 85374 102-B2
21100 MarC 85387 102-B2
21100 SURP 85387 102-B2
25000 BUCK 85387 102-B2
27400 BUCK 85390 102-B2
N SUNVIEW
- MESA 85205 703-E5
- MESA 85215 703-E5
900 MESA 85205 743-D1
N SUN VIEW PKWY
200 GIL 85234 782-D4
N SUNVIEW ST
1400 GIL 85234 782-D4
N SUN VILLAGE PKWY
13900 SURP 85374 535-A7
W SUN VILLAGE PKWY
13900 SURP 85374 535-A6
S SUNVISTA DR
23900 MarC 85248 901-B3
W SUNWARD DR
900 GIL 85233 822-A2
N SUNWAY DR
- GIL 85233 781-H5
S SUNWOOD CIR
500 MESA 85204 742-G7
W SUPAI DR
- GDYR 85338 (734-E1
See Page 733)
N SUPAI WY
3400 SCTS 85251 700-E2
E SUPERIOR AV
3600 PHX 85040 739-F4
W SUPERIOR AV
- GDYR 85338 (734-D3
See Page 733)
- PHX 85353 735-J3
- PHX 85353 736-A3
4900 PHX 85043 737-A3
W SUPER SABRE ST
14700 GLEN 85340 (654-F3
See Page 653)
14700 GLEN 85309 (654-F3
See Page 653)
15300 MarC 85340 (654-F3
See Page 653)
E SUPERSTITION BLVD
- APJT 85219 745-G5
3100 APJT 85219 746-B5
3100 PinC 85219 746-B5
N SUPERSTITION BLVD
200 CHAN 85225 821-J5
900 CHAN 85225 822-A4
W SUPERSTITION BLVD
300 APJT 85220 745-C5
E SUPERSTITION DR
20000 QC 85242 864-B4
W SUPERSTITION DR
16300 GDYR 85326 (854-B1
See Page 813)
17300 GDYR 85326 (853-J1
See Page 813)
SUPERSTITION FRWY
U.S.-60
- APJT - 785-A3
- APJT - 786-A3
- MarC - 784-F3
- MarC - 785-A3
- MESA - 781-C2
- MESA - 782-C1
- MESA - 783-C2
- MESA - 784-B2
- PinC - 785-A3
- TEMP - 780-C2
- TEMP - 781-C2
E SUPERSTITION LN
9500 SCTS 85262 (461-E1
See Page 421)
N SUPERSTITION LN
5800 PVAL 85253 660-B4
W SUPERSTITION WY
- SURP 85374 534-F6
S SUPERSTITION
MOUNTAIN DR
- APJT 85219 786-D6
- PinC 85219 786-F3
E SUPERSTITION
RANGE RD
- PinC 85219 826-H2
E SUPERSTITION
SPRINGS BLVD
6200 MESA 85206 783-F3
6800 MESA 85208 783-F3
SUPERSTITION
SPRINGS MALL CIR
1100 MESA 85206 783-F2
E SUPERSTITION
VIEW DR
- PinC 85219 746-D7
S SURF DR
500 GIL 85233 822-A2
N SURFSIDE DR
500 GIL 85233 782-A6
S SURFSIDE DR
- GIL 85233 782-A7
300 GIL 85233 822-A1
N SURPRISE FARMS DR
- SURP 85374 534-C7
- SURP 85374 (574-B1
See Page 573)
S SURPRISE FARMS DR
- SURP 85374 (574-C2
See Page 573)
E SURREY AV
- PHX 85022 578-H6
2800 PHX 85032 579-E6
4800 PHX 85254 580-A6
8800 SCTS 85260 581-B6
W SURREY AV
- ELMG 85335 575-D5
- PHX 85029 578-A6
3700 PHX 85029 577-H6
5100 GLEN 85304 577-B6
6700 MarC 85381 577-A6
6900 PEOR 85381 577-A6
7000 PEOR 85381 576-F5
W SURREY CIR
13000 PHX 85029 578-F6
E SURREY DR
5600 CVCK 85331 420-D5
E SUSAN LN
400 TEMP 85281 700-E7
N SUSSEX PL
14000 FTNH 85268 583-C6
E SUTHERLAND WY
9300 SCTS 85262 501-D1
W SUTTER LN
- MarC 85086 (378-B6
See Page 337)
W SUTTERS GOLD LN
10100 MarC 85351 576-B2
E SUTTON AV
3500 PHX 85032 579-F6
E SUTTON DR
7200 SCTS 85260 580-G6
8400 SCTS 85260 581-A6
N SUTTON DR
13300 SCTS 85260 581-E6
S SWALLOW CT
- MarC 85236 823-D4
W SWALLOW DR
12300 MarC 85375 535-F3
N SWALLOW LN
- MarC 85236 783-D6
600 GIL 85236 783-D5
S SWALLOW LN
- MarC 85236 823-D4
W SWAN CT
- CHAN 85248 861-C3
N SWAN DR
600 GIL 85236 783-E5
W SWAN DR
1000 CHAN 85248 861-D3
E SWEET ACACIA DR
8000 PinC 85219 786-F6
10000 SCTS 85255 501-E5
S SWEET BUSH LN
- PinC 85219 786-E4
E SWEETWATER AV
- SCTS 85268 582-G7
1800 PHX 85022 579-D6
2400 PHX 85032 579-D6
4800 PHX 85254 580-B6
4800 PHX 85032 580-B6
7200 SCTS 85254 580-F7
7200 SCTS 85260 580-F7
8400 SCTS 85260 581-A7
10400 SCTS 85259 581-H7
13600 SCTS 85259 582-E7
W SWEETWATER AV
- ELMG 85335 575-D5
200 PHX 85029 578-A6
3500 PHX 85029 577-G6
4100 PHX 85304 577-G6
5100 GLEN 85304 577-B6
6700 MarC 85381 577-B6
7100 PEOR 85381 576-F6
7100 PEOR 85381 577-B6
N SWEETWATER BAY DR
900 GIL 85234 782-G5
E SWILLING AV
100 WICK 85390 290-E2
E SWILLING RD
4400 PHX 85050 540-A2
4400 PHX 85050 539-J2
21700 PHX 85054 540-A2
S SYCAMORE
1600 MESA 85202 781-C2
N SYCAMORE CT
600 CHAN 85224 821-C3
W SYCAMORE CT
16000 SURP 85374 534-E6
E SYCAMORE DR
- GIL 85236 863-E6
15400 FTNH 85268 582-J7
15400 FTNH 85268 622-J1
15400 FTNH 85268 623-A1
N SYCAMORE DR
11600 FTNH 85268 623-A2
S SYCAMORE DR
1600 BUCK 85326 (692-C7
See Page 651)
1800 BUCK 85326 (732-C1
See Page 731)
E SYCAMORE LN
- GIL 85236 863-B3
N SYCAMORE PL
700 CHAN 85224 821-C3
3000 CHAN 85224 781-C7
3400 CHAN 85225 781-C7
S SYCAMORE PL
100 CHAN 85224 821-C7
700 CHAN 85224 861-C2
1500 CHAN 85248 861-C2
W SYCAMORE PL
800 CHAN 85225 781-D6
N SYCAMORE ST
- MESA 85201 741-C3
- MESA 85202 741-C5
S SYCAMORE ST
- MESA 85202 741-C5
1100 MESA 85202 781-C1
E SYLVAN AV
- MarC 85212 824-J3
W SYLVAN LN
200 WICK 85390 290-F3
S SYLVAN ST
200 WICK 85390 290-F3
W SYLVIA LN
- MarC 85390 290-B2
E SYLVIA ST
2200 PHX 85022 579-C7
2300 PHX 85032 579-D7
5600 PHX 85254 580-C7
N SYMER DR
- PHX 85331 460-A2

T

N TABASCO CIR
15800 FTNH 85268 582-H3
N TABOR
4200 MESA 85215 703-G2
N TABOR ST
3700 MESA 85215 703-G3
E TACONY DR
15500 FTNH 85268 622-J1
15500 FTNH 85268 623-A1
W TAD LN
15200 SURP 85374 534-G7
E TAFT AV
21600 MarC 85361 (452-J2
See Page 411)
21600 MarC 85361 (453-A2
See Page 413)
E TAHITIAN WY
1100 GIL 85234 782-J4
N TAHITIAN WY
1100 GIL 85234 782-J4
E TAHOE AV
7100 MESA 85212 823-G6
E TAILFEATHER DR
- SCTS 85255 541-A3
7200 SCTS 85255 540-H4
E TAILSPIN LN
7400 SCTS 85255 540-H4
8200 SCTS 85255 541-A5
TAINTER DR
200 LP 85340 655-A6
W TALARA WY
16200 SURP 85374 534-E3
N TALAVI BLVD
16600 GLEN 85306 577-E1
W TALAVI BLVD
5500 GLEN 85306 577-D1
S TALAVI LN
11200 PHX 85044 779-H7
N TALBOT CIR
1700 MESA 85208 784-E3
E TALIESIN DR
11000 SCTS 85259 621-G1
N TALIESIN DR
- SCTS 85259 621-G1
12800 SCTS 85259 581-G7
W TALISMAN RD
- MarC 85351 575-J3
10100 MarC 85351 576-A3
E TALLY HO DR
5900 CVCK 85331 420-D5
E TALON AV
7000 MESA 85212 823-G5
E TALON DR
- SCTS 85255 541-A5
N TALON TR
9500 FTNH 85268 622-G4
E TALOWA ST
3800 PHX 85044 819-F1
N TAMANAR DR
5000 PVAL 85253 660-E5
E TAMAR RD
1600 MarC 85086 419-C3
N TAMARACK LN
15000 FTNH 85268 583-C5
W TAMARAK LN
16200 SURP 85374 534-E4
W TAMARISK AV
1900 PHX 85041 738-D6
3500 PHX 85041 737-H5
7100 MarC 85043 736-H5
N TAMARISK CT
- CHAN 85224 821-B4
S TAMARISK DR
- CHAN 85248 861-A2
E TAMARISK ST
900 APJT 85219 745-F6
1700 PHX 85040 739-A6
N TAMARISK ST
600 CHAN 85224 821-B1
2600 CHAN 85224 781-A7
W TAMARISK ST
- PHX 85041 738-D6
- PHX 85040 738-E6
E TAMARISK WY
10500 SCTS 85262 (381-H6
See Page 341)
S TAMARRON WY
1300 CHAN 85249 901-J6
E TAMAYA ST
4000 PHX 85044 779-F7
E TAMBLO DR
5100 PHX 85044 819-J1
N TAMBOR
- MESA 85220 744-J4
S TAMBOR
- MarC 85212 824-H1
- MESA 85212 784-H7
- MESA 85212 824-J1
S TAMBOR CIR
- MarC 85212 824-H3
N TAMBOR PL
- MarC 85220 784-J1
11200 MESA 85220 784-J1
W TAMI LN
12300 SURP 85374 575-E1
S TAMMARON WY
- CHAN 85249 901-H5
E TAM O SHANTER DR
- PHX 85022 578-H5
W TAM O SHANTER DR
200 PHX 85023 578-G5
E TANDEM DR
5900 CVCK 85331 420-D5
S TANGELO AV
25200 MarC 85242 903-D6
W TANGELO DR
12900 MarC 85375 535-D2
N TANGERINE AV
3000 PHX 85018 700-C2
5800 SCTS 85018 700-C2
N TANGERINE DR
- CHAN 85226 820-E4
S TANGERINE DR
100 CHAN 85226 820-E7
800 CHAN 85226 860-E1
S TANGERINE LN
- GIL 85236 863-E6
W TANGERINE LN
- PHX 85051 617-J4
3300 PHX 85051 618-A4
N TANGLE RIDGE CT
- MarC 85086 (378-D5
See Page 337)
E TANGLEWOOD CIR
5000 CVCK 85331 460-B1
N TANGLEWOOD CIR
20300 MarC 85375 534-H3
N TANGLEWOOD CT
15000 FTNH 85268 583-B5
E TANGLEWOOD DR
1300 PHX 85048 818-J6
3100 PHX 85048 819-D6
N TANGLEWOOD DR
20400 MarC 85375 534-H3
S TANGLEWOOD DR
5000 CHAN 85248 901-E3
E TANGLEWOOD TR
- MarC 85085 (458-H1
See Page 417)
N TANGLEWOOD TR
33800 MarC 85331 460-A1
33800 PHX 85331 460-A1
W TANGRINE LN
6800 GLEN 85345 617-A4
S TANINA ST
200 GIL 85296 822-J1
E TANNERY CT
- GIL 85236 863-D5
E TANNERY RD
- GIL 85236 863-E5
E TANO CT
3600 PHX 85044 819-E2
E TANO ST
3800 PHX 85044 819-F2
N TANQUE VERDE CT
1600 CHAN 85224 821-A3
N TAN TARA DR
10200 MarC 85351 576-B4
N TAN TARA PT
13600 MarC 85351 576-A5
E TANYA RD
100 MarC 85086 (418-J2
See Page 417)
900 MarC 85086 419-A2
6600 CVCK 85331 420-F2
E TANYA TR
700 MarC 85086 (418-J2
See Page 417)
700 MarC 85086 419-A2
E TAOS DR
9500 SCTS 85262 421-D3
E TAPADERO DR
- SCTS 85255 541-C4
E TAPATIO DR
1100 PHX 85020 618-J2
1100 PHX 85020 619-A2
W TAPATIO DR
16200 SURP 85374 534-E3
E TAPATITO DR
10700 PHX 85020 618-J2

PHOENIX

INDEX

STREET
Block City ZIP Pg-Grid

W TOREADOR DR
12400 MarC 85375 535-E2
TORNASOL CIR
900 LP 85340 655-C5
S TORNILLO LN
- PinC 85219 786-D5
TORNO LN
900 LP 85340 655-C4
N TORO CT
23200 MarC 85375 495-A6
W TORONTO WY
- PHX 85043 736-J2
S TORRE MOLINOS CIR
1600 TEMP 85281 740-J5
S TORRENCE
500 MESA 85208 744-B7
TORREON DR E
900 LP 85340 655-C5
W TORREY PINES CIR
4900 PHX 85308 537-F7
E TORREY PINES LN
- MarC 85249 902-D4
1300 CHAN 85249 901-H4
1700 CHAN 85249 902-A4
E TORREY PINES PL
- CHAN 85249 902-A4
E TORREY POINT CIR
- MESA 85207 703-G1
E TORREY POINT ST
- MESA 85207 703-J2
W TORTOISE CT
11500 SURP 85374 535-H4
N TOTEM DR
21000 MarC 85375 535-D2
N TOURNAMENT DR
22000 MarC 85375 535-A1
23000 MarC 85375 495-B7
S TOURNAMENT LN
6200 CHAN 85249 901-J4
N TOVREA DR
5700 MarC 85340 (654-J2 See Page 653)
6500 GLEN 85309 (654-J1 See Page 653)
N TOWER AV
400 CHAN 85225 822-A3
S TOWER AV
- CHAN 85249 862-A1
- MarC 85249 901-J1
N TOWER CT
300 CHAN 85225 822-A6
N TOWER DR
11800 FTNH 85268 623-E1
N TOWER PL
700 CHAN 85225 822-A5
S TOWER PL
- CHAN 85249 862-A2
N TOWER RD
5900 BUCK 85373 (652-J1 See Page 651)
5900 BUCK 85373 653-B3
20700 BUCK 85340 653-B3
S TOWERS ST
6700 TEMP 85283 780-B5
E TOWN AND COUNTRY LN
1400 PHX 85014 659-A2
E TOWNE LN
4200 GIL 85236 783-E5
W TOWNELY AV
- GLEN 85302 617-B4
E TOWNLEY AV
- PHX 85020 618-H4
1300 PHX 85020 619-A4
W TOWNLEY AV
- GLEN 85345 617-A4
300 PHX 85021 618-C4
2900 PHX 85051 618-B4
3500 PHX 85051 617-H4
4200 PHX 85051 617-G4
4400 GLEN 85302 617-B4
8500 PEOR 85345 616-E4
11200 PEOR 85345 615-H4
W TOWNLEY CT
- MarC 85355 (613-G3 See Page 573)
E TRACY LN
2400 PHX 85032 579-D3
W TRACY LN
2000 PHX 85023 578-D3
E TRADEWIND DR
1200 GIL 85234 782-F7
W TRADING POST DR
14400 MarC 85375 535-A4
14400 MarC 85375 534-J3
W TRADITIONS LN
- SURP 85374 534-A6
N TRADITIONS LOOP RD
17300 SURP 85374 534-A6
TRADITIONS LOOP RD E
- SURP 85374 534-A5
W TRAFALGAR AV
8100 PHX 85033 656-F7
E TRAIL DR
9000 CARE 85377 421-C5
E TRAILBLAZER DR
4400 PHX 85050 540-A2
21500 PHX 85054 540-A2
N TRAIL BOSS
18100 SURP 85374 534-C5
N TRAIL HEAD
- CVCK 85331 419-H3
E TRAILHEAD CT
- PinC 85219 826-H3
E TRAILRIDGE CIR
- MESA 85207 703-G2
4100 MESA 85215 703-F2
E TRAILRIDGE DR
4000 MESA 85215 703-F2
N TRAIL RIDGE DR
19400 MarC 85375 535-A4
W TRAIL RIDGE DR
13900 MarC 85375 535-A3
W TRAILS DR
7100 GLEN 85308 536-J3
7100 GLEN 85308 537-A3
N TRAILS END
26400 MarC 85263 503-H5
E TRAILS END DR
- SCTS 85255 541-C4
E TRAILS END PL
1000 CHAN 85225 821-H6
N TRANQUIL TR
37000 CARE 85377 420-J4
E TRANQUILITY WY
9600 MarC 85248 901-B2
N TRANQUILO LN
27800 MarC 85263 503-H3

E TRANQUILO WY
18400 MarC 85263 503-H3
N TRAVIS
- MESA 85207 704-E6
N TRAVIS CIR
- MESA 85207 704-E7
E TRAVOIS TR
7400 CARE 85377 420-H3
E TREASURE CV
1300 GIL 85234 782-G4
E TREASURE PL
9700 PinC 85219 786-H5
N TREE LINED TR
36400 CARE 85377 421-D5
E TREMAINE AV
100 GIL 85234 782-E5
3800 GIL 85236 783-D6
W TREMAINE AV
800 GIL 85233 782-A5
1100 GIL 85233 781-J6
E TREMAINE CT
- MarC 85236 783-F6
3600 GIL 85236 783-C6
E TREMAINE DR
- CHAN 85225 781-G5
- CHAN 85233 781-G5
16400 GIL 85234 783-B6
16800 MarC 85234 783-B6
W TREMAINE DR
1900 GIL 85233 781-G5
E TREMAINE ST
4000 GIL 85236 783-D5
E TRENT AV
7000 MESA 85212 823-G6
N TRENTON
- MESA 85207 704-E7
W TRES HOMBRES CT
16400 SURP 85374 534-D6
E TREVINO DR
15800 FTNH 85268 623-C4
S TREVINO DR
26600 MarC 85248 900-J6
W TREVINO DR
- GDYR 85338 (654-H7 See Page 653)
- GDYR 85338 (694-H1 See Page 653)
N TREVINO PL
2400 MESA 85215 703-D6
N TREVOR
1600 MESA 85201 701-F7
1600 MESA 85201 741-F1
N TRIBUTARY WY
19100 SURP 85374 534-F4
W TRIGGER
17200 SURP 85374 534-B7
S TRIGGER CT
1000 PinC 85219 746-D7
1000 PinC 85219 786-C1
E TRIGGER WY
- GIL 85236 863-B3
W TRIUMPH CT
- MarC 85086 (378-A5 See Page 337)
W TROCAR AV
15700 GDYR 85338 (734-D4 See Page 733)
E TROJAN CT
16900 FTNH 85268 623-D2
TRONTERA CIR
200 LP 85340 655-B7
E TROON MOUNTAIN DR
11000 SCTS 85255 501-G4
E TROON NORTH DR
9300 SCTS 85262 501-D1
29200 SCTS 85262 (461-E7 See Page 421)
E TROON VISTA DR
11400 SCTS 85255 541-H1
S TROPHY CT
- MarC 85236 903-D3
W TROPICANA CIR
10400 MarC 85351 576-A3
10600 MarC 85351 575-J3
W TROSPER ST
200 GBND 85337 (1090-A2 See Page 1049)
N TROVAS DR
19800 SURP 85374 534-E3
W TROY ST
8300 PEOR 85382 536-F6
E TRUITT AV
7000 MESA 85212 823-G5
S TRURO DR
9700 MarC 85248 901-B4
N TUBAC TR
40100 CARE 85377 421-A1
N TUCANA CT
1200 GIL 85234 783-B3
S TUCANA CT
- GIL 85236 823-B1
- MarC 85236 823-B7
N TUCANA LN
800 GIL 85234 783-B4
S TUCANA LN
- GIL 85236 823-A2
- MarC 85236 823-B6
- MarC 85236 863-B2
TUCKEY LN
- SCTS 85250 661-A2
E TUCKEY LN
- PHX 85012 658-H2
300 PHX 85014 658-H2
1200 PHX 85014 659-A2
1600 PHX 85016 659-B2
6700 SCTS 85250 660-F2
W TUCKEY LN
700 PHX 85013 658-E2
1100 PHX 85015 658-C2
2800 PHX 85017 658-A2
3300 PHX 85017 657-H2
3500 PHX 85019 657-G2
4900 GLEN 85301 657-B1
6600 GLEN 85303 656-G1
6600 GLEN 85305 656-D1
6900 GLEN 85303 657-A1
13100 MarC 85307 655-C1
E TUCSON RD
7600 SCTS 85258 660-G1
W TUFA ST
2000 APJT 85220 745-B5
E TULANE DR
100 TEMP 85283 780-E3
W TULANE DR
800 TEMP 85283 780-B3
S TULIP
2400 MESA 85208 784-A5
W TULIP CT
12300 MarC 85375 535-F7

N TULLEY ST
2300 MESA 85215 703-E6
E TULSA CT
- GIL 85296 822-F5
E TULSA ST
- GIL 85236 822-J5
- GIL 85236 823-A5
- GIL 85296 822-F5
400 CHAN 85225 821-G5
1500 CHAN 85225 822-A5
W TULSA ST
- CHAN 85225 822-C5
- CHAN 85225 821-D5
1200 CHAN 85224 821-A5
3400 CHAN 85226 820-C5
E TUMACACORI WY
8200 CARE 85377 421-B1
8400 CARE 85262 (381-B7 See Page 341)
8400 CARE 85377 (381-B7 See Page 341)
8400 SCTS 85262 (381-B7 See Page 341)
8400 SCTS 85262 421-C1
N TUMBLEBROOK WY
13800 MarC 85351 576-C5
N TUMBLEWEED
17500 SURP 85374 534-C6
E TUMBLEWEED CIR
4900 MarC 85331 460-B1
W TUMBLEWEED CIR
100 GIL 85233 822-C1
S TUMBLEWEED CT
- CHAN 85248 861-E6
E TUMBLEWEED DR
- PHX 85331 460-A1
7400 SCTS 85262 460-H1
15700 FTNH 85268 583-A6
S TUMBLEWEED DR
- CHAN 85248 861-E7
S TUMBLEWEED LN
- CHAN 85248 861-E4
S TUMBLEWEED RD
1900 CHAN 85248 861-E3
W TUMBLEWEED RD
500 GIL 85233 822-A1
N TUMBLEWEED TR
- PinC 85242 865-C7
W TUMBLEWOOD DR
7700 PEOR 85382 576-E2
10200 MarC 85351 576-A2
S TUM TUM CT
6900 PinC 85219 826-H1
E TUNDER CIR
5100 PHX 85044 819-J1
E TUNDER DR
5100 PHX 85044 819-J1
E TUNIS CT
500 PHX 85022 538-J7
E TURNBERRY RD
10400 SCTS 85255 501-F6
N TURNER RD
300 MarC 85326 (691-D3 See Page 651)
500 MarC 85373 (691-D3 See Page 651)
1600 BUCK 85373 651-D6
1600 BUCK 85373 (691-D3 See Page 651)
S TURNER RD
1400 BUCK 85326 (691-D7 See Page 651)
1600 MarC 85326 (691-D7 See Page 651)
1600 MarC 85326 731-D1
7600 MarC 85322 (771-D3 See Page 731)
7600 MarC 85326 (771-D3 See Page 731)
E TURNEY AV
700 PHX 85014 658-J6
1600 PHX 85014 659-A7
1600 PHX 85016 659-A7
3300 PHX 85018 659-F7
8200 SCTS 85251 660-J7
8400 SCTS 85251 661-A7
W TURNEY AV
- PHX 85013 658-F6
1800 PHX 85015 658-C6
2700 PHX 85017 658-A6
3300 PHX 85017 657-J6
3600 PHX 85019 657-H6
4400 PHX 85033 657-A6
4400 PHX 85037 655-H6
4400 PHX 85037 656-A6
5300 PHX 85031 657-C6
7100 PHX 85033 656-F6
E TURQUOISE ARC
12200 SCTS 85259 622-A4
E TURQUOISE AV
1500 PHX 85020 619-A3
2200 PHX 85028 619-C3
4800 PVAL 85253 620-A3
5200 PHX 85253 620-B3
6400 SCTS 85253 620-D3
7300 SCTS 85258 620-G4
8300 SCTS 85258 621-A4
9800 SCTS 85259 622-A4
11600 SCTS 85259 621-J4
W TURQUOISE AV
4300 GLEN 85302 617-B3
6700 PEOR 85345 617-A3
6900 PEOR 85345 616-H3
S TURQUOISE DR
- MarC 85249 902-F5
3800 BUCK 85326 (732-A3 See Page 731)
N TURQUOISE LN
42400 MarC 85331 (382-A5 See Page 341)
N TURQUOISE HILLS DR
19800 MarC 85373 536-A4
N TURTLE BACK TR
30600 MarC 85390 290-G7
S TURTLE DOVE DR
10800 GDYR 85338 (774-A5 See Page 733)
W TURTLE HILL CT
- MarC 85086 (378-D6 See Page 337)
W TURTLE HILL DR
- MarC 85086 (378-D6 See Page 337)
S TUSAYAN CT
11600 PHX 85044 819-E1
N TUSCANY
- MESA 85207 703-J4
N TUSCANY CIR
- MESA 85207 703-J3

W TUSCANY WY
16200 SURP 85374 534-E3
N TUTHILL RD
1600 MarC 85326 (693-C1 See Page 653)
2300 BUCK 85326 (693-C1 See Page 653)
2900 BUCK 85340 653-C5
2900 BUCK 85340 (693-C1 See Page 653)
5500 BUCK 85373 (613-C7 See Page 573)
5500 BUCK 85373 653-C5
S TUTHILL RD
200 BUCK 85326 (693-C5 See Page 653)
200 MarC 85326 (693-C5 See Page 653)
9200 BUCK 85326 (773-D4 See Page 733)
9200 MarC 85326 (773-D4 See Page 733)
12800 MarC 85326 813-C1
14000 GDYR 85326 813-C5
16400 MarC 85326 (853-C3 See Page 813)
20400 GDYR 85326 (853-C3 See Page 813)
S TUZIGOOT CT
11800 PHX 85044 819-E1
E TUZIGOOT DR
3200 PHX 85040 819-D1
3200 PHX 85044 819-D1
E T V RD
- PHX 85040 778-J7
- PHX 85040 818-H2
- PHX 85048 818-H2
W TWAIN CT
- MarC 85086 (378-B7 See Page 337)
W TWAIN DR
- MarC 85086 (378-A7 See Page 337)
S TWEET
5800 MESA 85212 823-G6
S TWELVE OAKS BLVD
- CHAN 85226 820-E7
800 CHAN 85226 860-E1
N TWILIGHT CIR
- MESA 85207 703-G1
E TWILIGHT CT
10300 MarC 85248 901-D5
E TWILIGHT DR
10400 MarC 85248 901-D5
N TWILIGHT TR
36200 CARE 85377 421-C5
36200 SCTS 85262 421-C5
36200 SCTS 85377 421-C5
N TWILIGHT WY
- SURP 85374 534-G5
E TWILIGHT VIEW DR
- FTNH 85268 622-H5
E TWIN ACRES
- QC 85242 864-C6
E TWIN ACRES DR
12400 CHAN 85249 861-J6
21600 QC 85242 864-E6
N TWIN BUTTES DR
22500 MarC 85375 495-C7
TWIN BUTTES CEMETERY RD
- TEMP 85282 740-A6
N TWIN DEER RUN
12200 FTNH 85268 623-A1
S TWINING
5800 MESA 85212 823-G6
6400 MESA 85212 863-G1
W TWIN OAKS DR
10200 MarC 85351 576-A2
W TWIN PEAKS LN
2700 MarC 85087 (338-C5 See Page 337)
4100 MarC 85087 337-J5
TWISTED LEAF DR
- PinC 85219 786-E4
E TWO GUN CIR
15300 FTNH 85268 582-J3
W TWO GUNS TR
- SURP 85374 535-A6
S TYLER CT
600 CHAN 85226 820-D7
E TYLER ST
700 TEMP 85281 740-F4
E TYNDALL CIR
- MESA 85207 703-J2
6700 MESA 85215 703-G2
E TYNDALL ST
- MESA 85207 703-H2
E TYSON CT
- GIL 85236 823-A6
- GIL 85296 822-F6
1000 CHAN 85225 821-H5
E TYSON PL
1500 CHAN 85225 821-J6
1800 CHAN 85225 822-A6
W TYSON PL
3200 CHAN 85226 820-J5
E TYSON ST
- GIL 85296 822-F6
600 CHAN 85225 821-G5
W TYSON ST
- CHAN 85225 822-C6
800 CHAN 85225 821-D5
1200 CHAN 85224 821-A5
3400 CHAN 85226 820-F5

U

S UDALL
- MESA 85204 741-J5
N UDALL CIR
1300 MESA 85203 741-J2
W UDALL DR
- SURP 85374 533-J7
17900 SURP 85374 534-A7
S UDALL ST
500 MESA 85204 741-J7
N ULRICH WY
- SURP 85374 575-C2
W ULTRALIGHT LN
- PHX 85310 537-G2
E ULYSSES AV
6900 MESA 85212 823-G7
S UNA AV
900 TEMP 85281 740-G4
S UNA BUTTE DR
1200 TEMP 85281 740-G5
W UNA NOCHA CT
16400 SURP 85374 534-D6

E UNGER AV
6800 MESA 85212 823-F7
E UNION AV
6900 MESA 85212 823-G7
UNION DR
- TEMP 85281 740-E5
N UNION TR
- MarC 85086 (378-C6 See Page 337)
E UNION HILLS DR
- PHX 85022 538-H6
600 PHX 85024 538-H6
1000 PHX 85024 539-A6
1000 PHX 85022 539-A6
2400 PHX 85050 539-H6
2600 PHX 85032 539-H6
4600 PHX 85050 540-A6
4600 PHX 85032 540-A6
8000 SCTS 85255 540-J7
8200 SCTS 85255 541-A7
W UNION HILLS DR
- PHX 85022 538-C6
- PHX 85023 538-C6
200 PHX 85027 538-C6
2600 PHX 85053 538-C6
3500 PHX 85308 537-H6
3500 PHX 85308 538-C6
5100 GLEN 85308 537-B6
7100 GLEN 85308 536-G6
8100 PEOR 85308 536-G6
8300 PEOR 85382 536-G6
9100 PEOR 85373 536-A6
9200 MarC 85382 536-A6
9700 MarC 85373 536-A6
10700 PEOR 85373 535-H6
10700 MarC 85373 535-H6
11400 SURP 85373 535-H6
16700 SURP 85387 534-B5
16700 SURP 85374 534-B5
17900 SURP 85387 533-D5
17900 SURP 85374 533-D5
E UNITY AV
6800 MESA 85212 823-F7
N UNITY LN
- MarC 85086 (378-C6 See Page 337)
E UNIVERSITY DR
- MESA 85201 741-H4
- TEMP 85281 740-G4
200 PHX 85004 738-G3
400 MESA 85203 741-H4
600 MESA 85203 742-B4
700 PHX 85034 738-G3
700 PHX 85034 739-A3
2000 MESA 85213 742-B4
2100 TEMP 85281 741-A4
3200 PHX 85040 739-F4
3600 MESA 85205 742-H4
4200 MESA 85205 743-A4
5200 MESA 85205 743-E4
6800 MESA 85207 743-F4
7600 MESA 85207 744-B5
7600 MarC 85207 743-F4
7600 MarC 85207 744-B5
10000 MarC 85220 744-G5
10100 MESA 85220 744-G5
11400 MESA 85220 745-A5
11400 MarC 85220 745-A5
W UNIVERSITY DR
- MESA 85201 741-D4
- TEMP 85281 740-B4
2200 TEMP 85281 739-J4
4700 PHX 85281 739-J4
UNIVERSITY WY N
- PHX 85304 577-F5
UNIVERSITY WY S
- PHX 85304 577-F6
N UNKNOWN
7500 SCTS 85258 661-A1
S UNWIN CT
26600 MarC 85248 901-C6
N UP AND DOWN PL
36400 CARE 85377 420-J5
N UPLAND CIR
1500 MESA 85201 741-F1
W UPLAND DR
2600 CHAN 85224 821-A3
UPPER RATTLESNAKE
- MarC 85255 (424-G1 See Page 423)
E UPPER RIDGE WY
4200 MarC 85253 659-H1
4200 PVAL 85253 659-H1
E UPPER TRAIL CIR
- MESA 85207 703-G2
E UPSALA AV
6300 MESA 85212 823-F7
E UPTON AV
6200 MESA 85212 823-F7
E URAL AV
6800 MESA 85212 823-F7
E URBANA AV
6100 MESA 85212 823-F7
E URSALA AV
6800 MESA 85212 823-F7
S URSA MAJOR DR
- GDYR 85338 (774-A5 See Page 733)
E USERY PARK RD
9600 MarC 85207 704-F5
N USERY PASS RD
2000 MESA 85207 704-D5
2000 MESA 85207 744-D1
2800 MarC 85207 704-D5
3400 MarC 85290 664-F5
3400 MarC 85290 704-F1
E USHER AV
6100 MESA 85212 823-F7
E USHER CIR
6800 MESA 85212 823-F7
E UTAH AV
7400 MESA 85212 823-H6
8900 MarC 85248 900-J4
E UTE CIR
4500 PHX 85044 819-H1
W UTE CT
2600 MarC 85087 (338-D3 See Page 337)
UTE RD
5600 GLEN 85307 655-B1
E UTE ST
4400 PHX 85044 819-G1
W UTICA CT
14200 MarC 85375 535-A4
W UTICA DR
13600 MarC 85375 535-B5
E UTOPIA RD
300 PHX 85024 538-H5
1000 PHX 85024 539-A5
2400 PHX 85050 539-E5

W UTOPIA RD
- PEOR 85373 535-J5
- PEOR 85373 535-A5
100 PHX 85027 538-D5
5500 GLEN 85308 537-A5
7100 GLEN 85308 536-H5
8300 PEOR 85382 536-F4

V

S VACATION WY
23600 MarC 85248 901-B2
N VADO CT
24800 MarC 85263 503-H6
E VALDAI CIR
5900 MESA 85215 703-E1
N VALE
900 MESA 85201 741-E2
W VALE DR
4000 GDYR 85338 (654-E6 See Page 653)
8200 PHX 85033 656-F7
8200 PHX 85037 656-E7
S VALENCIA AV
25200 MarC 85242 903-E6
N VALENCIA CT
16400 SURP 85374 534-E4
E VALENCIA DR
- PHX 85040 779-B3
- PHX 85040 778-G2
N VALENCIA DR
300 CHAN 85226 820-G3
W VALENCIA DR
- PHX 85339 777-E2
100 PHX 85041 778-F2
N VALENCIA LN
2900 PHX 85018 700-B2
N VALENCIA PL
500 CHAN 85226 820-G4
S VALENCIA PL
- CHAN 85226 820-G6
4900 TEMP 85282 780-C3
S VALENCIA ST
400 MESA 85202 741-B6
W VALENTINE AV
- ELMG 85335 575-D5
N VALENTINE ST
- WICK 85390 290-F2
S VALENTINE ST
- WICK 85390 290-F2
W VALENTINE ST
11600 ELMG 85335 575-F5
E VALERIE DR
300 TEMP 85281 700-E7
S VALERIE DR
- CHAN 85249 902-A4
N VALERIE ST
4500 PHX 85013 658-G6
W VALERIE WY
- SURP 85374 533-J6
W VALHALLA CT
- MarC 85086 (378-E6 See Page 337)
N VALIANT
- MarC 85086 (378-D5 See Page 337)
N VALIANT CT
- MarC 85086 (378-C6 See Page 337)
E VALIENTE CIR
17300 MarC 85206 743-D7
E VALLA VISTA WY
1000 PHX 85014 658-H3
E VALLECITO DR
17200 FTNH 85268 583-E6
N VALLECITO DR
14000 FTNH 85268 583-E6
E VALLEJO CT
- MarC 85236 902-J4
- MarC 85236 903-A4
E VALLEJO ST
10800 MarC 85248 901-E3
13200 MarC 85249 902-B3
N VALLE VERDE
- MarC 85220 744-G5
- MESA 85220 744-G6
S VALLE VERDE
- MESA 85212 784-F6
- MESA 85220 744-G7
- MESA 85220 784-G1
S VALLE VERDE CIR
- MESA 85212 784-F6
E VALLE VISTA RD
5000 PHX 85018 660-A5
5100 PHX 85253 660-A5
N VALLEY DR
- APJT 85220 745-C4
4000 PinC 85220 745-C1
4200 PinC 85220 705-C6
11000 FTNH 85268 623-D3
S VALLEY DR
- APJT 85220 745-C7
- APJT 85220 785-C1
N VALLEY GN
4900 LP 85340 (654-J4 See Page 653)
W VALLEY RD
51000 MarC 85320 (284-J4 See Page 244)
E VALLEY TR
7100 PVAL 85253 660-F1
W VALLEY VW
14200 LP 85340 655-A4
14200 LP 85340 (654-J4 See Page 653)
E VALLEY WY
6000 CVCK 85331 420-E3
E VALLEY AUTO DR
- MESA 85206 782-J3
S VALLEY VIEW AV
10000 PHX 85041 778-D6
E VALLEY VIEW CIR
- CARE 85377 420-H2
E VALLEY VIEW DR
2400 PHX 85040 779-C4
4600 PHX 85044 779-J4
10400 PinC 85219 786-J3
W VALLEY VIEW DR
- PHX 85041 778-E4
E VALLEY VIEW RD
7200 SCTS 85250 660-F4
8400 SCTS 85250 661-A5
N VALLEY VIEW RD
35100 PinC 85242 904-D7
E VALLEY VIEW TR
7400 CARE 85377 420-H2
E VALLEY VISTA CIR
- MESA 85207 704-B2
E VALLEY VISTA DR
8000 SCTS 85250 660-H3

E VALLEY VISTA DR
8400 SCTS 85250 661-A3
N VALLEY VISTA DR
6100 SCTS 85250 661-A3
E VALLEY VISTA LN
3200 PVAL 85253 659-E3
4800 PVAL 85253 660-A3
7300 SCTS 85250 660-G3
N VALLEY VISTA LN
6000 SCTS 85250 660-H4
W VALLEY VISTA RD
- MarC 85373 573-C5
E VALLEY VISTA WY
5000 PVAL 85253 660-A4
E VALLOROSO DR
17300 FTNH 85268 583-E5
N VALLOROSO DR
14600 FTNH 85268 583-E5
VAL VERDE CIR E
700 LP 85340 655-C6
VAL VERDE CIR W
600 LP 85340 655-B6
N VAL VERDE DR
12100 FTNH 85268 622-J1
N VAL VISTA DR
- MarC 85256 662-H6
- MarC 85256 663-A5
- MarC 85256 702-H2
- GIL 85234 782-G6
- MESA 85205 742-H2
- MESA 85213 742-H2
1500 GIL 85204 782-G6
1600 MESA 85213 702-H5
1600 MESA 85205 702-H6
2000 MESA 85215 702-H6
3200 MarC 85215 702-H2
3200 MarC 85213 702-H2
S VAL VISTA DR
- GIL 85296 782-H2
- GIL 85296 822-G3
- MESA 85204 742-H7
- MESA 85206 742-H7
800 MESA 85204 782-H2
800 MESA 85206 782-H2
1200 MarC 85296 822-G7
4000 MarC 85296 862-G3
21200 MarC 85249 862-G7
22000 MarC 85249 902-G3
W VAL VISTA DR
2000 WICK 85390 290-A3
2100 WICK 85390 289-J3
N VAL VISTA RD
- PinC 85219 746-B3
5800 MarC 85256 663-A4
S VAL VISTA RD
- PinC 85219 746-B7
1600 PinC 85219 786-B1
N VAL VISTA PARK BLVD
800 GIL 85234 782-F5
E VALWOOD AV
6300 MESA 85212 823-F7
E VALWOOD CIR
6900 MESA 85212 823-F7
E VAN BUREN ST
- AVON 85323 695-B5
- GDYR 85338 695-B5
- PHX 85004 698-G6
700 PHX 85006 698-G6
700 PHX 85034 698-G6
1200 PHX 85008 700-B7
1200 TEMP 85008 700-B7
1200 TEMP 85281 700-B7
1400 PHX 85034 699-B6
1400 PHX 85006 699-B6
2400 PHX 85008 699-F6
5100 PHX 85008 700-B7
W VAN BUREN ST
- AVON 85323 695-G6
- PHX 85003 698-C6
200 PHX 85009 698-C6
700 PHX 85007 698-C6
2800 GDYR 85338 (694-H5 See Page 653)
3200 PHX 85009 697-F6
4300 PHX 85043 697-C6
6700 PHX 85043 696-F5
7500 TOL 85043 696-F5
8300 TOL 85353 696-F5
9900 AVON 85353 696-A6
9900 TOL 85323 696-A6
10100 AVON 85323 696-A6
10300 TOL 85323 695-G6
10300 TOL 85353 695-G6
10700 AVON 85353 695-G6
10700 MarC 85353 695-G6
14100 GDYR 85338 695-G6
17100 GDYR 85326 (693-F5 See Page 653)
17100 BUCK 85326 (694-A5 See Page 653)
17900 MarC 85326 (693-F5 See Page 653)
18700 BUCK 85326 (693-D5 See Page 653)
27400 MarC 85326 (691-B4 See Page 651)
28200 BUCK 85326 (691-B4 See Page 651)
E VANCE AV
7000 MESA 85212 863-G1
N VANDALIA DR
13200 FTNH 85268 583-B7
E VANDENBURG AV
7000 MESA 85212 863-G1
E VANGUARD ST
6600 MESA 85215 703-G1
N VANISHING TR
- SCTS 85262 (461-A2 See Page 421)
N VANISHING RAIN DR
- SCTS 85262 (381-E6 See Page 341)
N VAN NESS AV
2000 TEMP 85281 700-E7
E VAQUERO DR
7700 SCTS 85258 620-G6
N VAQUERO RD
1700 APJT 85219 745-H4
S VAQUERO RD
900 APJT 85219 745-H7
1200 APJT 85219 785-H2
E VAQUERO TR
7800 SCTS 85258 620-H6
W VARNEY RD
- ELMG 85335 615-E1
7900 PEOR 85345 616-F1
12500 ELMG 85335 575-D7
12900 ELMG 85379 575-D7

PHOENIX

INDEX

STREET
Block City ZIP Pg-Grid

E VAUGHN
- GIL 85234 783-C6
E VAUGHN AV
- GIL 85233 782-C6
- GIL 85234 782-C6
3600 GIL 85236 783-C6
15800 MarC 85234 782-J6
16200 GIL 85234 783-B6
16200 MarC 85234 783-A6
W VAUGHN AV
- GIL 85233 782-A6
1400 GIL 85233 781-H6
E VAUGHN CT
- GIL 85234 783-A6
E VAUGHN DR
600 TEMP 85283 780-E5
4300 PHX 85044 779-H5
E VAUGHN ST
- GIL 85234 782-J6
- GIL 85234 783-A6
200 TEMP 85283 780-E5
W VAUGHN ST
100 TEMP 85283 780-B5
E VECINO AV
- MESA 85212 863-G1
6800 MESA 85212 823-F7
E VECINO ST
10800 MarC 85248 901-E4
N VECINOS DR
4400 PHX 85018 660-B7
S VE ELLA CIR
1000 TEMP 85281 740-H4
N VEGA DR
22400 MarC 85375 495-B7
E VEGAS
- MESA 85220 744-G6
N VEGAS
- MESA 85220 744-G6
- MESA 85220 784-G1
S VEGAS
- MESA 85212 784-G6
N VELERO CT
- CHAN 85225 821-J6
S VELERO PL
- CHAN 85249 861-J2
N VELERO ST
300 CHAN 85225 821-J3
600 CHAN 85225 822-A3
600 GIL 85233 782-A5
S VELERO ST
400 CHAN 85225 821-J7
500 CHAN 85225 861-J1
W VELERO ST
800 GIL 85233 782-A6
W VELIANA WY
- PHX 85353 736-E2
N VELMA CIR
1100 GIL 85233 782-A4
N VELMA DR
- GIL 85233 781-J7
S VELMA DR
- MarC 85233 781-H7
- MarC 85233 821-J1
E VELOCITY WY
- MESA 85212 823-H7
- MESA 85212 863-H1
E VELVET DR
1800 TEMP 85284 780-H7
1800 TEMP 85284 820-H1
W VELVET DR
1500 TEMP 85284 780-A7
E VENADO DR
- MarC 85087 (338-J7
See Page 337)
- MarC 85087 (378-J1
See Page 337)
1100 MarC 85087 (379-B1
See Page 339)
N VENADO DR
13500 MarC 85375 535-C1
W VENADO DR
- MarC 85087 (338-H7
See Page 337)
E VENADO TR
- SCTS 85262 421-F1
E VENETIAN LN
15900 FTNH 85268 623-A3
W VENICE WY
3200 CHAN 85226 820-J4
E VENTANA AV
6900 MESA 85212 823-G7
W VENTANA DR
- PEOR 85373 536-A3
N VENTANA DR E
11000 PEOR 85373 535-J3
20400 PEOR 85373 536-A3
W VENTANA DR E
10800 PEOR 85373 535-J3
10800 PEOR 85373 536-A3
N VENTANA DR W
20300 PEOR 85373 535-J3
W VENTANA DR W
10900 PEOR 85373 535-J3
N VENTURA CT
- FTNH 85268 622-G3
S VENTURA DR
1600 TEMP 85281 740-E6
2000 TEMP 85282 740-E6
3200 TEMP 85282 780-E1
N VENTURA LN
1600 TEMP 85281 700-E7
W VENTURA ST
- SURP 85379 (574-H4
See Page 573)
SURP 85379 575-C4
11800 ELMG 85335 575-F4
N VENTURE CT
- MarC 85086 (378-A5
See Page 337)
W VENTURI DR
10700 MarC 85351 615-H3
E VENUE CIR
6600 MESA 85215 703-G2
E VENUE ST
6700 MESA 85215 703-G2
E VENUS DR
8900 CARE 85377 421-C6
W VENUS WY
1600 CHAN 85224 821-C6
4100 CHAN 85226 820-C6
E VERA LN
- TEMP 85284 820-D3
W VERA LN
- TEMP 85284 820-B3
N VERACRUZ PZ
15800 FTNH 85268 582-H3
E VERADA SOLANO DR
9200 SCTS 85255 501-C7
9200 SCTS 85255 541-C1

N VERANO CT
3100 CHAN 85224 781-D6
W VERANO CT
500 GIL 85233 822-B2
W VERANO PL
100 GIL 85233 822-B2
N VERANO WY
1000 CHAN 85224 821-D2
S VERBENA
2400 MESA 85208 784-A5
S VERBENA AV
- GIL 85236 863-E5
E VERBENA CT
3900 PHX 85044 819-F5
E VERBENA DR
700 PHX 85048 818-H5
2600 PHX 85048 819-C5
3400 PHX 85044 819-E5
15100 FTNH 85268 582-J7
E VERBENA LN
10200 SCTS 85260 581-E2
10800 SCTS 85259 581-G2
W VERBENA LN
- SURP 85374 534-F2
N VERBENA ST
13500 ELMG 85335 575-F4
S VERBENIA PL
- CHAN 85248 901-C2
W VERDE
4000 MarC 85086 417-J3
S VERDE CIR
- MESA 85212 784-D7
E VERDE DR
- SCTS 85262 460-H6
N VERDE DR
1100 CHAN 85224 781-D7
W VERDE DR
1600 WICK 85390 290-B3
E VERDE LN
300 PHX 85012 698-H2
700 TEMP 85284 780-E7
1300 PHX 85014 698-J2
1600 PHX 85014 699-A2
1600 PHX 85016 699-A2
3600 PHX 85018 699-C2
5100 PHX 85018 700-A2
7600 SCTS 85251 700-G3
W VERDE LN
- AVON 85340 695-C1
- TEMP 85284 780-C7
900 PHX 85013 698-F2
1500 PHX 85015 698-C2
2500 PHX 85017 698-B2
2900 PHX 85031 697-D2
3700 PHX 85019 697-H2
5900 PHX 85033 697-A2
6800 PHX 85033 696-F1
8500 PHX 85037 696-E2
14900 GDYR 85338 (694-E1
See Page 653)
N VERDE ST
15400 SURP 85374 575-E2
S VERDE ST
- MESA 85212 784-D6
N VERDE RIDGE DR
21000 MarC 85375 534-F1
W VERDE RIDGE DR
15800 MarC 85375 534-G2
N VERDE RIVER DR
12500 FTNH 85268 623-C1
12600 FTNH 85268 583-D7
N VERDE ROCA DR
17900 SURP 85374 534-E5
E VERDIN RD
3600 PHX 85044 819-E3
E VEREDA SOLANA DR
9600 SCTS 85255 501-D7
9600 SCTS 85255 541-D1
E VERLEA CIR
2300 TEMP 85282 740-G6
E VERLEA DR
1200 TEMP 85282 740-G6
W VERLEA LN
200 TEMP 85284 820-D3
N VERMEERSCH RD
38000 CVCK 85331 420-G3
S VERMEERSCH RD
3600 AVON 85323 735-C4
E VERMILLION CIR
6100 MESA 85215 703-E2
E VERMILLION ST
5900 MESA 85215 703-E2
E VERMONT AV
900 PHX 85014 658-J4
1300 PHX 85014 659-A4
2500 PHX 85016 659-E4
3200 PHX 85018 659-F4
6800 PVAL 85253 660-E5
W VERMONT AV
200 PHX 85013 658-F4
1900 PHX 85015 658-D4
2900 PHX 85017 658-A4
3300 PHX 85017 657-J4
3500 PHX 85019 657-J4
6200 GLEN 85301 657-B4
6700 GLEN 85303 657-A4
6900 GLEN 85303 656-F4
10100 PHX 85307 656-B4
E VERMONT AV N
4400 PHX 85018 659-H5
E VERMONT AV S
4400 PHX 85018 659-H5
E VERMONT CT
- MarC 85236 823-A7
E VERMONT DR
- GIL 85296 822-D7
- MarC 85236 823-B7
4300 MESA 85215 703-F2
N VERN PL
14200 FTNH 85268 583-B6
E VERNOA ST
- PinC 85242 905-D2
E VERNON AV
- PHX 85004 698-G3
3800 PHX 85008 699-G3
5400 PHX 85008 700-B3
5600 SCTS 85257 700-B3
8600 SCTS 85257 701-A4
W VERNON AV
- PHX 85003 698-F3
700 PHX 85007 698-E3
2300 PHX 85035 697-A3
3300 PHX 85009 697-G3
6800 PHX 85035 696-J3
8500 PHX 85037 696-E2
12300 AVON 85323 695-C2
13600 GDYR 85338 695-A2
N VERNON DR
100 CHAN 85225 822-B6

S VERNON DR
- CHAN 85225 862-B1
- CHAN 85249 902-A5
E VERNON ST
- MarC 85236 903-B2
E VERONA AV
6600 MESA 85212 863-G1
S VERONICA LN
- PinC 85219 786-H4
E VEST AV
16800 MarC 85236 823-C6
N VETERANS DR
21800 MarC 85375 534-J1
22300 MarC 85375 494-J7
N VIA AQUILA
- PHX 85086 (418-C6
See Page 417)
N VIA ARNOLDO
21800 MarC 85375 534-G1
N VIA AZUL
7900 SCTS 85258 620-H7
W VIA BONA FORTUNA
- PHX 85086 (418-C7
See Page 417)
E VIA BONITA
7800 SCTS 85258 620-H6
N VIA BONITA LN
- SURP 85374 534-E5
E VIA BUENA VISTA
5200 PVAL 85253 620-B5
N VIA BUENO
8100 SCTS 85258 620-J6
E VIA CABALLO
BLANCO
- PHX 85331 460-C4
W VIA CALABRIA
- PHX 85086 (418-C7
See Page 417)
N VIA CAMELLO
7800 SCTS 85258 660-H1
N VIA CAMELLO DEL
NORTE
7200 SCTS 85258 660-H1
7600 SCTS 85258 620-J7
N VIA CAMELLO DEL
SUR
7000 SCTS 85258 660-H1
7400 SCTS 85258 620-J7
E VIA CAMILA
- GDYR 85338 695-B4
W VIA CAMILLE
5200 GLEN 85306 577-D5
13800 ELMG 85335 575-D4
E VIA CAMPO
8000 SCTS 85258 620-J6
E VIA CASTA
7700 SCTS 85258 620-H7
N VIA COBRE CIR
- MarC 85290 704-A1
- MESA 85207 704-A1
W VIA CORTE DR
600 WICK 85390 290-D2
E VIA COSTA
7700 SCTS 85258 620-H6
W VIA CYNTHIA DR
4700 GLEN 85301 617-F7
N VIA DE ALEGRIA
7000 SCTS 85258 660-J1
N VIA DE AMIGOS
7000 SCTS 85258 660-J1
N VIA DE AMOR
7000 SCTS 85258 660-J2
E VIA DE ARBOLES
12400 MarC 85249 901-J3
12400 MarC 85249 902-A3
18400 QC 85236 903-H3
19200 QC 85242 903-J3
E VIA DE BELLEZA
7000 SCTS 85258 660-H2
8500 SCTS 85258 661-A2
N VIA DE CALMA
7700 SCTS 85258 620-J7
E VIA DE CERRO
8600 SCTS 85258 621-A7
E VIA DE COMMERCIO
8600 SCTS 85258 621-A7
E VIA DE CORTO
7600 SCTS 85258 620-G6
E VIA DE DORADO
8100 SCTS 85258 660-J1
E VIA DE ENCANTO
7100 SCTS 85258 661-A1
7200 SCTS 85258 660-J1
N VIA DE FONDA
7600 SCTS 85258 620-J7
N VIA DE FRONTERA
7700 SCTS 85258 620-J7
N VIA DE LA
CABALLA LN
22000 MarC 85375 535-A1
22400 MarC 85375 495-A7
N VIA DE LA CAMPANA
7100 SCTS 85258 661-A1
N VIA DE LA COMPANA
7000 SCTS 85258 661-A1
7600 SCTS 85258 621-A7
E VIA DE LA ENTRADA
7800 SCTS 85258 660-H1
E VIA DE LA ESCUELA
8000 SCTS 85258 620-J7
8300 SCTS 85258 660-J1
8500 SCTS 85258 661-A1
N VIA DE LA ESCUELA
7500 SCTS 85258 660-J1
E VIA DE LA GENTE
8300 SCTS 85258 660-J2
8600 SCTS 85258 661-A2
N VIA DE LAGO
7600 SCTS 85258 620-G6
E VIA DE LA LUNA
8300 SCTS 85258 660-J1
8700 SCTS 85258 621-A7
8700 SCTS 85258 661-A1
N VIA DE LA LUNA
7500 SCTS 85258 661-A1
7700 SCTS 85258 621-A7
N VIA DE LA MONTANA
7000 SCTS 85258 661-A1
7700 SCTS 85258 621-A7
E VIA DEL ARBOR
8000 SCTS 85258 660-F1
8600 SCTS 85258 661-A1
S VIA DEL ARROYO
22800 QC 85236 903-G2
N VIA DE LAS BRISAS
7700 SCTS 85258 621-A7
E VIA DE LA SENDERO
8500 SCTS 85258 661-A1
N VIA DE LA SENDERO
7000 SCTS 85258 661-A1

N VIA DE LA SENDERO
7700 SCTS 85258 621-A7
E VIA DE LAS FLORES
8300 SCTS 85258 620-J7
N VIA DE LA SOMBRE
7700 SCTS 85258 621-A7
E VIA DEL CIELO
5200 PVAL 85253 620-B5
N VIA DEL CIERZO
4900 PHX 85037 656-B5
W VIA DEL COUNTRY
CLUB TR
- PEOR 85382 496-A7
- PEOR 85382 536-A1
E VIA DEL DESERTO
8000 SCTS 85258 620-J7
8000 SCTS 85258 660-J1
W VIA DEL DESERTO
- PHX 85086 (418-B6
See Page 417)
N VIA DEL ELEMENTAL
7000 SCTS 85258 660-J1
7300 SCTS 85258 661-A1
E VIA DEL FUTURO
7700 SCTS 85258 660-H1
E VIA DE LINDO
7600 SCTS 85258 620-H6
E VIA DEL JARDIN
8400 SCTS 85258 620-J7
18600 QC 85236 903-G1
W VIA DELLA VISTA
- PHX 85086 (418-C6
See Page 417)
N VIA DEL MUNDO
7700 SCTS 85258 621-A7
E VIA DEL ORO
- MarC 85249 901-H2
- QC 85242 903-H2
- QC 85242 904-A2
17200 FTNH 85268 623-E1
17300 FTNH 85264 623-E1
18400 QC 85236 903-G2
E VIA DE LOS LIBROS
8000 SCTS 85258 620-J7
8300 SCTS 85258 660-J1
8500 SCTS 85258 661-A1
N VIA DE LOS LIBROS
7500 SCTS 85258 660-J1
N VIA DE LOS NINOS
7000 SCTS 85258 660-J2
7600 SCTS 85258 620-J7
7600 SCTS 85258 661-A1
E VIA DEL PALACIO
8500 SCTS 85258 661-A1
E VIA DEL PALO
- MarC 85249 901-H1
- QC 85242 903-J2
18600 QC 85236 903-G2
21300 QC 85242 904-A2
N VIA DEL PARAISO
7000 SCTS 85258 661-A1
7600 SCTS 85258 621-A7
E VIA DEL PARQUE
8400 SCTS 85258 620-J7
E VIA DEL PLACITO
7600 SCTS 85258 620-H6
E VIA DEL RANCHO
- MarC 85249 901-H1
- MarC 85249 902-G1
- QC 85242 903-H2
- QC 85242 904-A2
18600 QC 85236 903-G2
E VIA DEL REPOSO
7600 SCTS 85258 620-G6
E VIA DEL SOL
8600 SCTS 85255 541-B3
N VIA DEL SOL
- FTNH 85268 583-E7
7800 SCTS 85258 621-A7
12400 FTNH 85268 623-E1
W VIA DEL SOL
- PEOR 85373 536-A1
10500 PEOR 85382 536-A2
E VIA DEL SOL DR
8000 SCTS 85255 540-H2
8200 SCTS 85255 541-B2
N VIA DEL SOL DR
21800 SCTS 85255 541-B2
W VIA DEL SOL DR
3200 PHX 85027 538-A2
3500 PHX 85310 538-A2
3600 PHX 85310 537-J2
5900 GLEN 85310 537-A2
6500 GLEN 85308 537-B2
7300 GLEN 85310 536-J2
E VIA DE LUNA DR
8000 SCTS 85255 540-J1
8800 SCTS 85255 541-B2
W VIA DE LUNA DR
7100 GLEN 85310 537-A1
7300 GLEN 85310 536-J1
E VIA DEL VALLE
7900 SCTS 85258 620-H7
8000 SCTS 85258 660-F1
8600 SCTS 85258 661-A1
E VIA DEL VENCINO
8000 SCTS 85258 660-F1
E VIA DEL VERDE
- QC 85242 903-H2
18900 QC 85236 903-H2
N VIA DE MANANA
7000 SCTS 85258 661-A1
7600 SCTS 85258 621-A7
N VIA DE MAS
7100 SCTS 85258 660-J1
E VIA DE MCCORMICK
8600 SCTS 85258 621-A7
E VIA DE NEGOCIO
8600 SCTS 85258 621-A7
N VIA DE NEGOCIO
8000 SCTS 85258 621-A7
E VIA DE NORTHGATE
18400 MarC 85212 823-G2
E VIA DE OLIVOS
19200 QC 85242 903-J3
N VIA DE PAESIA
7000 SCTS 85258 660-J1
E VIA DE PALMAS
12000 MarC 85249 901-H3
12600 MarC 85249 902-A3
18400 QC 85236 903-G3
19200 QC 85242 903-J3
N VIA DE PAZ
7100 SCTS 85258 660-J1
W VIA DE PEDRO
MIGUEL
- PHX 85086 (418-C6
See Page 417)
N VIA DE PENASCO
12400 FTNH 85268 623-E1

N VIA DE PLATINA
7600 SCTS 85258 620-J7
E VIA DE RISA
8300 SCTS 85258 660-J1
8500 SCTS 85258 661-A1
E VIA DE SERENO
8200 SCTS 85258 660-J1
8500 SCTS 85258 661-A1
E VIA DE SIESTA
7000 SCTS 85258 661-A2
N VIA DE SIESTA
7100 SCTS 85258 661-A1
VIA DE VENTURA
- MarC 85258 621-B7
- SCTS 85258 621-B7
E VIA DE VENTURA
7600 SCTS 85258 620-J7
8100 SCTS 85258 621-A7
N VIA DE VIDA
7000 SCTS 85258 660-J2
E VIA DE VIVA
7700 SCTS 85258 620-H7
8200 SCTS 85258 660-J1
8500 SCTS 85258 661-A1
E VIA DONA RD
4400 PHX 85331 459-J7
4500 PHX 85331 460-A7
4500 PHX 85331 499-J1
7200 SCTS 85262 500-H1
8000 SCTS 85262 501-A1
12200 SCTS 85262 502-B1
13600 MarC 85255 502-F1
N VIA DON JUAN
7100 GLEN 85301 617-F7
E VIA DONNA DR
29100 PHX 85331 460-B7
E VIA DORADO
8300 SCTS 85258 660-J1
8500 SCTS 85258 661-A1
N VIA ELEMENTAL
7500 SCTS 85258 661-A1
7600 SCTS 85258 621-A7
E VIA ELENA ST
600 GDYR 85338 695-B5
W VIA ELENA ST
- GDYR 85338 695-C5
E VIA ESQUINA
19000 MarC 85263 (504-A5
See Page 503)
E VIA ESQUINA CIR
25700 MarC 85263 (504-A5
See Page 503)
E VIA ESTRELLA
2800 PHX 85028 619-D3
6000 PHX 85253 620-D3
E VIA ESTRELLA CT
7300 SCTS 85258 620-G3
E VIA HERMOSA
18500 MarC 85263 503-H6
19000 MarC 85263 (504-A6
See Page 503)
E VIA LAGUNA
18700 MarC 85263 503-J5
E VIA LA PLAYA
12400 FTNH 85268 623-E1
N VIA LA SERENA
8600 PVAL 85253 620-B5
E VIA LINDA
7900 SCTS 85258 620-J5
8300 SCTS 85258 621-C4
10600 SCTS 85259 621-H2
12000 SCTS 85259 622-C2
N VIA LINDA
8300 SCTS 85258 620-J6
E VIA LOS CABALLOS
4400 PHX 85028 619-J5
5200 PVAL 85253 620-B5
E VIA LOS RANCHOS
5700 PVAL 85253 620-C5
N VIA LUCIA MARIE
7100 GLEN 85301 617-F7
N VIA MANANA
22100 MarC 85375 534-H1
W VIA MANANA
13700 MarC 85375 535-A1
14300 MarC 85375 495-A7
14400 MarC 85375 494-J7
14400 MarC 85375 534-G1
E VIA MARIA ST
600 GDYR 85338 695-B5
E VIA MARINA
7800 SCTS 85258 620-H7
N VIA MIA
8300 SCTS 85258 620-H6
N VIA MONICA
7100 GLEN 85301 617-F1
7100 GLEN 85301 657-F1
E VIA MONTANA
300 MarC 85206 783-E1
E VIA MONTANA PZ
- MarC 85206 783-F1
E VIA MONTANA VISTA
3200 PHX 85028 619-F3
E VIA MONTOYA
8400 SCTS 85255 541-B2
N VIA MONTOYA
21800 MarC 85375 534-J1
22200 SCTS 85255 541-A2
W VIA MONTOYA
- PEOR 85382 536-G1
13700 MarC 85375 535-A1
14300 MarC 85375 534-H1
E VIA MONTOYA DR
- SCTS 85255 540-H2
4500 PHX 85050 539-J1
4600 PHX 85050 540-B2
5000 PHX 85054 540-B2
W VIA MONTOYA DR
3100 PHX 85027 538-A1
5900 GLEN 85310 537-A1
6300 GLEN 85308 537-C2
7300 GLEN 85310 536-J1
8300 PEOR 85382 536-A1
S VIA NORTE
2600 MarC 85206 743-F7
N VIA NUEVA
7000 SCTS 85258 660-H1
N VIA PALMA
8000 SCTS 85258 620-H7
E VIA PARK ST
- QC 85242 903-H4
E VIA PASEO DEL
NORTE
7400 SCTS 85258 660-J1
7500 SCTS 85258 661-A1
7600 SCTS 85258 621-A7
7600 SCTS 85258 620-J7
E VIA PASEO DEL SUR
8100 SCTS 85258 660-J2

N VIA PASEO DEL SUR
7100 SCTS 85258 660-J1
W VIA PERUGIA
- PHX 85086 (418-C7
See Page 417)
N VIA PUZZOLA
- PHX 85085 (418-C6
See Page 417)
- PHX 85086 (418-C6
See Page 417)
W VIA RIALTO AV
2300 MESA 85202 781-B2
N VIA RICO
8200 SCTS 85258 620-H6
E VIA RIO
7700 SCTS 85258 620-H7
W VIA RIVERA
2900 PHX 85053 578-B1
N VIA ROSA
8300 SCTS 85258 620-H6
E VIA ROSSMOOR BLVD
600 MarC 85206 783-F1
600 MESA 85206 783-F1
E VIA RUIDOSA
8400 SCTS 85258 620-J7
W VIA SAVELLI
- PHX 85086 (418-D6
See Page 417)
N VIA SERENA CIR
- MESA 85207 704-D6
E VIA SIERRA
7900 SCTS 85258 620-J7
VIA SIESTA
7500 SCTS 85258 661-A1
E VIA SONRISA
7100 SCTS 85258 660-H1
N VIA SONRISA
7200 SCTS 85258 660-H1
E VIA TAZ NORTE
8700 SCTS 85258 621-A7
E VIA TAZ SUR
8700 SCTS 85258 621-A7
N VIA TERCERO
22400 MarC 85375 494-J7
22900 MarC 85375 495-A7
W VIA TERCERO
13500 MarC 85375 495-A7
14300 MarC 85375 494-J7
N VIA TRAMONTO
- PHX 85086 (418-D7
See Page 417)
E VIA VENTOSA
22300 SCTS 85255 541-E1
N VIA VENTOSO
22200 SCTS 85255 541-E2
E VIA VERDE
8000 SCTS 85258 620-H7
E VIA VILLA ST
600 GDYR 85338 695-B5
E VICTOR RD
2000 GIL 85296 782-H7
E VICTOR HUGO AV
1200 PHX 85022 579-A6
2700 PHX 85032 579-A6
N VICTOR HUGO AV
13100 PHX 85032 579-D6
E VICTORIA DR
6100 CVCK 85331 420-E5
N VICTORIA DR
- CVCK 85331 420-E5
W VICTORIA LN
6300 CHAN 85226 820-B3
W VICTORIA SQ
200 PHX 85013 658-G4
E VICTORIA ST
10800 MarC 85248 901-E3
12000 CHAN 85249 901-J4
12000 MarC 85249 901-J4
12400 MarC 85249 902-B3
E VICTORY DR
600 APJT 85220 745-B5
2200 TEMP 85281 741-A4
W VICTORY LN
- PHX 85027 498-F7
E VICTORY ST
- PHX 85040 738-G4
1500 PHX 85034 739-A4
W VICTORY ST
- GDYR 85338 (734-D3
See Page 733)
16500 MarC 85338 (734-C3
See Page 733)
N VIDA CT
21800 MarC 85375 535-B1
N VIENNA CT
1100 CHAN 85226 820-H4
N VIENTO CT
- FTNH 85268 622-H2
S VIEW LN
- MarC 85236 903-C2
E VIEW CREST CIR
- MESA 85207 704-B2
E VIEWMONT CIR
5900 MESA 85215 703-E1
E VIEWMONT DR
4300 MESA 85215 703-F1
S VILLA CT
4800 TEMP 85282 780-J3
W VILLA RD
6900 PHX 85033 657-A7
E VILLA ST
1600 PHX 85006 699-A6
W VILLA ST
2900 PHX 85009 698-A5
5900 PHX 85043 697-C5
6900 PHX 85043 696-J5
E VILLA WY
7200 SCTS 85257 700-F6
N VILLA BELLA DR
15600 SURP 85374 534-F5
E VILLA CASSANDRA
- CVCK 85331 419-H7
E VILLA CASSANDRA
DR
8000 SCTS 85262 420-J7
8000 SCTS 85262 421-A7
W VILLA CASSANDRA
DR
- PHX 85086 (418-D7
See Page 417)
E VILLA CASSANDRA
WY
5000 CVCK 85331 420-B7
6200 CARE 85377 420-E7
8200 SCTS 85262 421-A7
W VILLA CHICA
2600 MESA 85202 781-A3
W VILLA CHULA
6900 GLEN 85310 497-A7
7200 GLEN 85310 496-J7

W VILLA CHULA
8200 MarC 85382 496-G7
8700 PEOR 85382 496-A7
10600 PEOR 85373 496-A7
E VILLA DEL RANCHO
17400 MarC 85236 903-C2
S VILLAGE BLVD
- GDYR 85338 (734-E3
See Page 733)
E VILLAGE CIDR
800 PHX 85022 578-J5
N VILLAGE DR
4400 PHX 85018 659-H5
16600 SURP 85374 535-E7
16600 SURP 85374 575-E1
W VILLAGE DR
- GLEN 85308 537-E7
- SURP 85374 533-J7
1900 PHX 85023 538-D7
2300 PHX 85023 578-C1
7400 GLEN 85308 536-J7
8300 PEOR 85382 536-F7
E VILLAGE PKWY
- GIL 85236 863-D6
W VILLAGE PKWY
8300 PEOR 85382 536-F5
W VILLAGE WY
1600 TEMP 85282 780-A1
W VILLA HERMOSA
6900 GLEN 85310 497-A7
7300 GLEN 85310 496-J7
8700 PEOR 85382 496-A7
W VILLA LINDA DR
- PHX 85310 498-A5
3700 PHX 85310 497-C5
W VILLA LINDA ST
8900 PEOR 85382 496-E5
8900 MarC 85382 496-E5
W VILLA LINDO
6600 PEOR 85382 497-A6
8100 PEOR 85382 496-G6
N VILLA MANANA
6500 PHX 85014 658-J2
E VILLA MARIA CIR
4200 PHX 85032 539-H7
E VILLA MARIA DR
100 PHX 85022 538-H7
500 PHX 85022 539-A7
2400 PHX 85032 539-E7
4600 PHX 85032 540-A7
N VILLA MARIA DR
2100 PHX 85022 539-C7
W VILLA MARIA DR
- PHX 85023 538-D6
2700 PHX 85053 538-A6
3600 PHX 85308 537-F6
3600 PHX 85308 538-A6
5400 GLEN 85308 537-C6
N VILLA MARIA PL
18000 PHX 85022 538-H7
E VILLA NUEVA
- LP 85340 655-C5
N VILLA NUEVA DR
100 LP 85340 655-C5
E VILLA PARK CT
- MarC 85236 902-J4
- MarC 85236 903-A4
E VILLA PARK ST
10800 MarC 85248 901-E4
13200 MarC 85249 902-B4
W VILLA RIDGE DR
13700 MarC 85375 535-B3
E VILLA RITA DR
- PHX 85022 538-H7
900 PHX 85022 539-A7
2400 PHX 85032 539-D7
4600 PHX 85032 540-A7
4800 PHX 85254 540-A7
W VILLA RITA DR
- PHX 85022 538-G7
- PHX 85023 538-C7
2700 PHX 85053 538-A6
3400 PHX 85308 538-A6
3500 PHX 85308 537-F6
5300 GLEN 85308 537-A6
7100 GLEN 85308 536-J6
8300 PEOR 85382 536-E6
9100 PEOR 85373 536-D6
S VILLAS CT
1300 CHAN 85248 861-C2
N VILLAS LN
1000 CHAN 85224 821-C2
2800 CHAN 85224 781-C7
S VILLAS LN
700 CHAN 85224 861-C1
1500 CHAN 85248 861-C2
N VILLA SERENO DR
400 WICK 85390 290-E1
W VILLA SERENO DR
400 WICK 85390 290-E1
E VILLA THERESA DR
- PHX 85022 538-H6
1000 PHX 85022 539-A6
2500 PHX 85032 539-D6
4800 PHX 85254 540-A6
W VILLA THERESA DR
100 PHX 85023 538-E6
2900 PHX 85053 538-A6
3600 PHX 85308 537-F6
5400 GLEN 85308 537-A6
7100 GLEN 85308 536-H6
S VILLA VISTA
- MarC 85206 783-G1
E VILLEROY CIR
6700 MESA 85215 703-G2
E VILLEROY ST
6600 MESA 85215 703-G2
S VINCENT
- MESA 85212 784-D4
N VINCENT CIR
- MarC 85207 744-E1
E VINE AV
- MESA 85210 741-H6
400 MESA 85204 741-J6
800 MESA 85204 742-A6
4600 MarC 85204 744-D7
11000 MarC 85220 744-H7
11000 MESA 85220 744-H7
11400 MarC 85220 745-A7
W VINE AV
200 MESA 85210 741-F6
1300 MESA 85202 741-D6
E VINE CIR
200 MESA 85210 741-H6
S VINE CT
1200 GIL 85233 822-B3
N VINE ST
200 CHAN 85225 821-E3
21300 MarC 85361 (453-A1
See Page 413)

STREET Block City ZIP Pg-Grid

S VINE ST
600 CHAN 85225 861-E1
1300 GIL 85233 822-B4
1500 CHAN 85248 861-E2
32300 MarC 85361 (453-A2
See Page 413)
E VINEDO LN
100 TEMP 85284 780-E7
W VINEDO LN
- TEMP 85284 780-D7
W VINEWOOD DR
16000 SURP 85374 534-E6
S VINEYARD
1700 MESA 85210 781-F2
S VINEYARD AV
1900 MESA 85210 781-F3
E VINEYARD RD
- PHX 85040 778-G1
1400 PHX 85040 779-A1
N VINEYARD RD
- PinC 85212 825-B4
- PinC 85212 865-B4
- PinC 85219 825-B4
- PinC 85220 825-B4
- PinC 85242 825-B4
37900 PinC 85242 905-B3
40800 PinC 85242 865-B4
W VINEYARD RD
- PHX 85041 777-G1
- PHX 85040 778-F1
- PHX 85041 778-C1
2000 TEMP 85282 780-A2
2100 TEMP 85282 779-J2
2700 PHX 85040 779-J2
5800 MarC 85339 777-A1
5800 PHX 85339 777-B1
10600 AVON 85353 775-H1
10600 MarC 85353 775-H1
14300 GDYR 85338 (734-G7
See Page 733)
N VINEYARD ST
400 MESA 85201 741-G3
S VINEYARD ST
- MESA 85210 741-F5
1000 MESA 85210 781-F1
W VINEYARD WY
1200 CHAN 85248 861-C2
E VINSON CIR
6700 MESA 85215 703-G2
W VINYARD RD
- PHX 85041 777-H1
E VIOLA LN
6600 CVCK 85331 420-F3
N VIOLA LN
38100 CVCK 85331 420-F3
E VIOLET DR
1600 PHX 85040 739-A6
S VIOLET DR
4600 PHX 85040 739-A6
N VIOLETTA DR
22400 SCTS 85255 541-F2
E VIRGINIA AV
- MarC 85203 702-B3
- MarC 85256 701-C3
- MESA 85203 702-B3
- PHX 85004 698-H3
700 PHX 85006 698-H3
1400 PHX 85006 699-A3
2300 PHX 85008 699-D3
4900 PHX 85008 700-A3
5500 PHX 85257 700-A3
6400 SCTS 85257 700-D3
8400 SCTS 85257 701-A3
8700 MarC 85257 701-A3
W VIRGINIA AV
- MarC 85323 695-F2
- PHX 85003 698-F3
- PHX 85004 698-F3
700 PHX 85007 698-E3
1900 PHX 85009 698-A2
2500 PHX 85035 697-B2
3200 PHX 85009 697-G2
6900 PHX 85035 696-F2
8400 PHX 85037 696-E2
12300 AVON 85323 695-C2
13200 GDYR 85338 695-B2
E VIRGINIA CIR
300 PHX 85004 698-H3
W VIRGINIA CIR
13700 GDYR 85338 695-A2
W VIRGINIA CT
13100 GDYR 85338 695-C2
E VIRGINIA ST
- MarC 85213 702-G4
- PinC 85219 746-C5
1500 APJT 85219 745-G5
2100 MESA 85213 702-E4
4400 MESA 85215 703-A4
W VIRGINIA ST
800 APJT 85220 745-A5
W VIRGO CT
11100 MarC 85351 575-H3
E VIRGO PL
- CHAN 85249 901-G3
- MarC 85249 902-A3
N VISADO CT
- MarC 85255 (462-F6
See Page 421)
S VISALIA ST
500 MESA 85202 741-B6
E VISAO DR
- SCTS 85262 460-H5
VISION WY
- PHX 85086 (377-J4
See Page 337)
S VISION QUEST CT
5000 PinC 85219 786-H5
E VISTA AV
600 PHX 85020 618-H7
1200 PHX 85020 619-A7
W VISTA AV
- GLEN 85303 616-J7
- GLEN 85307 616-A6
- PHX 85021 618-C7
2500 PHX 85051 618-B7
3500 PHX 85051 617-H7
4300 GLEN 85301 617-C7
8000 MarC 85303 616-G7
10700 MarC 85307 615-H6
E VISTA DR
- FTNH 85268 622-H3
- MarC 85250 661-C5
- MarC 85256 661-J5
- MarC 85256 662-A5
1900 PHX 85022 579-C4
2600 PHX 85032 579-D4
5200 PHX 85251 660-D5
6400 PVAL 85251 660-D5
6400 PVAL 85253 660-D5
7200 SCTS 85250 660-F5

E VISTA DR
7200 SCTS 85253 660-F5
8400 SCTS 85250 661-A5
9200 SCTS 85262 (461-C2
See Page 421)
N VISTA DR
- MarC 85390 290-A2
W VISTA DR
1500 WICK 85390 290-A4
VISTA LP
- PinC 85219 786-G4
S VISTA PL
- CHAN 85248 901-C2
N VISTA RD
- APJT 85219 745-G5
S VISTA RD
- APJT 85219 745-G7
1300 APJT 85219 785-G2
E VISTA BONITA DR
2100 PHX 85024 499-C7
8000 SCTS 85255 540-H1
8500 SCTS 85255 541-A1
W VISTA BONITA DR
- PHX 85027 498-A7
E VISTA CANYON CIR
- MESA 85207 704-B2
S VISTA DEL CERRO
2600 MarC 85206 743-E7
E VISTA DEL CERRO DR
100 TEMP 85281 740-D5
E VISTA DEL LAGO
8300 SCTS 85255 541-A1
N VISTA DEL LAGO
12900 FTNH 85268 583-E7
N VISTA DEL SOL
- MESA 85207 703-J7
500 MESA 85207 743-J4
S VISTA DEL SOL
2700 MESA 85212 783-J5
E VISTA DE VALLE
8200 SCTS 85255 541-A1
N VISTA DE VALLE
8200 SCTS 85255 541-A1
S VISTA DR
3100 CHAN 85248 861-D5
S VISTA GRANDE
5200 PHX 85041 738-C7
N VISTA GRANDE CT
12400 MarC 85351 576-C6
W VISTA GRANDE LN
15600 SURP 85374 534-G3
W VISTA NORTH DR
16100 MarC 85375 534-F1
W VISTA PASEO DR
100 LP 85340 655-A5
S VISTA PL
3500 CHAN 85248 861-C6
W VISTA PL
1300 CHAN 85248 861-C7
S VISTA POINT CIR
- PinC 85219 786-H7
N VISTA RANCH RD
15800 SURP 85374 (574-E1
See Page 573)
E VISTA RICA ST
5300 PVAL 85253 620-B6
E VISTA VAL VERDE
4400 PHX 85331 459-J6
N VISTA VERDE
- FTNH 85268 622-J5
- FTNH 85268 623-A5
E VISTA VERDE DR
13000 MarC 85249 902-B3
N VISTA VERDE DR
1000 LP 85340 655-C5
E VISTAVIEW CT
- SCTS 85268 622-H1
E VITA VERDE CT
- MarC 85236 902-J3
- MarC 85236 903-A3
N VIVA DR
22500 MarC 85375 495-A7
E VOAX DR
10500 MarC 85248 901-D3
E VOGEL AV
- PHX 85020 618-G3
1200 PHX 85020 619-A3
2200 PHX 85028 619-C3
9700 SCTS 85258 621-D4
W VOGEL AV
- PHX 85021 618-E3
3100 PHX 85051 618-A3
3400 PHX 85051 617-J3
4900 GLEN 85302 617-B3
6700 PEOR 85345 617-A3
7100 PEOR 85345 616-C3
W VOGEL LN
3800 PHX 85051 617-J3
4300 GLEN 85302 617-F3
E VOLANTE AV
6900 MESA 85212 863-G1
E VOLANTE CIR
6900 MESA 85212 863-F1
E VOLTAIRE AV
100 PHX 85022 578-H5
1200 PHX 85022 579-A5
2600 PHX 85032 579-D5
4700 PHX 85032 580-A6
4800 PHX 85254 580-A6
8000 SCTS 85260 580-J6
8200 SCTS 85260 581-A6
N VOLTAIRE AV
13300 SCTS 85260 581-E6
W VOLTAIRE AV
- ELMG 85335 575-D5
1600 PHX 85029 578-A5
3500 PHX 85029 577-H5
6900 PEOR 85381 577-A5
7100 PEOR 85381 576-F5
E VOLTAIRE DR
9300 SCTS 85260 581-D6
W VOLTAIRE DR
5200 GLEN 85304 577-B5
E VOSLER AV
6900 MESA 85212 863-G1
E VOSLER CIR
6900 MESA 85212 863-F1
N VOYAGER DR
- GIL 85234 782-J4
- GIL 85296 782-H7
1100 MarC 85234 782-J4
S VOYAGER DR
500 GIL 85296 822-H2
S VOYAGER ST
- GIL 85296 822-G6
N VULTURE MINE RD
- YavC - 250-A7
- MarC 85390 290-A2
- WICK 85390 290-A2

N VULTURE MINE RD
1200 WICK 85390 250-A7
46000 MarC 85390 289-J5
55000 MarC 85390 250-A7
15400 MarC 85320 102-A2
15400 MarC 85354 102-A2
S VULTURE MINE RD
- WICK 85390 290-A4
W VULTURE MOUNTAIN CT
11600 SURP 85374 535-G4
W VULTURE PEAK SCHOOL LP
- WICK 85390 289-J4
- WICK 85390 290-A4
VULTURE RUN RD
- YavC - 250-A5

W

W WACKER RD
7900 PEOR 85381 576-G5
W WADDELL RD
13100 SURP 85379 575-B4
13100 MarC 85379 575-B4
13900 SURP 85379 (574-F4
See Page 573)
13900 MarC 85379 (574-A4
See Page 573)
18000 MarC 85379 573-H4
WADDELL CSR
- PEOR - (416-D2
See Page 415)
- PEOR - (456-F2
See Page 415)
S WADE CT
- GIL 85236 863-C2
N WADE DR
900 GIL 85236 783-C4
S WADE DR
300 GIL 85236 783-C6
W WADE LN
15900 GDYR 85338 (694-E4
See Page 653)
W WAGNER CT
600 GIL 85233 822-A3
S WAGNER DR
900 GIL 85233 822-A3
W WAGNER DR
1100 GIL 85233 821-H3
E WAGON CIR
- GIL 85236 863-D4
- SCTS 85262 (461-D1
See Page 421)
E WAGON CT
- GIL 85236 863-D4
WAGON BOX RD
- YavC - 250-E1
E WAGONER RD
- PHX 85022 538-H6
900 PHX 85022 539-A6
2500 PHX 85032 539-D6
4900 PHX 85254 540-A7
W WAGONER RD
- PHX 85023 538-D6
2800 PHX 85053 538-A6
3600 PHX 85308 537-F6
3600 PHX 85308 538-A6
5400 GLEN 85308 537-A6
7500 GLEN 85308 536-H6
E WAGONER ST
1900 PHX 85022 539-C6
N WAGON WHEEL
2100 APJT 85219 745-J3
S WAGON WHEEL
1000 APJT 85219 745-J7
E WAGON WHEEL DR
- PHX 85008 699-J6
- PHX 85020 618-H7
1200 PHX 85020 619-A7
N WAGON WHEEL DR
7500 PHX 85020 618-H7
22400 MarC 85375 495-C7
S WAGON WHEEL DR
- CHAN 85249 861-G2
W WAGON WHEEL DR
500 PHX 85021 618-F7
4000 PHX 85051 617-G7
10700 MarC 85307 615-J6
13500 MarC 85375 495-C7
13500 MarC 85375 535-A1
14400 MarC 85375 534-J1
N WAGON WHEEL LN
47800 MarC 85087 (338-C5
See Page 337)
N WAGON WHEEL RD
- QC 85242 903-J7
8600 PinC 85242 903-J7
E WAHALLA LN
900 PHX 85024 538-J4
1000 PHX 85024 539-A4
2800 PHX 85050 539-E4
W WAHALLA LN
- PHX 85024 538-G4
- PHX 85027 538-A4
3600 PHX 85308 537-F4
5400 GLEN 85308 537-A4
7500 GLEN 85308 536-H4
W WAIKIKI DR
10900 MarC 85351 575-J3
W WAITE PL
5000 GLEN 85301 617-E6
E WAITS FOR NO ONE RD
- MarC 85331 499-J2
S WAKIAL LP
12400 PHX 85044 819-H3
W WAKONDA LN
500 PHX 85023 578-G4
N WALAPAI CIR
11600 FTNH 85268 623-C2
E WALATANIN LN
- PHX 85023 578-F3
E WALATOWA ST
4000 PHX 85040 779-G7
4000 PHX 85044 779-G7
W WALATOWA ST
- PHX 85041 778-A6
W WALDEN CT
- MarC 85086 (378-A7
See Page 337)
W WALDEN DR
3000 MarC 85086 (378-B7
See Page 337)
W WALDEN WY
- MarC 85086 (378-B7
See Page 337)
WALKER RD
- PinC - 901-C7

E WALKING STICK WY
- PinC 85219 786-J5
W WALKING STICK WY
- SURP 85374 534-H5
E WALLACE AV
2600 PHX 85032 579-D1
5000 PHX 85254 580-B2
S WALNUT DR
2300 CHAN 85248 861-C4
E WALNUT LN
15300 FTNH 85268 582-J3
E WALNUT RD
- GIL 85236 863-D6
E WALNUT ST
1200 MarC 85337 (1090-D4
See Page 1049)
N WALNUT ST
32800 MarC 85361 (453-A1
See Page 413)
S WALNUT ST
32000 MarC 85361 (453-A2
See Page 413)
N WALNUT CREEK CT
- MarC 85263 (504-A3
See Page 503)
WALPAI RD
5500 GLEN 85307 615-C7
5500 GLEN 85307 655-C1
N WALSH DR
10800 FTNH 85268 623-D3
E WALTANN LN
- PHX 85022 578-H3
1600 PHX 85022 579-B3
2400 PHX 85032 579-D3
4800 PHX 85254 580-A3
W WALTANN LN
- PHX 85023 578-C3
3000 PHX 85053 578-A3
3500 PHX 85053 577-J3
4300 PHX 85306 577-F3
5100 GLEN 85306 577-E3
E WALTER RD
30000 MarC 85390 290-H5
W WALTER WY
- PHX 85027 498-A7
W WALTON WY
700 CHAN 85226 820-F4
E WAMPUM WY
7200 CARE 85377 420-H4
S WANDA DR
800 GIL 85296 822-H3
W WANDA LYNN LN
6700 GLEN 85382 577-A2
W WANDER LN
2700 MarC 85087 (338-B5
See Page 337)
E WARBLER RD
- MarC 85236 863-B4
N WARBLER WY
11600 FTNH 85268 623-D2
S WARCLOUD CT
11600 PHX 85044 819-E1
W WARHAWK ST
- MarC 85340 (654-H3
See Page 653)
N WARNER DR
800 APJT 85220 745-A3
4200 PinC 85220 705-A7
4200 PinC 85220 745-A3
S WARNER DR
400 APJT 85220 745-A7
800 APJT 85220 785-A1
E WARNER RD
- PHX 85044 819-H2
- CHAN 85225 821-G2
- GIL 85296 822-D2
- MarC 85296 822-G2
- TEMP 85284 820-F2
16000 GIL 85236 822-G2
16000 GIL 85236 823-C2
16400 MarC 85236 823-C2
18400 MarC 85212 823-F2
19200 MarC 85212 824-B2
W WARNER RD
- CHAN 85224 820-B2
- PHX 85284 819-J2
- TEMP 85284 819-J2
- CHAN 85225 821-E2
- GIL 85233 822-A2
- GIL 85296 822-B2
- TEMP 85284 820-B2
900 CHAN 85224 821-A2
4800 GIL 85233 821-J2
E WARNER ST
1600 PHX 85040 739-A5
10100 MarC 85220 744-F6
10300 MESA 85220 744-G6
W WARNER ST
- PHX 85043 737-B4
3600 PHX 85043 736-H4
12500 AVON 85323 735-D4
E WARNER ELLIOT LP
4200 PHX 85044 779-G7
4200 PHX 85044 819-G1
S WARNER ELLIOT LP
12000 PHX 85044 819-G2
S WARNER RANCH DR
8800 TEMP 85284 820-D3
W WARNER RANCH DR
100 TEMP 85284 820-C3
S WARPAINT CT
12200 PHX 85044 819-E2
S WARPAINT DR
11600 PHX 85044 819-E1
13000 PHX 85048 819-D2
N WARREN
- MarC 85207 744-E2
S WARREN
- MESA 85212 784-D4
N WARREN CIR
- MarC 85207 744-E2
W WARREN DR
- MarC 85086 (378-B7
See Page 337)
W WARREN LN
- MarC 85086 (378-A7
See Page 337)
W WARREN ST
200 GBND 85337 (1090-A2
See Page 1049)
E WASHBOARD CREEK WY
- SCTS 85255 541-E4
E WASHINGTON AV
- GIL 85234 783-B7
- GIL 85236 783-C7
200 GIL 85234 782-D7
N WASHINGTON AV
- GIL 85234 782-D7

N WASHINGTON AV
100 GBND 85337 (1090-C3
See Page 1049)
S WASHINGTON AV
400 GBND 85337 (1090-C3
See Page 1049)
W WASHINGTON AV
- GIL 85233 782-A7
1200 GIL 85233 781-J7
E WASHINGTON CT
- GIL 85234 783-A7
- GIL 85236 783-C7
E WASHINGTON ST
- GIL 85236 783-D7
- PHX 85004 698-H7
- PHX 85034 699-A7
300 TEMP 85281 740-D1
700 PHX 85034 698-H7
800 AVON 85323 695-C6
4800 PHX 85034 700-A7
10600 MarC 85234 783-A7
16200 GIL 85234 783-A7
N WASHINGTON ST
- WICK 85390 290-E2
100 CHAN 85225 821-F6
3000 CHAN 85225 781-G7
S WASHINGTON ST
- WICK 85390 290-F2
100 CHAN 85225 821-F7
700 CHAN 85225 861-F1
W WASHINGTON ST
- AVON 85353 695-E6
- GDYR 85338 (694-D5
See Page 653)
- PHX 85003 698-E7
- TEMP 85281 740-B1
100 PHX 85043 697-A6
600 PHX 85007 698-E7
1900 PHX 85009 698-A6
2000 PHX 85034 700-B7
2000 TEMP 85281 700-B7
3200 PHX 85009 697-G6
6700 PHX 85043 696-J6
7500 TOL 85043 696-G6
8200 PEOR 85345 616-B2
8300 TOL 85353 696-A6
N WA-SU-JA ST
- MarC 85264 583-H4
E WATEKA CT
- GIL 85236 863-D5
N WATERBURY RD
2600 MarC 85207 704-B6
E WATERCRESS LN
1700 GIL 85234 782-G5
W WATERFALL CANYON RD
- MarC 85373 573-B6
E WATERFORD CIR
8500 MESA 85242 864-A3
W WATERFORD DR
- SURP 85374 534-G5
S WATERFRONT DR
2000 CHAN 85248 861-A7
E WATERMAN CT
- MarC 85236 863-A2
N WATERMAN LN
4500 PVAL 85028 619-J6
E WATERMAN ST
- GIL 85236 863-C2
E WATERMAN WY
- GIL 85236 863-B2
- MarC 85236 863-A2
N WATERMANN LN
2200 APJT 85220 745-B3
S WATERMANN LN
13200 MarC 85326 813-D1
W WATERMELON RD
29300 GBND 85337 (1050-C7
See Page 1049)
30700 GBND 85337 1049-G7
30700 MarC 85337 1049-G7
30700 MarC 85337 (1050-C7
See Page 1049)
E WATER TANK RD
- GIL 85296 822-C1
- MarC 85296 822-C1
E WATERVIEW DR
- MarC 85249 902-C5
1700 CHAN 85249 901-J5
1700 CHAN 85249 902-A5
E WATERVIEW PL
1300 CHAN 85249 901-J5
S WATERVIEW PL
1200 CHAN 85249 901-H5
E WATFORD CT
11000 MarC 85248 901-F5
E WATFORD DR
10800 MarC 85248 901-E5
E WATFORD WY
9700 MarC 85248 901-B5
E WATKINS AV
1000 BUCK 85326 (772-B1
See Page 731)
E WATKINS DR
800 AVON 85323 695-C5
E WATKINS ST
- PHX 85004 738-G3
700 PHX 85034 738-J3
1400 PHX 85034 739-A3
W WATKINS ST
- PHX 85043 736-F2
- PHX 85353 736-E2
- PHX 85003 738-F3
700 PHX 85007 738-D3
4700 PHX 85043 737-E2
15600 GDYR 85338 (734-D2
See Page 733)
16500 MarC 85338 (734-C2
See Page 733)
20300 BUCK 85326 733-B1
21900 BUCK 85326 (732-G1
See Page 731)
22700 MarC 85326 (732-A1
See Page 731)
W WATSON CIR
- SURP 85379 (574-H4
See Page 573)
E WATSON CT
6000 TEMP 85283 780-J4
E WATSON DR
400 TEMP 85283 780-E4
W WATSON DR
800 TEMP 85283 780-B4
W WATSON LN
- SURP 85379 (574-F4
See Page 573)
- SURP 85379 575-C4
4400 PHX 85306 577-G4
7700 PEOR 85381 576-H4

N WATSON RD
1000 MarC 85326 (692-E3
See Page 651)
1000 BUCK 85326 (692-E3
See Page 651)
S WATSON RD
900 BUCK 85326 (692-E5
See Page 651)
900 MarC 85326 (692-E5
See Page 651)
2000 MarC 85326 (732-E3
See Page 731)
4400 BUCK 85326 (732-E7
See Page 731)
7600 MarC 85326 (772-E4
See Page 731)
8400 BUCK 85326 (772-E2
See Page 731)
S WATTLEWOOD
- MESA 85212 784-H4
S WAVERLY WY
5200 TEMP 85283 780-F3
N WAVYLEAF AV
17200 SURP 85374 534-H6
WAX WING CT
- FTNH 85268 582-G5
E WAXWING DR
18900 MarC 85263 503-J4
S WAYFARER
200 MESA 85204 742-E6
1300 MESA 85204 782-E1
E WAYLAND DR
- PHX 85040 738-J7
E WAYLAND RD
1200 PHX 85040 738-J7
4100 PHX 85040 739-G7
W WAYLAND RD
1700 PHX 85041 738-C7
S WAYNE DR
- CHAN 85225 822-B7
- CHAN 85225 862-B1
- CHAN 85249 862-A2
- MarC 85249 902-A3
W WAYNE LN
- MarC 85086 (378-C6
See Page 337)
W WAYSIDE GARNET DR
- MarC 85335 575-G1
- SURP 85335 575-G1
- SURP 85335 575-G1
W WEATHERBY DR
- SURP 85374 534-B6
W WEATHERBY PL
- CHAN 85248 861-E3
W WEATHERBY WY
- CHAN 85248 861-A3
E WEATHERVANE LN
1500 TEMP 85283 780-G3
S WEAVER DR
- APJT 85220 785-C1
300 APJT 85220 745-C6
E WEAVER RD
4000 PHX 85050 539-J2
4400 PHX 85050 540-A2
N WEAVER ST
700 WICK 85390 290-E1
S WEAVERS A NEEDLE TR
- PinC 85219 786-G7
E WEBER DR
600 TEMP 85281 740-F1
N WEBER DR
- CHAN 85284 819-J4
1000 CHAN 85284 820-A3
S WEBER DR
100 CHAN 85226 819-J7
16800 MarC 85226 819-J7
16800 MarC 85226 859-J1
W WEBSTER CT
- MarC 85086 (378-A7
See Page 337)
N WEDGEWOOD CIR
1100 MESA 85203 741-J2
N WEDGEWOOD DR
900 MESA 85203 741-J3
W WEDGEWOOD DR
8700 PEOR 85382 576-E1
10600 MarC 85351 576-A1
10800 MarC 85351 575-J1
N WEIDNER ST
100 GBND 85337 (1090-A3
See Page 1049)
W WEINBERG RD
400 MarC 85342 (412-D4
See Page 411)
N WELD CIR
1100 MESA 85203 742-A2
E WELDON AV
- PHX 85012 698-G1
300 PHX 85014 698-J1
1300 PHX 85014 699-A1
1600 PHX 85016 699-A1
3200 PHX 85018 699-E1
4900 PHX 85018 700-A1
6300 SCTS 85251 700-D1
8600 SCTS 85251 701-A1
8700 MarC 85251 701-A1
W WELDON AV
- GDYR 85338 (654-J7
See Page 653)
- GDYR 85338 655-A7
- PHX 85013 698-E1
1300 PHX 85015 698-C1
2700 PHX 85017 698-A1
3100 AVON 85340 655-C7
3400 PHX 85017 657-J7
3800 PHX 85033 656-F7
4300 PHX 85031 657-D7
6400 PHX 85033 657-A7
8500 PHX 85037 656-D7
N WELK DR
18200 MarC 85373 536-A4
W WELK DR
10600 MarC 85373 536-A7
10700 MarC 85373 535-J7
W WELL ST
12100 ELMG 85335 575-E4
E WELLAND RD
800 PHX 85041 778-E5
W WELLINGBOROUGH RD
- SURP 85374 534-D5
W WELLS CT
- MarC 85086 (378-C6
See Page 337)
N WELLS FARGO AV
3300 SCTS 85251 700-F1
4300 SCTS 85251 660-F7
W WELLS FARGO AV
1000 APJT 85220 745-C7

E WELSH TR
8300 SCTS 85258 620-J3
8300 SCTS 85258 621-A3
12000 SCTS 85259 622-A3
S WENDLER DR
- TEMP 85284 819-J1
- TEMP 85284 820-A1
1700 TEMP 85282 780-A2
N WENDOVER DR
13800 FTNH 85268 583-B6
W WENDOVER DR
14400 SURP 85374 534-J6
E WESCOTT DR
400 PHX 85024 538-H6
1000 PHX 85024 539-B6
2400 PHX 85050 539-D6
N WESCOTT DR
19000 PEOR 85382 536-G5
W WESCOTT DR
200 PHX 85027 538-A5
3500 PHX 85308 537-F5
3500 PHX 85308 538-A5
5300 GLEN 85308 537-A5
7100 GLEN 85308 536-H5
8300 PEOR 85382 536-C5
S WESLEY
- MESA 85212 784-F6
- MESA 85220 784-F3
S WESLEY CIR
- MESA 85212 784-F6
E WESLEYAN DR
400 TEMP 85282 740-E7
2400 TEMP 85282 741-A7
N WEST RD
48200 MarC 85320 (284-G7
See Page 244)
S WEST RD
- WICK 85390 290-A3
W WEST RD
- PHX 85041 738-F5
W WESTAR DR
- GDYR 85326 (774-A7
See Page 733)
- GDYR 85326 813-J1
- GDYR 85326 (814-A1
See Page 813)
W WESTBROOK DR
8300 PEOR 85382 536-F4
N WESTBROOK LN
6000 MarC 85340 (654-H2
See Page 653)
N WESTBROOK PKWY
8900 PEOR 85382 536-E4
W WESTBROOK PKWY
9100 PEOR 85382 536-C5
E WESTBROOKE RD
1000 PinC 85242 865-D6
W WESTBROOKE RD
- PinC 85242 865-A6
E WESTBY DR
16600 FTNH 85268 583-C6
E WESTCHESTER AV
300 TEMP 85283 780-F4
W WESTCHESTER AV
800 TEMP 85283 780-B4
E WESTCHESTER DR
1000 CHAN 85249 901-H5
1700 CHAN 85249 902-A5
W WESTCOTT DR
5100 GLEN 85308 537-E5
W WESTCOURT WY
2000 TEMP 85282 739-J6
2000 TEMP 85282 740-A6
E WESTERN AV
- AVON 85323 695-B7
- GDYR 85338 695-B7
100 AVON 85338 695-B7
W WESTERN AV
- GDYR 85323 695-A7
- AVON 85323 695-B7
W WESTERN DR
1900 CHAN 85224 781-B6
WESTERN CSR
- CHAN - 780-J6
- CHAN - 781-A6
- GIL - 782-A6
- MarC - 777-J6
- MarC - 778-C5
- MarC - 817-F1
- MESA - 780-J6
- MESA - 781-A6
- PHX - 777-J6
- PHX - 778-F2
- PHX - 779-D2
- TEMP - 779-F2
- TEMP - 780-C3
E WESTERN HILLS ST
- MESA 85207 703-J2
S WESTERN SKIES DR
800 GIL 85296 822-F2
E WESTERN SKY LN
- SCTS 85262 421-E7
E WESTERN STAR BLVD
4000 PHX 85040 779-G6
4000 PHX 85044 779-H6
S WESTERN STAR BLVD
- GDYR 85326 (773-H4
See Page 733)
- GDYR 85338 (773-H4
See Page 733)
S WESTFALL AV
5700 TEMP 85283 780-B4
9500 TEMP 85284 820-B3
S WESTFALL DR
200 TEMP 85281 740-C3
3400 TEMP 85282 780-B1
W WESTFALL WY
18000 SURP 85374 533-J6
18000 SURP 85374 534-A6
W WESTGATE DR
- SURP 85374 535-C7
12300 MarC 85375 535-D7
E WESTLAND DR
6000 SCTS 85331 460-D2
7200 SCTS 85262 460-H2
7900 SCTS 85262 (461-B2
See Page 421)
E WESTLAND RD
- PHX 85085 459-H1
- PHX 85331 459-H1
4800 MarC 85331 460-B1
4900 CHAN 85331 460-B1
N WESTLAND RD
- MarC 85331 419-J7
- MarC 85331 459-J1
- PHX 85331 419-J7
- PHX 85331 459-J1
W WESTMINSTER DR
- SURP 85374 534-D6

STREET Block City ZIP Pg-Grid

W WINNWOOD AV
5600 GLEN 85304 617-D1
E WINONA ST
3400 PHX 85044 819-E3
E WINSLOW AV
3800 PHX 85040 739-G4
W WINSLOW AV
- PHX 85043 737-A3
- PHX 85353 736-A3
11100 MarC 85353 735-G3
12600 AVON 85323 735-D3
E WINSTON DR
- PHX 85040 778-G4
1600 PHX 85040 779-A4
4600 PHX 85044 779-J4
W WINSTON DR
- MarC 85339 777-D3
- PHX 85339 777-E3
100 PHX 85041 778-F3
N WINSTON LN
14600 FTNH 85268 583-C5
E WINTER DR
100 PHX 85020 618-H6
1200 PHX 85020 619-A6
N WINTER DR
7800 PHX 85020 619-A6
S WINTER LN
- GIL 85236 863-E4
N WINTERGREEN DR
20400 MarC 85375 535-B3
N WINTERGREEN WY
3700 AVON 85323 655-H7
N WINTERHAVEN
200 MESA 85213 742-E4
2000 MESA 85213 702-E6
S WINTERHAVEN
200 MESA 85204 742-E6
N WINTERHAVEN CIR
800 MESA 85213 742-E3
N WINTERHAVEN LN
- SURP 85374 534-F4
S WINTERSBURG RD
2900 MarC 85354 102-A3
E WINTER SUN DR
- SCTS 85262 421-F5
N WINTHROP
2100 MESA 85213 702-F6
S WINTHROP
200 MESA 85204 742-F6
1400 MESA 85204 782-F2
N WINTHROP CIR
200 MESA 85213 742-F2
2700 MESA 85213 702-F5
S WINTHROP CIR
800 MESA 85204 742-F7
S WINTHROP ST
500 GIL 85296 822-E2
E WINTU WY
4700 PHX 85044 779-H7
4700 PHX 85044 819-H1
E WINWOOD LN
- SCTS 85255 540-J3
W WISCONSIN AV
11100 YNTN 85335 575-H5
N WISDOM WY
- MarC 85086 (378-B7
See Page 337)
- MarC 85086 (418-B1
See Page 417)
W WISTERIA CT
1200 CHAN 85248 861-C5
W WISTERIA DR
1100 CHAN 85248 861-B5
E WODDEN LN
- MarC 85264 583-H4
N WOLF ST
4600 PHX 85017 658-A5
W WOLF ST
5300 PHX 85031 657-D5
5900 PHX 85033 657-A5
6900 PHX 85033 656-H5
8600 PHX 85037 656-E5
E WOLFBERRY CIR
- SCTS 85255 501-C4
8000 PinC 85219 786-F6
E WOLF CANYON CIR
- MESA 85207 703-J2
E WOLF CANYON ST
- MESA 85207 703-J2
W WOLFLEY DR
12700 ELMG 85335 615-D1
12900 ELMG 85379 615-D1
W WOLF RUN DR
- MarC 85086 (378-D5
See Page 337)
W WOLFTRAP RD
900 MarC 85087 (338-G5
See Page 337)
N WOLVERINE PASS RD
3900 PinC 85219 745-F1
4100 PinC 85219 705-F7
W WONDERVIEW DR
3900 PHX 85019 657-H5
E WONDERVIEW RD
4900 PHX 85018 660-B6
E WOOD AV
10000 MarC 85208 744-F6
10000 MarC 85220 744-F6
10200 MESA 85220 744-F6
E WOOD DR
- MarC 85249 901-H2
- MarC 85249 902-C3
- PHX 85022 578-H6
7600 SCTS 85260 580-H6
8300 SCTS 85260 581-C6
N WOOD DR
13000 PHX 85029 577-J6
13000 PHX 85029 578-A6
W WOOD DR
- CHAN 85248 901-F3
- PHX 85304 577-F5
- PHX 85029 578-A6
3500 PHX 85029 577-H6
5100 GLEN 85304 577-C6
8100 PEOR 85381 576-F5
W WOOD LN
- PHX 85043 736-G4
E WOOD PL
- MarC 85249 902-B3
E WOOD RD
9700 SCTS 85260 581-D7
E WOOD ST
1200 PHX 85040 738-J5
1400 PHX 85040 739-A5
W WOOD ST
- PHX 85043 737-B4
25100 BUCK 85326 (732-A3
See Page 731)
N WOODBURNE DR
800 CHAN 85224 821-A4
3100 CHAN 85224 781-A6
W WOODBURY LN
- SURP 85374 534-H5
N WOODHALL DR
2400 MESA 85215 703-C6
E WOODLAND AV
1000 PHX 85034 698-H6
8500 MESA 85242 864-B3
W WOODLAND AV
- AVON 85323 695-D6
700 PHX 85003 698-E6
700 PHX 85007 698-E6
N WOODLAND CT
8500 SCTS 85258 620-G5
E WOODLAND DR
2300 PHX 85048 819-B6
W WOODLANDS AV
300 GDYR 85338 (694-D5
See Page 653)
E WOODMAN DR
200 TEMP 85283 780-E5
W WOODMAN DR
600 TEMP 85283 780-B5
N WOODMERE FAIRWAY
4800 SCTS 85251 660-G6
5100 SCTS 85250 660-G5
N WOODPECKER BAY
11200 FTNH 85268 623-D3
E WOODRIDGE DR
4300 PHX 85032 579-H1
5200 PHX 85254 580-B1
W WOODRIDGE DR
- SURP 85374 534-G6
2900 PHX 85053 578-B1
3700 PHX 85308 577-H1
N WOODROSE AV
17000 SURP 85374 534-H6
N WOODROSE CT
17300 SURP 85374 534-H7
N WOODRUFF
- MESA 85207 704-B7
S WOODRUFF
2900 MESA 85212 784-A6
S WOODRUFF CIR
2000 MESA 85212 784-A6
E WOODSAGE LN
7400 SCTS 85258 620-G5
S WOODSHED CT
- GIL 85236 863-D4
S WOODSHED RD
- GIL 85236 863-D4
E WOODSHIRE CV
7400 SCTS 85258 620-G6
N WOODSHIRE PL
8500 SCTS 85258 620-G6
N WOODSIDE CT
1100 CHAN 85224 821-A3
N WOODSIDE DR
800 CHAN 85224 820-J4
800 CHAN 85224 821-A3
13600 FTNH 85268 583-D6
W WOODSIDE DR
13500 MarC 85375 535-B4
E WOODSIDE LN
- GIL 85236 863-C2
N WOODSIDE LN
13900 FTNH 85268 583-D6
N WOODSIDE RD
1400 CHAN 85224 821-A3
E WOODSIDE ST
- GIL 85236 863-B2
E WOODSIDE WY
- GIL 85236 863-C2
- MarC 85236 863-B2
E WOODSMAN PL
- CHAN 85249 861-J1
- CHAN 85249 862-A2
E WOODSTOCK RD
4100 PHX 85331 459-H3
4300 MarC 85331 460-A3
4300 PHX 85331 460-C3
E WOODWARD DR
- PHX 85004 698-G3
E WOODY ST
3900 MESA 85205 742-H5
N WORLEY LN
- SURP 85374 575-C1
N WORTMAN WY
7100 MarC 85253 659-H1
7400 MarC 85253 619-H7
W WRANGLER
17200 SURP 85374 534-B5
E WRANGLER CT
- GIL 85236 863-D4
15400 FTNH 85268 582-J4
W WRANGLER DR
9600 MarC 85373 536-C7
E WRANGLER RD
2300 MarC 85086 419-D5
N WRANGLER RD
25400 SCTS 85255 501-A5
E WREN CIR
5100 MESA 85215 703-C6
N WREN CIR
8600 PHX 85028 619-J5
N WREN CT
- FTNH 85268 583-A5
N WREN DR
900 GIL 85236 783-E5
N WRIGHT WY
2700 MESA 85215 703-D5
W WT ROAD F
- MarC 85373 573-B6
N WUSICH ST
16400 SURP 85374 575-E1
E WYATT CT
- GIL 85236 863-D2
N WYATT DR
600 CHAN 85226 820-A4
E WYATT WY
- GIL 85236 863-D1
N WYCLIFF CIR
1400 MESA 85201 741-E1
S WYCLIFF CIR
2900 MESA 85210 781-E6
S WYLIE
- MESA 85212 784-E6
S WYLIE CIR
- MESA 85212 784-E6
N WYNONA WY
18700 SURP 85374 534-E5
W WYOMING
9600 PEOR 85345 616-C1
S WYOMING AV
25400 MarC 85248 901-A4

X

S XAVIER CT
10700 GDYR 85338 (774-A5
See Page 733)

Y

E YAHOO TR
5100 CVCK 85331 460-B1
5100 MarC 85331 460-B1
S YAKI CT
12200 PHX 85044 819-E1
N YALE
600 MESA 85213 742-E2
2100 MESA 85213 702-F6
S YALE
200 MESA 85204 742-E6
1200 MESA 85204 782-E2
S YALE CIR
200 GIL 85296 822-D1
E YALE DR
700 TEMP 85283 780-E4
N YALE DR
200 MESA 85213 742-E4
300 GIL 85234 782-D5
W YALE DR
- MarC 85283 780-C4
500 TEMP 85283 780-B4
E YALE ST
1400 PHX 85006 698-J3
1400 PHX 85006 699-A3
2300 PHX 85008 699-F3
4900 PHX 85008 700-A3
W YALE ST
9000 PHX 85037 696-D2
E YAMU KIVA CIR
17500 FTNH 85268 583-E5
E YANEZ AV
- BUCK 85326 (772-B2
See Page 731)
E YAQUI CT
16700 FTNH 85268 623-C2
S YAQUI DR
500 WICK 85390 290-A4
S YAQUI LN
3200 PinC 85219 786-H3
W YAVAPAI LN
- AVON 85353 735-E1
E YAVAPAI RD
17500 FTNH 85268 583-G5
17500 MarC 85264 583-G5
17500 MarC 85268 583-G5
E YAVAPAI ST
100 WICK 85390 290-F2
1100 PHX 85034 738-J1
W YAVAPAI ST
- GDYR 85338 (694-E7
See Page 653)
- MarC 85353 735-G1
- PHX 85003 738-F1
- WICK 85390 290-E2
600 PHX 85004 738-H1
1500 PHX 85007 738-E1
1900 PHX 85009 738-B1
W YAVAPI ST
- GDYR 85326 (694-A7
See Page 653)
E YAWEPE ST
4000 PHX 85044 779-G7
E YEARLING DR
10500 SCTS 85255 501-F5
E YEARLING RD
100 MarC 85024 498-H4
8200 SCTS 85255 501-A5
W YEARLING RD
- PEOR 85382 496-D4
- PEOR 85382 497-B4
- MarC 85024 498-G4
- MarC 85027 498-E4
11300 MarC 85373 495-H4
E YELLOW BELL DR
25700 SCTS 85255 501-F5
N YELLOWSTONE CIR
21600 MarC 85375 535-A1
N YELLOWSTONE CT
21500 MarC 85375 535-A1
E YELLOWSTONE PL
15600 FTNH 85268 583-A3
S YELLOW WOOD
- MESA 85212 784-J4
N YERBA BUENA WY
14200 FTNH 85268 583-D5
E YOLANTHA ST
5300 CVCK 85331 460-C1
N YORK CIR
200 MESA 85213 742-F2
S YORK CIR
300 MESA 85204 742-F6
N YORK ST
500 MESA 85213 742-F2
W YORKSHIRE DR
2500 PHX 85027 538-B5
3300 PHX 85308 538-B5
3500 PHX 85308 537-H5
19800 SURP 85387 533-D4
N YORKTOWN CT
- MarC 85086 (378-D6
See Page 337)
N YORKTOWN TR
- MarC 85086 (378-D6
See Page 337)
W YOSEMITE CT
14000 MarC 85375 535-B4
W YOSEMITE DR
14100 MarC 85375 535-A3
14500 MarC 85375 534-H3
N YOUNG
700 MESA 85203 742-C3
W YOUNG ST
- SURP 85374 534-C7
12700 SURP 85374 575-B1
15600 SURP 85374 (574-E1
See Page 573)
W YOUNGTOWN AV
11100 YNTN 85335 575-H7
E YOWY ST
4000 PHX 85044 779-G7
N YUCATAN CT
22800 MarC 85375 494-J7
S YUCCA
1700 MESA 85202 781-C2
N YUCCA CIR
500 MESA 85201 741-C3
S YUCCA CIR
26200 MarC 85248 901-A5
W YUCCA CIR
1900 MESA 85201 741-C4
N YUCCA CT
2100 CHAN 85224 821-B1
W YUCCA CT
11600 SURP 85374 535-G7
E YUCCA DR
15600 FTNH 85268 583-A5
N YUCCA DR
- GBND 85337 (1090-C3
See Page 1049)
900 MarC 85390 290-B4
900 WICK 85390 290-B4
S YUCCA DR
- GBND 85337 (1090-C3
See Page 1049)
- WICK 85390 290-B4
32600 MarC 85390 290-B6
W YUCCA DR
- TEMP 85282 779-J1
- WICK 85390 290-A2
8700 PEOR 85345 616-E1
32200 MarC 85390 290-A1
E YUCCA LN
11600 MarC 85331 (382-A4
See Page 341)
S YUCCA PL
1000 CHAN 85248 861-B1
E YUCCA RD
5600 CVCK 85331 420-D1
N YUCCA RD
5500 PVAL 85253 660-C3
E YUCCA ST
1200 PHX 85020 618-J1
1200 PHX 85020 619-A1
2300 PHX 85028 619-C1
5000 PHX 85254 620-A2
9400 SCTS 85260 621-B2
10800 SCTS 85259 621-G2
12800 SCTS 85259 622-C2
N YUCCA ST
400 CHAN 85224 821-B1
2600 CHAN 85224 781-B6
S YUCCA ST
- CHAN 85224 821-B7
1500 CHAN 85248 861-B2
3000 MESA 85202 781-B6
W YUCCA ST
1500 PHX 85029 618-A1
3400 PHX 85029 617-H1
4300 PHX 85304 617-G1
5000 GLEN 85304 617-B1
6700 PEOR 85345 617-A1
7100 PEOR 85345 616-D1
E YUCCA WY
- SCTS 85259 621-J2
- SCTS 85259 622-A2
E YUCCA BLOSSOM CIR
8600 PinC 85219 786-F6
E YUCCA BLOSSOM DR
8600 PinC 85219 786-F6
E YUKON DR
1700 PHX 85024 539-B4
3300 PHX 85050 539-B4
N YUKON DR
20800 MarC 85375 535-A3
20800 MarC 85375 534-J2
W YUKON DR
- PEOR 85308 536-G4
- PHX 85308 537-H4
500 PHX 85027 538-D4
9700 PEOR 85382 536-B3
10800 PEOR 85373 535-J4
10800 PEOR 85373 536-A4
14300 MarC 85375 535-A2
14400 MarC 85375 534-J1
N YUMA
37300 MarC 85086 417-J4
W YUMA
4100 MarC 85086 417-J4
S YUMA DR
800 WICK 85390 290-A4
N YUMA RD
- SCTS 85258 660-H1
W YUMA RD
- GDYR 85338 695-A7
- MarC 85338 695-A7
1200 BUCK 85326 (692-E6
See Page 651)
14000 GDYR 85338 (694-B7
See Page 653)
14000 MarC 85338 (694-G7
See Page 653)
17500 GDYR 85326 (694-B7
See Page 653)
17500 MarC 85326 (694-B7
See Page 653)
17500 GDYR 85326 (693-F7
See Page 653)
17500 MarC 85326 (693-F7
See Page 653)
18700 BUCK 85326 (693-F7
See Page 653)
23500 MarC 85326 (692-E6
See Page 651)
25000 MarC 85326 (691-J7
See Page 651)
25100 BUCK 85326 (691-J7
See Page 651)
E YUMA ST
- PHX 85004 738-G1
1100 PHX 85034 738-J1
2500 PHX 85034 739-C2
4900 PHX 85044 819-H1
W YUMA ST
- MarC 85353 735-G1
- PHX 85003 738-F1
- PHX 85004 738-F1
900 PHX 85007 738-D1
2100 PHX 85009 738-A1
3100 PHX 85009 737-J1
6500 PHX 85043 737-F1
11100 AVON 85353 735-E1
E YUMA FRANK RD
- MarC 85264 583-H4
E YUSUCU ST
5400 GUAD 85283 780-A4
S YUTA ST
10800 PHX 85044 779-G7
E YVONNE LN
- TEMP 85284 820-E3
W YVONNE LN
1200 TEMP 85284 820-A3

Z

E ZABEL MINE RD
30200 MarC 85390 290-H4
W ZABEL MINE RD
30300 MarC 85390 290-H4
W ZACHARY DR
- PHX 85027 538-B3
E ZAHARIAS DR
17300 FTNH 85268 623-E2
W ZAK RD
- PHX 85043 736-H2
N ZAMORA PZ
15200 FTNH 85268 582-H4
N ZANE GREY LN
16200 FTNH 85268 583-A3
E ZAPATA DR
15000 FTNH 85268 582-H5
N ZAPATA DR
14800 FTNH 85268 582-J4
E ZENITH LN
- PHX 85331 459-J1
- PHX 85331 460-A1
5000 CVCK 85331 460-B1
5000 MarC 85331 460-B1
W ZENNIA CT
- SURP 85374 534-F2
N ZEPHYR CT
18400 MarC 85375 535-B5
N ZEPHYR DR
10800 FTNH 85268 623-D3
E ZIA ST
4000 PHX 85044 819-G1
S ZINNIA
2100 MESA 85208 784-A4
S ZINNIA AV
2000 MESA 85208 784-A4
S ZINNIA CIR
2400 MESA 85208 784-A5
N ZINNIA CT
18800 MarC 85375 535-E5
N ZION DR
19800 MarC 85375 535-D4
W ZOE ELLA WY
5500 GLEN 85306 577-B3
6700 GLEN 85382 577-A3
N ZORITA PZ
14800 FTNH 85268 582-H5
N ZORRILLO DR
44600 MarC 85087 (378-H1
See Page 337)
44800 MarC 85087 (338-H7
See Page 337)
ZUNI CIR
2700 GLEN 85307 615-C7
E ZUNI CIR
9500 MarC 85248 901-B6
E ZUNI CT
4400 PHX 85044 819-G2
N ZUNI PKWY
14400 SURP 85374 534-J7
S ZUNI RD
- MarC 85326 (773-D7
See Page 733)
13400 MarC 85326 813-D1
N ZUNI ST
200 GBND 85337 (1090-A3
See Page 1049)
N ZUNI TR
17000 SURP 85374 534-J7
17000 SURP 85374 535-A7
W ZUNI TR
14400 SURP 85374 534-J7

#

E 1ST AV
- MESA 85210 741-H5
100 MESA 85207 743-G5
400 MESA 85204 741-J5
700 MESA 85204 742-A5
2000 APJT 85219 745-G6
6600 SCTS 85251 700-E1
7900 MarC 85208 744-A6
7900 MESA 85208 744-A6
N 1ST AV
- PHX 85003 698-G2
100 AVON 85323 695-B7
100 PHX 85013 658-G1
2900 PHX 85013 698-G2
7000 PHX 85021 658-G1
7700 PHX 85021 618-G3
13000 PHX 85029 578-G6
13900 ELMG 85335 575-E4
14600 PHX 85023 578-H1
17400 PHX 85023 538-H6
18700 PHX 85027 538-H3
50300 MarC 85320 (284-H4
See Page 244)
S 1ST AV
- GDYR 85338 (773-J4
See Page 733)
- PHX 85003 698-G7
600 PHX 85003 738-G1
700 AVON 85323 735-B2
3400 PHX 85041 738-F4
6200 PHX 85041 778-G1
15400 PHX 85045 818-F4
15500 PHX 85048 818-F5
W 1ST AV
- MESA 85210 741-F5
700 ELMG 85335 615-F1
1800 MESA 85202 741-C5
1800 APJT 85220 745-B6
1ST AV E
200 BUCK 85326 (732-B7
See Page 731)
200 MarC 85326 (732-B7
See Page 731)
1ST AV W
200 BUCK 85326 (732-A7
See Page 731)
E 1ST DR
100 AVON 85323 735-B2
N 1ST DR
5300 PHX 85013 658-G4
8100 PHX 85021 618-G5
16200 PHX 85023 578-G1
17400 PHX 85023 538-G7
20800 PHX 85027 538-H3
S 1ST DR
1100 AVON 85323 735-B2
7600 PHX 85041 778-F3
16700 PHX 85045 818-E7
N 1ST LN
16600 PHX 85023 578-G2
20800 PHX 85027 538-G3
E 1ST PL
- PHX 85012 658-G1
600 MESA 85203 741-J5
700 MESA 85203 742-A5
2600 MESA 85213 742-E5
N 1ST PL
100 PHX 85012 658-G1
3100 PHX 85012 698-G1
7200 PHX 85020 618-H6
7200 PHX 85020 658-H1
13000 PHX 85022 578-H1
17600 PHX 85022 538-H7
50500 MarC 85320 (284-J4
See Page 244)
S 1ST PL
15500 PHX 85048 818-F5
W 1ST PL
600 MESA 85201 741-B4
E 1ST ST
- MESA 85201 741-H5
300 MESA 85203 741-J5
700 MESA 85203 742-A5
1800 MarC 85281 740-H3
1800 TEMP 85281 740-H3
2100 TEMP 85281 741-A3
2100 MESA 85281 741-A3
2500 MESA 85213 742-E5
6500 SCTS 85251 700-E1
10300 MarC 85220 744-G5
N 1ST ST
- AVON 85323 695-B6
- PHX 85004 698-G4
4700 PHX 85012 658-G4
7100 PHX 85020 658-G1
7300 PHX 85020 618-G3
12800 PHX 85022 578-H2
17600 PHX 85022 538-H6
37800 MarC 85086 (418-J3
See Page 417)
50200 MarC 85320 (284-H4
See Page 244)
S 1ST ST
- AVON 85323 695-B7
- ELMG 85335 575-F7
- ELMG 85335 615-F1
- TEMP 85281 740-B3
- AVON 85323 735-B1
100 PHX 85004 698-G7
200 PHX 85040 778-G1
600 PHX 85004 738-G1
700 GBND 85337 (1090-D4
See Page 1049)
700 MarC 85337 (1090-D4
See Page 1049)
6000 PHX 85040 738-G7
15400 PHX 85048 818-F4
15600 PHX 85045 818-F6
W 1ST ST
- MESA 85201 741-B5
- TEMP 85281 740-A3
2000 TEMP 85281 739-J3
E 2ND AV
- MESA 85210 741-H6
100 APJT 85219 745-E6
100 MESA 85207 743-G5
400 MESA 85204 741-J5
700 MESA 85204 742-A6
4700 PinC 85219 746-B6
7900 MarC 85208 744-A6
N 2ND AV
- PHX 85027 538-H2
100 PHX 85003 698-G6
100 PHX 85023 538-G7
200 PHX 85013 658-G1
300 AVON 85323 695-B7
3400 PHX 85013 698-G1
7000 PHX 85021 658-G1
7300 PHX 85021 618-G4
13000 PHX 85029 578-G6
13900 ELMG 85335 575-E4
14200 PHX 85023 578-G1
50300 MarC 85320 (284-H4
See Page 244)
S 2ND AV
300 PHX 85003 698-G7
600 PHX 85003 738-G1
4400 PHX 85041 738-F6
6000 PHX 85041 778-F1
16600 PHX 85045 818-F4
W 2ND AV
- PHX 85029 578-G6
100 MESA 85210 741-F5
1200 APJT 85220 745-C6
1800 MESA 85202 741-C6
2ND AV E
100 BUCK 85326 (732-B7
See Page 731)
100 MarC 85326 (732-B7
See Page 731)
2ND AV W
100 BUCK 85326 (732-A7
See Page 731)
N 2ND DR
4200 PHX 85013 658-G4
7000 PHX 85021 658-G1
7300 PHX 85021 618-G4
14600 PHX 85023 578-G1
18000 PHX 85023 538-G6
18800 PHX 85027 538-G4
W 2ND DR
7600 PHX 85021 618-G7
N 2ND LN
16600 PHX 85023 578-G1
E 2ND PL
600 MESA 85203 741-J4
600 MESA 85203 742-A4
N 2ND PL
300 AVON 85323 695-B7
3300 PHX 85012 698-G1
4000 PHX 85012 658-H1
7100 PHX 85020 658-H1
8300 PHX 85020 618-H3
12600 PHX 85022 578-H1
17400 PHX 85022 538-H6
S 2ND PL
1700 PHX 85004 738-G2
16400 PHX 85048 818-F7
W 2ND PL
400 MESA 85201 741-C4
E 2ND ST
- MESA 85201 741-H4
400 MESA 85203 741-J5
800 MESA 85203 742-B4
2600 MESA 85213 742-E5
6500 SCTS 85251 700-E1
N 2ND ST
- AVON 85323 695-B6
- PHX 85004 698-G3
100 BUCK 85326 (772-A1
See Page 731)
100 PHX 85022 578-H1
2900 PHX 85012 698-G1
4000 PHX 85012 658-G1
7000 PHX 85020 658-H1
7300 PHX 85020 618-H3
17400 PHX 85022 538-H6
33700 MarC 85085 (458-J1
See Page 417)
50600 MarC 85320 (284-J4
See Page 244)
S 2ND ST
- PHX 85048 818-F4
- PHX 85004 698-G7
100 AVON 85323 735-B1
100 BUCK 85326 (772-A2
See Page 731)
100 PHX 85040 778-G1
100 ELMG 85335 615-F1
200 ELMG 85335 575-F7
600 PHX 85004 738-G1
700 MarC 85337 (1090-D4
See Page 1049)
4400 PHX 85040 738-G6
W 2ND ST
- MESA 85201 741-C4
- TEMP 85281 740-B3
10700 AVON 85353 735-H1
N 2ND WY
8800 PHX 85020 618-H3
38500 MarC 85086 (418-J2
See Page 417)
E 3RD AV
200 MESA 85207 743-G5
400 MESA 85204 741-J6
700 MESA 85204 742-A6
5600 PinC 85219 746-D6
5700 SCTS 85251 660-F7
7900 MarC 85208 744-A6
N 3RD AV
- AVON 85323 695-A7
- PHX 85003 698-F3
100 PHX 85013 658-G2
200 PHX 85023 578-G1
2900 PHX 85013 698-F1
7000 PHX 85021 658-G1
7300 PHX 85021 618-G4
13200 PHX 85029 578-G6
13900 ELMG 85335 575-E4
17800 PHX 85023 538-G1
18800 PHX 85027 538-G2
34000 MarC 85085 (418-H7
See Page 417)
34000 MarC 85086 (418-H1
See Page 417)
40200 MarC 85086 (378-H7
See Page 337)
43300 MarC 85087 (378-H3
See Page 337)
52200 MarC 85320 (284-H4
See Page 244)
S 3RD AV
- PHX 85045 818-F4
- AVON 85323 695-B7
- AVON 85323 735-B1
- PHX 85003 698-F7
600 PHX 85003 738-F1
3400 PHX 85041 738-F4
6000 PHX 85041 778-F1
W 3RD AV
100 MESA 85210 741-G6
800 APJT 85220 745-D6
3RD AV E
100 MarC 85326 (732-B7
See Page 731)
100 BUCK 85326 (732-B7
See Page 731)
3RD AV W
100 BUCK 85326 (732-A7
See Page 731)
E 3RD DR
- MESA 85210 741-H6
400 MESA 85204 741-J6
2000 MESA 85204 742-D6
N 3RD DR
200 PHX 85023 578-G1
6600 PHX 85013 658-G2
9000 PHX 85021 618-G3
18800 PHX 85027 538-G4
S 3RD DR
700 PHX 85003 738-F1
E 3RD PL
- MESA 85201 741-H4
300 MESA 85203 742-A4
400 MESA 85203 741-J4
N 3RD PL
100 AVON 85323 695-A7
300 PHX 85012 658-H1
13200 PHX 85022 578-H1
17800 PHX 85022 538-H6
S 3RD PL
3400 PHX 85040 738-G4
8400 PHX 85040 778-G3
16600 PHX 85048 818-G7
W 3RD PL
- MESA 85201 741-C4
300 AVON 85323 695-A7
E 3RD ST
200 PHX 85040 738-G4
400 MESA 85203 741-J4
600 MESA 85203 742-A4
1800 TEMP 85281 740-H3
1900 MarC 85281 740-H3
6500 SCTS 85251 700-E1
N 3RD ST
- AVON 85323 695-B6
- PHX 85004 698-G3
100 BUCK 85326 (772-A1
See Page 731)
2900 PHX 85012 698-H1
3800 PHX 85012 658-H3
7000 PHX 85020 658-H1
7200 PHX 85020 618-H4
13000 PHX 85022 578-H1
17400 PHX 85022 538-H6
19400 PHX 85024 538-H5
25800 MarC 85024 498-H4
26300 PHX 85024 498-H4
26300 PHX 85085 498-H4
34000 MarC 85086 (418-J1
See Page 417)
39800 MarC 85086 (378-J5
See Page 337)
50300 MarC 85320 (284-J4
See Page 244)
S 3RD ST
- AVON 85323 695-B7
- PHX 85004 698-G7
- AVON 85323 735-B1
100 BUCK 85326 (772-A2
See Page 731)
200 ELMG 85335 615-F1
200 ELMG 85335 575-F7
600 PHX 85004 738-G1
3200 PHX 85040 738-G4
6000 PHX 85040 778-G1
15600 PHX 85048 818-G6
W 3RD ST
- TEMP 85281 740-B3
400 MESA 85201 741-C4
10800 AVON 85353 735-H1

STREET
Block City ZIP Pg-Grid

N 3RD WY
13200 PHX 85022 578-H6
S 3RD WY
8300 PHX 85040 778-G3
E 4TH AV
300 APJT 85219 745-E6
4700 PinC 85219 746-B7
6800 MESA 85207 743-G5
7200 SCTS 85251 660-F7
8000 MarC 85208 744-A6
10800 MarC 85220 744-J6
11400 MarC 85220 745-A6
19500 MarC 85208 743-G5
N 4TH AV
- PHX 85003 698-F6
3100 PHX 85013 698-F1
5500 PHX 85013 658-G1
7600 PHX 85021 618-G3
13900 ELMG 85335 575-E4
15800 PHX 85023 578-G2
17400 PHX 85023 538-G7
18600 PHX 85027 538-G3
N 4TH AV NW
4100 PHX 85013 658-F7
S 4TH AV
- AVON 85323 695-A7
- AVON 85323 735-A1
- PHX 85003 698-F7
600 PHX 85003 738-F1
4800 PHX 85041 738-F6
6000 PHX 85041 778-F1
15400 PHX 85045 818-F4
W 4TH AV
800 APJT 85220 745-A6
4TH AV E
100 BUCK 85326 (732-B7 See Page 731)
100 MarC 85326 (732-B7 See Page 731)
4TH AV W
100 BUCK 85326 (732-A7 See Page 731)
N 4TH DR
6200 PHX 85013 658-F2
7300 PHX 85021 618-G5
7300 PHX 85021 658-G2
15800 PHX 85023 578-G2
18600 PHX 85027 538-G4
S 4TH DR
15200 PHX 85045 818-E4
E 4TH PL
400 MESA 85203 741-J4
800 MESA 85203 742-A4
N 4TH PL
5700 PHX 85012 658-H2
7800 PHX 85020 618-H6
17800 PHX 85022 538-H7
19200 PHX 85024 538-H5
S 4TH PL
4800 PHX 85040 738-G6
8300 PHX 85040 778-G3
W 4TH PL
400 MESA 85201 741-C4
E 4TH ST
6500 SCTS 85251 700-E1
N 4TH ST
100 BUCK 85326 (772-A1 See Page 731)
200 PHX 85004 698-G5
300 AVON 85323 695-B6
500 BUCK 85326 (732-A7 See Page 731)
3800 PHX 85012 658-H1
3800 PHX 85012 698-H1
7000 PHX 85020 658-H1
8100 PHX 85020 618-H4
15200 PHX 85022 578-H1
17600 PHX 85022 538-H7
18600 PHX 85024 538-H5
37800 MarC 85086 (418-J2 See Page 417)
49400 MarC 85320 (284-J4 See Page 244)
S 4TH ST
- AVON 85323 695-B7
- AVON 85323 735-B1
100 BUCK 85326 (772-A2 See Page 731)
200 PHX 85004 698-G7
400 ELMG 85335 615-F1
700 PHX 85004 738-G1
4100 PHX 85040 738-G5
8000 PHX 85040 778-G3
9100 MarC 85326 (772-A3 See Page 731)
15900 PHX 85048 818-G4
W 4TH ST
1200 TEMP 85281 740-A3
2100 TEMP 85281 739-J3
10700 AVON 85353 735-H1
E 5TH AV
- MESA 85210 741-H6
800 MESA 85204 742-A6
4300 SCTS 85251 660-F7
5400 PinC 85219 746-C7
6800 SCTS 85251 700-E1
6900 MESA 85207 743-G5
7900 MarC 85208 743-G5
7900 MarC 85208 744-A6
11300 MarC 85220 744-J6
11400 MarC 85220 745-A6
N 5TH AV
- PHX 85003 698-F3
500 PHX 85013 658-F2
3400 PHX 85013 698-F1
7600 PHX 85021 618-G3
13000 PHX 85029 578-G6
13900 ELMG 85335 575-E4
15200 PHX 85023 578-G1
17600 PHX 85023 538-G6
18600 PHX 85027 538-G3
35100 MarC 85086 (418-H6 See Page 417)
N 5TH AV NW
4100 PHX 85013 658-F7
S 5TH AV
- AVON 85338 735-A2
- PHX 85003 698-F7
300 AVON 85323 735-A1
600 PHX 85003 738-F1
5200 PHX 85041 738-F6
6000 PHX 85041 778-F1
15600 PHX 85045 818-E5
W 5TH AV
100 ELMG 85335 615-F1
400 APJT 85220 745-A6
600 MESA 85210 741-F6
5TH AV E
100 MarC 85326 (732-B7 See Page 731)
7400 BUCK 85326 (732-B7 See Page 731)
5TH AV W
100 BUCK 85326 (732-A7 See Page 731)
N 5TH DR
5500 PHX 85013 658-F4
15800 PHX 85023 578-G2
18300 PHX 85023 538-G6
19400 PHX 85027 538-G3
S 5TH DR
8400 PHX 85041 778-F4
N 5TH LN
5500 PHX 85013 658-F4
15000 PHX 85023 578-G3
W 5TH LN
600 PHX 85023 578-G3
E 5TH PL
100 MESA 85201 741-H4
N 5TH PL
500 MESA 85201 741-H4
600 PHX 85012 658-H3
1000 PHX 85004 698-H5
14400 PHX 85022 578-H4
17600 PHX 85022 538-H6
19200 PHX 85024 538-J5
S 5TH PL
7500 PHX 85040 778-G3
W 5TH PL
300 MESA 85201 741-D3
1500 TEMP 85281 740-A3
2100 TEMP 85281 739-J3
E 5TH ST
- MESA 85201 741-H4
- TEMP 85281 740-E3
800 MESA 85203 742-A4
2100 TEMP 85281 741-A3
6500 SCTS 85251 700-E1
N 5TH ST
- AVON 85323 695-C6
- PHX 85004 698-H2
100 BUCK 85326 (772-A1 See Page 731)
500 PHX 85022 578-H1
2900 PHX 85012 698-H1
4500 PHX 85012 658-H5
7300 PHX 85020 618-H4
17800 PHX 85022 538-H7
18600 PHX 85024 538-H5
26100 MarC 85024 498-J4
38000 MarC 85086 (418-J3 See Page 417)
S 5TH ST
- AVON 85323 695-C7
- PHX 85004 698-H7
100 AVON 85323 735-B1
100 BUCK 85326 (772-A2 See Page 731)
300 PHX 85048 818-G4
600 PHX 85004 738-H2
600 ELMG 85335 615-F1
3200 PHX 85040 738-G5
8000 PHX 85040 778-G3
W 5TH ST
- TEMP 85281 740-B3
200 MESA 85201 741-C4
E 6TH AV
- PinC 85219 746-B7
- MESA 85210 741-H6
800 MESA 85204 742-B7
2400 APJT 85219 745-H7
6900 MESA 85207 743-G5
7100 SCTS 85251 660-F7
7900 MarC 85208 743-G5
7900 MarC 85208 744-A6
11200 MarC 85220 744-J7
11400 MarC 85220 745-A7
N 6TH AV
- PHX 85003 698-F6
2900 PHX 85013 698-F1
3700 PHX 85013 658-F2
7000 PHX 85021 658-F1
7600 PHX 85021 618-F7
15800 PHX 85023 578-G1
17600 PHX 85023 538-G7
N 6TH AV NW
4100 PHX 85013 658-F7
S 6TH AV
- PHX 85003 698-F7
300 AVON 85323 735-A1
400 PHX 85003 738-F1
3800 PHX 85041 738-F5
6000 PHX 85041 778-F1
15700 PHX 85045 818-E5
W 6TH AV
- MESA 85210 741-F6
100 ELMG 85335 615-F1
1200 MESA 85202 741-C6
6TH AV E
100 MarC 85326 (732-B6 See Page 731)
W 6TH AV W
100 BUCK 85326 (732-A7 See Page 731)
N 6TH CIR
15000 PHX 85023 578-G3
E 6TH DR
400 MESA 85204 741-J7
N 6TH DR
300 PHX 85021 618-F3
4100 PHX 85013 658-F7
15800 PHX 85023 578-G2
17900 PHX 85023 538-G7
18800 PHX 85027 538-G3
S 6TH DR
400 PHX 85003 698-F7
400 PHX 85003 738-F1
15400 PHX 85045 818-E5
W 6TH DR
400 MESA 85210 741-F7
1200 MESA 85202 741-C7
N 6TH LN
600 PHX 85023 578-G3
E 6TH PL
- MESA 85201 741-H3
600 MESA 85203 741-J3
600 MESA 85203 742-A3
N 6TH PL
1100 AVON 85323 695-C6
7200 PHX 85020 658-H1
7200 PHX 85020 618-H5
14200 PHX 85022 578-J1
17400 PHX 85022 538-J7
19400 PHX 85024 538-J5
S 6TH PL
14800 PHX 85048 818-G5
W 6TH PL
- MESA 85201 741-D3
E 6TH ST
- TEMP 85281 740-D3
- MESA 85201 741-J3
400 MESA 85203 741-J3
600 MESA 85203 742-A4
2100 TEMP 85281 741-A4
6500 SCTS 85251 700-E2
N 6TH ST
- AVON 85323 695-C6
500 PHX 85004 698-H5
3800 PHX 85012 658-H4
3800 PHX 85012 698-H1
7700 PHX 85020 618-H3
14400 PHX 85022 578-H1
17400 PHX 85022 538-H7
19000 PHX 85024 538-J5
44600 MarC 85087 (378-J1 See Page 337)
45600 MarC 85087 (338-J7 See Page 337)
49200 MarC 85320 (285-A5 See Page 244)
S 6TH ST
- AVON 85323 695-C7
100 AVON 85323 735-C1
600 ELMG 85335 615-F1
1000 PHX 85004 738-H1
4400 PHX 85040 738-H6
8000 PHX 85040 778-G3
15500 PHX 85048 818-G5
W 6TH ST
- TEMP 85281 740-B3
200 MESA 85201 741-C3
N 6TH WY
- PHX 85013 658-F2
600 PHX 85012 658-H2
7200 PHX 85020 658-H1
7200 PHX 85020 618-H7
S 6TH WY
14800 PHX 85048 818-G4
E 7TH AV
- MESA 85210 741-H7
800 MESA 85204 742-A7
1700 APJT 85219 745-G7
6900 MESA 85207 743-G5
N 7TH AV
- PHX 85003 698-F3
- PHX 85007 698-F3
2900 PHX 85013 698-F3
3800 PHX 85013 658-F3
7000 PHX 85021 658-F3
7200 PHX 85021 618-F3
10600 PHX 85029 618-F3
15400 PHX 85023 578-G1
17200 PHX 85023 538-G5
18600 PHX 85027 538-G3
24200 MarC 85027 498-G4
34600 MarC 85085 (418-G5 See Page 417)
34600 MarC 85086 (418-G3 See Page 417)
39400 MarC 85086 (378-G7 See Page 337)
42600 MarC 85087 (378-H2 See Page 337)
48700 MarC 85087 (338-H3 See Page 337)
S 7TH AV
- PHX 85003 698-F7
- PHX 85007 698-F7
600 PHX 85003 738-F3
600 PHX 85007 738-F3
3000 PHX 85041 738-F6
6000 PHX 85041 778-F1
W 7TH AV
100 ELMG 85335 615-F1
600 MESA 85210 741-F7
1200 MESA 85202 741-C7
7TH AV E
100 MarC 85326 (732-B6 See Page 731)
7TH AV W
100 BUCK 85326 (732-A7 See Page 731)
E 7TH DR
- MESA 85210 741-H7
400 MESA 85204 741-J7
700 MESA 85204 742-A7
N 7TH DR
5600 PHX 85013 658-F2
13200 PHX 85029 578-F6
15000 PHX 85023 578-G2
18000 PHX 85023 538-G6
18600 PHX 85027 538-G5
S 7TH DR
- PHX 85041 778-E4
15400 PHX 85045 818-E5
W 7TH DR
1200 MESA 85202 741-D7
N 7TH LN
16100 PHX 85023 578-F2
S 7TH LN
16000 PHX 85045 818-E6
E 7TH PL
400 MESA 85203 741-J3
600 MESA 85203 742-A3
N 7TH PL
700 PHX 85022 538-J7
1000 PHX 85006 698-H5
1100 AVON 85323 695-C6
7300 PHX 85020 618-J2
14600 PHX 85022 578-J1
18800 PHX 85024 538-J3
S 7TH PL
4400 PHX 85040 738-H5
7100 PHX 85040 778-H2
14600 PHX 85048 818-G4
W 7TH PL
- MESA 85201 741-D3
1300 TEMP 85281 740-B3
E 7TH ST
- TEMP 85281 740-D4
600 MESA 85203 741-J3
600 MESA 85203 742-A3
N 7TH ST
- MarC 85085 (458-J1 See Page 417)
- MarC 85087 (379-A2 See Page 339)
- PHX 85034 698-H5
- PHX 85004 698-H3
100 AVON 85323 695-C6
100 BUCK 85326 (772-B1 See Page 731)
300 PHX 85006 698-H3
2900 PHX 85012 698-H3
2900 PHX 85014 698-H3
3700 PHX 85012 658-H4
4100 PHX 85014 658-H4
7000 PHX 85020 658-H4
7300 PHX 85020 618-H1
11200 PHX 85020 578-H7
12100 PHX 85022 578-J3
17400 PHX 85022 538-J4
18500 PHX 85024 538-J1
22600 MarC 85024 498-J6
22600 PHX 85024 498-J6
34600 MarC 85085 (418-J4 See Page 417)
34600 MarC 85086 (418-J1 See Page 417)
38600 MarC 85086 419-A1
39400 MarC 85086 (378-J7 See Page 337)
39400 MarC 85086 (379-A5 See Page 339)
49100 MarC 85320 (285-A5 See Page 244)
S 7TH ST
- AVON 85323 695-C7
- PHX 85034 698-H7
- PHX 85004 698-H7
100 AVON 85323 735-C1
100 BUCK 85326 (772-B2 See Page 731)
600 PHX 85004 738-H4
600 PHX 85034 738-H4
600 ELMG 85335 615-F1
3200 PHX 85040 738-H4
6000 PHX 85040 778-H1
14200 PHX 85048 818-G4
W 7TH ST
- MESA 85201 741-D3
400 TEMP 85281 740-B3
2100 TEMP 85281 739-J3
N 7TH WY
17200 PHX 85022 578-J1
17400 PHX 85022 538-J7
19400 PHX 85024 538-J5
S 7TH WY
14800 PHX 85048 818-G4
E 8TH AV
- MESA 85210 741-H7
400 MESA 85204 741-J7
600 MESA 85204 742-C7
6900 MESA 85207 743-G5
N 8TH AV
- PHX 85007 698-F3
2900 PHX 85013 698-F1
3800 PHX 85013 658-F2
7000 PHX 85021 658-F1
7200 PHX 85021 618-F2
12800 PHX 85029 578-F6
15000 PHX 85023 578-F1
17400 PHX 85023 538-G7
19000 PHX 85027 538-G4
S 8TH AV
- PHX 85007 698-F7
700 PHX 85007 738-F1
3700 PHX 85041 738-E5
9400 PHX 85041 778-E5
W 8TH AV
- MESA 85210 741-F7
100 ELMG 85335 615-F1
1200 MESA 85202 741-B7
E 8TH DR
- MESA 85210 741-H7
N 8TH DR
5600 PHX 85013 658-F4
15200 PHX 85023 578-F3
S 8TH DR
- PHX 85041 778-E4
E 8TH PL
800 MESA 85203 742-A3
N 8TH PL
800 PHX 85022 538-J7
800 PHX 85024 538-J4
1600 AVON 85323 695-C5
4500 PHX 85014 658-H1
8200 PHX 85020 618-J3
13400 PHX 85022 578-J1
S 8TH PL
600 PHX 85034 738-H1
4400 PHX 85040 738-H6
6000 PHX 85040 778-H1
14000 PHX 85048 818-G3
W 8TH PL
- MESA 85201 741-F3
E 8TH ST
- MESA 85201 741-H3
- PHX 85014 698-H2
400 MESA 85203 741-H3
600 MESA 85203 742-A3
900 TEMP 85281 740-G4
N 8TH ST
100 BUCK 85326 (772-B1 See Page 731)
200 PHX 85034 698-H6
500 PHX 85022 578-J1
800 PHX 85022 538-J6
900 PHX 85006 698-H3
3600 PHX 85014 698-H1
3800 PHX 85014 658-H6
7300 PHX 85020 618-J2
19400 PHX 85024 538-J5
39000 MarC 85086 419-A2
S 8TH ST
- PHX 85034 698-H7
100 BUCK 85326 (772-B2 See Page 731)
600 PHX 85034 738-H1
1000 ELMG 85335 615-F1
4400 PHX 85040 738-H6
6800 PHX 85040 778-H2
14000 PHX 85048 818-G4
W 8TH ST
- MESA 85201 741-C3
2200 TEMP 85281 741-C3
2200 MESA 85201 741-C3
N 8TH WY
14900 PHX 85022 578-J4
E 9TH AV
- MESA 85210 741-H7
400 APJT 85219 745-E7
400 MESA 85204 741-J7
600 MESA 85204 742-A7
7000 MESA 85207 743-G4
N 9TH AV
- PHX 85007 698-F4
2900 PHX 85013 698-F2
4100 PHX 85013 658-F3
7200 PHX 85021 618-F3
7200 PHX 85021 658-F3
15600 PHX 85023 578-F1
17400 PHX 85023 538-F6
18600 PHX 85027 538-G2
S 9TH AV
- PHX 85007 698-F7
600 PHX 85007 738-F1
3800 PHX 85041 738-E5
6800 PHX 85041 778-E2
W 9TH AV
100 MESA 85210 741-G7
100 ELMG 85335 615-F1
700 PHX 85021 618-F6
1700 APJT 85220 745-B7
E 9TH DR
200 MESA 85210 741-H7
900 MESA 85204 742-A7
N 9TH DR
10600 PHX 85029 618-F2
E 9TH PL
- MESA 85201 741-H3
800 MESA 85203 742-A3
N 9TH PL
- MarC 85086 419-A3
900 PHX 85022 538-J7
3400 PHX 85014 698-H1
3700 PHX 85014 658-J3
7300 PHX 85020 618-J2
15400 PHX 85022 578-J2
19400 PHX 85024 538-J3
S 9TH PL
600 PHX 85034 738-H1
5600 PHX 85040 738-H7
7100 PHX 85040 778-H2
14000 PHX 85048 818-H3
W 9TH PL
- MESA 85201 741-E3
W 9TH PL N
200 MESA 85201 741-G2
W 9TH PL S
200 MESA 85201 741-G3
E 9TH ST
100 TEMP 85281 740-D4
800 MESA 85203 742-A3
800 AVON 85323 695-C5
N 9TH ST
- PHX 85034 698-H6
100 BUCK 85326 (772-B1 See Page 731)
300 PHX 85006 698-H3
900 PHX 85022 578-J1
3700 PHX 85014 658-H5
3700 PHX 85014 698-H1
7100 PHX 85020 658-J1
8200 PHX 85020 618-H1
11300 PHX 85020 578-J7
17200 PHX 85022 538-J7
18400 PHX 85024 538-J3
35200 MarC 85086 419-A2
S 9TH ST
- PHX 85034 698-H7
100 BUCK 85326 (772-B2 See Page 731)
800 PHX 85034 738-H1
900 PHX 85048 818-H5
2300 PHX 85040 778-H1
3500 PHX 85040 738-H5
W 9TH ST
- TEMP 85281 740-C4
- MESA 85201 741-E3
N 9TH WY
14600 PHX 85022 578-J4
S 9TH WY
- PHX 85040 778-H3
600 PHX 85034 738-H1
16100 PHX 85048 818-G6
E 10TH AV
- MESA 85210 741-H7
300 MESA 85207 743-H4
400 APJT 85219 745-E7
400 MESA 85204 741-H7
400 MESA 85204 781-J1
600 MESA 85204 782-A1
1000 MESA 85204 782-A7
4900 PinC 85219 746-B7
N 10TH AV
- PHX 85007 698-E5
900 PHX 85023 538-F6
900 PHX 85013 658-F1
3300 PHX 85013 698-F1
7000 PHX 85021 658-F1
7200 PHX 85021 618-F3
13000 PHX 85029 578-F6
15000 PHX 85023 578-F2
18600 PHX 85027 538-F3
S 10TH AV
- PHX 85007 698-E7
700 PHX 85007 738-E1
9200 PHX 85041 778-E5
16800 PHX 85045 818-E7
W 10TH AV
- MESA 85210 741-G7
100 ELMG 85335 615-F1
1700 APJT 85220 745-B7
E 10TH DR
100 MESA 85210 781-H1
200 MESA 85204 781-J1
800 MESA 85204 782-A1
N 10TH DR
5600 PHX 85013 658-F4
7000 PHX 85021 658-F1
9200 PHX 85021 618-F4
10600 PHX 85029 618-F2
16600 PHX 85023 578-F2
18200 PHX 85023 538-F6
S 10TH DR
9400 PHX 85041 778-E5
W 10TH DR
- MESA 85210 781-G1
E 10TH PL
400 MESA 85203 741-J3
800 MESA 85203 742-A2
1000 PHX 85022 578-J2
N 10TH PL
200 PHX 85034 698-J1
900 PHX 85020 618-J2
3600 PHX 85014 698-J1
3800 PHX 85014 658-J1
7000 PHX 85020 658-J1
13400 PHX 85022 578-J2
17600 PHX 85022 538-J7
19200 PHX 85024 538-J4
S 10TH PL
400 PHX 85034 698-H7
400 PHX 85034 738-H1
15900 PHX 85048 818-H6
W 10TH PL
200 MESA 85201 741-E2
1000 TEMP 85281 740-A4
2200 TEMP 85281 739-J4
E 10TH ST
- TEMP 85281 740-D4
400 MESA 85201 741-J3
400 MESA 85203 741-J3
800 MESA 85203 742-A3
1000 PHX 85022 538-J6
2100 TEMP 85281 741-A4
N 10TH ST
- PHX 85034 698-H6
400 PHX 85006 698-H6
3700 PHX 85014 698-J1
3800 PHX 85014 658-J3
7000 PHX 85020 658-J3
7200 PHX 85020 618-J1
14200 PHX 85022 578-J1
17600 PHX 85022 538-J7
18600 PHX 85024 538-J3
33000 MarC 85085 459-A2
33800 MarC 85085 419-A7
33800 MarC 85086 419-A1
39400 MarC 85086 (379-A5 See Page 339)
43700 MarC 85087 (379-A1 See Page 339)
S 10TH ST
100 PHX 85034 698-H7
900 PHX 85034 738-H1
4600 PHX 85040 738-H6
6000 PHX 85040 778-H1
14000 PHX 85048 818-H3
W 10TH ST
- TEMP 85281 740-A4
400 MESA 85201 741-F2
N 10TH WY
6000 PHX 85014 658-J3
14600 PHX 85022 578-J4
S 10TH WY
- PHX 85040 778-H4
E 11TH AV
400 MESA 85204 781-J1
800 MESA 85204 782-A1
N 11TH AV
- PHX 85007 698-E2
2900 PHX 85013 698-F1
3800 PHX 85013 658-F1
7000 PHX 85021 658-F1
7200 PHX 85021 618-F3
10400 PHX 85029 618-F2
13200 PHX 85029 578-F6
15400 PHX 85023 578-F2
17800 PHX 85023 538-F7
20600 PHX 85027 538-F2
24200 MarC 85027 498-F4
35400 MarC 85086 (418-G4 See Page 417)
35400 PHX 85086 (418-G4 See Page 417)
42600 MarC 85087 (378-G3 See Page 337)
46800 MarC 85087 (338-G6 See Page 337)
S 11TH AV
100 PHX 85007 698-E7
600 PHX 85007 738-E3
4600 PHX 85041 738-E6
6200 PHX 85041 778-E1
16600 PHX 85045 818-E7
W 11TH AV
- MESA 85210 781-G1
100 ELMG 85335 615-F1
1800 APJT 85220 745-B7
N 11TH DR
1100 PHX 85021 618-F7
5600 PHX 85013 658-F2
18200 PHX 85023 538-F7
19000 PHX 85027 538-F6
S 11TH DR
9400 PHX 85041 778-E1
W 11TH DR
- MESA 85210 781-G1
S 11TH LN
9400 PHX 85041 778-E5
E 11TH PL
1100 PHX 85022 539-A7
N 11TH PL
300 PHX 85006 698-J4
4200 PHX 85014 658-J1
7000 PHX 85020 658-J1
7300 PHX 85020 618-J2
13800 PHX 85022 578-J3
16200 PHX 85022 579-A2
18600 PHX 85024 539-A6
S 11TH PL
- PHX 85040 778-H4
14400 PHX 85048 818-H4
W 11TH PL
800 MESA 85201 741-F2
E 11TH ST
- TEMP 85281 740-D4
1000 PHX 85014 658-J3
1100 PHX 85020 618-J2
N 11TH ST
- PHX 85034 698-J6
300 PHX 85006 698-J4
1000 PHX 85020 618-J1
3400 PHX 85014 698-J1
3800 PHX 85014 658-J1
6700 PHX 85020 658-J1
13800 PHX 85022 578-J2
17600 PHX 85022 539-A7
19400 PHX 85024 539-A5
20600 PHX 85024 538-J3
S 11TH ST
- PHX 85034 698-H7
400 PHX 85034 738-H1
4200 PHX 85040 738-J5
6000 PHX 85040 778-J1
W 11TH ST
- TEMP 85281 740-B4
800 MESA 85201 741-E2
N 11TH WY
300 PHX 85006 698-J6
5700 PHX 85014 658-J3
7000 PHX 85020 658-J1
7300 PHX 85020 618-J7
14200 PHX 85022 578-J5
S 11TH WY
16000 PHX 85048 818-H7
E 12TH AV
200 APJT 85219 745-E7
4900 PinC 85219 786-C1
N 12TH AV
- PHX 85007 698-E3
3800 PHX 85013 658-F1
7200 PHX 85021 618-F6
7200 PHX 85021 658-F1
12800 PHX 85029 578-F6
15400 PHX 85023 578-F1
18200 PHX 85023 538-F6
18600 PHX 85027 538-F2
S 12TH AV
- PHX 85007 698-E7
1000 ELMG 85335 615-F1
1200 PHX 85007 738-E1
5200 PHX 85041 738-E6
9400 PHX 85041 778-E5
16600 PHX 85045 818-E7
W 12TH AV
700 APJT 85220 745-A7
N 12TH CT
10300 PHX 85020 619-A3
N 12TH DR
1200 PHX 85013 658-F4
14200 PHX 85022 579-A5
19000 PHX 85027 538-F6
S 12TH DR
- PHX 85041 778-E1
4400 PHX 85041 738-E5
N 12TH PL
1100 PHX 85020 618-J2
1100 PHX 85020 619-A1
1200 PHX 85022 579-A2
3400 PHX 85014 698-J1
4600 PHX 85014 658-J2
7100 PHX 85020 658-J1
18000 PHX 85022 539-A6
18800 PHX 85024 539-A4
S 12TH PL
700 PHX 85034 738-J1
5800 PHX 85040 738-J7
6000 PHX 85040 778-J1
14000 PHX 85048 818-H4
W 12TH PL
700 TEMP 85281 740-A4
E 12TH ST
1600 TEMP 85281 740-H5
N 12TH ST
- PHX 85034 698-J6
300 PHX 85006 698-J4
1100 PHX 85014 658-J3
1200 PHX 85022 579-A1
1200 PHX 85024 539-A4
1200 PHX 85022 539-A7
3400 PHX 85014 698-J1
7000 PHX 85020 658-J3
7200 PHX 85020 618-J2
14800 PHX 85022 578-J4
33000 MarC 85085 459-A2
33800 MarC 85085 419-A4
34600 MarC 85086 419-A1
39400 MarC 85086 (379-B7 See Page 339)
42800 MarC 85087 (379-B1 See Page 339)
45000 MarC 85087 339-B7
S 12TH ST
- PHX 85034 698-J7
900 PHX 85034 738-J2
3600 PHX 85040 738-J4
6000 PHX 85040 778-J1
14200 PHX 85048 818-H4
W 12TH ST
- TEMP 85281 740-B4
2400 TEMP 85281 739-J4
N 12TH TER
- PHX 85020 619-A1
N 12TH WY
- PHX 85020 618-J2
6700 PHX 85014 658-J2
7000 PHX 85020 658-J1
10300 PHX 85020 619-A1
13600 PHX 85022 579-A5
18300 PHX 85022 539-A6
S 12TH WY
1200 PHX 85048 818-H7
5200 PHX 85040 738-J7
E 13TH AV
3000 APJT 85219 785-H1
N 13TH AV
- PHX 85007 698-E4
900 PHX 85027 538-F3
1000 MarC 85087 (378-G3 See Page 337)
1200 PHX 85023 578-F1
3300 PHX 85013 698-E1
3800 PHX 85013 658-E2
7500 PHX 85021 618-F3
10600 PHX 85029 618-F2
17200 PHX 85023 538-F7
24600 MarC 85027 498-F5
46800 MarC 85087 (338-G3 See Page 337)
S 13TH AV
100 PHX 85007 698-E7
600 PHX 85007 738-E1
5200 PHX 85041 738-E6
9400 PHX 85041 778-E1
15400 PHX 85045 818-E5
W 13TH AV
1100 PHX 85021 618-F7
1600 APJT 85221 745-B7
N 13TH DR
5000 PHX 85013 658-E2
7300 PHX 85021 618-E7
18600 PHX 85027 538-F4
S 13TH DR
- PHX 85041 778-E1
15400 PHX 85045 818-D6
N 13TH LN
13000 PHX 85029 578-F6
N 13TH PL
300 MESA 85201 741-G2
300 PHX 85006 698-J5
1200 PHX 85020 619-A3
3900 PHX 85014 658-J5
3900 PHX 85014 698-J1
5000 PHX 85014 659-A2
7000 PHX 85020 659-A1
13100 PHX 85022 579-A1
17800 PHX 85022 539-A6
19000 PHX 85024 539-A6
S 13TH PL
1100 PHX 85034 738-J2
5200 PHX 85040 738-J7
6000 PHX 85040 778-J1
14200 PHX 85048 818-H4
W 13TH PL
1300 TEMP 85281 740-B5
E 13TH ST
- TEMP 85281 740-D5
N 13TH ST
- PHX 85034 698-J7
300 PHX 85006 698-J4
1200 PHX 85022 539-A5
1300 PHX 85022 579-A1
4600 PHX 85014 658-J4
6200 PHX 85014 659-A2
7000 PHX 85020 659-A1
7500 PHX 85020 619-A1
8100 PHX 85020 618-J6
17800 PHX 85022 539-A6
S 13TH ST
- PHX 85034 698-J7
1100 PHX 85034 738-J2

STREET Block City ZIP Pg-Grid

STREET
Block City ZIP Pg-Grid

N 24TH LN
- PHX 85086 (418-D7
See Page 417)
3000 PHX 85015 698-C1
14200 PHX 85023 578-D1
N 24TH PKWY
6100 PHX 85016 659-D3
N 24TH PL
- PHX 85034 699-C7
1000 PHX 85008 699-C3
2500 PHX 85016 659-C2
2900 PHX 85016 699-C2
6800 PHX 85020 659-C1
9800 PHX 85028 619-D2
14600 PHX 85032 579-D2
17500 PHX 85032 539-D7
19000 PHX 85050 539-D6
22700 PHX 85024 539-D1
S 24TH PL
4000 PHX 85040 739-C5
8000 PHX 85040 779-C1
14700 PHX 85048 819-B4
N 24TH ST
- PHX 85034 699-C3
300 PHX 85006 699-C3
300 PHX 85008 699-C3
800 MESA 85213 742-E1
1800 MESA 85213 702-E6
2300 PHX 85016 659-C3
2300 PHX 85028 619-C2
2900 PHX 85016 699-C3
7600 PHX 85020 619-C7
11800 PHX 85028 579-D7
12200 PHX 85032 579-D7
12600 PHX 85022 579-D7
22700 PHX 85024 539-D1
34600 MarC 85086 419-D5
43200 MarC 85087 (379-E3
See Page 339)
S 24TH ST
- PHX 85034 699-C7
300 MESA 85204 742-E7
400 PHX 85034 739-C3
900 MESA 85204 782-E1
2300 PHX 85040 779-C2
3600 PHX 85040 739-C6
14600 PHX 85048 819-B4
W 24TH ST
600 TEMP 85282 740-C6
N 24TH WY
9300 PHX 85028 619-C4
19600 PHX 85050 539-D4
S 24TH WY
2500 PHX 85048 819-B4
8000 PHX 85040 779-C3
N 25TH AV
- PHX 85009 698-B4
2500 PHX 85023 578-C2
8400 PHX 85021 618-C3
10600 PHX 85029 618-C1
11600 PHX 85029 578-C5
17400 PHX 85023 538-C6
22200 PHX 85027 538-C1
37800 MarC 85086 (418-D2
See Page 417)
38300 PHX 85086 (418-D6
See Page 417)
48800 MarC 85087 (338-D3
See Page 337)
S 25TH AV
- PHX 85009 698-B7
800 PHX 85009 738-B1
4400 PHX 85041 738-B5
8400 PHX 85041 778-B3
N 25TH DR
- PHX 85085 498-D2
1600 PHX 85009 698-B4
2900 PHX 85017 698-B1
5700 PHX 85017 658-C1
7000 PHX 85051 618-C7
7000 PHX 85051 658-C1
9800 PHX 85021 618-C3
13200 PHX 85029 578-C5
15400 PHX 85023 578-C2
S 25TH DR
- PHX 85041 778-B6
N 25TH LN
- PHX 85086 (418-D7
See Page 417)
7200 PHX 85051 618-C7
13200 PHX 85029 578-C6
15400 PHX 85023 578-C3
E 25TH PL
19400 PHX 85050 539-D5
N 25TH PL
1000 PHX 85008 699-C3
2400 PHX 85016 659-C4
2400 PHX 85028 619-D1
2900 PHX 85016 699-C2
12000 PHX 85028 579-D7
12100 PHX 85032 579-D3
17600 PHX 85032 539-D7
18600 PHX 85050 539-D5
22800 PHX 85024 539-D1
23000 PHX 85024 499-D7
S 25TH PL
8000 PHX 85040 779-C3
14400 PHX 85048 819-C4
E 25TH ST
2500 MESA 85213 742-E2
N 25TH ST
- PHX 85034 699-C7
200 MESA 85213 742-E1
1000 PHX 85008 699-C3
2000 MESA 85213 702-E7
2400 PHX 85032 579-D2
2400 PHX 85050 539-D5
2500 PHX 85032 539-D7
2900 PHX 85016 699-C1
4100 PHX 85016 659-D2
9400 PHX 85028 619-D1
23200 PHX 85024 499-D7
36600 MarC 85086 419-E5
S 25TH ST
- PHX 85034 699-C7
3900 PHX 85040 739-C5
7400 PHX 85040 779-C2
14600 PHX 85048 819-C4
N 25TH WY
3400 PHX 85016 699-D1
18000 PHX 85032 539-D7
18400 PHX 85050 539-D6
S 25TH WY
14600 PHX 85048 819-C4
E 26TH AV
- PinC 85219 785-G2
4800 PinC 85219 786-B2
N 26TH AV
- PHX 85085 498-C2
- PHX 85086 (418-C6
See Page 417)
- PHX 85009 698-B4
2500 PHX 85023 578-C1
2900 PHX 85017 698-B2
4500 PHX 85017 658-B3
7100 PHX 85051 618-C6
7100 PHX 85051 658-C1
8500 PHX 85021 618-C5
13000 PHX 85029 578-C5
20600 PHX 85027 538-C1
49000 MarC 85087 (338-D3
See Page 337)
S 26TH AV
- PHX 85009 698-B7
10400 PHX 85041 778-B6
N 26TH CIR
- MESA 85213 702-E7
S 26TH CT
15600 PHX 85048 819-C6
N 26TH DR
- PHX 85086 (418-C6
See Page 417)
2900 PHX 85017 698-B1
6700 PHX 85017 658-B1
7000 PHX 85051 618-B7
7000 PHX 85051 658-B1
9800 PHX 85021 618-C3
12200 PHX 85029 578-C6
14000 PHX 85023 578-C4
N 26TH LN
7200 PHX 85051 618-B7
13000 PHX 85029 578-C5
14000 PHX 85023 578-C4
N 26TH PL
1600 PHX 85008 699-D4
2600 PHX 85032 579-D5
3100 PHX 85016 699-D1
9600 PHX 85028 619-D1
18200 PHX 85032 539-D7
S 26TH PL
- PHX 85040 779-C2
2500 PHX 85034 739-C3
15400 PHX 85048 819-C5
N 26TH ST
300 MESA 85213 742-E1
1000 PHX 85008 699-D2
2200 MESA 85213 702-E6
2500 PHX 85016 659-D2
2500 PHX 85032 579-D1
2900 PHX 85016 699-D1
6800 PHX 85020 659-D2
9400 PHX 85028 619-D2
17400 PHX 85032 539-D7
10000 PHX 85050 539-D5
23200 PHX 85024 499-D7
37000 MarC 85086 419-E2
37100 MarC 85331 419-E2
38000 CVCK 85331 (379-E7
See Page 339)
38000 CVCK 85331 419-E2
S 26TH ST
- PHX 85034 699-C7
500 MESA 85204 742-E7
1000 MESA 85204 782-E1
1200 PHX 85034 739-C1
3800 PHX 85040 739-C5
6000 PHX 85040 779-C1
15200 PHX 85048 819-B5
N 26TH WY
11200 PHX 85028 619-D1
12200 PHX 85032 579-D7
S 26TH WY
- PHX 85040 779-C3
14900 PHX 85048 819-C5
N 27TH AV
- PHX 85085 (418-C7
See Page 417)
- PHX 85085 (458-C1
See Page 417)
- PHX 85009 698-B4
2600 PHX 85027 538-C1
2900 PHX 85017 698-B4
3800 PHX 85017 658-B4
7000 PHX 85051 618-B2
7000 PHX 85051 658-B4
17600 PHX 85053 538-C7
36300 PHX 85086 (418-C7
See Page 417)
37800 MarC 85086 (418-C3
See Page 417)
47400 MarC 85087 (338-D3
See Page 337)
S 27TH AV
- PHX 85009 698-B7
800 PHX 85009 738-B2
4400 MarC 85041 738-B6
4400 PHX 85041 738-B6
6000 MarC 85041 778-B2
6000 PHX 85041 778-B2
8500 MarC 85339 778-A3
8500 PHX 85339 778-A3
N 27TH CT
- PHX 85086 (418-C6
See Page 417)
14000 PHX 85032 579-E5
N 27TH DR
- PHX 85085 (418-C7
See Page 417)
- PHX 85086 (418-C7
See Page 417)
- PHX 85009 698-B5
2700 PHX 85053 578-B3
4100 PHX 85017 658-B1
8200 PHX 85051 618-B2
12500 PHX 85029 578-B6
17800 PHX 85053 538-C7
S 27TH DR
- PHX 85009 698-B7
11000 MarC 85339 778-A7
N 27TH LN
- PHX 85086 (418-C6
See Page 417)
1000 PHX 85009 698-B4
17600 PHX 85053 538-B7
22300 PHX 85027 538-C1
N 27TH PL
1000 PHX 85008 699-D3
2700 PHX 85028 579-D7
2700 PHX 85032 579-D1
2700 PHX 85028 619-D1
3100 PHX 85016 699-D3
4700 PHX 85016 659-D6
19800 PHX 85050 539-E4
S 27TH PL
- PHX 85040 779-C1
2700 PHX 85048 819-C5
5600 PHX 85040 739-D7
N 27TH ST
- PHX 85034 699-D7
1000 PHX 85008 699-D5
2600 PHX 85050 539-D5
2600 PHX 85028 579-D7
2700 PHX 85016 659-D2
2900 PHX 85016 699-D2
9600 PHX 85028 619-D1
12200 PHX 85032 579-D3
17400 PHX 85032 539-D7
S 27TH ST
- PHX 85034 699-D7
1200 PHX 85034 739-D1
3800 PHX 85040 739-C5
8400 PHX 85040 779-C1
14800 PHX 85048 819-C5
N 27TH WY
2600 PHX 85032 579-D7
17800 PHX 85032 539-E6
S 27TH WY
- PHX 85040 779-C3
14800 PHX 85048 819-C5
E 28TH AV
4800 PinC 85219 786-B2
N 28TH AV
- PHX 85009 698-B2
3100 PHX 85017 698-B1
3800 PHX 85017 658-B5
7000 PHX 85051 658-B1
8000 PHX 85051 618-B4
10600 PHX 85029 618-B2
12600 PHX 85029 578-B6
14400 PHX 85053 578-B1
17200 PHX 85053 538-B7
21900 PHX 85027 538-C1
S 28TH AV
- PHX 85009 698-B7
600 PHX 85009 738-B1
2700 MarC 85339 778-A6
N 28TH DR
- PHX 85009 698-A5
4100 PHX 85017 658-B1
7000 PHX 85051 658-B1
7200 PHX 85051 618-B2
10600 PHX 85029 618-B2
11200 PHX 85029 578-B7
14100 PHX 85053 578-B3
17200 PHX 85053 538-B6
S 28TH DR
- PHX 85009 698-A7
1600 PHX 85009 738-A2
11200 MarC 85339 778-A7
11200 PHX 85339 778-A7
N 28TH LN
7500 PHX 85051 618-B7
E 28TH PL
2800 PHX 85028 619-D3
N 28TH PL
400 PHX 85008 699-D3
2000 MESA 85213 702-F7
2600 PHX 85016 699-D2
2800 PHX 85028 619-E3
2800 PHX 85032 579-E2
4400 PHX 85016 659-D3
18200 PHX 85032 539-E6
18800 PHX 85050 539-E4
S 28TH PL
- PHX 85040 779-C3
5200 PHX 85040 739-D7
15700 PHX 85048 819-C6
N 28TH ST
- PHX 85034 699-D6
300 PHX 85008 699-D4
2700 PHX 85032 579-E1
2700 PHX 85016 619-D1
2800 PHX 85016 699-D2
2800 PHX 85016 659-D2
11800 PHX 85028 579-E5
17500 PHX 85032 539-E7
18600 PHX 85050 539-E4
36200 MarC 85086 419-E5
36200 CVCK 85086 419-E5
36200 CVCK 85331 419-E5
S 28TH ST
- PHX 85034 739-D1
- PHX 85034 699-D7
2700 PHX 85048 819-C5
2900 PHX 85040 779-D1
3600 PHX 85040 739-D5
N 28TH WY
- PHX 85050 539-E6
4300 PHX 85016 659-D7
9800 PHX 85028 619-E3
12600 PHX 85032 579-E2
N 29TH AV
100 PHX 85009 698-A4
2800 MarC 85087 (338-C4
See Page 337)
2800 PHX 85053 578-B1
3100 PHX 85017 698-B1
3800 PHX 85017 658-B1
7000 PHX 85051 658-B1
7100 PHX 85051 618-B3
11600 PHX 85029 618-B1
11800 PHX 85029 578-B6
17200 PHX 85053 538-B6
18600 PHX 85027 538-B1
23400 PHX 85027 498-B6
36200 MarC 85086 (418-C2
See Page 417)
36200 PHX 85086 (418-C5
See Page 417)
S 29TH AV
- PHX 85009 698-A7
700 PHX 85009 738-A1
7600 MarC 85339 778-A3
N 29TH DR
- PHX 85086 (418-C5
See Page 417)
100 PHX 85009 698-A4
2900 PHX 85017 698-B2
4100 PHX 85017 658-B1
7100 PHX 85051 658-B1
7200 PHX 85051 618-B5
12400 PHX 85029 578-B6
14000 PHX 85053 578-B1
17800 PHX 85053 538-B6
20600 PHX 85027 538-B1
S 29TH DR
- PHX 85009 698-A7
11200 MarC 85339 778-A7
11200 PHX 85339 778-A7
N 29TH LN
- PHX 85086 (418-C6
See Page 417)
6800 PHX 85017 658-B1
16400 PHX 85053 578-B2
S 29TH LN
- PHX 85009 737-J2
- PHX 85009 738-A2
N 29TH PL
1000 PHX 85008 699-D3
1800 MESA 85213 702-F7
1800 MESA 85213 742-F1
2900 PHX 85016 699-D3
4300 PHX 85016 659-D2
9800 PHX 85028 619-E1
12000 PHX 85028 579-E7
12400 PHX 85032 579-E2
18600 PHX 85032 539-E6
18600 PHX 85050 539-E4
S 29TH PL
- GIL 85296 782-F7
- GIL 85296 822-F1
200 MarC 85296 822-F1
16600 PHX 85048 819-C7
N 29TH ST
- PHX 85034 699-D7
400 MESA 85213 742-F4
400 PHX 85008 699-D3
2800 PHX 85032 579-E3
2900 PHX 85016 699-D3
2900 PHX 85028 619-E1
4300 PHX 85016 659-D2
12000 PHX 85028 579-E6
17800 PHX 85032 539-E7
19000 PHX 85050 539-E4
S 29TH ST
- PHX 85034 699-D7
4800 PHX 85040 739-D6
15200 PHX 85048 819-C5
N 29TH WY
16400 PHX 85032 579-E2
19400 PHX 85050 539-E4
S 29TH WY
- PHX 85040 779-D3
16800 PHX 85048 819-C7
E 30TH AV
4900 PinC 85219 786-B3
5300 PinC 85219 786-B3
N 30TH AV
- PHX 85085 498-B1
- PHX 85086 (418-C5
See Page 417)
- PHX 85009 698-A3
2900 PHX 85017 698-A2
2900 PHX 85027 538-B1
3800 PHX 85017 658-A1
7000 PHX 85051 658-A1
7200 PHX 85051 618-A4
10600 PHX 85029 618-B1
12000 PHX 85029 578-B6
13800 PHX 85053 578-B2
17600 PHX 85053 538-B6
47900 MarC 85087 (338-C4
See Page 337)
S 30TH AV
- PHX 85009 698-A7
800 PHX 85009 738-A1
2900 MarC 85339 778-A6
S 30TH CIR
600 MESA 85204 742-F7
N 30TH CT
6300 PHX 85016 659-E3
N 30TH DR
- PHX 85085 498-B1
- PHX 85086 (418-B5
See Page 417)
- PHX 85009 698-A4
4100 PHX 85017 658-A1
7200 PHX 85051 618-A4
11600 PHX 85029 618-B1
11800 PHX 85029 578-B6
13800 PHX 85053 578-B1
14100 PHX 85032 579-E5
20200 PHX 85027 538-B1
S 30TH DR
- PHX 85009 698-A7
800 PHX 85009 738-A1
9600 MarC 85339 778-A5
W 30TH DR
3000 PHX 85029 618-B2
3000 PHX 85051 618-B2
N 30TH LN
- PHX 85085 498-B2
- PHX 85086 (418-B6
See Page 417)
1300 PHX 85009 698-A4
2900 PHX 85027 538-B2
6600 PHX 85017 658-A2
7200 PHX 85051 618-A7
11400 PHX 85029 618-B1
13800 PHX 85053 578-B5
17500 PHX 85053 538-B6
N 30TH PL
300 PHX 85008 699-E3
3000 PHX 85028 619-E1
4500 PHX 85016 659-D3
11800 PHX 85028 579-E6
13200 PHX 85032 579-E4
17800 PHX 85032 539-E7
18500 PHX 85050 539-E4
S 30TH PL
14800 PHX 85048 819-D5
N 30TH ST
- PHX 85034 699-D6
300 PHX 85008 699-D5
1700 MESA 85213 742-F1
2000 MESA 85213 702-F7
2900 PHX 85016 699-E2
2900 PHX 85032 579-E1
4000 PHX 85016 659-E4
9800 PHX 85028 619-E2
11800 PHX 85028 579-E7
17500 PHX 85032 539-E6
18600 PHX 85050 539-E4
S 30TH ST
- GIL 85296 782-F7
- GIL 85296 822-F1
- PHX 85034 699-D7
300 MarC 85296 822-F1
400 MESA 85204 742-F6
1200 MESA 85204 782-F2
3600 PHX 85040 739-D5
6200 PHX 85040 779-D1
14800 PHX 85048 819-C5
N 30TH WY
3000 PHX 85050 539-E4
6200 PHX 85016 659-E2
17800 PHX 85016 539-E7
S 30TH WY
16800 PHX 85048 819-D7
N 31ST AV
- PHX 85027 498-B2
- PHX 85086 (418-B5
See Page 417)
- PHX 85009 698-A5
2900 PHX 85017 698-A2
3000 PHX 85085 498-B1
3900 PHX 85017 658-A2
7000 PHX 85051 658-A1
7100 PHX 85051 618-A3
10600 PHX 85029 618-A1
11600 PHX 85029 578-B6
13800 PHX 85053 578-B1
17200 PHX 85053 538-B6
18600 PHX 85027 538-B2
36200 MarC 85086 (418-B2
See Page 417)
47400 MarC 85087 (338-C4
See Page 337)
S 31ST AV
- PHX 85009 698-A7
700 PHX 85009 738-A1
9700 MarC 85339 777-J5
S 31ST CIR
600 MESA 85204 742-F7
N 31ST CT
6300 PHX 85016 659-E3
N 31ST DR
- PHX 85027 498-B7
- PHX 85085 498-B2
- PHX 85086 (418-B6
See Page 417)
3100 PHX 85053 578-B1
3100 PHX 85051 618-A5
4100 PHX 85017 658-A1
7100 PHX 85051 658-A1
10800 PHX 85029 618-A1
11600 PHX 85029 578-B5
17800 PHX 85053 538-B6
18600 PHX 85027 538-B1
N 31ST LN
- PHX 85085 498-B1
- PHX 85086 (418-B5
See Page 417)
5500 PHX 85017 658-A1
8100 PHX 85051 618-A5
11600 PHX 85029 578-A4
11600 PHX 85029 618-A1
14600 PHX 85053 578-A1
17800 PHX 85053 538-B6
19200 PHX 85027 538-B5
N 31ST PL
- MESA 85213 742-G1
1300 PHX 85008 699-E3
4200 PHX 85016 659-E2
10000 PHX 85028 619-E1
13200 PHX 85032 579-E6
18000 PHX 85032 539-F7
19000 PHX 85050 539-F4
S 31ST PL
5200 PHX 85040 739-D7
13800 PHX 85048 819-D3
E 31ST ST
14800 MarC 85296 822-F2
N 31ST ST
- MESA 85213 742-G1
800 PHX 85008 699-E3
3000 PHX 85032 579-E6
3000 PHX 85028 619-E1
3400 PHX 85016 699-E1
4100 PHX 85016 659-E2
11800 PHX 85028 579-E7
12600 PHX 85032 579-E2
19000 PHX 85050 539-E4
S 31ST ST
400 MESA 85204 742-F6
1200 MESA 85204 782-F1
4800 PHX 85040 739-D6
11600 MarC 85296 822-F2
12200 GIL 85296 822-F2
15100 PHX 85048 819-D5
N 31ST WY
3100 PHX 85032 579-E6
4600 PHX 85016 659-E2
19400 PHX 85050 539-F4
S 31ST WY
14600 PHX 85048 819-D4
E 32ND AV
- APJT 85219 785-G3
- PinC 85219 785-G3
4900 APJT 85219 786-B3
5000 PinC 85219 786-B3
N 32ND AV
- PHX 85027 498-B7
- PHX 85085 498-B1
300 PHX 85009 698-A2
3100 PHX 85053 578-A1
3200 PHX 85051 618-A2
3200 PHX 85029 578-A6
3700 PHX 85017 658-A1
3700 PHX 85017 698-A1
7000 PHX 85051 658-A1
10400 PHX 85029 618-A1
17400 PHX 85053 538-A6
18800 PHX 85027 538-A1
S 32ND AV
900 PHX 85009 737-J2
N 32ND CIR
10600 PHX 85029 618-A2
N 32ND DR
- PHX 85027 498-B7
- PHX 85085 498-B2
3200 PHX 85053 578-A3
3200 PHX 85029 578-A6
3200 PHX 85051 618-A5
4800 PHX 85017 658-A1
10600 PHX 85029 618-A1
18400 PHX 85053 538-A6
19200 PHX 85027 538-A3
S 32ND DR
100 PHX 85009 697-J7
1900 PHX 85009 737-J2
N 32ND LN
- PHX 85027 498-B3
- PHX 85085 498-B1
10600 PHX 85029 618-A2
14600 PHX 85053 578-A3
18000 PHX 85053 538-A6
19200 PHX 85027 538-A1
20000 PHX 85050 539-F4
N 32ND PL
- PHX 85034 699-E7
300 PHX 85008 699-E3
2800 PHX 85018 699-E1
3200 PHX 85032 579-F3
4000 PHX 85018 659-E4
5700 PVAL 85253 659-E4
9200 PHX 85028 619-F1
17600 PHX 85032 539-F7
18800 PHX 85050 539-F4
S 32ND PL
- PHX 85040 779-E2
400 MESA 85204 742-G6
4800 PHX 85040 739-E6
13600 PHX 85048 819-D4
13600 PHX 85044 819-D3
N 32ND ST
- PHX 85050 499-F7
- PHX 85034 699-E4
300 PHX 85008 699-E4
1200 MESA 85213 742-G1
1800 MESA 85213 702-G6
2800 PHX 85050 539-F3
2900 PHX 85016 699-E4
2900 PHX 85018 699-E4
3100 PHX 85032 579-F1
4000 PHX 85016 659-E7
4000 PHX 85018 659-E7
5500 PVAL 85253 659-E7
5500 PHX 85253 659-E7
5500 PVAL 85016 659-E7
8800 PHX 85028 619-E3
11800 PHX 85028 579-F4
14200 PHX 85022 579-F4
17700 PHX 85032 539-F6
34600 CVCK 85331 419-F6
40200 CVCK 85331 (379-G7
See Page 339)
S 32ND ST
- MarC 85326 899-B3
- PHX 85034 739-D3
- PHX 85034 699-E7
400 MESA 85204 742-G7
900 MESA 85204 782-G2
3200 PHX 85040 739-E5
6000 PHX 85040 779-E2
13600 PHX 85048 819-D3
14400 PHX 85044 819-D4
17100 PHX 85326 819-D7
N 32ND WY
1700 PHX 85008 699-E4
3100 PHX 85018 699-E1
4000 PHX 85018 659-E6
11400 PHX 85028 619-F1
15800 PHX 85032 579-F1
17600 PHX 85032 539-F7
19000 PHX 85050 539-F5
S 32ND WY
16400 PHX 85048 819-D7
N 33RD AV
- PHX 85009 697-J2
1000 PHX 85009 698-A4
2900 PHX 85017 698-A1
3000 PHX 85017 698-A1
3300 PHX 85029 578-A6
3700 PHX 85017 658-A3
7000 PHX 85051 658-A1
7100 PHX 85051 618-A3
10600 PHX 85029 618-A1
13800 PHX 85053 578-A5
17800 PHX 85053 538-A7
18400 PHX 85027 538-A2
26600 PHX 85085 498-B1
36200 MarC 85086 (418-B2
See Page 417)
36200 PHX 85086 (418-B2
See Page 417)
S 33RD AV
900 PHX 85009 697-J7
900 PHX 85009 737-J1
4300 MarC 85041 737-J5
9200 MarC 85339 777-J4
9200 PHX 85339 777-J4
N 33RD CIR
11800 PHX 85029 578-A7
S 33RD CT
11400 PHX 85044 819-D3
N 33RD DR
- PHX 85085 498-A1
3000 PHX 85017 697-J2
4100 PHX 85017 657-J4
4100 PHX 85017 658-A1
7600 PHX 85051 618-A3
10800 PHX 85029 618-A1
12200 PHX 85029 578-A6
13800 PHX 85053 578-A2
17800 PHX 85053 538-A6
18600 PHX 85027 538-A1
N 33RD LN
- PHX 85086 (418-B6
See Page 417)
3300 PHX 85085 498-A1
8200 PHX 85051 618-A5
16200 PHX 85053 578-A2
17400 PHX 85053 538-A7
18800 PHX 85027 538-A1
N 33RD PL
1700 PHX 85008 699-E3
2800 PHX 85018 699-E1
3300 PHX 85028 619-F2
3300 PHX 85018 659-E6
3400 PHX 85032 579-F1
5700 PVAL 85253 659-F4
17600 PHX 85032 539-F7
18600 PHX 85050 539-F4
S 33RD PL
400 MESA 85204 742-G6
900 MESA 85204 782-G1
4600 PHX 85040 739-E6
15500 PHX 85048 819-D6
N 33RD ST
500 PHX 85008 699-E3
2800 PHX 85018 699-E1
3200 PHX 85018 659-E5
3200 PHX 85032 579-F1
3200 PVAL 85253 659-E3
9600 PHX 85028 619-F1
17600 PHX 85032 539-F5
19400 PHX 85050 539-F5
S 33RD ST
- PHX 85034 699-E7
4400 PHX 85040 739-E6
13500 PHX 85044 819-D3
13500 PHX 85048 819-D4
N 33RD WY
9000 PHX 85028 619-F4
16200 PHX 85032 579-F2
16700 PHX 85032 539-F7
18900 PHX 85050 539-F6
S 33RD WY
14000 PHX 85044 819-D4
15800 PHX 85048 819-E6
N 33TH AV
17000 PHX 85053 538-A7
E 34TH AV
1800 PinC 85219 785-G3
5200 PinC 85219 786-C3
N 34TH AV
- PHX 85085 498-A1
1000 PHX 85009 697-J3
3400 PHX 85017 657-J4
3600 PHX 85017 697-J3
6200 PHX 85051 658-A1
7000 PHX 85051 618-A1
7200 PHX 85051 617-J7
7600 PHX 85051 618-A3
11000 PHX 85029 618-A1
13000 PHX 85029 578-A6
13800 PHX 85053 578-A1
17800 PHX 85053 538-A6
18600 PHX 85027 538-A2
S 34TH AV
900 PHX 85009 737-J1
W 34TH AV
3400 PHX 85017 658-A2
S 34TH CT
12800 PHX 85044 819-E2
N 34TH DR
400 PHX 85009 697-J2
2900 PHX 85017 697-J1
4300 PHX 85017 657-J2
7600 PHX 85051 617-J5
9600 PHX 85051 618-A3
11200 PHX 85029 618-A1
13000 PHX 85029 578-A6
14000 PHX 85053 578-A1
17600 PHX 85053 538-A6
18800 PHX 85027 538-A1
N 34TH LN
6300 PHX 85017 657-J2
9500 PHX 85051 617-J3
10000 PHX 85051 618-A3
17400 PHX 85053 538-A6
21800 PHX 85027 538-A1
E 34TH PL
3400 PHX 85028 619-F4
N 34TH PL
2000 PHX 85008 699-F4
2800 MESA 85213 702-H5
2900 PHX 85018 699-F1
4000 PHX 85018 659-F5
6100 PVAL 85253 659-F2
9000 PHX 85028 619-F2
12000 PHX 85028 579-F7
12600 PHX 85032 579-F3
17800 PHX 85032 539-F7
18600 PHX 85050 539-F5
S 34TH PL
500 MESA 85204 742-G7
5700 PHX 85040 739-E7
8000 PHX 85040 779-E3
12600 PHX 85044 819-E2
17000 PHX 85048 819-E7
E 34TH ST
3300 PHX 85028 619-F2
3400 PHX 85044 819-E2
17600 PHX 85032 539-F7
17600 PHX 85032 579-F1
N 34TH ST
300 PHX 85008 699-E3
3000 PHX 85018 699-F1
3400 PHX 85028 619-F1
4000 PHX 85018 659-F5
5800 PVAL 85253 659-F3
12000 PHX 85028 579-F7
12200 PHX 85032 579-F1
17600 PHX 85032 539-F7
18600 PHX 85050 539-F4
S 34TH ST
- PHX 85034 699-F7
400 MESA 85204 742-G6
900 MESA 85204 782-G1
4000 PHX 85040 739-E5
13400 PHX 85044 819-E3
15600 PHX 85048 819-E6
N 34TH WY
3400 PHX 85050 539-F6
9400 PHX 85028 619-F4
14000 PHX 85032 579-F1
17800 PHX 85032 539-G7
S 34TH WY
3400 PHX 85048 819-E6
13200 PHX 85044 819-E3
E 35TH AV
- APJT 85219 785-G3
N 35TH AV
- PHX 85050 539-F5
- PHX 85009 697-J3
2900 PHX 85019 697-J3
2900 PHX 85017 697-J3
3300 MarC 85087 (338-B1
See Page 337)
3600 PHX 85019 657-J6
3600 PHX 85017 657-J3
7000 PHX 85051 657-J3
7100 PHX 85051 617-J6
10600 PHX 85029 617-J1
11500 PHX 85029 618-A1
11700 PHX 85029 578-A5
13800 PHX 85053 578-A2
17000 PHX 85308 578-A2
17200 PHX 85308 538-A5
17200 PHX 85053 538-A5
18600 PHX 85027 538-A5
22400 PHX 85310 538-A5
22800 PHX 85310 498-A6
22800 PHX 85027 498-A6
27300 PHX 85085 498-A6
38600 MarC 85086 (418-A2
See Page 417)
S 35TH AV
- PHX 85009 697-J7
800 PHX 85009 737-J4
3600 PHX 85041 737-J4
4400 MarC 85041 737-J4
6000 MarC 85041 777-J1
6000 PHX 85041 777-J1
7600 PHX 85339 777-H4
9200 MarC 85339 777-H7
N 35TH CIR
1100 MESA 85213 742-H2
S 35TH CIR
500 MESA 85204 742-H7
14000 PHX 85044 819-E4
S 35TH CT
13200 PHX 85044 819-E3
N 35TH DR
1300 PHX 85009 697-J3
3000 PHX 85019 697-J1
3500 PHX 85019 657-J2
3500 PHX 85029 617-J1
3500 PHX 85310 498-A5
3500 PHX 85308 538-A3
7200 PHX 85051 617-J3
12400 PHX 85029 577-J6
14000 PHX 85053 578-A1
17200 PHX 85308 578-A1
22000 PHX 85310 538-A2
23400 PHX 85310 497-J7
S 35TH DR
4800 PHX 85041 737-J6
N 35TH LN
9600 PHX 85051 617-J3
13800 PHX 85053 577-J1
16300 PHX 85053 578-A2

Block	City	ZIP	Pg-Grid
N 35TH LN			
22000	PHX	85310	538-A2
W 35TH LN			
3500	PHX	85053	577-J1
3500	PHX	85053	578-A1
E 35TH PL			
3400	PHX	85028	619-F4
N 35TH PL			
1800	PHX	85008	699-F3
3400	PHX	85018	699-F1
3400	PHX	85032	579-F1
4100	PHX	85018	659-F5
6200	PVAL	85253	659-F3
9200	PHX	85028	619-F1
11800	PHX	85028	579-F7
17800	PHX	85032	539-G7
18600	PHX	85050	539-G5
S 35TH PL			
500	MESA	85204	742-H6
900	MESA	85204	782-H1
4600	PHX	85040	739-F6
12600	PHX	85044	819-E2
N 35TH ST			
200	PHX	85008	699-F4
2700	MESA	85213	702-H5
2900	PHX	85018	699-F1
3400	PHX	85050	539-F5
3500	PHX	85032	579-F1
3500	PHX	85018	659-F1
6100	PVAL	85253	659-F2
9400	PHX	85028	619-F1
17600	PHX	85032	539-G7
S 35TH ST			
2800	PHX	85034	739-F4
4600	PHX	85040	739-E6
8000	PHX	85040	779-E3
12000	PHX	85044	819-E1
16000	PHX	85048	819-E6
N 35TH WY			
3500	PHX	85032	579-F1
4100	PHX	85018	659-F6
17600	PHX	85032	539-G7
19000	PHX	85050	539-G6
S 35TH WY			
15600	PHX	85048	819-E6
E 36TH AV			
-	PinC	85219	785-G4
5200	PinC	85219	786-B3
5200	APJT	85219	786-B3
N 36TH AV			
-	PHX	85310	537-J2
-	PHX	85310	538-A2
300	PHX	85009	697-J2
3100	PHX	85019	697-J1
3500	PHX	85019	657-J3
3600	PHX	85029	617-J1
7100	PHX	85051	657-J1
7100	PHX	85051	617-J2
11600	PHX	85029	577-J5
13800	PHX	85053	577-J1
16000	PHX	85053	578-A2
17200	PHX	85308	577-J1
17400	PHX	85308	537-J2
17400	PHX	85308	538-A2
23400	PHX	85310	497-J5
23800	PHX	85310	498-A5
27700	PHX	85085	498-A2
S 36TH AV			
4400	PHX	85041	737-H6
W 36TH AV			
1500	PinC	85220	785-B3
1500	APJT	85220	785-B3
N 36TH CIR			
21600	PHX	85308	537-J2
N 36TH CT			
17000	PHX	85032	579-F1
N 36TH DR			
1300	PHX	85009	697-J3
3000	PHX	85019	697-J1
3600	PHX	85029	577-J5
4400	PHX	85019	657-J1
7200	PHX	85051	617-J2
11200	PHX	85029	617-J1
13800	PHX	85053	577-J1
17200	PHX	85308	577-J1
17400	PHX	85308	537-J3
17400	PHX	85308	538-A7
21800	PHX	85310	537-J2
23600	PHX	85310	497-J5
24000	PHX	85310	498-A6
S 36TH DR			
700	PHX	85009	697-H7
900	PHX	85009	737-H1
4400	PHX	85041	737-H6
N 36TH LN			
-	PHX	85310	537-J2
7200	PHX	85051	617-J7
12600	PHX	85029	577-J6
17000	PHX	85308	577-J1
17200	PHX	85308	537-J6
W 36TH LN			
3600	PHX	85308	577-J1
N 36TH PL			
-	CVCK	85331	419-G7
1600	MESA	85205	742-H1
1800	PHX	85008	699-F3
3500	PHX	85032	579-G3
3600	PHX	85028	619-G1
3600	PHX	85050	539-G3
4300	PHX	85018	659-F6
12000	PHX	85028	579-G7
17600	PHX	85032	539-G7
S 36TH PL			
4800	PHX	85040	739-F6
13200	PHX	85044	819-E3
16400	PHX	85048	819-E7
N 36TH ST			
-	PHX	85331	419-G7
300	PHX	85008	699-F3
2900	PHX	85018	699-F3
3500	PHX	85032	579-G1
3600	PHX	85018	659-F1
3600	PHX	85028	619-F2
5400	PVAL	85253	659-F4
7600	PHX	85018	619-G7
12000	PHX	85028	579-F6
17600	PHX	85032	539-G7
18600	PHX	85050	539-G5
36100	CVCK	85331	419-H5
S 36TH ST			
-	PHX	85034	699-F7
400	PHX	85034	739-F1
2800	PHX	85040	739-F4
6000	PHX	85040	779-F1
12300	PHX	85044	819-E3
15800	PHX	85048	819-E6
N 36TH WY			
3600	PHX	85050	539-G5
14000	PHX	85032	579-G5
S 36TH WY			
13100	PHX	85044	819-E3
16600	PHX	85048	819-E7
E 37TH AV			
-	PinC	85219	785-G4
N 37TH AV			
-	PHX	85009	697-H4
2900	PHX	85019	697-H2
4300	PHX	85019	657-J2
7000	PHX	85051	657-J2
7200	PHX	85051	617-J2
10400	PHX	85029	617-J1
11600	PHX	85029	577-J5
13800	PHX	85053	577-J1
17000	PHX	85308	577-J1
17200	PHX	85308	537-J2
24400	PHX	85310	497-J6
27400	PHX	85085	498-A2
S 37TH AV			
400	PHX	85009	697-H7
3200	PHX	85009	737-H3
4600	PHX	85041	737-H6
11100	MarC	85339	777-H7
N 37TH CT			
3700	PHX	85032	579-G7
S 37TH CT			
12500	PHX	85044	819-E2
N 37TH DR			
300	PHX	85009	697-H2
3000	PHX	85019	697-H1
3700	PHX	85051	617-J2
3700	PHX	85053	577-J1
3700	PHX	85019	657-J1
7100	PHX	85051	657-J1
10600	PHX	85029	617-J1
12600	PHX	85029	577-J5
17000	PHX	85308	577-J1
18000	PHX	85308	537-J2
24000	PHX	85310	497-J5
24100	PHX	85310	498-A6
S 37TH DR			
700	PHX	85009	697-H7
900	PHX	85009	737-H1
4800	PHX	85041	737-H6
W 37TH DR			
3700	PHX	85019	697-H2
N 37TH LN			
600	PHX	85009	697-H5
3000	PHX	85019	697-H2
15400	PHX	85053	577-J2
20400	PHX	85308	537-J3
24300	PHX	85310	498-A6
24400	PHX	85310	497-J5
N 37TH PL			
1800	PHX	85008	699-F3
3600	PHX	85032	579-G2
3800	PHX	85018	699-F3
4500	PHX	85018	659-G5
5200	PVAL	85253	659-G3
10600	PHX	85028	619-G1
18800	PHX	85050	539-G4
S 37TH PL			
4400	PHX	85040	739-F6
12800	PHX	85044	819-F2
16600	PHX	85048	819-E7
N 37TH ST			
200	PHX	85008	699-F4
600	MESA	85205	742-H4
2900	PHX	85018	699-F2
3600	PHX	85032	579-G3
3600	PHX	85028	619-G1
4200	PHX	85018	659-F2
4500	SCTS	85251	660-E7
5700	PVAL	85253	659-F4
18600	PHX	85050	539-G6
S 37TH ST			
-	PHX	85034	699-F7
500	MESA	85206	742-H7
1100	MESA	85206	782-H1
2600	PHX	85034	739-F3
2600	PHX	85040	739-F5
6400	PHX	85040	779-F1
13000	PHX	85044	819-E2
16600	PHX	85048	819-E7
N 37TH WY			
2300	PHX	85008	699-F3
3700	PHX	85032	579-G4
10600	PHX	85028	619-G1
19400	PHX	85050	539-G4
S 37TH WY			
13600	PHX	85044	819-F3
15600	PHX	85048	819-E6
E 38TH AV			
-	PinC	85219	785-G4
N 38TH AV			
300	PHX	85009	697-H3
2900	PHX	85019	697-H1
3800	PHX	85019	657-H2
3800	PHX	85053	577-J1
7000	PHX	85051	657-H1
7100	PHX	85051	617-J3
10600	PHX	85029	617-J1
12600	PHX	85029	577-J6
17000	PHX	85308	577-J1
17300	PHX	85308	537-J2
23600	PHX	85310	497-J5
S 38TH AV			
4400	PHX	85041	737-H6
N 38TH CIR			
14800	PHX	85053	577-J4
N 38TH DR			
1300	PHX	85009	697-H4
3000	PHX	85019	697-H1
3500	PHX	85051	617-J2
4100	PHX	85019	657-H1
11000	PHX	85029	617-J1
12600	PHX	85029	577-J6
13800	PHX	85053	577-J1
17800	PHX	85308	537-J3
23600	PHX	85310	497-J5
S 38TH DR			
-	PHX	85041	777-H2
4400	PHX	85041	737-H5
N 38TH LN			
1300	PHX	85009	697-H3
3700	PHX	85029	577-J6
5700	PHX	85019	657-H3
10300	PHX	85051	617-J2
16800	PHX	85053	577-J1
23800	PHX	85310	497-J5
S 38TH LN			
-	PHX	85041	777-H2
W 38TH LN			
3800	PHX	85019	697-H1
N 38TH PL			
-	PHX	85050	539-H4
1600	PHX	85008	699-G3
2800	MESA	85215	702-J5
3800	PHX	85032	579-G2
4000	PHX	85018	659-G5
N 38TH PL			
4000	PHX	85018	699-G3
10800	PHX	85028	619-G1
S 38TH PL			
3800	PHX	85040	779-F2
3800	PHX	85044	819-F2
4400	PHX	85040	739-F6
15900	PHX	85048	819-F7
N 38TH ST			
-	MESA	85205	742-H1
200	PHX	85008	699-G3
2300	MESA	85215	702-J6
2900	PHX	85018	699-G1
3600	PHX	85018	659-G6
3700	PHX	85032	579-G3
3800	PVAL	85253	659-G3
9000	PHX	85028	619-G1
18600	PHX	85050	539-G4
S 38TH ST			
-	MESA	85206	742-H6
900	MESA	85206	782-H1
2600	PHX	85034	739-F4
2800	PHX	85040	739-F4
5600	PHX	85040	779-F1
12500	PHX	85044	819-F2
15600	PHX	85048	819-F6
N 38TH TER			
24300	PHX	85310	497-J5
N 38TH WY			
600	MESA	85205	742-J3
2000	PHX	85008	699-G4
12600	PHX	85032	579-G2
S 38TH WY			
-	PHX	85040	779-F3
13600	PHX	85044	819-G3
15900	PHX	85048	819-F6
E 39TH AV			
-	PinC	85219	785-G4
N 39TH AV			
-	PHX	85009	697-H4
2900	PHX	85019	697-H1
3600	PHX	85019	657-H1
3800	PHX	85051	617-H5
7000	PHX	85051	657-H1
10600	PHX	85029	617-H1
11600	PHX	85029	577-J5
13800	PHX	85053	577-J2
16800	PHX	85308	577-J2
17200	PHX	85308	537-J3
24400	PHX	85310	497-J4
27400	PHX	85085	497-J2
S 39TH AV			
-	PHX	85339	777-H3
400	PHX	85009	697-H7
700	PHX	85009	737-H1
4800	MarC	85041	737-H7
4800	PHX	85041	737-H7
6200	MarC	85041	777-H1
6200	PHX	85041	777-H1
W 39TH AV			
3800	PHX	85308	537-J2
N 39TH CIR			
700	MESA	85205	742-J3
2200	MESA	85215	702-J7
S 39TH CIR			
100	MESA	85206	742-H5
N 39TH DR			
300	PHX	85009	697-H2
2900	PHX	85019	697-H1
3900	PHX	85308	577-J1
3900	PHX	85308	537-J2
4700	PHX	85019	657-H4
7300	PHX	85051	617-H2
10800	PHX	85029	617-H1
12000	PHX	85029	577-H6
14000	PHX	85053	577-J1
23400	PHX	85310	497-J7
S 39TH DR			
6400	PHX	85041	777-H1
N 39TH LN			
2000	PHX	85009	697-H2
5000	PHX	85019	657-H5
10000	PHX	85051	617-H2
11400	PHX	85029	617-H1
12800	PHX	85029	577-H6
13800	PHX	85053	577-H5
23400	PHX	85310	497-J6
S 39TH LN			
-	PHX	85041	777-G1
N 39TH PL			
-	CVCK	85331	419-H7
2000	PHX	85008	699-G3
3800	PHX	85050	539-H4
3900	PHX	85028	619-G1
4500	PHX	85018	659-G6
12200	PHX	85032	579-G4
S 39TH PL			
6400	PHX	85040	779-G1
13000	PHX	85044	819-F2
16000	PHX	85048	819-F6
E 39TH ST			
3800	PHX	85028	619-G2
N 39TH ST			
1500	GIL	85234	782-H3
1800	MESA	85205	702-J7
1800	MESA	85205	742-J1
1800	PHX	85008	699-G3
2300	MESA	85215	702-J6
2900	PHX	85018	699-G1
3800	PHX	85028	619-G1
4100	PHX	85018	659-G6
5800	PVAL	85253	659-G3
12200	PHX	85032	579-G3
18600	PHX	85050	539-H4
S 39TH ST			
-	PHX	85040	779-F3
-	MESA	85206	742-H5
1100	MESA	85206	782-H2
2800	PHX	85034	739-G4
2800	PHX	85040	739-G4
13200	PHX	85044	819-F3
16000	PHX	85048	819-F6
N 39TH WY			
400	MESA	85205	742-J3
10600	PHX	85028	619-G2
12200	PHX	85032	579-G5
18600	PHX	85050	539-H4
S 39TH WY			
13600	PHX	85044	819-F3
16600	PHX	85048	819-F7
N 40TH AV			
300	PHX	85009	697-H2
2900	PHX	85019	697-H1
3600	PHX	85019	657-H4
4000	PHX	85051	617-H2
10600	PHX	85029	617-H1
11600	PHX	85029	577-H5
13800	PHX	85053	577-H1
17000	PHX	85308	577-J1
17800	PHX	85308	537-J4
N 40TH AV			
23400	PHX	85310	497-J5
S 40TH AV			
600	PHX	85009	697-H7
900	PHX	85009	737-G1
6400	PHX	85041	777-G1
N 40TH CT			
11400	PHX	85028	619-H1
N 40TH DR			
2000	PHX	85009	697-H2
2900	PHX	85019	697-H1
4000	PHX	85029	617-H1
4000	PHX	85019	657-H2
7300	PHX	85051	617-H2
11600	PHX	85029	577-H6
17000	PHX	85308	577-H1
17400	PHX	85308	537-H2
23800	PHX	85310	497-J4
S 40TH DR			
-	PHX	85041	777-G1
N 40TH LN			
2900	PHX	85019	697-H2
5300	PHX	85019	657-H4
9800	PHX	85051	617-H2
15000	PHX	85053	577-H2
N 4OTH LN			
12200	PHX	85029	577-H7
N 4OTH LN			
17800	PHX	85308	537-H3
23400	PHX	85310	497-J4
S 40TH LN			
-	PHX	85041	777-G2
N 40TH PL			
-	PHX	85034	699-G6
700	PHX	85008	699-G6
3400	PHX	85018	699-G1
4000	PHX	85018	659-G6
4300	PHX	85050	539-J1
6200	PVAL	85253	659-H2
10200	PHX	85028	619-H1
12600	PHX	85032	579-H2
17700	PHX	85032	539-H7
25800	PHX	85050	499-H4
30200	PHX	85331	499-H3
S 40TH PL			
-	PHX	85034	699-G7
4000	PHX	85044	819-F2
5200	PHX	85040	739-G7
6100	PHX	85040	779-G1
10600	PHX	85044	779-F6
15800	PHX	85048	819-F6
N 40TH ST			
-	MESA	85215	703-A4
-	PHX	85034	699-G5
300	PHX	85008	699-G4
800	MESA	85205	742-J1
2300	MESA	85215	702-J4
2900	PHX	85018	699-G4
3800	PHX	85253	659-G5
3800	PHX	85018	659-G1
3900	PHX	85028	619-G4
3900	PHX	85050	539-J2
5200	PVAL	85253	659-G2
5800	PVAL	85018	659-G1
6800	MarC	85018	659-G1
6800	MarC	85253	659-G1
12000	PHX	85028	579-H2
12100	PHX	85032	579-H2
17600	PHX	85032	539-H7
25800	PHX	85050	499-H4
26100	PHX	85085	499-H2
27400	MarC	85331	499-H2
28100	MarC	85085	499-H2
30000	PHX	85085	459-H5
30000	PHX	85331	459-H5
31800	MarC	85331	459-H5
32200	MarC	85085	459-H5
S 40TH ST			
-	MESA	85206	742-J6
-	PHX	85034	699-G7
400	PHX	85034	739-G3
2700	PHX	85040	739-G5
3800	PHX	85040	779-G1
12400	PHX	85044	819-F2
15600	PHX	85048	819-F6
N 40TH WY			
4300	PHX	85050	539-J2
11200	PHX	85028	619-H1
12000	PHX	85028	579-H6
12800	PHX	85032	579-H2
30100	PHX	85331	459-H6
S 40TH WY			
4000	PHX	85044	819-F5
6600	PHX	85040	779-G1
16000	PHX	85048	819-F6
N 41ST AV			
-	PHX	85009	697-G3
3000	PHX	85019	697-H1
4000	PHX	85053	577-H3
5200	PHX	85019	657-H1
7000	PHX	85051	657-H1
7100	PHX	85051	617-H2
10800	PHX	85029	617-H1
11600	PHX	85029	577-H5
17000	PHX	85308	577-H1
17200	PHX	85308	537-H3
23400	PHX	85310	497-H4
47100	MarC	85087	337-J5
S 41ST AV			
-	PHX	85339	777-G2
200	PHX	85009	697-G7
900	PHX	85009	737-G1
5600	MarC	85041	737-G7
6000	PHX	85041	737-G7
6200	PHX	85041	777-G2
S 41ST CIR			
6000	PHX	85040	779-G1
N 41ST CT			
13800	PHX	85053	577-H5
14400	PHX	85032	579-H4
N 41ST DR			
-	PHX	85086	(377-J4 See Page 337)
300	PHX	85009	697-G3
3000	PHX	85019	697-G1
4100	PHX	85019	657-H1
7200	PHX	85051	617-H2
10800	PHX	85029	617-H1
11600	PHX	85029	577-H6
13800	PHX	85053	577-H2
17400	PHX	85308	537-H5
23600	PHX	85310	497-H3
S 41ST DR			
5600	MarC	85041	737-G7
6200	PHX	85041	737-G7
6200	PHX	85041	777-G1
N 41ST LN			
-	PHX	85310	497-H3
1900	PHX	85009	697-G3
3500	PHX	85019	697-G1
N 41ST LN			
4100	PHX	85029	577-H7
4100	PHX	85053	577-H5
6700	PHX	85019	657-H1
7100	PHX	85051	617-H2
7100	PHX	85051	657-H1
11600	PHX	85029	617-H1
18200	PHX	85308	537-H3
S 41ST LN			
-	PHX	85041	777-G2
N 41ST PL			
300	PHX	85008	699-G4
3100	PHX	85018	699-H1
4100	PHX	85018	659-H4
4100	PHX	85032	579-H1
4100	PHX	85331	459-J5
6000	PVAL	85018	659-H3
10600	PHX	85028	619-H1
17600	PHX	85032	539-H7
18600	PHX	85050	539-H5
26000	PHX	85050	499-H4
26600	PHX	85331	499-H3
S 41ST PL			
-	PHX	85034	699-G7
4100	PHX	85044	819-F2
5200	PHX	85040	739-G7
6000	PHX	85040	779-G1
10400	PHX	85044	779-G6
16000	PHX	85048	819-F6
N 41ST ST			
-	PHX	85034	699-G6
400	PHX	85008	699-G4
3100	PHX	85018	699-G2
3900	PHX	85018	659-G5
4000	PHX	85331	459-H5
5900	PVAL	85018	659-G3
6500	PVAL	85253	659-H2
10600	PHX	85028	619-H1
12600	PHX	85032	579-H2
17800	PHX	85032	539-H7
18600	PHX	85050	539-J2
22500	PHX	85050	540-A1
25800	PHX	85050	499-H4
26600	PHX	85331	499-H3
28200	MarC	85331	499-H1
S 41ST ST			
-	PHX	85034	739-G1
-	PHX	85326	819-F7
-	PHX	85034	699-G7
900	MESA	85206	742-J7
900	MESA	85206	782-J1
4000	PHX	85040	739-G5
5800	PHX	85040	779-G1
12600	PHX	85044	819-F2
16000	PHX	85048	819-F6
N 41ST WY			
25800	PHX	85050	499-H4
26600	PHX	85331	499-H3
30600	PHX	85331	459-J5
S 41ST WY			
-	PHX	85326	819-F7
5600	PHX	85040	739-G7
7000	PHX	85040	779-G1
13600	PHX	85044	819-F3
N 42ND AV			
300	PHX	85009	697-G2
2900	PHX	85019	697-G1
3500	PHX	85019	657-G1
4100	PHX	85029	577-H6
4100	PHX	85053	577-H1
4200	PHX	85051	617-H2
10800	PHX	85029	617-H1
17000	PHX	85308	577-H1
17800	PHX	85308	537-H3
23400	PHX	85310	497-H5
S 42ND AV			
-	PHX	85041	777-G1
5600	MarC	85041	737-G7
N 42ND CIR			
18800	PHX	85308	537-H5
N 42ND CT			
26700	PHX	85331	499-J3
N 42ND DR			
1000	PHX	85009	697-G3
2900	PHX	85019	697-G1
5100	PHX	85019	657-G1
7500	PHX	85051	617-H2
10800	PHX	85029	617-H1
11600	PHX	85029	577-H6
13800	PHX	85053	577-H1
17600	PHX	85308	537-H6
23400	PHX	85310	497-H3
S 42ND DR			
-	PHX	85041	777-G1
5600	MarC	85041	737-G7
N 42ND LN			
3000	PHX	85019	697-G1
5200	PHX	85019	657-G1
7500	PHX	85051	617-G6
13800	PHX	85053	577-H5
17200	PHX	85308	577-H1
17200	PHX	85308	537-H5
24600	PHX	85310	497-H4
S 42ND LN			
-	PHX	85041	777-G1
E 42ND PL			
-	PHX	85331	459-J3
N 42ND PL			
3600	PHX	85018	699-H1
4000	PHX	85018	659-H5
4100	PHX	85331	459-H5
4400	PHX	85050	540-A1
10400	PHX	85028	619-H2
12400	PHX	85032	579-H1
17600	PHX	85032	539-H6
18600	PHX	85050	539-H6
26400	PHX	85050	499-H4
26700	PHX	85331	499-J3
S 42ND PL			
3600	PHX	85040	739-G5
4200	PHX	85048	819-G7
6600	PHX	85040	779-G1
10600	PHX	85044	779-G6
12800	PHX	85044	819-G2
N 42ND ST			
400	PHX	85008	699-G4
2800	PHX	85018	699-G4
4100	PHX	85018	659-H4
4100	PHX	85331	499-H3
4100	PHX	85032	579-H1
4200	PHX	85331	459-J3
6000	PVAL	85018	659-H3
6200	PVAL	85253	659-H3
9400	PHX	85028	619-H2
17600	PHX	85032	539-H7
18600	PHX	85050	539-H6
26200	PHX	85050	499-H4
27200	MarC	85331	499-J2
S 42ND ST			
-	PHX	85326	819-G7
S 42ND ST			
-	PHX	85034	699-G7
2700	PHX	85034	739-G4
2800	PHX	85040	739-G4
4200	PHX	85048	819-G6
5800	PHX	85040	779-G1
10600	PHX	85044	779-G6
12800	PHX	85044	819-G2
N 42ND WY			
2800	PHX	85008	699-H3
5200	PHX	85019	657-G4
14800	PHX	85032	579-H4
18600	PHX	85050	539-H6
26400	PHX	85050	499-J4
26600	PHX	85331	499-J3
31000	PHX	85331	459-J5
S 42ND WY			
6600	PHX	85040	779-G1
13600	PHX	85044	819-G3
S 42RD PL			
-	PHX	85034	699-H7
N 43RD AV			
-	PHX	85086	(377-J3 See Page 337)
-	PHX	85087	(377-J3 See Page 337)
-	PHX	85009	697-G4
-	PHX	85043	697-G4
1600	PHX	85035	697-G4
2900	PHX	85031	697-G4
2900	PHX	85019	697-G4
3500	PHX	85031	657-G7
3500	PHX	85019	657-G2
5000	GLEN	85301	657-G2
6700	GLEN	85019	657-G2
7000	PHX	85051	657-G2
7100	GLEN	85301	617-G6
7100	PHX	85051	617-G2
8000	GLEN	85302	617-G2
8000	PHX	85302	617-G2
10000	GLEN	85051	617-G2
10600	GLEN	85029	617-G2
10600	PHX	85029	617-G2
10600	PHX	85304	617-G2
11600	PHX	85029	577-H4
12000	PHX	85304	577-H4
13800	PHX	85053	577-H1
13800	PHX	85306	577-H4
17000	PHX	85308	537-H5
17000	PHX	85308	577-H1
21900	PHX	85310	497-H3
21900	PHX	85310	537-G1
47500	MarC	85087	337-J5
S 43RD AV			
-	PHX	85009	697-G7
-	PHX	85043	697-G7
400	PHX	85043	737-G1
400	PHX	85009	737-G1
1300	PHX	85339	777-G1
4700	MarC	85041	737-G4
4700	MarC	85339	737-G7
6000	PHX	85339	737-G7
6000	PHX	85041	737-G7
6300	PHX	85041	777-G1
8400	MarC	85339	777-F5
11800	MarC	85339	817-F1
N 43RD CIR			
20000	PHX	85308	537-G4
N 43RD CT			
26000	PHX	85050	499-J4
S 43RD CT			
7000	PHX	85040	779-H2
10000	PHX	85044	779-G6
N 43RD DR			
2500	PHX	85035	697-G3
3100	PHX	85031	697-G1
4300	PHX	85308	537-H4
7300	GLEN	85301	617-G7
8100	GLEN	85302	617-G3
10800	PHX	85304	617-G1
11600	PHX	85304	577-G6
14000	PHX	85306	577-H2
23400	PHX	85310	497-H5
N 43RD LN			
3000	PHX	85031	697-G1
8700	GLEN	85302	617-G3
12400	PHX	85304	577-G7
16200	PHX	85306	577-H2
19800	PHX	85308	537-H4
N 43RD PL			
-	PHX	85050	539-J2
1200	PHX	85008	699-H5
2900	PHX	85018	699-H1
4100	PHX	85018	659-H5
4300	PHX	85032	579-H1
4400	PHX	85050	540-A1
6500	PVAL	85253	659-H2
9400	PHX	85028	619-H3
17800	PHX	85032	539-J7
25800	PHX	85050	499-H4
29700	PHX	85331	459-J5
S 43RD PL			
4000	PHX	85040	739-H5
6000	PHX	85040	779-G1
9200	PHX	85044	779-G6
14200	PHX	85044	819-G4
15600	PHX	85048	819-G6
N 43RD ST			
1600	PHX	85008	699-H4
3400	PHX	85018	699-H1
4100	PHX	85018	659-H5
4200	PHX	85028	619-H1
4300	PHX	85032	539-H7
4400	PHX	85050	539-J2
6000	PVAL	85018	659-H3
13200	PHX	85032	579-H1
22500	PHX	85050	540-A1
26600	PHX	85331	499-J3
29200	PHX	85331	459-J1
32200	MarC	85331	459-J3
S 43RD ST			
-	PHX	85326	819-G7
100	PHX	85034	699-H7
6000	PHX	85040	779-H1
10100	PHX	85044	779-G6
13000	PHX	85044	819-G3
15800	PHX	85048	819-G7
N 43RD WY			
9600	PHX	85028	619-H4
14100	PHX	85032	579-H4
17800	PHX	85032	539-J7
25800	PHX	85050	499-J4
29800	PHX	85331	459-J6
S 43RD WY			
7000	PHX	85040	779-H2
10000	PHX	85044	779-G6
15600	PHX	85048	819-G6
N 44TH AV			
400	PHX	85043	697-G1
2300	PHX	85035	697-G2
N 44TH AV			
3600	PHX	85031	697-G1
3600	PHX	85031	657-G6
6400	GLEN	85301	657-G2
7200	GLEN	85301	617-G7
8500	GLEN	85302	617-G3
10800	PHX	85304	617-G1
11800	PHX	85304	577-G6
17800	PHX	85308	537-G4
23400	PHX	85310	497-H4
S 44TH AV			
11600	MarC	85339	777-F7
11800	MarC	85339	817-F1
N 44TH CT			
10600	PHX	85028	619-J2
26600	PHX	85331	499-J3
S 44TH CT			
6800	PHX	85040	779-H2
10400	PHX	85044	779-H6
12200	PHX	85044	819-H1
N 44TH DR			
2500	PHX	85035	697-G3
3600	PHX	85031	657-G7
3600	PHX	85031	697-G3
4400	PHX	85308	537-G4
7300	GLEN	85301	617-G6
9800	GLEN	85302	617-G2
10800	PHX	85304	617-G2
11800	PHX	85304	577-G6
14000	PHX	85306	577-G4
23400	PHX	85310	497-H4
S 44TH DR			
10400	MarC	85339	777-F6
W 44TH DR			
-	PHX	85310	497-H4
N 44TH LN			
2900	PHX	85031	697-G1
8800	GLEN	85302	617-G4
10800	PHX	85304	617-G1
12400	PHX	85304	577-G6
19000	PHX	85308	537-G4
23800	PHX	85310	497-G4
E 44TH PL			
4400	PHX	85008	699-H4
4400	PHX	85028	619-J3
4400	PHX	85040	739-H5
N 44TH PL			
-	PHX	85040	739-H6
1900	PHX	85008	699-H4
3400	PHX	85018	699-H1
4000	PHX	85018	659-H4
4300	PHX	85331	459-J1
4400	PVAL	85253	659-H3
4400	PHX	85032	579-J1
7600	GLEN	85301	617-G6
10400	PHX	85028	619-J2
18400	PHX	85032	539-J7
18600	PHX	85050	539-J3
22000	PHX	85050	540-A2
26200	PHX	85050	499-J4
26700	PHX	85331	499-J3
S 44TH PL			
-	PHX	85326	819-G7
4000	PHX	85040	739-H5
4400	PHX	85040	779-H1
10000	PHX	85044	779-G6
12800	PHX	85044	819-G2
16000	PHX	85048	819-G6
N 44TH ST			
200	PHX	85008	699-H4
200	PHX	85034	699-H4
2900	PHX	85018	699-H4
3900	PHX	85018	659-H5
4300	PHX	85331	459-J4
4300	PHX	85331	499-J3
4300	PHX	85032	539-J7
4400	PHX	85050	539-J2
4500	PHX	85050	540-A1
5900	PVAL	85018	659-H5
6000	PVAL	85253	659-H5
9600	PHX	85028	619-H2
13000	PHX	85032	579-J4
26100	PHX	85050	499-J4
26800	MarC	85331	499-J2
31400	MarC	85331	459-J4
S 44TH ST			
-	PHX	85326	819-G7
2600	PHX	85034	739-H4
2800	PHX	85040	739-H4
4400	PHX	85044	779-H5
6000	PHX	85040	779-H1
11400	PHX	85044	819-G1
15500	PHX	85048	819-G6
N 44TH WY			
10600	PHX	85028	619-J1
18400	PHX	85032	539-J7
25800	PHX	85050	499-J4
31200	PHX	85331	459-J2
S 44TH WY			
4000	PHX	85040	739-H5
6800	PHX	85040	779-H1
10200	PHX	85044	779-H6
13000	PHX	85044	819-G3
16000	PHX	85048	819-G6
N 45TH AV			
-	PHX	85043	697-F6
1600	PHX	85035	697-F4
3400	PHX	85031	697-G1
3500	PHX	85031	657-F6
4300	PHX	85306	577-G2
5500	GLEN	85301	657-G1
7100	GLEN	85301	617-G7
8000	GLEN	85302	617-G2
10800	PHX	85304	617-G1
11600	PHX	85304	577-G6
17000	PHX	85308	577-G1
17000	PHX	85308	537-G5
23400	PHX	85310	497-G5
S 45TH AV			
-	PHX	85043	697-F7
1100	PHX	85043	737-F1
8800	MarC	85339	777-F3
11700	MarC	85339	817-F1
N 45TH CIR			
7500	GLEN	85301	617-G7
19000	PHX	85308	537-G5
S 45TH CT			
11400	PHX	85044	819-G1
N 45TH DR			
2000	PHX	85035	697-F2
2900	PHX	85031	697-F1
4000	PHX	85031	657-F7
4500	GLEN	85304	617-G1
4500	PHX	85308	537-G5
5600	GLEN	85301	657-G2
7600	GLEN	85301	617-G7
8500	GLEN	85302	617-G5
11800	PHX	85304	577-G6
14200	PHX	85306	577-G2
23800	PHX	85310	497-G3

PHOENIX INDEX

STREET
Block City ZIP Pg-Grid

STREET Block City ZIP Pg-Grid

STREET
Block City ZIP Pg-Grid

N 171ST AV
28200 SURP 85375 (454-C7 See Page 413)

N 171ST DR
- MarC 85355 (654-B1 See Page 653)
9000 MarC 85355 (614-B2 See Page 573)
10400 MarC 85379 (614-B2 See Page 573)

S 171ST DR
- GDYR 85326 (694-B7 See Page 653)
- GDYR 85326 (734-B1 See Page 733)

S 171ST LN
- GDYR 85326 (694-B7 See Page 653)

N 172ND AV
- MarC 85355 (654-B1 See Page 653)

S 172ND AV
- GDYR 85326 (734-B1 See Page 733)

S 172ND DR
- GDYR 85326 (734-B1 See Page 733)

S 172ND LN
- GDYR 85326 (694-A7 See Page 653)
- GDYR 85326 (734-A1 See Page 733)

S 172ND ST
7600 MarC 85234 783-C5
7600 MESA 85234 783-C5
7600 MarC 85236 783-C5
7600 MESA 85236 783-C5
8200 GIL 85234 783-C5
8200 GIL 85236 783-C7
10800 MarC 85236 823-C1
16400 MarC 85236 863-C1
22300 MarC 85236 903-C2

N 173RD AV
7000 MarC 85355 (614-B2 See Page 573)
28200 SURP 85375 (454-C7 See Page 413)

S 173RD AV
- GDYR 85326 (694-A7 See Page 653)
- GDYR 85326 (734-A1 See Page 733)
- MarC 85326 (734-A1 See Page 733)
18700 GDYR 85326 (854-A3 See Page 813)

S 173RD DR
- GDYR 85326 (694-A7 See Page 653)
- GDYR 85326 (734-A1 See Page 733)

S 173RD LN
- GDYR 85326 (694-A7 See Page 653)
- GDYR 85326 (734-A1 See Page 733)

S 173RD ST
- MarC 85242 903-C5

S 174TH AV
- GDYR 85326 (694-A7 See Page 653)
- GDYR 85326 (734-A1 See Page 733)
- GDYR 85338 (774-B6 See Page 733)

S 174TH DR
- GDYR 85326 (694-A7 See Page 653)
- GDYR 85326 (734-A1 See Page 733)

S 174TH LN
- GDYR 85326 (694-A7 See Page 653)
- GDYR 85326 (734-A1 See Page 733)

N 174TH ST
17400 MarC 85263 503-F3

S 174TH ST
- MarC 85242 903-C5
8000 MarC 85236 783-D4
10400 GIL 85236 783-D7

N 175TH AV
- GDYR 85326 (774-B7 See Page 733)
6000 MarC 85355 (654-A1 See Page 653)
6200 MarC 85355 (614-B2 See Page 573)
12200 MarC 85379 (574-B4 See Page 573)

S 175TH AV
- GDYR 85326 (774-B7 See Page 733)
- GDYR 85326 (814-B1 See Page 813)
- GDYR 85338 (774-B4 See Page 733)
3500 GDYR 85326 (734-A4 See Page 733)
3500 MarC 85326 (734-A4 See Page 733)
18800 GDYR 85326 (853-J3 See Page 813)
23500 MarC 85326 (853-J6 See Page 813)

S 175TH DR
- GDYR 85326 (774-B7 See Page 733)
- GDYR 85326 (814-B1 See Page 813)
- GDYR 85338 (774-B4 See Page 733)
1200 MarC 85326 (694-A7 See Page 653)
1200 MarC 85326 (734-A1 See Page 733)
1200 GDYR 85326 (694-A7 See Page 653)

S 175TH LN
- GDYR 85326 (774-A7 See Page 733)
- GDYR 85326 (814-A1 See Page 813)
- GDYR 85338 (774-A6 See Page 733)
1200 MarC 85326 (694-A7 See Page 653)
1500 MarC 85326 (734-A1 See Page 733)

N 176TH AV
- GDYR 85326 (774-A7 See Page 733)
28600 SURP 85375 (454-B6 See Page 413)

S 176TH AV
- GDYR 85326 (814-A1 See Page 813)
1600 MarC 85326 (734-A1 See Page 733)

N 176TH DR
10200 MarC 85355 (614-A1 See Page 573)

S 176TH DR
- GDYR 85326 (814-A1 See Page 813)

S 176TH LN
- GDYR 85326 (774-A7 See Page 733)
- GDYR 85326 (814-A1 See Page 813)

N 176TH ST
- MarC 85263 (463-F6 See Page 423)
26600 MarC 85263 503-F3

N 177TH AV
7000 MarC 85355 (614-A6 See Page 573)
26600 MarC 85375 (454-A6 See Page 413)
26600 MarC 85375 494-A1
28900 SURP 85375 (454-A6 See Page 413)

S 177TH AV
- GDYR 85326 (774-A7 See Page 733)
- GDYR 85326 (814-A1 See Page 813)
1200 MarC 85326 (693-J7 See Page 653)
1500 MarC 85326 733-J1
18800 GDYR 85326 (853-J2 See Page 813)

N 177TH DR
22100 SURP 85387 534-B1
22100 SURP 85387 494-B7

S 177TH LN
- GDYR 85326 (774-A7 See Page 733)
- GDYR 85326 (814-A1 See Page 813)

N 178TH AV
10200 MarC 85355 (614-A1 See Page 573)
21800 SURP 85387 494-A7
21800 SURP 85387 534-A1

S 178TH AV
1500 MarC 85326 (693-J7 See Page 653)
1500 MarC 85326 733-J1

S 178TH PL
- MarC 85236 903-E1
- QC 85236 903-E1

S 178TH ST
12400 MarC 85236 823-E3

N 179TH AV
29800 MarC 85375 (454-A4 See Page 413)

N 180TH AV
- GDYR 85338 (694-E1 See Page 653)
1400 GDYR 85326 (693-J3 See Page 653)
13800 MarC 85379 (574-A4 See Page 573)

N 180TH DR
- MarC 85326 (693-J4 See Page 653)
1400 GDYR 85326 (693-J3 See Page 653)

S 180TH DR
- MarC 85326 (693-J5 See Page 653)

N 180TH LN
1400 GDYR 85326 (693-J3 See Page 653)

N 180TH ST
400 GIL 85236 783-E6

S 180TH ST
12400 MarC 85236 823-E3
22800 MarC 85236 903-E2

N 181ST AV
- MarC 85326 (693-J5 See Page 653)
1400 GDYR 85326 (693-J3 See Page 653)
6200 MarC 85355 653-J1
6500 MarC 85355 (613-J2 See Page 573)
13800 MarC 85379 573-J4
24200 SURP 85387 494-A5
24800 SURP 85361 494-A5

S 181ST AV
200 MarC 85326 (693-H6 See Page 653)

N 181ST DR
1100 MarC 85326 (693-J4 See Page 653)
1400 GDYR 85326 (693-J3 See Page 653)

N 181ST LN
1400 GDYR 85326 (693-H3 See Page 653)

S 181ST ST
25700 MarC 85242 903-E5

N 182ND AV
10400 MarC 85355 (613-J1 See Page 573)
13800 MarC 85379 573-J3

S 182ND AV
- GDYR 85338 (773-J4 See Page 733)

N 182ND DR
1100 MarC 85326 (693-H4 See Page 653)

S 182ND DR
- GDYR 85338 (773-J5 See Page 733)

S 182ND ST
22800 MarC 85236 903-E2

N 183RD AV
1000 MarC 85326 (693-H4 See Page 653)
5000 MarC 85340 653-H2
5000 MarC 85355 653-H2
6500 MarC 85355 (613-J1 See Page 573)
12200 MarC 85379 573-J4
22800 SURP 85387 493-J5

S 183RD AV
2800 GDYR 85326 733-H3
2800 MarC 85326 733-H3
17900 GDYR 85326 813-G7
17900 GDYR 85326 (853-G1 See Page 813)

N 183RD DR
1000 MarC 85326 (693-H4 See Page 653)
1100 GDYR 85326 (693-H4 See Page 653)

S 183RD LN
- GDYR 85338 (773-H4 See Page 733)

N 184TH AV
13800 MarC 85379 573-J3
24200 SURP 85387 493-J5

S 184TH AV
- GDYR 85326 (773-H4 See Page 733)

S 184TH PL
24000 QC 85236 903-F3

N 185TH AV
1000 MarC 85326 (693-H4 See Page 653)
1100 GDYR 85326 (693-H4 See Page 653)
6000 MarC 85355 653-H1
6500 MarC 85355 (613-H1 See Page 573)
13800 MarC 85379 573-H3
23000 SURP 85387 493-J5

S 185TH AV
- GDYR 85326 (773-H4 See Page 733)

S 185TH DR
- GDYR 85326 (773-H4 See Page 733)

N 186TH AV
13800 MarC 85379 573-H4

S 186TH AV
12400 GDYR 85326 (773-H4 See Page 733)
12400 MarC 85326 (773-H7 See Page 733)
12800 MarC 85326 813-H1

N 186TH DR
1200 MarC 85326 (693-G4 See Page 653)

S 186TH LN
- GDYR 85326 (773-H4 See Page 733)

S 186TH ST
22800 QC 85236 903-F2

N 187TH AV
14400 MarC 85373 573-H3
14400 SURP 85373 573-H3
22400 MarC 85387 493-H5
22400 SURP 85387 493-H5
29700 MarC 85375 (453-H1 See Page 413)
33000 MarC 85375 413-H4
36200 MarC 85342 413-H3

S 187TH AV
13400 GDYR 85326 813-G1
13400 MarC 85326 813-G1
18000 GDYR 85326 (853-F2 See Page 813)
18000 MarC 85326 (853-F2 See Page 813)

S 188TH AV
12400 MarC 85326 (773-G7 See Page 733)
12800 MarC 85326 813-G1

S 188TH ST
23600 QC 85236 903-G3

N 189TH AV
1000 MarC 85326 (693-G4 See Page 653)

S 189TH AV
12400 MarC 85326 (773-G7 See Page 733)

S 190TH AV
13100 MarC 85326 813-G1

N 191ST AV
300 MarC 85326 (693-F3 See Page 653)
300 BUCK 85326 (693-F4 See Page 653)
2900 MarC 85340 653-F7
2900 MarC 85340 (693-F3 See Page 653)
26600 MarC 85361 493-G1

S 191ST AV
12900 MarC 85326 813-F1
13400 MarC 85326 (773-G7 See Page 733)
18700 MarC 85326 (853-E2 See Page 813)

S 191ST ST
24900 QC 85236 903-G4

N 192ND AV
- MarC 85355 (613-G3 See Page 573)
600 MarC 85326 (693-F3 See Page 653)
3500 MarC 85340 653-F7

S 192ND AV
13800 MarC 85326 813-F1

N 193RD AV
- MarC 85355 (613-G3 See Page 573)
600 MarC 85326 (693-F3 See Page 653)
2900 MarC 85340 (693-F1 See Page 653)
4100 MarC 85340 653-F5
23800 MarC 85387 493-G4
24200 MarC 85361 493-G1
27800 MarC 85361 (453-G7 See Page 413)

N 193RD DR
- MarC 85355 (613-G3 See Page 573)
2900 MarC 85340 (693-F1 See Page 653)

S 193RD DR
11200 MarC 85326 (773-F6 See Page 733)

S 193RD PL
- QC 85242 903-H1

S 193RD ST
22400 QC 85242 903-H1

N 194TH AV
600 BUCK 85326 (693-E3 See Page 653)
600 MarC 85326 (693-E3 See Page 653)

S 194TH DR
11200 MarC 85326 (773-F6 See Page 733)

S 194TH PL
- QC 85242 903-H1

S 194TH ST
22600 QC 85242 903-H1

S 194TH WY
- QC 85242 903-J1

N 195TH AV
16900 SURP 85374 533-F6
21700 MarC 85387 493-F5
21700 MarC 85387 533-F1
25000 MarC 85361 493-F5
27800 MarC 85361 (453-F7 See Page 413)
29400 MarC 85375 (453-F2 See Page 413)
36200 MarC 85342 413-F3

S 195TH AV
19600 MarC 85326 (853-D3 See Page 813)
20400 GDYR 85326 (853-D3 See Page 813)

N 195TH DR
- MarC 85340 653-E6

S 195TH DR
- MarC 85326 733-E2

S 195TH PL
- QC 85242 903-J1

S 195TH ST
- QC 85242 903-J1

N 196TH AV
5100 MarC 85340 653-E3

S 196TH CIR
- QC 85242 903-J1

S 196TH DR
- MarC 85326 733-E2

N 196TH LN
- MarC 85340 653-E7

S 196TH ST
23100 QC 85242 903-J1

N 197TH AV
- MarC 85340 653-E5
25000 MarC 85361 493-F4

S 197TH CIR
- QC 85242 903-J1

N 197TH CT
- MarC 85340 653-E7

N 197TH LN
- BUCK 85340 653-E6
- MarC 85340 653-E6

S 197TH PL
23300 QC 85242 903-J1

S 197TH ST
- QC 85242 903-J2

S 198TH CIR
- QC 85242 903-J1

S 198TH DR
- MarC 85326 733-D2

S 198TH ST
- QC 85242 863-J6
25100 QC 85242 903-J5

N 199TH AV
- BUCK 85340 653-D4
1600 MarC 85326 (693-D2 See Page 653)
5000 MarC 85340 653-D4
18600 SURP 85387 533-E4
25000 MarC 85361 493-E3

S 199TH CIR
- QC 85242 904-A1

S 199TH PL
- QC 85242 904-A2

S 199TH ST
- QC 85242 904-A1

S 199TH WY
- QC 85242 863-J7
- QC 85242 864-A7

N 200TH AV
1600 MarC 85326 (693-D2 See Page 653)
5200 MarC 85340 653-D3

N 201ST AV
1600 MarC 85326 (693-D2 See Page 653)

S 201ST ST
- QC 85242 904-A2

S 201ST WY
- QC 85242 904-A2

N 202ND AV
1600 MarC 85326 (693-C2 See Page 653)
5000 MarC 85340 653-C3

S 202ND PL
11600 MarC 85212 824-B2

S 202ND ST
22100 QC 85242 904-A2
25900 MarC 85242 904-A6

N 203RD AV
- MarC 85361 413-D7
17800 SURP 85374 533-D5
18600 SURP 85387 533-D5
20200 MarC 85361 (453-D1 See Page 413)
26600 MarC 85361 493-D1
30200 MarC 85375 (453-D1 See Page 413)

S 203RD AV
1400 MarC 85326 (693-C7 See Page 653)
1400 MarC 85326 733-C3
7500 MarC 85326 (773-D2 See Page 733)
18800 MarC 85326 (853-B2 See Page 813)

S 203RD ST
- QC 85242 864-B7
- QC 85242 904-B1

N 204TH AV
26600 MarC 85361 493-D1
27600 MarC 85361 (453-D7 See Page 413)

S 204TH AV
14000 MarC 85326 813-C2

N 204TH PL
26600 MarC 85361 493-D1
27800 MarC 85361 (453-C7 See Page 413)

S 204TH ST
- QC 85242 904-B3
18800 QC 85242 864-B4
25900 MarC 85242 904-B6

N 204TH WY
27600 MarC 85361 (453-D7 See Page 413)
27600 MarC 85361 493-D1

N 205TH AV
26600 MarC 85361 493-C1
28400 MarC 85361 (453-D6 See Page 413)

S 205TH AV
11000 MarC 85326 (773-C7 See Page 733)
14000 MarC 85326 813-C1

S 205TH PL
- QC 85242 904-B1

N 206TH AV
26600 MarC 85361 493-C2
29800 MarC 85361 (453-C5 See Page 413)

N 207TH AV
20200 MarC 85387 533-C2
24500 MarC 85387 493-C4
26600 MarC 85361 493-C1
27800 MarC 85361 (453-C5 See Page 413)

S 207TH AV
7600 MarC 85326 (773-C2 See Page 733)
13600 MarC 85326 813-B2

N 207TH CT
27300 MarC 85361 493-C1

S 208TH PL
22000 QC 85242 904-C1

S 208TH ST
22100 QC 85242 904-C1

S 209TH AV
12000 MarC 85326 (773-B7 See Page 733)
12800 MarC 85326 813-B2

S 209TH ST
- QC 85242 864-C6
22100 QC 85242 904-C1

S 210TH ST
- QC 85242 904-C5

N 211TH AV
17800 MarC 85374 533-B3
17800 MarC 85387 533-B3
19000 SURP 85387 533-B3
21800 MarC 85387 493-B6
21800 SURP 85387 493-B6
25000 MarC 85361 493-B1
25000 SURP 85361 493-B3
27400 MarC 85361 (453-B5 See Page 413)
33000 MarC 85361 413-B4
36200 MarC 85342 413-B4

S 211TH ST
- QC 85242 864-C6
- QC 85242 904-D5

S 212TH ST
- QC 85242 864-D6

S 213TH AV
10800 MarC 85326 (773-A6 See Page 733)

S 213TH ST
- QC 85242 904-D2

S 214TH WY
22200 QC 85242 904-D2

N 215TH AV
33000 MarC 85361 413-A7
33000 MarC 85361 (453-A1 See Page 413)

S 215TH AV
10800 MarC 85326 (773-A5 See Page 733)

S 215TH ST
22600 QC 85242 904-E1

S 216TH ST
21500 QC 85242 904-E1

S 217TH PL
20800 QC 85242 864-E6

N 219TH AV
21800 MarC 85361 (452-J1 See Page 411)

S 220TH LN
2400 BUCK 85326 (732-J1 See Page 731)

N 221ST AV
27400 MarC 85361 (452-J4 See Page 411)

S 221ST AV
2000 BUCK 85326 (732-J1 See Page 731)

S 222ND AV
2000 BUCK 85326 (732-H1 See Page 731)
11500 MarC 85326 (772-H6 See Page 731)

S 222ND ST
15600 MarC 85242 824-G7
15600 MarC 85242 864-F1

N 223RD AV
26600 MarC 85361 (452-H2 See Page 411)

S 223RD AV
1200 BUCK 85326 (692-H7 See Page 651)
1200 BUCK 85326 (732-H1 See Page 731)

N 223RD DR
33000 MarC 85361 (452-H1 See Page 411)
33200 MarC 85361 (412-H7 See Page 411)

N 224TH AV
22400 MarC 85361 (412-H7 See Page 411)
33000 MarC 85361 (452-H1 See Page 411)

S 224TH AV
2000 BUCK 85326 (732-H1 See Page 731)

N 224TH LN
33200 MarC 85361 (412-H7 See Page 411)

N 225TH AV
22500 MarC 85361 (412-H7 See Page 411)
28000 MarC 85361 (452-H3 See Page 411)

S 225TH AV
2600 BUCK 85326 (732-G1 See Page 731)

S 225TH LN
2000 BUCK 85326 (732-G1 See Page 731)

N 226TH DR
1100 BUCK 85326 (692-G3 See Page 651)
28200 MarC 85361 (452-G7 See Page 411)

S 226TH DR
2200 BUCK 85326 (732-G1 See Page 731)

N 227TH AV
27400 MarC 85361 (452-G3 See Page 411)

S 227TH AV
2000 MarC 85326 (732-G1 See Page 731)

N 227TH LN
1000 BUCK 85326 (692-G3 See Page 651)

S 228TH AV
2700 MarC 85326 (732-G1 See Page 731)

S 228TH DR
2100 MarC 85326 (732-G1 See Page 731)

W 228TH DR
22800 MarC 85326 (732-G1 See Page 731)

S 228TH ST
22000 MarC 85242 904-H1

N 229TH AV
1200 BUCK 85326 (692-G3 See Page 651)
28200 MarC 85361 (452-G3 See Page 411)

S 229TH AV
2000 MarC 85326 (732-F1 See Page 731)

S 229TH DR
2300 MarC 85326 (732-F1 See Page 731)

N 230TH AV
1000 BUCK 85326 (692-F3 See Page 651)

N 231ST AV
1000 BUCK 85326 (692-F3 See Page 651)
26600 MarC 85361 (452-F1 See Page 411)
32200 MarC 85342 (452-F1 See Page 411)

S 231ST AV
2000 MarC 85326 (732-F1 See Page 731)

N 232ND AV
1100 BUCK 85326 (692-F3 See Page 651)

S 232ND AV
23100 MarC 85326 (732-F1 See Page 731)

N 233RD AV
1000 BUCK 85326 (692-F3 See Page 651)
1200 MarC 85326 (692-F3 See Page 651)

S 233RD AV
2200 MarC 85326 (732-E1 See Page 731)

N 233RD LN
1400 BUCK 85326 (692-E3 See Page 651)
1400 MarC 85326 (692-E3 See Page 651)

N 234TH AV
1000 BUCK 85326 (692-E3 See Page 651)

S 234TH AV
2100 MarC 85326 (732-E1 See Page 731)

N 235TH AV
1000 BUCK 85326 (692-E3 See Page 651)
22700 MarC 85342 (412-F2 See Page 411)
26600 MarC 85361 (452-E4 See Page 411)
26600 SURP 85361 (452-E7 See Page 411)
38000 MarC 85342 (372-F6 See Page 331)

N 237TH AV
- MarC 85342 (412-E2 See Page 411)
27700 MarC 85361 (452-E7 See Page 411)

N 239TH AV
27200 MarC 85361 (452-D7 See Page 411)

S 239TH AV
7500 BUCK 85326 (772-D2 See Page 731)
7500 MarC 85326 (732-D7 See Page 731)
7500 MarC 85326 (772-D2 See Page 731)
7500 BUCK 85326 (732-D7 See Page 731)

N 243RD AV
26600 MarC 85361 (452-C2 See Page 411)
33000 MarC 85342 (412-C7 See Page 411)
33000 MarC 85342 (452-C2 See Page 411)

S 247TH AV
1200 BUCK 85326 (692-B7 See Page 651)
2000 MarC 85326 (692-B7 See Page 651)
2000 MarC 85326 (732-B1 See Page 731)
2000 BUCK 85326 (732-B1 See Page 731)

S 248TH AV
2100 MarC 85326 (732-B1 See Page 731)

S 249TH AV
2100 MarC 85326 (732-B1 See Page 731)

S 250TH AV
2000 BUCK 85326 (692-A7 See Page 651)
2000 MarC 85326 (692-A7 See Page 651)
2000 MarC 85326 (732-A1 See Page 731)
2400 BUCK 85326 (732-A1 See Page 731)

N 251ST AV
28200 MarC 85361 (452-A6 See Page 411)

N 252ND AV
- MarC 85361 (452-A7 See Page 411)

N 253RD AV
- MarC 85342 (372-A5 See Page 331)

S 253RD AV
8000 MarC 85326 (771-J1 See Page 731)

N 255TH AV
600 MarC 85326 (691-J6 See Page 651)
28200 MarC 85361 (451-J5 See Page 411)

N 257TH AV
800 MarC 85326 (691-J6 See Page 651)

N 259TH AV
28200 MarC 85361 (451-H2 See Page 411)
31300 MarC 85342 411-H5
31300 MarC 85361 411-H5

N 266TH AV
500 MarC 85326 (691-J6 See Page 651)

N 267TH AV
26600 MarC 85361 (451-F6 See Page 411)
26600 MarC 85390 (451-F6 See Page 411)

N 277TH AV
4100 BUCK 85373 651-D5

N 289TH AV
1300 MarC 85326 (691-A2 See Page 651)

N 324TH AV
51100 MarC 85390 290-C5

N 326TH AV
- WICK 85390 290-B4

S 326TH AV
51000 MarC 85390 290-B5

N 328TH AV
50600 MarC 85390 290-B4

N 329TH AV
- WICK 85390 290-A5
32800 MarC 85390 290-A5

330TH AV
- YavC - 250-A5

N 330TH DR
53000 MarC 85390 290-A3

N 332ND AV
50400 MarC 85390 290-A6

N 334TH AV
50300 MarC 85390 289-J3
52400 WICK 85390 289-J3

N 335TH AV
50000 MarC 85390 289-J4
50000 WICK 85390 289-J4

N 337TH AV
52200 MarC 85390 289-H4
52400 WICK 85390 289-H4

N 339TH AV
- MarC 85390 289-H4

N 491ST AV
47600 MarC 85320 (285-E6 See Page 244)

N 507TH AV
47400 MarC 85320 (285-A7 See Page 244)

N 508TH AV
47800 MarC 85320 (285-A7 See Page 244)

N 509TH AV
48600 MarC 85320 (285-A6 See Page 244)

N 510TH AV
47800 MarC 85320 (284-J7 See Page 244)

N 511TH AV
48600 MarC 85320 (284-J6 See Page 244)

N 513TH AV
48100 MarC 85320 (284-J6 See Page 244)

N 514TH AV
47800 MarC 85320 (284-H7 See Page 244)

N 516TH AV
47400 MarC 85320 (284-H7 See Page 244)

N 518TH AV
- MarC 85320 (284-G7 See Page 244)

N 523RD AV
- MarC 85320 244-G3

N 531ST AV
- MarC 85320 244-E3

S 555TH AV
- MarC 85354 105-C1

S 571ST AV
45300 MarC 85354 105-C1

I-8 FRWY
- MarC - 105-C1
- MarC - 106-A1
- GBND - 106-A1
- MarC - (1089-J4 See Page 1049)
- GBND - (1089-G4 See Page 1049)
- MarC - (1090-A4 See Page 1049)
- GBND - (1090-E6 See Page 1049)

I-10 FRWY
- AVON - 695-J4
- BUCK - 102-B3
- BUCK - (691-A6 See Page 651)
- BUCK - (692-J4 See Page 651)
- BUCK - (693-D3 See Page 653)
- GDYR - 102-B3
- GDYR - (693-G3 See Page 653)
- GDYR - (694-A3 See Page 653)
- GDYR - 695-A4
- MarC - 101-C2
- MarC - 102-A2
- MarC - (691-C6 See Page 651)
- MarC - (692-J4 See Page 651)
- MarC - (693-G3 See Page 653)
- MarC - 695-G4

I-10 MARICOPA FRWY
- CHAN - 819-J5
- GUAD - 780-A5
- MarC - 819-J5
- MarC - 859-J1
- MarC - 860-A3
- MarC - 900-D1
- PHX - 739-D4
- PHX - 779-J7
- PHX - 780-A5
- PHX - 819-J5
- PHX - 859-J1

STREET Block City ZIP Pg-Grid

AIRPORTS

FEATURE NAME	Address City, ZIP Code	PAGE-GRID
CHANDLER MUNICIPAL	2380 S STINSON WY, CHAN, 85249	861 - J5
DEER VALLEY	W DEER VALLEY RD & N 19TH AV, PHX, 85027	538 - F1
GILA BEND MUNICIPAL (SEE PAGE 1049)	PIMA ST & GILA BEND AIRPORT, GBND, 85337	1090 - G2
GLENDALE MUNICIPAL	6801 N GLEN HARBOR BLVD, GLEN, 85307	655 - J1
MCGILL ULTRALIGHT FIELD	W PINNACLE PEAK RD & N 43RD AV, PHX, 85310	537 - F2
MESA MUNICIPAL FALCON FIELD	4800 E FALCON DR, MESA, 85215	703 - B7
PAPAGO ARMY AIRFIELD	E OAK ST & N 52ND ST, PHX, 85008	700 - A4
PEGASUS AIRPARK	N ELLSWORTH RD & E PEGASUS PKW, QC, 85242	904 - D6
PHOENIX GOODYEAR MUNICIPAL	1658 S LITCHFIELD RD, GDYR, 85338	735 - A1
PLEASANT VALLEY (SEE PAGE 415)	CAREFREE & PLEASANT VLY ARPT, PEOR, 85382	416 - F6
SCOTTSDALE MUNICIPAL	15000 N AIRPORT DR, SCTS, 85260	580 - H4
SKY HARBOR INTL	3400 E SKY HARBOR BLVD, PHX, 85034	739 - D3
SKYRANCH	8302 E CAVE CREEK RD, CARE, 85377	421 - A5
STELLAR AIRPARK	W CHANDLER BL & S STELLAR PKWY, CHAN, 85226	820 - G6
WICKENBURG MUNICIPAL	SABIN BROWN RD & WICKENBURG WY, WICK, 85390	289 - G2
WILLIAMS GATEWAY	6001 S POWER RD, MESA, 85212	823 - H6

BUILDINGS

FEATURE NAME	Address City, ZIP Code	PAGE-GRID
300 CLARENDON BLDG	300 W CLARENDON AV, PHX, 85013	698 - F1
505 2ND ST BLDG	505 N 2ND ST, PHX, 85004	698 - G6
1001 CENTRAL BLDG	1001 N CENTRAL AV, PHX, 85004	698 - G5
2120 CENTRAL BLDG	2120 N CENTRAL AV, PHX, 85003	698 - G3
2400 CENTRAL BLDG	2400 N CENTRAL AV, PHX, 85003	698 - G3
2700 CENTRAL BLDG	2700 N CENTRAL AV, PHX, 85003	698 - G2
3800 TOWER	3800 N CENTRAL AV, PHX, 85013	698 - G1
ARIZONA BANK BLDG	302 N 1ST AV, PHX, 85003	698 - G6
ARIZONA TITLE	111 W MONROE ST, PHX, 85003	698 - G6
BANK OF AMERICA BLDG	101 N 1ST AV, PHX, 85003	698 - G6
BANK ONE BLDG	201 N CENTRAL AV, PHX, 85004	698 - G6
CAPITAL CTR	W JEFFERSON ST & S 15TH AVE, PHX, 85007	698 - E7
DIAL TOWER	1850 N CENTRAL AV, PHX, 85003	698 - G4
FARM & HOME BLDG	300 W OSBORN RD, PHX, 85013	698 - F1
FINANCIAL CTR	3443 N CENTRAL AV, PHX, 85012	698 - G1
FIRST INTERSTATE TOWER	3550 N CENTRAL AV, PHX, 85013	698 - G1
GENERAL MOTORS PROVING GROUNDS	S ELLSWORTH RD & E PECOS RD, MarC, 85212	824 - D5
GREAT AMERICAN TOWER	3200 N CENTRAL AV, PHX, 85013	698 - G1
GREATER ARIZONA SAVINGS	N CENTRAL AVE & W ADAMS ST, PHX, 85003	698 - G6
GREYHOUND TOWER	111 W CLARENDON AV, PHX, 85013	698 - G1
INTER-TEL COURTYARD CENTRE	202 E MCDOWELL RD, PHX, 85004	698 - G4
LAWYERS TITLE BLDG	2200 N CENTRAL AV, PHX, 85003	698 - G3
LUHRS TOWER COMPLEX	11 W JEFFERSON ST, PHX, 85003	698 - G7
MIDTOWNE BUSINESS CENTRE III	202 E EARLL DR, PHX, 85012	698 - G2
NATL BANK PLAZA	3101 N CENTRAL AV, PHX, 85012	698 - G2
NORWEST TOWER	3300 N CENTRAL AV, PHX, 85013	698 - G1
PHELPS DODGE TOWER	2600 N CENTRAL AV, PHX, 85003	698 - G3
PHOENIX CTR	E MORELAND ST & N 3RD ST, PHX, 85004	698 - G5
PHOENIX CORPORATE TOWER	3003 N CENTRAL AV, PHX, 85012	698 - G2
PHOENIX TOWERS	E MONTE VISTA RD & N CENTRAL A, PHX, 85004	698 - G3
PHOENIX TOWNE HOUSE	100 W CLARENDON AV, PHX, 85013	658 - G7
RENAISSANCE SQUARE	2 N CENTRAL AV, PHX, 85003	698 - G6
SECURITY CTR	W VAN BUREN ST & N CENTRAL AVE, PHX, 85003	698 - G6
TRANSAMERICA TITLE	N 1ST ST & W ADAMS ST, PHX, 85003	698 - G6
U-HAUL TOWERS	2727 N CENTRAL AV, PHX, 85004	698 - G2
VALLEY CTR	W VAN BUREN ST & N CENTRAL AVE, PHX, 85003	698 - G6
WELLS FARGO PLAZA	W WASHINGTON ST & N 1ST AV, PHX, 85003	698 - G7

BUILDINGS - GOVERNMENTAL

FEATURE NAME	Address City, ZIP Code	PAGE-GRID
ARIZONA DEPT OF HEALTH SERVICES	1740 W ADAMS ST, PHX, 85007	698 - D6
ARIZONA PUB SERVICE	N 1ST ST & E TAYLOR ST, PHX, 85004	698 - G6
CAPITOL ANNEX	W ADAMS ST & N 17TH AV, PHX, 85007	698 - D6
COUNTY ADMIN BLDG	301 W JEFFERSON ST, PHX, 85003	698 - F7
COUNTY COURT BLDG	201 W JEFFERSON ST, PHX, 85003	698 - F7
FEDERAL BLDG & US COURTHOUSE	230 N 1ST AV, PHX, 85003	698 - F6
HIGHWAY DEPARTMENT	206 S 17TH AV, PHX, 85007	698 - D7
MARICOPA CO DEPARTMENT OF HEALTH	1845 E ROOSEVELT ST, PHX, 85006	699 - A5
MUNICIPAL BLDG	S 3RD AVE & W WASHINGTON ST, PHX, 85003	698 - F7
MUNICIPAL BLDG ANNEX	N 3RD AV & W WASHINGTON ST, PHX, 85003	698 - F7
OFFICE OF ATTORNEY GENERAL	W WASHINGTON ST & S 14TH AV, PHX, 85007	698 - E7
POLICE & PUB SAFETY BLDG	W WASHINGTON AV & N 7TH AVE, PHX, 85003	698 - F6
SCOTTSDALE COURT HOUSE	3629 N CIVIC CENTER BLVD, SCTS, 85251	700 - G1
STATE CAPITOL	1700 W WASHINGTON ST, PHX, 85007	698 - D7
STATE COURTS BLDG	W JEFFERSON ST & S 15TH AV, PHX, 85007	698 - E7

CEMETERIES

FEATURE NAME	Address City, ZIP Code	PAGE-GRID
BETH EL CEM	W VAN BUREN ST & N 27TH AV, PHX, 85009	698 - B5
BETH ISRAEL MEM CEM	305 S 35TH AV, PHX, 85009	697 - J7
DOUBLE BUTTE CEM	2525 W BROADWAY RD, TEMP, 85282	739 - J6
EAST RESTHAVEN PK CEM	4310 E SOUTHERN AV, PHX, 85040	739 - G7
GLENDALE MEM PK	7844 N 61ST AV, GLEN, 85301	617 - C6
GREEN ACRES CEM	401 N HAYDEN RD, SCTS, 85257	700 - H6
GREENWOOD MEMORY LAWN CEM	2300 W VAN BUREN ST, PHX, 85009	698 - B5
HANSEN DESERT HILLS MEM PK	6500 E BELL RD, PHX, 85054	580 - E1
HAZELTON, LOUIS B CEM (SEE PAGE 731)	W BROADWAY RD, MarC, 85326	732 - F3
HOLY CROSS CEM	N 99TH AV & W THOMAS RD, AVON, 85323	696 - B2
MESA CITY CEM	N CENTER ST & E 14TH ST, MESA, 85201	741 - H2
MTN VIEW MEM GARDENS	7900 E APACHE TR, MarC, 85207	743 - J5
NATL MEM CEM OF ARIZONA	23029 CAVE CREEK RD, PHX, 85050	539 - F1
PARADISE MEM GARDENS	9300 E SHEA BLVD, SCTS, 85260	621 - C2
PHOENIX MEM PK	200 W BEARDSLEY RD, PHX, 85027	538 - G4
PIONEER-MILITARY MEM PK	S 15TH AV & W MADISON ST, PHX, 85007	698 - E7
QUEEN OF HEAVEN CEM	1500 E BASELINE RD, MESA, 85204	782 - B3
RESTHAVEN PK CEM	6290 W NORTHERN AV, GLEN, 85302	617 - B5
SAINT FRANCIS CATHOLIC CEM	5005 E OAK ST, PHX, 85008	699 - J3
SUNLAND MEM PK	15826 N DEL WEBB BLVD, MarC, 85351	576 - A2
SUNWEST CEM	15399 NW GRAND AV, ELMG, 85335	575 - E3
TWIN BUTTES CEM	W BROADWAY RD, TEMP, 85282	740 - A6
VALLEY OF THE SUN MEM PK	W CHANDLER HEIGHTS RD, MarC, 85248	901 - E2

CHAMBERS OF COMMERCE

FEATURE NAME	Address City, ZIP Code	PAGE-GRID
APACHE JUNCTION	112 E 2ND AV, APJT, 85219	745 - E6
BUCKEYE VALLEY (SEE PAGE 731)	508 E MONROE AV, BUCK, 85326	772 - A1
CAREFREE-CAVE CREEK	748 E EASY ST, CARE, 85377	420 - H4
CHANDLER	218 N ARIZONA AV, CHAN, 85225	821 - F6
FOUNTAIN HILLS	16837 E PALISADES BLVD, FTNH, 85268	583 - D7
GILBERT	202 N GILBERT RD, GIL, 85234	782 - C5
GLENDALE	7501 N 59TH AV, GLEN, 85301	657 - C1
MESA	120 N CENTER ST, MESA, 85201	741 - H5
PEORIA	8355 W PEORIA AV, PEOR, 85345	616 - F2
PHOENIX	201 N CENTRAL AV, PHX, 85003	698 - G6
SCOTTSDALE	7343 E MAIN ST, SCTS, 85251	700 - F1
TEMPE	990 E APACHE BLVD, TEMP, 85281	740 - F5
VISITORS BUREAU	400 E VAN BUREN ST, PHX, 85004	698 - H6

CITY HALLS

FEATURE NAME	Address City, ZIP Code	PAGE-GRID
APACHE JUNCTION	1001 N IDAHO RD, APJT, 85219	745 - E5
AVONDALE	525 N CENTRAL AV, AVON, 85323	695 - B7
BUCKEYE (SEE PAGE 731)	100 N APACHE RD, BUCK, 85326	772 - C1
CAREFREE	11 SUNDIAL CIR, CARE, 85377	420 - H4
CAVE CREEK	37622 N CAVE CREEK RD, CVCK, 85331	420 - D4
CHANDLER	55 N ARIZONA PL, CHAN, 85225	821 - F6
EL MIRAGE	14405 N PALM ST, ELMG, 85335	575 - F4
FOUNTAIN HILLS	16836 E PALISADES BLVD, FTNH, 85268	583 - D7
GILA BEND (SEE PAGE 1049)	644 W PIMA ST, GBND, 85337	1089 - J3
GILBERT	1025 S GILBERT RD, GIL, 85296	822 - C3
GLENDALE	5850 W GLENDALE AV, GLEN, 85301	657 - C1
GOODYEAR	119 N LITCHFIELD RD, GDYR, 85338	695 - A7
GUADALUPE	9050 S AVD DEL YAQUI, GUAD, 85283	780 - A4
LITCHFIELD PK	214 W WIGWARM BLVD, LP, 85340	655 - A6
MESA	20 E MAIN ST, MESA, 85201	741 - H5
PARADISE VALLEY	6401 E LINCOLN DR, PVAL, 85253	660 - D3
PEORIA	8401 W MONROE ST, PEOR, 85345	616 - F2
PHOENIX	200 W WASHINGTON ST, PHX, 85003	698 - G7
QUEEN CREEK	22350 S ELLSWORTH RD, QC, 85242	904 - C1
SCOTTSDALE	3939 N CIVIC CENTER BLVD, SCTS, 85251	700 - G1
SURPRISE	12425 W BELL RD, SURP, 85374	535 - E7
TEMPE	31 E 5TH ST, TEMP, 85281	740 - D3
TOLLESON	9555 W VAN BUREN ST, TOL, 85353	696 - C6
WICKENBURG	155 N TEGNER ST, WICK, 85390	290 - F2
YOUNGTOWN	12030 W ALABAMA AV, YNTN, 85335	575 - H7

COLLEGES & UNIVERSITIES

FEATURE NAME	Address City, ZIP Code	PAGE-GRID
AMERICAN GRADUATE OF INTL MGMNT	15249 N 59TH AV, GLEN, 85306	577 - D3
ARIZONA STATE UNIV	E UNIVERSITY DR & N RURAL RD, TEMP, 85281	740 - E4
ASU EAST CAMPUS	7001 E WILLIAMS FIELD RD, MESA, 85212	823 - G6
ASU RESEARCH PK	8750 S SCIENCE DR, TEMP, 85284	820 - J1
ASU WEST CAMPUS	4701 W THUNDERBIRD RD, PHX, 85304	577 - F5
CENTRAL ARIZONA COLLEGE SUPRSTN MTN	273 OLD WEST HWY, APJT, 85219	745 - E6
CHANDLER-GILBERT COMM COLLEGE	2626 E PECOS RD, CHAN, 85225	862 - B1
ESTRELLA MTN COMM COLLEGE	3000 N DYSART RD, AVON, 85340	695 - C1
GATEWAY COMM COLLEGE	108 N 40TH ST, PHX, 85034	699 - G7
GLENDALE COMM COLLEGE	6000 W OLIVE AV, GLEN, 85302	617 - C3
GRAND CANYON UNIV	3300 W CAMELBACK RD, PHX, 85017	658 - A5
MESA COMM COLLEGE	1833 W SOUTHERN AV, MESA, 85202	781 - C1
OTTAWA UNIV	2340 W MISSION LN, PHX, 85021	618 - C4
PARADISE VALLEY COM COLLEGE	18401 N 32ND ST, PHX, 85032	539 - F7
PHOENIX COLLEGE	1202 W THOMAS RD, PHX, 85013	698 - E2
RIO SALADO COMM COLLEGE	2323 W 14TH ST, TEMP, 85281	739 - J5
SCOTTSDALE COMM COLLEGE	9000 E CHAPARRAL RD, MarC, 85250	661 - B5
SOUTH MTN COM COLLEGE	7050 S 24TH ST, PHX, 85040	779 - B2
UNIV OF PHOENIX	4605 E ELWOOD ST, PHX, 85040	739 - H5

DEPARTMENT OF MOTOR VEHICLES

FEATURE NAME	Address City, ZIP Code	PAGE-GRID
AVONDALE	1452 N ELISEO C FELIX JR WY, AVON, 85323	695 - C5
BUCKEYE (SEE PAGE 731)	100 N APACHE RD, BUCK, 85326	772 - C1
CHANDLER	50 S BECK AV, CHAN, 85226	820 - B6
GLENDALE	5890 W BEVERLY AV, GLEN, 85306	577 - D2
GOODYEAR COM DRIVERS LIC- (SEE PAGE 653)	14370 W VAN BUREN ST, GDYR, 85338	694 - J5
MESA	1840 S MESA DR, MESA, 85210	781 - H3
MESA EAST	7631 E MAIN ST, MESA, 85208	743 - J5
NORTH SCOTTSDALE	7339 E PARADISE LN, SCTS, 85260	580 - G3
NORTHWEST	20626 N 26TH AV, PHX, 85027	538 - C3
PHOENIX	4005 N 51ST AV, PHX, 85031	657 - E7
PHOENIX MAIN	1801 W JEFFERSON ST, PHX, 85007	698 - D7
SOUTH MTN	221 E OLYMPIC DR, PHX, 85040	778 - G3
SURPRISE	13009 W BELL RD, SURP, 85374	535 - D7
TEMPE	1703 E LARKSPUR LN, TEMP, 85281	700 - H7

ENTERTAINMENT & SPORTS

FEATURE NAME	Address City, ZIP Code	PAGE-GRID
AMERICA WEST ARENA	201 E JEFFERSON ST, PHX, 85004	698 - G7
APACHE GREYHOUND PK	2551 W APACHE TR, APJT, 85220	745 - A6
ARIZONA STATE FAIRGROUND	1826 W MCDOWELL RD, PHX, 85007	698 - D3
BANK ONE BALLPARK	S 4TH ST & E JACKSON ST, PHX, 85004	698 - H7
BIG SURF	1500 N MCCLINTOCK RD, TEMP, 85281	700 - H7
BLACK MTN BMX RACE PK	N CAVE BUTTES DAM RD, MarC, 85024	499 - A6
CANYON RACEWAY (SEE PAGE 415)	9777 W CAREFREE HWY, PEOR, 85382	416 - D7
CASTLES & COASTERS	9445 N METRO PKWY E, PHX, 85051	618 - B3
COMPADRE STADIUM	4001 S ALMA SCHOOL RD, CHAN, 85248	861 - C7
ENCHANTED ISLAND AMUSEMENT PK	1202 W ENCANTO BLVD, PHX, 85007	698 - E3
FIDDLESTICKS FAMILY FUNPARK	8800 E INDIAN BEND RD, MarC, 85258	661 - A1
FIREBIRD INTL RACEWAY	20000 S MARICOPA RD, MarC, 85326	859 - J4
GOLFLAND SUNSPLASH	155 W HAMPTON AV, MESA, 85210	781 - G2
HOHOKAM PK	1235 N CENTER ST, MESA, 85201	741 - H2
MANZANITA SPEEDWAY	3412 W BROADWAY RD, MarC, 85041	737 - J5
MARYVALE STADIUM	3600 N 51ST AV, PHX, 85031	657 - E7
PACKARD STADIUM	PACKARD DR & RIO SALTADO PKWY, TEMP, 85281	740 - F3
PEORIA STADIUM	16101 N 83RD AV, PEOR, 85382	576 - G2
PHOENIX CIVIC PLAZA CONV CTR	225 E ADAMS ST, PHX, 85004	698 - G6
PHOENIX GREYHOUND PK	3801 E WASHINGTON ST, PHX, 85034	699 - G7
PHOENIX INTL RACEWAY	S 115TH AV & OLD BASELINE RD, AVON, 85353	775 - E2
PHOENIX MUNICIPAL STADIUM	5999 E VAN BUREN ST, PHX, 85008	700 - C7
PHOENIX RACEWAY PK	W HAPPY VALLEY RD & N 195TH AV, MarC, 85361	493 - G3
RAWHIDE 1880S WESTERN TOWN	N SCOTTSDALE RD & WILLIAMS DR, SCTS, 85255	540 - G1
RODEO GROUNDS	LOST DUTCHMAN BLVD & TOMAHAWK, APJT, 85219	745 - F3
ROSE MOFFORD SPORTS COMPLEX	N 25TH AV & W PEORIA AV, PHX, 85021	618 - C3
SCOTTSDALE STADIUM	7408 E OSBORN RD, SCTS, 85251	700 - G2

FEATURE NAME	Address City, ZIP Code	PAGE-GRID
SUN DEVIL STADIUM	E 5TH ST & S STADIUM DR, TEMP, 85281	740 - E3
TEMPE DIABLO STADIUM COMPLEX	S 48TH ST & W ALAMEDA DR, TEMP, 85282	739 - J6
TURF PARADISE RACE COURSE	1501 W BELL RD, PHX, 85023	578 - E1
VETERANS MEM COLISEUM	N 17TH AV & W PALM LN, PHX, 85007	698 - D4
VICTORY LANE SPORTS COMPLEX	22603 N 43RD AV, PHX, 85310	537 - H1
WATERWORLD	4243 W PINNACLE PEAK RD, PHX, 85310	497 - H7
WELLS FARGO ARENA	E 6TH ST & S STADIUM DR, TEMP, 85281	740 - E3
WEST WORLD OF SCOTTSDALE	16601 N PIMA RD, SCTS, 85260	581 - C3

GOLF COURSES

FEATURE NAME	Address City, ZIP Code	PAGE-GRID
500 CLUB GC, THE	4707 W PINNACLE PEAK RD, PHX, 85310	497 - F7
ADOBE DAM GC	3847 W PINNACLE PEAK RD, PHX, 85310	497 - J7
AHWATUKEE CC	12432 S 48TH ST, PHX, 85044	819 - H2
ALTA MESA CC	1460 N ALTA MESA DR, MESA, 85205	743 - D1
ANCALA CC	11700 E VIA LINDA, SCTS, 85259	621 - J2
ANTHEM GOLF & CC (SEE PAGE 337)	W ANTHEM CLUB DR, MarC, 85086	378 - C5
APACHE CREEK GC	S IRONWOOD DR & US HWY 60, APJT, 85220	785 - C3
APACHE SUN GC	E PIMA RD & N SUBURBAN AV, PinC, 85242	865 - C6
APACHE WELLS CC	5601 E HERMOSA VISTA DR, MESA, 85215	703 - D6
ARIZONA BILTMORE CC	2400 E MISSOURI AV, PHX, 85016	659 - D5
ARIZONA CC	5668 E ORANGE BLOSSOM LN, PHX, 85018	700 - B2
ARIZONA GOLF RESORT	425 S POWER RD, MESA, 85208	743 - G7
ARIZONA TRADITIONS GC	17225 N CITRUS RD, SURP, 85374	534 - A6
ARROWHEAD CC	19888 N 73RD AV, GLEN, 85308	536 - J5
ASU KARSTEN GC	1125 E RIO SALADO PKWY, TEMP, 85281	740 - F3
BELLAIR GC	17233 N 45TH AV, PHX, 85308	537 - G7
BOULDERS CLUB, THE	34631 N TOM DARLINGTON DR, CARE, 85377	420 - H6
BRIARWOOD CC	20800 N 135TH AV, MarC, 85375	535 - C2
CAMELBACK GC	7847 N MOCKINGBIRD LN, PVAL, 85253	620 - C4
CAVE CREEK MUNICIPAL GC	15202 N 19TH AV, PHX, 85023	578 - D4
CHUPAROSA GC	21515 E CHUPAROSA CIR, QC, 85242	904 - D1
CLUB AT DC RANCH	9290 E THOMPSON PEAK PKWY, SCTS, 85255	541 - D3
CLUB TERRAVITA GC	34034 N 69TH WY, SCTS, 85262	460 - F1
CLUB WEST GC	16400 S 14TH AV, PHX, 85045	818 - E6
CONTINENTAL GC	7920 E OSBORN RD, SCTS, 85251	700 - H1
CORONADO GC	2829 N MILLER RD, SCTS, 85257	700 - G3
COTTONFIELDS GC	5740 W BASELINE RD, PHX, 85339	777 - C1
COTTONWOOD CC	25630 S BRENTWOOD DR, MarC, 85248	901 - B4
COYOTE LAKES GC	18800 N COYOTE LAKES PKWY, SURP, 85374	535 - G5
COYOTE RIDGE GC	8411 N 107TH AV, PEOR, 85345	616 - A5
CYPRESS GC	10801 E MCDOWELL RD, MarC, 85256	701 - F5
DEER VALLEY GC	13975 W DEER VALLEY RD, MarC, 85375	535 - B1
DESERT CANYON GC	10440 N INDIAN WELLS DR, FTNH, 85268	623 - C3
DESERT FOREST GC	37207 N MULE TRAIN RD, CARE, 85377	421 - A4
DESERT HIGHLANDS GC	10040 E HAPPY VALLEY RD, SCTS, 85255	501 - E5
DESERT MTN GC	10333 E ROCKAWAY HILLS, SCTS, 85262	421 - G1
DESERT SANDS GC	1922 S 74TH ST, MESA, 85208	783 - H3
DESERT SPRINGS GC	19900 N REMINGTON DR, SURP, 85374	534 - F4
DESERT TRAILS GC	22525 N EXECUTIVE WY, MarC, 85375	534 - H1
DOBSON RANCH GC	2155 S DOBSON RD, MESA, 85202	781 - B4
DREAMLAND VILLA GC	5641 E ALBANY ST, MarC, 85205	743 - D5
EAGLE MTN GC	14915 E EAGLE MOUNTAIN PKWY, FTNH, 85268	622 - H4
EAGLES NEST AT PEBBLE CREEK- (SEE PAGE 653)	3645 W CLUBHOUSE DR, GDYR, 85338	654 - G7
ECHO MESA GC	20349 N ECHO MESA DR, MarC, 85375	535 - B3
EL CARO GC	2222 W ROYAL PALM RD, PHX, 85021	618 - D5
ENCANTO MUNICIPAL GC	2300 N 17TH AV, PHX, 85007	698 - D2
ESTANCIA GC	27998 N 99TH PL, SCTS, 85255	501 - E2
ESTRELLA MTN GC (SEE PAGE 733)	15205 W VINEYARD RD, GDYR, 85338	734 - F7
FALCON GC (SEE PAGE 653)	15152 W CAMELBACK RD, MarC, 85340	654 - G3
FIESTA LAKES GC	1415 S WESTWOOD CIR, MESA, 85210	781 - E2
FOOTHILLS GC	2201 E CLUBHOUSE DR, PHX, 85048	818 - J6
FOUNTAIN OF THE SUN CC	500 S 80TH ST, MESA, 85208	743 - J7
GAINEY RANCH GC	7600 E GAINEY CLUB DR, SCTS, 85258	620 - G4
GLEN LAKES MUNICIPAL GC	5450 W NORTHERN AV, GLEN, 85302	617 - D5
GRANDVIEW GC	14260 W MEEKER BLVD, MarC, 85375	535 - A4
GRAYHAWK GC	8620 E THOMPSON PEAK PKWY, SCTS, 85255	541 - A3
GREENFIELD LAKES GC	2484 E WARNER RD, GIL, 85236	823 - A1
HAPPY TRAILS GOLF RESORT	17200 W BELL RD, SURP, 85374	534 - B6
HILLCREST GC	20002 N STAR RIDGE DR, MarC, 85375	535 - C3
IRONWOOD GC	550 W CHAMPAGNE DR, CHAN, 85248	901 - E2
KEN MCDONALD GC	800 E DIVOT DR, TEMP, 85283	780 - D5
KIERLAND GC	15636 CLUBGATE DR, PHX, 85254	580 - F3
KOKOPELLI GOLF RESORT	1800 W GUADALUPE RD, GIL, 85233	781 - H5
LAKES AT AHWATUKEE	13431 S 44TH ST, PHX, 85044	819 - G2
LAKES AT WESTBROOK VILLAGE, THE	19260 N WESTBROOK PKWY, PEOR, 85382	536 - D4
LAKES WEST GC	10433 TALISMAN RD, MarC, 85351	575 - J3
LAS SENDAS GC	7555 E EAGLE CREST DR, MESA, 85207	703 - J2
LEGEND AT ARROWHEAD, THE	21027 N 67TH AV, GLEN, 85308	537 - C3
LEGEND TRAIL GC	9462 W LEGENDARY LN, SCTS, 85262	421 - D7
LEISURE WORLD CC	908 S POWER RD, MarC, 85206	783 - D1
LINKS AT QUEEN CREEK, THE	E OCOTILLO RD & N VINEYARD RD, PinC, 85242	905 - C2
MARYVALE MUNICIPAL GC	5902 W INDIAN SCHOOL RD, PHX, 85033	657 - B6
MCCORMICK RANCH GC	7505 E MCCORMICK PKWY, SCTS, 85258	620 - H6
MESA CC	660 W FAIRWAY DR, MESA, 85201	741 - F1
MOON VALLEY CC	151 W MOON VALLEY DR, PHX, 85023	578 - G5
MTN SHADOWS GC	5641 E LINCOLN DR, PVAL, 85253	660 - B3
OAKWOOD GC	25612 E E J ROBSON BLVD, MarC, 85248	901 - B3
OCOTILLO GC	3751 S CLUBHOUSE DR, CHAN, 85248	861 - C6
ORANGE TREE GOLF RESORT	10601 N 56TH ST, PHX, 85254	620 - C2
PAINTED MTN GC	6210 E MCKELLIPS RD, MESA, 85215	703 - E7
PALM BROOK CC	9350 W GREENWAY RD, MarC, 85351	576 - D2
PALM VALLEY GC	2211 N LITCHFIELD RD, GDYR, 85338	695 - B2
PALO VERDE CC	10801 E SAN TAN BLVD, MarC, 85248	901 - E5
PALO VERDE GC	6215 N 15TH AV, PHX, 85013	658 - E2
PAPAGO MUNICIPAL GC	5595 E MORELAND ST, PHX, 85008	700 - B6
PARADISE PEAK WEST GC	3901 E PINNACLE PEAK RD, PHX, 85050	499 - G7
PARADISE VALLEY CC	7101 N TATUM BLVD, PVAL, 85253	660 - A2
PARADISE VALLEY PK GC	3505 E UNION HILLS DR, PHX, 85032	539 - G7
PAVILION LAKES GC	8870 E INDIAN BEND RD, MarC, 85258	661 - B1
PEBBLEBROOK GC	18836 N 128TH AV, MarC, 85375	535 - D5
PEPPERWOOD GC	647 W BASELINE RD, TEMP, 85283	780 - C3
PHOENICIAN GC	6000 E CAMELBACK RD, PHX, 85018	660 - D6
PHOENIX CC	2901 N 7TH ST, MarC, 85014	698 - J2
PINNACLE PEAK CC	8701 E PINNACLE PEAK RD, SCTS, 85255	541 - A1
POINTE GC AT LOOKOUT MTN	11111 N 7TH ST, PHX, 85022	578 - J6
POINTE GC AT SOUTH MTN	7777 S POINTE PKWY, PHX, 85040	779 - J4
PUEBLO CC	11201 N EL MIRAGE RD, ELMG, 85335	615 - F1
QUAIL RUN GC	9774 W ALABAMA AV, MarC, 85351	576 - C7
RANCHO MANANA GC	5734 E RANCHO MANANA BLVD, CVCK, 85331	420 - D3
RAVEN GC AT SOUTH MTN	3636 E BASELINE RD, PHX, 85040	779 - E2
RED MTN RANCH CC	6425 E TETON CIR, MESA, 85215	703 - F3
RIO SALADO GC	1490 E WEBER DR, TEMP, 85281	740 - G1
RIVERVIEW GC	2202 W 8TH ST, MESA, 85201	741 - B3
ROLLING HILLS GC	1415 N MILL AV, TEMP, 85281	740 - D1
ROYAL PALMS GC	1415 E MCKELLIPS RD, MESA, 85203	702 - B7
SAN MARCOS CC	N SAN MARCOS DR & W BUFFALO ST, CHAN, 85225	821 - D6
SCOTTSDALE CC	7702 E SHEA BLVD, SCTS, 85260	620 - H2
SHALIMAR GC	2032 E GOLF AV, TEMP, 85282	740 - J7
SPRINGFIELD GOLF RESORT	1200 E SAINT ANDREWS BLVD, CHAN, 85249	901 - H5
STARDUST GC	12702 W STARDUST BLVD, MarC, 85375	535 - E3
STONECREEK GC	4435 E PARADISE VILLAGE PKWY, PHX, 85028	619 - J1
SUNBIRD GOLF RESORT	6250 E SUNBIRD BLVD, CHAN, 85249	901 - J5
SUN CITY CC	9433 N 107TH AV, MarC, 85351	615 - J3
SUN CITY NORTH GC	12650 N 107TH AV, MarC, 85351	575 - J6
SUN CITY RIVER VIEW GC	16401 N DEL WEBB BLVD, MarC, 85351	576 - A1
SUN CITY SOUTH GC	11000 N 103RD AV, MarC, 85351	616 - B1
SUN LAKES CC	25425 E SUN LAKES BLVD, MarC, 85248	901 - A5
SUNLAND VILLAGE GC	725 S ROCHESTER, MESA, 85206	743 - B7
SUNRIDGE CANYON GC	13100 N SUNRIDGE DR, FTNH, 85268	582 - J7
SUN VILLAGE GC	14300 W BELL RD, SURP, 85374	535 - A7
SUPERSTITION SPRINGS GC	6542 E BASELINE RD, GIL, 85236	783 - F4
TATUM RANCH GC	29888 N TATUM RANCH DR, PHX, 85331	459 - J6
THUNDERBIRD CC	701 E THUNDERBIRD TR, PHX, 85040	778 - H5
TOKA STICKS GC	6001 S POWER RD, MESA, 85212	823 - G5
TONTO VERDE GC	18401 E EL CIRCULO DR, MarC, 85263	503 - H4
TOURNAMENT PLAYERS CLUB OF SCOTTSDALE	17020 N HAYDEN RD, SCTS, 85255	580 - H2
TRAIL RIDGE GC	21021 N 151ST AV, MarC, 85375	534 - J2
TROON CC	25000 N WINDY WALK DR, SCTS, 85255	501 - F5
TROON NORTH GC	10320 E DYNAMITE BLVD, SCTS, 85255	501 - D1
UNION HILLS CC	9860 W LINDGREN AV, MarC, 85373	536 - C6
VIEW POINT GOLF RESORT	650 N HAWES RD, MESA, 85207	744 - B4
VILLA DE PAZ GC	4220 N 103RD AV, PHX, 85037	656 - A6
VILLA MONTEREY GC	8100 E CAMELBACK RD, SCTS, 85251	660 - H6
VISTAS AT WESTBROOK VILLAGE, THE	18823 N COUNRTY CLUB PKWY, PEOR, 85382	536 - F5
WESTERN SKIES GC	1245 E WARNER RD, GIL, 85296	822 - G2
WICKENBURG CC	N COUNTRY CLUB DR, MarC, 85390	290 - B1
WIGWAM CC	451 N LITCHFIELD RD, LP, 85340	655 - A5
WILLOWCREEK GC	10600 W BOSWELL BLVD, MarC, 85373	536 - A6

HOSPITALS

FEATURE NAME	Address City, ZIP Code	PAGE-GRID
ARIZONA STATE HOSP	2500 E VAN BUREN ST, PHX, 85008	699 - D6
ARROWHEAD COMM HOSP AND MED	18701 N 67TH AV, GLEN, 85308	537 - B5
BOSWELL, WALTER O MEM HOSP	10401 W THUNDERBIRD BLVD, MarC, 85351	576 - A5
CHANDLER REGL HOSP	475 S DOBSON RD, CHAN, 85224	821 - C7
COMM HOSP MED CTR	6501 N 19TH AV, PHX, 85015	658 - D2
DESERT FOOTHILLS MED CTR	34115 N SCOTTSDALE RD, SCTS, 85262	460 - G1
DESERT SAMARITAN MED CTR	2225 W SOUTHERN AV, MESA, 85202	781 - B1
GOOD SAMARITAN REGL MED CTR	1111 E MCDOWELL RD, PHX, 85006	698 - J4
HAYDEN, CARL T VA MED CTR	650 E INDIAN SCHOOL RD, PHX, 85012	658 - H7
LINCOLN, JOHN C HEALTH NETWORK	250 E DUNLAP AV, PHX, 85020	618 - H4
MARICOPA MED CTR	2601 E ROOSEVELT ST, PHX, 85008	699 - C5
MARYVALE HOSP MED CTR	5102 W CAMPBELL AV, PHX, 85031	657 - E6
MAYO CLINIC HOSP	5777 E MAYO BLVD, PHX, 85054	540 - C6
MAYO CLINIC SCOTTSDALE	13400 E SHEA BLVD, SCTS, 85259	622 - D2
MESA GENERAL HOSP MED CTR	515 N MESA DR, MESA, 85203	741 - J4
MESA LUTHERAN HOSP	525 W BROWN RD, MESA, 85201	741 - G2
OWENS, JESSE MEM MED CTR	325 E BASELINE RD, PHX, 85040	778 - G2
PARADISE VALLEY HOSP	3929 E BELL RD, PHX, 85032	579 - G2
PHOENIX BAPTIST HOSP AND MED CTR	2000 W BETHANY HOME RD, PHX, 85015	658 - D3
PHOENIX CHILDRENS HOSP	1111 E MCDOWELL RD, PHX, 85006	698 - H4
PHOENIX MEM HEALTH SYSTEM	1201 S 7TH AV, PHX, 85003	738 - F1
PHOENIX REGL MED CTR	1947 E THOMAS RD, PHX, 85006	699 - B2
SAINT JOSEPHS HOSP & MED CTR	350 W THOMAS RD, PHX, 85013	698 - F2
SAINT LUKES MED CTR	1800 E VAN BUREN ST, PHX, 85006	699 - A6
SCOTTSDALE HEALTHCARE OSBORN	7400 E OSBORN RD, SCTS, 85251	700 - F1
SCOTTSDALE HEALTHCARE-SHEA	9003 E SHEA BLVD, SCTS, 85258	621 - B3
TEMPE SAINT LUKES HOSP	1500 S MILL AV, TEMP, 85281	740 - D5
THUNDERBIRD SAMARITAN MED CTR	5555 W THUNDERBIRD RD, GLEN, 85304	577 - D5
US PUB HLTH SERVICE PHX INDIAN MED-CTR	4212 N 16TH ST, PHX, 85014	659 - A7
VALLEY LUTHERAN HOSP	6644 E BAYWOOD AV, MESA, 85206	743 - F6
VENCOR HOSP PHOENIX	40 E INDIANOLA AV, PHX, 85012	658 - G7
WEBB, DEL E MEM HOSP	14502 W MEEKER BLVD, MarC, 85375	534 - J4
WICKENBURG REGL HOSP	520 W ROSE LN, WICK, 85390	290 - E1

HOTELS

FEATURE NAME	Address City, ZIP Code	PAGE-GRID
ARIZONA GOLF RESORT & CONFERENCE CTR	425 S POWER RD, MESA, 85208	743 - G6
BEST WESTERN GRACE INN AT AHWATUKEE	10831 S 51ST ST, MarC, 85044	779 - J7
BEST WESTERN PAPAGO INN & RESORT	7017 E MCDOWELL RD, SCTS, 85257	700 - F5
BEST WESTERN TEMPE	670 N SCOTTSDALE RD, TEMP, 85281	740 - F2
BOULDERS RESORT & CLUB, THE	34631 N TOM DARLINGTON DR, SCTS, 85262	420 - G7
BUTTES, THE	2000 W WESTCOURT WY, TEMP, 85282	739 - J6
COURTYARD BY MARRIOTT	1221 S WESTWOOD, MESA, 85210	781 - E1
COURTYARD BY MARRIOTT CAMELBACK	2101 E CAMELBACK RD, PHX, 85016	659 - B5
COURTYARD BY MARRIOTT PHOENIX	2621 S 47TH ST, PHX, 85034	739 - H3
COURTYARD BY MARRIOTT PHX METROCTR	9631 N BLACK CANYON HWY, PHX, 85021	618 - C3
COURTYARD BY MARRIOTT SCOTTSDALE	13444 E SHEA BLVD, SCTS, 85259	622 - D3
COURTYARD BY MARRIOTT SCOTTSDALE N	17010 N SCOTTSDALE RD, PHX, 85254	580 - G1
CROWNE PLAZA DOWNTOWN PHOENIX	100 N 1ST ST, PHX, 85004	698 - G6
CROWNE PLAZA PHOENIX METROCENTER	2532 W PEORIA AV, PHX, 85029	618 - C2
DOBSON RANCH INN RESORT	1666 S DOBSON RD, MESA, 85202	781 - B2
DOUBLETREE GUEST SUITES AT PHX GTWY-CTR	320 N 44TH ST, PHX, 85008	699 - H6
DOUBLETREE LA POSADA RESORT	4949 E LINCOLN DR, PVAL, 85253	660 - A3
DOUBLETREE PARADISE VALLEY RESORT	5401 N SCOTTSDALE RD, PVAL, 85250	660 - F5
EMBASSY SUITES 44TH STREET	1515 N 44TH ST, PHX, 85008	699 - H5

PHOENIX
INDEX

PHOENIX

INDEX

FEATURE NAME Address City, ZIP Code	PAGE-GRID
M C O CORPORATION E PALISADES BL & N LA MONTANA, FTNH, 85268	583 - C7
MERVYNS S RURAL RD & E SOUTHERN AV, TEMP, 85282	780 - F1
MESA SOUTH CTR S GILBERT RD & E SOUTHERN AV, MESA, 85204	782 - D1
METROCTR TRANSIT CENTER 415 N METRO PKWY W, PHX, 85051	618 - A3
MICRO SEMI CORPORATION E THOMAS RD & N PIMA RD, SCTS, 85251	701 - A3
MILLER PLAZA E CAMELBACK RD & N MILLER RD, SCTS, 85251	660 - G7
MTN VIEW LUTHERAN CHURCH S 48TH ST & E CHEYENNE DR, PHX, 85044	779 - H7
ORANGE TREE PLAZA E MCKELLIPS RD & N GILBERT RD, MESA, 85203	702 - D7
PARADISE VALLEY COMM COLLEGE PK N 32ND ST & E UNION HILLS DR, PHX, 85032	539 - F6
PARADISE VALLEY TRANSIT CTR 4623 E PARADISE VILLAGE PKWY, PHX, 85032	579 - J6
PARK & RIDE E CHICAGO ST & S COLORADO ST, CHAN, 85225	821 - G7
PEORIA COMM CTR W JEFFERSON ST & N 84TH AV, PEOR, 85345	616 - F2
PEPPER RIDGE PLAZA W BASELINE RD & S HARDY DR, TEMP, 85283	780 - C3
PIONEER PK E MAIN ST & N HOBSON, MESA, 85203	741 - J5
PRICE CLUB N HAYDEN RD & N 83RD PL, SCTS, 85260	580 - J4
RIVERIA PLAZA E UNIVERSITY DR & N GILBERT RD, MESA, 85203	742 - D4
SAFEWAY N ARIZONA AV & E RAY RD, CHAN, 85225	821 - F4
SAINT CATHERINES CHURCH S CENTRAL AV & W LYNNE AV, PHX, 85041	778 - G1
SMITHS FOOD & DRUG CTR N 19TH AV & W BELL RD, PHX, 85023	578 - E1
SMITTYS E MCDOWELL RD & N GRANITE REEF, SCTS, 85257	700 - J5
SMITTYS E SHEA BLVD & N TATUM BLVD, PHX, 85028	619 - J2
SMITTYS PLAZA S CENTRAL AV & E BASELINE RD, PHX, 85040	778 - G2
SOUTHERN BUSINESS PK E SOUTHERN AV & S 16TH ST, PHX, 85040	739 - A7
SOUTHWEST SUPER MARKET GLENDALE AV & 51ST AV, GLEN, 85301	657 - E1
SUN BOWL PLAZA WEST N 107TH AV & W PEORIA AV, MarC, 85351	615 - J2
SUNDOME 19403 N R H JOHNSON BLVD, MarC, 85375	535 - B4
SUNNYSLOPE TRANSIT CTR 8927 N 3RD ST, PHX, 85020	618 - H4
SUPERSTITION SPRINGS CTR 6555 E SOUTHERN AV, MESA, 85206	783 - F1
SURPRISE W SMOKEY DR & N VILLAGE DR, SURP, 85374	575 - E1
TARGET SHOPPING CTR S MCCLINTOCK DR & E BASELINE, TEMP, 85282	780 - H3
TEMPE CHURCH OF CHRIST 2424 S MILL AV, TEMP, 85282	740 - D7
TEMPLE BETH SHALOM E BROADWAY RD & S LESUEUR, MESA, 85204	741 - J6
THUNDERBIRD FAIRLANES W INDIAN SCHOOL RD & N 24TH AV, PHX, 85015	658 - C7
TRINITY CHURCH 7800 PAS DL SUR, SCTS, 85258	660 - J1
TRUE VALUE HARDWARE S CENTRAL AV & E BROADWAY RD, PHX, 85040	738 - G5

PARKS & RECREATION

FEATURE NAME	PAGE-GRID
ACACIA PK, PHX	578 - B4
ACOMA PK, PHX	577 - J4
ACOMA PK, GLEN	577 - E4
ADOBE DAM REC AREA, PHX	497 - G7
AGUA LINDA PK, SCTS	661 - A4
ALICIA PK, PHX	618 - D5
ALKIRE PK, PHX	738 - D2
ALLEN, JOHN PK, GIL	782 - D7
ALTADENA PK, PHX	619 - G1
ALTA MESA PK, MESA	743 - D1
AMBERWOOD PK, CHAN	821 - A3
ANTHEM COMM PK, MarC- (SEE PAGE 337)	378 - A5
APACHE PK, SCTS	700 - J5
APACHE PK, CHAN	821 - E3
APACHE PK, PEOR	536 - F6
ARCADIA PK, PHX	700 - B1
ARMSTRONG PK, CHAN	821 - G6
ARREDONDO PK, TEMP	780 - G2
ARROWHEAD LAKES PK, GLEN	537 - E3
ARROWHEAD MEADOWS PK, CHAN	821 - C5
ARROWHEAD SHORES PK, PEOR	576 - F2
AUTRY, GENE PK, MESA	702 - J7
AVERY, BEN REC AREA, PHX	417 - H6
AZTEC PK, SCTS	581 - E6
BARRIOS UNIDOS PK, PHX	738 - J2
BENEDICT PK, TEMP	780 - C4
BICENTENNIAL PK, GLEN	656 - J4
BICENTENNIAL PK, SURP	575 - E1
BIRCHETT PK, TEMP	740 - D5
BOLIN MEM PK, PHX	698 - D6
BONSALL PK NORTH, GLEN	657 - C3
BONSALL PK SOUTH, GLEN	657 - C3
BRAEWOOD PK, PEOR	616 - E1
BROOKS CROSSING PK, CHAN	821 - C3
BUCKEYE HILLS PK, MarC	811 - C6
BUCKEYE PK, BUCK (SEE PAGE 731)	772 - B1
BUFFALO RIDGE PK, PHX	539 - B5
BURLESON PK, GBND (SEE PAGE 1049)	1090 - B2
BUTLER PK, GLEN	617 - D4
CACTUS PK, PHX	577 - J7
CACTUS PK, SCTS	580 - G7
CALBRISA PK, PEOR	576 - E3
CAMELBACK MTN ECHO CYN REC AREA, PVAL	660 - A5
CAMPBELL PK, TEMP	820 - B3
CANAL PK, TEMP	700 - E7
CANDLELIGHT PK, MESA	742 - B2
CARMEL PK, GLEN	537 - E5
CARRIAGE LANE PK, MESA	781 - A6
CASHION COMM PK, AVON	735 - H1
CASHMAN PK, PHX	540 - A2
CAVE CREEK PK, PHX	578 - C6
CAVE CREEK REC AREA, CVCK	419 - H2
CELAYA PK, TEMP	780 - C5
CENTRAL PK, PHX	738 - G1
CHANDLER, A J PK, CHAN	821 - F6
CHANDLER SPORTS COMPLEX, CHAN	901 - D1
CHAPARRAL PK, SCTS	660 - H4
CHAPARRAL PK, MESA	742 - D1
CHAPPARAL PK, GLEN	537 - D7
CHAVEZ, CESAR PK, PHX	777 - H2
CHELSEA PK, MESA	742 - J6
CHESTNUTT PK, SCTS	660 - J7

FEATURE NAME	PAGE-GRID
CHOLLA COVE PK, PHX	619 - H1
CHOLLA PK, GLEN	617 - E1
CHOLLA PK, SCTS	621 - H2
CHRISTY COVE PK, PHX	619 - C2
CIELITO PK, PHX	657 - J6
CIRCLE G BASIN, GIL	782 - E5
CIRCLE K PK, PHX	778 - J3
CITY PK, AVON	695 - B7
CITY PK, CHAN	781 - B6
CLARK PK, TEMP	740 - C5
CLAVELITO PK, GLEN	657 - E1
COFFELT LAMOREAUX PK, PHX	738 - D1
COFFINGER PK, WICK	290 - E2
COLDWATER PK, AVON	695 - D7
COLE PK, TEMP	780 - J2
COLTER PK, PHX	658 - F5
COMANCHE PK, SCTS	620 - J7
CONOCIDO PK, PHX	578 - A2
CONSTELLATION PK, WICK	290 - H2
CORBELL PK, TEMP	780 - F6
CORONADO PK, PHX	698 - J4
CORTEZ PK, PHX	618 - A4
COUNTRY GABLES PK, GLEN	577 - E3
COUNTRY GABLES PK, PHX	578 - A4
COUNTRYSIDE PK, MESA	782 - F1
COYOTE BASIN PK, PHX	539 - D4
CROSSED ARROWS PK, PHX	580 - D4
CROSSROADS PK, GIL	822 - H3
CYPRUS PK, TEMP	780 - G1
DALEY PK, TEMP	740 - E5
DAUMLER PK, TEMP	741 - A7
DEER VALLEY PK, PHX	538 - D5
DELICIAS PK, GLEN	617 - F7
DESERT BREEZE PK, CHAN	820 - F5
DESERT FOOTHILLS PK, PHX	818 - H5
DESERT GARDENS PK, GLEN	657 - A1
DESERT HORIZON PK, PHX	580 - B3
DESERT MIRAGE PK, GLEN	656 - E2
DESERT ROSE PK, GLEN	577 - C1
DESERT STAR PK, PHX	696 - E3
DESERT STORM PK, PHX	659 - A5
DESERT VALLEY PK, GLEN	577 - C6
DESERT WEST PK, PHX	697 - A2
DESERT WILLOW PK, PHX	459 - H5
DESSIE LORENZ PK, AVON	735 - B1
DISCOVERY PK, GLEN	656 - G2
DOBSON PK, CHAN	861 - C4
DOBSON RANCH PK, MESA	781 - B4
DOS LAGOS PK, GLEN	537 - C5
DWIGHT PK, TEMP	780 - C1
EASTLAKE PK, PHX	699 - A7
EDISON PK, PHX	699 - B5
EHRHARDT PK, TEMP	781 - B2
ELDORADO PK, SCTS	700 - G4
ELLSWORTH PK, MESA	742 - A5
EL OSO PK, PHX	656 - H7
EL PRADO PK, PHX	778 - D1
EL REPOSO PK, PHX	778 - G1
EMERALD PK, MESA	782 - C2
ENCANTO PK, PHX	698 - E3
ENSENADA PK, MESA	743 - F3
ESCALANTE PK, TEMP	740 - J4
ESCOBEDO PK, MESA	741 - H4
ESTEBAN PK, PHX	739 - E7
ESTRADA PK, TEMP	820 - G1
ESTRELLA MTN PK, GDYR- (SEE PAGE 733)	774 - G4
ESTRELLA VISTA PK, GDYR- (SEE PAGE 733)	734 - E2
EVERGREEN PK, MESA	741 - G4
FALCON FIELD PK, MESA	703 - B7
FALCON HILL PK, MESA	743 - H1
FALCON PK, PHX	697 - J5
FITCH PK, MESA	741 - H3
FLOYD GAINES PK, SURP	575 - E1
FOLLEY PK, CHAN	821 - G7
FOOTHILLS PK, GLEN	537 - D5
FOUNTAIN PARK, THE, FTNH	583 - D7
FOWLER PK, GLEN	615 - B7
FRED CAMPBELL PK, AVON	695 - B6
FREESTONE PK, GIL	782 - F6
GAICKI PK, TEMP	780 - G4
GATEWAY PK, MESA	741 - J5
GAZELLE MEADOWS PK, CHAN	821 - G5
GENTRY, BILL PK, ELMG	575 - E4
GOLDEN HILLS PK, MESA	743 - H7
GOODWIN PK, TEMP	820 - G3
GRANADA PK, PHX	659 - B2
GRANT PK, PHX	738 - F1
GRAYHAWK NEIGHBORHOOD PK, SCTS	540 - H4
GREENBRIAR PK, GLEN	537 - A7
GREENFIELD PK, MESA	742 - J7
GREEN VALLEY PK, PHX	738 - J3
GROVERS PK, PHX	539 - C7
GUERRERO ROTARY PK, MESA	741 - G7
HANCE, MARGARET T PK, PHX	698 - G5
HANGER PK, TEMP	820 - E3
HARELSON PK, TEMP	820 - D3
HARMON PK, PHX	738 - F2
HARMONY PK, MESA	782 - F2
HARTER PK, CHAN	820 - H5
HAYDEN BUTTE PK, TEMP	740 - D3
HAYDEN PK, PHX	738 - F5
HAYES, CB MEM PK, PEOR	616 - J3
HERBERGER, GR PK, PHX	700 - B1
HERITAGE PK, GLEN	617 - D3
HERITAGE PK, MESA	781 - H2
HERITAGE SQUARE PK, PHX	698 - H6
HERMOSA VISTA PK, MESA	702 - F6
HERMOSO PK, PHX	739 - B7
HIDDEN MEADOWS PK, GLEN	536 - J7
HILLCREST PK, GLEN	537 - A1
HOHOKAM PIMA NATL MONUMENT, PinC	900 - E7
HOLIDAY PK, PHX	657 - A5
HOLMES PK, MESA	782 - J2
HOOPES PK, CHAN	821 - E1
HORIZON PK, SCTS	581 - C4
HORIZON PK, GLEN	617 - F5
HOSHONI PK, PHX	617 - H5
HUDSON PK, TEMP	740 - G5
INDIAN BEND PK, TEMP	700 - G7
INDIAN SCHOOL PK, SCTS	660 - H7
IRONWOOD PK, SCTS	541 - C7
JACKRABBIT PK, CHAN	822 - A5
JACKRABBIT PK, PHX	580 - C2
JAYCEE PK, TEMP	740 - C3
JEFFERSON PK, MESA	743 - G6
JOHN TEETS PK, PHX	499 - J4
JOYCE PK, TEMP	780 - E2
KACHINA PK, PHX	659 - H6
KINGSBOROUGH PK, MESA	782 - D2
KINGS PK, GLEN	577 - E1
KIWANIS COMM PK, TEMP	780 - D4
KIWANIS PK, PEOR	576 - H6
KLEINMAN PK, MESA	741 - E7
LADMO PK, PHX	697 - G1

FEATURE NAME	PAGE-GRID
LAKE PLEASANT PK, PEOR- (SEE PAGE 335)	336 - A2
LA MIRADA DESERT PK, SCTS	501 - B7
LA PRADERA PK, PHX	657 - H1
LAWRENCE PK, GLEN	657 - C1
LEWIS PK, PHX	738 - J1
LIBRARY PK, PHX	698 - E7
LINDO PK, PHX	738 - C6
LIONS PK, GLEN	617 - B6
LITTLE CANYON PK, PHX	658 - A4
LOOKOUT MTN PK, PHX	579 - B4
LOS ALAMOS PK, MESA	742 - F4
LOS OLIVOS PK, PHX	659 - D7
LOST DUTCHMAN STATE PK, PinC	706 - C7
MADISON PK, PHX	659 - A7
MAGGIO RANCH PK, CHAN	821 - C6
MAGUIRE PK, WICK	290 - D3
MA-HA-TUAK PK, PHX	778 - E5
MANISTEE RANCH PK, GLEN	617 - E6
MARIPOSA PK, PHX	618 - A7
MARIVUE PK, PHX	697 - D1
MARYVALE PK, PHX	657 - E6
MCCORMICK RAILROAD PK, SCTS	660 - F2
MCDOWELL MTN PK, MarC	542 - G4
MCDOWELL MTN RANCH PK, SCTS	581 - E4
MCQUEEN PK, GIL	781 - J6
MEADOWGREEN PK, MESA	742 - F7
MESCAL PK, SCTS	620 - F2
MEYER PK, TEMP	740 - G7
MISSION PK, GLEN	617 - F3
MITCHELL PK, TEMP	740 - C4
MOEUR PK, TEMP	740 - D2
MONDO PK, GLEN	617 - D3
MONROE PK, PEOR	616 - E2
MONTARA PK, GLEN	617 - B2
MONTEREY PK, MESA	783 - G5
MONTEREY PK, PHX	698 - H3
MOON VALLEY PK, PHX	578 - G3
MTN VIEW PK, AVON	735 - B2
MTN VIEW PK, SCTS	621 - A4
MTN VIEW PK, PHX	618 - F3
MTN VIEW PK, MESA	742 - F3
MTN VIEW PK, CHAN	820 - E7
MTN VISTA PK, PHX	819 - J3
MULTI-USE TRAIL AREA, APJT	745 - C2
MURPHY PK, PEOR	616 - J2
MURPHY PK, GLEN	657 - C1
NAVARRETE PK, CHAN	821 - E5
NEVITT PK, PHX	779 - H1
NEW WORLD PK, GLEN	617 - F4
NORTHSIGHT PK, SCTS	581 - A6
NORTON PK, PHX	618 - J4
NUESTRO PK, PHX	738 - H2
NUEVE PK, PHX	738 - H6
OASIS PK, MarC	744 - G7
OKEMAH PK, PHX	739 - F5
ONEIL PK, GLEN	657 - B4
OPTIMIST PK, TEMP	780 - H4
ORME PK, PHX	697 - F1
OSBORN PK, SCTS	700 - G2
PAGE PK, GIL	782 - C7
PAIUTE PK, SCTS	700 - D2
PALMA PK, PHX	618 - J4
PALMER PK, TEMP	780 - D2
PALOMINO PK, PHX	579 - E3
PALO VERDE PK, MESA	781 - C6
PAPAGO PK, PHX	700 - C6
PAPAGO SPORTS COMPLEX, PHX	700 - D4
PARADISE COVE PK, PHX	579 - G2
PARADISE VALLEY PK, PHX	579 - G1
PARK OF CANALS, MESA	742 - A1
PASADENA PK, GLEN	656 - E4
PASEO RACQUET CTR, GLEN	577 - C4
PATRIOTS PK, PHX	698 - G7
PECOS RANCH PK, CHAN	861 - C2
PEQUENO PK, MESA	743 - A4
PERRY PK, PHX	699 - E3
PETERSON PK, TEMP	780 - A1
PIERCE PK, PHX	699 - H4
PIMA PK, SCTS	701 - A3
PIMA PK, CHAN	821 - J5
PINE VIEW PK, CHAN	820 - D5
PINNACLE PEAK PK, SCTS	501 - E3
PIONEER PK, MESA	741 - J5
PLAYA MARGARITA PK, PHX	737 - H6
PORTER PK, MESA	741 - J3
PRICE PK, CHAN	820 - H7
PRINCESS PK, MESA	743 - A2
PROSPECTOR PK, APJT	745 - F2
RANCHO DEL MAR PK, MESA	781 - E5
REACH REC AREA, PHX	540 - B6
REDDEN PK, TEMP	780 - F6
RED MTN DIST PK, MESA	744 - A2
REED PK, MESA	742 - C6
RIO MONTANA PK, SCTS	622 - C2
RIO SALADO PK, PHX	738 - J4
RIVERVIEW PK, MESA	741 - C2
ROADRUNNER PK, PHX	579 - F7
RODEO PK, GIL	822 - G5
ROESLEY PK, PHX	738 - E6
ROSE LANE PK, GLEN	657 - E2
ROTARY PK, SCTS	620 - H5
ROTARY PK, TEMP	780 - H2
ROYAL PALM PK, PHX	618 - E5
SAHUARO RANCH PK, GLEN	617 - C2
SANDPIPER PK, PHX	580 - E5
SANDS PK, GLEN	617 - D7
SAN MARCOS PK, CHAN	821 - E7
SAN TAN PK, CHAN	822 - B7
SCOTTSDALE RANCH PK, SCTS	621 - E4
SCUDDER PK, TEMP	780 - F4
SELLEH PK, TEMP	740 - H6
SERENO PK, PHX	580 - C6
SHAWNEE PK, CHAN	821 - C1
SHEEPHERDERS PK, MESA	702 - E5
SHERWOOD PK, MESA	782 - A2
SHOSHONE PK, SCTS	660 - J1
SIERRA VERDE PK, GLEN	537 - A3
SILVA, MARY A PK, GLEN	657 - G4
SILVERGATE PK, MESA	742 - D7
SKYLINE COMM PK, MESA	744 - F7
SMITH PK, PHX	697 - G7
SOLANO PK, PHX	658 - E4
SONORAN HILLS PK, SCTS	540 - H1
SONRISA PK, PHX	580 - A7
SOUTH MTN PK, PHX	778 - F6
STAPLEY PK, MESA	741 - J6
STARLIGHT PK, PHX	696 - G1
STONEBROOK PK, SURP	534 - J6
STONEGATE EQUESTRIAN PK, SCTS	622 - A4
STONEGATE PK, CHAN	821 - G3
STROUD PK, TEMP	780 - H6
SUENO PK, PHX	697 - G3
SUMIDA PK, PHX	619 - B7
SUMMIT PK, MESA	703 - F4
SUNBURST PARADISE PK, PHX	577 - G2

FEATURE NAME Address City, ZIP Code	PAGE-GRID
SUNDANCE PK, CHAN	820 - C4
SUNNYSIDE PK, GLEN	617 - C1
SUNNYSLOPE HERGERGER PK, PHX	618 - G4
SUNNYSLOPE PK, PEOR	616 - J3
SUNRAY PK, PHX	819 - F4
SUNSET PALMS PK, GLEN	577 - E6
SUNSET PK, GLEN	617 - G3
SUNVIEW BASIN, GIL	782 - D4
SUPERSTITION PK, APJT	745 - E5
SURREY PK, PHX	577 - J6
SVOB PK, TEMP	779 - J1
SWEETWATER PK, PHX	579 - H6
SWEETWATER PK, PEOR	576 - J6
TELEPHONE PIONEER PK, PHX	538 - D7
TEMPE BEACH PK, TEMP	740 - D2
TERRA-RAY PK, CHAN	820 - F4
THUNDERBIRD PK, SCTS	581 - B6
THUNDERBIRD PK, GLEN	497 - D7
TIERRA BUENA PK, GLEN	577 - D2
TONTO NATL FOREST, MarC	664 - E4
TOWNSEND PK, PHX	698 - H4
UNIV PK, PHX	698 - E6
USERY MTN REC AREA, MarC	704 - F6
VARNEY PK, PEOR	576 - G7
VENTUROSO PK, PHX	579 - F5
VERDE PK, PHX	698 - H6
VETERANS MEM PK, APJT	745 - E5
VISTA ALLEGRE PK, GIL	782 - D4
VISTA CANYON PK, PHX	819 - C6
VISTA DEL CAMINO PK, SCTS	700 - G5
VISTA MONTEREY PK, MESA	742 - H3
WACKER PK, PEOR	576 - G5
WAGGONER PK, TEMP	820 - F1
WASHINGTON PK, PHX	658 - C2
WASHINGTON PK, PEOR	616 - F2
WATER PK, GIL	782 - J6
WERNER PK, PHX	538 - G7
WESTERN STAR PK, PHX	779 - G6
WESTGREEN PK, PEOR	616 - E5
WESTOWN PK, PHX	578 - A6
WEST PLAZA PK, PHX	657 - G2
WHITE TANK MTN REGL PK, MarC	533 - A7
WHITMAN PK, MESA	741 - G1
WILLOW PK, PHX	698 - B6
WINDMILLS WEST PK, CHAN	820 - H3
WINDROSE PK, PEOR	576 - F6
WOODGLEN PK, MESA	781 - E4
ZUNI PK, SCTS	661 - A1

PERFORMING ARTS

FEATURE NAME Address City, ZIP Code	PAGE-GRID
BLOCKBUSTER DESERT SKY PAVILION 2121 N 83RD AV, PHX, 85035	696 - G3
CELEBRITY THEATRE 440 N 32ND ST, PHX, 85008	699 - E6
CHANDLER CTR FOR THE ARTS 250 N ARIZONA AV, CHAN, 85225	821 - F6
ETHINGTON THEATER 3200 W CAMELBACK RD, PHX, 85017	658 - A5
GRADY GAMMAGE MEM AUDITORIUM MYRTLE AV & 11TH ST, TEMP, 85281	740 - D4
HERBERGER THEATER CTR 222 E MONROE ST, PHX, 85004	698 - G6
MESA AMPHITHEATRE 251 N CENTER ST, MESA, 85201	741 - H4
MESA ARTS CTR 155 N CENTER ST, MESA, 85201	741 - H4
NELSON FINE ARTS COMPLEX S MYRTLE AV & E 10TH ST, TEMP, 85281	740 - E4
ORPHEUM THEATER 203 W ADAMS ST, PHX, 85003	698 - F6
PHOENIX SYMPHONY HALL 225 E ADAMS ST, PHX, 85004	698 - G6
PHOENIX THEATER 100 E MCDOWELL RD, PHX, 85004	698 - G4
RED RIVER MUSIC HALL 730 N MILL AV, TEMP, 85281	740 - D1
SCOTTSDALE CTR FOR THE PERF ARTS 7380 E 2ND ST, SCTS, 85251	700 - F1
STAGEBRUSH THEATRE 7020 E 2ND ST, SCTS, 85251	700 - F1
SUNDOME 19403 N R H JOHNSON BLVD, MarC, 85375	535 - B4
TEMPE LITTLE THEATRE 132 E 6TH ST, TEMP, 85281	740 - D3
WEB THEATRE 600 E VAN BUREN ST, PHX, 85004	698 - H6

POINTS OF INTEREST

FEATURE NAME Address City, ZIP Code	PAGE-GRID
CASINO ARIZONA 9700 E INDIAN BEND RD, MarC, 85258	661 - C2
CASINO ARIZONA II HWY 101 & E MCKELLIPS RD, MarC, 85256	701 - B6
DOWNTOWN PHOENIX YMCA 350 N 1ST AV, PHX, 85003	698 - G6
FORT MCDOWELL CASINO FORT MCDOWELL RD & HWY 87, MarC, 85264	623 - H3
GILA RIVER CASINO-VEE QUIVA 6443 N W DUSTY LN & W RAY RD L, MarC, 85339	817 - E3
GILA RIVER CASINO-WILD HORSE S MARICOPA RD, MarC, 85326	859 - H4
OUT OF AFRICA 2 N FORT MCDOWELL RD, MarC, 85264	623 - H4
PHOENIX ZOO 455 N GALVIN PKWY, PHX, 85008	700 - C7
PUEBLO GRANDE RUINS E WASHINGTON ST & S 44TH ST, PHX, 85034	699 - H7
WILDLIFE WORLD ZOO (SEE PAGE 573) 16501 W NORTHERN AV, MarC, 85340	614 - D5

POINTS OF INTEREST - HISTORIC

FEATURE NAME Address City, ZIP Code	PAGE-GRID
CARVER, GEORGE WASHINGTON HOUSE 415 E GRANT ST, PHX, 85004	738 - G1
GOLDFIELD GHOST TOWN & MINE 4650 E MAMMOTH MINE RD, PinC, 85219	706 - B7
HOHOKAM PETROGLYPHS W GREENWAY RD & N 19TH AV, PHX, 85023	578 - E3
MYSTERY CASTLE 800 E MINERAL RD, PHX, 85040	778 - H5
OLD MARICOPA COUNTY COURTHOUSE 125 W WASHINGTON ST, PHX, 85003	698 - G7
PUEBLO GRANDE RUINS E WASHINGTON ST & S 44TH ST, PHX, 85034	699 - H7
ROSSON HOUSE 139 N 6TH ST, PHX, 85004	698 - H6
SAINT MARYS BASILICA E MONROE ST & N 3RD ST, PHX, 85004	698 - G6
TALIESIN WEST FRANK LLOYD WRIGHT & 108TH ST, SCTS, 85259	581 - G6
WRIGLEY MANSION 2501 E TELAWA TR, PHX, 85016	659 - D3

POST OFFICES

FEATURE NAME Address City, ZIP Code	PAGE-GRID
AHWATUKEE STA 11010 S 51ST ST, PHX, 85044	779 - J7
AIR PK ANNEX 8175 E EVANS DR, SCTS, 85260	580 - J5
ANDERSEN SPRINGS STA 1900 W CARLA VISTA DR, CHAN, 85224	821 - B5
APACHE BLVD CARRIER 1962 E APACHE BLVD, TEMP, 85281	740 - H5
APACHE JUNCTION 151 W SUPERSTITION BLVD, APJT, 85220	745 - E5
ARCADIA STA 3920 E THOMAS RD, PHX, 85018	699 - G2
ARROWHEAD STA 19801 N 59TH AV, GLEN, 85308	537 - D4
AVONDALE 401 W WESTERN AV, AVON, 85323	695 - A7
BUCKEYE (SEE PAGE 731) 51 E MONROE AV, BUCK, 85326	772 - A1
CACTUS STA 2901 E GREENWAY RD, PHX, 85032	579 - E3
CAPITAL STA 2 S 35TH AV, PHX, 85009	697 - J7
CAREFREE 100 E EASY ST, CARE, 85377	420 - H4
CASHION 12615 S 111TH DR, AVON, 85353	735 - H1
CAVE CREEK 6061 E CAVE CREEK RD, CVCK, 85331	420 - E3
CHANDLER HEIGHTS STA S POWER RD & E SAN TAN BLVD, MarC, 85242	903 - F6
CHANDLER MAIN 101 N COLORADO ST, CHAN, 85225	821 - G6
COMMERCE STA S CENTRAL AV & W JEFFERSON ST, PHX, 85003	698 - G7
DESERT STA 6644 E BROADWAY RD, MESA, 85206	743 - F6
DOBSON STA 2415 W BROADWAY RD, MESA, 85202	741 - B6
EL MIRAGE 11925 W THUNDERBIRD RD, ELMG, 85335	575 - G5
FALCON FIELD STA 5155 E EAGLE DR, MESA, 85215	703 - C6
FOUNTAIN HILLS 16605 E AV OF THE FOUNTAINS, FTNH, 85268	583 - C7
GILA BEND (SEE PAGE 1049) W PIMA ST & N EUCLID AV, GBND, 85337	1090 - B3
GILBERT 137 E ELLIOT RD, GIL, 85296	782 - D7
GLENDALE MIAN 6537 N 55TH AV, GLEN, 85301	657 - D2
HIGLEY 16912 E RAY RD, MarC, 85236	823 - B4
HOPI STA 8790 E VIA D VENTURA, SCTS, 85258	621 - A7
INDIAN STA 741 E HIGHLAND AV, PHX, 85014	658 - H6
LAVEEN W DOBBINS RD & S 51ST AV, MarC, 85339	777 - E4
LITCHFIELD PK 591 W PLAZA CIR, AVON, 85340	655 - B7
MARYVALE STA 4415 N MARYVALE PKWY, PHX, 85031	657 - E6
MCDOWELL STA 2650 E MCDOWELL RD, PHX, 85008	699 - D4
MESA MAIN 135 N CENTER ST, MESA, 85201	741 - H5
MTN VIEW STA 2747 E UNIVERSITY DR, MESA, 85213	742 - F4
NORTHEAST STA 5021 N 20TH ST, PHX, 85016	659 - B5
NORTHWEST STA 2727 W CAMELBACK RD, PHX, 85017	658 - B5
OSBORN STA 3905 N 7TH AV, PHX, 85013	658 - F7
PAPAGO ANNEX 7460 E MCDOWELL RD, SCTS, 85257	700 - G5
PAPAGO RETAIL 7750 E MCDOWELL RD, SCTS, 85257	700 - G5
PECOS STA 16825 S DESERT FOOTHILLS PKWY, PHX, 85048	818 - G7
PEORIA ANNEX 8380 W EMILE ZOLA AV, PEOR, 85381	576 - F5
PEORIA 10700 N 85TH AV, PEOR, 85345	616 - F2
PEORIA STA 5955 W PEORIA AV, GLEN, 85302	617 - C2
PHOENIX DOWNTOWN STA 522 N CENTRAL AV, PHX, 85003	698 - G6
PHOENIX MAIN 4949 E VAN BUREN ST, PHX, 85034	699 - J7
PIONEER STA 167 S STAPLEY DR, MESA, 85204	742 - B6
QUEEN CREEK 22048 S ELLSWORTH RD, QC, 85242	904 - C1
REMOTE ENCODING CTR 5260 W PHELPS RD, GLEN, 85306	577 - E1
RIO SALADO STA 1441 E BUCKEYE RD, PHX, 85034	739 - A1
SCOTTSDALE MAIN 7242 E OSBORN RD, SCTS, 85251	700 - F2
SHAW BUTTE STA 12208 N 19TH AV, PHX, 85029	578 - D7
SHERWOOD STA 325 S LINDSAY RD, MESA, 85204	742 - F6
SIERRA ADOBE STA 1902 W UNION HILLS DR, PHX, 85027	538 - E6
SOUTH CENTRAL STA 432 E SOUTHERN AV, PHX, 85040	738 - G7
SOUTH MTN STA 6825 S 7TH ST, PHX, 85040	778 - H1
SUN CITY 9802 W BELL RD, MarC, 85373	576 - C1
SUN CITY WEST 19437 N 139TH AV, MarC, 85375	535 - B5
SUNNYSLOPE STA 9635 N 7TH ST, PHX, 85020	618 - H3
TEMPE DOWNTOWN STA 500 S MILL AV, TEMP, 85281	740 - D3
TEMPE MAIN 233 E SOUTHERN AV, TEMP, 85282	780 - E1
TOLLESON 8805 W VAN BUREN ST, TOL, 85353	696 - D6
WASHINGTON STA 8155 N BLACK CANYON HWY, PHX, 85021	618 - C6
WICKENBURG N FRONTIER ST & W APACHE ST, WICK, 85390	290 - F2
YOUNGTOWN 11129 W ARIZONA AV, YNTN, 85335	575 - H7

SCHOOLS - PRIVATE ELEMENTARY

FEATURE NAME Address City, ZIP Code	PAGE-GRID
ALL SAINTS EPISCOPAL DAY 6300 N CENTRAL AV, PHX, 85013	658 - G2
CAMELBACK DESERT 6050 N INVERGORDON RD, PVAL, 85253	660 - D3
CAMELBACK THUNDERBIRD 7440 E SUTTON DR, SCTS, 85260	580 - G6
CAROUSEL LEARNING CTR 3302 W BELL RD, PHX, 85053	578 - A1
CHANDLER CHRISTIAN 301 N HARTFORD ST, CHAN, 85225	821 - E6
CHRISTIAN CHALLENGE ACADEMY 2030 N 36TH ST, PHX, 85008	699 - F4
CHRIST LUTHERAN 3901 E INDIAN SCHOOL RD, PHX, 85019	657 - H7
CHRIST THE KING 109 E DANA AV, MESA, 85204	742 - C5
EMMANUEL LUTHERAN 715 W SOUTHERN AV, TEMP, 85282	780 - C1
EMMAUS LUTHERAN 3841 W SWEETWATER AV, PHX, 85029	577 - J6
GRACE CHRISTIAN 2940 W BETHANY HOME RD, PHX, 85017	658 - B3
GRACE COMM CHRISTIAN 1200 E SOUTHERN AV, TEMP, 85282	780 - F1
GRACE LUTHERAN 7161 N 56TH AV, GLEN, 85301	617 - D7
JOY COMM 21000 N 75TH ST, GLEN, 85308	536 - J3
JUDSON 6704 N MOCKINGBIRD LN, PVAL, 85253	660 - E2
KHALSA 346 E CORONADO RD, PHX, 85004	698 - H4
KIDDIE CARE 1830 N COUNTRY CLUB DR, MESA, 85201	741 - G1
LIGHT & LIFE CHRISTIAN 4002 N 18TH AV, PHX, 85015	658 - D7
LINCOLN LEARNING CTR 303 E EVA ST, PHX, 85020	618 - H4
MARTIN LUTHER -PHOENIX 1830 W GLENROSA AV, PHX, 85015	658 - D6
MEXICAN GOSPEL MISSION 2925 W POLK ST, PHX, 85009	698 - A6
MOST HOLY TRINITY 535 E ALICE AV, PHX, 85020	618 - H5
NEW WORLD EDUCATION CTR 1313 N 2ND ST, PHX, 85004	698 - G5
NORTHWEST CHRISTIAN ACADEMY 14240 N 43RD AV, PHX, 85306	577 - H5
NORTHWEST COMM CHRISTIAN 16615 N 43RD AV, PHX, 85053	577 - H1
OUR LADY OF MOUNT CARMEL 2117 S RURAL RD, TEMP, 85282	740 - F6
OUR LADY OF PERPETUAL HELP 3801 N MILLER RD, SCTS, 85251	700 - G1
OUR LADY OF PERPETUAL HELP 7521 N 57TH AV, GLEN, 85301	617 - D7
PHOENIX CHRISTIAN GRADE 2425 N 26TH ST, PHX, 85008	699 - D3
PHOENIX COUNTRY DAY 3901 E STANFORD DR, PVAL, 85253	659 - G4
PHOENIX HEBREW ACADEMY 515 E BETHANY HOME RD, PHX, 85012	658 - H3
PILGRIM LUTHERAN 3257 E UNIVERSITY DR, MESA, 85213	742 - G4
QUEEN OF PEACE 109 N MACDONALD ST, MESA, 85201	741 - G5
RANCHO SOLANO 240 W MISSOURI AV, PHX, 85013	658 - G4
RANCHO SOLANO 3 3540 W UNION HILLS DR, PHX, 85308	538 - A6
REDEEMER CHRISTIAN 719 N STAPLEY DR, MESA, 85203	742 - B3
SAINT AGNES 2311 E PALM LN, PHX, 85006	699 - C4
SAINT CATHERINE OF SIENA 6413 S CENTRAL AV, PHX, 85040	778 - G1
SAINT DANIEL THE PROPHET 7923 E LATHAM ST, SCTS, 85257	700 - H6
SAINT FRANCIS XAVIER 4715 N CENTRAL AV, PHX, 85012	658 - G6
SAINT GREGORY 3440 N 18TH AV, PHX, 85015	698 - D1
SAINT JEROME 10815 N 35TH AV, PHX, 85029	618 - A2
SAINT LOUIS THE KING 4331 W MARYLAND AV, GLEN, 85301	657 - G2
SAINT MARYS/BASHA CATHOLIC 200 W GALVESTON ST, CHAN, 85225	821 - F5
SAINT MATHEW 2038 W VAN BUREN ST, PHX, 85009	698 - C6
SAINTS SIMON & JUDE 6351 N 27TH AV, PHX, 85017	658 - B2
SAINT TERESA 5001 E THOMAS RD, PHX, 85008	700 - A3
SAINT THOMAS THE APOSTLE 4510 N 24TH ST, PHX, 85016	659 - C6
SCOTTSDALE CHRISTIAN ACADEMY 14400 N TATUM BLVD, PHX, 85032	579 - J5
SOUTH MTN ACADEMY 7139 S 10TH ST, PHX, 85040	778 - J2
TEMPE MONTESSORI 410 S EL DORADO RD, MESA, 85202	741 - A6
TRI-CITY CHRISTIAN ACADEMY 2150 E SOUTHERN AV, TEMP, 85282	780 - J1
VALLEY CATHEDRAL CHRISTIAN 6225 N CENTRAL AV, PHX, 85012	658 - G3

SCHOOLS - PRIVATE HIGH

FEATURE NAME Address City, ZIP Code	PAGE-GRID
ARIZONA LUTHERAN ACADEMY 6036 S 27TH ST, PHX, 85041	738 - A7
BOUREGADE CATHOLIC 4602 N 31ST AV, PHX, 85017	658 - A6
BROPHY COLLEGE PREP 4701 N CENTRAL AV, PHX, 85012	658 - G6
GETHSEMANE LUTHERAN 1035 E GUADALUPE RD, TEMP, 85283	780 - E5
GRACE CHRISTIAN 2940 W BETHANY HOME RD, PHX, 85017	658 - B3
JUDSON 6704 N MOCKINGBIRD LN, PVAL, 85253	660 - E2
MEXICAN GOSPEL MISSION 2925 W POLK ST, PHX, 85009	698 - A6
NEW WAY 1300 N 77TH ST, SCTS, 85257	700 - G5
NEW WORLD EDUCATION CTR 1313 N 2ND ST, PHX, 85004	698 - G4
NORTHWEST CHRISTIAN ACADEMY 14240 N 43RD AV, PHX, 85306	577 - G5
NORTHWEST COMM CHRISTIAN 16615 N 43RD AV, PHX, 85053	577 - H1
PHOENIX CHRISTIAN JR SR 1751 W INDIAN SCHOOL RD, PHX, 85015	658 - D7
PHOENIX COUNTRY DAY 3901 E STANFORD DR, PVAL, 85253	659 - G4
PHOENIX JEWISH STUDY 32 W COOLIDGE ST, PHX, 85013	658 - G6

SCHOOLS - PUBLIC ELEMENTARY

SCHOOLS - PUBLIC HIGH

FEATURE NAME	Address City, ZIP Code	PAGE-GRID
CENTRAL	4525 N CENTRAL AV, PHX, 85012	658 - G6
CHANDLER	350 N ARIZONA AV, CHAN, 85225	821 - F6
CHAPARRAL	6935 E GOLD DUST AV, SCTS, 85253	620 - F3
CHAVEZ, CESAR	3921 W BASELINE RD, PHX, 85339	777 - H2
CORONA DEL SOL	1001 E KNOX RD, TEMP, 85284	820 - E3
CORONADO	2501 N 74TH ST, SCTS, 85257	700 - G3
CORTEZ	8828 N 31ST AV, PHX, 85051	618 - A4
DEER VALLEY	18424 N 51ST AV, GLEN, 85308	537 - E6
DESERT MTN	12575 E VIA LINDA, SCTS, 85259	622 - B2
DESERT VISTA	16440 S 32ND ST, PHX, 85048	819 - D7
DESIDERATA ALTERNATIVE	512 E PIERCE ST, PHX, 85004	698 - H6
DOBSON	1501 W GUADALUPE RD, MESA, 85202	781 - C5
DYSART	11405 N DYSART RD, ELMG, 85335	575 - D7
EAST VALLEY INSTITUTE OF TECHNOLOGY	1601 W MAIN ST, MESA, 85202	741 - D5
FOUNTAIN HILLS	16100 E PALISADES BLVD, FTNH, 85268	583 - B6
GILA BEND (SEE PAGE 1049)	308 N MARTIN AV, GBND, 85337	1090 - B2
GILBERT	1101 E ELLIOT RD, GIL, 85296	782 - F7
GLENDALE	6216 W GLENDALE AV, GLEN, 85301	657 - B1
GOLDWATER	2820 W ROSE GARDEN LN, PHX, 85027	538 - C3
GREENWAY	3930 W GREENWAY RD, PHX, 85053	577 - H3
HAMILTON	3700 S ARIZONA AV, CHAN, 85248	861 - F6
HAYDEN	3333 W ROOSEVELT ST, PHX, 85009	697 - J5
HIGHLAND	4301 E GUADALUPE RD, GIL, 85236	783 - E5
HORIZON	5601 E GREENWAY RD, PHX, 85254	580 - C4
INDEPENDENCE	6602 N 75TH AV, GLEN, 85303	656 - H1
IRONWOOD	6051 W SWEETWATER AV, GLEN, 85304	577 - C6
MARCOS DE NIZA	6000 S LAKESHORE DR, TEMP, 85283	780 - F4
MARYVALE	3415 N 59TH AV, PHX, 85031	657 - C7
MCCLINTOCK	1830 E DEL RIO DR, TEMP, 85282	740 - H7
MESA	1630 E SOUTHERN AV, MESA, 85204	782 - C1
MESA VISTA	266 S CENTER ST, MESA, 85210	741 - G6
MESQUITE	500 S MCQUEEN RD, GIL, 85225	821 - H1
METRO TECH VOCATIONAL INSTITUTE	1900 W THOMAS RD, PHX, 85015	698 - D2
MILLENNIUM (SEE PAGE 653)	14802 W INDIAN SCHOOL RD, GDYR, 85338	654 - H6
MOON VALLEY	3625 W CACTUS RD, PHX, 85029	577 - J7
MTN POINTE	4201 E KNOX RD, PHX, 85044	819 - G3
MTN RIDGE	22800 N 67TH ST, GLEN, 85310	537 - B1
MTN VIEW	2700 E BROWN RD, MESA, 85213	742 - E2
NORTH CANYON	1700 E UNION HILLS DR, PHX, 85024	539 - B6
NORTH	1101 E THOMAS RD, PHX, 85006	698 - J2
PARADISE VALLEY	3950 E BELL RD, PHX, 85032	579 - G1
PEORIA	11200 N 83RD AV, PEOR, 85345	616 - F1
PHOENIX ALTERNATIVE EDUCATION CTR	735 E FILLMORE ST, PHX, 85006	698 - H6
POLARIS	3950 E BELL RD, PHX, 85032	579 - G1
QUEEN CREEK	20435 S ELLSWORTH RD, QC, 85242	864 - C6
RED MTN	7301 E BROWN RD, MESA, 85207	743 - H2
SAGUARO	6250 N 82ND ST, SCTS, 85250	660 - H3
SHADOW MTN	2902 E SHEA BLVD, PHX, 85028	619 - E2
SKYLINE	845 S CRISMON RD, MESA, 85220	784 - F1
SOUTH MTN	5401 S 7TH ST, PHX, 85040	738 - H7
STAR TEC PRO CTR R	3950 E BELL RD, PHX, 85032	579 - G1
SUNNYSLOPE	35 W DUNLAP AV, PHX, 85021	618 - G4
SUNRISE MTN	21200 N 83RD AV, PEOR, 85382	536 - G3
TAPP	1601 W MAIN ST, MESA, 85202	741 - D5
TEMPE	1730 S MILL AV, TEMP, 85281	740 - D5
THUNDERBIRD	1750 W THUNDERBIRD RD, PHX, 85023	578 - E5
TOLLESON UNION	9419 W VAN BUREN ST, TOL, 85353	696 - C6
WASHINGTON	2217 W GLENDALE AV, PHX, 85015	658 - C1
WEST VALLEY	3160 N 33RD AV, PHX, 85017	698 - A1
WESTVIEW	10850 W GARDEN LAKES PKWY, AVON, 85323	655 - J7
WESTWOOD	945 W 8TH ST, MESA, 85201	741 - F3
WICKENBURG	251 S TEGNER ST, WICK, 85390	290 - F2
WILSON CHARTER	3005 E FILLMORE ST, PHX, 85008	699 - E6

SCHOOLS - PUBLIC JUNIOR HIGH

FEATURE NAME	Address City, ZIP Code	PAGE-GRID
ANDERSEN	1255 N DOBSON RD, CHAN, 85224	821 - B3
APACHE JUNCTION	W SOUTHERN AV & S SAN MARCOS D, APJT, 85220	785 - D2
AVONDALE	1406 N CENTRAL AV, AVON, 85323	695 - B6
BOGLE	1600 W QUEEN CREEK RD, CHAN, 85248	861 - C5
BORMAN	3637 N 55TH AV, PHX, 85031	657 - D7
BRIMHALL	4949 E SOUTHERN AV, MESA, 85206	783 - B1
CARSON	525 N WESTWOOD, MESA, 85201	741 - E3
CHOLLA	3120 W CHOLLA ST, PHX, 85029	618 - A1
CONNOLLY	2002 E CONCORDA DR, TEMP, 85282	740 - J6
CREIGHTON	2820 E MCDOWELL RD, PHX, 85008	699 - D4
DESERT FOOTHILLS	3333 W BANFF LN, PHX, 85053	578 - A4
DESERT SANDS	6308 W CAMPBELL AV, PHX, 85033	657 - B6
ESTRELLA	3733 N 75TH AV, PHX, 85033	656 - H7
FEES	1600 E WATSON DR, TEMP, 85283	780 - G4
FOUNTAIN HILLS	16100 E PALISADES BLVD, FTNH, 85268	583 - B6
FREMONT	1001 N POWER RD, MESA, 85207	743 - G3
GILBERT	1016 N BURK ST, GIL, 85234	782 - D4
GILLILAND	1025 S BECK AV, TEMP, 85281	740 - B4
GREENFIELD	101 S GREENFIELD RD, GIL, 85236	782 - J7
GREENFIELD	7009 S 10TH ST, PHX, 85040	778 - H2
HENDRIX	1550 W SUMMIT PL, CHAN, 85224	781 - C6
HIGHLAND	6915 E GUADALUPE RD, MESA, 85212	783 - F5
ISAAC	3402 W MCDOWELL RD, PHX, 85009	697 - J4
JULIAN	2149 E CARVER DR, PHX, 85040	739 - B6
KINO	848 N HORNE ST, MESA, 85203	742 - A3
KYRENE DEL PUEBLO	360 S TWELVE OAKS BLVD, CHAN, 85226	820 - E7
MADISON #1	5525 N 16TH ST, PHX, 85016	659 - A4
MADISON MEADOWS	225 W OCOTILLO RD, PHX, 85013	658 - G2
MCKEMY	2250 S COLLEGE AV, TEMP, 85282	740 - E6
MESA	828 E BROADWAY RD, MESA, 85204	742 - A6
MESQUITE	130 W MESQUITE ST, GIL, 85233	822 - C1
MTNS SKY	16225 N 7TH AV, PHX, 85023	578 - G2
PALO VERDE	7502 N 39TH AV, PHX, 85051	617 - H7
PHOENIX PREP ACADEMY	735 E FILLMORE ST, PHX, 85006	698 - H6
POSTON	2433 E ADOBE RD, MESA, 85213	742 - E3
POWELL	855 W 8TH AV, MESA, 85210	741 - F7
POWER LEARNING CTR	7038 E ADOBE RD, MESA, 85207	743 - G3
RHODES	1860 S LONGMORE ST, MESA, 85202	781 - C3
ROYAL PALM	8520 N 19TH AV, PHX, 85021	618 - D5
SHEPHERD	1407 N ALTA MESA DR, MESA, 85205	743 - D2
STAPLEY	3250 E HERMOSA VISTA DR, MESA, 85213	702 - G6
TAYLOR	705 S 32ND ST, MESA, 85204	742 - G7
TOLLESON	9401 W GARFIELD ST, TOL, 85353	696 - C5
TONTO	7501 E OAK ST, SCTS, 85257	700 - G4
UNDERDOWN	1642 S 107TH AV, AVON, 85353	735 - J1
WEST VALLEY	4641 W MARYLAND AV, GLEN, 85301	657 - F2
WILLIS	401 S MCQUEEN RD, CHAN, 85225	821 - H7

SCHOOLS - PUBLIC MIDDLE

FEATURE NAME	Address City, ZIP Code	PAGE-GRID
AKIMEL A-AL	2720 E LIBERTY LN, PHX, 85048	819 - C7
ANDALUCIA	4730 W CAMPBELL AV, PHX, 85031	657 - F6
BARCELONA	6530 N 44TH AV, GLEN, 85301	657 - G2
BARCELONA MONTEBELLO	W MONTEBELLO AV & N 27TH AV, PHX, 85017	658 - B3
CHALLENGER	6905 W MARYLAND AV, GLEN, 85303	657 - A2
COCOPAH	6615 E CHOLLA ST, SCTS, 85254	620 - E2
CORDOVA	5631 N 35TH AV, PHX, 85017	657 - J4
DEER VALLEY	21100 N 27TH AV, PHX, 85027	538 - C2
DESERT ARROYO	33401 N 56TH ST, SCTS, 85331	460 - D2
DESERT CANYON	10203 E MCDOWELL MTN RANCH RD, SCTS, 85260	581 - E4
DESERT MTN (SEE PAGE 417)	35959 N 7TH AV, MarC, 85086	418 - H6
DESERT SHADOWS	5858 E SWEETWATER AV, PHX, 85254	580 - C6
DESERT SHADOWS	801 W SOUTHERN AV, APJT, 85220	785 - C2
DESERT SKY	5130 W GROVERS AV, GLEN, 85308	537 - F7
DON MENSENDICK	5535 N 67TH AV, GLEN, 85301	657 - A4
DYSART	11405 N DYSART RD, ELMG, 85335	575 - D7
EAST VALLEY	122 N COUNTRY CLUB DR, MESA, 85201	741 - G5
EXPLORER	22401 N 40TH ST, PHX, 85050	539 - J2
GRANADA EAST	3022 W CAMPBELL AV, PHX, 85017	658 - A6
GREENWAY	3002 E GREENWAY RD, PHX, 85032	579 - E4
INGLESIDE	5402 E OSBORN RD, PHX, 85018	700 - B1
KYRENE ALTADENA	14620 S DESERT FOOTHILLS PKWY, PHX, 85048	818 - H4
KYRENE APRENDE	777 N DESERT BREEZE BLVD E, CHAN, 85226	820 - F4
KYRENE CENTENNIAL	13808 S 36TH ST, PHX, 85032	579 - G5
KYRENE	1050 E CARVER RD, TEMP, 85284	820 - F1
LANDMARK	5730 W MYRTLE AV, GLEN, 85301	617 - D7
LONGVIEW	1209 E INDIAN SCHOOL RD, PHX, 85014	658 - J7
MCKELLIPS	325 E MCKELLIPS RD, MESA, 85201	701 - J7
MOHAVE	5520 N 86TH ST, SCTS, 85250	660 - J5
MTNSIDE	11256 N 128TH ST, SCTS, 85259	622 - B2
OSBORN	1102 W HIGHLAND AV, PHX, 85013	658 - E6
PUEBLO DEL SOL	3449 N 39TH AV, PHX, 85019	697 - H1
QUEEN CREEK	20435 S ELLSWORTH RD, QC, 85242	864 - C6
SANTA MARIA	7250 W LOWER BUCKEYE RD, PHX, 85043	736 - H2
SHEA	2728 E SHEA BLVD, PHX, 85028	619 - D2
SIMPSON R E	5330 N 23RD AV, PHX, 85015	658 - C4
SUNRISE	4960 E ACOMA DR, PHX, 85254	580 - A4
SUPAI	6720 E CONTINENTAL DR, SCTS, 85257	700 - E6
THUNDER MTN	3700 E 16TH AV, APJT, 85219	785 - J1
VISTA DEL SUR	3908 W SOUTH MOUNTAIN AV, PHX, 85339	777 - G3
VISTA VERDE	2826 E GROVERS AV, PHX, 85032	539 - E7
VULTURE PEAK	925 VULTURE MINE RD, WICK, 85390	289 - J4
WESTERN SKY (SEE PAGE 653)	4095 N 144TH AV, GDYR, 85338	654 - J6
WILSON	2929 E FILLMORE ST, PHX, 85008	699 - D6

SHOPPING - COMMUNITY

FEATURE NAME	Address City, ZIP Code	PAGE-GRID
AHWATUKEE FOOTHILLS TOWNE CTR	4601 E RAY RD, PHX, 85044	819 - H4
ALMA-ELLIOT SQUARE	941 W ELLIOT RD, CHAN, 85225	781 - D7
ANCALA VILLAGE SHOPPING CTR	VIA LINDA & FL WRIGHT BLVD, SCTS, 85259	621 - H2
APACHE/MERIDIAN PLAZA	APACHE JUNCTION & MERIDIAN DR, APJT, 85220	745 - A6
APACHE PLAZA	E MAIN ST & S POWER RD, MESA, 85208	743 - G5
ARIZONA CTR	400 E VAN BUREN ST, PHX, 85004	698 - G6
ARROWHEAD CROSSING	W BELL RD & N 77TH AV, PEOR, 85382	576 - J1
ARROWHEAD MALL	N 99TH AV & W PEORIA AVE, PEOR, 85345	616 - C1
BELL CANYON PAVILLIONS	W BELL RD & I-17, PHX, 85053	578 - B1
BELL TOWNE CENTRE	E BELL RD & N 7TH ST, PHX, 85022	578 - H1
BELL WEST PLAZA	N 33RD AV & W BELL RD, PHX, 85053	578 - A1
BILTMORE PLAZA SHOPPING CTR	N 32ND ST & E CAMELBACK RD, PHX, 85016	659 - E5
BORGATA OF SCOTTSDALE, THE	SCOTTSDALE RD & ROSE LN, SCTS, 85253	660 - F3
BROWN & GILBERT PLAZA	E BROWN RD & S GILBERT RD, MESA, 85203	742 - D2
BUCKHORN CTR	MAIN ST & N RECKER RD, MESA, 85205	743 - E5
CAMELBACK & MILLER PLAZA	MILLER RD & CAMELBACK RD, SCTS, 85251	660 - G7
CENTRAL PLACE SHOPPING CTR	S CENTRAL AV & E BASELINE RD, PHX, 85040	778 - G2
CHANDLER MERCADO	2031 N ARIZONA AV, CHAN, 85225	821 - F2
CHAPARRAL PLAZA	HAYDEN RD & CHAPARRAL RD, SCTS, 85250	660 - H6
CINEMA PK SHOPPING CTR	7TH ST & MISSOURI AV, PHX, 85014	658 - H4
COLLEGE PK CTR	E BASELINE RD & S RURAL RD, TEMP, 85282	780 - E2
COLLEGE PK SHOPPING CTR	CAMELBACK RD & 35TH AV, PHX, 85017	657 - J5
COOPER VILLAGE	6704 E BROADWAY RD, MESA, 85206	743 - G6
CORNERSTONE, THE	S RURAL RD & E UNIVERSITY DR, TEMP, 85281	740 - F4
COSTCO PLAZA	S PRIEST DR & W ELLIOT RD, TEMP, 85284	780 - A7
CROSSROADS TOWNE CTR	R H JOHNSON BLVD & BELL RD, SURP, 85374	535 - D7
DEER VALLEY CTR	N 43RD AV & W THUNDERBIRD RD, PHX, 85029	577 - H5
DEER VALLEY TOWNE CTR	N 31ST AV & FRWY 101, PHX, 85027	538 - B4
DESERT PALMS POWER CTR	N 38TH ST & E THOMAS RD, PHX, 85008	699 - G2
DESERT SKY FESTIVAL	N 75TH AV & W THOMAS RD, PHX, 85035	696 - H2
DESERT VILLAGE SHOPPING CTR	PINNNACLE PEAK RD & PIMA RD, SCTS, 85255	541 - B1
EAST THUNDERBIRD SQUARE	SCOTTSDALE & THUNDERBIRD RDS, PHX, 85254	580 - F5
EL PEDREGAL	CAREFREE HWY & SCOTTSDALE RD, SCTS, 85262	460 - G1
FACTORY STORES OF AMERICA	2050 S ROSLYN, MESA, 85208	783 - F3
FIESTA VILLAGE	W SOUTHERN AV & ALMA SCHOOL RD, MESA, 85202	781 - D1
FOOTHILLS PK PLACE	E RAY RD & S 48TH ST, PHX, 85044	819 - H3
FOUNTAIN HILLS PLAZA	16605 E PALISADES BLVD, FTNH, 85268	583 - C7
GILBERT TOWNE CENTRE	N GILBERT RD & W GUADALUPE RD, GIL, 85234	782 - C5
GLENDALE GALLERIA	N 59TH AV & W PEORIA AV, GLEN, 85304	617 - D2
GOODYEAR VILLAGE STORE	LITCHFIELD RD & VAN BUREN ST, GDYR, 85338	695 - A5
GRAND CTR	107TH AV & GRAND AV, MarC, 85351	575 - J6
GREENWAY PK PLAZA	E GREENWAY RD & N 32ND ST, PHX, 85032	579 - F3
GREENWAY TERRACE	W GREENWAY RD & N 99TH AV, MarC, 85351	576 - C3
GROVES POWER CTR	S PRIEST DR & W ELLIOT RD, TEMP, 85283	780 - A6

SHOPPING - REGIONAL

TRANSPORTATION